ECONOMIC REPORT

OF THE

PRESIDENT

TRANSMITTED TO THE CONGRESS
FEBRUARY 2012

TOGETHER WITH
THE ANNUAL REPORT
OF THE
COUNCIL OF ECONOMIC ADVISERS

UNITED STATES GOVERNMENT PRINTING OFFICE
WASHINGTON : 2012

For sale by the Superintendent of Documents, U.S. Government Printing Office
Internet: bookstore.gpo.gov Phone: toll free (866) 512-1800; DC area (202) 512-1800
Fax: (202) 512-2104 Mail: Stop IDCC, Washington, DC 20402-0001
ISBN 978-0-16-090181-2

CONTENTS

Page

---

*For a detailed table of contents of the Council's Report, see page 11.

ECONOMIC REPORT
OF THE
PRESIDENT

ECONOMIC REPORT OF THE PRESIDENT

To the Congress of the United States:

One of the fundamental tenets of the American economy has been that if you work hard, you can do well enough to raise a family, own a home, send your kids to college, and put a little money away for retirement. That's the promise of America.

The defining issue of our time is how to keep that promise alive. We can either settle for a country where a shrinking number of people do very well while a growing number of Americans barely get by, or we can restore an economy where everyone gets a fair shot, everyone does their fair share, and everyone plays by the same set of rules.

Long before the recession that began in December 2007, job growth was insufficient for our growing population. Manufacturing jobs were leaving our shores. Technology made businesses more efficient, but also made some jobs obsolete. The few at the top saw their incomes rise like never before, but most hardworking Americans struggled with costs that were growing, paychecks that were not, and personal debt that kept piling up.

In 2008, the house of cards collapsed. We learned that mortgages had been sold to people who could not afford them or did not understand them. Banks had made huge bets and doled out big bonuses with other people's money. Regulators had looked the other way, or did not have the authority to stop the bad behavior. It was wrong. It was irresponsible. And it plunged our economy into a crisis that put millions out of work, saddled us with more debt, and left innocent, hardworking Americans holding the bag.

In the year before I took office, we lost nearly 5 million private sector jobs. And we lost almost another 4 million before our policies were in full effect.

Those are the facts. But so are these: In the last 23 months, businesses have created 3.7 million jobs. Last year, they created the most jobs since 2005. American manufacturers are hiring again, creating jobs for the first time since the late 1990s. And we have put in place new rules to hold Wall Street accountable, so a crisis like this never happens again.

Some, however, still advocate going back to the same economic policies that stacked the deck against middle-class Americans for way too many years. And their philosophy is simple: We are better off when everybody is left to fend for themselves and play by their own rules.

That philosophy is wrong. The more Americans who succeed, the more America succeeds. These are not Democratic values or Republican values. They are American values. And we have to reclaim them.

This is a make-or-break moment for the middle class, and for all those who are working to get into the middle class. It is a moment when we can go back to the ways of the past—to growing deficits, stagnant incomes and job growth, declining opportunity, and rising inequality—or we can make a break from the past. We can build an economy by restoring our greatest strengths: American manufacturing, American energy, skills for American workers, and a renewal of American values—an economy built to last.

When it comes to the deficit, we have already agreed to more than $2 trillion in cuts and savings. But we need to do more, and that means making choices. Right now, we are poised to spend nearly $1 trillion more on what was supposed to be a temporary tax break for the wealthiest 2 percent of Americans. Right now, because of loopholes and shelters in the tax code, a quarter of all millionaires pay lower tax rates than millions of middle-class households. I believe that tax reform should follow the Buffett Rule. If you make more than $1 million a year, you should not pay less than 30 percent in taxes. In fact, if you are earning a million dollars a year, you should not get special tax subsidies or deductions. On the other hand, if you make under $250,000 a year, like 98 percent of American families do, your taxes should not go up.

Americans know that this generation's success is only possible because past generations felt a responsibility to each other, and to the future of their country. Now it is our turn. Now it falls to us to live up to that same sense of shared responsibility.

This year's *Economic Report of the President*, prepared by the Council of Economic Advisers, describes the emergency rescue measures taken to end the recession and support the ongoing recovery, and lays out a blueprint for an economy built to last. It explains how we are restoring our strengths as a Nation—our innovative economy, our strong manufacturing base, and our workers—by investing in the technologies of the future, in companies that create jobs here in America, and in education and training programs that will prepare our workers for the jobs of tomorrow. We must ensure that these investments benefit everyone and increase opportunity for all Americans or we risk threatening one of the features that defines us as a Nation—that America is a country in which anyone can do well, regardless of how they start out.

No one built this country on their own. This Nation is great because we built it together. If we remember that truth today, join together in common purpose, and maintain our common resolve, then I am as confident as ever that our economic future is hopeful and strong.

THE WHITE HOUSE
FEBRUARY 2012

THE ANNUAL REPORT
OF THE
COUNCIL OF ECONOMIC ADVISERS

LETTER OF TRANSMITTAL

Council of Economic Advisers
Washington, D.C., February 17, 2012

Mr. President:

The Council of Economic Advisers herewith submits its 2012 Annual Report in accordance of the Employment Act of 1946 as amended by the Full Employment and Balanced Growth Act of 1978.

Sincerely,

Alan B. Krueger
Chairman

Katharine G. Abraham
Member

Carl Shapiro
Member

C O N T E N T S

Page

APPENDIXES

FIGURES

TABLES

BOXES

DATA WATCH

ECONOMICS APPLICATIONS

CHAPTER 1

TO RECOVER, REBALANCE, AND REBUILD

The problems that caused the deep recession that began at the end of 2007 and lasted until mid-2009 were a long time in the making and will not be solved overnight. But in 2011, the Nation continued to recover from the Great Recession and to make progress toward building a stronger foundation for more balanced and sustainable economic growth in the future. The economy has expanded for 10 straight quarters. As a result of this growth, by the third quarter of 2011, the real gross domestic product (GDP) of the United States had surpassed its peak level at the start of the 2007–09 recession. Sustaining and strengthening the ongoing recovery remains a top priority for the Obama Administration, while seeking to address the fundamental imbalances and other problems that had built up for decades and erupted with the financial and economic crisis in 2008.

The pace of the recovery has not been faster because of the severity of the financial and economic crisis and the unique nature of the problems that led to the crisis in the first place. These problems included excess borrowing in the run-up to the financial crisis that subsequently caused massive deleveraging by households, a massive loss of wealth during the financial crisis that continues to constrain consumption, and excess residential home building during the housing boom that continues to cause weakness in residential construction and the housing sector.

Fundamentally, many of the problems that have plagued the economy in the past decade can be traced to weak income growth for middle-class workers. This can be seen in Figure 1-1, which displays the median household's income each year after adjusting for inflation. Income growth was stagnant for middle-income earners in the 2001–07 period and, as is common, declined in the recessions at the end and beginning of the decade. Had income grown at the same average annual rate in the first decade of the 2000s as it did in the 1990s, middle-income households would have greatly improved their financial situation.

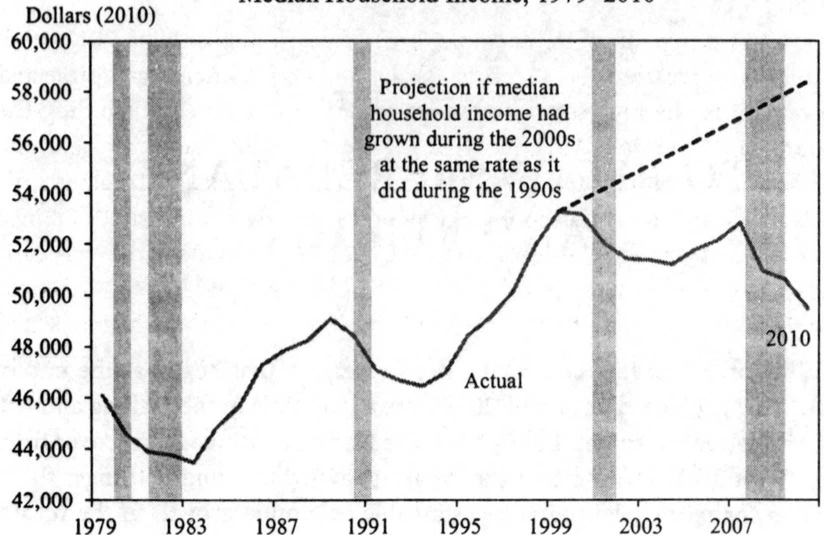

Note: Shading denotes recession.
Source: CEA calculations and Census Bureau.

A related phenomenon is that the size of the middle class has shrunk. This disturbing trend has taken place over several decades. While those at the top of the income distribution have seen strong income growth, many in the middle and at the bottom have struggled. Many economists have argued that, when confronted with easy credit and nontransparent terms, many families borrowed at an unsustainable rate to make up for the weak income growth they experienced in the 2000s. Strengthening and expanding the middle class, and adequately reforming the financial sector, are therefore at the root of the Obama Administration's strategy to reestablish an economy that is built to last.

In addition to lingering effects of the financial crisis and the long-standing problem of weak income growth for the middle class, the recovery in 2011 faced additional shocks from natural disasters in Asia, unrest in the Middle East that caused oil prices to spike, self-inflicted wounds to confidence from the contentious debt ceiling debate over the summer, and stress in European debt markets. Despite these encumbrances—and with the support, in part, of measures the President signed into law in December 2010, including the payroll tax cut, the extension of unemployment insurance, and 100 percent business expensing—private-sector employment has increased for 23 straight months, and the unemployment rate fell from a high of 10.0 percent in October 2009 to 8.3 percent in January 2012. Over the course of

2011, the unemployment rate fell by 0.9 percentage points, the largest drop in any year since 1994. Most of that decline occurred in the last three months of 2011.

The sharp drop in unemployment toward the end of 2011 took economic forecasters by surprise, because unemployment was projected to remain in the high-8-percent range by many forecasters, including the Council of Economic Advisers (CEA). As part of the Budget process, the CEA, together with the Office of Management and Budget and Treasury officials, made its forecast of economic outcomes in mid-November 2011. Since that forecast was locked down, the reported unemployment rate has now fallen by 0.7 percentage points, and the advance estimate of GDP growth for the fourth quarter of 2011 exceeded what most forecasters had expected in November. In view of the new information, the consensus of Blue Chip forecasters lowered its forecast of the unemployment rate for the end of 2012 by about 0.8 percentage point, to 8.1 percent. The more optimistic private forecasters expect the rate to be below 8.0 percent at the end of the year. In Chapter 2, the *Report* illustrates the latest forecasting range for the unemployment rate. One of the reasons for the range of forecasting uncertainty is that it is unclear how many of the President's job creation initiatives Congress will enact in the coming year. Respected private forecasters have estimated that a continuation of the 2 percentage point payroll tax cut and extended unemployment insurance benefits through the remainder of 2012 could significantly boost economic growth and job creation.

The Administration's economic strategy continues to be to: 1) pursue avenues to raise demand for U.S. goods and services in the short run to support the ongoing recovery and put more people back to work; 2) develop credible policies to return to a fiscally sustainable path in the intermediate and long term; and 3) invest in education, innovation, research, domestic energy, and infrastructure in order to build a stronger foundation for future economic growth and an expanding middle class. Put simply, the Nation needs to recover, rebalance, and rebuild. As described in this *Report*, in many instances, when Congress has not acted, the President has taken steps to implement this agenda.

Recovering from the Great Recession

When President Obama took office on January 20, 2009, the U.S. economy was contracting at an alarming rate, and employment was falling by more than 700,000 jobs a month. The plunge in economic activity was even deeper than the Bureau of Economic Analysis initially reported: revised estimates showed that the economy contracted at an 8.9 percent annualized

Economic statistics are central to understanding how the economy is working—whether consumer spending is growing or shrinking, the extent to which businesses are investing in equipment and software, the number of people currently employed, and the wages they are earning, among many other examples. This year's *Economic Report of the President* highlights the role that accurate and timely economic measurement plays in supporting sound economic decisions by policymakers, businesses, and families. In a series of Data Watch boxes, the *Report* offers examples of recently developed data series that shed light on economic performance, significant gaps in available economic data, and opportunities for improvements in the Nation's economic measures.

The growing integration of technology in our daily lives has created an abundance of new possibilities for producing better and more timely data based on nontraditional sources of information. As Census Bureau Director Robert Groves has written, "(t)he volume of data generated outside the government statistical systems is increasing much faster than the volume of data collected by the statistical systems; almost all of these data are digitized in electronic files" (Groves 2012). Nontraditional sources of information include both digital administrative data (e.g., tax records and records related to participation in government transfer programs) and records generated in the private sector (e.g., data from Internet searches, scanner data and social media data).

There is a long history of using administrative records to produce economic statistics—under strict standards of confidentiality. The Obama Administration has endeavored to create new databases that track student performance across different stages of education, as well as the performance of postsecondary educational institutions. Once these databases have been developed, analyses of the outcomes achieved by students with different educational experiences will help to guide improvements in instructional quality and college choice.

Innovative statistics based on electronic records compiled as a byproduct of commercial activity also can be informative. Adding series based on Google Trends to economic forecasting models, for example, can improve those models' predictive power. The number of search queries for a particular make of automobiles in the last two weeks of a month, for instance, turns out to be a good predictor of sales of that car, and the number of searches for real estate agencies is one of the best predictors of current home sales (Choi and Varian 2009).

Unlike government survey data, data based on electronic records generated for commercial or administrative purposes may not be nationally representative, and expanding access to these records, even for purely statistical purposes, can pose privacy concerns that must be addressed. But their use also has the potential to improve and enrich existing official statistics. The Bureau of Economic Analysis, for example, plans to use credit card data to improve its statistics on international travel services. The Census Bureau is exploring the use of administrative data on receipt of government benefits to improve estimates of income in its household surveys. Other uses of both commercial and administrative data to improve official statistics can easily be imagined. Government statistical agencies can play a vital role in this burgeoning field by providing survey data to improve the representativeness of nonsurvey data, and the Federal statistical agencies can improve their measures by integrating private-sector information. Progress in this area will ultimately lead to better informed decisions by policymakers, businesses, and families.

rate in the last quarter of 2008, from the initial advanced estimate of 3.8 percent, the largest quarterly downward revision in history. The Administration immediately took bold steps to turn around an economy in free fall. It worked to stem the job losses and put people back to work through the American Recovery and Reinvestment Act of 2009 (the Recovery Act), and it shored up the banking system and stabilized the financial sector through a series of measures including stress tests for banks and rigorous requirements for banks to raise private capital and repay the government for funds from the Troubled Asset Relief Program, and it rescued the American auto industry.

Soon after the Recovery Act was passed, the contraction of GDP slowed markedly to –0.7 percent in the second quarter of 2009 from –6.7 percent in the preceding quarter. Economic growth turned positive in the third quarter of 2009, and the economy has grown at an annualized growth rate of 2.4 percent over the past 10 quarters.

The economy is continuing to recover from the most severe downturn since the Great Depression. Despite numerous adverse headwinds—both domestic and international—that threatened the recovery, the U.S. economy displayed notable resilience in 2011. Private nonfarm employment growth, shown in Figure 1-2, averaged 174,000 jobs per month in 2011, and 218,000 jobs per month over the past three months (ending in January 2012). Private employers added more than 2.1 million jobs in 2011, the most in any year since 2005. At $15.3 trillion dollars, real GDP now exceeds its pre-recession peak. Clearly, this improvement since the end of the recession represents real progress. Nevertheless, given the depth and severity of the Great Recession,

Data Watch 1-2: Revisions to Estimates of the Gross Domestic Product

The gross domestic product (GDP) is a summary measure of the Nation's economic activity, constructed as the sum of personal consumption, gross private investment, net exports, and government expenditures. The first estimate of GDP appears within a month after the end of the quarter to which it applies and is based, in part, on source data that are preliminary and incomplete. More complete data are available for the second estimate, published the following month, and the third estimate, released the month after that; each of these revisions incorporates new or revised information from private and public sources, including monthly and quarterly Census Bureau surveys. Annual revisions to the National Income and Product Accounts allow the Bureau of Economic Analysis (BEA) to catch up in an organized way with further revisions to the source data used to compute GDP and to incorporate additional data available only at yearly frequencies. About every five years, a benchmark revision incorporates data from the Economic Censuses (Landefeld, Seskin, and Fraumeni 2008).

Between 1983 and 2009, revisions in the annualized growth rate of real quarterly GDP between the first and latest available estimate averaged 1.2 percentage points in absolute value (Fixler, Greenaway-McGrevy, and Grimm 2011). A dramatic example is provided by the revisions to the GDP growth rate for the fourth quarter of 2008, which was originally reported as –3.8 percent and later revised down to –8.9 percent in the annual revision released in July 2011. This was the largest downward revision to the quarterly data ever reported. Taken as a whole, the revised data for 2008 and 2009 indicated that the recent recession was considerably more severe than originally reported.

While revisions to initial GDP estimates for the United States can be substantial, they are smaller than the average for other large developed economies (see, for example, Faust, Rogers, and Wright 2005). And despite sometimes sizable revisions, early estimates of quarterly GDP growth generally do a good job of capturing increases or decreases in growth rates, as well as the timing of cyclical peaks and troughs (Fixler and Grimm 2005). Further, research has found that there is only limited potential to improve the initial GDP estimates given the contemporaneous information available to the BEA (Dynan and Elmendorf 2001; McKenzie, Tosetto, and Fixler 2008).

Still, more accurate early estimates of GDP would be helpful to policymakers and businesses. Improving the quality and timeliness of the source data available to the BEA is the best way to accomplish this objective.

stronger economic growth and faster job gains are needed to make full use of the Nation's human and physical resources.

On the whole, the pace of real GDP growth so far during this recovery has been almost as fast as was the case at a similar stage of the recoveries following the 1991 and 2001 recessions, which is noteworthy progress given that the earlier recoveries received a strong boost from residential home building and State and local government spending. Because of the excess home and office construction during the housing bubble, construction of structures has been notably weak so far in this recovery. In addition, once Recovery Act funds began to phase out, State and local governments cut spending and laid off workers at a faster pace. Both of these developments are unprecedented headwinds that were not present during other postwar recoveries.

As has been the pattern in recent recoveries, job growth has lagged a resumption of economic growth. Job growth started in February 2010, 8 months after the official conclusion of the 2007–09 recession, versus 11 months after the end of the 1991 recession and 21 months after the end of the 2001 recession. From February 2010 through January 2012 (months 8 through 31 after the official end of the recession), private-sector employers added a net total of 3.7 million jobs. Over the comparable period of the recovery from the 1991 recession, businesses added 3.0 million jobs (from November 1991 to October 1993), and over the comparable period of the

Figure 1-2
Change in Nonfarm Payrolls, 2007–2011

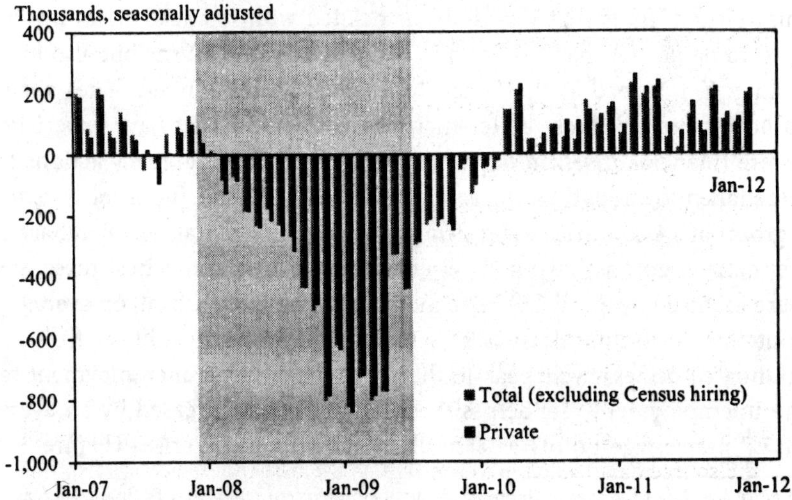

Note: Shading denotes recession.
Source: Bureau of Labor Statistics.

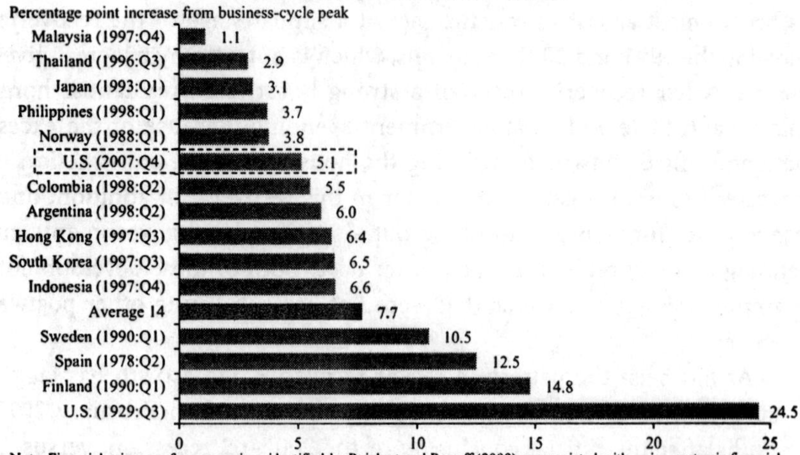

Note: Financial crises are from recessions identified by Reinhart and Rogoff (2009) as associated with major, systemic financial crises. Each data point represents the increase from the business-cycle peak to the subsequent peak in the unemployment rate. U.S. business-cycle peaks are defined by the National Bureau of Economic Research, and the business-cycle peaks of other countries refer to the peaks of real GDP. Unemployment rates for Argentina, Colombia, Indonesia, Malaysia, and Thailand are based on annual data. "Average 14" excludes the 2007–2009 U.S. recession.
Source: Reinhart and Rogoff (2009); National Bureau of Economic Research; International Monetary Fund, World Economic Outlook and International Financial Statistics; Moore (1961); national sources; CEA calculations.

recovery from the 2001 recession, businesses added 1.1 million jobs (July 2002 to June 2004).

The catastrophic financial crisis that exacerbated the economic downturn during the second half of 2008 is an important reason why the pace of the recovery has not been stronger. As discussed in Chapter 2, previous research finds that recessions associated with financial crises not only tend to be deeper than other types of economic downturns but also longer lasting. Yet, as bad as the Great Recession was, the United States appears to have fared relatively better than other countries that have experienced severe financial crises, in large part because of the emergency actions that were taken to strengthen the economy and stabilize the financial system. In a group of 14 countries identified by the economists Carmen Reinhart and Kenneth Rogoff as having experienced severe financial crises, these crises were followed by a real GDP decline of more than 10 percent, on average. In contrast, U.S. output decreased by substantially less. In addition, from each country's business cycle peak to their subsequent peak unemployment rate, the unemployment rate across these 14 countries increased by an average of 7.7 percentage points as a result of their financial crises (Figure 1-3).[1]

---

[1] Figure 1-3 shows the average increase in the unemployment rate across 14 financial crisis recessions, regardless of how many quarters it took the unemployment rate to reach its peak. Figure 2-4, in contrast, shows the average rise in the unemployment rate in each quarter elapsed from the beginning of each recession.

Although still a large increase relative to previous postwar recessions, the U.S. unemployment rate rose by 5.1 percentage points from the last quarter of 2007 to the fourth quarter of 2009, about 2.6 points less than the average country's experience.

The financial crisis was precipitated largely by lax credit standards, inadequate oversight, excessive debt, and a boom-and-bust cycle in housing prices, which led to unsustainable expansions in residential construction and consumer spending. Chapter 4 highlights the challenges that remain in the housing market, deriving primarily from institutional frictions, and explains the Administration's initiatives for addressing many of the inter-linked housing market problems.

Rebalancing at Home and Abroad

Once economic recovery began in mid-2009, the Obama Administration took steps to restore balance to the U.S. economy to help prevent the sorts of excesses that led to the financial crisis that erupted in 2008. In June 2009, the President presented his proposals for Wall Street reform. Those proposals began a process that culminated at the end of July 2010 with President Obama signing the Wall Street Reform and Consumer Protection Act of 2010.

Progress is being made on rebalancing the sources of economic growth as well. Business investment has begun to rebound. The mix of business investment has shifted from residential and structures toward equipment and software, the types of investments that expand capacity, help workers become more productive, and build a foundation for sustainable growth. Exports as a share of GDP have also grown by 13 percent since the end of the recession. The growth in exports puts the United States on track to meet the President's goal of doubling exports by the end of 2014.

More rebalancing is needed, and the adjustment process may continue to cause headwinds for the recovery. As Chapter 3 details, government balance sheets need to shift by both cutting unnecessary spending and raising revenue to continue needed investments in the future. In September 2011, President Obama submitted a balanced plan to the Joint Select Committee on Deficit Reduction that would have reduced the deficit by $4 trillion over 10 years with a mix of spending cuts and additional revenue, and the President remains committed to pursuing a balanced approach to put America on a sustainable fiscal path.

Finally, rebalancing in the economy is required so that the gains of economic growth provide more opportunity for the middle class and those struggling to get into the middle class. One step in this direction is provided by the landmark Affordable Care Act, which will provide premium assistance tax credits for those without access to affordable health insurance to obtain coverage. The new law will also begin to lower the rate of health care cost growth. Additionally, improvements in K–12 education and greater access to postsecondary education will provide more opportunity for middle-class families and those struggling to get into the middle class.

Restoring Fiscal Responsibility

In the late 1990s, the Federal Government was generating budget surpluses, both annually and throughout the 10-year budget window, as well as actually paying down the national debt. Since 2001, Federal debt has been growing unsustainably, primarily as a result of the 2001 and 2003 tax cuts that were skewed toward the wealthiest, increased military operations, the unfunded Medicare prescription drug benefit, and slow job and economic growth. Although safety net stabilizers and job creation measures in the short term are important to keep the recovery gaining momentum, the long-term Federal debt must be reduced.

Chapter 3 details how Federal debt shifted sharply from a downward to an upward path to reach today's unsustainable heights, and what the options are for reducing the long-term debt. Recognizing the economic risks associated with increased budget deficits, the Administration and Congress agreed on a $1 trillion deficit reduction package in the Budget Control Act of 2011—with an additional $1.2 trillion to $1.5 trillion in further reductions scheduled to follow. In his Fiscal Year 2013 Budget, the President has proposed a balanced approach that recognizes the need to prioritize spending initiatives while aligning revenues with current spending.

REBUILDING A STRONGER ECONOMY

President Obama has emphasized that the United States can out-educate, out-innovate, and out-build the rest of the world. Accomplishing this goal will require a Federal Government that lives within its means and makes targeted cuts to government spending while maintaining essential safety net services. But it will also require continuing to invest in the Nation's future—training and educating workers; increasing the commitment to research and technology; and building new roads and bridges, high-speed rail, and high-speed Internet. In cities and towns throughout America, the benefits of these investments are clear.

Investments in education, innovation, clean energy, and infrastructure are an essential down payment on the future. These investments today will be the foundation of long-term output and employment growth in the future, robust wage growth for all Americans, and improvements in the quality of life. As emphasized, the Nation can afford these investments only by getting its fiscal house in order. The Federal Government has to live within its means to make room for things it absolutely needs, without jeopardizing essential safety net programs or the ability to make investments for the future. That is why President Obama urged Congress to find common ground so that government policies can, with the private sector, accelerate, not impede, economic growth and sharpen America's competitive edge in the world.

Measured GDP growth is not the only contributor to the quality of life that Americans seek to enjoy. Government investments as well as regulatory policies can improve well-being by correcting market failures and protecting safety, health, and environmental quality. In fashioning long-term policies, the Nation should not overlook those factors that contribute to well-being even if they are not fully captured in economic statistics.

Jobs and Income: Today and Tomorrow

Problems that were building in the labor market for well over a decade were amplified by the Great Recession. Chapter 6 explains where the labor market is today and distinguishes between the effects of the recession and longer-term trends in employment and income that predated the recession. The goals of current policies are twofold: to increase job growth in the near term, and to prepare Americans of all ages for the jobs of the future. The chapter discusses the President's job creation proposals and the key role they can play in supporting job growth in the near term.

One notable long-term trend that can be stopped is the sharp decline in manufacturing jobs. From 2000 to 2007, the economy lost nearly 4 million manufacturing jobs, as these positions migrated overseas. Another 2 million manufacturing jobs were lost during the 2007–09 recession. Thanks, in part, to the President's efforts to rescue the American auto industry, manufacturing companies have been adding jobs for the first time since the late 1990s. On net, 400,000 manufacturing jobs have been added in the past two years. The auto industry was central to the rebound in manufacturing: although the auto industry accounts for only 6 percent of industrial production, it is responsible for 23 percent of the increase in industrial production since the end of the recession.

As discussed in Chapter 5 and Chapter 6, a number of companies have indicated that they are bringing jobs back to the United States because of the Nation's high productivity and growing cost advantages. The President has laid out a bold agenda to support this trend and to encourage more manufacturing production at home.

Investments in education will build on America's highly productive workforce and are essential to prepare today's children for the jobs of tomorrow. Increasing educational attainment for low-income children would substantially improve their chances of moving up the rungs of the ladder of opportunity. As shown in Figure 1-4, the average earnings of college-educated workers has risen to a level twice as high as that of workers with only a high school diploma. And the unemployment rate of college graduates is about half of the national average. Yet while the benefits of education have grown, the growth in the relative share of college-educated American workers has slowed since 1980 (Goldin and Katz 2008). In the last few years, however, there has been an increase in school enrollment, and the President has set a goal for the United States to have the highest share of 25- to 34-year-olds with a college degree of any country by 2020. Chapter 6 lays out the strides the Obama Administration has made in bettering the education system at every level, making higher education more affordable, and improving job training programs.

Making sure American workers have the right set of skills is also critical for a revival of manufacturing jobs and jobs in other high-paying sectors. The United States has a comparative advantage in high-technology, innovative sectors, but jobs in such sectors require a highly skilled workforce. As technology changes, advanced manufacturing products can become an even more important segment of the U.S. economy. Cars, for example, are now a highly advanced product: fully 30 percent of the value of many automobiles is derived from computer software, electronic components, and intellectual property, according to industry estimates. Thus, the President's education and job training strategy is a necessary complement to proposals to strengthen the manufacturing sector.

Preserving and Modernizing the Safety Net

The recession highlighted the need for a strong safety net as millions of Americans, through no fault of their own, lost their jobs and saw their savings decline. In addition to cushioning the shock of income loss, safety net programs are important for long-term growth because they help maintain consumer demand in a downturn and make it easier for entrepreneurs to take risks, knowing that if they fail, they will have access to a minimum level of support.

As the economy has undergone major changes, the safety net has not always adapted with it. Chapter 7 describes this changing landscape and the steps the Administration has taken to modernize the safety net for a more dynamic economy and more mobile workforce. The President has already reformed health care to give millions more Americans access to care and to

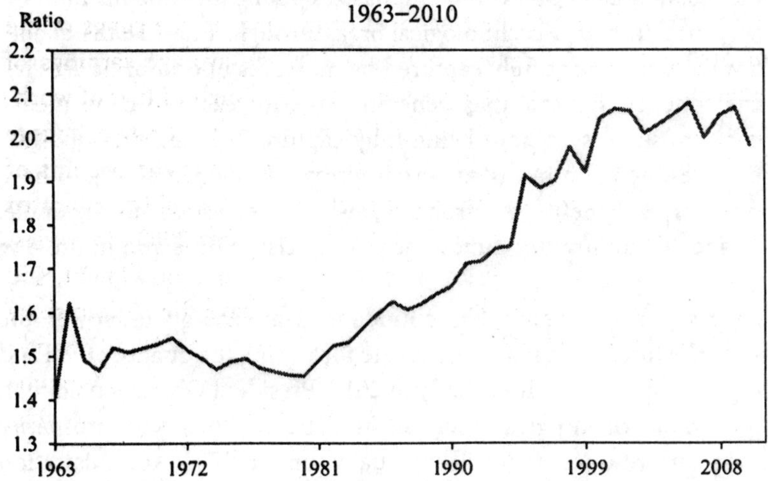

Source: CEA calculations using March Current Population Survey data for workers aged 25–65 who worked at least 35 hours a week and for at least 50 weeks in the calendar year. Before 1992, education groups are defined based on the highest grade of school or year of college completed. Beginning in 1992, groups are defined based on the highest degree or diploma earned. Earnings are deflated using the CPI-U. Calculations are based on survey data collected in March of each year and reflect average wage and salary income for the previous calendar year.

bring down costs. He has also called for the largest changes to the unemployment insurance program in 60 years and proposes to improve retirement preparedness by broadening the reach of individual retirement accounts, simplifying financial decisions for retirement savers and retirees, and promoting financial literacy.

Improving the Quality of Life through Smart Regulation, Innovation, Clean Energy, and Public Investment

Rebuilding the American economy entails investments in the foundations of economic growth—education, infrastructure, and research and development. Government investments in innovation and infrastructure and smart government regulations improve the quality of life and help the economy to operate more efficiently.

The President has reduced burdensome regulations, where possible, but smart regulations have also enabled Americans to live longer, healthier, and more productive lives. As discussed in Chapter 8, the Obama Administration has made significant reforms to the regulatory system to better measure relevant costs and benefits and to establish a review process that will result in continual improvement of the regulatory architecture.

A focus on quality of life also emphasizes public investments in innovation and infrastructure. Technological breakthroughs improve the quality of life in ways that are not fully captured by measures of economic activity. Cellular telephones, for example, generate large increases in convenience that benefit consumers without being fully captured in measures of GDP. Similarly, investments in infrastructure improve productivity but also have other, even larger benefits. A strong infrastructure system, for example, facilitates shorter commuting times, increasing leisure time and improving well-being.

Ensuring that America has abundant clean energy to power the economy of the future is also a prerequisite for raising the quality of life and enhancing the Nation's security. Early in 2011, President Obama noted that, "The United States of America cannot afford to bet our long-term prosperity and security on a resource that will eventually run out." The Administration laid out a *Blueprint for a Secure Energy Future*, a comprehensive strategy that focuses on three key areas: developing and securing America's energy supplies, including oil and natural gas; providing consumers with choices to reduce costs and save energy; and innovating our way to a clean energy future. This past year has seen remarkable progress toward reaching many of these energy goals. In 2011, domestic oil production was the highest it has been in the past eight years and natural gas production reached an all-time high. At the same time, the Administration has advanced common-sense new standards to ensure the safe and responsible development of these resources.

Conclusion

The U.S. economy has been expanding for two and a half years, but the pace of economic growth and job growth has not been fast enough given the deep hole that was created by the sharp recession that started at the end of 2007. The economic challenges that the United States faces are the direct result of problems that took years to build up and that came to a boil in the financial and economic crisis of 2007–09. While actions taken to prevent a deeper recession and to strengthen the recovery have made a difference, the Nation is still recovering from that profound crisis and the problems that led to it. Because household income for vast swaths of the middle class had stagnated, many families borrowed to support their consumption and to buy houses that later fell in value. Families are now paying down debt, which is restraining consumption and economic growth. Meanwhile, because of the collapse of the housing boom, builders have been reluctant to build new homes, and construction workers had a 16.4 percent unemployment rate in 2011. And the government budget moved from surplus and debt reduction at the end of the 1990s to deficit and increasing debt in the early 2000s, as the priorities in Washington at that time shifted to increased spending to prosecute two wars while cutting taxes in a skewed and inefficient way.

These are the Nation's principal economic challenges, not uncertainty about economic policies, taxes, or regulations. To economists, the solution to these problems is clear: the Nation needs to raise demand for its goods and services in the short run to strengthen and sustain the economic recovery and put more people back to work, while pursuing credible policies to return to a fiscally sustainable path in the intermediate and long term *and* investing more in education, innovation, clean domestic energy, research and development, and infrastructure to raise long-run growth and expand the middle class.

C H A P T E R   2

THE YEAR IN REVIEW AND THE YEARS AHEAD

The U.S. economy continued to recover in 2011 from the deep recession that began at the end of 2007. The real value of goods and services produced in the economy, as measured by gross domestic product adjusted for changes in prices (real GDP), has now grown in each of the past 10 quarters. In the third quarter of 2011, real output surpassed the level last reached at the business-cycle peak in the fourth quarter of 2007. Employment continued to expand in 2011, and the private sector created more than 3 million new jobs in 2010 and 2011, about in line with the recovery from the 1991 recession and faster than the recovery from the 2001 recession.

However, the level of unemployment remains too high, and the pace of the recovery in output and employment would in all likelihood be faster if it were not for the lingering effects of the financial crisis. The destruction of household wealth during the financial crisis and the deep recession that followed appears to have restrained the growth of consumption during the recovery, particularly in services. Investment in new residential construction also remains much weaker than in typical recoveries, a reflection of soft demand since the recession as well as the vast amount of overbuilding of houses during the years leading up to the crisis. Growth in other components of demand, such as business investment and exports, has followed trajectories more typical of business-cycle recoveries, and in some cases has been even stronger than average.

To put the current U.S. recovery in historical and international context, this chapter presents an overview of the influential work by Charles Kindleberger (1978) and Carmen Reinhart and Kenneth Rogoff (2009), who argue that recessions associated with financial crises are typically deeper than normal downturns and that the recoveries that follow tend to take longer. As severe as the recession was, the drop in U.S. real GDP after the financial crisis of 2008 was smaller than the average decline in recessions associated with other severe, systemic financial crises in various countries over the past 40 years. Similarly, the rise in U.S. unemployment was less extreme than the average experience following these financial crises, and it peaked earlier. As of January 2012, the unemployment rate has fallen by 1.7 percentage points since peaking in October 2009.

This chapter also reviews the developments of 2011 for individual sectors of the U.S. economy. In the household sector, credit conditions continued to improve, and purchases of durable goods—such as motor vehicles—rose at a robust pace. Households continued to work down debt in 2011. As noted, growth in consumption remained somewhat restrained, however, as households continued to pay down debt and growth in nominal income slowed. In the business sector, investment in equipment and software posted solid gains in 2011, and global demand for U.S. goods and services was strong. The growth in U.S. exports supported job creation in 2011 as well as the continued expansion of manufacturing output. Conditions in residential real estate markets continued to stabilize in 2011, with a modest uptick toward the end of the year, but demand for new housing remained weak. Spending by State and local governments was also severely restrained in 2011 by tight budgets. Much of the weakness in these areas can be tied directly to the financial crisis and the problems that precipitated the crisis.

An Economy in Recovery: Key Events of 2011

Real GDP rose 1.6 percent over the four quarters of 2011 after having risen 3.1 percent in 2010. Output expanded at an annual rate of only 0.8 percent in the first half of the year, when a series of shocks—among them a sharp rise in the price of oil due to turmoil in the Middle East—appeared to reduce consumer and business sentiment and dampen economic activity. As the effects of the transitory shocks waned in the second half of the year, real GDP growth picked up to an average annual rate of 2.3 percent (Figure 2-1).

Nonfarm private payroll employment expanded by 2.1 million jobs during the twelve months of 2011, having added 1.3 million jobs in the last 10 months of 2010. The recovery in payroll employment, like that in real output, was uneven over the months of 2011. Payrolls expanded moderately near the beginning of the year, but job creation slowed in the spring and summer before picking up again in the fall. The unemployment rate fell over the course of the year, from 9.4 percent in December 2010 to 8.5 percent in December 2011, and then to 8.3 percent in January 2012.

A Series of Global Shocks and Revised GDP Data. A succession of global shocks turned 2011 into a turbulent year for the U.S. economy. The collapse of Libyan crude oil production during that nation's revolution caused world oil markets to tighten near the beginning of the year. The price

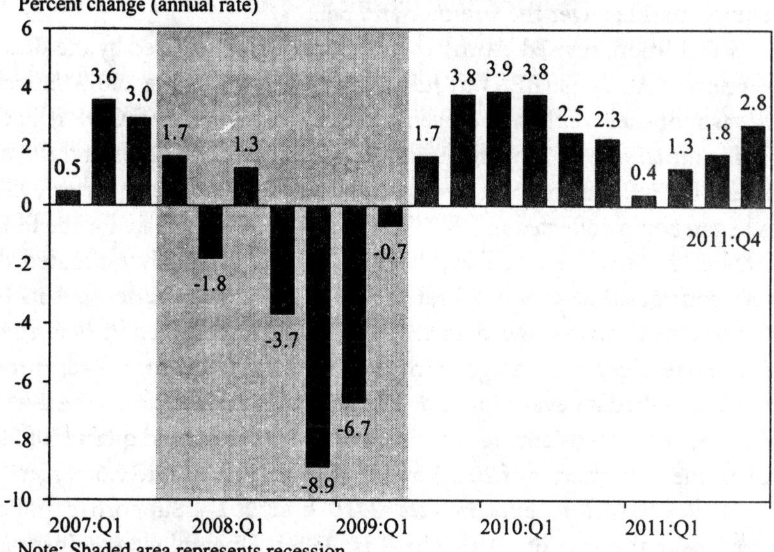

Note: Shaded area represents recession.
Source: Bureau of Economic Analysis, National Income and Product Accounts.

refiners paid for crude oil rose from an average of $78 a barrel in the second half of 2010 to $101 a barrel in the first half of 2011. The $23 per-barrel increase led to higher gasoline prices, eroded the real purchasing power of disposable personal income by more than $50 billion at an annual rate, and dampened consumer confidence. Consumers appear to have reacted with a combination of reduced spending on other goods and services and a lower saving rate than might otherwise have been the case. The 2 percentage point cut in the payroll tax for workers that President Obama proposed and the Congress passed near the end of 2010 helped offset the impact of higher oil prices.

Another supply shock hit the world economy in March 2011, when an earthquake struck northeastern Japan and set off a tsunami, a disaster that resulted in a devastating human toll and required a massive rebuilding effort. Economic activity across the globe slowed because damage to Japan's electrical grid disrupted industrial output throughout the country. As a result, global supply chains in some industries faced shortages of key parts. In the United States, vehicle assembly plants were forced to cut production when supplies of critical parts produced in Japan became scarce. U.S. motor vehicle production fell 21.2 percent at an annual rate in the second quarter before rebounding in the third and fourth quarters.

In the summer, concerns mounted over sovereign debts and financial institutions in Europe and the likelihood of a global slowdown in economic growth. In addition, the contentious debate in Congress over raising the statutory debt ceiling kept financial markets on edge and appeared to weigh on equity markets over the summer and fall.

In addition, revised estimates of U.S. real GDP released by the Bureau of Economic Analysis (BEA) in July 2011 revealed that the 2007–09 recession was more severe than had been originally reported. Real GDP fell at an average annual rate of 7.8 percent in the fourth quarter of 2008 and the first quarter of 2009, the sharpest two-quarter contraction since quarterly GDP data began being collected in 1947. The change to the estimate for the fourth quarter of 2008 was particularly stark. The BEA originally estimated that output contracted at an annual rate of 3.8 percent that quarter, but its July 2011 revised estimate showed an 8.9 percent rate of contraction. The downward change of 5.1 percentage points was the largest downward adjustment to the quarterly data ever reported. The BEA also revised down the average annual rate of growth during the recovery (from the second quarter of 2009 through the first quarter of 2011) by 0.2 percentage point, to 2.6 percent.

Policy Developments in late 2010 and 2011. Supportive policies enacted near the end of 2010—the Tax Relief, Unemployment Insurance Reauthorization, and Job Creation Act (TRUIRJCA)—cushioned the adverse shocks experienced in 2011. Provisions in the legislation included a 2 percentage point reduction in workers' payroll taxes and a continuation of the extended and emergency unemployment benefit programs through the end of 2011. In the absence of this legislation, real GDP growth over the four quarters of 2011 would have been lower by 0.9 to 2.8 percentage points, according to the Congressional Budget Office (CBO 2011b). Because the legislative package was constructed to be temporary (including mostly one- and two-year provisions), it had little effect on the long-term deficit.

The American Recovery and Reinvestment Act (Recovery Act), enacted in early 2009 when real GDP was contracting at an annual rate of more than 6 percent and employment was falling by more than 700,000 jobs a month, also continued to support the level of real GDP in 2011, although its effect, which had been designed to be strongest during 2009 and 2010, was gradually declining. In 2011, Recovery Act–related outlays, obligations, and tax cuts totaled $117 billion, down from $350 billion a year earlier, as measured in the National Income and Product Accounts. The Council of Economic Advisers (CEA 2011) estimates that the Recovery Act increased GDP as of the second quarter of 2011, relative to what it otherwise would have been, by 2.0 to 2.9 percent and raised employment by between 2.2 million and 4.2 million jobs. The CBO and outside analysts have also presented estimates in this range.

In 2011, the Administration proposed additional steps to strengthen and sustain the economic recovery in the wake of world events that posed increasing risks to growth. Before a joint session of Congress on September 8, 2011, the President proposed the American Jobs Act to strengthen the current recovery and spur the creation of new jobs. The American Jobs Act incorporated a number of proposals that some independent economists estimated could have boosted payrolls by 1.3 million to 1.9 million jobs by the end of 2012 (for example, Macroeconomic Advisers 2011). Equally important, the American Jobs Act would not have added to the long-term Federal Budget deficit. The CBO (2011a) estimated that revenue raisers recommended by the President in September would have more than offset the cost of the proposed tax cuts and investments. Specifically, the bill proposed limiting deductions and exclusions for upper-income taxpayers, taxing carried interest earned on private equity and hedge fund investments at the same rate as ordinary income, and eliminating certain tax provisions for oil and gas production companies.

The full American Jobs Act did not pass Congress in the form that the President proposed. Nevertheless, the President kept pressing for measures to support economic growth and job creation and will keep doing so until every American looking for work can get a job. In November, the President won enactment of one element of the American Jobs Act: a new tax credit for America's veterans that provides up to $5,600 to businesses that hire veterans who have been unemployed for more than 26 weeks and $9,600 for businesses that hire a veteran with a service-related disability.

And, in the waning days of 2011, the President signed into law a 2-month extension of the 2 percentage point reduction in workers' payroll taxes and of the emergency and extended unemployment insurance programs. Those initiatives were mostly paid for by an increase in guarantee fees charged to lenders by Fannie Mae and Freddie Mac. The President has called on Congress to extend these policies for the entire calendar year. The extension of the payroll tax cut for the rest of 2012 would help approximately 160 million full-time and part-time workers and provide a typical worker with an additional $40 in each bi-weekly paycheck. The full-year extension of unemployment insurance programs would prevent 5 million unemployed workers from exhausting benefits this year and help support the equivalent of about 500,000 cumulative job-years of employment by the end of 2014 as these benefits are spent.

Policy actions by the Federal Reserve also supported the recovery in 2011. Monetary policy remained accommodative throughout the year, with the Federal Open Market Committee (FOMC) maintaining a target range for the federal funds rate of 0 to 0.25 percent. During the first half of the year, the FOMC continued to advise that economic conditions were "likely to warrant exceptionally low levels for the federal funds rate for an extended period." In June, the Federal Reserve completed the program first announced in November 2010 under which it purchased $600 billion of longer-term Treasury securities, and the FOMC maintained its policy of reinvesting principal payments from its holdings of debt and mortgage-backed securities issued by Fannie Mae and Freddie Mac.

The FOMC took steps in the second half of 2011 and in the early part of 2012 to further ease conditions in financial markets and to provide additional support to the recovery. In the statement released following its August 2011 meeting, the FOMC said that it expected economic conditions to warrant exceptionally low levels for the federal funds rate at least through mid-2013. In January 2012, the committee extended this period until at least late-2014. The committee voted at its September 2011 meeting to extend the average maturity of the Federal Reserve's holdings of Treasury securities in order to lower longer-term interest rates. In response to the escalation of the sovereign debt crisis in Europe, the FOMC approved an extension of the temporary U.S. dollar liquidity swap arrangements with a number of foreign central banks in June and again in November.[1]

An Economy in Recovery: The Lingering Effects of Financial Crises

The 2007–08 financial crisis and the drop in economic activity during the recession were unprecedented. In the two and a half years that have elapsed since the official end of the recession, real U.S. GDP has risen 6.2 percent, enough to recoup the 5.1 percent loss of real output recorded during the recession. The pace of GDP growth during the recovery has been almost the same as the rates of growth observed during the recoveries that followed the 1991 and 2001 recessions (Figure 2-2), although private employment has grown at a faster pace than in the 2001 recession.

A major reason that the rate of real GDP growth has not been faster during the current recovery involves the lingering effects of the financial crisis. As argued by Kindleberger (1978) and Reinhart and Rogoff (2009), recessions linked with financial crises tend to be deeper than other recessions, and the subsequent recoveries take longer. Hall (2010) and Woodford (2010) argue that recessions around financial crises are worse, in part,

---

[1] The Federal Reserve receives collateral in the form of foreign currency during the life of the transaction. The exchange rate used for the transaction is based on the market exchange rate at the time of the transaction. The swap is unwound at the same exchange rate, so the Fed is not exposed to any currency risk resulting from the transaction.

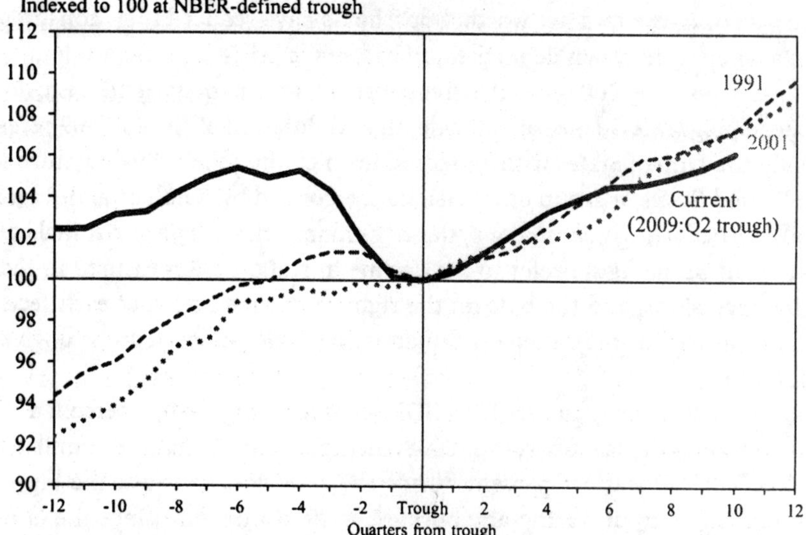

Source: Bureau of Economic Analysis, National Income and Product Accounts; National Bureau of Economic Research; CEA calculations.

because the critical intermediation role played by the financial sector is disrupted. Financial crises also tend to spread across countries, temporarily reducing the volume of world trade and restraining growth of output during the recovery, as noted by Reinhart and Rogoff (2009) and IMF (2009). Housing slumps are also typically associated with slower growth during recoveries (Howard, Martin, and Wilson 2011).

Some sectors of the U.S. economy are recovering at a moderate pace, while growth in other sectors continues to be restrained by the lingering effects of the financial crisis. In the current recovery, real U.S. exports have risen at a robust pace and have exceeded their average rate of growth in the preceding eight recoveries. Business fixed investment has been about as strong in the current recovery as in the average U.S. recovery. Real residential investment, in contrast, had barely returned to its level at the business-cycle trough by the very end of 2011, whereas this type of investment in a typical U.S. recovery would have increased roughly 34 percent over a comparable period. In addition, real expenditures by State and local governments have continued to decline, on balance, during the current recovery, instead of rising, as they had in every other postwar recovery.

Personal consumption expenditures have risen more slowly in the current recovery than in the average U.S. recovery. The slower recovery in consumer spending may partly reflect the sharp losses in household net worth caused by the financial crisis and the high levels of consumer debt—including mortgage debt—taken on during the period leading up to the financial crisis. After the collapse in house prices destroyed large amounts of household net worth, households have reduced their consumption as they work down debt taken on before the crisis.

To put the 2007–09 U.S. recession in international and historical contexts, Figure 2-3 compares the depth and duration of the 2007-09 recession in the United States with 14 recessions including the 1929 downturn in the United States, a group of recessions categorized by Reinhart and Rogoff (2009) as occurring near major systemic banking crises.[2] The horizontal bars on the left of the figure refer to the decline in real output measured in each of the recessions, and the bars on the right report the length of each recession, measured as the number of quarters between the peak and trough of real output.

While the drop in real U.S. GDP reached as high as 8.9 percent at an annual rate in the last quarter of 2008, the figure shows that the cumulative decline in GDP was 5.1 percent during the recession. This was the biggest drop in U.S. output during any business-cycle contraction since the Great Depression, although it was less drastic than the declines in output experienced in most other financial crises, and well below the average decline of 10.2 percent. The duration of the recent U.S. downturn, which measured six quarters, was about 10 percent shorter than the average. The breadth and speed of the emergency economic recovery measures that were put in place to address the financial and economic crisis, including the Recovery Act and Financial Stability Plan, as well as extraordinary actions by the Federal Reserve Board, are the main reasons why the economy avoided a steeper and more prolonged decline, with growth returning by the middle of 2009.

Figure 2-4 compares the rise in the unemployment rate in the United States between the fourth quarter of 2007 and January 2012 with the average rise in unemployment following the business-cycle peaks for the 14 financial crises shown in Figure 2-3. Between the fourth quarter of 2007 and the fourth quarter of 2009, the U.S. unemployment rate rose more sharply than the average cumulative rise over the first 8 quarters after these business-cycle peaks, but then it peaked and declined over the next two years—an outcome less severe than the average rise in unemployment around other financial crises. If the United States had followed the path of the average country during a financial crisis recession, the unemployment rate would have been 10.4 percent in January 2012 instead of 8.3 percent.

---

[2] The crises shown in Figure 2-3 are the major, systemic banking crises included in Reinhart and Rogoff (2009) Table 14-3. The analysis here differs from Reinhart and Rogoff (2009) in that we use seasonally adjusted quarterly real GDP rather than annual real GDP per capita.

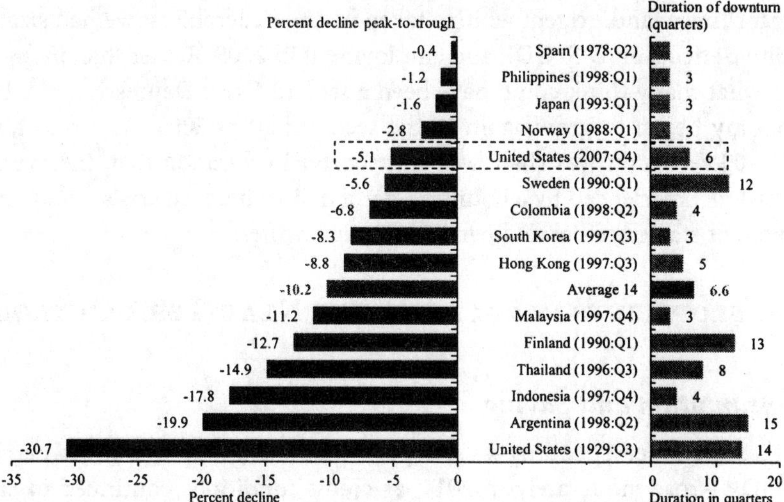

Note: Financial crisis dates are from Reinhart and Rogoff (2009). U.S. business cycles are defined by the National Bureau of Economic Research, and the business cycles of other countries refer to the peaks and troughs of real GDP. "Average 14" excludes current U.S. cycle.
Source: Reinhart and Rogoff (2009); National Bureau of Economic Research; International Monetary Fund, World Economic Outlook (2010) and data from authors; Gordon and Krenn (2010); national sources; CEA calculations.

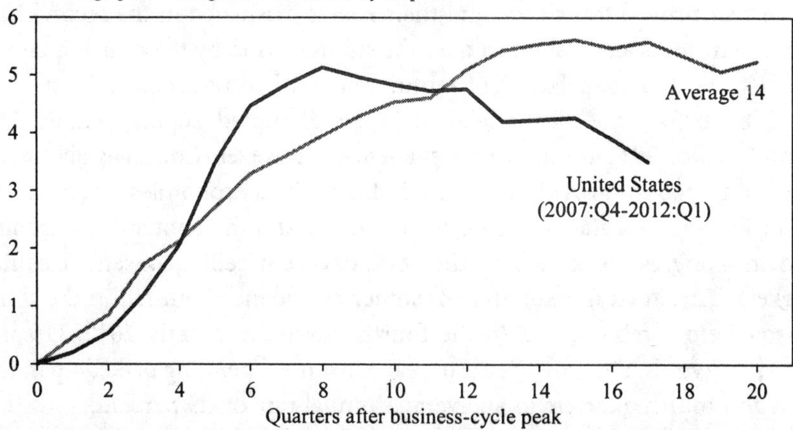

Note: "Average 14" shows the average rise in the unemployment rate in each quarter after the business-cycle peaks identified by Reinhart and Rogoff (2009) as being associated with major, systemic financial crises. Financial crises are shown in Figure 2-3. U.S. business-cycle peaks are defined by the National Bureau of Economic Research, and the business-cycle peaks of other countries refer to the peaks of real GDP. Quarterly unemployment rates for Argentina, Colombia, Indonesia, Malaysia, and Thailand are based on annual data. The 2012:Q1 value for the United States is through January 2012.
Source: Reinhart and Rogoff (2009); National Bureau of Economic Research; International Monetary Fund, International Financial Statistics, World Economic Outlook (2010), and data from authors; Moore (1961); national sources; CEA calculations.

According to analysis by the Congressional Budget Office and private-sector forecasters, the Recovery Act, the Financial Stability Plan, and the extraordinary and exigent actions taken by the Federal Reserve had sizable, positive effects on U.S. GDP and employment in 2009. Rather than plunging into what many think could have been a second Great Depression, the U.S. economy began to grow again in the second half of 2009. As a result, the 2007–09 recession was shallower and shorter in duration than the average recession experienced by a country after a major financial crisis, and unemployment started to come down sooner and swifter.

DEVELOPMENTS IN 2011 AND THE NEAR-TERM OUTLOOK

Consumption and Saving

Consumer spending—a category that makes up about 70 percent of GDP—rose moderately in 2011, as credit conditions continued to ease, household liabilities fell relative to income, and the labor market continued to recover. Gains over the year were uneven, however, in the face of upheavals at the beginning of the year. Partly reflecting these shocks, real consumer spending rose at an annual rate of only 1.4 percent in the first half of 2011, having increased more than 3 percent at an annual rate in the second half of 2010. The slowdown in spending growth would have been more severe in the absence of the workers' payroll tax cut, which offset oil price shocks early in the year and supported household consumption.

The disturbances that slowed consumption growth in the early part of the year proved transitory, and their effects dissipated in the second half of the year; oil prices stabilized over the summer, and by the fourth quarter, production (and availability) of motor vehicles had returned to levels that prevailed before the earthquake in Japan disrupted supply chains. The second half of 2011 brought new challenges, however. Concerns about the weakening pace of growth in several industrialized economies—most notably in Europe—escalated during the summer, and the contentious debates held in Congress over raising the statutory debt ceiling unsettled equity markets. The stock market and consumer confidence both fell in the third quarter before rebounding in the fourth quarter and early 2012. Despite these headwinds, the growth rate of real consumer spending picked up in the third and fourth quarters to an average annual rate of 1.9 percent.

Several key developments in 2011 shaped the contours of consumer spending.

Household Income in 2011. Nominal personal income grew 3.9 percent during the four quarters of 2011, a somewhat slower pace of growth than in 2010. Growth in nominal personal income was held down in 2011 by a slowdown in job growth near the middle of the year. Real disposable personal income, which is personal income less personal taxes and adjusted for price changes, edged down 0.1 percent over the four quarters of 2011 after having risen 3.5 percent in the year-earlier period. The purchasing power of wages and salaries was curtailed somewhat in 2011 by a run-up in food and energy prices in the first half of the year, which appeared to have passed through to the prices of some other goods and services as well. As noted, tax policies passed near the end of 2010 helped cushion some of the effects of these price increases on consumers while providing an additional boost to income. The Administration seeks to extend the workers' payroll tax cut in 2012 and to provide additional immediate support for aggregate demand through the continuation of extended unemployment insurance benefits and other measures initially proposed in the American Jobs Act.

Household Wealth and Saving in 2011. The wealth-to-income ratio, depicted in Figure 2-5, declined in the third quarter of 2011 after rising, on balance, since the beginning of 2009. The consumption rate (shown in the figure as the share of disposable income consumed) tends to fluctuate with the wealth-to-income ratio. As a rule of thumb, a one dollar drop in wealth tends to reduce annual consumer spending by about two to five cents, although the source of the wealth change (housing or equities, for example)

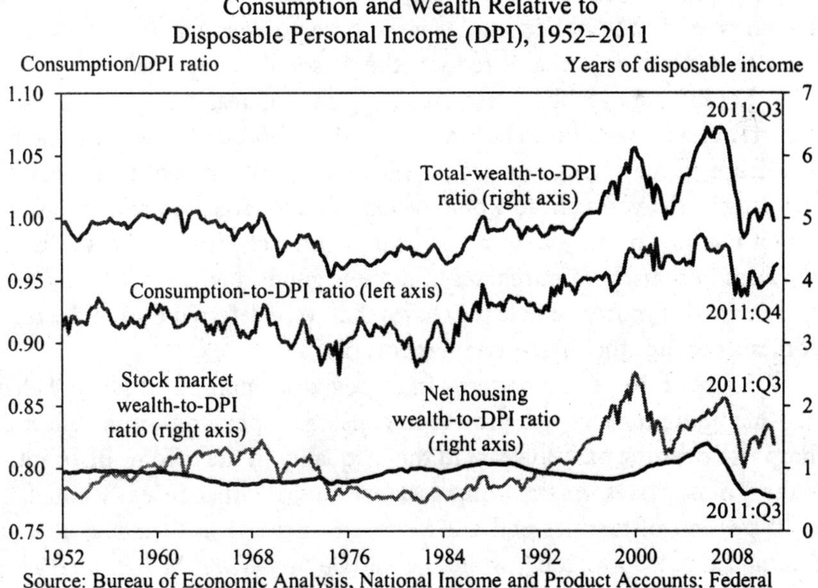

Figure 2-5
Consumption and Wealth Relative to
Disposable Personal Income (DPI), 1952–2011

Source: Bureau of Economic Analysis, National Income and Product Accounts; Federal Reserve Board, Z.1; CEA calculations.

also may matter. The decline in the wealth-to-income ratio from the second quarter of 2007 to its low point in the first quarter of 2009 amounted to 1.8 years of income. (In other words, household wealth declined by the amount of income earned in 1.8 years). The drop in the wealth-to-income ratio over this period was the deepest sustained decline since 1952, when these data began to be compiled. Of the total decline, 1.1 years were lost from the decline in stock market wealth, and about 0.6 year from net housing wealth. All told, a drop in wealth of this magnitude could be expected to reduce personal consumption expenditures by about 6.7 percent.

Equity prices fell during the summer of 2011 before regaining most of the losses toward the end of the year. Driven in part by the rise in uncertainty during the debt ceiling debate as well as external events in Japan and Europe, consumer sentiment also dropped to low levels in the summer before partially rebounding toward year's end.

Households continued to work down their debt through the third quarter of 2011 (the latest data available as this report goes to press). The personal saving rate—expressed in the National Income and Product Accounts as a share of disposable personal income—fluctuated around 5 percent for the first half of 2011, about the same rate as in 2010 but below the average rate of about 6 percent observed in the first half of 2009. The personal saving rate fell in the second half of 2011 to 3.8 percent, a decline from the first half of 2011 that may have partially reflected the pick up in purchases of consumer durables, especially new vehicles. Purchases of new motor vehicles, are counted as a consumption outlay in the National Income and Product Accounts even though households view these purchases as investment, and so a rise in vehicle purchases reduces the personal saving rate.

Looking ahead, the personal saving rate appears roughly consistent at current levels with household wealth. As a consequence, while some further drops in the saving rate are possible, the growth rate of real consumer spending in the years ahead would be expected to largely mirror the growth rate of income, barring a dramatic change in asset prices. Even so, further increases in household purchases of durable goods, perhaps reflecting pent-up demand for motor vehicle purchases that were deferred during the recession, may reduce the saving rate temporarily.

Some of the recent patterns in aggregate spending and saving behavior—including the sluggish growth in consumer spending—may reflect the sharp rise over the past 30 years in the inequality in the income distribution in the United States. As the Congressional Budget Office recently noted, the top 1 percent of families had a 278 percent increase in their real after-tax income from 1979 to 2007, while the middle 60 percent had an increase of less than 40 percent. As a result of these trends, the very top income earners have pulled much further ahead of everyone else. (See Chapter 6 for a discussion of shifts in the income distribution.)

The effects of this dramatic shift in the income distribution on aggregate demand are hard to document, although some of the spending patterns in the Consumer Expenditure Survey reveal evidence of the increasing inequality of income. For example, the share of income spent on luxury goods and services, such as entertainment, relative to necessities, such as food, is higher for high-income households than for low-income households, and this gap has widened over time (Aguiar and Bils 2011).

Several authors have argued that increases in inequality have likely adversely affected the economy.[3] For example, the rise in income inequality may have reduced aggregate demand, because the highest income earners typically spend a lower share of their income—at least over intermediate horizons—than do other income groups. The following calculation illustrates the potential magnitude of this effect. As shown in recent research by Piketty and Saez (2003, 2010), the share of all income going to the top 1 percent has risen sharply over the past three decades, rising by 13.5 percentage points, from 10 percent to 23.5 percent, between 1979 and 2007. This is the equivalent of about $1.2 trillion of annual income in 2007. Research on the saving rate (or marginal propensity to consume) of families at the very top of the income distribution is scarce, but one study (Dynan, Skinner, and Zeldes 2004) implies that the top 1 percent of households save about half of their total current income, while the population at large has a saving rate of about 10 percent of their total income.[4] This finding implies that if another $1.2 trillion had been earned by the bottom 99 percent instead of the top 1 percent of income earners, annual consumption could have been about $480 billion—or about 5 percent—higher.

There are many caveats to this calculation, because the marginal propensity to consume is not well established for the extreme upper end of the income distribution. In addition, aggregate consumption may not have been reduced by a full 5 percent because the dramatic shift in the income distribution likely led many households to accrue more debt. In his book *Fault Lines*, Raghuram Rajan (Rajan 2010) argues that slow income growth for the middle class led, in part, to the rising levels of debt and the overleveraging that played a central role in the 2007–08 financial crisis.[5]

---

[3] See Rajan (2010) and Reich (2010). Kaldor (1956) provides some early research in this area.

[4] The saving rate cited here refers to the change in real net worth as a share of real pre-tax income, a measure that differs from the personal saving rate reported in the National Income and Product Accounts.

[5] Note that the increase in leverage by the middle class may explain why the aggregate saving rate did not rise despite the shift in income to high savers.

Increases in the inequality of income have been developing for some time, but their effects on aggregate demand may have become more pronounced in the wake of the financial crisis. Increasing levels of debt during 1979–2007 may have masked the influence of the rising inequality of incomes on aggregate consumer spending, because increased access to credit card debt, other consumer loans, and mortgage loans allowed the growth of purchases to outpace the growth of income for most income groups. With the onset of the recession and financial crisis, however, the scope for this level of borrowing came to an abrupt end. Access to credit, particularly for mortgages, was severely restricted, and the average consumer was left with elevated levels of debt taken on before the crisis. Since the crisis, the process of deleveraging appears to have reduced consumption below what it would have been otherwise. By targeting support to a broad group of American workers—including those with a higher propensity to spend additional income—the measures the President put forward in the American Jobs Act, like the payroll tax cut and extension of unemployment benefits, are likely to have a greater impact on consumption and aggregate demand than alternative measures.

Other Influences on Consumption in 2011. For the second consecutive year, lending standards eased, as reported in the Federal Reserve's senior loan officer survey, and consumer credit expanded modestly over the first three quarters of 2011. The level of overall household debt fell in 2011, reflecting a decline in mortgage debt. The decline in real household debt outstanding in the current recovery has been unprecedented, which suggests that the process of deleveraging has played a sizable role in household consumption decisions in recent years.

Reflecting, in part, the improvement in credit availability since 2009, household consumption of durable goods, including items such as new and used automobiles as well as household electronics, furniture, and other appliances has risen at a solid pace in the current recovery and somewhat more strongly than the rates of growth observed during the recoveries that followed the 1991 and 2001 recessions. Household consumption of nondurable goods and services, in contrast, has risen at a slower pace in the current recovery than in most previous U.S. recoveries. Real consumer spending on services has increased only 2.9 percent so far in the current recovery, whereas this type of spending grew by an average of 10.7 percent over the first ten quarters of the previous eight recoveries. Consumer spending on services has been particularly weak in categories such as housing services, financial services, and insurance, likely reflecting the continuing effects of the financial crisis, and on categories that are more discretionary, such as recreation and gambling.[6]

Restrained demand for services may have implications for the labor market, because the production of services accounts for about two-thirds of U.S. GDP and a larger share of U.S. employment. (For a discussion of the measurement of services see Data Watch 2-1.) Although it is difficult to tie final consumption of a particular type of good or service to employment in that industry (the purchase of a new motor vehicle creates jobs in a number of service industries, for example), jobs in service-producing sectors accounted for about 68 percent of total nonfarm payroll employment in 2007.[7]

Developments in Housing Markets

After posting steep declines during the 2007-09 recession, activity in the housing sector remained at subdued levels in the first half of 2011 before edging up in the second half of the year. New housing starts were about 607,000 units in 2011, an increase of 3.7 percent from the level in 2010. New housing starts remain well below the long-run trend in U.S. housing demand. According to researchers at the Joint Center for Housing Studies at Harvard University, projected rates of household formation and immigration for the period 2010 through 2020 are consistent with housing starts in the range of 1.6 million to 1.9 million units a year (Masnick, McCue, and Belsky 2010). Activity in the housing sector is likely to remain below these levels for some time, however, as new construction continues to be restrained by a sizable overhang of vacant properties for sale.

House prices, discussed in more detail in Chapter 4, fell 4.7 percent, on net, during the twelve months of 2011, according to the CoreLogic home price index. Distressed sales—which include short sales and sales of properties owned by lenders (real-estate owned, or REO)—remained a headwind in 2011: CoreLogic estimates that 1.6 million properties were seriously delinquent, in foreclosure, or owned by lenders in October 2011, equal to about five months of supply at the current pace of sales. The modest rates of growth in personal income and the tighter mortgage underwriting standards observed in recent years also kept sales and starts below their long-run trend levels.

---

[6] Consumption of services is more difficult to measure than is consumption of goods, and estimates for 2011 may be revised considerably when the Services Annual Survey is incorporated into the *National Income and Product Accounts*. Nonetheless, the pattern of weaker-than-normal growth in services consumption in the current recovery has been quite pronounced through 2010, a period for which estimates reflect the latest annual survey.

[7] Industries counted in this figure include professional and business services, education and health services, leisure and hospitality, other services, and government services.

coverage of services in the Economic Census and marking substantial improvement relative to even just a few years ago.

Measurement of real activity in the service sector requires appropriate price deflators for service outputs. In 1990, the Producer Price Index (PPI) covered less than 5 percent of U.S. service output. Today, thanks to a concerted effort by the Bureau of Labor Statistics, PPI deflators are available for more than three-quarters of domestically provided services. This has translated directly into more accurate estimates of real GDP.

Nevertheless, as the U.S. economy continues to evolve, the work of accurately measuring service activity grows accordingly. Despite recent innovations in the collection of primary source data, there are still conceptual issues pertaining to the appraisal and definition of services that remain unresolved. As an example, improvements in health care have contributed to longer life spans and better quality of life, but there is not a consensus about how to value and incorporate these benefits in a national income accounting framework. Similarly, industries such as finance largely produce intangible outputs that are difficult even to identify, much less quantify. Furthermore, although estimates of international trade in services are now more detailed than was the case before the 1980s, the statistics still could and should be improved. Data on the prices of traded services are extremely limited, and even the most disaggregated data collected by the BEA on services extend to only 36 categories, in contrast to thousands of categories for manufactured goods. Continued research and investment in the development of data on services are needed to ensure timely and accurate measurement of the U.S. economy.

Although home prices in some parts of the country have stabilized, CoreLogic estimates that more than 20 percent of homeowners with mortgages remained underwater at the end of the third quarter of 2011 (that is, the value of the mortgage exceeds the house price). The share of mortgages in the foreclosure process remained elevated by historical standards in 2011 and changed little from the level in 2010, as reported by the Mortgage Bankers Association.

For a description of the Administration's housing policy proposals, see Chapter 4.

Business Fixed Investment

Business fixed investment grew at a solid 7.3 percent annual rate during the four quarters of 2011, after rising 11.1 percent at an annual rate in the four quarters of 2010. Among the two main components of business fixed investment, spending on equipment and software investment grew 9.0 percent over the four quarters of 2011, and investment in nonresidential structures increased 2.7 percent.

Within equipment and software, purchases of transportation equipment rose at a brisk 22.7 percent annual rate over the four quarters of 2011, after having surged at a 68.1 percent annual rate in 2010. Business outlays on information technology rose at a 4.1 percent annual rate over the four quarters of 2011, a third consecutive year of solid growth. Investment in industrial equipment also grew notably, posting a four-quarter increase of 15.2 percent. (For more information on how investment is defined, see Data Watch 2-2.)

Investment growth among the categories of nonresidential structures was mixed in 2011. On one hand, investment in mining and drilling structures was strong, reflecting elevated oil prices as well as some advances in technology that have enabled drilling at new sites. (See Chapter 8.) Investment in commercial and health care structures, on the other hand, edged down over the four quarters of 2011.

The strength of business fixed investment since mid-2009 reflects several developments. Investment fell sharply during the recession, and, as the prospects for sales have begun to improve, businesses have invested in recent years to replace aging equipment. In addition, the Administration's 100 percent business expensing policy boosted business investment by allowing firms to take an immediate deduction on investments made in new equipment in 2011. The President has proposed extending this provision into 2012.

Business investment may be positioned to grow rapidly if demand accelerates because corporations have plenty of internal funds (Figure 2-6). Corporate profits continued to rise in 2011 and were above their pre-recession level, while corporate dividends have returned roughly to pre-recession levels. Largely as a result, corporate cash flow, a measure that includes undistributed profits and depreciation and represents the internal funds available for investment, has also risen substantially during the recovery. A large share of these investable funds has been channeled to financial investments rather than to new physical capital, as can be seen by the rising level of liquid assets held by nonfinancial corporations.

Manufacturing Output

The real output of U.S. factories rose 3.7 percent over the twelve months of 2011 after having risen 6.4 percent in 2010, according to the manufacturing component of the industrial production index published

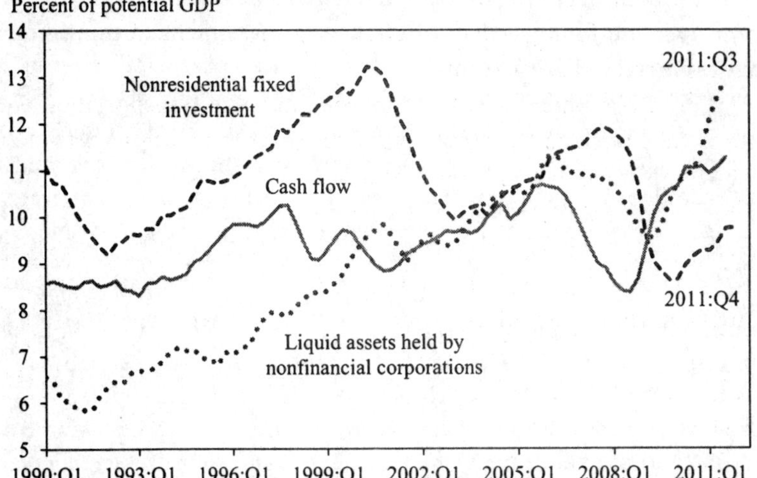

Note: Potential GDP is a CBO estimate. Cash flow, from the National Income and Product Accounts, and nonfinancial liquid assets are plotted using three-quarter moving averages.
Source: Bureau of Economic Analysis, National Income and Product Accounts; Federal Reserve Board (Flow of Funds L.102); Congressional Budget Office.

by the Federal Reserve Board. The manufacturing sector has been growing faster than the rest of the economy during the recovery, with real output rising at an average annual rate of 5.7 percent since its low in June of 2009—its fastest pace of growth in a decade.

The rise in manufacturing output during the recovery has provided a considerable boost to the U.S. economy. Following two decades of shrinking employment—a trend that reflected both increases in automation and the lower labor costs in emerging-market economies—manufacturers in the United States have added more than 400,000 jobs since employment in the sector reached its low in January 2010. These numbers reflect an emerging trend of some companies bringing jobs back to the United States, as discussed in the special report, *Investing in America: Building an Economy that Lasts* (White House 2012). This nascent trend likely reflects, in part, the improvement in unit labor costs in the United States relative to many of our trading partners in recent years. (See Chapter 5 for more discussion of the rising competitiveness of U.S. industry.)

The robust gains in manufacturing output during the recovery appear to reflect rising investment demand for domestically-produced capital goods from both domestic and foreign customers. The rebound of the U.S. motor vehicle industry has played a particularly large role, with the production of motor vehicles and parts directly accounting for about 23 percent of the increase in manufacturing output since mid-2009. As U.S. demand for new

Data Watch 2-2: Investment in Intangibles

Investment can be defined as devoting resources to produce a durable asset that will yield a future flow of services. Until recently, measures of investment in the National Income and Product Accounts (NIPAs) were restricted to investments in physical capital such as buildings, machinery, and equipment; new residential construction; and net additions to inventories. In today's knowledge economy, however, intangible assets such as computer software and scientific innovations make increasingly important contributions to economic growth.

The Bureau of Economic Analysis (BEA) has begun to incorporate investments in intangible capital into the NIPAs. The first step in this direction, taken in 1999, was to treat spending on computer software as an investment outlay, which enters GDP directly, rather than as a business expense, which is considered an intermediate input rather than a part of final demand; the treatment of government spending on computer software was changed at the same time. Because business and government spending on computer software had been growing rapidly compared to other types of spending, these changes raised the measured growth rate of GDP slightly. In 2013, BEA plans to begin treating spending on scientific research and development as an investment rather than an expense; had this treatment been in effect historically, it too would have raised the average measured rate of growth of GDP in recent decades.

Some researchers have argued that investment in intangibles should be defined even more broadly (Corrado, Hulten, and Sichel 2009; Corrado and Hulten 2010). In addition to research and development that builds on a scientific base of knowledge, for example, there is an argument for treating as investment the money firms spend on other sorts of new product development, such as the development of new motion pictures or new financial services products. Businesses also spend money on strategic planning, the implementation of new business processes, and employee training, all of which may add significantly to future productivity and thus arguably should be treated as investment as well. Taking an even broader perspective, time and money devoted to formal education add to the human capital of the American workforce and thus to its future productivity. While accounting accurately for the value of these investments poses some difficult measurement challenges (Abraham 2010), their importance to future economic growth should not be overlooked. According to some research (Krueger 1999), returns on human capital generate the lion's share of national income.

vehicles has recovered, the Detroit auto companies along with the foreign-domiciled auto companies have been expanding U.S. production to serve both U.S. and foreign markets. Over the past two years, the entire U.S. auto industry—including dealerships and suppliers of auto parts—has added nearly 160,000 jobs. General Motors was the world's top-selling automaker in 2011, Ford is investing in new American plants, and sales at Chrysler grew faster in 2011 than in recent years.

In addition to rescuing the American auto industry, the Administration has more broadly supported American manufacturing through its efforts to reduce barriers for American businesses to sell products all over the world. To build on the progress already made, the President laid out in his 2012 State of the Union address a Blueprint for an America Built to Last, which included proposals to encourage companies to create manufacturing jobs in the United States while removing tax deductions for shipping jobs overseas.

Business Inventories

Businesses continued to build inventories during 2011, and inventories in the manufacturing and trade sectors remained lean relative to sales. Inventory investment—measured as the change in inventories from one quarter to the next—is typically an important contributor to the changes in real GDP during recessions and the early stages of recoveries.

Over the course of 2011, real inventory investment stepped up in the first quarter and then slowed in the second and third quarters, but closed out the year on a high note. The slower pace of inventory investment in the second quarter reflected, in part, the reduced rate of motor vehicle production caused by disruptions to the flow of auto parts following the earthquake and tsunami in Japan. Altogether, real inventory investment added roughly 0.2 percentage point to real GDP growth between the fourth quarter of 2010 and the fourth quarter of 2011.

Government Outlays, Consumption, and Investment

The Federal budget deficit during Fiscal Year 2011—which ended on September 30—was $1.3 trillion, roughly unchanged from the year before. As a share of GDP, the deficit fell to 8.7 percent in FY 2011 from 9.0 percent in FY 2010. Federal receipts rose 6.5 percent during FY 2011, largely driven by a 21.5 percent increase in individual income tax receipts. Corporate tax receipts fell 5.4 percent in FY 2011, partly reflecting the introduction of 100 percent depreciation for business equipment investment in calendar year 2011 (up from 50 percent in calendar year 2010), which pulls forward deductions that businesses would otherwise receive over several years. Corporate tax receipts in FY 2011 were only about half what they were in FY 2007, even as domestic corporate profits (excluding Federal Reserve Banks) were roughly unchanged.[8] In contrast, individual income tax receipts in FY 2011 were more than 90 percent of their FY 2007 level.

Federal outlays rose 4.2 percent in FY 2011 from FY 2010 but remained steady as a share of GDP at 24.1 percent. According to the CBO, approximately half of the year-over-year increase in Federal outlays reflects re-evaluations of the cumulative cost of the Troubled Asset Relief Program (TARP).[9] The President's FY 2013 Budget estimates that the cumulative cost of TARP will be $67.8 billion, well below the Administration's 2009 estimate of $341 billion.

Nominal spending on defense grew more slowly in FY 2011 than in recent years. Combined total spending on Social Security, Medicare, and Medicaid rose in FY 2011, though at a slower pace than the average over the past three years. According to the Department of Labor, extended unemployment benefits and emergency unemployment benefits are on track to be about $60 billion in 2011, following total benefits of $80 billion in 2010. The past three years of unemployment benefits stabilized consumer spending at a level higher than would have occurred absent this income support. In addition, the 2 percentage point reduction in payroll taxes through the end of 2011 lowered tax liabilities by about $114 billion.

During the four quarters of calendar year 2011, real Federal expenditures on consumption and gross investment, as measured in the National Income and Product Accounts, declined 3.3 percent; federal defense spending fell 3.7 percent over the four quarters of 2011, and federal nondefense spending declined 2.6 percent.

As projected in the Administration's FY 2013 Budget, which includes demand-supporting initiatives for FY 2012 that have not yet been approved by the Congress, the deficit as a share of GDP will fall from 8.7 percent in FY 2011 to 5.5 percent in FY 2013, and to 3.4 percent in FY 2015. The full-employment deficit as a share of GDP (the budget deficit that would exist if the economy were at full employment) would be roughly unchanged in FY 2012 and fall by about 3 percentage points in FY 2013 and by another 1.5 percentage points in FY 2014. This fiscal consolidation will restrain the

---

[8] The divergence of corporate profits and corporate tax receipts between 2007 and 2011 reflects changes in tax policy and differences in how profits in the National Income and Product Accounts (NIPA) and corporate taxable income are calculated. Business credits for corporations have increased between 2007 and 2011. The components of NIPA profits that are not counted in taxable income include capital gains, bad debt, and Federal Reserve profits.

[9] The CBO (2011c) estimates the net present value of the cumulative cost of TARP each year and—if costs are revised down—records the changes in these valuations in the Budget as a negative outlay. The CBO adjusted down the total cost of the program in FY 2010 and FY 2011, but the downward adjustment in FY 2011 was smaller than in FY 2010.

growth of demand in those years, but an increase in private-sector demand in those years is projected to fill in the gap.

Looking further ahead, the deficit reduction from the cuts mandated by the Budget Control Act of 2011 and the expiration of the tax cuts on upper-income Americans enacted between 2001 and 2003, combined with the winding down of operations in Afghanistan and Iraq, will bring deficits down to approximately 2.8 percent of GDP near the end of the 10-year budget window. Policy changes recommended in the FY 2013 Budget put the debt on a stable or declining path as a share of the economy and would—if enacted—place the budget in a fiscally sustainable position in the ten-year budget window.

State and Local Governments

State and local governments remained under severe fiscal pressure in 2011, and, as noted, declines in this sector's revenues have forced sharper declines in real State and local consumption and gross investment than in earlier U.S. recoveries. Although nominal State and local government tax receipts continued to increase in 2011, Federal funds from the Recovery Act—which helped support State and local governments during 2009 and 2010—declined, and employment continued to contract.

State and local tax revenues rose about 4 percent, or $50 billion, during the four quarters through the third quarter of 2011, roughly the same pace as during the year-earlier period. About half of the rise came from personal income taxes. State and local taxes on production and imports—a category that includes sales and property taxes—increased about $32 billion over this period, while corporate taxes were down $8 billion. Federal grants-in-aid to the states plunged $87.8 billion during the four quarters of 2011 after rising notably during 2009 and 2010; both the earlier increase and the 2011 decline were attributable to the Recovery Act, which was designed to offer temporary support to State and local governments.

Current State and local government expenditures—which include transfers to individuals as well as government consumption—fell 0.2 percent over the four quarters of 2011, following a 4.4 percent increase in the year-earlier period. Reflecting, in part, the decline in Federal grants-in-aid between the third quarters of 2010 and 2011, the operating position of State and local governments deteriorated to an aggregate deficit of $83 billion by the third quarter of 2011, the fourth consecutive year of operating deficits for the State and local sector.

Employment in State and local government declined by 235,000 in 2011, and employment in the sector fell 660,000 from its peak in August

2008 to December 2011. About 36 percent of the jobs lost over this period were in education.

Real investment by State and local governments in structures, such as schools, roads, and bridges, fell 9.9 percent during the four quarters of 2011, a decline notably steeper than those of the preceding three years. Some of the decline is attributable to the expiration of the Build America Bonds program at the end of 2010. Part of the Recovery Act, the program subsidized municipal bonds issued for infrastructure development and helped finance $181 billion worth of capital projects, including schools, bridges, and hospitals (Department of Treasury 2011).

State and local governments have made tough budget decisions during the past four years. They will likely continue doing so in 2012 as Federal transfers diminish, and past declines in house prices erode the property tax base. The Administration took important steps in 2010 and 2011 to help State and local governments maintain critical services in public safety and education. In addition to the grants-in-aid components of the Recovery Act, the Administration eased the burden on State and local governments in August 2010 by establishing a new teacher job fund and by extending the enhanced Federal matching formula for certain social services and medical insurance expenditures covered by the States. In 2011, the President proposed additional funds as part of the American Jobs Act to prevent layoffs of teachers, police, and firefighters. To support infrastructure investment, the Administration also included funds in the American Jobs Act to modernize more than 35,000 schools.

Real Exports and Imports

Real exports grew 5.2 percent during the four quarters of 2011 after jumping 8.8 percent in 2010. As noted, the rebound in exports since the trough of the recession has been strong and reflects rising demand for U.S. goods and services abroad. Total exports rose at an average rate of almost 16 percent per year between 2009 and the twelve-month period that ended in November 2011, an increase that creates jobs for U.S. workers and puts U.S. exports on track to meet the President's goal of doubling nominal exports between 2009 and the end of 2014. Meeting this goal depends, in part, on healthy growth of the world economy; world growth, however, may falter in the near term for reasons related to the sovereign debt crisis in Europe. Maintaining robust exports is a key to building an American economy that can prosper in the global economy in the years to come (see Chapter 5).

Real imports also grew in 2011, expanding 3.8 percent over the four quarters of the year. The rise in real imports over the past year likely reflects the increase in consumer spending on goods, the rise in real business fixed investment, and the continued recovery in industrial production in 2011.

All told, real net exports—exports less imports—made a small positive contribution to the rise in real GDP over the four quarters of 2011, after subtracting from real GDP growth in the year-earlier period.

Labor Market Trends

The job market continued to heal in 2011, adding a total of 1.8 million jobs. The private-sector added 2.1 million jobs during the twelve months of 2011, while State and local government employment fell by 235,000. The growth in private-sector jobs was the strongest since 2005. Private sector payroll employment has grown in each month since February 2010, and lay-offs—as measured by the four-week average of initial claims for unemployment insurance—have come down considerably over this period (Figure 2-7). The four-week average of initial claims continued to recede through the end of January 2012.

Private-sector job growth during the current recovery has been similar to that in the 1991 recovery and faster than that in the 2001 recovery, as illustrated in Figure 2-8. As is typical, the recovery in jobs since 2009 has lagged the recovery in output. Growth in private nonfarm jobs in the current recovery began nine months after the business-cycle trough. By comparison,

Figure 2-7
Weekly Initial Unemployment Insurance Claims, 2004–2012

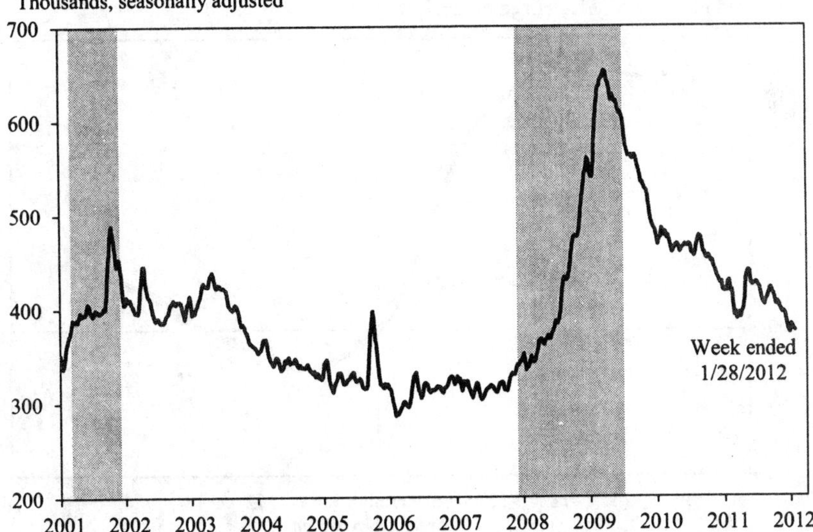

Note: Four-week moving average. Shading denotes recession.
Source: Department of Labor, Employment and Training Administration.

payrolls first began expanding consistently twelve months into the 1990–91 recovery, and sustained private-sector job growth in the 2001 recovery did not begin until 21 months after the official end date of the recession. Thus, although the 2007–09 recession lasted longer and featured job losses much deeper than those in the recessions of 1990–91 and 2001, recovery in the labor market began somewhat sooner.

Nonetheless, the steep rate of job loss during the recession has left the rate of unemployment high. During the recovery the unemployment rate receded from its peak of 10.0 percent in October 2009 to 8.3 percent by January 2012. The unemployment rate dropped by 0.6 percentage point between October 2011 and January 2012 (Figure 2-9). Other measures of labor market slack—such as the "U-6" unemployment rate published by the Bureau of Labor Statistics—have also declined over the past year. The U-6 measure includes in the pool of unemployed workers those who are under-employed or are marginally attached to the labor force, that is, would like a job but are not currently searching for work. The U-6 unemployment rate in January 2012 was a percentage point below its year-earlier level.

In addition to tracking the number of jobs added in 2011, other margins of labor market adjustment such as the workweek also contain important information about the pace of the recovery. At the business-cycle peak in the fourth quarter of 2007, the workweek for all private-sector employees

Figure 2-8
Private Nonfarm Employment During Recoveries

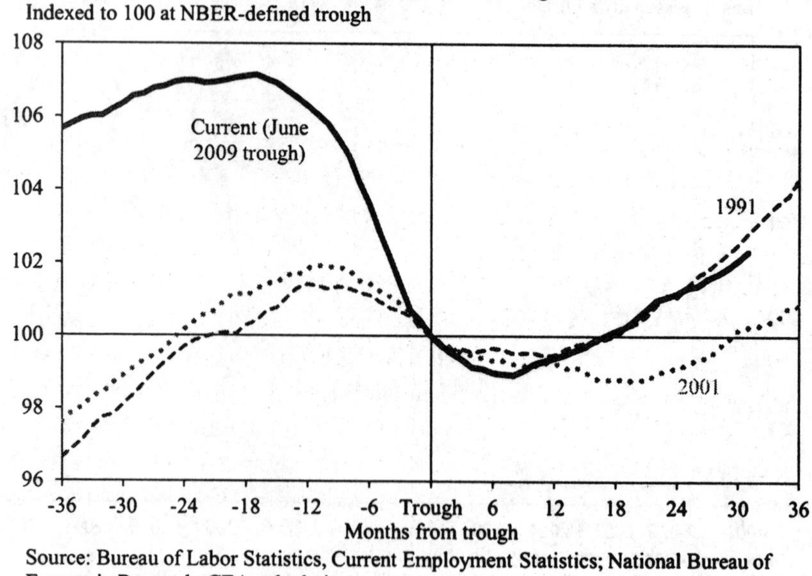

Source: Bureau of Labor Statistics, Current Employment Statistics; National Bureau of Economic Research; CEA calculations.

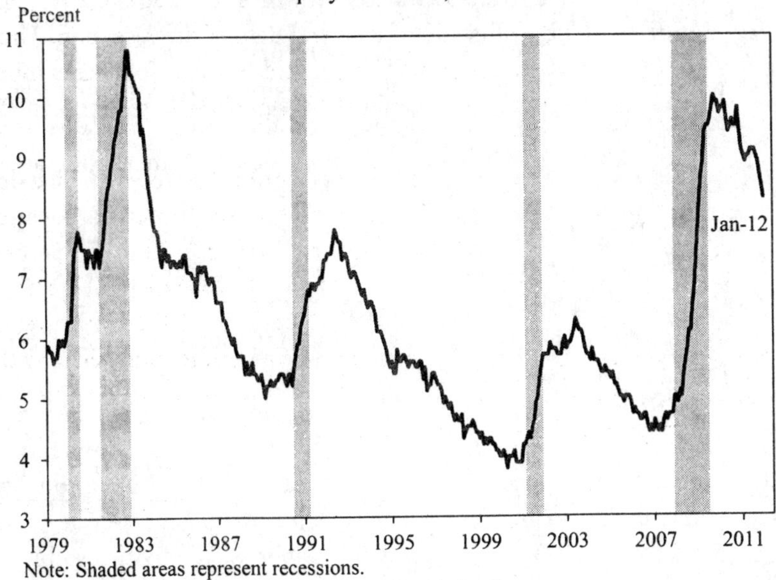

Note: Shaded areas represent recessions.
Source: Bureau of Labor Statistics, Current Population Survey.

averaged 34.6 hours. By the second quarter of 2009, it had shortened 0.8 hour. By the fourth quarter of 2011, the workweek increased to 34.4 hours, recovering most of the hours lost during the recession. A 0.1 hour lengthening of the workweek is roughly equivalent, in terms of labor input, to an increase in employment of more than 300,000 jobs.

Wages, Labor Productivity, and Prices

Hourly compensation rose at about the same pace in 2011 as in 2010. The employment cost index for private-sector workers, including wages and benefits, rose 2.1 percent over the twelve months of 2011, roughly the same as the year-earlier increase. Nominal hourly compensation in the nonfarm business sector—a measure based primarily on compensation in the National Income and Product Accounts—rose 1.7 percent during the four quarters of 2011, up slightly from the pace during 2010 but well below the average increase of about 4.0 percent in 2006 and 2007.

Labor productivity in the nonfarm business sector (that is, real output per hour worked) rose about 0.5 percent during the four quarters of 2011, a slower pace of growth than during the preceding two years. Averaged over the nearly four years since the business-cycle peak, labor productivity grew at a 1.8 percent annual rate.

Consumer prices—as measured by the consumer price index (CPI)—rose almost 3 percent during the twelve months of 2011, 1.6 percentage points more than they did in 2010 (Figure 2-10). The cost of food, crude oil, and many other commodities rose sharply in the first half of 2011, and some of these increases were passed through to consumer prices for food and energy products. Excluding food and energy products, the core CPI rose a more moderate 2.2 percent during the 12 months of 2011 after rising at an unusually slow pace of 0.8 percent in 2010.

Over the second half of 2011, overall consumer price inflation fell considerably as the price pressures from the earlier increases in energy and commodity prices waned. After rising at an annual rate of 3.8 percent in the first six months of the year, consumer price inflation fell to 2.2 percent between June and December.

Most of the inflation in nonfarm business prices during the past four years has been due to a rise in the price markup over unit labor costs rather than to rising unit labor costs. Hourly compensation has risen at a roughly 2 percent annual rate during the four years since the business-cycle peak, but this growth has been offset by growth of labor productivity also by an annual rate of about 2 percent during the same period, leaving unit labor costs essentially unchanged. Over the long run, prices of nonfarm business output rise in a roughly parallel fashion to unit labor costs, so the markup of prices relative to unit labor costs has been flat, although it has certainly fluctuated in the short run. As can be seen in Figure 2-11, this long-term property of the U.S. economy appears to have broken down over the past decade. The markup has now risen to its highest level in post–World War II history, with much of that increase taking place over the past four years. Because the markup of prices over unit labor costs is the inverse of the labor share of output, saying that an increase in the price markup is the highest in postwar history is equivalent to saying that the labor share of output has fallen to its lowest level.

The Administration expects consumer prices to rise slightly below 2 percent a year for the next few years, edging up to a 2.1 percent annual rate in the long run. The long-run projection is in line with the levels of inflation deemed by the Federal Reserve as consistent with stable prices and full employment, and only slightly below survey measures of long-run inflation expectations and the 5-year forward inflation rate implied by the yields on inflation-protected Treasury securities.[10] Moreover, because slack in the labor market remains, the economy has considerable room to expand without increasing price pressures.

---

[10] The Survey of Professional Forecasters projects the CPI will grow at an average annual rate of 2.5 percent from 2011 through 2020.

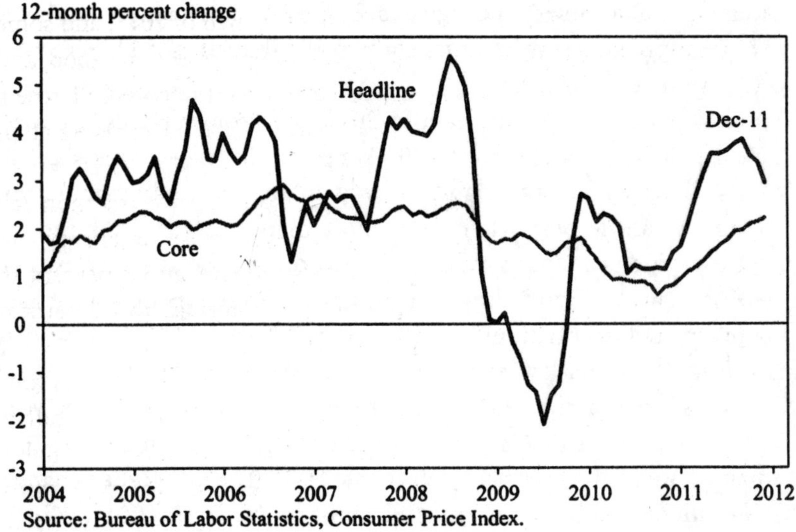

Figure 2-10
Consumer Price Inflation, 2004–2011

Source: Bureau of Labor Statistics, Consumer Price Index.

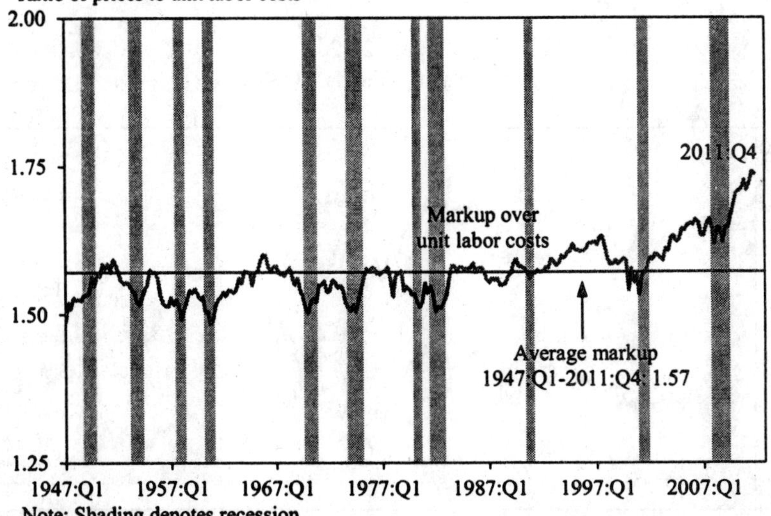

Figure 2-11
Price Markup over Unit Labor Costs, Nonfarm Business, 1947–2011

Note: Shading denotes recession.
Source: Bureau of Economic Analysis, National Income and Product Accounts; Bureau of
Labor Statistics, Productivity and Costs; CEA calculations.

Financial Markets

The past year was a volatile one for financial markets. Concerns that had arisen late in 2009 over sovereign debt in Greece and Portugal continued into 2011 and spread to several larger countries in the European Union, with effects that were felt worldwide.

Following a 12.8 percent gain in 2010, U.S. equity prices—as measured by the Standard and Poor's 500 Composite Index—were essentially flat in 2011. External factors weighed heavily on investor sentiment at times over the course of the year. After rising more than 8 percent from the end of 2010 through April, equity values plunged during the summer, reflecting the uncertainty surrounding the European sovereign debt problems and the protracted negotiations over raising the statutory U.S. Federal debt ceiling. Measures of market volatility—such as the Market Volatility Index (VIX)—rose sharply in mid-2011 before retreating near the end of the year. The VIX reached levels in 2011 that were about equal to those in mid-2009 but remained well below record levels in late 2008. The day-to-day changes in the S&P index exceeded 1 percentage point on 96 days in 2011, 20 days more than in 2010. In 2005 and 2006, swings in the S&P index exceeded a percentage point only 30 times per year on average.

Yields on 10-year Treasury notes were 1.98 percent in December 2011, down from 3.29 percent in December 2010 (Figure 2-12). Ten-year yields rose to a monthly high of 3.58 percent in February of 2011, as investors

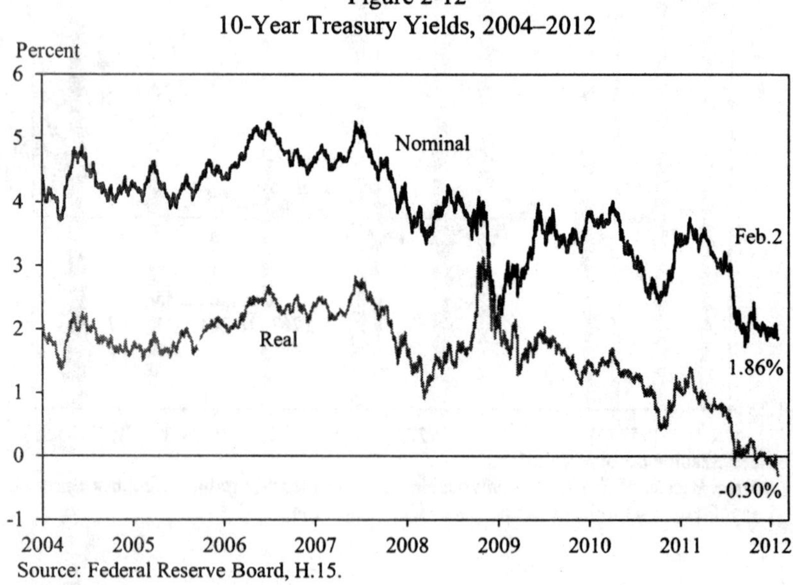

Figure 2-12
10-Year Treasury Yields, 2004–2012

Source: Federal Reserve Board, H.15.

elevated their outlook for the U.S. economy. Renewed concerns about sovereign debt issues in Europe, however, triggered a flight to safety that pushed down long-term rates, on balance, during the remainder of 2011. The Federal Reserve System's program to lengthen the maturity of the portfolio of their U.S. government debt also held down long-term rates. Over the final five months of the year, 10-year Treasury yields fluctuated around 2 percent, and real long-term interest rates at the same maturity, as indicated by the market for Treasury Inflation-Protected Securities, fluctuated around zero.

When the Administration's economic forecast was finalized in mid-November 2011, interest rates, both short- and long-term, were recognized as being in the low end of their historical range. Yet, in light of the Federal Reserve's August 9 announcement that "economic conditions … are likely to warrant exceptionally low levels for the federal funds rate at least through mid-2013," the Administration did not foresee any material changes in short-term interest rates over the near term. Thus, the Administration's projected path for 91-day Treasury bills, calibrated from rates in the market for federal funds futures, anticipated that these rates would remain extremely low until the second half of 2013. The FOMC forecasted in January 2012 that these rates would remain low at least through late 2014.

Small Businesses and the Recovery

Small firms—with fewer than 500 employees—account for about half of private-sector nonfarm employment. Between 1993 and 2010, more than half of firms in the private sector had 1 to 4 employees, and nearly 98 percent had fewer than 100 employees. Figure 2-13 illustrates that small firms experienced proportionately larger job losses than large firms during the recession and until early 2010. Similarly, the number of bank loans to small firms fell dramatically during the recession and—although it has stabilized since—still has not returned to pre-recession levels (see Figure 2-14). In 13 consecutive quarters between 2007:Q1 and 2010:Q1, respondents to the Federal Reserve's Senior Loan Officer Opinion Survey reported that credit tightened or remained tight for small firms (those with less than $50 million in annual sales) and that, since 2010, credit standards for large firms eased at a faster rate than for small firms.

Small firms depend more on banks for financing than do larger firms, in part because larger firms have access to other forms of finance, including public debt and equity markets, typically unavailable to small firms. Petersen and Rajan (1994) have documented the critical relationship between banks and small firms and showed that over half of financing for small firms came

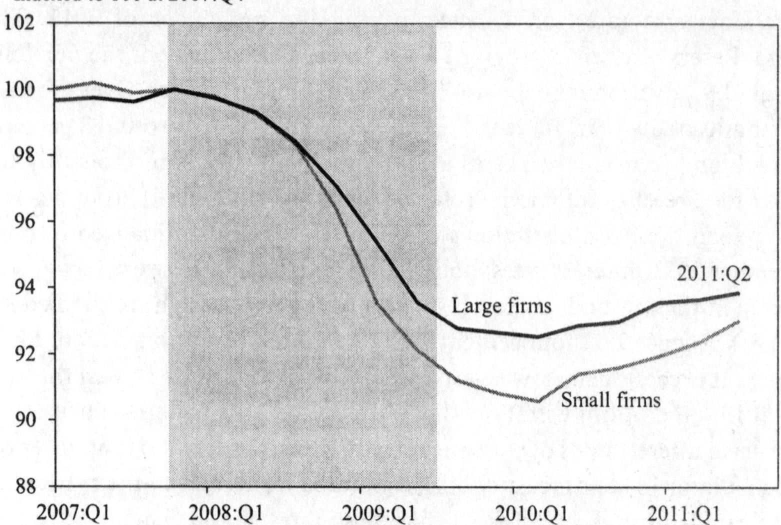

Note: Small firms have fewer than 500 employees. Shaded area denotes recession.
Source: Bureau of Labor Statistics, Business Employment Dynamics.

from bank finance.[11] Economists have modeled a link between the supply of credit and macroeconomic activity (Bernanke 1983; Holmstrom and Tirole 1997; and Peek and Rosengren 2000). Credit conditions have been shown to affect a variety of specific macroeconomic outcomes, including investment spending, inventories, and economic growth and development (Fazzari, Hubbard, and Petersen 1988; King and Levine 1993; Kashyap, Lamont, and Stein 1994; Levine and Zervos 1998; Rajan and Zingales 1998; and Guiso, Sapienza, and Zingales 2004). Gertler and Gilchrist (1994) find that smaller manufacturing firms respond more to money supply conditions than larger firms, and Kroszner, Laeven, and Klingebiel (2007) use cross-country evidence to show that banking crises negatively affect bank-dependent firms more than they affect firms less dependent on bank finance.

The credit-contraction hypothesis has been used to explain the steeper loss of employment in small firms. Until recently, however, the literature from the recent financial crisis has largely been unable to disentangle the contributions of credit-supply and aggregate-demand conditions. Duygan-Bump, Levkov, and Montoriol-Garriga (2011) use data from the Current Population Survey, Compustat, and the National Survey of Small Business

---

[11] Small firms in their paper are the smallest 10 percent of the sample measured by the book value of assets. Their sample, which is drawn from the Federal Reserve's National Survey of Small Business Finances conducted in 1988 and 1989, contains 3,404 firms with fewer than 500 employees.

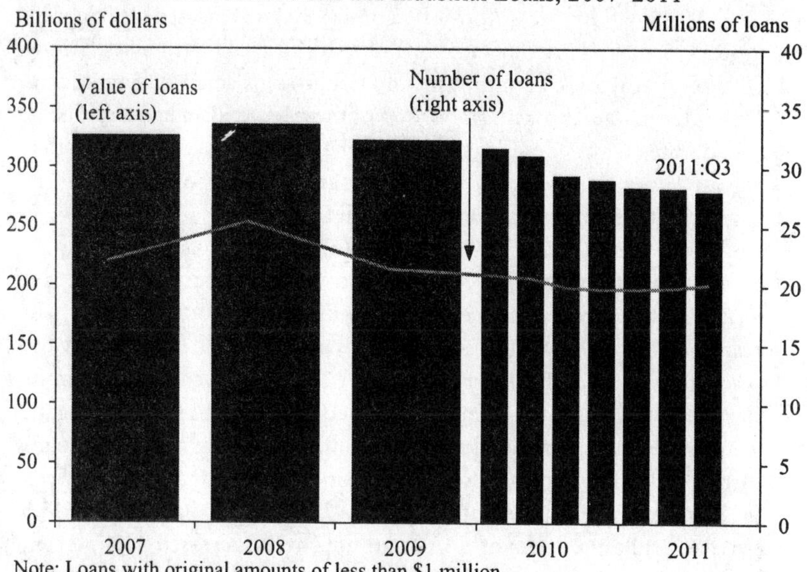

Note: Loans with original amounts of less than $1 million.
Source: Federal Deposit Insurance Corporation, Statistics on Banking.

Finances to separate the contributions of these two factors. They find that, as in previous recessions involving banking crises, following the crisis of 2007–09, the likelihood of becoming unemployed was greater in sectors that were more dependent on external finance. Further, among firms highly dependent on banks for financing, the likelihood that an employee will become unemployed is greater in small firms (defined as those with 99 or fewer employees).[12] The authors do not observe such a divergence in unemployment incidence in firms with low dependence on external finance.

Prior to the financial crisis, the share of lending to small businesses by the largest banks—those with assets of over $50 billion—had risen substantially (Corner and Bhaskar 2010). Since 2009, however, financing has been constrained and it remains so for small firms seeking funding. Simultaneously, the data show that other financial institutions—smaller banks, credit unions, and other alternative lenders—and government-sponsored programs have filled part of this gap. Between January and December 2011, Biz2Credit, a private firm that matches over 1.5 million small businesses seeking loans to nearly 500 lenders and loan intermediaries, reports that loan-approval rates by large banks fell 3.1 percentage points, while increasing 3.6 percentage points at small banks, 8.5 percentage points

---

[12] This evidence does not address whether the credit-supply conditions are due to factors related to lower credit quality.

Box 2-1: SBA's Role in Financing Small Firms During the Recovery

The Small Business Administration (SBA) was created by Congress in 1953 to aid and provide technical support for small businesses.[1] Many SBA programs seek to minimize the riskiness of small-business loans for lenders by guaranteeing a portion of these loans against default. SBA collaborates with federal agencies and the White House to ensure that at least 23 percent of Federal Government contract opportunities, worth nearly $100 billion, are available to small businesses.

Traditional SBA programs, the 7(a) and 504 loans, target small firms. These programs have been found to have a positive impact on local economic performance (Craig, Jackson, and Thomson 2005). In response to ongoing tight credit conditions facing small firms during the recovery, the Small Business Jobs Act of 2010 increased the loan limits for SBA loan guarantees. The limits for equipment and real estate loans were increased permanently and the limits for working capital loans through the SBA Express program were increased temporarily. Between FY2010 and FY2011, the number of SBA loans approved increased 12.5 percent, while the value of SBA loans approved increased 45.4 percent (see box figure). SBA increased overall lending supported to $30.5 billion in FY 2011, the highest ever lending year in its 60-year history.[2]

Recent economic research shows that new and young firms contribute disproportionately to job growth in the U.S. (see Chapter 6). The Obama Administration has created the Startup America initiative to support the role that startups play in economic growth and job creation. The initiative aims to accelerate high-growth entrepreneurship through policies that unlock access to capital for high-growth companies, create mentoring programs, accelerate lab-to-market innovation, and make government work better for entrepreneurs.

As a part of the Startup America initiative, SBA is improving access to capital for high-growth small businesses. The SBA has launched two new Small Business Investment Company (SBIC) programs, each seeking to guarantee an additional $1 billion in private investment within five years: the Early-Stage Innovation Fund for seed- and early-stage companies and the Impact Investment Fund for companies in areas of national priority, including underserved markets and emerging

---

[1] The Small Business Administration's definition of a small business uses guidelines that reflect, among other things, sales, employment levels, and sector of economic activity. These guidelines are available online at http://www.sba.gov/sites/default/files/Size_Standards_Table.pdf.

[2] Lending supported includes gross loan approvals for SBA's 7(a) and 504 programs as well as third-party loans that are made by commercial lenders as part of the 504 funding package. The box figure depicts the value of loans 7(a) and 504 loans approved, which will be smaller than the value of loans supported.

sectors, such as energy and education. SBA licensed the first SBIC Impact Investment Fund in Michigan in July 2011. The InvestMichigan! Mezzanine Fund, with resources of $130 million, is a public-private partnership between SBA, Dow Chemical Company, and Michigan Growth Capital Partners that will be managed privately and will focus on funding new and small firms with plans to expand their operations and create jobs. SBA also deepened its commitment to underserved markets in 2011 with the implementation of the Underserved Markets Initiative, which will disseminate SBA resources to youth, rural, veteran, low-income, and other communities.

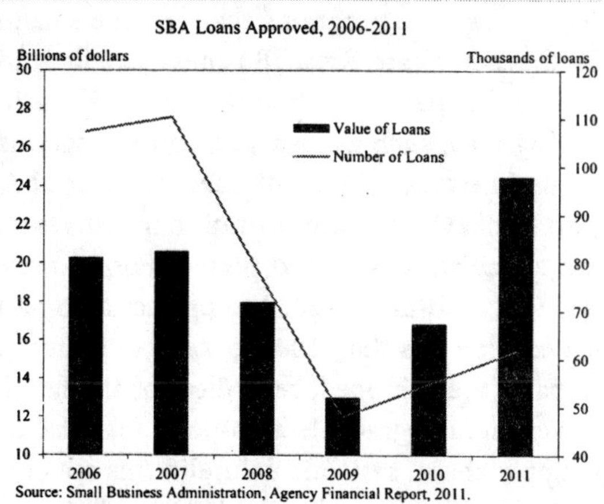

Source: Small Business Administration, Agency Financial Report, 2011.

SBA augmented its role as a coordinator of federal agencies in supporting small businesses in 2011. As is common after financial crises, small firms are experiencing difficulties managing cash flow due to adverse credit conditions. To improve access to working capital for thousands of small firms, in September, President Obama issued an executive order to institute the QuickPay program, which requires an agency to pay its contractors within 15 days and, at a maximum, within 30 days. As with the QuickPay program, SBA plays a coordinating role for the Small Business Innovation Research (SBIR) program, which focuses on small high-technology firms and includes 11 granting agencies. Evidence suggests that SBA and SBIR involvement make a difference to young firms. Between 1983 and 1997 awardees of the SBIR program subsequently had substantially higher employment and sales growth compared to a matched sample of similar firms (Lerner 1999). In December, Congress passed a long-term reauthorization of the SBIR program that will increase its funding.

at credit unions, and 12.9 percentage points at other alternative lenders, such as CDFIs, microlenders, and accounts-receivable financiers.[13]

In 2009, the Obama Administration increased the amount of capital invested in financial institutions and other entities to support small-business lending. This lending evolved along two lines: investing capital directly into financial institutions that provide small business loans and adding funding to new and existing programs that provide credit support to small business loans. In terms of direct investment that strengthened small-business lending, the Administration invested more than $11 billion in over 1,000 financial institutions, most of which were small banks but also including credit unions, Community Development Financial Institutions (CDFIs), and business loan funds. The programs that provide small-business credit support include the new State Small Business Credit Initiative (SSBCI), which is expected to channel $15 billion in new small-business lending, as well as existing programs, such as loan-guarantee programs housed at the Small Business Administration (SBA), the Department of Agriculture, and the Export-Import Bank. Other Administration initiatives also helped small firms gain access to capital at a critical period. For example, the Financial Stability program was modified in 2009 to protect auto parts suppliers, 82 percent of which employ less than 100 workers, to ensure that they would be paid for any parts they shipped, regardless of the fate of the recipient car company. Given the integral role auto-parts manufacturers play in the manufacturing supply chain, systemic failure in this sector would have had a substantial effect on the auto industry, the manufacturing supply chain, output, and employment.[14]

By the end of FY2011, marked increases in these capital-access programs were partly due to the introduction of two new programs administered by Treasury—the Small Business Lending Fund (SBLF) and the SSBCI—and increases in the scope of the aforementioned loan-guarantee programs. As of the beginning of January, institutions participating in the SBLF have increased lending to small businesses by roughly $3.5 billion over their baseline, and, in Fiscal Year 2011, SBA supported over $30 billion in loans. (Box 2-1 further describes the Administration's efforts to address credit constraints among small businesses through the SBA's loan-guarantee programs administered through bank finance and Startup America.)

The most recent data on the expectations of small businesses concerning financing and future job growth suggest that these efforts, along with

---

[13] Small firms in the Biz2Credit sample are firms with fewer than 500 employees and under $6 million in annual revenue. Loan-approval rates are based on a random sample of 1,000 firms in the Biz2Credit database reported each month between January 2011 and December 2011.

[14] It is estimated that intervention in the auto industry broadly averted a loss of approximately 1.1 million jobs and hundreds of small businesses (White House 2010).

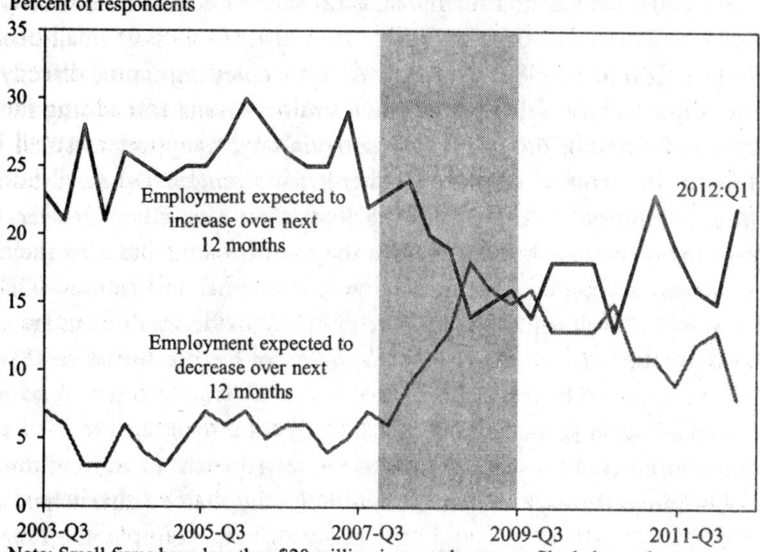

Note: Small firms have less than $20 million in annual revenue. Shaded area denotes recession.
Source: Wells Fargo/Gallup Small Business Survey cited in Jacobe (2012).

the ongoing economic recovery, are having a positive effect. Small-business owners who responded to the Wells Fargo-Gallup survey conducted from January 9 to 13, 2012, for example, report being more optimistic than at any time since July 2008. This sentiment is largely attributed to sharp increases in their expectations related to their firms' financial situation, i.e., revenue and cash flow.[15] Moreover, respondents' hiring plans have become more optimistic than at any point since January 2008, as Figure 2-15 illustrates. In early 2012, more small businesses expected to add new employees in the next 12 months (22 percent) than expected to let them go (8 percent). This is the biggest margin by which small businesses' expectations for increasing jobs have exceeded those for decreasing jobs since the start of the financial crisis in 2008.

THE LONG-TERM OUTLOOK

Looking ahead, the Administration projects that the economic recovery that began in 2009 will continue and gather speed (Table 2-1). In the economic forecast, which was used to estimate the FY 2013 Budget, inflation

---

[15] The Wells Fargo-Gallup telephone survey was based on a nationally representative sample of 604 firms extracted from the Dun & Bradstreet database of firms earning $20 million in annual revenue or less. See Jacobe (2012).

remains moderate, interest rates rise gradually, and the rate of unemploy-ment recedes. The Administration projects real GDP growth to rise to 3 percent in 2012 and 2013 after growing 1.6 percent during the four quarters of 2011.

The Administration also expects the employment situation to continue to improve in coming years: The Administration's unemployment rate forecast—also completed in mid-November 2011, when the latest-available reading on the unemployment rate was 9.0 percent for October, is shown in the first column of Table 2-2. The Budget forecast does not reflect the improvement in the job market since the forecast was finalized. Since that forecast was completed, the unemployment rate has fallen to 8.3 percent, beginning 2012 well below the 8.9 percent unemployment rate that had been forecast for the year as a whole. This should not be interpreted as a projection that the unemployment rate will rise: instead, it is the result of an out-of date forecast. The second, third, and fourth columns of Table 2-2 show a range of forecasts that were completed more recently so as to illustrate a plausible range through which the unemployment rate is likely to evolve.

Table 2-1
Administration Economic Forecast

	Nominal GDP	Real GDP (chain-type)	GDP price index (chain-type)	Con-sumer price index (CPI-U)	Interest rate, 91-day Treasury bills (percent)	Interest rate, 10-year Treasury notes (percent)
	Percent change, Q4-to-Q4				Level, calendar year	
2010 (actual)	4.7	3.1	1.6	1.2	0.1	3.2
2011	4.0	1.7	2.2	3.6	0.1	2.8
2012	4.6	3.0	1.6	1.9	0.1	2.8
2013	4.7	3.0	1.6	1.9	0.2	3.5
2014	5.8	4.0	1.7	2.0	1.4	3.9
2015	6.1	4.2	1.8	2.0	2.7	4.4
2016	5.8	3.9	1.8	2.1	3.8	4.7
2017	5.7	3.8	1.8	2.1	4.1	5.0
2018	4.6	2.8	1.8	2.1	4.1	5.1
2019	4.4	2.6	1.8	2.1	4.1	5.1
2020	4.3	2.5	1.8	2.1	4.1	5.1
2021	4.3	2.5	1.8	2.1	4.1	5.3
2022	4.3	2.5	1.8	2.1	4.1	5.3

Note: 2011-2022 forecasts were based on data available as of November 15, 2011, and were used for the FY 2013 Budget. The interest rate on 91-day T-bills is measured on a secondary-market discount basis.

Source: The forecast was done jointly by the Council of Economic Advisers, the Department of Commerce (Bureau of Economic Analysis), the Department of the Treasury, and the Office of Management and Budget.

Table 2-2
Alternative Labor Market Forecasts, as of February 2012

| | Unemployment rate (percent) | | | | Nonfarm payroll employment[e] (average monthly change, Q4-to-Q4, thousands) Feb-2012 |
| | Annual average | | | Fourth quarter | |
	FY 2013 Budget[a] Nov-2011	CBO[b] Dec-2011	Blue Chip[c] low-high Feb-2012	FOMC[d] low-high Jan-2012	
2011	9.0	9.0	—	—	146
2012	8.9	8.8	8.0 – 8.6	8.2 – 8.5	167
2013	8.6	9.1	7.4 – 8.4	7.4 – 8.1	220
2014	8.1	8.7	—	6.7 – 7.6	264
2015	7.3	7.4	—	—	284
2016	6.5	6.3	—	—	259
2017	5.8	5.7	—	—	251
2018	5.5	5.5	—	—	131
2019	5.4	5.5	—	—	101
2020	5.4	5.4	—	—	92
2021	5.4	5.4	—	—	97
2022	5.4	5.3	—	—	89

[a] The Administration Budget forecast (done jointly by the Council of Economic Advisers, the Office of Management and Budget, the Department of the Treasury, and the Department of Commerce) was based on data available as of November 15, 2011.

[b] The Congressional Budget Office forecast was completed in early December.

[c] The Blue Chip Economic Indicators for February 2012 was based on a survey of more than 50 professional forecasters conducted on February 6-7, 2012. The high-10 and low-10 forecasts are the average of the ten highest and ten lowest forecasts.

[d] The high and low end of the central tendency of the Federal Open Market Committee announced on January 25, 2012.

[e] Based on data available on February 5, 2012.

Source: Aspen Publishers, Blue Chip Economic Indicators; Federal Reserve, Federal Open Market Committee.

In early February, the ten forecasters with the lowest unemployment rate forecasts on the Blue Chip panel of professional forecasters projected that the unemployment rate would average 8.0 percent in 2012 and 7.4 percent in 2013 while the highest ten projected 8.6 and 8.4 percent for those two years. Similarly, the members of the Federal Reserve's Open Market Committee projected a central-tendency band of 8.2 percent to 8.5 percent for the fourth quarter of 2012 and 7.4 to 8.1 percent for 2013. And it should be noted that the CBO and FOMC forecasts are somewhat out of date in view of the encouraging January labor market report.

The Council of Economic Advisers' forecast for the gain in payroll employment was finalized in early February, after the labor market report was released showing growth of 157,000, 203,000, and 243,000 in November, December, and January, respectively. Looking ahead, the average monthly change in payroll employment is projected to rise from 146,000 in 2011 to about 167,000 in 2012. At this pace, two million jobs will be created during 2012, an increase from the 1.8 million created last year.

Despite shocks that slowed growth in 2011, the Administration expects an upturn in economic growth. With the economy now operating below its capacity and many resources still underutilized, we forecast that the recovery will continue to gain strength.

Growth in GDP over the Long Term

The growth rate of the economy over the long run is determined by the growth of its supply-side components, although growth rates over shorter periods can vary considerably. The growth rate that characterizes the long-run trend in real U.S. GDP—or potential GDP—plays an important role in guiding the Administration's long-run forecast, because actual GDP tends to gravitate toward its potential in the long run. Between 2011:Q3 and 2022:Q4—the projection period for the FY 2013 Budget—potential real GDP is projected to grow at a 2.5 percent annual rate.

Table 2-3 shows the Administration's forecast for the contribution of each supply-side factor to the growth in potential real GDP. The factors include the population, the rate of labor force participation, the employed share of the labor force, the ratio of nonfarm business employment to household employment, the workweek, labor productivity, and the ratio of real GDP to nonfarm output. Each column in Table 2-3 shows the average annual growth rate for each component over a specific period of time: The first column shows the long-run average growth rates between the business-cycle peak of 1953 and the business-cycle peak of 2007, with business-cycle peaks chosen as end points to remove the substantial fluc-tuations within cycles and to reveal long-run trends. The second column shows average growth rates between 2007:Q4 and 2011:Q3, a period that includes the 2007-09 recession and the recovery so far. The third column shows the Administration's projection for the 11-year period from 2011:Q3 to 2022:Q4, and the fourth column shows average projected growth rates between 2007:Q4 and 2022:Q4, a blended forecast period over which the effects of the recession and recovery are offsetting.

The working-age population is projected to grow 1.0 percent a year, on average, over the projection period (line 1, column 3), the same rate of growth that is projected by the Census Bureau. Over this same period, the labor force participation rate is projected to decline 0.1 percent a year (line 2, column 3), primarily because of longstanding demographic trends. The projected moderate decline in the labor force participation rate reflects the balance of opposing influences. The entry of the baby-boom generation into its retirement years is expected to reduce the participation rate in the

Table 2-3

Components of Actual and Potential Real GDP Growth, 1952–2022

Component	Growth rate[a]			
	History, peak-to-peak	Recent history, since peak	Forecast	History and forecast, since peak
	1953:Q2 to 2007:Q4[b]	2007:Q4 to 2011:Q3	2011:Q3 to 2022:Q4	2007:Q4 to 2022:Q4
1 Civilian noninstitutional population aged 16+	1.4	1.1	1.0	1.0
2 Labor force participation rate	0.2	–0.8	–0.1	–0.3
3 Employed share of the labor force	–0.0	–1.2	0.4	–0.0
4 Ratio of nonfarm business employment to household employment	0.0	–1.0	0.1	–0.2
5 Average weekly hours (nonfarm business)	–0.3	–0.1	0.0	–0.0
6 Output per hour (productivity, nonfarm business)	2.1	1.9	2.3	2.2
7 Ratio of real GDP to nonfarm business output	–0.2	0.2	–0.5	–0.3
8 Sum: Actual real GDP	3.2	0.1	3.1	2.4
9 Memo: Potential real GDP	3.2	2.5	2.5	2.5

[a] All contributions are in percentage points at an annual rate.

[b] 1953:Q2 and 2007:Q4 are business-cycle peaks.

Note: Population, labor force, and household employment have been adjusted for discontinuities in the population series. Nonfarm business employment, workweek, and productivity come from the Labor Productivity and Costs database maintained by the Bureau of Labor Statistics.

Source: Bureau of Labor Statistics, Current Population Survey, Labor Productivity and Costs; Bureau of Economic Analysis, National Income and Product Accounts; Department of the Treasury; Office of Management and Budget; CEA calculations.

coming years, but some of this reduction is projected to be offset as the labor market improves. The labor force participation rate may also receive a boost during the forecast period from the recent increase in the share of young adults enrolled in school. The share of young adults aged 16 to 24 enrolled in school rose well above its trend between January 2008 and December 2011, sufficient to account for the entire decline in the labor force participation rate for this age group over this period (Figure 2-16). As these young adults complete their education, they are expected to re-enter the labor force. Taking into account all of these effects, the labor force participation rate is projected to recede about 0.1 percent a year between now and 2022.

The employed share of the labor force—which is equal to 1 minus the unemployment rate—is expected to increase 0.4 percent per year over the next 11 years (line 3, column 3) but to be nearly unchanged, on balance, between 2007 and 2022 (line 3, column 4).[16] Because of the recession, the employed share of the labor force has contributed negatively to GDP growth

---

[16] To be precise, changes in the employment ratio reduce growth in real GDP by 0.04 percentage point per year between 2007:Q4 and 2022:Q4, because the unemployment rate in 2007:Q4 (4.8 percent) was below the level consistent with stable inflation, which is expected to remain stable at around 5.4 percent from 2007 through the end of the projection period.

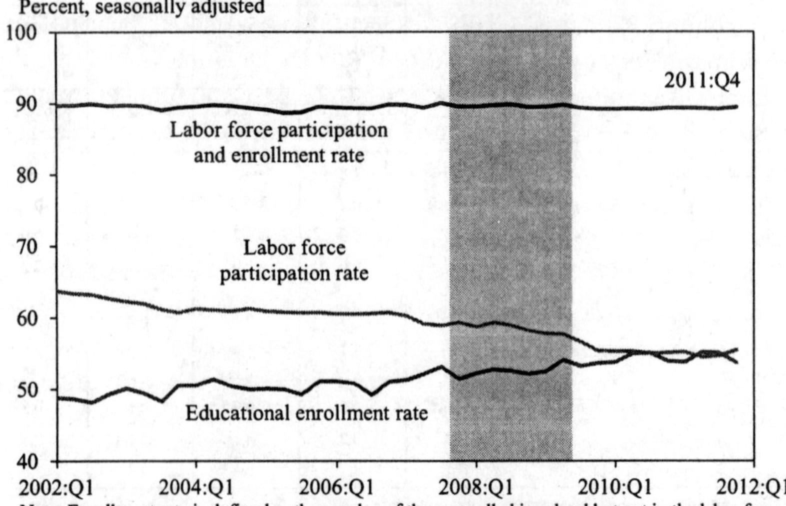

Note: Enrollment rate is defined as the number of those enrolled in school but not in the labor force as a share of the population. Shading denotes recession.
Source: Bureau of Labor Statistics; CEA calculations.

during the past four years, but the contribution is projected to turn positive during the projection period.

The workweek is projected to remain roughly unchanged during the projection period (line 5, column 3) even though it has declined 0.3 percent a year, on average, over the long run (line 5, column 1). The workweek is expected to hold steady as a natural labor-market adaptation to the anticipated decline in the labor force participation rate.

Labor productivity is projected to increase 2.3 percent a year over the forecast horizon (line 6, column 3), a slight increase over the average growth rate from 1953–2007 (line 6, column 1). The elevated rate of long-term unemployment poses some risk to the projection insofar as the human capital of workers may deteriorate with prolonged unemployment. On the other hand, higher rates of school enrollment among young adults in recent years, as noted, should contribute to productivity growth in the coming years.

The ratio of real GDP to nonfarm business output is expected to subtract from GDP growth over the projection period (line 7, column 3), consistent with its long-run trend. The nonfarm business sector generally grows faster than other sectors, such as government, households, and nonprofit institutions, reflecting an accounting convention that holds productivity growth to zero for government.

Summing each of these pieces, real GDP is projected to rise at an average 3.1 percent a year over the projection period (line 8, column 3), notably faster than the 2.5 percent annual growth rate for potential real GDP (line 9, column 3). Actual GDP is expected to grow faster than potential GDP primarily because of the projected rise in the employment rate (line 3, column 3) as millions of workers who are currently unemployed find jobs. Smoothing through the effects of the recent business cycle, real GDP is expected to rise 2.4 percent a year, on average, over the 15-year period from 2007 to 2022, just short of the growth rate of potential real GDP of 2.5 percent because the economy in 2007 is estimated to have been above its trend.

Real potential GDP is projected to rise 2.5 percent a year in 2007–2022 (line 8, column 4), more slowly than the long-term historical growth rate of 3.2 percent a year (line 8, column 1). The projected slowdown in real potential GDP growth reflects the lower projected growth rate of the working-age population and the aging of the baby-boom cohort into retirement. The effects of the financial crisis and the 2007–09 recession, in contrast, are expected to have little effect on the level of potential real GDP by the end of the projection, because the recession is not expected to permanently reduce any of the demographically-determined elements of long-term growth.

An important question addressed in the budget outlook, however, is how quickly real GDP will return to its potential level. In the Administration's 2013 Budget forecast, the U.S. economy catches up to potential real GDP in the second half of the forecast period. The historical record supports this forecast. The full recovery of real GDP during the decade following the Great Depression suggests that the U.S. economy can recover from a severe shock to return to this underlying trend level.

Conclusion

The U.S. economy continued to recover in 2011 from the severe effects of the financial crisis and the deep recession that followed. The rise in real GDP since the beginning of the recovery has been roughly similar to the trend in both following the 1991 and 2001 recessions, while private payroll growth came sooner and more swiftly than in the beginning of the recovery from the 2001 recession. The housing market began to show signs of life in 2011, and is likely to have a positive effect on the economy, though from a low base.

As 2012 begins, the recovery appears most likely to proceed at a moderate pace over the coming year, with the gains in output and employment increasing in subsequent years, as credit conditions continue to ease and confidence improves. Ensuring this outcome requires policies that both restore balance to the economy by increasing aggregate demand and guard against the types of excesses that led to the crisis in the first place. With millions of Americans still unemployed, much work remains to restore the U.S. economy to full health. Only a prolonged and robust expansion can eliminate the large jobs deficit that opened up during the recession, and the economy as a whole has considerable room to grow. The fact that private job growth has closely tracked the pattern of the early 1990s expansion is encouraging, and highlights the importance of sustaining the recovery.

❧

C H A P T E R 3

RESTORING FISCAL RESPONSIBILITY

When President Obama took office three years ago, the Administration was given an annual deficit of $1.3 trillion and a projected 10-year fiscal shortfall of more than $8 trillion.[1] The Administration has taken many steps to restore fiscal responsibility because large and sustained fiscal imbalances pose one of the Nation's greatest economic challenges. Policymakers are charged with the dual imperative of safeguarding the ongoing economic recovery while simultaneously ensuring that future generations are not burdened with excessive debt and that future government borrowing does not unduly crowd out private investment. In the near term, sharp deficit reduction serves as a drag on aggregate demand and threatens to disrupt ongoing economic growth. In the long term, persistent budget deficits can reduce national saving, raise interest rates, and discourage private domestic investment, even in an economy as dynamic and robust as our own. These seemingly conflicting concerns make deficit reduction a crucial but delicate endeavor.

Recognizing the economic risks associated with sustained large budget deficits, the Obama Administration has made deficit reduction a priority. In February 2010, the President signed the Statutory Pay-As-You-Go Act, a law that restored the commonsense principle of paying for permanent mandatory spending or tax changes—a rule that had lapsed or been waived during the previous decade. In March 2010, the President signed the Affordable Care Act, which both expands health coverage and directly addresses one of the key drivers of the long-term deficits, rising health care costs. Last summer, the President and Congress enacted a $1 trillion deficit-reduction package in the Budget Control Act of 2011, with a minimum $1.2 trillion

---

[1] In this chapter only, unless otherwise noted, budget deficits and spending programs are reported in fiscal years and tax receipts are reported in calendar years.

in further reductions scheduled to follow. As a way forward, the President has laid out a balanced plan that would—in combination with the Budget Control Act and other deficit reduction measures taken since the beginning of 2011—cut the 10-year deficit by more than $4 trillion, bring the budget into primary balance so that revenues cover all noninterest expenditures, and reduce debt as a share of the economy. These steps represent a radical departure from the budget policies of the previous administration, which included a series of sweeping tax cuts skewed toward the wealthiest, establishment of the Medicare prescription drug benefit program, and wars in Iraq and Afghanistan—all enacted without being offset by cuts or additional revenue raised elsewhere in the budget.

This chapter highlights the sources of budget deficits and public debt, describes projected budget outlooks, and outlines the Administration's deficit-reduction plan, a balanced approach that recognizes the need to prioritize spending initiatives while aligning revenues with current spending by asking the highest-income Americans to contribute to deficit reduction, as well as closing loopholes for corporations and special interests. The President's plan acknowledges that balancing the budget on the spending side of the ledger alone would hurt programs that help the middle class and those trying to get into it and put at risk other national priorities, such as investment in infrastructure and education.

The prospective fiscal imbalances have been decades in the making. Restoring balance will necessitate bold and difficult reforms in government programs. Although the Affordable Care Act and the Budget Control Act were the most aggressive Federal deficit-reduction legislation in years, much work remains to be done. Because budget projections show continued fiscal imbalances, it is critical for Congress to work with the Administration to return the Nation to a sound fiscal outlook.

DETERMINANTS OF CURRENT DEFICITS

Under current law and established budget policy, which are reflected in the adjusted baseline of the Office of Management and Budget (OMB), the annual budget would improve rapidly as the economy recovers, falling from $1.3 trillion in 2011 (8.7 percent of GDP) to $662 billion in 2014 (3.9 percent of GDP). Despite these projected improvements, the deficits moving forward are expected to remain at unsustainable levels absent additional policy actions. The fiscal shortfall is not primarily driven by countercyclical policies enacted in response to the Great Recession. Instead, recent deficits are principally the result of spending policies enacted during the previous administration, sweeping tax cuts initiated in 2001 and 2003,[2] and economic conditions. While temporary policies designed to increase aggregate demand, improve business investment, and jump-start employment contributed to annual deficits immediately following the financial crisis, they are less costly than the previous decade's spending and tax policies; most importantly, they are temporary emergency measures projected to have a minimal effect on annual budget deficits going forward.

As noted, spending policies enacted in the early part of the previous decade are one of the primary causes of recent deficits. Wars in Iraq and Afghanistan, substantially more costly than initially announced by the previous administration, added $1.3 trillion in military spending between September 2001 and December 2011. The Medicare Part D prescription drug benefit, enacted in 2003, has raised Medicare spending by over $250 billion through calendar year 2011. Increased interest costs associated with these programs have driven deficits even higher.

Tax cuts initiated in the previous decade, including those for the wealthiest individuals, have helped drive down tax revenues to historical lows. In particular, sweeping cuts in income and estate taxes, initially enacted in 2001 and 2003, have reduced revenue and increased interest costs by nearly $3.0 trillion between 2001 and 2011 (Ruffing and Horney 2011). In 2011, Federal tax receipts amounted to just 14.4 percent of GDP, far below the postwar average of 17.7 percent. Part of this revenue shortfall is attributable to temporary tax cuts designed to aid the economy and create jobs, and part to the slow rebound of wages, investment income, and corporate profits—the income base from which tax receipts are primarily derived. But several ongoing tax policy trends that long predated the financial crisis have also put downward pressure on tax revenue.

By comparison, policies enacted to revitalize the economy and stabilize the financial system have contributed only moderately to deficits over the past several years, with a substantially waning impact after 2012. The American Recovery and Reinvestment Act (the Recovery Act) of 2009 cost $833 billion overall, while the most recent Troubled Asset Relief Program (TARP) cost estimate is just $68 billion. Other countercyclical measures, including the 2 percentage point payroll tax reduction for workers, have also carried relatively small costs, which have often been offset by other budget measures. For example, the Temporary Payroll Tax Cut Continuation Act of 2011, which temporarily extended the payroll tax cut, unemployment

---

[2] These policies contributed to a historic gap between projected and realized budget outcomes. In 2001, following several years of budget surpluses, the Congressional Budget Office projected a cumulative surplus of $5.6 trillion between 2001 and 2011 (CBO 2001). No surplus was realized after 2001, and a cumulative deficit of $6.5 trillion accumulated between 2001 and 2011.

benefits, and certain about-to-expire Medicare provisions regarding physician payments, included offsets that made the bill deficit neutral.

Figure 3-1 compares the incremental cost of various post-2001 determinants of the deficit, including the wars in Iraq and Afghanistan, economic downturns, 2001 and 2003 tax cuts, financial stabilization measures, and economic stimulus initiatives. What the figure does not show is the path the deficit would have taken had the Great Recession persisted. The projections in the figure, based on Congressional Budget Office (CBO) data, incorporate both the direct economic growth owing to countercyclical measures undertaken by the Obama Administration and the subsequent projected economic recovery. If economic growth had turned negative instead of growing throughout 2009–11, or if the financial system had remained in turmoil, the tax base would have eroded further and the fiscal crisis would have been more severe.

The connection between unused countercyclical fiscal policy and stunted economic growth has been shown time and again. From the Great Depression, to Japan's Lost Decade, to international attempts to enact austerity measures during economic recessions, research has shown that in the absence of countercyclical measures, recessions become even more severe (Auerbach and Gale 2010). As painful as the past three years have been

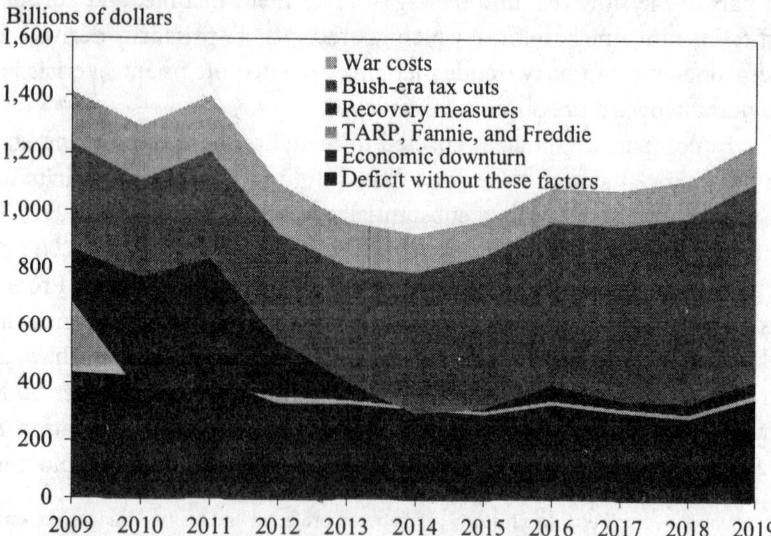

Figure 3-1

Selected Components of Deficit Projections: 2009–2019

Note: Based on CBO budget projections. CBO employs different economic assumptions and methodology than OMB. As a result, the projections presented in this figure may differ from those presented by OMB.

Source: Ruffing and Horney (2011).

for the U.S. economy, countercyclical measures brought the downturn to a quicker end and have reinforced the recovery.

While demographic trends and rising health care costs pose serious challenges on the spending side of the ledger, the failure of tax revenue to match Federal spending remains a primary concern.

Falling Effective Tax Rates on Upper-Income Taxpayers

Effective tax rates, also known as average tax rates, are simply the amount of taxes paid as a share of total income. In contrast, marginal rates are defined as the taxes paid on an additional dollar of earnings. Tax preferences, such as preferential rates for investment income or deductions for particular activities, can drive effective tax rates far below marginal tax rates. As a result, effective tax rates have varied over time with periodic tax reforms and a shift in the composition of income among high earners toward business and capital income. Several of the President's tax policy initiatives, including the American Opportunity Tax Credit, the expansion of refundable tax credits for families with children, and the cut in the payroll tax, have provided tax relief for middle-income Americans.

In order to isolate the effects of changing tax policy on effective tax rates, a useful exercise is to track effective tax rates holding income characteristics constant. Under this methodology, as indicated in Figure 3-2, effective tax rates on middle-income Americans rose slightly in the 1960s and 1970s, and then remained mostly flat between 1980 and the start of the Obama Presidency. Effective tax rates for the top 1 percent have varied moderately over the past five decades, peaking in about 1980 before falling back to lower levels between the late 1980s and the present. In stark contrast, the wealthiest taxpayers have seen their effective tax rate plummet over the past five decades because of changes in Federal tax policies. The wealthiest 1-in-1,000 taxpayers pay barely a quarter of their income in Federal taxes today—half of what they would have contributed in 1960.

Although trends in effective tax rates are attributable to a variety of factors, the tax cuts initiated under the previous administration had a notable impact. When the Economic Growth and Tax Relief Reconciliation Act of 2001 cut statutory income tax rates, high-income taxpayers benefited disproportionately, in large part because of the cut in the top rate from 39.6 percent to 35.0 percent. Two years later, in 2003, preferential rates on long-term capital gains and dividends were cut to historical lows of 15 percent, again resulting in large benefits for the upper-income taxpayers who realize the bulk of investment income.

Treasury data show clearly that high-income families benefited the most from the 2001 and 2003 tax law changes. For example, as Figure 3-3

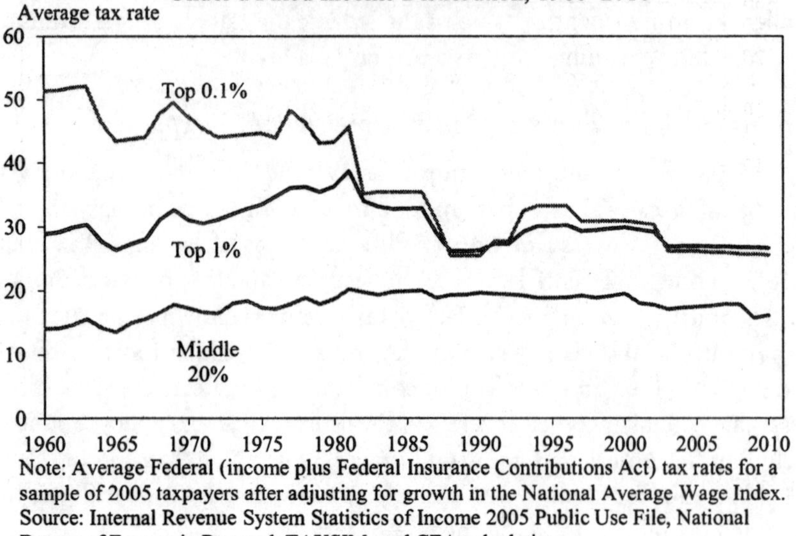

Note: Average Federal (income plus Federal Insurance Contributions Act) tax rates for a sample of 2005 taxpayers after adjusting for growth in the National Average Wage Index. Source: Internal Revenue System Statistics of Income 2005 Public Use File, National Bureau of Economic Research TAXSIM, and CEA calculations.

illustrates, between 2000 and 2008, income tax rates fell more for the top 1 percent and top 0.1 percent of the income distribution than for the middle-income quintile. Average individual income tax rates fell by 4.7 percentage points for families in the top 0.1 percent, but only by 3.7 percent for middle-income families.

To help reduce the deficit consistent with the notion of shared responsibility, the President's Fiscal Year 2013 Budget proposes to let the tax breaks expire for income above $250,000 a year, reversing a decade-long trend of unequal tax benefits for the wealthy, while making the tax cuts for those families making $250,000 or less permanent.

Heterogeneity in Effective Tax Rates among High-Income Taxpayers

The gradual drop in effective tax rates on high-income taxpayers is only part of the story. Effective tax rates on these taxpayers also vary widely because of the tax code's differing treatment of various sources of income, allowances for changing the timing of taxes paid, and various deductions and credits. For example, a high-income taxpayer who is compensated primarily with cash wages might remit in excess of 30 percent of income in payroll and income taxes, while a high-income taxpayer who receives a large share of compensation in the form of interest in an investment fund (known as "carried interest") would have a far lower tax rate.

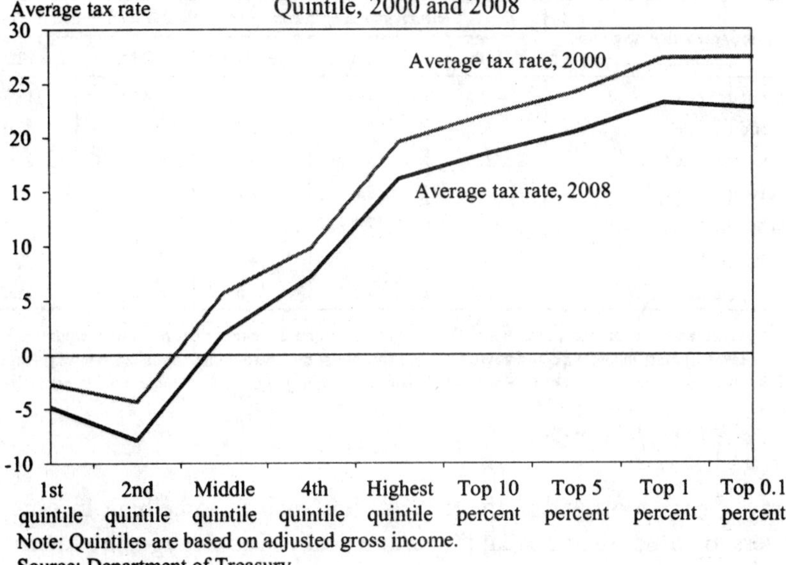

Note: Quintiles are based on adjusted gross income.
Source: Department of Treasury.

In 2012, among taxpayers in the highest income quintile, effective tax rates (including income, payroll, and corporate taxes) are expected to vary between 12.1 percent for those at the 10th percentile (in terms of effective tax rates) to 29.3 percent for those at the 90th percentile. That is, 10 percent of all high-income taxpayers are expected to pay less than 12.1 percent of their income in Federal taxes and another 10 percent are expected to pay more than 29.3 percent (the remaining 80 percent will pay somewhere in between the two rates). For the top 1 percent of taxpayers, the variation in rates is even starker. Among those in the top 1 percent, one in ten taxpayers is expected to pay less than 8.7 percent of their income in taxes, while another one in ten is expected to pay 34.6 percent or more (see Table 3-1).

The variation is perhaps most evident at the very top of the income distribution. In 2008, the most recent year for which data are available, 30 of the 400 highest-earning taxpayers (7.5 percent) paid less than 10 percent of their income in Federal income taxes, while 59 (14.8 percent) paid in excess of 30 percent.

Addressing the Role Of Exclusions and Deductions in Effective Tax Burdens

As noted, effective tax rates vary widely because of myriad deductions, exemptions, and preferences in the tax code. Moreover, particular streams of income are excluded from taxation entirely. But, as noted, the expanding

Table 3-1

Distribution of Average Federal Tax Rates

Family cash income group	Average rate at each breakpoint in the rate distribution				
	10th	25th	Median	75th	90th
Lowest quintile	−13.7	0.0	5.4	13.1	15.5
Second quintile	−8.7	0.5	7.2	17.0	20.9
Middle quintile	1.7	5.4	13.3	20.4	23.5
Fourth quintile	7.2	12.1	17.2	22.3	26.2
Highest quintile	12.1	17.4	21.9	26.0	29.3
Total	0.0	5.0	14.5	20.7	25.0
Top 1 percent	8.7	21.2	29.6	32.3	34.6

Note: Calculations assume 2012 tax law with an AMT patch and 2012 income levels, and includes individual income tax, corporate income tax, and payroll tax. For the lowest income quintile, the calculation of average rates and the distribution of average rates do not include families with negative income. These families are included in the total.

Source: Department of Treasury.

array of such tools within the tax code has enabled some high-income tax-payers to reduce their tax liability dramatically. Decades ago, the Alternative Minimum Tax (AMT) was enacted in an attempt to combat the low rates paid by some high-income taxpayers, but its poor design has caused it to fall primarily on upper-middle-income families from high-tax states, as well as on those with many children (Burman 2007). In addition, because the value of a deduction or exclusion is a function of a taxpayer's marginal tax rate, deductions and exclusions from taxable income are typically worth much more to high-income households—as much as two to three times more—than to low- and middle-income ones.

As a way to combat this "upside-down" system of tax incentives, the President has proposed several principles for tax reform. The President's proposed Buffett rule would ensure that Americans making more than $1 million a year would pay no less a share of their income than middle-income families pay—in particular, no less than 30 percent of their income—in taxes. In addition, the President has proposed tax reform that would ensure fair incentives for the middle class, helping to equalize the value of tax expenditures across the income distribution. (For information on how to evaluate effective tax rates based on their progressivity, see Economics Application Box 3-1).

THE FISCAL OUTLOOK

Without the pro-growth policies of the past three years, future budget shortfalls would be even more severe. Moreover, the policies presented in the Administration's Fiscal Year 2013 Budget significantly improve projected medium-term deficits relative to an adjusted policy baseline, and projected long-term public debt continues to rapidly decline over the course of the Obama Administration.

Medium-Term Budget Projections

Under the OMB adjusted baseline, medium-term deficits gradually decline as a share of GDP—projected deficits fall from 8.7 percent of GDP in 2011 to 4.7 percent of GDP in 2022, as Figure 3-4 indicates. This adjusted baseline represents a medium-term scenario in which current policies continue throughout the decade. The scenario includes the continued indexation of AMT parameters, extension of the 2001 and 2003 tax cuts, and extension of the estate tax parameters at their current levels, as well as a continuation of current levels of spending for Overseas Contingency Operations and physician pay rates under Medicare.

This improved fiscal outlook is due in large part to a recovering economy and the fiscal steps the Administration has already taken, including the Affordable Care Act and the Budget Control Act. Nonetheless, this adjusted baseline remains problematic and represents a fundamental imbalance between government spending and revenues. The President's plan to rebalance revenue streams and spending priorities is detailed later in the chapter.

Figure 3-4
Projected Medium-Term Budget Deficits, 2011–2022

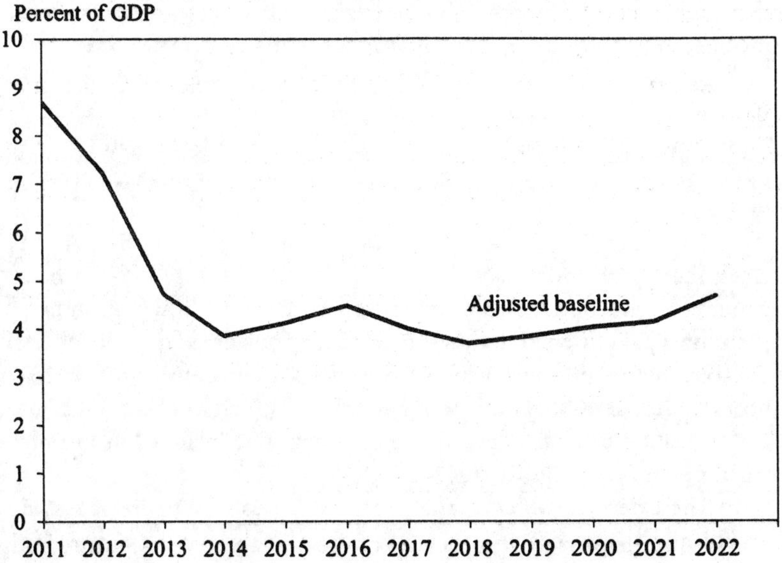

Note: See text for policies incorporated in OMB's adjusted baseline.
Source: Office of Management and Budget (2012a).

Tax changes are typically evaluated based on several key criteria, including efficiency, simplicity, ease of compliance and administration, impact on economic activity, and progressivity. Progressivity is the measure of how a particular policy affects households with differing levels of income or resources. Fairness is the essence of progressivity; many taxes—particularly income taxes—are designed to ensure a lighter tax burden for households with less income and lower ability to pay.

Economists typically define a progressive tax as one that has average tax rates that increase with income; under a progressive tax code, higher-income taxpayers devote a higher share of their income to taxes than other taxpayers. A progressive tax change is one that lowers average tax rates more for low- and middle-income households relative to others or raises average tax rates more for high-income households relative to others. For example, the recent 2 percentage point cut in the payroll tax is considered progressive because it reduces average tax rates more for low- and middle-income families compared to high-income families.

Other measures of progressivity, such as measures that refer strictly to dollar changes in taxes paid or to the percentage change in taxes paid, can be misleading. For example, a tax cut might reduce taxes paid by low-income households from $100 to $50 (a change of 50 percent), and reduce taxes paid by high-income households from $500,000 to $400,000 (a change of just 20 percent). Some might argue that this change is progressive because it reduces taxes paid by low-income households by proportionately more than it reduces taxes paid by high-income households, but this measure is actually inconclusive because it tells us nothing about the change in average tax rates. Along these same lines, metrics that focus on the share of taxes paid are not useful because they do not incorporate information on average tax rates by income group.

The definition of income or well-being can also be important when measuring progressivity. Some forms of compensation—such as employer contributions to a retirement account or health insurance premiums paid by an employer—may not be considered income for tax purposes but might in principle be considered as income for measuring taxpayer resources. Similarly, income transfers such as unemployment compensation or Social Security benefits could be included in income when measuring progressivity.

The extent to which the tax code equalizes income is expressed graphically by the Lorenz curve in the box, which shows the cumulative distribution of income before and after taxes. The 45 degree line represents a perfectly equal distribution of income; the closer the Lorenz curve to that line of equality, the more equal the distribution of income. A progressive tax code is one that shifts the income distribution closer to the 45 degree line. In 2007, the tax code helped to improve the progressivity of the income distribution, as illustrated by the graph, by making after-tax income more equal than before-tax income. However, even the after-tax Lorenz curve was well below the 45 degree line, meaning that the distribution of after-tax income was highly skewed towards the highest-income taxpayers.

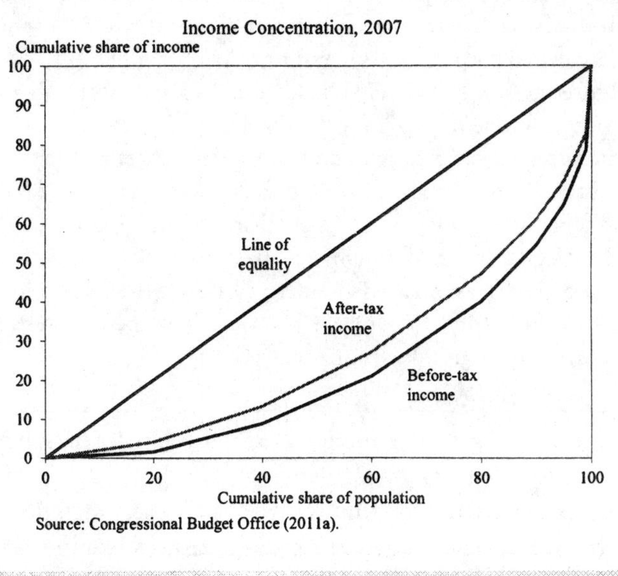

Source: Congressional Budget Office (2011a).

The Vital Role of Economic Growth in Future Fiscal Outcomes

Budget discipline is nearly impossible to achieve in practice without healthy economic growth. Budget outcomes are sensitive to weak economic conditions. Deteriorating economic conditions resulting from the financial crisis are one of the most important determinants of projected medium-term deficits, accounting for $3.9 trillion in expected deficits between 2009 and 2019 (as shown earlier in Figure 3-1). OMB (2012b) projects that a 1 percentage point drop in GDP growth in 2012, not matched with a subsequent boost in GDP in later years, would increase the deficit by $720 billion over 10 years. Similarly, CBO (2011b) projects that an ongoing 0.1 percentage point

> ### Data Watch 3-1: Data from the IRS Statistics of Income Division
>
> The Statistics of Income (SOI) Division of the Treasury Department's Internal Revenue Service produces informative annual statistics. The resulting information is an important input to the National Income and Product Accounts and has been invaluable for the evaluation of economic and tax policies, as well as for business decisions.
>
> One advantage of SOI statistics is that they are available for a long period of time: historical data series cover the period from 1916 to the present. Of particular interest are tabulations of selected items by county and ZIP Code, such as migration patterns. Extensive data also are available on businesses, including corporations, partnerships, and sole proprietorships. In response to increased globalization, for example, SOI produces regular reports on both foreign-owned U.S. corporations and U.S.-owned corporations operating in other counties.
>
> More than 14,000 detailed tables and regular reports are available to the public online through the Tax Stats pages located at www.irs.gov. Periodic special reports have examined topics such as pensions, foreign earned income, and noncash charitable contributions. Users may create custom tables using a table wizard application. Importantly, SOI painstakingly safeguards the confidentiality and anonymity of the underlying information it draws on. Statistics derived from the SOI provide a rich source of information for policymakers, business people, researchers, and public interest groups, among others.

decrease in real GDP growth compared to its baseline forecast will add $310 billion to the projected 2012–2021 deficit.

The link between economic growth and fiscal stability is, in fact, central to the rationale for countercyclical measures like the Recovery Act and the American Jobs Act. Although the countercyclical measures in these bills may impose an initial fiscal cost,[3] the cost can be considered a down payment on future economic growth, which in turn can lead to a more stable fiscal policy. Economic growth leads to a sound fiscal outlook.

Improvement in Long-Run Budget Projections

Although the need for long-run deficit reduction is evident, recent Administration policies have already helped to partially close the long-run fiscal imbalance. As noted, the Budget Control Act of 2011 reduced Federal spending by $1 trillion over the next decade by making cuts to discretionary spending, with an additional $1.2 trillion in deficit reduction scheduled to

---

[3] The President's proposed American Jobs Act is deficit-neutral; all provisions are more than fully paid for.

come. The Administration regards this legislation as a down payment on deficit reduction, and last fall proposed to Congress an additional $3 trillion deficit-reduction package that would, by the middle of this decade, mean that current spending is no longer adding to the debt, and that debt is falling as a share of the economy.

Health care legislation passed in 2010 is a key factor to gains in long-run deficit reduction. The Affordable Care Act addressed the Nation's most profound long-run budget challenge by limiting the growth in health care costs in several ways. (Chapter 7 discusses Health Insurance Exchanges as well as other provisions of the Affordable Care Act and existing health programs.) The Act includes Medicare payment reforms that will restrain spending growth by rewarding improvements in health care productivity. It established the Center for Medicare and Medicaid Innovation, which will fund and test new strategies for providing high-quality care more efficiently, and the Independent Payment Advisory Board, which will recommend policies to reduce the growth in Medicare spending, without limiting beneficiaries' access to care. The projections presented in this chapter assume that the provisions of the Affordable Care Act are fully implemented, limiting Medicare costs in the long run compared with previous law. The Medicare Trustees estimate these gains to be substantial, slowing the average long-range annual growth in Medicare spending per enrollee to just 0.2 percentage point a year above the growth in GDP per capita. This growth rate is significantly smaller than previous Medicare Trustee projections—a reduction that is largely attributable to the Affordable Care Act. These trends indicate that in the absence of recent health care reform, long-run budget projections would be substantially worse.

The Importance of Restoring Fiscal Sustainability

Reducing the deficit while the economy continues to recover requires a delicate balance. Looming fiscal shortfalls can seem a distant concern in the face of high unemployment and sluggish economic growth. But as a result of continued growth since 2009 and a gradual recovery from the financial crisis of 2008, the Administration maintains its view that short-term economic support and long-term fiscal responsibility can be complementary policies. Although reducing the deficit is a difficult task, it is critical to the Nation's future. As the debt-to-GDP ratio has steadily risen, economists have become increasingly concerned about the consequences of persistent deficits.

Not all types of deficit spending yield identical effects on the budget. The net economic effect of budget deficits depends critically on the characteristics of the underlying spending. Public borrowing to finance productive investment, including investment in infrastructure, technology, and education, can yield positive fiscal returns in the future. A more productive private sector will lead to higher profits and stronger wage growth, which will ultimately prove to boost revenues and reduce spending in later years. As such, government spending that makes the private sector more productive is distinctly different from spending devoted to consumption in the current period.

Prolonged fiscal shortfalls also tend to raise interest rates. Today's historically low interest rates may make that link between interest rates and deficits seem tenuous, but in typical economic circumstances, budget deficits drive interest rates higher by increasing the demand for saving. The consensus view among economists is that a 1 percent increase in the deficit relative to GDP leads to a 20- to 60- basis-point rise in interest rates (Gale and Orszag 2003). Higher interest rates depress interest-sensitive consumption (such as housing and durable goods) and diminish asset values and household wealth.

Of perhaps greater concern is the potential for prolonged budget deficits to impact domestic private investment via elevated interest rates. All else equal, higher interest rates can divert savings away from productive domestic investment towards government securities; higher interest rates also encourage domestic and foreign savers to increase their net investment in the United States. Thus, higher budget deficits can be financed by a combination of reduced domestic private-sector investment, increased domestic saving, and additional lending by foreign investors. Although there is no consensus among economists on the relative share of each of these factors, studies often assume that about 25 percent of the increase in the budget deficit is met with increased private-sector saving (Elmendorf and Liebman 2000) and about 20 to 40 percent through increased foreign lending (Engen and Hubbard 2005).

An active research agenda has considered how government debt affects the economy. According to research by economists Carmen Reinhart and Kenneth Rogoff (2010), "high debt/GDP levels (90 percent and above) are associated with notably lower growth outcomes." Several aspects of this finding warrant mention. First, although slow growth and debt are correlated, high debt does not necessarily cause stagnant growth. In fact, some have theorized that stagnant growth leads to higher levels of debt, rather than the other way around (Irons and Bivens 2010). Second, some question whether the 90 percent threshold is appropriate for the largest economy in the world, especially given the ongoing appetite of foreign and domestic investors for Treasury debt and the relative attractiveness of investment in the United States. Finally, some have argued that the key factor in measuring the impact of debt on the economy is debt held by the public, rather than total debt (including intragovernmental debt; see Data Watch 3-2 for further explanation).

Although the precise impact of government debt on economic growth is subject to debate, economists agree that confidence is paramount in the relationship between government debt and financial markets. A long-term commitment to sound fiscal policies will reassure investors that the government can service its debt. More importantly, sound fiscal policy and a commitment to living within our means and investing in the future will ensure better access to capital by domestic investors, as well as higher standards of living for future generations.

THE PRESIDENT'S BALANCED APPROACH TO DEFICIT REDUCTION

The President's proposed framework for deficit reduction, laid out in the Fiscal Year 2013 Budget, represents a balanced approach along several dimensions. Deficit-reduction measures are phased in gradually to avoid disrupting the economic recovery. Ineffective spending programs are eliminated, while tax expenditures on the Nation's wealthiest taxpayers are limited. Targeted investment initiatives, including those for education, infrastructure, and personal saving, are paid for by eliminating ineffective tax cuts to high-income taxpayers. Most importantly, the President's Budget charts a sustainable fiscal course, ensuring that the budget deficit will fall to a sustainable level in the next 10 years and beyond. In sum, the President's Budget represents a critical first step toward a stable and prosperous economic future and ensures that the American economy will remain competitive and vibrant for decades.

The cornerstone of the President's approach to deficit reduction—and perhaps the way in which it differs most from plans offered by others—is the balance it strikes between sustainable tax revenues and spending cuts. A deficit-reduction framework based on spending cuts alone would preclude the provision of basic protections provided to the Nation's most vulnerable citizens and investment in the Nation's future. The balanced approach of the President's Budget preserves the basic functions of the Federal Government. Medicare and Medicaid are strengthened, ensuring health care for the nation's elderly, low-income families, and individuals with disabilities. Social Security continues to provide a reliable, steady stream of income for retirees. The military continues to receive funding to serve American interests at home and abroad. Veterans continue to receive the support they

Differences in government accounting practices and in the types of assets held by central governments complicate the comparison of government debt across countries. These complications can lead to confusion over the most appropriate measure of government debt and the relative levels of debt for different countries.

One source of misunderstanding is the distinction between public debt and total government debt. Public debt refers to government debt held by private investors, including individuals, pension funds, mutual funds, and corporations. Total government debt is the sum of public debt and intragovernmental debt—government debt held in government accounts, such as government securities held in the U.S. Social Security and Medicare trust funds. Economists widely recognize public debt as the more relevant measure since it is government borrowing from the private sector that can be expected to interact with credit markets.

In most Organisation for Economic Co-operation and Development (OECD) countries, there is little intragovernmental debt. In the United States and Canada, however, budgetary conventions give rise to large accumulations of such debt. At the end of December 2011, U.S. debt totaled $15.2 trillion, of which $10.5 trillion was held by the public and $4.8 trillion was intragovernmental debt. Intragovernmental debt is similarly important in Canada. Including intragovernmental debt when making international comparisons leads to an exaggerated impression of government indebtedness in the United States and Canada relative to other OECD nations.

A second source of confusion is the distinction between gross debt and net debt. The OECD measures gross debt as total liabilities outstanding, including securities issued on behalf of the government (such as Treasury securities), currency, and liabilities to government employee pension funds. Net debt is measured as gross debt minus government-owned financial assets. The importance of this distinction varies across countries. In Japan, for example, the difference is stark: gross government debt equaled 220 percent of GDP in 2010, while net government debt was just 117 percent of GDP.

A final source of misunderstanding concerns the particular government sector being measured. The OECD presents measures of general government debt, which encompasses debt at all levels of government, including State and local governments in the United States, and central government debt. Both of these measures carry economic significance, but the distinction matters insofar as central governments generally are not liable for debt incurred by other levels of government.

deserve. Investments in education, infrastructure, and innovation continue to be a priority. Many other deficit-reduction plans fall short in these areas.

While the President's Budget makes and maintains critical investments in areas important to growth and competitiveness, it also institutes broadly shared sacrifices to reduce the deficit. The Administration proposes to achieve $1 trillion in discretionary spending savings over the next 10 years through the budgetary caps established by the Budget Control Act; $30 billion in deficit reduction through cutting or consolidating ineffective, duplicative, or outdated Federal programs; adopting a new defense strategy that cuts defense spending by 9 percent relative to the Fiscal Year 2012 Budget; limiting funding for Overseas Contingency Operations to $450 billion through 2021; a $60 billion fee on large financial firms; adjustments to the Medicare and Medicaid programs to make them more efficient and cost-effective; and a reform of the Federal civilian workers' retirement plan that saves $21 billion over the next decade.

As the President's deficit-reduction strategy cuts long-run deficits, it also supports the economic recovery. The cornerstone of this support is the American Jobs Act, one of the boldest pieces of pro-employment legislation in decades. At the end of 2011, the President signed into law several key parts of the American Jobs Act, including a short-term extension of both the payroll tax cut and extended unemployment benefits that were set to expire at the end of 2011. Extending the payroll tax cut into 2012 added an average of $40 to each paycheck of 160 million American workers. If continued through 2012 as the President favors, extended unemployment benefits will save 5 million job seekers from depleting their benefits and will create nearly 500,000 jobs through 2014 as workers spend their extra income. To bolster labor market conditions and spur near-term economic growth, the President proposes pushing ahead with elements of the American Jobs Act and with additional job-creating measures. Among those proposals are an initial $50 billion investment in roads, rails, and runways through surface transportation reauthorization legislation; aid to states and localities to rehire teachers and first responders; additional incentives for Americans to invest in energy-saving home improvements through the Homestar Bill; incentives to private industry to upgrade offices, stores, universities, hospitals, and commercial buildings through the Better Buildings Initiative; a 10 percent income tax credit to encourage small businesses to hire new employees and to increase wages; the halting of an automatic increase in student loan interest to ease the burden on students; funds to modernize at least 35,000 schools; a renewed Build America Bonds program to help finance the modernization and upgrading of America's infrastructure; reauthorization of Clean Energy Manufacturing Tax Credits to spur the creation of manufacturing jobs in the advanced energy technology sector; continuation of provisions to allow businesses to write off the full amount of new investments next year; and enactment of Project Rebuild, a series of policies aimed at connecting unemployed workers in distressed communities with efforts to rehabilitate residential and commercial properties.

The President's deficit-reduction framework also calls for tax reform that will simplify the tax code and lower rates, cut unfair and unnecessary tax expenditures, increase growth and job creation in the United States, observe the Buffett rule, and raise $1.5 trillion from the highest-income Americans to be devoted to deficit reduction. To begin a national conversation about tax reform, the President has offered a detailed set of measures to close specific tax loopholes, broaden the tax base, and allow the high–income tax cuts of the past decade to expire. With this conversation, the President's Budget begins to reclaim the Nation's fiscal future and restore fiscal responsibility by making balanced and necessary policy decisions.

CHAPTER 4

STABILIZING AND HEALING THE HOUSING MARKET

The recession that began at the end of 2007 is inextricably linked with the bursting of the housing bubble that had built up over the previous decade. The ensuing shock to financial markets, and the more than $7 trillion in lost housing wealth, prolonged and deepened the downturn and has been a headwind for the economic recovery. Although the housing market is showing signs of stabilization, the healing process is not complete in many parts of the country.

The bursting of the bubble was a culmination of a multiyear process of rapid growth in house prices fueled by excess capital flows into the United States. These flows were converted into home mortgages by various financial intermediaries using lax underwriting standards and channeled through the financial system with an increasingly complex web of mortgage securitizations. These trends, in turn, created unmoored expectations of continuous price growth that caused a spike in residential construction. The overheated housing market ultimately proved to be unsustainable, and the return to more realistic levels has been very painful for the economy. As this process continues to unfold, responsible policies are needed to assist the market in its transition to a new, sustainable equilibrium supported by a prudent and robust financial framework. In this context, healing the housing market requires laying the foundation for balanced and sustainable growth, while repairing and improving the housing finance system that helped inflate the housing bubble.

The effects of the drop in housing prices have been amplified by the uniqueness of housing as a financial asset class. Indeed, housing is the single most important asset for a majority of American households. Houses generate a steady stream of consumption services for their owners, as well as enabling them to send their children to local schools and use neighborhood amenities ranging from parks to retail stores to hospitals. They also create demand and jobs as homeowners furnish their homes and invest in their maintenance. By virtue of their tangibility, houses also serve as an important form of collateral for other borrowing purposes, notably startup financing for small businesses. Housing collateral attracts lender financing, making housing the most levered asset in household portfolios and closely linking the health of the housing market to that of the broader financial sector. Consequently, declines in housing wealth can have a far greater effect on the economy than equivalent losses in other financial assets, such as equities.

Setting the housing market back on track is a key step on the road to recovery. Yet housing presents several particular challenges, many of which derive from an array of institutional frictions in housing finance markets that have been exposed by the enormous scale and scope of home price declines and from very long lags in the adjustment in the stock of housing. This chapter highlights some of these challenges. They include a poorly functioning system for loss mitigation of nonperforming mortgages and effective disposition of mortgaged properties; inadequate origination of mortgage credit; and obstacles to refinancing, including the widespread phenomenon of negative equity. These deficiencies form a mutually reinforcing adverse feedback system in which negative equity raises the likelihood of delinquencies that often result in a drawn-out foreclosure process, eventually concluding with distressed sales that exert further downward pressure on home prices and thereby deepen the amount of negative equity. The large overhang of unresolved properties in distress, along with mortgage debt in excess of home value, further feeds this negative dynamic by depressing price expectations of potential homebuyers and lenders. Left unchecked, this dynamic creates a dangerous possibility for housing prices to overshoot and fall below their fundamental values, posing a difficult hurdle for sustained economic recovery.

Some have argued that the best course of action is to rely on the market alone to work out the problems of struggling homeowners, negative equity, and foreclosed properties through liquidation. This approach disregards the risk of overshooting the bottom, and it fails to recognize the many complex incentive conflicts that exist between purely private parties, such as homeowners, investors, and mortgage servicers. These conflicts and the need to recognize and allocate housing losses to various economic actors, present a serious collective action problem, the resolution of which by the market has been sluggish, at best, over the past several years. Perhaps most important, a *laissez-faire* approach also disregards the spillover effects of large numbers of delinquencies and foreclosures on local housing markets, the financial system, and the toll they exact on American families and the economy in general.

The alternative to sitting back and waiting for these enormous challenges to work themselves out slowly and painfully is for the Government to engage in a series of coordinated, measured, and multifaceted policy actions. This approach involves working in conjunction with market participants and housing regulators to address the lingering effects of the bursting of the housing bubble, as suggested, for instance, in a recent Federal Reserve Board white paper (2012). This chapter describes a set of existing and proposed policy initiatives that target many of the interlinked housing market problems. Some of these policies are pursued through Government agencies, such as the Federal Housing Administration (FHA), the Department of Housing and Urban Development (HUD), and the Department of the Treasury. Others are undertaken in conjunction with private investors, and still others are carried out together with the government-sponsored enterprises (GSEs), Fannie Mae and Freddie Mac, under the supervision of their regulator, the Federal Housing Finance Agency (FHFA).

THE HOUSING CRISIS AND THE INITIAL POLICY RESPONSES

After growing at a rapid pace through the early years of the new century, home price appreciation ground to a halt in the summer of 2006. This change in the path of housing prices triggered an initial wave of subprime mortgage defaults, and the resulting losses quickly propagated through the global financial system, bringing it to the brink of collapse and ushering in a deep recession. By the beginning of 2009, nationwide measures of home prices had declined for 30 straight months, falling by a total of nearly 28 percent. This drop in the national average masks significant regional variation. In some states, like Florida and Nevada, where prices had gone up the fastest, housing prices plummeted by 35 to 50 percent from their peak. Price drops in some other states were much milder.

Overall, as shown in Figure 4-1, the decline in inflation-adjusted home prices was unprecedented in the post-World War I U.S. economic experience in both its severity and its geographic scope. Some of the regional housing recessions—notably in California and New England in the early 1990s—generated sharp and long-lasting price declines, but neither was as steep and prolonged as the current episode. And during the Great Depression, the only other instance of nationwide price declines since WWI, much of the comparably-sized decline in nominal home prices was offset by a concurrent drop in general price levels, so the decline in *real* housing values was only about one-quarter as large as the one we recently experienced.

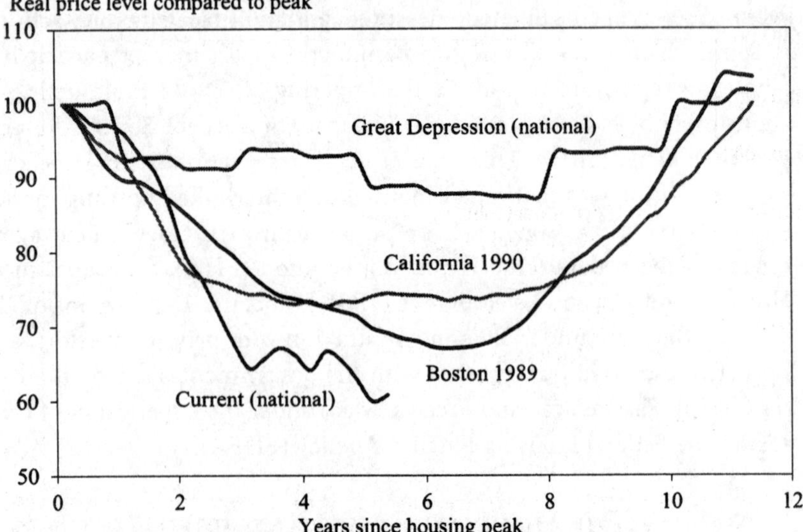

Source: S&P/Case-Shiller Home Price Index; the Great Depression time series from Shiller (2005).

The unprecedented and ultimately unsustainable nature of housing market trends before 2007 is further highlighted in Figure 4-2. The dashed line depicts annualized growth in real levels of mortgage debt per home-owner household between 1991 and the third quarter of 2011. Mortgage debt balances grew at a rapid pace from 2001 to 2007, one that far exceeded growth in real income during this period. There were many factors behind the escalating household debt. In part, it reflected rising home prices and growing household leverage driven by extraction of home equity and shrinking down payment requirements. As households continued to accumulate mortgage debt in the expectation of ongoing housing appreciation, housing was becoming less and less affordable, as evidenced by the price-to-rent ratio series (the sold line) in the same figure. After remaining in a narrow range between 100 and 120 percent for nearly two decades, the price-to-rent ratio accelerated rapidly to peak at 186 percent in the first quarter of 2006.

Once the bubble burst, falling prices and poor economic conditions resulted in steep increases in delinquencies and foreclosures across a broad spectrum of American homeowners. By the first quarter of 2009, non-performance rates among prime borrowers rose nearly threefold relative to their level in the first quarter of 2005 (from 2.2 to 6.1 percent), while those for subprime loans spiked to nearly 25 percent, from 10.6 percent four years earlier. About 1.7 million homes were at some stage of the foreclosure

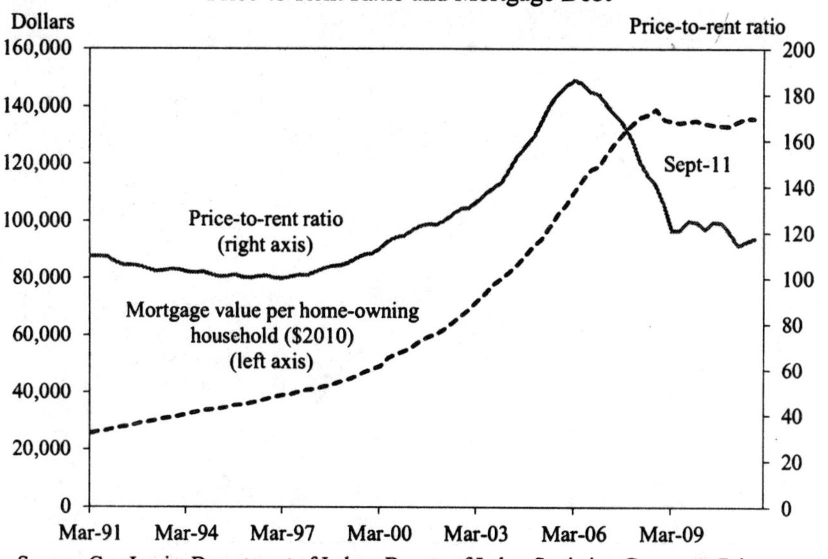

Source: CoreLogic; Department of Labor; Bureau of Labor Statistics, Consumer Price Index.

process, and nearly 7 percent of total mortgage debt was seriously delinquent (more than 90 days past due). Market participants were deeply pessimistic about the future path for housing prices—the Case-Shiller index futures contracts traded in January of 2009 suggested that house prices were expected to fall an additional 10 percent by September 2010 (the dashed line in Figure 4-3). Other housing futures contracts traded in over-the-counter markets (not shown) were even more downbeat.

Initial Policy Responses to the Crisis

The broad meltdown in the financial sector called for a series of emergency responses by the Executive Branch, the Legislative Branch, and the Federal Reserve. The Federal Reserve undertook a series of aggressive monetary policy actions and launched a number of programs to support liquidity and lending activity in key financial markets. Congress passed the Housing and Economic Recovery Act (HERA) in July of 2008, which established the Federal Housing Finance Agency, the new regulator of the GSEs with greatly expanded powers. The HERA was followed by the Emergency Economic Stabilization Act in October of 2008, which established the Troubled Asset Relief Program.

In one of its first major policy actions, the Obama Administration implemented the Financial Stability Plan in February 2009. A key part of

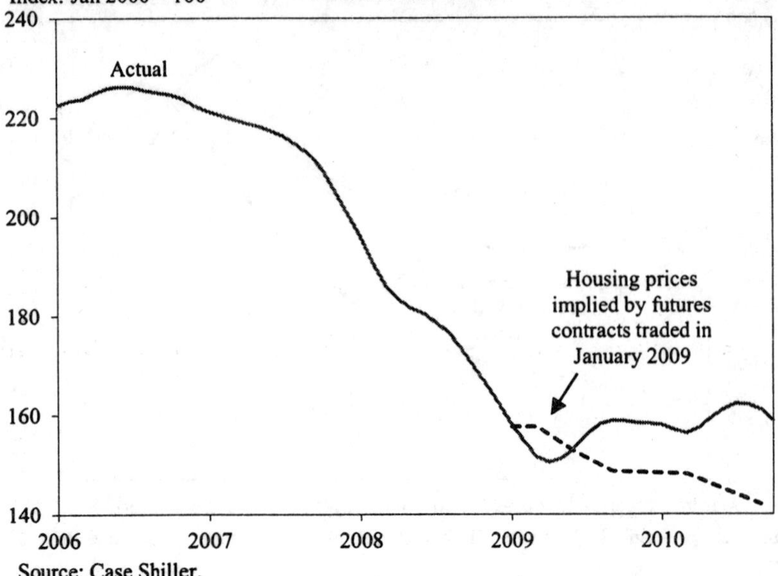

Source: Case Shiller.

the plan focused on maintaining the flow of housing credit and helping responsible homeowners stay in their homes through the Making Home Affordable (MHA) program. In particular, the Treasury Department made an increased funding commitment to Fannie Mae and Freddie Mac, which had been placed in conservatorship six months earlier. The Federal Reserve, which had previously announced a program to purchase up to $600 billion of GSE debt and mortgage-backed securities, expanded the planned size of the program to $1.75 trillion in March 2009. These actions have resulted in economically meaningful and long-lasting reductions in mortgage interest rates (Gagnon et al. 2010) and credit availability (Fuster and Willen 2010).

To help responsible households take advantage of these lower rates, the MHA included the Home Affordable Refinance Program (HARP), which was intended to enhance refinancing opportunities for borrowers who had insufficient equity in their homes. While HARP helped homeowners to hold onto their homes through more sustainable mortgages, other components of the MHA focused on restructuring mortgages of borrowers struggling to stay current on their loans. In particular, the Home Affordable Modification Program (HAMP) provided a streamlined approach to modification of delinquent loans and offered monetary incentives and procedural safe harbors to industry participants. To help communities manage the destruction caused when the housing market collapsed, the American Recovery and

Reinvestment Act of 2009 (the Recovery Act) provided additional support to the housing market by extending HUD's Neighborhood Stabilization Program, which began under HERA. This program allocated funds to state and local governments and nonprofit organizations to mitigate foreclosures and to pursue innovative local approaches to deal with the economic effects of abandoned properties. The Recovery Act extended the first-time home-buyer credit established under HERA and increased it to $8,000. This program was extended further by the Workers, Homeownership, and Business Assistance Act of 2009.

To date, these initial responses to the housing crisis have assisted several million households. The most recent housing scorecard released by the Department of the Treasury and HUD indicated that, as of December 2011, more than 930,000 homeowners had received permanent modifications under HAMP, putting the program on pace to reach the 1 million threshold early in 2012. Of equal importance, HAMP provided a template for major servicers to follow in conducting their own modifications outside of the program. To date, servicers have undertaken nearly 2.7 million so-called "proprietary" modifications, many of which would not have occurred without the standards established by HAMP. The scorecard also highlights 998,000 loans refinanced though HARP, as well as nearly 1.2 million bor-rowers helped through various FHA loss mitigation interventions. These programs have faced challenges from a number of structural problems in housing markets. These problems include incentive conflicts that arose when loan servicing was separated from loan ownership in mortgage secu-ritizations, as well as uncertainty about legal liability in loan origination and loss mitigation practices. These problems have been greatly exacerbated by erosion in collateral values, which have increasingly fallen below the value of associated loans and put more than one in five mortgage borrowers "under water." These dramatic declines in collateral necessitate eventual recognition of economic losses and allocation of such losses to various economic actors. As policymakers have increasingly focused on addressing these deficiencies, each of these original MHA programs has undergone substantial modifica-tion, described more fully in the following sections.

Negative Equity: An Unprecedented and Pervasive Problem

As noted, widespread declines in housing prices resulted in more than a $7 trillion fall in aggregate housing wealth. These losses were borne to at least some extent by most homeowners. For some homeowners, however, falling prices not only wiped out their housing wealth in its entirety but also pushed the value of their homes below the value of outstanding mortgages. The resulting "negative" equity, which is estimated to total $700 billion, has become one of the legacy hallmarks of the housing price bubble. This negative equity resulted from large home price declines combined with a number of other factors. According to recent estimates, as many as 10.7 million (or 22 percent of) borrowers are under water. The aggregate negative equity is unequally distributed across the nation. Six states with the highest incidence of negative equity—Arizona, California, Florida, Georgia, Michigan, and Nevada—account for more than half of all underwater borrowers and of the aggregate amount of negative equity (Figure 4-4). All of these states have experienced steep declines in house prices.

Negative equity has been associated with a number of problems over and above those caused by the more widespread loss in housing wealth. Underwater borrowers find it difficult, if not impossible, to take advantage of record low interest rates through refinancing, because lenders and investors are unwilling to take on uncollateralized credit risk. The inability to refinance prevents households from lowering their monthly mortgage payments. It also undermines the effectiveness of monetary policy that aims to lower borrowing costs to businesses and households and thus encourage greater economic activity. (For more on the decision to refinance, see Economics Application Box 4-1).

Underwater households have weakened incentives to invest in their property, since the expected gains from their investment are likely going to be absorbed by the lender. As a result, underwater households underinvest

Figure 4-4
The Distribution of Underwater Mortgages By State, 2011

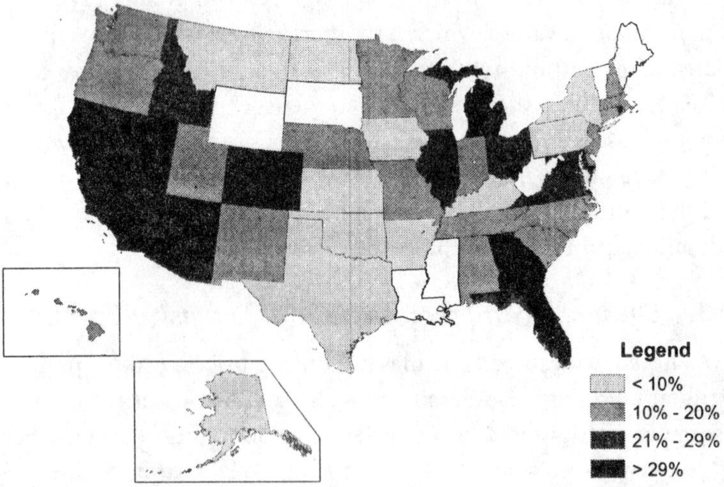

Source: CoreLogic.

in home improvements and maintenance, which leads to the overall decline in the quality of the nation's housing stock (Melzer 2010).

Negative equity has also been associated with heightened realized default rates. Several recent academic and industry studies have found that the higher their negative equity, the more likely households are to become delinquent (Bajari, Chu, and Park 2010; Elul et al. 2010). Recent work by Federal Reserve Board economists (Bhutta, Dokko, and Shan 2010) shows that a household's equity position amplifies the effect of unemployment shocks on default and that this interaction grows in strength with the degree of negative equity. (For more on data challenges in evaluating the financial situation of homeowners, see Data Watch 4-1). Household delinquency and the ensuing foreclosures are very costly, as they disrupt the social fabric of neighborhoods and cause lenders to engage in an expensive and drawn-out process of liquidation. Moreover, foreclosures not only lower the value of the foreclosed property itself; they also have a sizable spillover effect on valuations of neighboring homes. According f to a recent academic study (Campbell, Giglio, and Pathak 2011), each foreclosure within a 0.1 mile radius of a given house lowers its predicted sale price by 7.2 percent.

Negative equity also poses a roadblock for efficient reallocation of housing resources. Families naturally buy and sell houses over their life cycle and in response to shocks such as illness or divorce. The necessity to write a sizable check to the lender upon sale makes it effectively impossible for liquidity-constrained households to trade their houses without credit-impairing actions such as delinquency; deed-in-lieu, in which a borrower returns the property to the lender; or short sale, in which a house is sold for less than the balance of debts secured by the property. Negative equity also has the potential to limit underwater borrowers' ability to pursue employ-ment opportunities in other geographic areas. The empirical evidence to date, however, has largely suggested that the adverse effect of negative equity on labor mobility—the so-called "house lock effect"—is fairly limited.

MACROECONOMIC EFFECTS OF HOUSING MARKET WEAKNESS

The housing sector plays an important role in determining the health of the broader economy. Two aspects of this relationship are particularly important—the effect of housing wealth on household consumption and the direct contribution of residential construction to gross domestic product (GDP).

The computation and comparison of net present values is the main idea behind a broad range of online calculators designed to answer the question of whether refinancing makes sense. An example can be found on Jack Guttentag's Mortgage Professor's Website at http://www.mtgprofessor.com/calculators/Calculator3a.html. Some mortgage brokers are fond of making use of simple rules of thumb as a shortcut for using the NPV approach. For example, they may suggest that "the new mortgage rate has to be 1 percentage point lower to justify refinancing with typical closing costs." Recent estimates of such rule-of-thumb threshold differences in interest rates have varied between 1 and 1.5 percentage points.

One often overlooked cost of refinancing has not yet been mentioned. By refinancing today, one generally forgoes the opportunity to refinance in the future if interest rates were to drop a bit further. Suppose you determine that refinancing a 5.75 percent loan into a 4.5 percent loan is advantageous from an NPV standpoint. Then refinancing the original loan into a 4.25 percent loan would be even more beneficial, but refinancing from a 4.5 percent loan would not. This difference between payments at 4.5 percent and 4.25 percent is essentially the value of the forgone option to delay refinancing. The value of preserving this option has fluctuated over time, because it clearly depends on the volatility of interest rates, the economic outlook, and the ability to maintain access to credit markets-a nontrivial concern for today's borrowers.

In recent work, Sumit Agarwal, John Driscoll and David Laibson (2007) calculated the optimal interest rate differential at which to refinance that explicitly takes into account the aforementioned option value (these calculations can be found at http://zwicke.nber.org/refinance/). Take, for example, a family that plans to stay in their house for 10 years, has a $250,000 mortgage at 6 percent interest rate and has a marginal tax rate of 28 percent. For this family, assuming an upfront fee of 1 percentage point of mortgage value (1 point) and cash closing costs of $2,000, refinancing is optimal if the interest rate on the new mortgage is 4.6 percent or less. Unlike the simple rule of thumb, this calculation takes into account family expectations of the future inflation rate, interest rate volatility, and how long they plan to stay in the house—the option value determinants—which affect the ultimate recommendation.

Consumption Effects

The standard approach in economics has been to assume that households consume about the same fraction of the increase in their wealth each year, regardless of its source. Numerous econometric studies have come up with a range of estimates that relate changes in household consumption to changes in wealth (Poterba 2000). Although there is no single agreed-upon value, the consensus range is fairly narrow—the fraction of each additional dollar in wealth consumed in a given year (what economists call the marginal propensity to consume out of wealth, or MPC) is estimated to be roughly between three and five cents. Applying the lower of these estimates to the $7.25 trillion in housing wealth losses to date implies consumption losses of $218 billion a year, or 1.5 percent of GDP. Under standard Okun's law assumptions, this GDP impact, in turn, translates into a 0.75 percentage point increase in the unemployment rate. The severity of losses experienced during the recession that began in December of 2007 in both national output and in labor markets makes these estimates appear too small.

One of the possible explanations for this puzzle may be that declines in housing wealth have a more profound effect on consumption than equivalent declines in other forms of wealth. Case, Quigley, and Shiller (2005, 2011) find strong empirical evidence in support of this hypothesis by exploiting substantial variation across states in house price paths and holdings of equity assets. In particular, they relate quarterly growth rates in house prices and equity holdings to quarterly growth rates in state-level retail sales and find that the consumption response is more sensitive to changes in housing wealth than to changes in stock market wealth. It is noteworthy that both the level of the response and the difference between sensitivities to financial and housing wealth shocks increase substantially once the recent experience is incorporated in the data (the 2011 study includes data from 2000 through 2010.)

Why would households respond more to housing wealth shocks? Part of the likely answer has to do with the very different distributions of ownership of various financial asset classes. Most financial assets other than liquidity-restricted retirement plans are heavily concentrated at the top of the wealth distribution. In contrast, holdings of housing assets are much more uniformly spread across different wealth, income, and demographic strata. At the peak of the housing market in the third quarter of 2006, home ownership stood near a record high at 69 percent. Although home ownership rates among African American and Hispanic households were noticeably lower (49 percent and 50 percent, respectively), they vastly exceed ownership rates of all other financial assets other than bank accounts for these two groups. Perhaps more important, housing assets make up a much

Data Watch 4-1: Need for a Comprehensive Source of Data on Mortgage Debt and Performance

There are currently four basic sources of loan-level data on mortgage debt: the Home Mortgage Disclosure Act (HMDA) database, data reported by mortgage servicers, credit bureau data, and public records data. Each of these sources provides insight about mortgage holdings, but the existing system is inadequate for measuring the extent and ownership of financial obligations backed by residential real estate.

The HMDA database contains data required to be publicly reported for all mortgages. It is useful for measuring long-term trends in mortgage application volumes and originations, but contains little information on loan terms or performance following origination. Further, HMDA data are released only annually with a significant lag. In contrast, proprietary data sets from loan servicers, such as Lender Processing Services (LPS) and CoreLogic, have useful information on loan characteristics and performance but underrepresent certain loan and investor types. They also have little detail on borrower income or credit scores following origination and lack information on other debt obligations, including those collateralized by the same real estate.

The credit bureau data track borrower credit scores and performance on multiple debt obligations over time, but tell us little about loan terms and mortgage contract type and nothing about the employment status and current income of homeowners. Public records contain legal notices of property-related transactions, such as mortgage origination and foreclosure, but they contain little information beyond the reason for creating the record, loan amount, and an associated property identifier.

Linking these data sources to produce a more comprehensive database is a challenging undertaking, but a pilot version developed by a team of researchers at Freddie Mac and the Federal Reserve Board has laid a strong foundation for this effort. A combined database could make available critical statistics on the health of the housing market. For example, it could establish a link between first- and second-lien mortgages on the same property, providing key information on the overall extent of borrowers' leverage in different housing markets. This, in turn, would enable better risk management by first-lien lenders and private investors, as well as better design and implementation of government and private-sector loss mitigation programs. In addition, by utilizing statistical sampling techniques, such a database could correct for known biases across different data sources. Reliance on sampling also could reduce operational burden, allowing for more timely reporting.

larger fraction of wealth among lower income households. Whereas housing accounted for nearly two-thirds of the overall assets of households in the bottom half of the wealth distribution in 2007, it constituted only 25 percent of assets for those in the top decile, and only 10 percent for those in the top percentile. Shocks to housing wealth not only affect more households than other wealth shocks; they also apply disproportionately to those at the lower end of the wealth distribution.

A Pew Research Center report issued in July 2011 provides a stark illustration of these trends, concentrating on the disparate effects of the burst housing bubble on the wealth of minority and white households. Because home equity accounts for a much greater share of household wealth among minorities—59 percent for African Americans and 65 percent for Hispanics in 2005, compared with 44 percent for whites—minority households experienced much greater losses from the housing downturn. These losses were further compounded by the uneven geographic distribution of house price declines. As underscored by the Pew report, more than 40 percent of the nation's Hispanic households resided in the five states with the steepest price drops—Arizona, California, Florida, Michigan and Nevada—while only about one in five of all white and African American households resided in those states. For Hispanics in those five states, declining home prices have nearly wiped out household net worth, with median values collapsing from about $51,000 in 2005 to just $6,000 in 2009.

These trends matter to consumption because empirical research has pointed out systematic differences in marginal propensities to consume across income groups. For example, studies that analyzed the consumption effects of the 2001 and 2008 tax rebates using actual household expenditure data found that low-income households and those with low liquid wealth spent considerably higher fractions of these rebates. These effects were identified in credit card data (Agarwal, Liu, and Souleles 2007), the multiple-category Consumer Expenditure Survey (Johnson, Parker, and Souleles 2006), and automobile purchases (Parker et al. 2011). The fact that housing wealth losses were concentrated among the subset of households most responsive to such shocks may account in part for the magnitude of the observed declines in consumption. Indeed, a recent study by Mian, Rao, and Sufi (2011) shows that households with low levels of nonhousing financial assets experienced much greater declines in consumption for a given decline in home prices.

A growing economics literature highlights the importance of household debt balances in influencing the severity of economic slumps. Most of the growth in household debt between 2002 and 2006 can be traced to mortgage-related borrowing, which increased by nearly $5 trillion (or 94 percent of the total increase) over this period. As housing values collapsed, many households found their balance sheets tilting heavily toward debt. Household efforts to bring their balance sheets closer to equilibrium leverage can potentially proceed along several avenues. Households can default on their debt obligations. They can accelerate repayment of their debts. Or they can repair their asset base through more aggressive saving. Collectively, these approaches are often referred to as deleveraging.

A series of empirical papers attempts to quantify the effect of such deleveraging on consumption (Mian and Sufi 2010; Mian, Rao, and Sufi 2011). These papers broadly suggest that the levered nature of household housing assets amplified the effect of pure wealth losses from the crash in housing prices. The studies compared the consumption response in counties with different pre-recession levels of household debt and found that counties with the highest debt levels experienced much larger and longer-lasting drops in consumption than counties with low debt levels. This finding held true for consumer durables, such as automobiles, appliances, and furniture, as well as for consumption of groceries. These counties also exhibit patterns consistent with deleveraging, as increases in the numbers of defaults, and debt paybacks by non-defaulters are much higher in high-debt counties than in low-debt ones. These trends in consumption in turn affect local employment, particularly in sectors that produce locally consumed goods and services, such as restaurants and retail establishments (Mian and Sufi 2011). Figure 4-5 illustrates the divergence in employment trends in such nontradable industry sectors for high- and low-debt counties. In contrast, the traded goods sectors (not shown) display no such divergence, suggesting that the run-up in debt and bursting of the housing bubble have caused the contraction in aggregate demand.

Aside from the consumption effects of debt reduction or increases in savings needed to deleverage, households with impaired balance sheets may also have difficulty obtaining credit, which would further affect their consumption (Hall 2010). Before the crisis, the ability to use home equity as loan collateral served as an important source of financing for household purchases of goods and services. For example, Doms, Dunn, and Vine (2008) find that the increasing ease of tapping home equity credit in the early 2000s allowed homeowners to use their housing wealth to finance various forms of consumption. Another example of the pernicious effects of over-leveraging on access to credit, discussed earlier, is the inability of homeowners with low or negative equity stakes to refinance into low-interest mortgages. Moreover, reductions in the collateral value of houses have a negative effect on the economic recovery by restricting one of the primary channels for financing startup businesses.

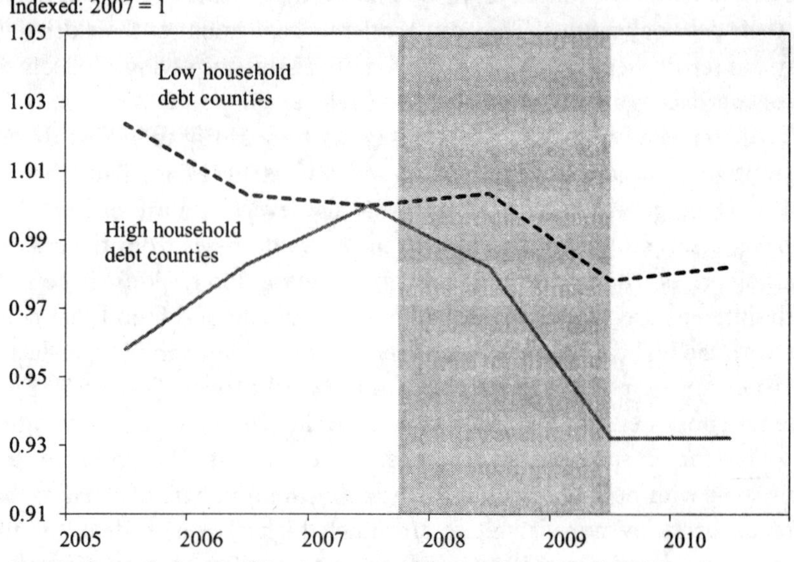

Source: Quarterly Census of Employment and Wages; Mian and Sufi (2011).

Residential Construction and Home Ownership Patterns

As discussed in Chapter 2, residential construction in 2011 remained at very subdued, albeit stable, levels. Starts of new housing units averaged a little over 600,000, roughly in line with the levels observed in 2009 and 2010. Housing starts of both single- and multi-family structures remain far below their peak 2006 levels of 2 million units, weighed down by the cyclical weakness in demand, the slow pace of household formation, high inventories of vacant properties for sale, and tight financing conditions for homebuilders.

In addition to cyclical headwinds, residential construction has been impeded by the need to reallocate the nation's housing stock from owner-occupied to rental units, as a growing number of households exited the ranks of homeowners through foreclosures. Recent research by Federal Reserve economists analyzes the moving decisions of homeowners who went through foreclosure between 1999 and 2010 (Molloy and Shan 2011). This study finds that post-foreclosure households do not tend to move in with others to defray their living expenses. Rather, the overwhelming majority of them (76 percent) end up renting single-family housing units.

This evidence suggests that many of the newly foreclosed households will continue to exhibit strong preference for single-family structures. However, the conversion of an owner-occupied house to a rental property takes a certain amount of time, especially if the home is repossessed at the conclusion of the foreclosure process. Repossessed homes need to be sold, often rehabilitated, and then marketed to potential renters. This process is made all the more difficult by tight credit conditions for financing investment properties, evidenced by historically high shares of all-cash purchases and by execution problems in amassing property portfolios necessary to realize any economies of scale through multiple foreclosure auctions.

In the meantime, prices in rental markets have been trending upward, pointing to the critical importance of efficient conversion of foreclosed properties and providing some of the necessary impetus for this process. A well-functioning mechanism for disposition and conversion of distressed properties into rental units has the potential to ease the downward pressure on owner-occupied house prices by removing a part of bank-owned and shadow inventory of soon-to-be-foreclosed properties from the sales market. (See the Data Watch 4-2 for discussion of challenges in measuring home sales.)

Demand for rental housing is likely to grow at a healthy rate over the next few years, creating an ongoing need to convert existing homes to rental. First, household formation is poised to accelerate. As numerous observers have pointed out, household formation slowed dramatically during the 2007–09 recession and has only recently begun to grow. Data from the Census Bureau show formation of fewer than 400,000 new households in both 2009 and 2010, well below the 2002–07 annual average of 1.3 million. The primary part of this trend is cyclical, deriving both from high unemployment rates among the young and from a substantial drop-off in immigration. A 2010 study done for the Mortgage Bankers Association (Painter 2010) suggests that historically, as economic conditions improved, individuals who delayed forming households during recession years were more likely to turn to rental markets to fulfill their housing needs.

Second, credit conditions have tightened considerably in recent years. Successful mortgage applicants have substantially higher average credit scores and are required to put up larger down payments than was the case in the era of rapidly rising house prices. For potential homebuyers who are unable to put down 20 percent of the purchase price, loans through the FHA and the U.S. Departments of Veterans Affairs (VA) and Agriculture have become the primary and, in many cases, only avenues for mortgage financing—providing a vital counter-cyclical buffer to sustain access to credit through the crisis. Consequently, the agencies' market share has risen rapidly, with the FHA accounting for nearly 40 percent of all house purchase loans in 2010. Among minority households, in particular, the FHA and VA loans became the predominant form of financing for home purchase. Between 2005 and 2010, the share of FHA/VA loans has skyrocketed from

15 percent to 80 percent of all purchase mortgages originated to African-American households and from 8 percent to 75 percent of all purchase mortgages originated to Hispanic households. During the past three years, at least 60 percent of all first-time home buyers financed their purchases with FHA or VA loans. Young households surveyed by Fannie Mae repeatedly cite an insufficiently strong "credit history" and "not having enough for a down payment" as two of the biggest obstacles to homeownership.

Third, younger households that just experienced a historic decline in housing prices may be less optimistic about homeownership. Recent research (Malmendier and Nagel 2011) showed that households coming of age during periods of sizable declines in the equity market stayed away from equity ownership in the future. For such households, a longer lifetime perspective could not offset the dramatic price declines experienced early in life, which thus tended to have a strong and long-lasting influence on subsequent economic behavior. It is premature to say whether a similar "Depression babies" effect is applicable to today's young renters. The scant survey evidence available on this question is mixed. On one hand, the Fannie Mae surveys indicate that the majority of young households continue to regard housing as a good financial investment and homeownership as a desirable goal. On the other hand, a series of special supplements to the Michigan Survey of Consumer Sentiment suggest that younger households hold more pessimistic views of homeownership, although this result is limited to a subset of responders with personal knowledge of someone who experienced foreclosure or substantial home price declines (Bracha and Jamison 2011).

In sum, the weakness in the housing sector continues to weigh heavily on macroeconomic performance. The enormity of losses in housing wealth and the uneven distribution of those losses in the population, along with the substantial weakening of household balance sheets burdened by debt overhang, have an outsized effect on consumption. High unresolved inventories of distressed properties, along with a concurrent need for large-scale rebalancing of the housing stock, contribute to ongoing difficulties in the residential construction sector.

These challenges are compounded by several structural problems in housing markets that have been exposed by the crisis. Understanding and addressing these institutional frictions represents a necessary step in formulating appropriate policy actions.

Structural Problems in Housing Market

The shock to the housing market laid bare serious deficiencies in the existing infrastructure for servicing delinquent mortgage loans, liquidating foreclosed properties, and adjudicating legal disputes between various parties. These deficiencies have impaired the effectiveness of loss mitigation efforts and may also be affecting borrowers' ability to access mortgage credit.

Adjudicating Legal Disputes

Rapid growth in the volume and complexity of securitized mortgage credit during the bubble years outpaced developments in case law adjudicating legal liability for representations and warranties associated with loan underwriting. The resulting legal uncertainty has the potential to impede origination of new mortgage credit if it unnecessarily adds to lender liability vis-à-vis mortgage investors.

During the standard loan origination process an underwriter provides legally binding representations and warranties (R&W) backing the veracity of collected information. Representations and warranties encompass such crucial elements of the loan application as borrower income, available assets, and the appraised value of the house. Within a specified period of time following securitization, an agent of the investors (the Trustee) conducts a postsale audit of loan documentation. If the Trustee finds R&W violations on a particular loan, the originator is obligated to buy back that loan from the securitized pool. A similar audit may be conducted in the event of mortgage default, when the discovery of R&W violations on defaulted loans would also result in the investor "putting back" the loan to the originator. These put-back rights create a liability for originators that is designed to serve an important quality control function: the originator must bear the risk of loss on defaulted loans with R&W violations.

As the number of intermediaries between the underwriter and loan investor grew, the transmission of this liability by each party along the chain became less well understood, and quality control standards became more difficult to enforce. For example, many financial institutions increasingly relied on independent mortgage brokers to carry out customer prospecting and loan underwriting, especially in urban and minority-dominated neighborhoods that have been historically underserved by traditional lenders. Because mortgage brokers did not have sufficient capital to originate and hold a substantial number of loans, they quickly sold their mortgages to a larger financial institution, which, in turn, would securitize the resulting loan portfolio in broader capital markets. In effect, mortgage brokers functioned as independent contractors for banks that would eventually securitize these loans. In a twist on a common description of mortgage securitization, "originate-to-distribute," this business model was labeled as "outsource-to-originate-to-distribute."

In theory, established financial institutions that securitized loans had ample incentives to exercise due diligence. They retained liability for representations and warranties, and carried reputational risk, as well as the risk that they might not be able to pass faulty loans back to the originating mortgage brokers. Yet, there is empirical evidence that at least some banks actively securitized loans originated by mortgage brokers with little or no documentation—the so-called "liar" loans that can be easily falsified (Jiang, Nelson, and Vytlacil 2011). The lengthening of the chain of financial intermediaries made the evaluation and assignment of liability for faulty underwriting processes considerably more complicated.

The complexity of the claims, and the sheer number of lawsuits that are being litigated on a loan-by-loan basis, suggest that court resolution will take considerable time, which poses a challenge to stabilizing the housing market and accelerating a recovery.

Incentive Conflicts

Before securitization became prevalent, the majority of mortgages was funded directly by banks and other deposit-taking financial institutions. These loans were held on lenders' own balance sheets and were typically serviced by them as well. Securitization of mortgage credit either through GSEs or private label issuers allowed the expansion of funding to broader capital markets. As a result, bank-funded (or portfolio) mortgages became less prevalent, ceding ground to GSE and private-label securitizations (PLS). By 2007, the share of aggregate residential mortgage debt held on portfolio had fallen to 37 percent from 48 percent in 1992, while that held by the PLS investors nearly quadrupled to 19 percent over the same time period. Investors in mortgage-backed securities relied on third-party servicers to collect monthly payments, transmit those payments to various investor classes, and mitigate losses on nonperforming mortgages.

The separation of mortgage ownership and servicing gave rise to a number of incentive conflicts between loan investors and their servicers, which made problem mortgages more difficult to address. These relationships are generally governed by "pooling and servicing agreements" (PSAs) that specify permissible actions servicers may take in dealing with delinquent loans. Although the overriding PSA principle is maximization of the value of the loan pool, some litigation was necessary to clarify this principle. Even now that the principle has been established, it can be interpreted in several different ways, particularly for mortgage pools with multiple investor classes or tranches. In particular, junior investors that are second in line (or lower) to receive flows generated by mortgage pools have an incentive to legally challenge modification actions that curtail overall cash flows. The resulting internecine "tranche warfare" discourages servicer actions. Indeed, some observers have argued that servicers tailor their loss mitigation practices to minimize the risk of litigation by their investors. Because loan modification is an expensive and uncertain undertaking, servicers may have an incentive to pursue foreclosures as the least legally contentious option. Indeed, recent research found evidence of considerably lower likelihood of modifications for privately securitized mortgages than for portfolio-held loans where no conflicts of interest are present (Piskorski, Seru, and Vig 2010; Agarwal et al. 2011).

Moreover, because servicer compensation is based on the unpaid principal balance of performing loans, their incentives are skewed toward modification practices that favor reductions in interest rates and adding unpaid loan balances (or arrears) to the principal, even when that is not the most effective approach to ensuring long-term performance of the loan. These incentive conflicts, coupled with the absence of established legal precedent, effectively limited early modification efforts on securitized mortgages to three alternatives: adding arrears to principal and either lowering the interest rate or freezing it on adjustable-rate mortgages (Agarwal et al. 2011).

The unveiling of the Home Affordable Modification Program in early 2009 substantially changed the playing field for loan modifications. By establishing a standardized approach to modifying mortgage contracts that explicitly maximized the return to investors as a group, the program reduced the exposure of servicers performing such modifications to investor lawsuits. The HAMP standards have served as a catalyst for spurring rapid growth in mortgage modification efforts across the industry. As servicers built up their distressed loan infrastructure to accommodate HAMP, they also switched their own modification focus to more aggressive methods that emphasize loan affordability.

Policy Actions

Both the complexity of the existing challenges in the housing market and the importance to the broader economy of resolving these challenges call for a robust and multifaceted menu of policy actions. Over the past three years, the Administration's housing policy has continued to expand to fit the circumstances, building on the experience of the early responses to the crisis. The Administration is pursuing additional innovative approaches designed to help households refinance their mortgages and maintain access to credit, to avoid unnecessary and costly foreclosures, to stabilize housing prices, and to help communities rebuild after experiencing a wave of foreclosures and erosion in property values.

Building on the Experience of Existing Programs

A number of program modifications are focused on counteracting the corrosive effects of negative equity. These modifications also seek to overcome a set of institutional hurdles that have thus far limited the effectiveness of certain policy actions. In particular, the Administration worked with the Federal Housing Finance Agency and private market participants to improve HARP—the existing refinancing program for borrowers with insufficient or negative equity in their homes whose mortgages are guaranteed by Fannie Mae or Freddie Mac. The revised program guidelines announced in November 2011 expand the pool of eligible borrowers by removing limits on loan-to-value ratios and extending the program deadline until December 2013. The program also lowers refinancing costs by reducing unnecessary pricing overlays and negotiating favorable pricing on some of the major closing cost items, such as title insurance. The revised HARP also addresses some of the difficult institutional hurdles, such as coordination problems with second-lien holders and mortgage insurers. The changes also lower some of the representation and warranty requirements for existing loan servicers, thereby encouraging greater lender participation. In a bid to further increase use of HARP, the revised program allows servicers to solicit some potentially eligible borrowers directly. Furthermore, major lenders have committed to dedicate additional origination capacity and resources to refinancing HARP borrowers.

Whereas changes in HARP were aimed at dulling the adverse effects of negative equity on the ability of currently performing borrowers to refinance their loans, other HAMP initiatives tackled the issues posed by negative equity in modifying loans of delinquent borrowers. In particular, the Principal Reduction Alternative (PRA), announced in October 2010, augments the original HAMP focus on affordability with elimination of a portion of the mortgage balance. The PRA builds on the insight that high levels of negative equity contribute to mortgage default over and above the effects of loan affordability. Consequently, modifications of delinquent loans with high loan-to-value (LTV) ratios may be more effective if they include a principal reduction component. The PRA requires servicers of non-GSE loans to evaluate the benefit of principal reduction for loans that exceed the appraised value of the house by 15 percent or more (that is, have LTV ratios above 115 percent) in making their HAMP determinations. To encourage servicers to use the PRA, HAMP provides monetary incentives for investors to write down principal. At the same time, the PRA seeks to lessen the risk of moral hazard by implementing principal write-down in three annual installments and making it conditional on continuous performance of the modified mortgage. Under this earned principal reduction structure, a borrower has a strong incentive to remain current, which enhances the net present value of the PRA modifications to investors. To further encourage investors to evaluate the use of principal reduction in modifying problem loans, the Treasury has recently announced a tripling of the PRA monetary incentives. The Treasury also offered to extend PRA incentives to Fannie Mae- and Freddie Mac-insured loans.

The pace of PRA modifications has picked up appreciably in the past few months, with more than one in four HAMP modifications receiving principal reductions. According to the latest Treasury report, more than 36,000 permanent modifications that include principal reduction had been implemented by the end of November 2011 (Department of the Treasury 2011). The median PRA loan had an LTV ratio of 158 percent before modification and a target ratio after modification of 115 percent. The median amount of principal forgiveness for active permanent PRA modifications was about $66,000. Because servicers are not required to offer principal reduction and usually may do so only when permitted by the loan investor, the growing use of the program suggests increasing acceptance of principal reduction as an effective loss mitigation tool by private investors.

Similar acceptance is echoed in servicer actions on private, non-HAMP, modifications. Several servicers have shifted their focus to principal reduction for deeply underwater delinquent loans held in securitization trusts. These reductions are typically earned over time to encourage borrowers to maintain loan performance. Principal reductions are also often coupled with a shared appreciation component that exchanges forgiven principal for an equity stake in the property. If the market value of the house in a future sale or refinancing exceeds its value at the time of principal reduction, the borrower shares a part of the appreciation with the lender. Much like the earned principal reduction, shared appreciation effectively raises the borrower's costs of defaulting to qualify for principal forgiveness.

Another HAMP-related initiative recently announced by the Department of the Treasury expands the reach of the program by broadening eligibility. One of the reasons many borrowers have not been able to take advantage of the program is that eligibility was tied to first-lien mortgages. Some borrowers with high medical debts, for example, but relatively average mortgage burdens, did not previously qualify for the program. By expanding eligibility, the changes aim to extend loan modifications to such borrowers and lower the number of preventable foreclosures.

The Administration has also expanded housing assistance for unemployed or underemployed homeowners. To help out-of-work homeowners avoid foreclosure, these programs generally provide for a period of forbearance of all or part of the monthly mortgage payment. In July of 2011, as the length of unemployment spells continued to exceed forbearance periods for many of the unemployed homeowners, the FHA and the Treasury announced the extension of forbearance to 12 months. This change applies to mortgage servicers that participate in the HAMP's unemployment initiative program (HAMP UP), as well as to the FHA Special Forbearance program. Following the Administration's lead, two major lenders and the GSEs have recently announced their commitment to provide up to 12 months of mortgage payment forbearance to unemployed borrowers.

Mortgage payment assistance for unemployed or underemployed homeowners has become a prominent feature of state level programs developed under the Hardest Hit Fund (HHF). The President announced the establishment of the Fund in February 2010 to provide targeted aid to families in states that have been hit hard by the economic and housing market downturn. HHF currently provides assistance to homeowners in 18 states and the District of Columbia. The specific programs are designed by state housing finance agencies and take into account local market conditions. In addition to helping unemployed borrowers, HHF programs commonly include efforts to fund innovative approaches to modification of delinquent mortgages and to allow homeowners to transition into more affordable places of residence.

Furthermore, in June of 2011 HUD launched the Emergency Homeowners Loan Program (EHLP) which provided $1 billion in interest-free loans to help keep borrowers in non-HHF states who are unemployed, or who suffer from a severe medical condition, from losing their homes. The EHLP is available to borrowers with a long track record of staying current on their mortgages but who find their ability to continue doing so compromised by job loss or illness. EHLP loans are secured by a junior lien note on the homeowner's principal residence, and the balance on these loans is forgiven in 20 percent increments for each year the borrower remains current on regular mortgage payments.

The Administration's Project Rebuild, introduced as part of the American Jobs Act in September 2011, is another example of building on the experience of existing housing programs. While the revised HARP and the HAMP PRA focus on negative equity, Project Rebuild addresses the damaging effects of foreclosed or abandoned homes on neighborhood property values, economic prospects, and social fabric. Project Rebuild seeks to integrate and expand strategies proven successful under the Neighborhood Stabilization Program to deal with vacant and foreclosed properties. In particular, it explicitly allows federal funding to support for-profit development subject to HUD oversight. It also extends rehabilitation efforts to commercial as well as residential properties. Project Rebuild further calls for expanding support for land banks that work at the local level to acquire, hold, and redevelop distressed properties. Federal funds granted under the project would provide land banks with capital infusions that can be leveraged with private-sector investments to finance long-term redevelopment strategies.

New Levers in Housing Policy

Refinancing. The Administration has called on Congress to pass legislation that will enable more homeowners to refinance their mortgages at today's historically low interest rates. First, the HARP program is available only to homeowners whose loans are owned or guaranteed by the GSEs. This restriction has left some borrowers unable to refinance their loans only because their mortgages were kept on the originating bank's books or were securitized in the private, as opposed to the GSE, market—events largely outside of a borrower's control. To remove this arbitrary distinction, the Administration proposes that the FHA be authorized to offer streamlined refinancing to non-GSE borrowers with standard mortgage contracts. To limit risks to the taxpayers, the proposal emulates HARP in requiring eligible borrowers to have remained current on their mortgages and to meet certain underwriting standards. Another risk-management component of the proposal includes capping the loan-to-value ratio of eligible loans.

Second, while enhancements to HARP announced in November of 2011 will increase the reach of the program, more can be done to reduce the barriers to refinancing of GSE-backed loans. Such steps would include harmonizing underwriting requirements for mortgages with LTV ratios below and above 80 percent; further reducing loan fees because GSEs do not acquire any new credit risk by refinancing these loans; fully aligning the treatment of representations and warranties for refinancing with the existing or new mortgage servicers; and removing remaining differences in HARP requirements that still exist between Fannie Mae and Freddie Mac. These changes are aimed at streamlining the operational requirements of the HARP program and making it more accessible to a greater number of borrowers. By leveling the playing field between existing and new servicers, the proposed changes also seek to harness competitive forces to bring more interest savings to borrowers.

Third, the Administration's proposal helps address the problem of negative equity by providing a pathway for responsible homeowners who refinance their mortgages to rebuild their equity more quickly. Under this option, home owners would refinance into a shorter-maturity (20-year, for example) mortgage and commit to deploying the savings from refinancing to rebuilding equity in their homes. As an example, consider a borrower who has a 6.5 percent mortgage originated in 2006 with an outstanding balance of $200,000, whose house is worth $160,000 (a loan-to-value ratio of 125). This borrower could lower the monthly payment by $166 by refinancing into a 20-year mortgage at 3.75 percent. Should the borrower choose to keep their mortgage payment at its original level and direct the $166 in savings to principal reduction, the outstanding mortgage balance would decline to $152,000 in five years. Under the proposal, underwater borrowers would have the choice of pursuing this pathway to rebuild their home equity. To assist borrowers who make this choice, the proposal directs the GSEs and the FHA to cover the closing costs of their refinanced loans.

Servicing standards. The experience of the past few years showed that the Nation is not well served by the patchwork of rules that govern the mortgage servicing system. To improve accountability and align incentives in the mortgage servicing industry, the Administration recently released a unified framework of servicing standards—the Homeowner Bill of Rights— that is designed to better serve borrowers, investors, and the overall housing market. The Administration will work closely with the Consumer Financial Protection Bureau (CFPB) and other independent regulators, Congress, and other stakeholders to create a more robust and comprehensive set of rules driven by a set of core principles outlined in the framework. These principles include full disclosure of all fees provided in understandable language upfront, with any changes disclosed before they go into effect. The framework also requires servicers to implement standards and practices that minimize conflicts of interest, such as those that exist between multiple investor classes and those that arise when the servicer simultaneously owns a secondary lien on the property. To make loss mitigation actions more timely and effective, servicers are required to contact homeowners who have demonstrated hardship or fallen delinquent, and provide them with a comprehensive set of options to avoid foreclosure. Servicers must further allow homeowners the right to appeal denials for mortgage modification to an independent third party and provide homeowners who find themselves in economic distress with access to a customer service employee with a complete record of previous communications with that homeowner. To minimize inappropriate foreclosure actions, servicers may schedule a fore-closure sale only after they have certified in writing that all loss mitigation alternatives have been considered. To ensure compliance, servicers must maintain strong controls over servicing and loss mitigation operations and subject these controls to periodic independent audits. The Homeowner Bill of Rights is meant to provide an enforceable set of rules, not just guidance, for the servicing industry.

Conversion of Repossessed Properties into Rental Units. An orderly, fair process for disposition of foreclosed properties remains a key objective of housing policy. Given the ongoing reduction in rates of homeownership, many foreclosed properties will have to be converted to rental units, a process that typically involves rehabilitation. The demand for this type of housing stock will come mainly from private investors whose activity to date has been hampered by execution problems in putting together property portfolios through a series of small-scale acquisitions. Tight credit conditions for financing investment properties have further limited the ability of private investors to fill the gap in demand.

To counteract these problems, the FHFA, with the Departments of Treasury and Housing and Urban Development, initiated a process to manage the sale of REO properties held by Fannie Mae, Freddie Mac and the FHA. The goal of this effort is to allow private investors to bid on acquiring pools of REO properties in exchange for a commitment to rehabilitate and manage the properties as rental units. Bulk purchases will make it easier for investors to achieve economies of scale as they implement their individual business strategies. Qualified bidders must demonstrate evidence of property management experience and adequate capital resources, as well as agree to abide by property usage restrictions. For instance, antiflipping provisions establish minimum time periods that an investor must hold the property before seeking to sell it, and minimum reinvestment requirements impose certain quality standards for rented properties.

In many ways, the REO-to-rental conversion program seeks to build on the best practices established by successful policy interventions during the crisis. The program focuses on leveraging the expertise and financial resources of private investors, while preserving value for the taxpayers. It looks to avoid rigid top-down solutions, allowing for customization at the local level. And it makes use of the unique position of the GSEs and FHA as owners of large nationwide inventories of distressed properties to provide a large-scale, transparent, and predictable mechanism for converting these properties to better suit local housing demands. Furthermore, the process is intended to help the industry develop a viable framework for acquiring and managing large-scale scattered-site rental portfolios. Similar to the HAMP experience, this framework may well help establish industry standards.

CONCLUSION

Developments in the housing market played a central role in the financial crisis and the ensuing recession, and they continue to present a headwind for the economic recovery. Although housing markets are stabilizing in many regions, the healing process will inevitably take time. This is a reflection of both the magnitude of the recent housing price collapse and the many institutional obstacles on the path to a new equilibrium. Getting to the end of this path will require unwinding accumulated inventories of foreclosed homes, whether by finding new owners or by converting them to rental units. It will require enabling more homeowners to refinance their mortgages at today's low interest rates. It will require resolving multiple conflicts of interest in the modification of delinquent loans and providing meaningful assistance to unemployed homeowners as they search for new jobs that would allow them to remain in their homes. It will require restoring access to credit for responsible borrowers and repairing household balance sheets hard hit by erosion of home equity. And it will require working out legal uncertainties and fixing up mortgage finance markets.

Instead of waiting for these processes to play themselves out slowly and painfully, the Administration has embarked on a series of multifaceted and fiscally responsible actions in partnership with private market participants and housing regulators to proactively repair the housing market and ease the transition to a new and stable equilibrium. The new policy initiatives seek to enable refinancing, to unlock access to credit for responsible underwater homeowners, to reallocate foreclosed properties to the rental market, to prevent unnecessary foreclosures for borrowers struggling with temporary loss of income, to implement sustainable modifications of delinquent loans, and to repair the frayed infrastructure of mortgage servicing and mortgage finance.

❧

C H A P T E R   5

INTERNATIONAL TRADE AND FINANCE

Over the past year, global economic growth has slowed, largely due to a range of challenges in the advanced economies. These adverse shocks are, for the most part, unrelated to policies or business decisions undertaken within the borders of the United States. Nevertheless, in an integrated global economy, the United States cannot fully escape their impact.

One could hardly begin with a starker example of an adverse shock to the world economy than the massive earthquake that struck Japan's northeastern coast on March 11. This earthquake was the most powerful to have hit Japan in recorded history, triggering tsunami waves that leveled towns and claimed nearly 16,000 lives. Alongside the devastating human toll, the disaster also had a major impact on the Japanese economy. The International Monetary Fund (IMF) estimates that the Japanese economy contracted by 0.9 percent in 2011. The economic impact also extended far beyond Japan's borders. For months afterward, supply chains around the world, especially in the automotive industry, were disrupted by production slowdowns and parts shortages.

While Japan's severe economic slowdown in 2011 was driven by a natural disaster, those elsewhere in the developed world were largely a product of forces outside of nature. Slow growth has exacerbated sovereign debt and deficit problems in Europe, and austerity measures put into place in response have impeded near-term growth in a number of euro-area countries. In January, the IMF reported that the euro area's gross domestic product (GDP) grew 1.6 percent in 2011, down from 1.9 percent in 2010, and predicted that the euro area would contract by 0.5 percent in 2012. Growth in the United Kingdom has also slowed significantly, in part reflecting tight fiscal policies, and is estimated by the IMF to have been only 0.9 percent in 2011. With the European Union, Japan, and the United States collectively accounting for almost 60 percent of global GDP, slower growth

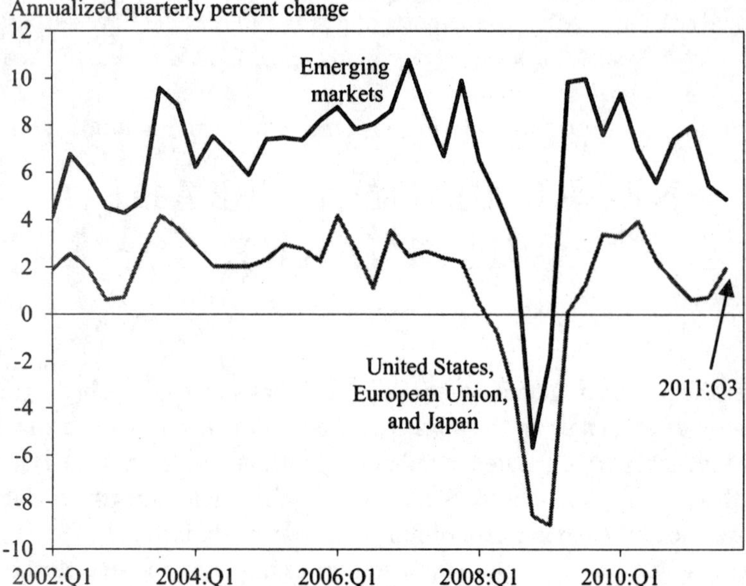

Note: Weights come from each nation's share of GDP within each aggregate.
Source: Country sources; International Monetary Fund, World Economic Outlook,
September 2011; CEA calculations.

in these economies was sufficient to lower growth at the global level in 2011,
as Figure 5-1 illustrates.

In the face of the broad-based slowdown in economic growth in the
developed economies, growth in emerging markets also decelerated.[1] Slower
growth in import demand in the large economies meant slower export
growth in emerging markets.[2] For example, growth in China is decelerating
because of a decline in export growth as well as a slowdown in domestic real
estate investment. Although the IMF predicts China is likely to grow more
than 8 percent in 2012, its slowdown contributes to the loss of momentum
in global growth.

---

[1] The growth slowdown in some emerging markets also reflected the impact of policy
tightening in some countries to prevent overheating. As the year progressed, concerns about
overheating tended to give way to concerns about the economic slowdown in the developed
countries.

[2] The emerging markets aggregate in Figure 5-1 includes Argentina, Brazil, Chile, China,
Colombia, Hong Kong, India, Indonesia, Israel, Malaysia, Mexico, Peru, Russia, Singapore,
South Africa, South Korea, Taiwan, Thailand, Turkey, Ukraine, and Venezuela. Seventeen
member states of the European Union (the EU-27) use the euro. They are Austria, Belgium,
Cyprus, Estonia, Finland, France, Germany, Greece, Ireland, Italy, Luxembourg, Malta,
Netherlands, Portugal, the Slovak Republic, Slovenia, and Spain.

Viewed in the context of these external challenges, the growth of U.S. exports over the past year has been a particular bright spot. Despite a slowing global economy, America's exports of goods and services have surpassed their pre-crisis peaks and have been growing more than fast enough to meet the President's goal of doubling the 2009 export level by the end of 2014. Many factors are contributing to this fast pace of growth, including continued productivity growth in manufacturing, a shift in unit labor costs that favors U.S. businesses over those in other advanced countries, and technological innovation in the energy sector, which is improving America's trade balance in petroleum products. A possible further weakening of foreign demand conditions, however, could pose a risk to future U.S. export growth.

Global economic events could also affect the U.S. economy through financial links between the United States and the rest of the world. These links have increased dramatically in recent decades. U.S.-owned assets abroad and foreign-owned assets in the United States increased more than six-fold between 1994 and 2010.

"Global rebalancing" has been a major theme of U.S. international economic policy since the beginning of the Obama Administration. In the years before the global financial crisis erupted in 2008, large asymmetries had developed in the global economy. Several countries characterized by large, persistent current account surpluses, including Germany, Japan, and China, relied too heavily on unsustainable growth in net exports to drive economic growth. Several other countries characterized by large, persistent current account deficits, including the United States, relied on unsustainable growth in household consumption and construction of residential real estate. A more symmetric, better balanced pattern of growth is needed throughout the major economies. In the United States, future growth must be driven less by consumption and more by net exports and investment. Conversely, countries that have traditionally run large current account surpluses need to rely more on domestic consumption and less heavily on net exports. So far, the United States has made significant progress toward rebalancing. For progress to continue, however, U.S. exports must grow even more, and consumption in the surplus countries must increase.

THE EURO-AREA CRISIS AND ITS IMPLICATIONS FOR THE UNITED STATES

A key potential risk in 2012 to the U.S. and global economic recoveries remains the sovereign-debt and banking crises in Europe. Economic and fiscal conditions vary greatly among the 17 economies in the euro area, as illustrated in Figure 5-2. Although there is significant heterogeneity among

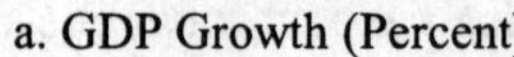

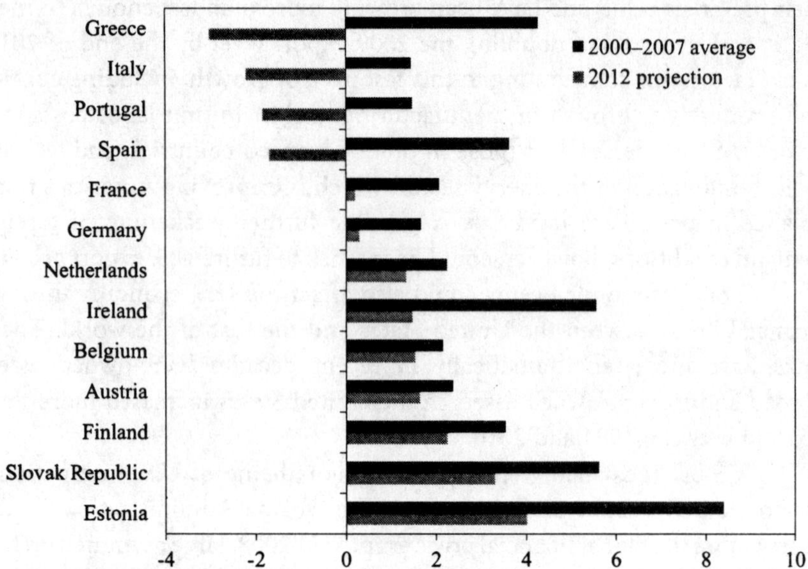

Note: Projections include revisions as of January 2012.
Source: International Monetary Fund, World Economic Outlook, September 2011.

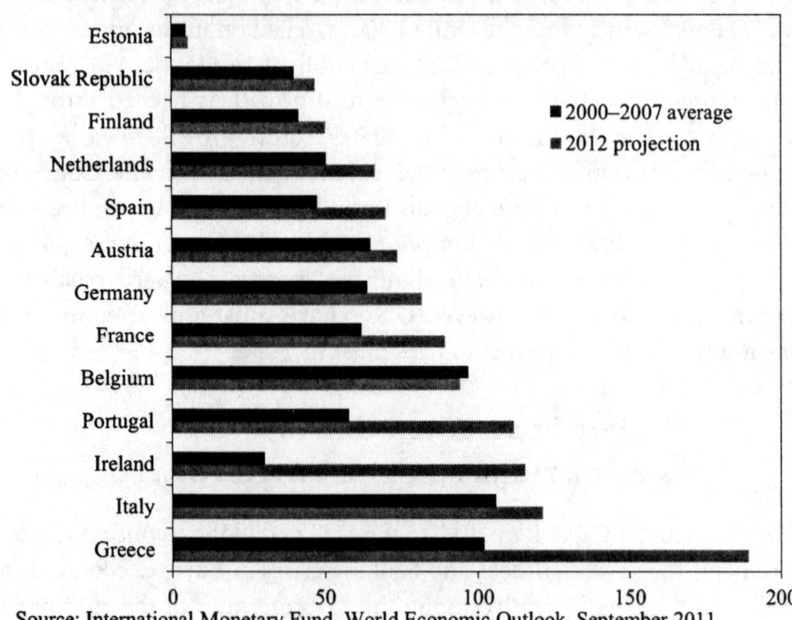

Source: International Monetary Fund, World Economic Outlook, September 2011.

euro-area economies, economic and fiscal conditions in most of them deteriorated throughout 2011. In 2012, the economies of Estonia, Finland, and the Slovak Republic are predicted to grow by more than 2 percent, but those in Greece, Italy, Portugal, and Spain are predicted to shrink by more than 1.5 percent. Similarly, the ratio of general government gross debt to GDP is projected to be roughly 70 percent or below in Estonia, Finland, the Netherlands, the Slovak Republic, and Spain and above 110 percent in Greece, Ireland, Italy, and Portugal.

Economic research shows that there are many determinants of sovereign credit risk or sovereign borrowing costs, including individual factors (Berg and Sachs 1988) and global financial factors (Eichengreen and Mody 2000; Longstaff et al. 2011). Since early 2010, both sets of factors raised borrowing costs for some smaller and a few larger economies in the euro area. The European Commission (EC) and the IMF negotiated assistance programs for Ireland (November 2010), Portugal (May 2011), and Greece (May 2010, July 2011, and October 2011). In October 2011, the sovereign-debt crisis intensified in Italy and Spain, the third- and fourth-largest economies in the euro area.[3]

In response to the marked increase in sovereign borrowing costs, the European Central Bank (ECB) intervened, resuming its Securities Markets Program, in an effort designed to lower sovereign bond yields by purchasing government debt in secondary markets. European leaders and institutions have also introduced and expanded various measures to inhibit contagion, such as the European Financial Stability Facility. While these measures have helped contain the sovereign-debt crisis in Europe, significant risks remain. Market participants are expressing ongoing concerns about the fiscal conditions of Italy and Spain, as well as Greece and Portugal, in part because of fears that economic growth in these countries is likely to be sluggish for a prolonged period, exacerbating their fiscal situation.

European banks are among the largest holders of European government debt. (See Financial Stability Oversight Council 2011 for a discussion of the interconnections between U.S. banks, European banks, and European government debt.) As concerns about sovereign debt rose, spreads widened on sovereign bond yields relative to German bond yields in June 2011 (as highlighted in Figure 5-3), leading to deteriorating conditions of both solvency and liquidity among European banks. Toward the end of 2011, many European banks were facing shortened maturities and higher costs of funding in the interbank market, an important source of bank liquidity.

In December 2011, after two successive cuts in interest rates, the ECB took major steps to provide increased liquidity to euro-area banks. Among

---

[3] Assistance programs for Greece negotiated in 2011 have not yet been implemented.

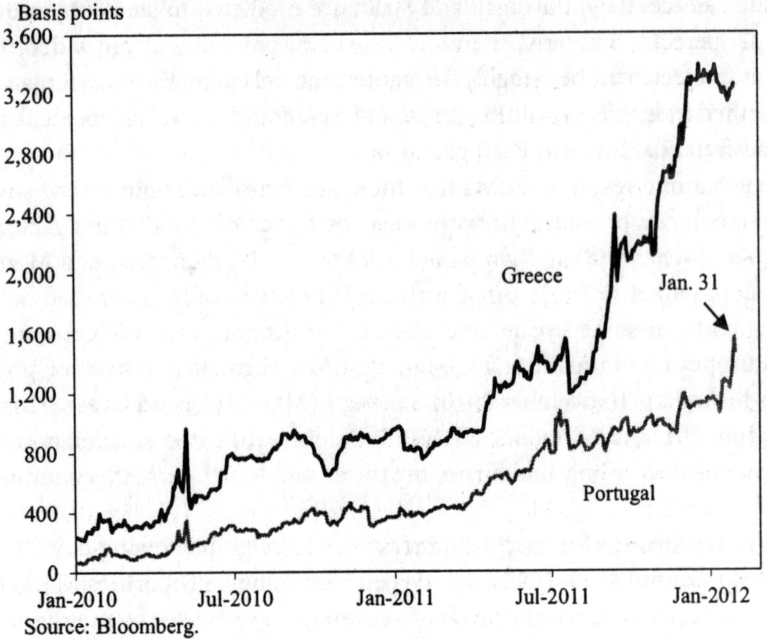

Source: Bloomberg.

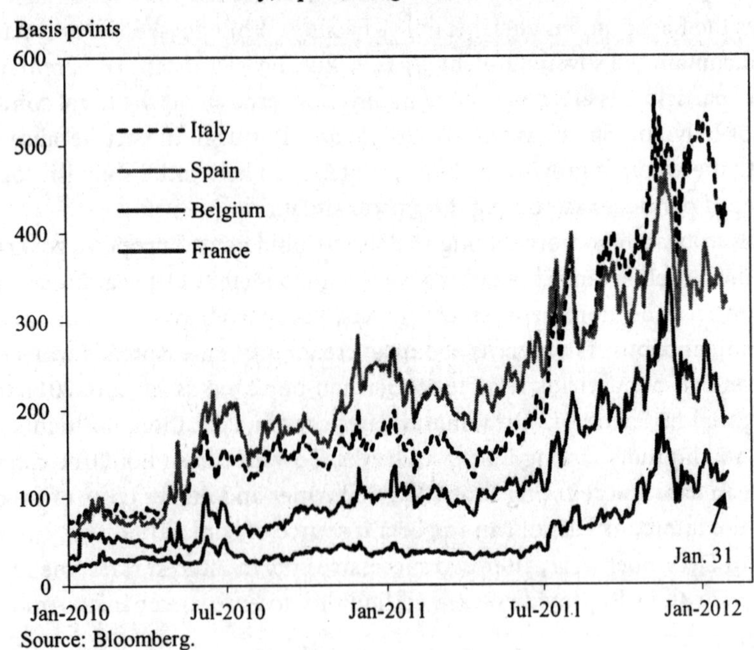

Source: Bloomberg.

other measures, the ECB's new longer-term refinancing operation extended the maturity of loans offered to banks from one year to three years, and the ECB eased collateral requirements for those loans. The Federal Reserve also extended and reduced the cost of dollar liquidity swap arrangements to the ECB, as it had done during the credit freeze of 2008–09. A currency liquidity swap is an agreement between two or more parties to exchange a set amount of a given currency for another currency at a given price until a specific date in the future. In this case, the Federal Reserve provides dollars for periods ranging from overnight to as long as three months in exchange for the currency of the foreign central bank. In turn, the foreign central bank can lend the dollars during the specified period in its local markets, helping to relieve funding pressures in those markets and to prevent the spread of strains to markets elsewhere.

Given the interconnectedness of European and U.S. banks and the presence of branches, agencies, and subsidiaries of European banks in the United States, adverse financial conditions in Europe can be transmitted to American financial institutions. According to the Federal Reserve's Senior Loan Officer Opinion Survey, several European branches tightened standards on commercial and industrial (C&I) loans over the second half of 2011, in contrast to U.S. and other foreign banks. The C&I loans on the books of European branches in the United States have in fact declined noticeably since the middle of 2011. Such financial data are being monitored closely. One of the goals of recent financial oversight embedded in the Dodd-Frank Wall Street Reform and Consumer Protection Act is to reduce systemic risk by increasing transparency. Among other things, the new law supports trading of financial instruments on central exchanges, including derivatives. (For a discussion of the role of the Office of Financial Research in fostering transparency, see Data Watch 5-1.)

Similarly, trade and investment links between the United States and Europe are broad and deep, and, in recent years, of growing importance relative to the rest of the world. Europe is a significant destination for U.S. exports, accounting for more than 20 percent of U.S. goods exports and nearly 40 percent of U.S. service exports. In addition, sales by European affiliates of U.S. multinational firms totaled $3.1 trillion in 2008, making up more than half of the $6.1 trillion in total sales abroad by U.S. multinational firms. Furthermore, Europe is the leading foreign source of investment and jobs in America, accounting for $173.2 billion, or 76 percent, of all foreign direct investment (FDI) inflows into the United States in 2010.

Data Watch 5-1: The Significance of the Office of Financial Research (OFR) in Combating Global Risks to the U.S. Financial System

The recent financial crisis presented a stark example of the need for comprehensive data on the financial system. While the initial catalyst for the financial crisis was a decline in U.S. housing prices that in 2007 led to a dramatic rise in subprime mortgage defaults (Brunnermeier 2009), neither market participants nor policymakers were aware of the extent to which leverage, reliance on ultra-cheap short-term funding, and a web of interconnected transactions and claims had built up in the financial system prior to that time. It became clear that investors had placed too high a value on the underlying homes, real estate, and other assets that were supposed to stand behind their investments. Consequently, as defaults on mortgages multiplied, they triggered a wholesale flight from related financial securities, which spread across countries and financial markets. The inadequacy of information available to assess risks properly magnified that flight from risk (Squam Lake Working Group 2009). The resulting credit crunch ultimately triggered a global economic recession from which many countries are still recovering.

Responding to the devastating effects of the financial crisis, on July 21, 2010, Congress enacted the Dodd-Frank Wall Street Reform and Consumer Protection Act (PL 111-203). The creation of the OFR in that Act addresses two glaring deficiencies in the financial data infrastructure that were revealed by the crisis. First, the OFR is charged with increasing the availability of financial information so that policymakers can better identify, analyze and monitor potential risks to the U.S. financial system. Critically, given the interconnectedness of global financial markets, this legislation permits the acquisition of data from financial institutions related to their activities globally that may pose a threat to the financial stability of the United States. Second, OFR is charged with improving the quality of financial information, in part by standardizing the types and formats of data that are reported to regulators. Standardized data would make it easier for policymakers to accurately evaluate whether a financial institution or group of institutions—located either domestically or abroad—or certain financial activities in which they may be engaged pose a threat to the U.S. financial system.

Over the past eighteen months, the OFR has laid the critical groundwork for enhancing both the quantity and the quality of financial information that is available to U.S. policymakers. The OFR is in the midst of comprehensively cataloguing the data that are currently held and collected by U.S. financial regulators. Concurrently, the OFR will collaborate with the member agencies of the Financial Stability Oversight Council to identify and fill deficiencies in the collection of data on financial markets. Likewise, the OFR has taken an important step toward enhancing the quality of the financial data infrastructure through the promotion of a global Legal Entity Identifier (LEI) for financial institutions. At the G-20 Cannes Summit, leaders supported the development of a global LEI and tasked the Financial Stability Board with coordinating this work. U.S. policymakers have partnered with the global financial services industry, foreign regulators, and associations such as the International Organization for Standardization to develop and begin to implement a universal standard for identifying counterparties to financial transactions (Department of Treasury 2011). In time, further initiatives will be undertaken to meet the information needs of regulators in fulfilling the mandate of the Dodd-Frank Wall Street Reform Act and responding to potential threats to the financial stability of the United States.

Outlook for Europe and Implications for the U.S. Economy

As noted, the crisis in Europe has slowed both current and predicted growth. The IMF estimates that euro-area growth in 2011 was 1.6 percent, but for 2012, the IMF forecasts that economies in the euro area will contract by 0.5 percent.

Faltering consumer confidence in Europe has spread to countries outside the euro area. Britain's Nationwide Consumer Confidence Index fell for the fifth month in a row in November 2011, reaching an all-time low of 36 points, compared with a historical average of 77. Economic growth projections for the European Union for 2012 are lower than for 2011: -0.1 percent in 2012 compared with 1.6 percent for 2011 (IMF 2012). A slowdown in Europe could affect the U.S. economy through two channels in addition to the finance channel mentioned above: trade and direct investment.

Exports. The share of U.S. goods exports to Europe has been over 20 percent for decades. A severe financial episode in Europe could reduce exports from businesses throughout the United States. As is the case with flows of inward investment, exports to Europe are distributed broadly across the United States, as displayed in Figure 5-4. The European Union is the destination for more than 20 percent of total goods exports from Alabama, Connecticut, Indiana, Massachusetts, South Carolina, and West Virginia. Exports range from cars, aircraft, and semiconductors, to coal, gold, soybeans, kaolin, and live chickens. Moreover, export data for commodities underestimate the extent of U.S. trade with Europe because, as noted, more than one-third of U.S. service exports go to Europe. Shrinking purchases of

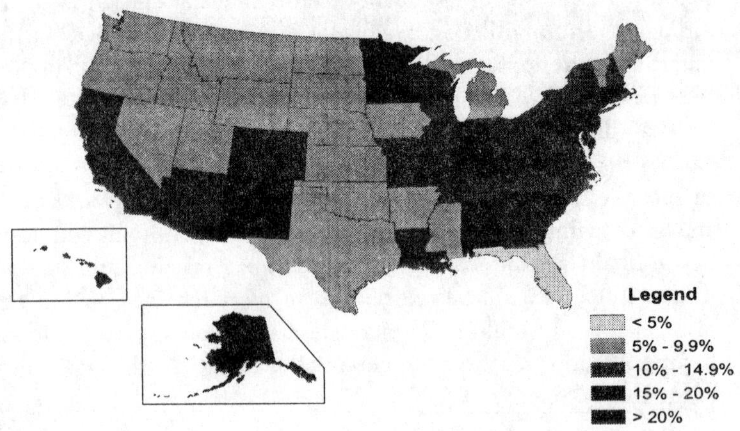

Note: This map depicts the state from which the product is last shipped, which is not necessarily the state in which the product is produced. Products with multiple stages of production often move across state boundaries more than once before leaving the country. Source: U.S. Census Bureau, Foreign Trade Data.

American goods and services by Europeans could have a significant impact on U.S. employment in several states.

Foreign Direct Investment. Declines in output, profit, and investor confidence in Europe could have an adverse effect on the ability and willingness of European firms to invest in American firms and jobs. The United States received more than $228 billion in FDI from all foreign sources in 2010, over 75 percent of which came from Europe. Between 2004 and 2010, FDI flowed into every state, with Texas receiving the most, followed by Alaska, California, New York, Indiana, Illinois, Ohio, Alabama, South Carolina, and Georgia.

International Cooperation in Resolving Crises

The data in Figure 5-3 starkly reflect growing concerns of market participants regarding the scope and magnitude of euro-area bank and sovereign-credit risk. In the last decade, systemic risk related to financial crises has received more attention in the economics literature, including studies by Allen and Gale (2000), Kaminsky, Reinhart, and Vegh (2003), Frankel and Wei (2005), Reinhart and Rogoff (2009), and Ang and Longstaff (2011).

While Europe has the capacity to take responsibility for addressing its crisis through decisive policy action and a credible financial backstop, the United States has made clear that the international community has a strong interest in the successful resolution of the crisis. The Administration is engaging with European governments both bilaterally and in multilateral forums. The United States has also been involved in the response to the crisis through its role in the IMF.

The Administration continues to urge movement along several dimensions in Europe: robust implementation of countries' agreed fiscal and structural reform programs, in the context of steps that euro-area leaders have outlined to reform fiscal governance in the euro area; a more substantial financial firewall to ensure that governments can borrow at sustainable interest rates while executing policies to strengthen the foundations for growth and to reduce their debts; and measures to ensure that European banks have sufficient liquidity and are adequately capitalized to maintain the full confidence of depositors and creditors.

Global and U.S. economic performance will depend, in part, on the swift resolution of problems in the euro area. In such times of global economic and financial disequilibrium, U.S. coordination with international partners remains essential.

FOREIGN DIRECT INVESTMENT, INTERNATIONAL TRADE, AND THE U.S. ECONOMY

Experience and economic theory suggest that a global economy can provide enormous advantages for American workers, consumers, and firms. In the absence of international trade and investment, a country can consume only what it produces, it can invest only what it saves, it can use only the technology that it creates, and it can take advantage of only those natural resources within its borders. Countries that have deliberately cut themselves off from international trade and investment for extensive periods of time have paid a stiff price in forgone opportunities for investment, consumption, and growth. North Korea, a nation that has pursued this kind of isolation assiduously, illustrates this point in a powerful and tragic way. Before Kim Il-Sung seized power in northern Korea, it was at least as rich as southern Korea. Today, per capita GDP in South Korea is over 17 times higher than that of North Korea.

One of America's achievements after World War II was helping to build the open and integrated global trading and investment system that now incorporates almost all of the world's economies. Of course, this system brings challenges, along with opportunities. The Obama Administration has focused on meeting the challenges of this system in ways that enable American workers and firms to make the most of the rich opportunities provided by a more open global trading and investment system. At the same time, the Administration has sought to ensure, through strong enforcement efforts, that other countries play by the rules of the system, and it has sought to protect those who are potentially adversely affected by global competition with a stronger safety net and an improved training and reemployment system (discussed in Chapters 6 and 7).

Investment in the United States by Foreign Companies

The United States had the largest annual flow of inbound FDI of any economy in the world in every year between 2006 and 2010. By 2010, the cumulative FDI stock in the United States had reached nearly $3.5 trillion—more than three times the FDI stock in each of the next three largest recipients (Hong Kong, France, and the United Kingdom) and more than five times China's cumulative inbound FDI stock ($579 billion). Given the rapid GDP growth of large emerging markets such as Brazil, India, and China, both before and after the global financial crisis, it is not surprising that these countries and other emerging markets are absorbing an increasing fraction of the world's FDI. Nevertheless, their inflows remained substantially below those into the United States throughout this period.

Like trade flows, FDI flows tend to be procyclical, rising when the global economy expands and contracting when it shrinks. In late 2008 and 2009, as the global economy sank into its deepest postwar recession, FDI inflows around the world contracted (Figure 5-5); by 2009, total FDI flows were roughly 60 percent of their 2007 levels. Nonetheless, the United States remained the largest destination for new FDI inflows. As both the U.S. and global economies recovered from the recession, FDI inflows into the United States increased 49 percent from 2009 to 2010. Then, as global growth slowed again in 2011, FDI into the United States also decelerated. Through the third quarter of 2011, FDI inflows into the United States were running roughly 4 percent below 2010 levels.

If the global economy returns to normal growth rates, FDI inflows into the United States will likely resume their growth. The Nation continues to offer a set of "fundamental attractors" to foreign investors that other countries struggle to match. One such attractor is the sheer size of America's domestic market. In 2010, America's GDP was nearly two-and-a-half times larger than that of China, the world's second-largest economy. The United States also offers potential investors a strong rule of law, a highly skilled, motivated workforce, a highly developed financial system, and effective protection of property rights. The United States continues to lead the world in key technologies, attracting investment by firms eager to conduct world-class research in close proximity to the world's top universities. For all of these reasons, leading companies around the world continue to be attracted to investment opportunities within the borders of the United States.

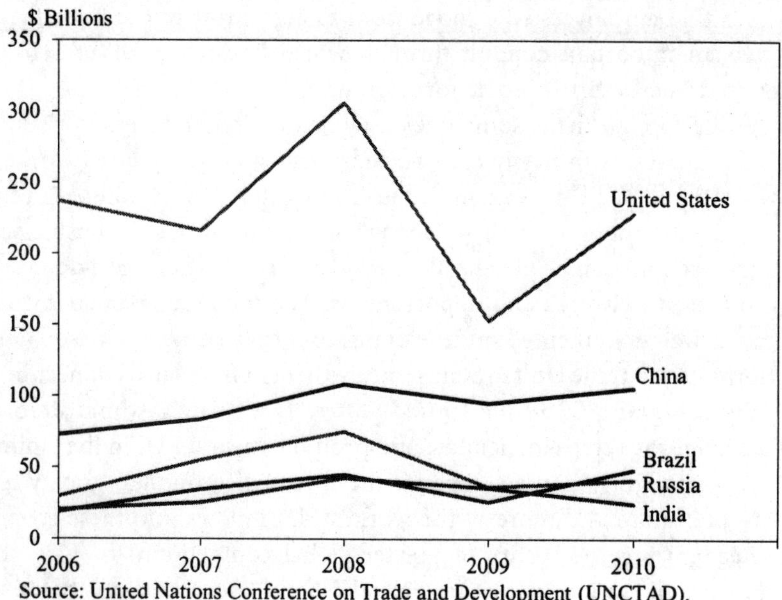

Source: United Nations Conference on Trade and Development (UNCTAD).

The Benefits of FDI. U.S. affiliates of foreign firms make significant contributions to U.S. employment, output, investment, research and development (R&D), and exports. The Bureau of Economic Analysis (BEA) of the U.S. Department of Commerce surveys the activities of foreign-owned affiliates in the United States. According to its data, in 2008, subsidiaries of foreign companies accounted for nearly 5 percent of U.S. private-sector jobs, more than 11 percent of all U.S. private capital investment, more than 14 percent of all U.S. private-sector R&D, and 19 percent of all U.S. goods exported. In that year, the U.S. employees of these global companies earned an average annual compensation of about $73,000—about one-third more than the economy-wide average.

Economic research shows that the benefits of foreign investment are even greater than these measures indicate. When foreign subsidiaries use advanced technologies and effective management to achieve high levels of productivity in their U.S. operations, the benefits can "spill over" to their American competitors (Keller and Yeaple 2009). As U.S. firms increasingly interact in their home market with highly productive foreign subsidiaries, the U.S. firms may be able to learn from their competitors' strengths. Keller and Yeaple find that 14 percent of the aggregate productivity growth between 1987 and 1996 (a period of rapidly rising FDI in the United States) resulted from FDI-related productivity spillovers. These spillovers were particularly valuable for small firms, which do not routinely encounter these competitors in markets outside the United States. One reason proximity matters is that employees who move from foreign firms to domestic firms are often an important conduit through which knowledge diffuses from foreign to domestic firms (Poole forthcoming).

While foreign firms sometimes establish entirely new enterprises in the United States, with newly constructed plants and newly hired workers (known as "greenfield" investment), they more often gain a foothold in the U.S. market by merging with or acquiring existing domestic businesses. These transactions can be beneficial. Finally, FDI can help connect domestic firms to export networks and opportunities. The importance of such connections is well documented in developing countries (Aitken, Hanson, and Harrison 1997), but the United States can also benefit from such connections.

Encouraging FDI in the United States. The Obama Administration has taken vigorous steps to facilitate and promote inward FDI in the United States. As emerging markets expand, the forces of economic gravity are likely to pull more and more of the world's FDI inflows into these economies. Recognizing the reality of greater global competition for FDI, the Obama Administration has set up SelectUSA, a "one-stop shop" based in the Department of Commerce that helps both foreign and U.S. investors find the best options for their prospective businesses within the borders of the United States. SelectUSA is the first systematic Federal Government initiative to identify, inform, assist, and attract potential investors to the United States. It is also finding ways to partner with state and local economic development agencies, so that governments at all levels can coordinate efforts to attract investment. In the United States, state, local, and regional economic development organizations (EDOs) facilitate business investment attraction, retention, and expansion. SelectUSA can help these organizations compete more successfully with alternative production sites outside the United States; it can also function as an important resource for these organizations on international investment issues.

SelectUSA's activities cover a broad range of investment promotion functions. Staff respond to investment inquiries, help connect investors to appropriate federal and state agencies, and educate investors regarding relevant U.S. policies and procedures. SelectUSA staff and senior leadership also serve as ombudsmen for the investment community in Washington, working across the Federal Government to address investor concerns and issues involving federal agencies. Finally, SelectUSA works with U.S. EDO officials and U.S. embassies and consulates to organize events abroad that enable U.S. locales to promote themselves as a destination for FDI. President Obama has recently called for a substantial increase in support for SelectUSA, proposing

$12 million in new resources and an increase in staff to 35 full-time employees. Complementing this investment, President Obama has proposed to increase the presence of the Department of Commerce's U.S. and Foreign Commercial Service officers in key markets. These new officers will enhance the ability of the U.S. global network of embassies and consulates to promote FDI in the United States.

President Obama has also called for tax reforms that will help attract more FDI. These proposals include a decrease in the United States' corporate income tax rate, as well as additional tax incentives for firms that manufacture, conduct R&D, or invest in the capability to produce clean energy products within the borders of the United States. At the same time, the President's proposals eliminate incentives for U.S. firms to move jobs and production offshore. By complementing the United States' fundamental attractors with well-targeted FDI promotion efforts, the Federal Government can help ensure that the United States remains a premier destination for foreign direct investment for many years to come.

The National Export Initiative

In his January 2010 State of the Union address, President Obama set a goal of doubling U.S. exports of goods and services in five years, meaning that nominal exports would double from their 2009 level of $1.58 trillion to an annual level of $3.16 trillion by the end of 2014. To meet that goal, nominal U.S. exports must grow an average of 15 percent a year. So far, exports have grown even faster, putting the U.S. economy on track to meet the President's goal. In fact, the United States is currently ahead of schedule, despite the recent global trade slowdown. Over the 12 months ending in November 2011, total U.S. exports of goods and services exceeded $2.08 trillion, surpassing the pre-crisis peak level of $1.7 trillion and establishing a historical record. Current data suggest that the ratio of exports to GDP nearly reached 14 percent in 2011, another historical record.

Anatomy of Recent Growth in Goods Exports. U.S. trade data provide an interesting picture of the markets and goods in which America's export growth has been concentrated since the global financial crisis. Table 5-1 ranks U.S. export goods categories in order of the biggest increases in export value between the first half of 2009 and the first half of 2011. The top 10 categories collectively account for 72 percent of the total value increase in exports between the two periods.

The biggest increases have been concentrated in manufacturing industries characterized by high technology and capital intensity and in primary products, reflecting America's abundant endowments of human and physical capital, its technological prowess, and its natural-resource wealth.

Between the first half of 2009 and the first half of 2011, the United States increased its exports of vehicles by more than $26 billion (83 percent); its exports of engines, appliances, and general machinery by more than $25 billion (35 percent); and its exports of electrical machinery by more than $19 billion (33 percent). Exports of plastics, organic chemicals, and steel and ferrous metals increased by 53 percent, 57 percent, and 78 percent, respectively. These data point to America's competitiveness in important sectors of manufacturing.

At the same time, the data reaffirm the United States' strength as an exporter of natural-resource-intensive goods. Exports of mineral fuels and oils (a commodity dominated by shale oil) surged by 150 percent, or more than $35 billion, over the two-year period. That surge stems from technological breakthroughs in horizontal drilling and hydraulic fracturing that are allowing U.S. producers to extract oil from previously unusable areas; these technological developments are reviewed further in Chapter 8. Fuel exports have grown so much that the United States became a net exporter in 2011, for the first time in decades. The United States remains the world's largest importer of crude oil, and U.S. net imports of crude remain large relative to net exports of fuel products, but increased domestic production is offsetting some crude oil imports. Exports of gold, diamonds, and precious metals grew 94 percent, reflecting the high prices of those commodities on international markets.

Exports of cereals grew 77 percent, reflecting America's strength as a producer of agricultural commodities. This strength is also reflected in the impressive growth of total agricultural exports, a broader category not shown in the table, which increased by 51.8 percent over the same period, an expansion of $24 billion in dollar terms. The U.S. Department of Agriculture reports that U.S. agricultural exports reached a record high of $137.4 billion in Fiscal Year 2011, and that America's agricultural sector recorded a trade surplus of $42 billion over that period. America's ranchers, farmers, and producers are benefiting from the Administration's focus on free trade agreements and increased market access abroad.

Trends Driving Growth in Goods Exports. The sharp growth in goods exports reflects, in part, the impact of recovering from the depth of the global financial and economic crisis. It also reflects the impact of coordinated Federal Government action flowing from the President's National Export Initiative. These actions amplify the positive influence of longer-term trends that are enhancing the competitiveness of the U.S. tradable goods sector, particularly in manufacturing. U.S. workers are more productive than those of any other G-20 economy, and U.S. productivity growth has been especially strong in the manufacturing sector. However, highly productive

Table 5-1
Growth in U.S. Goods Exports, by Product

Product	HS-code	Export growth, 2009:H1–2011:H1		12-month sum (Sept. 2010–Aug. 2011) ($ Billions)
		Change ($ Billions)	Change (%)	
Mineral fuels (including shale oil)	27	35.8	150	113.3
Vehicles and parts	87	26.3	83	112.7
Engines, appliances, and general machinery	84	25.7	35	198.7
Electrical machinery and equipment accessories	85	19.1	33	157.3
Precious metals and gems	71	16.6	94	64.9
Plastics	39	10.2	53	57.5
Organic chemicals	29	8.0	57	44.4
Optical equipment and medical devices	90	7.4	24	78.0
Cereals	10	6.7	77	27.8
Iron and steel	72	5.5	78	23.8

Note: Export growth is measured between the first half of 2009 (2009:H1) and the first half of 2011 (2011:H1).
Source: U.S. International Trade Commission.

U.S. workers can be placed at a competitive disadvantage because of low labor costs abroad. This disadvantage was especially severe in the early years of the 2000s when the enduring effects of earlier financial crises in many parts of the world depressed production costs in much of Asia, Brazil, Russia, and elsewhere.

Since then, continued robust productivity growth in the United States, particularly in the manufacturing sector, has been reinforced by a gradual realignment of the currencies of many U.S. trading partners. The result has been a sharp improvement in relative unit labor costs in the United States. For example, the U.S. Bureau of Labor Statistics (BLS) tracks changes over time in the unit labor cost of manufacturing in the United States and in key trading partners. U.S. hourly compensation in manufacturing has grown over the past decade, but rapid productivity growth in the United States has reduced the cost of producing a unit of manufactured output. Meanwhile, measured in U.S. dollars, the cost of producing a unit of manufactured output in key trading partners has risen, in some cases substantially. Of the 19 economies tracked by the BLS, only Taiwan managed to improve its unit labor cost position more than the United States did.[4] Figure 5-6 displays changes in manufacturing unit labor costs for some of the key economies tracked by the BLS.

---

[4] Although the BLS does not track Chinese unit labor costs, it has tracked an index of import prices from China since 2003, and the most recent movements in this index suggest that Chinese unit labor costs are also rising.

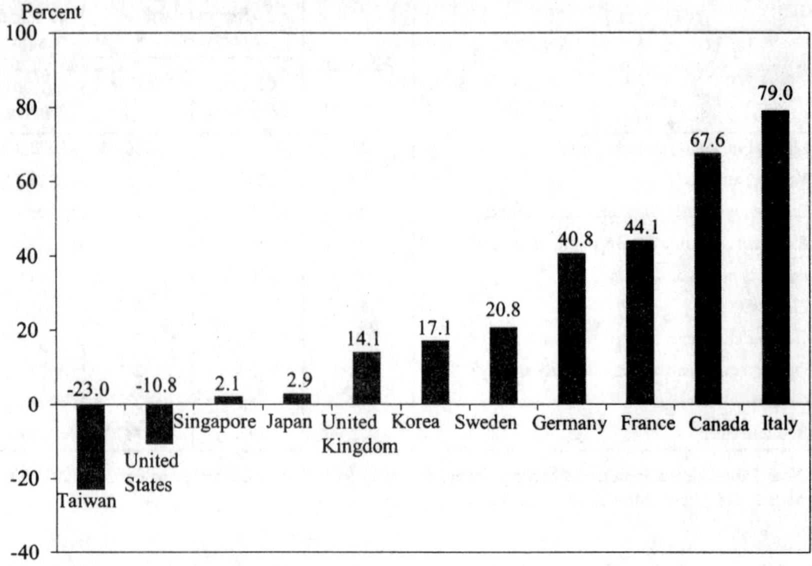

Source: Bureau of Labor Statistics.

The impact of these shifts can be seen in a number of industries including the auto industry. As U.S. auto demand recovers, the Big 3 domestic auto companies and the foreign-domiciled companies have been expanding U.S. production. This expansion is designed not only to serve the U.S. market but also to use U.S. production sites as an export platform from which to serve other markets within the Americas and beyond. Ford has announced intentions to increase investment in the United States, both to serve the U.S. market and to export. Such plans include insourcing production of its F-650 and F-750 medium-duty trucks to Ohio from Mexico; it also reportedly plans to move manufacture of components like transmission oil pumps from China to Michigan.

Improved competitiveness also appears to be reflected in employment data. U.S. manufacturers have added jobs for two consecutive years, something that had not happened since the late 1990s. Manufacturing employment has grown faster in the United States than in any other leading developed economy since the start of the recovery. As of the most recent period for which comprehensive data are available, the United States has added more net manufacturing jobs since the start of 2010 than the rest of the Group of 7 countries put together, with over 300,000 created since December 2009. While the economy is still far from recovering all the manufacturing jobs lost during the recession, signs suggest that the United

States may be experiencing a manufacturing revival. Between 2010:Q1 and 2011:Q3, manufacturing employment rose 2.5 percent in the United States compared with 2.4 percent in Germany and 1.8 percent in Canada.

In some industries, the advantage created by high U.S. productivity is reinforced by the additional advantage of abundant, domestic, low-cost natural gas. Only a few years ago, leaders of the domestic organic chemical industry predicted that shortages in natural gas would dramatically raise the domestic price of natural gas, one of their key inputs. Without adequate domestic supplies of natural gas at reasonable prices, it seemed likely that chemical production would have to shift overseas.

Since the mid-2000s, however, the discovery of new natural gas reserves, such as those within the Marcellus Shale Formation, and the development of hydraulic fracturing techniques to extract natural gas from these reserves have led to rapidly growing domestic production and relatively low domestic prices for households and downstream industrial users. By keeping domestic energy costs relatively low, the increased supply from this resource supports energy-intensive manufacturing in the United States. In fact, companies such as Dow Chemical and Westlake Chemical have announced intentions to make major investments in new U.S. facilities over the next several years. In the longer run, the scale of America's natural gas endowment appears to be large enough that exports of natural gas to other major markets could be economically viable. The Obama Administration is taking steps to ensure that this resource is developed in a safe and environmentally responsible way.

However, in most of the manufacturing industries where American firms continue to enjoy robust export sales, U.S. producers rely principally on high productivity, rather than inexpensive inputs, to offset the higher wages and other labor compensation they pay their U.S. workers. The openness and competitive intensity of the American economy have been a key source of our national strength, since they have increased the efficiency of U.S. firms and industries. (See Hsieh and Klenow 2009, 2011 for recent research.) As a consequence, even extremely low wages in developing countries are not sufficient to provide a commanding cost advantage with respect to U.S. firms, at least in some product categories.

Exports can also be measured by looking at major destination markets. Table 5-2 ranks destination markets by the increase in value of exports between the first half of 2009 and the first half of 2011. The top 10 markets collectively accounted for 70 percent of the total increase in export value. Export flows to Canada and Mexico increased by nearly $80 billion. Much of the rest of the U.S. export expansion was driven by exports to Asia. Even the tsunami-battered Japanese economy purchased nearly $8 billion more

Market	Export growth, 2009:H1–2011:H1		12-month sum (Sept. 2010–Aug. 2011) ($ Billions)
	Change ($ Billions)	Change (%)	
Canada	43.1	45	272.2
Mexico	36.3	62	187.1
China, Mainland	19.2	63	102.2
Euro Area	16.1	20	193.2
Republic of Korea	9.0	72	42.1
Brazil	8.4	71	40.2
Japan	7.7	31	64.3
Hong Kong	6.9	71	31.9
Taiwan	6.0	80	27.5
Singapore	5.0	51	30.5

Note: Export growth is measured between the first half of 2009 (2009:H1) and the first half of 2011 (2011:H1).
Source: U.S. International Trade Commission.

in U.S. exports in the first half of 2011 than it did in the first half of 2009. Outside of North America and Asia, Brazil continued to display its emerging economic importance, absorbing a 71 percent increase in U.S. exports that, in dollar terms, slightly exceeded export growth to Japan.

The Role of Services in Export Growth and America's Current Account Balance

While export growth is critical, exports are just one component of the current account balance, the most comprehensive measure of the Nation's exchange of goods and services with the rest of the world. The main components of the current account include exports and imports of goods, exports and imports of services, and the income balance—the difference between the income American firms earn from their foreign businesses and the income foreign firms earn from their U.S. businesses.

A look at the recent history of the U.S. current account balance and its key components reveals some interesting patterns. Although U.S. exports of goods are at historical highs, reflecting in part the improved competitiveness of American manufacturers, the U.S. trade deficit in goods (which does not include trade in services) has nevertheless widened significantly since early 2009, as an expanding economy has boosted demand for imports (Figure 5-7). The trajectory of the U.S. current account, however, is following a different path now than it did in the previous recovery, and the difference primarily reflects the impact of the other two main elements of the current account—services trade and the U.S. income balance.

From the early 2000s through 2006, the current account balance tracked the trade balance in goods quite closely. The two series began to diverge in late 2007. The balance on goods remained in deep deficit, but the trade surplus in services began to increase, and the income balance grew even more rapidly. When the global financial crisis hit in earnest in the third quarter of 2008, U.S. growth and import demand dried up, and the two series moved closely together (this time rapidly toward balance) through early 2009. Then, as financial markets stabilized and growth resumed, a gap opened up once again. The balance on goods deteriorated, but the services surplus expanded and the income balance grew even more sharply, largely offsetting the declining balance in goods and keeping the current account relatively stable. More recently, the goods trade balance appears to have broadly stabilized, whereas the services surplus and the income balance continue to grow. With a need to further strengthen the current account balance, federal policymakers recognize the need not only to encourage exports of goods, but also to expand the important role that services trade can play in that process.

The Prospects for Trade Growth in Services. Like most other advanced economies, U.S. GDP is dominated by service industries. According to the Bureau of Economic Analysis, services, broadly defined, account for more than 60 percent of U.S. GDP. However, the role of business services within

Figure 5-7
U.S. Current Account Balance and Its Components, 2000–2011

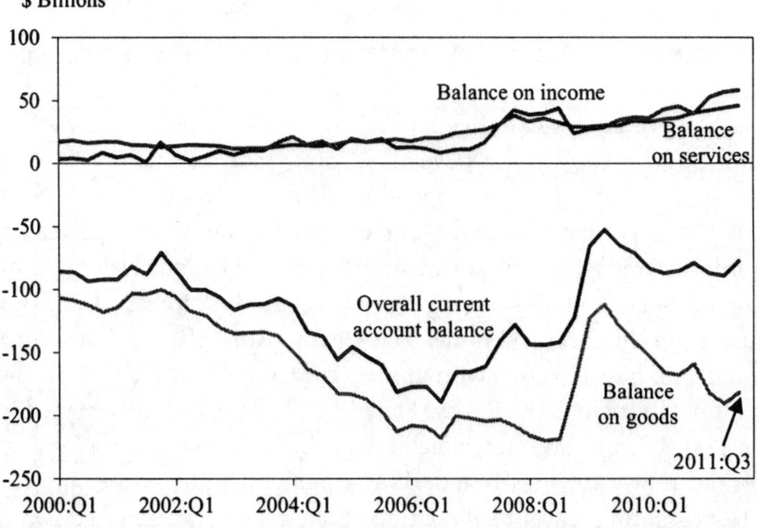

Note: The current account balance above includes goods, services, and income, but does not include unilateral transfers.
Source: Bureau of Economic Analysis.

the U.S. economy is less widely recognized. In 2007, a year unaffected by the recent severe downturn and gradual recovery, business services, a collection of industries that includes finance, engineering services, research and development services, and software production, employed 25 percent of the U.S. workforce according to data from the Economic Census. The share of employment in business services was substantially larger than in the entire manufacturing sector in that year (10 percent), and the average wage in business services, $56,000, was significantly higher than in manufacturing ($46,000) (Jensen 2011).

While services remain more difficult to trade than goods, advances in communications technologies and the growing ease and declining expense of international travel are making business services increasingly tradable across countries. As this trend gained strength, employment in the business service sector increased almost 30 percent between 1997 and 2007, while manufacturing employment decreased more than 20 percent. Most tradable business services rely intensively on highly skilled experts, which the United States has in large numbers. In other words, the growing tradability of business services plays to America's comparative advantage. Some evidence of this potential is apparent when one looks at the broader context of America's trade across the full range of service industries.

Services exports have expanded dramatically, growing by 114 percent between 1997 and 2010, according to official data. They now account for nearly 30 percent of total U.S. exports. Imports of services have also expanded rapidly, but the U.S. surplus in services trade, already large, has more than tripled since 2003.

What are the categories of services exports, and what is their relative contribution to the surplus? Figure 5-8 depicts the aggregate service trade flows in the five main categories tracked by official statistics and measures their contribution to America's overall services trade surplus.

Travel exports reflect the spending of foreign tourists and business travelers to the United States who purchase goods and services here, while travel imports reflect purchases made by U.S. residents traveling abroad. The United States remains among the world's leading tourist destinations and runs a surplus in travel trade. The Obama Administration has sought to expand U.S. travel exports with unprecedented federal action to promote international tourism in the United States. In 2010, the President signed into law the Travel Promotion Act, which established the Corporation for Travel Promotion, now known as Brand USA, a public-private partnership dedicated to promoting travel to the United States. The State Department has also increased its visa-processing capacity in priority countries like Brazil

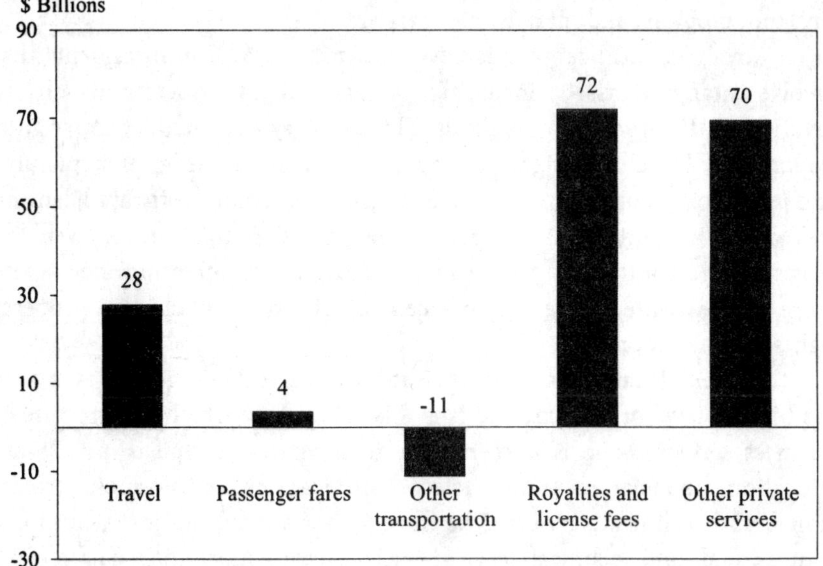

Source: Bureau of Economic Analysis.

and China to ensure that the United States benefits from the rapid expansion of outbound tourism from these emerging markets.

Moreover, on January 19, the President established a Task Force on Travel and Competitiveness that will develop a National Travel and Tourism Strategy with a goal of making the United States the world's top travel and tourism destination. The benefits of that strategy include not only the potential increase in travel exports, but also lower travel imports as it will provide Americans with more and better choices of travel and tourism destinations within the United States. Because of their value as public goods, the government has an important role in ensuring that national treasures such as Yellowstone National Park and the Statue of Liberty are appropriately maintained and made accessible to domestic and international tourists. While there are many private, state, and local destinations in the United States, public expenditures on the National Park System (NPS) are much lower than the benefits they provide to all Americans, even to those who are not necessarily planning a vacation or visit to one of the 397 destinations that make up the NPS (National Research Council 1996). This provides yet another example of the ways in which investments in the environment yield benefits for the economy (Chapter 8).

In the category of passenger fares, exports are those received by U.S. carriers from foreign residents; imports are those paid by U.S. residents to foreign carriers. Other transportation exports and imports include U.S. international transactions arising from the transportation of goods by ocean, air, land, pipeline, and inland water carriers.

Royalties and license fees cover transactions with nonresidents that involve intangible assets, including patents and trade secrets, which are involved in the production of goods. This category also includes copyrights, trademarks, franchises, rights to reproduce or distribute motion pictures and television recordings, rights to broadcast live events, software licensing fees, and other intellectual property rights. In 2010, this category was the largest single contributor to the services surplus, highlighting the importance to the United States of enforcement of strong intellectual property rights in other countries.[5]

The final category, other private services (OPS), generates by far the highest level of exports, and it is this category in which the promise of business services exports is seen. The main services included in OPS are education, financial, insurance, telecommunications, and business, professional, and technical services. The most important subcategory—business, professional, and technical services—accounts for more than half of OPS exports. Altogether, OPS exports expanded by about 150 percent from 2000 through 2010—a compound average growth rate of nearly 10 percent a year.

The additional detail on service exports and imports presented in Table 5-3 and Table 5-4 underlines two important facts about U.S. services trade. First, the other advanced industrial countries are still America's dominant trading partners in this sector, both as markets and as suppliers. As rapid economic growth raises income levels in large emerging markets, however, U.S. service export flows to these countries are likely to grow. Second, as noted, the surplus in services is disproportionately driven by two categories—other private services and royalties and licensing—that are skill-intensive and thus conform to America's comparative advantage as a technologically advanced nation with an abundant supply of highly educated workers. This supply of skilled workers and the broader role that education plays in the U.S. labor market is discussed in Chapter 6.

In addition to exporting services, U.S. firms provide services through affiliates in foreign markets. Over the past decade, services provided through affiliates have grown rapidly, and in 2009, the most recent year for which comprehensive data are available, services supplied through the foreign affiliates of U.S. firms totaled $1.1 trillion. Of course, U.S. customers also

---

[5] In fact, the official numbers for royalty and license fees may understate, perhaps substantially, America's receipts for the use of its intangible assets. A report submitted last year by leading international economists (Feenstra et al. 2010) noted the ability of multinational corporations to effectively locate their intellectual property in low-tax jurisdictions, minimizing their global tax liability as well as measured U.S. royalties and license fees.

purchase services from the U.S. affiliates of foreign firms. These purchases totaled $668.8 billion in 2009. The difference between services received from and supplied to the United States via the channel of affiliate sales was $407.6 billion, providing yet another reflection of America's comparative advantage in this domain (Koncz-Bruner and Flatness 2011).

Policy Initiatives to Support Export Growth in Goods and Services

Recent economic research has focused on U.S. firm productivity and the fixed cost of exporting as fundamental determinants of U.S. exports at the firm and product level (Bernard et al. 2003; Melitz 2003). Fixed costs for firms are associated not only with the decision to begin exporting but also with the decision to export to a specific country. Before significant exports to a given country can begin, a prospective exporting firm must develop a strategy that allows it to compete successfully against experienced rivals in that country, which operates under a different legal system and may use a different language. Successful exporters must invest considerable management attention and time to developing this strategy before they can begin to earn any returns from exporting. The costs of serving a particular foreign market may also increase if the firm's products and complementary services must be significantly altered to meet the demands and tastes of customers in that market. Exporters also must incur the costs of finding distribution channels in the foreign country and the ongoing costs of transporting their goods across national borders and contending with tariff or nontariff barriers to trade. These costs are worth incurring only if the firm is dynamic and productive enough to have a high probability of success.

Federal programs exist to help firms deal with these costs. While private firms must take the lead in crafting their export strategies, the Department of Commerce's International Trade Administration maintains offices of trade professionals in more than 100 U.S. communities and 77 foreign countries to help U.S. firms become export-ready, identify target markets, and navigate the demands of foreign regulation and cultural differences. The Federal Government can also use effective multilateral, bilateral, or regional trade negotiations to reduce the costs imposed on U.S. firms by foreign tariff and nontariff barriers. It can also seek to ensure that American firms face a level playing field by insisting that U.S. trading partners honor their treaty commitments regarding market access for U.S. firms. Finally, in circumstances in which a particular exporter faces financing constraints or the threat of subsidized finance for international competitors, the Federal Government can seek to alleviate these constraints and counter foreign

Table 5-3

Cross-Border Services Exports by Type and Country, 2010

Country	2010 Exports ($ Millions)					
	Total private services	Travel	Passenger fares	Other transportation	Royalties and license fees	Other private services
All countries	530,274	103,505	30,931	39,936	105,583	250,320
Total for the top 10 countries	290,680	59,489	19,659	20,395	65,607	125,530
Canada	50,521	16,641	4,182	2,984	8,287	18,427
United Kingdom	48,535	8,765	2,801	3,641	6,864	26,464
Japan	44,750	10,198	4,360	3,555	10,721	15,916
Ireland	24,840	1,033	280	300	12,850	10,377
Germany	24,118	4,534	1,248	2,779	6,181	9,376
Mexico	24,110	6,117	2,612	1,226	2,526	11,629
China	21,135	3,780	1,225	2,296	3,333	10,501
Switzerland	20,313	1,043	320	1,169	8,281	9,500
Brazil	16,515	4,236	1,683	998	3,123	6,475
France	15,843	3,142	948	1,447	3,441	6,865
Other countries	239,594	44,016	11,272	19,541	39,976	124,790

Source: Bureau of Economic Analysis.

Table 5-4

Cross-Border Services Imports by Type and Country, 2010

Country	2010 Imports ($ Millions)					
	Total private services	Travel	Passenger fares	Other transportation	Royalties and license fees	Other private services
All countries	368,036	75,507	27,279	51,202	33,450	180,598
Total for the top 10 countries	215,078	33,704	11,410	25,382	25,071	119,511
Canada	39,652	4,324	3,705	3,107	3,031	25,485
United Kingdom	31,740	245	—	974	16	30,505
Japan	25,579	6,539	501	4,404	1,036	13,099
Ireland	23,541	3,278	1,331	5,670	7,817	5,445
Germany	22,476	2,606	2,562	3,632	3,187	10,489
Mexico	19,665	630	399	1,748	5,272	11,616
China	15,067	2,409	1,473	1,887	4,016	5,282
Switzerland	13,730	8,999	697	904	379	2,751
Brazil	13,661	2,108	207	156	141	11,049
France	9,967	2,566	535	2,900	176	3,790
Other countries	152,958	41,803	15,869	25,820	8,379	61,087

Source: Bureau of Economic Analysis.

government efforts. Over the past three years, the Obama Administration has placed renewed emphasis on all of these policy domains.

Free Trade Agreements with Colombia, Panama, and Korea. The Obama Administration has worked to restore the Nation's economic stability and support jobs for more Americans with the expansion of smart, responsible trade policy. From day one, the Obama Administration has insisted on higher standards for trade agreements. The President moved to address important concerns that the Administration, certain stakeholders, and Members of Congress had with respect to the situations in Colombia, Panama, and Korea. This domestic consultation and further consultations with U.S. trading partners took time, as did negotiations with Congress to ensure that the passage of the free trade agreements was accompanied by a strengthening of America's Trade Adjustment Assistance program for workers adversely impacted by international competition and by an extension of key trade preference programs. Once this process was complete, Congress passed the three agreements in quick succession in the fall of 2011, marking the biggest step forward in American trade liberalization in nearly two decades. Of the three agreements, the most economically significant was the Korea–United States free trade agreement, which was expected to boost annual U.S. goods exports to Korea by as much as $11 billion. The agreement also included Korean commitments expected to result in considerable expansion of U.S. services exports.

The Trans-Pacific Partnership. In November 2009, President Obama announced the Administration's intention to participate in Trans-Pacific Partnership (TPP) negotiations to conclude a free trade agreement with key trading partners in the Asia-Pacific region. The agreement aims to set a new and higher standard for regional free trade agreements, not only addressing the traditional core issues in such agreements but broadening the scope to include regulatory coherence and priorities for small and medium-size enterprises. In addition to the United States, the other countries participating in the negotiations currently include Australia, Brunei Darussalam, Chile, Malaysia, New Zealand, Peru, Singapore, and Vietnam.

At the November 2011 APEC meeting in Honolulu, TPP leaders announced the broad outlines of a TPP agreement. In addition to existing negotiating partners, Japan, Canada, and Mexico have formally expressed their interest in joining TPP negotiations. While no decision has been made yet by the TPP countries regarding expanding negotiations, interest by Japan, Canada, and Mexico in the TPP demonstrates the economic and strategic importance of this initiative to the Asia-Pacific region.

Support for Small Exporters. In a world of imperfect financial markets, the costs of financing export operations pose an additional barrier for smaller firms. Given that export opportunities can come to small exporters with significant risks attached, domestic financial institutions may regard a small firm that is highly dependent on exports as a riskier (and therefore less creditworthy) borrower than one with an exclusively domestic focus. The relatively modest financing needs of small exporters are a further disincentive to private financial institutions, which would have to engage in time-consuming assessments of the firm, its products, and the country-specific risks involved in a transaction to originate only a small loan with limited value for the lending institution. Unless it is obvious to the lender that the firm has excellent prospects for significant export growth, and brings with it the near certainty of rapid expansion in loan volume, the money a private bank can make on such a transaction is limited relative to the transaction costs themselves.

To address these issues the Federal Government has directed the Export-Import Bank of the United States to proactively support small and medium-size firms. First established in the 1930s to finance U.S. international trade when and where private-sector financing was difficult or unreasonably costly to obtain, the Ex-Im Bank has historically focused much of its lending activity on larger, established exporters. The Obama Administration, however, has encouraged the bank to substantially increase lending to smaller firms, and in Fiscal Year 2010, the Ex-Im Bank authorized $5 billion—20 percent of its total authorizations—to support small businesses as primary exporters. The Ex-Im Bank approved 3,091 transactions involving small business exporters—88 percent of total authorizations. In the same year, the bank issued 2,524 insurance policies to small business exporters, 90 percent of such policies for the year. The bank also authorized a record $2.2 billion in working-capital guarantees, 70 percent of which supported small business.

Financial support for the expanding international activities of small business extends beyond the Ex-Im Bank. The Overseas Private Investment Corporation (OPIC), the U.S. Government's development finance institution, extends medium- to long-term financing through direct loans, loan guaranties, political risk insurance, and support for investment funds to eligible investment projects in developing and emerging markets, where conventional financial institutions often are reluctant or unable to lend. In Fiscal Year 2011, 78 percent of OPIC's projects, representing nearly $1 billion in commitments, involved American small and medium-sized businesses.[6]

---

[6] The Ex-Im Bank and OPIC follow the Small Business Administration's definition of a small business, using guidelines that reflect, among other things, sales, employment levels, and sector of economic activity. These guidelines are available online at http://www.sba.gov/sites/default/files/Size_Standards_Table.pdf.

Promoting U.S. Economic Interests Abroad. Even as it seeks to open up new markets for American business through new trade agreements, the Obama Administration is also working to protect American commercial interests under existing trade agreements. An historic victory came in May 2011, when the World Trade Organization (WTO) issued a final ruling siding with the United States in its case against the European Union over illegal subsidies to Airbus. After decades of dispute and more than five years of official proceedings, the WTO ruled that the EU governments had provided $18 billion in illegal subsidies to Airbus and ordered them removed by the end of the year. U.S. Trade Representative Ron Kirk hailed the ruling, saying, "The WTO Appellate Body has confirmed without a doubt that Airbus received massive subsidies for more than 40 years and that these subsidies have greatly harmed the United States, including causing Boeing to lose sales and market share in key markets throughout the world." If the European Union fails to comply with the WTO directive, the United States can seek the right to impose countermeasures.

In its ongoing dialogue with China, the Obama Administration secured a strong commitment from Chinese President Hu Jintao that China would stop discriminating against U.S. technologies and intellectual property in its government procurement plans. The Administration is monitoring developments closely to ensure that market realities conform to central government directives. The United States has filed a WTO case against China, challenging the troubling imposition by China of antidumping and countervailing duties against imports of U.S. chicken "broiler products." The Administration scored another major victory in January 2012 when the WTO's Appellate Body upheld a WTO panel ruling condemning Chinese export quotas and duties on certain key industrial raw materials as a violation of China's WTO commitments. These actions add to a series of cases in which the Federal Government has taken action at the WTO to protect U.S. economic interests jeopardized by Chinese policy in areas such as steel products, electronic payment services, and wind power equipment.

In November 2011, the United States gained China's confirmation through bilateral negotiations that it would not require foreign electric vehicle manufacturers to transfer technology to Chinese enterprises or to establish Chinese brands as a condition for investing and selling in China. One year earlier, the United States successfully persuaded China to adopt transparent and non-discriminatory technology standards for its emerging smart grid market and to remain technologically neutral with regard to the development of third-generation and future technologies for its telecommunications market.

Several of America's trading partners, including China, have effectively imposed bans on U.S. meat product exports. These bans have no scientific basis, and the Administration has been trying to bring these bans to an end as soon as possible. In 2011, agreements were reached to resume exports to Chile and Egypt. Fifty-seven countries have removed their avian influenza bans on imports of poultry products from the United States since 2008. Most of the countries that imposed bans on the import of U.S. swine, pork, and pork products in the wake of international concern over the H1N1 virus have removed those bans.

With strong support from the United States, Russia concluded negotiations to join the WTO in December 2011. In supporting Russia's WTO accession, the Obama Administration has laid the basis for a more effective, rules-based approach to managing U.S. trade relations with the largest economy not yet inside the WTO system. The Administration will be working with Congress to end application of the "Jackson-Vanik" amendment to Russia so that the United States can enjoy all of the benefits of Russia's membership in the WTO and U.S. companies and workers can compete on a level playing field with those of other WTO Members in exporting products and services to Russia.[7]

To further enhance the Federal Government's ability to protect the Nation's commercial interests, the President is creating and seeking funding for a new Trade Enforcement Unit, which will significantly enhance the Administration's capabilities to aggressively challenge unfair trade practices under international and domestic trade rules. The President is also proposing to improve trade inspection capabilities of the Customs and Border Patrol and the Food and Drug Administration, to increase the likelihood of stopping counterfeit, pirated, or unsafe goods before they enter the U.S. market. Certain countries, including China, aggressively use subsidized capital to promote their exports, and appear to offer such export financing on better terms than allowed under current international best practices. In response, the Administration will actively employ its existing authorities so that the Ex-Im Bank can provide U.S. firms competing for domestic or third-country sales with matching financial support to counter foreign noncompetitive official financing that fails to observe international best practices.

The IMF estimates that sub-Saharan Africa will grow by 5.5 percent in 2012, faster than advanced, emerging, and developing economies as a whole. Between 2000 and 2010, five of the 10 fastest-growing economies in the world were in sub-Saharan Africa, and trade between Africa and the

---

[7] The Jackson-Vanik amendment is a provision in the 1974 Trade Act that denies most favored nation status to certain countries that restrict emigration. It was introduced during the Cold War, partly as a response to efforts by the Soviet Union to restrict emigration.

rest of the world increased more than 200 percent. Central to the United States' economic policy for Africa is the African Growth and Opportunity Act (AGOA), which provides duty-free access to a broad range of exports from 37 eligible sub-Saharan African countries. To help African countries make the most of AGOA's trade benefits, the United States funds technical assistance work at Regional Trade Hubs. The United States also fosters investment by negotiating Bilateral Investment Treaties (BITs) with African countries. In 2009, the United States launched BIT negotiations with Mauritius, and, in 2011, the U.S. Senate ratified the U.S.-Rwanda BIT.

In agriculture and other sectors, the U.S. Agency for International Development uses public-private partnerships to build new markets and has been recognized by the Organisation for Economic Co-operation and Development as the best among its peers with respect to private-sector engagement. The Millennium Challenge Corporation (MCC) is partnering with American and local businesses. From helping the Port of Cotonou in Benin cut its average customs-clearance time in half to facilitating an American company's efforts to provide much-needed power to Tanzania's national grid, the MCC is investing in infrastructure to expand trade, commerce, and development across the African continent. Other agencies—including OPIC and the Ex-Im Bank—have significantly increased their investment in Africa. These activities are consistent with the goals of President Obama's Presidential Policy Directive on Global Development signed in September 2010 that establishes a new model for U.S. development efforts.

Tax Reform to Promote American Competitiveness. The Administration's proposed reform of the U.S. corporate income tax seeks to enhance American competitiveness, promote investment in the United States, and support continued robust growth of American exports. As part of a comprehensive tax reform plan, the President has proposed a reduction in the U.S. corporate income tax rate, with additional incentives available for firms that manufacture, conduct research and development, or invest in the capability to produce clean energy products within the borders of the United States. At the same time, the President addresses longstanding features of the American corporate tax system that encourage some companies to move jobs and production overseas.

Increasing Market Access for Services. As noted, the United States has a strong comparative advantage in services. The global market for services trade, however, remains far more closed than the global market for manufactured goods. The long history of extensive trade in goods, the relatively simple nature of many barriers (tariffs and quotas) to such trade, and the cumulative result of six decades of multilateral, bilateral, and regional trade liberalization efforts have resulted in a global economy in which formal barriers to trade in manufactured goods are reasonably low, especially in the advanced industrial countries.

The barriers to trade in services are more complex and harder to quantify. Hufbauer, Schott, and Wong (2010) review a number of methodologies for quantifying the barriers to trade in services and present new estimates at the country level of the tariff equivalents of these barriers. Their findings suggest that the aggregate level of discrimination against services imports in important emerging markets such as China, India, and Indonesia is equivalent to a tariff on these imports of more than 60 percent. The size of these barriers may not be surprising—extensive international trade in services is a recent phenomenon, and diplomatic efforts to open services markets are just beginning—but these barriers deprive American firms of critical export opportunities to rapidly emerging markets in an area where their international comparative advantage is the strongest.

America's productive exporters of services cannot solve this problem on their own. The President is committed to negotiating effectively and aggressively for increased liberalization of services trade. The Administration has already made progress in bilateral and regional trade agreements, but the largest emerging-market economies have not yet been fully engaged in these initiatives. The primary multilateral means for seeking greater services market access has been through negotiations pursuant to the General Agreement on Trade in Services (GATS) and, to a lesser degree, the WTO Agreement on Government Procurement. While taking existing GATS disciplines and market access commitments into account, the United States is also pursuing additional pathways to services liberalization, including a new, multiparty agreement open to any country ready to take on high standards and address new issues such as trade in the digital economy. Other advanced countries and progressive developing countries are likely to share the U.S. interest in pushing for greater liberalization of services trade and may be willing partners in this effort.

Recent scholarship demonstrates that services liberalization is in the interest of countries that are importing services as well as those that are exporting services. Better access to world-class services raises productivity and living standards in emerging-market economies. Interesting evidence on this point comes from a randomized experiment in India (Bloom et al. 2011). Researchers based at Stanford University and the World Bank randomly selected a set of Indian textile factories to receive a complimentary five-month program of consulting services from a leading international firm. Upon arriving in these factories, the researchers and consultants found that productivity was hampered by poor management practices. Over the next five months, the consultants worked with the firms to implement standard management practices proven to have enhanced productivity, output, and profitability in the West. When the project ended, the "treated" factories had cut defects roughly in half, substantially reduced inventories, and increased output, while the control factories saw little change. The authors calculate that these performance improvements increased profits by about $350,000 a year. These are sufficiently large increases that the firms would have made enough money from the consulting projects to be able to pay the consultants commercial rates for their engagement in the projects.

Given the magnitude of the improvement, why had the firms not adopted these practices earlier? The researchers' results suggest that informational barriers were the primary factor explaining the lack of adoption. What is true for India is likely to be true throughout the developing world. By reducing barriers to trade in services, developing countries can help their own firms move toward the productivity frontier achieved in the West.

CONCLUSION

Over the course of 2011, the pace of growth in the global economy slowed, posing challenges for the U.S. recovery. Nevertheless, U.S. exports have climbed to record high levels, the current account deficit narrowed to 2.9 percent of GDP in the third quarter, and the economy has begun to rebalance its sources of growth, laying the foundation for sustained future expansion. The greatest threats to continued progress in these domains lie beyond America's borders. Provided Europe's debt crisis can be resolved, America's export growth and progress toward rebalancing are likely to continue at a brisk pace. Other developments in the global economy, notably the continued expansion of international trade in services and the interest of major trading partners in new U.S. trade initiatives, provide a foundation of new opportunities on which the U.S. economy can build in the years to come.

CHAPTER 6

JOBS AND INCOME: TODAY AND TOMORROW

Recessions caused by financial crises typically cause large declines in aggregate demand, as households that have borrowed excessively during the boom years bring down their debt during and after the recession. This deleveraging cycle takes time and disrupts the labor market, because reductions in consumer spending mean that employers require fewer workers to satisfy customer demand. Long-term problems that have been building over several decades pose a further set of challenges for the labor market. Inequality was sharply rising and earnings were stagnant for middle-income families for many years before the latest recession. And job growth from the end of the 2001 recession through 2007 was the weakest for any recovery in more than five decades. The Great Recession exacerbated these problems.

Despite the severe damage caused by the recession that began in December 2007, the labor market is gradually improving. Sustained private-sector job growth resumed more quickly after the official end of the 2007–09 recession than it did after the two previous recessions (Figure 6-1). Private employers have now added jobs, on net, every month since February 2010. In 2011, 2.1 million private-sector jobs were added to the economy, the most in any year since 2005. But, given the depth of the 2007–09 recession, the recovery has not yet resulted in enough new jobs to replace all of those that were lost.

Continuing the recovery is essential to putting more Americans back to work. And even as the economy and job market recover, long-term trends that predate the recession continue to pose a challenge for American families and businesses. Responding to these challenges, the President has proposed measures that independent economists predict would create millions of jobs. To make sure that Americans are equipped to compete in the economy of the future, the President has also taken steps to improve K–12 education and to make college more accessible and affordable for middle-class families,

Monthly Change in Private-Sector Employment, 1980–2012

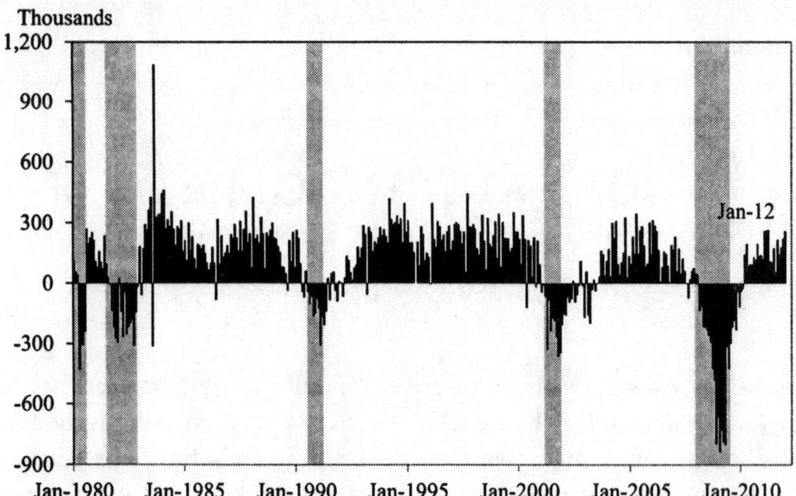

Note: The large fluctuations in private-sector employment in 1983 were due to strike activity. Shading denotes recession.
Source: Department of Labor, Bureau of Labor Statistics.

actions that should help to mitigate the long-term trend of growing income inequality.

JOBS AND EMPLOYMENT

The traditional pattern has been that as both the U.S. economy and population have grown, so too has the number of jobs filled by American workers. Between January 1980 and July 1990, from business-cycle peak to business-cycle peak, total U.S. employment grew by an average of 151,000 net new payroll jobs a month; it grew even more quickly, at a rate of 178,000 payroll jobs a month, between July 1990 and March 2001, again from business-cycle peak to business-cycle peak. But this long-term pattern of job growth changed around the turn of the millennium. Between March 2001 and December 2007, the economy added a monthly average of only 68,000 total jobs and only 50,000 private-sector jobs. U.S. job creation slowed even as productivity growth remained relatively strong, and even as other developed countries, such as the United Kingdom and Canada, maintained robust job growth.

Against this backdrop of weak employment growth beginning in about 2000, the economy fell into recession in December 2007 and began to shed jobs at the end of 2008 at a rate unprecedented in the postwar era.

During 2008 and 2009, the economy lost an average of 361,000 jobs a month, reaching a high of 818,000 jobs in January 2009. As the recession continued, the unemployment rate doubled, from 5.0 percent in April 2008 to a peak of 10.0 percent in October 2009, a rate not seen since 1983 (Figure 6-2).

Soon after the President signed the American Recovery and Reinvestment Act (Recovery Act) on February 17, 2009, the pace of job loss slowed. The private sector has added jobs in each of the past 23 months, registering a cumulative gain of 3.7 million jobs since February 2010, including 2.1 million jobs in 2011. Private-sector job growth has averaged 159,000 jobs per month since February 2010, and 218,000 jobs per month in the last three months (ending in January 2012).

The recession has had a large and continuing negative fiscal impact on State and local governments, however, and they continue to shed workers, thus offsetting some of the private-sector job growth. Nonetheless, with the support provided by the Recovery Act and by the payroll tax cut and unemployment insurance extensions contained in the Tax Relief, Unemployment Insurance Reauthorization, and Job Creation Act of 2010, the U.S. economy has added jobs in every month since February 2010, excluding temporary Census hires. The continuing recovery has brought the unemployment rate down from a peak of 10.0 percent in October 2009 to 8.3 percent in January

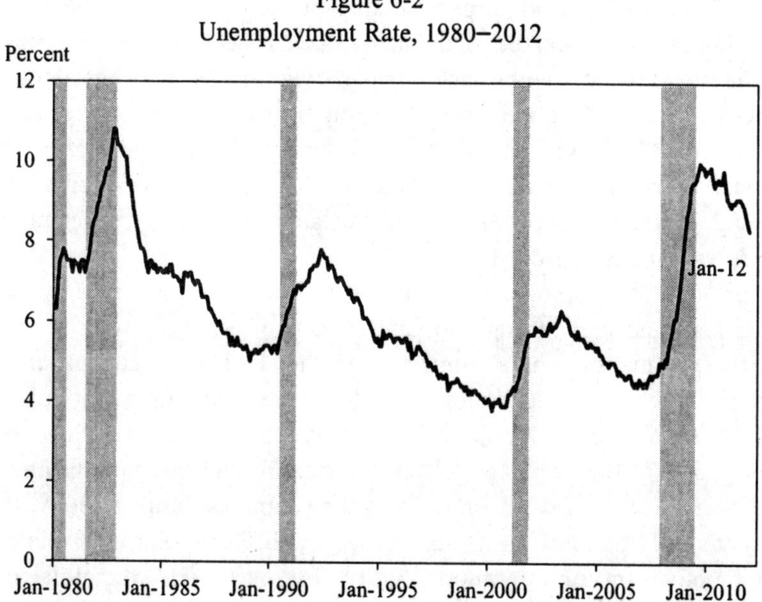

Figure 6-2
Unemployment Rate, 1980–2012

Note: Shading denotes recession.
Source: Department of Labor, Bureau of Labor Statistics.

2012. The 0.9 percentage point decline in the unemployment rate that occurred in 2011 is the largest in any calendar year since 1994.

The pace of the recovery has varied across sectors of the economy, with those sectors most harmed by the financial crisis the slowest to recover. Since February 2010, when the private sector began consistently adding jobs, job growth has been strong in industries such as education and health services (+717,000 jobs as of January 2012); trade, transportation, and utilities (+683,000 jobs); and manufacturing (+400,000), but is still weak in some sectors, notably construction (+43,000 jobs) and State and local government (-456,000 jobs). The continued weakness in these two sectors reflects the severity of the financial crisis and the recession's impact on the housing market and on government revenues.

The pace of recovery has also differed across demographic groups. The Hispanic unemployment rate reached a peak of 13.1 percent twice, first in August 2009 and then again in November 2010. The unemployment rate for African Americans reached 16.7 percent in March 2010 and then again as recently as August 2011. The unemployment rates for Hispanics and African Americans as of January 2012 are well below their respective peaks—down 2.6 percentage points for Hispanics and 3.1 percentage points for African Americans—but still remain elevated.

Trends in the labor force participation rate and in the employment-to-population ratio that pre-date the recession, and were exacerbated by the recession, are a continuing concern. After trending upward for most of the post-World-War-II period, largely because of increases in the fraction of women in the labor force, the participation rate has been in a secular decline since the late 1990s, driven by declining participation of Americans between the ages of 16 and 54, as well as by the aging of the workforce. These same developments have also lowered the employment-to-population ratio. The labor force participation rate fell further in the recession. As discussed in Chapter 2, many of those who have left the labor force since the beginning of the recession have enrolled in school.

Extended unemployment insurance benefits have encouraged workers who lost their jobs through no fault of their own to keep searching for work, thereby maintaining a connection to the labor force. Helping more Americans get back to work more quickly remains the top priority of the Administration's economic policy. That is why, in September 2011, President Obama proposed the American Jobs Act to support and speed up the ongoing recovery for American workers and their families. More recently, the President's 2012 State of the Union Address and Fiscal Year 2013 Budget laid out a blueprint for an economy built to last on American manufacturing, American energy, skills for American workers, and American values.

The Dynamics of Labor Market Trends

Underlying the changes in employment is a dynamic process through which firms are born and die, jobs are gained and lost, and workers transition in and out of employment and between jobs. These labor market dynamics have strong cyclical properties that have been very much at work during and since the recession, but secular trends are also changing the functioning of the U.S. labor market over the long run.

Job Dynamics

The job market is dynamic, with new firms entering and others exiting, and some growing and others contracting. The dynamic job market is supported by a safety net that helps to protect workers when job transitions do not occur smoothly and that gives entrepreneurs a backstop when they take risks with potentially high payoffs in future productivity. The importance of the many facets of the safety net is discussed in detail in Chapter 7.

These job dynamics are characterized by gross flows of job gains and job losses across firms. Gross job gains are measured as jobs created in new and expanding firms, while gross job losses are measured as jobs that disappear in firms that are contracting or closing.[1] Net job growth in a given period is the difference between gross job gains and gross job losses:

$$NET_t = G_t - L_t$$

where

$$G_t = \sum_{i \in C} (N_{it} - N_{it-1}) \quad \text{and} \quad L_t = \sum_{i \in D} (N_{it-1} - N_{it}),$$

and NET_t is the net number of jobs created by firms in the economy in period t; G_t is the amount of gross job gains in the period; L_t is the amount of gross job losses; i is a firm; C is the set of firms that are either new or have grown in period t; D is the set of firms that have either exited or contracted in period t; and N is the number of jobs.

To calculate the rates of net job growth, gross job gains, and gross job losses, each of these values is divided by overall employment in the economy

---

[1] Alternative measures of gross job gains and gross job losses use units of observation other than the firm, such as the establishment, generally a physical location of business activity where goods and services are produced. Using units smaller than firms leads to higher rates of gross gains and losses because jobs that flow across the units within a firm are counted in the gross measures.

averaged between one period and the next period. So, for example, the rate of gross job gains in period t is:[2]

$$GR_t = \frac{G_t}{0.5 * (N_t + N_{t-1})}.$$

Recent work by economists using the Business Dynamic Statistics (BDS) data at the U.S. Census Bureau demonstrates the tremendous dynamism of private-sector employment in the United States (Haltiwanger, Jarmin, and Miranda 2010; Haltiwanger 2011). Between 1980 and 2009 (the most recent year of BDS data), approximately 17 percent of all jobs in the private sector in an average year were added in that year at new or expanding firms; approximately 15 percent of jobs in an average year were gone by the next year because firms closed or contracted. While both large and small firms contribute to gross job gains and losses, small firms tend to gain and lose jobs disproportionately and to account disproportionately for net job growth.

Recent research suggests that an important part of the explanation for the disproportionate amount of both gross job gains and gross job losses accounted for by small firms is that they tend to be young. Put differently, startups and other young firms drive the large rates of job gains and losses in small firms. Between 1980 and 2009, for example, 18.2 percent of overall gross job gains each year were in new firms—mostly small new firms—even though new firms accounted for only 3.1 percent of employment (Data Watch 6-1). These numbers make clear the importance and contribution of America's entrepreneurs to the dynamism of the economy.

The annual average rates of job gains and losses between 1980 and 2009 mask two important features of heterogeneity across time—secular, or long-term, trends, and cyclical patterns. The rates of both gross gains and gross losses have been declining over time. Whereas, on average, 18.2 percent of private-sector jobs in the 1980s were newly created positions in startups or expanding firms, gross job gains fell to 16.8 percent of total private-sector employment in the 1990s and to 15.8 percent between 2000 and 2009 (Figure 6-3). Similarly, gross job losses were slightly more than 16.2 percent of overall private-sector employment in the 1980s but fell to 14.9 percent in the 1990s and then remained largely the same between 2000 and 2009. These secular declines also are apparent when one focuses more narrowly on startups. Gross job gains from startups accounted, on average,

---

[2] The data on U.S. firms capture gross flows over a 12-month period beginning and ending in March. So, for example, the rate of job gains in year t=2009 refers to information on jobs gained in firms between March 2008 and March 2009.

Research based on a new Census Bureau data set called the Longitudinal Business Database (LBD) has led to new discoveries about the important role that startups play in creating jobs. The LBD contains annual information on virtually the entire universe of U.S. nonfarm private businesses that paid Federal payroll and income taxes between 1976 and 2009, and it will continue to be updated as new data become available.

LBD data are available both at the level of the firm—a measurement unit combining all of the economic activity of a business that occurs under common operational control—and at the level of individual establishments—physical locations of economic activity where goods and services are produced. The initial data are derived from quarterly Internal Revenue Service filings that are compiled by the Census Bureau and augmented with data collected through the Census Bureau Economic Censuses and business surveys. The final LBD data set contains annual information on payroll, employment size, industry, and other key economic variables for both firms and establishments.

One of the key advances of the LBD is its ability to track the births and deaths of firms. When a new economic entity is reported in the administrative sources used to create the LBD, the Census Bureau determines whether that new economic entity is a new firm, a new establishment that is part of an existing firm, or an establishment that has undergone a change in legal form because of a merger, change in ownership, or some other similar change. Through this process, the Census Bureau is able to identify essentially all new private payroll startups.

The creation of the LBD has allowed researchers to study comprehensively the process of private-sector job gains and losses. One of the most important findings has been how important startups are to the dynamism of the U.S. economy. For example, Haltiwanger, Jarmin, and Miranda (2010) find that about 2.5 million net new private-sector jobs were gained in 2005. Firm startups created nearly 3.5 million net new jobs in that year, while all other firms together lost about 1 million jobs on net.

More information on the LBD is available from the Census Bureau at http://www.ces.census.gov/index.php/bds/bds_home. The Bureau of Labor Statistics has produced a separate database, the Business Employment Dynamics (BED), which tracks gross quarterly job gains and losses; more information about the BED is available at http://www.bls.gov/bdm.

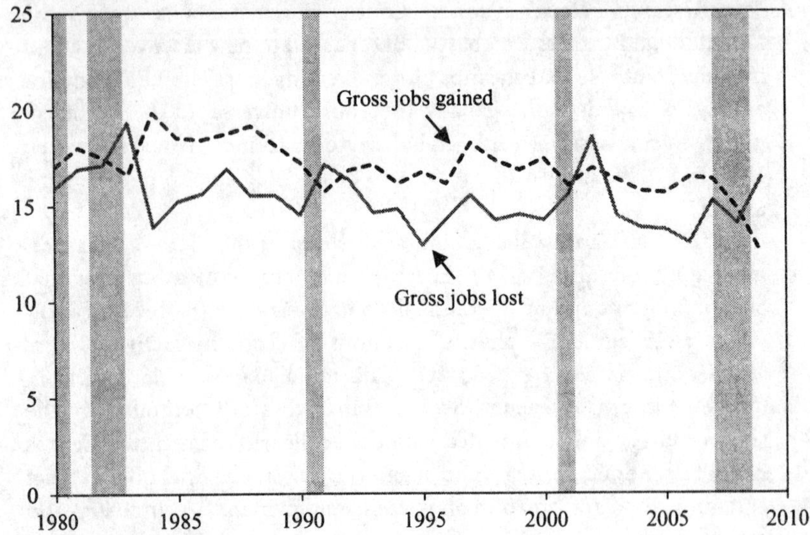

Note: Shading denotes recession.
Source: Census Bureau.

for 3.6 percent of the overall number of private-sector jobs in the 1980s but for only 2.7 percent between 2000 and 2009.

The rates of gross job gains and losses exhibit not only secular declines but cyclical patterns as well. Gross job gains are procyclical, increasing in expansions and declining in recessions, whereas gross job losses are countercyclical, increasing during recessions and declining in expansions. In the depths of the recent recession, gross job losses rose sharply, but the decline in gross job gains was even more notable.

An alternative data set produced by the Bureau of Labor Statistics (BLS) offers more frequent and more recent data than the BDS. The Business Employment Dynamics (BED) reports quarterly data on payroll employment at the level of the Employer Identification Number (EIN). An EIN is a tax-reporting construct rather than an economic construct, but the unit of observation in the BED consists in most cases of all of the operations of a particular firm located within a given U.S. state. Movements in gross job gains and losses in the BED on an annualized basis since its 1990 inception are broadly similar to those in the BDS; most important, the BED also shows a trend decline in gross gain and loss rates since 2000.

The quarter-to-quarter movements shown in Figure 6-4, which are based on BED data through the second quarter of 2011 (the most recent quarter of data available), show a large increase in the rate of gross job losses toward the beginning of the recession; the rate reached a peak in the

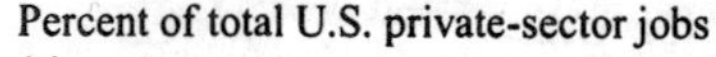

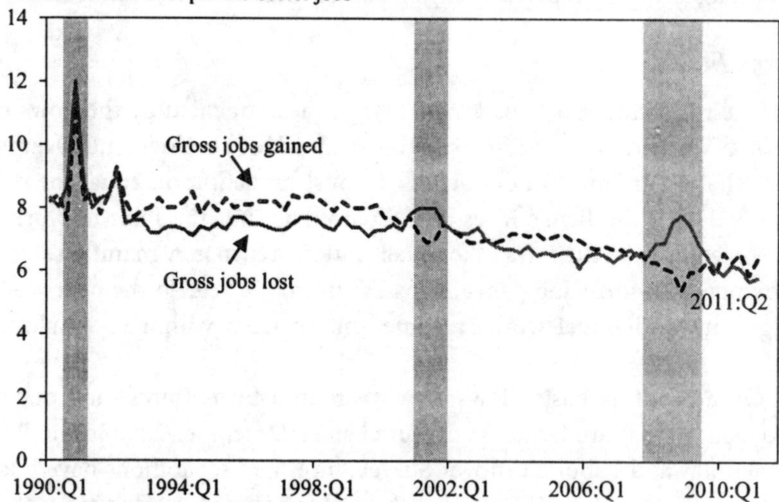

Note: Shading denotes recession.
Source: Department of Labor, Bureau of Labor Statistics.

first quarter of 2009, and then returned to approximately the pre-recession trend by the beginning of 2010. The BED data also show a precipitous fall in the rate of gross job gains during the recession, and although that decline reversed and gross job gains exceeded gross job losses by the second quarter of 2010, the gains so far have resulted in too few new jobs to accommodate the large number of individuals who lost jobs in the 2007–09 recession.

Now that researchers have documented the long-term secular slow-down in job gains and losses, the underlying reasons for the slowdown and its implications for the future of the U.S. economy are fast becoming the subject of an active debate. One possible reason for the slowdown in job reallocation is the aging of the population. Older workers may be less likely to become entrepreneurs, and research has documented a positive correlation between worker age and job tenure (Davis et al. 2007; Krueger 2010). But while the U.S. population is indeed aging, it is and will remain much younger than the population in the countries of Western Europe. So, to the extent that aging can explain part of the slowdown in job flows in the United States, other countries can be expected to experience slowdowns as well. Further research is needed to better understand the secular trends in job flows in the United States, and international comparisons could be helpful in this regard.

Because of the importance of entrepreneurship to the vitality of the economy, the President last year launched Startup America, a national campaign to improve the environment for high-growth entrepreneurs by expanding their access to capital and connecting them with mentors, helping the Nation's veterans start businesses, reducing barriers to entrepreneurship, and fostering entrepreneurship in communities.

Worker Flows

The reallocation of jobs across firms is accompanied by the flows of individual workers between firms and in and out of employment. Overall, the net change in employment at a firm must by definition equal the difference between the firm's hires and separations. But the rates of worker flows are larger than the rates of job reallocation: a firm may maintain stable employment (no gross job gains or losses) from one year to the next while having many individual workers come and go from within its employee ranks.

On a monthly basis, flows of workers into firms (hires) and out of firms (separations) are large. As captured since December 2000 in the BLS Job Openings and Labor Turnover Survey, hires and separations have both averaged more than 4.7 million a month and have tended to track each other closely over time. As Figure 6-5 illustrates, firm hires and separations before the start of the recession in 2007 were notably below the levels observed before the start of the 2001 recession.

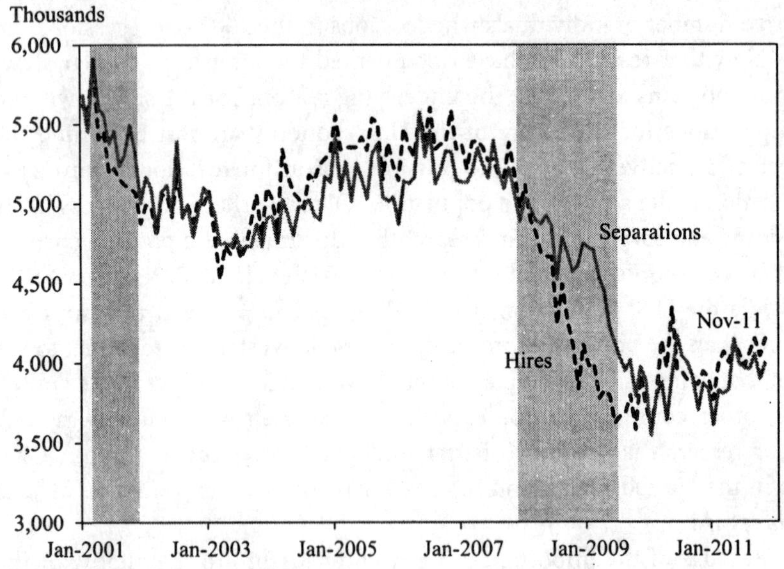

Figure 6-5
Hires and Separations, 2001–2011

Note: Shading denotes recession.
Source: Department of Labor, Bureau of Labor Statistics.

As the U.S. economy fell into recession in December 2007, worker flows slowed notably, with large monthly declines in the number of separations, and even more precipitous monthly declines in the number of hires. A decline in separations during a recession may seem counterintuitive, but it is attributable to a large decline in the frequency of workers quitting their jobs; quits are usually a sign of workers leaving jobs voluntarily for better opportunities. So while layoffs were increasing over this period, the decline in quits swamped the increase in layoffs. Overall, the economy on net was shedding jobs at a very fast pace during the recession because the decline in hiring in absolute numbers was larger than the decline in separations. Hires and separations both began to rise in the second quarter of 2010, but both remained below pre-recession levels at the end of 2011.

One can also study flows of workers into and out of employment, unemployment, and the labor force. Perhaps most important over time are the flows into and out of unemployment, which can be calculated using the Current Population Survey (CPS). Because of the structure of the CPS, in any given month three-quarters of the sample members have also been interviewed in the previous month, making it possible to use these repeat respondents to follow transitions into and out of unemployment. The BLS has been constructing these flows each month since 1990 in a manner that also matches up with the level of reported unemployment. Figure 6-6

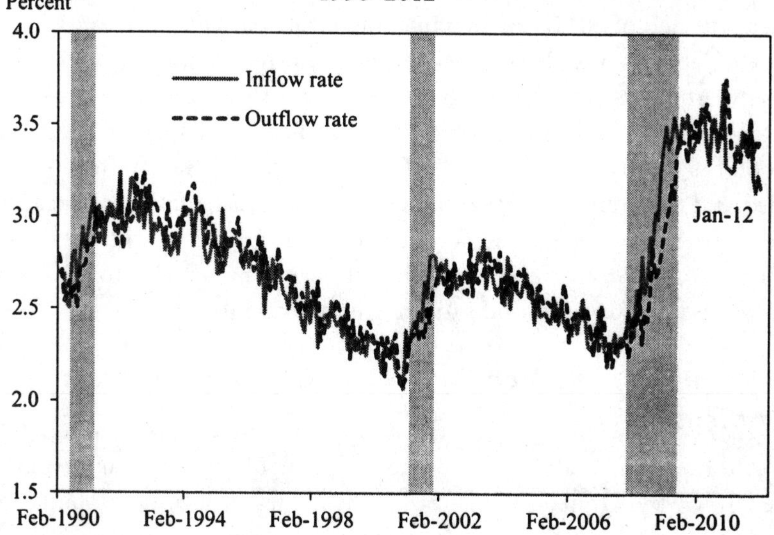

Figure 6-6
Flows into and out of Unemployment as Percent of the Labor Force,
1990–2012

Note: Shading denotes recession.
Source: Department of Labor, Bureau of Labor Statistics.

displays the extent of inflows and outflows as a percent of the total labor force for each month from the start of 1990 through January 2012.

Although the BLS labor force flow series goes back only to 1990 and is dominated by strong cyclical movements, the data in Figure 6-6 through the end of 2007 suggest a secular decline in both the inflow and outflow rate. A similar decline has also been documented elsewhere (see, for example, Davis, Faberman, and Haltiwanger 2006) for years before 1990, using alternative methods of calculating unemployment inflows and outflows. As with job flows, the aging of the population may account for some of these secular declines, because older workers tend to leave jobs less often than younger workers and, when they do, are more likely to leave the labor force permanently. But the declining flows into and out of unemployment also may reflect other forces that have lowered the rates of gross job gains and losses over the past three decades.

As the recession began, monthly inflows and outflows from unemployment both stood at approximately 2.4 percent of the labor force. Both began to rise steeply, but the inflow rate rose more quickly than the outflow rate, increasing the unemployment rate to levels not seen in approximately 30 years. Put differently, both the increase in the monthly average probability of a worker entering unemployment and the decrease in the monthly average probability of an unemployed worker exiting unemployment have, as in a typical recession, contributed to the observed rise in unemployment (Elsby, Michaels, and Solon 2009). Since March 2009, unemployment inflow and outflow rates, measured as a share of the labor force, each have been over 3 percent. Because the outflow rate was notably higher than the inflow rate near the end of 2011, the unemployment rate has fallen.

The labor market is still recovering from the cyclical impacts of the recession. And it is still subject to the long-term slower trend in gross job gains and losses, as well as to the long-term decline in the share of the population that is employed. In the face of these trends, the Administration has pursued and continues to pursue robust policies to foster faster job creation in the short run, as well as an economic environment in which existing firms have reasons to increase employment, new firms are able to grow and innovate, and workers can find satisfying employment.

Earnings and Income Mobility over the Career and between Generations

Although the Nation's labor market is highly dynamic in terms of worker flows, the United States has had low rates of income mobility for decades, both across the career and across generations.

Low rates of income mobility across the career are especially notable for men, whose higher rates of labor force attachment make them much less likely than women to have years with zero earnings. Kopczuk, Saez, and Song (2010) show that the annual earnings of a man averaged across 11 years early in his working career are highly predictive of his annual earnings averaged across 11 years later in his working career. For example, a man in one of the bottom two quintiles of the income distribution early in his lifetime has less than a 10 percent chance of rising to the top quintile 20 years later.

Family (or individual) incomes in one generation are also highly correlated with family (or individual) incomes in the next generation. In other words, the children of parents who are poor are more likely than the children of well-off parents to be poor when they grow up. A common measure of mobility across generations is the intergenerational elasticity (IGE) of earnings or income, which is defined as the percentage difference in a child's income associated with a 1 percent difference in the parent's income.[3] These IGE estimates are sensitive to several measurement issues, particularly fluctuations in incomes from year to year. Studies based on U.S. data that deal appropriately with these measurement issues suggest that plausible estimates of the average IGE between fathers and sons are between 0.4 and 0.6. An IGE of 0.4 means that if one father earned 20 percent more than another over their lifetime, the first father's son on average would earn 8 percent more than the second father's son; an IGE of 0.6 means that the first father's son would earn 12 percent more on average than the second father's son. That is, the higher the IGE is, the lower economic mobility is between the generations.

Data limitations make it difficult to infer whether the IGE or the correlation between parents' and children's income has changed significantly over time (Data Watch 6-2). Lee and Solon (2009) conclude that the IGE in the United States was fairly stable for cohorts born between 1952 and 1975, while Aaronson and Mazumder (2008) present evidence suggesting that it has increased in the past 30 years, implying that intergenerational mobility has fallen. None of the available research has suggested a decline in the IGE over time. Moreover, the widening of income inequality has meant that it is harder for someone born into the bottom to move to the middle or the top of the income distribution.

The high degree of persistence in incomes between generations in the United States is especially noteworthy in the context of cross-country comparisons. Corak (2011) makes such a comparison and finds that the average

---

[3] IGEs most commonly have been estimated as the regression coefficient resulting from a linear regression of the logarithm of the income (or earnings) of a child on a measure of the logarithm of income (or earnings) of a parent or family.

estimated IGE of 0.47 for men in the United States, while lower than the IGE for countries such as the United Kingdom (0.50) and South Africa (0.69), is much higher than the IGE for men in countries such as Sweden (0.27), Norway (0.17), Finland (0.18), and Denmark (0.15). Jäntti et al. (2006) also compare IGEs for men's incomes in some of the same countries and report similar estimates.[4]

While many factors contribute to cross-country differences in intergenerational mobility, one clear pattern is that countries with more intergenerational mobility also tend to have lower point-in-time income inequality. Figure 6-7 plots the relationship across 13 industrialized countries between the IGE of the earnings of fathers and sons as reported in Corak (2011)

---

[4] One exception is that Jäntti et al. report a somewhat lower IGE (0.31) for the United Kingdom, below that of the United States but still well above those in Nordic countries. Following the literature, this discussion focuses on IGEs for men, because in many countries the inconsistent labor force participation of women complicates the estimation of their IGEs.

and the Gini coefficient of after-tax 1985 income as reported in the OECD statistical database. The Gini coefficient, shown along the horizontal axis of the figure, is a common measure of income inequality; higher values mean higher levels of income inequality. Higher IGEs along the vertical axis mean less intergenerational mobility. The United States appears in the upper right part of Figure 6-7, indicating both high inequality and low intergenerational mobility.

As other research has shown, the finding of a positive relationship between IGE and inequality—a relationship that Krueger (2012) has referred to as "the Great Gatsby Curve"—is robust to alternative choices of countries, intergenerational mobility measures, and year in which income inequality is measured (see, for example, Corak 2011; Andrews and Leigh 2009; OECD 2010). This robust relationship suggests that at least some of the same mechanisms that drive income inequality also drive intergenerational mobility. For example, a rise in the rate of return to schooling can be expected to lead to both a rise in point-in-time income inequality and a decline in intergenerational mobility because educational attainment is positively correlated across generations.

The educational system also may contribute to the pattern in Figure 6-7. Research has found a strong negative correlation between spending on public education and IGEs across countries (Ichino, Karabarounis, and

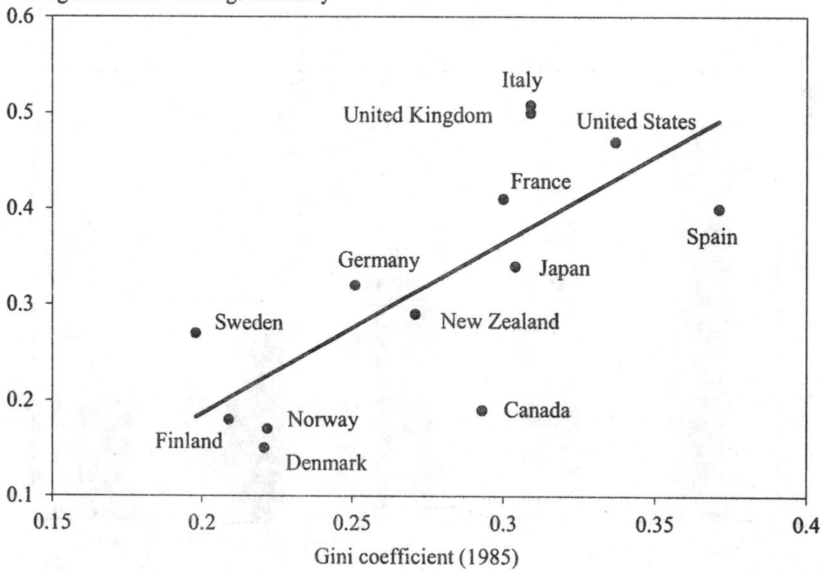

Figure 6-7

The Great Gatsby Curve: Inequality and Intergenerational Mobility

Source: Corak (2011) and OECD.

Moretti 2011). This pattern suggests that public investments in supporting children may help to reduce persistent inequality across generations. Similarly, the OECD has concluded that educational policies ranging from support for early childhood education to measures that support postsecondary education for students from low-income backgrounds can increase intergenerational income mobility (OECD 2010). As discussed later in this chapter, the Administration has taken multiple steps to improve the quality of education and to provide opportunities for all students to earn a postsecondary credential or degree.

Overall Trends in Income and Rising Inequality

Irrespective of the persistence in income across generations, the rungs on the ladder of the income distribution in the United States have moved farther apart, and income growth has been stagnant for the middle class for a decade.

One indicator of the evolution of income over time is annual real median household income, which rose in the United States from the late 1960s through the late 1990s, was stagnant in the first part of the 2000s, and then, as is typical during recessions and their aftermath, fell between 2007 and 2010 (the last year for which data are available).

Figure 6-8
Percent of Households with Annual Income
within 50 Percent of the Median

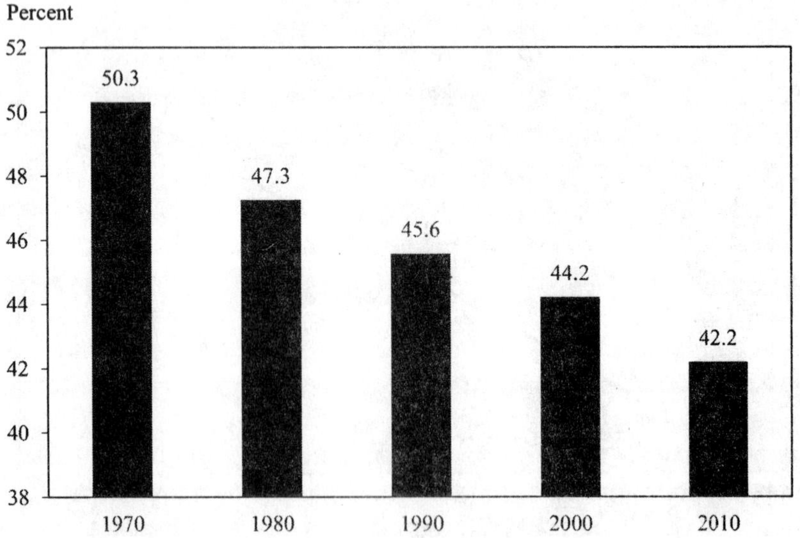

Source: Department of Labor, Bureau of Labor Statistics; CEA calculations.

Growth in Real After-Tax Income, 1979–2007

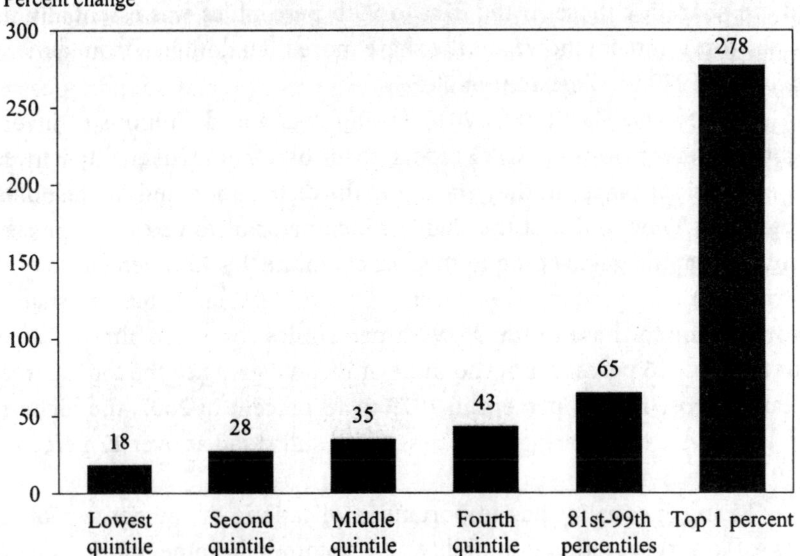

Source: Congressional Budget Office.

Rising income inequality is another major development in the United States economy (see, for example, Autor, Katz, and Kearney 2008; Card and DiNardo 2002; CEA 1997). Growing dispersion of household incomes, a manifestation of growing dispersion of earnings, means that fewer and fewer households have incomes in the middle band of the income distribution. This can be seen clearly in Figure 6-8. In 1970, just over 50 percent of households had incomes within 50 percent of the median; that share fell to just over 44 percent in 2000 and to just over 42 percent in 2010.

Another way to look at changes in the distribution of income is to examine the rates of income growth for households at different income levels. A report released by the Congressional Budget Office (CBO) in October 2011 examines real growth in after-tax (and transfer) household income from 1979 through 2007 across quintiles and the top 1 percent of the income distribution. Figure 6-9, reproducing information from the CBO report, provides stark evidence of the rise in inequality, showing that real after-tax incomes grew by just 18 percent over nearly 30 years for those in the bottom income quintile and rose only somewhat more rapidly for those in the middle 60 percent of the distribution, but grew by a stunning 278 percent for those in the top 1 percent of the distribution.

As a result of these divergent growth rates, increasingly more income has been concentrated at the top and less at the bottom of the income distribution. The CBO reports that the share of total after-tax household income for the bottom four income quintiles was lower in 2007 than it was in 1979, and the share for those in the 81st to 99th percentiles was essentially flat. For the top 1 percent, however, the share more than doubled, from almost 8 percent in 1979 to 17 percent in 2007.

Piketty and Saez (2003, 2010), using data and definitions of income slightly different from the CBO report, focus on income inequality between those at various places in the very top of the distribution and the rest of the population. They find that the share of income prior to taxes and transfers excluding capital gains going to the earners in the 90–95th percentile of the distribution barely changed between 1979 and 2010 and that the share of income going to those in the 95–99th percentiles rose from almost 13 percent to about 16 percent. But the share of income going to the top 1 percent of earners rose from 8 percent in 1979 to 18 percent in 2007, the highest it had been since the Roaring Twenties, and it still stood at over 17 percent in 2010 (Figure 6-10).

Rising inequality has important implications in the context of low rates of intergenerational mobility. As incomes become more unequal, larger increases in household income are necessary for families to move from a lower part of the income distribution to a higher part—for example, from a level of household income that classifies a family as living in poverty to one that puts it in the middle of the distribution. Low rates of economic

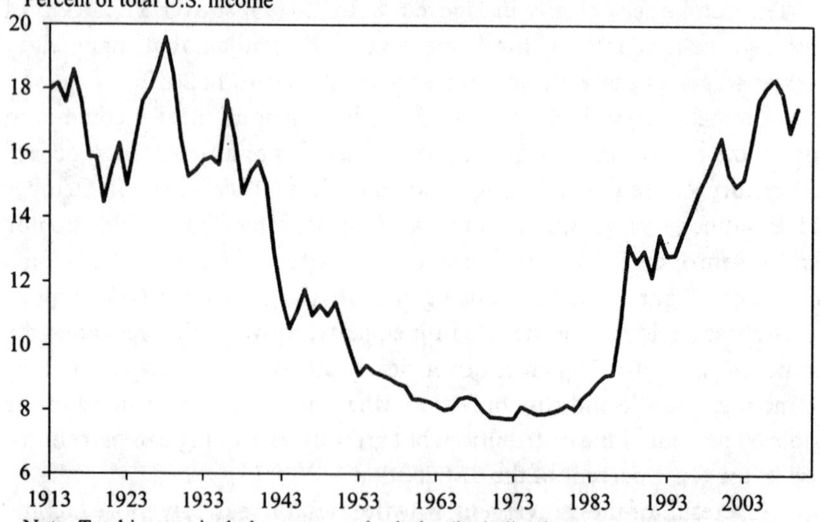

Figure 6-10
Share of Total U.S. Income Earned by Top 1 Percent, 1913–2010

Note: Total income includes wages and salaries (including bonuses and stock-option exercises), pensions, profits, farm income, dividends, interest, and rental income.
Source: Piketty and Saez (2003, 2010); authors provided an estimate for 2010 based on partial returns.

mobility across generations imply that children born in poverty are more likely to remain in poverty as adults, while children born to higher-income parents are more likely to have higher incomes as adults. As long as income inequality is increasing, those adult children will find themselves even farther away from the middle class than their parents were. Perhaps even more worrisome, the Great Gatsby curve in Figure 6-7 suggests that a rise in inequality for the current generation of families could lead to a slowdown in economic mobility for the next generation.

The confluence of rising inequality and low economic mobility over the past three decades poses a real threat to the future of the United States as a land of opportunity. Social and economic mobility across generations are at risk of declining unless concerted efforts are devoted to providing more opportunities for those born into lower-income households.

Long-Term Unemployment

The upheaval in the labor market brought on by the recession that started in late 2007 is primarily a cyclical phenomenon. A major challenge, especially given the long-term changes in the labor market that were under-way even before the recession, is how to prevent these cyclical dislocations from having permanent effects on workers' prospects. This means that pathways for the long-term unemployed to return to the workforce are a particular priority The protracted high level of unemployment has led to large numbers of long-term unemployed workers—those who have been out of work for more than 26 weeks. Currently, 5.5 million workers—more than two-fifths of all unemployed individuals—have been jobless for more than 26 weeks, and over 1.8 million have been without a job for more than two years.

Historically, as depicted in Figure 6-11, the share of the unemployed that has been unemployed for more than 26 weeks has been quite cyclical, starting at a relatively low point right before a recession, growing thereafter, and usually peaking many months into the recovery before gradually declin-ing. Another useful measure of unemployment duration is the median dura-tion—the amount of time that the person in the middle of the distribution has spent unemployed to date. Typically, this measure has been similarly cyclical, and as a result of the 2007–09 recession it remains elevated at 21.1 weeks.

A long period of joblessness is obviously first and foremost a serious hardship for the individuals involved. The loss of income due to unemploy-ment can wreak havoc on households' finances, often necessitating liquida-tion of savings. Households with unemployed members are more likely to fall behind on their bills and to suffer foreclosure or bankruptcy; foreclosures

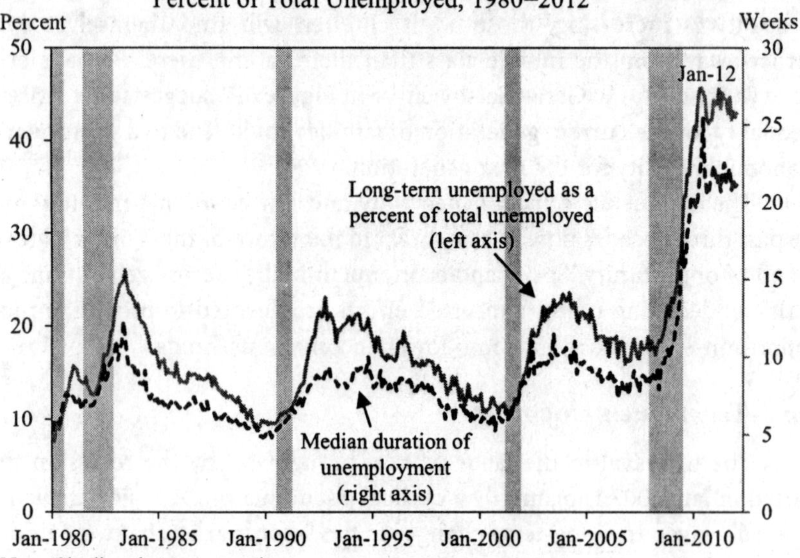

Figure 6-11

Median Duration of Unemployment and Long-Term Unemployed as a
Percent of Total Unemployed, 1980–2012

Note: Shading denotes recession.
Source: Department of Labor, Bureau of Labor Statistics.

also can have adverse effects on the prices of neighboring homes. To help
the long-term unemployed keep their homes, the Administration created
a version of the Home Affordable Modification Program (HAMP) for the
unemployed, called HAMP UP, in which unemployed homeowners were
given a three month forbearance period on their mortgage payments. In July
2011, this forbearance period was extended to 12 months.

Income losses associated with job loss can persist even after reemployment. Recent research examined male workers age 50 or younger with
at least three years of tenure who lost their jobs in mass layoffs (defined as
employment decreases of at least 30 percent over two years at their place of
employment) between 1980 and 2005. The researchers concluded that job
displacement led to a loss of 1.7 years of earnings, on average, accumulated
over 20 years. Moreover, job displacement led to an average accumulated
earnings loss of 2.8 years if the job was lost when the unemployment rate was
above 8 percent, but the earnings loss was only half as large—1.4 years—if
the job was lost when the unemployment rate was below 6 percent (Davis
and von Wachter 2011).

In addition to the mortgage forbearance program mentioned above,
the Administration has supported the long-term unemployed by calling
for extended unemployment compensation, which provides much-needed
income to these workers and their families while the recipient searches for
work. As explained in Chapter 7, continued extensions of the Emergency

Unemployment Compensation and Extended Benefits programs through 2012 are vital to those who remain unemployed. Additionally, the American Jobs Act proposal for extending unemployment benefits also included significant reforms to the unemployment insurance system designed to speed the return of benefit recipients to work.

As part of his Fiscal Year 2013 Budget, the President is proposing a $12.5 billion Pathways Back to Work Fund to provide employment opportunities for vulnerable youth, low-income adults, and the long-term unemployed, and an expanded community college initiative to support state and community college partnerships with business to give workers the skills employers need. The President also is proposing to streamline training and employment services for dislocated workers, improving access to critical supports for getting the unemployed back into employment.

PREPARING FOR TOMORROW'S LABOR MARKET

Even as the Administration remains focused on strengthening and sustaining the recovery from the recession, the President continues to address the longer-term challenges in the structure of the American economy and labor market. To ensure that American workers are prepared to meet the evolving needs of employers, the Nation's education and training system must provide the workers of tomorrow with the skills they will need for the jobs of tomorrow. At the same time, jobs and workplaces also must evolve to enable workers to fulfill family and other nonwork responsibilities (Box 6-1). This section describes what the jobs of tomorrow are likely to look like, why educating workers is a cornerstone of economic opportunity and growth, and how the Administration's policies are working to prepare Americans for the jobs of tomorrow.

Education and the Workers of Tomorrow

The rise in wage and income inequality over recent decades is largely attributable to long-lasting structural changes in the U.S. economy. Among the changes are technological advances that have increased employer demand for a relatively more highly educated workforce, a slowdown in the expansion of educational attainment, and increased competition from overseas for many lower-paid jobs. Another is a decline in the share of the workforce covered by collective bargaining agreements and the decline in the real value of the minimum wage, both of which historically helped protect the wages of lower-paid workers.[5]

---

[5] Extensive reviews of existing research can be found in Acemoglu and Autor (2011) and Autor and Katz (1999).

American household life has changed dramatically over the past half century in ways that have caused many workers to face conflicts between their work and personal lives. Women are now the majority recipients of bachelor's and advanced degrees and compose nearly 50 percent of the workforce. Families rely increasingly on women's earnings to make ends meet. In addition to managing care of children, both men and women juggle elder caregiving responsibilities with work. In 2008, approximately 43.5 million Americans served as unpaid caregivers to a family member over the age of 50. Workplace flexibility is also important for older Americans themselves. In 2011, the first of the baby boomers turned age 65. Workplace flexibility policies, such as part-time work or job sharing, facilitate a phased retirement that helps older workers transition slowly out of the workforce, allowing them to take care of their health needs and maintain their economic security while moving toward retirement.

Workplace flexibility can be expanded by increasing workers' control over when, where, and how much they work. These goals can be achieved through a variety of different arrangements that allow workers to continue making productive contributions to the workforce while also attending to family and other responsibilities. Arrangements range from job sharing, to phased retirement of older workers, to telecommuting. Workplace flexibility policies not only help employees balance work and family responsibilities but also can improve employers' bottom lines.

As in all business decisions, the critical considerations for employers in adoption of flexible workplace policies are the benefits and costs. Almost one-third of firms cite costs or limited funds as obstacles to implementing workplace flexibility arrangements. On the benefit side, however, as documented in CEA (2010), these practices can reduce turnover and improve recruitment, increasing the productivity of an employer's workforce. Moreover, flexible workplace practices are associated with improved employee health and decreased absenteeism, a major cost for employers. The CEA study estimated that wholesale adoption of flexible workplace policies could save as much as $15 billion a year through greater productivity, lower turnover, and reduced absenteeism. Should more firms adopt such practices, the benefits to society, in the form of reduced traffic, improved employment outcomes, and more efficient allocation of workers to employers, could be even greater than the gains to individual firms and workers (Galinsky et al. 2011).

Although the academic literature has identified numerous benefits from flexible workplace practices, along a variety of dimensions, the adoption rates for these practices differ across industries and employers of different sizes. Goldin and Katz (2011) explored the prevalence of flexible workplace arrangements across industries and found that, although these practices are gaining in popularity, some industries lag behind, in particular the business and financial sectors. Overall, the CEA study reported that more than half of employers report allowing some workers to periodically change their starting and quitting times. However, only 28 percent of full-time workers and 39 percent of part-time workers report actually having flexible work hours. Even if some employers offer more flexible workplace arrangements, there remains the concern that their employees may not be taking advantage of those arrangements because either, in the case of unpaid leave, they cannot afford to bring home a smaller paycheck, or, in the case of paid leave, they are afraid to take leave for fear of missing out on advancements or not being viewed as a "team player."

A lack of data has hindered deeper understanding of the benefits and costs of flexibility, as well as knowledge about who is taking advantage of that flexibility. The largest, most detailed source of data, a survey of employers, provides information on practices that is now three years old and does not contain information for the smallest firms. The only nationally representative data from workers are seven years old and provide little information on the prevalence of flexible practices. While the existing evidence has demonstrated a strong connection between flexibility and productivity, additional research exploring the mechanism through which flexibility influences worker's job satisfaction and firms' profits would better inform policymakers and managers alike. In the summer of 2012, the results of a module added to the American Time Use Survey will provide expanded information about workplace flexibility from the workers' perspective. The module asks survey respondents about their access to leave and flexible scheduling, how they use such policies to balance their work and personal responsibilities, and whether they fail to take advantage of existing policies because of a fear of negative consequences. These data will add to the existing knowledge base on workplace flexibility. Although the literature is small, the best available evidence suggests that adoption of more flexible practices can boost productivity, improve morale, and benefit the U.S. economy—all while strengthening families.

Because these structural changes have shifted demand toward a workforce with relatively more education, a substantial fraction of the overall increase in wage and income inequality is related to a growing divergence in earnings between those with more years of education and those with fewer years of education, as depicted in Figure 6-12.

For example, in 2010, workers with a bachelor's degree or higher earned nearly twice as much as those with a high school degree, a premium that has risen since 1980, when college graduates earned 45 percent more than high school graduates. In fact, even long before the most recent recession, the average real annual earnings of those with a high school degree or less fell below the levels of the 1970s.

One important way to help stem the tide of rising inequality, and potentially to ameliorate the effects of low intergenerational economic mobility, is to increase the number of workers who obtain postsecondary education and earn higher wages as a result. For this reason, President Obama has set the ambitious goal of returning the United States, by 2020, to the world's top spot in the share of 25- to 34-year-olds with a college degree.

Increasing the number of workers who obtain postsecondary education is also vital for meeting the changing skill needs of firms. The BLS Employment Projections Program produces forecasts of employment by industry, occupation, and education on an approximately biennial basis. The industry employment forecasts are based on incorporating projections of the size of the labor force into a model of output growth across U.S. industries. These detailed industry employment forecasts are then mapped into projections of employment growth by occupation, and then into forecasts of growth in employment by education group. Beginning with the newly released projections for 2010–20, the BLS is projecting employment growth by education group by assigning to each occupation the typical level of formal education needed to enter the occupation, and then aggregating by education group the projected employment growth in the occupations requiring that level of education. As shown in Figure 6-13, the BLS projects that in the coming years, jobs requiring education beyond a high school degree will grow by more than the average, while occupations requiring at most a high school diploma will grow by less than the average. For example, between 2010 and 2020, employment in jobs that require an associate's degree is projected to grow by 18.0 percent, 3.7 percentage points more than the average projected employment growth of 14.3 percent. Much of the divergence in employment growth across education groups is driven by the projected growth of sectors such as health care and education that intensively utilize workers in occupations that typically require education beyond a high school diploma.

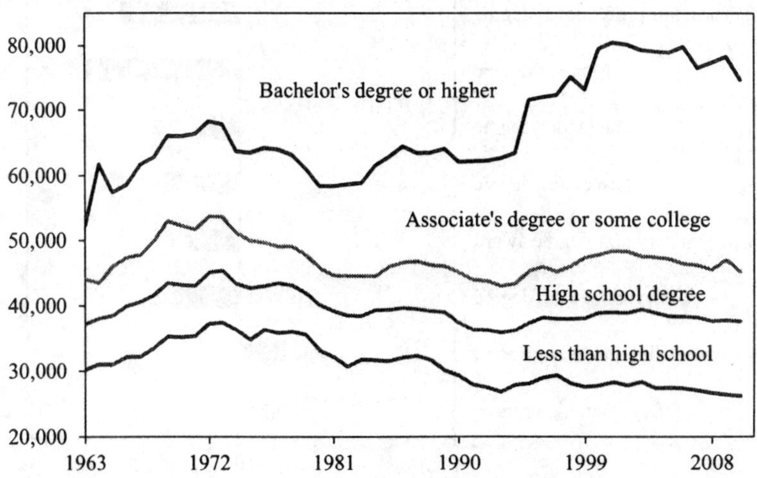

Note: The sample includes workers aged 25–65 who worked at least 35 hours a week and for at least 50 weeks in the calendar year. Before 1992, education groups are defined based on the highest grade of school or year of college completed. Beginning in 1992, groups are defined based on the highest degree or diploma earned. Earnings are deflated using the CPI-U. Calculations are based on survey data collected in March of each year and reflect average wage and salary income for the previous calendar year.
Source: CEA calculations using March Current Population Survey

Information that tracks the changing skill needs of firms can help Americans make informed career decisions. In addition to the statistics published by the BLS on existing and projected jobs by industry, occupation, and education, the potential exists to harness new data sources to gain a deeper understanding of what skills are in high demand. For example, the more than 50 million U.S.-based members of LinkedIn, an online professional networking company, typically provide to LinkedIn their job titles and the companies they work for, and upon joining, many members also provide information on their past work history. LinkedIn classifies members' jobs by industry and occupation, often at a more detailed level than is available in government statistics. The resulting information can be used to track changes over time in the industries and occupations in which LinkedIn's members work and to identify emerging sectors and job titles. LinkedIn's members are not a nationally representative sample of the U.S. workforce, but because they tend to work in sectors of the economy that require higher levels of education, the information embodied in the changing distribution of the industries and occupations in which members are employed has the potential to inform the decisions of individuals considering specific educational and career paths.

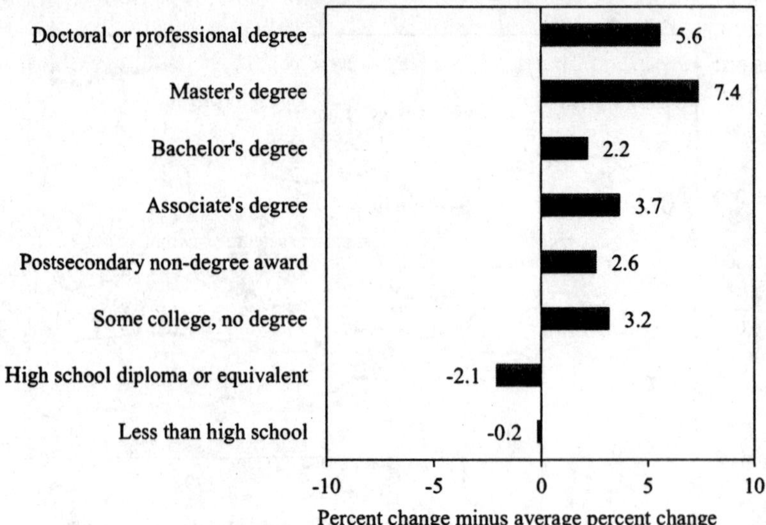

Source: Department of Labor, Bureau of Labor Statistics.

LinkedIn has produced initial tabulations from among its U.S. members of the growth rate of employment in industries and occupations since 2007. These tabulations are for a longitudinal sample of individuals, based on aggregated historical data from their resumes and other information that they provide, LinkedIn reports that two of the fastest-growing industries among their members between 2007 and 2011 were the Internet and oil and energy; two of the fastest-shrinking industries were newspapers and construction. Among the fastest-growing occupations were social media (including jobs titles such as social media manager, social media marketing manager, and social media specialist) and digital technology (including digital producer, digital product manager, digital strategist, and digital sales manager); LinkedIn reports that teachers and middle-management positions were among the shrinking occupations.

One of the main drivers of the increasing relative demand for workers with more education and training is the continuing shift toward using machines or computers to perform the routine tasks once done by workers. Although the BLS, assuming a continuation of these trends, projects that the number of manufacturing jobs will decline between 2010 and 2020, the U.S. manufacturing sector has added more than 400,000 net new jobs since the beginning of 2010, the first sustained job growth in manufacturing since the late 1990s.

Some of the recent growth in manufacturing jobs is the direct result of firms that are choosing to produce goods in the United States rather than using overseas labor. The Administration is supporting this "insourcing" with new tax proposals that eliminate tax advantages for moving jobs overseas and reward companies that choose to invest in or bring jobs back to the United States. In addition, the President has proposed measures to revitalize the manufacturing sector. These measures include initiatives to help develop and produce advanced technologies, ensuring clean energy technologies that will fuel the 21st century economy are built in the United States; funding to help catalyze partnerships between universities and industries to develop new technologies for manufacturing products and processes; the creation of a new Interagency Trade Enforcement Center to challenge unfair trading practices; and tax incentives to promote job growth in communities hard-hit by factory closings.

Increasing Educational Attainment

To prepare for the jobs of tomorrow, it is essential to invest in the American workforce and to increase the number of young people who attain a college degree. Meeting the President's college completion goal for 25- to 34-year-olds requires investments in early, primary, and secondary education to increase the number of students who are college-ready when they graduate from high school. Meeting the goal also requires policies and programs that make college more affordable and accessible.

Teachers in the Nation's public schools are crucial to preparing children for the jobs of tomorrow. During the depths of the recession, however, many State and local governments were forced to make cuts, resulting in the loss of more than 200,000 education jobs over the past three years. Had it not been for the combined $40 billion in targeted assistance through the Recovery Act's State Fiscal Stabilization Fund and the Education Jobs Fund, the cuts would have been worse: these programs provided the resources to support 420,000 teacher job-years. Given the continued need to prevent teacher layoffs and to rehire many of the teachers who lost their jobs during the recession, the President's FY 2013 Budget proposes a $25 billion teacher stabilization fund.

The Administration also has made improving the quality of education a priority and has taken an innovative approach, using grant competitions and evaluations to fund promising practices and learn more about what works, from early childhood education through high school. A key part of this effort has been Race to the Top grants, established as part of the Recovery Act. Competitive grants have been awarded to states to undertake innovative reform in four areas of K–12 education: implementing rigorous standards and assessments; using data to improve instruction and decisionmaking; recruiting and retaining effective teachers and principals; and turning around the lowest-performing schools. Race to the Top grants have catalyzed widespread reform even in states that did not win an award.

In 2011, Race to the Top funds were also used for Early Learning Challenge grants to promote evidence-based evaluation of programs, develop strategies for families and parents to assess the quality of early learning programs, and create age-appropriate curricula and assessment systems. The Early Learning Challenge fund announced nine state grant winners in December 2011. As with the K–12 Race to the Top competition, although not all proposals were funded, the framework of providing competitive grants to states to formulate their own solutions focused local conversations on education reform. The Early Learning Challenge grants complement the Administration's major investments in improving a cornerstone of early childhood education, the Head Start and Early Head Start programs, by increasing funding by $2.1 billion in two years through the Recovery Act, by nearly doubling the number of children and families served by Early Head Start, and by taking key steps to increase Head Start Center program quality and accountability. Notably, the Department of Health and Human Services has begun implementing new regulations that, for the first time, require current grantees that do not meet quality benchmarks to compete for continued funding.

In addition to Race to the Top, the Administration has funded other important innovations in education. The Investing in Innovation Fund supports projects in K–12 education that test, validate, and scale up promising strategies and interventions that raise overall student achievement, close the achievement gap, and improve outcomes for high-need students. The Promise Neighborhoods initiative supports cradle-to-career wraparound services to improve educational outcomes for students in distressed high-poverty neighborhoods. The President's 2012 State of the Union Address challenged all states to do what 21 states have already done: require all students to graduate from high school or stay in school until age 18. Raising the compulsory schooling age increases average educational attainment and, for those induced to stay in school longer, leads to higher earnings when those students become adults. In view of the positive externalities from schooling, economists Milton and Rose Friedman wrote, "What kind of governmental action is justified…? The most obvious is to require that each child receive a minimum amount of schooling of a specified kind" (Friedman and Friedman 1962).

The President has committed to continued investments in America's education system. Beyond making investments to help all students prepare for college, the Administration is working to make college affordable for American families. In recent years, published college tuitions have risen sharply, posing a threat to the Nation's growing need for workers with college-level skills. The Administration has made college accessibility and affordability a top priority. Through the Recovery Act and the Health Care and Education Reconciliation Act passed in 2010, the Administration raised the maximum Pell Grant award from $4,731 in 2008 to $5,550 in 2010, and the FY 2013 Budget calls for the maximum to increase to $5,635 for the 2013–14 school year. Some 8.1 million college students received an average of $3,700 in Pell Grants in 2009–10. These figures are up sharply from the year before President Obama took office, when 5.5 million college students received an average of $2,650 apiece in Pell aid, and the President remains committed to protecting these historic increases in Pell Grant awards.

In addition, the American Opportunity Tax Credit (AOTC), established through the Recovery Act, provides up to $2,500 a year for college tuition and related expenses for American families. Compared with the Hope Scholarship that it largely replaces, the AOTC offers a higher maximum benefit; can be claimed for up to four, rather than only two, years of undergraduate education; has a higher income eligibility cutoff, making the credit available to more middle-class families; and is partially refundable, thereby also reaching lower-income families. This credit is estimated to have benefited 9.4 million students and their families in 2011. In December 2010, the President signed an extension of the AOTC through the end of 2012, and his FY 2013 Budget request proposes to make the AOTC permanent.

Data from the College Board (2011) demonstrate the effectiveness of these Administration initiatives to keep college affordable (see also CEA 2011). The estimated average net price for full-time students attending public four-year institutions increased by only about $60 between 2007–08 and 2011–12, and the estimated average net price for full-time students attending public two-year and private nonprofit four-year institutions actually fell.

To build on the successes of Pell expansions and the AOTC as well as lessons from K–12 education reform, the President has proposed a Race to the Top for College Completion and Affordability to make public colleges more affordable and a better value and to drive reforms that will help more students complete their degrees on time. The FY 2013 Budget also proposes reforms to the distribution of campus based-aid to reward colleges that are serving low-income students, setting tuitions responsibly, and offering a quality education that prepares students to obtain employment and repay their loans. Finally, the Budget proposes a new First in the World Fund that introduces an evidence-based framework, modeled after the Investing in Innovation initiative, to develop, validate, and scale up effective approaches in higher education. (For a discussion of financing the cost of college, see Economics Applications Box 6-1.)

Federally Supported Job Training

The education of workers does not end when they complete formal schooling and enter the labor market. As the economy evolves, workers often need to develop new skills to meet the changing demands of firms. In many cases, firms partner with their workers to help them acquire new skills, but for workers who have lost their jobs or are seeking to change fields or careers, this option may not be available. Providing such workers with opportunities for training is especially important in today's economy given the continued high rates of unemployment that are the direct result of the recession, and it will remain important in ensuring a skilled workforce well into the future.

The Federal Government funds two main training programs for adults—the Trade Adjustment Assistance (TAA) program and the Workforce Investment Act (WIA) formula grant program. The WIA Adult and Dislocated Programs have by far the largest reach, serving 8.6 million participants in 2010 (the most recent year for which data are available) at a total annual cost of $3.8 billion.[6] Created in 1998, the WIA system provides reemployment and training services to adults who are economically disadvantaged and to workers who have been displaced from their jobs. Importantly, WIA moved the design and management of job training programs to the local level by creating "one-stop" employment centers where job seekers can access all employment services of the Department of Labor. WIA provides both short-term services, including job search assistance and basic skills assessments, and longer-term services that involve more substantial career counseling as well as training services. Program participants work with a case worker to choose the menu of services that best meets their needs, although limited funds mean not all participants have access to all services deemed appropriate. Research suggests that the average WIA participant benefits from the program, although the quality of the services provided is somewhat uneven. One recent study found that, on average, WIA training programs for adults boosted employment and earnings, although there was substantial variation across states and across participants depending on which WIA program they were in and what kind of services they received (Heinrich, Mueser, and Troske 2008). Growing evidence from studies of state programs, particularly studies that track participants for a longer

---

[6] Other smaller programs serving many fewer participants include the Employment Services Program and the Adult Basic Education Program. In addition, WIA also has a small program that serves economically disadvantaged youth.

Economics Application Box 6-1: Calculating the Cost of College

The decision to attend college is one of life's most important decisions. Individuals with a college degree earn substantially more throughout their working lives than otherwise similar non-degree holders, on average, but the dollar costs of college can be high and many students accumulate substantial debt. In addition, there is an "opportunity cost" of college—students are unable to work for pay while performing school-related tasks.

One key piece of information that a prospective student should have is the actual dollar price of college that the student is likely to pay. The published costs of a year of college do not tell the full story. Many students receive Federal assistance, and individual colleges and universities often have their own need-based aid programs, as well as merit scholarships.

The Department of Education has two particularly useful tools for prospective college students who would like to understand better what they are likely to pay in tuition, room and board, expenses, and fees. While the exact financial aid available to any particular student depends on a number of factors including household size, household income, and asset net worth, the Department of Education's FAFSA4caster (http://fafsa4caster.ed.gov/) can help students learn how much aid might be available. Using the College Navigator tool (https://nces.ed.gov/collegenavigator/), a prospective college student can learn how Federal, state and local, and institutional aid affect net prices at specific colleges.

A menu-driven format allows a prospective student to select a college or set of colleges (say, by geography or type of degree) and discover the average net price paid by students of various income levels at each college on the prospective student's list. The average net prices across schools can vary widely and can deviate substantially from the published costs. For example, information from the College Calculator shows that, for households with income between $48,000 and $75,000, the average annual cost of attending one of the top ten national universities (as ranked by *U.S. News and World Report*) in 2009–10 was $52,796. The average net price for those who received aid at one of those institutions, however, was a substantially lower $9,340. Meanwhile, large state schools with much lower published costs than the private universities can have higher net costs. For households in the $48,000–$75,000 income range that received aid, the average annual net cost (including the costs of living on campus) in 2009–10 at the top ten largest public universities was $13,486.

period of time, shows that training for adults can have large positive effects on earnings. Combining classroom learning with more hands-on training usually has led to the largest and most lasting impacts (Hotz, Imbens, and Klerman 2006; Dyke et al. 2006).

The Trade Adjustment Assistance program was established in 1963 and has undergone numerous changes since its inception, but its basic purpose remains to provide training to workers displaced as the result of foreign competition. Eligible workers receive the same kinds of reemployment and training services offered to WIA participants, but more generous funding allows them to receive training for a longer period of time. Moreover, TAA provides income supplements to regular unemployment insurance benefits as well as an allowance for relocation. If the displaced worker is over 50 years old and finds a new job paying less than $50,000 a year, TAA also provides the worker the option to receive wage insurance in the amount of half the difference between his or her old and new wage (up to a cap of $10,000) for up to two years.

Recognizing the importance of job training to American workers and their families, the President has proposed a major initiative to provide workers with the tools and skills they need to find new jobs—by forging new partnerships between community colleges and businesses to train 2 million skilled workers and by streamlining access to training and employment services for dislocated workers.

The current system does not treat all workers who were dislocated because of economic shifts equally. As noted above, workers in trade-impacted industries are eligible for extensive income support, training, and reemployment services under the TAA, while those who lose their jobs for other reasons receive less generous assistance. In this increasingly global economy, it is difficult to distinguish between trade, technology, outsourcing, consumer trends, and other economic shifts that cause displacement. The President believes that dislocated workers should be able to access a single program, visit a single location or go to a single web site to find information about and assistance with job and training opportunities in their community. Ensuring that displaced workers have the information and training they need to successfully return to work is important not only for those who have lost their jobs as a result of the 2007–09 recession, but also for those who will be in need of these services in the future.

Conclusion

The 2007–09 recession severely disrupted a labor market that was already under stress from decades of rising inequality, stagnant middle-class incomes, and weak job growth in the 2001–07 recovery period. The job market has been recovering gradually since the end of the recession, and the Administration continues to make strengthening and sustaining the recovery in the job market a top priority. The policies proposed by the Administration will promote continued economic growth and job creation by supporting aggregate demand through an extension of the 2 percentage point payroll tax cut, the continuation of extended unemployment insurance benefits, investments in infrastructure, and assistance to states and localities to retain school teachers and first responders. Investments in expanded reemployment services and training for low-skilled and displaced workers will help get Americans back to work. And the President's proposals to invest in elementary and secondary education and to make college more affordable will lay the foundation for a stronger economy in the future.

✤

C H A P T E R   7

PRESERVING AND MODERNIZING THE SAFETY NET

Today's dynamic, global economy, driven by rapid technological change, offers abundant benefits and opportunities—but also entails many risks. The Great Recession has made clearer than ever that a strong and flexible economy requires a robust safety net to protect families against major risks and to reduce the likelihood that temporary economic shocks will inflict permanent harm on families and the economy.

In the first weeks after President Obama was inaugurated, the President and the Congress enacted policies to expand and strengthen the safety net in response to the ongoing economic crisis. The American Recovery and Reinvestment Act of 2009 (the Recovery Act) provided increased funding for a number of key safety net programs, including unemployment insurance (UI), Temporary Assistance for Needy Families (TANF), Medicaid, and the Earned Income Tax Credit (EITC). These and other safety net programs have been critical in cushioning American families from the effects of the Great Recession and in stabilizing the economy by supporting aggregate demand.

One way to gauge the impact of the safety net is to consider the number of American families that would have been in poverty were it not for the support provided by specific programs. These effects are significant. In 2010, the official poverty rate was 15.1 percent, which translates to roughly 46 million people living in poverty. According to U.S. Census Bureau estimates, were it not for unemployment insurance benefits, 3.2 million more Americans would have been in poverty in 2010. This figure includes about 2.3 million nonelderly adults, 900,000 children, and 100,000 adults age 65 and older. Among families participating in the program, the receipt of UI benefits has the effect of cutting the poverty rate roughly in half (Gabe and Whittaker 2011).

Data Watch 7-1: The Census Bureau's Supplemental Poverty Measure

The official poverty measure was developed in the 1960s. According to this measure, a family is considered to be poor if its before-tax income falls below a "poverty line" that varies according to family size and composition.

In 2011, the Census Bureau released an alternative to the official poverty measure that presents a more complete picture of poverty and of the effects of policies to support low-income families. This Supplemental Poverty Measure (SPM), developed early in the Obama Administration, is based on an approach recommended in 1995 by the National Academy of Sciences. Like the official poverty measure, the supplemental measure compares the resources available to a household with a threshold level of income that takes into account household composition. It differs from the official measure, however, both in how it calculates resources and in how it sets the thresholds. The supplemental measure adds in-kind assistance such as nutritional assistance and subsidized housing to household resources and subtracts necessary expenses such as taxes, child care, and other work-related expenses, as well as medical out-of-pocket costs. Its thresholds are calculated differently than those for the official poverty line, and they reflect geographic differences in housing costs.

Overall, 16.0 percent of all Americans were estimated to be in poverty in 2010 according to the supplemental measure, compared with 15.2 percent using the official methodology.[a] Differences between the two measures vary across demographic groups. For example, because they disproportionately benefit from programs like the Earned Income Tax Credit (EITC) and the Supplemental Nutrition Assistance Program (SNAP), children are more likely to be in poverty according to the official measure, which does not account for support from these programs. By contrast, the poverty rate for elderly Americans is higher according to the supplemental measure, since unlike the official measure, it subtracts out-of-pocket medical expenses from income.

The supplemental poverty measure allows researchers to isolate more accurately the effects of a specific policy, source of income, or category of expense on the prevalence of poverty. Among the programs studied by the Census Bureau, the EITC has the largest antipoverty effect; according to the supplemental measure, in the absence of the tax credit, an additional 6.1 million people would have been in poverty in 2010. Accounting for medical out-of-pocket expenses in the supplemental measure, on the other hand, moved 10 million individuals into poverty in 2010.

---

[a] This official estimate differs from the usual published rate (of 15.1 percent) as unrelated individuals under 15 years of age are included in the universe.

The official definition of poverty does not account for the effect of taxes paid and tax credits, such as the Earned Income Tax Credit. Nor does it incorporate the value of in-kind benefits. As a result, the official measure does not reflect the benefit that American families receive from the EITC or important safety net programs, such as the Supplemental Nutrition Assistance Program (SNAP), on the official poverty rate. However, such a calculation is possible using an alternative measure of poverty, known as the Supplemental Poverty Measure (Data Watch 7-1). Using the supplemental measure, the Census Bureau estimated that in the absence of the EITC another 6.1 million Americans, nearly half of them children, would have been in poverty in 2010. In that same year, SNAP benefits lifted 2.9 million adults and 2.2 million children out of poverty. Considered all together, it is estimated that the social insurance and means-tested transfer programs that make up the safety net reduce the number of Americans falling below the poverty line by more than half (Ziliak 2011).

Safety net programs can improve economic efficiency by supplementing private markets if they fail to provide adequate insurance against major economic risks. A fundamental market failure common to both insurance and annuity markets is adverse selection, which arises when consumers know more than insurers about their own risk—their expected medical claims, their likelihood of becoming unemployed, or their expected longevity (Rothschild and Stiglitz 1976). If insurance or annuity contracts are priced according to the average risk in a population, coverage will be attractive to those who know that they are at high risk and unattractive to those who know that they are at low risk. To the extent that high-risk consumers are more likely to purchase insurance, the cost of coverage will rise, which in turn will make coverage even less attractive to their low-risk counterparts. The gravity of the adverse selection problem will vary across types of insurance and, for a given type, across market segments. Some types of insurance, such as unemployment insurance, have virtually no private market. Private health insurance and annuity markets exist, though not without substantial support from tax and regulatory policies; even with this support, coverage remains costly and incomplete.

In addition to addressing specific types of market failure, a strong safety net can promote growth and entrepreneurship. By providing a basic level of security, well-designed safety net programs help create an environment that encourages people to engage in value-creating activities such as changing jobs or starting a new business. A strong safety net is especially important in a global economy in which international trade and financial integration can bring both substantial benefits and increased risk. Robust cross-country evidence finds that economies that have stronger safety nets also tend to pursue more efficient economic policies (Rodrik 1998). Safety net programs also protect workers and their families from the labor market disruptions that can arise from technological change and other sources of fluctuation in demand. Finally, safety net programs can be an important component of automatic stabilizers—providing expansions in aggregate demand that help counteract the weakening of the economy during economic downturns.

An effective and efficient safety net must adapt and evolve in response to changes in technology and economic conditions. This chapter provides an overview of the key components of the safety net in the United States, emphasizing recent policy developments and proposals to keep the nation's safety net strong.

Unemployment Insurance

Unemployment insurance has long been an essential component of the safety net for workers who have lost a job through no fault of their own. In the recent period of high unemployment, the basic UI program and emergency extensions have provided critical support for millions of American families. In 2010, almost 10 percent of households received UI benefits—and that share is expected to fall back toward the pre-recession average of about 4 percent as the economy recovers.

Unemployment insurance is a joint Federal-state program that covers nearly all civilian workers. During normal economic times, workers and employers contribute to state systems that pay benefits to unemployed workers for up to 26 weeks. During periods of high unemployment, extended benefits (EB) are available to workers who have exhausted regular UI benefits, with the costs normally shared between the Federal Government and states. Benefits are determined as a function of past wages, up to a cap. Although key program parameters vary across states, on average UI benefits replace roughly half of a recipient's lost earnings. In 2011, the average weekly benefit was roughly $300.

Historically the Federal Government has funded benefits for extended periods while the economy recovers from a serious downturn. It did so once during the 1950s, once during the 1960s, twice during the 1970s, and once each during the early 1980s, the 1990s, and the early 2000s. In each instance since the 1970s, extended benefits have been reauthorized, usually multiple times, in reaction to continued weakness in the labor market. In June 2008, Congress enacted the Emergency Unemployment Compensation (EUC) Program that added 13 weeks of Federally funded UI benefits. As the labor market continued to deteriorate, Congress extended the program for workers in the hardest-hit states several times. In addition, starting in February 2009, Congress provided full Federal funding of extended jobless benefits. Together these policies allow workers in high-unemployment states to qualify for up to 99 weeks of benefits.

The Economics of Unemployment Insurance

Unemployment insurance benefits enable workers to minimize disruptions in spending caused by unanticipated income shocks (Baily 1978). Economic research indicates that this consumption-smoothing effect is important. According to one study, in the absence of UI, a typical family whose household head becomes unemployed lowers spending on food by 22 percent, while a family receiving UI benefits spends only 7 percent less on food (Gruber 1997). In addition to helping families whose income has been reduced due to job loss, by providing income to families that they can spend, UI benefits mitigate the impact of the recession on the broader economy.

These benefits must be weighed against the cost of longer spells of unemployment potentially induced by the availability of UI—although in the current environment, any effect on spell length is likely to be comparatively small. Theoretical models of labor supply and job search predict that unemployed workers covered by more generous UI systems can take longer to find a new job (see, for example, Mortensen 1977). More recent work has shown that it is important to distinguish among reasons why UI increases the duration of unemployment. Traditionally, economists have interpreted the relationship between UI and duration in the context of a worker's choice between work and leisure, assuming that UI reduces the effort devoted to job search. An alternative view, given that a large fraction of unemployed workers have limited assets, is that UI benefits allow workers to meet their basic needs while they search for a job that is a good match for their talents (Chetty 2008). Better matches generally translate to higher wages (leading to higher tax revenues), increased job satisfaction, and greater employment stability (which reduces employers' hiring costs).

The empirical research literature on the relationship between UI benefits and unemployment duration is sizable. Recent research suggests that UI benefits have small effects on unemployment duration even when the economy is strong (Card and Levine 2000). In periods of high unemployment, the consumption-smoothing benefit of UI will be especially valuable to workers, and any negative effects on worker search effort will be less important because of the scarcity of jobs (Kroft and Notowidigdo 2011; Schmieder, von Wachter, and Bender 2012). Consistent with this premise, research suggests that the recent expansion of extended and emergency benefits has had a minimal effect on the duration of unemployment spells and the unemployment rate (Farber and Valletta 2011; Rothstein 2011; Daly et al. 2012). Moreover, to the extent that the extension of benefits has affected the measured unemployment rate, it has done so not by reducing the probability that unemployed workers look for and find jobs, but by reducing the number of unemployed workers who have given up on searching for a new job (Rothstein 2011). This finding is important in light of evidence suggesting that during periods of high unemployment, many older workers who exhaust their UI benefits end up applying for Social Security Disability Insurance (Rutledge 2011).

Recent Trends in UI Receipt and Its Effect on Household Income

The share of households receiving UI rose from 4.1 percent in 2007 to 9.6 percent in 2010. Over the same period, the average annual amount received by households benefiting from UI rose from $4,400 to $8,340, mainly because of longer duration of benefit receipt but also because of the extra $25 in weekly benefits provided through FY 2010 by the Recovery Act. This money was crucial to keeping many families in their homes and able to pay other household expenses. As noted, UI lifts millions of families out of poverty. However, because a large share of benefits flows to middle-income workers, these antipoverty effects understate the economic impact of the program on participants. Households that received UI benefits in 2010 had a median income of $55,000 the previous year, which is only slightly less than the median income of working households that did not receive UI. Among all recipients, UI payments represented 23 percent of household income in 2010. The share of income represented by UI ranged from 15 percent for multiple-earner households without children to almost 36 percent for households with a single worker and no children (Figure 7-1).[1]

In addition to providing income insurance to families of unemployed workers, the UI system helps the economy as a whole (Auerbach and Feenberg 2000). Unemployment insurance is an automatic stabilizer that leans against the negative cycle of increased unemployment leading to reduced consumption, which leads to a further decline in economic activity. Since unemployed workers tend to spend rather than save their benefits, the impact on aggregate demand is fairly immediate. Because of the way that the emergency and extended benefits programs increase economic activity, they generate partially offsetting income and payroll tax revenues for the Federal Government and help state and local budgets by increasing sales tax revenues. In addition, without the income support provided by these

---

[1] Because previous research suggests that recipients tend to understate the amount of unemployment benefits they receive (Meyer, Mok, and Sullivan 2009), these figures can be seen as lower-bound estimates of the effect of UI on household income.

Share of Household Income from Unemployment Insurance among
Recipients in 2010, by Household Type

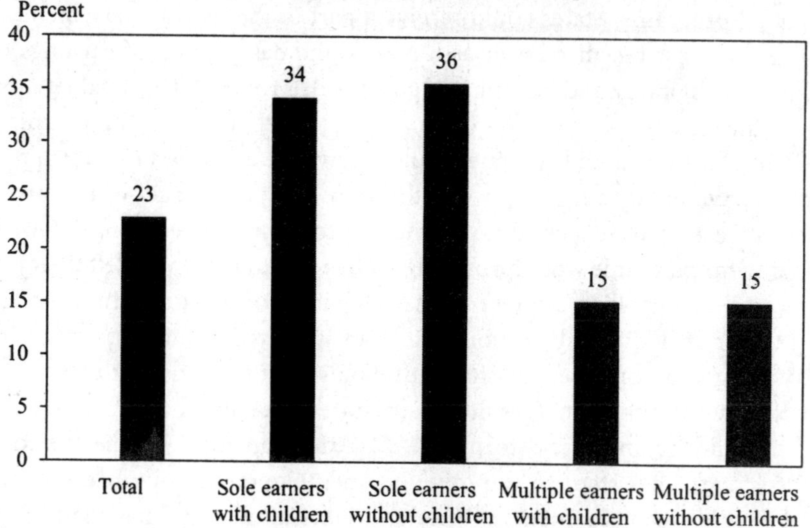

Source: Current Population Survey, Annual Social and Economic Supplement.

programs, more families would draw on other public programs. For these reasons, the Congressional Budget Office notes that extending UI benefits is the most timely and cost-effective policy for increasing economic activity and employment (CBO 2011).

Policy Innovations

The U.S. unemployment insurance system dates to the Great Depression of the 1930s. Originally, most covered workers were employed in manufacturing. At its inception, the UI system allowed for income smoothing for workers who would ultimately return to their old job or one like it. Research based on data from the early 1980s suggests that at that time 60 percent of UI spells ended with the worker being recalled to his or her original job (Corson and Nicholson 1983; Katz and Meyer 1991). Today, temporary layoffs are less common; increasingly, workers receiving UI benefits have been dislocated as the result of structural changes in the economy and must find a new industry or occupation. In many cases, wages in the new jobs these workers find are significantly lower than their former wages. Thus, workers today need income support while they are searching for a new job, but they also need training, job search support, and other assistance to help ease what can be a difficult transition.

The first step to modernize the unemployment insurance program was taken in the UI Modernization Act, a part of the Recovery Act. The UI Modernization Act made $7 billion available to states that made reforms to their UI programs. States could receive a part of the incentive payment for using the most recent quarter as a part of the base period of earnings on which UI eligibility and benefit amounts are determined. This made it more likely that recent labor market entrants would meet the minimum earnings threshold for UI eligibility. States could receive the other part of their apportioned payment by adopting two of the following policies: allowing workers who were employed part-time previously to continue receiving UI while looking for part-time work, providing UI benefits to those who left their jobs for certain compelling family reasons, allowing workers to continue receiving UI for an additional six months if in an approved training program, and providing additional benefits for households with more dependents. These small incentive payments resulted in 36 states changing their UI laws.

Building on these reforms, in the American Jobs Act the President called for further steps to improve the unemployment insurance program and expand reemployment services and job training, and has made these reforms a part of the FY 2013 Budget proposal. Although most UI policy innovations target workers who have already lost their jobs, another important policy goal is to reduce the number of workers who are laid off in the first place. One promising initiative is work-sharing. Under a work-sharing arrangement, workers whose hours are reduced in lieu of temporary layoffs receive partial UI benefits while remaining on the job and keeping their skills sharp. By allowing employers to retain skilled workers at reduced hours rather than laying them off, work-sharing makes it easier and less costly for employers to scale up production when orders increase. Twenty-four states now have work-sharing programs, and in the American Jobs Act, President Obama proposed incentives to help expand the program to more states.

Workers who have been laid off need help finding a new job. The American Jobs Act included the Reemployment NOW program, a set of reforms to help UI claimants get back to work more quickly. The FY 2013 Budget continues this support. As a part of this initiative, the Administration has proposed requiring states to provide reemployment services, such as career and job search counseling, skills assessments, and assistance in identifying helpful resources to EUC recipients to speed their return to work. Face-to-face contacts also provide an opportunity to assess recipients' eligibility for UI benefits. Research suggests that these services can lower program costs by reducing spells of UI receipt and eliminating payments to ineligible individuals (Black et al. 2003).

Because entrepreneurship is key to a dynamic economy, a modern UI system should make it easier for displaced workers to start their own businesses. The Administration has proposed allowing states to use Reemployment NOW funds to expand Self-Employment Assistance programs that pay UI benefits to recipients who are working full-time to establish a new business. Seven states already permit a similar use of unemployment insurance benefits. Under this program, entrepreneurship training would be facilitated through One-Stop Centers in collaboration with the Small Business Administration. A demonstration project, Growing America Through Entrepreneurship (Project GATE), provided training and one-on-one counseling to anyone interested in creating, sustaining, or expanding a small business. A recent study found that GATE had a positive effect on new business starts for unemployed participants and higher total earnings after five years than a comparison group (Michaelides and Benus 2010).

For jobless workers seeking to change occupations, lack of experience can be a significant barrier. With Reemployment NOW funds, states could experiment with Bridge to Work programs, which would allow EUC recipients to get short-term work-based experience that helps them maintain or enhance their skills. Under this program, private employers would be able to take on EUC recipients for up to 38 hours a week for a trial period of up to eight weeks with the workers receiving compensation through the EUC program. In addition, all program participants would be covered by workers' compensation and be guaranteed at least the minimum wage.

Finally, to support state creativity and flexibility, upon approval of the Secretary of Labor, states would be permitted to use Reemployment NOW funds to implement their own innovative strategies for connecting the long-term unemployed to employment opportunities.

In addition to these efforts that build upon the existing Federally-financed unemployment compensation system to help with getting the long-term unemployed back to work, the President's Budget includes other important and complementary initiatives that will contribute to the goal of ensuring that every American who wants a job can find one. As discussed in Chapter 6, these initiatives include streamlining training and employment services so that job seekers can visit a single location or go to a single web site to find the help they need; providing a universal core set of services to serve all dislocated workers; and introducing a new Pathways Back to Work fund to support employment opportunities for low-income youth, low-income adults and the long-term unemployed.

Several means-tested programs also provide support to American families, especially those who have experienced adverse economic shocks. Table 7-1 reports the number of participants and Federal cost of several important programs. One of the largest Federal programs targeted at low-income families is the Earned Income Tax Credit, a refundable tax credit for low-income workers. The assistance is available only to those with earnings, and the amount of the credit increases with a worker's earned income up to a maximum level and then phases out at higher income levels. The maximum benefit amount increases with the number of children in the family, and the income level at which the credit begins to phase out differs according to taxpayer filing status (single or married couple filing jointly). As part of the Recovery Act, Congress created a new category with a higher credit for taxpayers with three or more children, providing those families as much as $600 extra, and increased the income level at which the credit phases out for married couples filing jointly by $3,000 over 2008 levels. The Tax Relief and Job Creation Act of 2010 extended these changes through 2012. Over 26 million working families and individuals received the EITC on their 2010 tax return, with the average claimant receiving $2,220.

The benefits of the EITC go beyond the amount of the credit received. Studies have found that the EITC increases participation in the labor market (Eissa and Liebman 1996; Meyer and Rosenbaum 2000), improves maternal health outcomes (Evans and Garthwaite 2010) and helps low-income individuals acquire additional experience that contributes to higher earnings growth (Dahl, DeLeire, and Schwabish 2009).

The Supplemental Nutrition Assistance Program (SNAP) is another critical safety net program targeted at low-income families. SNAP benefits are funded by the Federal Government and administered by states. Families and individuals qualify if their income and assets are sufficiently low. Participants usually receive their benefits on electronic benefit transfer cards that can be used only to purchase food. Nondisabled adults who have no dependents and who are not working or participating in a work training program can usually receive SNAP benefits only for three months over a three-year period.

Roughly half of all SNAP participants were children, and more than three-quarters of all participant households included a child, an elderly person, or a disabled nonelderly person. Roughly a quarter of all children participated. In FY 2010, the average household participating in the SNAP program received monthly benefits worth $287; 40 percent of participating

Number of Participants and Total Federal Expenditures for Safety Net Programs, 2010

	Participants (millions)	Federal expenditures (billions of dollars)
Social insurance		
Medicare	47.5	522.8
Old Age and Survivors Insurance	43.8	584.9
Unemployment insurance	10.4	158.3
Social Security Disability Insurance	10.2	127.7
Means-tested transfers and credits		
Medicaid/Children's Health Insurance Program	58.3	281.9
Supplemental Nutrition Assistance Program	40.3	68.3
Earned Income Tax Credit	26.8	59.5
Supplemental Security Income	7.9	47.8
Public and assisted housing	4.7	37.9
Temporary Assistance for Needy Families	4.4	18.1

Note: Recipients are counts of individuals except for recipients of EITC (tax filing units) and housing (families). Expenditures for UI, Medicaid/CHIP, SNAP, and TANF are for fiscal year 2010, and the number of recipients is the average of point-in-time recipients over fiscal year 2010. Public and assisted housing includes only programs operated by the Department of Housing and Urban Development, and recipients and expenditures are for fiscal year 2010. The number of SSI recipients is as of December 2010. For all other programs, the number of recipients represents those participating at any point in the (calendar) year. Federal expenditures include grants to states.

Source: Center for Medicare and Medicaid Services, Social Security Administration, Department of Labor, Office of Management and Budget, Medicaid Payment Advisory Commission, Department of Agriculture, Internal Revenue Service, Department of Health and Human Services, Department of Housing and Urban Development.

households received the maximum benefit for their family size—for example, $668 a month for a family of four.

Both participation and expenditures are strongly countercyclical in the SNAP program, increasing during economic contractions and decreasing during expansions. Current projections are that SNAP enrollment will begin falling next year, as the economy continues to recover. Thus, like UI, SNAP not only provides direct benefits to participant households, but also has a stabilizing effect on the economy by limiting declines in consumption during economic downturns.

The Recovery Act established the Emergency Contingency Fund for state Temporary Aid for Needy Families programs, which provided $5 billion to states for increased spending for basic assistance, nonrecurrent short-term benefits, or subsidized employment. States expanded efforts in all three areas, including committing $1.3 billion to the largest targeted employment initiative in the history of welfare reform. Thirty-nine states in addition to the District of Columbia, Puerto Rico, and the Virgin Islands established subsidized employment programs, with an estimated 260,000 job slots created for adults and youth, many of them involving subsidies that created jobs with private sector employers. While most of these subsidized employment efforts were not sustained at previous levels after Recovery Act funding ended, many jurisdictions have maintained programs at a smaller scale. Based in part on the success of this initiative, the President has proposed the Pathways Back to Work Fund (discussed in Chapter 6) that would provide employment opportunities for low-income individuals and the long-term unemployed.

Housing is the largest component of virtually every family's budget, especially low-income families. The Federal safety net includes several programs designed to ensure that financial stress does not result in home-lessness. Stable housing allows families to weather labor market shocks and is a precondition for children's educational success. In addition to the 2.3 million families assisted by the Department of Housing and Urban Development's project-based rental assistance and public housing pro-grams, the largest Federal program aimed at low-income households is the Housing Choice Voucher program. The Housing Choice Voucher program served 2.1 million families in FY 2010, of which 90 percent included chil-dren, the elderly, or individuals with disabilities. As discussed in Chapter 4, the Administration has also developed new programs that help unemployed homeowners avoid foreclosure.

Two other programs that are critical to the safety net provide benefits to Americans with disabilities. Social Security Disability Insurance (SSDI) is a social insurance program designed to offset the loss of wages of workers with long-term health conditions that prevent "substantial gainful activity." Individuals with adequate Social Security–covered employment history, or children (disabled before age 22) of a retired, deceased, or disabled worker entitled to Social Security benefits, are covered by the program. Beneficiaries receive a cash benefit based on their income before becoming disabled, adjusted upward by wage inflation. In December 2010, more than 10 million people received SSDI benefits. Recipients become eligible for Medicare after two years, offsetting the loss of employer-sponsored health insurance.

A second Federal program that assists persons with disabilities is Supplemental Security Income (SSI), a means-tested entitlement program that provides cash benefits to needy aged, blind, or disabled individuals. In December 2010, roughly 7.9 million Americans received SSI benefits; of that total, about 6.6 million qualified on the basis of a disability. The program is a particularly important source of income for older working-age adults: roughly one-quarter of all participants are between the ages of 50 and 64.

A recent study illustrates how critical these programs are to their participants (DeCesaro and Hemmeter 2008). Using data from 2002, the study shows that nearly a quarter of SSDI and roughly half of SSI beneficia-ries had family incomes that fell below the Federal poverty level. However, the programs play an important role in keeping their beneficiaries out of extreme poverty, which is defined as having an income below 50 percent of the Federal poverty threshold. According to this study, the majority of SSDI recipients relied on that program for at least 75 percent of their income. While only 5 percent of SSI beneficiaries were in extreme poverty, taking away SSI benefits would have raised that figure above 40 percent.

HEALTH INSURANCE

In March 2010, the President signed into law the Patient Protection and Affordable Care Act (the Affordable Care Act). When fully implemented, the Affordable Care Act will significantly strengthen the health care safety net, substantially increasing the number of Americans with health insurance and providing new protections and benefits to those who are already insured. The Affordable Care Act builds on and maintains the strengths of the current private system of employer-sponsored health coverage and insurance provided through Medicare, Medicaid, and the Children's Health Insurance Program (CHIP). Therefore, the changes brought about by the new law need to be considered in the context of the current system.

The Economics of Employer-Sponsored Health Insurance

One of the defining features of the U.S. health care system is the central role played by employers. Today, roughly nine in ten Americans with private health insurance obtain their coverage through the workplace, either through their own employer or through the employer of a family member. Employer-sponsored insurance is generally much less costly for workers—who pay for coverage through reductions in their wages as well as direct premium contributions—than coverage purchased directly in the individual market. There are three main sources of savings.

First, employer-sponsored group coverage greatly mitigates the problem of adverse selection. Because employer-sponsored groups are formed for reasons other than purchasing health insurance, they represent stable risk pools. Employer policies themselves contribute to this stability and to the spreading of risks. Within firms, the amount that employees are required to contribute toward premiums generally does not vary with health risk. Common employer and insurer policies—such as limiting periods when employees can sign up for coverage and requiring a minimum employee participation rate—prevent employees from declining coverage when they are healthy and joining the plan only when they need medical care.

A stable risk pool translates to lower administrative costs as insurers need to devote fewer resources to underwriting. Administrative savings also come from economies of scale in marketing and administration. Because important costs vary with the number of contracts rather than the number of individuals covered by a contract, it is less expensive on a per-person basis to sell to a group of 1,000 than to sell to 1,000 individuals.

Third, because employer expenditures on health insurance premiums are exempt from Federal and state income taxes and Social Security payroll taxes, employer-sponsored insurance can effectively be purchased with pretax dollars. For a typical worker in the 15 percent tax bracket, the tax exclusion reduces the cost of insurance by roughly one third (Gruber 2010). Overall, the estimated FY 2011 tax expenditure associated with the exemption from Federal taxes is $282 billion.

Although the cost savings associated with employer provision of insurance can be large, the savings are not evenly distributed among employers. The advantages of more efficient risk pooling and economies of scale in marketing and administration increase with firm size. The value of the tax exemption is not explicitly tied to firm size, but because compensation tends to be higher in larger firms, this advantage is correlated with size as well. As a result, the larger the firm, the greater the probability it will offer health insurance. Figure 7-2 illustrates that, whereas nearly all firms with more than 50 employees offer health benefits, less than half of those with 2 to 24 employees do. Between 2000 and 2010, the share of private sector establishments with fewer than 50 workers that offer health insurance benefits declined from 47.2 percent to 39.2 percent.

Firm size affects more than just whether workers are offered coverage. Among firms that offer insurance, large firms are substantially more likely to offer a choice of plans: more than 80 percent of private sector establishments with 1,000 or more employees offered a choice of health insurance options in 2010, compared with 18 percent of establishments with 50 or fewer employees. Employees who have a choice of plans tend to report greater satisfaction with their insurance coverage and their health care (Schone and Cooper 2001). And some very large firms have actively promoted strategies to improve health care quality and patient safety.

Over the past two decades, rising health care costs have eroded the accessibility of employer-sponsored health insurance, especially for middle-class families who experienced relatively little income growth over that period. Figure 7-3 plots the percentage of workers who lack health insurance (left axis) against an estimate of their per capita health spending divided by their median income (right axis). Because the growth in health spending is a principal determinant of rising insurance premiums, this ratio can be seen to capture changes in the affordability of health insurance. The figure indicates that during the 1980s insurance became less affordable as health care costs

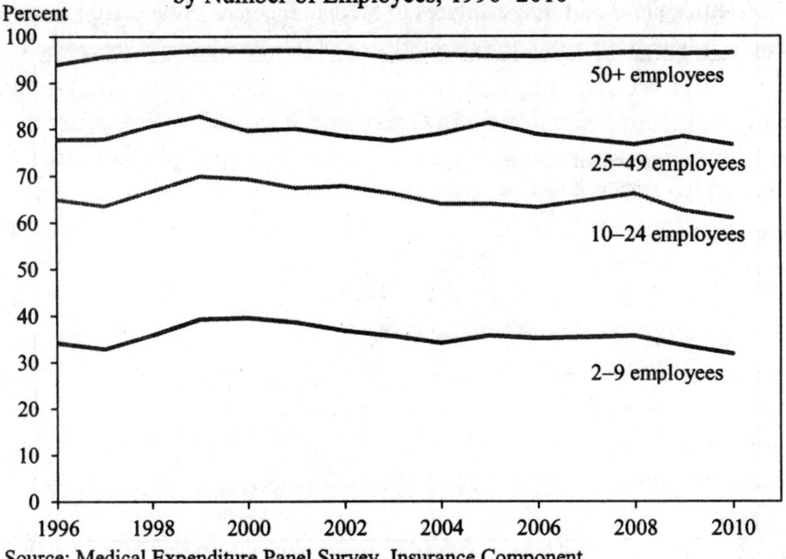

Source: Medical Expenditure Panel Survey, Insurance Component.

grew faster than median incomes and the percentage of workers without coverage grew. In the mid-1990s, health care spending grew less rapidly and a strong economy caused median income to rise. As a result of this confluence, the affordability index remained relatively constant, and insurance coverage stabilized. However, health care cost growth picked up again in the late 1990s and has outstripped income growth for the past decade, causing coverage to decline once again.

Medicaid and CHIP: A Health Care Safety Net for Children

As insurance coverage has declined among working-age adults over the past two decades, coverage among children has actually increased because of expanded eligibility for public programs. Until the mid-1980s, Medicaid eligibility was tied to eligibility for Aid to Families with Dependent Children, the cash welfare program. Starting in 1986, the two programs were delinked, and income eligibility limits for Medicaid were increased. The most significant eligibility expansions came as part of the Omnibus Budget Reconciliation Acts of 1989 and 1990. As the data in Figure 7-4 depict, with these expansions the share of children without health insurance began to decline, even as the share of uninsured adults rose. By 1997, while 18 percent of nonelderly adults were uninsured, the share of children who were uninsured was 14 percent.

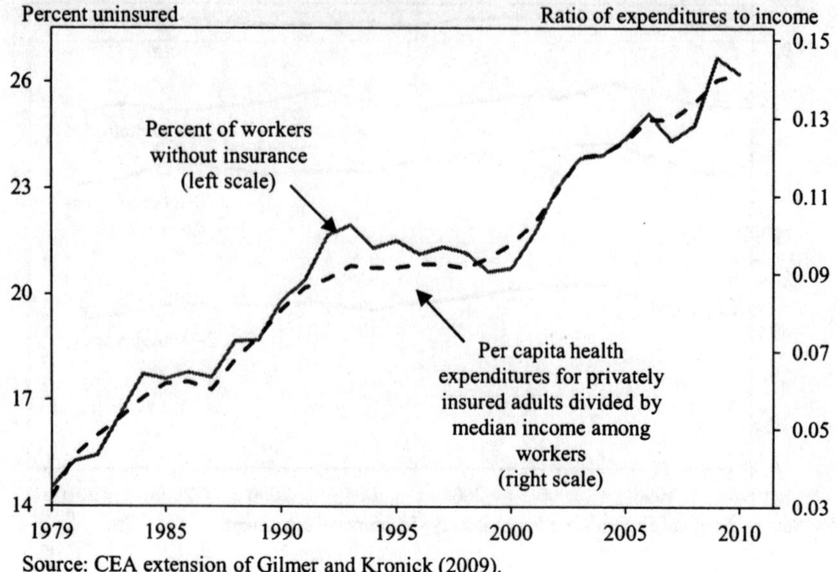

Source: CEA extension of Gilmer and Kronick (2009).

That same year, Congress established the State Children's Health Insurance Program (initially referred to as SCHIP, now CHIP) as part of the Balanced Budget Act of 1997. Like Medicaid, CHIP is funded jointly by states and the Federal Government, although CHIP allows states more flexibility in designing their programs. States began implementing CHIP in late 1997, and by 2000 every state program was up and running. Today, the income eligibility limit in 47 states and the District of Columbia is 200 percent of the Federal poverty level or greater. As a result of Medicaid and CHIP, the percentage of children who are uninsured has fallen since the late 1990s and is now less than half the adult rate.

President Obama has built on the success of Medicaid and CHIP by making these programs even stronger. In the early days of the Administration, the President signed the Children's Health Insurance Program Reauthorization Act of 2009, which extended funding for CHIP through September 2013. This legislation also introduced administrative reforms that improve program effectiveness, including new performance bonuses for states that successfully increase coverage by streamlining eligibility and enrollment procedures. Also in 2009, the Recovery Act provided additional support to states by boosting the Federal share of Medicaid at a time when program enrollment was increasing and state budgets were in crisis. Between 2008 and June 2011, over

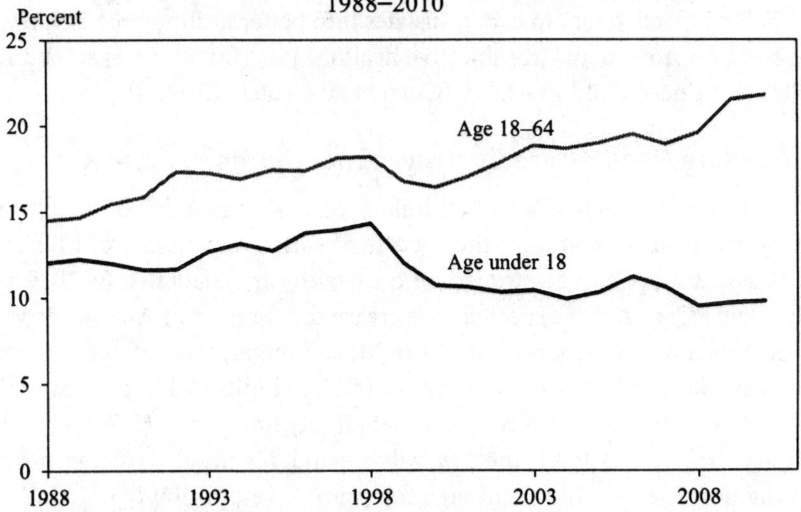

Note: Data for 1988 to 1998 adjusted to reflect CPS's 2011 revision to the health insurance editing process.
Source: Current Population Survey, Annual Social and Economic Supplement.

4.4 million children gained coverage through Medicaid and CHIP. In 2010, the Affordable Care Act extended funding for CHIP through 2015.

Because of Medicaid and CHIP, insurance coverage of children tends to be less sensitive to changes in macroeconomic conditions than that of adults. Research suggests that, holding other factors constant, a 1 percentage point increase in the national unemployment rate translates to almost a 1 point decrease in the percentage of nonelderly adults and children covered by employer-sponsored insurance (Holahan and Garrett 2009). Without a strong public insurance safety net for adults, more than half of the working-age Americans who lose employer-sponsored insurance during an economic downturn end up uninsured. For children, however, the loss of private coverage is mostly offset by an increase in public insurance. This discrepancy between the experience of adults and children will change with the full implementation of the Affordable Care Act, described below.

Many studies indicate that the expansion of Medicaid and CHIP has also significantly improved access to health care. One study using data from the 1980s and early 1990s found that eligibility for public insurance roughly halved the probability that a child failed to have at least one physician visit a year (Currie and Gruber 1996a). Other research shows that increased Medicaid eligibility for children leads to an increase in hospitalizations overall, but a decrease in "preventable" admissions (that is, those that are avoidable if a child receives appropriate primary care) (Dafny and Gruber 2005). Improved access to care translates into better health outcomes, ranging from improvements in subjective health status (Currie, Decker, and Lin 2008) to reduced child mortality (Currie and Gruber 1996a, 1996b).

Expanding Health Care Coverage: The Affordable Care Act

The Affordable Care Act builds on the strengths of employer-sponsored insurance and on the success of earlier expansions of Medicaid and CHIP to expand and strengthen the health care safety net. By 2019, the Affordable Care Act is expected to increase the number of Americans with health insurance by more than 30 million. Roughly half of the coverage gain will come from raising Medicaid eligibility limits to 133 percent of the Federal poverty level. Because income eligibility limits for CHIP in all states already exceed this level, the law will expand Medicaid coverage mainly among nonelderly adults. Although the primary responsibility for administering Medicaid will remain with the states, funding for the expanded coverage will come almost entirely from the Federal Government.

Most of the remaining coverage gains will come from private insurance purchased through state-level Affordable Insurance Exchanges. Individuals and families with incomes up to 400 percent of the Federal poverty level who do not have access to affordable employer-sponsored coverage that meets a minimum value will be eligible for premium tax credits that they can use to purchase coverage through an Exchange. These new tax credits are targeted at lower- and middle-income families who currently receive little or no benefit from the large tax subsidies that implicitly support the system of employer-sponsored insurance. The Affordable Care Act also establishes a Small Business Health Insurance Options Program (SHOP) in each state that gives small employers and their employees access to private health insurance plans and small business health insurance tax credits as well.

The state-level Exchanges will extend to workers at small firms, the self-employed, part-time workers, and nonworkers many of the advantages of employer-sponsored insurance already enjoyed by employees of large firms: more efficient risk pooling and greater administrative economies of scale than are available in the current individual and small group market. Within an Exchange, consumers and employers will be able to choose from a broad menu of plans. To improve consumer choices, Exchanges will provide transparent information on premiums, benefits, cost-sharing, and plan quality—information that will help cut the high consumer search costs that push up premiums in the small group and individual health insurance markets (Cebul et al. 2011). By creating a marketplace in which consumers can easily compare plans on the basis of price and quality, the Exchanges should increase competition among insurers. Considerable evidence from large employers shows that when employees are given a choice of health plans and clear information about premiums and benefits, they switch plans in response to small differences in premiums (Buchmueller 2009).

The Affordable Care Act establishes new consumer protections for health insurance coverage purchased either through an Exchange or in the outside individual or small group market, many of which are already in effect today. Insurers will not be allowed to deny or limit coverage on the basis of an individual's health status. Within certain limits, premiums may vary by age, geography, and smoking status, but not by individual health status, gender, or other factors. The Act also includes a requirement that individuals who can afford insurance maintain minimum essential coverage. These market reforms fill an important gap in the health care safety net.

Provisions of the Affordable Care Act Now in Place

Many of the insurance market reforms, along with the expansion of Medicaid and the creation of the Exchanges, will not take effect until 2014. Some provisions of the Affordable Care Act, however, have already been put into place. Insurers are now prohibited from retroactively cancelling coverage because of honest mistakes made on the application. The Act also eliminates lifetime dollar limits on essential health benefits and restricts the use of annual dollar limits. (Annual benefit limits will be eliminated completely by 2014.) Since July 2010, consumers who are uninsured and unable to get insurance because of a pre-existing condition can find subsidized coverage through the Pre-Existing Condition Insurance Plan. This temporary program gives uninsured individuals with costly conditions access to affordable insurance until the full set of consumer protections takes effect in 2014. As of the end of 2011, 45,000 individuals were enrolled.

Another coverage-related provision of the law that is already in force allows young adults to remain on their parents' private insurance policies until they reach age 26. This policy targets a population that is disproportionately uninsured. Although one reason large numbers of young adults have no health insurance is that people in this age group tend to be in good health and do not perceive a need for health care (the "young invincibles" hypothesis), a second important reason is lack of access to affordable coverage, because many young adults have not yet settled into full-time jobs that offer health benefits. As a result, the probability of being uninsured jumps between the ages of 18 and 19, as many young adults lose coverage under their parents' employer-sponsored insurance. This loss of coverage translates to a significantly lower use of health care services (Anderson, Dobkin, and Gross 2012).

The dependent coverage provision of the Affordable Care Act took effect on September 23, 2010. Data from several independent sources indicate that the policy has significantly increased the insurance coverage of young adults. Figure 7-5 presents data from one such source, the National Health Interview Survey, highlighting the change in insurance coverage for youth age 19 to 25 in comparison to a slightly older group, age 26 to 35. Because these two groups should face roughly similar labor market conditions, the experience of the older group provides a sense of what would have happened to the younger group had this provision of the Affordable Care Act not gone into effect.

Estimates from the third quarter of 2010 show that 35.6 percent of the younger group was uninsured, compared with 27.7 percent of the older group. Between the third quarter of 2010 and the second quarter of 2011, insurance coverage was essentially unchanged for the older group. In contrast, among the younger group the share uninsured fell 8.3 percentage points. This change translates to a gain in health insurance coverage for approximately 2.5 million people. Because even before this policy, college students were able to stay on their parents' insurance plans or obtain coverage through their school, the coverage gains arising from the Affordable

Figure 7-5
Percentage of Young Adults Without Health Insurance,
2010 Q3 and 2011 Q2

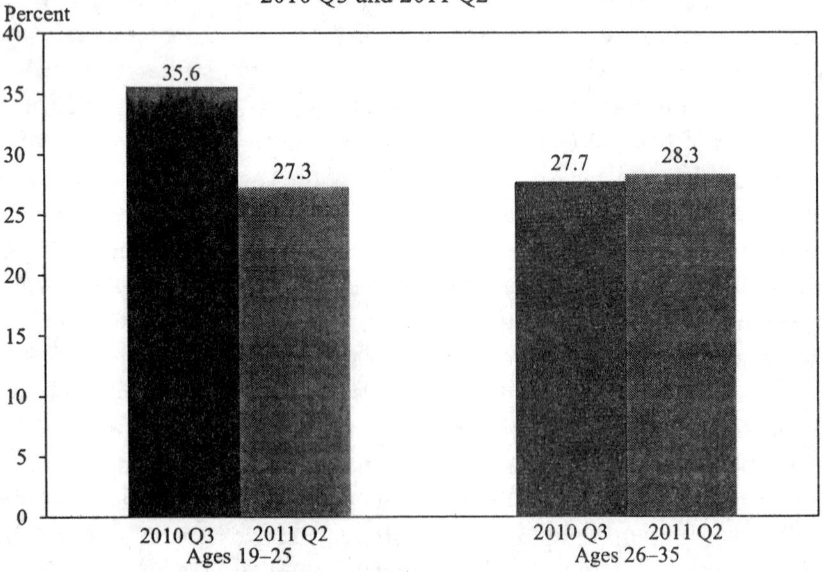

Source: National Health Interview Survey.

Care Act have been concentrated among non-students and recent graduates. Many of these newly insured young adults are from lower middle-class families who are working to maintain their position in the economy in the face of not only the recent economic downturn, but long-run forces that have been working against the middle class for decades.

The Economic Benefits of Expanding Insurance Coverage

Expansion in health insurance coverage from the ACA can be expected to positively affect access to care, health, and financial security. These effects and the impact of other provisions of the Affordable Care Act will be important topics of research (see Data Watch 7-2).

Research on previous coverage expansions suggests that health insurance can significantly improve all three outcomes. As noted, considerable research has examined the benefits of health insurance for children. One recent study (Finkelstein et al. 2011) examines the effect of insurance coverage on low-income adults. The study, which uses data from Oregon's Medicaid program, has two especially notable features. First, its population sample is similar to the group that will gain Medicaid coverage as a result of the Affordable Care Act. Second, because of budgetary constraints, access to Medicaid coverage was determined randomly by a lottery, in the same way patients are assigned to treatment and control groups in a randomized control trial. As a result, the study avoids the fundamental problems of inference inherent to observational studies.

The study finds that in the program's first year insurance coverage significantly increased the use of outpatient and inpatient care and of prescription drugs. The added care led to increases in the share of men and women screened for high cholesterol and high blood sugar and in the share of women receiving mammograms and Pap tests. The study also noted significant gains in several self-reported measures of physical and mental health. These findings are especially striking because the health benefits of improved access to care are likely to grow over time.

In addition to improving access to appropriate care, health insurance protects individuals and families from the financial risk associated with uncertain and potentially catastrophic medical costs. Today few uninsured families have the resources to cover the cost of a serious illness. According to one recent study, about a third of uninsured families have no financial assets at all, and the average uninsured family can afford to pay only 12 percent of the cost of a single hospitalization (Chappel, Kronick, and Glied 2011). The Oregon study used several financial outcomes to assess economic benefits of insurance. It found that individuals with health insurance were less likely to have unpaid bills sent to a collection agency and that they were significantly

Data Watch 7-2: Health Data for Policy

Health policy formulation and evaluation requires high-quality data on a broad range of outcomes. Federal surveys have provided the basis for a large research literature that informed the design of the Affordable Care Act. These surveys along with other Federal data programs will be important resources for monitoring the impact of the Act.

One objective of the Affordable Care Act is to substantially increase the number of Americans with health insurance. The National Health Interview Survey (NHIS) sponsored by the Department of Health and Human Services (HHS) and three other surveys conducted by the Census Bureau—the Current Population Survey's Annual Social and Economic Supplement, the Survey of Income and Program Participation, and the American Community Survey—provide data on various aspects of insurance coverage. Increased insurance coverage should lead to improved access to care and improved population health. The NHIS and another HHS survey, the Household Component of the Medical Expenditure Panel Survey (MEPS), combine information on insurance coverage with information on medical care utilization and health status. Another component of the MEPS surveys employers on key features of the health insurance they offer employees. Additional information on utilization comes from HHS surveys of health care providers, including office-based physicians, ambulatory care facilities, and hospitals.

Two Federal data programs—the National Health Expenditure Accounts, produced by the Centers for Medicare and Medicaid Services, and the National Income and Product Accounts, produced by the Bureau of Economic Analysis—provide independent estimates of national health spending. Efforts also are under way at the Bureau of Labor Statistics to improve the collection of health data to better measure health sector prices and productivity (Bradley et al. 2010). Current initiatives by Federal agencies and academic researchers are aimed at developing data systems that support disease-based estimates of health spending (Aizcorbe, Retus, and Smith 2008). Research in this area focusing on selected conditions has shown that disease-based measures allow for a more nuanced understanding of what drives the growth in health spending. The results suggest that failing to account for changes in the inputs used to treat a particular condition and for improvements in health outcomes leads to an overestimate of health care inflation and an underestimate of productivity gains in the health sector (Aizcorbe and Nestoriak 2011). Whether this conclusion can be generalized is the subject of ongoing research.

less likely to report having to borrow money or skip paying other bills to pay medical expenses. These findings are consistent with earlier research showing that the advent of Medicare in 1965 generated large benefits in the form of reduced exposure to out-of-pocket medical expenditure risk (Finkelstein and McKnight 2008).

The benefits of the Affordable Care Act's coverage expansion are likely to spill over to the labor market as well. Because small firms cannot offer health insurance that matches in cost and quality the insurance offered by larger firms, they often find it difficult to compete with large firms in attracting and retaining workers. Similarly, the lack of affordable insurance options in the individual health insurance market poses a barrier to workers who would like to start their own business, work part-time, or retire before they are eligible for Medicare. Indeed, numerous studies find that the link between health insurance and full-time employment distorts decisions regarding labor supply, job mobility, and retirement (Gruber and Madrian 2004). By improving the health insurance options available to small employers and expanding the availability of affordable individual coverage, the Affordable Care Act should greatly reduce if not eliminate these distortions.

The Affordable Care Act and Medicare

Given the high and uncertain medical expenses faced by seniors, the health insurance coverage that Medicare provides for individuals age 65 and older is a critical component of the health care safety net. The inability of private markets alone to provide adequate health insurance coverage for seniors is a classic example of adverse selection (Akerlof 1970). Indeed, before Medicare was enacted in 1965, only an estimated one-quarter of seniors had meaningful private insurance (Finkelstein 2007). Today Medicare covers roughly 40 million elderly Americans and 8 million people under age 65 who qualify on the basis of disability.

Although the Affordable Care Act's coverage expansions and insurance market reforms are targeted at nonelderly Americans, the new law has important implications for Medicare as well. It provides new benefits to seniors by eliminating cost sharing for recommended preventive services, adds an annual wellness visit, and reduces out-of-pocket costs for prescription drugs in the Medicare Part D coverage gap. By the end of 2011, more than 24 million elderly Americans have benefited from the elimination of cost sharing for preventive benefits, and 3.6 million beneficiaries have received $2.1 billion in drug discounts.

The Affordable Care Act also puts in place several strategies for reducing the growth in Medicare spending. Such efforts to "bend the cost curve" are essential to maintaining the long-run fiscal status of the program and reducing long-run Federal budget deficits. The Act includes important changes in the way Medicare pays doctors, hospitals, and other health care providers to create strong incentives for providers to redesign the way they deliver care, both to improve health and to use scarce resources more efficiently. The Medicare Shared Savings Program, for example, encourages physicians, hospitals, and other organizations to form Accountable Care Organizations (ACOs) to provide cost-effective, coordinated care to Medicare beneficiaries. Both the Shared Savings program and a similar Affordable Care Act initiative developed through the Center for Medicare and Medicaid Innovation (the Innovation Center) reward ACOs that are able to reduce the growth in health care spending while achieving high standards for clinical quality and patient satisfaction.

The mission of the Innovation Center is to help transform the Medicare, Medicaid, and CHIP programs to deliver better health care, better health, and reduced costs. The center's portfolio of initiatives includes demonstration projects that test new strategies for providing higher-quality health care more efficiently. These strategies include models of enhanced primary care; the use of episode-based bundled payments to improve care coordination; and a challenge grant program that will award up to $1 billion in grants to applicants who will implement the most compelling ideas for delivering better health, improved care, and lower costs to people enrolled in Medicare, Medicaid, and CHIP. Because of Medicare's outsized role as a purchaser of health care, these initiatives are likely to spur similar innovations by private insurers.

RETIREMENT SECURITY

For older Americans, retirement savings in combination with Social Security benefits are a critical element of the safety net. These savings and benefits together allow retirees to maintain the living standards they had during their working lives and to protect themselves against downturns in the financial markets, unexpectedly high health care costs, and the risk of running down one's assets. In addition, some Americans elect to accumulate additional savings in hopes of bequeathing assets to their heirs. From a broader societal perspective, private retirement savings fuel capital accumulation. Capital thus accumulated leads to greater investment, which in turn leads to a more productive workforce and stronger economic growth. In this sense, saving not only bolsters the standard of living in retirement for participating workers but also raises the quality of life for future generations.

Over the years, policymakers have implemented a variety of policies to encourage capital accumulation, to protect retired households against economic shocks, and to increase the likelihood that Americans enjoy the same quality of life during retirement that they enjoyed during their working years. The most prominent of these programs is Old Age and Survivors' Insurance, also known as Social Security, which pays retiree benefits to more than 95 percent of elderly individuals in the United States. Social Security is the nation's retirement security bedrock, paying out $596.7 billion to 44.4 million beneficiaries in 2011—an average annual benefit of $13,561. Social Security payments, combined with private savings and employer-provided retirement benefits, provide sufficient income to enjoy a comfortable retirement, and for many others, make the difference between meeting basic needs and living in poverty. In 2010 Social Security income lifted an estimated 13.8 million elderly Americans out of poverty. The program also provides a key safety net for survivors of deceased workers, helping roughly 6 million surviving spouses and children.

Even as Social Security helps provide a stable source of income in retirement, tax preferences for retirement saving give working-age households greater incentive to accumulate assets toward retirement. Most tax-preferred accounts allow workers and their employers to make pre-tax contributions to a retirement account and also allow earnings on those contributions to accumulate tax-free; other accounts allow after-tax contributions to grow and be withdrawn tax-free. Many American households have responded to these tax incentives by building assets toward retirement, with total balances in defined-contribution and individual retirement accounts (IRAs) rising to nearly $9.2 trillion in 2010. The overall tax expenditure for the principal retirement saving incentives is substantial, totaling almost $120 billion in fiscal year 2010.

Declining Retirement Preparedness

Despite the availability of tax-related incentives to spur saving, many households have not accumulated sufficient assets to overcome the potential risks faced in retirement. By some estimates, the proportion of households with adequate retirement saving has been in decline for decades. As illustrated in Figure 7-6, the share of households "at risk" of experiencing marked declines in consumption in retirement rose from 31 percent in 1983 to 51 percent in 2009, with much of the recent change owing to declining housing values.[2] For members of Generation X (individuals born between

---

[2] These estimates are based on the National Retirement Risk Index (NRRI) produced by the Center for Retirement Research at Boston College. For each household, the NRRI estimates household income in retirement (based on projected assets at retirement) as a share of pre-retirement earnings; this percentage represents the replacement rate of pre-retirement earnings. Each household is assigned a benchmark "adequate" replacement rate; households that are more than 10 percent below the benchmark are deemed to be "at risk."

the mid-1960s and 1972), the situation is even more troubling, with nearly three in five households in that age group in danger of becoming unable to maintain their living standard in retirement (Munnell, Webb, and Golub-Sass 2009).

Although retirement preparedness has been in decline in the aggregate, specific demographic groups are particularly vulnerable. Single individuals and low-income households are all especially likely to enter retirement with insufficient assets. For example, one estimate for 2009 identified 60 percent of low-income households as inadequate savers, compared with 42 percent of high-income households (Munnell, Webb, and Golub-Sass 2009). Another estimate found that 60.2 percent of single men had insufficient retirement wealth to maintain preretirement consumption, compared with 45.2 percent of married couples (Haveman et al. 2006).

Recent economic shocks have impacted individuals nearing retirement. Between 2007 and 2009, Americans aged 55 to 64 saw their real median household income decline by 5 percent and their median net worth fall 15 percent—from $258,000 to $222,000 (Bricker et al. 2011). In addition, the value of housing—a key source of wealth for older Americans—has dropped 34 percent since the housing market's peak in April 2006. The value of financial assets also declined precipitously following the financial crisis and has yet to rebound fully to pre-recession levels. The combination of declining asset values and lower income has further weakened retirement preparedness.

Challenges to the Retirement Safety Net

Several developments have contributed to the problem of inadequate retirement saving. A first-order concern is declining participation in employer-sponsored retirement plans. Between 2000 and 2010, the share of private sector workers between the ages of 21 and 64 who participated in an employer-sponsored retirement plan fell from 48 percent to 39 percent.

The past several decades have also seen changes in the nature of private employer retirement plans. The share of private-sector workers covered by defined-benefit pension plans fell from 38 percent in 1980 to 20 percent in 2008 as many private employers switched to defined-contribution plans like 401(k) plans. Section 401(k) and other defined-contribution plans offer workers particular benefits, such as portability, high potential for growth, and flexibility. However, the shift to 401(k) plans (and to a lesser degree a shift from traditional defined-benefit pensions to hybrid defined-benefit plans such as cash balance plans) has also transferred substantial risk away from employers, placing greater responsibility on workers to accumulate and manage assets and exposing them to greater financial risk.

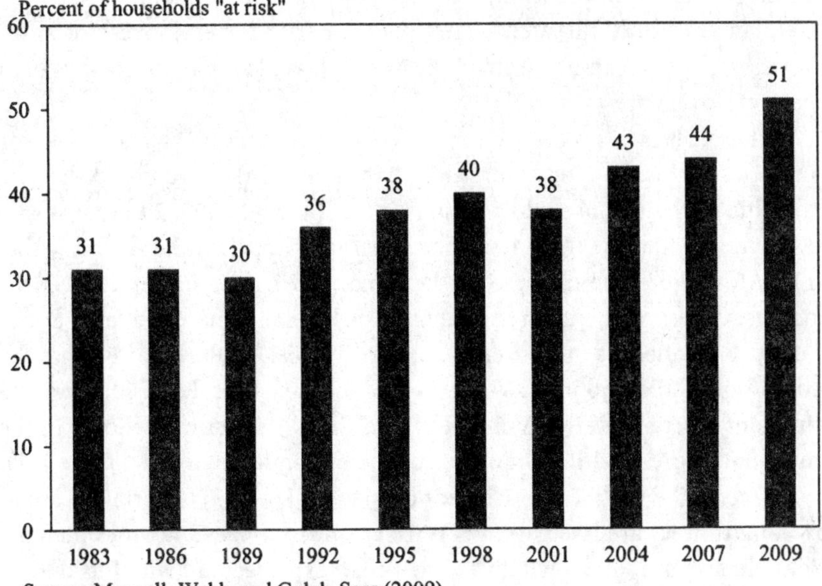

Source: Munnell, Webb, and Golub-Sass (2009).

To take full advantage of the wide array of incentives for retirement saving, workers must assess complex details associated with establishing an account, making contributions, managing investments, and eventually making withdrawals. In the face of complex saving and investment decisions, some workers put off enrolling in employer-sponsored retirement programs or taking advantage of tax-preferred saving vehicles outside of employment. Such delays are costly in terms of lifetime asset accumulation. (See Economics Application Box 7-1 for more information on common mistakes made by retirement savers.)

Another challenge to the retirement safety net is the uneven distribution of the benefits of the tax code's generous incentives for retirement saving. Because these tax incentives are often provided as a deduction or exclusion from income, they are most valuable for taxpayers in higher tax brackets. In the aggregate, these incentives flow disproportionately to upper-income households; almost 80 percent of the total tax benefit is projected to go in 2012 to the richest 20 percent of households and more than 40 percent to households in the top 5 percent of the income distribution (Toder, Harris, and Lim 2011).

The availability of employer-sponsored retirement saving options also varies by firm size. As with health insurance, small employers face significant challenges in establishing retirement plans. High per-participant administrative costs, frequent employee turnover, uncertain revenues, and lack of familiarity with plan design and characteristics all discourage small business owners from providing retirement plans. Their inability to provide these plans not only threatens retirement security for employees of small businesses but also can make small businesses less attractive to workers than larger employers are.

These obstacles to retirement saving keep account balances low for many households. In 2011, more than half of all workers reported that the total value of their household's savings is less than $25,000; 29 percent said they have less than $1,000 in savings (Helman, Copeland, and VanDerhei 2011). Although some of these workers may participate in defined-benefit pensions, others will enter retirement with little income outside of Social Security. One analysis of households aged 65 to 69 in 2008 showed that the median household had just $15,000 in financial assets and $5,000 in private retirement assets (Poterba, Venti, and Wise 2011). Most households in the sample had more wealth in housing equity than in liquid assets (Table 7-2).

One of the toughest retirement challenges involves uncertainty about how long retirees are likely to live. With extended longevity comes the possibility that an individual will live longer than expected and will thus outlive his or her accumulated assets. This possibility increases as the time between retirement and expected age of death lengthens. In 1970 a worker retiring at age 65 could expect to live another 15.2 years; by 2008 that figure had grown to 18.7 years. Although extending life expectancy is an exceptional achievement for the United States, it also increasingly exposes retirees to the risk of outliving their assets outside of Social Security. In 2010, just 17 percent of Americans aged 65 to 69 relied on Social Security for more than 90 percent of their income, but the share almost doubled, to 33 percent, for Americans age 80 and older (Figure 7-7).

Another serious risk is costly health shocks. Even with the protection provided by Medicare, many retirees face high out-of-pocket health expenditures, diminishing their retirement assets and threatening their well-being. Recent research estimates that for a 65-year-old couple, the expected present value of lifetime out-of-pocket medical costs exceeds $250,000, with a 5 percent risk that expenses will exceed $570,000 (Webb and Zhivan 2010). As discussed in Data Watch 7-1, out-of-pocket health costs can push retirees into poverty.

The risk of large health expenditures and the possibility of outliving one's assets force retirees to face difficult decisions about how much of their assets to consume in any given year. Uncertainty about lifespan, inflation, investment return, and unexpected medical expenses makes the "decumulation decision"—how much to withdraw from accumulated

Table 7-2
Distribution of Wealth Components for Households Aged 65–69, 2008
Thousands of dollars

Percentile	Financial assets	Personal retirement account assets	Financial + personal retirement account	Housing equity	Defined-benefit pension	Social Security	Net worth
10	0.0	0.0	0.0	0.0	0.0	0.0	197.0
20	0.3	0.0	0.8	5.0	0.0	154.3	297.3
30	2.0	0.0	5.5	42.0	0.0	214.5	413.6
40	6.0	0.0	20.0	80.0	0.0	267.9	564.0
50	15.0	5.0	52.0	120.0	0.0	315.3	731.1
60	32.0	28.8	104.0	162.0	25.3	379.0	898.4
70	70.0	75.0	195.0	229.5	116.8	463.3	1,146.4
80	145.0	142.0	375.0	349.2	238.5	542.9	1,483.4
90	358.0	347.0	711.0	585.0	468.9	643.1	2,103.0

Source: Poterba, Venti, and Wise (2011).

saving—exceptionally complicated. Retirees who live longer than expected might find themselves with insufficient assets in the later years of life, at a time when they are most vulnerable and in need of a reliable stream of income. While private annuities can serve to mitigate many of these risks, annuities markets face a host of obstacles including regulatory barriers,

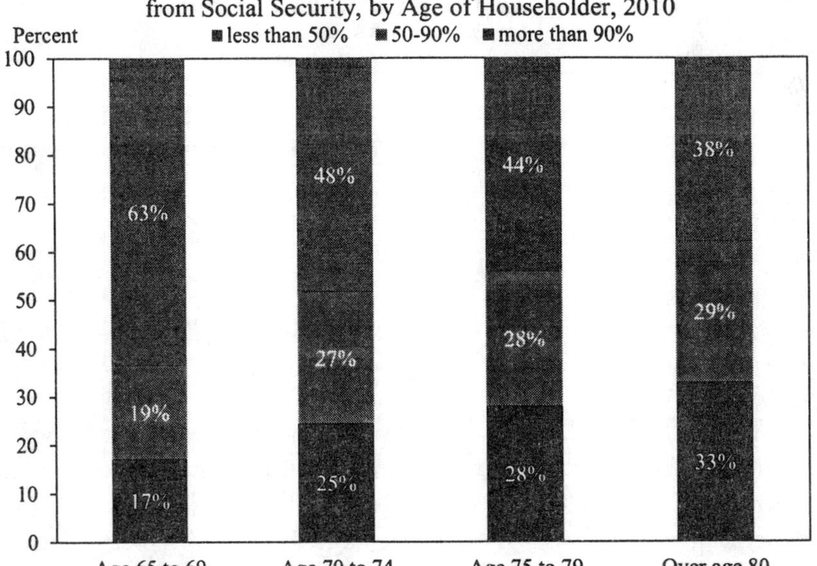

Figure 7-7
Percent of Individuals with Various Shares of Family Income
from Social Security, by Age of Householder, 2010

Source: Current Population Survey, Annual Social and Economic Supplement.

Failing to participate in an employer-sponsored retirement plan. Some employer-sponsored retirement plans provide an employer match for money that an employee deposits into a retirement account. Taking advantage of an employer match is one of the best ways to leverage retirement contributions and rapidly accumulate saving. Many workers, especially new hires and young employees, however, leave this "free money" on the table by failing to sign up for a retirement plan. In 2001, only 57.5 percent of workers aged 20–29 participated in a company retirement plan even when one was offered (Kawachi, Smith, and Toder 2006).

Failing to diversify retirement savings. Investment needs and risk appetites vary across households. However, concentrating all assets in one particular type of investment can prove risky, especially if that asset is stock in an employee's company. One study found that in 2002, nearly 4 million workers invested in excess of 80 percent of their employer retirement plan assets in own-company stock (Mitchell and Utkus 2002). In general, investors can protect themselves against risk by spreading their assets across various types of investments.

Losing investment returns to high fees. High fees can inhibit rapid accumulation of retirement wealth. Savers should pay attention to all investment fees, including those charged at purchase of a mutual fund, ongoing fees, fees charged by brokers and registered investment advisors, and fees charged on the purchase of annuity products. Although these fees are ordinarily charged for legitimate services provided, investors should incorporate the cost of fees in their purchase decisions.

Cashing-out retirement savings. When workers leave a job, some fail to rollover their pension wealth into an IRA and pay a penalty for cashing out their retirement savings. These leakages in retirement savings make it difficult to arrive at retirement with adequate amounts of savings. In 2006, workers aged 15 to 60 cashed out $74 billion in retirement assets when changing jobs (GAO 2009).

Failing to protect against longevity and health care risk in old age. As lifespans increase, more Americans will face the prospect of running out of money in old age. Planning for and protecting against the risk of outliving family assets as well as the need for long-term care is an essential part of the retirement security picture.

behavioral aversion to annuities, and inadequate savings to purchase an annuity (Benartzi, Previtero, and Thaler 2011).

Policies to Address Retirement Saving Challenges

The President has proposed several policies to bolster Americans' retirement saving behavior and lead to a more secure retirement for millions of families. Perhaps the most significant policy is the establishment of automatic IRAs for tens of millions of workers. This proposal builds on a broad literature showing that automatic enrollment can dramatically increase participation rates in workplace retirement plans. For example, Madrian and Shea (2001) show that the participation rate after one year of employment at a large corporation increased from 37.4 percent to 85.9 percent following the adoption of automatic enrollment.

The President's proposal would require most firms without qualified employee retirement plans to offer employees an automatic IRA option. By default, automatic IRA contributions would be funded by payroll deductions equal to 3 percent of pay, unless employees opted out of the program or elected to contribute a different amount. Firms would not contribute on behalf of the employee, and companies offering the automatic IRA to workers could claim a tax credit for the employer's associated expenses up to $500 for the first year and $250 for the second year along with an additional tax credit of $25 per employee—up to a maximum of $250 a year for six years.

The automatic IRA would transform the retirement saving landscape. Employees who previously accumulated little or nothing toward retirement would begin accumulating assets immediately. Upward of 40 million workers, all previously ineligible for workplace retirement saving plans, would be covered by the new proposal. About 80 percent of these workers would be low- and middle-income employees with less than $50,000 in annual wages, indicating that the IRA would primarily be targeted at workers who are more likely to have accumulated little savings.

The Administration also proposes to increase the tax credit for small businesses that adopt, for the first time, a qualified employee retirement plan. Under current law, small businesses can receive up to $500 in tax credits—each year for up to three years—for establishing an employee retirement plan. The President proposes to double the maximum credit to $1,000 annually to provide a stronger incentive for small employers to establish workplace retirement plans.

The Administration's Budget eases the compliance burden for retirement savings by exempting retirees with modest accumulated saving from minimum required distribution (MRDs) rules. MRDs are established to ensure that retirees with high accumulated retirement assets direct those assets towards retirement, and not use retirement accounts to shelter their income from estate taxes. The Administration proposes to exempt retirees with less than $75,000 in retirement savings from these rules. This move would simplify tax compliance for millions of elderly Americans, who would no longer need to calculate the amount and timing of their minimum required payouts. It would give millions of seniors greater freedom of choice as to when and how rapidly to spend their limited assets in retirement, while also adding flexibility to purchase lifetime income products—such as longevity annuities—that might violate MRD regulations.

The Administration has made a commitment to financial literacy as a means of assisting Americans in making sound decisions regarding saving and investment. In 2010, the President signed an Executive Order creating the President's Advisory Council on Financial Capability to assist the American people in understanding financial matters and making informed financial decisions. In addition, the Wall Street Reform and Consumer Protection Act of 2010 created the Consumer Financial Protection Bureau, which is charged with educating consumers about financial matters and enabling them to make sound financial decisions. And, in 2011, the Financial Literacy and Education Commission, established to coordinate Federal efforts to promote financial literacy, developed a new national strategy to enable Federal agencies to coordinate and promote all the Federal initiatives aimed at helping Americans make better financial choices.

Taken together, these policies will lead to a more inclusive retirement saving landscape. Workers who would defer retirement saving because of financial inertia or behavioral obstacles will automatically be put on a path toward better saving. Easing MRD rules will simplify financial decisions in retirement for millions of elderly Americans. A coordinated national financial literacy campaign will help Americans become more active savers and will lead to improved investment decisions and smarter consumer behavior. More active saving, coupled with improved investment behavior, will increase the level of assets earmarked for retirement saving, leading to a more stable retirement for millions of Americans.

Conclusion

A strong and dynamic economy requires a robust and modern safety net to protect families against economic shocks and to provide a level of security that promotes entrepreneurship and economic growth. The challenging economic times of the past decade have made clear the important role that public policy can play in this area. In particular, unemployment insurance benefits, the Earned Income Tax Credit, and the Supplemental

Nutrition Assistance Program have kept millions of American families out of poverty. Medicaid and the Children's Health Insurance Program have ensured that children are able to maintain health insurance coverage even if their parents lose access to employer-sponsored plans.

New policy initiatives will further strengthen the safety net. Although the current system of unemployment insurance has provided critical support for dislocated workers, the system can be modernized and improved. The President has proposed a number of innovative programs that would make it easier for jobless workers to invest in new skills or even start their own businesses. These proposals build on current programs that have been proven to work.

The Affordable Care Act represents the most significant improvement in the health care safety net since the advent of Medicare and Medicaid in the mid-1960s. By 2019, the Act is expected to increase the number of Americans with health insurance by over 30 million, and it will put in place new consumer protections ensuring that health insurance coverage remains available and affordable for all Americans regardless of an individual's health status or medical history.

In the area of retirement security, the President has proposed a number of policies that will boost retirement savings, making it more likely that Americans will enter retirement with adequate assets to maintain their desired level of consumption. These efforts to strengthen the safety net will provide tangible benefits for the economy and families in the coming decades.

CHAPTER 8

IMPROVING THE QUALITY OF LIFE THROUGH SMART REGULATION, INNOVATION, CLEAN ENERGY, AND PUBLIC INVESTMENT

Recent years have seen an unprecedented number of official efforts to improve, develop, and implement new measures of the quality of life and economic performance. Much of the groundwork for these efforts was laid in two important National Research Council reports. *Nature's Numbers*, published in 1999, considered how to expand the national income accounts that track the country's economic activity to properly take into account the environment and natural resources. *Beyond the Market*, published in 2005, proposed ways to integrate nonmarket activity into the accounts.

This work has implications for economic policy. Carefully designed regulations can promote economic growth and improve the Nation's quality of life. Water pollution, for example, can cause illness and destroy the livelihood of fishermen and others who rely on a healthy ecosystem to earn a living. Pollution, as Robert Kennedy noted, does not subtract from the gross domestic product. Appropriately balanced efforts to restrict harmful pollution can improve economic performance along with the health and safety of Americans.

The theme of this chapter is that, properly measured, both economic growth and the Nation's well-being can be increased by smart regulation, innovation and public investment in such fields as medical research, clean domestic energy and transportation infrastructure.

A Smart Approach to Regulations

For more than a century, the United States has been a world leader in protecting the health and safety of its citizens through well-chosen regulations. Fuchs (1998 and 2010) attributes gains in life expectancy prior to World War II to improvements in "nonmedical factors: nutrition, sanitation, housing, and public health measures." For example, in response to yellow fever and cholera outbreaks caused by water pollution, the Rivers and Harbors Act of 1899 gave the Army Corps of Engineers the authority to regulate the discharge into waterways of "refuse matter of any kind or description." Similarly, public health concerns about unsanitary meat packing conditions and patent medicines containing narcotics gave rise to the Pure Food and Drug Act of 1906, which authorized the Food and Drug Administration (FDA) to inspect food and drug products and regulate their sale. In 1900, roughly one in every 200 Americans was addicted to narcotics found in patent medicines (DOJ n.d.). Following the disclosure requirements in the Pure Food and Drug Act, sales of patent medicines containing those substances fell by nearly a third (Musto 1999).

As society evolves and technology changes, such basic protections afforded to citizens through regulation are updated and improved. Today, the water pollution controls provided for in the Rivers and Harbors Act have been incorporated into more expansive provisions in the Clean Water Act of 1972 and the Safe Drinking Water Act of 1974, which enable the Environmental Protection Agency (EPA) to promulgate regulations with the goal of making U.S. waters safe for drinking, swimming, and fishing. Similarly, the Pure Food and Drug Act of 1906 was amended by the Food, Drug, and Cosmetic Act of 1938 to give the FDA the authority to require evidence of safety for new drugs and to tighten food quality standards. It was amended again in 1962 to require manufacturers to prove drug effectiveness (Randall 2001). Most recently, the Food Safety Modernization Act of 2010 further improved the safety of food sold in the United States by, among other provisions, giving the FDA the authority to directly issue mandatory food recalls, requiring food processors to have plans in place for addressing safety risks, and requiring importers to verify food safety.

Measuring the benefits of regulations for the quality of life is a formidable task. Some forms of regulation have a positive effect on economic growth, for example, by improving the health and vitality of the workforce, by promoting stable and efficient operation of financial markets, by speeding the adoption of energy-saving technologies, by improving educational outcomes, or by upgrading the operation of the transportation system. Much of the benefit from those types of regulations eventually translates into increases in GDP. In other cases, such as the protection of the National Park System, safeguards against invasive species, or cleaner lakes for swimming and fishing, the benefits of regulation help the economy, but are less easily charted in the national accounts. For example, increased tourism or higher returns to commercial fishing resulting from cleaner water would be reflected in GDP, whereas the public's increased appreciation of that cleaner water would not be.

Designing Smart Regulations

On January 18, 2011, President Obama issued Executive Order 13563, "Improving Regulation and Regulatory Review," which lays out a balanced approach to regulation—to protect the health and safety of the American people in a way that maximizes net benefits to society, that uses the best information available, and that avoids unnecessary or overly burdensome requirements. The President called for an agency-wide review to reduce burdensome regulations. Underlying that approach is a belief that a smart, effective regulatory system depends on careful analysis of costs and benefits, both before and after regulatory action, including an informed public discussion. The Executive order directs the Office of Information and Regulatory Affairs (OIRA) of the Office of Management and Budget (OMB) to provide oversight, transparency, and discipline for executive agencies in the regulatory process, and coordinates that interagency review of rulemakings to ensure that regulations are consistent with applicable law. The net benefits of regulations finalized in 2011 are expected to be at their highest level in the last 10 years. And monetized savings from the retrospective review of regulations called for in the new Executive order are likely to exceed $10 billion over the next five years.

Many of those regulations are intended to improve the quality of life by correcting market failures that lead to unsafe living or working environments. Effective regulations put into place rules that correct for significant market failures and thus achieve greater social benefits. "Smart regulations" are those that maximize the net benefits of a regulatory action to society. Benefit-cost analysis attempts to quantify and assign dollar values to the various effects of a regulation, which can be used to determine how it can reach its goal in the most efficient manner—that is, how it can generate the largest net benefits (the difference between total benefits and total costs) to society. Such information is useful for both policymakers and the public, even when economic efficiency is neither the only nor the overriding public policy objective, as in the case of protecting privacy.

Benefit-cost analysis is used to estimate likely future benefits and costs of a proposed regulation, but it can also be used to "look back" at existing regulations, based on evidence about the actual, realized benefits and costs of those regulations. Such retrospective analyses can be used both to improve existing regulations and to better evaluate new ones.

Smart regulations thus seek to use the best information available in order to maximize net benefits by setting regulatory stringency at the most efficient level—the point at which the incremental benefits are equal to the incremental costs. For example, even though the marginal costs of seat belt standards increased over time (front-seat shoulder and rear-seat lap belts were mandated for cars in 1968 and for light trucks and vans in 1971, and three-point belts were required in the mid-1970s), those costs were far outweighed by the corresponding number of lives saved per year by seat belts (DOT 2004; Kahane 2004). The buckle-up laws of the mid-1980s raised the number of lives saved by wearing seat belts to 6,000 a year by 1988–90, and subsequent increases in belt use raised the annual number of lives saved to more than 15,000 in each year from 2003 to 2007. All together, between 1975 and 2009, seat belt regulations saved an estimated 268,000 lives (Kahane 2004; DOT 2009). (For another example of how benefit-cost analysis works, see Economics Application Box 8-1.)

Smart Regulations in Practice

Benefit-cost analysis has long been used to evaluate regulations within the Federal Government. For example, the Flood Control Act of 1936 declared that "the Federal Government should improve or participate in the improvement of navigable waters or their tributaries including watersheds thereof, for flood-control purposes if the benefits to whomsoever they may accrue are in excess of the estimated costs, and if the lives and social security of people are otherwise adversely affected."

The use of benefit-cost analysis in evaluating Federal regulations has become widespread since 1981, when President Reagan issued Executive Order 12291, formally requiring that "regulatory action shall not be undertaken unless the potential benefits to society for the regulation outweigh the potential costs to society and that regulatory objectives shall be chosen to maximize the net benefits to society." President Clinton issued Executive Order 12866, which focused OIRA oversight on "significant" rules and increased transparency. As noted earlier, President Obama issued Executive Order 13563, which reaffirms the principles in Executive Order 12866 and outlines a regulatory strategy to support continued economic growth and job creation. In particular, Executive Order 13563 offers new directions for regulatory review, including a requirement that agencies "use the best available techniques to quantify anticipated present and future benefits and costs as accurately as possible" while authorizing consideration of "values that are difficult or impossible to quantify, including equity, human dignity, fairness, and distributive impacts."

Based on the quantified benefits and costs in current regulations, smart regulations are generating the highest level of net benefits for U.S. citizens in the last decade. In calendar year 2011, the Administration completed 740 regulatory reviews, 336 of which were interim final or final rules from executive agencies. Of the interim final and final rules reviewed, 18 percent were "economically significant," meaning that they are anticipated to have an effect on the economy of more than $100 million in any given year. Those economically significant rules are expected to result in $15 billion in costs and $116 billion in benefits annually (in 2001 dollars). Over the past three calendar years, the annualized net benefits of completed rules have totaled about $155 billion. In 2011 alone, annualized net benefits totaled more than $101 billion. Those figures reflect an estimate of not only purely monetary savings, but also an estimate of the monetary value of prevented deaths, illnesses, and injuries. Figure 8-1 shows the benefits and costs of regulations, which are detailed in the agencies' Regulatory Impact Assessments for each economically significant rule and summarized annually in OMB's annual Regulatory-Right-to-Know report to Congress.

Data and estimation methods have improved substantially over time, as have modeling tools for projecting a regulation's effect into the future. For

Figure 8-1

Benefits and Costs of Regulations, 2001–2011

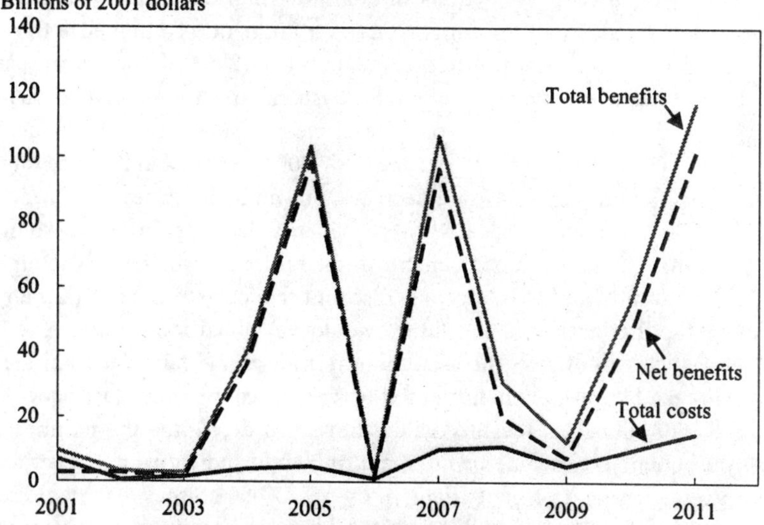

Note: Total benefits, total costs, and net benefits are based on the midpoints of agency estimates for regulations completed during the calendar year.
Source: Office of Information and Regulatory Affairs.

How do policymakers determine whether a regulation is a smart regulation? For example, in 2007, the Department of Transportation (DOT) decided to require that all new passenger vehicles weighing less than 10,000 pounds be equipped with electronic stability control (ESC) systems, which reduce crashes by improving braking in critical situations when the driver is beginning to lose control. This rule will increase the fraction of new vehicles with ESC from 29 percent in 2006 to 100 percent in 2012. How did the DOT decide this was a smart regulation?

First, the DOT identified what is arguably a market failure: a relatively affordable technology existed that lowered the risk of a crash, but it was not being offered by some manufacturers and, when offered the choice, many consumers declined. This market failure was caused by asymmetric information (drivers purchasing a vehicle could not fully assess the protection afforded by ESC systems) and by a negative externality (consumers purchasing a car without an ESC system did not fully account for the risks of a crash to others).[a]

Second, the DOT then examined the likely costs and benefits of equipping all passenger cars and light trucks/vans with ESC by model year 2012. Approximately 17 million vehicles will be subject to this regulation; however, DOT estimates that as of 2011, manufacturers would have installed ESC in 71 percent of their fleet absent the rulemaking. Therefore, both the benefits and costs were calculated by raising ESC installation from that baseline of 71 percent to 100 percent. The benefits of the rule include reductions in fatalities, injuries, property damage, and travel delays, all resulting from fewer accidents. To monetize those benefits, the DOT multiplied the total number of loss-of-control crashes by the average effectiveness of ESC systems and found that 67,000–91,000 crashes would be avoided each year. Using historical accident data, DOT estimated that a decline of 67,000 crashes would reduce total annual fatalities by 1,547 and decrease total annual injuries by 46,896.[b]

The monetary value of those benefits depends on the discount rate, that is, on how much benefits in the future are worth today (a high discount rate implies that people discount the future more and thus any benefits that accrue in the future would be valued less today). At a 7 percent discount rate, the reduction in injuries and fatalities translates into $6.4 billion in benefits; at a 3 percent discount rate, those benefits are $8.0 billion, as the Box Table shows. To determine the noninjury component of benefits, the DOT multiplied the individual unit costs for travel delays and property damage by the 67,000 crashes that would be prevented by the rule, yielding $247 million in benefits at the discount rate of 7 percent.

Annual Costs and Benefits by Discount Rate
Millions of 2005 dollars

	3% discount	7% discount
Injury and fatality benefits	$7,965	$6,360
Savings from reduced property damage and travel delays	309	247
Total benefits	8,274	6,607
Vehicle costs	985	985
Fuel costs	27	22
Total costs	1,012	1,007
Net benefits	7,262	5,600

Note: Vehicle costs are not discounted, because they occur when the vehicle is purchased, whereas benefits occur over the vehicle's lifetime and are discounted back to the time of purchase.
Source: Department of Transportation, National Highway Traffic Safety Administration (2007).

The DOT determined that production costs would rise by between $111 and $479 for each affected vehicle, depending on whether the vehicle was already equipped with anti-lock braking systems, a necessary component of ESC. The expected costs of the standard above the baseline total $985 million. Because the average weight of passenger cars is expected to increase by 2.1 pounds as a result of the new equipment, the lifetime fuel use of those vehicles is expected to go up by 2.6 gallons. At discount rates of 7 percent and 3 percent, the total additional fuel costs are $21.8 million and $26.8 million, respectively. Summing vehicle and fuel costs gave the total costs of the regulation: about $1.0 billion. Net benefits, then, are the difference between total costs and total benefits, or between $5.6 billion and $7.3 billion each year for the lower range of accident prevention.

---

[a] For further discussion of market failures and automobile safety standards, see Mannering and Winston (1995), Arnould and Grabowski (1981) and Viscusi and Gayer (2002).

[b] The appropriateness of including private benefits net of private costs in a benefit-cost analysis varies from rule to rule. By including private net benefits—the value of reducing injuries and fatalities of the consumers minus the purchase cost of the technology—the DOT is making the implicit assumption that consumers have made a suboptimal purchasing decision (one of the market failures being addressed by the regulation). However, if consumers do not face an information problem, a traditional approach would assume that consumers have made the purchasing decision that maximizes their welfare. If this were the case, it would be inappropriate to include those private net benefits in the analysis. For further discussion, see Gayer (2011).

example, the health benefits from reducing different air pollutants over different time periods and populations have been estimated by epidemiologists using air quality monitoring data and various health endpoints (EPA 2011a). Improvements in computing power and data records now allow air quality modelers to forecast the effects of regulatory actions on future air quality under different scenarios. Combining those estimates allows policymakers to weigh the expected health results of a given air quality regulation with the expected costs associated with the controls required by the rule.

A peer-reviewed study by the EPA using the Criteria Air Pollutant Modeling System estimated that the Clean Air Act prevented more than 160,000 premature deaths, 54,000 cases of chronic bronchitis, 130,000 non-fatal heart attacks, and 1.7 million cases of asthma exacerbation between 1990 and 2010. Those adverse health outcomes could have led to 86,000 emergency room visits for respiratory problems, 3.2 million lost school days, and 13 million lost work days (EPA 2011b).

Some health benefits from Clean Air Act regulations will likely raise economic growth indirectly and over time through intermediate factors. For example, a healthier population will arguably be a more productive one, a change that can be measured in improved labor productivity. A growing consensus has identified certain of those intermediate drivers of growth, including increased human capital, capital investment, research and development, economic competition, physical infrastructure, and good governance. Some evidence strongly suggests that regulations promoting educational attainment may improve human capital accumulation, thereby increasing economic growth over time (for example, see Cohen and Soto 2007). Other studies show a positive link between increased life expectancy and economic growth. A survey of the existing literature on health and economic outcomes (Bloom et al. 2004) finds in cross-country analysis that a one-year increase in life expectancy generates a 4 percent increase in economic output, controlling for other variables. Similarly, Murphy and Topel (2006) find that progress made battling various diseases after 1970 added about $3.2 trillion a year to national wealth.

Retrospective Analysis

The prospective benefit-cost analysis that goes into crafting smart, efficient regulations is necessarily fraught with uncertainty. Prospective analysis requires that the costs and benefits of a regulation be identified and quantified before (*ex-ante*) the regulation is implemented. Only after a regulation has gone into effect can its actual (*ex-post*) effects become known (see Data Watch 8-1).[1]

Changes in technology often make pollution abatement cheaper. For example, the actual costs to utilities of the cap-and-trade system for sulfur dioxide allowances set up by the Clean Air Act Amendments of 1990 were much lower than had been predicted. Scrubbing technologies turned out to be more efficient at removing sulfur dioxide from emissions, and power plants were able to blend a higher percentage of cheaper, low-sulfur coal than had initially been assumed. Moreover, the benefits of reducing sulfur dioxide emissions have since been found to be much larger than originally thought. As a result, subsequent regulations for utilities have tightened controls on those emissions.

Similarly, during the 1970s, automobile technologies were improved by new pollution standards. Regulators were phasing lead out of gasoline, and again the costs of the regulation were overestimated and the benefits underestimated. Lead impairs brain development in children and has been linked to serious health problems in adults such as hypertension, heart attacks, and premature death (Lovei 1998). Concern about high blood lead concentrations in the U.S. population led the EPA to begin in 1974 to phase in a stringent standard reducing the amount of lead allowed in the gasoline supply. Subsequent studies found that the annual benefits of banning lead in gasoline would be more than $6 billion (in 1983 dollars), but would cost around $500 million a year (Schwartz 1985). Harrington, Morgenstern, and Nelson (1999) note that those costs may have been overstated, but that it was difficult to disentangle the effects of a phase-out of leaded gasoline from the much larger effect of changes in oil markets around that time. Research also found that the benefits of lowering lead exposure were greater than initially thought. The EPA's 1985 benefit estimate implied that reducing mean blood lead concentrations in the population by 1 microgram per deciliter (or 1 µg/dl) was worth at least $3.5 billion a year (Schwartz 1994). By 1994, however, researchers were finding that a reduction of 1 µg/dl in mean blood lead concentrations resulted in much greater benefits than earlier estimates—as high as $17.2 billion a year (1989 dollars) (Schwartz 1994). The phase-out of leaded gasoline was completed in 1995; by then the average blood lead concentration was approximately 2.3 µg/dl, down from more than 15 µg/dl in the early 1970s (Weaver 1999).

---

[1] Retrospective analyses of benefits and costs are also subject to uncertainty, because they require evaluation of a counterfactual scenario in which the rule was not adopted. Identifying that counterfactual is often difficult, in part because changes that occurred due to the rule are difficult to distinguish from changes that the industry would have adopted voluntarily.

Data Watch 8-1: The Value of Information—the PACE Survey

One of the few data sources for benchmarking costs of air and water pollution controls is the Pollution Abatement Costs and Expenditures (PACE) survey, which recently has been funded by the Environmental Protection Agency (EPA) and administered by the Census Bureau. From 1973 to 1994, the PACE survey was administered annually to nearly 20,000 manufacturing and mining facilities and electric utilities. Since 1994, because of resource constraints, the Census Bureau has conducted this survey only twice (for 1999 and 2005). To estimate the overall regulatory burden facing American manufacturers, the PACE survey collects data on overall pollution abatement expenditures by manufacturers for treatment, prevention, recycling, and disposal, rather than trying to allocate costs to specific regulations. It is the only survey that measures environmental compliance costs at both the individual and aggregate levels (Ross et al. 2004).

Pollution equipment expenditures have fallen over time, on average accounting for 7 percent of all investments made by manufacturing industries in the early 1990s and 4 percent in 2005. There is considerable variation in spending across industries, but given that pollution levels (and the negative externalities associated with pollution) also vary by industry, that is neither surprising nor necessarily suboptimal.

The EPA has used PACE data to estimate the cost of both past and proposed regulations (see for example, Gallaher, Morgan and Shadbegian 2008). Academics have used the data set to investigate the relationship between EPA regulations and economic outcomes. For example, Levinson (1999) used the PACE data to develop a new index of state environmental compliance costs. Similarly, Shadbegian and Gray (2005) examined the relationship between of pollution abatement and productivity. And Becker (2005) found expenditures on environmental compliance for small facilities differ from larger facilities.

"Look-Back" Initiative

President Obama's Executive Order 13563, issued in 2011, directed executive agencies to conduct retrospective reviews of their regulations to determine whether any of the agencies' regulations should be modified, streamlined, expanded, or repealed. This Executive order was followed by Executive Order 13579, which called on independent agencies to conduct such retrospective reviews to the extent possible. Look-back exercises enable regulatory agencies to learn whether they can increase net benefits by modifying existing regulations, expanding regulations, or even eliminating existing regulations that may turn out to be ineffective or duplicative.

Incorporating *ex-post* benefits and costs of regulations is the key goal of the new Executive order requiring agencies to conduct retrospective reviews of their regulations. In the past, agencies have undertaken such reviews in certain situations but only on an *ad hoc* basis. The new Executive order aims to improve regulatory analyses by providing a formalized process for incorporating new information into regulations and for gaining insight into the costs and benefits borne by the private sector in practice.

The President's regulatory look-back initiative has produced more than 500 reform proposals, detailed in 26 agency plans, and monetized savings from this review are likely to exceed $10 billion over the next five years. A number of recent actions eliminate or streamline unjustified or excessive regulations, and the Administration has put in place an improved regulatory system that will generate more current and accurate information on regulatory costs and benefits. Moreover, pursuant to Executive Order 13579, issued in July 2011, some of the major independent regulatory agencies have also issued preliminary retrospective review plans for public comment.[2] Five examples illustrate the effectiveness of the look-back initiatives.

First, the Occupational Safety and Health Administration (OSHA), has announced a final rule that will eliminate redundant reporting burdens; the regulation is expected to save employers 1.9 million hours and $40 million annually. OSHA also plans to finalize a rule projected to result in more than $585 million in savings each year by making U.S. hazard classifications and labels consistent with other nations.

Second, since the 1970s, the EPA has treated milk as "oil" subject to regulations designed to prevent oil spills. In response to feedback from the agriculture community and the President's Executive order, the EPA recently concluded that the rules placed unjustifiable burdens on dairy farmers and decided to exempt milk from those regulations. That exemption will save the dairy industry, including many small businesses, as much as $148 million per year.

Third, to reduce burdens on railroads, the Department of Transportation has proposed to refine its requirements for tracks that are to be equipped with positive train controls. This equipment can automatically control a train in emergency circumstances, reducing the risk of an accident. The potential refinements would eliminate the need for costly wayside components and mitigation measures along as much as 10,000 miles of track where they are not needed for safety. The initial 5-year savings are expected to be as high as $335 million, with total 20-year savings of up to $778 million.

---

[2] Specific retrospective analyses by executive and independent agencies can generally be found on the relevant websites; for example, the Federal Trade Commission provides information on its retrospective review process at http://www.ftc.gov/ftc/regreview/index.shtml.

Fourth, the EPA has proposed to eliminate a requirement for air pollution vapor recovery systems at local gas stations in many states, on the ground that modern vehicles already have effective air pollution control technologies. The anticipated annual savings from eliminating the requirement are estimated to be as high as $87 million.

Fifth, the Health and Human Services Department has proposed or finalized several rules that reduce regulatory burdens and restrictions on doctors and hospitals and that are expected to save more than $5 billion over the next five years.

There are many other look-back efforts—in all, the initial round of retrospective proposals is expected to eliminate millions of hours of required paperwork for individuals, businesses, and State and local governments and to save billions of dollars.

Improvements in Everyday Life

Every time Americans drive a car, take a breath, swim in a lake, or take a medication they are benefiting from regulations. As noted, such improvements in quality of life often show up in national accounts only as a fraction of their total benefit to society. For example, although the growth and size of the pharmaceutical industry are reflected in GDP, the value of assurances given to the U.S. public that the medicines they are taking have been tested and verified to be effective and safe goes far beyond the measured value of that sector to the national economy.

Similarly, the Clean Water Act and its associated permitting requirements have reduced effluent discharge into U.S. streams, lakes, and estuaries. Putting a price tag on the benefits of being able to swim, fish, and boat in those bodies of water is difficult. Regardless of the value, some of those benefits (for example, increasing expenditures on fishing equipment and recreation) will show up in a calculation of GDP, while many others (such as reducing the level of fecal coliform in the water) will not. The EPA estimates the benefits of reducing discharge of conventional pollutants to U.S. rivers and streams to be approximately $11 billion annually (Bingham et al. 2000).

The EPA's Superfund program, which identifies, investigates, and cleans the Nation's most contaminated hazardous waste sites, has also improved public health. Since 1980 the Superfund program has prevented millions of people from being exposed to hazardous substances by requiring protective and containment measures and the removal from industrial sites of many millions of tons of material contaminated with toxic chemicals such as lead, arsenic, mercury, and benzene (EPA 2011c). Studies have shown that Superfund cleanups have lowered the risk of acute poisoning, improved infant health, and decreased the risk of cancer (Currie, Greenstone, and

Moretti 2011; and EPA 2011c). Those improvements are generally not captured well in GDP for any given year.

Even though smart regulations can impose restrictions on the private
sector, as Figure 8-2 illustrates, the resulting benefits do not come at the
cost of prosperity or sacrifices in U.S. standards of living. Over a period of
decades, air quality has improved while the economy has grown; indeed, the
demand for clean air and water has risen along with income across countries
(see for example, Grossman and Krueger 1995; and World Bank 1992).
Even though those benefits do not show up directly in GDP measures, they
are consistent with increases in conventional (albeit incomplete) measures
of growth. Per capita GDP has shown substantial growth between 1980 and
2010, rising by 65 percent, while at the same time per capita emissions of
criteria pollutants (lead, carbon monoxide, sulfur dioxide, nitrogen oxides,
particulate matter, and ozone) have declined by nearly 75 percent. Similar
achievements have been made in other areas as well. The number of fatalities on U.S. roads per million vehicle miles traveled (VMT) has declined by
67 percent between 1980 and 2010, while VMT per capita increased by 44
percent, reflecting the effectiveness of road and vehicle safety regulations.

INNOVATION

Innovation, loosely defined as the introduction of a new or improved
product, service, or process, is the primary source of long-run increases in
productivity and human welfare (Grossman and Helpman 1991). When new
ideas are integrated into the economy, they offer new possibilities for both
production and consumption. Innovation comes in two general forms: process and product innovation. Process innovations involve new or improved
methods of production or distribution, often as firms seek to reduce costs.
The cost savings are reflected in conventional accounting statistics as greater
productivity. Over time, rising productivity drives the growth in the amount
of output that the economy can produce. By contrast, product innovations
introduce new or improved products or services into the marketplace. As
noted, consumers benefit from product innovations in ways that conventional accounting statistics do not adequately measure.

Although there is no perfect measure of the importance of innovation
to an economy, by many measures innovation has played an increasingly
important role in the U.S. economy in recent decades. For example, the
industries classified by the OECD as "knowledge- and technology-intensive"
have steadily increased as a share of the U.S. economy, from 34 percent
of GDP in 1992 to 40 percent in 2010, according to the National Science
Foundation (2010; 2012).

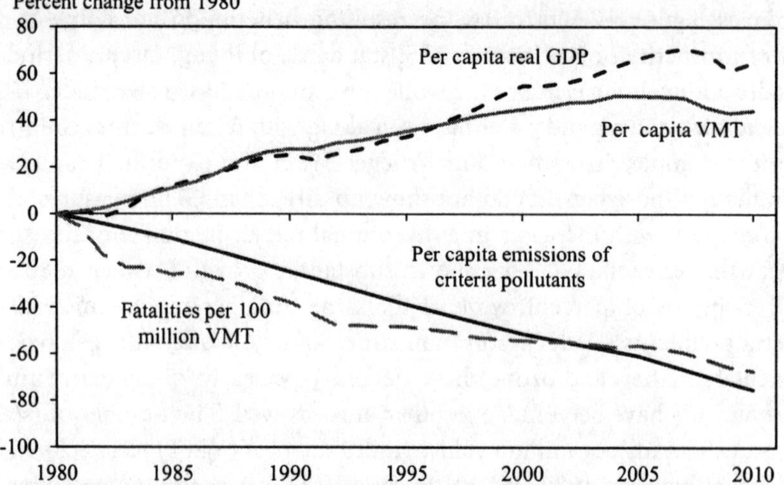

Note: VMT is vehicle miles traveled. Criteria emissions are linearly interpolated from 5-year interval data between 1980 and 2010.
Source: National Highway Traffic Safety Administration; Federal Highway Administration; Environmental Protection Agency; Bureau of Economic Analysis.

Private-sector competition is the primary driver of innovation. Firms in innovative industries must continually work to improve their products or increase their efficiency to avoid losing market share to competitors. Businesses that successfully invest in innovations are rewarded in the marketplace. Incentives for businesses to invest in innovation are often less than optimal from the perspective of society as a whole, however, primarily because the innovator may not be able to capture all of the benefits generated by the innovation. The positive spillovers from innovation mean that the private returns from innovation will often be less than the social returns, particularly when it comes to basic research. Private firms have limited incentive to conduct basic scientific research from which they generally can capture only a small fraction of the value that emerges from that research. As a result, private markets may lead to underinvestment in basic science and limited diffusion of scientific advances.

Because private incentives to invest in innovation are often inadequate, public-sector support for innovation has important benefits. Government can promote innovation in many ways. By operating a well-functioning system of intellectual property rights, the government can help innovators earn returns commensurate with the social value of their innovations. Government can increase investment in innovation through research and development (R&D) expenditures, both by direct funding and by tax incentives. It can facilitate the commercialization of innovations by removing barriers that prevent the private sector from transforming inventions into marketable products. It can provide infrastructure necessary for innovation, for example by allocating spectrum to support the growth of wireless broadband, itself an important platform for innovation in mobile devices, applications, and services. The government can also target innovation initiatives to areas of key public importance, including education, health care, and energy. This section of the chapter discusses these issues and describes some of the Federal Government's current efforts to promote innovation in the U.S. economy.

Measuring Innovation

Innovation's crucial role in economic growth and welfare has prompted efforts to improve the tools to measure it. One longstanding approach to measuring innovation is to infer that any economic growth *not* attributable to additional capital and labor must be due to some sort of "technical change." This so-called "Solow residual" approach (Solow 1957), however, leaves unanswered many questions about the nature of the technical change.

Data on patenting activity can provide a useful, if imperfect, measure of innovation. Although many innovations are kept secret to preserve competitive advantage, many others are made public through patent filings. The innovations for which patents are granted vary greatly in their significance, however, and a raw count of patents cannot account for these differences. Moreover, increases in patent activity over time may be attributable, at least in part, to more aggressive patenting of marginal innovations rather than increases in innovation itself (Hall and Ziedonis 2001). To address these limitations, studies of innovation have often relied on measures of patent citations. For example, the number of times a firm's patents are cited by other patent applications is more closely correlated with the firm's market value than is the raw number of patents it holds (Hall et al. 2001).

New measurement efforts have focused on the funds allocated to R&D within the economy. Historically, R&D has been treated as an intermediate input to the production process and is therefore excluded from GDP estimates. Beginning in 2013, the GDP estimates produced by the Bureau of Economic Analysis (BEA) will include R&D under the category of investment, increasing measured GDP. Spending on R&D is large and growing; if the new definition had been in effect earlier, current-dollar GDP in 2007 would have been, on average 2.7, percent higher, and R&D would have accounted for 6.3 percent of real GDP growth between 1998 and 2007.

In addition, to help improve understanding of the role of R&D in fostering innovation, the Census Bureau and the National Science Foundation (NSF) have introduced the Business R&D and Innovation Survey. This new survey combines firm-level data on R&D expenditures with measures of new or improved products or processes and patenting and licensing activity. The first group of 40,000 for-profit firms was surveyed in 2009, and some preliminary findings have been reported. For example, the NSF reports that companies that invest in R&D exhibit far higher rates of innovation than other firms (Boroush 2010).

Measuring innovation is particularly challenging in the growing medical care sector. For example, medical science has established that aspirin—an old and inexpensive product—can substantially reduce heart attack risk. Patients have seen enormous benefits from that scientific advancement, but those benefits are not captured by estimates of GDP. The National Institute on Aging has sponsored research on the development of national health accounts that would gauge the population's health status and measure how medical care and other factors affect health.

Intellectual Property Rights and Patent Reform

Innovation is spurred in part by the desire to reap rewards for developing new products and services that people will value. The central purpose of intellectual property (IP) rights, which include patents, trademarks, and copyrights, is to promote innovation by giving IP owners the right to exclude others from making use of their novel product or service. Well-designed IP rights enhance the private returns to innovation and bring them closer to the social returns, thereby increasing the incentives to invest in socially valuable innovation. As President Lincoln famously said, the patent system "added the fuel of interest to the fire of genius" (Edwards 2006).[3]

The United States has long had a robust system of IP rights. In fact, one of the powers explicitly given Congress in the Constitution is "To promote the Progress of Science and useful Arts, by securing for limited Times to Authors and Inventors the exclusive Right to their respective Writings and Discoveries." In recent years, however, many observers have raised concerns about the U.S. patent system. For example, the Federal Trade Commission (FTC 2003) describes concerns that the patent system has failed to keep up with the challenges posed by the growth of the knowledge-based economy. Similarly, the National Academy of Science (NRC 2004) describes unease among academics and practitioners that "the escalation in the number of patents, possibly encouraged by a lowering of the threshold to their

---

[3] President Lincoln was himself an inventor. He was granted patent no. 6469 in 1849 for a flotation system for lifting riverboats stuck on sandbars.

acquisition, was creating thickets of rights that could impede innovation." Shapiro (2008) sees the core problem as being that, in some circumstances, "the patent system predictably provides excessive rewards to patent holders." The opportunity for excessive returns can arise when patents are issued for technologies that are not genuinely novel or when a patent covers a small component of a complex product that allows the patent's owner to extract royalties disproportionate to the incremental value of the component. Some empirical evidence suggests that, at least in certain industries, greater patenting activity has in fact led to *reduced* R&D intensity (Hunt and Bessen 2004).

To address concerns about the performance of the patent system, President Obama, on September 16, 2011, signed into law the America Invents Act, the most significant reform of U.S. patent law since 1952. By allowing third parties to provide the patent office with additional information that may be helpful in assessing the novelty of an invention for which a patent application has been filed, the new law will reduce the number of improperly issued patents and thus increase "patent quality." The law will also reduce unnecessary litigation by creating new ways of resolving patent disputes more quickly and cheaply, allowing inventors to invest with more confidence in the validity of their IP rights while reducing the drag on innovation caused by improperly granted patents. The law will also reduce wait times for patent applicants by giving the U.S. Patent and Trademark Office more resources to reduce the backlog of applications and by creating a "fast-track option" for time-sensitive patent applications such as those from fast-growing startups or entrepreneurs seeking venture capital. Last, the new law will harmonize the American patent system with patent systems in the rest of the world by adopting a "first inventor to file" system. This change will make the U.S. system more efficient and predictable, allowing innovative entrepreneurs to market their products more easily in the United States while simultaneously exporting them abroad.

Private and Public Investments in R&D

R&D is a critical driver of innovation. Investments aimed at creating new knowledge or applying existing knowledge in new ways are often a necessary precursor to developing new or improved products or processes or entire new industries. Although innovative activities extend far beyond conventional R&D, and innovations arise in industries that perform little R&D as such, investing in R&D is generally an important element of innovative activity.

A large body of research confirms that investments in R&D increase productivity growth (CBO 2005). Other research demonstrates that the social returns to R&D investment are generally substantially greater than the private returns. For example, Nordhaus (2004) concludes that "only a minuscule fraction of the social returns from technological advances over the 1948–2001 period was captured by producers, indicating that most of the benefits of technological change are passed on to consumers." (See also Hall, Mairesse, and Mohnen 2009; Bloom, Schankerman, and Van Reenen 2010; and Jones and Williams 1998.) These findings support the conclusion that R&D investments often have important positive spillover effects that prevent private firms from fully capturing the benefits of their innovations, thus giving them inadequate incentives to invest in R&D. In addition, Hall (2002) finds evidence that capital market imperfections may lead to underinvestment in R&D even in the absence of these spillovers. In short, economics research provides persuasive support for a robust government role in promoting R&D.

The United States is a world leader in R&D investments. With an estimated $400 billion in public and private expenditures in 2009, the United States invested more in R&D than China, Japan, and Germany combined. Moreover, R&D spending as a share of the U.S. economy has been increasing in recent years, with the ratio of R&D spending to GDP reaching nearly 2.9 percent in 2009, the highest since the 1960s. During that interval, however, the composition of U.S. R&D spending shifted dramatically. During the 1950s and 1960s, the majority of total R&D expenditures was federally funded; today nonfederal sources predominate. Private industry investments have consistently accounted for about 90 percent of all nonfederal R&D expenditures.

Despite the increasing role of private-sector investment in R&D, public support for R&D remains critically important, particularly in basic research, which aims to expand scientific knowledge and thus does not generally have immediate commercial applications. Private firms can thus find it especially difficult to capture the benefits that stem from this research, and the positive spillover effects of basic research can be especially large. For example, NSF-funded basic research into the principle of nuclear magnetic resonance ultimately led to the development of magnetic resonance imaging (MRI) machines, a medical imaging technology that has significantly improved diagnosis for cancer and other conditions. Not surprisingly, the Federal Government is a strong supporter of basic research. In 2008, while the Federal Government accounted for only 15 percent of U.S. development expenditures and less than one-third of applied research expenditures, it accounted for nearly 60 percent of the Nation's basic research expenditures.

Overall, the Federal Government provides substantial support for R&D. In 2009, when the Recovery Act helped Federal R&D spending reach 1.18 percent of GDP, the U.S. Government invested a greater share of GDP in R&D than did the government of any other OECD country. Even in other years, the U.S. Government's R&D investments relative to GDP have substantially exceeded the OECD average. Although this largely reflects U.S. dominance in military R&D (national defense has historically accounted for more than half of Federal R&D expenditures), many defense-related innovations ultimately have significant benefits in the private sector. Research into communications networks by the Defense Advanced Research Projects Agency, for example, ultimately led to the emergence of the Internet.

Recognizing the importance of R&D for innovation, in April 2009, the President set the goal of devoting more than 3 percent of GDP to R&D, both public and private—a share that surpasses the record of almost 2.9 percent set in 1964 at the height of the space race. In its effort to reach this goal, the Administration has supported large increases in Federal R&D funding. The Recovery Act's investment of $18.3 billion in research funding was part of the largest annual increase in R&D funding in U.S. history. The President's Fiscal Year 2013 Budget has proposed additional support for science and basic research, making progress toward the goal of doubling funding for three key basic research agencies—the National Science Foundation, the Office of Science in the Department of Energy, and the National Institute of Standards and Technology. A particular success story is the Small Business Innovation Research (SBIR) and Small Business Technology Transfer (SBTT) programs, competitive programs that provide about $2.5 billion annually to the most promising research projects at small firms. From 2002 to 2006, about one-fourth of the "top 100" innovations selected by *R&D Magazine* came from companies that had received an SBIR grant at some point in their history. Recognizing the importance of continuing these successes, on December 31, 2011, President Obama signed a bill reauthorizing the SBIR and SBTT programs for the next six years.

In addition to direct Federal funding for R&D, the Administration has promoted incentives to support private R&D investment. The Research and Experimentation tax credit, for example, enacted in 1981, provides a tax credit based on qualified research expenses to encourage businesses to increase their investments. Subsidizing this activity through the tax system allows the private sector, rather than the government, to choose the research projects and the method for conducting the research. Recent studies show that the credit is a cost-effective way to encourage research spending (U.S. Treasury 2011). On September 8, 2010, the President proposed to expand and simplify the credit and to make it permanent; that proposal is also included in the President's FY 2013 Budget. The proposal will further enhance private firms' incentives to invest in research and will provide businesses with assurance that the credit will be available for the duration of long-term research projects.

Commercialization

An important stage in the process of innovation is commercialization of new technologies. New inventions and new knowledge alone will have little effect on economic welfare unless they are converted into marketable products or processes that change how firms do business. One obstacle to realizing the economic benefits of innovation is the difficulty in transferring new ideas from universities and Federal laboratories to the marketplace. For example, recent empirical studies point to substantial frictions attributable to licensing costs and show large gains in innovation when these frictions are reduced (Williams 2010). Other researchers have found that universities often adopt technology transfer policies that constrain the volume of innovations brought into the marketplace (Litan, Mitchell, and Reddy 2007).

As the President announced in January 2011, one of the goals of the Administration's "Startup America" campaign is to foster innovation by increasing the rate of technology transfer. Since then, the Administration has announced a number of initiatives in support of this goal. In October 2011, the President issued a Presidential Memorandum directing the heads of Executive departments and agencies to take action to accelerate technology transfer and commercialization of Federal research in support of high-growth businesses. The National Center for Advancing Translational Sciences at the National Institutes of Health assists biomedical entrepreneurs by identifying barriers to commercialization and speeding development of new drugs and diagnostics. The Administration's National Bioeconomy Blueprint lays out a number of steps designed to advance biological research innovations, including reforms to speed commercialization and open new markets. The NSF's Innovation Corps program is a public-private partnership that will connect NSF-funded researchers with private-sector mentors who will help to transform the results of scientific research into commercially successful technologies. The Department of Energy (DOE) launched a program called "America's Next Top Energy Innovator," which offers startup companies low-cost and streamlined procedures for licensing new energy technologies patented by DOE labs. Together, the Administration's "lab-to-market" initiatives will encourage universities and government research centers to streamline their technology transfer procedures, support additional government-industry collaboration, and encourage the commercialization of novel technologies flowing from research programs—in short, they will facilitate the commercialization phase of the process of innovation.

Wireless Broadband and Spectrum Policy

Information and communication technology (ICT) is vitally important to the U.S. economy. A large body of research has linked economic growth in recent decades with ICT expansion. For example, Roller and Waverman (2001) estimate that one-third of the growth in per capita GDP in 21 developed economies from 1970 to 1990 is attributable to investments in telecommunications infrastructure. Similarly, Bloom, Sadun, and van Reenen (2007) note that the great majority of growth in U.S. productivity since the mid-1990s has been in sectors that either intensively use or produce information technologies.[4]

Wireless broadband is a form of ICT that can transform many different areas of the American economy by providing a platform for innovation, in areas ranging from media-rich consumer products to health care and education technologies. Much of the investment necessary to realize the potential of wireless broadband will come from the private sector. According to the Census Bureau, total capital spending by wireless telecommunications carriers has exceeded $20 billion in each year since 2000 (U.S. Census Bureau 2011). Public support is necessary in some important areas, including developing a nationwide wireless broadband network for public safety and extending wireless broadband services into rural communities, both of which are discussed in this chapter in the section on infrastructure. Another important way that the government can help to support the growth of wireless broadband is by making more spectrum available, both for licensed and unlicensed use. With the proliferation of smartphones, tablets, and other mobile devices with Internet access, mobile data traffic has been growing tremendously, more than doubling between 2009 and 2010, and industry forecasters expect data traffic to continue to grow rapidly (Cisco 2011). To accommodate this surging demand, wireless carriers will need access to additional spectrum.

In early 2011, President Obama introduced his National Wireless Initiative. The proposal aims to nearly double the spectrum available for wireless broadband in the next 10 years by freeing up 500 megahertz (MHz) of spectrum currently allocated to other uses. Some of this spectrum will be shifted away from Federal Government uses, in part by finding ways to make more efficient use of the remaining Federal and shared spectrum. Any changes in the use of Federal spectrum will be designed to ensure that there is no harmful interference with public safety needs or other critical public uses of the spectrum. Doubling the spectrum for wireless broadband will

---

[4] Jorgenson et al. (2008) estimate that ICT accounted for 59 percent of productivity growth during 1995–2000 and 38 percent during 2000–2006. Most recently, Brynjolfsson and Saunders (2010) conclude that most U.S. productivity growth since 1995 can be attributed to ICT.

also require changes in commercially licensed spectrum. Shifting to wireless broadband a portion of the spectrum now licensed for over-the-air television broadcasting will yield substantial economic benefits. To ensure that commercially held spectrum is reallocated efficiently and that the economic benefits are widely shared, the Administration supports using "voluntary incentive auctions" to guide the reallocation. These auctions will allow existing licensees to receive a portion of the auction proceeds in exchange for voluntarily making their spectrum available for wireless broadband. The auctions will also generate substantial revenues for the U.S. Treasury, providing support for important goals, including deficit reduction, R&D for emerging wireless technologies, and a nationwide interoperable wireless broadband network for public safety.

CLEAN & SECURE ENERGY

In his State of the Union address, President Obama, noted that, "This country needs an all-out, all-of-the-above strategy that develops every available source of American energy. A strategy that's cleaner, cheaper, and full of new jobs." The President has outlined goals that will set the United States on a path toward lowering its dependence on oil and developing cleaner domestic energy sources that reduce emissions of air pollutants. Those include goals to continue focusing on increasing responsible domestic oil and gas production, to reduce foreign oil imports by a third by 2025, and to increase the share of electricity generated from clean energy sources—including nuclear power, natural gas, clean coal, and renewables like wind and solar—to 80 percent by 2035.

The President has outlined a *Blueprint for a Secure Energy Future* to guide the Nation's transition to a clean and secure energy economy. While the market provides key signals that greatly influence energy production and consumption decisions, energy markets are subject to market failures, so the government has an important role to play in guiding the mix of energy supplies and uses that is best for the Nation. The government also has a role to play in increasing energy security, reducing air pollution, promoting clean energy through investments in innovation and infrastructure, and establishing rules of the road that promote a cleaner and more secure energy future.

Enhancing Energy Security

The short-run demand for energy is relatively inelastic, so consumers will bear the brunt of sudden, unexpected energy supply disruptions in the form of price increases, causing them to reduce their consumption of other goods and services, or reduce savings. Elevated global energy prices can, in turn, slow economic growth. Promoting the development of alternative energies and energy-efficient technologies reduces the economy's vulnerability to international energy supply shocks and improves energy security. Oil consumption per thousand dollars of real GDP has fallen by about half since 1980 (from almost one barrel per thousand dollars of GDP in 1980 to about 0.5 barrel per thousand dollars of GDP in 2010). Despite progress in reducing the "petroleum intensity" of the economy, vulnerability to increases in the global market price of crude oil remains. We can improve energy security by lowering demand for petroleum and by increasing the supply of domestic conventional and alternative energy.

Reducing Demand

During the past year, the Administration has pursued a course that reduces demand for petroleum. In November, EPA and DOT proposed new fuel economy standards for vehicle model years 2017–2025, building on the successful programs for the 2011 and 2012–2016 model years. These standards will save consumers money at the pump, dramatically reduce the Nation's dependence on oil, and increase investment in new technologies and new manufacturing here in the United States. Under the proposed rules, fuel economy standards from the DOT, greenhouse gas (GHG) emission standards from the EPA, and State of California regulations will be harmonized and auto companies will be able to rely on well-defined regulatory targets to help steer their investments in producing advanced vehicles. Annualized costs of the rule are expected to be between $6.4 billion and $10.6 billion; annualized fuel savings are expected to range between $20.3 billion and $26.7 billion (2009 dollars). Additional annualized benefits from improved health, greater energy security, and lower GHG emissions are expected to range between $5.4 billion and $6.4 billion. Taken together, the fuel economy standards proposed for model years 2011–2025 are projected to reduce oil consumption by over 2.2 million barrels per day by 2025, and save consumers $1.7 trillion in fuel costs.

The President has also proposed a new tax incentive to offset half of the incremental cost of dedicated alternative-fuel commercial vehicles, such as natural gas and electric trucks, for a five-year period. In addition, the President has proposed transforming the individual tax credit for consumers who purchase advanced vehicles into a rebate.

Increasing Domestic Energy Supplies

The Nation has pursued strategies to safely increase domestic energy sources. As part of this focus, the President is committed to advancing the responsible production of domestic oil and natural gas resources. Thanks to higher domestic production and lower imports, dependence on foreign oil is being reduced. In 2010, for the first time in over a decade, the United States relied on net imports for less than half of the oil we consumed; in 2011, import dependence declined even further, to 45 percent. Since 2007, the United States has been the leading natural gas producer in the world.

To help ensure safe and responsible development of abundant natural gas resources, the Administration is taking a number of steps, including: exploring home grown technologies and methods to improve safety and environmental performance of shale gas production; encouraging greater use of natural gas in transportation; and requiring disclosure of chemicals used in hydraulic fracturing on public lands. As Box 8-1 describes, the development of unconventional oil and gas deposits across the United States illustrates how American enterprise and innovation in horizontal drilling and hydraulic fracturing, combined with government-supported research, have unlocked vast new domestic oil and gas resources.

The United States has also increased the amount of ethanol and biodiesel blended into the nation's fuel supply. In 2011, ethanol and bio-diesel production in the United States were estimated by the U.S. Energy Information Administration (EIA) to be roughly 14 billion gallons and 920 million gallons, respectively (EIA 2012). That represented about 10 percent of U.S. gasoline demand and 2 percent of diesel demand for 2011. In March 2011, the President set the goal of breaking ground on at least four commercial-scale cellulosic or advanced bio-refineries over the next two years, and we are on track to exceed that goal. In addition, the Administration announced a partnership between the Departments of Agriculture, Energy and the Navy to invest in multiple domestic commercial or pre-commercial scale bio-refineries to produce advanced "drop-in" biofuels, substitutes for diesel and jet fuel.

Reducing Emissions

The Administration has taken historic steps to address air pollution from stationary sources such as aging coal-fired power plants. The Mercury and Air Toxics Standard (MATS) regulation announced by the EPA in December, for example, will reduce emissions of sulfur dioxide, mercury and other toxic air pollution and generate between $27 billion and $80 billion in net benefits annually by improving people's health.

In addition, to create a market for innovative technologies that will encourage the deployment of clean energy and the benefits that come with it, such as reduced emissions of air pollutants and greenhouse gases, the President has proposed a Clean Energy Standard (CES).

A CES works by giving electric power plants clean energy credits for electricity they generate from clean energy. Utilities that serve retail customers are responsible for making sure they have enough clean energy credits to meet their target. Utilities that generate more clean energy than needed to meet their target can bank their extra credits for later use, or sell them to other companies. Under the President's proposal, the target would increase over time, so that by 2035, 80 percent of the country's electricity would be generated from clean sources. This flexible approach would harness private-sector incentives to minimize the cost of generating electricity from clean energy sources.

Because of cleaner power plants, greater use of alternative fuels, and more energy-efficient vehicles, buildings, and appliances, EIA (2012) expects per capita emissions of carbon dioxide in the United States to fall over time, by an average of 0.8 percent a year between 2010 and 2035.

Supporting Clean Energy R&D and Infrastructure

Public investments in innovation and infrastructure are critical to solving the twin objectives of increasing energy security and reducing GHG emissions. Private-sector investment in energy R&D and infrastructure will be less than optimal because the positive externalities from such investments prevent private firms from fully capturing the benefits. Support for innovation is a key piece of the *Blueprint* strategy, which involves creating markets for clean technologies that are ready to deploy and funding cutting-edge research to deliver the next generation of technologies. In addition, investments in modernizing the energy infrastructure with advanced technologies will help to increase efficiency and reduce waste. Innovation and adoption of new technologies will be critical to improving energy efficiency and shifting the Nation's energy use toward low-carbon energy generation.

Among the DOE offices that provide support for clean energy innovation is the Advanced Research Projects Agency-Energy (ARPA-E), an organization modeled after the Defense Advanced Research Projects Agency. ARPA-E provides funds to develop advanced energy technologies that reduce energy-related emissions and increase energy efficiency, focusing on transformational energy research that the private sector by itself is unlikely to support. The Obama Administration funded ARPA-E for the first time with $400 million as part of the Recovery Act. This funding, along with subsequent appropriations, has been used to support about 180 projects, including technologies for plug-in electric vehicles, batteries that convert wind power into a steady power source, and microorganisms that produce liquid biofuels from sunlight and carbon dioxide. The President's Fiscal Year 2013 Budget proposes $350 million in new funding for ARPA-E to continue

Box 8-1: Developing Domestic Energy: Shale Gas and Shale Oil

Shale gas and shale oil (also known as "tight" oil) are deposits trapped inside formations of fine-grained sedimentary rocks, or shale. As recently as a decade ago many of these deposits were viewed as uneconomical to extract. Now they are being profitably extracted, leading to a boom in production from these unconventional oil and gas deposits.

The President has been clear about the importance of domestic oil and gas production, including the central role responsible natural gas development will play in our energy future, increasing energy independence, and supporting jobs.

The percent of new wells directed to shale gas and oil deposits surged from 13 percent in 2005 to 57 percent in 2011. That dramatic increase is in large part due to rising energy prices in the early 2000s, which made it profitable for oil and gas companies to pursue higher cost reserves. But it is also due in part to R&D investments made by the Department of Energy (DOE). Between 1978 and 1992, the DOE invested about $137 million in the Eastern Gas Shale program, which helped develop and demonstrate directional and horizontal drilling technology.

Horizontal drilling allows multiple wells to be completed from one drilling pad by drilling vertically for several thousand feet and then drilling horizontally. Hydraulic fracturing pumps water, chemicals and sand into the well to fracture the surrounding rock, releasing trapped natural gas and oil, allowing more gas and oil to be captured (see figure). From 2006 through 2010 the average annual growth rate of shale gas production was 48 percent. By 2035 shale gas is expected to make up 49 percent of total U.S. natural gas production, up from 23 percent in 2010 (EIA 2012). Increased supply has caused wholesale natural gas prices to fall more than 75 percent from their peak in October 2005 through October 2011. This led to a 67 percent drop in prices charged for natural gas used to generate electricity and a 34 percent decline in residential natural gas prices.

Domestic oil production also grew in 2009 and 2010, in part due to horizontal drilling methods. That growth helped improve America's energy security. We reduced our imports of crude oil, from 10.1 million barrels per day in 2005 to an estimated 8.9 million barrels per day in 2011. EIA (2012) projects that domestic oil production will continue to increase through 2020. We are also exporting more refined petroleum products than ever: between the first half of 2009 and the first half of 2011, exports of mineral fuels and oils jumped 150 percent, an increase valued at more than $35 billion (see Chapter 5). In addition, the United States is at the forefront of exporting extraction technologies and related services to other countries interested in tapping their own unconventional oil and gas reserves.

This expansion of natural gas and oil production has also supported jobs for thousands of Americans. Bureau of Labor Statistics (BLS) data show that oil and gas extraction and drilling services jobs have grown by 100,000 between 2005 and 2010, with much of that increase tied to horizontal drilling for shale gas and oil. The industry also indirectly supports many more jobs, including jobs associated with the transportation, processing, and distribution of oil and natural gas products. Furthermore, downstream industries, such as the chemical and plastics sectors that use natural gas as an important input, benefit from the expanded supply of natural gas.

Such tremendous growth also comes with the responsibility to develop these new resources safely. A number of concerns have been raised regarding the potential adverse environmental impacts associated with current shale gas extraction practices, particularly the use of hydraulic fracturing. The Obama Administration is taking a number of steps to ensure that the United States can realize the economic benefits of its natural gas resources in a an environmentally responsible way. An important part of this effort consists of targeted research coordinated between the DOE, the Department of the Interior, and the Environmental Protection Agency to assess and address potential impacts of natural gas and oil development using hydraulic fracturing and to identify innovative ways to reduce adverse environmental impacts. For example, the DOE is actively involved in research exploring improved methods to treat the water used in shale gas extraction so it can be reused or disposed of safely. The Administration is committed to ensuring that natural gas and oil extraction will be pursued in a prudent manner that is safe for the environment.

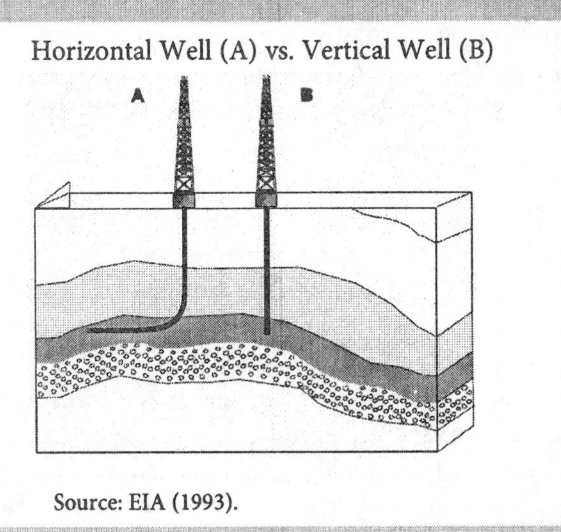

Source: EIA (1993).

to support breakthrough clean energy research in areas such as solar energy, energy storage, carbon capture and storage, and advanced biofuels.

An important part of the effort to transition to a clean energy future is the "SunShot Initiative" announced by the DOE in February 2011. This initiative supports innovation to reduce the cost of solar energy by 75 percent by 2020, making unsubsidized solar energy cost-competitive with other forms of energy. Achieving the goal will require major innovations in the ways solar technologies are conceived, designed, manufactured, and installed. SunShot is investing in solar technology and manufacturing improvements and working to reduce installation and permitting costs. According to DOE (2011) analysis, by reducing the cost of solar electricity to about six cents per kilowatt hour, SunShot has the potential to increase the share of electricity generation from solar photovoltaics to 15 percent by 2030.

As the United States transitions to a clean energy future, an important way to improve energy efficiency, reliability, and security is to upgrade the electricity transmission and distribution infrastructure to make greater use of advanced technology and to incorporate real-time communications, monitoring, and control systems. Transforming the electricity infrastructure into a "smart grid" could lead to substantial cost savings and efficiencies, help avoid blackouts, and improve the integration of renewable energy sources on the grid. The Recovery Act included $4.5 billion in grid modernization investments, matched by contributions of more than $5.5 billion from the private sector. Building on these investments, the Administration announced a number of new initiatives to support the development and deployment of smart-grid technologies, including $250 million in loans to deploy smart-grid technology in rural areas under the Rural Utility Service. In June 2011, the White House released a report by the National Science and Technology Council, "A Policy Framework for the 21st Century Grid: Enabling Our Secure Energy Future," outlining policy recommendations that build on existing smart-grid investments to foster continued modernization of electricity infrastructure.

In addition to efforts to support smart grid development, the Administration has announced efforts to improve Federal coordination and ensure timely review of proposed renewable energy projects and transmission lines through the formation of two interagency Rapid Response Teams, one for transmission and one for renewables. The Rapid Response Team for Transmission is focused on seven pilot project transmission lines which cross through 12 states. These projects were selected from lists produced through independent stakeholder processes. When built, these seven pilot projects will help increase electric reliability and integrate renewable energy into the grid. The agencies participating in the Renewable Energy Rapid

Response Team have all made significant strides toward the deployment of renewable energy through the development of better government processes to issue permits for renewable energy projects.

INFRASTRUCTURE

As emphasized, energy infrastructure is critical for developing our domestic clean energy potential. Infrastructure also includes transportation systems like roads, railways, ports and airports; information and communications networks; and schools, parks, and other public facilities. As economic activity grows, the infrastructure that supports it must grow as well. Moreover, physical infrastructure deteriorates over time and requires ongoing investment for maintenance. If investments to maintain, upgrade, and expand infrastructure do not keep pace with the growth in demand, the result is congestion: too many hours sitting in traffic or in an airplane stalled on the tarmac, too many dropped calls, slow Internet connections. Such disruptions impose substantial economic costs through wasted time and resources and diminished quality of life. As a result, efficient infrastructure investments can have a significant positive impact on economic welfare.

The State of the Nation's Infrastructure

The value of the U.S. transportation capital stock steadily increased from 2004 to 2009, reaching more than $6 trillion in 2009 (the most recently reported year). The greatest percentage increase in mileage for any mode of transportation from 2004 to 2009 was in light transit rail track, which increased by 24 percent, followed by commuter rail track, which increased by 10 percent. At the same time, the overall condition of many parts of the Nation's transportation infrastructure remained disappointing. In 2008, nearly 21 percent of urban interstate highways and 35 percent of urban collector roads were in poor or mediocre condition, according to the Bureau of Transportation Statistics. Moreover, in 2009 nearly 71,200 bridges—more than 10 percent of all U.S. bridges—were rated as structurally deficient.

The current disappointing state of transportation infrastructure is partly reflected in rising levels of congestion on many parts of the transportation system, particularly urban roadways. According to the Texas Traffic Institute's (TTI) *Urban Mobility Report*, traffic congestion in urban areas in 2010 accounted for 4.8 billion hours of travel delay and 1.9 billion gallons of wasted fuel, for an aggregate congestion cost of more than $100 billion, an increase of more than 25 percent over 2000 in constant (inflation-adjusted) dollars (Schrank, Lomax, and Eisele 2011). If current trends continue, TTI projects that the total cost of congestion in U.S. urban areas could grow by a further 32 percent in real terms by 2015. These estimates likely understate the real effects of congestion on welfare because they do not take into account the reduction in quality of life that results from additional time spent commuting. Studies of how individuals experience the activities of daily life have found that commuting is among the least enjoyable and most stressful (Kahneman et al. 2004, Stutzer and Frey 2004).

The U.S. electricity grid is also showing signs of strain, with investment in capacity generally lagging behind growth in demand. According to the DOE (2008), growth in peak demand for electricity has exceeded transmission growth by almost 25 percent every year since 1982. Power outages and interruptions have become more frequent and are now affecting more consumers. The DOE reported that 41 percent more outages affected 50,000 or more consumers in the second half of the 1990s than in the first half, and the average outage affected 15 percent more consumers. By 2008, power outages and interruptions cost Americans an estimated $150 billion each year.

Broadband is another important category of infrastructure where the United States faces significant investment needs. Described by the Federal Communications Commission as "the great infrastructure challenge of the early 21st century" (FCC 2010), broadband's growth over the past decade has been substantial. Thanks to significant investments by telecommunications and cable companies, 95 percent of the U.S. population had access to wired broadband service in 2010, and industry analysts project that by 2013, wireless providers will offer such service to about 94 percent of the population. (Atkinson et al. 2011). At the same time, many households, particularly in rural areas, continue to have Internet access only at much slower speeds. As discussed, perhaps the most significant challenge to the Nation's broadband infrastructure is the threat of growing congestion on wireless networks.

Overall, evidence is growing that the United States has been underinvesting in many kinds of infrastructure. For example, the Nation invests annually approximately 2 percent of GDP on infrastructure, compared with 9 percent and 5 percent, respectively, for China and Europe. In addition, compared with other OECD countries, Americans are relatively dissatisfied with their local public infrastructure systems, according to the Gallup World Poll. Americans' satisfaction with public transit ranks 25th out of 32 OECD nations, and satisfaction with roads and highways ranks 17th out of 32. Many observers, including the American Society of Civil Engineers (2009), have concluded that the United States faces a substantial need for infrastructure investment over the next five years. Although the optimal level of infrastructure investment is difficult to quantify precisely, the evidence strongly suggests that the United States has not been investing adequately to meet future infrastructure needs.

Government and Private Sector Roles in Infrastructure

In the United States some kinds of infrastructure, including most roadways and public transit systems, are typically owned and financed by government; other kinds, such as freight railways and telecommunications networks, are largely privately owned. In part, these patterns of ownership reflect historical accident. In choosing how much public support for infrastructure to provide and how to finance it, the United States, like other nations, faces questions about how best to balance the roles of the public and private sectors in infrastructure investment. Two key economic principles are whether it is costly or difficult for a private owner or investor to earn a return by monetizing access to the network, through tolls or user fees, and whether important positive spillover benefits from infrastructure investment would prevent private investors from fully capturing the overall economic benefit, even if there were a dedicated revenue stream from users.

The most important potential positive spillover effect is that many infrastructure investments improve economic efficiency, increase productivity, and promote rapid economic growth. Through these effects, as a large body of research has shown, investments in infrastructure can substantially improve the long-run performance of an economy. For example, Munnell (1992) reviews the evidence on infrastructure investment and economic growth and concludes that, "in addition to providing immediate economic stimulus, public infrastructure investment has a significant positive effect on output and growth." Gramlich's (1994) review of the same research cautions that the rates of return on investments vary widely across different types of infrastructure and highlights the need for policies that direct public investment toward projects with the highest social return. More recent studies have found further evidence that public infrastructure investment often offers considerable returns, in some cases higher than those from private capital investment. This research is reviewed in a U.S. Treasury-CEA report (2010).

In addition to their long-run benefits on economic growth and productivity, investments in infrastructure can also provide short-run benefits during times when economic resources are underutilized, by supporting employment in construction and in materials production. These short-run effects depend on the state of the overall economy. When the economy is operating at or close to its full potential, the new employment generated by infrastructure projects generally requires diverting workers from other productive activities, and the expenditure of public funds may similarly divert funds from other investment opportunities. Certain infrastructure investments may still be justified during such times, but the opportunity costs of diverting economic resources from other activities reduce the net benefits of such investments.

By contrast, today the economy is gradually recovering from the most serious economic crisis since the Great Depression and is operating significantly below its full potential, with unemployment still unacceptably high. In 2011, over 1.8 million workers in the construction industry were jobless, with an industry unemployment rate of 16.4 percent. In these circumstances, public infrastructure projects create net jobs for workers. With excess capacity widely available in the economy, increased public spending on construction materials and increased private spending by newly hired workers are unlikely to divert goods or materials from other uses. Similarly, with interest rates exceptionally low, there is little risk that Federal investment will crowd out private investment, and more infrastructure investments will yield a positive rate of return. Moreover, State and local governments, which typically fund a significant portion of infrastructure spending, have been forced to cut back on spending because of revenue shortfalls since the recession of 2007–09. Recent macroeconomic research confirms the intuition that the expansionary effect of Federal investment spending is likely to be significantly greater during times of substantial slack in the economy. For example, Auerbach and Gorodnichenko (2010) find that expansionary fiscal policy is substantially more effective during recessions than during expansions. Overall, with so many resources sitting idle, the opportunity costs of using those resources for infrastructure investment are greatly reduced. Moreover, postponing necessary infrastructure investments until after the economy has rebounded would have the undesirable effect of occupying productive resources just when the private sector needs them most.

Financing Infrastructure Investments

Government funding for infrastructure draws on a number of different sources, including Federal disbursements of Highway Trust Fund revenues and State and local issues of municipal bonds. Recent years have seen increased interest in alternative financing mechanisms that may expand the pool of available capital and improve the efficiency of project selection. A common theme in these alternative approaches is the goal of attracting more private capital for direct or indirect investment in transportation infrastructure. Increased reliance on the private sector to finance transportation infrastructure investments can help increase funding for those investments and may also improve the efficiency of project selection and drive greater returns on investment. For example, to attract private financing, many projects incorporate a dedicated revenue stream, often from user fees or other forms of usage-based pricing. Because these revenue streams link investment returns directly to user demand, they can help to guide capital toward the most efficient projects. In general, innovative financing mechanisms can engage the private sector in infrastructure investments with important public benefits. In particular, this chapter considers three innovative approaches to private-sector engagement: public-private partnerships, particularly in the area of rail freight; Build America Bonds (BABs) as an alternative to municipal bonds that can attract new sources of private funding into the market for financing infrastructure projects; and a National Infrastructure Bank that has the potential to leverage private capital into projects of national significance.

Public-Private Partnerships. In the United States, most investment in freight railway infrastructure is privately financed, because it is largely owned by the rail carriers themselves. However, even in a network based on private ownership, important public benefits can be realized through investments that improve the flow of freight across the railway network. The benefits of diverting freight efficiently from trucks to rails, for example, include reduced highway congestion, greater safety, and reduced pollution. Public-private partnerships between State and Federal agencies and the rail carriers can be an efficient way to promote such investments. For example, the Chicago Region Environmental and Transportation Efficiency program is a public-private partnership between the U.S. Department of Transportation, the State of Illinois, the City of Chicago, Metra commuter rail, and Class I railroad companies. The partnership, formed to develop and implement a set of multimodal infrastructure improvements to untangle congestion choke points in the Chicago transportation hub, involves significant financial cooperation between the private railroad industry and public government entities.

Build America Bonds. Introduced in 2009, BABs are taxable bonds for which the U.S. Treasury Department pays a direct subsidy to the issuer to offset borrowing costs for public capital infrastructure projects. These bonds can function as an attractive alternative to municipal bonds, which deliver a borrowing subsidy only indirectly through the Federal tax exemption to investors for interest earnings. BABs appeal to a broader class of investors than tax-exempt municipal bonds, including nonprofits, pension funds, and many other institutional investors. Since the inception of the program in April 2009, BABs have had a very strong reception from both issuers and investors. They have supported more than $181 billion of financing, in 2,275 transactions in all 50 states, the District of Columbia, and two territories, for new public capital infrastructure projects such as schools, bridges, and hospitals. An empirical study by the Treasury Department (2011) found that State and local governments that issued BABs realized considerable savings relative to the cost of issuing tax-exempt bonds. The study also found that expanding the BABs program would lead to continued savings on borrowing costs for State and local governments. Although the initial program expired at the end of December 2010, the President's Fiscal Year 2013 Budget has proposed extending the program for two years at a subsidy rate of 30 percent and extending it permanently thereafter at a revenue-neutral subsidy rate of 28 percent. The Administration has also proposed expanding the program to include a broader range of eligible municipal projects.

National Infrastructure Bank. Another new approach to increasing private-sector participation in infrastructure investment is a National Infrastructure Bank, as President Obama has proposed as part of the American Jobs Act. The proposed bank would help increase overall investment in infrastructure by attracting private capital to co-invest in specific infrastructure projects and would help improve the efficiency of infrastructure investment by relying on a merit-based selection process for projects. To ensure substantial leverage of private capital, the bank would finance no more than 50 percent of the total costs of any project. It would fill in an important gap in the Nation's infrastructure funding system by focusing on projects of national or regional significance, whose effects cross over state and jurisdictional lines. Such projects are often at a disadvantage under current financing mechanisms, including state-level infrastructure banks and bonds issued by State and local governments. As a result, the National Infrastructure Bank would be a valuable complement to existing sources of funding and would improve the efficiency of U.S. infrastructure investment.

Recent and Current Federal Infrastructure Initiatives

Infrastructure investment has been an important priority throughout the Obama Administration. As discussed above, the modernization of the electricity grid is a key element of the effort to transition to a clean energy future. This subsection reviews some of the Administration's other recent and current initiatives to support infrastructure investment.

Transportation. The Recovery Act of 2009 provided over $48 billion to fund transportation infrastructure investments. In 2010, the Federal Highway Administration announced that it had finished obligating more than $26 billion of that amount for 12,000 road, highway, and bridge projects, and in June 2010, President Obama visited Columbus, Ohio, to commemorate the breaking of ground on the 10,000th such project. The Recovery Act also provided funds for investments in the Nation's air and sea transportation infrastructure, including $1.3 billion to construct new runways and improve air traffic control facilities and equipment, as well as more than $18 billion to support transit and high-speed rail. Many of these and other recently completed transportation infrastructure investments have already produced substantial economic benefits for the American people, including increased flows of traffic in congested areas, improved highway safety, expansion of public transit service into new communities, and rehabilitation and maintenance of aging infrastructure.

Despite these substantial achievements, there is still a pressing need to revitalize America's infrastructure networks. Recognizing this need, President Obama has proposed $50 billion in immediate investments in transportation infrastructure as part of the American Jobs Act. The proposal includes investments to speed up the permitting process, to make highways safer and more efficient, to repair and modernize public transit systems, to improve intercity passenger rail service and airports, to develop high-speed rail corridors, to support innovative multi-modal transportation programs, and to modernize the air traffic system by investing in the Next Generation Air Transportation System, or NextGen. The President also supports a robust renewal of surface transportation programs, now scheduled to expire on March 31, 2012, to keep existing and planned transportation projects moving forward.

Broadband. The Recovery Act provided $7.2 billion to upgrade the Nation's broadband infrastructure, including $4.7 billion for broadband infrastructure programs at the Department of Commerce's National Telecommunications and Information Administration (NTIA) and $2.5 billion for the Department of Agriculture's Rural Utilities Service (RUS) to expand broadband access in rural areas. These two programs together received more than 3,800 applications requesting more than $52 billion in support for potential projects in all 50 states and territories. When the final awards were announced in September 2010, NTIA had awarded approximately $4 billion for 233 projects throughout the country. The funds will support the construction or upgrade of approximately 120,000 miles of broadband infrastructure and will improve broadband access for approximately 24,000 community institutions, including schools, libraries, and health care facilities. In addition, RUS has awarded more than $3.5 billion in grants and loans for 320 broadband projects, which will provide broadband access for 2.8 million households and 364,000 businesses in rural areas.

As part of the National Wireless Initiative, the President has called for investment in a state-of-the-art nationwide wireless broadband network for public safety communications. Developing and deploying such a system would help enable interoperability at the national level, making first responders more effective when they are called on to cross jurisdictional lines. An interoperable network would also reduce the costs of the assorted interoperability measures now being used, ranging from swapping radios to using Internet-based gateways to patch together noninteroperable systems. Moreover, deploying a single nationwide network would realize important scale economies, eliminating duplicative operating and maintenance costs and enabling public safety entities to obtain commercially supplied devices and equipment at substantially lower cost than they can today. Finally, with clear, nationwide standards that help make public safety communication systems interoperable across jurisdictions and vendors, software and hardware developers will find it more economical to invest in innovative public safety devices and applications, further enhancing the effectiveness of first responders.

CONCLUSION

Through smart regulation, innovation, promotion of clean domestic energy, and public investment, the Federal Government helps Americans every day, improving safety and health, laying the groundwork for technological breakthroughs, and putting into place the infrastructure that facilitates commerce and travel and raises productivity. The benefits of these activities are not fully reflected in standard measures of economic activity such as GDP, but they do significantly improve the quality of life and our economy.

Jan Tinbergen (1976), the first winner of the Nobel Prize in economics, commented that, "progress in our understanding can only be based on our push for measurement of phenomena previously thought to be non-measurable." Spurred by the creation of new measurement techniques and the need to improve conventional measures of well-being, several recent official efforts have aimed at expanding the boundaries of measurement of the quality of life. As this year's *Economic Report of the President* suggests, further innovation and advances in measurement through improvements to traditional economic indicators and the development of new indicators of societal well-being will help bring about further improvements in the Nation's quality of life and the economy.

REFERENCES

Chapter 1
To Recover, Rebalance, and Rebuild

Choi, Hyunyoung, and Hal R. Varian. 2009. "Predicting the Present with Google Trends." Mountain View: Google. April.

Dynan, Karen E., and Douglas W. Elmendorf. 2001. "Do Provisional Estimates of Output Miss Economic Turning Points?" Finance and Economics Discussion Series 2011-32. Washington: Board of Governors of the Federal Reserve System. December.

Faust, Jon, John H. Rogers, and Jonathan H. Wright. 2005. "New and Noise in G-7 GDP Announcements." *Journal of Money, Credit and Banking* 37, no. 3: 403–19.

Fixler, Dennis J., Ryan Greenaway-McGrevy, and Bruce T. Grimm. 2011. "Revisions to GDP, GDI and Their Major Components." *Survey of Current Business* 91, no. 7: 9–31.

Fixler, Dennis J., and Bruce T. Grimm. 2005. "Reliability of the NIPA Estimates of U.S. Economic Activity." *Survey of Current Business* 85, no.2: 8–19.

Goldin, Claudia, and Lawrence F. Katz. 2008. *The Race Between Education and Technology.* Cambridge, MA: Belknap Press of Harvard University Press.

Groves, Robert M., 2012. "National Statistical Offices: Independent, Identical, Simultaneous Actions Thousands of Miles Apart," Director's Blog, U.S. Census Bureau. February.

Landefeld, J. Steven, Eugene P. Seskin, and Barbara M. Fraumeni. 2008. "Taking the Pulse of the Economy: Measuring GDP." *Journal of Economic Perspectives* 22, no. 2: 193–216.

McKenzie, Richard, Elena Tosetto, and Dennis Fixler. 2008. "Assessing the Efficiency of Early Release Estimates of Economic Statistics." Working Paper. Paris: Organisation for Economic Co-operation and Development.

Moore, Geoffrey H., editor. 1961. *Business Cycle Indicators, Volume II.* Princeton University Press.

Reinhart, Carmen M., and Kenneth S. Rogoff. 2009. *This Time is Different: Eight Centuries of Financial Folly.* Princeton University Press.

CHAPTER 2
THE YEAR IN REVIEW AND THE YEARS AHEAD

Abraham, Katharine G. 2010. "Accounting for Investments in Formal Education." *Survey of Current Business* 90, no. 6: 42-53.

Aguiar, Mark A., and Mark Bils. 2011. "Has Consumption Inequality Mirrored Income Inequality?" Working Paper 16807. Cambridge, MA: National Bureau of Economic Research. February.

Bernanke, Ben S. 1983. "Non-Monetary Effects of the Financial Crisis in the Propagation of the Great Depression." *American Economic Review* 73, no. 3: 257–76.

CBO (Congressional Budget Office). 2011a. "S. 1549, American Jobs Act of 2011." Cost estimate for bill as introduced. October.

______. 2011b. "The Budget and Economic Outlook: Fiscal Years 2011 to 2021." January.

______. 2011c. "The Budget and Economic Outlook: An Update." August.

CEA (Council of Economic Advisers). 2011. "The Economic Impact of the American Recovery and Reinvestment Act of 2009." Eighth Quarterly Report to Congress. December.

Corrado, Carol A. and Charles R. Hulten. 2010. "How Do You Measure a 'Technological Revolution'?" *American Economic Review* 100, no. 5: 99–104.

Corrado, Carol A., Charles R. Hulten and Daniel Sichel. 2009. "Intangible Capital and U.S. Economic Growth." *Review of Income and Wealth* 55, no. 3: 661–85.

Corner, Gary S., and Rajeev S. Bhaskar. 2010. "The Demographics of Decline in Small-Business Lending." *Central Banker* (Spring) (Federal Reserve Bank of St. Louis).

Craig, Ben R., William E. Jackson III, and James B. Thomson. 2005. "Small Firm Finance, Credit Rationing, and the Impact of SBA-Guaranteed Lending on Local Economic Growth." *Journal of Small Business Management* 45, no. 1: 116–32.

Department of the Treasury. 2011. "Treasury Analysis of Build America Bonds Issuance and Savings." May (www.treasury.gov/initiatives/recovery/Documents/BABs%20Report.pdf).

Duygan-Bump, Burcu, Alexey Levkov, and Judit Montoriol-Garriga. 2011. "Financing Constraints and Unemployment: Evidence from the Great Recession." Working Paper QAU10-6. Federal Reserve Bank of Boston.

Dynan, Karen E., Jonathan Skinner, and Stephen P. Zeldes. 2004. "Do the Rich Save More?" *Journal of Political Economy* 112, no. 2: 397–444.

Fazzari, Steven, R. Glenn Hubbard, and Bruce Petersen. 1988. "Investment, Financing Decisions, and Tax Policy." *American Economic Review* 78, no. 2: 200–05.

Gertler, Mark, and Simon Gilchrist. 1994. "Monetary Policy, Business Cycles and the Behavior of Small Manufacturing Firms." *Quarterly Journal of Economics* 109, no. 2: 309–40.

Gordon, Robert J., and Robert Krenn. 2010. "The End of the Great Depression 1939–41: Policy Contributions and Fiscal Multipliers." Working Paper 16380. Cambridge, MA: National Bureau of Economic Research. September.

Guiso, Luigi, Paola Sapienza, and Luigi Zingales. 2004. "Does Local Financial Development Matter?" *Quarterly Journal of Economics* 119, no. 3: 929–69.

Hall, Robert E. 2010. "Why Does the Economy Fall to Pieces after a Financial Crisis?" *Journal of Economic Perspectives* 24, no. 4: 3–20.

Holmstrom, Bengt, and Jean Tirole. 1997. "Financial Intermediation, Loanable Funds, and the Real Sector." *Quarterly Journal of Economics* 112, no. 3: 663–91.

Howard, Greg, Robert Martin, and Beth Anne Wilson. 2011. "Are Recoveries from Banking and Financial Crises Really So Different?" International Finance Discussion Papers D2011-19. Washington: Board of Governors of the Federal Reserve System. August.

IMF (International Monetary Fund). 2009. "From Recession to Recovery: How Soon and How Strong?" In *World Economic Outlook: April 2009*. Washington.

______. 2010. "Unemployment Dynamics during Recessions and Recoveries: Okun's Law and Beyond." In *World Economic Outlook: April 2010*. Washington.

Jacobe, Dennis. 2012. Testimony before the United States House of Representatives, Committee on Small Business. Hearing on *The Path to Job Creation: The State of American Small Business*. February 1.

Kaldor, Nicholas. 1956. "Alternative Theories of Distribution." *Review of Economic Studies* 23, no. 2: 83–100.

Kashyap, Anil K., Owen A. Lamont, and Jeremy C. Stein. 1994. "Credit Conditions and the Cyclical Behavior of Inventories." *Quarterly Journal of Economics* 109, no. 3: 565–92.

Kindleberger, Charles P. 1978. *Manias, Panics and Crashes: A History of Financial Crises*. New York: Basic Books.

King, Robert G., and Ross Levine. 1993. "Finance and Growth: Schumpeter Might Be Right." *Quarterly Journal of Economics* 108, no. 3: 717–37.

Kroszner, Randall S., Luc Laeven, and Daniela Klingebiel. 2007. "Banking Crises, Financial Dependence, and Growth." *Journal of Financial Economics* 84, no. 1: 187–228.

Krueger, Alan B. 1999. "Measuring Labor's Share." Papers and Proceedings of the One Hundred

Eleventh Annual Meeting of the American Economic Association, *American Economic Review* 89, no. 2: 45-51.

Lerner, Josh. 1999. "The Government as Venture Capitalist: The Long-Run Effects of the SBIR Program. *Journal of Business* 72, no. 3: 285–318.

Levine, Ross, and Sara Zervos. 1998. "Stock Markets, Banks, and Economic Growth." *American Economic Review* 88, no. 3: 537–58.

Macroeconomic Advisers. 2011. "American Jobs Act: A Significant Boost to GDP and

Employment." September (http://macroadvisers.blogspot.com/2011/09/american-jobs-act-significant-boost-to.html).

Masnick, George S., Daniel McCue, and Eric S. Belsky. 2010. "Updated 2010–2020 Household and New Home Demand Projections." Harvard

University Joint Center for Housing Studies. September (http://jchs. harvard.edu/sites/jchs.harvard.edu/files/w10-9_masnick_mccue_ belsky.pdf).

Moore, Geoffrey H., editor. 1961. *Business Cycle Indicators, Volume II.* Princeton University Press.

Peek, Joe, and Eric S. Rosengren. 2000. "Collateral Damage: Effects of the Japanese Bank Crisis on Real Activity in the United States." *American Economic Review* 90, no. 1: 30–45.

Petersen, Mitchell A., and Raghuram G. Rajan. 1994. "The Benefits of Lending Relationships: Evidence from Small Business Data." *Journal of Finance* 49, no. 1: 3–37.

Piketty, Thomas, and Emmanuel Saez. 2003. "Income Inequality in the United States, 1913–1998." *Quarterly Journal of Economics* 118, no. 1: 1–39.

______. 2010. Data update to "Income Inequality in the United States, 1913– 1998" (http://elsa.berkeley.edu/~saez/TabFig2008.xls).

Rajan, Raghuram G. 2010. *Fault Lines: How Hidden Fractures Still Threaten the World Economy.* Princeton University Press.

Rajan, Raghuram G., and Luigi Zingales. 1998. "Financial Dependence and Growth." *American Economic Review* 88, no. 3: 559–86.

Reich, Robert B. 2010. *Aftershock: The Next Economy and America's Future.* New York: Random House.

Reinhart, Carmen M., and Kenneth S. Rogoff. 2009. *This Time is Different: Eight Centuries of Financial Folly.* Princeton University Press.

White House. 2010. "Rebuilding the American Auto Industry." July (www. whitehouse.gov/files/documents/20100729-autos-report-final.pdf).

______. 2012. "Investing in America: Building an Economy that Lasts." January (www.whitehouse.gov/sites/default/files/investing_in_ america_report_final.pdf). January.

Woodford, Michael. 2010. "Financial Intermediation and Macroeconomic Analysis." *Journal of Economic Perspectives* 24, no. 4: 21–44.

CHAPTER 3
RESTORING FISCAL RESPONSIBILITY

Auerbach, Alan J., and William G. Gale. 2010. "Activist Fiscal Policy to Stabilize Economic Activity." *Financial Policy and Economic Stability*, 327–74. Federal Reserve Bank of Kansas City.

Burman, Leonard. 2007. "The Alternative Minimum Tax: Assault on the Middle Class." *Milken Institute Review* 12, no. 4: 12–23.

CBO (Congressional Budget Office). 2001. "The Budget and Economic Outlook: Fiscal Years 2002–2011." January.

______. 2011a. "Trends in Distribution of Household Income between 1979 and 2007." October.

______. 2011b. "The Budget and Economic Outlook: Fiscal Years 2011 to 2021." January.

Elmendorf, Douglas W., and Jeffrey Liebman. 2000. "Social Security Reform and National Saving in an Era of Budget Surpluses." *Brookings Papers on Economic Activity* 31, no. 2: 1–71. Washington: Brookings Institution.

Engen, Eric M., and R. Glenn Hubbard. 2005. "Federal Government Debt and Interest Rates." *NBER Macroeconomics Annual*, vol. 19, edited by Mark Gertler and Kenneth Rogoff, pp. 83–160. Cambridge, MA: National Bureau of Economic Research.

Gale, William G., and Peter R. Orszag. 2003. "Economic Effects of Sustained Budget Deficits." *National Tax Journal* 56, no. 3: 463–85.

Irons, John, and Josh Bivens. 2010. "Government Debt and Economic Growth." Briefing Paper 271. Washington: Economic Policy Institute. July.

OMB (Office of Management and Budget). 2012a. "Budget of the United States Government, Fiscal Year 2013."

______. 2012b. "Analytical Perspectives, Budget of the United States, Fiscal Year 2013."

Reinhart, Carmen M., and Kenneth S. Rogoff. 2010. "Growth in a Time of Debt." *American Economic Review* 100, no. 2: 573–78.

Ruffing, Kathy, and James R. Horney. 2011. "Economic Downturn and Bush Policies Continue to Drive Large Projected Deficits." Washington: Center on Budget and Policy Priorities. May.

Agarwal, Sumit, John Driscoll, and David Laibson. 2007. "Optimal Mortgage Refinancing: A Closed Form Solution." Working Paper 13487. Cambridge, MA: National Bureau of Economic Research. October.

Agarwal, Sumit, Chunlin Liu, and Nicholas Souleles. 2007. "The Reaction of Consumer Spending and Debt to Tax Rebates: Evidence from Consumer Credit Data." *Journal of Political Economy* 115, no. 6: 986–1019.

Agarwal, Sumit, et al. 2011. "The Role of Securitization in Mortgage Renegotiation." *Journal of Financial Economics* 102, no. 3: 559–78.

Bajari, Patrick, Chenghuan Chu, and Minjung Park. 2010. "An Empirical Model of Subprime Mortgage Default from 2000 to 2007." Working Paper 14625. Cambridge, MA: National Bureau of Economic Research. December.

Bhutta, Neil, Jane Dokko, and Hui Shan. 2010. "The Depth of Negative Equity and Mortgage Default Decisions." Washington: Federal Reserve Board. May.

Bracha, Anat, and Julian C. Jamison. 2011. "Shifting Confidence in Home Ownership: The Great Recession." Federal Reserve Bank of Boston. October.

Campbell, John, Stefano Giglio, and Parag Pathak. 2011. "Forced Sales and House Prices." *American Economic Review* 101, no. 5: 2108–31.

Case, Karl, John Quigley, and Robert Shiller. 2005. "Comparing Wealth Effects: The Stock Market versus the Housing Market." *Advances in Macroeconomics* 5, no. 1, article 1.

______. 2011. "Wealth Effects Revisited 1978–2009." Working Paper 16848. Cambridge, MA: National Bureau of Economic Research. March.

Department of the Treasury. 2011. "November 2011 Making Home Affordable Report" (www.treasury.gov/initiatives/financial-stability/results/MHA-Reports/Documents/FINAL_Nov%202011%20MHA%20Report.pdf).

Doms, Mark, Wendy Dunn, and Daniel Vine. 2008. "Changes in Housing Wealth and Consumption: Did the Linkage Increase in the 2000s?" Working Paper. Washington: Federal Reserve System. October.

Elul, Ronel, et al. 2010. "What 'Triggers' Mortgage Default?" Federal Reserve Bank of Philadelphia. April.

Federal Reserve Board of Governors. 2012. "The U.S. Housing Market: Current Conditions and Policy Considerations." Washington. January.

Fuster, Andreas, and Paul Willen. 2010 "$1.25 Trillion Is Still Real Money: Some Facts about the Effects of the Federal Reserve's Mortgage Market Investments." Federal Reserve Bank of Boston. August.

Gagnon, Joseph, et al. 2010. "Large-Scale Asset Purchases by the Federal Reserve: Did They Work?" Federal Reserve Bank of New York. March.

Hall, Robert. 2010. "Why Does the Economy Fall to Pieces after a Financial Crisis?" *Journal of Economic Perspectives* 24, no. 4: 3–20.

Jiang, Wen, Ashlyn Nelson, and Edwart Vytlacil, 2011. "Liar's Loan? Effects of Origination Channel and Information Falsification on Mortgage Delinquency." Columbia University. April.

Johnson, David, Jonathan Parker, and Nicholas Souleles. 2006. "Household Expenditure and the Income Tax Rebates of 2001." *American Economic Review* 96, no. 5: 1589–1610.

Molloy, Raven, and Hui Shan. 2011. "The Post-Foreclosure Experience of U.S. Households." Finance and Economics Discussion Series 2011-32. Washington: Board of Governors of the Federal Reserve System. May.

Malmendier, Ulrike, and Stefan Nagel. 2011. "Depression Babies: Do Macroeconomic Experiences Affect Risk Taking?" *Quarterly Journal of Economics* 126, no. 1: 373–416.

Melzer, Brian. 2010. "Mortgage Debt Overhang: Reduced Investment by Homeowners with Negative Equity." Northwestern University. August.

Mian, Atif, and Amir Sufi. 2010. "Household Leverage and the Recession of 2007 to 2009." Working Paper 15896. Cambridge, MA: National Bureau of Economic Research. April.

______. 2011. "What Explains High Unemployment? The Deleveraging–Aggregate Demand Hypothesis." University of California, Berkeley. October.

Mian, Atif, Kamalesh Rao, and Amir Sufi. 2011. "Household Balance Sheets, Consumption, and *the Economic Slump.*" *University of Chicago.* November.

Painter, Gary. 2010. "What Happens to Household Formation in a Recession?" Report prepared for the Mortgage Bankers Association. University of Southern California. April.

Parker, Jonathan, et al. 2011. "Consumer Spending and the Economic Stimulus Payments of 2008." Working Paper No. 16684. Cambridge, MA: National Bureau of Economic Research. January.

Pew Research Center. 2011. "Twenty-to-One: Wealth Gaps Rise to Record Highs between Whites, Blacks, and Hispanics." Washington (www. pewsocialtrends.org/2011/07/26/wealth-gaps-rise-to-record-highs-between-whites-blacks-hispanics/).

Piskorski, Tomasz, Amit Seru, and Vikrant Vig. 2010. "Securitization and Distressed Loan Renegotiation: Evidence from Subprime Mortgage Crisis." *Journal of Financial Economics* 97, no. 3: 369–97.

Poterba, James. 2000. "Stock Market Wealth and Consumption." *Journal of Economic Perspectives* 14, no. 2: 99–118.

Shiller, Robert. 2005. *Irrational Exuberance.* 2d ed. Princeton University Press. (www.econ.yale.edu/~shiller/data/Fig2-1.xls).

CHAPTER 5
INTERNATIONAL TRADE AND FINANCE

Aitken, Brian, Gordon Hanson, and Ann Harrison. 1997. "Spillovers, Foreign Direct Investment, and Export Behavior." *Journal of International Economics* 43, no. 1-2: 103–32.

Allen, Franklin, and Douglas Gale. 2000. "Financial Contagion." *Journal of Political Economy* 108, no. 1: 1–33.

Ang, Andrew, and Francis A. Longstaff. 2011. "Systemic Sovereign Credit Risk: Lessons from the U.S. and Europe." Working Paper 16982. Cambridge, MA: National Bureau of Economic Research.

Berg, Andrew, and Jeffrey Sachs. 1988. "The Debt Crisis Structural Explanations of Country Performance." *Journal of Development Economics* 29, no. 3: 271–306.

Bernard, Andrew, et al. 2003. "Plants and Productivity in International Trade." *American Economic Review* 93, no. 4: 1268–90.

Bloom, Nicholas, et al. 2011. "Does Management Matter? Evidence from India." Working Paper 16658. Cambridge, MA: National Bureau of Economic Research. January.

Brunnermeier, Markus K. 2009. "Deciphering the Liquidity and Credit Crunch 2007–2008." *Journal of Economic Perspectives* 23, no. 1: 77–100.

Department of Treasury. 2011. "Legal Entity Identifier (LEI) – Timeline of Major Events" (www.treasury.gov/press-center/press-releases/Documents/081211%20LEI%20Major%20Timeline%20of%20Events.pdf).

Eichengreen, Barry, and Ashoka Mody. 2000. "Lending Booms, Reserves and the Sustainability of Short-Term Debt: Inferences from the Pricing of Syndicated Bank Loans." *Journal of Development Economics* 63, no. 1: 5–44.

Feenstra, Robert, et al. 2010. "Report on the State of Available Data for the Study of International Trade and Investment." Working Paper 16254. Cambridge, MA: National Bureau of Economic Research.

Financial Stability Oversight Council. 2011. *Annual Report.* Washington. July.

Frankel, Jeffrey A., and Shang-Jin Wei. 2005. "Managing Macroeconomic Crises: Policy Lessons." In *Managing Macroeconomic Volatility and Crises: A Practitioner's Guide*, edited by J. Aizenman and B. Pinto. Cambridge University Press.

Hsieh, Chang-Tai, and Peter J. Klenow. 2009. "Misallocation and Manufacturing TFP in China and India." *Quarterly Journal of Economics* 124, no. 4: 1403–48.

______. 2011. "The Life Cycle of Plants in India and Mexico." Chicago Booth Research Paper 11-38. University of Chicago. September.

Hufbauer, Gary, Jeffrey Schott, and Woan Foong Wong. 2010. *Figuring Out the Doha Round.* Washington: Peterson Institute for International Economics.

International Monetary Fund. 2011. *World Economic Outlook.* Washington. September.

______. 2012. *World Economic Outlook (Update).* Washington. January (www.imf.org/external/pubs/ft/weo/2012/update/01/index.htm).

Jensen, J. Bradford. 2011. *Global Trade in Services: Fear, Facts, and Offshoring.* Washington: Peterson Institute for International Economics.

Kaminsky, Graciela L., Carmen M. Reinhart, and Carlos A. Vegh. 2003. "The Unholy Trinity of Financial Contagion." *Journal of Economic Perspectives* 17, no. 4: 51–74.

Keller, Wolfgang, and Stephen Yeaple. 2009. "Multinational Enterprises, International Trade, and Productivity Growth: Firm-Level Evidence from the United States." *Review of Economics and Statistics* 91, no. 4: 821–31.

Koncz-Bruner, Jennifer, and Anne Flatness. 2011. "U.S. International Services: Cross-Border Trade in 2010 and Services Supplied through Affiliates in 2009." Bureau of Economic Analysis, Department of Commerce. (www.bea.gov/scb/pdf/2011/10%20October/1011_services%20text.pdf).

Longstaff, Francis A., et al. 2011. "How Sovereign Is Sovereign Credit Risk?" *American Economic Journal: Macroeconomics* 3, no. 2: 75–103.

Melitz, Marc J. 2003. "The Impact of Trade on Intra-Industry Reallocations and Aggregate Industry Productivity." *Econometrica* 71, no. 6: 1695–725.

National Research Council. 1996. *River Resource Management in the Grand Canyon.* Washington: National Academies Press.

Poole, Jennifer. Forthcoming. "Knowledge Transfers from Multinationals to Domestic Firms: Evidence from Worker Mobility." *Review of Economics and Statistics.*

Reinhart, Carmen M., and Kenneth S. Rogoff. 2009. *This Time is Different: Eight Centuries of Financial Folly.* Princeton University Press.

Squam Lake Working Group on Financial Regulation. 2009. "A New Information Infrastructure for Financial Markets." Center for Geoeconomic Studies Working Paper. New York: Council on Foreign Relations.

Chapter 6
Jobs and Income: Today and Tomorrow

Aaronson, Daniel, and Bhashkar Mazumder. 2008. "Intergenerational Economic Mobility in the U.S., 1940 to 2000." *Journal of Human Resources* 43, no. 1: 139–72.

Acemoglu, Daron, and David Autor. 2011. "Skills, Tasks, and Technologies: Implications for Employment and Earnings." In *Handbook of Labor*

Economics 4B, edited by Orley Ashenfelter and David Card, pp. 1043–171. London: Elsevier.

Andrews, Dan, and Andrew Leigh. 2009. "More Inequality, Less Social Mobility." *Applied Economics Letters* 16: 1489–92.

Autor, David H., and Lawrence F. Katz. 1999. "Changes in the Wage Structure and Earnings Inequality." *Handbook of Labor Economics* 3, edited by Orley Ashenfelter and David Card, pp. 1463–555. London: Elsevier.

Autor, David H., Lawrence F. Katz, and Melissa S. Kearney. 2008. "Trends in U.S. Wage Inequality: Revising the Revisionists." *Review of Economics and Statistics* 90, no. 2: 300–23.

Card, David E., and John E. DiNardo. 2002. "Skill-Biased Technological Change and Rising Wage Inequality: Some Problems and Puzzles." *Journal of Labor Economics* 20, no. 4: 733–83.

CBO (Congressional Budget Office). 2011. "Trends in the Distribution of Household Income between 1979 and 2007." October.

CEA (Council of Economic Advisers). 1997. *Economic Report of the President.* February.

______. 2010. *Work-Life Balance and the Economics of Workplace Flexibility.* March.

______. 2011. *Making College More Affordable: Implications of New Data.* October.

College Board Advocacy and Policy Center. 2011. "Trends in College Pricing." Trends in Higher Education Series. New York.

Corak, Miles. 2011. "Inequality from Generation to Generation: The United States in Comparison" (http://milescorak.files. wordpress.com/2012/01/inequality-from-generation-to-gener-ation-the-united-states-in-comparison-v2.pdf) (forthcoming in Economics of Inequality, Poverty and Discrimination in the 21st Century, edited by Robert S. Rycroft. Santa Barbara, CA: ABC-Clio Publishers).

Davis, Steven J., R. Jason Faberman, and John Haltiwanger. 2006. "The Flow Approach to Labor Markets: New Data Sources and Micro-Macro Links." *Journal of Economic Perspectives* 20, no. 3: 3–26.

Davis, Steven J., and Till von Wachter. 2011. "Recessions and the Costs of Job Loss." *Brookings Papers on Economic Activity* 2: 1–70. Washington: Brookings Institution.

Davis, Steven J., et al. 2007. "Volatility and Dispersion in Business Growth Rates: Publicly Traded versus Privately Held Firms." *NBER Macroeconomics Annual 2006* 21: 107–80.

Dyke, Andrew, et al. 2006. "The Effects of Welfare-to-Work Program Activities on Labor Market Outcomes." *Journal of Labor Economics* 24, no. 3: 567–607.

Elsby, Michael W. L., Ryan Michaels, and Gary Solon. 2009. "The Ins and Outs of Cyclical Unemployment." *American Economic Journal: Macroeconomics* 1, no. 1: 84–110.

Friedman, Milton, and Rose D. Friedman. 1962. *Capitalism and Freedom.* University of Chicago Press.

Galinsky, Ellen, et al. 2011. "Workplace Flexibility: From Research to Action." *Future of Children: Work and Family* 21, no. 2: 141–61.

Goldin, Claudia, and Lawrence F. Katz. 2011. "The Cost of Workplace Flexibility for High-Powered Professionals." *Annals of the American Academy of Political and Social Science* 638, no. 1: 45–67.

Grusky, David B., and Erin Cumberworth. 2010. "A National Protocol for Measuring Intergenerational Mobility?" Presentation at a workshop on Advancing Social Science Theory: The Importance of Common Metrics, National Academy of Science, Washington, February 25–26.

Haltiwanger, John. 2011. "Job Creation and Firm Dynamics in the U.S." *Innovation Policy and the Economy* 12, edited by Josh Lerner and Scott Stern, ch. 2. University of Chicago Press.

Haltiwanger, J, R. Jarmin, and J. Miranda. 2010. "Who Creates Jobs? Small vs. Large vs. Young." Working Paper 16300. Cambridge, MA: National Bureau of Economic Research (forthcoming in *Review of Economics and Statistics*).

Heinrich, Carolyn J., Peter R. Mueser, and Kenneth R. Troske. 2008. "Workforce Investment Act Non-Experimental Net Impact Evaluation." Report to U.S. Department of Labor. Columbia, MD: IMPAQ International. December.

Hotz, V. Joseph, Guido W. Imbens, and Jacob A. Klerman. 2006. "Evaluating the Differential Effects of Alternative Welfare-to-Work Training Components: A Re-analysis of the California GAIN Program." *Journal of Labor Economics* 24, no. 3: 521–66.

Ichino, Andrea, Loukas Karabarounis, and Enrico Moretti. 2011. "The Political Economy of Intergenerational Income Mobility." *Economic Inquiry* 49, no. 1: 47–69.

Jäntti, Markus, et al. 2006. "American Exceptionalism in a New Light: A Comparison of Intergenerational Earnings Mobility in the Nordic Countries, the United Kingdom and the United States." IZA Discussion Paper 1938. Bonn: Institute for the Study of Labor.

Kopczuk, Wojciech, Emmanuel Saez, and Jae Song. 2010. "Earnings Inequality and Mobility in the United States: Evidence from Social Security Data since 1937." *Quarterly Journal of Economics* 125, no. 1: 91–128.

Krueger, Alan B. 2010. "Avoiding Another Lost Decade: How to Promote Job Creation." Testimony before the Joint Economic Committee, United States Congress, May 5 (http://jec.senate.gov/public/?a=Files. Serve&File_id=6f298a71-cac8-44fa-95cb-7a47fcae63ee).

______. 2012. "The Rise and Consequences of Inequality in the United States." Remarks delivered to the Center for American Progress. Washington. January 12 (www.americanprogress.org/events/2012/01/pdf/ krueger.pdf).

Lee, Chul-In, and Gary Solon. 2009. "Trends in Intergenerational Income Mobility." *Review of Economics and Statistics* 91, no. 4: 766–72.

Mazumder, Bhashkar. 2005. "Fortunate Sons: New Estimates of Intergenerational Mobility in the United States Using Social Security Earnings Data." *Review of Economics and Statistics* 87, no. 2: 235–55.

OECD (Organisation for Economic Co-operation and Development). 2010. "A Family Affair: Intergenerational Social Mobility across OECD Countries." *Economic Policy Reforms: Going for Growth 2010*, pp. 181–98. Paris.

Piketty, Thomas, and Emmanuel Saez. 2003. "Income Inequality in the United States, 1913–1998." *Quarterly Journal of Economics* 118, no. 1: 1–39.

______. 2010. Data update to "Income Inequality in the United States, 1913–1998" (http://elsa.berkeley.edu/~saez/TabFig2008.xls).

CHAPTER 7
PRESERVING AND MODERNIZING THE SAFETY NET

Aizcorbe, Ana, and Nicole Nestoriak. 2011. "Changing Mix of Medical Care Services: Stylized Facts and Implications for Price Indexes." *Journal of Health Economics* 30, no. 3: 568–74.

Aizcorbe, Ana M., Bonnie A. Retus, and Shelly Smith. 2008. "Toward a Health Care Satellite Account." *Survey of Current Business* 88, no. 5: 24–30.

Akerlof, George A. 1970. "The Market for 'Lemons': Quality Uncertainty and the Market Mechanism." *Quarterly Journal of Economics* 84, no. 3: 488–500.

Anderson, Michael L., Carlos Dobkin, and Tal Gross. 2012. "The Effect of Health Insurance Coverage on the Use of Medical Services." *American Economic Journal: Economic Policy* (forthcoming).

Auerbach, Alan, and Daniel Feenberg. 2000. "The Significance of Federal Taxes as Automatic Stabilizers." Journal of Economic Perspectives 14, no. 3: 37–56.

Baily, Martin N. 1978. "Some Aspects of Optimal Unemployment Insurance." *Journal of Public Economics* 10: 379–402.

Benartzi, Shlomo, Alessandro Previtero, and Richard H. Thaler. 2011. "Annuitization Puzzles." *Journal of Economic Perspectives* 25, no. 4: 143–64.

Black, Dan A., et al. 2003. "Is the Threat of Reemployment Services More Effective than the Services Themselves? Evidence from Random Assignment in the UI System." *American Economic Review* 93, no. 4: 1313–27.

Bradley, Ralph, et al. 2010. "Producing Disease-Based Price Indexes." *Monthly Labor Review* 133: 20–28.

Bricker, Jesse, et al. 2011. "Surveying the Aftermath of the Storm: Changes in Family Finances from 2007 to 2009." Finance and Economics Discussion Series 2011-17. Washington: Federal Reserve Board.

Buchmueller, Thomas. 2009. "Consumer-Oriented Health Care Reform Strategies: A Review of the Evidence on Managed Competition and Consumer-Directed Health Insurance." *Milbank Quarterly* 87, no. 4: 820–41.

Card, David, and Phillip B. Levine. 2000. "Extended Benefits and the Duration of UI Spells: Evidence from the New Jersey Extended Benefit Program." *Journal of Public Economics* 78, no. 1-2: 107–38.

CBO (Congressional Budget Office). 2011. "Policies for Increasing Economic Growth and Employment in 2012 and 2013." Testimony by Douglas W. Elmendorf, director. Prepared for the Committee on the Budget, United States Senate.

Cebul, Randall D., et al. 2011. "Unhealthy Insurance Markets: Search Frictions and the Cost and Quality of Health Insurance." *American Economic Review* 101, no. 5: 1842–71.

Chappel, Andre, Richard Kronick, and Sherry Glied. 2011. "The Value of Health Insurance: Few of the Uninsured Have Adequate Resources to Pay Potential Hospital Bills." ASPE Research Brief. Department of Health and Human Services. May.

Chetty, Raj. 2008. "Moral Hazard vs. Liquidity and Optimal Unemployment." *Journal of Political Economy* 116, no. 2: 173–234.

Corson, Walter, and Walter Nicholson. 1983. "An Analysis of UI Recipients' Unemployment Spells." Unemployment Insurance Occasional Paper 83-1. Department of Labor, Employment and Training Administration.

Currie, Janet, and Jonathan Gruber. 1996a. "Health Insurance Eligibility, Utilization of Medical Care, and Child Health." *Quarterly Journal of Economics* 111, no. 2: 431–66.

______. 1996b. "Saving Babies: The Efficacy and Cost of Recent Expansions of Medicaid Eligibility for Pregnant Women." *Journal of Political Economy* 104, no. 6: 1263–96.

Currie, Janet, Sandra Decker, and Wanchuan Lin. 2008. "Has Public Health Insurance for Older Children Reduced Disparities in Access to Care and Health Outcomes?" *Journal of Health Economics* 27, no. 6: 1567–81.

Dafny, Leemore, and Jonathan Gruber. 2005. "Public Insurance and Child Hospitalizations: Access and Efficiency Effects." *Journal of Public Economics* 89, no.1: 109–29.

Dahl, Molly, Thomas DeLeire, and Jonathan A. Schwabish. 2009. "Stepping Stone or Dead End? The Effect of the EITC on Earnings Growth." *National Tax Journal* 62: 329–46.

Daly, Mary, et al. 2012. "A Rising Natural Rate of Unemployment: Transitory or Permanent." *Journal of Economic Perspectives* (forthcoming).

DeCesaro, Anne, and Jeffrey Hemmeter. 2008. "Characteristics of Noninstitutionalized DI and SSI Program Participants." Note 2008-02. Social Security Administration Research and Statistics.

Eissa, Nada, and Jeffrey Liebman. 1996. "Labor Supply Response to the Earned Income Tax Credit." *Quarterly Journal of Economics* 111, no. 2: 605–37.

Evans, William N., and Craig L. Garthwaite. 2010. "Giving Mom a Break: The Impact of Higher EITC Payments on Maternal Health." Working Paper 16296. Cambridge, MA: National Bureau of Economic Research. August.

Farber, Henry S., and Robert Valletta. 2011. "Extended Unemployment Insurance and Unemployment Duration in the Great Recession: The U.S. Experience." Princeton University and Federal Reserve Bank of San Francisco. June.

Finkelstein, Amy. 2007. "The Aggregate Effects of Health Insurance: Evidence from the Introduction of Medicare." *Quarterly Journal of Economics* 122, no. 1: 1–37.

Finkelstein, Amy, and Robin McKnight. 2008. "What Did Medicare Do? The Initial Impact of Medicare on Mortality and Out-of-Pocket Medical Spending." *Journal of Public Economics* 92, no. 7: 1644–68.

Finkelstein, Amy, et al. 2011. "The Oregon Health Insurance Experiment: Evidence from the First Year." Working Paper 17190. Cambridge, MA: National Bureau of Economic Research. July.

GAO (Government Accountability Office). 2009. "401(K) Plans: Policy Changes Could Reduce the Long-Term Effects of Leakage on Workers' Retirement Savings." GAO-09-715. September.

Gabe, Thomas, and Julie M. Whittaker. 2011. "Antipoverty Effects of Unemployment Insurance." Congressional Research Service. April.

Gilmer, Todd, and Richard Kronick. 2009. "Hard Times and Health Insurance: How Many Americans Will Be Uninsured by 2010?" *Health Affairs* 28, no. 4: w573–w577.

Gruber, Jonathan. 1997. "The Consumption Smoothing Benefits of Unemployment Insurance." *American Economic Review* 87, no. 1: 192–205.

_____. 2010. "The Tax Exclusion for Employer-Sponsored Health Insurance." Working Paper 15766. Cambridge, MA: National Bureau of Economic Research. February.

Gruber, Jonathan, and Brigette C. Madrian. 2004. "Health Insurance, Labor Supply, and Job Mobility: A Critical Review of the Literature." In *Health Policy and the Uninsured*, edited by Catherine G. McLaughlin, pp. 97–178. Washington: Urban Institute Press.

Haveman, Robert, et al. 2006. "Do Newly Retired Workers in the United States Have Sufficient Resources to Maintain Well-Being?" *Economic Inquiry* 44, no. 2: 249–64.

Helman, Ruth, Craig Copeland, and Jack VanDerhei. 2011. "The 2011 Retirement Confidence Survey: Confidence Drops to Record Lows, Reflecting 'the New Normal.'" EBRI Issue Brief 355. Washington: Employee Research Institute. March.

Holahan, John, and Bowen Garrett. 2009. "Rising Unemployment, Medicaid and the Uninsured." Washington: Kaiser Family Foundation. January.

Katz, Lawrence F., and Bruce D. Meyer. 1991. "Unemployment Insurance, Recall Expectations, and Unemployment Outcomes." Working Paper 2594. Cambridge, MA: National Bureau of Economic Research. February.

Kawachi, Janette, Karen E. Smith, and Eric J. Toder. 2006. "Making Maximum Use of Tax-Deferred Retirement Accounts." Washington: Urban Institute. March.

Kroft, Kory, and Matthew J. Notowidigdo. 2011. "Should Unemployment Insurance Vary with the Unemployment Rate? Theory and Evidence." Working Paper 17173. Cambridge, MA: National Bureau of Economic Research. June.

Madrian, Brigitte and Dennis Shea. 2001. "The Power of Suggestion: Inertia in 401(k) Participation and Savings Behavior." *Quarterly Journal of Economics* 116, no. 4: 1149–87.

Meyer, Bruce D., and Dan T. Rosenbaum. 2000. "Making Single Mothers Work: Recent Tax and Welfare Policy and Its Effects." Working Paper 7491. Cambridge, MA: National Bureau of Economic Research. January.

Meyer, Bruce D., Wallace K. C. Mok, and James X. Sullivan. 2009. "The Under-Reporting of Transfers in Household Surveys: Its Nature and

Consequences." Working Paper 15181. Cambridge, MA: National Bureau of Economic Research. July.

Michaelides, Marios, and Jacob Benus. 2010. "Are Self-Employment Training Programs Effective? Evidence from Project GATE." IMPAQ International and University of Maryland–College Park for the U.S. Department of Labor.

Mitchell, Olivia S., and Stephen P. Utkus. 2002. "Company Stock and Retirement Plan Diversification." Working Paper 2002-4. Philadelphia: Pension Research Council. March.

Mortensen, Dale T. 1977. "Unemployment Insurance and Job Search Decisions." *Industrial and Labor Relations Review* 30, no. 4: 505–17.

Munnell, Alicia H., Anthony Webb, and Francesca Golub-Sass. 2009. "The National Retirement Risk Index: After the Crash." *Issue in Brief* 9-22. Chestnut Hill, MA: Center for Retirement Research at Boston College. October.

Poterba, James M., Steven F. Venti, and David A. Wise. 2011. "The Composition and Draw-Down of Wealth in Retirement." Working Paper 17536. Cambridge, MA: National Bureau of Economic Research. October.

Rodrik, Dani. 1998. "Why Do More Open Economies Have Bigger Governments?" *Journal of Political Economy* 106, no. 5: 997–1032.

Rothschild, Michael, and Joseph Stiglitz. 1976. "Equilibrium in Competitive Insurance Markets: An Essay on the Economics of Imperfect Information." *Quarterly Journal of Economics* 90, no. 4: 629–49.

Rothstein, Jesse. 2011. "Unemployment Insurance and Job Search in the Great Recession." Working Paper 17534. Cambridge, MA: National Bureau of Economic Research. October.

Rutledge, Matthew. 2011. "The Impact of Unemployment Insurance Extensions on Disability Insurance Application and Allowance Rates." Working Paper 2011-17. Chestnut Hill, MA: Center for Retirement Research at Boston College. October.

Schmieder, Johannes F., Till von Wachter, and Stefan Bender. 2012. "The Effects of Extended Unemployment Insurance over the Business Cycle: Regression Discontinuity Estimates over 20 Years." *Quarterly Journal of Economics* (forthcoming).

Schone, Barbara Steinberg, and Philip Cooper. 2001. "Assessing the Impact of Health Plan Choice." *Health Affairs* 20, no. 1: 267–75.

Toder, Eric J., Benjamin H. Harris, and Katherine Lim. 2011. "Distributional Effects of Tax Expenditures in the United States." In *Tax Expenditures: State of the Art,* edited by Lisa Philipps, Neil Brooks, and Jinyan Li. Toronto: Canadian Tax Foundation.

Webb, Anthony, and Natalia Zhivan. 2010. "How Much Is Enough? The Distribution of Lifetime Health Care Costs." Working Paper 2010-1. Chestnut Hill, MA: Center for Retirement Research at Boston College. February.

Ziliak, James P. 2011. "Recent Developments in Antipoverty Policies in the United States." Discussion Paper DP2011-01. University of Kentucky Center for Poverty Research. September.

CHAPTER 8
IMPROVING THE QUALITY OF LIFE THROUGH SMART REGULATION, INNOVATION, CLEAN ENERGY, AND PUBLIC INVESTMENT

American Society of Civil Engineers. 2009. "2009 Report Card for America's Infrastructure." (www.asce.org/PPLContent.aspx?id=2147484137).

Arnould, Richard J., and Henry Grabowski. 1981. "Auto Safety Regulation: An Analysis of Market Failure." *Bell Journal of Economics* 12, no. 1: 27–48.

Atkinson, Robert C., et al. 2011. "Broadband in America 2nd Edition: Where It Is and Where It Is Going." Columbia University, Columbia Institute for Tele-Information. May.

Auerbach, Alan J., and Yuriy Gorodnichenko. 2010. "Measuring the Output Responses to Fiscal Policy." Working Paper 16311. Cambridge, MA: National Bureau of Economic Research. August.

Becker, Randy A. 2005. "Air Pollution Abatement Costs under the Clean Air Act: Evidence from the PACE Survey." *Journal of Environmental Economics and Management* 50, no. 1: 144–69.

Bingham, Tayler H., et al. 2000. *A Benefits Assessment of Water Pollution Control Programs Since 1972: Part 1, The Benefits of Point Source Controls for Conventional Pollutants in Rivers and Streams.* Final Report. Research Triangle Park, N.C. Report for U.S. EPA, contract 68-C6-0021 prepared by RTI.

Bloom, David E., David Canning, and Jaypee Sevilla. 2004. "The Effect of Health on Economic Growth: A Production Function Approach." *World Development* 32, no. 1: 1–13.

Bloom, Nicholas, Mark Schankerman, and John van Reenen. 2010. "Identifying Technology Spillovers and Product Market Rivalry." CEP Discussion Paper 0675. Centre for Economic Performance, LSE. February.

Bloom, Nicholas, Raffaella Sadun, and John Van Reenen. 2007. "American Do I.T. Better: U.S. Multinationals and the Productivity Miracle." CEP Discussion Paper 788. London School of Economics and Political Science, Centre for Economic Performance. April.

Boroush, Mark. 2010. "NSF Releases New Statistics on Business Innovation." National Science Foundation, Directorate for Social, Behavioral, and Economic Sciences. October. (www.nsf.gov/statistics/infbrief/nsf11300/nsf11300.pdf).

Brynjolfsson, Erik, and Adam Saunders. 2010. *Wired for Innovation: How Information Technology Is Reshaping the Economy.* MIT Press.

CBO (Congressional Budget Office). 2005. "R&D and Productivity Growth: A Background Paper." June.

Cisco Systems. 2011. "Cisco Visual Networking Index: Global Mobile Data Traffic Forecast Update, 2010–2015." White paper. San Jose, CA. February.

Cohen, Daniel, and Marcelo Soto. 2007. "Growth and Human Capital: Good Data, Good Results." Paris: OECD Development Centre. December.

Currie, Janet, Michael Greenstone, and Enrico Moretti. 2011. "Superfund Cleanups and Infant Health." Working Paper 16844. Cambridge, MA: National Bureau of Economic Research.

DOE (U.S. Department of Energy). 2008. "20 Percent Wind Energy by 2030: Increasing Wind Energy's Contribution to U.S. Electricity Supply." December.

______. 2011. "SunShot: Making Solar Energy Cost Competitive Throughout the United States." June.

DOJ (Department of Justice). No date. "Fact 6: Legalization of Drugs Will Lead to Increased Use and Increased Levels of Addiction. Legalization Has Been Tried Before, and Failed Miserably." (www.justice.gov/dea/demand/speakout/06so.htm).

DOT (Department of Transportation). 2004. "Cost and Weight Added by the Federal Motor Vehicle Safety Standards for Model Years 1968-2001 in Passenger Cars and Light Trucks." National Highway Traffic Safety Administration. (http://www.nhtsa.gov/cars/rules/regrev/evaluate/pdf/809834Part1.pdf).

______. National Highway Traffic Safety Administration. 2007. "FMVSS No. 126 Electronic Stability Control Systems." Final Regulatory Impact Analysis. March.

______. National Highway Traffic Safety Administration. 2009. "Traffic Safety Facts: 2009 Data." (http://www-nrd.nhtsa.dot.gov/Pubs/811390.PDF).

Edwards, Owen. 2006. "Inventive Abe." *Smithsonian Magazine* (October).

EIA (U.S. Energy Information Administration). 1993. "Drilling Sideways—A Review of Horizontal Well Technology and Its Domestic Application." April.

______. 2012. *Annual Energy Outlook 2010 Early Release.* January.

EPA (Environmental Protection Agency). 2011a. "Policy Assessment for the Review of the Particulate Matter National Ambient Air Quality Standards." (www.epa.gov/ttn/naaqs/standards/pm/data/20110419pmpafinal.pdf).

______. 2011b. "The Benefits and Costs of the Clean Air Act from 1990 to 2020." Final Report. Office of Air and Radiation. March.

______. 2011c. "Beneficial Effects of the Superfund Program." March. (www.epa.gov/superfund/accomp/pdfs/SFBenefits-031011-Ver1.pdf).

FCC (Federal Communications Commission). 2010. *Connecting America: The National Broadband Plan.* (http://download.broadband.gov/plan/national-broadband-plan.pdf).

FTC (Federal Trade Commission). 2003. "To Promote Innovation: The Proper Balance of Competition and Patent Law and Policy." October.

Fuchs, Victor R. 1998. *Who Shall Live?* New York: Basic.

______. 2010. "New Priorities for Future Biomedical Innovations." *New England Journal of Medicine* 363, no. 8: 704–06

Gallaher, M. P., C. L. Morgan, and R. J. Shadbegian. 2008. "Redesign of the 2005 Pollution Abatement Costs and Expenditure Survey." *Journal of Economic and Social Measurement* 33, no. 4: 1–50.

Gayer, Ted. 2011. "A Better Approach to Environmental Regulation: Getting the Costs and Benefits Right." Discussion Paper 2011-06. Washington: The Hamilton Project. May.

Gramlich, Edward M. 1994. "Infrastructure Investment: A Review Essay." *Journal of Economic Literature* 32, no. 3: 1176–96.

Gray, Wayne B., and Ronald J. Shadbegian. 2005. "Assessing Multi-Dimensional Performance: Environmental and Economic Outcomes." Working Paper Series. U. S. Census Bureau, Center for Economic Studies. May.

Grossman, Gene M., and Alan B. Krueger. 1995. "Economic Growth and the Environment." *Quarterly Journal of Economics* 110, no. 2: 353–77.

Grossman, Gene M., and Elhanan Helpman. 1991. *Innovation and Growth in the Global Economy*. MIT Press.

Hall, Bronwyn H. 2002. "The Financing of Research and Development." Working Paper 8773. Cambridge, MA: National Bureau of Economic Research. February.

Hall, Bronwyn H., Adam Jaffe, and Manuel Trajtenberg. 2001. "Market Value and Patent Citations: A First Look." May. (www.card.iastate.edu/research/stp/papers/hall-jaffe-trajtenberg.pdf).

Hall, Bronwyn H., Jacques Mairesse, and Pierre Mohnen. 2009. "Measuring the Returns to R&D." Working Paper 15622. Cambridge, MA: National Bureau of Economic Research. December.

Hall, Bronwyn H. and Rosemarie Ham Ziedonis. 2001. "The Patent Paradox Revisited: An Empirical Study of Patenting in the U.S. Semiconductor industry, 1979–1995." *RAND Journal of Economics* 32, no. 1: 101–28.

Harrington, Winston, Richard D. Morgenstern, and Peter Nelson. 1999. "On the Accuracy of Regulatory Cost Estimates." Discussion Paper 99-18. Washington: Resources for the Future. January.

Hunt, Robert, and James Bessen. 2004. "The Software Patent Experiment." *Q3 2004 Business Review*. Federal Reserve Bank of Philadelphia.

Jones, Charles I., and John C. Williams. 1998. "Too Much of a Good Thing? The Economics of Investment in R&D." *Journal of Economic Growth* 5, no. 1: 65–85.

Jorgenson, Dale W., Mun S. Ho, and Kevin J. Stiroh. 2008. "A Retrospective Look at the U.S. Productivity Growth Resurgence." *Journal of Economic Perspectives* 22, no. 1: 3–24.

Kahane, Charles J. 2004. "Lives Saved by the Federal Motor Vehicle Safety Standards and Other Vehicle Safety Technologies, 1960–2002." DOT HS 809 833. Department of Transportation. October.

Kahneman, Daniel, et al. 2004. "A Survey Method for Characterizing Daily Life Experience: The Day Reconstruction Method." *Science* 306, no. 5702: 1776–80.

Levinson, Arik. 1999. "An Industry-Adjusted Index of State Environmental Compliance Costs." Working Paper 7297. Cambridge, MA: National Bureau for Economic Research.

Litan, Robert E., Lesa Mitchell, and E. J. Reedy. 2007. "Commercializing University Innovations: Alternative Approaches." *Innovation Policy and the Economy*, vol. 8, edited by Adam B. Jaffe, Josh Lerner, and Scott Stern, pp. 31–57. University of Chicago Press for the National Bureau of Economic Research.

Lovei, Magda. 1998. "Phasing Out Lead From Gasoline: Worldwide Experience and Policy Implications." Technical Paper 297. Washington: World Bank.

Mannering, Fred, and Clifford Winston. 1995. "Automobile Air Bags in the 1990s: Market Failure or Market Efficiency?" *Journal of Law and Economics* 38, no. 2: 265–79.

Munnel, Alicia Haydock. 1992. "Infrastructure Investment and Economic Growth." *Journal of Economic Perspectives* 6, no. 4: 189–98.

Murphy, Kevin M., and Robert H. Topel. 2006. "The Value of Health and Longevity." *Journal of Political Economy* 114, no. 5: 871–904.

Musto, David F. 1999. *The American Disease: Origins of Narcotic Control.* New York: Oxford University Press.

Nordhaus, William D. 2004. "Schumpeterian Profits in the American Economy: Theory and Measurement." Working Paper 10433. Cambridge, MA: National Bureau of Economic Research. April.

NRC (National Research Council). 1999. *Nature's Numbers: Expanding the National Economic Accounts to Include the Environment.* Washington: National Academies Press.

______. 2004. A Patent System for the 21st Century. Washington: National Academies Press.

______. 2005. *Beyond the Market: Designing Nonmarket Accounts for the United States.* Washington: National Academies Press.

NSF (National Science Foundation). 2010. "Science and Engineering Indicators 2010." NSB 10-01. Arlington, VA.

______. 2012. "Industry, Technology, and the Global Marketplace" in *Science and Engineering Indicators 2012*. January. (www.nsf.gov/statistics/seind12/pdf/c06.pdf).

Randall, Blanchard. 2001. "The U.S. Drug Approval Process: A Primer." Congressional Research Service. July.

Robert M. Solow. 1957. "Technical Change and the Aggregate Production Function." *Review of Economics and Statistics* 39, no. 3: 312–20.

Roller, Lars-Hendrik, and Leonard Waverman. 2001. "Telecommunications Infrastructure and Economic Development: A Simultaneous Approach." *American Economic Review* 91, no. 4: 909–23.

Ross, Martin T., et al. 2004. "PACE Survey: Background, Applications, and Data Quality Issues." NCEE Working Paper 200409. National Center for Environmental Economics, U.S. Environmental Protection Agency. July.

Schrank, David, Tim Lomax, and Bill Eisele. 2011. *Urban Mobility Report*. Texas Transportation Institute. September. (http://tti.tamu.edu/documents/mobility-report-2011.pdf).

Schwartz, Joel. 1994. "Societal Benefits of Reducing Lead Exposure." *Environmental Research* 66, no. 1: 105–24.

Schwartz, Joel et al. 1985. *Costs and Benefits of Reducing Lead in Gasoline: Final Regulatory Impact Analysis*. Environmental Protection Agency. February.

Shadbegian, Ronald J., and Wayne B. Gray. 2005. "Assessing Multi-Dimensional Performance: Environmental and Economic Outcomes." Working Paper 05-03. Center for Economic Studies, U.S. Census Bureau.

Shapiro, Carl. 2008. "Patent Reform: Aligning Reward and Contribution." In *Innovation Policy and the Economy*, vol. 8, edited by Adam B. Jaffe, Josh Lerner, and Scott Stern, pp. 111–56. University of Chicago Press for the National Bureau of Economic Research.

Stutzer, Alois, and Bruno S. Frey. 2004. "Stress that Doesn't Pay: The Commuting Paradox." IZA Discussion Paper 1278. Bonn: Institute for the Study of Labor. August.

Solow, Robert M. 1957. "Technical Change and the Aggregate Production Function." *Review of Economics and Statistics* 39, no. 3: 312–20.

Tinbergen, Jan. 1976. "The Demand-Supply Theory of Incomes Tested by 1970 Census Figures." *Review of Income and Wealth* 22, no. 2: 199–202.

U.S. Census Bureau. 2011. Annual Capital Expenditures Survey.

U.S. Department of Transportation, Research and Innovative Technology Administration, Bureau of Transportation Statistics. 2011. *Transportation Statistics Annual Report 2010.* Washington, DC.

U.S. Department of the Treasury. 2011. "Investing in U.S. Competitiveness: The Benefits of Enhancing the Research and Experimentation (R&E) Tax Credit." A Report from the Office of Tax Policy. March 25.

______. 2011. "Treasury Analysis of Build America Bonds Issuance and Savings." May 16.

U.S. Department of the Treasury with the President's Council of Economic Advisers. 2010. "An Economic Analysis of Infrastructure Investment." October 11.

Viscusi, W. Kip, and Ted Gayer. 2002. "Safety at Any Price?" *Regulation* 25, no. 3: 54–63.

Weaver, C. S. 1999. *Implementer's Guide to Phasing Out Lead in Gasoline.* Environmental Protection Agency, Office of International Activities.

White House. 2011. "Blueprint for a Secure Energy Future." March 30. (www.whitehouse.gov/sites/default/files/blueprint_secure_energy_future.pdf).

Williams. Heidi L. 2010. "Intellectual Property Rights and Innovation: Evidence from the Human Genome." Working Paper 16212. National Bureau of Economic Research. July.

World Bank. 1992. *World Development Report 1992.* New York: Oxford University Press.

REPORT TO THE PRESIDENT ON THE ACTIVITIES OF THE COUNCIL OF ECONOMIC ADVISERS DURING 2011

COUNCIL OF ECONOMIC ADVISERS
Washington, D.C., December 31, 2011

MR. PRESIDENT:

The Council of Economic Advisers submits this report on its activities during calendar year 2011 in accordance with the requirements of the Congress, as set forth in section 10(d) of the Employment Act of 1946 as amended by the Full Employment and Balanced Growth Act of 1978.

Sincerely,

Alan B. Krueger, *Chairman*
Katharine G. Abraham, *Member*
Carl Shapiro, *Member*

Name	Position	Oath of office date	Separation date
Edwin G. Nourse	Chairman	August 9, 1946	November 1, 1949
Leon H. Keyserling	Vice Chairman	August 9, 1946	
	Acting Chairman	November 2, 1949	
	Chairman	May 10, 1950	January 20, 1953
John D. Clark	Member	August 9, 1946	
	Vice Chairman	May 10, 1950	February 11, 1953
Roy Blough	Member	June 29, 1950	August 20, 1952
Robert C. Turner	Member	September 8, 1952	January 20, 1953
Arthur F. Burns	Chairman	March 19, 1953	December 1, 1956
Neil H. Jacoby	Member	September 15, 1953	February 9, 1955
Walter W. Stewart	Member	December 2, 1953	April 29, 1955
Raymond J. Saulnier	Member	April 4, 1955	
	Chairman	December 3, 1956	January 20, 1961
Joseph S. Davis	Member	May 2, 1955	October 31, 1958
Paul W. McCracken	Member	December 3, 1956	January 31, 1959
Karl Brandt	Member	November 1, 1958	January 20, 1961
Henry C. Wallich	Member	May 7, 1959	January 20, 1961
Walter W. Heller	Chairman	January 29, 1961	November 15, 1964
James Tobin	Member	January 29, 1961	July 31, 1962
Kermit Gordon	Member	January 29, 1961	December 27, 1962
Gardner Ackley	Member	August 3, 1962	
	Chairman	November 16, 1964	February 15, 1968
John P. Lewis	Member	May 17, 1963	August 31, 1964
Otto Eckstein	Member	September 2, 1964	February 1, 1966
Arthur M. Okun	Member	November 16, 1964	
	Chairman	February 15, 1968	January 20, 1969
James S. Duesenberry	Member	February 2, 1966	June 30, 1968
Merton J. Peck	Member	February 15, 1968	January 20, 1969
Warren L. Smith	Member	July 1, 1968	January 20, 1969
Paul W. McCracken	Chairman	February 4, 1969	December 31, 1971
Hendrik S. Houthakker	Member	February 4, 1969	July 15, 1971
Herbert Stein	Member	February 4, 1969	
	Chairman	January 1, 1972	August 31, 1974
Ezra Solomon	Member	September 9, 1971	March 26, 1973
Marina v.N. Whitman	Member	March 13, 1972	August 15, 1973
Gary L. Seevers	Member	July 23, 1973	April 15, 1975
William J. Fellner	Member	October 31, 1973	February 25, 1975
Alan Greenspan	Chairman	September 4, 1974	January 20, 1977
Paul W. MacAvoy	Member	June 13, 1975	November 15, 1976
Burton G. Malkiel	Member	July 22, 1975	January 20, 1977
Charles L. Schultze	Chairman	January 22, 1977	January 20, 1981
William D. Nordhaus	Member	March 18, 1977	February 4, 1979
Lyle E. Gramley	Member	March 18, 1977	May 27, 1980
George C. Eads	Member	June 6, 1979	January 20, 1981
Stephen M. Goldfeld	Member	August 20, 1980	January 20, 1981

Council Members and Their Dates of Service

Name	Position	Oath of office date	Separation date
Murray L. Weidenbaum	Chairman	February 27, 1981	August 25, 1982
William A. Niskanen	Member	June 12, 1981	March 30, 1985
Jerry L. Jordan	Member	July 14, 1981	July 31, 1982
Martin Feldstein	Chairman	October 14, 1982	July 10, 1984
William Poole	Member	December 10, 1982	January 20, 1985
Beryl W. Sprinkel	Chairman	April 18, 1985	January 20, 1989
Thomas Gale Moore	Member	July 1, 1985	May 1, 1989
Michael L. Mussa	Member	August 18, 1986	September 19, 1988
Michael J. Boskin	Chairman	February 2, 1989	January 12, 1993
John B. Taylor	Member	June 9, 1989	August 2, 1991
Richard L. Schmalensee	Member	October 3, 1989	June 21, 1991
David F. Bradford	Member	November 13, 1991	January 20, 1993
Paul Wonnacott	Member	November 13, 1991	January 20, 1993
Laura D'Andrea Tyson	Chair	February 5, 1993	April 22, 1995
Alan S. Blinder	Member	July 27, 1993	June 26, 1994
Joseph E. Stiglitz	Member	July 27, 1993	
	Chairman	June 28, 1995	February 10, 1997
Martin N. Baily	Member	June 30, 1995	August 30, 1996
Alicia H. Munnell	Member	January 29, 1996	August 1, 1997
Janet L. Yellen	Chair	February 18, 1997	August 3, 1999
Jeffrey A. Frankel	Member	April 23, 1997	March 2, 1999
Rebecca M. Blank	Member	October 22, 1998	July 9, 1999
Martin N. Baily	Chairman	August 12, 1999	January 19, 2001
Robert Z. Lawrence	Member	August 12, 1999	January 12, 2001
Kathryn L. Shaw	Member	May 31, 2000	January 19, 2001
R. Glenn Hubbard	Chairman	May 11, 2001	February 28, 2003
Mark B. McClellan	Member	July 25, 2001	November 13, 2002
Randall S. Kroszner	Member	November 30, 2001	July 1, 2003
N. Gregory Mankiw	Chairman	May 29, 2003	February 18, 2005
Kristin J. Forbes	Member	November 21, 2003	June 3, 2005
Harvey S. Rosen	Member	November 21, 2003	
	Chairman	February 23, 2005	June 10, 2005
Ben S. Bernanke	Chairman	June 21, 2005	January 31, 2006
Katherine Baicker	Member	November 18, 2005	July 11, 2007
Matthew J. Slaughter	Member	November 18, 2005	March 1, 2007
Edward P. Lazear	Chairman	February 27, 2006	January 20, 2009
Donald B. Marron	Member	July 17, 2008	January 20, 2009
Christina D. Romer	Chair	January 29, 2009	September 3, 2010
Austan D. Goolsbee	Member	March 11, 2009	
	Chairman	September 10, 2010	August 5, 2011
Cecilia Elena Rouse	Member	March 11, 2009	February 28, 2011
Katharine G. Abraham	Member	April 19, 2011	
Carl Shapiro	Member	April 19, 2011	
Alan B. Krueger	Chairman	November 7, 2011	

Report to the President on the Activities of the Council of Economic Advisers During 2011

The Council of Economic Advisers was established by the Employment Act of 1946 to provide the President with objective economic analysis and advice on the development and implementation of a wide range of domestic and international economic policy issues. The Council is comprised of a Chairman and two members appointed by the President and confirmed by the United States Senate.

The Chairman of the Council

Alan B. Krueger was nominated as Chairman of the Council by the President on August 29, 2011. He was confirmed by the Senate on November 3, 2011. Chairman Krueger is on leave of absence from Princeton University, where he is the Bendheim Professor of Economics and Public Affairs. He previously served as the Assistant Secretary for Economic Policy and Chief Economist at the U.S Department of the Treasury.

The Chairman is a member of the President's Cabinet and is responsible for communicating the Council's views on economic matters directly to the President through personal discussions and written reports. Chairman Krueger represents the Council at Presidential economic briefings, daily White House senior staff meetings, budget meetings, Cabinet meetings, a variety of inter-agency meetings, and other formal and informal meetings with the President, the Vice President, and other senior government officials. He also meets frequently with members of Congress well as with business, academic and labor leaders to discuss economic policy issues.

Austan D. Goolsbee resigned as Chairman on August 5, 2011 to return to the University of Chicago, where he is the Robert P. Gwinn Professor of Economics at the Booth School of Business.

The Members of the Council

Katharine G. Abraham was confirmed by the U.S. Senate as a Member of the Council on April 14, 2011. Dr. Abraham is on a leave of absence from the University of Maryland, where she is a faculty associate in the Maryland Population Research Center and a professor in the Joint Program in Survey Methodology. Dr. Abraham served as the Commissioner of the Bureau of Labor Statistics from 1993 to 2001.

Carl Shapiro was confirmed by the U.S. Senate as a Member of the Council on April 14, 2011. Dr. Shapiro is on leave from the University of California at Berkeley, where he is the Transamerica Professor of Business Strategy at the Haas School of Business and Professor of Economics in the Department of Economics. Dr. Shapiro served from 2009 to 2011 as Deputy Assistant Attorney General for Economics at the Antitrust Division of the United States Department of Justice.

Cecilia E. Rouse resigned as Member of the Council on February 28 to return to Princeton University, where she is the Lawrence and Shirley Katzman and Lewis and Anna Ernst Professor in the Economics of Education and Professor of Economics and Public Affairs.

Areas of Activities

A central function of the Council is to advise the President on all economic issues and developments. In the past year, as with the two prior years, advising the President on targeted policies to spur job creation and evaluating the effects of the policies on the economy have been a priority.

The Council works closely with various government agencies, including the National Economic Council, the Office of Management and Budget, White House senior staff, and other officials and engages in discussions on numerous policy matters. In the area of international economic policy, the Council coordinates with other units of the White House, the Treasury Department, the State Department, the Commerce Department, and the Federal Reserve on matters related to the global financial system.

Among the specific economic policy areas that received attention in 2011 were: housing policies, including foreclosure mitigation and prevention and refinancing; implementation of the Affordable Care Act; income inequality; individual and corporate taxation; college affordability; small business lending; regional development; intellectual property and innovation; infrastructure investment; regulatory measures; trade policies; unemployment insurance; job training; and policies to promote the international competitiveness of American manufacturing companies. The Council also worked on several issues related to the quality of the data available for assessing economic conditions.

The Council prepares for the President, the Vice President, and the White House senior staff a daily economic briefing memo analyzing current economic developments, and almost-daily memos on key economic data releases. Chairman Krueger has also been preparing monthly briefings on the state of the economy.

The Council, the Department of Treasury, and the Office of Management and Budget—the Administration's economic "troika"—are responsible for producing the economic forecasts that underlie the Administration's budget proposals. The Council initiates the forecasting process twice each year, consulting with a wide variety of outside sources, including leading private sector forecasters and other government agencies.

The Council was an active participant in the trade policy process, participating in the Trade Policy Staff Committee and the Trade Policy Review Group. The Council provided analysis and opinions on a range of trade-related issues involving the enforcement of existing trade agreements, reviews of current U.S. trade policies, and consideration of future policies. The Council also participated on the Trade Promotion Coordinating Committee, helping to examine the ways in which exports may support economic growth in the years to come. In the area of investment and security, the Council participated on the Committee on Foreign Investment in the United States (CFIUS), reviewing individual cases before the committee.

Council Members and staff regularly met with economists, policy officials, and government officials from other countries to discuss issues relating to the global economy. The Council's role also included policy development and planning for the G-20 Summit in Los Cabos, Mexico, and the G-8 Summit in Chicago.

The Council is a leading participant in the Organisation for Economic Co-operation and Development (OECD), an important forum for economic cooperation among high-income industrial economies. The Council coordinated and oversaw the OECD's review of the U.S. economy. Dr. Krueger is chairman of the OECD's Economic Policy Committee, and Council members and staff participate actively in working-party meetings on macroeconomic policy and coordination and contribute to the OECD's research agenda.

The Council issued a series of reports in 2011. Quarterly reports to Congress on the effects of the Recovery Act on overall economic activity were issued in March, July, and December. In June, the Council released a report on U.S. Inbound Foreign Direct Investment. The Council was also the primary contributor to White House reports released on educational technology in September and two more reports related to education in October—one on the effect the American Jobs Act would have on teaching jobs and another on college affordability. In November, the Council led the preparation of a White House report on the economic benefits of infrastructure. In December, the Council was the primary contributor to a White House report issued on the effects of temporary unemployment insurance extensions on the U.S. economy.

The Council continued its efforts to improve the public's understanding of economic developments and of the Administration's economic policies through briefings with the economic and financial press, speeches, discussions with outside economists, presentations to outside organizations, and regular updates on major data releases on the CEA blog. The Chairman and Members also regularly met to exchange views on the economy with the Chairman and Members of the Board of Governors of the Federal Reserve System.

Public Information

The Council's annual *Economic Report of the President* is an important vehicle for presenting the Administration's domestic and international economic policies. It is available for purchase through the Government Printing Office, and is viewable on the Internet at www.gpo.gov/erp.

The Council prepared numerous reports in 2011, and the Chairman and Members gave numerous public speeches. The reports, texts of speeches, and written statements accompanying testimony are available at the Council's website, www.whitehouse.gov/cea. Finally, the Council publishes the monthly *Economic Indicators*, which is available on-line at www.gpo.gov/economicindicators.

The Staff of the Council of Economic Advisers

The staff of the Council consists of the senior staff, senior economists, staff economists, research economists, research assistants, and the administrative and support staff. The staff at the end of 2011 was:

Senior Staff

David P. Vandivier. . . . . Chief of Staff

Judith K. Hellerstein . . . . Chief Economist

Steven N. Braun . . . . Director of Macroeconomic
Forecasting

Adrienne Pilot . . . . Director of Statistical Office

Senior Economists

Gene Amromin .... Housing, Public Finance

Lee G. Branstetter .... International Trade and Investment, Innovation, and Manufacturing

Thomas C. Buchmueller .... Health

Lisa D. Cook .... International Finance, Entrepreneurship, Innovation and Development

Benjamin H. Harris .... Tax, Budget and Retirement

Robert Johansson .... Energy, Environment, Agriculture, Regulation

Craig T. Peters .... Industrial Organization, Infrastructure, Innovation, Regulation

Charles R. Pierret .... Labor and Education

Daniel J. Vine .... Macroeconomics

Staff Economists

Jeffrey A. Borowitz .... Housing, Labor, Education

Andres Bustamante .... International Finance, Development, Entrepreneurship

Colleen M. Carey .... Health, Industrial Organization, Public Finance

David Cho .... Macroeconomics

Judd N. L. Cramer .... Labor and Immigration

Reid B. Stevens .... Energy, Environment, Regulation

Research Economists

Pedro Spivakovsky-Gonzalez ...... International Economics and Trade

Julia H. Yoo .... Public Finance, Housing, Macroeconomics

Research Assistants

Matthew L. Aks .... Macroeconomics

Sandra M. Levy .... Energy, Environment, Regulation

Carter Mundell .... Education, Labor, Health

Seth H. Werfel .... International Finance and Innovation

Statistical Office

The Statistical Office gathers, administers, and produces statistical information for the Council. Duties include preparing the statistical appendix to the *Economic Report of the President* and the monthly publication *Economic Indicators*. The staff also creates background materials for economic analysis and verifies statistical content in Presidential memoranda. The Office serves as the Council's liaison to the statistical community.

Brian A. Amorosi . . . . Statistical Analyst

Lindsay M. Kuberka . . . . Statistical Analyst

Ms. Kuberka is on detail from the Census Bureau.

Administrative Office

The Administrative Office provides general support for the Council's activities. This includes financial management, ethics compliance, human resource management, travel, operations of facilities, security, information technology, and telecommunications management support.

Archana A. Snyder . . . . Director of Finance and
Administration

Doris T. Searles . . . . Information Management Specialist

Office of the Chairman

Andres Bustamante . . . . Special Assistant to the Chairman
and Staff Economist

Paige Shevlin . . . . Special Assistant to the Chairman

Michael P. Bourgeois . . . . Special Assistant to the Members

Staff Support

Sharon K. Thomas . . . . Administrative Support and
Executive Assistant to the Chief
Economist, Senior Economists

Interns

Student interns provide invaluable help with research projects, day-to-day operations, and fact-checking. Interns during the year were: Noam Angrist, Dan Aloisio, David Bard, Obafemi Elegbede, Rahul Garabadu, Jeanne Jeong, Juliette Lu, Suril Kantaria, Sarah McGhee, Jeremy Patashnik, Benjamin Pyle, Clare Quinn, Sid Shankar, Daniel Seder, Alex T. Stein, Elizabeth Sundheim, and Lucas Zucker.

Departures in 2011

Jay C. Shambaugh left his position as Chief Economist of the Council in June, and he is presently on faculty at Georgetown University's McDonough School of Business. In October, Nan Gibson left her position as Executive Director and Adam Hitchcock left his position as Chief of Staff in August.

The senior economists who resigned in 2011(with the institutions to which they returned after leaving the Council in parentheses) were: Chad Bown (World Bank); Aaron Chatterji (Duke Fuqua School of Business); Thomas Davidoff (Sauder School of Business, UBC); Benjamin F. Jones (Northwestern University, Kellogg School); Lisa Kahn (Yale School of Management); Arik Levinson (Georgetown University); Helen Levy (University of Michigan School of Public Health); Matthew Magura (Department of Justice); Nicholas Mastronardi (US Air Force Academy); and Paul Smith (Federal Reserve Board).

The staff economists who departed in 2011 were Douglas Campbell, Hoan Soo Lee, Sayeh Nikpay, James O'Brien, Jamin Speer, and Owen Zidar. Those who served as research assistants at the Council and resigned were Ravi Deedwania, Nicholas Hagerty, and Kia McLeod.

Brittany Heyd, Meryl Holt, Eric Lesser, and Matthew Tully all served in the Office of the Chairman and resigned in 2011 to pursue other endeavors.

Several long-term staff members departed as well. Dagmara Mocala Mathews left her position as Program Analyst after almost 10 dedicated years of service in the Statistical Office. There were two retirements at the Council in 2011. They are Rosemary M. Rogers, who served as the Administrative Officer and Lisa D. Branch who served as Executive Assistant to the Members. Mrs. Rogers devoted 30 years to working in the Executive Branch, with almost 20 of those years at the Council. Ms. Branch devoted 34 years to working in the Executive Branch, with 25 of those years at the Council. Their dedication, loyalty and diligence in serving the Council, Chairs, Members, staff and the people of the United States will be missed tremendously.

STATISTICAL TABLES RELATING TO INCOME, EMPLOYMENT, AND PRODUCTION

C O N T E N T S

AGRICULTURE—*Continued*

INTERNATIONAL STATISTICS

General Notes

Detail in these tables may not add to totals because of rounding.

Because of the formula used for calculating real gross domestic product (GDP), the chained (2005) dollar estimates for the detailed components do not add to the chained-dollar value of GDP or to any intermediate aggregate. The Department of Commerce (Bureau of Economic Analysis) no longer publishes chained-dollar estimates prior to 1995, except for selected series.

Unless otherwise noted, all dollar figures are in current dollars.

Symbols used:
p Preliminary.
... Not available (also, not applicable).

Data in these tables reflect revisions made by the source agencies through January 27, 2012. In particular, tables containing national income and product accounts (NIPA) estimates reflect revisions released by the Department of Commerce in July 2011.

TABLE B–1. Gross domestic product, 1963–2011

[Billions of dollars, except as noted; quarterly data at seasonally adjusted annual rates]

Year or quarter	Gross domestic product	Personal consumption expenditures			Gross private domestic investment						
		Total	Goods	Services	Total	Fixed investment					Change in private inventories
						Total	Nonresidential			Residential	
							Total	Structures	Equipment and software		
1963	617.8	382.7	198.2	184.6	93.8	88.1	56.0	21.2	34.8	32.1	5.6
1964	663.6	411.5	212.3	199.2	102.1	97.2	63.0	23.7	39.2	34.3	4.8
1965	719.1	443.8	229.7	214.1	118.2	109.0	74.8	28.3	46.5	34.2	9.2
1966	787.7	480.9	249.6	231.3	131.3	117.7	85.4	31.3	54.0	32.3	13.6
1967	832.4	507.8	259.0	248.8	128.6	118.7	86.4	31.5	54.9	32.4	9.9
1968	909.8	558.0	284.6	273.4	141.2	132.1	93.4	33.6	59.9	38.7	9.1
1969	984.4	605.1	304.7	300.4	156.4	147.3	104.7	37.7	67.0	42.6	9.2
1970	1,038.3	648.3	318.8	329.5	152.4	150.4	109.0	40.3	68.7	41.4	2.0
1971	1,126.8	701.6	342.1	359.5	178.2	169.9	114.1	42.7	71.5	55.8	8.3
1972	1,237.9	770.2	373.8	396.4	207.6	198.5	128.8	47.2	81.7	69.7	9.1
1973	1,382.3	852.0	416.6	435.4	244.5	228.6	153.3	55.0	98.3	75.3	15.9
1974	1,499.5	932.9	451.5	481.4	249.4	235.4	169.5	61.2	108.2	66.0	14.0
1975	1,637.7	1,033.8	491.3	542.5	230.2	236.5	173.7	61.4	112.4	62.7	–6.3
1976	1,824.6	1,151.3	546.3	604.9	292.0	274.8	192.4	65.9	126.4	82.5	17.1
1977	2,030.1	1,277.8	600.4	677.4	361.3	339.0	228.7	74.6	154.1	110.3	22.3
1978	2,293.8	1,427.6	663.6	764.1	438.0	412.2	280.6	93.6	187.0	131.6	25.8
1979	2,562.2	1,591.2	737.9	853.2	492.9	474.9	333.9	117.7	216.2	141.0	18.0
1980	2,788.1	1,755.8	799.8	956.0	479.3	485.6	362.4	136.2	226.2	123.2	–6.3
1981	3,126.8	1,939.5	869.4	1,070.1	572.4	542.6	420.0	167.3	252.7	122.6	29.8
1982	3,253.2	2,075.5	899.3	1,176.2	517.2	532.1	426.5	177.6	248.9	105.7	–14.9
1983	3,534.6	2,288.6	973.8	1,314.8	564.3	570.1	417.2	154.3	262.9	152.9	–5.8
1984	3,930.9	2,501.1	1,063.7	1,437.4	735.6	670.2	489.6	177.4	312.2	180.6	65.4
1985	4,217.5	2,717.6	1,137.6	1,580.0	736.2	714.4	526.2	194.5	331.7	188.2	21.8
1986	4,460.1	2,896.7	1,195.6	1,701.1	746.5	739.9	519.8	176.5	343.3	220.1	6.6
1987	4,736.4	3,097.0	1,256.3	1,840.7	785.0	757.8	524.1	174.2	349.9	233.7	27.1
1988	5,100.4	3,350.1	1,337.3	2,012.7	821.6	803.1	563.8	182.8	381.0	239.3	18.5
1989	5,482.1	3,594.5	1,423.8	2,170.7	874.9	847.3	607.7	193.7	414.0	239.5	27.7
1990	5,800.5	3,835.5	1,491.3	2,344.2	861.0	846.4	622.4	202.9	419.5	224.0	14.5
1991	5,992.1	3,980.1	1,497.4	2,482.6	802.9	803.3	598.2	183.6	414.6	205.1	–.4
1992	6,342.3	4,236.9	1,563.3	2,673.6	864.8	848.5	612.1	172.6	439.6	236.3	16.3
1993	6,667.4	4,483.6	1,642.3	2,841.2	953.3	932.5	666.6	177.2	489.4	266.0	20.8
1994	7,085.2	4,750.8	1,746.6	3,004.3	1,097.3	1,033.5	731.4	186.8	544.6	302.1	63.8
1995	7,414.7	4,987.3	1,815.5	3,171.7	1,144.0	1,112.9	810.0	207.3	602.8	302.9	31.2
1996	7,838.5	5,273.6	1,917.7	3,355.9	1,240.2	1,209.4	875.4	224.6	650.8	334.1	30.8
1997	8,332.4	5,570.6	2,006.8	3,563.9	1,388.7	1,317.7	968.6	250.3	718.3	349.1	71.0
1998	8,793.5	5,918.5	2,110.0	3,808.5	1,510.8	1,447.1	1,061.1	275.1	786.0	385.9	63.7
1999	9,353.5	6,342.8	2,290.0	4,052.8	1,641.5	1,580.7	1,154.9	283.9	871.0	425.8	60.8
2000	9,951.5	6,830.4	2,459.1	4,371.2	1,772.2	1,717.7	1,268.7	318.1	950.5	449.0	54.5
2001	10,286.2	7,148.8	2,534.0	4,614.8	1,661.9	1,700.2	1,227.8	329.7	898.1	472.4	–38.3
2002	10,642.3	7,439.2	2,610.0	4,829.2	1,647.0	1,634.9	1,125.4	282.8	842.7	509.5	12.0
2003	11,142.2	7,804.1	2,728.0	5,076.1	1,729.7	1,713.3	1,135.7	281.9	853.8	577.6	16.4
2004	11,853.3	8,270.6	2,892.1	5,378.5	1,968.6	1,903.6	1,223.0	306.7	916.4	680.6	64.9
2005	12,623.0	8,803.5	3,076.7	5,726.8	2,172.3	2,122.3	1,347.3	351.8	995.6	775.0	50.0
2006	13,377.2	9,301.0	3,224.7	6,076.3	2,327.1	2,267.2	1,505.3	433.7	1,071.7	761.9	60.0
2007	14,028.7	9,772.3	3,363.9	6,408.3	2,295.2	2,266.1	1,637.5	524.9	1,112.6	628.7	29.1
2008	14,291.5	10,035.5	3,381.7	6,653.8	2,087.6	2,128.7	1,656.3	586.3	1,070.0	472.4	–41.1
2009	13,939.0	9,866.1	3,197.5	6,668.7	1,546.8	1,707.6	1,353.0	449.9	903.0	354.7	–160.8
2010	14,526.5	10,245.5	3,387.0	6,858.5	1,795.1	1,728.2	1,390.1	374.4	1,015.7	338.1	66.9
2011 *p*	15,087.7	10,722.6	3,645.2	7,077.4	1,913.6	1,866.4	1,529.2	407.8	1,121.4	337.2	47.2
2008: I	14,273.9	10,018.5	3,422.3	6,596.2	2,185.7	2,205.2	1,689.3	570.9	1,118.4	515.9	–19.5
II	14,415.5	10,126.5	3,466.9	6,659.6	2,165.4	2,183.7	1,689.0	589.6	1,099.4	494.6	–18.3
III	14,395.1	10,135.8	3,456.1	6,679.7	2,086.3	2,130.5	1,665.9	594.7	1,071.2	464.6	–44.1
IV	14,081.7	9,861.3	3,181.4	6,679.9	1,913.0	1,995.5	1,580.9	590.0	990.9	414.6	–82.5
2009: I	13,893.7	9,781.7	3,130.7	6,651.0	1,620.1	1,799.6	1,430.6	527.4	903.2	369.0	–179.5
II	13,854.1	9,781.6	3,143.6	6,638.0	1,493.8	1,694.3	1,351.9	461.4	890.5	342.4	–200.5
III	13,920.5	9,911.1	3,245.6	6,665.5	1,481.2	1,678.3	1,324.3	424.8	899.5	353.9	–197.1
IV	14,087.4	9,990.0	3,270.0	6,720.1	1,592.2	1,658.3	1,305.1	386.1	918.9	353.2	–66.1
2010: I	14,277.9	10,103.7	3,338.1	6,765.6	1,702.3	1,658.0	1,318.7	361.2	957.5	339.3	44.3
II	14,467.8	10,184.8	3,340.1	6,844.7	1,809.7	1,731.6	1,377.1	370.2	1,006.9	354.5	78.1
III	14,605.5	10,276.6	3,386.5	6,890.1	1,850.5	1,743.8	1,416.5	376.6	1,039.9	327.3	106.7
IV	14,755.0	10,417.1	3,483.4	6,933.7	1,818.0	1,779.3	1,447.9	389.6	1,058.3	331.3	38.7
2011: I	14,867.8	10,571.7	3,592.2	6,979.4	1,853.1	1,791.1	1,460.5	379.5	1,081.0	330.6	62.0
II	15,012.8	10,676.0	3,622.7	7,053.3	1,895.3	1,841.7	1,506.0	405.2	1,100.8	335.7	53.6
III	15,176.1	10,784.5	3,661.2	7,123.2	1,906.6	1,905.8	1,568.7	424.8	1,143.9	337.0	.8
IV *p*	15,294.3	10,858.1	3,704.5	7,153.6	1,999.7	1,927.1	1,581.5	421.7	1,159.9	345.6	72.6

See next page for continuation of table.

[Billions of dollars, except as noted; quarterly data at seasonally adjusted annual rates]

Year or quarter	Net exports of goods and services			Government consumption expenditures and gross investment					Final sales of domestic product	Gross domestic purchases [1]	Addendum: Gross national product [2]	Percent change from preceding period	
	Net exports	Exports	Imports	Total	Federal			State and local				Gross domestic product	Gross domestic purchases [1]
					Total	National defense	Non-defense						
1963	4.9	31.1	26.1	136.4	76.9	61.0	15.9	59.5	612.1	612.8	622.2	5.5	5.4
1964	6.9	35.0	28.1	143.2	78.4	60.2	18.2	64.8	658.8	656.7	668.6	7.4	7.2
1965	5.6	37.1	31.5	151.4	80.4	60.6	19.8	71.0	709.9	713.5	724.4	8.4	8.6
1966	3.9	40.9	37.1	171.6	92.4	71.7	20.8	79.2	774.1	783.8	792.8	9.5	9.9
1967	3.6	43.5	39.9	192.5	104.6	83.4	21.2	87.9	822.6	828.9	837.8	5.7	5.7
1968	1.4	47.9	46.6	209.3	111.3	89.2	22.0	98.0	900.8	908.5	915.9	9.3	9.6
1969	1.4	51.9	50.5	221.4	113.3	89.5	23.8	108.2	975.3	983.0	990.5	8.2	8.2
1970	4.0	59.7	55.8	233.7	113.4	87.6	25.8	120.3	1,036.3	1,034.4	1,044.7	5.5	5.2
1971	.6	63.0	62.3	246.4	113.6	84.6	29.1	132.8	1,118.6	1,126.2	1,134.4	8.5	8.9
1972	−3.4	70.8	74.2	263.4	119.6	86.9	32.7	143.8	1,228.8	1,241.3	1,246.4	9.9	10.2
1973	4.1	95.3	91.2	281.7	122.5	88.1	34.3	159.2	1,366.4	1,378.2	1,394.9	11.7	11.0
1974	−.8	126.7	127.5	317.9	134.5	95.6	39.0	183.4	1,485.5	1,500.3	1,515.0	8.5	8.9
1975	16.0	138.7	122.7	357.7	149.0	103.9	45.1	208.7	1,644.0	1,621.7	1,650.7	9.2	8.1
1976	−1.6	149.5	151.1	383.0	159.7	111.1	48.6	223.3	1,807.5	1,826.2	1,841.4	11.4	12.6
1977	−23.1	159.4	182.4	414.1	175.4	120.9	54.5	238.7	2,007.8	2,053.2	2,050.4	11.3	12.4
1978	−25.4	186.9	212.3	453.6	190.9	130.5	60.4	262.7	2,268.0	2,319.1	2,315.3	13.0	13.0
1979	−22.5	230.1	252.7	500.7	210.6	145.2	65.4	290.2	2,544.2	2,584.8	2,594.2	11.7	11.5
1980	−13.1	280.8	293.8	566.1	243.7	168.0	75.8	322.4	2,794.5	2,801.2	2,822.3	8.8	8.4
1981	−12.5	305.2	317.8	627.5	280.2	196.2	83.9	347.3	3,097.0	3,139.4	3,159.8	12.1	12.1
1982	−20.0	283.2	303.2	680.4	310.8	225.9	84.9	369.7	3,268.1	3,273.2	3,289.7	4.0	4.3
1983	−51.7	277.0	328.6	733.4	342.9	250.6	92.3	390.5	3,540.4	3,586.3	3,571.7	8.7	9.6
1984	−102.7	302.4	405.1	796.9	374.3	281.5	92.7	422.6	3,865.5	4,033.6	3,967.2	11.2	12.5
1985	−115.2	302.0	417.2	878.9	412.8	311.2	101.6	466.1	4,195.6	4,332.7	4,244.0	7.3	7.4
1986	−132.5	320.3	452.9	949.3	438.4	330.8	107.6	510.9	4,453.5	4,592.6	4,477.7	5.8	6.0
1987	−145.0	363.8	508.7	999.4	459.5	350.0	109.6	539.9	4,709.2	4,881.3	4,754.0	6.2	6.3
1988	−110.1	443.9	554.0	1,038.9	461.6	354.7	106.8	577.3	5,081.9	5,210.5	5,123.8	7.7	6.7
1989	−87.9	503.1	591.0	1,100.6	481.4	362.1	119.3	619.2	5,454.5	5,570.0	5,508.1	7.5	6.9
1990	−77.6	552.1	629.7	1,181.7	507.5	373.9	133.6	674.2	5,786.0	5,878.1	5,835.0	5.8	5.5
1991	−27.0	596.6	623.5	1,236.1	526.6	383.1	143.4	709.5	5,992.5	6,019.1	6,022.0	3.3	2.4
1992	−32.8	635.0	667.8	1,273.5	532.9	376.8	156.1	740.6	6,326.0	6,375.1	6,371.4	5.8	5.9
1993	−64.4	655.6	720.0	1,294.8	525.0	363.0	162.0	769.8	6,646.5	6,731.7	6,698.5	5.1	5.6
1994	−92.7	720.7	813.4	1,329.8	518.6	353.8	164.8	811.2	7,021.4	7,177.9	7,109.2	6.3	6.6
1995	−90.7	811.9	902.6	1,374.0	518.8	348.8	170.0	855.3	7,383.5	7,505.3	7,444.3	4.7	4.6
1996	−96.3	867.7	964.0	1,421.0	527.0	354.8	172.2	894.0	7,807.7	7,934.8	7,870.1	5.7	5.7
1997	−101.4	954.4	1,055.8	1,474.4	531.0	349.8	181.1	943.5	8,261.4	8,433.7	8,355.8	6.3	6.3
1998	−161.8	953.9	1,115.7	1,526.1	531.0	346.1	184.9	995.0	8,729.8	8,955.3	8,810.8	5.5	6.2
1999	−262.1	989.3	1,251.4	1,631.3	554.9	361.1	193.8	1,076.3	9,292.7	9,615.6	9,381.3	6.4	7.4
2000	−382.1	1,093.2	1,475.3	1,731.0	576.1	371.0	205.0	1,154.9	9,896.9	10,333.5	9,989.2	6.4	7.5
2001	−371.0	1,027.7	1,398.7	1,846.4	611.7	393.0	218.7	1,234.7	10,324.5	10,657.2	10,338.1	3.4	3.1
2002	−427.2	1,003.0	1,430.2	1,983.3	680.6	437.7	242.9	1,302.7	10,630.3	11,069.5	10,691.4	3.5	3.9
2003	−504.1	1,041.0	1,545.1	2,112.6	756.5	497.9	258.5	1,356.1	11,125.8	11,646.3	11,210.9	4.7	5.2
2004	−618.7	1,180.2	1,798.9	2,232.8	824.6	550.8	273.9	1,408.2	11,788.3	12,471.9	11,944.5	6.4	7.1
2005	−722.7	1,305.1	2,027.8	2,369.9	876.3	589.0	287.3	1,493.6	12,573.0	13,345.7	12,720.1	6.5	7.0
2006	−769.3	1,471.0	2,240.3	2,518.4	931.7	624.9	306.8	1,586.7	13,317.3	14,146.5	13,449.6	6.0	6.0
2007	−713.1	1,661.7	2,374.8	2,674.2	976.3	662.3	314.0	1,697.9	13,999.6	14,741.7	14,151.9	4.9	4.2
2008	−709.7	1,846.8	2,556.5	2,878.1	1,080.1	737.8	342.3	1,798.0	14,332.7	15,001.3	14,460.7	1.9	1.8
2009	−391.5	1,583.0	1,974.6	2,917.5	1,142.7	774.9	367.8	1,774.8	14,099.8	14,330.5	14,091.2	−2.5	−4.5
2010	−516.9	1,839.8	2,356.7	3,002.8	1,222.8	819.2	403.6	1,780.0	14,459.6	15,043.4	14,715.9	4.2	5.0
2011 *p*	−578.2	2,087.6	2,665.8	3,029.7	1,232.7	824.8	407.9	1,797.0	15,040.5	15,665.9	....	3.9	4.1
2008: I	−742.3	1,819.3	2,561.6	2,812.0	1,042.7	706.0	336.7	1,769.3	14,293.4	15,016.2	14,452.5	.6	1.9
II	−746.1	1,922.8	2,668.9	2,869.6	1,066.0	724.7	341.3	1,803.7	14,433.8	15,161.5	14,596.8	4.0	3.9
III	−756.9	1,933.8	2,690.6	2,929.8	1,100.6	758.4	342.1	1,829.2	14,439.2	15,151.9	14,594.0	−.6	−.3
IV	−593.7	1,711.1	2,304.8	2,901.1	1,111.2	762.1	349.0	1,789.9	14,164.2	14,675.4	14,199.5	−8.4	−12.0
2009: I	−383.5	1,522.2	1,905.7	2,875.5	1,105.3	747.7	357.7	1,770.1	14,073.3	14,277.3	14,026.4	−5.2	−10.4
II	−338.3	1,520.8	1,859.1	2,916.9	1,137.2	771.6	365.7	1,779.7	14,054.6	14,192.4	13,994.4	−1.1	−2.4
III	−406.7	1,590.3	1,997.0	2,935.0	1,157.7	789.0	368.6	1,777.3	14,117.6	14,327.2	14,084.2	1.9	3.9
IV	−437.6	1,699.0	2,136.5	2,942.7	1,170.6	791.4	379.2	1,772.1	14,153.5	14,525.0	14,259.8	4.9	5.6
2010: I	−495.8	1,749.5	2,245.3	2,967.7	1,195.2	803.5	391.6	1,772.6	14,233.6	14,773.7	14,447.4	5.5	7.0
II	−531.2	1,813.8	2,345.0	3,004.6	1,224.5	818.0	406.5	1,780.1	14,389.8	14,999.0	14,664.0	5.4	6.2
III	−540.3	1,860.6	2,400.9	3,018.7	1,237.5	831.3	406.2	1,781.2	14,498.8	15,145.8	14,812.8	3.9	4.0
IV	−500.2	1,935.3	2,435.5	3,020.2	1,234.3	823.9	410.3	1,786.0	14,716.3	15,255.2	14,939.4	4.2	2.9
2011: I	−571.3	2,024.1	2,595.4	3,014.4	1,219.9	809.0	410.9	1,794.4	14,805.8	15,439.1	15,094.9	3.1	4.9
II	−597.1	2,085.3	2,682.4	3,038.6	1,237.1	830.6	406.5	1,801.5	14,959.2	15,609.9	15,274.0	4.0	4.5
III	−562.3	2,119.2	2,681.6	3,047.3	1,248.9	844.0	404.9	1,798.5	15,175.3	15,738.4	15,443.4	4.4	3.3
IV *p*	−582.1	2,121.6	2,703.6	3,018.6	1,225.0	815.6	409.4	1,793.7	15,221.7	15,876.3	....	3.2	3.6

[1] Gross domestic product (GDP) less exports of goods and services plus imports of goods and services.

[2] GDP plus net income receipts from rest of the world.

Source: Department of Commerce (Bureau of Economic Analysis).

Table B-2. Real gross domestic product, 1963–2011

[Billions of chained (2005) dollars, except as noted; quarterly data at seasonally adjusted annual rates]

Year or quarter	Gross domestic product	Personal consumption expenditures			Gross private domestic investment							
		Total	Goods	Services	Total	Fixed investment						Change in private inventories
						Total	Nonresidential			Residential		
							Total	Structures	Equipment and software			
1963	3,204.0	1,989.0	....	....	353.0	....	....	....	....	....	....	....
1964	3,389.4	2,107.5	....	....	382.1	....	....	....	....	....	....	....
1965	3,607.0	2,240.8	....	....	435.7	....	....	....	....	....	....	....
1966	3,842.1	2,367.9	....	....	474.1	....	....	....	....	....	....	....
1967	3,939.2	2,438.8	....	....	452.4	....	....	....	....	....	....	....
1968	4,129.9	2,579.6	....	....	478.7	....	....	....	....	....	....	....
1969	4,258.2	2,676.2	....	....	506.6	....	....	....	....	....	....	....
1970	4,266.3	2,738.9	....	....	473.4	....	....	....	....	....	....	....
1971	4,409.5	2,843.3	....	....	527.3	....	....	....	....	....	....	....
1972	4,643.8	3,018.1	....	....	589.8	....	....	....	....	....	....	....
1973	4,912.8	3,167.7	....	....	658.9	....	....	....	....	....	....	....
1974	4,885.7	3,141.4	....	....	610.3	....	....	....	....	....	....	....
1975	4,875.4	3,212.6	....	....	502.2	....	....	....	....	....	....	....
1976	5,136.9	3,391.5	....	....	603.7	....	....	....	....	....	....	....
1977	5,373.1	3,534.3	....	....	694.9	....	....	....	....	....	....	....
1978	5,672.8	3,690.1	....	....	778.7	....	....	....	....	....	....	....
1979	5,850.1	3,777.8	....	....	803.5	....	....	....	....	....	....	....
1980	5,834.0	3,764.5	....	....	715.2	....	....	....	....	....	....	....
1981	5,982.1	3,821.6	....	....	779.6	....	....	....	....	....	....	....
1982	5,865.9	3,874.9	....	....	670.3	....	....	....	....	....	....	....
1983	6,130.9	4,096.4	....	....	732.8	....	....	....	....	....	....	....
1984	6,571.5	4,313.6	....	....	948.7	....	....	....	....	....	....	....
1985	6,843.4	4,538.3	....	....	939.8	....	....	....	....	....	....	....
1986	7,080.5	4,722.4	....	....	933.5	....	....	....	....	....	....	....
1987	7,307.0	4,868.0	....	....	962.2	....	....	....	....	....	....	....
1988	7,607.4	5,064.3	....	....	984.9	....	....	....	....	....	....	....
1989	7,879.2	5,207.5	....	....	1,024.4	....	....	....	....	....	....	....
1990	8,027.1	5,313.7	....	....	989.9	....	....	....	....	....	....	....
1991	8,008.3	5,321.7	....	....	909.4	....	....	....	....	....	....	....
1992	8,280.0	5,503.2	....	....	983.1	....	....	....	....	....	....	....
1993	8,516.2	5,698.6	....	....	1,070.9	....	....	....	....	....	....	....
1994	8,863.1	5,916.2	....	....	1,216.4	....	....	....	....	....	....	....
1995	9,086.0	6,076.2	1,896.0	4,208.5	1,254.3	1,231.2	787.9	342.0	489.4	456.1	32.1
1996	9,425.8	6,288.3	1,980.9	4,331.7	1,365.3	1,341.6	861.5	361.4	541.4	492.5	31.2
1997	9,845.9	6,520.4	2,075.3	4,465.3	1,535.2	1,465.4	965.5	387.9	615.9	501.8	77.4
1998	10,274.7	6,862.3	2,215.5	4,662.1	1,688.9	1,624.4	1,081.4	407.7	705.2	540.4	71.6
1999	10,770.7	7,237.6	2,392.0	4,853.1	1,837.6	1,775.5	1,194.3	408.2	805.0	574.2	68.5
2000	11,216.4	7,604.6	2,518.2	5,093.6	1,963.1	1,906.8	1,311.3	440.0	889.2	580.0	60.2
2001	11,337.5	7,810.3	2,597.3	5,219.1	1,825.2	1,870.7	1,274.8	433.3	860.6	583.3	−41.8
2002	11,543.1	8,018.3	2,702.9	5,318.5	1,800.4	1,791.5	1,173.7	356.6	824.2	613.8	12.8
2003	11,836.4	8,244.5	2,827.2	5,418.2	1,870.1	1,854.7	1,189.6	343.0	850.0	664.3	17.3
2004	12,246.9	8,515.8	2,953.3	5,562.7	2,058.2	1,992.5	1,263.0	346.7	917.3	729.5	66.3
2005	12,623.0	8,803.5	3,076.7	5,726.8	2,172.3	2,122.3	1,347.3	351.8	995.6	775.0	50.0
2006	12,958.5	9,054.5	3,178.9	5,875.6	2,231.8	2,172.7	1,455.5	384.0	1,071.1	718.2	59.4
2007	13,206.4	9,262.9	3,273.5	5,990.2	2,159.5	2,130.6	1,550.0	438.2	1,106.8	584.2	27.7
2008	13,161.9	9,211.7	3,192.9	6,017.0	1,939.8	1,978.6	1,537.6	466.4	1,059.4	444.4	−36.3
2009	12,703.1	9,037.5	3,098.0	5,935.5	1,454.2	1,606.3	1,263.2	367.3	889.7	345.6	−144.9
2010	13,088.0	9,220.9	3,230.7	5,991.8	1,714.9	1,648.4	1,319.2	309.1	1,019.4	330.8	58.8
2011 ^p	13,313.4	9,421.1	3,351.9	6,075.4	1,795.2	1,757.8	1,432.4	321.8	1,124.1	326.2	35.6
2008: I	13,266.8	9,289.1	3,249.0	6,039.7	2,055.7	2,066.4	1,589.1	463.8	1,117.2	481.3	−12.5
II	13,310.5	9,285.8	3,252.7	6,032.9	2,024.0	2,039.1	1,580.0	474.4	1,094.6	462.8	−14.2
III	13,186.9	9,196.0	3,187.9	6,006.5	1,934.7	1,973.5	1,539.2	469.9	1,056.8	437.8	−38.1
IV	12,883.5	9,076.0	3,082.0	5,988.8	1,744.6	1,835.4	1,442.3	457.5	969.0	395.8	−80.3
2009: I	12,663.2	9,040.9	3,082.6	5,953.5	1,490.4	1,665.5	1,312.9	415.3	883.7	354.9	−161.6
II	12,641.3	8,998.5	3,064.3	5,928.6	1,397.2	1,589.8	1,257.6	375.4	874.2	334.3	−183.0
III	12,694.5	9,050.3	3,120.7	5,926.8	1,407.3	1,592.6	1,247.0	354.9	888.0	348.2	−178.7
IV	12,813.5	9,060.2	3,124.6	5,932.9	1,522.0	1,577.5	1,235.2	323.7	912.9	344.8	−56.5
2010: I	12,937.7	9,121.2	3,173.3	5,947.4	1,630.0	1,582.0	1,253.3	301.5	958.8	330.8	39.9
II	13,058.5	9,186.9	3,202.9	5,984.3	1,728.3	1,654.0	1,308.0	306.9	1,010.1	348.2	64.6
III	13,139.6	9,247.1	3,240.8	6,008.1	1,766.8	1,663.5	1,343.6	310.1	1,044.1	321.1	92.3
IV	13,216.1	9,328.4	3,306.0	6,027.5	1,734.5	1,693.9	1,371.9	318.0	1,064.5	323.1	38.3
2011: I	13,227.9	9,376.7	3,344.4	6,039.1	1,750.9	1,699.0	1,378.9	305.9	1,086.9	321.1	49.1
II	13,271.8	9,392.7	3,331.2	6,067.0	1,778.4	1,736.7	1,413.2	321.9	1,103.5	324.4	39.1
III	13,331.6	9,433.5	3,342.7	6,096.1	1,784.2	1,790.4	1,465.6	332.9	1,145.7	325.4	−2.0
IV ^p	13,422.4	9,481.3	3,389.2	6,099.4	1,867.4	1,805.0	1,471.9	326.7	1,160.3	333.9	56.0

See next page for continuation of table.

[Billions of chained (2005) dollars, except as noted; quarterly data at seasonally adjusted annual rates]

Year or quarter	Net exports of goods and services			Government consumption expenditures and gross investment					Final sales of domestic product	Gross domestic purchases [1]	Addendum: Gross national product [2]	Percent change from preceding period	
	Net exports	Exports	Imports	Total	Federal			State and local				Gross domestic product	Gross domestic purchases [1]
					Total	National defense	Non-defense						
1963	....	111.4	130.0	996.1	....	....	....	....	3,199.9	3,246.0	3,230.1	4.4	4.2
1964	....	124.5	136.9	1,018.0	....	....	....	....	3,390.8	3,423.4	3,417.5	5.8	5.5
1965	....	128.0	151.5	1,048.7	....	....	....	....	3,587.6	3,656.1	3,636.4	6.4	6.8
1966	....	136.9	174.0	1,141.1	....	....	....	....	3,803.4	3,907.0	3,869.8	6.5	6.9
1967	....	140.0	186.7	1,228.7	....	....	....	....	3,920.0	4,014.8	3,967.7	2.5	2.8
1968	....	151.0	214.5	1,267.2	....	....	....	....	4,115.8	4,222.1	4,160.6	4.8	5.2
1969	....	158.3	226.7	1,264.3	....	....	....	....	4,245.0	4,355.0	4,288.0	3.1	3.1
1970	....	175.3	236.4	1,233.7	....	....	....	....	4,284.3	4,348.3	4,295.8	.2	–.2
1971	....	178.3	249.0	1,206.9	....	....	....	....	4,403.6	4,503.1	4,442.2	3.4	3.6
1972	....	191.7	277.0	1,198.1	....	....	....	....	4,636.7	4,751.8	4,678.9	5.3	5.5
1973	....	227.8	289.9	1,193.9	....	....	....	....	4,884.0	4,987.0	4,960.3	5.8	5.0
1974	....	245.8	283.3	1,224.0	....	....	....	....	4,870.0	4,922.1	4,939.8	–.6	–1.3
1975	....	244.3	251.8	1,251.6	....	....	....	....	4,922.1	4,867.9	4,917.2	–.2	–1.1
1976	....	255.0	301.1	1,257.2	....	....	....	....	5,115.9	5,184.8	5,186.8	5.4	6.5
1977	....	261.1	334.0	1,271.0	....	....	....	....	5,340.3	5,459.8	5,429.1	4.6	5.3
1978	....	288.6	362.9	1,308.4	....	....	....	....	5,634.9	5,758.4	5,728.4	5.6	5.5
1979	....	317.2	369.0	1,332.8	....	....	....	....	5,836.2	5,898.3	5,925.2	3.1	2.4
1980	....	351.4	344.5	1,358.8	....	....	....	....	5,873.6	5,784.8	5,908.3	–.3	–1.9
1981	....	355.7	353.5	1,371.2	....	....	....	....	5,954.4	5,939.7	6,047.3	2.5	2.7
1982	....	328.5	349.1	1,395.3	....	....	....	....	5,918.2	5,860.4	5,934.0	–1.9	–1.3
1983	....	320.1	393.1	1,446.3	....	....	....	....	6,167.6	6,203.1	6,197.1	4.5	5.8
1984	....	346.2	488.8	1,494.9	....	....	....	....	6,490.0	6,739.7	6,634.1	7.2	8.7
1985	....	356.7	520.5	1,599.0	....	....	....	....	6,833.1	7,039.4	6,888.0	4.1	4.4
1986	....	384.1	565.0	1,696.2	....	....	....	....	7,092.7	7,297.2	7,110.4	3.5	3.7
1987	....	425.4	598.4	1,737.1	....	....	....	....	7,289.9	7,512.1	7,335.9	3.2	2.9
1988	....	493.5	621.9	1,758.9	....	....	....	....	7,601.3	7,752.2	7,643.9	4.1	3.2
1989	....	550.2	649.3	1,806.8	....	....	....	....	7,860.8	7,984.2	7,917.3	3.6	3.0
1990	....	599.7	672.6	1,864.0	....	....	....	....	8,025.8	8,097.8	8,075.0	1.9	1.4
1991	....	639.5	671.6	1,884.4	....	....	....	....	8,027.9	8,027.8	8,048.8	–.2	–.9
1992	....	683.5	718.7	1,893.2	....	....	....	....	8,277.2	8,302.7	8,319.4	3.4	3.4
1993	....	705.9	780.8	1,878.2	....	....	....	....	8,508.0	8,585.7	8,556.0	2.9	3.4
1994	....	767.4	873.9	1,878.0	....	....	....	....	8,801.7	8,968.5	8,893.0	4.1	4.5
1995	–98.8	845.1	943.9	1,888.9	704.1	476.8	227.5	1,183.6	9,065.4	9,181.3	9,121.7	2.5	2.4
1996	–110.7	915.3	1,026.0	1,907.9	696.0	470.4	225.7	1,211.1	9,404.4	9,534.0	9,463.1	3.7	3.8
1997	–139.8	1,024.3	1,164.1	1,943.8	689.1	457.2	231.9	1,254.3	9,774.2	9,984.4	9,873.4	4.5	4.7
1998	–252.5	1,047.7	1,300.2	1,985.0	681.4	447.5	233.7	1,303.8	10,208.3	10,531.1	10,295.3	4.4	5.5
1999	–356.4	1,093.4	1,449.9	2,056.1	694.6	455.8	238.7	1,361.8	10,706.5	11,131.8	10,802.9	4.8	5.7
2000	–451.3	1,187.4	1,638.7	2,097.8	698.1	453.5	244.4	1,400.1	11,158.0	11,671.6	11,259.2	4.1	4.8
2001	–471.8	1,120.8	1,592.6	2,178.3	726.5	470.7	255.5	1,452.3	11,382.0	11,815.8	11,395.0	1.1	1.2
2002	–548.5	1,098.3	1,646.8	2,279.6	779.5	505.3	273.9	1,500.6	11,533.6	12,097.5	11,597.1	1.8	2.4
2003	–603.7	1,116.0	1,719.7	2,330.5	831.1	549.2	281.7	1,499.7	11,820.5	12,444.7	11,909.9	2.5	2.9
2004	–687.9	1,222.5	1,910.4	2,362.0	865.0	580.4	284.6	1,497.1	12,181.3	12,935.5	12,341.6	3.5	3.9
2005	–722.7	1,305.1	2,027.8	2,369.9	876.3	589.0	287.3	1,493.6	12,573.0	13,345.7	12,720.1	3.1	3.2
2006	–729.4	1,422.1	2,151.5	2,402.1	894.9	598.4	296.6	1,507.2	12,899.3	13,688.1	13,028.3	2.7	2.6
2007	–648.8	1,554.4	2,203.2	2,434.2	906.1	611.8	294.2	1,528.1	13,177.5	13,855.3	13,322.0	1.9	1.2
2008	–494.8	1,649.3	2,144.0	2,497.4	971.1	657.7	313.3	1,528.1	13,200.5	13,653.1	13,316.9	–.3	–1.5
2009	–358.8	1,494.0	1,852.8	2,539.6	1,029.5	695.6	333.8	1,514.2	12,852.7	13,051.6	12,843.2	–3.5	–4.4
2010	–421.8	1,663.2	2,085.0	2,556.8	1,075.9	718.3	357.7	1,487.0	13,028.9	13,500.4	13,261.0	3.0	3.4
2011 [p]	–412.3	1,776.3	2,188.7	2,502.0	1,054.7	701.4	353.3	1,453.4	13,281.8	13,717.2	....	1.7	1.6
2008: I	–550.2	1,643.9	2,194.1	2,473.9	943.8	634.7	309.1	1,530.9	13,277.8	13,818.0	13,431.7	–1.8	–2.1
II	–486.2	1,693.9	2,180.1	2,484.5	955.1	643.1	312.1	1,530.5	13,325.9	13,794.5	13,476.6	1.3	–.7
III	–464.6	1,678.7	2,143.2	2,510.7	982.0	669.7	312.0	1,530.8	13,225.6	13,646.5	13,367.4	–3.7	–4.2
IV	–478.0	1,580.6	2,058.6	2,520.5	1,003.5	683.2	320.2	1,520.1	12,972.9	13,353.3	12,991.9	–8.9	–8.3
2009: I	–404.2	1,451.1	1,855.3	2,509.6	995.2	669.9	325.3	1,517.2	12,836.0	13,057.0	12,785.6	–6.7	–8.6
II	–331.8	1,449.4	1,781.2	2,546.0	1,029.2	695.7	333.4	1,520.7	12,830.0	12,964.0	12,770.7	–.7	–2.8
III	–352.4	1,497.3	1,849.7	2,554.2	1,043.9	709.5	334.3	1,514.9	12,875.1	13,035.7	12,844.9	1.7	2.2
IV	–346.9	1,578.3	1,925.2	2,548.5	1,049.6	707.3	342.2	1,503.9	12,869.5	13,149.6	12,971.6	3.8	3.5
2010: I	–376.8	1,606.2	1,983.0	2,540.6	1,056.9	708.2	348.7	1,489.2	12,895.9	13,304.1	13,092.9	3.9	4.8
II	–437.4	1,645.0	2,082.4	2,564.0	1,079.4	718.6	360.8	1,490.8	12,992.2	13,486.8	13,238.4	3.8	5.6
III	–458.7	1,684.8	2,143.5	2,570.3	1,087.8	728.6	359.2	1,488.9	13,046.0	13,589.6	13,328.9	2.5	3.1
IV	–414.2	1,716.8	2,131.0	2,552.1	1,079.6	717.7	361.9	1,478.9	13,181.6	13,621.2	13,383.9	2.3	.9
2011: I	–424.4	1,749.6	2,173.9	2,513.9	1,053.3	694.0	359.4	1,466.4	13,182.8	13,644.2	13,432.2	.4	.7
II	–416.4	1,765.0	2,181.4	2,508.2	1,058.3	705.9	352.4	1,456.1	13,236.2	13,679.9	13,504.2	1.3	1.0
III	–402.8	1,785.2	2,187.9	2,507.6	1,063.7	714.6	349.0	1,450.4	13,340.9	13,725.3	13,567.9	1.8	1.3
IV [p]	–405.8	1,805.6	2,211.5	2,478.5	1,043.7	691.1	352.6	1,440.7	13,367.4	13,819.5	....	2.8	2.8

[1] Gross domestic product (GDP) less exports of goods and services plus imports of goods and services.
[2] GDP plus net income receipts from rest of the world.

Source: Department of Commerce (Bureau of Economic Analysis).

[Quarterly data are seasonally adjusted]

Year or quarter	Index numbers, 2005=100					Percent change from preceding period [1]				
	Gross domestic product (GDP)			Personal consumption expenditures (PCE)		Gross domestic product (GDP)			Personal consumption expenditures (PCE)	
	Real GDP (chain-type quantity index)	GDP chain-type price index	GDP implicit price deflator	PCE chain-type price index	PCE less food and energy price index	Real GDP (chain-type quantity index)	GDP chain-type price index	GDP implicit price deflator	PCE chain-type price index	PCE less food and energy price index
1963	25.382	19.290	19.281	19.254	19.788	4.4	1.1	1.1	1.2	1.3
1964	26.851	19.589	19.580	19.536	20.091	5.8	1.6	1.6	1.5	1.5
1965	28.575	19.945	19.936	19.819	20.345	6.4	1.8	1.8	1.4	1.3
1966	30.437	20.511	20.502	20.322	20.805	6.5	2.8	2.8	2.5	2.3
1967	31.206	21.142	21.133	20.834	21.442	2.5	3.1	3.1	2.5	3.1
1968	32.717	22.040	22.031	21.645	22.362	4.8	4.2	4.2	3.9	4.3
1969	33.733	23.130	23.119	22.626	23.412	3.1	4.9	4.9	4.5	4.7
1970	33.798	24.349	24.338	23.685	24.510	.2	5.3	5.3	4.7	4.7
1971	34.932	25.567	25.554	24.692	25.664	3.4	5.0	5.0	4.3	4.7
1972	36.788	26.670	26.657	25.536	26.493	5.3	4.3	4.3	3.4	3.2
1973	38.920	28.148	28.136	26.913	27.505	5.8	5.5	5.5	5.4	3.8
1974	38.705	30.695	30.690	29.716	29.687	–.6	9.0	9.1	10.4	7.9
1975	38.623	33.606	33.591	32.198	32.174	–.2	9.5	9.5	8.4	8.4
1976	40.695	35.535	35.519	33.966	34.130	5.4	5.7	5.7	5.5	6.1
1977	42.566	37.796	37.783	36.171	36.320	4.6	6.4	6.4	6.5	6.4
1978	44.940	40.447	40.435	38.705	38.749	5.6	7.0	7.0	7.0	6.7
1979	46.345	43.811	43.798	42.137	41.569	3.1	8.3	8.3	8.9	7.3
1980	46.217	47.817	47.791	46.663	45.377	–.3	9.1	9.1	10.7	9.2
1981	47.390	52.326	52.270	50.833	49.342	2.5	9.4	9.4	8.9	8.7
1982	46.470	55.514	55.459	53.640	52.526	–1.9	6.1	6.1	5.5	6.5
1983	48.570	57.705	57.652	55.948	55.247	4.5	3.9	4.0	4.3	5.2
1984	52.060	59.874	59.817	58.065	57.541	7.2	3.8	3.8	3.8	4.2
1985	54.214	61.686	61.628	59.965	59.724	4.1	3.0	3.0	3.3	3.8
1986	56.092	63.057	62.991	61.427	61.974	3.5	2.2	2.2	2.4	3.8
1987	57.887	64.818	64.819	63.618	64.331	3.2	2.8	2.9	3.6	3.8
1988	60.266	67.047	67.046	66.151	67.120	4.1	3.4	3.4	4.0	4.3
1989	62.420	69.579	69.577	69.025	69.889	3.6	3.8	3.8	4.3	4.1
1990	63.591	72.274	72.262	72.180	72.872	1.9	3.9	3.9	4.6	4.3
1991	63.442	74.826	74.824	74.789	75.709	–.2	3.5	3.5	3.6	3.9
1992	65.595	76.602	76.598	76.989	78.256	3.4	2.4	2.4	2.9	3.4
1993	67.466	78.288	78.290	78.679	80.106	2.9	2.2	2.2	2.2	2.4
1994	70.214	79.935	79.940	80.302	81.875	4.1	2.1	2.1	2.1	2.2
1995	71.980	81.602	81.606	82.078	83.761	2.5	2.1	2.1	2.2	2.3
1996	74.672	83.154	83.159	83.864	85.386	3.7	1.9	1.9	2.2	1.9
1997	78.000	84.627	84.628	85.433	87.022	4.5	1.8	1.8	1.9	1.9
1998	81.397	85.580	85.584	86.246	88.284	4.4	1.1	1.1	1.0	1.5
1999	85.326	86.840	86.842	87.636	89.597	4.8	1.5	1.5	1.6	1.5
2000	88.857	88.724	88.723	89.818	91.154	4.1	2.2	2.2	2.5	1.7
2001	89.816	90.731	90.727	91.530	92.783	1.1	2.3	2.3	1.9	1.8
2002	91.445	92.192	92.196	92.778	94.390	1.8	1.6	1.6	1.4	1.7
2003	93.769	94.134	94.135	94.658	95.823	2.5	2.1	2.1	2.0	1.5
2004	97.021	96.784	96.786	97.121	97.815	3.5	2.8	2.8	2.6	2.1
2005	100.000	100.000	100.000	100.000	100.000	3.1	3.3	3.3	3.0	2.2
2006	102.658	103.237	103.231	102.723	102.265	2.7	3.2	3.2	2.7	2.3
2007	104.622	106.231	106.227	105.499	104.631	1.9	2.9	2.9	2.7	2.3
2008	104.270	108.565	108.582	108.943	107.020	–.3	2.2	2.2	3.3	2.3
2009	100.635	109.732	109.729	109.169	108.691	–3.5	1.1	1.1	.2	1.6
2010	103.684	111.000	110.992	111.112	110.208	3.0	1.2	1.2	1.8	1.4
2011 ᴾ	105.470	113.307	113.327	113.815	111.790	1.7	2.1	2.1	2.4	1.4
2008: I	105.101	107.623	107.591	107.852	106.208	–1.8	2.5	2.4	3.9	2.5
II	105.447	108.282	108.302	109.052	106.844	1.3	2.5	2.7	4.5	2.4
III	104.468	109.107	109.162	110.218	107.384	–3.7	3.1	3.2	4.3	2.0
IV	102.064	109.247	109.300	108.650	107.644	–8.9	.5	.5	–5.6	1.0
2009: I	100.319	109.709	109.717	108.194	107.913	–6.7	1.7	1.5	–1.7	1.0
II	100.145	109.589	109.594	108.703	108.475	–.7	–.4	–.4	1.9	2.1
III	100.567	109.662	109.658	109.513	108.888	1.7	.3	.2	3.0	1.5
IV	101.509	109.969	109.943	110.265	109.488	3.8	1.1	1.0	2.8	2.2
2010: I	102.494	110.370	110.358	110.774	109.796	3.9	1.5	1.5	1.9	1.1
II	103.450	110.770	110.793	110.864	110.147	3.8	1.5	1.6	.3	1.3
III	104.093	111.162	111.156	111.136	110.353	2.5	1.4	1.3	1.0	.8
IV	104.699	111.699	111.644	111.673	110.534	2.3	1.9	1.8	1.9	.7
2011: I	104.792	112.390	112.398	112.747	110.963	.4	2.5	2.7	3.9	1.6
II	105.140	113.091	113.118	113.666	111.585	1.3	2.5	2.6	3.3	2.3
III	105.614	113.811	113.836	114.324	112.156	1.8	2.6	2.6	2.3	2.1
IV ᴾ	106.334	113.935	113.946	114.524	112.454	2.8	.4	.4	.7	1.1

[1] Quarterly percent changes are at annual rates.

Source: Department of Commerce (Bureau of Economic Analysis).

[Percent change from preceding period; quarterly data at seasonally adjusted annual rates]

Year or quarter	Gross domestic product	Personal consumption expenditures			Gross private domestic investment					Exports and imports of goods and services		Government consumption expenditures and gross investment		
					Nonresidential fixed									
		Total	Goods	Services	Total	Structures	Equipment and software	Residential fixed		Exports	Imports	Total	Federal	State and local
1963	4.4	4.1	4.0	4.2	5.6	1.2	8.4	11.8		7.2	2.7	2.6	0.1	6.0
1964	5.8	6.0	6.0	6.0	11.9	10.4	12.8	5.8		11.8	5.3	2.2	−1.3	6.8
1965	6.4	6.3	7.1	5.5	17.4	15.9	18.3	−2.9		2.8	10.6	3.0	.0	6.7
1966	6.5	5.7	6.3	5.0	12.5	6.8	16.0	−8.9		6.9	14.9	8.8	11.1	6.3
1967	2.5	3.0	2.0	4.1	−1.3	−2.5	−.7	−3.1		2.3	7.3	7.7	10.0	5.1
1968	4.8	5.8	6.2	5.3	4.5	1.4	6.2	13.6		7.9	14.9	3.1	.8	5.9
1969	3.1	3.7	3.1	4.5	7.6	5.4	8.8	3.0		4.8	5.7	−.2	−3.4	3.4
1970	.2	2.3	.8	3.9	−.5	.3	−1.0	−6.0		10.7	4.3	−2.4	−7.4	2.8
1971	3.4	3.8	4.2	3.5	.0	−1.6	1.0	27.4		1.7	5.3	−2.2	−7.7	3.1
1972	5.3	6.1	6.5	5.8	9.2	3.1	12.9	17.8		7.5	11.3	−.7	−4.1	2.2
1973	5.8	5.0	5.2	4.7	14.5	8.2	18.3	−.6		18.9	4.6	−.4	−4.2	2.9
1974	−.6	−.8	−3.6	1.9	.8	−2.2	2.6	−20.6		7.9	−2.3	2.5	.9	3.8
1975	−.2	2.3	.7	3.8	−9.9	−10.5	−9.5	−13.0		−.6	−11.1	2.3	.3	3.7
1976	5.4	5.6	7.0	4.3	4.9	2.4	6.3	23.5		4.4	19.6	.4	.0	.7
1977	4.6	4.2	4.3	4.1	11.3	4.1	15.1	21.5		2.4	10.9	1.1	2.1	.4
1978	5.6	4.4	4.1	4.7	15.0	14.4	15.2	6.3		10.5	8.7	2.9	2.5	3.3
1979	3.1	2.4	1.6	3.1	10.1	12.7	8.7	−3.7		9.9	1.7	1.9	2.4	1.5
1980	−.3	−.4	−2.5	1.5	−.3	5.9	−3.6	−21.2		10.8	−6.6	1.9	4.7	−.1
1981	2.5	1.5	1.2	1.8	5.7	8.0	4.3	−8.0		1.2	2.6	.9	4.8	−2.0
1982	−1.9	1.4	.7	1.9	−3.8	−1.6	−5.2	−18.2		−7.6	−1.3	1.8	3.9	.0
1983	4.5	5.7	6.4	5.2	−1.3	−10.8	5.4	41.4		−2.6	12.6	3.7	6.6	1.2
1984	7.2	5.3	7.2	3.9	17.6	13.9	19.8	14.8		8.2	24.3	3.4	3.1	3.6
1985	4.1	5.2	5.3	5.2	6.6	7.1	6.4	1.6		3.0	6.5	7.0	7.8	6.2
1986	3.5	4.1	5.6	3.0	−2.9	−11.0	1.9	12.3		7.7	8.5	6.1	5.7	6.4
1987	3.2	3.1	1.8	4.0	−.1	−2.9	1.4	2.0		10.8	5.9	2.4	3.6	1.4
1988	4.1	4.0	3.7	4.2	5.2	.7	7.5	−1.0		16.0	3.9	1.3	−1.6	3.7
1989	3.6	2.8	2.5	3.0	5.6	2.0	7.3	−3.0		11.5	4.4	2.7	1.6	3.7
1990	1.9	2.0	.6	3.0	.5	1.5	.0	−8.6		9.0	3.6	3.2	2.0	4.1
1991	−.2	.2	−2.0	1.5	−5.4	−11.1	−2.6	−9.6		6.6	−.2	1.1	−.2	2.1
1992	3.4	3.4	3.2	3.6	3.2	−6.0	7.3	13.8		6.9	7.0	.5	−1.8	2.2
1993	2.9	3.6	4.2	3.2	8.7	−.6	12.5	8.2		3.3	8.6	−.8	−3.9	1.5
1994	4.1	3.8	5.3	3.0	9.2	1.8	11.9	9.7		8.7	11.9	.0	−3.8	2.6
1995	2.5	2.7	3.0	2.5	10.5	6.4	12.0	−3.3		10.1	8.0	.6	−2.7	2.7
1996	3.7	3.5	4.5	2.9	9.3	5.7	10.6	8.0		8.3	8.7	1.0	−1.2	2.3
1997	4.5	3.7	4.8	3.1	12.1	7.3	13.8	1.9		11.9	13.5	1.9	−1.0	3.6
1998	4.4	5.2	6.8	4.4	12.0	5.1	14.5	7.7		2.3	11.7	2.1	−1.1	3.9
1999	4.8	5.5	8.0	4.1	10.4	.1	14.1	6.3		4.4	11.5	3.6	1.9	4.5
2000	4.1	5.1	5.3	5.0	9.8	7.8	10.5	1.0		8.6	13.0	2.0	.5	2.8
2001	1.1	2.7	3.1	2.5	−2.8	−1.5	−3.2	.6		−5.6	−2.8	3.8	4.1	3.7
2002	1.8	2.7	4.1	1.9	−7.9	−17.7	−4.2	5.2		−2.0	3.4	4.7	7.3	3.3
2003	2.5	2.8	4.6	1.9	1.4	−3.8	3.1	8.2		1.6	4.4	2.2	6.6	−.1
2004	3.5	3.3	4.5	2.7	6.2	1.1	7.9	9.8		9.5	11.1	1.4	4.1	−.2
2005	3.1	3.4	4.2	3.0	6.7	1.4	8.5	6.2		6.7	6.1	.3	1.3	−.2
2006	2.7	2.9	3.3	2.6	8.0	9.2	7.6	−7.3		9.0	6.1	1.4	2.1	.9
2007	1.9	2.3	3.0	1.9	6.5	14.1	3.3	−18.7		9.3	2.4	1.3	1.2	1.4
2008	−.3	−.6	−2.5	.4	−.8	6.4	−4.3	−23.9		6.1	−2.7	2.6	7.2	.0
2009	−3.5	−1.9	−3.0	−1.4	−17.8	−21.2	−16.0	−22.2		−9.4	−13.6	1.7	6.0	−.9
2010	3.0	2.0	4.3	.9	4.4	−15.8	14.6	−4.3		11.3	12.5	.7	4.5	−1.8
2011 p	1.7	2.2	3.8	1.4	8.6	4.1	10.3	−1.4		6.8	5.0	−2.1	−2.0	−2.3
2008: I	−1.8	−1.0	−5.6	1.5	−.8	.8	−1.7	−28.5		5.5	1.4	3.1	9.7	−.6
II	1.3	−.1	.5	−.5	−2.3	9.4	−7.9	−14.5		12.7	−2.5	1.7	4.9	−.1
III	−3.7	−3.8	−7.7	−1.7	−9.9	−3.7	−13.1	−20.0		−3.5	−6.6	4.3	11.7	.1
IV	−8.9	−5.1	−12.6	−1.2	−22.9	−10.2	−29.3	−33.2		−21.4	−14.9	1.6	9.1	−2.8
2009: I	−6.7	−1.5	.1	−2.3	−31.3	−32.1	−30.8	−35.4		−29.0	−34.0	−1.7	−3.3	−.8
II	−.7	−1.9	−2.3	−1.7	−15.8	−33.3	−4.2	−21.3		−.5	−15.0	5.9	14.4	.9
III	1.7	2.3	7.6	−.1	−3.3	−20.1	6.4	17.8		13.9	16.3	1.3	5.9	−1.5
IV	3.8	.4	.5	.4	−3.7	−30.8	11.7	−3.8		23.5	17.4	−.9	2.2	−2.9
2010: I	3.9	2.7	6.4	1.0	6.0	−24.7	21.7	−15.3		7.2	12.5	−1.2	2.8	−3.9
II	3.8	2.9	3.8	2.5	18.6	7.5	23.2	22.8		10.0	21.6	3.7	8.8	.4
III	2.5	2.6	4.8	1.6	11.3	4.2	14.1	−27.7		10.0	12.3	1.0	3.2	−.5
IV	2.3	3.6	8.3	1.3	8.7	10.5	8.1	2.5		7.8	−2.3	−2.8	−3.0	−2.7
2011: I	.4	2.1	4.7	.8	2.1	−14.3	8.7	−2.4		7.9	8.3	−5.9	−9.4	−3.4
II	1.3	.7	−1.6	1.9	10.3	22.6	6.2	4.2		3.6	1.4	−.9	1.9	−2.8
III	1.8	1.7	1.4	1.9	15.7	14.4	16.2	1.3		4.7	1.2	−.1	2.1	−1.6
IV p	2.8	2.0	5.7	.2	1.7	−7.2	5.2	10.9		4.7	4.4	−4.6	−7.3	−2.6

Note: Percent changes based on unrounded data.

Source: Department of Commerce (Bureau of Economic Analysis).

[Percentage points, except as noted; quarterly data at seasonally adjusted annual rates]

Year or quarter	Gross domestic product (percent change)	Personal consumption expenditures			Gross private domestic investment						
		Total	Goods	Services	Total	Fixed investment					Change in private inventories
						Total	Nonresidential			Residential	
							Total	Structures	Equipment and software		
1963	4.4	2.56	1.29	1.27	1.00	1.08	0.50	0.04	0.46	0.58	−0.08
1964	5.8	3.69	1.91	1.78	1.25	1.37	1.07	.36	.71	.30	−.13
1965	6.4	3.91	2.26	1.66	2.16	1.50	1.65	.57	1.07	−.15	.66
1966	6.5	3.50	2.02	1.48	1.44	.87	1.29	.27	1.02	−.43	.58
1967	2.5	1.82	.62	1.21	−.76	−.28	−.15	−.10	−.05	−.13	−.49
1968	4.8	3.51	1.92	1.59	.90	.99	.46	.05	.41	.53	−.10
1969	3.1	2.29	.95	1.34	.90	.90	.78	.20	.58	.13	.00
1970	.2	1.44	.24	1.19	−1.04	−.31	−.06	.01	−.07	−.26	−.73
1971	3.4	2.37	1.27	1.10	1.67	1.10	.00	−.06	.07	1.10	.58
1972	5.3	3.81	1.97	1.84	1.87	1.81	.93	.12	.81	.89	.06
1973	5.8	3.08	1.57	1.51	1.96	1.47	1.50	.31	1.19	−.04	.50
1974	−.6	−.52	−1.12	.60	−1.31	−1.04	.09	−.09	.18	−1.13	−.27
1975	−.2	1.40	.20	1.20	−2.98	−1.71	−1.14	−.43	−.70	−.57	−1.27
1976	5.4	3.51	2.08	1.43	2.84	1.42	.52	.09	.43	.90	1.41
1977	4.6	2.66	1.28	1.38	2.43	2.18	1.19	.15	1.04	.99	.25
1978	5.6	2.77	1.22	1.56	2.16	2.04	1.69	.54	1.15	.35	.12
1979	3.1	1.48	.47	1.02	.61	1.02	1.23	.53	.71	−.21	−.41
1980	−.3	−.22	−.74	.52	−2.12	−1.21	−.03	.27	−.30	−1.17	−.91
1981	2.5	.95	.34	.62	1.55	.39	.74	.40	.34	−.35	1.16
1982	−1.9	.86	.19	.67	−2.55	−1.21	−.50	−.09	−.42	−.71	−1.34
1983	4.5	3.65	1.74	1.91	1.45	1.17	−.17	−.57	.41	1.33	.29
1984	7.2	3.43	1.97	1.47	4.63	2.68	2.05	.60	1.45	.64	1.95
1985	4.1	3.32	1.41	1.90	−.17	.89	.82	.32	.50	.07	−1.06
1986	3.5	2.62	1.49	1.13	−.12	.20	−.36	−.50	.15	.55	−.32
1987	3.2	2.01	.48	1.53	.51	.09	−.01	−.11	.10	.10	.42
1988	4.1	2.64	.98	1.66	.39	.53	.58	.02	.55	−.05	−.14
1989	3.6	1.86	.66	1.20	.64	.47	.61	.07	.54	−.14	.17
1990	1.9	1.34	.16	1.18	−.53	−.32	.05	.05	.00	−.37	−.21
1991	−.2	.10	−.51	.61	−1.20	−.94	−.57	−.39	−.18	−.37	−.26
1992	3.4	2.27	.78	1.49	1.07	.79	.31	−.18	.50	.47	.29
1993	2.9	2.37	1.02	1.35	1.21	1.14	.83	−.02	.85	.31	.07
1994	4.1	2.57	1.29	1.27	1.94	1.30	.91	.05	.86	.39	.63
1995	2.5	1.81	.73	1.08	.48	.94	1.08	.17	.91	−.14	−.46
1996	3.7	2.35	1.09	1.26	1.35	1.33	1.01	.16	.85	.33	.02
1997	4.5	2.48	1.16	1.33	1.95	1.41	1.33	.21	1.12	.08	.54
1998	4.4	3.50	1.61	1.90	1.65	1.70	1.38	.16	1.22	.32	−.05
1999	4.8	3.68	1.90	1.78	1.50	1.52	1.24	.00	1.24	.28	−.02
2000	4.1	3.44	1.29	2.15	1.19	1.24	1.20	.24	.96	.05	−.05
2001	1.1	1.85	.77	1.09	−1.24	−.32	−.35	−.05	−.30	.03	−.92
2002	1.8	1.85	.99	.86	−.22	−.70	−.94	−.58	−.36	.24	.48
2003	2.5	1.97	1.12	.85	.60	.54	.14	−.10	.24	.40	.06
2004	3.5	2.30	1.09	1.22	1.57	1.15	.63	.03	.60	.52	.42
2005	3.1	2.35	1.01	1.34	.93	1.05	.69	.04	.65	.36	−.13
2006	2.7	1.98	.80	1.18	.47	.40	.86	.27	.59	−.46	.07
2007	1.9	1.60	.71	.89	−.56	−.33	.73	.46	.26	−1.05	−.23
2008	−.3	−.39	−.59	.21	−1.66	−1.15	−.09	.24	−.34	−1.05	−.51
2009	−3.5	−1.32	−.69	−.63	−3.61	−2.77	−2.05	−.85	−1.20	−.72	−.84
2010	3.0	1.44	.99	.46	1.96	.32	.42	−.51	.93	−.11	1.64
2011 ᵖ	1.7	1.53	.87	.66	.58	.79	.82	.11	.71	−.03	−.20
2008: I	−1.8	−.70	−1.37	.67	−2.02	−1.36	−.10	.03	−.13	−1.26	−.66
II	1.3	−.08	.12	−.20	−.94	−.80	−.25	.37	−.63	−.55	−.14
III	−3.7	−2.67	−1.89	−.78	−2.63	−1.91	−1.18	−.14	−1.04	−.73	−.73
IV	−8.9	−3.53	−3.04	−.49	−5.59	−4.05	−2.84	−.41	−2.43	−1.21	−1.54
2009: I	−6.7	−1.02	.05	−1.07	−7.76	−5.09	−3.90	−1.47	−2.43	−1.19	−2.66
II	−.7	−1.28	−.52	−.76	−2.84	−2.26	−1.66	−1.41	−.25	−.60	−.58
III	1.7	1.66	1.70	−.04	.35	.13	−.29	−.71	.42	.42	.21
IV	3.8	.33	.12	.21	3.51	−.42	−.33	−1.07	.74	−.10	3.93
2010: I	3.9	1.92	1.45	.47	3.25	.15	.56	−.76	1.32	−.41	3.10
II	3.8	2.05	.87	1.18	2.92	2.12	1.62	.18	1.45	.50	.79
III	2.5	1.85	1.09	.75	1.14	.28	1.04	.10	.94	−.76	.86
IV	2.3	2.48	1.87	.61	−.91	.88	.82	.26	.56	.06	−1.79
2011: I	.4	1.47	1.10	.36	.47	.15	.20	−.40	.60	−.06	.32
II	1.3	.49	−.38	.87	.79	1.07	.98	.54	.44	.09	−.28
III	1.8	1.24	.33	.90	.17	1.52	1.49	.37	1.12	.03	−1.35
IV ᵖ	2.8	1.45	1.34	.10	2.35	.41	.18	−.21	.39	.23	1.94

See next page for continuation of table.

[Percentage points, except as noted; quarterly data at seasonally adjusted annual rates]

| Year or quarter | Net exports | Net exports of goods and services | | | | | | Government consumption expenditures and gross investment | | | | |
| | | Exports | | | Imports | | | Total | Federal | | | State and local |
		Total	Goods	Services	Total	Goods	Services		Total	National defense	Non-defense	
1963	0.24	0.35	0.29	0.06	−0.12	−0.12	0.00	0.58	0.01	−0.25	0.26	0.57
1964	.36	.59	.52	.07	−.23	−.19	−.04	.49	−.17	−.39	.23	.65
1965	−.30	.15	.02	.13	−.45	−.41	−.04	.65	−.01	−.19	.19	.66
1966	−.29	.36	.27	.09	−.65	−.49	−.16	1.87	1.24	1.21	.03	.63
1967	−.22	.12	.02	.10	−.34	−.17	−.16	1.68	1.17	1.19	−.02	.51
1968	−.30	.41	.30	.10	−.71	−.68	−.03	.73	.10	.16	−.06	.63
1969	−.04	.25	.20	.05	−.29	−.20	−.09	−.05	−.42	−.49	.06	.37
1970	.34	.56	.44	.12	−.22	−.15	−.07	−.55	−.86	−.83	−.03	.31
1971	−.19	.10	−.02	.11	−.29	−.33	.04	−.50	−.85	−.97	.12	.36
1972	−.21	.42	.43	−.01	−.63	−.57	−.06	−.16	−.42	−.60	.18	.26
1973	.82	1.12	1.01	.11	−.29	−.34	.05	−.08	−.41	−.39	−.02	.33
1974	.75	.58	.46	.12	.18	.17	.00	.52	.08	−.05	.13	.44
1975	.89	−.05	−.16	.10	.94	.87	.07	.48	.03	−.06	.09	.45
1976	−1.08	.37	.31	.05	−1.45	−1.35	−.10	.10	.00	−.02	.03	.09
1977	−.72	.20	.08	.11	−.92	−.84	−.07	.23	.19	.07	.12	.04
1978	.05	.82	.68	.15	−.78	−.67	−.11	.60	.22	.05	.16	.38
1979	.66	.82	.77	.06	−.16	−.14	−.02	.37	.20	.17	.03	.17
1980	1.68	.97	.86	.11	.71	.67	.04	.38	.39	.25	.14	−.01
1981	−.15	.12	−.09	.21	−.27	−.18	−.09	.19	.42	.38	.04	−.23
1982	−.60	−.73	−.67	−.06	.12	.20	−.08	.35	.35	.48	−.13	.01
1983	−1.35	−.22	−.19	−.03	−1.13	−1.01	−.13	.76	.63	.50	.13	.13
1984	−1.58	.63	.46	.17	−2.21	−1.83	−.39	.70	.30	.35	−.05	.40
1985	−.42	.23	.20	.02	−.65	−.52	−.13	1.41	.74	.60	.14	.67
1986	−.30	.54	.26	.28	−.84	−.82	−.02	1.27	.55	.47	.08	.71
1987	.16	.77	.56	.21	−.61	−.39	−.22	.51	.35	.35	.00	.17
1988	.82	1.24	1.04	.20	−.43	−.36	−.07	.26	−.16	−.03	−.12	.42
1989	.52	.99	.75	.24	−.48	−.38	−.09	.55	.14	−.03	.17	.41
1990	.43	.81	.56	.26	−.38	−.26	−.13	.64	.18	.00	.18	.46
1991	.64	.63	.46	.16	.02	−.04	.05	.22	−.02	−.07	.05	.24
1992	−.05	.68	.52	.16	−.72	−.78	.06	.10	−.16	−.32	.16	.26
1993	−.57	.32	.23	.10	−.90	−.85	−.05	−.16	−.33	−.31	−.02	.17
1994	−.43	.85	.67	.19	−1.28	−1.18	−.10	.00	−.30	−.27	−.04	.30
1995	.11	1.03	.85	.19	−.92	−.86	−.06	.11	−.20	−.19	−.01	.30
1996	−.15	.90	.68	.22	−1.04	−.94	−.10	.19	−.08	−.06	−.02	.27
1997	−.32	1.30	1.11	.19	−1.62	−1.44	−.17	.34	−.07	−.13	.06	.41
1998	−1.18	.26	.18	.08	−1.43	−1.21	−.22	.38	−.07	−.09	.02	.45
1999	−.99	.47	.29	.18	−1.45	−1.31	−.14	.63	.12	.07	.04	.51
2000	−.85	.91	.82	.08	−1.76	−1.52	−.24	.36	.03	−.02	.05	.33
2001	−.20	−.61	−.48	−.13	.41	.39	.02	.67	.24	.14	.09	.43
2002	−.65	−.20	−.25	.05	−.46	−.42	−.04	.84	.44	.28	.15	.40
2003	−.45	.15	.12	.03	−.60	−.56	−.04	.42	.43	.36	.07	−.01
2004	−.66	.90	.56	.34	−1.55	−1.29	−.26	.26	.28	.26	.02	−.02
2005	−.27	.67	.52	.15	−.95	−.87	−.07	.06	.09	.07	.02	−.03
2006	−.06	.93	.68	.25	−.98	−.81	−.18	.26	.15	.07	.07	.11
2007	.62	1.03	.75	.28	−.40	−.37	−.04	.25	.09	.11	−.02	.17
2008	1.21	.73	.53	.20	.47	.57	−.10	.50	.50	.36	.15	.00
2009	1.11	−1.18	−1.04	−.13	2.29	2.19	.10	.34	.45	.30	.16	−.11
2010	−.51	1.31	1.12	.19	−1.82	−1.74	−.08	.14	.37	.18	.19	−.23
2011 _p_	.05	.88	.68	.20	−.82	−.79	−.03	−.45	−.17	−.13	−.03	−.28
2008: I	.38	.65	.75	−.10	−.28	.05	−.33	.58	.66	.38	.28	−.08
II	2.00	1.56	1.21	.35	.44	.31	.13	.34	.35	.27	.09	−.01
III	.79	−.47	−.22	−.24	1.25	1.47	−.21	.85	.84	.85	−.01	.01
IV	−.12	−2.97	−2.75	−.21	2.84	2.98	−.14	.35	.69	.44	.25	−.34
2009: I	2.44	−3.82	−3.25	−.57	6.26	5.63	.63	−.33	−.25	−.40	.15	−.08
II	2.21	−.02	−.20	.18	2.24	2.15	.09	1.21	1.09	.84	.25	.12
III	−.59	1.49	1.48	.01	−2.08	−1.98	−.10	.28	.48	.45	.03	−.19
IV	.15	2.51	2.01	.49	−2.36	−2.36	.00	−.18	.18	−.07	.25	−.37
2010: I	−.97	.86	.96	−.10	−1.83	−1.71	−.12	−.26	.23	.03	.21	−.49
II	−1.94	1.19	.97	.23	−3.13	−3.05	−.08	.77	.71	.33	.38	.05
III	−.68	1.21	.75	.46	−1.89	−1.58	−.31	.20	.26	.31	−.05	−.06
IV	1.37	.98	.79	.18	.39	.08	.31	−.58	−.26	−.34	.09	−.33
2011: I	−.34	1.01	.94	.07	−1.35	−1.29	−.06	−1.23	−.82	−.74	−.08	−.41
II	.24	.48	.24	.24	−.24	−.23	−.01	−.18	.16	.37	−.22	−.34
III	.43	.64	.48	.16	−.21	−.08	−.13	−.02	.17	.27	−.10	−.19
IV _p_	−.11	.64	.48	.16	−.75	−.60	−.15	−.93	−.62	−.73	.11	−.32

Source: Department of Commerce (Bureau of Economic Analysis).

Table B-6. Chain-type quantity indexes for gross domestic product, 1963–2011

[Index numbers, 2005=100; quarterly data seasonally adjusted]

Year or quarter	Gross domestic product	Personal consumption expenditures			Gross private domestic investment					
		Total	Goods	Services	Total	Fixed investment				Resi-dential
						Total	Nonresidential			
							Total	Structures	Equip-ment and software	
1963	25.382	22.593	21.701	22.543	16.249	16.306	12.247	51.986	6.476	32.142
1964	26.851	23.939	22.994	23.885	17.589	17.882	13.701	57.399	7.303	34.011
1965	28.575	25.453	24.623	25.204	20.058	19.708	16.088	66.553	8.641	33.017
1966	30.437	26.897	26.184	26.453	21.825	20.838	18.100	71.109	10.024	30.063
1967	31.206	27.703	26.697	27.541	20.827	20.453	17.856	69.313	9.958	29.117
1968	32.717	29.301	28.350	29.009	22.039	21.881	18.654	70.299	10.578	33.086
1969	33.733	30.399	29.216	30.303	23.323	23.242	20.070	74.096	11.513	34.063
1970	33.798	31.112	29.447	31.487	21.791	22.754	19.963	74.300	11.399	32.026
1971	34.932	32.297	30.679	32.574	24.275	24.477	19.964	73.082	11.512	40.808
1972	36.788	34.283	32.685	34.458	27.150	27.420	21.797	75.359	12.997	48.061
1973	38.920	35.982	34.378	36.091	30.331	29.926	24.968	81.520	15.381	47.752
1974	38.705	35.683	33.124	36.783	28.097	28.055	25.177	79.755	15.774	37.895
1975	38.623	36.492	33.349	38.164	23.120	25.042	22.689	71.355	14.272	32.975
1976	40.695	38.525	35.684	39.802	27.791	27.511	23.800	73.073	15.164	40.740
1977	42.566	40.146	37.215	41.447	31.989	31.465	26.486	76.079	17.449	49.486
1978	44.940	41.916	38.753	43.375	35.846	35.274	30.450	87.058	20.106	52.602
1979	46.345	42.912	39.373	44.700	36.989	37.265	33.517	98.098	21.861	50.672
1980	46.217	42.761	38.376	45.389	32.926	34.844	33.429	103.837	21.075	39.949
1981	47.390	43.410	38.830	46.203	35.886	35.623	35.333	112.161	21.971	36.747
1982	46.470	44.015	39.101	47.103	30.859	33.125	34.003	110.325	20.829	30.075
1983	48.570	46.531	41.589	49.568	33.733	35.541	33.563	98.404	21.950	42.524
1984	52.060	48.998	44.586	51.508	43.672	41.543	39.486	112.125	26.303	48.836
1985	54.214	51.551	46.931	54.173	43.266	43.729	42.103	120.095	27.974	49.608
1986	56.092	53.642	49.556	55.784	42.971	44.237	40.901	106.935	28.504	55.696
1987	57.887	55.297	50.448	58.007	44.295	44.480	40.870	103.859	28.895	56.807
1988	60.266	57.525	52.322	60.469	45.337	45.947	43.008	104.539	31.074	56.231
1989	62.420	59.152	53.643	62.301	47.156	47.328	45.409	106.616	33.351	54.524
1990	63.591	60.359	53.975	64.151	45.569	46.340	45.633	108.187	33.361	49.819
1991	63.442	60.450	52.904	65.110	41.862	43.335	43.186	96.150	32.504	45.032
1992	65.595	62.511	54.571	67.431	45.254	45.904	44.565	90.354	34.873	51.263
1993	67.466	64.731	56.838	69.589	49.299	49.839	48.456	89.768	39.226	55.450
1994	70.214	67.203	59.836	71.666	55.998	54.500	52.915	91.405	43.904	60.840
1995	71.980	69.021	61.623	73.488	57.743	58.010	58.478	97.235	49.158	58.850
1996	74.672	71.429	64.383	75.640	62.851	63.213	63.940	102.744	54.383	63.550
1997	78.000	74.066	67.453	77.973	70.672	69.045	71.658	110.280	61.861	64.751
1998	81.397	77.950	72.010	81.409	77.747	76.537	80.264	115.911	70.837	69.732
1999	85.326	82.213	77.745	84.744	84.592	83.658	88.640	116.049	80.857	74.092
2000	88.857	86.382	81.847	88.944	90.371	89.843	97.327	125.101	89.320	74.834
2001	89.816	88.718	84.417	91.134	84.023	88.142	94.614	123.191	86.438	75.258
2002	91.445	91.080	87.848	92.870	82.879	84.412	87.112	101.377	82.789	79.204
2003	93.769	93.650	91.890	94.611	86.090	87.390	88.290	97.514	85.377	85.712
2004	97.021	96.731	95.988	97.134	94.749	93.880	93.740	98.571	92.138	94.130
2005	100.000	100.000	100.000	100.000	100.000	100.000	100.000	100.000	100.000	100.000
2006	102.658	102.850	103.322	102.599	102.742	102.375	108.027	109.180	107.590	92.667
2007	104.622	105.218	106.394	104.599	99.412	100.390	115.039	124.578	111.168	75.379
2008	104.270	104.637	103.776	105.067	89.296	93.228	114.125	132.595	106.411	57.345
2009	100.635	102.657	100.693	103.644	66.944	75.688	93.755	104.426	89.367	44.587
2010	103.684	104.741	105.006	104.628	78.945	77.667	97.913	87.883	102.393	42.681
2011 _p_	105.470	107.015	108.944	106.087	82.642	82.822	106.314	91.497	112.909	42.091
2008: I	105.101	105.515	105.599	105.465	94.633	97.363	117.944	131.860	112.220	62.104
II	105.447	105.478	105.719	105.344	93.176	96.078	117.269	134.869	109.945	59.721
III	104.468	104.458	103.615	104.884	89.061	92.989	114.238	133.594	106.148	56.484
IV	102.064	103.096	100.171	104.576	80.314	86.480	107.050	130.057	97.330	51.072
2009: I	100.319	102.696	100.190	103.958	68.610	78.473	97.447	118.078	88.760	45.790
II	100.145	102.215	99.597	103.524	64.317	74.910	93.341	106.721	87.812	43.133
III	100.567	102.803	101.430	103.493	64.782	75.041	92.556	100.894	89.194	44.932
IV	101.509	102.915	101.555	103.599	70.067	74.327	91.678	92.013	91.700	44.495
2010: I	102.494	103.608	103.139	103.853	75.037	74.541	93.023	85.704	96.309	42.680
II	103.450	104.355	104.100	104.496	79.562	77.935	97.081	87.261	101.463	44.933
III	104.093	105.038	105.333	104.912	81.333	78.380	99.725	88.169	104.873	41.427
IV	104.699	105.962	107.452	105.250	79.848	79.812	101.822	90.399	106.925	41.684
2011: I	104.792	106.511	108.700	105.453	80.600	80.052	102.342	86.974	109.174	41.428
II	105.140	106.693	108.272	105.941	81.869	81.829	104.889	91.511	110.839	41.855
III	105.614	107.156	108.646	106.449	82.135	84.362	108.782	94.631	115.077	41.991
IV _p_	106.334	107.699	110.157	106.506	85.964	85.046	109.244	92.874	116.546	43.090

See next page for continuation of table.

[Index numbers, 2005=100; quarterly data seasonally adjusted]

Year or quarter	Exports of goods and services			Imports of goods and services			Government consumption expenditures and gross investment				
								Federal			State and local
	Total	Goods	Services	Total	Goods	Services	Total	Total	National defense	Non-defense	
1963	8.535	8.074	9.605	6.411	5.035	14.943	42.032	60.526	72.838	36.946	30.552
1964	9.540	9.180	10.180	6.752	5.367	15.328	42.958	59.725	69.951	40.157	32.626
1965	9.807	9.228	11.215	7.471	6.127	15.779	44.250	59.697	68.481	42.878	34.813
1966	10.487	9.870	11.986	8.581	7.093	17.783	48.149	66.303	78.306	43.320	36.998
1967	10.728	9.916	12.932	9.206	7.466	19.957	51.844	72.903	88.567	42.913	38.868
1968	11.572	10.701	13.925	10.578	9.009	20.315	53.472	73.491	90.001	41.897	41.168
1969	12.131	11.262	14.442	11.181	9.502	21.596	53.347	70.969	85.556	43.019	42.557
1970	13.435	12.546	15.729	11.658	9.874	22.722	52.059	65.738	77.800	42.567	43.738
1971	13.663	12.497	16.942	12.280	10.702	22.075	50.926	60.677	68.981	44.575	45.077
1972	14.689	13.840	16.835	13.662	12.158	23.011	50.556	58.197	63.588	47.722	46.068
1973	17.458	17.020	18.025	14.296	13.016	22.235	50.379	55.748	60.061	47.429	47.381
1974	18.837	18.371	19.432	13.972	12.654	22.210	51.648	56.243	59.595	49.891	49.164
1975	18.718	17.944	20.626	12.419	11.059	21.247	52.812	56.426	59.030	51.594	50.970
1976	19.536	18.796	21.236	14.848	13.560	22.714	53.049	56.453	58.828	52.085	51.346
1977	20.006	19.042	22.606	16.471	15.213	23.846	53.630	57.647	59.511	54.324	51.532
1978	22.115	21.170	24.496	17.898	16.577	25.546	55.210	59.092	60.019	57.700	53.216
1979	24.307	23.671	25.250	18.195	16.861	25.897	56.241	60.519	61.845	58.309	53.998
1980	26.925	26.492	26.826	16.987	15.610	25.319	57.337	63.390	64.541	61.573	53.958
1981	27.256	26.205	29.683	17.433	15.931	26.778	57.860	66.420	68.628	62.396	52.873
1982	25.173	23.837	28.860	17.214	15.531	28.205	58.876	68.989	73.814	59.402	52.898
1983	24.524	23.151	28.380	19.386	17.641	30.483	61.027	73.561	79.110	62.471	53.514
1984	26.526	24.982	30.911	24.105	21.908	38.126	63.078	75.829	82.971	61.279	55.444
1985	27.331	25.903	31.279	25.669	23.279	41.026	67.471	81.771	90.002	64.900	58.879
1986	29.429	27.233	35.820	27.863	25.665	41.488	71.573	86.407	95.766	67.130	62.669
1987	32.594	30.252	39.390	29.511	26.855	46.378	73.300	89.477	100.301	67.081	63.575
1988	37.815	35.953	42.939	30.671	27.943	47.954	74.220	88.010	99.826	63.499	65.933
1989	42.161	40.237	47.375	32.022	29.146	50.278	76.240	89.379	99.335	68.795	68.340
1990	45.954	43.623	52.372	33.168	29.995	53.564	78.655	91.185	99.305	74.465	71.112
1991	49.005	46.633	55.505	33.118	30.130	52.173	79.514	91.000	98.214	76.170	72.585
1992	52.370	50.122	58.496	35.440	32.971	50.768	79.885	89.351	93.351	81.218	74.156
1993	54.086	51.756	60.437	38.505	36.270	52.124	79.253	85.842	88.401	80.687	75.244
1994	58.802	56.790	64.275	43.098	41.114	54.901	79.245	82.555	84.072	79.525	77.197
1995	64.755	63.436	68.316	46.547	44.817	56.556	79.705	80.353	80.936	79.207	79.247
1996	70.133	69.031	73.101	50.595	49.018	59.514	80.507	79.423	79.856	78.577	81.090
1997	78.490	78.955	77.436	57.409	56.082	64.687	82.020	78.641	77.618	80.737	83.980
1998	80.281	80.717	79.303	64.119	62.727	71.721	83.759	77.758	75.978	81.374	87.291
1999	83.785	83.788	83.857	71.500	70.549	76.569	86.761	79.270	77.386	83.095	91.179
2000	90.985	93.080	86.102	80.813	80.018	84.955	88.519	79.661	76.986	85.066	93.744
2001	85.880	87.318	82.534	78.540	77.464	84.292	91.917	82.901	79.908	88.945	97.236
2002	84.160	84.176	84.115	81.213	80.341	85.837	96.192	88.953	85.782	95.357	100.473
2003	85.514	85.687	85.107	84.806	84.302	87.474	98.336	94.839	93.243	98.071	100.408
2004	93.677	92.995	95.237	94.212	93.637	97.252	99.668	98.710	98.535	99.067	100.234
2005	100.000	100.000	100.000	100.000	100.000	100.000	100.000	100.000	100.000	100.000	100.000
2006	108.969	109.425	107.935	106.099	105.920	107.059	101.359	102.127	101.588	103.237	100.910
2007	119.108	120.090	116.885	108.652	108.674	108.539	102.713	103.399	103.867	102.420	102.311
2008	126.376	127.691	123.395	105.733	104.500	112.488	105.381	110.819	111.649	109.081	102.310
2009	114.479	112.417	119.041	91.372	88.174	108.576	107.161	117.479	118.090	116.200	101.378
2010	127.444	128.564	125.030	102.821	101.248	111.742	107.886	122.782	121.942	124.508	99.557
2011 *p*	136.112	138.256	131.392	107.934	107.118	112.937	105.577	120.363	119.076	123.004	97.308
2008: I	125.966	127.394	122.720	108.203	107.516	111.891	104.391	107.703	107.756	107.602	102.501
II	129.793	131.666	125.544	107.511	106.907	110.696	104.838	108.996	109.173	108.640	102.473
III	128.631	130.878	123.540	105.698	104.396	112.908	105.941	112.058	113.693	108.622	102.490
IV	121.112	120.825	121.774	101.518	99.182	114.459	106.356	114.518	115.975	111.459	101.776
2009: I	111.191	108.530	117.044	91.492	88.340	108.490	105.895	113.570	113.724	113.237	101.583
II	111.058	107.723	118.392	87.838	84.079	107.816	107.431	117.445	118.106	116.062	101.817
III	114.728	113.062	118.433	91.215	87.919	108.940	107.779	119.128	120.457	116.365	101.424
IV	120.941	120.352	122.297	94.941	92.357	109.060	107.537	119.772	120.073	119.137	100.689
2010: I	123.074	123.835	121.464	97.789	95.522	110.303	107.205	120.614	120.233	121.391	99.704
II	126.049	127.341	123.262	102.695	101.199	111.197	108.193	123.177	121.992	125.618	99.814
III	129.101	130.096	126.961	105.708	104.206	114.282	108.457	124.138	123.698	125.038	99.689
IV	131.551	132.984	128.433	105.091	104.065	111.185	107.691	123.197	121.846	125.985	99.020
2011: I	134.061	136.363	128.977	107.207	106.464	111.798	106.076	120.195	117.822	125.111	98.177
II	135.240	137.206	130.926	107.573	106.875	111.918	105.837	120.769	119.841	122.665	97.488
III	136.789	138.874	132.204	107.897	107.020	113.243	105.812	121.385	121.311	121.494	97.107
IV *p*	138.358	140.579	133.463	109.058	108.113	114.788	104.582	119.101	117.332	122.745	96.461

Source: Department of Commerce (Bureau of Economic Analysis).

TABLE B–7. Chain-type price indexes for gross domestic product, 1963–2011

[Index numbers, 2005=100, except as noted; quarterly data seasonally adjusted]

Year or quarter	Gross domestic product	Personal consumption expenditures			Gross private domestic investment					
					Total	Fixed investment				
						Total	Nonresidential			Residential
		Total	Goods	Services			Total	Structures	Equipment and software	
1963	19.290	19.254	29.689	14.305	26.560	25.485	33.971	11.636	53.975	12.901
1964	19.589	19.536	30.013	14.572	26.710	25.640	34.142	11.801	53.952	13.003
1965	19.945	19.819	30.328	14.845	27.136	26.077	34.532	12.143	54.001	13.372
1966	20.511	20.322	30.996	15.276	27.692	26.626	35.047	12.580	54.144	13.857
1967	21.142	20.834	31.542	15.785	28.424	27.372	35.939	12.973	55.344	14.339
1968	22.040	21.645	32.642	16.467	29.485	28.472	37.203	13.621	56.831	15.100
1969	23.130	22.626	33.907	17.324	30.883	29.877	38.740	14.518	58.411	16.144
1970	24.349	23.685	35.200	18.285	32.190	31.162	40.571	15.473	60.560	16.666
1971	25.567	24.692	36.258	19.284	33.794	32.731	42.479	16.664	62.360	17.632
1972	26.670	25.536	37.186	20.102	35.206	34.135	43.914	17.863	63.112	18.703
1973	28.148	26.913	39.404	21.077	37.107	36.020	45.605	19.247	64.184	20.359
1974	30.695	29.716	44.322	22.866	40.797	39.568	50.008	21.910	68.917	22.460
1975	33.606	32.198	47.903	24.834	45.833	44.525	56.893	24.534	79.100	24.547
1976	35.535	33.966	49.777	26.556	48.366	47.106	60.048	25.741	83.754	26.124
1977	37.796	36.171	52.435	28.558	51.994	50.803	64.157	27.973	88.730	28.759
1978	40.447	38.705	55.653	30.777	56.235	55.094	68.453	30.675	93.412	32.281
1979	43.811	42.137	60.916	33.350	61.323	60.088	74.013	34.238	99.335	35.902
1980	47.817	46.663	67.737	36.802	67.080	65.710	80.541	37.421	107.819	39.789
1981	52.326	50.833	72.769	40.555	73.422	71.816	88.316	42.567	115.524	43.036
1982	55.514	53.640	74.753	43.709	77.180	75.747	93.181	45.927	120.030	45.340
1983	57.705	55.948	76.102	46.429	76.987	75.628	92.350	44.757	120.284	46.380
1984	59.874	58.065	77.541	48.846	77.538	76.070	92.127	45.147	119.234	47.713
1985	61.686	59.965	78.785	51.049	78.332	77.028	92.850	46.219	119.090	48.944
1986	63.057	61.427	78.417	53.375	80.029	78.870	94.427	47.106	120.976	50.994
1987	64.818	63.618	80.939	55.409	81.561	80.332	95.275	47.863	121.637	53.079
1988	67.047	66.151	83.072	58.123	83.424	82.415	97.392	49.895	123.155	54.913
1989	69.579	69.025	86.268	60.840	85.418	84.410	99.435	51.848	124.695	56.680
1990	72.274	72.180	89.801	63.808	87.064	86.125	101.339	53.522	126.310	58.011
1991	74.826	74.789	91.996	66.581	88.302	87.404	102.906	54.491	128.112	58.771
1992	76.602	76.989	93.106	69.236	87.993	87.152	102.048	54.502	126.605	59.486
1993	78.288	78.679	93.915	71.294	88.997	88.163	102.100	56.103	125.322	61.890
1994	79.935	80.302	94.870	73.200	90.157	89.352	102.592	58.089	124.604	64.069
1995	81.602	82.078	95.757	75.365	91.173	90.393	102.811	60.601	123.163	66.403
1996	83.154	83.864	96.809	77.473	90.786	90.149	101.612	62.141	120.199	67.828
1997	84.627	85.433	96.696	79.812	90.449	89.921	100.326	64.516	116.639	69.557
1998	85.580	86.246	95.237	81.689	89.435	89.085	98.125	67.480	111.454	71.412
1999	86.840	87.636	95.735	83.509	89.315	89.029	96.704	69.559	108.195	74.151
2000	88.724	89.818	97.655	85.818	90.283	90.083	96.750	72.298	106.893	77.415
2001	90.731	91.530	97.563	88.422	91.080	90.888	96.317	76.087	104.364	80.994
2002	92.192	92.778	96.563	90.801	91.451	91.261	95.889	79.292	102.240	83.002
2003	94.134	94.658	96.492	93.686	92.483	92.374	95.471	82.174	100.450	86.953
2004	96.784	97.121	97.929	96.688	95.633	95.543	96.837	88.441	99.900	93.297
2005	100.000	100.000	100.000	100.000	100.000	100.000	100.000	100.000	100.000	100.000
2006	103.237	102.723	101.441	103.414	104.302	104.347	103.425	112.922	100.049	106.081
2007	106.231	105.499	102.764	106.981	106.313	106.360	105.645	119.780	100.525	107.612
2008	108.565	108.943	105.912	110.584	107.501	107.587	107.717	125.706	101.000	106.296
2009	109.732	109.169	103.209	112.353	106.401	106.305	107.106	122.490	101.496	102.637
2010	111.000	111.112	104.837	114.465	104.743	104.843	105.373	121.117	99.634	102.214
2011 ᵖ	113.307	113.815	108.750	116.493	106.432	106.161	106.734	126.597	99.745	103.367
2008: I	107.623	107.852	105.356	109.211	106.487	106.687	106.261	123.025	100.070	107.250
II	108.282	109.052	106.609	110.386	106.815	107.048	106.846	124.220	100.396	106.941
III	109.107	110.218	108.437	111.204	107.447	107.912	108.183	126.538	101.313	106.196
IV	109.247	108.650	103.248	111.536	109.254	108.699	109.578	129.041	102.222	104.799
2009: I	109.709	108.194	101.575	111.715	108.646	108.062	108.968	127.209	102.182	104.023
II	109.589	108.703	102.597	111.964	106.872	106.595	107.525	123.194	101.851	102.451
III	109.662	109.513	104.007	112.463	105.274	105.410	106.238	120.003	101.295	101.643
IV	109.969	110.265	104.657	113.269	104.811	105.154	105.694	119.555	100.657	102.430
2010: I	110.370	110.774	105.196	113.758	104.507	104.818	105.237	119.947	99.860	102.568
II	110.770	110.864	104.286	114.380	104.510	104.693	105.293	120.647	99.677	101.784
III	111.162	111.136	104.497	114.682	104.755	104.826	105.424	121.399	99.595	101.941
IV	111.699	111.673	105.367	115.037	105.199	105.035	105.536	122.475	99.406	102.563
2011: I	112.390	112.747	107.412	115.574	105.755	105.412	105.909	123.982	99.446	102.958
II	113.091	113.666	108.752	116.260	106.342	106.039	106.560	125.835	99.743	103.479
III	113.811	114.324	109.530	116.852	106.646	106.433	107.027	127.565	99.838	103.551
IV ᵖ	113.935	114.524	109.304	117.286	106.983	106.759	107.442	129.008	99.953	103.482

See next page for continuation of table.

[Index numbers, 2005=100, except as noted; quarterly data seasonally adjusted]

Year or quarter	Exports and imports of goods and services		Government consumption expenditures and gross investment					Final sales of domestic product	Gross domestic purchases [1]		Percent change [2]		
				Federal			State and local				Gross domestic product	Gross domestic purchases [1]	
	Exports	Imports	Total	Total	National defense	Non-defense			Total	Less food and energy		Total	Less food and energy
1963	27.898	20.102	13.690	14.506	14.209	15.037	13.028	19.141	18.887		1.1	1.2	
1964	28.128	20.526	14.070	14.995	14.620	15.798	13.293	19.440	19.191		1.6	1.6	
1965	29.023	20.812	14.444	15.379	15.024	16.104	13.662	19.798	19.524		1.8	1.7	
1966	29.900	21.297	15.044	15.914	15.535	16.708	14.334	20.363	20.071		2.8	2.8	
1967	31.045	21.379	15.671	16.386	15.994	17.215	15.137	20.996	20.654		3.1	2.9	
1968	31.723	21.704	16.520	17.287	16.834	18.327	15.945	21.898	21.526		4.2	4.2	
1969	32.796	22.270	17.517	18.226	17.757	19.284	17.013	22.988	22.582		4.9	4.9	
1970	34.053	23.587	18.945	19.699	19.116	21.143	18.411	24.203	23.798		5.3	5.4	
1971	35.310	25.035	20.421	21.383	20.810	22.746	19.720	25.415	25.021		5.0	5.1	
1972	36.956	26.789	21.989	23.471	23.209	23.892	20.896	26.516	26.134		4.3	4.4	
1973	41.816	31.446	23.594	25.080	24.911	25.231	22.495	27.992	27.647		5.5	5.8	
1974	51.517	44.989	25.977	27.315	27.223	27.245	24.970	30.519	30.484		9.0	10.3	
1975	56.781	48.734	28.586	30.158	29.880	30.505	27.410	33.418	33.328		9.5	9.3	
1976	58.645	50.201	30.469	32.302	32.057	32.549	29.114	35.350	35.238		5.7	5.7	
1977	61.033	54.624	32.583	34.742	34.486	34.993	31.005	37.614	37.617		6.4	6.8	
1978	64.752	58.482	34.670	36.888	36.908	36.514	33.042	40.266	40.286		7.0	7.1	
1979	72.545	68.483	37.575	39.727	39.853	39.100	35.976	43.614	43.833		8.3	8.8	
1980	79.903	85.301	41.669	43.900	44.179	42.906	40.002	47.598	48.448		9.1	10.5	
1981	85.810	89.886	45.768	48.165	48.542	46.917	43.975	52.074	52.909		9.4	9.2	
1982	86.204	86.855	48.775	51.434	51.953	49.825	46.786	55.280	55.906	55.408	6.1	5.7	
1983	86.544	83.601	50.717	53.218	53.775	51.501	48.857	57.464	57.865	57.569	3.9	3.5	3.9
1984	87.347	82.879	53.319	56.358	57.603	52.779	51.034	59.624	59.904	59.704	3.8	3.5	3.7
1985	84.674	80.157	54.974	57.635	58.696	54.574	53.002	61.466	61.605	61.577	3.0	2.8	3.1
1986	83.406	80.154	55.977	57.938	58.642	55.915	54.577	62.856	63.000	63.464	2.2	2.3	3.1
1987	85.516	85.008	57.541	58.642	59.236	56.953	56.884	64.607	64.798	65.506	2.8	3.1	3.2
1988	89.945	89.074	59.074	59.884	60.326	58.679	58.621	66.865	67.215	67.900	3.4	3.4	3.7
1989	91.443	91.021	60.924	61.504	61.882	60.497	60.654	69.397	69.765	70.346	3.8	3.8	3.6
1990	92.063	93.630	63.405	63.548	63.917	62.568	63.474	72.102	72.601	73.043	3.9	4.1	3.8
1991	93.283	92.848	65.606	66.070	66.222	65.672	65.443	74.655	74.980	75.539	3.5	3.3	3.4
1992	92.904	92.922	67.276	68.101	68.522	67.034	66.856	76.436	76.788	77.520	2.4	2.4	2.6
1993	92.879	92.210	68.949	69.830	69.712	70.002	68.494	78.123	78.404	79.228	2.2	2.1	2.2
1994	93.914	93.075	70.819	71.725	71.438	72.267	70.351	79.775	80.029	80.947	2.1	2.1	2.2
1995	96.070	95.625	72.753	73.717	73.161	74.830	72.252	81.449	81.743	82.722	2.1	2.1	2.2
1996	94.799	93.958	74.488	75.763	75.431	76.406	73.806	83.024	83.220	84.077	1.9	1.8	1.6
1997	93.174	90.691	75.854	77.047	76.517	78.095	75.219	84.522	84.468	85.344	1.8	1.5	1.5
1998	91.042	85.809	76.879	77.931	77.328	79.120	76.320	85.516	85.034	86.171	1.1	.7	1.0
1999	90.477	86.311	79.337	79.886	79.225	81.188	79.036	86.795	86.377	87.463	1.5	1.6	1.5
2000	92.069	90.027	82.513	82.524	81.821	83.907	82.482	88.698	88.537	89.243	2.2	2.5	2.0
2001	91.696	87.824	84.764	84.201	83.484	85.612	85.019	90.709	90.198	90.851	2.3	1.9	1.8
2002	91.322	86.846	87.003	87.318	86.624	88.689	86.810	92.168	91.498	92.384	1.6	1.4	1.7
2003	93.282	89.851	90.650	91.024	90.659	91.774	90.425	94.123	93.584	94.214	2.1	2.3	2.0
2004	96.539	94.164	94.531	95.335	94.895	96.234	94.062	96.774	96.415	96.779	2.8	3.0	2.7
2005	100.000	100.000	100.000	100.000	100.000	100.000	100.000	100.000	100.000	100.000	3.3	3.7	3.3
2006	103.440	104.131	104.842	104.107	104.421	103.468	105.276	103.240	103.354	103.127	3.2	3.4	3.1
2007	106.900	107.785	109.863	107.753	108.249	106.743	111.112	106.238	106.402	105.938	2.9	2.9	2.7
2008	111.975	119.237	115.245	111.225	112.187	109.240	117.666	108.576	109.858	108.719	2.2	3.2	2.6
2009	105.959	106.571	114.883	111.000	111.402	110.188	117.214	109.703	109.803	109.580	1.1	−.1	.8
2010	110.617	113.032	117.445	113.653	114.046	112.860	119.704	110.981	111.438	110.898	1.2	1.5	1.2
2011 *p*	117.546	121.774	121.093	116.878	117.593	115.456	123.646	113.242	114.186	112.874	2.1	2.5	1.8
2008: I	110.731	116.791	113.673	110.488	111.240	108.936	115.571	107.647	108.703	107.751	2.5	4.1	3.4
II	113.584	122.490	115.506	111.605	112.696	109.353	117.848	108.309	109.893	108.576	2.5	4.5	3.1
III	115.264	125.623	116.698	112.080	113.251	109.654	119.496	109.171	110.982	109.291	3.1	4.0	2.7
IV	108.320	112.045	115.103	110.726	111.561	109.017	117.750	109.179	109.852	109.256	.5	−4.0	−.1
2009: I	104.944	102.793	114.581	111.065	111.610	109.961	116.666	109.637	109.340	109.249	1.7	−1.9	.0
II	104.967	104.443	114.572	110.502	110.902	109.690	117.030	109.544	109.472	109.424	−.4	.5	.6
III	106.249	108.027	114.908	110.898	111.202	110.285	117.326	109.652	109.913	109.592	.3	1.6	.6
IV	107.674	111.019	115.470	111.537	111.892	110.817	117.835	109.979	110.485	110.056	1.1	2.1	1.7
2010: I	108.955	113.252	116.812	113.080	113.455	112.321	119.030	110.375	111.057	110.490	1.5	2.1	1.6
II	110.295	112.610	117.182	113.444	113.834	112.655	119.404	110.761	111.190	110.783	1.5	.5	1.1
III	110.461	111.994	117.444	113.759	114.093	113.083	119.627	111.140	111.456	110.991	1.4	1.0	.8
IV	112.757	114.271	118.341	114.331	114.802	113.380	120.757	111.647	112.048	111.326	1.9	2.1	1.2
2011: I	115.725	119.370	119.910	115.827	116.576	114.333	122.372	112.315	113.147	111.987	2.5	4.0	2.4
II	118.182	122.949	121.146	116.902	117.672	115.367	123.721	113.021	114.081	112.734	2.5	3.3	2.7
III	118.747	122.543	121.523	117.413	118.119	116.011	123.997	113.754	114.642	113.239	2.6	2.0	1.8
IV *p*	117.529	122.236	121.794	117.372	118.005	116.115	124.494	113.876	114.873	113.535	.4	.8	1.0

[1] Gross domestic product (GDP) less exports of goods and services plus imports of goods and services.
[2] Quarterly percent changes are at annual rates.

Source: Department of Commerce (Bureau of Economic Analysis).

Table B-8. Gross domestic product by major type of product, 1963–2011

[Billions of dollars; quarterly data at seasonally adjusted annual rates]

Year or quarter	Gross domestic product	Final sales of domestic product	Change in private inventories	Goods Total: Total	Goods Total: Final sales	Goods Total: Change in private inventories	Durable goods: Final sales	Durable goods: Change in private inventories[1]	Nondurable goods: Final sales	Nondurable goods: Change in private inventories[1]	Services[2]	Structures
1963	617.8	612.1	5.6	258.5	252.9	5.6	108.6	2.6	144.3	3.0	286.6	72.7
1964	663.6	658.8	4.8	277.8	273.0	4.8	119.3	3.8	153.7	1.0	307.4	78.4
1965	719.1	709.9	9.2	304.3	295.1	9.2	131.6	6.2	163.5	3.0	330.1	84.7
1966	787.7	774.1	13.6	337.1	323.5	13.6	145.4	10.0	178.0	3.6	362.6	88.0
1967	832.4	822.6	9.9	345.4	335.5	9.9	150.0	4.8	185.5	5.0	397.5	89.6
1968	909.8	900.8	9.1	370.8	361.7	9.1	162.8	4.5	198.9	4.5	439.1	100.0
1969	984.4	975.3	9.2	397.6	388.4	9.2	175.7	6.0	212.7	3.2	478.6	108.3
1970	1,038.3	1,036.3	2.0	408.7	406.7	2.0	178.6	-.2	228.2	2.2	519.9	109.7
1971	1,126.8	1,118.6	8.3	432.6	424.4	8.3	186.7	2.9	237.7	5.3	565.8	128.4
1972	1,237.9	1,228.8	9.1	472.0	462.9	9.1	208.4	6.4	254.5	2.7	619.0	146.9
1973	1,382.3	1,366.4	15.9	547.1	531.2	15.9	243.6	13.0	287.6	2.9	672.2	162.9
1974	1,499.5	1,485.5	14.0	588.0	574.0	14.0	262.4	10.9	311.7	3.1	745.8	165.6
1975	1,637.7	1,644.0	-6.3	628.6	634.8	-6.3	293.2	-7.5	341.6	1.2	842.4	166.7
1976	1,824.6	1,807.5	17.1	706.6	689.5	17.1	330.9	10.8	358.6	6.3	926.8	191.2
1977	2,030.1	2,007.8	22.3	773.5	751.2	22.3	374.6	9.5	376.6	12.8	1,029.9	226.8
1978	2,293.8	2,268.0	25.8	872.6	846.8	25.8	424.9	18.2	422.0	7.6	1,147.2	273.9
1979	2,562.2	2,544.2	18.0	977.2	959.2	18.0	483.9	12.8	475.3	5.2	1,271.7	313.3
1980	2,788.1	2,794.5	-6.3	1,035.2	1,041.5	-6.3	512.3	-2.3	529.2	-4.0	1,431.6	321.3
1981	3,126.8	3,097.0	29.8	1,167.3	1,137.5	29.8	554.8	7.3	582.6	22.5	1,606.9	352.6
1982	3,253.2	3,268.1	-14.9	1,148.8	1,163.7	-14.9	552.5	-16.0	611.2	1.1	1,759.9	344.5
1983	3,534.6	3,540.4	-5.8	1,226.9	1,232.6	-5.8	592.3	2.5	640.3	-8.2	1,939.1	368.7
1984	3,930.9	3,865.5	65.4	1,402.2	1,336.8	65.4	665.9	41.4	670.9	24.0	2,102.9	425.8
1985	4,217.5	4,195.6	21.8	1,452.8	1,431.0	21.8	727.9	4.4	703.1	17.4	2,305.9	458.7
1986	4,460.1	4,453.5	6.6	1,491.2	1,484.7	6.6	758.3	-1.9	726.4	8.4	2,488.7	480.1
1987	4,736.4	4,709.2	27.1	1,570.7	1,543.6	27.1	785.3	22.9	758.3	4.2	2,668.0	497.6
1988	5,100.4	5,081.9	18.5	1,703.7	1,685.2	18.5	863.3	22.7	821.9	-4.3	2,881.7	515.0
1989	5,482.1	5,454.5	27.7	1,851.9	1,824.2	27.7	939.7	20.0	884.5	7.7	3,101.2	529.0
1990	5,800.5	5,786.0	14.5	1,923.1	1,908.5	14.5	973.2	7.7	935.3	6.8	3,343.9	533.5
1991	5,992.1	5,992.5	-.4	1,943.5	1,943.9	-.4	967.6	-13.6	976.3	13.2	3,548.6	499.9
1992	6,342.3	6,326.0	16.3	2,031.5	2,015.1	16.3	1,010.7	-3.0	1,004.4	19.3	3,788.1	522.7
1993	6,667.4	6,646.5	20.8	2,124.2	2,103.4	20.8	1,072.9	17.1	1,030.4	3.7	3,985.1	558.1
1994	7,085.2	7,021.4	63.8	2,290.7	2,226.9	63.8	1,149.8	35.7	1,077.1	28.1	4,187.2	607.3
1995	7,414.7	7,383.5	31.2	2,379.5	2,348.3	31.2	1,225.9	33.6	1,122.4	-2.4	4,396.7	638.5
1996	7,838.5	7,807.7	30.8	2,516.3	2,485.5	30.8	1,321.0	19.1	1,164.5	11.7	4,625.5	696.7
1997	8,332.4	8,261.4	71.0	2,701.2	2,630.2	71.0	1,430.7	40.0	1,199.5	31.0	4,882.5	748.6
1998	8,793.5	8,729.8	63.7	2,819.2	2,755.5	63.7	1,524.2	39.3	1,231.3	24.4	5,159.7	814.5
1999	9,353.5	9,292.7	60.8	2,990.1	2,929.3	60.8	1,633.8	37.4	1,295.5	23.4	5,485.1	878.2
2000	9,951.5	9,896.9	54.5	3,124.5	3,070.0	54.5	1,734.4	35.6	1,335.6	19.0	5,878.0	949.0
2001	10,286.2	10,324.5	-38.3	3,077.6	3,115.9	-38.3	1,731.5	-44.4	1,384.4	6.2	6,208.7	999.9
2002	10,642.3	10,630.3	12.0	3,101.2	3,089.1	12.0	1,678.9	17.7	1,410.3	-5.6	6,535.5	1,005.7
2003	11,142.2	11,125.8	16.4	3,170.7	3,154.3	16.4	1,699.3	13.0	1,455.0	3.3	6,891.2	1,080.4
2004	11,853.3	11,788.3	64.9	3,333.8	3,268.9	64.9	1,759.3	37.3	1,509.6	27.6	7,304.9	1,214.5
2005	12,623.0	12,573.0	50.0	3,475.7	3,425.8	50.0	1,873.8	35.2	1,552.0	14.7	7,783.8	1,363.4
2006	13,377.2	13,317.5	60.0	3,663.7	3,603.7	60.0	1,973.4	25.9	1,630.3	34.0	8,260.8	1,452.7
2007	14,028.7	13,999.6	29.1	3,844.1	3,815.0	29.1	2,087.3	11.2	1,727.7	17.9	8,751.8	1,432.8
2008	14,291.5	14,332.7	-41.1	3,758.6	3,799.7	-41.1	2,043.1	-23.1	1,756.6	-18.0	9,174.0	1,359.0
2009	13,939.0	14,099.8	-160.8	3,617.0	3,777.8	-160.8	1,911.4	-113.6	1,866.4	-47.2	9,211.9	1,110.1
2010	14,526.5	14,459.6	66.9	4,009.9	3,943.0	66.9	2,006.0	45.5	1,937.0	21.4	9,508.6	1,008.0
2011 ᵖ	15,087.7	15,040.5	47.2	4,256.0	4,208.8	47.2	2,153.6	32.3	2,055.2	14.9	9,811.8	1,020.0
2008: I	14,273.9	14,293.4	-19.5	3,825.3	3,844.8	-19.5	2,101.3	-16.0	1,743.5	-3.5	9,074.1	1,374.6
II	14,415.5	14,433.8	-18.3	3,847.5	3,865.8	-18.3	2,090.2	-34.2	1,775.6	15.9	9,185.5	1,382.4
III	14,395.1	14,439.2	-44.1	3,789.8	3,833.9	-44.1	2,058.1	-7.1	1,775.8	-37.0	9,240.1	1,365.2
IV	14,081.7	14,164.2	-82.5	3,571.9	3,654.4	-82.5	1,922.8	-35.1	1,731.6	-47.5	9,196.2	1,313.6
2009: I	13,893.7	14,073.3	-179.5	3,539.7	3,719.2	-179.5	1,900.3	-142.1	1,818.9	-37.4	9,148.1	1,205.9
II	13,854.1	14,054.6	-200.5	3,567.3	3,767.8	-200.5	1,903.4	-144.1	1,864.4	-56.4	9,172.4	1,114.4
III	13,920.5	14,117.6	-197.1	3,617.4	3,814.5	-197.1	1,929.6	-118.8	1,884.9	-78.3	9,217.8	1,085.4
IV	14,087.4	14,153.5	-66.1	3,743.7	3,809.8	-66.1	1,912.4	-49.4	1,897.4	-16.7	9,309.2	1,034.6
2010: I	14,277.9	14,233.6	44.3	3,909.7	3,865.4	44.3	1,953.1	32.4	1,912.3	11.9	9,382.1	986.1
II	14,467.8	14,389.8	78.1	3,953.8	3,875.8	78.1	1,982.2	62.8	1,893.6	15.3	9,491.3	1,022.7
III	14,605.5	14,498.8	106.7	4,050.0	3,943.4	106.7	2,015.0	69.2	1,928.4	37.5	9,549.1	1,006.4
IV	14,755.0	14,716.3	38.7	4,126.1	4,087.4	38.7	2,073.6	17.7	2,013.8	21.0	9,612.1	1,016.8
2011: I	14,867.8	14,805.8	62.0	4,193.8	4,131.8	62.0	2,094.1	42.7	2,037.7	19.3	9,684.1	989.9
II	15,012.8	14,959.2	53.6	4,199.4	4,145.8	53.6	2,119.9	34.2	2,025.9	19.4	9,800.4	1,013.0
III	15,176.1	15,175.3	.8	4,262.2	4,261.4	.8	2,184.5	34.2	2,076.9	-33.4	9,877.2	1,036.7
IV ᵖ	15,294.3	15,221.7	72.6	4,368.7	4,296.1	72.6	2,215.9	18.2	2,080.2	54.4	9,885.4	1,040.2

[1] Estimates for durable and nondurable goods for 1996 and earlier periods are based on the Standard Industrial Classification (SIC); later estimates are based on the North American Industry Classification System (NAICS).

[2] Includes government consumption expenditures, which are for services (such as education and national defense) produced by government. In current dollars, these services are valued at their cost of production.

Source: Department of Commerce (Bureau of Economic Analysis).

[Billions of chained (2005) dollars; quarterly data at seasonally adjusted annual rates]

Year or quarter	Gross domestic product	Final sales of domestic product	Change in private inventories	Goods — Total — Total	Goods — Total — Final sales	Goods — Total — Change in private inventories	Goods — Durable goods — Final sales	Goods — Durable goods — Change in private inventories [1]	Goods — Nondurable goods — Final sales	Goods — Nondurable goods — Change in private inventories [1]	Services [2]	Structures
1963	3,204.0	3,199.9	20.3	673.0							2,090.5	591.7
1964	3,389.4	3,390.8	17.3	718.1							2,189.6	631.5
1965	3,607.0	3,587.6	32.9	778.4							2,299.2	663.1
1966	3,842.1	3,803.4	47.1	846.0							2,441.1	663.9
1967	3,939.2	3,920.0	33.9	848.3							2,577.0	654.2
1968	4,129.9	4,115.8	30.8	882.2							2,712.9	694.5
1969	4,258.2	4,245.0	30.3	912.6							2,801.0	703.3
1970	4,266.3	4,284.3	5.6	905.0							2,858.4	673.0
1971	4,409.5	4,403.6	25.0	931.8							2,927.0	735.5
1972	4,643.8	4,636.7	25.7	995.5							3,034.9	790.2
1973	4,912.8	4,884.0	39.0	1,101.4							3,125.7	807.1
1974	4,885.7	4,870.0	29.1	1,090.8							3,194.8	723.4
1975	4,875.4	4,922.1	−12.8	1,063.5							3,309.3	657.6
1976	5,136.9	5,115.9	34.3	1,147.0							3,400.4	719.2
1977	5,373.1	5,340.3	43.1	1,202.1							3,517.3	787.2
1978	5,672.8	5,634.9	45.6	1,282.9							3,651.8	862.8
1979	5,850.1	5,836.2	28.0	1,335.9							3,740.4	887.4
1980	5,834.0	5,873.6	−9.3	1,324.2							3,811.4	823.0
1981	5,982.1	5,954.4	39.0	1,384.0							3,887.6	811.9
1982	5,865.9	5,918.2	−19.7	1,312.8							3,957.1	742.6
1983	6,130.9	6,167.6	−7.7	1,369.5							4,120.4	796.3
1984	6,571.5	6,490.0	78.3	1,539.3							4,234.4	903.9
1985	6,843.4	6,833.1	25.4	1,576.1							4,449.0	951.0
1986	7,080.5	7,092.7	8.5	1,622.2							4,635.5	965.1
1987	7,307.0	7,289.9	33.2	1,687.5							4,785.6	969.3
1988	7,607.4	7,601.3	21.9	1,792.5							4,961.7	967.6
1989	7,879.2	7,860.8	30.6	1,894.4							5,115.1	961.0
1990	8,027.1	8,025.8	16.6	1,914.2							5,269.7	941.9
1991	8,008.3	8,027.9	−1.4	1,881.9							5,363.4	869.1
1992	8,280.0	8,277.2	17.9	1,958.7							5,522.0	902.4
1993	8,516.2	8,508.0	22.3	2,034.1							5,648.3	930.5
1994	8,863.1	8,801.7	69.3	2,177.1							5,781.5	978.4
1995	9,086.0	9,065.4	32.1	2,257.1	2,234.2	32.1	1,017.9	31.4	1,259.3	−3.3	5,902.9	988.9
1996	9,425.8	9,404.4	31.2	2,380.4	2,356.6	31.2	1,105.4	17.9	1,286.0	12.5	6,045.7	1,053.1
1997	9,845.9	9,774.2	77.4	2,566.0	2,502.1	77.4	1,216.7	40.2	1,309.2	36.1	6,208.7	1,097.8
1998	10,274.7	10,208.3	71.6	2,714.7	2,654.8	71.6	1,334.8	40.6	1,333.6	29.5	6,422.2	1,155.1
1999	10,770.7	10,706.5	68.5	2,905.1	2,847.0	68.5	1,469.2	39.5	1,384.2	27.7	6,664.0	1,202.2
2000	11,216.4	11,158.0	60.2	3,046.9	2,993.5	60.2	1,582.7	37.7	1,411.0	21.4	6,919.2	1,245.3
2001	11,337.5	11,382.0	−41.8	2,997.7	3,034.2	−41.8	1,606.7	−46.4	1,427.4	7.3	7,095.8	1,254.1
2002	11,543.1	11,533.6	12.8	3,049.9	3,038.0	12.8	1,588.8	18.1	1,451.0	−6.4	7,276.1	1,223.2
2003	11,836.4	11,820.5	17.3	3,160.3	3,142.4	17.3	1,658.0	13.5	1,485.2	3.6	7,415.9	1,263.6
2004	12,246.9	12,181.3	66.3	3,324.4	3,259.1	66.3	1,750.4	38.1	1,508.8	28.1	7,598.2	1,325.6
2005	12,623.0	12,573.0	50.0	3,475.7	3,425.8	50.0	1,873.8	35.2	1,552.0	14.7	7,783.8	1,363.4
2006	12,958.5	12,899.3	59.4	3,659.1	3,599.9	59.4	1,989.5	25.2	1,610.6	34.1	7,961.0	1,341.1
2007	13,206.4	13,177.5	27.7	3,819.6	3,792.1	27.7	2,133.1	10.8	1,660.7	16.9	8,131.5	1,267.0
2008	13,161.9	13,200.5	−36.3	3,789.7	3,834.7	−36.3	2,129.9	−21.1	1,704.8	−15.5	8,216.6	1,169.9
2009	12,703.1	12,852.7	−144.9	3,566.6	3,732.1	−144.9	1,994.5	−105.9	1,730.4	−41.2	8,173.1	971.9
2010	13,088.0	13,028.9	58.8	3,984.2	3,921.9	58.8	2,128.4	41.5	1,789.9	18.6	8,261.2	886.5
2011 p	13,313.4	13,281.8	35.6	4,162.9	4,131.4	35.6	2,302.9	28.2	1,833.7	9.1	8,339.6	869.0
2008: I	13,266.8	13,277.8	−12.5	3,862.0	3,877.2	−12.5	2,176.0	−14.8	1,702.8	1.6	8,226.7	1,196.0
II	13,310.5	13,325.9	−14.2	3,905.1	3,924.9	−14.2	2,189.4	−30.5	1,736.3	13.8	8,231.0	1,196.5
III	13,186.9	13,225.6	−38.1	3,822.0	3,867.0	−38.1	2,150.2	−5.8	1,717.0	−30.8	8,211.6	1,170.9
IV	12,883.5	12,972.9	−80.3	3,569.6	3,669.9	−80.3	2,004.0	−33.3	1,663.1	−46.4	8,197.3	1,116.3
2009: I	12,663.2	12,836.0	−161.6	3,471.1	3,661.8	−161.6	1,974.0	−132.6	1,682.6	−32.2	8,159.3	1,031.6
II	12,641.3	12,830.0	−183.0	3,502.7	3,710.8	−183.0	1,979.3	−135.1	1,723.9	−50.6	8,168.7	973.7
III	12,694.5	12,875.1	−178.7	3,569.9	3,769.3	−178.7	2,020.1	−110.3	1,742.6	−70.0	8,169.7	964.2
IV	12,813.5	12,869.5	−56.5	3,722.8	3,786.6	−56.5	2,004.6	−45.6	1,772.6	−12.0	8,194.8	918.1
2010: I	12,937.7	12,895.9	39.9	3,903.4	3,859.9	39.9	2,061.4	30.0	1,790.9	11.1	8,201.4	872.0
II	13,058.5	12,992.2	64.6	3,941.5	3,871.2	64.6	2,100.9	57.1	1,766.6	9.6	8,253.9	902.9
III	13,139.6	13,046.0	92.3	4,016.9	3,916.6	92.3	2,140.2	62.6	1,774.4	31.5	8,284.5	884.3
IV	13,216.1	13,181.6	38.3	4,075.1	4,040.1	38.3	2,211.2	16.4	1,827.5	22.3	8,305.0	886.6
2011: I	13,227.9	13,182.8	49.1	4,124.5	4,078.0	49.1	2,240.2	37.4	1,837.6	13.9	8,303.5	856.0
II	13,271.8	13,236.2	39.1	4,118.1	4,082.0	39.1	2,266.6	29.8	1,819.0	11.1	8,341.0	866.5
III	13,331.6	13,340.9	−2.0	4,140.6	4,154.6	−2.0	2,334.2	29.8	1,828.6	−27.2	8,366.7	878.8
IV p	13,422.4	13,367.4	56.0	4,268.4	4,211.0	56.0	2,370.7	15.9	1,849.5	38.7	8,347.2	874.8

[1] Estimates for durable and nondurable goods for 1996 and earlier periods are based on the Standard Industrial Classification (SIC); later estimates are based on the North American Industry Classification System (NAICS).

[2] Includes government consumption expenditures, which are for services (such as education and national defense) produced by government. In current dollars, these services are valued at their cost of production.

Source: Department of Commerce (Bureau of Economic Analysis).

[Billions of dollars; quarterly data at seasonally adjusted annual rates]

| Year or quarter | Gross domestic product | Business[1] | | | Households and institutions | | | General government[3] | | | Addendum: Gross housing value added |
		Total	Nonfarm[1]	Farm	Total	Households	Nonprofit institutions serving households[2]	Total	Federal	State and local	
1963	617.8	488.0	469.5	18.5	54.3	39.1	15.2	75.5	38.4	37.1	48.9
1964	663.6	524.9	507.5	17.3	57.7	41.2	16.5	81.1	40.7	40.4	51.6
1965	719.1	570.7	550.7	19.9	61.8	43.6	18.2	86.6	42.4	44.2	54.9
1966	787.7	624.3	603.5	20.8	66.6	46.2	20.4	96.8	47.2	49.6	58.2
1967	832.4	653.6	633.5	20.1	71.8	49.1	22.7	107.0	51.5	55.5	62.1
1968	909.8	713.5	693.0	20.5	77.5	51.9	25.6	118.8	56.3	62.5	65.9
1969	984.4	769.1	746.3	22.8	85.4	56.0	29.4	130.0	59.9	70.0	71.3
1970	1,038.3	802.2	778.5	23.7	92.6	59.8	32.8	143.5	64.0	79.5	76.7
1971	1,126.8	868.3	842.9	25.4	102.2	65.5	36.7	156.4	67.7	88.6	83.9
1972	1,237.9	957.1	927.5	29.7	111.4	70.8	40.5	169.4	71.5	97.9	91.1
1973	1,382.3	1,077.4	1,030.6	46.8	121.7	76.5	45.2	183.2	73.9	109.3	98.3
1974	1,499.5	1,164.5	1,120.3	44.2	133.6	83.0	50.6	201.3	79.6	121.8	106.8
1975	1,637.7	1,265.8	1,220.1	45.6	147.5	90.8	56.7	224.5	87.3	137.2	117.2
1976	1,824.6	1,420.7	1,377.7	43.0	160.5	98.7	61.8	243.5	93.8	149.7	126.6
1977	2,030.1	1,590.0	1,546.5	43.5	175.5	107.9	67.6	264.6	102.0	162.6	140.5
1978	2,293.8	1,809.4	1,758.7	50.7	196.9	121.3	75.6	287.5	109.7	177.8	155.5
1979	2,562.2	2,028.5	1,968.4	60.1	220.8	136.0	84.8	313.0	117.6	195.4	172.9
1980	2,788.1	2,186.1	2,134.7	51.4	253.5	156.5	97.0	348.5	131.2	217.3	199.8
1981	3,126.8	2,454.0	2,389.0	65.0	287.5	177.8	109.7	385.3	147.4	237.9	228.8
1982	3,253.2	2,514.9	2,454.5	60.4	319.3	196.7	122.7	419.0	161.2	257.7	255.7
1983	3,534.6	2,741.1	2,696.2	44.9	348.2	212.5	135.6	445.4	171.2	274.1	277.7
1984	3,930.9	3,065.5	3,001.3	64.2	380.3	231.0	149.3	485.1	192.1	293.1	301.3
1985	4,217.5	3,283.9	3,220.5	63.4	410.1	250.3	159.8	523.4	205.0	318.4	333.1
1986	4,460.1	3,461.5	3,402.1	59.5	442.3	268.0	174.3	556.3	212.6	343.7	359.7
1987	4,736.4	3,662.0	3,600.5	61.5	482.8	288.0	194.8	591.5	223.3	368.2	385.5
1988	5,100.4	3,940.2	3,879.4	60.7	529.7	313.1	216.6	630.6	234.8	395.8	415.3
1989	5,482.1	4,235.7	4,162.0	73.8	574.2	337.2	237.0	672.2	246.4	425.8	443.4
1990	5,800.5	4,453.9	4,376.6	77.3	624.0	363.3	260.6	722.7	258.8	463.9	477.8
1991	5,992.1	4,558.6	4,488.0	70.6	665.9	383.7	282.2	767.6	274.8	492.8	508.1
1992	6,342.3	4,829.2	4,748.9	80.4	711.1	405.3	305.9	801.9	282.0	519.9	538.6
1993	6,667.4	5,084.1	5,012.7	71.4	752.1	428.3	323.8	831.2	285.2	546.0	562.9
1994	7,085.2	5,425.2	5,341.3	83.9	800.0	461.3	338.7	859.9	285.2	574.7	602.6
1995	7,414.7	5,677.8	5,608.7	69.1	852.1	492.2	359.9	884.8	283.6	601.2	640.7
1996	7,838.5	6,030.2	5,936.9	93.3	897.0	519.8	377.2	911.3	287.6	623.7	671.3
1997	8,332.4	6,442.8	6,354.9	87.9	949.2	550.9	398.3	940.3	290.0	650.3	708.6
1998	8,793.5	6,810.8	6,731.6	79.2	1,010.1	583.9	426.3	972.5	292.2	680.3	745.3
1999	9,353.5	7,249.0	7,177.8	71.2	1,082.9	628.4	454.5	1,021.6	300.4	721.2	798.3
2000	9,951.5	7,715.5	7,641.9	73.6	1,157.2	673.5	483.7	1,078.8	315.1	763.7	849.9
2001	10,286.2	7,913.6	7,837.4	76.2	1,232.9	719.5	513.4	1,139.6	324.9	814.7	904.4
2002	10,642.3	8,132.8	8,060.5	72.3	1,298.0	746.0	552.1	1,211.4	351.8	859.6	932.5
2003	11,142.2	8,502.8	8,410.4	92.4	1,347.2	762.7	584.5	1,292.2	382.9	909.3	938.2
2004	11,853.3	9,070.1	8,951.9	118.3	1,423.8	806.0	617.7	1,359.3	412.0	947.3	988.7
2005	12,623.0	9,680.1	9,578.0	102.0	1,506.4	864.4	642.0	1,436.5	438.7	997.7	1,054.0
2006	13,377.2	10,262.4	10,169.4	93.1	1,602.9	924.8	678.1	1,512.0	460.6	1,051.3	1,130.8
2007	14,028.7	10,738.3	10,623.4	114.9	1,685.8	968.1	717.8	1,604.6	486.0	1,118.6	1,200.6
2008	14,291.5	10,787.8	10,657.4	130.5	1,805.7	1,042.8	762.9	1,698.0	517.7	1,180.3	1,299.7
2009	13,939.0	10,338.8	10,225.7	113.1	1,836.0	1,046.9	789.1	1,764.1	553.2	1,210.9	1,321.2
2010	14,526.5	10,879.1	10,746.5	132.6	1,838.4	1,033.6	804.8	1,809.1	589.6	1,219.5	1,314.5
2011 [p]	15,087.7	11,381.8	11,230.4	151.4	1,867.5	1,037.3	830.1	1,838.5	608.6	1,230.0	1,330.3
2008: I	14,273.9	10,842.8	10,699.7	143.2	1,764.9	1,016.1	748.7	1,666.2	506.9	1,159.3	1,262.6
II	14,415.5	10,926.9	10,791.9	135.1	1,802.3	1,045.6	756.7	1,686.2	514.6	1,171.7	1,299.3
III	14,395.1	10,869.0	10,746.2	122.8	1,816.0	1,050.1	765.9	1,710.0	521.9	1,188.0	1,310.3
IV	14,081.7	10,512.6	10,391.9	120.7	1,839.6	1,059.2	780.4	1,729.6	527.4	1,202.2	1,326.8
2009: I	13,893.7	10,316.8	10,206.7	110.1	1,828.4	1,050.3	778.1	1,748.5	543.9	1,204.6	1,319.8
II	13,854.1	10,259.2	10,146.7	112.6	1,832.6	1,043.9	788.7	1,762.2	550.5	1,211.6	1,317.6
III	13,920.5	10,312.2	10,198.5	113.7	1,839.2	1,049.8	789.5	1,769.1	555.8	1,213.3	1,325.9
IV	14,087.4	10,467.1	10,350.9	116.2	1,843.6	1,043.5	800.1	1,776.8	562.6	1,214.2	1,321.4
2010: I	14,277.9	10,646.1	10,524.4	121.7	1,833.9	1,039.3	794.7	1,797.9	580.9	1,217.0	1,319.6
II	14,467.8	10,820.7	10,697.1	123.6	1,835.2	1,033.0	802.3	1,811.9	592.2	1,219.8	1,313.5
III	14,605.5	10,950.7	10,809.6	141.1	1,843.9	1,031.5	812.4	1,810.9	591.3	1,219.6	1,312.8
IV	14,755.0	11,098.9	10,954.7	144.1	1,840.5	1,030.6	810.0	1,815.6	593.8	1,221.8	1,312.3
2011: I	14,867.8	11,188.9	11,038.0	150.9	1,851.9	1,035.1	816.8	1,827.0	601.9	1,225.2	1,321.5
II	15,012.8	11,315.1	11,161.4	153.6	1,861.6	1,036.7	824.9	1,836.1	607.2	1,228.9	1,327.4
III	15,176.1	11,462.7	11,307.4	155.3	1,871.5	1,035.9	835.6	1,841.9	611.0	1,231.0	1,330.4
IV [p]	15,294.3	11,560.5	11,414.7	145.8	1,884.8	1,041.6	843.2	1,849.0	614.2	1,234.8	1,341.7

[1] Gross domestic business value added equals gross domestic product excluding gross value added of households and institutions and of general government. Nonfarm value added equals gross domestic business value added excluding gross farm value added.

[2] Equals compensation of employees of nonprofit institutions, the rental value of nonresidential fixed assets owned and used by nonprofit institutions serving households, and rental income of persons for tenant-occupied housing owned by nonprofit institutions.

[3] Equals compensation of general government employees plus general government consumption of fixed capital.

Source: Department of Commerce (Bureau of Economic Analysis).

[Billions of chained (2005) dollars; quarterly data at seasonally adjusted annual rates]

Year or quarter	Gross domestic product	Business [1] Total	Nonfarm [1]	Farm	Households and institutions Total	House-holds	Nonprofit institutions serving house-holds [2]	General government [3] Total	Federal	State and local	Adden-dum: Gross housing value added
1963	3,204.0	2,186.8	2,152.8	25.7	384.0	226.9	152.6	742.8	396.7	356.1	278.9
1964	3,389.4	2,325.4	2,297.1	24.9	399.9	236.0	159.4	768.4	400.7	377.5	291.6
1965	3,607.0	2,489.6	2,459.8	26.5	419.7	246.9	168.6	794.2	403.4	400.5	307.1
1966	3,842.1	2,658.0	2,635.6	25.5	438.9	256.8	178.5	843.9	429.9	424.2	320.9
1967	3,939.2	2,708.9	2,681.0	27.6	457.1	267.1	186.6	888.7	457.9	442.1	335.6
1968	4,129.9	2,843.7	2,821.6	26.6	480.1	274.6	204.9	923.6	465.7	468.6	348.3
1969	4,258.2	2,930.7	2,907.6	27.5	501.2	285.9	214.9	947.2	467.1	490.0	364.6
1970	4,266.3	2,930.0	2,904.4	28.3	510.2	292.6	216.7	950.8	447.1	511.7	376.6
1971	4,409.5	3,042.6	3,014.8	29.8	531.7	305.9	224.5	952.4	426.5	532.5	393.6
1972	4,643.8	3,238.5	3,215.2	29.8	554.8	319.1	234.4	950.6	405.8	550.9	412.5
1973	4,912.8	3,465.5	3,450.9	29.5	574.6	330.6	242.7	954.9	390.7	570.2	427.8
1974	4,885.7	3,413.7	3,400.3	28.8	597.7	345.0	251.0	974.4	389.4	590.9	448.5
1975	4,875.4	3,381.8	3,344.8	34.3	617.9	354.2	262.5	990.1	387.3	608.9	462.2
1976	5,136.9	3,605.2	3,579.3	32.7	628.2	360.9	265.8	998.7	387.9	616.9	469.3
1977	5,373.1	3,805.8	3,778.7	34.5	637.5	365.0	271.3	1,009.2	389.0	626.4	481.2
1978	5,672.8	4,045.6	4,027.9	33.3	666.4	387.4	276.7	1,028.3	393.9	641.0	503.2
1979	5,850.1	4,179.9	4,155.0	36.3	695.3	405.0	287.8	1,039.5	393.5	652.4	523.0
1980	5,834.0	4,132.8	4,110.3	35.2	730.9	430.6	297.1	1,054.4	399.7	661.2	555.0
1981	5,982.1	4,247.7	4,197.8	46.5	754.1	444.1	306.8	1,060.2	405.9	660.9	576.7
1982	5,865.9	4,119.1	4,062.4	48.8	778.9	452.1	324.3	1,071.0	412.5	665.2	592.3
1983	6,130.9	4,341.0	4,323.6	31.9	801.0	460.5	338.5	1,077.9	422.0	662.5	605.4
1984	6,571.5	4,717.9	4,679.3	43.3	826.8	476.4	348.3	1,091.3	431.6	666.4	624.6
1985	6,843.4	4,937.0	4,880.9	52.9	841.2	487.4	351.2	1,122.5	443.9	685.6	649.1
1986	7,080.5	5,121.2	5,070.4	50.8	863.4	493.7	368.0	1,150.1	451.8	705.4	661.1
1987	7,307.0	5,289.8	5,239.3	51.3	895.8	506.8	388.0	1,175.3	463.6	719.0	676.8
1988	7,607.4	5,516.6	5,478.3	45.6	937.2	525.7	411.1	1,205.8	469.3	743.6	696.4
1989	7,879.2	5,720.9	5,671.7	52.3	974.8	542.0	432.9	1,234.6	475.1	766.4	712.2
1990	8,027.1	5,808.8	5,753.4	56.0	1,009.6	555.7	454.9	1,266.2	483.8	789.2	730.2
1991	8,008.3	5,757.9	5,700.5	56.9	1,038.5	572.0	467.4	1,279.4	486.7	799.4	754.6
1992	8,280.0	5,985.1	5,914.6	66.2	1,071.4	589.0	483.5	1,283.7	476.5	813.0	776.7
1993	8,516.2	6,178.1	6,121.3	57.8	1,106.9	603.5	504.9	1,286.5	467.4	824.2	789.1
1994	8,863.1	6,481.0	6,407.0	70.5	1,140.0	631.9	508.7	1,286.8	452.2	838.5	821.7
1995	9,086.0	6,663.3	6,610.4	56.4	1,175.5	651.3	524.8	1,287.7	435.1	855.1	846.9
1996	9,425.8	6,966.8	6,901.6	65.3	1,199.8	665.4	535.0	1,289.8	423.2	868.4	860.4
1997	9,845.9	7,327.5	7,253.2	72.5	1,240.5	687.6	553.5	1,299.6	415.2	885.6	885.6
1998	10,274.7	7,693.8	7,624.8	69.4	1,280.2	703.7	577.8	1,314.3	410.4	904.6	900.9
1999	10,770.7	8,123.7	8,051.5	72.8	1,325.5	740.3	585.3	1,326.3	407.1	919.5	942.3
2000	11,216.4	8,491.4	8,408.3	83.5	1,376.2	774.1	601.8	1,349.4	410.5	939.0	977.8
2001	11,337.5	8,559.5	8,482.3	77.7	1,407.0	793.1	613.4	1,373.7	412.1	961.3	997.8
2002	11,543.1	8,726.8	8,646.1	81.2	1,417.3	789.9	627.7	1,401.4	420.2	980.9	988.5
2003	11,836.4	9,001.6	8,910.5	91.6	1,417.8	787.1	631.1	1,418.2	431.5	986.7	969.3
2004	12,246.9	9,363.0	9,265.1	97.9	1,457.4	821.7	635.9	1,426.8	435.8	991.0	1,008.4
2005	12,623.0	9,680.1	9,578.0	102.0	1,506.4	864.4	642.0	1,436.5	438.7	997.7	1,054.0
2006	12,958.5	9,974.0	9,874.6	99.1	1,539.8	898.0	642.0	1,445.0	438.4	1,006.5	1,098.6
2007	13,206.4	10,172.5	10,082.1	90.3	1,571.9	914.2	657.8	1,462.5	441.8	1,020.8	1,132.4
2008	13,161.9	10,038.4	9,934.2	101.7	1,628.6	954.8	674.2	1,492.3	459.0	1,033.3	1,183.9
2009	12,703.1	9,550.3	9,430.8	117.1	1,623.0	944.8	678.3	1,520.1	485.9	1,034.6	1,184.6
2010	13,088.0	9,923.9	9,804.7	116.5	1,630.6	943.2	687.2	1,527.9	503.7	1,025.0	1,189.5
2011 _p_	13,313.4	10,153.1	10,055.7	99.3	1,635.2	934.5	699.8	1,522.6	508.9	1,014.6	1,187.3
2008: I	13,266.8	10,182.9	10,077.1	102.5	1,603.9	938.1	666.1	1,479.6	449.6	1,030.1	1,161.3
II	13,310.5	10,189.0	10,087.5	99.4	1,634.4	961.0	673.9	1,486.1	454.5	1,031.5	1,188.5
III	13,186.9	10,049.3	9,952.9	95.0	1,636.9	958.7	678.6	1,498.0	462.2	1,035.8	1,189.7
IV	12,883.5	9,732.3	9,619.4	110.0	1,639.3	961.3	678.4	1,505.4	469.9	1,035.7	1,196.1
2009: I	12,663.2	9,518.9	9,402.3	114.0	1,623.4	947.0	676.6	1,511.5	475.1	1,036.7	1,182.2
II	12,641.3	9,493.9	9,375.7	115.6	1,615.9	939.4	676.6	1,521.2	485.6	1,036.0	1,178.0
III	12,694.5	9,535.7	9,408.3	126.2	1,625.6	946.5	679.2	1,522.9	489.7	1,033.7	1,187.9
IV	12,813.5	9,652.6	9,537.0	112.5	1,627.1	946.5	680.7	1,524.9	493.2	1,032.3	1,190.2
2010: I	12,937.7	9,773.3	9,657.6	112.6	1,630.3	947.0	683.3	1,526.7	498.5	1,028.9	1,192.9
II	13,058.5	9,886.9	9,766.6	117.3	1,632.1	946.1	686.0	1,533.1	507.0	1,026.8	1,192.4
III	13,139.6	9,977.9	9,851.7	123.2	1,630.2	941.6	688.3	1,526.7	504.3	1,023.2	1,188.4
IV	13,216.1	10,057.5	9,942.8	112.7	1,629.8	938.1	691.2	1,525.1	505.0	1,020.9	1,184.4
2011: I	13,227.9	10,065.9	9,964.0	102.4	1,633.7	940.1	693.1	1,524.6	507.4	1,018.1	1,189.2
II	13,271.8	10,107.9	10,009.6	99.9	1,638.4	940.0	697.7	1,522.5	508.4	1,014.9	1,192.3
III	13,331.6	10,175.1	10,079.2	98.2	1,633.4	929.2	702.9	1,520.9	508.7	1,013.1	1,183.1
IV _p_	13,422.4	10,263.4	10,169.8	96.8	1,635.4	928.7	705.4	1,522.3	511.0	1,012.2	1,184.6

[1] Gross domestic business value added equals gross domestic product excluding gross value added of households and institutions and of general government. Nonfarm value added equals gross domestic business value added excluding gross farm value added.

[2] Equals compensation of employees of nonprofit institutions, the rental value of nonresidential fixed assets owned and used by nonprofit institutions serving households, and rental income of persons for tenant-occupied housing owned by nonprofit institutions.

[3] Equals compensation of general government employees plus general government consumption of fixed capital.

Source: Department of Commerce (Bureau of Economic Analysis).

[Billions of dollars; except as noted]

Year	Gross domestic product	Private industries									
		Total private industries	Agriculture, forestry, fishing, and hunting	Mining	Construction	Manufacturing			Utilities	Wholesale trade	Retail trade
						Total manufacturing	Durable goods	Non-durable goods			
						Value added					
1980	2,788.1	2,404.8	62.1	90.8	131.5	558.3	339.2	219.2	61.0	186.3	198.3
1981	3,126.8	2,701.6	75.6	121.5	133.1	619.6	376.2	243.4	72.0	206.2	218.0
1982	3,253.2	2,791.4	71.6	118.5	131.0	606.5	359.2	247.3	83.2	206.6	226.9
1983	3,534.6	3,041.7	57.2	102.8	139.6	657.5	385.5	272.0	94.4	222.4	255.3
1984	3,930.9	3,393.0	77.0	107.2	160.7	731.8	451.0	280.7	105.7	249.8	286.8
1985	4,217.5	3,634.6	76.6	106.2	177.0	751.4	458.6	292.8	113.0	269.2	309.1
1986	4,460.1	3,840.4	73.7	70.3	197.2	777.4	468.4	308.9	117.5	279.3	331.4
1987	4,736.4	4,077.9	78.8	73.1	210.1	823.1	492.5	330.6	125.8	285.6	345.7
1988	5,100.4	4,395.3	78.1	74.1	226.5	900.2	537.9	362.2	125.1	314.3	366.8
1989	5,482.1	4,729.7	91.6	78.6	238.6	950.2	562.4	387.7	138.2	335.7	390.7
1990	5,800.5	4,994.3	95.7	88.4	243.6	968.9	558.9	410.1	145.5	347.7	400.4
1991	5,992.1	5,133.2	88.3	79.5	228.8	976.7	554.2	422.5	153.8	362.6	407.9
1992	6,342.3	5,442.0	99.3	73.6	233.2	1,016.7	574.5	442.2	159.7	380.1	430.0
1993	6,667.4	5,735.9	90.6	74.4	250.4	1,058.9	603.0	456.0	164.3	402.5	462.9
1994	7,085.2	6,119.9	105.6	75.9	277.2	1,127.3	650.2	477.1	171.2	444.5	500.5
1995	7,414.7	6,420.0	91.3	76.7	294.2	1,180.9	675.4	505.5	175.3	460.2	525.0
1996	7,838.5	6,812.6	114.2	90.0	320.9	1,208.5	705.0	503.5	173.4	492.5	556.8
1997	8,332.4	7,271.0	108.4	94.8	346.7	1,277.3	748.9	528.3	169.9	524.9	589.9
1998	8,793.5	7,694.4	100.3	81.0	383.7	1,326.7	781.2	545.6	165.1	557.3	626.9
1999	9,353.5	8,199.6	92.8	82.0	428.4	1,368.1	802.4	565.6	172.7	579.1	653.4
2000	9,951.5	8,736.1	95.6	108.9	467.3	1,415.6	839.1	576.5	173.9	617.7	686.2
2001	10,286.2	9,010.8	98.6	119.3	490.5	1,343.9	758.8	585.2	177.6	613.3	703.9
2002	10,642.3	9,289.3	94.4	109.5	494.3	1,355.5	767.8	587.8	181.0	614.9	731.2
2003	11,142.2	9,706.9	115.5	134.9	516.1	1,374.3	766.4	607.9	192.0	638.1	769.5
2004	11,853.3	10,345.6	142.7	159.3	554.2	1,482.7	822.0	660.6	208.0	684.2	795.1
2005	12,623.0	11,037.1	127.1	192.3	612.5	1,569.3	878.3	691.0	205.9	725.5	837.6
2006	13,377.2	11,709.4	122.5	229.8	651.0	1,648.4	921.3	727.1	236.0	769.7	875.8
2007	14,028.7	12,268.8	144.5	254.5	653.8	1,698.0	939.9	758.1	248.6	816.7	887.9
2008	14,291.5	12,437.1	159.4	319.2	614.2	1,628.5	904.1	724.4	257.7	824.1	848.6
2009	13,939.0	12,018.1	140.0	213.4	541.9	1,540.2	800.4	739.8	258.3	768.5	837.2
2010	14,526.5	12,558.0	157.0	239.5	511.6	1,701.9	914.5	787.4	264.9	797.3	884.9
	Percent	Industry value added as a percentage of GDP (percent)									
1980	100.0	86.3	2.2	3.3	4.7	20.0	12.2	7.9	2.2	6.7	7.1
1981	100.0	86.4	2.4	3.9	4.3	19.8	12.0	7.8	2.3	6.6	7.0
1982	100.0	85.8	2.2	3.6	4.0	18.6	11.0	7.6	2.6	6.4	7.0
1983	100.0	86.1	1.6	2.9	3.9	18.6	10.9	7.7	2.7	6.3	7.2
1984	100.0	86.3	2.0	2.7	4.1	18.6	11.5	7.1	2.7	6.4	7.3
1985	100.0	86.2	1.8	2.5	4.2	17.8	10.9	6.9	2.7	6.4	7.3
1986	100.0	86.1	1.7	1.6	4.4	17.4	10.5	6.9	2.6	6.3	7.4
1987	100.0	86.1	1.7	1.5	4.4	17.4	10.4	7.0	2.7	6.0	7.3
1988	100.0	86.2	1.5	1.5	4.4	17.6	10.5	7.1	2.5	6.2	7.2
1989	100.0	86.3	1.7	1.4	4.4	17.3	10.3	7.1	2.5	6.1	7.1
1990	100.0	86.1	1.6	1.5	4.2	16.7	9.6	7.1	2.5	6.0	6.9
1991	100.0	85.7	1.5	1.3	3.8	16.3	9.2	7.1	2.6	6.1	6.8
1992	100.0	85.8	1.6	1.2	3.7	16.0	9.1	7.0	2.5	6.0	6.8
1993	100.0	86.0	1.4	1.1	3.8	15.9	9.0	6.8	2.5	6.0	6.9
1994	100.0	86.4	1.5	1.1	3.9	15.9	9.2	6.7	2.4	6.3	7.1
1995	100.0	86.6	1.2	1.0	4.0	15.9	9.1	6.8	2.4	6.2	7.1
1996	100.0	86.9	1.5	1.1	4.1	15.4	9.0	6.4	2.2	6.3	7.1
1997	100.0	87.3	1.3	1.1	4.2	15.3	9.0	6.3	2.0	6.3	7.1
1998	100.0	87.5	1.1	.9	4.4	15.1	8.9	6.2	1.9	6.3	7.1
1999	100.0	87.7	1.0	.9	4.6	14.6	8.6	6.0	1.8	6.2	7.0
2000	100.0	87.8	1.0	1.1	4.7	14.2	8.4	5.8	1.7	6.2	6.9
2001	100.0	87.6	1.0	1.2	4.8	13.1	7.4	5.7	1.7	6.0	6.8
2002	100.0	87.3	.9	1.0	4.6	12.7	7.2	5.5	1.7	5.8	6.9
2003	100.0	87.1	1.0	1.2	4.6	12.3	6.9	5.5	1.7	5.7	6.9
2004	100.0	87.3	1.2	1.3	4.7	12.5	6.9	5.6	1.8	5.8	6.7
2005	100.0	87.4	1.0	1.5	4.9	12.4	7.0	5.5	1.6	5.7	6.6
2006	100.0	87.5	.9	1.7	4.9	12.3	6.9	5.4	·1.8	5.8	6.5
2007	100.0	87.5	1.0	1.8	4.7	12.1	6.7	5.4	1.8	5.8	6.3
2008	100.0	87.0	1.1	2.2	4.3	11.4	6.3	5.1	1.8	5.8	5.9
2009	100.0	86.2	1.0	1.5	3.9	11.0	5.7	5.3	1.9	5.5	6.0
2010	100.0	86.4	1.1	1.6	3.5	11.7	6.3	5.4	1.8	5.5	6.1

[1] Consists of agriculture, forestry, fishing, and hunting; mining; construction; and manufacturing.

[2] Consists of utilities; wholesale trade; retail trade; transportation and warehousing; information; finance, insurance, real estate, rental, and leasing; professional and business services; educational services, health care, and social assistance; arts, entertainment, recreation, accommodation, and food services; and other services, except government.

Note: Data shown in Tables B–12 and B–13 are consistent with the 2011 flexible annual revision of the industry accounts released in December 2011. For details see *Survey of Current Business*, December 2011.

See next page for continuation of table.

[Billions of dollars; except as noted]

Year	Transportation and warehousing	Information	Finance, insurance, real estate, rental, and leasing	Professional and business services	Educational services, health care, and social assistance	Arts, entertainment, recreation, accommodation, and food services	Other services, except government	Government	Private goods-producing industries [1]	Private services-producing industries [2]
					Value added					
1980	102.6	108.3	446.8	173.1	134.1	83.0	68.5	383.3	842.8	1,562.0
1981	110.1	123.5	502.8	197.3	152.9	92.9	76.0	425.2	949.9	1,751.7
1982	106.3	135.3	544.7	213.2	169.2	100.0	78.3	461.8	927.7	1,863.7
1983	118.0	152.5	611.6	242.4	189.7	111.5	86.8	492.9	957.1	2,084.6
1984	131.4	160.0	677.5	280.9	207.1	120.8	96.3	537.9	1,076.7	2,316.3
1985	137.1	176.4	739.4	316.3	225.4	132.0	105.3	582.9	1,111.2	2,523.4
1986	147.0	185.6	804.0	352.4	245.2	144.0	115.3	619.7	1,118.6	2,721.8
1987	152.6	197.4	850.3	384.5	277.7	152.3	121.1	658.4	1,185.0	2,892.9
1988	161.4	205.4	915.7	424.3	301.5	168.8	133.0	705.1	1,278.8	3,116.5
1989	166.3	222.4	981.0	470.4	337.4	184.0	144.8	752.4	1,358.9	3,370.8
1990	172.8	235.6	1,049.2	516.5	376.7	199.6	153.9	806.2	1,396.5	3,597.7
1991	182.3	244.3	1,109.8	524.0	413.4	205.9	155.9	858.9	1,373.2	3,760.0
1992	192.0	260.5	1,192.1	566.6	452.9	219.0	166.3	900.3	1,422.8	4,019.2
1993	206.4	279.6	1,259.3	600.9	476.4	230.9	178.3	931.4	1,474.3	4,261.6
1994	223.7	299.4	1,321.6	639.7	500.2	242.3	190.7	965.3	1,586.1	4,533.8
1995	231.7	311.5	1,405.7	687.3	523.9	255.3	200.7	994.6	1,643.1	4,776.9
1996	241.3	338.6	1,490.3	756.5	545.4	272.8	211.2	1,025.9	1,733.6	5,079.0
1997	261.8	349.4	1,610.6	842.1	571.4	300.3	223.8	1,061.3	1,827.2	5,443.8
1998	275.6	386.1	1,696.8	927.0	601.2	321.1	245.6	1,099.1	1,891.7	5,802.7
1999	287.1	438.5	1,834.0	1,010.2	638.5	355.4	259.3	1,153.9	1,971.3	6,228.3
2000	301.4	417.8	1,997.7	1,116.8	678.0	381.6	277.6	1,215.4	2,087.4	6,648.7
2001	302.6	451.1	2,154.8	1,170.7	729.2	391.2	264.2	1,275.4	2,052.3	6,958.5
2002	302.4	499.7	2,222.3	1,198.3	789.8	411.1	285.0	1,353.0	2,053.7	7,235.6
2003	319.8	506.6	2,316.5	1,260.0	847.1	427.8	288.8	1,435.3	2,140.8	7,566.1
2004	347.0	558.8	2,400.4	1,347.5	906.1	458.7	300.8	1,507.7	2,338.9	8,006.6
2005	369.5	586.5	2,598.8	1,460.2	953.5	485.4	313.0	1,585.9	2,501.2	8,535.8
2006	394.0	590.6	2,765.3	1,567.2	1,015.3	512.4	331.6	1,667.8	2,651.6	9,057.8
2007	404.9	635.5	2,857.0	1,697.6	1,076.9	549.0	343.8	1,759.9	2,750.9	9,517.9
2008	415.0	636.8	2,916.6	1,783.2	1,153.9	537.3	342.7	1,854.4	2,721.2	9,715.9
2009	391.7	615.4	2,964.5	1,678.1	1,210.4	517.6	340.8	1,920.9	2,435.5	9,582.6
2010	402.5	623.5	3,007.2	1,782.8	1,272.3	555.8	356.8	1,968.5	2,610.1	9,948.0
				Industry value added as a percentage of GDP (percent)						
1980	3.7	3.9	16.0	6.2	4.8	3.0	2.5	13.7	30.2	56.0
1981	3.5	4.0	16.1	6.3	4.9	3.0	2.4	13.6	30.4	56.0
1982	3.3	4.2	16.7	6.6	5.2	3.1	2.4	14.2	28.5	57.3
1983	3.3	4.3	17.3	6.9	5.4	3.2	2.5	13.9	27.1	59.0
1984	3.3	4.1	17.2	7.1	5.3	3.1	2.4	13.7	27.4	58.9
1985	3.3	4.2	17.5	7.5	5.3	3.1	2.5	13.8	26.3	59.8
1986	3.3	4.2	18.0	7.9	5.5	3.2	2.6	13.9	25.1	61.0
1987	3.2	4.2	18.0	8.1	5.9	3.2	2.6	13.9	25.0	61.1
1988	3.2	4.0	18.0	8.3	5.9	3.3	2.6	13.8	25.1	61.1
1989	3.0	4.1	17.9	8.6	6.2	3.4	2.6	13.7	24.8	61.5
1990	3.0	4.1	18.1	8.9	6.5	3.4	2.7	13.9	24.1	62.0
1991	3.0	4.1	18.5	8.7	6.9	3.4	2.6	14.3	22.9	62.8
1992	3.0	4.1	18.8	8.9	7.1	3.5	2.6	14.2	22.4	63.4
1993	3.1	4.2	18.9	9.0	7.1	3.5	2.7	14.0	22.1	63.9
1994	3.2	4.2	18.7	9.0	7.1	3.4	2.7	13.6	22.4	64.0
1995	3.1	4.2	19.0	9.3	7.1	3.4	2.7	13.4	22.2	64.4
1996	3.1	4.3	19.0	9.7	7.0	3.5	2.7	13.1	22.1	64.8
1997	3.1	4.2	19.3	10.1	6.9	3.6	2.7	12.7	21.9	65.3
1998	3.1	4.4	19.3	10.5	6.8	3.7	2.8	12.5	21.5	66.0
1999	3.1	4.7	19.6	10.8	6.8	3.8	2.8	12.3	21.1	66.6
2000	3.0	4.2	20.1	11.2	6.8	3.8	2.8	12.2	21.0	66.8
2001	2.9	4.4	20.9	11.4	7.1	3.8	2.6	12.4	20.0	67.6
2002	2.8	4.7	20.9	11.3	7.4	3.9	2.7	12.7	19.3	68.0
2003	2.9	4.5	20.8	11.3	7.6	3.8	2.6	12.9	19.2	67.9
2004	2.9	4.7	20.3	11.4	7.6	3.9	2.5	12.7	19.7	67.5
2005	2.9	4.6	20.6	11.6	7.6	3.8	2.5	12.6	19.8	67.6
2006	2.9	4.4	20.7	11.7	7.6	3.8	2.5	12.5	19.8	67.7
2007	2.9	4.5	20.4	12.1	7.7	3.9	2.5	12.5	19.6	67.8
2008	2.9	4.5	20.4	12.5	8.1	3.8	2.4	13.0	19.0	68.0
2009	2.8	4.4	21.3	12.0	8.7	3.7	2.4	13.8	17.5	68.7
2010	2.8	4.3	20.7	12.3	8.8	3.8	2.5	13.6	18.0	68.5

Note (cont'd): Value added is the contribution of each private industry and of government to GDP. Value added is equal to an industry's gross output minus its intermediate inputs. Current-dollar value added is calculated as the sum of distributions by an industry to its labor and capital, which are derived from the components of gross domestic income.

Value added industry data shown in Tables B–12 and B–13 are based on the 2002 North American Industry Classification System (NAICS).

Source: Department of Commerce (Bureau of Economic Analysis).

Year	Gross domestic product	Total private industries	Agriculture, forestry, fishing, and hunting	Mining	Construction	Manufacturing Total manufacturing	Durable goods	Nondurable goods	Utilities	Wholesale trade	Retail trade
Chain-type quantity indexes for value added (2005=100)
1980	46.217	44.227	38.449	115.603	75.146	43.142	33.516	61.448	59.058	28.963	34.293
1981	47.390	45.387	48.384	114.882	68.529	45.199	34.438	66.320	58.963	30.726	35.287
1982	46.470	44.282	51.011	109.757	60.546	41.913	31.046	64.152	57.737	30.871	35.240
1983	48.570	46.325	36.388	104.252	62.785	45.226	33.064	70.536	60.798	32.224	38.504
1984	52.060	49.753	47.087	114.545	70.655	49.545	38.389	70.782	66.262	34.845	42.183
1985	54.214	51.961	55.753	121.137	75.849	51.109	39.540	73.192	70.538	36.656	44.468
1986	56.092	53.470	54.881	116.810	77.499	51.078	39.836	72.251	74.025	40.323	47.777
1987	57.887	55.466	56.750	122.364	79.148	54.843	42.637	77.950	82.732	39.192	46.100
1988	60.266	58.098	50.675	136.911	82.976	58.683	46.870	80.123	82.022	41.306	50.726
1989	62.420	60.243	56.742	132.276	85.326	59.359	47.610	80.544	90.437	43.307	52.973
1990	63.591	61.264	60.074	130.787	84.779	58.575	46.726	80.093	95.576	42.692	53.825
1991	63.442	61.161	60.756	133.113	78.616	57.674	45.243	80.651	96.834	44.438	53.661
1992	65.595	63.537	67.964	129.022	80.403	59.597	46.187	84.672	97.689	48.490	56.467
1993	67.466	65.296	58.983	131.161	82.649	61.987	48.129	87.853	96.434	49.957	59.225
1994	70.214	68.374	70.448	142.428	87.293	66.078	51.830	92.380	99.397	53.134	63.523
1995	71.980	70.112	59.555	143.474	88.224	68.798	55.832	91.805	102.620	52.901	66.714
1996	74.672	73.146	66.286	133.682	92.982	70.997	59.253	91.157	101.716	57.783	72.881
1997	78.000	76.840	71.591	138.097	95.170	75.261	64.194	93.699	97.108	64.068	79.185
1998	81.397	80.541	69.837	148.848	98.277	79.022	70.550	92.120	95.007	74.157	84.195
1999	85.326	84.778	73.031	137.847	103.607	83.268	75.962	94.101	104.692	78.059	86.596
2000	88.857	88.667	81.603	121.027	106.961	88.584	84.443	93.958	108.309	83.510	89.942
2001	89.816	89.792	78.861	136.785	104.536	84.499	79.298	91.571	93.854	87.671	92.731
2002	91.445	91.300	82.079	138.414	100.882	86.606	82.246	92.420	97.378	88.479	95.770
2003	93.769	93.464	90.644	120.511	101.161	89.347	85.053	95.052	100.904	93.901	97.961
2004	97.021	96.945	96.510	119.237	101.134	96.658	93.004	101.453	104.815	98.912	97.982
2005	100.000	100.000	100.000	100.000	100.000	100.000	100.000	100.000	100.000	100.000	100.000
2006	102.658	102.980	100.756	108.435	96.982	104.159	106.663	101.069	100.539	102.995	102.176
2007	104.622	104.953	93.149	111.427	91.606	107.847	110.655	104.394	104.004	108.619	102.473
2008	104.270	103.909	101.279	107.236	85.547	101.545	108.932	93.038	108.818	107.416	96.613
2009	100.635	99.343	112.225	129.626	74.474	92.000	92.746	90.535	96.381	92.866	94.284
2010	103.684	102.877	108.774	121.680	72.127	102.328	108.529	95.142	99.554	96.473	103.764
Percent change from year earlier
1980	-0.3	-0.6	-1.2	10.4	-5.6	-5.2	-5.3	-5.0	-6.7	-0.7	-5.6
1981	2.5	2.6	25.8	-.6	-8.8	4.8	2.8	7.9	-.2	6.1	2.9
1982	-1.9	-2.4	5.4	-4.5	-11.6	-7.3	-9.8	-3.3	-2.1	.5	-.1
1983	4.5	4.6	-28.7	-5.0	3.7	7.9	6.5	10.0	5.3	4.4	9.3
1984	7.2	7.4	29.4	9.9	12.5	9.5	16.1	.3	9.0	8.1	9.6
1985	4.1	4.4	18.4	5.8	7.4	3.2	3.0	3.4	6.5	5.2	5.4
1986	3.5	2.9	-1.6	-3.6	2.2	-.1	.7	-1.3	4.9	10.0	7.4
1987	3.2	3.7	3.4	4.8	2.1	7.4	7.0	7.9	11.8	-2.8	-3.5
1988	4.1	4.7	-10.7	11.9	4.8	7.0	9.9	2.8	-.9	5.4	10.0
1989	3.6	3.7	12.0	-3.4	2.8	1.2	1.6	.5	10.3	4.8	4.4
1990	1.9	1.7	5.9	-1.1	-.6	-1.3	-1.9	-.6	5.7	-1.4	1.6
1991	-.2	-.2	1.1	1.8	-7.3	-1.5	-3.2	.7	1.3	4.1	-.3
1992	3.4	3.9	11.9	-3.1	2.3	3.3	2.1	5.0	.9	9.1	5.2
1993	2.9	2.8	-13.2	1.7	2.8	4.0	4.2	3.8	-1.3	3.0	4.9
1994	4.1	4.7	19.4	8.6	5.6	6.6	7.7	5.2	3.1	6.4	7.3
1995	2.5	2.5	-15.5	.7	1.1	4.1	7.7	-.6	3.2	-.4	5.0
1996	3.7	4.3	11.3	-6.8	5.4	3.2	6.1	-.7	-.9	9.2	9.2
1997	4.5	5.1	8.0	3.3	2.4	6.0	8.3	2.8	-4.5	10.9	8.6
1998	4.4	4.8	-2.5	7.8	3.3	5.0	9.9	-1.7	-2.2	15.7	6.3
1999	4.8	5.3	4.6	-7.4	5.4	5.4	7.7	2.2	10.2	5.3	2.9
2000	4.1	4.6	11.7	-12.2	3.2	6.4	11.2	-.2	3.5	7.0	3.9
2001	1.1	1.3	-3.4	13.0	-2.3	-4.6	-6.1	-2.5	-13.3	5.0	3.1
2002	1.8	1.7	4.1	1.2	-3.5	2.5	3.7	.9	3.8	.9	3.3
2003	2.5	2.4	10.4	-12.9	.3	3.2	3.4	2.8	3.6	6.1	2.3
2004	3.5	3.7	6.5	-1.1	.0	8.2	9.3	6.7	3.9	5.3	.0
2005	3.1	3.2	3.6	-16.1	-1.1	3.5	7.5	-1.4	-4.6	1.1	2.1
2006	2.7	3.0	.8	8.4	-3.0	4.2	6.7	1.1	.5	3.0	2.2
2007	1.9	1.9	-7.5	2.8	-5.5	3.5	3.7	3.3	3.4	5.5	.3
2008	-.3	-1.0	8.7	-3.8	-6.6	-5.8	-1.6	-10.9	4.6	-1.1	-5.7
2009	-3.5	-4.4	10.8	20.9	-12.9	-9.4	-14.9	-2.7	-11.4	-13.5	-2.4
2010	3.0	3.6	-3.1	-6.1	-3.2	11.2	17.0	5.1	3.3	3.9	10.1

[1] Consists of agriculture, forestry, fishing, and hunting; mining; construction; and manufacturing.

[2] Consists of utilities; wholesale trade; retail trade; transportation and warehousing; information; finance, insurance, real estate, rental, and leasing; professional and business services; educational services, health care, and social assistance; arts, entertainment, recreation, accommodation, and food services; and other services, except government.

See next page for continuation of table.

Year	Transportation and warehousing	Information	Finance, insurance, real estate, rental, and leasing	Professional and business services	Educational services, health care, and social assistance	Arts, entertainment, recreation, accommodation, and food services	Other services, except government	Government	Private goods-producing industries [1]	Private services-producing industries [2]
	Private industries—Continued									
	Chain-type quantity indexes for value added (2005=100)									
1980	41.818	30.378	48.277	34.690	56.112	44.619	75.952	74.868	50.611	42.038
1981	40.790	32.049	48.938	35.550	57.200	46.189	73.651	75.162	52.361	42.951
1982	38.832	31.956	49.393	35.428	57.034	47.380	70.878	75.297	48.901	42.869
1983	43.831	34.198	50.583	37.922	59.229	51.042	74.147	75.976	50.241	45.236
1984	45.938	33.874	52.452	42.010	60.919	53.218	78.074	76.794	55.880	47.804
1985	46.619	34.821	53.847	45.365	62.423	55.848	80.627	78.818	58.708	49.789
1986	46.696	34.983	54.648	48.917	63.597	59.483	82.446	80.650	58.664	51.881
1987	48.989	37.356	56.560	51.538	67.638	59.082	83.865	82.216	62.184	53.341
1988	50.432	38.579	58.607	54.138	68.238	62.454	87.958	84.340	65.702	55.673
1989	52.397	41.288	60.088	57.635	70.866	64.701	91.973	86.397	66.909	58.155
1990	55.147	42.649	61.497	60.141	73.463	66.671	93.971	88.511	66.431	59.704
1991	57.664	43.057	62.438	58.046	75.173	64.814	91.234	88.991	64.989	60.060
1992	61.325	45.429	64.388	59.787	77.453	67.092	93.331	89.513	67.163	62.511
1993	64.042	47.837	66.268	61.282	77.728	69.166	96.564	89.512	68.816	64.309
1994	69.180	50.285	67.851	63.418	78.052	71.235	101.126	89.780	73.841	66.769
1995	71.236	52.034	69.615	65.656	79.293	73.630	103.010	89.719	75.400	68.566
1996	75.138	55.321	71.251	70.179	80.204	76.742	103.940	90.120	78.077	71.717
1997	79.006	56.402	74.419	75.051	81.559	80.225	102.674	91.101	82.210	75.282
1998	78.063	62.107	76.667	79.327	82.657	82.504	108.399	92.284	85.786	79.023
1999	80.801	70.528	81.686	82.819	84.776	87.572	109.304	93.395	89.880	83.304
2000	86.201	67.832	87.064	86.923	86.688	91.104	110.957	95.142	94.368	87.019
2001	83.090	72.885	92.351	89.035	88.822	89.691	99.325	95.941	91.430	89.318
2002	81.948	80.958	92.155	89.688	92.487	91.313	102.420	97.802	92.368	90.987
2003	86.133	82.501	93.538	92.228	95.460	93.634	100.428	98.749	94.040	93.288
2004	93.911	92.679	94.519	95.440	98.332	97.751	100.685	99.445	99.161	96.307
2005	100.000	100.000	100.000	100.000	100.000	100.000	100.000	100.000	100.000	100.000
2006	104.049	101.530	104.035	103.229	103.265	102.563	101.704	100.437	102.528	103.112
2007	105.231	109.310	105.125	106.140	104.978	105.614	101.659	101.209	103.194	105.471
2008	106.182	111.156	104.357	110.288	109.833	100.271	97.388	103.008	97.973	105.673
2009	93.455	107.166	105.553	102.660	110.915	92.642	92.399	103.940	91.739	101.586
2010	96.695	110.347	105.311	106.587	114.020	99.866	94.327	104.525	96.834	104.683
	Percent change from year earlier									
1980	−2.3	8.4	5.0	2.6	3.6	−3.6	0.9	1.7	−3.6	1.1
1981	−2.5	5.5	1.4	2.5	1.9	3.5	−3.0	.4	3.5	2.2
1982	−4.8	−.3	.9	−.3	−.3	2.6	−3.8	.2	−6.6	−.2
1983	12.9	7.0	2.4	7.0	3.8	7.7	4.6	.9	2.7	5.5
1984	4.8	−.9	3.7	10.8	2.9	4.3	5.3	1.1	11.2	5.7
1985	1.5	2.8	2.7	8.0	2.5	4.9	3.3	2.6	5.1	4.2
1986	.2	.5	1.5	7.8	1.9	6.5	2.3	2.3	−.1	4.2
1987	4.9	6.8	3.5	5.4	6.4	−.7	1.7	1.9	6.0	2.8
1988	2.9	3.3	3.6	5.0	.9	5.7	4.9	2.6	5.7	4.4
1989	3.9	7.0	2.5	6.5	3.9	3.6	4.6	2.4	1.8	4.5
1990	5.2	3.3	2.3	4.3	3.7	3.0	2.2	2.4	−.7	2.7
1991	4.6	1.0	1.5	−3.5	2.3	−2.8	−2.9	.5	−2.2	.6
1992	6.3	5.5	3.1	3.0	3.0	3.5	2.3	.6	3.3	4.1
1993	4.4	5.3	2.9	2.5	.4	3.1	3.5	.0	2.5	2.9
1994	8.0	5.1	2.4	3.5	.4	3.0	4.7	.3	7.3	3.8
1995	3.0	3.5	2.6	3.5	1.6	3.4	1.9	−.1	2.1	2.7
1996	5.5	6.3	2.4	6.9	1.1	4.2	.9	.4	3.6	4.6
1997	5.1	2.0	4.4	6.9	1.7	4.5	−1.2	1.1	5.3	5.0
1998	−1.2	10.1	3.0	5.7	1.3	2.8	5.6	1.3	4.3	5.0
1999	3.5	13.6	6.5	4.4	2.6	6.1	.8	1.2	4.8	5.4
2000	6.7	−3.8	6.6	5.0	2.3	4.0	1.5	1.9	5.0	4.5
2001	−3.6	7.5	6.1	2.4	2.5	−1.6	−10.5	.8	−3.1	2.6
2002	−1.4	11.1	−.2	.7	4.1	1.8	3.1	1.9	1.0	1.9
2003	5.1	1.9	1.5	2.8	3.2	2.5	−1.9	1.0	1.8	2.5
2004	9.0	12.3	1.0	3.5	3.0	4.4	.3	.7	5.4	3.2
2005	6.5	7.9	5.8	4.8	1.7	2.3	−.7	.6	.8	3.8
2006	4.0	1.5	4.0	3.2	3.3	2.6	1.7	.4	2.5	3.1
2007	1.1	7.7	1.0	2.8	1.7	3.0	.0	.8	.6	2.3
2008	.9	1.7	−.7	3.9	4.6	−5.1	−4.2	1.8	−5.1	.2
2009	−12.0	−3.6	1.1	−6.9	1.0	−7.6	−5.1	.9	−6.4	−3.9
2010	3.5	3.0	−.2	3.8	2.8	7.8	2.1	.6	5.6	3.0

Note: Data are based on the 2002 North American Industry Classification System (NAICS).
See Note, Table B–12.

Source: Department of Commerce (Bureau of Economic Analysis).

[Billions of dollars; quarterly data at seasonally adjusted annual rates]

Year or quarter	Gross value added of nonfinancial corporate business [1]	Consumption of fixed capital	Net value added						Addenda					
			Total	Compensation of employees	Taxes on production and imports less subsidies	Net operating surplus						Profits before tax	Inventory valuation adjustment	Capital consumption adjustment
						Total	Net interest and miscellaneous payments	Business current transfer payments	Corporate profits with inventory valuation and capital consumption adjustments					
									Total	Taxes on corporate income	Profits after tax [2]			
1963	329.9	25.6	304.3	210.1	31.7	62.5	4.7	1.7	56.1	22.8	33.4	49.7	0.1	6.4
1964	356.1	27.0	329.0	225.7	33.9	69.5	5.2	2.0	62.4	23.9	38.5	55.9	−.5	7.0
1965	391.2	29.1	362.1	245.4	36.0	80.7	5.8	2.2	72.7	27.1	45.5	66.1	−1.2	7.8
1966	429.0	31.9	397.1	272.9	37.0	87.2	7.0	2.7	77.5	29.5	48.0	71.4	−2.1	8.1
1967	451.2	35.2	416.0	291.1	39.3	85.6	8.4	2.8	74.4	27.8	46.5	67.6	−1.6	8.3
1968	497.8	38.7	459.1	321.9	45.5	91.7	9.7	3.1	78.9	33.5	45.4	74.0	−3.7	8.6
1969	540.5	42.9	497.5	357.1	50.2	90.3	12.7	3.2	74.4	33.3	41.0	71.2	−5.9	9.1
1970	558.3	47.5	510.8	376.5	54.2	80.1	16.6	3.3	60.2	27.3	32.9	58.5	−6.6	8.3
1971	603.0	52.0	551.1	399.4	59.5	92.1	17.6	3.7	70.8	30.0	40.8	67.4	−4.6	8.0
1972	669.4	56.5	613.0	443.9	63.7	105.4	18.6	4.0	82.8	33.8	49.0	79.5	−6.6	9.9
1973	750.8	63.1	687.6	502.2	70.1	115.4	21.8	4.7	88.9	40.4	48.5	99.5	−19.6	9.0
1974	809.8	74.2	735.7	552.2	74.4	109.1	27.5	4.1	77.5	42.8	34.6	110.2	−38.2	5.5
1975	876.7	88.6	788.0	575.5	80.2	132.4	28.4	5.0	98.9	41.9	57.0	110.7	−10.5	−1.2
1976	989.7	97.8	892.0	651.4	86.7	153.9	26.0	7.0	121.0	53.5	67.5	138.2	−14.1	−3.2
1977	1,119.4	110.1	1,009.2	735.3	94.6	179.3	28.5	9.0	141.9	60.6	81.3	159.5	−15.7	−1.9
1978	1,272.7	125.1	1,147.5	845.1	102.7	199.7	33.4	9.5	156.8	67.6	89.2	183.7	−23.7	−3.2
1979	1,414.4	144.3	1,270.2	958.4	108.8	203.0	41.8	9.5	151.8	70.6	81.2	197.2	−40.1	−5.3
1980	1,534.5	166.7	1,367.8	1,047.2	121.5	199.1	54.2	10.2	134.7	68.2	66.5	184.1	−42.1	−7.2
1981	1,742.2	192.4	1,549.8	1,157.6	146.7	245.5	67.2	11.4	166.8	66.0	100.8	185.0	−24.6	6.5
1982	1,802.6	212.8	1,589.8	1,200.4	152.9	236.5	77.4	8.8	150.2	48.8	101.5	140.0	−7.5	17.8
1983	1,929.1	219.3	1,709.8	1,263.1	168.0	278.7	77.0	10.5	191.2	61.7	129.5	163.4	−7.4	35.2
1984	2,161.4	228.8	1,932.6	1,400.0	185.0	347.5	86.0	11.7	249.8	75.9	173.9	197.6	−4.0	56.2
1985	2,293.9	244.0	2,049.9	1,496.1	196.6	357.2	91.5	16.1	249.6	71.1	178.6	173.5	.0	76.2
1986	2,383.2	258.0	2,125.2	1,575.4	204.6	345.2	98.5	27.3	219.5	76.2	143.2	149.7	7.1	62.7
1987	2,551.0	270.0	2,280.9	1,678.4	216.8	385.6	95.9	29.9	259.9	94.2	165.7	213.5	−16.2	62.6
1988	2,765.4	287.3	2,478.1	1,804.7	233.8	439.6	107.9	27.4	304.3	104.0	200.3	264.1	−22.2	62.3
1989	2,899.2	303.9	2,595.3	1,905.7	248.2	441.5	133.9	24.0	283.5	101.2	182.3	243.1	−16.3	56.7
1990	3,035.2	321.0	2,714.2	2,005.5	263.5	445.2	143.1	25.4	276.7	98.5	178.3	243.3	−12.9	46.3
1991	3,104.1	336.1	2,768.0	2,044.8	285.7	437.5	139.6	26.6	271.3	88.6	182.7	226.8	4.9	39.6
1992	3,241.1	344.1	2,897.0	2,152.9	302.5	441.6	114.2	31.3	296.1	94.4	201.7	258.6	−2.8	40.3
1993	3,398.4	359.0	3,039.3	2,244.0	318.0	477.3	99.8	30.1	347.5	108.0	239.5	308.7	−4.0	42.9
1994	3,677.6	380.1	3,297.5	2,382.1	347.8	567.5	98.8	35.3	433.5	132.4	301.1	391.9	−12.4	54.0
1995	3,888.0	408.3	3,479.7	2,511.5	354.2	614.0	112.7	30.7	470.6	140.3	330.3	431.2	−18.3	57.6
1996	4,119.4	435.1	3,684.4	2,631.3	365.6	687.5	112.1	38.0	537.4	152.9	384.5	471.3	3.1	63.0
1997	4,412.5	466.9	3,945.6	2,814.6	381.0	750.0	124.7	39.2	586.2	161.4	424.8	506.8	14.1	65.3
1998	4,668.3	499.9	4,168.5	3,049.7	393.1	725.7	146.8	35.2	543.7	158.7	385.1	460.5	15.7	67.5
1999	4,955.5	539.3	4,416.3	3,256.5	414.6	745.1	164.5	47.1	533.5	171.4	362.1	468.6	−4.0	68.9
2000	5,279.4	590.1	4,689.4	3,541.8	439.4	708.2	192.8	47.9	467.5	170.2	297.3	432.5	−16.8	51.8
2001	5,252.5	632.0	4,620.5	3,559.4	434.5	626.7	197.7	58.9	370.1	111.2	258.8	315.1	8.0	47.0
2002	5,307.7	654.5	4,653.1	3,544.2	461.9	647.1	163.7	56.3	427.2	97.1	330.1	342.3	−2.6	87.5
2003	5,503.7	669.0	4,834.7	3,651.3	484.2	699.2	147.9	65.2	486.1	132.9	353.2	425.9	−11.3	71.5
2004	5,877.5	695.6	5,181.9	3,786.7	517.7	877.5	134.4	65.5	677.5	187.0	490.6	662.1	−34.3	49.7
2005	6,302.8	743.0	5,559.8	3,976.3	558.4	1,025.1	148.2	79.3	797.6	271.9	525.8	957.1	−30.7	−128.8
2006	6,740.3	800.9	5,939.4	4,182.3	593.3	1,163.7	164.0	75.8	923.9	307.6	616.2	1,117.9	−38.0	−156.0
2007	6,946.0	840.1	6,106.0	4,361.0	607.7	1,137.4	232.3	69.1	835.9	293.8	542.2	1,042.0	−47.2	−158.8
2008	6,991.4	864.3	6,127.1	4,441.2	615.2	1,070.8	257.7	58.1	755.0	227.4	527.7	831.2	−44.5	−31.7
2009	6,592.0	862.2	5,729.8	4,178.2	587.4	964.2	243.7	78.3	642.1	175.0	467.1	693.5	.6	−52.0
2010	6,902.0	856.8	6,045.2	4,263.0	614.3	1,167.8	130.9	85.4	951.5	229.3	722.3	942.8	−39.1	47.8
2011 ᵖ	....	890.1	....	4,440.7	639.8	....	....	87.1	....	....	....	....	....	126.3
2008: I	6,955.8	852.2	6,103.6	4,456.3	613.4	1,033.9	251.5	57.9	724.5	248.0	476.5	884.8	−131.3	−29.1
II	6,964.7	858.8	6,105.9	4,450.2	620.5	1,035.2	248.7	54.6	731.8	252.8	479.1	916.5	−155.4	−29.3
III	7,094.8	869.6	6,225.2	4,445.9	619.9	1,159.4	254.5	54.1	850.9	255.3	595.5	957.1	−72.7	−33.5
IV	6,950.5	876.6	6,073.8	4,412.3	606.9	1,054.6	275.9	65.7	713.0	153.5	559.5	566.2	181.6	−34.8
2009: I	6,650.3	874.2	5,776.1	4,210.8	584.5	980.7	286.2	74.6	619.9	164.6	455.4	607.9	76.5	−64.4
II	6,534.6	864.5	5,670.1	4,178.9	586.5	904.7	255.2	83.4	566.1	156.7	409.4	604.2	15.9	−54.0
III	6,533.4	856.4	5,677.0	4,156.0	581.6	939.4	228.3	75.8	635.2	169.8	465.4	701.9	−20.7	−46.0
IV	6,649.7	853.8	5,796.0	4,167.0	597.1	1,031.8	205.2	79.4	747.2	209.0	538.2	859.9	−69.3	−43.4
2010: I	6,811.1	850.3	5,960.7	4,188.9	607.3	1,164.5	166.7	84.5	913.3	233.4	680.0	976.6	−28.4	−34.9
II	6,876.6	853.9	6,022.6	4,247.5	612.3	1,162.8	135.5	84.8	942.5	232.0	710.5	984.3	−5.6	−36.2
III	6,953.9	857.7	6,096.2	4,299.8	617.1	1,179.4	114.9	86.7	977.8	239.4	738.3	961.5	−32.0	48.3
IV	6,966.5	865.4	6,101.1	4,315.9	620.7	1,164.6	106.5	85.5	972.6	212.4	760.2	848.9	−90.3	214.1
2011: I	7,078.3	873.4	6,205.0	4,386.5	633.2	1,185.3	106.6	86.3	992.3	238.5	753.8	974.8	−116.0	133.6
II	7,216.5	885.4	6,331.1	4,426.3	641.2	1,263.6	103.0	87.5	1,073.1	252.2	821.0	1,006.3	−60.4	127.2
III	7,269.9	896.3	6,373.6	4,450.5	640.9	1,282.1	104.5	86.7	1,091.0	250.1	840.9	1,013.4	−45.5	123.1
IV ᵖ	....	905.5	....	4,499.7	644.0	....	....	87.9	....	....	....	....	....	121.4

[1] Estimates for nonfinancial corporate business for 2000 and earlier periods are based on the Standard Industrial Classification (SIC); later estimates are based on the North American Industry Classification System (NAICS).
[2] With inventory valuation and capital consumption adjustments.

Source: Department of Commerce (Bureau of Economic Analysis).

TABLE B–15. Gross value added and price, costs, and profits of nonfinancial corporate business, 1963–2011

[Quarterly data at seasonally adjusted annual rates]

Year or quarter	Gross value added of nonfinancial corporate business (billions of dollars)[1]		Price per unit of real gross value added of nonfinancial corporate business (dollars)[1,2]									
				Compensation of employees (unit labor cost)	Unit nonlabor cost				Corporate profits with inventory valuation and capital consumption adjustments[4]		
	Current dollars	Chained (2005) dollars	Total		Total	Consumption of fixed capital	Taxes on production and imports[3]	Net interest and miscellaneous payments	Total	Taxes on corporate income	Profits after tax[5]
1963	329.9	1,277.9	0.258	0.164	0.050	0.020	0.026	0.004	0.044	0.018	0.026
1964	356.1	1,368.1	.260	.165	.050	.020	.026	.004	.046	.017	.028
1965	391.2	1,481.8	.264	.166	.050	.020	.026	.004	.049	.018	.031
1966	429.0	1,588.1	.270	.172	.049	.020	.025	.004	.049	.019	.030
1967	451.2	1,630.9	.277	.178	.053	.022	.026	.005	.046	.017	.029
1968	497.8	1,736.7	.287	.185	.056	.022	.028	.006	.045	.019	.026
1969	540.5	1,806.9	.299	.198	.061	.024	.030	.007	.041	.018	.023
1970	558.3	1,792.4	.311	.210	.067	.026	.032	.009	.034	.015	.018
1971	603.0	1,866.3	.323	.214	.071	.028	.034	.009	.038	.016	.022
1972	669.4	2,009.0	.333	.221	.071	.028	.034	.009	.041	.017	.024
1973	750.8	2,132.7	.352	.235	.075	.030	.035	.010	.042	.019	.023
1974	809.8	2,099.0	.386	.263	.085	.035	.037	.013	.037	.020	.016
1975	876.7	2,068.2	.424	.278	.098	.043	.041	.014	.048	.020	.028
1976	989.7	2,237.2	.442	.291	.098	.044	.042	.012	.054	.024	.030
1977	1,119.4	2,402.9	.466	.306	.101	.046	.043	.012	.059	.025	.034
1978	1,272.7	2,560.2	.497	.330	.106	.049	.044	.013	.061	.026	.035
1979	1,414.4	2,640.4	.536	.363	.116	.055	.045	.016	.057	.027	.031
1980	1,534.5	2,613.4	.587	.401	.135	.064	.050	.021	.052	.026	.025
1981	1,742.2	2,717.8	.641	.426	.154	.071	.058	.025	.061	.024	.037
1982	1,802.6	2,653.0	.679	.452	.170	.080	.061	.029	.057	.018	.038
1983	1,929.1	2,781.1	.694	.454	.171	.079	.064	.028	.069	.022	.047
1984	2,161.4	3,027.7	.714	.462	.169	.076	.065	.028	.083	.025	.057
1985	2,293.9	3,157.9	.726	.474	.173	.077	.067	.029	.079	.023	.057
1986	2,383.2	3,235.5	.737	.487	.182	.080	.072	.030	.068	.024	.044
1987	2,551.0	3,402.5	.750	.493	.180	.079	.073	.028	.076	.028	.049
1988	2,765.4	3,599.1	.768	.501	.183	.080	.073	.030	.085	.029	.056
1989	2,899.2	3,658.8	.792	.521	.194	.083	.074	.037	.077	.028	.050
1990	3,035.2	3,713.1	.817	.540	.203	.086	.078	.039	.075	.027	.048
1991	3,104.1	3,695.4	.840	.553	.214	.091	.085	.038	.073	.024	.049
1992	3,241.1	3,804.9	.852	.566	.208	.090	.088	.030	.078	.025	.053
1993	3,398.4	3,905.0	.870	.575	.207	.092	.089	.026	.089	.028	.061
1994	3,677.6	4,155.3	.885	.573	.207	.091	.092	.024	.104	.032	.072
1995	3,888.0	4,349.0	.894	.577	.209	.094	.089	.026	.108	.032	.076
1996	4,119.4	4,588.6	.898	.573	.207	.095	.088	.024	.117	.033	.084
1997	4,412.5	4,887.8	.903	.576	.208	.096	.086	.026	.120	.033	.087
1998	4,668.3	5,167.3	.903	.590	.208	.097	.083	.028	.105	.031	.075
1999	4,955.5	5,452.4	.909	.597	.214	.099	.085	.030	.098	.031	.066
2000	5,279.4	5,745.7	.919	.616	.222	.103	.085	.034	.081	.030	.052
2001	5,252.5	5,637.8	.932	.631	.235	.112	.088	.035	.066	.020	.046
2002	5,307.7	5,675.5	.935	.624	.235	.115	.091	.029	.075	.017	.058
2003	5,503.7	5,818.1	.946	.628	.234	.115	.094	.025	.084	.023	.061
2004	5,877.5	6,085.1	.966	.622	.232	.114	.096	.022	.111	.031	.081
2005	6,302.8	6,302.8	1.000	.631	.243	.118	.101	.024	.127	.043	.083
2006	6,740.3	6,543.2	1.030	.639	.249	.122	.102	.025	.141	.047	.094
2007	6,946.0	6,606.4	1.051	.660	.264	.127	.102	.035	.127	.044	.082
2008	6,991.4	6,515.9	1.073	.682	.276	.133	.103	.040	.116	.035	.081
2009	6,592.0	6,036.5	1.092	.692	.293	.143	.110	.040	.106	.029	.077
2010	6,902.0	6,329.5	1.090	.674	.267	.135	.111	.021	.150	.036	.114
2008: I	6,955.8	6,557.3	1.061	.680	.270	.130	.102	.038	.110	.038	.073
II	6,964.7	6,538.7	1.065	.681	.272	.131	.103	.038	.112	.039	.073
III	7,094.8	6,585.9	1.077	.675	.273	.132	.102	.039	.129	.039	.090
IV	6,950.5	6,381.8	1.089	.691	.285	.137	.105	.043	.112	.024	.088
2009: I	6,650.3	6,035.2	1.102	.698	.301	.145	.109	.047	.103	.027	.075
II	6,534.6	5,966.1	1.095	.700	.300	.145	.112	.043	.095	.026	.069
III	6,533.4	6,006.1	1.088	.692	.290	.143	.109	.038	.106	.028	.077
IV	6,649.7	6,138.4	1.083	.679	.282	.139	.110	.033	.122	.034	.088
2010: I	6,811.1	6,288.7	1.083	.666	.272	.135	.110	.027	.145	.037	.108
II	6,876.6	6,329.3	1.086	.671	.266	.135	.110	.021	.149	.037	.112
III	6,953.9	6,361.5	1.093	.676	.264	.135	.111	.018	.154	.038	.116
IV	6,966.5	6,338.4	1.099	.681	.265	.137	.111	.017	.153	.034	.120
2011: I	7,078.3	6,407.9	1.105	.685	.265	.136	.112	.017	.155	.037	.118
II	7,216.5	6,504.1	1.110	.681	.264	.136	.112	.016	.165	.039	.126
III	7,269.9	6,491.6	1.120	.686	.266	.138	.112	.016	.168	.039	.130

[1] Estimates for nonfinancial corporate business for 2000 and earlier periods are based on the Standard Industrial Classification (SIC); later estimates are based on the North American Industry Classification System (NAICS).
[2] The implicit price deflator for gross value added of nonfinancial corporate business divided by 100.
[3] Less subsidies plus business current transfer payments.
[4] Unit profits from current production.
[5] With inventory valuation and capital consumption adjustments.

Source: Department of Commerce (Bureau of Economic Analysis).

[Billions of dollars; quarterly data at seasonally adjusted annual rates]

Year or quarter	Personal consumption expenditures	Goods						Services					Addendum: Personal consumption expenditures excluding food and energy [2]
		Total	Durable		Nondurable			Total	Household consumption expenditures				
			Total [1]	Motor vehicles and parts	Total [1]	Food and beverages purchased for off-premises consumption	Gasoline and other energy goods		Total [1]	Housing and utilities	Health care	Financial services and insurance	
1963	382.7	198.2	54.2	24.2	143.9	65.9	16.9	184.6	178.6	68.2	21.0	15.9	290.0
1964	411.5	212.3	59.6	25.8	152.7	69.5	17.7	199.2	192.5	72.1	24.2	17.7	313.8
1965	443.8	229.7	66.4	29.6	163.3	74.4	19.1	214.1	206.9	76.6	26.0	19.4	339.3
1966	480.9	249.6	71.7	29.9	177.9	80.6	20.7	231.3	223.5	81.2	28.7	21.3	368.1
1967	507.8	259.0	74.0	29.6	185.0	82.6	21.9	248.8	240.4	86.3	31.9	22.8	391.1
1968	558.0	284.6	84.8	35.4	199.8	88.8	23.2	273.4	264.0	92.7	36.6	25.8	432.9
1969	605.1	304.7	90.5	37.4	214.2	95.4	25.0	300.4	290.4	101.0	42.1	28.5	470.8
1970	648.3	318.8	90.0	34.5	228.8	103.5	26.3	329.5	318.4	109.4	47.7	31.1	503.3
1971	701.6	342.1	102.4	43.2	239.7	107.1	27.6	359.5	347.2	120.0	53.7	34.1	550.1
1972	770.2	373.8	116.4	49.4	257.4	114.5	29.4	396.4	382.8	131.2	59.8	38.3	607.9
1973	852.0	416.6	130.5	54.4	286.1	126.7	34.3	435.4	420.7	143.5	67.2	41.5	670.9
1974	932.9	451.5	130.2	48.2	321.4	143.0	43.8	481.4	465.0	158.6	76.1	45.9	722.4
1975	1,033.8	491.3	142.2	52.6	349.2	156.6	48.0	542.5	524.4	176.5	89.0	54.0	800.6
1976	1,151.3	546.3	168.6	68.2	377.7	167.3	53.0	604.9	584.9	194.7	101.8	59.3	898.3
1977	1,277.8	600.4	192.0	79.8	408.4	179.8	57.8	677.4	655.6	217.8	115.7	67.8	1,002.5
1978	1,427.6	663.6	213.3	89.2	450.2	196.1	61.5	764.1	739.6	244.3	131.2	80.6	1,127.8
1979	1,591.2	737.9	226.3	90.2	511.6	218.4	80.4	853.2	825.4	273.4	148.8	87.6	1,245.4
1980	1,755.8	799.8	226.4	84.4	573.4	239.2	101.9	956.0	924.1	311.8	171.7	95.6	1,358.3
1981	1,939.5	869.4	243.9	93.0	625.4	255.3	113.4	1,070.1	1,033.9	352.0	201.9	102.0	1,507.1
1982	2,075.5	899.3	253.0	100.0	646.3	267.1	108.4	1,176.2	1,136.1	387.0	225.2	116.3	1,627.2
1983	2,288.6	973.8	295.0	122.9	678.8	277.0	106.5	1,314.8	1,271.9	421.2	253.1	145.9	1,824.2
1984	2,501.1	1,063.7	342.2	147.2	721.5	291.1	108.2	1,437.4	1,389.8	458.3	276.5	156.6	2,016.9
1985	2,717.6	1,137.6	380.4	170.1	757.2	303.0	110.5	1,580.0	1,529.7	500.7	302.2	180.5	2,215.1
1986	2,896.7	1,195.6	421.4	187.5	774.2	316.4	91.2	1,701.1	1,645.8	535.7	330.2	196.7	2,401.8
1987	3,097.0	1,256.3	442.0	188.2	814.3	324.3	96.4	1,840.7	1,782.1	571.8	366.0	207.1	2,587.3
1988	3,350.1	1,337.3	475.1	202.2	862.3	342.8	99.9	2,012.7	1,946.0	614.5	410.1	219.4	2,813.2
1989	3,594.5	1,423.8	494.3	207.8	929.5	365.4	110.4	2,170.7	2,099.0	65[illegible]	451.2	235.7	3,019.8
1990	3,835.5	1,491.3	497.1	205.1	994.2	391.2	124.2	2,344.2	2,264.5	696.4	506.2	253.2	3,221.3
1991	3,980.1	1,497.4	477.2	185.7	1,020.3	403.0	121.1	2,482.6	2,398.4	735.5	555.8	282.0	3,351.1
1992	4,236.9	1,563.3	508.1	204.8	1,055.2	404.5	125.0	2,673.6	2,581.3	771.2	612.8	311.8	3,601.1
1993	4,483.6	1,642.3	551.5	224.7	1,090.8	413.5	126.9	2,841.2	2,746.6	814.5	648.8	341.0	3,828.2
1994	4,750.8	1,746.6	607.2	249.8	1,139.4	432.1	129.2	3,004.3	2,901.9	866.5	680.5	349.0	4,072.3
1995	4,987.3	1,815.5	635.7	255.7	1,179.8	443.7	133.4	3,171.7	3,064.6	913.8	719.9	364.7	4,291.9
1996	5,273.6	1,917.7	676.3	273.5	1,241.4	461.9	144.7	3,355.9	3,240.2	961.2	752.1	393.6	4,542.0
1997	5,570.6	2,006.8	715.5	293.1	1,291.2	474.8	147.7	3,563.9	3,451.6	1,009.9	790.9	431.3	4,821.6
1998	5,918.5	2,110.0	780.0	320.2	1,330.0	486.5	133.4	3,808.5	3,677.5	1,065.2	832.0	469.6	5,173.5
1999	6,342.8	2,290.0	857.4	350.7	1,432.6	513.6	148.8	4,052.8	3,907.4	1,125.0	863.6	514.2	5,554.6
2000	6,830.4	2,459.1	915.8	363.2	1,543.4	537.5	188.8	4,371.2	4,205.9	1,198.6	918.4	570.0	5,966.4
2001	7,148.8	2,534.0	946.3	383.3	1,587.7	559.7	183.6	4,614.8	4,428.6	1,287.7	996.6	562.8	6,255.9
2002	7,439.2	2,610.0	992.1	401.3	1,617.9	569.6	174.6	4,829.2	4,624.2	1,334.8	1,082.9	576.2	6,549.4
2003	7,804.1	2,728.0	1,019.9	401.0	1,708.1	587.5	209.5	5,076.1	4,864.8	1,393.9	1,148.2	602.5	6,846.7
2004	8,270.6	2,892.1	1,072.9	403.9	1,819.3	613.0	249.4	5,378.5	5,169.1	1,462.4	1,228.5	651.7	7,240.0
2005	8,803.5	3,076.7	1,123.4	408.2	1,953.4	644.5	303.8	5,726.8	5,515.1	1,582.6	1,308.9	698.4	7,665.3
2006	9,301.0	3,224.7	1,155.0	394.8	2,069.8	674.2	335.2	6,076.3	5,836.3	1,686.2	1,373.7	732.6	8,090.7
2007	9,772.3	3,363.9	1,188.4	399.9	2,175.5	711.2	364.8	6,408.3	6,154.4	1,756.2	1,457.7	790.3	8,485.9
2008	10,035.5	3,381.7	1,108.9	339.3	2,272.8	746.4	410.5	6,653.8	6,369.3	1,831.0	1,532.6	807.0	8,655.0
2009	9,866.1	3,197.5	1,029.6	316.5	2,167.8	746.0	299.4	6,668.7	6,388.4	1,871.6	1,604.2	747.8	8,605.3
2010	10,245.5	3,387.0	1,085.5	340.1	2,301.5	766.4	354.1	6,858.5	6,578.3	1,893.2	1,667.4	780.2	8,901.3
2011 ᵖ	10,722.6	3,645.2	1,161.9	378.3	2,483.3	809.0	427.4	7,077.4	6,791.9	1,921.2	1,728.8	804.6	9,263.2
2008: I	10,018.5	3,422.3	1,163.0	378.9	2,259.4	732.5	418.3	6,596.2	6,325.0	1,802.0	1,513.0	817.0	8,649.7
II	10,126.5	3,466.9	1,146.6	354.1	2,320.3	749.2	444.0	6,659.6	6,377.8	1,825.2	1,526.5	819.7	8,707.0
III	10,135.8	3,456.1	1,106.6	332.6	2,349.4	757.1	466.9	6,679.7	6,389.2	1,838.6	1,539.0	807.7	8,688.2
IV	9,861.3	3,181.4	1,019.3	291.5	2,162.2	746.7	312.6	6,679.9	6,385.1	1,858.4	1,552.0	783.6	8,574.9
2009: I	9,781.7	3,130.7	1,020.1	303.0	2,110.6	741.3	261.4	6,651.0	6,366.9	1,867.2	1,571.8	753.8	8,556.7
II	9,781.6	3,143.6	1,009.5	303.5	2,134.1	743.8	275.5	6,638.0	6,361.3	1,866.7	1,596.2	744.3	8,550.9
III	9,911.1	3,245.6	1,050.1	339.2	2,195.5	746.4	321.5	6,665.5	6,386.7	1,872.1	1,615.4	741.9	8,632.2
IV	9,990.0	3,270.0	1,038.8	320.5	2,231.1	752.6	339.3	6,720.1	6,438.7	1,880.3	1,633.5	751.2	8,681.3
2010: I	10,103.7	3,338.1	1,058.0	323.1	2,280.1	761.5	359.5	6,765.6	6,484.0	1,883.6	1,632.9	770.5	8,763.5
II	10,184.8	3,340.1	1,071.7	330.6	2,268.3	759.4	337.0	6,844.7	6,562.3	1,887.1	1,659.1	788.6	8,868.2
III	10,276.6	3,386.5	1,087.5	339.6	2,299.0	766.4	345.9	6,890.1	6,610.9	1,900.8	1,677.1	779.2	8,934.2
IV	10,417.1	3,483.4	1,124.7	367.1	2,358.7	778.2	374.1	6,933.7	6,656.0	1,901.1	1,700.4	782.7	9,039.3
2011: I	10,571.7	3,592.2	1,154.5	383.0	2,437.8	792.0	420.2	6,979.4	6,700.0	1,901.7	1,708.1	795.7	9,141.4
II	10,676.0	3,622.7	1,143.8	363.4	2,478.9	806.7	431.5	7,053.3	6,771.6	1,913.3	1,729.5	803.1	9,215.2
III	10,784.5	3,661.2	1,158.3	368.7	2,503.0	815.8	434.5	7,123.2	6,834.4	1,937.7	1,734.4	811.9	9,299.8
IV ᵖ	10,858.1	3,704.5	1,190.9	397.9	2,513.6	821.5	423.5	7,153.6	6,861.5	1,932.0	1,743.2	807.6	9,395.5

[1] Includes other items not shown separately.

[2] Food consists of food and beverages purchased for off-premises consumption; food services, which include purchased meals and beverages, are not classified as food.

Source: Department of Commerce (Bureau of Economic Analysis).

TABLE B–17. Real personal consumption expenditures, 1995–2011

[Billions of chained (2005) dollars; quarterly data at seasonally adjusted annual rates]

Year or quarter	Personal consumption expenditures	Goods Total	Goods Durable Total[1]	Goods Durable Motor vehicles and parts	Goods Nondurable Total[1]	Goods Nondurable Food and beverages purchased for off-premises consumption	Goods Nondurable Gasoline and other energy goods	Services Total	Services Household consumption expenditures Total[1]	Housing and utilities	Health care	Financial services and insurance	Addendum: Personal consumption expenditures excluding food and energy[2]
1995	6,076.2	1,896.0	510.5	255.6	1,437.7	548.4	264.3	4,208.5	4,068.9	1,234.8	947.6	489.9	5,123.9
1996	6,288.3	1,980.9	548.6	268.0	1,479.2	553.9	268.5	4,331.7	4,183.6	1,261.6	967.2	508.2	5,319.4
1997	6,520.4	2,075.3	593.3	286.1	1,522.7	558.8	273.9	4,465.3	4,327.6	1,290.3	997.2	525.7	5,540.7
1998	6,862.3	2,215.5	665.6	316.0	1,580.2	565.5	283.7	4,662.1	4,511.0	1,329.7	1,029.6	559.1	5,860.1
1999	7,237.6	2,392.0	752.0	345.1	1,660.7	587.3	292.4	4,853.1	4,690.8	1,371.7	1,045.7	606.2	6,199.5
2000	7,604.6	2,518.2	818.0	356.1	1,714.5	600.5	287.1	5,093.6	4,918.2	1,413.6	1,081.6	666.0	6,545.5
2001	7,810.3	2,597.3	862.4	374.3	1,745.4	607.5	289.2	5,219.1	5,029.3	1,451.4	1,135.6	661.3	6,742.5
2002	8,018.3	2,702.9	927.9	394.0	1,780.1	608.9	294.0	5,318.5	5,109.8	1,461.9	1,202.4	658.9	6,938.6
2003	8,244.5	2,827.2	989.1	404.8	1,840.7	616.5	301.9	5,418.2	5,199.4	1,480.2	1,228.3	659.2	7,145.2
2004	8,515.8	2,953.3	1,060.9	410.4	1,892.8	623.9	305.9	5,562.7	5,345.1	1,512.8	1,267.4	675.5	7,401.8
2005	8,803.5	3,076.7	1,123.4	408.2	1,953.4	644.5	303.8	5,726.8	5,515.1	1,582.6	1,308.9	698.4	7,665.3
2006	9,054.5	3,178.9	1,174.2	394.4	2,005.0	663.0	296.9	5,875.6	5,640.6	1,616.8	1,333.0	716.4	7,911.5
2007	9,262.9	3,273.5	1,232.4	401.4	2,042.9	673.2	294.4	5,990.2	5,745.2	1,626.6	1,364.0	739.8	8,110.4
2008	9,211.7	3,192.9	1,171.8	346.8	2,019.1	666.0	280.6	6,017.0	5,745.6	1,637.8	1,396.5	732.3	8,087.2
2009	9,037.5	3,098.0	1,108.3	322.5	1,983.4	657.3	281.1	5,935.5	5,660.5	1,654.9	1,423.1	676.1	7,917.2
2010	9,220.9	3,230.7	1,188.3	330.1	2,041.3	673.1	281.3	5,991.8	5,714.0	1,669.2	1,442.9	667.8	8,076.8
2011 [p]	9,421.1	3,351.9	1,284.5	356.5	2,077.0	683.6	269.4	6,075.4	5,798.1	1,670.7	1,471.9	678.0	8,286.3
2008: I	9,289.1	3,249.0	1,218.7	381.9	2,032.1	672.9	286.3	6,039.7	5,775.9	1,637.3	1,385.7	746.3	8,143.9
II	9,285.8	3,252.7	1,209.8	360.7	2,043.5	674.5	282.7	6,032.9	5,765.1	1,637.0	1,395.7	738.3	8,148.9
III	9,196.0	3,187.9	1,170.8	340.8	2,015.4	666.5	273.4	6,006.5	5,734.4	1,630.9	1,401.9	732.2	8,090.4
IV	9,076.0	3,082.0	1,088.0	303.8	1,985.3	650.2	280.0	5,988.8	5,707.1	1,646.1	1,402.5	712.5	7,965.7
2009: I	9,040.9	3,082.6	1,094.6	316.2	1,980.3	647.0	284.9	5,953.5	5,676.3	1,650.0	1,409.1	693.1	7,929.2
II	8,998.5	3,064.3	1,083.4	312.4	1,972.8	654.8	281.2	5,928.6	5,657.0	1,651.3	1,421.6	679.7	7,882.9
III	9,050.3	3,120.7	1,134.5	344.5	1,982.7	660.8	279.3	5,926.8	5,653.5	1,656.6	1,429.1	670.6	7,927.7
IV	9,060.2	3,124.6	1,120.8	316.7	1,997.7	666.8	279.1	5,932.9	5,655.2	1,661.5	1,432.8	661.0	7,929.1
2010: I	9,121.2	3,173.3	1,147.5	315.9	2,021.1	671.6	281.8	5,947.4	5,668.1	1,663.6	1,424.1	667.0	7,981.7
II	9,186.9	3,202.9	1,169.3	321.4	2,030.8	667.2	282.1	5,984.3	5,702.6	1,665.7	1,438.2	670.8	8,051.4
III	9,247.1	3,240.8	1,194.1	328.0	2,045.8	672.8	282.7	6,008.1	5,730.6	1,675.3	1,446.9	665.9	8,096.2
IV	9,328.4	3,306.0	1,242.4	354.9	2,067.4	680.8	278.4	6,027.5	5,754.7	1,672.2	1,462.3	667.6	8,178.0
2011: I	9,376.7	3,344.4	1,277.4	368.2	2,075.4	682.1	274.2	6,039.1	5,765.9	1,666.0	1,464.3	674.7	8,238.4
II	9,392.7	3,331.2	1,260.2	342.1	2,076.6	684.1	268.5	6,067.0	5,793.2	1,669.1	1,474.5	676.9	8,258.7
III	9,433.5	3,342.7	1,277.8	343.5	2,073.7	683.9	267.5	6,096.1	5,816.6	1,680.4	1,472.3	682.8	8,292.0
IV [p]	9,481.3	3,389.2	1,322.7	372.1	2,082.2	684.1	267.2	6,099.4	5,816.9	1,667.2	1,476.4	677.7	8,356.0

[1] Includes other items not shown separately.

[2] Food consists of food and beverages purchased for off-premises consumption; food services, which include purchased meals and beverages, are not classified as food.

Note: See Table B–2 for data for total personal consumption expenditures for 1963–94.

Source: Department of Commerce (Bureau of Economic Analysis).

[Billions of dollars; quarterly data at seasonally adjusted annual rates]

Year or quarter	Private fixed invest-ment	Total non-resi-den-tial	Struc-tures	Equipment and software								Total resi-den-tial [1]	Residential Structures	
				Total	Information processing equipment and software				Indus-trial equip-ment	Trans-por-tation equip-ment	Other equip-ment		Total [1]	Single family
					Total	Com-puters and periph-eral equip-ment	Soft-ware	Other						
1963	88.1	56.0	21.2	34.8	6.5	0.7	0.4	5.4	10.0	9.4	8.8	32.1	31.5	16.0
1964	97.2	63.0	23.7	39.2	7.4	.9	.5	5.9	11.4	10.6	9.9	34.3	33.6	17.6
1965	109.0	74.8	28.3	46.5	8.5	1.2	.7	6.7	13.7	13.2	11.0	34.2	33.5	17.8
1966	117.7	85.4	31.3	54.0	10.7	1.7	1.0	8.0	16.2	14.5	12.7	32.3	31.6	16.6
1967	118.7	86.4	31.5	54.9	11.3	1.9	1.2	8.2	16.9	14.3	12.4	32.4	31.6	16.8
1968	132.1	93.4	33.6	59.9	11.9	1.9	1.3	8.7	17.3	17.6	13.0	38.7	37.9	19.5
1969	147.3	104.7	37.7	67.0	14.6	2.4	1.8	10.4	19.1	18.9	14.4	42.6	41.6	19.7
1970	150.4	109.0	40.3	68.7	16.6	2.7	2.3	11.6	20.3	16.2	15.6	41.4	40.2	17.5
1971	169.9	114.1	42.7	71.5	17.3	2.8	2.4	12.2	19.5	18.4	16.3	55.8	54.5	25.8
1972	198.5	128.8	47.2	81.7	19.5	3.5	2.8	13.2	21.4	21.8	19.0	69.7	68.1	32.8
1973	228.6	153.3	55.0	98.3	23.1	3.5	3.2	16.3	26.0	26.6	22.6	75.3	73.6	35.2
1974	235.4	169.5	61.2	108.2	27.0	3.9	3.9	19.2	30.7	26.3	24.3	66.0	64.1	29.7
1975	236.5	173.7	61.4	112.4	28.5	3.6	4.8	20.2	31.3	25.2	27.4	62.7	60.8	29.6
1976	274.8	192.4	65.9	126.4	32.7	4.4	5.2	23.1	34.1	30.0	29.6	82.5	80.4	43.9
1977	339.0	228.7	74.6	154.1	39.2	5.7	5.5	28.0	39.4	39.3	36.3	110.3	107.9	62.2
1978	412.2	280.6	93.6	187.0	48.7	7.6	6.3	34.8	47.7	47.3	43.2	131.6	128.9	72.8
1979	474.9	333.9	117.7	216.2	58.5	10.2	8.1	40.2	56.2	53.6	47.9	141.0	137.8	72.3
1980	485.6	362.4	136.2	226.2	68.8	12.5	9.8	46.4	60.7	48.4	48.3	123.2	119.8	52.9
1981	542.6	420.0	167.3	252.7	81.5	17.1	11.8	52.5	65.5	50.6	55.2	122.6	118.9	52.0
1982	532.1	426.5	177.6	248.9	88.3	18.9	14.0	55.3	62.7	46.8	51.2	105.7	102.0	41.5
1983	570.1	417.2	154.3	262.9	100.1	23.9	16.4	59.8	58.9	53.5	50.4	152.9	148.6	72.5
1984	670.2	489.6	177.4	312.2	121.5	31.6	20.4	69.6	68.1	64.4	58.1	180.6	175.9	86.4
1985	714.4	526.2	194.5	331.7	130.3	33.7	23.8	72.9	72.5	69.0	59.9	188.2	183.1	87.4
1986	739.9	519.8	176.5	343.3	136.8	33.4	25.6	77.7	75.4	70.5	60.7	220.1	214.6	104.1
1987	757.8	524.1	174.2	349.9	141.2	35.8	29.0	76.4	76.7	68.1	63.9	233.7	227.9	117.2
1988	803.1	563.8	182.8	381.0	154.9	38.0	34.2	82.8	84.2	72.9	69.0	239.3	233.2	120.1
1989	847.3	607.7	193.7	414.0	172.6	43.1	41.9	87.6	93.3	67.9	80.2	239.5	233.4	120.9
1990	846.4	622.4	202.9	419.5	177.2	38.6	47.6	90.9	92.1	70.0	80.2	224.0	218.0	112.9
1991	803.3	598.2	183.6	414.6	182.9	37.7	53.7	91.5	89.3	71.5	70.8	205.1	199.4	99.4
1992	848.5	612.1	172.6	439.6	199.9	44.0	57.9	98.1	93.0	74.7	72.0	236.3	230.4	122.0
1993	932.5	666.6	177.2	489.4	217.6	47.9	64.3	105.4	102.2	89.4	80.2	266.0	259.9	140.1
1994	1,033.5	731.4	186.8	544.6	235.2	52.4	68.3	114.6	113.6	107.7	88.1	302.1	295.9	162.3
1995	1,112.9	810.0	207.3	602.8	263.0	66.1	74.6	122.3	129.0	116.1	94.7	302.9	296.5	153.5
1996	1,209.4	875.4	224.6	650.8	290.1	72.8	85.5	131.9	136.5	123.2	101.0	334.1	327.7	170.8
1997	1,317.7	968.6	250.3	718.3	330.3	81.4	107.5	141.4	140.4	135.5	112.1	349.1	342.8	175.2
1998	1,447.1	1,061.1	275.1	786.0	366.1	87.9	126.0	152.2	147.4	147.1	125.4	385.9	379.2	199.4
1999	1,580.7	1,154.9	283.9	871.0	417.1	97.2	157.3	162.5	149.1	174.4	130.4	425.8	418.5	223.8
2000	1,717.7	1,268.7	318.1	950.5	478.2	103.2	184.5	190.6	162.9	170.8	138.6	449.0	441.2	236.8
2001	1,700.2	1,227.8	329.7	898.1	452.5	87.6	186.6	178.4	151.9	154.2	139.5	472.4	464.4	249.1
2002	1,634.9	1,125.4	282.8	842.7	419.8	79.7	183.0	157.0	141.7	141.6	139.6	509.5	501.3	265.9
2003	1,713.3	1,135.7	281.9	853.8	430.9	77.6	191.3	162.0	142.6	132.9	147.5	577.6	569.1	310.6
2004	1,903.6	1,223.0	306.7	916.4	455.3	80.2	205.7	169.4	142.0	161.1	157.9	680.6	671.4	377.6
2005	2,122.3	1,347.3	351.8	995.6	475.3	78.9	218.0	178.4	159.6	181.7	178.9	775.0	765.2	433.5
2006	2,267.2	1,505.3	433.7	1,071.7	505.2	84.9	229.8	190.6	178.4	198.2	189.8	761.9	751.6	416.0
2007	2,266.1	1,637.5	524.9	1,112.6	536.6	87.0	245.0	204.6	193.0	190.2	192.8	628.7	618.4	305.2
2008	2,128.7	1,656.3	586.3	1,070.0	536.4	84.9	257.2	194.3	194.5	146.9	192.2	472.4	462.7	185.8
2009	1,707.6	1,353.0	449.9	903.0	504.0	75.6	253.2	175.2	156.2	77.8	165.1	354.7	345.9	105.3
2010	1,728.2	1,390.1	374.4	1,015.7	543.8	93.8	257.9	192.1	168.6	122.7	180.5	338.1	329.2	112.6
2011 ᵖ	1,866.4	1,529.2	407.8	1,121.4	566.7	103.6	272.5	190.7	195.9	156.8	202.0	337.2	328.2	106.8
2008: I	2,205.2	1,689.3	570.9	1,118.4	550.3	90.6	256.0	203.6	194.5	183.6	190.1	515.9	505.9	221.3
II	2,183.7	1,689.0	589.6	1,099.4	550.2	90.8	258.2	201.2	196.7	161.6	191.0	494.6	484.6	202.1
III	2,130.5	1,665.9	594.7	1,071.2	538.6	84.1	259.5	195.1	197.5	138.9	196.2	464.6	454.8	174.0
IV	1,995.5	1,580.9	590.0	990.9	506.4	74.2	255.2	177.0	189.2	103.6	191.7	414.6	405.3	145.7
2009: I	1,799.6	1,430.6	527.4	903.2	491.9	71.3	250.3	170.3	162.6	72.2	176.4	369.0	360.1	112.1
II	1,694.3	1,351.9	461.4	890.5	492.7	71.6	252.3	168.8	155.2	79.0	163.6	342.4	333.8	92.9
III	1,678.3	1,324.3	424.8	899.5	507.3	74.6	252.6	180.0	153.2	78.8	160.3	353.9	345.3	105.0
IV	1,658.3	1,305.1	386.1	918.9	524.2	84.9	257.6	181.7	153.6	81.2	159.9	353.2	344.5	111.3
2010: I	1,658.0	1,318.7	361.2	957.5	528.4	86.6	254.8	187.0	154.5	104.4	170.2	339.3	330.5	114.4
II	1,731.6	1,377.1	370.2	1,006.9	539.8	94.1	255.1	190.5	169.1	120.7	177.4	354.5	345.5	118.7
III	1,743.8	1,416.5	376.6	1,039.9	548.0	95.3	258.6	194.0	172.9	132.8	186.3	327.3	318.4	110.7
IV	1,779.3	1,447.9	389.6	1,058.3	559.3	99.3	263.2	196.8	178.0	133.1	187.9	331.3	322.5	106.6
2011: I	1,791.1	1,460.5	379.5	1,081.0	557.9	95.6	265.1	197.3	185.0	145.4	192.7	330.6	321.7	106.9
II	1,841.7	1,506.0	405.2	1,100.8	567.6	103.9	270.4	193.3	186.5	152.0	194.6	335.7	326.7	105.2
III	1,905.8	1,568.7	424.8	1,143.9	567.4	105.1	275.5	186.8	201.2	163.1	212.3	337.0	327.8	106.3
IV ᵖ	1,927.1	1,581.5	421.7	1,159.9	573.9	109.7	279.0	185.2	211.0	166.7	208.2	345.6	336.3	109.0

[1] Includes other items not shown separately.

Source: Department of Commerce (Bureau of Economic Analysis).

[Billions of chained (2005) dollars; quarterly data at seasonally adjusted annual rates]

Year or quarter	Private fixed invest-ment	Total non-resi-den-tial	Struc-tures	Equipment and software Total	Information processing equipment and software Total	Com-puters and periph-eral equip-ment [1]	Soft-ware	Other	Indus-trial equip-ment	Trans-por-tation equip-ment	Other equip-ment	Total resi-den-tial [2]	Total [2]	Single family
1995	1,231.2	787.9	342.0	489.4	147.3	....	66.9	90.1	145.5	131.5	110.6	456.1	450.1	240.2
1996	1,341.6	861.5	361.4	541.4	176.5	....	78.5	98.7	150.9	136.8	114.8	492.5	486.8	262.4
1997	1,465.4	965.5	387.9	615.9	217.6	....	101.7	107.2	154.1	148.2	125.9	501.8	496.3	261.6
1998	1,624.4	1,081.4	407.7	705.2	267.1	....	122.8	120.7	160.8	162.0	138.8	540.4	534.5	290.1
1999	1,775.5	1,194.3	408.2	805.0	327.2	....	151.5	134.6	161.8	190.3	142.4	574.2	567.5	311.5
2000	1,906.8	1,311.3	440.0	889.2	386.2	....	172.4	162.0	175.8	186.2	150.4	580.0	572.6	315.0
2001	1,870.7	1,274.8	433.3	860.6	384.5	....	173.7	157.0	162.8	169.6	149.3	583.3	575.6	315.4
2002	1,791.5	1,173.7	356.6	824.2	373.9	....	173.4	142.7	151.9	154.2	148.2	613.8	605.9	327.7
2003	1,854.7	1,189.6	343.0	850.0	403.7	....	185.6	155.1	151.6	140.4	155.0	664.3	655.9	362.6
2004	1,992.5	1,263.0	346.7	917.3	443.1	....	204.6	168.1	147.4	162.3	164.4	729.5	720.1	406.1
2005	2,122.3	1,347.3	351.8	995.6	475.3	....	218.0	178.4	159.6	181.7	178.9	775.0	765.2	433.5
2006	2,172.7	1,455.5	384.0	1,071.1	516.3	....	227.1	192.8	172.9	196.5	185.5	718.2	708.1	391.1
2007	2,130.6	1,550.0	438.2	1,106.8	558.2	....	240.9	208.4	179.9	185.8	184.2	584.2	574.2	284.0
2008	1,978.6	1,537.6	466.4	1,059.4	569.7	....	250.8	202.4	172.9	142.7	177.8	444.4	434.9	178.4
2009	1,606.3	1,263.2	367.3	889.7	548.3	....	249.1	186.1	137.1	70.7	145.6	345.6	336.9	105.5
2010	1,648.4	1,319.2	309.1	1,019.4	602.6	....	256.1	207.3	146.6	119.3	162.6	330.8	321.5	114.7
2011 _p_	1,757.8	1,432.4	321.8	1,124.1	638.4	....	271.2	208.6	165.4	149.4	179.5	326.2	316.5	108.1
2008: I	2,066.4	1,589.1	463.8	1,117.2	583.0	....	251.0	211.8	176.9	180.6	180.0	481.3	471.6	209.6
II	2,039.1	1,580.0	474.4	1,094.6	583.3	....	251.4	209.8	175.6	158.2	181.1	462.8	453.0	193.2
III	1,973.5	1,539.2	469.9	1,056.8	571.7	....	251.9	203.3	173.1	133.6	181.9	437.8	428.3	168.4
IV	1,835.4	1,442.3	457.5	969.0	540.7	....	248.8	184.8	165.8	98.3	168.3	395.8	386.9	142.4
2009: I	1,665.5	1,312.9	415.3	883.7	529.9	....	244.8	180.0	142.8	65.5	154.4	354.9	346.2	109.8
II	1,589.8	1,257.6	375.4	874.2	535.5	....	247.8	179.8	136.5	69.8	143.5	334.3	325.9	93.3
III	1,592.6	1,247.0	354.9	888.0	553.7	....	249.8	190.8	134.5	70.6	142.3	348.2	339.6	106.9
IV	1,577.5	1,235.2	323.7	912.9	574.1	....	253.9	193.7	134.5	76.7	142.3	344.8	336.0	112.2
2010: I	1,582.0	1,253.3	301.5	958.8	581.2	....	252.0	200.3	135.1	101.8	153.8	330.8	321.7	115.6
II	1,654.0	1,308.0	306.9	1,010.1	596.1	....	252.9	204.8	147.3	117.6	160.5	348.2	338.9	121.8
III	1,663.5	1,343.6	310.1	1,044.1	608.5	....	257.2	209.9	150.1	129.1	167.1	321.1	311.8	113.1
IV	1,693.9	1,371.9	318.0	1,064.5	624.5	....	262.4	214.4	153.7	128.9	168.9	323.1	313.6	108.1
2011: I	1,699.0	1,378.9	305.9	1,086.9	625.0	....	263.7	215.2	158.1	139.6	174.0	321.1	311.5	108.4
II	1,736.7	1,413.2	321.9	1,103.5	638.4	....	268.9	211.5	157.7	144.6	173.8	324.4	314.8	106.7
III	1,790.4	1,465.6	332.9	1,145.7	640.2	....	274.1	204.3	169.0	155.2	187.9	325.4	315.7	107.6
IV _p_	1,805.0	1,471.9	326.7	1,160.3	650.0	....	277.9	203.2	177.0	158.1	182.2	333.9	324.1	109.8

[1] Because computers exhibit rapid changes in prices relative to other prices in the economy, the chained-dollar estimates should not be used to measure the component's relative importance or its contribution to the growth rate of more aggregate series. The quantity index for computers can be used to accurately measure the real growth rate of this series. For information on this component, see _Survey of Current Business_ Table 5.3.1 (for growth rates), Table 5.3.2 (for contributions), and Table 5.3.3 (for quantity indexes).

[2] Includes other items not shown separately.

Source: Department of Commerce (Bureau of Economic Analysis).

[Billions of dollars; quarterly data at seasonally adjusted annual rates]

Year or quarter	Total	Government consumption expenditures and gross investment												
		Federal										State and local			
		Total	National defense					Nondefense				Total	Consumption expenditures	Gross investment	
			Total	Consumption expenditures	Gross investment		Total	Consumption expenditures	Gross investment					Structures	Equipment and software
					Structures	Equipment and software			Structures	Equipment and software					
1963	136.4	76.9	61.0	48.3	1.6	11.0	15.9	12.4	2.3	1.2	59.5	41.9	16.0	1.5
1964	143.2	78.4	60.2	48.8	1.3	10.2	18.2	14.0	2.5	1.6	64.8	45.8	17.2	1.8
1965	151.4	80.4	60.6	50.6	1.1	8.9	19.8	15.1	2.8	1.9	71.0	50.2	19.0	1.9
1966	171.6	92.4	71.7	59.9	1.3	10.5	20.8	15.9	2.8	2.1	79.2	56.1	21.0	2.1
1967	192.5	104.6	83.4	69.9	1.2	12.3	21.2	17.0	2.2	1.9	87.9	62.6	23.0	2.3
1968	209.3	111.3	89.2	77.1	1.2	10.9	22.0	18.2	2.1	1.7	98.0	70.4	25.2	2.4
1969	221.4	113.3	89.5	78.1	1.5	9.9	23.8	20.2	1.9	1.7	108.2	79.8	25.6	2.7
1970	233.7	113.4	87.6	76.5	1.3	9.8	25.8	22.1	2.1	1.7	120.3	91.5	25.8	3.0
1971	246.4	113.6	84.6	77.1	1.8	5.7	29.1	24.9	2.5	1.7	132.8	102.7	27.0	3.1
1972	263.4	119.6	86.9	79.5	1.8	5.7	32.7	28.2	2.7	1.8	143.8	113.2	27.1	3.5
1973	281.7	122.5	88.1	79.4	2.1	6.6	34.3	29.4	3.1	1.8	159.2	126.0	29.1	4.1
1974	317.9	134.5	95.6	84.5	2.2	8.9	39.0	33.4	3.4	2.2	183.4	143.7	34.7	4.9
1975	357.7	149.0	103.9	90.9	2.3	10.7	45.1	38.7	4.1	2.4	208.7	165.1	38.1	5.5
1976	383.0	159.7	111.1	95.8	2.1	13.2	48.6	41.4	4.6	2.7	223.3	179.5	38.1	5.7
1977	414.1	175.4	120.9	104.2	2.4	14.4	54.5	46.5	5.0	3.0	238.7	195.9	36.9	5.9
1978	453.6	190.9	130.5	112.7	2.5	15.3	60.4	50.6	6.1	3.7	262.7	213.2	42.8	6.6
1979	500.7	210.6	145.2	123.8	2.5	18.9	65.4	55.1	6.3	4.0	290.2	233.3	49.0	7.8
1980	566.1	243.7	168.0	143.7	3.2	21.1	75.8	63.8	7.1	4.9	322.4	258.4	55.1	8.9
1981	627.5	280.2	196.2	167.3	3.2	25.7	83.9	71.0	7.7	5.3	347.3	282.3	55.4	9.5
1982	680.4	310.8	225.9	191.1	4.0	30.8	84.9	72.1	6.8	6.0	369.7	304.9	54.2	10.6
1983	733.4	342.9	250.6	208.7	4.8	37.1	92.3	77.7	6.7	7.8	390.5	324.1	54.2	12.2
1984	796.9	374.3	281.5	232.8	4.9	43.8	92.7	77.1	7.0	8.7	422.6	347.7	60.5	14.4
1985	878.9	412.8	311.2	253.7	6.2	51.3	101.6	84.7	7.3	9.6	466.1	381.8	67.6	16.8
1986	949.3	438.4	330.8	267.9	6.8	56.1	107.6	90.1	8.0	9.5	510.9	418.1	74.2	18.6
1987	999.4	459.5	350.0	283.6	7.7	58.8	109.6	90.1	9.0	10.4	539.9	441.4	78.8	19.6
1988	1,038.9	461.6	354.7	293.5	7.4	53.9	106.8	88.3	6.8	11.7	577.3	471.0	84.8	21.5
1989	1,100.6	481.4	362.1	299.4	6.4	56.3	119.3	99.1	6.9	13.4	619.2	504.5	88.7	26.0
1990	1,181.7	507.5	373.9	308.0	6.1	59.8	133.6	111.0	8.0	14.6	674.2	547.0	98.5	28.7
1991	1,236.1	526.6	383.1	319.7	4.6	58.8	143.4	118.6	9.2	15.7	709.5	577.5	103.2	28.9
1992	1,273.5	532.9	376.8	315.2	5.2	56.3	156.1	128.9	10.3	16.9	740.6	606.2	104.2	30.1
1993	1,294.8	525.0	363.0	307.5	5.3	50.1	162.0	133.7	11.2	17.0	769.8	634.2	104.5	31.2
1994	1,329.8	518.6	353.8	300.8	5.8	47.2	164.8	139.9	10.2	14.7	811.2	668.2	108.7	34.3
1995	1,374.0	518.8	348.8	297.0	6.7	45.1	170.0	143.2	10.8	16.0	855.3	701.3	117.3	36.7
1996	1,421.0	527.0	354.8	303.2	6.3	45.4	172.2	143.4	11.3	17.5	894.0	730.2	126.8	36.9
1997	1,474.4	531.0	349.8	304.5	6.1	39.2	181.1	153.0	9.9	18.2	943.5	764.5	139.5	39.4
1998	1,526.1	531.0	346.1	300.3	5.8	39.9	184.9	154.3	10.8	19.9	995.0	808.6	143.6	42.9
1999	1,631.3	554.9	361.1	313.0	5.4	42.8	193.8	160.3	10.7	22.7	1,076.3	870.6	159.7	46.1
2000	1,731.0	576.1	371.0	321.8	5.4	43.8	205.0	174.2	8.3	22.6	1,154.9	930.6	176.0	48.3
2001	1,846.4	611.7	393.0	342.0	5.3	45.6	218.7	188.1	8.1	22.5	1,234.7	994.2	192.3	48.2
2002	1,983.3	680.6	437.7	380.7	5.8	51.2	242.9	209.8	9.9	23.2	1,302.7	1,049.4	205.8	47.5
2003	2,112.6	756.5	497.9	435.2	7.3	55.4	258.5	225.1	10.3	23.1	1,356.1	1,096.5	211.8	47.8
2004	2,232.8	824.6	550.8	481.2	7.1	62.4	273.9	240.2	9.1	24.6	1,408.2	1,139.1	220.2	48.9
2005	2,369.9	876.3	589.0	514.8	7.5	66.8	287.3	251.0	8.3	28.0	1,493.6	1,212.0	230.8	50.8
2006	2,518.4	931.7	624.9	543.9	8.1	72.9	306.8	267.1	9.5	30.2	1,586.7	1,282.3	249.9	54.5
2007	2,674.2	976.3	662.3	575.4	10.1	76.9	314.0	273.5	11.1	29.4	1,697.9	1,368.9	268.4	60.7
2008	2,878.1	1,080.1	737.8	633.3	13.7	90.9	342.3	298.5	11.4	32.4	1,798.0	1,449.2	285.0	63.8
2009	2,917.5	1,142.7	774.9	664.1	17.3	93.5	367.8	322.5	12.4	32.9	1,774.8	1,425.5	284.5	64.8
2010	3,002.8	1,222.8	819.2	702.1	17.3	99.8	403.6	351.9	16.3	35.4	1,780.0	1,443.5	270.8	65.7
2011 p	3,029.7	1,232.7	824.8	717.0	14.8	93.0	407.9	355.5	15.4	37.0	1,797.0	1,475.0	253.8	68.3
2008: I	2,812.0	1,042.7	706.0	614.2	10.2	81.6	336.7	294.4	10.5	31.8	1,769.3	1,428.4	277.1	63.8
II	2,869.6	1,066.0	724.7	620.9	13.1	90.7	341.3	297.8	10.9	32.6	1,803.7	1,455.1	284.3	64.3
III	2,929.8	1,100.6	758.4	648.5	14.9	95.0	342.1	297.7	11.7	32.8	1,829.2	1,475.6	289.1	64.5
IV	2,901.1	1,111.2	762.1	649.6	16.4	96.2	349.0	303.9	12.5	32.7	1,789.9	1,437.8	289.4	62.7
2009: I	2,875.5	1,105.3	747.7	641.9	16.9	88.9	357.7	313.3	12.1	32.3	1,770.1	1,417.1	289.4	63.6
II	2,916.9	1,137.2	771.6	659.5	17.0	95.0	365.7	321.7	11.5	32.5	1,779.7	1,424.6	290.7	64.5
III	2,935.0	1,157.7	789.0	674.6	17.9	96.5	368.6	323.2	12.5	32.9	1,777.3	1,427.6	284.9	64.8
IV	2,942.7	1,170.6	791.4	680.5	17.4	93.5	379.2	331.9	13.6	33.8	1,772.1	1,432.7	273.0	66.4
2010: I	2,967.7	1,195.2	803.5	691.0	16.6	96.0	391.6	342.9	14.2	34.6	1,772.6	1,443.1	263.7	65.8
II	3,004.6	1,224.5	818.0	701.6	17.2	99.3	406.5	354.4	17.0	35.1	1,780.1	1,441.8	272.8	65.6
III	3,018.7	1,237.5	831.3	713.1	18.0	100.2	406.2	353.6	16.7	35.8	1,781.2	1,438.9	276.6	65.7
IV	3,020.2	1,234.3	823.9	702.7	17.5	103.7	410.3	356.9	17.1	36.3	1,786.0	1,450.1	270.0	65.8
2011: I	3,014.4	1,219.9	809.0	701.0	15.5	92.6	410.9	358.1	16.4	36.4	1,794.4	1,471.7	256.8	66.0
II	3,038.6	1,237.1	830.6	723.4	14.4	92.9	406.5	354.1	16.0	36.3	1,801.5	1,482.9	250.6	68.0
III	3,047.3	1,248.9	844.0	733.2	15.9	94.9	404.9	351.7	15.2	37.9	1,798.5	1,476.1	252.9	69.5
IV p	3,018.6	1,225.0	815.6	710.6	13.3	91.6	409.4	357.9	14.0	37.5	1,793.7	1,469.2	254.8	69.6

Source: Department of Commerce (Bureau of Economic Analysis).

TABLE B–21. Real government consumption expenditures and gross investment by type, 1995–2011

[Billions of chained (2005) dollars; quarterly data at seasonally adjusted annual rates]

Year or quarter	Total	Government consumption expenditures and gross investment												
		Federal										State and local		
		Total	National defense				Nondefense				Total	Consumption expenditures	Gross investment	
			Total	Consumption expenditures	Gross investment		Total	Consumption expenditures	Gross investment				Structures	Equipment and software
					Structures	Equipment and software			Structures	Equipment and software				
1995	1,888.9	704.1	476.8	424.5	10.1	43.7	227.5	201.2	15.7	13.7	1,183.6	983.0	175.4	29.1
1996	1,907.9	696.0	470.4	418.5	9.2	43.8	225.7	196.2	15.9	15.5	1,211.1	1,001.0	184.3	29.9
1997	1,943.8	689.1	457.2	412.2	8.7	38.9	231.9	203.2	13.8	16.6	1,254.3	1,027.7	196.7	33.1
1998	1,985.0	681.4	447.5	401.2	8.1	40.1	233.7	201.2	14.5	18.7	1,303.8	1,070.8	196.5	37.7
1999	2,056.1	694.6	455.8	407.6	7.2	42.4	238.7	202.9	14.0	21.7	1,361.8	1,109.5	210.9	41.8
2000	2,097.8	698.1	453.5	403.9	6.9	43.6	244.4	212.4	10.4	21.5	1,400.1	1,133.7	222.2	44.3
2001	2,178.3	726.5	470.7	418.5	6.5	46.3	255.5	224.2	9.8	21.6	1,452.3	1,172.6	234.8	45.3
2002	2,279.6	779.5	505.3	445.8	7.0	52.7	273.9	239.7	11.8	22.7	1,500.6	1,211.3	244.2	45.8
2003	2,330.5	831.1	549.2	484.1	8.5	57.0	281.7	247.1	11.9	23.0	1,499.7	1,207.5	245.5	47.2
2004	2,362.0	865.0	580.4	509.4	7.8	63.3	284.6	250.2	9.9	24.6	1,497.1	1,207.4	241.3	48.6
2005	2,369.9	876.3	589.0	514.8	7.5	66.8	287.3	251.0	8.3	28.0	1,493.6	1,212.0	230.8	50.8
2006	2,402.1	894.9	598.4	519.1	7.5	71.9	296.6	257.5	8.8	30.3	1,507.2	1,220.7	231.4	55.2
2007	2,434.2	906.1	611.8	528.0	8.8	75.1	294.2	254.7	9.8	29.7	1,528.1	1,239.8	227.6	61.6
2008	2,497.4	971.1	657.7	559.6	11.5	87.0	313.3	271.0	9.6	33.0	1,528.1	1,237.1	227.9	64.4
2009	2,539.6	1,029.5	695.6	591.5	14.6	89.7	333.8	289.7	10.4	33.7	1,514.2	1,228.9	222.2	64.8
2010	2,556.8	1,075.9	718.3	609.0	14.7	94.9	357.7	307.5	13.7	36.3	1,487.0	1,213.0	210.6	66.2
2011 ᵖ	2,502.0	1,054.7	701.4	602.2	12.2	86.7	353.3	303.0	12.6	37.9	1,453.4	1,199.0	190.4	68.6
2008: I	2,473.9	943.8	634.7	547.3	8.7	78.9	309.1	268.0	9.0	32.3	1,530.9	1,240.7	226.8	64.9
II	2,484.5	955.1	643.1	545.6	11.0	87.0	312.1	270.0	9.3	33.0	1,530.5	1,236.6	230.0	65.2
III	2,510.7	982.0	669.7	567.2	12.5	90.5	312.0	269.2	9.8	33.2	1,530.8	1,237.2	229.9	65.0
IV	2,520.5	1,003.5	683.2	578.4	13.7	91.4	320.2	276.7	10.2	33.3	1,520.1	1,233.9	224.8	62.6
2009: I	2,509.6	995.2	669.9	570.7	14.0	85.3	325.3	282.3	9.9	33.1	1,517.2	1,232.6	222.8	63.4
II	2,546.0	1,029.2	695.7	590.3	14.3	91.4	333.4	290.5	9.6	33.3	1,520.7	1,231.7	226.1	64.3
III	2,554.2	1,043.9	709.5	601.9	15.2	92.7	334.3	289.8	10.5	33.9	1,514.9	1,227.1	224.4	64.9
IV	2,548.5	1,049.6	707.3	603.0	14.8	89.5	342.2	296.1	11.5	34.5	1,503.9	1,224.3	215.4	66.7
2010: I	2,540.6	1,056.9	708.2	602.7	14.1	91.6	348.7	301.2	12.0	35.3	1,489.2	1,219.1	207.0	66.1
II	2,564.0	1,079.4	718.6	609.8	14.7	94.4	360.8	310.3	14.4	35.9	1,490.8	1,214.8	212.8	65.9
III	2,570.3	1,087.8	728.6	618.1	15.4	95.5	359.2	308.3	14.1	36.6	1,488.9	1,210.8	214.6	66.1
IV	2,552.1	1,079.6	717.7	605.3	14.8	98.3	361.9	310.3	14.3	37.2	1,478.9	1,207.4	208.1	66.5
2011: I	2,513.9	1,053.3	694.0	594.0	13.0	86.9	359.4	308.4	13.6	37.3	1,466.4	1,207.4	196.3	66.5
II	2,508.2	1,058.3	705.9	607.1	12.0	86.6	352.4	302.1	13.2	37.2	1,456.1	1,203.2	189.3	68.3
III	2,507.6	1,063.7	714.6	613.1	13.2	88.0	349.0	298.3	12.4	38.7	1,450.4	1,197.2	188.6	69.6
IV ᵖ	2,478.5	1,043.7	691.1	594.7	10.9	85.3	352.6	303.3	11.3	38.4	1,440.7	1,188.4	187.6	69.8

Note: See Table B–2 for data for total government consumption expenditures and gross investment for 1963–94.

Source: Department of Commerce (Bureau of Economic Analysis).

TABLE B-22. Private inventories and domestic final sales by industry, 1963–2011

[Billions of dollars, except as noted; seasonally adjusted]

| Quarter | Private inventories [1] | | | | | | | | Final sales of domestic business [3] | Ratio of private inventories to final sales of domestic business | |
	Total [2]	Farm	Mining, utilities, and construction [2]	Manufacturing	Wholesale trade	Retail trade	Other industries [2]	Non-farm [2]		Total	Non-farm
Fourth quarter:											
1963	149.9	44.4		55.1	19.5	23.9	7.1	105.5	37.9	3.95	2.78
1964	154.5	42.2		58.6	20.8	25.2	7.7	112.2	40.8	3.79	2.75
1965	169.4	47.2		63.4	22.5	28.0	8.3	122.2	44.9	3.77	2.72
1966	185.6	47.3		73.0	25.8	30.6	8.9	138.3	47.4	3.92	2.92
1967	194.8	45.7		79.9	28.1	30.9	10.1	149.1	49.9	3.90	2.99
1968	208.1	48.8		85.1	29.3	34.2	10.6	159.3	55.0	3.79	2.90
1969	227.4	52.8		92.6	32.5	37.5	12.0	174.6	58.7	3.88	2.98
1970	235.7	52.4		95.5	36.4	38.5	12.9	183.3	61.9	3.81	2.96
1971	253.7	59.3		96.6	39.4	44.7	13.7	194.4	67.5	3.76	2.88
1972	283.6	73.7		102.1	43.1	49.8	14.8	209.9	75.7	3.74	2.77
1973	351.5	102.2		121.5	51.7	58.4	17.7	249.4	83.7	4.20	2.98
1974	405.6	87.6		162.6	66.9	63.9	24.7	318.1	89.8	4.52	3.54
1975	408.5	89.5		162.2	66.5	64.4	25.9	319.0	101.1	4.04	3.16
1976	439.6	85.3		178.7	74.1	73.0	28.5	354.2	111.2	3.95	3.19
1977	482.0	90.6		193.2	84.0	80.9	33.3	391.4	124.0	3.89	3.16
1978	570.9	119.3		219.8	99.0	94.1	38.8	451.7	143.6	3.98	3.15
1979	667.6	134.9		261.8	119.5	104.7	46.6	532.6	159.4	4.19	3.34
1980	739.0	140.3		293.4	139.4	111.7	54.1	598.7	174.1	4.24	3.44
1981	779.1	127.4		313.1	148.8	123.2	66.6	651.7	186.7	4.17	3.49
1982	773.9	131.3		304.6	147.9	123.2	66.8	642.6	194.8	3.97	3.30
1983	796.9	131.7		308.9	153.4	137.6	65.2	665.1	215.7	3.69	3.08
1984	869.0	131.4		344.5	169.1	157.0	66.9	737.6	233.6	3.72	3.16
1985	875.9	125.8		333.3	175.9	171.4	69.5	750.2	249.5	3.51	3.01
1986	858.0	113.0		320.6	182.0	176.2	66.3	745.1	264.2	3.25	2.82
1987	924.2	119.9		339.6	195.8	199.1	69.9	804.4	277.7	3.33	2.90
1988	999.7	130.7		372.4	213.9	213.2	69.5	869.1	304.1	3.29	2.86
1989	1,044.3	129.6		390.5	222.8	231.4	70.1	914.7	322.8	3.23	2.83
1990	1,082.0	133.1		404.5	236.8	236.6	71.0	948.9	335.9	3.22	2.82
1991	1,057.2	123.2		384.1	239.2	240.2	70.5	934.0	345.7	3.06	2.70
1992	1,082.6	133.1		377.6	248.3	249.4	74.3	949.5	370.9	2.92	2.56
1993	1,116.0	132.3		380.1	258.6	268.6	76.5	983.7	391.4	2.85	2.51
1994	1,194.5	134.5		404.3	281.5	293.6	80.6	1,060.0	413.9	2.89	2.56
1995	1,257.2	131.1		424.5	303.7	312.2	85.6	1,126.1	436.0	2.88	2.58
NAICS:											
1996	1,284.7	136.6	31.1	421.0	285.1	328.7	82.1	1,148.1	465.6	2.76	2.47
1997	1,327.3	136.9	33.0	432.0	302.5	335.9	87.1	1,190.4	492.2	2.70	2.42
1998	1,341.6	120.5	36.6	432.3	312.0	349.2	91.1	1,221.1	525.8	2.55	2.32
1999	1,432.7	124.3	38.5	457.6	334.8	377.7	99.8	1,308.4	557.2	2.57	2.35
2000	1,524.0	132.1	42.3	476.5	357.7	400.8	114.6	1,391.8	588.3	2.59	2.37
2001	1,447.3	126.2	45.3	440.9	335.8	386.0	113.0	1,321.1	603.0	2.40	2.19
2002	1,489.1	135.9	46.5	443.7	343.2	408.0	111.8	1,353.2	608.5	2.45	2.22
2003	1,545.7	151.0	54.7	447.6	352.6	425.5	114.3	1,394.7	646.2	2.39	2.16
2004	1,681.5	157.2	64.1	487.2	388.9	460.9	123.2	1,524.3	683.4	2.46	2.23
2005	1,804.6	165.2	81.7	531.5	422.8	473.7	129.8	1,639.4	727.5	2.48	2.25
2006	1,917.1	165.1	90.7	575.7	456.4	491.6	137.7	1,752.0	769.6	2.49	2.28
2007	2,077.5	188.3	95.6	635.6	497.2	511.8	148.9	1,889.2	807.0	2.57	2.34
2008: I	2,146.8	197.8	101.3	670.4	515.8	508.9	152.6	1,949.0	803.4	2.67	2.43
II	2,232.2	213.5	111.1	703.0	539.6	509.9	155.1	2,018.7	810.3	2.75	2.49
III	2,203.2	206.7	111.3	681.8	537.1	508.3	158.0	1,996.5	804.8	2.74	2.48
IV	2,024.3	185.4	94.0	604.5	496.9	488.9	154.6	1,838.9	782.5	2.59	2.35
2009: I	1,949.4	181.2	88.9	585.3	472.7	471.5	149.8	1,768.2	775.8	2.51	2.28
II	1,901.6	176.1	85.6	577.0	457.5	458.0	147.5	1,725.5	769.8	2.47	2.24
III	1,863.4	171.1	84.7	572.1	441.2	447.4	146.9	1,692.3	772.8	2.41	2.19
IV	1,883.6	173.0	83.5	582.1	449.0	448.1	147.8	1,710.6	772.9	2.44	2.21
2010: I	1,926.4	183.5	84.2	595.4	457.6	455.9	149.8	1,742.9	777.0	2.48	2.24
II	1,938.9	183.4	83.0	595.2	462.7	464.9	149.7	1,755.5	787.0	2.46	2.23
III	2,001.3	195.1	82.2	608.6	489.4	475.6	150.3	1,806.2	794.1	2.52	2.27
IV	2,084.5	214.8	82.3	640.9	515.8	477.3	153.6	1,869.7	812.0	2.57	2.30
2011: I	2,189.6	237.7	85.3	680.5	541.6	485.8	158.6	1,951.9	816.5	2.68	2.39
II	2,211.6	230.0	88.0	690.7	557.8	484.7	160.4	1,981.6	825.4	2.68	2.40
III	2,225.8	234.8	89.0	689.5	566.0	486.3	160.1	1,991.0	840.3	2.65	2.37
IV [p]	2,246.4	233.0	90.9	701.4	573.4	485.6	162.1	2,013.4	845.8	2.66	2.38

[1] Inventories at end of quarter. Quarter-to-quarter change calculated from this table is not the current-dollar change in private inventories component of gross domestic product (GDP). The former is the difference between two inventory stocks, each valued at its respective end-of-quarter prices. The latter is the change in the physical volume of inventories valued at average prices of the quarter. In addition, changes calculated from this table are at quarterly rates, whereas change in private inventories is stated at annual rates.

[2] Inventories of construction, mining, and utilities establishments are included in other industries through 1995.

[3] Quarterly totals at monthly rates. Final sales of domestic business equals final sales of domestic product less gross output of general government, gross value added of nonprofit institutions, compensation paid to domestic workers, and imputed rental of owner-occupied nonfarm housing. Includes a small amount of final sales by farm and by government enterprises.

Note: The industry classification of inventories is on an establishment basis. Estimates through 1995 are based on the Standard Industrial Classification (SIC). Beginning with 1996, estimates are based on the North American Industry Classification System (NAICS).

Source: Department of Commerce (Bureau of Economic Analysis).

[Billions of chained (2005) dollars, except as noted; seasonally adjusted]

| Quarter | Private inventories [1] | | | | | | | | Final sales of domestic business [3] | Ratio of private inventories to final sales of domestic business | |
	Total [2]	Farm	Mining, utilities, and construction [2]	Manufacturing	Wholesale trade	Retail trade	Other industries [2]	Non-farm [2]		Total	Non-farm
Fourth quarter:											
1963	540.6	139.0		187.8	77.5	77.0	42.1	385.5	166.1	3.25	2.32
1964	557.9	135.1		198.2	82.2	81.1	44.7	407.3	176.1	3.17	2.31
1965	590.8	137.7		212.2	87.8	89.3	46.6	437.8	191.3	3.09	2.29
1966	637.9	136.3		240.6	99.5	96.6	47.9	487.9	195.4	3.26	2.50
1967	671.8	138.8		259.6	107.7	96.6	53.5	519.5	200.3	3.35	2.59
1968	702.6	142.9		271.5	111.5	104.8	55.1	545.9	211.2	3.33	2.58
1969	732.9	142.9		284.1	119.7	112.1	57.9	576.8	215.5	3.40	2.68
1970	738.5	140.5		284.0	128.7	112.2	58.6	585.5	218.1	3.39	2.68
1971	763.5	144.6		280.6	135.5	127.4	60.7	606.1	229.3	3.33	2.64
1972	789.1	145.0		288.3	141.6	137.3	63.7	632.8	248.4	3.18	2.55
1973	828.1	146.8		309.6	145.4	148.4	67.0	673.3	257.1	3.22	2.62
1974	857.2	142.4		333.0	158.9	146.2	71.4	712.3	247.5	3.46	2.88
1975	844.4	148.2		324.6	152.1	138.8	73.3	690.9	259.3	3.26	2.66
1976	878.7	146.6		340.1	162.2	149.5	74.0	728.5	272.0	3.23	2.68
1977	921.8	153.9		349.6	175.3	158.1	79.6	764.2	286.4	3.22	2.67
1978	967.4	155.9		365.6	189.3	168.7	84.4	809.1	307.8	3.14	2.63
1979	995.4	160.2		379.7	198.7	168.6	84.3	832.8	315.0	3.16	2.64
1980	986.0	153.0		380.1	204.0	163.8	82.9	832.4	314.7	3.13	2.65
1981	1,025.0	163.1		385.2	209.8	172.8	92.3	860.6	312.4	3.28	2.75
1982	1,005.3	170.6		367.9	207.2	168.9	89.4	833.3	311.2	3.23	2.68
1983	997.7	153.1		367.5	206.3	182.7	88.3	844.0	334.7	2.98	2.52
1984	1,075.9	159.4		399.4	222.8	205.0	89.7	916.3	353.1	3.05	2.60
1985	1,101.3	166.5		392.4	229.2	220.8	94.8	934.7	369.4	2.98	2.53
1986	1,109.8	164.2		388.3	237.7	224.3	98.3	945.1	383.3	2.90	2.47
1987	1,143.0	155.1		397.6	245.4	246.1	100.8	986.2	393.8	2.90	2.50
1988	1,164.9	142.0		416.2	254.9	253.9	99.3	1,021.6	414.2	2.81	2.47
1989	1,195.6	142.0		431.8	258.5	268.8	94.8	1,052.4	426.4	2.80	2.47
1990	1,212.1	148.6		441.6	267.2	267.2	91.2	1,066.4	427.7	2.83	2.49
1991	1,210.7	146.7		434.2	271.5	267.7	94.8	1,066.8	427.4	2.83	2.50
1992	1,228.6	153.8		429.0	280.3	272.5	97.7	1,077.7	450.6	2.73	2.39
1993	1,250.8	146.3		432.9	286.5	288.3	101.2	1,107.6	466.3	2.68	2.38
1994	1,320.1	160.0		446.3	302.7	309.4	106.1	1,163.4	484.9	2.72	2.40
1995	1,352.2	147.0		461.7	316.2	321.9	108.6	1,207.7	502.7	2.69	2.40
NAICS:											
1996	1,383.4	155.3	47.6	465.7	298.0	335.3	87.6	1,230.9	528.6	2.62	2.33
1997	1,460.8	159.0	50.1	490.0	324.9	349.5	93.2	1,304.4	550.7	2.65	2.37
1998	1,532.4	160.6	59.1	507.6	348.6	364.7	99.0	1,373.9	585.4	2.62	2.35
1999	1,600.9	156.9	57.1	523.8	369.7	390.5	106.6	1,444.7	615.6	2.60	2.35
2000	1,661.1	155.2	54.3	531.9	390.4	411.1	119.3	1,505.9	638.0	2.60	2.36
2001	1,619.4	155.3	65.1	505.7	376.8	400.5	119.1	1,464.4	644.2	2.51	2.27
2002	1,632.1	152.2	61.0	500.5	376.7	424.2	118.0	1,480.0	644.8	2.53	2.30
2003	1,649.5	152.4	68.2	492.0	376.3	441.5	119.6	1,497.2	676.3	2.44	2.21
2004	1,715.8	160.3	69.6	498.0	396.8	465.2	126.0	1,555.6	696.6	2.46	2.23
2005	1,765.8	160.4	73.4	519.0	415.0	469.8	128.3	1,605.4	718.7	2.46	2.23
2006	1,825.2	156.7	90.3	536.0	428.3	480.6	132.9	1,668.6	744.4	2.45	2.24
2007	1,852.9	155.9	90.3	551.4	432.8	484.8	137.2	1,697.3	766.1	2.42	2.22
2008: I	1,849.8	154.1	88.5	558.0	434.0	476.5	137.4	1,696.1	760.7	2.43	2.23
II	1,846.2	155.0	87.2	552.9	440.5	471.8	137.2	1,691.6	764.3	2.42	2.21
III	1,836.7	156.3	86.6	544.5	442.5	467.8	137.4	1,680.5	753.1	2.44	2.23
IV	1,816.6	156.9	81.8	537.3	441.7	458.3	138.8	1,659.7	730.4	2.49	2.27
2009: I	1,776.3	156.9	81.7	528.1	425.0	444.8	137.6	1,619.1	719.0	2.47	2.25
II	1,730.5	156.7	81.2	517.6	407.1	429.9	135.9	1,573.4	716.0	2.42	2.20
III	1,685.8	155.5	79.5	507.1	389.3	417.6	134.8	1,529.9	718.9	2.35	2.13
IV	1,671.7	155.4	74.8	505.9	387.0	412.5	134.0	1,515.9	717.7	2.33	2.11
2010: I	1,681.7	156.5	72.3	509.0	390.5	417.0	134.2	1,524.8	719.6	2.34	2.12
II	1,697.8	156.7	72.5	510.2	397.2	425.1	134.1	1,540.8	726.1	2.34	2.12
III	1,720.9	155.3	71.0	516.2	409.8	432.2	134.4	1,565.5	730.1	2.36	2.14
IV	1,730.5	154.0	70.6	526.1	413.9	428.8	134.7	1,576.6	742.9	2.33	2.12
2011: I	1,742.8	152.1	70.3	534.5	419.5	428.6	135.7	1,591.6	744.1	2.34	2.14
II	1,752.6	149.9	70.9	540.5	429.2	423.5	136.0	1,604.3	747.8	2.34	2.15
III	1,752.1	148.4	70.7	543.3	430.9	420.3	135.9	1,605.7	755.4	2.32	2.13
IV *p*	1,766.1	147.2	72.9	551.9	437.1	417.9	136.6	1,621.6	760.3	2.32	2.13

[1] Inventories at end of quarter. Quarter-to-quarter changes calculated from this table are at quarterly rates, whereas the change in private inventories component of gross domestic product (GDP) is stated at annual rates.

[2] Inventories of construction, mining, and utilities establishments are included in other industries through 1995.

[3] Quarterly totals at monthly rates. Final sales of domestic business equals final sales of domestic product less gross output of general government, gross value added of nonprofit institutions, compensation paid to domestic workers, and imputed rental of owner-occupied nonfarm housing. Includes a small amount of final sales by farm and by government enterprises.

Note: The industry classification of inventories is on an establishment basis. Estimates through 1995 are based on the Standard Industrial Classification (SIC). Beginning with 1996, estimates are based on the North American Industry Classification System (NAICS).
See *Survey of Current Business*, Tables 5.7.6A and 5.7.6B, for detailed information on calculation of the chained (2005) dollar inventory series.

Source: Department of Commerce (Bureau of Economic Analysis).

[Billions of dollars; quarterly data at seasonally adjusted annual rates]

Year or quarter	Current receipts from rest of the world					Current payments to rest of the world									Balance on current account, NIPA [2]
	Total	Exports of goods and services			Income receipts	Total	Imports of goods and services			Income payments	Current taxes and transfer payments to rest of the world (net)				
		Total	Goods [1]	Services [1]			Total	Goods [1]	Services [1]		Total	From persons (net)	From government (net)	From business (net)	
1963	37.6	31.1	23.3	7.7	6.5	32.7	26.1	17.7	8.4	2.1	4.5	0.7	3.7	0.1	4.9
1964	42.3	35.0	26.7	8.3	7.2	34.8	28.1	19.4	8.7	2.3	4.4	.7	3.5	.2	7.5
1965	45.0	37.1	27.8	9.4	7.9	38.9	31.5	22.2	9.3	2.6	4.7	.8	3.8	.2	6.2
1966	49.0	40.9	30.7	10.2	8.1	45.2	37.1	26.3	10.7	3.0	5.1	.8	4.1	.2	3.8
1967	52.1	43.5	32.2	11.3	8.7	48.7	39.9	27.8	12.2	3.3	5.5	1.0	4.2	.2	3.5
1968	58.0	47.9	35.3	12.6	10.1	56.5	46.6	33.9	12.6	4.0	5.9	1.0	4.6	.3	1.5
1969	63.7	51.9	38.3	13.7	11.8	62.1	50.5	36.8	13.7	5.7	5.9	1.1	4.5	.3	1.6
1970	72.5	59.7	44.5	15.2	12.8	68.8	55.8	40.9	14.9	6.4	6.6	1.3	4.9	.4	3.7
1971	77.0	63.0	45.6	17.4	14.0	76.7	62.3	46.6	15.8	6.4	7.9	1.4	6.1	.4	.3
1972	87.1	70.8	51.8	19.0	16.3	91.2	74.2	56.9	17.3	7.7	9.2	1.4	7.4	.5	−4.0
1973	118.8	95.3	73.9	21.3	23.5	109.9	91.2	71.8	19.3	10.9	7.9	1.6	5.6	.7	8.9
1974	156.5	126.7	101.0	25.7	29.8	150.5	127.5	104.5	22.9	14.3	8.7	1.4	6.4	1.0	6.0
1975	166.7	138.7	109.6	29.1	28.0	146.9	122.7	99.0	23.7	15.0	9.1	1.3	7.1	.7	19.8
1976	181.9	149.5	117.8	31.7	32.4	174.8	151.1	124.6	26.5	15.5	8.1	1.4	5.7	1.1	7.1
1977	196.6	159.4	123.7	35.7	37.2	207.5	182.4	152.6	29.8	16.9	8.1	1.4	5.3	1.4	−10.9
1978	233.1	186.9	145.4	41.5	46.3	245.8	212.3	177.4	34.8	24.7	8.8	1.6	5.9	1.4	−12.6
1979	298.5	230.1	184.0	46.1	68.3	299.6	252.7	212.8	39.9	36.4	10.6	1.7	6.8	2.0	−1.2
1980	359.9	280.8	225.8	55.0	79.1	351.4	293.8	248.6	45.3	44.9	12.6	2.0	8.3	2.4	8.5
1981	397.3	305.2	239.1	66.1	92.0	393.9	317.8	267.8	49.9	59.1	17.0	5.6	8.3	3.2	3.4
1982	384.2	283.2	215.0	68.2	101.0	387.5	303.2	250.5	52.6	64.5	19.8	6.7	9.7	3.4	−3.3
1983	378.9	277.0	207.3	69.7	101.9	413.9	328.6	272.7	56.0	64.8	20.5	7.0	10.1	3.4	−35.1
1984	424.2	302.4	225.6	76.7	121.9	514.3	405.1	336.3	68.8	85.6	23.6	7.9	12.2	3.5	−90.1
1985	414.5	302.0	222.2	79.8	112.4	528.8	417.2	343.3	73.9	85.9	25.7	8.3	14.4	2.9	−114.3
1986	431.3	320.3	226.0	94.3	111.0	574.0	452.9	370.0	82.9	93.4	27.8	9.1	15.4	3.2	−142.7
1987	486.6	363.8	257.5	106.2	122.8	640.7	508.7	414.8	93.9	105.2	26.8	10.0	13.4	3.4	−154.1
1988	595.5	443.9	325.8	118.1	151.6	711.2	554.0	452.1	101.9	128.3	29.0	10.8	13.7	4.5	−115.7
1989	680.3	503.1	369.4	133.8	177.2	772.7	591.0	484.8	106.2	151.2	30.4	11.6	14.2	4.6	−92.4
1990	740.6	552.1	396.6	155.5	188.5	815.6	629.7	508.1	121.7	154.1	31.7	12.2	14.7	4.8	−74.9
1991	764.7	596.6	423.6	173.0	168.1	756.9	623.5	500.7	122.8	138.2	−4.9	14.1	−24.0	5.0	7.9
1992	786.8	635.0	448.0	187.0	151.8	832.4	667.8	544.9	122.9	122.7	41.9	14.5	22.0	5.4	−45.6
1993	810.8	655.6	459.9	195.7	155.2	889.4	720.0	592.8	127.2	124.0	45.4	17.1	22.9	5.4	−78.6
1994	904.8	720.7	510.1	210.6	184.1	1,019.5	813.4	676.8	136.6	160.0	46.1	18.9	21.1	6.0	−114.7
1995	1,041.1	811.9	583.3	228.6	229.3	1,146.2	902.6	757.4	145.1	199.6	44.1	20.3	15.6	8.2	−105.1
1996	1,113.5	867.7	618.3	249.3	245.8	1,227.6	964.0	807.4	156.5	214.2	49.5	22.6	20.0	6.9	−114.1
1997	1,233.9	954.4	687.7	266.7	279.5	1,363.3	1,055.8	885.7	170.1	256.1	51.4	25.7	16.7	9.1	−129.3
1998	1,240.1	953.9	680.9	273.0	286.2	1,444.6	1,115.7	930.8	184.9	268.9	60.0	29.7	17.4	13.0	−204.5
1999	1,308.8	989.3	697.2	292.1	319.5	1,600.7	1,251.4	1,047.7	203.7	291.7	57.6	32.2	18.0	7.4	−291.9
2000	1,473.7	1,093.2	784.3	308.9	380.5	1,884.1	1,475.3	1,246.5	228.8	342.8	66.1	34.6	20.0	11.4	−410.4
2001	1,350.8	1,027.7	731.2	296.5	323.0	1,742.4	1,398.7	1,171.7	227.0	271.1	72.6	38.1	16.2	18.3	−391.6
2002	1,316.5	1,003.0	700.3	302.7	313.5	1,768.1	1,430.2	1,193.9	236.3	264.4	73.5	40.6	21.6	11.3	−451.6
2003	1,394.4	1,041.0	726.8	314.2	353.3	1,910.5	1,545.1	1,289.3	255.9	284.6	80.7	41.2	25.8	13.7	−516.1
2004	1,628.8	1,180.2	817.0	363.2	448.6	2,253.4	1,798.9	1,501.7	297.3	357.4	97.1	43.6	27.2	26.3	−624.6
2005	1,878.1	1,305.1	906.1	399.0	573.0	2,618.6	2,027.8	1,708.0	319.8	475.9	115.0	48.4	35.3	31.3	−740.5
2006	2,192.1	1,471.0	1,024.4	446.6	721.1	2,990.5	2,240.3	1,884.9	355.4	648.6	101.5	51.6	28.8	21.1	−798.4
2007	2,532.7	1,661.7	1,162.0	499.7	871.0	3,248.7	2,374.8	2,000.7	374.0	747.7	126.2	59.3	36.1	30.8	−716.0
2008	2,702.9	1,846.8	1,297.5	549.3	856.1	3,381.9	2,556.5	2,146.3	410.1	686.9	138.4	66.2	37.1	35.2	−679.0
2009	2,222.8	1,583.0	1,064.7	518.4	639.8	2,600.3	1,974.6	1,587.3	387.3	487.5	138.2	67.4	49.8	21.0	−377.4
2010	2,542.7	1,839.8	1,277.8	562.0	702.9	3,021.8	2,356.7	1,947.3	409.4	513.5	151.6	72.9	55.7	23.1	−479.2
2011 ᵖ	....	2,087.6	1,474.4	613.2	....	....	2,665.8	2,239.5	426.2	....	149.3	73.8	54.0	21.6	....
2008: I	2,724.9	1,819.3	1,279.1	540.2	905.6	3,434.2	2,561.6	2,162.3	399.4	726.9	145.6	64.8	42.8	38.0	−709.3
II	2,822.1	1,922.8	1,363.7	559.1	899.3	3,528.8	2,668.9	2,261.9	407.0	718.0	141.9	67.7	39.1	35.0	−706.6
III	2,809.1	1,933.8	1,374.5	559.3	875.3	3,505.0	2,690.6	2,270.0	420.7	676.3	138.0	69.8	35.6	32.6	−695.9
IV	2,455.3	1,711.1	1,172.6	538.6	744.2	3,059.5	2,304.8	1,891.3	413.5	626.4	128.2	62.4	30.8	35.1	−604.1
2009: I	2,146.7	1,522.2	1,013.5	508.7	624.6	2,529.1	1,905.7	1,521.7	384.0	491.9	131.5	66.2	39.4	26.0	−382.4
II	2,142.0	1,520.8	1,011.3	509.5	621.2	2,479.6	1,859.1	1,478.2	380.8	480.8	139.7	66.0	53.5	20.2	−337.7
III	2,227.2	1,590.3	1,074.8	515.5	636.9	2,617.7	1,997.0	1,608.4	388.6	473.2	147.6	67.8	61.6	18.2	−390.6
IV	2,375.5	1,699.0	1,159.1	539.9	676.5	2,774.6	2,136.5	1,740.7	395.8	504.2	133.9	69.6	44.5	19.8	−399.1
2010: I	2,423.5	1,749.5	1,208.7	540.8	674.0	2,905.4	2,245.3	1,844.0	401.3	504.6	155.5	71.9	60.0	23.6	−481.9
II	2,512.9	1,813.8	1,259.7	554.2	699.0	2,995.0	2,345.0	1,939.7	405.3	502.8	147.2	72.9	51.1	23.2	−482.2
III	2,569.5	1,860.6	1,288.9	571.6	708.9	3,057.4	2,400.9	1,982.7	418.2	501.6	155.0	74.3	56.0	24.7	−487.9
IV	2,664.7	1,935.3	1,353.8	581.5	729.4	3,129.4	2,435.5	2,022.8	412.7	545.0	148.9	72.5	55.7	20.8	−464.7
2011: I	2,776.2	2,024.1	1,431.0	593.2	752.1	3,269.7	2,595.4	2,176.2	419.3	525.0	149.3	73.5	54.5	21.4	−493.5
II	2,888.5	2,085.3	1,473.5	611.7	803.2	3,381.5	2,682.4	2,257.3	425.1	542.0	157.1	73.5	62.0	21.5	−493.0
III	2,911.5	2,119.2	1,496.6	622.6	792.2	3,353.7	2,681.6	2,251.9	429.7	524.9	147.2	73.8	51.3	22.1	−442.2
IV ᵖ	....	2,121.6	1,496.4	625.1	....	....	2,703.6	2,272.7	431.0	....	143.7	74.2	48.0	21.4	....

[1] Certain goods, primarily military equipment purchased and sold by the Federal Government, are included in services. Beginning with 1986, repairs and alterations of equipment were reclassified from goods to services.

[2] National income and product accounts (NIPA).

Source: Department of Commerce (Bureau of Economic Analysis).

[Billions of chained (2005) dollars; quarterly data at seasonally adjusted annual rates]

Year or quarter	Exports of goods and services					Imports of goods and services				
	Total	Goods [1]			Services [1]	Total	Goods [1]			Services [1]
		Total	Durable goods	Non-durable goods			Total	Durable goods	Non-durable goods	
1995	845.1	574.8	363.0	216.2	272.6	943.9	765.5	422.3	360.0	180.9
1996	915.3	625.5	404.8	223.4	291.7	1,026.0	837.2	467.5	384.1	190.3
1997	1,024.3	715.4	478.0	237.9	308.9	1,164.1	957.9	544.6	424.1	206.9
1998	1,047.7	731.4	493.4	237.6	316.4	1,300.2	1,071.4	616.4	462.9	229.4
1999	1,093.4	759.2	517.0	240.8	334.6	1,449.9	1,205.0	706.2	500.2	244.9
2000	1,187.4	843.4	583.7	256.5	343.5	1,638.7	1,366.7	813.7	549.2	271.7
2001	1,120.8	791.2	535.1	255.2	329.3	1,592.6	1,323.1	763.4	564.2	269.6
2002	1,098.3	762.7	504.8	259.1	335.6	1,646.8	1,372.2	795.4	580.2	274.5
2003	1,116.0	776.4	513.7	263.8	339.6	1,719.7	1,439.9	829.7	615.2	279.8
2004	1,222.5	842.6	570.7	272.2	380.0	1,910.4	1,599.3	944.6	655.8	311.0
2005	1,305.1	906.1	624.9	281.2	399.0	2,027.8	1,708.0	1,025.4	682.6	319.8
2006	1,422.1	991.5	692.0	299.6	430.6	2,151.5	1,809.1	1,115.6	694.5	342.4
2007	1,554.4	1,088.1	756.1	331.9	466.3	2,203.2	1,856.1	1,141.2	715.7	347.1
2008	1,649.3	1,157.0	795.8	359.8	492.3	2,144.0	1,784.8	1,099.3	686.6	359.8
2009	1,494.0	1,018.6	660.2	351.2	474.9	1,852.8	1,506.0	870.6	626.2	347.2
2010	1,663.2	1,164.9	771.6	387.2	498.8	2,085.0	1,729.3	1,065.7	661.9	357.4
2011 *p*	1,776.3	1,252.7	847.8	402.4	524.2	2,188.7	1,829.6	1,164.8	670.7	361.2
2008: I	1,643.9	1,154.3	794.8	358.3	489.6	2,194.1	1,836.4	1,145.7	695.2	357.8
II	1,693.9	1,193.0	825.1	367.5	500.9	2,180.1	1,825.9	1,142.9	688.9	354.0
III	1,678.7	1,185.9	821.8	364.0	492.9	2,143.3	1,783.1	1,107.4	679.0	361.1
IV	1,580.6	1,094.8	741.5	349.5	485.8	2,058.6	1,694.0	1,001.2	683.4	366.1
2009: I	1,451.1	983.4	644.0	333.4	467.0	1,855.3	1,508.8	848.8	648.8	347.0
II	1,449.4	976.1	625.3	343.3	472.3	1,781.2	1,436.1	812.8	612.8	344.8
III	1,497.3	1,024.4	661.6	355.3	472.5	1,849.7	1,501.6	873.4	619.1	348.4
IV	1,578.3	1,090.5	710.0	372.9	487.9	1,925.2	1,577.4	947.5	624.3	348.8
2010: I	1,606.2	1,122.1	730.5	383.9	484.6	1,983.0	1,631.5	986.7	639.9	352.8
II	1,645.0	1,153.8	767.9	380.3	491.8	2,082.4	1,728.5	1,060.2	665.7	355.6
III	1,684.8	1,178.8	786.3	387.1	506.5	2,143.5	1,779.8	1,099.4	679.0	365.5
IV	1,716.8	1,204.9	801.8	397.3	512.4	2,131.0	1,777.4	1,116.6	662.8	355.6
2011: I	1,749.6	1,235.6	826.3	404.2	514.6	2,173.9	1,818.4	1,155.4	668.1	357.5
II	1,765.0	1,243.2	843.5	397.8	522.4	2,181.4	1,825.4	1,151.3	676.8	357.9
III	1,785.2	1,258.3	861.8	396.8	527.5	2,187.9	1,827.9	1,169.0	666.4	362.2
IV *p*	1,805.6	1,273.8	859.6	411.0	532.5	2,211.5	1,846.5	1,183.7	671.3	367.1

[1] Certain goods, primarily military equipment purchased and sold by the Federal Government, are included in services. Beginning with 1986, repairs and alterations of equipment were reclassified from goods to services.

Note: See Table B–2 for data for total exports of goods and services and total imports of goods and services for 1963–94.

Source: Department of Commerce (Bureau of Economic Analysis).

TABLE B–26. Relation of gross domestic product, gross national product, net national product, and national income, 1963–2011

[Billions of dollars; quarterly data at seasonally adjusted annual rates]

Year or quarter	Gross domestic product	Plus: Income receipts from rest of the world	Less: Income payments to rest of the world	Equals: Gross national product	Less: Consumption of fixed capital			Equals: Net national product	Less: Statistical discrepancy	Equals: National income
					Total	Private	Government			
1963	617.8	6.5	2.1	622.2	63.3	45.9	17.5	558.9	−0.8	559.7
1964	663.6	7.2	2.3	668.6	66.4	48.3	18.1	602.2	.8	601.4
1965	719.1	7.9	2.6	724.4	70.7	51.9	18.9	653.7	1.5	652.2
1966	787.7	8.1	3.0	792.8	76.5	56.5	20.0	716.3	6.2	710.1
1967	832.4	8.7	3.3	837.8	82.9	61.6	21.4	754.9	4.5	750.4
1968	909.8	10.1	4.0	915.9	90.4	67.4	23.0	825.5	4.3	821.2
1969	984.4	11.8	5.7	990.5	99.2	74.5	24.7	891.4	2.9	888.5
1970	1,038.3	12.8	6.4	1,044.7	108.3	81.7	26.6	936.4	6.9	929.5
1971	1,126.8	14.0	6.4	1,134.4	117.8	89.5	28.2	1,016.6	11.0	1,005.6
1972	1,237.9	16.3	7.7	1,246.4	127.2	97.7	29.4	1,119.3	8.9	1,110.3
1973	1,382.3	23.5	10.9	1,394.9	140.8	109.5	31.3	1,254.1	8.0	1,246.1
1974	1,499.5	29.8	14.3	1,515.0	163.7	127.8	35.9	1,351.3	9.8	1,341.5
1975	1,637.7	28.0	15.0	1,650.7	190.4	150.4	39.9	1,460.3	16.3	1,444.0
1976	1,824.6	32.4	15.5	1,841.4	208.2	165.5	42.6	1,633.3	23.5	1,609.8
1977	2,030.1	37.2	16.9	2,050.4	231.8	186.1	45.6	1,818.6	21.2	1,797.4
1978	2,293.8	46.3	24.7	2,315.3	261.4	212.0	49.5	2,053.9	26.1	2,027.9
1979	2,562.2	68.3	36.4	2,594.2	298.9	244.5	54.4	2,295.3	47.0	2,248.3
1980	2,788.1	79.1	44.9	2,822.3	344.1	282.3	61.8	2,478.2	45.3	2,433.0
1981	3,126.8	92.0	59.1	3,159.8	393.3	323.2	70.1	2,766.4	36.6	2,729.8
1982	3,253.2	101.0	64.5	3,289.7	433.5	356.4	77.1	2,856.2	4.8	2,851.4
1983	3,534.6	101.9	64.8	3,571.7	451.1	369.5	81.6	3,120.6	49.7	3,070.9
1984	3,930.9	121.9	85.6	3,967.2	474.3	387.5	86.9	3,492.8	31.5	3,461.3
1985	4,217.5	112.4	85.9	4,244.0	505.4	412.8	92.7	3,738.6	42.3	3,696.3
1986	4,460.1	111.0	93.4	4,477.7	538.5	439.1	99.4	3,939.2	67.7	3,871.5
1987	4,736.4	122.8	105.2	4,754.0	571.1	464.5	106.6	4,182.9	32.9	4,150.0
1988	5,100.4	151.6	128.3	5,123.8	611.0	497.1	113.9	4,512.8	−9.5	4,522.3
1989	5,482.1	177.2	151.2	5,508.1	651.5	529.6	121.8	4,856.6	56.1	4,800.5
1990	5,800.5	188.5	154.1	5,835.0	691.2	560.4	130.8	5,143.7	84.2	5,059.5
1991	5,992.1	168.1	138.2	6,022.0	724.4	585.4	138.9	5,297.6	79.7	5,217.9
1992	6,342.3	151.8	122.7	6,371.4	744.4	599.9	144.5	5,627.1	110.0	5,517.1
1993	6,667.4	155.2	124.0	6,698.5	778.0	626.4	151.6	5,920.5	135.8	5,784.7
1994	7,085.2	184.1	160.0	7,109.2	819.2	661.0	158.2	6,290.1	108.8	6,181.3
1995	7,414.7	229.3	199.6	7,444.3	869.5	704.6	164.8	6,574.9	52.5	6,522.3
1996	7,838.5	245.8	214.2	7,870.1	912.5	743.4	169.2	6,957.6	25.9	6,931.7
1997	8,332.4	279.5	256.1	8,355.8	963.8	789.7	174.1	7,392.0	−14.0	7,406.0
1998	8,793.5	286.2	268.9	8,810.8	1,020.5	841.6	179.0	7,790.3	−85.3	7,875.6
1999	9,353.5	319.5	291.7	9,381.3	1,094.4	907.2	187.2	8,286.9	−71.1	8,358.0
2000	9,951.5	380.5	342.8	9,989.2	1,184.3	986.8	197.5	8,804.9	−134.0	8,938.9
2001	10,286.2	323.0	271.1	10,338.1	1,256.2	1,051.6	204.6	9,081.9	−103.4	9,185.2
2002	10,642.3	313.5	264.4	10,691.4	1,305.0	1,094.0	210.9	9,386.4	−22.1	9,408.5
2003	11,142.2	353.3	284.6	11,210.9	1,354.1	1,135.9	218.1	9,856.9	16.7	9,840.2
2004	11,853.3	448.6	357.4	11,944.5	1,432.8	1,200.9	231.9	10,511.7	−22.3	10,534.0
2005	12,623.0	573.0	475.9	12,720.1	1,541.4	1,290.8	250.6	11,178.7	−95.1	11,273.8
2006	13,377.2	721.1	648.6	13,449.6	1,660.7	1,391.4	269.3	11,789.0	−242.3	12,031.2
2007	14,028.7	871.0	747.7	14,151.9	1,767.5	1,476.2	291.3	12,384.4	−12.0	12,396.4
2008	14,291.5	856.1	686.9	14,460.7	1,854.1	1,542.9	311.2	12,606.6	−2.4	12,609.1
2009	13,939.0	639.8	487.5	14,091.2	1,866.2	1,542.4	323.7	12,225.0	77.4	12,147.6
2010	14,526.5	702.9	513.5	14,715.9	1,874.9	1,540.9	334.0	12,841.0	.8	12,840.1
2011 ᵖ	15,087.7	....	....	....	1,950.0	1,597.8	352.2	....	....	....
2008: I	14,273.9	905.6	726.9	14,452.5	1,817.4	1,515.0	302.4	12,635.1	−58.8	12,693.9
II	14,415.5	899.3	718.0	14,596.8	1,842.7	1,534.6	308.1	12,754.0	29.1	12,724.9
III	14,395.1	875.3	676.3	14,594.0	1,869.6	1,555.5	314.1	12,724.4	−8.6	12,733.1
IV	14,081.7	744.2	626.4	14,199.5	1,886.5	1,566.5	320.0	12,313.0	28.5	12,284.4
2009: I	13,893.7	624.6	491.9	14,026.4	1,885.2	1,562.6	322.6	12,141.2	42.1	12,099.2
II	13,854.1	621.2	480.8	13,994.4	1,868.4	1,545.2	323.2	12,126.1	90.3	12,035.7
III	13,920.5	636.9	473.2	14,084.2	1,854.1	1,530.5	323.6	12,230.1	104.1	12,126.1
IV	14,087.4	676.5	504.2	14,259.8	1,857.1	1,531.4	325.6	12,402.7	73.2	12,329.5
2010: I	14,277.9	674.0	504.6	14,447.4	1,858.6	1,529.6	329.0	12,588.8	−7.2	12,595.9
II	14,467.8	699.0	502.8	14,664.0	1,866.9	1,534.4	332.5	12,797.2	−6.6	12,803.7
III	14,605.5	708.9	501.6	14,812.8	1,878.2	1,542.6	335.5	12,934.7	−7.4	12,942.1
IV	14,755.0	729.4	545.0	14,939.4	1,896.1	1,557.0	339.1	13,043.3	24.5	13,018.8
2011: I	14,867.8	752.1	525.0	15,094.9	1,914.3	1,570.5	343.8	13,180.6	−52.0	13,232.6
II	15,012.8	803.2	542.0	15,274.0	1,939.9	1,590.5	349.4	13,334.1	−10.0	13,344.1
III	15,176.1	792.2	524.9	15,443.4	1,962.8	1,607.6	355.2	13,480.5	49.6	13,430.9
IV ᵖ	15,294.3	....	....	....	1,983.0	1,622.5	360.4	....	....	....

Source: Department of Commerce (Bureau of Economic Analysis).

[Billions of dollars; quarterly data at seasonally adjusted annual rates]

Year or quarter	National income	Less: Corporate profits with inventory valuation and capital consumption adjustments	Less: Taxes on production and imports less subsidies	Less: Contributions for government social insurance, domestic	Less: Net interest and miscellaneous payments on assets	Less: Business current transfer payments (net)	Less: Current surplus of government enterprises	Less: Wage accruals less disbursements	Plus: Personal income receipts on assets	Plus: Personal current transfer receipts	Equals: Personal income
1963	559.7	68.3	51.2	21.7	15.2	2.7	1.4	0.0	47.9	32.2	479.5
1964	601.4	75.5	54.5	22.4	17.4	3.1	1.3	.0	53.8	33.5	514.3
1965	652.2	86.5	57.7	23.4	19.6	3.6	1.3	.0	59.4	36.2	555.5
1966	710.1	92.5	59.3	31.3	22.4	3.5	1.0	.0	64.1	39.6	603.8
1967	750.4	90.2	64.1	34.9	25.5	3.8	.9	.0	69.0	48.0	648.1
1968	821.2	97.3	72.2	38.7	27.1	4.3	1.2	.0	75.2	56.1	711.7
1969	888.5	94.5	79.3	44.1	32.7	4.9	1.0	.0	84.1	62.3	778.3
1970	929.5	82.5	86.6	46.4	39.1	4.5	.0	.0	93.5	74.7	838.6
1971	1,005.6	96.1	95.8	51.2	43.9	4.3	−.2	.6	101.0	88.1	903.1
1972	1,110.3	111.4	101.3	59.2	47.9	4.9	.5	.0	109.6	97.9	992.6
1973	1,246.1	124.5	112.0	75.5	55.2	6.0	−.4	−.1	124.7	112.6	1,110.5
1974	1,341.5	115.1	121.6	85.2	70.8	7.1	−.9	−.5	146.4	133.3	1,222.7
1975	1,444.0	133.3	130.8	89.3	81.6	9.4	−3.2	.1	162.2	170.0	1,334.9
1976	1,609.8	161.6	141.3	101.3	85.5	9.5	−1.8	.1	178.4	184.0	1,474.7
1977	1,797.4	191.8	152.6	113.1	101.1	8.5	−2.7	.1	205.3	194.2	1,632.5
1978	2,027.9	218.4	162.0	131.3	115.0	10.8	−2.2	.3	234.8	209.6	1,836.7
1979	2,248.3	225.4	171.6	152.7	138.9	13.3	−2.9	−.2	274.7	235.3	2,059.5
1980	2,433.0	201.4	190.5	166.2	181.8	14.7	−5.1	.0	338.7	279.5	2,301.5
1981	2,729.8	223.3	224.2	195.7	232.3	17.9	−5.6	.1	421.9	318.4	2,582.3
1982	2,851.4	205.7	225.9	208.9	271.1	20.6	−4.5	.0	488.4	354.8	2,766.8
1983	3,070.9	259.8	242.0	226.0	285.3	22.6	−3.2	−.4	529.6	383.7	2,952.2
1984	3,461.3	318.6	268.7	257.5	327.1	30.3	−1.9	.2	607.9	400.1	3,268.9
1985	3,696.3	332.5	286.8	281.4	341.5	35.2	.6	−.2	653.2	424.9	3,496.7
1986	3,871.5	314.1	298.5	303.4	367.1	36.9	.9	.0	694.5	451.0	3,696.0
1987	4,150.0	367.8	317.3	323.1	366.7	34.1	.2	.0	715.8	467.6	3,924.4
1988	4,522.3	426.6	345.0	361.5	385.3	33.6	2.6	.0	767.0	496.5	4,231.2
1989	4,800.5	425.6	371.4	385.2	434.1	39.2	4.9	.0	874.8	542.6	4,557.5
1990	5,059.5	434.4	398.0	410.1	444.2	40.1	1.6	.1	920.8	594.9	4,846.7
1991	5,217.9	457.3	429.6	430.2	418.2	39.9	5.7	−.1	928.6	665.9	5,031.5
1992	5,517.1	496.2	453.3	455.0	387.7	40.7	8.2	−15.8	909.7	745.8	5,347.3
1993	5,784.7	543.7	466.4	477.4	364.6	40.5	8.7	6.4	900.5	790.8	5,568.1
1994	6,181.3	628.2	512.7	508.2	362.2	41.9	9.6	17.6	947.7	826.4	5,874.8
1995	6,522.3	716.2	523.1	532.8	358.3	45.8	13.1	16.4	1,005.4	878.9	6,200.9
1996	6,931.7	801.5	545.5	555.1	371.1	53.8	14.4	3.6	1,080.7	924.1	6,591.6
1997	7,406.0	884.8	577.8	587.2	407.6	51.3	14.1	−2.9	1,165.5	949.2	7,000.7
1998	7,875.6	812.4	603.1	624.7	479.3	65.2	13.3	−.7	1,269.2	977.9	7,525.4
1999	8,358.0	856.3	628.4	661.3	481.4	69.0	14.1	5.2	1,246.8	1,021.6	7,910.8
2000	8,938.9	819.2	662.7	705.8	539.3	87.0	9.1	.0	1,360.7	1,083.0	8,559.4
2001	9,185.2	784.2	669.0	733.2	544.4	101.3	4.0	.0	1,346.0	1,188.1	8,883.3
2002	9,408.5	872.2	721.4	751.5	506.4	82.4	6.3	.0	1,309.6	1,282.1	9,060.1
2003	9,840.2	977.8	757.7	778.9	504.1	76.1	7.0	15.0	1,312.9	1,341.7	9,378.1
2004	10,534.0	1,246.9	817.0	827.3	461.6	81.7	1.2	−15.0	1,408.5	1,415.5	9,937.2
2005	11,273.8	1,456.1	869.3	872.7	543.0	95.9	−3.5	5.0	1,542.0	1,508.6	10,485.9
2006	12,031.2	1,608.3	935.5	921.8	652.2	83.0	−4.2	1.3	1,829.7	1,605.0	11,268.1
2007	12,396.4	1,510.6	972.6	959.5	731.6	103.3	−11.8	−6.3	2,057.0	1,718.5	11,912.3
2008	12,609.1	1,248.4	985.7	987.3	870.1	123.0	−16.0	−5.0	2,165.4	1,879.2	12,460.2
2009	12,147.6	1,362.0	958.2	964.1	656.7	132.0	−14.9	5.0	1,707.7	2,138.1	11,930.2
2010	12,840.1	1,800.1	996.7	986.8	564.3	136.7	−15.7	.0	1,721.2	2,281.2	12,373.5
2011 [p]	....	....	1,035.2	920.1	535.8	134.4	−14.6	.0	1,790.7	2,336.0	12,961.0
2008: I	12,693.9	1,360.0	983.2	989.8	843.7	120.8	−15.2	.0	2,205.0	1,798.9	12,415.6
II	12,724.9	1,333.7	995.4	986.6	875.1	117.3	−15.9	.0	2,203.1	1,936.1	12,571.7
III	12,733.1	1,328.6	994.2	988.7	878.0	116.1	−16.1	.0	2,197.5	1,872.2	12,513.3
IV	12,284.4	971.2	970.1	984.2	883.7	137.8	−16.8	−20.0	2,056.0	1,909.7	12,340.0
2009: I	12,099.2	1,175.2	951.7	966.0	782.9	137.0	−16.8	20.0	1,851.5	2,029.8	11,964.4
II	12,035.7	1,262.3	955.0	966.9	656.4	141.5	−15.3	.0	1,707.5	2,167.7	11,944.1
III	12,126.1	1,438.8	952.0	962.1	596.6	122.2	−14.0	.0	1,635.7	2,170.1	11,874.1
IV	12,329.5	1,571.6	974.2	961.5	591.0	127.5	−13.6	.0	1,636.0	2,184.9	11,938.2
2010: I	12,595.9	1,724.2	984.5	976.0	589.1	134.6	−14.7	.0	1,693.3	2,242.1	12,137.7
II	12,803.7	1,785.8	993.8	985.7	569.2	135.7	−15.5	.0	1,724.5	2,252.1	12,325.6
III	12,942.1	1,833.1	1,002.0	991.5	550.1	140.9	−16.0	.0	1,723.4	2,289.4	12,453.2
IV	13,018.8	1,857.4	1,006.4	994.1	548.7	135.7	−16.5	.0	1,743.5	2,341.2	12,577.6
2011: I	13,232.6	1,876.4	1,027.3	911.5	556.6	134.7	−15.6	.0	1,777.2	2,328.1	12,846.9
II	13,344.1	1,937.6	1,038.5	917.4	525.6	133.9	−14.6	.0	1,802.3	2,347.3	12,955.3
III	13,430.9	1,970.1	1,035.8	921.2	535.7	133.7	−14.5	.0	1,794.2	2,336.6	12,979.6
IV [p]	....	....	1,039.0	930.2	525.1	135.4	−13.9	.0	1,789.1	2,331.9	13,062.2

Source: Department of Commerce (Bureau of Economic Analysis).

TABLE B–28. National income by type of income, 1963–2011

[Billions of dollars; quarterly data at seasonally adjusted annual rates]

Year or quarter	National income	Compensation of employees							Proprietors' income with inventory valuation and capital consumption adjustments			Rental income of persons with capital consumption adjustment
		Total	Wage and salary accruals			Supplements to wages and salaries			Total	Farm	Non-farm	
			Total	Government	Other	Total	Employer contributions for employee pension and insurance funds	Employer contributions for government social insurance				
1963	559.7	345.2	314.9	60.0	254.8	30.4	18.0	12.4	56.5	11.0	45.5	19.3
1964	601.4	370.7	337.8	64.9	272.9	32.9	20.3	12.6	59.4	9.8	49.6	19.4
1965	652.2	399.5	363.8	69.9	293.8	35.7	22.7	13.1	63.9	12.0	51.9	19.9
1966	710.1	442.7	400.3	78.4	321.9	42.3	25.5	16.8	68.2	13.0	55.2	20.5
1967	750.4	475.1	429.0	86.5	342.5	46.1	28.1	18.0	69.8	11.6	58.2	20.9
1968	821.2	524.3	472.0	96.7	375.3	52.3	32.4	20.0	74.2	11.7	62.5	20.6
1969	888.5	577.6	518.3	105.6	412.7	59.3	36.5	22.8	77.5	12.8	64.7	20.9
1970	929.5	617.2	551.6	117.2	434.3	65.7	41.8	23.8	78.5	12.9	65.6	21.1
1971	1,005.6	658.9	584.5	126.8	457.8	74.4	47.9	26.4	84.7	13.4	71.3	22.2
1972	1,110.3	725.1	638.8	137.9	500.9	86.4	55.2	31.2	96.0	17.0	79.0	23.1
1973	1,246.1	811.2	708.8	148.8	560.0	102.5	62.7	39.8	113.6	29.1	84.6	23.9
1974	1,341.5	890.2	772.3	160.5	611.8	118.0	73.3	44.7	113.5	23.5	90.0	24.0
1975	1,444.0	949.1	814.8	176.2	638.6	134.3	87.6	46.7	119.6	22.0	97.6	23.4
1976	1,609.8	1,059.3	899.7	188.9	710.8	159.6	105.2	54.4	132.2	17.2	115.0	22.1
1977	1,797.4	1,180.5	994.2	202.6	791.6	186.4	125.3	61.1	146.0	16.0	130.1	19.6
1978	2,027.9	1,335.5	1,120.6	220.0	900.6	214.9	143.4	71.5	167.5	19.9	147.6	20.9
1979	2,248.3	1,498.3	1,253.3	237.1	1,016.2	245.0	162.4	82.6	181.1	22.2	159.0	22.6
1980	2,433.0	1,647.6	1,373.4	261.5	1,112.0	274.2	185.2	88.9	173.5	11.7	161.8	28.5
1981	2,729.8	1,819.7	1,511.4	285.8	1,225.5	308.3	204.7	103.6	181.6	19.0	162.6	36.5
1982	2,851.4	1,919.6	1,587.5	307.5	1,280.0	332.1	222.4	109.8	174.8	13.3	161.5	38.1
1983	3,070.9	2,035.5	1,677.5	324.8	1,352.7	358.0	238.1	119.9	190.7	6.2	184.5	38.2
1984	3,461.3	2,245.4	1,844.9	348.1	1,496.8	400.5	261.5	139.0	233.1	20.9	212.1	40.0
1985	3,696.3	2,411.7	1,982.6	373.9	1,608.7	429.2	281.5	147.7	246.1	21.0	225.1	41.9
1986	3,871.5	2,557.7	2,102.3	397.2	1,705.1	455.3	297.5	157.9	262.6	22.8	239.7	33.8
1987	4,150.0	2,735.6	2,256.3	423.1	1,833.1	479.4	313.1	166.3	294.2	28.9	265.3	34.2
1988	4,522.3	2,954.2	2,439.8	452.0	1,987.7	514.4	329.7	184.6	334.8	26.8	308.0	40.2
1989	4,800.5	3,131.3	2,583.1	481.1	2,101.9	548.3	354.6	193.7	351.6	33.0	318.6	42.4
1990	5,059.5	3,326.3	2,741.2	519.0	2,222.2	585.1	378.6	206.5	365.1	32.2	333.0	49.8
1991	5,217.9	3,438.3	2,814.5	548.8	2,265.7	623.9	408.7	215.1	367.3	27.5	339.8	61.6
1992	5,517.1	3,631.4	2,957.8	572.0	2,385.8	673.6	445.2	228.4	414.9	35.8	379.1	84.6
1993	5,784.7	3,797.1	3,083.0	589.0	2,494.0	714.1	474.4	239.7	449.6	32.0	417.6	114.1
1994	6,181.3	3,998.5	3,248.5	609.5	2,639.0	750.1	495.9	254.1	485.1	35.6	449.5	142.9
1995	6,522.3	4,195.2	3,434.4	629.0	2,805.4	760.8	496.7	264.1	516.0	23.4	492.6	154.6
1996	6,931.7	4,391.4	3,620.0	648.1	2,971.9	771.4	496.6	274.8	583.7	38.4	545.2	170.4
1997	7,406.0	4,665.6	3,873.6	671.8	3,201.8	792.0	502.4	289.6	628.2	32.6	595.6	176.5
1998	7,875.6	5,023.2	4,180.9	701.2	3,479.7	842.3	535.1	307.2	687.5	28.9	658.7	191.5
1999	8,358.0	5,353.9	4,465.2	733.7	3,731.5	888.8	565.4	323.3	746.8	28.5	718.3	208.2
2000	8,938.9	5,788.8	4,827.7	779.7	4,048.0	961.2	615.9	345.2	817.5	29.6	787.8	215.3
2001	9,185.2	5,979.3	4,952.2	821.9	4,130.3	1,027.1	669.1	358.0	870.7	30.5	840.2	232.4
2002	9,408.5	6,110.8	4,997.3	873.1	4,124.2	1,113.5	747.4	366.1	890.3	18.5	871.8	218.7
2003	9,840.2	6,382.6	5,154.6	913.3	4,241.3	1,228.0	845.6	382.4	930.6	36.5	894.1	204.2
2004	10,534.0	6,693.4	5,410.7	952.8	4,457.9	1,282.7	874.6	408.1	1,033.8	49.7	984.1	198.4
2005	11,273.8	7,065.0	5,706.0	991.5	4,714.5	1,359.1	931.6	427.5	1,069.8	43.9	1,025.9	178.2
2006	12,031.2	7,477.0	6,070.1	1,035.2	5,035.0	1,406.9	960.1	446.7	1,133.0	29.3	1,103.6	146.5
2007	12,396.4	7,855.9	6,415.5	1,089.0	5,326.4	1,440.4	980.5	459.9	1,090.4	37.8	1,052.6	143.7
2008	12,609.1	8,068.3	6,545.9	1,144.1	5,401.8	1,522.5	1,052.4	470.1	1,097.9	51.8	1,046.1	231.6
2009	12,147.6	7,806.4	6,275.3	1,175.3	5,100.0	1,531.1	1,073.1	458.0	941.2	39.2	902.0	305.9
2010	12,840.1	7,971.4	6,408.2	1,190.8	5,217.4	1,563.1	1,089.9	473.2	1,036.4	52.2	984.2	350.2
2011 p	....	8,242.4	6,636.3	1,190.3	5,446.0	1,606.1	1,111.0	495.1	1,107.8	64.9	1,042.9	404.2
2008: I	12,693.9	8,099.0	6,600.5	1,127.6	5,472.9	1,498.5	1,026.7	471.8	1,113.7	60.5	1,053.1	188.9
II	12,724.9	8,073.4	6,554.9	1,137.9	5,417.1	1,518.5	1,048.8	469.7	1,127.2	55.3	1,071.9	218.5
III	12,733.1	8,084.7	6,550.6	1,151.0	5,399.6	1,534.1	1,063.5	470.6	1,104.0	46.6	1,057.4	243.5
IV	12,284.4	8,016.1	6,477.4	1,160.0	5,317.4	1,538.7	1,070.5	468.3	1,046.7	44.6	1,002.1	275.6
2009: I	12,099.2	7,830.1	6,300.5	1,168.9	5,131.5	1,529.6	1,071.0	458.6	960.2	37.1	923.1	278.8
II	12,035.7	7,809.2	6,278.2	1,175.9	5,102.2	1,531.1	1,071.7	459.4	926.9	38.7	888.2	299.7
III	12,126.1	7,781.9	6,251.3	1,177.1	5,074.2	1,530.6	1,073.5	457.1	929.3	39.5	889.9	319.3
IV	12,329.5	7,804.4	6,271.4	1,179.2	5,092.2	1,533.0	1,076.2	456.8	948.5	41.4	907.0	325.9
2010: I	12,595.9	7,852.5	6,301.6	1,188.6	5,113.0	1,550.9	1,083.4	467.5	981.7	44.6	937.1	344.1
II	12,803.7	7,960.0	6,399.8	1,196.3	5,203.5	1,560.2	1,087.6	472.6	1,025.6	45.8	979.7	349.1
III	12,942.1	8,022.2	6,454.5	1,189.9	5,264.7	1,567.7	1,092.0	475.7	1,057.0	58.3	998.7	352.8
IV	13,018.8	8,050.8	6,477.0	1,188.6	5,288.4	1,573.7	1,096.8	476.9	1,081.5	60.1	1,021.4	354.8
2011: I	13,232.6	8,172.5	6,578.2	1,191.1	5,387.1	1,594.4	1,103.0	491.4	1,095.6	66.1	1,029.5	385.0
II	13,344.1	8,219.7	6,617.1	1,191.9	5,425.2	1,602.7	1,108.7	494.0	1,106.5	67.3	1,039.2	396.9
III	13,430.9	8,250.0	6,641.9	1,189.3	5,452.6	1,608.1	1,112.6	495.5	1,113.7	67.5	1,046.2	406.3
IV p	....	8,327.4	6,708.0	1,188.9	5,519.1	1,619.4	1,119.7	499.7	1,115.5	58.7	1,056.8	428.6

See next page for continuation of table.

[Billions of dollars; quarterly data at seasonally adjusted annual rates]

Year or quarter	Corporate profits with inventory valuation and capital consumption adjustments								Capital consumption adjustment	Net interest and miscellaneous payments	Taxes on production and imports	Less: Subsidies	Business current transfer payments (net)	Current surplus of government enterprises
	Total	Profits with inventory valuation adjustment and without capital consumption adjustment						Inventory valuation adjustment						
		Total	Profits											
			Profits before tax	Taxes on corporate income	Profits after tax									
					Total	Net dividends	Undistributed profits							
1963	68.3	62.1	62.1	26.4	35.7	16.2	19.5	0.1	6.2	15.2	53.4	2.2	2.7	1.4
1964	75.5	68.6	69.1	28.2	40.9	18.2	22.7	−.5	6.9	17.4	57.3	2.7	3.1	1.3
1965	86.5	78.9	80.2	31.1	49.1	20.2	28.9	−1.2	7.6	19.6	60.7	3.0	3.6	1.3
1966	92.5	84.6	86.7	33.9	52.8	20.7	32.1	−2.1	8.0	22.4	63.2	3.9	3.5	1.0
1967	90.2	82.0	83.5	32.9	50.6	21.5	29.1	−1.6	8.2	25.5	67.9	3.8	3.8	.9
1968	97.3	88.8	92.4	39.6	52.8	23.5	29.3	−3.7	8.5	27.1	76.4	4.2	4.3	1.2
1969	94.5	85.5	91.4	40.0	51.4	24.2	27.2	−5.9	9.0	32.7	83.9	4.5	4.9	1.0
1970	82.5	74.4	81.0	34.8	46.2	24.3	21.9	−6.6	8.1	39.1	91.4	4.8	4.5	.0
1971	96.1	88.3	92.9	38.2	54.7	25.0	29.7	−4.6	7.8	43.9	100.5	4.7	4.3	−.2
1972	111.4	101.6	108.2	42.3	65.9	26.8	39.0	−6.6	9.8	47.9	107.9	6.6	4.9	.5
1973	124.5	115.4	135.0	50.0	85.0	29.9	55.1	−19.6	9.1	55.2	117.2	5.2	6.0	−.4
1974	115.1	109.6	147.8	52.8	95.0	33.2	61.8	−38.2	5.6	70.8	124.9	3.3	7.1	−.9
1975	133.3	135.0	145.5	51.6	93.9	33.0	60.9	−10.5	−1.7	81.6	135.3	4.5	9.4	−3.2
1976	161.6	165.6	179.7	65.3	114.5	39.0	75.4	−14.1	−4.0	85.5	146.4	5.1	9.5	−1.8
1977	191.8	194.8	210.5	74.4	136.1	44.8	91.3	−15.7	−3.0	101.1	159.7	7.1	8.5	−2.7
1978	218.4	222.4	246.1	84.9	161.3	50.8	110.5	−23.7	−4.0	115.0	170.9	8.9	10.8	−2.2
1979	225.4	232.0	272.1	90.0	182.1	57.5	124.6	−40.1	−6.6	138.9	180.1	8.5	13.3	−2.9
1980	201.4	211.4	253.5	87.2	166.4	64.1	102.3	−42.1	−10.0	181.8	200.3	9.8	14.7	−5.1
1981	223.3	219.1	243.7	84.3	159.4	73.8	85.6	−24.6	4.2	232.3	235.6	11.5	17.9	−5.6
1982	205.7	191.1	198.6	66.5	132.1	77.7	54.4	−7.5	14.6	271.1	240.9	15.0	20.6	−4.5
1983	259.8	226.6	234.0	80.6	153.4	83.5	69.9	−7.4	33.3	285.3	263.3	21.3	22.6	−3.2
1984	318.6	264.6	268.6	97.5	171.1	90.8	80.3	−4.0	54.0	327.1	289.8	21.1	30.3	−1.9
1985	332.5	257.5	257.5	99.4	158.1	97.6	60.5	.0	75.1	341.5	308.1	21.4	35.2	.6
1986	314.1	253.0	246.0	109.7	136.3	106.2	30.1	7.1	61.1	367.1	323.4	24.9	36.9	.9
1987	367.8	306.9	323.1	130.4	192.7	112.3	80.3	−16.2	61.0	366.7	347.5	30.3	34.1	.2
1988	426.6	367.7	389.9	141.6	248.3	129.9	118.4	−22.2	58.9	385.3	374.5	29.5	33.6	2.6
1989	425.6	374.1	390.5	146.1	244.4	158.0	86.4	−16.3	51.5	434.1	398.9	27.4	39.2	4.9
1990	434.4	398.8	411.7	145.4	266.3	169.1	97.2	−12.9	35.7	444.2	425.0	27.0	40.1	1.6
1991	457.3	430.3	425.4	138.6	286.8	180.7	106.1	4.9	27.0	418.2	457.1	27.5	39.9	5.7
1992	496.2	471.6	474.4	148.7	325.7	188.0	137.7	−2.8	24.6	387.7	483.4	30.1	40.7	8.2
1993	543.7	515.0	519.0	171.0	348.0	202.9	145.1	−4.0	28.7	364.6	503.1	36.7	40.5	8.7
1994	628.2	586.6	599.0	193.1	405.9	235.7	170.2	−12.4	41.6	362.2	545.2	32.5	41.9	9.6
1995	716.2	666.0	684.3	217.8	466.5	254.4	212.1	−18.3	50.2	358.3	557.9	34.8	45.8	13.1
1996	801.5	743.8	740.7	231.5	509.3	297.7	211.5	3.1	57.7	371.1	580.8	35.2	53.8	14.4
1997	884.8	815.9	801.8	245.4	556.3	331.2	225.1	14.1	69.0	407.6	611.6	33.8	51.3	14.1
1998	812.4	738.6	722.9	248.4	474.5	351.5	123.1	15.7	73.8	479.3	639.5	36.4	65.2	13.3
1999	856.3	776.6	780.5	258.8	521.7	337.4	184.3	−4.0	79.7	481.4	673.6	45.2	69.0	14.1
2000	819.2	755.7	772.5	265.1	507.4	377.9	129.5	−16.8	63.6	539.3	708.6	45.8	87.0	9.1
2001	784.2	720.8	712.7	203.3	509.4	370.9	138.5	8.0	63.4	544.4	727.7	58.7	101.3	4.0
2002	872.2	762.8	765.3	192.3	573.0	399.3	173.8	−2.6	109.4	506.4	762.8	41.4	82.4	6.3
2003	977.8	892.2	903.5	243.8	659.7	424.9	234.8	−11.3	85.6	504.1	806.8	49.1	76.1	7.0
2004	1,246.9	1,195.1	1,229.4	306.1	923.3	550.3	373.0	−34.3	51.8	461.6	863.4	46.4	81.7	1.2
2005	1,456.1	1,609.5	1,640.2	412.4	1,227.8	557.3	670.5	−30.7	−153.4	543.0	930.2	60.9	95.9	−3.5
2006	1,608.3	1,784.7	1,822.7	473.3	1,349.5	704.8	644.7	−38.0	−176.4	652.2	986.8	51.4	83.0	−4.2
2007	1,510.6	1,691.1	1,738.4	445.5	1,292.9	794.5	498.4	−47.2	−180.5	731.6	1,027.2	54.6	103.3	−11.8
2008	1,248.4	1,315.5	1,359.9	309.0	1,050.9	786.9	264.0	−44.5	−67.1	870.1	1,038.6	52.9	123.0	−16.0
2009	1,362.0	1,456.3	1,455.7	272.4	1,183.3	620.0	563.3	.6	−94.3	656.7	1,017.9	59.7	132.0	−14.9
2010	1,800.1	1,780.4	1,819.5	411.1	1,408.4	737.3	671.1	−39.1	19.7	564.3	1,054.0	57.3	136.7	−15.7
2011 *p*	....	....	....	....	....	814.6	....	....	106.6	535.8	1,098.3	63.1	134.4	−14.6
2008: I	1,360.0	1,412.3	1,543.5	355.2	1,188.3	835.9	352.4	−131.3	−52.3	843.7	1,035.0	51.9	120.8	−15.2
II	1,333.7	1,397.0	1,552.4	344.1	1,208.3	803.4	404.9	−155.4	−63.2	875.1	1,047.3	51.9	117.3	−15.9
III	1,328.6	1,403.1	1,475.8	312.5	1,163.3	780.5	382.8	−72.7	−74.5	878.0	1,046.7	52.5	116.1	−16.1
IV	971.2	1,049.6	868.0	224.3	643.7	727.6	−84.0	181.6	−78.4	883.7	1,025.5	55.4	137.8	−16.8
2009: I	1,175.2	1,285.7	1,209.3	208.8	1,000.4	671.9	328.5	76.5	−110.5	782.9	1,008.0	56.4	137.0	−16.8
II	1,262.3	1,359.7	1,343.8	244.8	1,099.0	600.9	498.1	15.9	−97.4	654.4	1,011.8	56.8	141.5	−15.3
III	1,438.8	1,525.0	1,545.7	301.6	1,244.2	584.1	660.0	−20.7	−86.2	596.6	1,020.4	68.4	122.2	−14.0
IV	1,571.6	1,654.6	1,723.9	334.4	1,389.5	623.0	766.5	−69.3	−83.0	591.0	1,031.3	57.1	127.5	−13.6
2010: I	1,724.2	1,797.0	1,825.3	409.7	1,415.6	684.8	730.8	−28.4	−72.7	589.1	1,040.9	56.4	134.6	−14.7
II	1,785.8	1,859.9	1,865.5	399.6	1,465.9	729.3	736.6	−5.6	−74.1	569.2	1,050.6	56.8	135.7	−15.5
III	1,833.1	1,812.6	1,844.5	430.3	1,414.2	760.5	653.7	−32.0	20.5	550.1	1,059.0	57.0	140.9	−16.0
IV	1,857.4	1,652.2	1,742.5	404.7	1,337.8	774.8	563.0	−90.3	205.2	548.7	1,065.5	59.1	135.7	−16.5
2011: I	1,876.4	1,761.1	1,877.1	422.3	1,454.8	793.8	660.9	−116.0	115.4	556.6	1,087.4	60.0	134.7	−15.6
II	1,937.6	1,830.2	1,890.6	420.5	1,470.1	807.4	662.7	−60.4	107.3	525.6	1,101.1	62.7	133.9	−14.6
III	1,970.1	1,867.4	1,912.9	411.4	1,501.5	821.4	680.1	−45.5	102.7	535.7	1,100.0	64.2	133.7	−14.5
IV *p*	....	....	....	....	....	835.6	....	....	100.8	525.1	1,104.6	65.6	135.4	−13.9

Source: Department of Commerce (Bureau of Economic Analysis).

[Billions of dollars; quarterly data at seasonally adjusted annual rates]

Year or quarter	Personal income	Compensation of employees, received							Proprietors' income with inventory valuation and capital consumption adjustments			Rental income of persons with capital consumption adjustment
		Total	Wage and salary disbursements			Supplements to wages and salaries			Total	Farm	Non-farm	
			Total	Private industries	Government	Total	Employer contributions for employee pension and insurance funds	Employer contributions for government social insurance				
1963	479.5	345.2	314.9	254.8	60.0	30.4	18.0	12.4	56.5	11.0	45.5	19.3
1964	514.3	370.7	337.8	272.9	64.9	32.9	20.3	12.6	59.4	9.8	49.6	19.4
1965	555.5	399.5	363.8	293.8	69.9	35.7	22.7	13.1	63.9	12.0	51.9	19.9
1966	603.8	442.7	400.3	321.9	78.4	42.3	25.5	16.8	68.2	13.0	55.2	20.5
1967	648.1	475.1	429.0	342.5	86.5	46.1	28.1	18.0	69.8	11.6	58.2	20.9
1968	711.7	524.3	472.0	375.3	96.7	52.3	32.4	20.0	74.2	11.7	62.5	20.6
1969	778.3	577.6	518.3	412.7	105.6	59.3	36.5	22.8	77.5	12.8	64.7	20.9
1970	838.6	617.2	551.6	434.3	117.2	65.7	41.8	23.8	78.5	12.9	65.6	21.1
1971	903.1	658.3	584.0	457.4	126.6	74.4	47.9	26.4	84.7	13.4	71.3	22.2
1972	992.6	725.1	638.8	501.2	137.6	86.4	55.2	31.2	96.0	17.0	79.0	23.1
1973	1,110.5	811.3	708.8	560.0	148.8	102.5	62.7	39.8	113.6	29.1	84.6	23.9
1974	1,222.7	890.7	772.8	611.8	161.0	118.0	73.3	44.7	113.5	23.5	90.0	24.0
1975	1,334.9	949.0	814.7	638.6	176.1	134.3	87.6	46.7	119.6	22.0	97.6	23.4
1976	1,474.7	1,059.2	899.6	710.8	188.8	159.6	105.2	54.4	132.2	17.2	115.0	22.1
1977	1,632.5	1,180.4	994.1	791.6	202.5	186.4	125.3	61.1	146.0	16.0	130.1	19.6
1978	1,836.7	1,335.2	1,120.3	900.6	219.7	214.9	143.4	71.5	167.5	19.9	147.6	20.9
1979	2,059.5	1,498.5	1,253.5	1,016.2	237.3	245.0	162.4	82.6	181.1	22.2	159.0	22.6
1980	2,301.5	1,647.6	1,373.5	1,112.0	261.5	274.2	185.2	88.9	173.5	11.7	161.8	28.5
1981	2,582.3	1,819.6	1,511.3	1,225.5	285.8	308.3	204.7	103.6	181.6	19.0	162.6	36.5
1982	2,766.8	1,919.6	1,587.5	1,280.0	307.5	332.1	222.4	109.8	174.8	13.3	161.5	38.1
1983	2,952.2	2,036.0	1,678.0	1,352.7	325.2	358.0	238.1	119.9	190.7	6.2	184.5	38.2
1984	3,268.9	2,245.2	1,844.7	1,496.8	347.9	400.5	261.5	139.0	233.1	20.9	212.1	40.0
1985	3,496.7	2,412.0	1,982.8	1,608.7	374.1	429.2	281.5	147.7	246.1	21.0	225.1	41.9
1986	3,696.0	2,557.7	2,102.3	1,705.1	397.2	455.3	297.5	157.9	262.6	22.8	239.7	33.8
1987	3,924.4	2,735.6	2,256.3	1,833.1	423.1	479.4	313.1	166.3	294.2	28.9	265.3	34.2
1988	4,231.2	2,954.2	2,439.8	1,987.7	452.0	514.4	329.7	184.6	334.8	26.8	308.0	40.2
1989	4,557.5	3,131.3	2,583.1	2,101.9	481.1	548.3	354.6	193.7	351.6	33.0	318.6	42.4
1990	4,846.7	3,326.2	2,741.1	2,222.2	519.0	585.1	378.6	206.5	365.1	32.2	333.0	49.8
1991	5,031.5	3,438.4	2,814.5	2,265.7	548.8	623.9	408.7	215.1	367.3	27.5	339.8	61.6
1992	5,347.3	3,647.2	2,973.5	2,401.5	572.0	673.6	445.2	228.4	414.9	35.8	379.1	84.6
1993	5,568.1	3,790.6	3,076.6	2,487.6	589.0	714.1	474.4	239.7	449.6	32.0	417.6	114.1
1994	5,874.8	3,980.9	3,230.8	2,621.3	609.5	750.1	495.9	254.1	485.1	35.6	449.5	142.9
1995	6,200.9	4,178.8	3,418.0	2,789.0	629.0	760.8	496.7	264.1	516.0	23.4	492.6	154.6
1996	6,591.6	4,387.7	3,616.3	2,968.3	648.1	771.4	496.6	274.8	583.7	38.4	545.2	170.4
1997	7,000.7	4,668.6	3,876.6	3,204.8	671.8	792.0	502.4	289.6	628.2	32.6	595.6	176.5
1998	7,525.4	5,023.9	4,181.6	3,480.4	701.2	842.3	535.1	307.2	687.5	28.9	658.7	191.5
1999	7,910.8	5,348.8	4,460.0	3,726.3	733.7	888.8	565.4	323.3	746.8	28.5	718.3	208.2
2000	8,559.4	5,788.8	4,827.7	4,048.0	779.7	961.2	615.9	345.2	817.5	29.6	787.8	215.3
2001	8,883.3	5,979.3	4,952.2	4,130.3	821.9	1,027.1	669.1	358.0	870.7	30.5	840.2	232.4
2002	9,060.1	6,110.8	4,997.3	4,124.2	873.1	1,113.5	747.4	366.1	890.3	18.5	871.8	218.7
2003	9,378.1	6,367.6	5,139.6	4,226.3	913.3	1,228.0	845.6	382.4	930.6	36.5	894.1	204.2
2004	9,937.2	6,708.4	5,425.7	4,472.9	952.8	1,282.7	874.6	408.1	1,033.8	49.7	984.1	198.4
2005	10,485.9	7,060.0	5,701.0	4,709.5	991.5	1,359.1	931.6	427.5	1,069.8	43.9	1,025.9	178.2
2006	11,268.1	7,475.7	6,068.9	5,033.7	1,035.2	1,406.9	960.1	446.7	1,133.0	29.3	1,103.6	146.5
2007	11,912.3	7,862.2	6,421.7	5,332.7	1,089.0	1,440.4	980.5	459.9	1,090.4	37.8	1,052.6	143.7
2008	12,460.2	8,073.3	6,550.9	5,406.8	1,144.1	1,522.5	1,052.4	470.1	1,097.9	51.8	1,046.1	231.6
2009	11,930.2	7,801.4	6,270.3	5,095.0	1,175.3	1,531.1	1,073.1	458.0	941.2	39.2	902.0	305.9
2010	12,373.5	7,971.4	6,408.2	5,217.4	1,190.8	1,563.1	1,089.9	473.2	1,036.4	52.2	984.2	350.2
2011 p	12,961.0	8,242.4	6,636.3	5,446.0	1,190.3	1,606.1	1,111.0	495.1	1,107.8	64.9	1,042.9	404.2
2008: I	12,415.6	8,099.0	6,600.5	5,472.9	1,127.6	1,498.5	1,026.7	471.8	1,113.7	60.5	1,053.1	188.9
II	12,571.7	8,073.4	6,554.9	5,417.1	1,137.9	1,518.5	1,048.8	469.7	1,127.2	55.3	1,071.9	218.5
III	12,513.3	8,084.7	6,550.6	5,399.6	1,151.0	1,534.1	1,063.5	470.6	1,104.0	46.6	1,057.4	243.5
IV	12,340.0	8,036.1	6,497.4	5,337.4	1,160.0	1,538.7	1,070.5	468.3	1,046.7	44.6	1,002.1	275.6
2009: I	11,964.4	7,810.1	6,280.5	5,111.5	1,168.9	1,529.6	1,071.0	458.6	960.2	37.1	923.1	278.8
II	11,944.1	7,809.2	6,278.2	5,102.2	1,175.9	1,531.1	1,071.7	459.4	926.9	38.7	888.2	299.7
III	11,874.1	7,781.9	6,251.3	5,074.2	1,177.1	1,530.6	1,073.5	457.1	929.3	39.5	889.9	319.3
IV	11,938.2	7,804.4	6,271.4	5,092.2	1,179.2	1,533.0	1,076.2	456.8	948.5	41.4	907.0	325.9
2010: I	12,137.7	7,852.5	6,301.6	5,113.0	1,188.6	1,550.9	1,083.4	467.5	981.7	44.6	937.1	344.1
II	12,325.6	7,960.0	6,399.8	5,203.5	1,196.3	1,560.2	1,087.6	472.6	1,025.6	45.8	979.7	349.1
III	12,453.2	8,022.2	6,454.5	5,264.7	1,189.9	1,567.7	1,092.0	475.7	1,057.0	58.3	998.7	352.8
IV	12,577.6	8,050.8	6,477.0	5,288.4	1,188.6	1,573.7	1,096.8	476.9	1,081.5	60.1	1,021.4	354.8
2011: I	12,846.9	8,172.5	6,578.2	5,387.1	1,191.1	1,594.4	1,103.0	491.4	1,095.6	66.1	1,029.5	385.0
II	12,955.3	8,219.7	6,617.1	5,425.2	1,191.9	1,602.7	1,108.7	494.0	1,106.5	67.3	1,039.2	396.9
III	12,979.6	8,250.0	6,641.9	5,452.6	1,189.3	1,608.1	1,112.6	495.5	1,113.7	67.5	1,046.2	406.3
IV p	13,062.2	8,327.4	6,708.0	5,519.1	1,188.9	1,619.4	1,119.7	499.7	1,115.5	58.7	1,056.8	428.6

See next page for continuation of table.

[Billions of dollars; quarterly data at seasonally adjusted annual rates]

| Year or quarter | Personal income receipts on assets | | | Personal current transfer receipts | | | | | | | Other current transfer receipts, from business (net) | Less: Contributions for government social insurance, domestic |
| | Total | Personal interest income | Personal dividend income | Total | Government social benefits to persons | | | | | | | |
					Total [1]	Social security [2]	Medi-care [3]	Medicaid	Un-employ-ment insurance	Other		
1963	47.9	31.7	16.2	32.2	30.3	15.2	....	....	3.1	7.3	1.9	21.7
1964	53.8	35.6	18.2	33.5	31.3	16.0	....	....	2.8	7.9	2.2	22.4
1965	59.4	39.2	20.2	36.2	33.9	18.1	....	....	2.4	8.6	2.3	23.4
1966	64.1	43.4	20.7	39.6	37.5	19.8	1.0	1.9	1.9	8.1	2.1	31.3
1967	69.0	47.5	21.5	48.0	45.8	21.1	4.7	2.7	2.2	9.4	2.3	34.9
1968	75.2	51.6	23.5	56.1	53.3	24.6	5.9	4.0	2.2	10.8	2.8	38.7
1969	84.1	59.9	24.2	62.3	59.0	26.4	6.7	4.6	2.3	12.4	3.3	44.1
1970	93.5	69.2	24.3	74.7	71.7	31.4	7.3	5.5	4.2	16.0	2.9	46.4
1971	101.0	75.9	25.0	88.1	85.4	36.6	8.0	6.7	6.2	19.4	2.7	51.2
1972	109.6	82.8	26.8	97.9	94.8	40.9	8.8	8.2	6.0	21.4	3.1	59.2
1973	124.7	94.8	29.9	112.6	108.6	50.7	10.2	9.6	4.6	23.3	3.9	75.5
1974	146.4	113.2	33.2	133.3	128.6	57.6	12.7	11.2	7.0	28.4	4.7	85.2
1975	162.2	129.3	32.9	170.0	163.1	65.9	15.6	13.9	18.1	35.7	6.8	89.3
1976	178.4	139.5	39.0	184.0	177.3	74.5	18.8	15.5	16.4	38.4	6.7	101.3
1977	205.3	160.6	44.7	194.2	189.1	83.2	22.1	16.7	13.1	40.6	5.1	113.1
1978	234.8	184.0	50.7	209.6	203.2	91.4	25.5	18.6	9.4	44.6	6.5	131.3
1979	274.7	217.3	57.4	235.3	227.1	102.6	29.9	21.1	9.7	49.7	8.2	152.7
1980	338.7	274.7	64.0	279.5	270.8	118.6	36.2	23.9	16.1	61.4	8.6	166.2
1981	421.9	348.3	73.6	318.4	307.2	138.6	43.5	27.7	15.9	65.6	11.2	195.7
1982	488.4	410.8	77.6	354.8	342.4	153.7	50.9	30.2	25.2	66.1	12.4	208.9
1983	529.6	446.3	83.3	383.7	369.9	164.4	57.8	33.9	26.4	71.0	13.8	226.0
1984	607.9	517.2	90.6	400.1	380.4	173.0	64.7	36.6	16.0	73.8	19.7	257.5
1985	653.2	555.8	97.4	424.9	402.6	183.3	69.7	39.7	15.9	77.6	22.3	281.4
1986	694.5	588.4	106.0	451.0	428.0	193.6	75.3	43.6	16.5	82.4	22.9	303.4
1987	715.8	603.6	112.2	467.6	447.4	201.0	81.6	47.8	14.6	85.9	20.2	323.1
1988	767.0	637.3	129.7	496.5	475.9	213.9	86.3	53.0	13.3	92.6	20.6	361.5
1989	874.8	717.0	157.8	542.6	519.4	227.4	98.2	60.8	14.4	101.4	23.2	385.2
1990	920.8	751.9	168.8	594.9	572.7	244.1	107.6	73.1	18.2	111.9	22.2	410.1
1991	928.6	748.2	180.3	665.9	648.2	264.2	117.5	96.9	26.8	124.7	17.6	430.2
1992	909.7	722.2	187.6	745.8	729.5	281.8	132.6	116.2	39.6	140.6	16.3	455.0
1993	900.5	698.1	202.3	790.8	776.7	297.9	146.8	130.1	34.8	147.7	14.1	477.4
1994	947.7	712.7	235.0	826.4	813.1	312.2	164.4	139.4	23.9	153.5	13.3	508.2
1995	1,005.4	751.9	253.4	878.9	860.2	327.7	181.2	149.6	21.7	159.5	18.7	532.8
1996	1,080.7	784.4	296.4	924.1	901.2	342.0	194.9	158.2	22.3	162.4	22.9	555.1
1997	1,165.5	835.8	329.7	949.2	929.8	356.6	206.9	163.1	20.1	160.7	19.4	587.2
1998	1,269.2	919.3	349.8	977.9	951.9	369.2	205.6	170.2	19.7	164.0	26.0	624.7
1999	1,246.8	910.9	335.9	1,021.6	987.6	379.9	208.7	184.6	20.5	169.8	34.0	661.3
2000	1,360.7	984.2	376.5	1,083.0	1,040.6	401.4	219.1	199.5	20.7	174.3	42.4	705.8
2001	1,346.0	976.5	369.5	1,188.1	1,141.3	425.1	242.6	227.3	31.9	187.9	46.8	733.2
2002	1,309.6	911.9	397.7	1,282.1	1,247.9	446.9	259.2	250.1	53.5	208.8	34.2	751.5
2003	1,312.9	889.8	423.1	1,341.7	1,316.0	463.5	276.9	264.6	53.2	226.1	25.7	778.9
2004	1,408.5	860.2	548.3	1,415.5	1,398.6	485.5	304.7	289.7	36.4	248.3	16.9	827.3
2005	1,542.0	987.0	555.0	1,508.6	1,482.7	512.7	331.9	304.4	31.8	265.6	25.8	872.7
2006	1,829.7	1,127.5	702.2	1,605.0	1,583.6	544.1	399.2	299.0	30.4	272.1	21.4	921.8
2007	2,057.0	1,265.1	791.9	1,718.5	1,687.9	575.6	427.6	324.1	32.7	286.2	30.5	959.5
2008	2,165.4	1,382.0	783.4	1,879.2	1,842.4	605.5	461.6	338.2	50.9	341.1	36.8	987.3
2009	1,707.7	1,108.9	598.8	2,138.1	2,099.9	664.5	493.8	374.1	130.6	385.4	38.2	964.1
2010	1,721.2	1,003.4	717.7	2,281.2	2,242.9	690.2	518.4	405.4	138.7	432.4	38.3	986.8
2011 *p*	1,790.7	997.8	792.9	2,336.0	2,296.5	713.5	554.3	423.5	107.2	434.7	39.5	920.1
2008: I	2,205.0	1,372.0	832.9	1,798.9	1,762.1	597.3	452.4	331.4	36.7	300.1	36.8	989.8
II	2,203.1	1,402.7	800.4	1,936.1	1,899.5	602.9	457.3	338.4	37.8	418.4	36.6	986.6
III	2,197.5	1,420.0	777.5	1,872.2	1,835.5	608.9	464.1	340.9	58.0	318.2	36.7	988.7
IV	2,056.0	1,333.3	722.8	1,909.7	1,872.7	613.1	472.8	342.2	71.2	327.6	37.1	984.2
2009: I	1,851.5	1,194.9	656.6	2,029.8	1,992.0	651.8	482.5	362.0	101.1	344.9	37.8	966.0
II	1,707.5	1,129.7	577.8	2,167.7	2,129.4	662.4	491.7	373.3	127.9	423.6	38.2	966.9
III	1,635.7	1,073.1	562.6	2,170.1	2,131.7	667.9	498.4	383.1	144.8	385.4	38.4	962.1
IV	1,636.0	1,038.0	598.0	2,184.9	2,146.6	675.7	502.7	378.0	148.7	387.7	38.3	961.5
2010: I	1,693.3	1,026.1	667.2	2,242.1	2,204.1	678.6	505.6	386.6	152.8	424.8	38.0	976.0
II	1,724.5	1,014.1	710.4	2,252.1	2,214.1	688.3	511.5	389.8	137.4	429.9	38.0	985.7
III	1,723.4	983.9	739.4	2,289.4	2,251.4	693.9	521.4	405.2	135.8	436.1	37.9	991.5
IV	1,743.5	989.6	753.9	2,341.2	2,301.9	699.9	535.3	439.8	128.7	438.7	39.3	994.1
2011: I	1,777.2	1,004.7	772.5	2,328.1	2,288.6	703.1	547.8	432.1	117.5	426.9	39.5	911.5
II	1,802.3	1,015.9	786.4	2,347.3	2,307.9	712.2	553.9	437.4	108.8	432.7	39.4	917.4
III	1,794.2	994.8	799.4	2,336.6	2,297.2	716.3	557.8	416.4	103.0	438.6	39.4	921.2
IV *p*	1,789.1	975.7	813.4	2,331.9	2,292.3	722.3	557.9	408.0	99.3	440.5	39.6	930.2

[1] Includes Veterans' benefits, not shown seperately.

[2] Includes old-age, survivors, and disability insurance benefits that are distributed from the federal old-age and survivors insurance trust fund and the disability insurance trust fund.

[3] Includes hospital and supplementary medical insurance benefits that are distributed from the federal hospital insurance trust fund and the supplementary medical insurance trust fund.

Source: Department of Commerce (Bureau of Economic Analysis).

[Billions of dollars, except as noted; quarterly data at seasonally adjusted annual rates]

Year or quarter	Personal income	Less: Personal current taxes	Equals: Disposable personal income	Less: Personal outlays				Equals: Personal saving	Percent of disposable personal income [2]		
				Total	Personal consumption expenditures	Personal interest payments [1]	Personal current transfer payments		Personal outlays		Personal saving
									Total	Personal consumption expenditures	
1963	479.5	54.6	425.0	391.8	382.7	7.9	1.2	33.1	92.2	90.0	7.8
1964	514.3	52.1	462.3	421.7	411.5	8.9	1.3	40.5	91.2	89.0	8.8
1965	555.5	57.7	497.8	455.1	443.8	9.9	1.4	42.7	91.4	89.2	8.6
1966	603.8	66.4	537.4	493.1	480.9	10.7	1.6	44.3	91.8	89.5	8.2
1967	648.1	73.0	575.1	520.9	507.8	11.1	2.0	54.2	90.6	88.3	9.4
1968	711.7	87.0	624.7	572.2	558.0	12.2	2.0	52.5	91.6	89.3	8.4
1969	778.3	104.5	673.8	621.4	605.1	14.0	2.2	52.5	92.2	89.8	7.8
1970	838.6	103.1	735.5	666.1	648.3	15.2	2.6	69.4	90.6	88.1	9.4
1971	903.1	101.7	801.4	721.0	701.6	16.6	2.8	80.4	90.0	87.5	10.0
1972	992.6	123.6	869.0	791.5	770.2	18.1	3.2	77.5	91.1	88.6	8.9
1973	1,110.5	132.4	978.1	875.2	852.0	19.8	3.4	102.9	89.5	87.1	10.5
1974	1,222.7	151.0	1,071.7	957.5	932.9	21.2	3.4	114.2	89.3	87.0	10.7
1975	1,334.9	147.6	1,187.3	1,061.3	1,033.8	23.7	3.8	125.9	89.4	87.1	10.6
1976	1,474.7	172.3	1,302.3	1,179.6	1,151.3	23.9	4.4	122.8	90.6	88.4	9.4
1977	1,632.5	197.5	1,435.0	1,309.7	1,277.8	27.0	4.8	125.3	91.3	89.0	8.7
1978	1,836.7	229.4	1,607.3	1,465.0	1,427.6	31.9	5.4	142.4	91.1	88.8	8.9
1979	2,059.5	268.7	1,790.9	1,633.4	1,591.2	36.2	6.0	157.5	91.2	88.8	8.8
1980	2,301.5	298.9	2,002.7	1,806.4	1,755.8	43.6	6.9	196.3	90.2	87.7	9.8
1981	2,582.3	345.2	2,237.1	2,000.4	1,939.5	49.3	11.5	236.7	89.4	86.7	10.6
1982	2,766.8	354.1	2,412.7	2,148.8	2,075.5	59.5	13.8	263.9	89.1	86.0	10.9
1983	2,952.2	352.3	2,599.8	2,372.9	2,288.6	69.2	15.1	226.9	91.3	88.0	8.7
1984	3,268.9	377.4	2,891.5	2,595.2	2,501.1	77.0	17.1	296.3	89.8	86.5	10.2
1985	3,496.7	417.3	3,079.3	2,825.7	2,717.6	89.4	18.8	253.6	91.8	88.3	8.2
1986	3,696.0	437.2	3,258.8	3,012.4	2,896.7	94.5	21.1	246.5	92.4	88.9	7.6
1987	3,924.4	489.1	3,435.3	3,211.9	3,097.0	91.7	23.2	223.4	93.5	90.2	6.5
1988	4,231.2	504.9	3,726.3	3,469.7	3,350.1	94.0	25.6	256.6	93.1	89.9	6.9
1989	4,557.5	566.1	3,991.4	3,726.4	3,594.5	103.9	28.0	265.0	93.4	90.1	6.6
1990	4,846.7	592.7	4,254.0	3,977.3	3,835.5	111.3	30.6	276.7	93.5	90.2	6.5
1991	5,031.5	586.6	4,444.9	4,131.7	3,980.1	115.0	36.7	313.2	93.0	89.5	7.0
1992	5,347.3	610.5	4,736.7	4,388.7	4,236.9	111.3	40.5	348.1	92.7	89.4	7.3
1993	5,568.1	646.5	4,921.6	4,636.2	4,483.6	107.0	45.6	285.4	94.2	91.1	5.8
1994	5,874.8	690.5	5,184.3	4,913.6	4,750.8	113.0	49.8	270.7	94.8	91.6	5.2
1995	6,200.9	743.9	5,457.0	5,170.8	4,987.3	130.6	52.9	286.3	94.8	91.4	5.2
1996	6,591.6	832.0	5,759.6	5,478.5	5,273.6	147.3	57.6	281.1	95.1	91.6	4.9
1997	7,000.7	926.2	6,074.6	5,794.2	5,570.6	159.7	63.9	280.4	95.4	91.7	4.6
1998	7,525.4	1,026.4	6,498.9	6,157.5	5,918.5	169.5	69.5	341.5	94.7	91.1	5.3
1999	7,910.8	1,107.5	6,803.3	6,595.5	6,342.8	176.5	76.2	207.8	96.9	93.2	3.1
2000	8,559.4	1,232.3	7,327.2	7,114.1	6,830.4	200.3	83.4	213.1	97.1	93.2	2.9
2001	8,883.3	1,234.8	7,648.5	7,443.5	7,148.8	203.7	91.0	204.9	97.3	93.5	2.7
2002	9,060.1	1,050.4	8,009.7	7,727.5	7,439.2	191.3	97.0	282.2	96.5	92.9	3.5
2003	9,378.1	1,000.3	8,377.8	8,088.1	7,804.1	182.7	101.3	289.6	96.5	93.2	3.5
2004	9,937.2	1,047.8	8,889.4	8,571.2	8,270.6	190.3	110.3	318.2	96.4	93.0	3.6
2005	10,485.9	1,208.6	9,277.3	9,134.1	8,803.5	210.8	119.8	143.2	98.5	94.9	1.5
2006	11,268.1	1,352.4	9,915.7	9,659.1	9,301.0	230.1	128.0	256.6	97.4	93.8	2.6
2007	11,912.3	1,488.7	10,423.6	10,174.9	9,772.3	260.9	141.7	248.7	97.6	93.8	2.4
2008	12,460.2	1,435.7	11,024.5	10,432.2	10,035.5	245.6	151.0	592.3	94.6	91.0	5.4
2009	11,930.2	1,141.4	10,788.8	10,236.3	9,866.1	213.7	156.5	552.6	94.9	91.4	5.1
2010	12,373.5	1,193.9	11,179.7	10,586.9	10,245.5	173.4	168.0	592.8	94.7	91.6	5.3
2011 _p_	12,961.0	1,404.8	11,556.2	11,050.9	10,722.6	157.0	171.3	505.3	95.6	92.8	4.4
2008: I	12,415.6	1,536.0	10,879.6	10,424.5	10,018.5	256.9	149.1	455.0	95.8	92.1	4.2
II	12,571.7	1,351.8	11,220.0	10,529.4	10,126.5	250.7	152.1	690.6	93.8	90.3	6.2
III	12,513.3	1,432.1	11,081.2	10,538.4	10,135.8	247.9	154.7	542.8	95.1	91.5	4.9
IV	12,340.0	1,422.8	10,917.3	10,236.3	9,861.3	226.9	148.1	680.9	93.8	90.3	6.2
2009: I	11,964.4	1,198.0	10,766.3	10,155.2	9,781.7	220.5	153.0	611.1	94.3	90.9	5.7
II	11,944.1	1,120.3	10,823.8	10,153.4	9,781.6	217.6	154.2	670.3	93.8	90.4	6.2
III	11,874.1	1,120.6	10,753.5	10,285.3	9,911.1	216.6	157.6	468.2	95.6	92.2	4.4
IV	11,938.2	1,126.4	10,811.7	10,351.2	9,990.0	200.1	161.1	460.5	95.7	92.4	4.3
2010: I	12,137.7	1,146.4	10,991.3	10,457.2	10,103.7	188.3	165.2	534.1	95.1	91.9	4.9
II	12,325.6	1,175.4	11,150.2	10,527.0	10,184.8	174.4	167.8	623.3	94.4	91.3	5.6
III	12,453.2	1,212.8	11,240.4	10,614.8	10,276.6	168.1	170.1	625.6	94.4	91.4	5.6
IV	12,577.6	1,240.9	11,336.7	10,748.6	10,417.1	162.7	168.9	588.1	94.8	91.9	5.2
2011: I	12,846.9	1,365.9	11,481.0	10,902.1	10,571.7	160.3	170.1	578.9	95.0	92.1	5.0
II	12,955.3	1,396.2	11,559.2	11,002.6	10,676.0	155.9	170.7	556.5	95.2	92.4	4.8
III	12,979.6	1,408.5	11,571.1	11,114.6	10,784.5	158.4	171.6	456.5	96.1	93.2	3.9
IV _p_	13,062.2	1,448.5	11,613.8	11,184.5	10,858.1	153.4	173.0	429.3	96.3	93.5	3.7

[1] Consists of nonmortgage interest paid by households.
[2] Percents based on data in millions of dollars.

Source: Department of Commerce (Bureau of Economic Analysis).

[Quarterly data at seasonally adjusted annual rates, except as noted]

| Year or quarter | Disposable personal income | | | | Personal consumption expenditures | | | | Gross domestic product per capita (dollars) | | Population (thousands) [1] |
| | Total (billions of dollars) | | Per capita (dollars) | | Total (billions of dollars) | | Per capita (dollars) | | | | |
	Current dollars	Chained (2005) dollars	Current dollars	Chained (2005) dollars	Current dollars	Chained (2005) dollars	Current dollars	Chained (2005) dollars	Current dollars	Chained (2005) dollars	
1963	425.0	2,208.5	2,245	11,666	382.7	1,989.0	2,022	10,507	3,263	16,925	189,300
1964	462.3	2,367.6	2,408	12,336	411.5	2,107.5	2,144	10,980	3,458	17,660	191,927
1965	497.8	2,513.6	2,562	12,933	443.8	2,240.8	2,284	11,530	3,700	18,560	194,347
1966	537.4	2,646.1	2,733	13,460	480.9	2,367.9	2,446	12,044	4,007	19,543	196,599
1967	575.1	2,762.2	2,894	13,898	507.8	2,438.8	2,555	12,271	4,188	19,819	198,752
1968	624.7	2,887.9	3,112	14,386	558.0	2,579.6	2,780	12,850	4,532	20,573	200,745
1969	673.8	2,979.9	3,324	14,699	605.1	2,676.2	2,985	13,200	4,856	21,003	202,736
1970	735.5	3,107.3	3,586	15,151	648.3	2,738.9	3,161	13,355	5,063	20,802	205,089
1971	801.4	3,247.7	3,859	15,637	701.6	2,843.3	3,378	13,690	5,425	21,231	207,692
1972	869.0	3,405.2	4,140	16,221	770.2	3,018.1	3,669	14,377	5,897	22,121	209,924
1973	978.1	3,636.6	4,615	17,159	852.0	3,167.7	4,020	14,946	6,522	23,180	211,939
1974	1,071.7	3,608.6	5,010	16,871	932.9	3,141.4	4,362	14,686	7,010	22,841	213,898
1975	1,187.3	3,689.5	5,497	17,083	1,033.8	3,212.6	4,786	14,874	7,583	22,573	215,981
1976	1,302.3	3,836.6	5,972	17,592	1,151.3	3,391.5	5,279	15,551	8,366	23,555	218,086
1977	1,435.0	3,969.0	6,514	18,017	1,277.8	3,534.3	5,801	16,044	9,216	24,391	220,289
1978	1,607.3	4,154.6	7,220	18,662	1,427.6	3,690.1	6,413	16,575	10,303	25,481	222,629
1979	1,790.9	4,251.9	7,956	18,888	1,591.2	3,777.8	7,069	16,782	11,382	25,988	225,106
1980	2,002.7	4,293.7	8,794	18,855	1,755.8	3,764.5	7,710	16,531	12,243	25,618	227,726
1981	2,237.1	4,407.9	9,726	19,164	1,939.5	3,821.6	8,432	16,615	13,594	26,008	230,008
1982	2,412.7	4,504.4	10,390	19,397	2,075.5	3,874.9	8,938	16,686	14,009	25,260	232,218
1983	2,599.8	4,653.5	11,095	19,859	2,288.6	4,096.4	9,766	17,481	15,084	26,163	234,333
1984	2,891.5	4,986.9	12,232	21,096	2,501.1	4,313.6	10,580	18,247	16,629	27,799	236,394
1985	3,079.3	5,142.4	12,911	21,561	2,717.6	4,538.3	11,394	19,028	17,683	28,693	238,506
1986	3,258.8	5,312.6	13,540	22,073	2,896.7	4,722.4	12,036	19,621	18,531	29,418	240,683
1987	3,435.3	5,399.9	14,146	22,236	3,097.0	4,868.0	12,753	20,046	19,504	30,090	242,843
1988	3,726.3	5,633.0	15,206	22,986	3,350.1	5,064.3	13,670	20,665	20,813	31,043	245,061
1989	3,991.4	5,782.5	16,134	23,374	3,594.5	5,207.5	14,530	21,050	22,160	31,850	247,387
1990	4,254.0	5,893.6	17,004	23,557	3,835.5	5,313.7	15,331	21,240	23,185	32,085	250,181
1991	4,444.9	5,943.2	17,532	23,442	3,980.1	5,321.7	15,699	20,991	23,635	31,587	253,530
1992	4,736.7	6,152.5	18,436	23,947	4,236.9	5,503.2	16,491	21,420	24,686	32,228	256,922
1993	4,921.6	6,255.3	18,909	24,033	4,483.6	5,698.6	17,226	21,894	25,616	32,719	260,282
1994	5,184.3	6,456.0	19,678	24,505	4,750.8	5,916.2	18,033	22,456	26,893	33,642	263,455
1995	5,457.0	6,648.6	20,470	24,939	4,987.3	6,076.2	18,708	22,793	27,813	34,082	266,588
1996	5,759.6	6,867.8	21,355	25,463	5,273.6	6,288.3	19,553	23,315	29,062	34,948	269,714
1997	6,074.6	7,110.4	22,255	26,049	5,570.6	6,520.4	20,408	23,888	30,526	36,071	272,958
1998	6,498.9	7,535.4	23,534	27,287	5,918.5	6,862.3	21,432	24,850	31,843	37,207	276,154
1999	6,803.3	7,763.1	24,356	27,792	6,342.8	7,237.6	22,707	25,911	33,486	38,559	279,328
2000	7,327.2	8,157.8	25,946	28,888	6,830.4	7,604.6	24,187	26,929	35,239	39,718	282,398
2001	7,648.5	8,356.2	26,816	29,297	7,148.8	7,810.3	25,064	27,383	36,063	39,749	285,225
2002	8,009.7	8,633.2	27,816	29,981	7,439.2	8,018.3	25,835	27,846	36,958	40,087	287,955
2003	8,377.8	8,850.5	28,827	30,453	7,804.1	8,244.5	26,853	28,368	38,339	40,727	290,626
2004	8,889.4	9,152.9	30,312	31,211	8,270.6	8,515.8	28,202	29,038	40,419	41,761	293,262
2005	9,277.3	9,277.3	31,343	31,343	8,803.5	8,803.5	29,742	29,742	42,646	42,646	295,993
2006	9,915.7	9,652.8	33,183	32,303	9,301.0	9,054.5	31,126	30,301	44,767	43,366	298,818
2007	10,423.6	9,880.3	34,550	32,749	9,772.3	9,262.9	32,391	30,703	46,499	43,774	301,696
2008	11,024.5	10,119.5	36,200	33,229	10,035.5	9,211.7	32,953	30,248	46,928	43,219	304,543
2009	10,788.8	9,882.7	35,115	32,166	9,866.1	9,037.5	32,112	29,415	45,368	41,346	307,240
2010	11,179.7	10,061.6	36,090	32,481	10,245.5	9,220.9	33,074	29,767	46,894	42,250	309,774
2011 [p]	11,556.2	10,153.5	37,035	32,539	10,722.6	9,421.1	34,363	30,192	48,352	42,666	312,040
2008: I	10,879.6	10,087.4	35,848	33,238	10,018.5	9,289.1	33,011	30,607	47,032	43,714	303,494
II	11,220.0	10,288.5	36,888	33,826	10,126.5	9,285.8	33,293	30,529	47,394	43,761	304,160
III	11,081.2	10,053.7	36,343	32,974	10,135.8	9,196.0	33,243	30,160	47,212	43,250	304,902
IV	10,917.3	10,047.9	35,722	32,878	9,861.3	9,076.0	32,267	29,698	46,077	42,156	305,616
2009: I	10,766.3	9,951.0	35,157	32,494	9,781.7	9,040.9	31,942	29,523	45,369	41,351	306,237
II	10,823.8	9,957.3	35,272	32,448	9,781.6	8,998.5	31,876	29,324	45,147	41,195	306,866
III	10,753.5	9,819.6	34,962	31,926	9,911.1	9,050.3	32,224	29,425	45,259	41,273	307,573
IV	10,811.7	9,805.4	35,071	31,806	9,990.0	9,060.2	32,405	29,389	45,696	41,564	308,285
2010: I	10,991.3	9,922.5	35,582	32,122	10,103.7	9,121.2	32,709	29,528	46,222	41,883	308,899
II	11,150.2	10,057.8	36,032	32,501	10,184.8	9,186.9	32,912	29,687	46,752	42,198	309,457
III	11,240.4	10,114.4	36,251	32,620	10,276.6	9,247.1	33,143	29,823	47,104	42,376	310,070
IV	11,336.7	10,152.0	36,491	32,678	10,417.1	9,328.4	33,531	30,027	47,494	42,541	310,670
2011: I	11,481.0	10,183.2	36,895	32,724	10,571.7	9,376.7	33,972	30,132	47,778	42,508	311,184
II	11,559.2	10,169.7	37,082	32,625	10,676.0	9,392.7	34,249	30,132	48,162	42,577	311,717
III	11,571.1	10,121.6	37,048	32,407	10,784.5	9,433.5	34,529	30,204	48,590	42,684	312,330
IV [p]	11,613.8	10,141.2	37,113	32,407	10,858.1	9,481.3	34,698	30,299	48,874	42,893	312,930

[1] Population of the United States including Armed Forces overseas. Annual data are averages of quarterly data. Quarterly data are averages for the period.

Source: Department of Commerce (Bureau of Economic Analysis and Bureau of the Census).

Table B-32. Gross saving and investment, 1963–2011

[Billions of dollars, except as noted; quarterly data at seasonally adjusted annual rates]

Year or quarter	Total gross saving	Gross saving									Consumption of fixed capital		
		Net saving											
		Total net saving	Net private saving				Net government saving			Total	Private	Government
			Total	Personal saving	Undistributed corporate profits [1]	Wage accruals less disbursements	Total	Federal	State and local			
1963	133.2	69.8	58.8	33.1	25.7	0.0	11.0	5.3	5.7	63.3	45.9	17.5
1964	143.4	77.0	69.7	40.5	29.2	.0	7.3	.9	6.4	66.4	48.3	18.1
1965	158.5	87.7	78.0	42.7	35.3	.0	9.8	3.2	6.5	70.7	51.9	18.9
1966	168.7	92.3	82.3	44.3	38.0	.0	10.0	2.3	7.8	76.5	56.5	20.0
1967	170.6	87.6	89.9	54.2	35.8	.0	−2.3	−9.3	7.0	82.9	61.6	21.4
1968	182.0	91.6	86.6	52.5	34.1	.0	5.1	−2.4	7.5	90.4	67.4	23.0
1969	198.4	99.3	82.7	52.5	30.3	.0	16.5	8.6	8.0	99.2	74.5	24.7
1970	192.8	84.5	92.9	69.4	23.4	.0	−8.4	−15.5	7.1	108.3	81.7	26.6
1971	209.2	91.5	113.7	80.4	32.9	.4	−22.2	−28.7	6.5	117.8	89.5	28.2
1972	237.3	110.1	119.4	77.5	42.2	−.3	−9.3	−24.9	15.6	127.2	97.7	29.4
1973	292.2	151.4	147.5	102.9	44.6	.0	3.9	−11.8	15.7	140.8	109.5	31.3
1974	301.8	138.1	143.3	114.2	29.1	.0	−5.2	−14.5	9.3	163.7	127.8	35.9
1975	296.9	106.5	174.6	125.9	48.7	.0	−68.2	−70.6	2.5	190.4	150.4	39.9
1976	342.0	133.8	180.1	122.8	57.3	.0	−46.3	−53.7	7.4	208.2	165.5	42.6
1977	396.7	164.9	197.9	125.3	72.6	.0	−33.0	−46.1	13.1	231.8	186.1	45.6
1978	476.3	214.9	225.2	142.4	82.8	.0	−10.2	−28.9	18.7	261.4	212.0	49.5
1979	533.2	234.3	235.3	157.5	77.8	.0	−1.0	−14.0	13.0	298.9	244.5	54.4
1980	542.7	198.6	246.5	196.3	50.2	.0	−47.8	−56.6	8.8	344.1	282.3	61.8
1981	646.1	252.7	301.9	236.7	65.2	.0	−49.2	−56.8	7.6	393.3	323.2	70.1
1982	621.5	187.9	325.4	263.9	61.5	.0	−137.5	−135.3	−2.2	433.5	356.4	77.1
1983	602.4	151.3	322.6	226.9	95.7	.0	−171.4	−176.2	4.9	451.1	369.5	81.6
1984	753.4	279.0	426.5	296.3	130.3	.0	−147.5	−171.5	23.9	474.3	387.5	86.9
1985	738.4	232.9	389.2	253.6	135.6	.0	−156.3	−178.6	22.4	505.4	412.8	92.7
1986	709.3	170.8	344.7	246.5	98.3	.0	−173.9	−194.6	20.7	538.5	439.1	99.4
1987	782.3	211.2	348.5	223.4	125.1	.0	−137.4	−149.3	12.0	571.1	464.5	106.6
1988	901.5	290.5	411.7	256.6	155.1	.0	−121.2	−138.4	17.2	611.0	497.1	113.9
1989	924.1	272.7	386.5	265.0	121.5	.0	−113.8	−133.9	20.1	651.5	529.6	121.8
1990	917.6	226.4	396.7	276.7	120.0	.0	−170.3	−176.4	6.2	691.2	560.4	130.8
1991	951.3	227.0	451.2	313.2	138.0	.0	−224.2	−218.4	−5.8	724.4	585.4	138.9
1992	932.3	187.9	491.8	348.1	159.5	−15.8	−303.9	−302.5	−1.4	744.4	599.9	144.5
1993	958.4	180.4	461.6	285.4	169.7	6.4	−281.2	−280.2	−.9	778.0	626.4	151.6
1994	1,094.7	275.5	487.7	270.7	199.4	17.6	−212.2	−220.4	8.2	819.2	661.0	158.2
1995	1,219.0	349.6	546.6	286.3	243.9	16.4	−197.0	−206.2	9.2	869.5	704.6	164.8
1996	1,344.4	431.8	557.1	281.1	272.3	3.6	−125.3	−148.2	23.0	912.5	743.4	169.2
1997	1,525.7	561.9	585.7	280.4	308.2	−2.9	−23.8	−60.1	36.3	963.8	789.7	174.1
1998	1,654.4	633.9	553.4	341.5	212.6	−.7	80.5	33.6	46.9	1,020.5	841.6	179.0
1999	1,708.0	613.6	473.0	207.8	260.1	5.2	140.6	98.8	41.8	1,094.4	907.2	187.2
2000	1,800.1	615.8	389.4	213.1	176.3	.0	226.5	185.2	41.3	1,184.3	986.8	197.5
2001	1,695.7	439.4	414.9	204.9	210.0	.0	24.6	40.5	−15.9	1,256.2	1,051.6	204.6
2002	1,560.9	255.9	562.8	282.2	280.6	.0	−306.9	−252.8	−54.1	1,305.0	1,094.0	210.9
2003	1,552.6	198.6	613.8	289.6	309.2	15.0	−415.2	−376.4	−38.8	1,354.1	1,135.9	218.1
2004	1,738.7	305.9	693.7	318.2	390.5	−15.0	−387.8	−379.5	−8.4	1,432.8	1,200.9	231.9
2005	1,918.8	377.5	634.5	143.2	486.4	5.0	−257.1	−283.0	25.9	1,541.4	1,290.8	250.6
2006	2,196.1	535.4	688.1	256.6	430.3	1.3	−152.7	−203.8	51.0	1,660.7	1,391.4	269.3
2007	2,047.7	280.2	513.2	248.7	270.7	−6.3	−233.0	−245.2	12.2	1,767.5	1,476.2	291.3
2008	1,908.2	54.1	739.8	592.3	152.5	−5.0	−685.7	−613.5	−72.2	1,854.1	1,542.9	311.2
2009	1,597.3	−268.8	1,027.1	552.6	469.6	5.0	−1,296.0	−1,217.9	−78.0	1,866.2	1,542.4	323.7
2010	1,820.5	−54.5	1,244.5	592.8	651.7	.0	−1,299.0	−1,273.7	−25.3	1,874.9	1,540.9	334.0
2011 *p*	....	....	....	505.3	....	.0	....	....	....	1,950.0	1,597.8	352.2
2008: I	2,010.1	192.7	624.0	455.0	168.9	.0	−431.3	−388.8	−42.5	1,817.4	1,515.0	302.4
II	1,925.5	82.8	876.9	690.6	186.3	.0	−794.2	−764.4	−29.8	1,842.7	1,534.6	308.1
III	1,907.1	37.5	778.3	542.8	235.5	.0	−740.9	−639.1	−101.8	1,869.6	1,555.5	314.1
IV	1,790.1	−96.4	680.2	680.9	19.2	−20.0	−776.6	−661.7	−114.9	1,886.5	1,566.5	320.0
2009: I	1,698.7	−186.4	925.6	611.1	294.5	20.0	−1,112.1	−993.9	−118.1	1,885.2	1,562.6	322.6
II	1,577.0	−291.4	1,086.9	670.3	416.6	.0	−1,378.3	−1,303.0	−75.3	1,868.4	1,545.2	323.2
III	1,496.1	−358.0	1,021.3	468.2	553.1	.0	−1,379.4	−1,305.4	−74.0	1,854.1	1,530.5	323.6
IV	1,617.5	−239.5	1,074.7	460.5	614.2	.0	−1,314.2	−1,269.4	−44.8	1,857.1	1,531.4	325.6
2010: I	1,718.4	−140.2	1,163.9	534.1	629.7	.0	−1,304.0	−1,271.8	−32.3	1,858.6	1,529.6	329.0
II	1,840.9	−25.9	1,280.3	623.3	657.0	.0	−1,306.2	−1,278.0	−28.2	1,866.9	1,534.4	332.5
III	1,883.2	5.0	1,267.9	625.6	642.3	.0	−1,262.9	−1,257.7	−5.2	1,878.2	1,542.6	335.5
IV	1,839.3	−56.8	1,266.0	588.1	677.9	.0	−1,322.8	−1,287.3	−35.5	1,896.1	1,557.0	339.1
2011: I	1,895.2	−19.1	1,239.2	578.9	660.3	.0	−1,258.3	−1,201.1	−57.2	1,914.3	1,570.5	343.8
II	1,890.5	−49.4	1,266.2	556.5	709.6	.0	−1,315.6	−1,275.4	−40.2	1,939.9	1,590.5	349.4
III	1,901.1	−61.8	1,193.8	456.5	737.3	.0	−1,255.6	−1,172.4	−83.2	1,962.8	1,607.6	355.2
IV *p*	....	....	....	429.3	....	.0	....	....	....	1,983.0	1,622.5	360.4

[1] With inventory valuation and capital consumption adjustments.

See next page for continuation of table.

Table B–32. Gross saving and investment, 1963–2011—*Continued*

[Billions of dollars, except as noted; quarterly data at seasonally adjusted annual rates]

| Year or quarter | Gross domestic investment, capital account transactions, and net lending, NIPA [2] | | | | | | | Addenda: | | | | | | |
| | Gross domestic investment | | | | Capital account transactions (net) [4] | Net lending or net borrowing (–), NIPA [2,5] | Statistical discrepancy | Gross private saving | Gross government saving | | | Net domestic investment | Gross saving as a percent of gross national income | Net saving as a percent of gross national income |
	Total	Total	Gross private domestic investment	Gross government investment [3]					Total	Federal	State and local			
1963	132.3	127.4	93.8	33.6	....	4.9	–0.8	104.7	28.4	17.4	11.1	64.1	21.4	11.2
1964	144.2	136.7	102.1	34.6	....	7.5	.8	118.0	25.4	13.2	12.1	70.3	21.5	11.5
1965	160.0	153.8	118.2	35.6	....	6.2	1.5	129.8	28.6	15.9	12.8	83.1	21.9	12.1
1966	174.9	171.1	131.3	39.8	....	3.8	6.2	138.7	30.0	15.3	14.6	94.6	21.5	11.7
1967	175.1	171.6	128.6	43.0	....	3.5	4.5	151.5	19.1	4.5	14.5	88.6	20.5	10.5
1968	186.4	184.8	141.2	43.6	....	1.5	4.3	154.0	28.0	12.2	15.8	94.4	20.0	10.1
1969	201.3	199.7	156.4	43.3	0.0	1.6	2.9	157.2	41.2	23.9	17.3	100.5	20.1	10.0
1970	199.7	196.0	152.4	43.6	.0	3.7	6.9	174.6	18.2	.6	17.7	87.6	18.6	8.1
1971	220.2	219.9	178.2	41.8	.0	.3	11.0	203.2	6.0	–12.2	18.3	102.2	18.6	8.1
1972	246.2	250.2	207.6	42.6	.0	–4.1	8.9	217.1	20.2	–8.3	28.5	123.1	19.2	8.9
1973	300.2	291.3	244.5	46.8	.0	8.8	8.0	257.0	35.2	5.2	30.0	150.6	21.1	10.9
1974	311.6	305.7	249.4	56.3	.0	5.9	9.8	271.1	30.7	3.7	27.0	142.0	20.1	9.2
1975	313.2	293.3	230.2	63.1	.1	19.8	16.3	325.1	–28.2	–50.9	22.7	102.9	18.2	6.5
1976	365.4	358.4	292.0	66.4	.1	7.0	23.5	345.6	–3.7	–32.3	28.6	150.2	18.8	7.4
1977	417.9	428.8	361.3	67.5	.1	–11.0	21.2	384.1	12.6	–23.1	35.7	197.1	19.6	8.1
1978	502.4	515.0	438.0	77.1	.1	–12.7	26.1	437.1	39.2	–3.9	43.2	253.6	20.8	9.4
1979	580.2	581.4	492.9	88.5	.1	–1.3	47.0	479.7	53.5	13.0	40.5	282.4	20.9	9.2
1980	588.0	579.5	479.3	100.3	.1	8.4	45.3	528.8	14.0	–26.6	40.6	235.4	19.5	7.2
1981	682.6	679.3	572.4	106.9	.1	3.2	36.6	625.2	20.9	–23.0	43.8	285.9	20.7	8.1
1982	626.2	629.5	517.2	112.3	.1	–3.4	4.8	681.9	–60.4	–97.7	37.3	196.0	18.9	5.7
1983	652.1	687.2	564.3	122.9	.1	–35.2	49.7	692.2	–89.8	–135.6	45.8	236.0	17.1	4.3
1984	784.9	875.0	735.6	139.4	.1	–90.2	31.5	814.0	–60.6	–126.9	66.3	400.6	19.1	7.1
1985	780.7	895.0	736.2	158.8	.1	–114.5	42.3	802.0	–63.6	–130.6	67.0	389.5	17.6	5.5
1986	777.1	919.7	746.5	173.2	.1	–142.8	67.7	783.8	–74.5	–143.0	68.6	381.3	16.1	3.9
1987	815.1	969.2	785.0	184.3	.1	–154.2	32.9	813.0	–30.8	–94.2	63.4	398.1	16.6	4.5
1988	892.0	1,007.7	821.6	186.1	.1	–115.9	–9.5	908.8	–7.3	–79.3	72.0	396.7	17.6	5.7
1989	980.3	1,072.6	874.9	197.7	.3	–92.7	56.1	916.1	8.0	–70.6	78.7	421.2	17.0	5.0
1990	1,001.8	1,076.7	861.0	215.7	7.4	–82.3	84.2	957.1	–39.5	–108.7	69.2	385.5	16.0	3.9
1991	1,031.0	1,023.2	802.9	220.3	5.3	2.6	79.7	1,036.6	–85.3	–146.4	61.1	298.8	16.0	3.8
1992	1,042.3	1,087.9	864.8	223.1	–1.3	–44.3	110.0	1,091.7	–159.4	–227.9	68.5	343.5	14.9	3.0
1993	1,094.2	1,172.8	953.3	219.4	.9	–79.4	135.8	1,088.0	–129.5	–202.4	72.9	394.8	14.6	2.7
1994	1,203.5	1,318.2	1,097.3	220.9	1.3	–116.0	108.8	1,148.6	–53.9	–140.3	86.4	499.0	15.6	3.9
1995	1,271.6	1,376.6	1,144.0	232.6	.4	–105.5	52.5	1,251.2	–32.2	–124.5	92.3	507.2	16.5	4.7
1996	1,370.3	1,484.4	1,240.2	244.2	.2	–114.4	25.9	1,300.5	43.9	–66.3	110.2	571.9	17.1	5.5
1997	1,511.7	1,641.0	1,388.7	252.4	.5	–129.8	–14.0	1,375.4	150.3	22.4	127.9	677.2	18.2	6.7
1998	1,569.1	1,773.6	1,510.8	262.9	.2	–204.8	–85.3	1,394.9	259.5	116.4	143.1	753.1	18.6	7.1
1999	1,637.0	1,928.9	1,641.5	287.4	4.5	–296.4	–71.1	1,380.3	327.8	183.9	143.9	834.5	18.1	6.5
2000	1,666.2	2,076.5	1,772.2	304.3	.3	–410.7	–134.0	1,376.2	424.0	273.0	151.0	892.2	17.8	6.1
2001	1,592.3	1,984.0	1,661.9	322.0	–12.9	–378.7	–103.4	1,466.5	229.2	129.1	100.1	727.7	16.2	4.2
2002	1,538.9	1,990.4	1,647.0	343.5	.5	–452.1	–22.1	1,656.8	–95.9	–163.6	67.7	685.4	14.6	2.4
2003	1,569.3	2,085.4	1,729.7	355.8	2.1	–518.2	16.7	1,749.7	–197.1	–285.5	88.4	731.4	13.9	1.8
2004	1,716.3	2,340.9	1,968.6	372.4	–2.8	–621.8	–22.3	1,894.6	–155.9	–284.6	128.7	908.2	14.5	2.6
2005	1,823.8	2,564.3	2,172.3	392.0	–12.9	–727.7	–95.1	1,925.4	–6.5	–182.6	176.1	1,022.9	15.0	2.9
2006	1,953.8	2,752.2	2,327.1	425.1	2.1	–800.5	–242.3	2,079.5	116.5	–97.2	213.8	1,091.5	16.0	3.9
2007	2,035.7	2,751.7	2,295.2	456.5	–.1	–715.9	–12.0	1,989.4	58.3	–132.6	190.9	984.2	14.5	2.0
2008	1,905.8	2,584.8	2,087.6	497.2	–5.4	–673.6	–2.4	2,282.8	–374.6	–493.5	119.0	730.7	13.2	.4
2009	1,674.8	2,052.2	1,546.8	505.4	.6	–378.0	77.4	2,569.6	–972.3	–1,093.2	121.0	186.0	11.4	–1.9
2010	1,821.3	2,300.4	1,795.1	505.3	.7	–479.9	.8	2,785.4	–964.9	–1,143.6	178.7	425.5	12.4	–.4
2011 *p*	....	2,395.9	1,913.6	482.3	....	....	....	....	....	....	....	445.9	....	....
2008: I	1,951.4	2,660.6	2,185.7	475.0	.4	–709.7	–58.8	2,138.9	–128.8	–272.1	143.3	843.2	13.9	1.3
II	1,954.6	2,661.3	2,165.4	495.9	.4	–707.1	29.1	2,411.5	–486.0	–645.2	159.2	818.5	13.2	.6
III	1,898.4	2,594.3	2,086.3	508.0	–23.8	–672.1	–8.6	2,333.9	–426.8	–517.8	91.0	724.7	13.1	.3
IV	1,818.6	2,422.8	1,913.0	509.8	1.3	–605.5	28.5	2,246.7	–456.6	–539.0	82.4	536.3	12.6	–.7
2009: I	1,740.8	2,123.2	1,620.1	503.1	.4	–382.8	42.1	2,488.2	–789.5	–870.7	81.3	238.0	12.1	–1.3
II	1,667.3	2,005.0	1,493.8	511.2	.5	–338.1	90.3	2,632.1	–1,055.1	–1,178.9	123.8	136.6	11.3	–2.1
III	1,600.1	1,990.7	1,481.2	509.6	.6	–391.2	104.1	2,551.9	–1,055.8	–1,180.3	124.5	136.6	10.7	–2.6
IV	1,690.8	2,089.9	1,592.2	497.7	.7	–399.9	73.2	2,606.2	–988.6	–1,143.0	154.4	232.8	11.4	–1.7
2010: I	1,711.2	2,193.1	1,702.3	490.8	.5	–482.4	–7.2	2,693.5	–975.0	–1,143.8	168.8	334.5	11.9	–1.0
II	1,834.3	2,316.5	1,809.7	506.9	.5	–482.7	–6.6	2,814.6	–973.7	–1,148.6	174.9	449.7	12.5	–.2
III	1,875.7	2,363.6	1,850.5	513.1	1.2	–489.1	–7.4	2,810.5	–927.4	–1,127.2	199.8	485.5	12.7	.0
IV	1,863.8	2,328.5	1,818.0	510.5	.5	–465.3	24.5	2,823.0	–983.7	–1,154.9	171.3	432.4	12.3	–.4
2011: I	1,843.2	2,336.7	1,853.1	483.6	.5	–494.0	–52.0	2,809.7	–914.5	–1,066.5	152.0	422.4	12.5	–.1
II	1,880.5	2,373.5	1,895.3	478.2	3.7	–496.7	–10.0	2,856.6	–966.2	–1,138.6	172.4	433.6	12.4	–.3
III	1,950.7	2,392.9	1,906.6	486.3	.4	–442.7	49.6	2,801.4	–900.3	–1,033.2	132.9	430.1	12.3	–.4
IV *p*	....	2,480.6	1,999.7	480.9	....	....	....	....	....	....	....	497.6	....	....

[2] National income and product accounts (NIPA).
[3] For details on government investment, see Table B–20.
[4] Consists of capital transfers and the acquisition and disposal of nonproduced nonfinancial assets.
[5] Prior to 1982, equals the balance on current account, NIPA (see Table B–24).

Source: Department of Commerce (Bureau of Economic Analysis).

Race, Hispanic origin, and year	Families [1]						People below poverty level		Median money income (in 2010 dollars) of people 15 years old and over with income [2]			
	Number (millions)	Median money income (in 2010 dollars) [2]	Below poverty level				Number (millions)	Percent	Males		Females	
			Total		Female householder				All people	Year-round full-time workers	All people	Year-round full-time workers
			Number (millions)	Percent	Number (millions)	Percent						
TOTAL (all races) [3]												
1998	71.6	$62,433	7.2	10.0	3.8	29.9	34.5	12.7	$35,389	$48,427	$19,276	$35,874
1999 [4]	73.2	63,897	6.8	9.3	3.6	27.8	32.8	11.9	35,714	49,005	20,026	35,810
2000 [5]	73.8	64,232	6.4	8.7	3.3	25.4	31.6	11.3	35,885	49,240	20,338	36,873
2001	74.3	63,310	6.8	9.2	3.5	26.4	32.9	11.7	35,839	49,429	20,461	37,463
2002	75.6	62,634	7.2	9.6	3.6	26.5	34.6	12.1	35,435	49,093	20,375	37,534
2003	76.2	62,451	7.6	10.0	3.9	28.0	35.9	12.5	35,483	49,201	20,460	37,524
2004 [7]	76.9	62,402	7.8	10.2	4.0	28.3	37.0	12.7	35,224	48,096	20,393	37,071
2005	77.4	62,760	7.7	9.9	4.0	28.7	37.0	12.6	34,929	47,118	20,747	37,142
2006	78.5	63,161	7.7	9.8	4.1	28.3	36.5	12.3	34,891	48,617	21,643	37,837
2007	77.9	64,518	7.6	9.8	4.1	28.3	37.3	12.5	34,908	48,607	22,001	38,032
2008	78.9	62,299	8.1	10.3	4.2	28.7	39.8	13.2	33,580	48,383	21,131	37,152
2009 [8]	78.9	61,080	8.8	11.1	4.4	29.9	43.6	14.3	32,715	49,976	21,303	37,849
2010	78.6	60,395	9.2	11.7	4.7	31.6	46.2	15.1	32,137	50,063	20,831	38,531
WHITE												
1998	60.1	65,487	4.8	8.0	2.1	24.9	23.5	10.5	36,931	49,688	19,526	36,474
1999 [4]	61.1	66,839	4.4	7.3	1.9	22.5	22.2	9.8	37,508	51,311	20,089	36,639
2000 [5]	61.3	67,141	4.3	7.1	1.8	21.2	21.6	9.5	37,726	50,965	20,358	37,921
2001	61.6	66,586	4.6	7.4	1.9	22.4	22.7	9.9	37,242	50,234	20,508	37,992
2002 [6]	62.3	66,213	4.9	7.8	2.0	22.6	23.5	10.2	36,823	50,145	20,407	38,056
2003	62.6	66,112	5.1	8.1	2.2	24.0	24.3	10.5	36,432	49,959	20,654	38,163
2004 [7]	63.1	65,475	5.3	8.4	2.3	24.7	25.3	10.8	36,181	49,168	20,430	37,781
2005	63.4	66,248	5.1	8.0	2.3	25.3	24.9	10.6	35,939	48,802	20,850	38,084
2006	64.1	66,268	5.1	8.0	2.4	25.1	24.4	10.3	36,598	49,672	21,717	38,416
2007	63.6	67,749	5.0	7.9	2.3	24.7	25.1	10.5	36,953	49,670	22,155	38,622
2008	64.2	65,822	5.4	8.4	2.4	25.2	27.0	11.2	35,564	50,556	21,215	37,681
2009 [8]	64.1	63,577	6.0	9.3	2.7	27.3	29.8	12.3	34,305	51,192	21,467	38,577
2010	63.8	63,146	6.3	9.8	2.8	28.8	31.7	13.0	34,047	50,852	20,947	39,729
BLACK												
1998	8.5	39,279	2.0	23.4	1.6	40.8	9.1	26.1	25,810	36,698	17,549	31,878
1999 [4]	8.7	41,677	1.9	21.8	1.5	39.2	8.4	23.6	26,748	39,458	19,335	32,898
2000 [5]	8.7	42,638	1.7	19.3	1.3	34.3	8.0	22.5	27,023	38,603	20,107	32,602
2001	8.8	41,377	1.8	20.7	1.4	35.2	8.1	22.7	26,436	39,312	20,052	33,617
2002 [6]	8.9	40,631	1.9	21.5	1.4	35.8	8.6	24.1	26,131	38,700	20,275	33,480
2003	8.9	40,744	2.0	22.3	1.5	36.9	8.8	24.4	26,064	39,630	19,657	32,746
2004 [7]	8.9	40,571	2.0	22.8	1.5	37.6	9.0	24.7	26,191	36,614	20,037	33,642
2005	9.1	39,608	2.0	22.1	1.5	36.1	9.2	24.9	25,300	38,233	19,691	33,911
2006	9.3	41,384	2.0	21.6	1.5	36.6	9.0	24.3	27,104	38,365	20,658	33,454
2007	9.3	42,213	2.0	22.1	1.5	37.3	9.2	24.5	27,153	38,630	20,770	33,220
2008	9.4	40,383	2.1	22.0	1.5	37.2	9.4	24.7	25,573	39,100	20,452	32,593
2009 [8]	9.4	39,043	2.1	22.7	1.5	36.7	9.9	25.8	24,130	40,012	19,791	33,006
2010	9.4	38,500	2.3	24.2	1.7	38.7	10.7	27.4	23,203	37,611	19,700	33,987
HISPANIC (any race)												
1998	7.3	39,551	1.6	22.7	.8	43.7	8.1	25.6	23,053	30,063	14,510	26,472
1999 [4]	7.8	41,249	1.6	20.5	.7	39.3	7.9	22.7	23,380	29,726	14,886	26,198
2000 [5]	8.0	43,607	1.5	19.2	.7	36.4	7.7	21.5	24,687	30,608	15,507	26,837
2001	8.5	42,476	1.6	19.4	.7	37.0	8.0	21.4	24,864	31,122	15,496	27,061
2002	9.1	41,431	1.8	19.7	.7	35.3	8.6	21.8	25,090	31,677	16,197	27,093
2003	9.3	40,629	1.9	20.8	.8	37.0	9.1	22.5	24,958	31,313	16,172	27,340
2004 [7]	9.5	40,908	2.0	20.5	.9	38.9	9.1	21.9	24,882	31,048	16,682	28,043
2005	9.9	42,292	1.9	19.7	.9	38.9	9.4	21.8	24,670	30,117	16,793	27,946
2006	10.2	43,256	1.9	18.9	.9	36.0	9.2	20.6	25,361	31,978	17,041	27,785
2007	10.4	42,658	2.0	19.7	1.0	38.4	9.9	21.5	25,712	32,024	17,612	28,554
2008	10.5	40,978	2.2	21.3	1.0	39.2	11.0	23.2	24,307	31,614	16,625	27,788
2009 [8]	10.4	40,386	2.4	22.7	1.1	38.8	12.4	25.3	22,623	32,160	16,478	28,343
2010	10.7	39,538	2.6	24.0	1.2	42.3	13.2	26.6	22,233	31,671	16,269	28,944

[1] The term "family" refers to a group of two or more persons related by birth, marriage, or adoption and residing together. Every family must include a reference person.

[2] Adjusted by consumer price index research series (CPI-U-RS).

[3] Data for American Indians and Alaska natives, Asians, native Hawaiians and other Pacific Islanders, and those reporting two or more races are included in the total but not shown separately.

[4] Reflects implementation of Census 2000–based population controls comparable with succeeding years.

[5] Reflects household sample expansion.

[6] Beginning with data for 2002, the Current Population Survey allowed respondents to choose more than one race; for earlier years respondents could report only one race. Data shown are for "white alone" and for "black alone" race categories. ("Black" is also "black or African American.")

[7] For 2004, figures are revised to reflect a correction to the weights in the 2005 Annual Social and Economic Supplement.

[8] Beginning with data for 2009, the upper income interval used to calculate median incomes was expanded to $250,000 or more.

Note: Poverty thresholds are updated each year to reflect changes in the consumer price index (CPI-U).
For details see publication Series P–60 on the Current Population Survey and Annual Social and Economic Supplements.

Source: Department of Commerce (Bureau of the Census).

Table B–34. Population by age group, 1939–2011

[Thousands of persons]

July 1	Total	Age (years)						
		Under 5	5–15	16–19	20–24	25–44	45–64	65 and over
1939	130,880	10,418	25,179	9,822	11,519	39,354	25,823	8,764
1940	132,122	10,579	24,811	9,895	11,690	39,868	26,249	9,031
1941	133,402	10,850	24,516	9,840	11,807	40,383	26,718	9,288
1942	134,860	11,301	24,231	9,730	11,955	40,861	27,196	9,584
1943	136,739	12,016	24,093	9,607	12,064	41,420	27,671	9,867
1944	138,397	12,524	23,949	9,561	12,062	42,016	28,138	10,147
1945	139,928	12,979	23,907	9,361	12,036	42,521	28,630	10,494
1946	141,389	13,244	24,103	9,119	12,004	43,027	29,064	10,828
1947	144,126	14,406	24,468	9,097	11,814	43,657	29,498	11,185
1948	146,631	14,919	25,209	8,952	11,794	44,288	29,931	11,538
1949	149,188	15,607	25,852	8,788	11,700	44,916	30,405	11,921
1950	152,271	16,410	26,721	8,542	11,680	45,672	30,849	12,397
1951	154,878	17,333	27,279	8,446	11,552	46,103	31,362	12,803
1952	157,553	17,312	28,894	8,414	11,350	46,495	31,884	13,203
1953	160,184	17,638	30,227	8,460	11,062	46,786	32,394	13,617
1954	163,026	18,057	31,480	8,637	10,832	47,001	32,942	14,076
1955	165,931	18,566	32,682	8,744	10,714	47,194	33,506	14,525
1956	168,903	19,003	33,994	8,916	10,616	47,379	34,057	14,938
1957	171,984	19,494	35,272	9,195	10,603	47,440	34,591	15,388
1958	174,882	19,887	36,445	9,543	10,756	47,337	35,109	15,806
1959	177,830	20,175	37,368	10,215	10,969	47,192	35,663	16,248
1960	180,671	20,341	38,494	10,683	11,134	47,140	36,203	16,675
1961	183,691	20,522	39,765	11,025	11,483	47,084	36,722	17,089
1962	186,538	20,469	41,205	11,180	11,959	47,013	37,255	17,457
1963	189,242	20,342	41,626	12,007	12,714	46,994	37,782	17,778
1964	191,889	20,165	42,297	12,736	13,269	46,958	38,338	18,127
1965	194,303	19,824	42,938	13,516	13,746	46,912	38,916	18,451
1966	196,560	19,208	43,702	14,311	14,050	47,001	39,534	18,755
1967	198,712	18,563	44,244	14,200	15,248	47,194	40,193	19,071
1968	200,706	17,913	44,622	14,452	15,786	47,721	40,846	19,365
1969	202,677	17,376	44,840	14,800	16,480	48,064	41,437	19,680
1970	205,052	17,166	44,816	15,289	17,202	48,473	41,999	20,107
1971	207,661	17,244	44,591	15,688	18,159	48,936	42,482	20,561
1972	209,896	17,101	44,203	16,039	18,153	50,482	42,898	21,020
1973	211,909	16,851	43,582	16,446	18,521	51,749	43,235	21,525
1974	213,854	16,487	42,989	16,769	18,975	53,051	43,522	22,061
1975	215,973	16,121	42,508	17,017	19,527	54,302	43,801	22,696
1976	218,035	15,617	42,099	17,194	19,986	55,852	44,008	23,278
1977	220,239	15,564	41,298	17,276	20,499	57,561	44,150	23,892
1978	222,585	15,735	40,428	17,288	20,946	59,400	44,286	24,502
1979	225,055	16,063	39,552	17,242	21,297	61,379	44,390	25,134
1980	227,726	16,451	38,838	17,167	21,590	63,470	44,504	25,707
1981	229,966	16,893	38,144	16,812	21,869	65,528	44,500	26,221
1982	232,188	17,228	37,784	16,332	21,902	67,692	44,462	26,787
1983	234,307	17,547	37,526	15,823	21,844	69,733	44,474	27,361
1984	236,348	17,695	37,461	15,295	21,737	71,735	44,547	27,878
1985	238,466	17,842	37,450	15,005	21,478	73,673	44,602	28,416
1986	240,651	17,963	37,404	15,024	20,942	75,651	44,660	29,008
1987	242,804	18,052	37,333	15,215	20,385	77,338	44,854	29,626
1988	245,021	18,195	37,593	15,198	19,846	78,595	45,471	30,124
1989	247,342	18,508	37,972	14,913	19,442	79,943	45,882	30,682
1990	250,132	18,856	38,632	14,466	19,323	81,291	46,316	31,247
1991	253,493	19,208	39,349	13,992	19,414	82,844	46,874	31,812
1992	256,894	19,528	40,161	13,781	19,314	83,201	48,553	32,356
1993	260,255	19,729	40,904	13,953	19,101	83,766	49,899	32,902
1994	263,436	19,777	41,689	14,228	18,758	84,334	51,318	33,331
1995	266,557	19,627	42,510	14,522	18,391	84,933	52,806	33,769
1996	269,667	19,408	43,172	15,057	17,965	85,527	54,396	34,143
1997	272,912	19,233	43,833	15,433	17,992	85,737	56,283	34,402
1998	276,115	19,145	44,332	15,856	18,250	85,663	58,249	34,619
1999	279,295	19,136	44,755	16,164	18,672	85,408	60,362	34,798
2000 [1]	282,162	19,178	45,166	16,230	19,117	84,973	62,428	35,070
2001 [1]	284,969	19,298	45,236	16,372	19,757	84,523	64,492	35,290
2002 [1]	287,625	19,429	45,232	16,512	20,244	83,990	66,696	35,522
2003 [1]	290,108	19,592	45,209	16,625	20,592	83,398	68,829	35,864
2004 [1]	292,805	19,786	45,131	16,838	20,846	83,067	70,935	36,203
2005 [1]	295,517	19,917	45,059	17,029	20,960	82,764	73,137	36,650
2006 [1]	298,380	19,939	44,984	17,401	21,036	82,639	75,216	37,164
2007 [1]	301,231	20,126	44,920	17,703	21,078	82,510	77,068	37,826
2008 [1]	304,094	20,271	44,955	17,892	21,181	82,400	78,618	38,778
2009 [1]	306,772	20,245	45,103	17,933	21,384	82,211	80,273	39,623
2010 [1]	309,350	20,201	45,323	17,712	21,668	82,229	81,780	40,438
2011 [1]	311,592							

[1] Data for 2000–2011 reflect the results of the 2010 Census, and do not include Armed Forces overseas.

Note: Includes Armed Forces overseas beginning with 1940. Includes Alaska and Hawaii beginning with 1950.
All estimates are consistent with decennial census enumerations.

Source: Department of Commerce (Bureau of the Census).

[Monthly data seasonally adjusted, except as noted]

Year or month	Civilian noninstitutional population [1]	Civilian labor force					Not in labor force	Civilian labor force participation rate [2]	Civilian employment/population ratio [3]	Unemployment rate, civilian workers [4]
		Total	Employment			Unemployment				
			Total	Agricultural	Nonagricultural					
		Thousands of persons 14 years of age and over						Percent		
1929		49,180	47,630	10,450	37,180	1,550				3.2
1933		51,590	38,760	10,090	28,670	12,830				24.9
1939		55,230	45,750	9,610	36,140	9,480				17.2
1940	99,840	55,640	47,520	9,540	37,980	8,120	44,200	55.7	47.6	14.6
1941	99,900	55,910	50,350	9,100	41,250	5,560	43,990	56.0	50.4	9.9
1942	98,640	56,410	53,750	9,250	44,500	2,660	42,230	57.2	54.5	4.7
1943	94,640	55,540	54,470	9,080	45,390	1,070	39,100	58.7	57.6	1.9
1944	93,220	54,630	53,960	8,950	45,010	670	38,590	58.6	57.9	1.2
1945	94,090	53,860	52,820	8,580	44,240	1,040	40,230	57.2	56.1	1.9
1946	103,070	57,520	55,250	8,320	46,930	2,270	45,550	55.8	53.6	3.9
1947	106,018	60,168	57,812	8,256	49,557	2,356	45,850	56.8	54.5	3.9
		Thousands of persons 16 years of age and over								
1947	101,827	59,350	57,038	7,890	49,148	2,311	42,477	58.3	56.0	3.9
1948	103,068	60,621	58,343	7,629	50,714	2,276	42,447	58.8	56.6	3.8
1949	103,994	61,286	57,651	7,658	49,993	3,637	42,708	58.9	55.4	5.9
1950	104,995	62,208	58,918	7,160	51,758	3,288	42,787	59.2	56.1	5.3
1951	104,621	62,017	59,961	6,726	53,235	2,055	42,604	59.2	57.3	3.3
1952	105,231	62,138	60,250	6,500	53,749	1,883	43,093	59.0	57.3	3.0
1953 [5]	107,056	63,015	61,179	6,260	54,919	1,834	44,041	58.9	57.1	2.9
1954	108,321	63,643	60,109	6,205	53,904	3,532	44,678	58.8	55.5	5.5
1955	109,683	65,023	62,170	6,450	55,722	2,852	44,660	59.3	56.7	4.4
1956	110,954	66,552	63,799	6,283	57,514	2,750	44,402	60.0	57.5	4.1
1957	112,265	66,929	64,071	5,947	58,123	2,859	45,336	59.6	57.1	4.3
1958	113,727	67,639	63,036	5,586	57,450	4,602	46,088	59.5	55.4	6.8
1959	115,329	68,369	64,630	5,565	59,065	3,740	46,960	59.3	56.0	5.5
1960 [5]	117,245	69,628	65,778	5,458	60,318	3,852	47,617	59.4	56.1	5.5
1961	118,771	70,459	65,746	5,200	60,546	4,714	48,312	59.3	55.4	6.7
1962 [5]	120,153	70,614	66,702	4,944	61,759	3,911	49,539	58.8	55.5	5.5
1963	122,416	71,833	67,762	4,687	63,076	4,070	50,583	58.7	55.4	5.7
1964	124,485	73,091	69,305	4,523	64,782	3,786	51,394	58.7	55.7	5.2
1965	126,513	74,455	71,088	4,361	66,726	3,366	52,058	58.9	56.2	4.5
1966	128,058	75,770	72,895	3,979	68,915	2,875	52,288	59.2	56.9	3.8
1967	129,874	77,347	74,372	3,844	70,527	2,975	52,527	59.6	57.3	3.8
1968	132,028	78,737	75,920	3,817	72,103	2,817	53,291	59.6	57.5	3.6
1969	134,335	80,734	77,902	3,606	74,296	2,832	53,602	60.1	58.0	3.5
1970	137,085	82,771	78,678	3,463	75,215	4,093	54,315	60.4	57.4	4.9
1971	140,216	84,382	79,367	3,394	75,972	5,016	55,834	60.2	56.6	5.9
1972 [5]	144,126	87,034	82,153	3,484	78,669	4,882	57,091	60.4	57.0	5.6
1973 [5]	147,096	89,429	85,064	3,470	81,594	4,365	57,667	60.8	57.8	4.9
1974	150,120	91,949	86,794	3,515	83,279	5,156	58,171	61.3	57.8	5.6
1975	153,153	93,775	85,846	3,408	82,438	7,929	59,377	61.2	56.1	8.5
1976	156,150	96,158	88,752	3,331	85,421	7,406	59,991	61.6	56.8	7.7
1977	159,033	99,009	92,017	3,283	88,734	6,991	60,025	62.3	57.9	7.1
1978 [5]	161,910	102,251	96,048	3,387	92,661	6,202	59,659	63.2	59.3	6.1
1979	164,863	104,962	98,824	3,347	95,477	6,137	59,900	63.7	59.9	5.8
1980	167,745	106,940	99,303	3,364	95,938	7,637	60,806	63.8	59.2	7.1
1981	170,130	108,670	100,397	3,368	97,030	8,273	61,460	63.9	59.0	7.6
1982	172,271	110,204	99,526	3,401	96,125	10,678	62,067	64.0	57.8	9.7
1983	174,215	111,550	100,834	3,383	97,450	10,717	62,665	64.0	57.9	9.6
1984	176,383	113,544	105,005	3,321	101,685	8,539	62,839	64.4	59.5	7.5
1985	178,206	115,461	107,150	3,179	103,971	8,312	62,744	64.8	60.1	7.2
1986 [5]	180,587	117,834	109,597	3,163	106,434	8,237	62,752	65.3	60.7	7.0
1987	182,753	119,865	112,440	3,208	109,232	7,425	62,888	65.6	61.5	6.2
1988	184,613	121,669	114,968	3,169	111,800	6,701	62,944	65.9	62.3	5.5
1989	186,393	123,869	117,342	3,199	114,142	6,528	62,523	66.5	63.0	5.3
1990 [5]	189,164	125,840	118,793	3,223	115,570	7,047	63,324	66.5	62.8	5.6
1991	190,925	126,346	117,718	3,269	114,449	8,628	64,578	66.2	61.7	6.8
1992	192,805	128,105	118,492	3,247	115,245	9,613	64,700	66.4	61.5	7.5
1993	194,838	129,200	120,259	3,115	117,144	8,940	65,638	66.3	61.7	6.9
1994 [5]	196,814	131,056	123,060	3,409	119,651	7,996	65,758	66.6	62.5	6.1
1995	198,584	132,304	124,900	3,440	121,460	7,404	66,280	66.6	62.9	5.6
1996	200,591	133,943	126,708	3,443	123,264	7,236	66,647	66.8	63.2	5.4
1997 [5]	203,133	136,297	129,558	3,399	126,159	6,739	66,837	67.1	63.8	4.9
1998 [5]	205,220	137,673	131,463	3,378	128,085	6,210	67,547	67.1	64.1	4.5
1999 [5]	207,753	139,368	133,488	3,281	130,207	5,880	68,385	67.1	64.3	4.2

[1] Not seasonally adjusted.
[2] Civilian labor force as percent of civilian noninstitutional population.
[3] Civilian employment as percent of civilian noninstitutional population.
[4] Unemployed as percent of civilian labor force.

See next page for continuation of table.

[Monthly data seasonally adjusted, except as noted]

Year or month	Civilian noninstitutional population [1]	Civilian labor force					Not in labor force	Civilian labor force participation rate [2]	Civilian employment/ population ratio [3]	Unemployment rate, civilian workers [4]
		Total	Employment			Unemployment				
			Total	Agricultural	Nonagricultural					
	Thousands of persons 16 years of age and over							Percent		
2000 [5,6]	212,577	142,583	136,891	2,464	134,427	5,692	69,994	67.1	64.4	4.0
2001	215,092	143,734	136,933	2,299	134,635	6,801	71,359	66.8	63.7	4.7
2002	217,570	144,863	136,485	2,311	134,174	8,378	72,707	66.6	62.7	5.8
2003 [5]	221,168	146,510	137,736	2,275	135,461	8,774	74,658	66.2	62.3	6.0
2004 [5]	223,357	147,401	139,252	2,232	137,020	8,149	75,956	66.0	62.3	5.5
2005 [5]	226,082	149,320	141,730	2,197	139,532	7,591	76,762	66.0	62.7	5.1
2006 [5]	228,815	151,428	144,427	2,206	142,221	7,001	77,387	66.2	63.1	4.6
2007 [5]	231,867	153,124	146,047	2,095	143,952	7,078	78,743	66.0	63.0	4.6
2008 [5]	233,788	154,287	145,362	2,168	143,194	8,924	79,501	66.0	62.2	5.8
2009 [5]	235,801	154,142	139,877	2,103	137,775	14,265	81,659	65.4	59.3	9.3
2010 [5]	237,830	153,889	139,064	2,206	136,858	14,825	83,941	64.7	58.5	9.6
2011 [5]	239,618	153,617	139,869	2,254	137,615	13,747	86,001	64.1	58.4	8.9
2008: Jan [5]	232,616	154,075	146,397	2,204	144,187	7,678	78,541	66.2	62.9	5.0
Feb	232,809	153,648	146,157	2,188	143,965	7,491	79,162	66.0	62.8	4.9
Mar	232,995	153,925	146,108	2,172	143,946	7,816	79,070	66.1	62.7	5.1
Apr	233,198	153,761	146,130	2,109	143,902	7,631	79,437	65.9	62.7	5.0
May	233,405	154,325	145,929	2,113	143,748	8,395	79,080	66.1	62.5	5.4
June	233,627	154,316	145,738	2,121	143,631	8,578	79,311	66.1	62.4	5.6
July	233,864	154,480	145,530	2,138	143,467	8,950	79,384	66.1	62.2	5.8
Aug	234,107	154,646	145,196	2,151	143,066	9,450	79,460	66.1	62.0	6.1
Sept	234,360	154,559	145,059	2,238	142,814	9,501	79,801	65.9	61.9	6.1
Oct	234,612	154,875	144,792	2,207	142,691	10,083	79,737	66.0	61.7	6.5
Nov	234,828	154,622	144,078	2,212	141,836	10,544	80,206	65.8	61.4	6.8
Dec	235,035	154,626	143,328	2,202	141,107	11,299	80,408	65.8	61.0	7.3
2009: Jan [5]	234,739	154,236	142,187	2,143	140,069	12,049	80,502	65.7	60.6	7.8
Feb	234,913	154,521	141,660	2,124	139,558	12,860	80,392	65.8	60.3	8.3
Mar	235,086	154,143	140,754	2,027	138,756	13,389	80,942	65.6	59.9	8.7
Apr	235,271	154,450	140,654	2,124	138,484	13,796	80,822	65.6	59.8	8.9
May	235,452	154,800	140,294	2,149	138,075	14,505	80,652	65.7	59.6	9.4
June	235,655	154,730	140,003	2,150	137,839	14,727	80,925	65.7	59.4	9.5
July	235,870	154,538	139,891	2,135	137,719	14,646	81,332	65.5	59.3	9.5
Aug	236,087	154,319	139,458	2,099	137,318	14,861	81,768	65.4	59.1	9.6
Sept	236,322	153,786	138,775	2,046	136,755	15,012	82,536	65.1	58.7	9.8
Oct	236,550	153,822	138,401	2,058	136,446	15,421	82,728	65.0	58.5	10.0
Nov	236,743	153,833	138,607	2,111	136,481	15,227	82,909	65.0	58.5	9.9
Dec	236,924	153,091	137,968	2,078	135,877	15,124	83,833	64.6	58.2	9.9
2010: Jan [5]	236,832	153,454	138,500	2,121	136,464	14,953	83,379	64.8	58.5	9.7
Feb	236,998	153,704	138,665	2,295	136,459	15,039	83,295	64.9	58.5	9.8
Mar	237,159	153,964	138,836	2,202	136,702	15,128	83,195	64.9	58.5	9.8
Apr	237,329	154,528	139,306	2,247	137,026	15,221	82,801	65.1	58.7	9.9
May	237,499	154,216	139,340	2,205	137,074	14,876	83,284	64.9	58.7	9.6
June	237,690	153,653	139,137	2,120	136,968	14,517	84,037	64.6	58.5	9.4
July	237,890	153,748	139,139	2,188	136,776	14,609	84,142	64.6	58.5	9.5
Aug	238,099	154,073	139,338	2,182	137,080	14,735	84,026	64.7	58.5	9.6
Sept	238,322	153,918	139,344	2,184	137,233	14,574	84,404	64.6	58.5	9.5
Oct	238,530	153,709	139,072	2,373	136,816	14,636	84,822	64.4	58.3	9.5
Nov	238,715	154,041	138,937	2,206	136,686	15,104	84,674	64.5	58.2	9.8
Dec	238,889	153,613	139,220	2,173	137,036	14,393	85,276	64.3	58.3	9.4
2011: Jan [5]	238,704	153,250	139,330	2,252	137,156	13,919	85,454	64.2	58.4	9.1
Feb	238,851	153,302	139,551	2,247	137,388	13,751	85,550	64.2	58.4	9.0
Mar	239,000	153,392	139,764	2,244	137,619	13,628	85,608	64.2	58.5	8.9
Apr	239,146	153,420	139,628	2,090	137,505	13,792	85,726	64.2	58.4	9.0
May	239,313	153,700	139,808	2,244	137,508	13,892	85,613	64.2	58.4	9.0
June	239,489	153,409	139,385	2,224	137,125	14,024	86,080	64.1	58.2	9.1
July	239,671	153,358	139,450	2,250	136,993	13,908	86,313	64.0	58.2	9.1
Aug	239,871	153,674	139,754	2,373	137,290	13,920	86,198	64.1	58.3	9.1
Sept	240,071	154,004	140,107	2,268	137,932	13,897	86,067	64.1	58.4	9.0
Oct	240,269	154,057	140,297	2,257	138,167	13,759	86,213	64.1	58.4	8.9
Nov	240,441	153,937	140,614	2,262	138,304	13,323	86,503	64.0	58.5	8.7
Dec	240,584	153,887	140,790	2,349	138,411	13,097	86,697	64.0	58.5	8.5

[5] Not strictly comparable with earlier data due to population adjustments or other changes. See *Employment and Earnings* or population control adjustments to the Current Population Survey (CPS) at http://www.bls.gov/cps/documentation.htm#concepts for details on breaks in series.

[6] Beginning in 2000, data for agricultural employment are for agricultural and related industries; data for this series and for nonagricultural employment are not strictly comparable with data for earlier years. Because of independent seasonal adjustment for these two series, monthly data will not add to total civilian employment.

Note: Labor force data in Tables B–35 through B–44 are based on household interviews and relate to the calendar week including the 12th of the month. For definitions of terms, area samples used, historical comparability of the data, comparability with other series, etc., see *Employment and Earnings* or population control adjustments to the CPS at http://www.bls.gov/cps/documentation.htm#concepts.

Source: Department of Labor (Bureau of Labor Statistics).

TABLE B–36. Civilian employment and unemployment by sex and age, 1965–2011

[Thousands of persons 16 years of age and over; monthly data seasonally adjusted]

| Year or month | Civilian employment | | | | | | Unemployment | | | | | | |
| | Total | Males | | | Females | | | Total | Males | | | Females | | |
		Total	16–19 years	20 years and over	Total	16–19 years	20 years and over		Total	16–19 years	20 years and over	Total	16–19 years	20 years and over
1965	71,088	46,340	2,918	43,422	24,748	2,118	22,630	3,366	1,914	479	1,435	1,452	395	1,056
1966	72,895	46,919	3,253	43,668	25,976	2,468	23,510	2,875	1,551	432	1,120	1,324	405	921
1967	74,372	47,479	3,186	44,294	26,893	2,496	24,397	2,975	1,508	448	1,060	1,468	391	1,078
1968	75,920	48,114	3,255	44,859	27,807	2,526	25,281	2,817	1,419	426	993	1,397	412	985
1969	77,902	48,818	3,430	45,388	29,084	2,687	26,397	2,832	1,403	440	963	1,429	413	1,015
1970	78,678	48,990	3,409	45,581	29,688	2,735	26,952	4,093	2,238	599	1,638	1,855	506	1,349
1971	79,367	49,390	3,478	45,912	29,976	2,730	27,246	5,016	2,789	693	2,097	2,227	568	1,658
1972	82,153	50,896	3,765	47,130	31,257	2,980	28,276	4,882	2,659	711	1,948	2,222	598	1,625
1973	85,064	52,349	4,039	48,310	32,715	3,231	29,484	4,365	2,275	653	1,624	2,089	583	1,507
1974	86,794	53,024	4,103	48,922	33,769	3,345	30,424	5,156	2,714	757	1,957	2,441	665	1,777
1975	85,846	51,857	3,839	48,018	33,989	3,263	30,726	7,929	4,442	966	3,476	3,486	802	2,684
1976	88,752	53,138	3,947	49,190	35,615	3,389	32,226	7,406	4,036	939	3,098	3,369	780	2,588
1977	92,017	54,728	4,174	50,555	37,289	3,514	33,775	6,991	3,667	874	2,794	3,324	789	2,535
1978	96,048	56,479	4,336	52,143	39,569	3,734	35,836	6,202	3,142	813	2,328	3,061	769	2,292
1979	98,824	57,607	4,300	53,308	41,217	3,783	37,434	6,137	3,120	811	2,308	3,018	743	2,276
1980	99,303	57,186	4,085	53,101	42,117	3,625	38,492	7,637	4,267	913	3,353	3,370	755	2,615
1981	100,397	57,397	3,815	53,582	43,000	3,411	39,590	8,273	4,577	962	3,615	3,696	800	2,895
1982	99,526	56,271	3,379	52,891	43,256	3,170	40,086	10,678	6,179	1,090	5,089	4,499	886	3,613
1983	100,834	56,787	3,300	53,487	44,047	3,043	41,004	10,717	6,260	1,003	5,257	4,457	825	3,632
1984	105,005	59,091	3,322	55,769	45,915	3,122	42,793	8,539	4,744	812	3,932	3,794	687	3,107
1985	107,150	59,891	3,328	56,562	47,259	3,105	44,154	8,312	4,521	806	3,715	3,791	661	3,129
1986	109,597	60,892	3,323	57,569	48,706	3,149	45,556	8,237	4,530	779	3,751	3,707	675	3,032
1987	112,440	62,107	3,381	58,726	50,334	3,260	47,074	7,425	4,101	732	3,369	3,324	616	2,709
1988	114,968	63,273	3,492	59,781	51,696	3,313	48,383	6,701	3,655	667	2,987	3,046	558	2,487
1989	117,342	64,315	3,477	60,837	53,027	3,282	49,745	6,528	3,525	658	2,867	3,003	536	2,467
1990	118,793	65,104	3,427	61,678	53,689	3,154	50,535	7,047	3,906	667	3,239	3,140	544	2,596
1991	117,718	64,223	3,044	61,178	53,496	2,862	50,634	8,628	4,946	751	4,195	3,683	608	3,074
1992	118,492	64,440	2,944	61,496	54,052	2,724	51,328	9,613	5,523	806	4,717	4,090	621	3,469
1993	120,259	65,349	2,994	62,355	54,910	2,811	52,099	8,940	5,055	768	4,287	3,885	597	3,288
1994	123,060	66,450	3,156	63,294	56,610	3,005	53,606	7,996	4,367	740	3,627	3,629	580	3,049
1995	124,900	67,377	3,292	64,085	57,523	3,127	54,396	7,404	3,983	744	3,239	3,421	602	2,819
1996	126,708	68,207	3,310	64,897	58,501	3,190	55,311	7,236	3,880	733	3,146	3,356	573	2,783
1997	129,558	69,685	3,401	66,284	59,873	3,260	56,613	6,739	3,577	694	2,882	3,162	577	2,585
1998	131,463	70,693	3,558	67,135	60,771	3,493	57,278	6,210	3,266	686	2,580	2,944	519	2,424
1999	133,488	71,446	3,685	67,761	62,042	3,487	58,555	5,880	3,066	633	2,433	2,814	529	2,285
2000	136,891	73,305	3,671	69,634	63,586	3,519	60,067	5,692	2,975	599	2,376	2,717	483	2,235
2001	136,933	73,196	3,420	69,776	63,737	3,320	60,417	6,801	3,690	650	3,040	3,111	512	2,599
2002	136,485	72,903	3,169	69,734	63,582	3,162	60,420	8,378	4,597	700	3,896	3,781	553	3,228
2003	137,736	73,332	2,917	70,415	64,404	3,002	61,402	8,774	4,906	697	4,209	3,868	554	3,314
2004	139,252	74,524	2,952	71,572	64,728	2,955	61,773	8,149	4,456	664	3,791	3,694	543	3,150
2005	141,730	75,973	2,923	73,050	65,757	3,055	62,702	7,591	4,059	667	3,392	3,531	519	3,013
2006	144,427	77,502	3,071	74,431	66,925	3,091	63,834	7,001	3,753	622	3,131	3,247	496	2,751
2007	146,047	78,254	2,917	75,337	67,792	2,994	64,799	7,078	3,882	623	3,259	3,196	478	2,718
2008	145,362	77,486	2,736	74,750	67,876	2,837	65,039	8,924	5,033	736	4,297	3,891	549	3,342
2009	139,877	73,670	2,328	71,341	66,208	2,509	63,699	14,265	8,453	898	7,555	5,811	654	5,157
2010	139,064	73,359	2,129	71,230	65,705	2,249	63,456	14,825	8,626	863	7,763	6,199	665	5,534
2011	139,869	74,290	2,108	72,182	65,579	2,219	63,360	13,747	7,684	786	6,898	6,063	613	5,450
2010: Jan	138,500	72,644	2,116	70,529	65,856	2,314	63,542	14,953	8,879	921	7,958	6,075	630	5,444
Feb	138,665	72,811	2,165	70,645	65,854	2,313	63,541	15,039	8,861	862	7,999	6,178	666	5,512
Mar	138,836	73,103	2,174	70,929	65,733	2,307	63,426	15,128	8,913	924	7,989	6,215	666	5,549
Apr	139,306	73,536	2,184	71,352	65,770	2,317	63,453	15,221	8,890	896	7,994	6,332	657	5,674
May	139,340	73,587	2,170	71,416	65,753	2,262	63,491	14,876	8,562	855	7,707	6,314	756	5,558
June	139,137	73,386	2,048	71,338	65,751	2,218	63,533	14,517	8,560	851	7,709	5,957	639	5,318
July	139,139	73,534	2,131	71,403	65,604	2,206	63,399	14,609	8,493	869	7,624	6,116	649	5,467
Aug	139,338	73,632	2,094	71,538	65,706	2,300	63,406	14,735	8,561	856	7,705	6,174	670	5,504
Sept	139,344	73,590	2,044	71,545	65,754	2,214	63,540	14,574	8,459	829	7,629	6,116	652	5,464
Oct	139,072	73,522	2,112	71,410	65,551	2,199	63,352	14,636	8,324	867	7,457	6,312	730	5,582
Nov	138,937	73,360	2,232	71,128	65,577	2,177	63,400	15,104	8,644	802	7,842	6,460	628	5,832
Dec	139,220	73,607	2,113	71,494	65,613	2,184	63,429	14,393	8,202	813	7,390	6,191	638	5,553
2011: Jan	139,330	73,785	2,192	71,593	65,546	2,142	63,403	13,919	7,819	818	7,001	6,100	661	5,440
Feb	139,551	74,053	2,153	71,901	65,498	2,147	63,351	13,751	7,683	752	6,931	6,067	600	5,467
Mar	139,764	74,051	2,133	71,918	65,714	2,199	63,515	13,628	7,651	763	6,887	5,977	641	5,336
Apr	139,628	73,969	2,027	71,942	65,659	2,228	63,431	13,792	7,747	794	6,953	6,045	615	5,430
May	139,808	74,217	2,055	72,161	65,591	2,207	63,385	13,892	7,802	759	7,043	6,090	597	5,493
June	139,385	74,068	2,088	71,981	65,316	2,228	63,088	14,024	7,923	788	7,135	6,101	619	5,482
July	139,450	74,011	2,081	71,930	65,439	2,182	63,257	13,908	7,825	777	7,047	6,084	635	5,449
Aug	139,754	74,209	2,110	72,098	65,545	2,223	63,322	13,920	7,817	826	6,991	6,103	641	5,462
Sept	140,107	74,435	2,095	72,340	65,672	2,266	63,406	13,897	7,707	806	6,901	6,190	606	5,584
Oct	140,297	74,492	2,113	72,379	65,805	2,286	63,520	13,759	7,707	795	6,912	6,052	592	5,461
Nov	140,614	74,975	2,129	72,846	65,639	2,287	63,352	13,323	7,366	772	6,594	5,957	598	5,359
Dec	140,790	75,235	2,155	73,080	65,555	2,232	63,323	13,097	7,138	782	6,356	5,959	535	5,425

Note: See footnote 5 and Note, Table B–35.

Source: Department of Labor (Bureau of Labor Statistics).

[Thousands of persons 16 years of age and over; monthly data seasonally adjusted]

Year or month	All civilian workers	White[1]				Black and other[1]				Black or African American[1]			
		Total	Males	Females	Both sexes 16–19	Total	Males	Females	Both sexes 16–19	Total	Males	Females	Both sexes 16–19
1965	71,088	63,446	41,844	21,602	4,562	7,643	4,496	3,147	474	....	....	....	....
1966	72,895	65,021	42,331	22,690	5,176	7,877	4,588	3,289	545	....	....	....	....
1967	74,372	66,361	42,033	23,528	5,114	8,011	4,646	3,365	568	....	....	....	....
1968	75,920	67,750	43,411	24,339	5,195	8,169	4,702	3,467	584	....	....	....	....
1969	77,902	69,518	44,048	25,470	5,508	8,384	4,770	3,614	609	....	....	....	....
1970	78,678	70,217	44,178	26,039	5,571	8,464	4,813	3,650	574	....	....	....	....
1971	79,367	70,878	44,595	26,283	5,670	8,488	4,796	3,692	538	....	....	....	....
1972	82,153	73,370	45,944	27,426	6,173	8,783	4,952	3,832	573	7,802	4,368	3,433	509
1973	85,064	75,708	47,085	28,623	6,623	9,356	5,265	4,092	647	8,128	4,527	3,601	570
1974	86,794	77,184	47,674	29,511	6,796	9,610	5,352	4,258	652	8,203	4,527	3,677	554
1975	85,846	76,411	46,697	29,714	6,487	9,435	5,161	4,275	615	7,894	4,275	3,618	507
1976	88,752	78,853	47,775	31,078	6,724	9,899	5,363	4,536	611	8,227	4,404	3,823	508
1977	92,017	81,700	49,150	32,550	7,068	10,317	5,579	4,739	619	8,540	4,565	3,975	508
1978	96,048	84,936	50,544	34,392	7,367	11,112	5,936	5,177	703	9,102	4,796	4,307	571
1979	98,824	87,259	51,452	35,807	7,356	11,565	6,156	5,409	727	9,359	4,923	4,436	579
1980	99,303	87,715	51,127	36,587	7,021	11,588	6,059	5,529	689	9,313	4,798	4,515	547
1981	100,397	88,709	51,315	37,394	6,588	11,688	6,083	5,606	637	9,355	4,794	4,561	505
1982	99,526	87,903	50,287	37,615	5,984	11,624	5,983	5,641	565	9,189	4,637	4,552	428
1983	100,834	88,893	50,621	38,272	5,799	11,941	6,166	5,775	543	9,375	4,753	4,622	416
1984	105,005	92,120	52,462	39,659	5,836	12,885	6,629	6,256	607	10,119	5,124	4,995	474
1985	107,150	93,736	53,046	40,690	5,768	13,414	6,845	6,569	666	10,501	5,270	5,231	532
1986	109,597	95,660	53,785	41,876	5,792	13,937	7,107	6,830	681	10,814	5,428	5,386	536
1987	112,440	97,789	54,647	43,142	5,898	14,652	7,459	7,192	742	11,309	5,661	5,648	587
1988	114,968	99,812	55,550	44,262	6,030	15,156	7,722	7,434	774	11,658	5,824	5,834	601
1989	117,342	101,584	56,352	45,232	5,946	15,757	7,963	7,795	813	11,953	5,928	6,025	625
1990	118,793	102,261	56,703	45,558	5,779	16,533	8,401	8,131	801	12,175	5,995	6,180	598
1991	117,718	101,182	55,797	45,385	5,216	16,536	8,426	8,110	690	12,074	5,961	6,113	494
1992	118,492	101,669	55,959	45,710	4,985	16,823	8,482	8,342	684	12,151	5,930	6,221	492
1993	120,259	103,045	56,656	46,390	5,113	17,214	8,693	8,521	691	12,382	6,047	6,334	494
1994	123,060	105,190	57,452	47,738	5,398	17,870	8,998	8,872	763	12,835	6,241	6,595	552
1995	124,900	106,490	58,146	48,344	5,593	18,409	9,231	9,179	826	13,279	6,422	6,857	586
1996	126,708	107,808	58,888	48,920	5,667	18,900	9,319	9,580	832	13,542	6,456	7,086	613
1997	129,558	109,856	59,998	49,859	5,807	19,701	9,687	10,014	853	13,969	6,607	7,362	631
1998	131,463	110,931	60,604	50,327	6,089	20,532	10,089	10,443	962	14,556	6,871	7,685	736
1999	133,488	112,235	61,139	51,096	6,204	21,253	10,307	10,945	968	15,056	7,027	8,029	691
2000	136,891	114,424	62,289	52,136	6,160	....	....	....	....	15,156	7,082	8,073	711
2001	136,933	114,430	62,212	52,218	5,817	....	....	....	....	15,006	6,938	8,068	637
2002	136,485	114,013	61,849	52,164	5,441	....	....	....	....	14,872	6,959	7,914	611
2003	137,736	114,235	61,866	52,369	5,064	....	....	....	....	14,739	6,820	7,919	516
2004	139,252	115,239	62,712	52,527	5,039	....	....	....	....	14,909	6,912	7,997	520
2005	141,730	116,949	63,763	53,186	5,105	....	....	....	....	15,313	7,155	8,158	536
2006	144,427	118,833	64,883	53,950	5,215	....	....	....	....	15,765	7,354	8,410	618
2007	146,047	119,792	65,289	54,503	4,990	....	....	....	....	16,051	7,500	8,551	566
2008	145,362	119,126	64,624	54,501	4,697	....	....	....	....	15,953	7,398	8,554	541
2009	139,877	114,996	61,630	53,366	4,138	....	....	....	....	15,025	6,817	8,208	442
2010	139,064	114,168	61,252	52,916	3,733	....	....	....	....	15,010	6,865	8,145	386
2011	139,869	114,690	61,920	52,770	3,691	....	....	....	....	15,051	6,953	8,098	380
2010: Jan	138,500	114,013	60,741	53,272	3,748	....	....	....	....	14,846	6,759	8,087	442
Feb	138,665	113,935	60,904	53,031	3,801	....	....	....	....	14,906	6,759	8,146	400
Mar	138,836	114,120	61,113	53,006	3,790	....	....	....	....	14,922	6,783	8,139	415
Apr	139,306	114,349	61,366	52,983	3,859	....	....	....	....	15,014	6,882	8,131	418
May	139,340	114,311	61,444	52,866	3,741	....	....	....	....	15,194	6,983	8,211	422
June	139,137	114,212	61,312	52,901	3,632	....	....	....	....	15,038	6,842	8,196	370
July	139,139	114,326	61,484	52,842	3,712	....	....	....	....	14,965	6,879	8,086	382
Aug	139,338	114,421	61,479	52,942	3,747	....	....	....	....	14,994	6,896	8,098	375
Sept	139,344	114,456	61,509	52,947	3,673	....	....	....	....	14,911	6,827	8,084	314
Oct	139,072	113,992	61,265	52,728	3,696	....	....	....	....	15,094	6,923	8,171	362
Nov	138,937	113,771	61,059	52,712	3,768	....	....	....	....	15,125	6,929	8,197	373
Dec	139,220	114,150	61,353	52,797	3,671	....	....	....	....	15,098	6,910	8,188	363
2011: Jan	139,330	114,263	61,515	52,748	3,728	....	....	....	....	15,025	6,887	8,138	365
Feb	139,551	114,294	61,692	52,602	3,644	....	....	....	....	15,078	6,918	8,160	386
Mar	139,764	114,652	61,659	52,994	3,675	....	....	....	....	15,047	6,943	8,104	388
Apr	139,628	114,603	61,661	52,942	3,629	....	....	....	....	14,964	6,904	8,060	403
May	139,808	114,827	61,968	52,859	3,638	....	....	....	....	14,862	6,825	8,037	375
June	139,385	114,428	61,751	52,677	3,660	....	....	....	....	14,875	6,939	7,936	401
July	139,450	114,497	61,775	52,722	3,641	....	....	....	....	14,812	6,889	7,923	363
Aug	139,754	114,704	61,960	52,743	3,720	....	....	....	....	14,965	6,888	8,077	335
Sept	140,107	114,818	62,075	52,743	3,728	....	....	....	....	15,224	6,986	8,238	377
Oct	140,297	114,837	62,005	52,832	3,761	....	....	....	....	15,351	7,054	8,296	390
Nov	140,614	115,130	62,411	52,719	3,751	....	....	....	....	15,151	7,027	8,124	388
Dec	140,790	115,254	62,576	52,678	3,736	....	....	....	....	15,248	7,160	8,088	393

[1] Beginning in 2003, persons who selected this race group only. Prior to 2003, persons who selected more than one race were included in the group they identified as the main race. Data for "black or African American" were for "black" prior to 2003. Data discontinued for "black and other" series. See *Employment and Earnings* or concepts and methodology of the Current Population Survey (CPS) at http://www.bls.gov/cps/documentation.htm#concepts for details.

Note: Beginning with data for 2000, detail will not sum to total because data for all race groups are not shown here.
See footnote 5 and Note, Table B–35.

Source: Department of Labor (Bureau of Labor Statistics).

[Thousands of persons 16 years of age and over; monthly data seasonally adjusted]

Year or month	All civilian workers	White [1]				Black and other [1]				Black or African American [1]			
		Total	Males	Females	Both sexes 16–19	Total	Males	Females	Both sexes 16–19	Total	Males	Females	Both sexes 16–19
1965	3,366	2,691	1,556	1,135	705	678	360	318	171	....	....	....	....
1966	2,875	2,255	1,241	1,014	651	622	310	312	186	....	....	....	....
1967	2,975	2,338	1,208	1,130	635	638	300	338	203	....	....	....	....
1968	2,817	2,226	1,142	1,084	644	590	277	313	194	....	....	....	....
1969	2,832	2,260	1,137	1,123	660	571	267	304	193	....	....	....	....
1970	4,093	3,339	1,857	1,482	871	754	380	374	235	....	....	....	....
1971	5,016	4,085	2,309	1,777	1,011	930	481	450	249	....	....	....	....
1972	4,882	3,906	2,173	1,733	1,021	977	486	491	288	906	448	458	279
1973	4,365	3,442	1,836	1,606	955	924	440	484	280	846	395	451	262
1974	5,156	4,097	2,169	1,927	1,104	1,058	544	514	318	965	494	470	297
1975	7,929	6,421	3,627	2,794	1,413	1,507	815	692	355	1,369	741	629	330
1976	7,406	5,914	3,258	2,656	1,364	1,492	779	713	355	1,334	698	637	330
1977	6,991	5,441	2,883	2,558	1,284	1,550	784	766	379	1,393	698	695	354
1978	6,202	4,698	2,411	2,287	1,189	1,505	731	774	394	1,330	641	690	360
1979	6,137	4,664	2,405	2,260	1,193	1,473	714	759	362	1,319	636	683	333
1980	7,637	5,884	3,345	2,540	1,291	1,752	922	830	377	1,553	815	738	343
1981	8,273	6,343	3,580	2,762	1,374	1,930	997	933	388	1,731	891	840	357
1982	10,678	8,241	4,846	3,395	1,534	2,437	1,334	1,104	443	2,142	1,167	975	396
1983	10,717	8,128	4,859	3,270	1,387	2,588	1,401	1,187	441	2,272	1,213	1,059	392
1984	8,539	6,372	3,600	2,772	1,116	2,167	1,144	1,022	384	1,914	1,003	911	353
1985	8,312	6,191	3,426	2,765	1,074	2,121	1,095	1,026	394	1,864	951	913	357
1986	8,237	6,140	3,433	2,708	1,070	2,097	1,097	999	383	1,840	946	894	347
1987	7,425	5,501	3,132	2,369	995	1,924	969	955	353	1,684	826	858	312
1988	6,701	4,944	2,766	2,177	910	1,757	888	869	316	1,547	771	776	288
1989	6,528	4,770	2,636	2,135	863	1,757	889	868	331	1,544	773	772	300
1990	7,047	5,186	2,935	2,251	903	1,860	971	889	308	1,565	806	758	268
1991	8,628	6,560	3,859	2,701	1,029	2,068	1,087	981	330	1,723	890	833	280
1992	9,613	7,169	4,209	2,959	1,037	2,444	1,314	1,130	390	2,011	1,067	944	324
1993	8,940	6,655	3,828	2,827	992	2,285	1,227	1,058	373	1,844	971	872	313
1994	7,996	5,892	3,275	2,617	960	2,104	1,092	1,011	360	1,666	848	818	300
1995	7,404	5,459	2,999	2,460	952	1,945	984	961	394	1,538	762	777	325
1996	7,236	5,300	2,896	2,404	939	1,936	984	952	367	1,592	808	784	310
1997	6,739	4,836	2,641	2,195	912	1,903	935	967	359	1,560	747	813	302
1998	6,210	4,484	2,431	2,053	876	1,726	835	891	329	1,426	671	756	281
1999	5,880	4,273	2,274	1,999	844	1,606	792	814	318	1,309	626	684	268
2000	5,692	4,121	2,177	1,944	795	....	....	....	....	1,241	620	621	230
2001	6,801	4,969	2,754	2,215	845	....	....	....	....	1,416	709	706	260
2002	8,378	6,137	3,459	2,678	925	....	....	....	....	1,693	835	858	260
2003	8,774	6,311	3,643	2,668	909	....	....	....	....	1,787	891	895	255
2004	8,149	5,847	3,282	2,565	890	....	....	....	....	1,729	860	868	241
2005	7,591	5,350	2,931	2,419	845	....	....	....	....	1,700	844	856	267
2006	7,001	5,002	2,730	2,271	794	....	....	....	....	1,549	774	775	253
2007	7,078	5,143	2,869	2,274	805	....	....	....	....	1,445	752	693	235
2008	8,924	6,509	3,727	2,782	947	....	....	....	....	1,788	949	839	246
2009	14,265	10,648	6,421	4,227	1,157	....	....	....	....	2,606	1,448	1,159	288
2010	14,825	10,916	6,476	4,440	1,128	....	....	....	....	2,852	1,550	1,302	291
2011	13,747	9,889	5,631	4,257	1,024	....	....	....	....	2,831	1,502	1,329	267
2010: Jan	14,953	10,875	6,643	4,232	1,127	....	....	....	....	2,927	1,586	1,341	318
Feb	15,039	11,119	6,615	4,504	1,129	....	....	....	....	2,833	1,590	1,243	297
Mar	15,128	11,061	6,561	4,500	1,187	....	....	....	....	2,986	1,722	1,264	293
Apr	15,221	11,319	6,802	4,517	1,177	....	....	....	....	2,940	1,549	1,391	259
May	14,876	10,988	6,408	4,580	1,228	....	....	....	....	2,769	1,486	1,283	270
June	14,517	10,742	6,386	4,356	1,096	....	....	....	....	2,702	1,536	1,166	258
July	14,609	10,734	6,367	4,367	1,121	....	....	....	....	2,783	1,502	1,281	272
Aug	14,735	10,843	6,461	4,382	1,143	....	....	....	....	2,874	1,557	1,317	301
Sept	14,574	10,764	6,362	4,402	1,119	....	....	....	....	2,843	1,555	1,288	294
Oct	14,636	10,763	6,292	4,471	1,119	....	....	....	....	2,854	1,508	1,346	343
Nov	15,104	11,140	6,548	4,592	1,005	....	....	....	....	2,898	1,520	1,378	323
Dec	14,393	10,569	6,159	4,410	1,079	....	....	....	....	2,836	1,483	1,352	286
2011: Jan	13,919	10,029	5,744	4,284	1,087	....	....	....	....	2,804	1,501	1,304	296
Feb	13,751	9,979	5,676	4,303	992	....	....	....	....	2,745	1,447	1,298	241
Mar	13,628	9,837	5,612	4,225	1,007	....	....	....	....	2,782	1,500	1,282	280
Apr	13,792	10,039	5,755	4,284	1,031	....	....	....	....	2,883	1,530	1,353	283
May	13,892	9,985	5,669	4,316	929	....	....	....	....	2,868	1,550	1,318	259
June	14,024	10,098	5,819	4,278	1,019	....	....	....	....	2,865	1,508	1,358	265
July	13,908	10,061	5,745	4,315	1,092	....	....	....	....	2,803	1,487	1,316	233
Aug	13,920	9,901	5,646	4,255	1,097	....	....	....	....	2,992	1,625	1,367	289
Sept	13,897	9,883	5,593	4,290	1,002	....	....	....	....	2,872	1,502	1,371	291
Oct	13,759	9,967	5,743	4,224	1,040	....	....	....	....	2,716	1,431	1,285	234
Nov	13,323	9,522	5,350	4,172	1,015	....	....	....	....	2,783	1,474	1,308	255
Dec	13,097	9,288	5,175	4,113	952	....	....	....	....	2,862	1,481	1,382	286

[1] See footnote 1 and Note, Table B–37.

Note: See footnote 5 and Note, Table B–35.

Source: Department of Labor (Bureau of Labor Statistics).

[Percent [1]; monthly data seasonally adjusted]

Year or month	Labor force participation rate							Employment/population ratio						
	All civilian workers	Males	Females	Both sexes 16–19 years	White [2]	Black and other [2]	Black or African American [2]	All civilian workers	Males	Females	Both sexes 16–19 years	White [2]	Black and other [2]	Black or African American [2]
1965	58.9	80.7	39.3	45.7	58.4	62.9	....	56.2	77.5	37.1	38.9	56.0	57.8	....
1966	59.2	80.4	40.3	48.2	58.7	63.0	....	56.9	77.9	38.3	42.1	56.8	58.4	....
1967	59.6	80.4	41.1	48.4	59.2	62.8	....	57.3	78.0	39.0	42.2	57.2	58.2	....
1968	59.6	80.1	41.6	48.3	59.3	62.2	....	57.5	77.8	39.6	42.2	57.4	58.0	....
1969	60.1	79.8	42.7	49.4	59.9	62.1	....	58.0	77.6	40.7	43.4	58.0	58.1	....
1970	60.4	79.7	43.3	49.9	60.2	61.8	....	57.4	76.2	40.8	42.3	57.5	56.8	....
1971	60.2	79.1	43.4	49.7	60.1	60.9	....	56.6	74.9	40.4	41.3	56.8	54.9	....
1972	60.4	78.9	43.9	51.9	60.4	60.2	59.9	57.0	75.0	41.0	43.5	57.4	54.1	53.7
1973	60.8	78.8	44.7	53.7	60.8	60.5	60.2	57.8	75.5	42.0	45.9	58.2	55.0	54.5
1974	61.3	78.7	45.7	54.8	61.4	60.3	59.8	57.8	74.9	42.6	46.0	58.3	54.3	53.5
1975	61.2	77.9	46.3	54.0	61.5	59.6	58.8	56.1	71.7	42.0	43.3	56.7	51.4	50.1
1976	61.6	77.5	47.3	54.5	61.8	59.8	59.0	56.8	72.0	43.2	44.2	57.5	52.0	50.8
1977	62.3	77.7	48.4	56.0	62.5	60.4	59.8	57.9	72.8	44.5	46.1	58.6	52.5	51.4
1978	63.2	77.9	50.0	57.8	63.3	62.2	61.5	59.3	73.8	46.4	48.3	60.0	54.7	53.6
1979	63.7	77.8	50.9	57.9	63.9	62.2	61.4	59.9	73.8	47.5	48.5	60.6	55.2	53.8
1980	63.8	77.4	51.5	56.7	64.1	61.7	61.0	59.2	72.0	47.7	46.6	60.0	53.6	52.3
1981	63.9	77.0	52.1	55.4	64.3	61.3	60.8	59.0	71.3	48.0	44.6	60.0	52.6	51.3
1982	64.0	76.6	52.6	54.1	64.3	61.6	61.0	57.8	69.0	47.7	41.5	58.8	50.9	49.4
1983	64.0	76.4	52.9	53.5	64.3	62.1	61.5	57.9	68.8	48.0	41.5	58.9	51.0	49.5
1984	64.4	76.4	53.6	53.9	64.6	62.6	62.2	59.5	70.7	49.5	43.7	60.5	53.6	52.3
1985	64.8	76.3	54.5	54.5	65.0	63.3	62.9	60.1	70.9	50.4	44.4	61.0	54.7	53.4
1986	65.3	76.3	55.3	54.7	65.5	63.7	63.3	60.7	71.0	51.4	44.6	61.5	55.4	54.1
1987	65.6	76.2	56.0	54.7	65.8	64.3	63.8	61.5	71.5	52.5	45.5	62.3	56.8	55.6
1988	65.9	76.2	56.6	55.3	66.2	64.0	63.8	62.3	72.0	53.4	46.8	63.1	57.4	56.3
1989	66.5	76.4	57.4	55.9	66.7	64.7	64.2	63.0	72.5	54.3	47.5	63.8	58.2	56.9
1990	66.5	76.4	57.5	53.7	66.9	64.4	64.0	62.8	72.0	54.3	45.3	63.7	57.9	56.7
1991	66.2	75.8	57.4	51.6	66.6	63.8	63.3	61.7	70.4	53.7	42.0	62.6	56.7	55.4
1992	66.4	75.8	57.8	51.3	66.8	64.6	63.9	61.5	69.8	53.8	41.0	62.4	56.4	54.9
1993	66.3	75.4	57.9	51.5	66.8	63.8	63.2	61.7	70.0	54.1	41.7	62.7	56.3	55.0
1994	66.6	75.1	58.8	52.7	67.1	63.9	63.4	62.5	70.4	55.3	43.4	63.5	57.2	56.1
1995	66.6	75.0	58.9	53.5	67.1	64.3	63.7	62.9	70.8	55.6	44.2	63.8	58.1	57.1
1996	66.8	74.9	59.3	52.3	67.2	64.6	64.1	63.2	70.9	56.0	43.5	64.1	58.6	57.4
1997	67.1	75.0	59.8	51.6	67.5	65.2	64.7	63.8	71.3	56.8	43.4	64.6	59.4	58.2
1998	67.1	74.9	59.8	52.8	67.3	66.0	65.6	64.1	71.6	57.1	45.1	64.7	60.9	59.7
1999	67.1	74.7	60.0	52.0	67.3	65.9	65.8	64.3	71.6	57.4	44.7	64.8	61.3	60.6
2000	67.1	74.8	59.9	52.0	67.3	....	65.8	64.4	71.9	57.5	45.2	64.9	....	60.9
2001	66.8	74.4	59.8	49.6	67.0	....	65.3	63.7	70.9	57.0	42.3	64.2	....	59.7
2002	66.6	74.1	59.6	47.4	66.8	....	64.8	62.7	69.7	56.3	39.6	63.4	....	58.1
2003	66.2	73.5	59.5	44.5	66.5	....	64.3	62.3	68.9	56.1	36.8	63.0	....	57.4
2004	66.0	73.3	59.2	43.9	66.3	....	63.8	62.3	69.2	56.0	36.4	63.1	....	57.2
2005	66.0	73.3	59.3	43.7	66.3	....	64.2	62.7	69.6	56.2	36.5	63.4	....	57.7
2006	66.2	73.5	59.4	43.7	66.5	....	64.1	63.1	70.1	56.6	36.9	63.8	....	58.4
2007	66.0	73.2	59.3	41.3	66.4	....	63.7	63.0	69.8	56.6	34.8	63.6	....	58.4
2008	66.0	73.0	59.5	40.2	66.3	....	63.7	62.2	68.5	56.2	32.6	62.8	....	57.3
2009	65.4	72.0	59.2	37.5	65.8	....	62.4	59.3	64.5	54.4	28.4	60.2	....	53.2
2010	64.7	71.2	58.6	34.9	65.1	....	62.2	58.5	63.7	53.6	25.9	59.4	....	52.3
2011	64.1	70.5	58.1	34.1	64.5	....	61.4	58.4	63.9	53.2	25.8	59.4	....	51.7
2010: Jan	64.8	71.1	58.9	35.1	65.2	....	62.3	58.5	63.4	53.9	26.0	59.6	....	52.0
Feb	64.9	71.2	58.9	35.3	65.3	....	62.1	58.5	63.5	53.9	26.3	59.5	....	52.2
Mar	64.9	71.4	58.8	35.7	65.3	....	62.6	58.5	63.7	53.7	26.4	59.5	....	52.2
Apr	65.1	71.7	58.9	35.7	65.5	....	62.7	58.7	64.0	53.7	26.5	59.6	....	52.5
May	64.9	71.4	58.8	35.7	65.3	....	62.7	58.7	64.0	53.7	26.2	59.6	....	53.0
June	64.6	71.2	58.5	34.0	65.1	....	61.8	58.5	63.8	53.6	25.2	59.5	....	52.4
July	64.6	71.2	58.5	34.7	65.1	....	61.8	58.5	63.8	53.5	25.7	59.5	....	52.1
Aug	64.7	71.3	58.5	35.1	65.2	....	62.1	58.5	63.9	53.5	26.1	59.5	....	52.1
Sept	64.6	71.1	58.5	34.1	65.1	....	61.7	58.5	63.8	53.5	25.3	59.5	....	51.8
Oct	64.4	70.8	58.4	35.1	64.8	....	62.3	58.3	63.6	53.3	25.6	59.2	....	52.4
Nov	64.5	70.9	58.5	34.8	64.8	....	62.4	58.2	63.4	53.3	26.2	59.1	....	52.4
Dec	64.3	70.7	58.3	34.3	64.7	....	62.1	58.3	63.6	53.3	25.6	59.2	....	52.2
2011: Jan	64.2	70.5	58.3	34.5	64.6	....	61.6	58.4	63.7	53.3	25.7	59.4	....	51.9
Feb	64.2	70.5	58.2	33.5	64.5	....	61.5	58.4	63.9	53.3	25.5	59.3	....	52.0
Mar	64.2	70.4	58.3	34.1	64.6	....	61.5	58.5	63.8	53.4	25.7	59.5	....	51.9
Apr	64.2	70.4	58.3	33.7	64.7	....	61.5	58.4	63.7	53.3	25.3	59.5	....	51.5
May	64.2	70.6	58.2	33.5	64.7	....	61.0	58.4	63.9	53.3	25.4	59.5	....	51.1
June	64.1	70.5	58.0	34.1	64.5	....	61.0	58.2	63.7	53.0	25.7	59.3	....	51.1
July	64.0	70.3	58.0	33.9	64.5	....	60.5	58.2	63.6	53.1	25.4	59.3	....	50.9
Aug	64.1	70.4	58.1	34.6	64.5	....	61.6	58.3	63.7	53.1	25.9	59.4	....	51.3
Sept	64.1	70.5	58.2	34.5	64.5	....	62.0	58.4	63.9	53.2	26.1	59.4	....	52.1
Oct	64.1	70.5	58.1	34.6	64.5	....	61.8	58.4	63.9	53.2	26.3	59.3	....	52.5
Nov	64.0	70.5	57.9	34.6	64.4	....	61.3	58.5	64.2	53.1	26.4	59.5	....	51.8
Dec	64.0	70.5	57.8	34.2	64.3	....	61.8	58.5	64.4	53.0	26.3	59.5	....	52.1

[1] Civilian labor force or civilian employment as percent of civilian noninstitutional population in group specified.
[2] See footnote 1, Table B–37.

Note: Data relate to persons 16 years of age and over.
See footnote 5 and Note, Table B–35.

Source: Department of Labor (Bureau of Labor Statistics).

TABLE B–40. Civilian labor force participation rate by demographic characteristic, 1972–2011

[Percent [1]; monthly data seasonally adjusted]

Year or month	All civilian workers	White [2]							Black or African American [2]						
		Total	Males			Females			Total	Males			Females		
			Total	16–19 years	20 years and over	Total	16–19 years	20 years and over		Total	16–19 years	20 years and over	Total	16–19 years	20 years and over
1972	60.4	60.4	79.6	60.1	82.0	43.2	48.1	42.7	59.9	73.6	46.3	78.5	48.7	32.2	51.2
1973	60.8	60.8	79.4	62.0	81.6	44.1	50.1	43.5	60.2	73.4	45.7	78.4	49.3	34.2	51.6
1974	61.3	61.4	79.4	62.9	81.4	45.2	51.7	44.4	59.8	72.9	46.7	77.6	49.0	33.4	51.4
1975	61.2	61.5	78.7	61.9	80.7	45.9	51.5	45.3	58.8	70.9	42.6	76.0	49.8	32.9	51.1
1976	61.6	61.8	78.4	62.3	80.3	46.9	52.8	46.2	59.0	70.0	41.3	75.4	49.8	32.9	52.5
1977	62.3	62.5	78.5	64.0	80.2	48.0	54.5	47.3	59.8	70.6	43.2	75.6	50.8	32.9	53.6
1978	63.2	63.3	78.6	65.0	80.1	49.4	56.7	48.7	61.5	71.5	44.9	76.2	53.1	37.3	55.5
1979	63.7	63.9	78.6	64.8	80.1	50.5	57.4	49.8	61.4	71.3	43.6	76.3	53.1	36.8	55.4
1980	63.8	64.1	78.2	63.7	79.8	51.2	56.2	50.6	61.0	70.3	43.2	75.1	53.1	34.9	55.6
1981	63.9	64.3	77.9	62.4	79.5	51.9	55.4	51.5	60.8	70.0	41.6	74.5	53.5	34.0	56.0
1982	64.0	64.3	77.4	60.0	79.2	52.4	55.0	52.2	61.0	70.1	39.8	74.7	53.7	33.5	56.2
1983	64.0	64.3	77.1	59.4	78.9	52.7	54.5	52.5	61.5	70.6	39.9	75.2	54.2	33.0	56.8
1984	64.4	64.6	77.1	59.0	78.7	53.3	55.4	53.1	62.2	70.8	41.7	74.8	55.2	35.0	57.6
1985	64.8	65.0	77.0	59.7	78.5	54.1	55.2	54.0	62.9	70.8	44.6	74.4	56.5	37.9	58.6
1986	65.3	65.5	76.9	59.3	78.5	55.0	56.3	54.9	63.3	71.2	43.7	74.8	56.9	39.1	58.9
1987	65.6	65.8	76.8	59.0	78.4	55.7	56.5	55.6	63.8	71.1	43.6	74.7	58.0	39.6	60.0
1988	65.9	66.2	76.9	60.0	78.3	56.4	57.2	56.3	63.8	71.0	43.8	74.6	58.0	37.9	60.1
1989	66.5	66.7	77.1	61.0	78.5	57.2	57.1	57.2	64.2	71.0	44.6	74.4	58.7	40.4	60.6
1990	66.5	66.9	77.1	59.6	78.5	57.4	55.3	57.6	64.0	71.0	40.7	75.0	58.3	36.8	60.6
1991	66.2	66.6	76.5	57.3	78.0	57.4	54.1	57.6	63.3	70.4	37.3	74.6	57.5	33.5	60.0
1992	66.4	66.8	76.5	56.9	78.0	57.7	52.5	58.1	63.9	70.7	40.6	74.3	58.5	35.2	60.8
1993	66.3	66.8	76.2	56.6	77.7	58.0	53.5	58.3	63.2	69.6	39.5	73.2	57.9	34.6	60.2
1994	66.6	67.1	75.9	57.7	77.3	58.9	55.1	59.2	63.4	69.1	40.8	72.5	58.7	36.3	60.9
1995	66.6	67.1	75.7	58.5	77.1	59.0	55.5	59.2	63.7	69.0	40.1	72.5	59.5	39.8	61.4
1996	66.8	67.2	75.8	57.1	77.3	59.1	54.7	59.4	64.1	68.7	39.5	72.3	60.4	38.9	62.6
1997	67.1	67.5	75.9	56.1	77.5	59.5	54.1	59.9	64.7	68.3	37.4	72.2	61.7	39.9	64.0
1998	67.1	67.3	75.6	56.6	77.2	59.4	55.4	59.7	65.6	69.0	40.7	72.5	62.8	42.5	64.8
1999	67.1	67.3	75.6	56.4	77.2	59.6	54.5	59.9	65.8	68.7	38.6	72.4	63.5	38.8	66.1
2000	67.1	67.3	75.5	56.5	77.1	59.5	54.5	59.9	65.8	69.2	39.2	72.8	63.1	39.6	65.4
2001	66.8	67.0	75.1	53.7	76.9	59.4	52.4	59.9	65.3	68.4	37.9	72.1	62.8	37.3	65.2
2002	66.6	66.8	74.8	50.3	76.7	59.3	50.8	60.0	64.8	68.4	37.3	72.1	61.8	34.7	64.4
2003	66.2	66.5	74.2	47.5	76.3	59.2	47.9	59.9	64.3	67.3	31.1	71.5	61.9	33.7	64.6
2004	66.0	66.3	74.1	47.4	76.2	58.9	46.7	59.7	63.8	66.7	30.0	70.9	61.5	32.8	64.2
2005	66.0	66.3	74.1	46.2	76.2	58.9	47.6	59.7	64.2	67.3	32.6	71.3	61.6	32.2	64.4
2006	66.2	66.5	74.3	46.9	76.4	59.0	46.6	59.9	64.1	67.0	32.3	71.1	61.7	35.6	64.2
2007	66.0	66.4	74.0	44.3	76.3	59.0	44.6	60.1	63.7	66.8	29.4	71.2	61.1	31.2	64.0
2008	66.0	66.3	73.7	43.0	76.1	59.2	43.3	60.3	63.7	66.7	29.1	71.1	61.3	29.7	64.3
2009	65.4	65.8	72.8	40.3	75.3	59.1	40.9	60.4	62.4	65.0	26.4	69.6	60.3	27.9	63.4
2010	64.7	65.1	72.0	37.4	74.6	58.5	38.0	59.9	62.2	65.0	25.8	69.5	59.9	25.1	63.2
2011	64.1	64.5	71.3	36.1	73.9	58.0	37.5	59.4	61.4	64.2	25.7	68.4	59.1	24.2	62.2
2010: Jan	64.8	65.2	71.9	37.5	74.5	58.8	37.5	60.3	62.3	65.0	27.6	69.3	60.1	29.1	63.1
Feb	64.9	65.3	72.0	37.1	74.6	58.9	38.9	60.2	62.1	64.9	26.6	69.3	59.8	25.4	63.1
Mar	64.9	65.3	72.1	38.3	74.7	58.8	38.5	60.2	62.6	66.0	27.5	70.4	59.9	25.5	63.1
Apr	65.1	65.5	72.6	38.6	75.2	58.8	39.2	60.1	62.7	65.4	25.4	69.9	60.5	25.2	63.9
May	64.9	65.3	72.2	38.0	74.8	58.7	39.0	60.0	62.7	65.6	23.7	70.4	60.3	28.2	63.3
June	64.6	65.1	72.0	36.2	74.7	58.5	37.2	59.9	61.8	64.8	24.6	69.4	59.4	22.7	62.8
July	64.6	65.1	72.1	37.5	74.7	58.4	37.6	59.8	61.8	64.7	25.9	69.1	59.4	23.4	62.7
Aug	64.7	65.2	72.1	37.1	74.8	58.5	39.0	59.8	62.1	65.2	27.5	69.4	59.6	23.5	63.0
Sept	64.6	65.1	72.0	36.5	74.7	58.4	38.2	59.8	61.7	64.6	24.3	69.1	59.3	21.6	62.7
Oct	64.4	64.8	71.6	37.1	74.2	58.2	38.0	59.6	62.3	64.8	27.3	69.0	60.1	26.1	63.3
Nov	64.5	64.8	71.6	38.2	74.1	58.3	36.3	59.8	62.4	64.9	27.0	69.1	60.4	25.9	63.6
Dec	64.3	64.7	71.5	37.5	74.0	58.2	36.8	59.7	62.1	64.4	23.4	68.9	60.1	26.0	63.3
2011: Jan	64.2	64.6	71.2	37.6	73.7	58.2	37.2	59.6	61.6	64.1	26.5	68.3	59.5	24.0	62.7
Feb	64.2	64.5	71.3	36.0	73.9	58.0	36.0	59.5	61.5	63.9	24.4	68.2	59.6	23.6	62.8
Mar	64.2	64.6	71.1	35.7	73.8	58.3	37.1	59.8	61.5	64.4	25.6	68.6	59.0	25.5	62.1
Apr	64.2	64.7	71.2	35.2	73.9	58.3	37.4	59.7	61.5	64.3	25.8	68.5	59.2	26.8	62.1
May	64.2	64.7	71.4	34.2	74.2	58.2	37.1	59.7	61.0	63.7	26.2	67.8	58.7	22.6	62.0
June	64.1	64.5	71.3	35.7	74.0	58.0	37.4	59.4	61.0	64.2	26.4	68.3	58.3	24.9	61.3
July	64.0	64.5	71.2	36.1	73.8	58.0	37.8	59.4	60.5	63.6	23.9	67.9	57.9	22.1	61.1
Aug	64.1	64.5	71.2	37.4	73.8	58.0	37.9	59.3	61.6	64.6	26.2	68.7	59.1	22.1	62.4
Sept	64.1	64.5	71.3	36.2	73.9	58.0	37.8	59.3	62.0	64.3	26.3	68.3	60.1	25.4	63.2
Oct	64.1	64.5	71.3	36.9	73.9	57.9	38.3	59.3	61.8	64.2	24.0	68.5	59.9	24.5	63.0
Nov	64.0	64.4	71.3	36.4	73.9	57.8	38.3	59.1	61.3	64.2	24.1	68.5	58.9	26.0	61.8
Dec	64.0	64.3	71.2	36.1	73.8	57.6	37.4	59.0	61.8	65.2	29.2	69.0	59.1	23.9	62.2

[1] Civilian labor force as percent of civilian noninstitutional population in group specified.

[2] See footnote 1, Table B–37.

Note: Data relate to persons 16 years of age and over.

See footnote 5 and Note, Table B–35.

Source: Department of Labor (Bureau of Labor Statistics).

[Percent [1]; monthly data seasonally adjusted]

Year or month	All civilian workers	White [2] Total	White Males Total	White Males 16–19 years	White Males 20 years and over	White Females Total	White Females 16–19 years	White Females 20 years and over	Black or African American [2] Total	Black Males Total	Black Males 16–19 years	Black Males 20 years and over	Black Females Total	Black Females 16–19 years	Black Females 20 years and over
1972	57.0	57.4	76.0	51.5	79.0	40.7	41.3	40.6	53.7	66.8	31.6	73.0	43.0	19.2	46.5
1973	57.8	58.2	76.5	54.3	79.2	41.8	43.6	41.6	54.5	67.5	32.8	73.7	43.8	22.0	47.2
1974	57.8	58.3	75.9	54.4	78.6	42.4	44.3	42.2	53.5	65.8	31.4	71.9	43.5	20.9	46.9
1975	56.1	56.7	73.0	50.6	75.7	42.0	42.5	41.9	50.1	60.6	26.3	66.5	41.6	20.2	44.9
1976	56.8	57.5	73.4	51.5	76.0	43.2	44.2	43.1	50.8	60.6	25.8	66.8	42.8	19.2	46.4
1977	57.9	58.6	74.1	54.4	76.5	44.5	45.9	44.4	51.4	61.4	26.4	67.5	43.3	18.5	47.0
1978	59.3	60.0	75.0	56.3	77.2	46.3	48.5	46.1	53.6	63.3	28.5	69.1	45.8	22.1	49.3
1979	59.9	60.6	75.1	55.7	77.3	47.5	49.4	47.3	53.8	63.4	28.7	69.1	46.0	22.4	49.3
1980	59.2	60.0	73.4	53.4	75.6	47.8	47.9	47.8	52.3	60.4	27.0	65.8	45.7	21.0	49.1
1981	59.0	60.0	72.8	51.3	75.1	48.3	46.2	48.5	51.3	59.1	24.6	64.5	45.1	19.7	48.5
1982	57.8	58.8	70.6	47.0	73.0	48.1	44.6	48.4	49.4	56.0	20.3	61.4	44.2	17.7	47.5
1983	57.9	58.9	70.4	47.4	72.6	48.5	44.5	48.9	49.5	56.3	20.4	61.6	44.1	17.0	47.4
1984	59.5	60.5	72.1	49.1	74.3	49.8	47.0	50.0	52.3	59.2	23.9	64.1	46.7	20.1	49.8
1985	60.1	61.0	72.3	49.9	74.3	50.7	47.1	51.0	53.4	60.0	26.3	64.6	48.1	23.1	50.9
1986	60.7	61.5	72.3	49.6	74.3	51.7	47.9	52.0	54.1	60.6	26.5	65.1	48.8	23.8	51.6
1987	61.5	62.3	72.7	49.9	74.7	52.8	49.0	53.1	55.6	62.0	28.5	66.4	50.3	25.8	53.0
1988	62.3	63.1	73.2	51.7	75.1	53.8	50.2	54.0	56.3	62.7	29.4	67.1	51.2	25.8	53.9
1989	63.0	63.8	73.7	52.6	75.4	54.6	50.5	54.9	56.9	62.8	30.4	67.0	52.0	27.1	54.6
1990	62.8	63.7	73.3	51.0	75.1	54.7	48.3	55.2	56.7	62.6	27.7	67.1	51.9	25.8	54.7
1991	61.7	62.6	71.6	47.2	73.5	54.2	45.9	54.8	55.4	61.3	23.8	65.9	50.6	21.5	53.6
1992	61.5	62.4	71.1	46.4	73.1	54.2	44.2	54.9	54.9	59.9	23.6	64.3	50.8	22.1	53.6
1993	61.7	62.7	71.4	46.6	73.3	54.6	45.7	55.2	55.0	60.0	23.6	64.3	50.9	21.6	53.8
1994	62.5	63.5	71.8	48.3	73.6	55.8	47.5	56.4	56.1	60.8	25.4	65.0	52.3	24.5	55.0
1995	62.9	63.8	72.0	49.4	73.8	56.1	48.1	56.7	57.1	61.7	25.2	66.1	53.4	26.1	56.1
1996	63.2	64.1	72.3	48.2	74.2	56.3	47.6	57.0	57.4	61.1	24.9	65.5	54.4	27.1	57.1
1997	63.8	64.6	72.7	48.1	74.7	57.0	47.2	57.8	58.2	61.4	23.7	66.1	55.6	28.5	58.4
1998	64.1	64.7	72.7	48.6	74.7	57.1	49.3	57.7	59.7	62.9	28.4	67.1	57.2	31.8	59.7
1999	64.3	64.8	72.8	49.3	74.8	57.3	48.3	58.0	60.6	63.1	26.7	67.5	58.6	29.0	61.5
2000	64.4	64.9	73.0	49.5	74.9	57.4	48.8	58.0	60.9	63.6	28.9	67.7	58.6	30.6	61.3
2001	63.7	64.2	72.0	46.2	74.0	57.0	46.5	57.7	59.7	62.1	26.4	66.3	57.8	27.0	60.7
2002	62.7	63.4	70.8	42.3	73.1	56.4	44.1	57.3	58.1	61.1	25.6	65.2	55.8	24.9	58.7
2003	62.3	63.0	70.1	39.4	72.5	56.3	41.5	57.3	57.4	59.5	19.9	64.1	55.6	23.4	58.6
2004	62.3	63.1	70.4	39.7	72.8	56.1	40.3	57.2	57.2	59.3	19.3	63.9	55.5	23.6	58.5
2005	62.7	63.4	70.8	38.8	73.3	56.3	41.8	57.4	57.7	60.2	20.8	64.7	55.7	22.4	58.9
2006	63.1	63.8	71.3	40.0	73.7	56.6	41.1	57.7	58.4	60.6	21.7	65.2	56.5	26.4	59.4
2007	63.0	63.6	70.9	37.3	73.5	56.7	39.2	57.9	58.4	60.7	19.5	65.5	56.5	23.3	59.8
2008	62.2	62.8	69.7	34.8	72.4	56.3	37.1	57.7	57.3	59.1	18.7	63.9	55.8	21.7	59.1
2009	59.3	60.2	66.0	30.2	68.7	54.8	33.4	56.3	53.2	53.7	14.3	58.2	52.8	18.6	56.1
2010	58.5	59.4	65.1	27.6	67.9	54.0	30.4	55.6	52.3	53.1	14.1	57.5	51.7	14.9	55.1
2011	58.4	59.4	65.3	27.3	68.2	53.7	30.4	55.3	51.7	52.8	14.6	56.9	50.8	14.7	54.0
2010: Jan	58.5	59.6	64.8	27.1	67.7	54.5	30.6	56.2	52.0	52.6	14.8	57.0	51.6	18.1	54.7
Feb	58.5	59.5	64.9	27.6	67.8	54.2	31.0	55.9	52.2	52.5	14.7	56.9	51.9	15.2	55.4
Mar	58.5	59.5	65.1	27.9	67.9	54.2	30.7	55.8	52.2	52.7	14.3	57.1	51.8	16.7	55.1
Apr	58.7	59.6	65.3	28.2	68.2	54.1	31.6	55.7	52.5	53.4	16.1	57.6	51.7	15.2	55.1
May	58.7	59.6	65.4	27.9	68.2	54.0	30.1	55.7	53.0	54.1	15.2	58.5	52.2	16.5	55.5
June	58.5	59.5	65.2	26.4	68.1	54.0	30.0	55.7	52.4	52.9	13.7	57.4	52.0	14.2	55.5
July	58.5	59.5	65.3	27.7	68.2	53.9	30.0	55.6	52.1	53.1	14.1	57.5	51.3	14.7	54.7
Aug	58.5	59.5	65.3	27.2	68.1	54.0	31.2	55.5	52.1	53.2	13.7	57.6	51.3	14.6	54.7
Sept	58.5	59.5	65.3	26.8	68.1	54.0	30.5	55.6	51.8	52.6	12.7	57.1	51.1	11.1	54.8
Oct	58.3	59.2	64.9	27.7	67.7	53.7	30.0	55.3	52.4	53.3	13.0	57.7	51.6	14.4	55.0
Nov	58.2	59.1	64.7	29.3	67.3	53.7	29.6	55.3	52.4	53.2	13.8	57.6	51.7	14.5	55.1
Dec	58.3	59.2	65.0	27.8	67.7	53.7	29.6	55.3	52.2	53.0	13.7	57.4	51.6	13.9	55.1
2011: Jan	58.4	59.4	65.1	28.4	67.9	53.8	29.5	55.5	51.9	52.7	14.0	56.9	51.3	13.8	54.7
Feb	58.4	59.3	65.3	27.8	68.1	53.6	28.9	55.3	52.0	52.8	14.2	57.1	51.4	15.3	54.7
Mar	58.5	59.5	65.2	27.4	68.0	54.0	29.9	55.7	51.9	53.0	15.3	57.1	51.0	14.4	54.3
Apr	58.4	59.5	65.2	26.5	68.1	53.9	30.2	55.6	51.5	52.6	14.1	56.8	50.7	16.8	53.7
May	58.4	59.5	65.4	26.5	68.4	53.8	30.3	55.4	51.1	51.9	14.5	56.0	50.5	14.4	53.7
June	58.2	59.3	65.2	26.8	68.0	53.6	30.4	55.2	51.1	52.8	15.5	56.8	49.8	15.4	52.9
July	58.2	59.3	65.2	27.0	68.0	53.6	29.9	55.2	50.9	52.3	14.9	56.3	49.7	13.2	52.9
Aug	58.3	59.4	65.3	27.4	68.1	53.6	30.9	55.2	51.3	52.2	14.5	56.3	50.6	11.5	54.1
Sept	58.4	59.4	65.4	27.2	68.2	53.6	31.3	55.1	52.1	52.9	14.9	57.0	51.5	14.3	54.8
Oct	58.4	59.3	65.2	27.4	68.1	53.7	31.5	55.1	52.5	53.4	14.7	57.5	51.8	15.6	55.0
Nov	58.5	59.5	65.6	27.4	68.5	53.5	31.5	55.0	51.8	53.1	13.8	57.3	50.7	16.4	53.7
Dec	58.5	59.5	65.8	27.7	68.6	53.5	30.9	55.0	52.1	54.0	15.1	58.2	50.4	15.6	53.5

[1] Civilian employment as percent of civilian noninstitutional population in group specified.
[2] See footnote 1, Table B–37.

Note: Data relate to persons 16 years of age and over.
See footnote 5 and Note, Table B–35.

Source: Department of Labor (Bureau of Labor Statistics).

TABLE B–42. Civilian unemployment rate, 1965–2011

[Percent [1]; monthly data seasonally adjusted, except as noted]

Year or month	All civilian workers	Males			Females			Both sexes 16–19 years	By race				Hispanic or Latino ethnicity [4]	Married men, spouse present	Women who maintain families (NSA) [3]
		Total	16–19 years	20 years and over	Total	16–19 years	20 years and over		White [2]	Black and other [2]	Black or African American [2]	Asian (NSA) [2,3]			
1965	4.5	4.0	14.1	3.2	5.5	15.7	4.5	14.8	4.1	8.1	....	....	....	2.4	....
1966	3.8	3.2	11.7	2.5	4.8	14.1	3.8	12.8	3.4	7.3	....	....	....	1.9	....
1967	3.8	3.1	12.3	2.3	5.2	13.5	4.2	12.9	3.4	7.4	....	....	....	1.8	4.9
1968	3.6	2.9	11.6	2.2	4.8	14.0	3.8	12.7	3.2	6.7	....	....	....	1.6	4.4
1969	3.5	2.8	11.4	2.1	4.7	13.3	3.7	12.2	3.1	6.4	....	....	....	1.5	4.4
1970	4.9	4.4	15.0	3.5	5.9	15.6	4.8	15.3	4.5	8.2	....	....	....	2.6	5.4
1971	5.9	5.3	16.6	4.4	6.9	17.2	5.7	16.9	5.4	9.9	....	....	....	3.2	7.3
1972	5.6	5.0	15.9	4.0	6.6	16.7	5.4	16.2	5.1	10.0	10.4	....	....	2.8	7.2
1973	4.9	4.2	13.9	3.3	6.0	15.3	4.9	14.5	4.3	9.0	9.4	....	7.5	2.3	7.1
1974	5.6	4.9	15.6	3.8	6.7	16.6	5.5	16.0	5.0	9.9	10.5	....	8.1	2.7	7.0
1975	8.5	7.9	20.1	6.8	9.3	19.7	8.0	19.9	7.8	13.8	14.8	....	12.2	5.1	10.0
1976	7.7	7.1	19.2	5.9	8.6	18.7	7.4	19.0	7.0	13.1	14.0	....	11.5	4.2	10.1
1977	7.1	6.3	17.3	5.2	8.2	18.3	7.0	17.8	6.2	13.1	14.0	....	10.1	3.6	9.4
1978	6.1	5.3	15.8	4.3	7.2	17.1	6.0	16.4	5.2	11.9	12.8	....	9.1	2.8	8.5
1979	5.8	5.1	15.9	4.2	6.8	16.4	5.7	16.1	5.1	11.3	12.3	....	8.3	2.8	8.3
1980	7.1	6.9	18.3	5.9	7.4	17.2	6.4	17.8	6.3	13.1	14.3	....	10.1	4.2	9.2
1981	7.6	7.4	20.1	6.3	7.9	19.0	6.8	19.6	6.7	14.2	15.6	....	10.4	4.3	10.4
1982	9.7	9.9	24.4	8.8	9.4	21.9	8.3	23.2	8.6	17.3	18.9	....	13.8	6.5	11.7
1983	9.6	9.9	23.3	8.9	9.2	21.3	8.1	22.4	8.4	17.8	19.5	....	13.7	6.5	12.2
1984	7.5	7.4	19.6	6.6	7.6	18.0	6.8	18.9	6.5	14.4	15.9	....	10.7	4.6	10.3
1985	7.2	7.0	19.5	6.2	7.4	17.6	6.6	18.6	6.2	13.7	15.1	....	10.5	4.3	10.4
1986	7.0	6.9	19.0	6.1	7.1	17.6	6.2	18.3	6.0	13.1	14.5	....	10.6	4.4	9.8
1987	6.2	6.2	17.8	5.4	6.2	15.9	5.4	16.9	5.3	11.6	13.0	....	8.8	3.9	9.2
1988	5.5	5.5	16.0	4.8	5.6	14.4	4.9	15.3	4.7	10.4	11.7	....	8.2	3.3	8.1
1989	5.3	5.2	15.9	4.5	5.4	14.0	4.7	15.0	4.5	10.0	11.4	....	8.0	3.0	8.1
1990	5.6	5.7	16.3	5.0	5.5	14.7	4.9	15.5	4.8	10.1	11.4	....	8.2	3.4	8.3
1991	6.8	7.2	19.8	6.4	6.4	17.5	5.7	18.7	6.1	11.1	12.5	....	10.0	4.4	9.3
1992	7.5	7.9	21.5	7.1	7.0	18.6	6.3	20.1	6.6	12.7	14.2	....	11.6	5.1	10.0
1993	6.9	7.2	20.4	6.4	6.6	17.5	5.9	19.0	6.1	11.7	13.0	....	10.8	4.4	9.7
1994	6.1	6.2	19.0	5.4	6.0	16.2	5.4	17.6	5.3	10.5	11.5	....	9.9	3.7	8.9
1995	5.6	5.6	18.4	4.8	5.6	16.1	4.9	17.3	4.9	9.6	10.4	....	9.3	3.3	8.0
1996	5.4	5.4	18.1	4.6	5.4	15.2	4.8	16.7	4.7	9.3	10.5	....	8.9	3.0	8.2
1997	4.9	4.9	16.9	4.2	5.0	15.0	4.4	16.0	4.2	8.8	10.0	....	7.7	2.7	8.1
1998	4.5	4.4	16.2	3.7	4.6	12.9	4.1	14.6	3.9	7.8	8.9	....	7.2	2.4	7.2
1999	4.2	4.1	14.7	3.5	4.3	13.2	3.8	13.9	3.7	7.0	8.0	....	6.4	2.2	6.4
2000	4.0	3.9	14.0	3.3	4.1	12.1	3.6	13.1	3.5	....	7.6	3.6	5.7	2.0	5.9
2001	4.7	4.8	16.0	4.2	4.7	13.4	4.1	14.7	4.2	....	8.6	4.5	6.6	2.7	6.6
2002	5.8	5.9	18.1	5.3	5.6	14.9	5.1	16.5	5.1	....	10.2	5.9	7.5	3.6	8.0
2003	6.0	6.3	19.3	5.6	5.7	15.6	5.1	17.5	5.2	....	10.8	6.0	7.7	3.8	8.5
2004	5.5	5.6	18.4	5.0	5.4	15.5	4.9	17.0	4.8	....	10.4	4.4	7.0	3.1	8.0
2005	5.1	5.1	18.6	4.4	5.1	14.5	4.6	16.6	4.4	....	10.0	4.0	6.0	2.8	7.8
2006	4.6	4.6	16.9	4.0	4.6	13.8	4.1	15.4	4.0	....	8.9	3.0	5.2	2.4	7.1
2007	4.6	4.7	17.6	4.1	4.5	13.8	4.0	15.7	4.1	....	8.3	3.2	5.6	2.5	6.5
2008	5.8	6.1	21.2	5.4	5.4	16.2	4.9	18.7	5.2	....	10.1	4.0	7.6	3.4	8.0
2009	9.3	10.3	27.8	9.6	8.1	20.7	7.5	24.3	8.5	....	14.8	7.3	12.1	6.6	11.5
2010	9.6	10.5	28.8	9.8	8.6	22.8	8.0	25.9	8.7	....	16.0	7.5	12.5	6.8	12.3
2011	8.9	9.4	27.2	8.7	8.5	21.7	7.9	24.4	7.9	....	15.8	7.0	11.5	5.8	12.4
2010: Jan	9.7	10.9	30.3	10.1	8.4	21.4	7.9	25.9	8.7	....	16.5	8.4	12.6	6.8	12.3
Feb	9.8	10.8	28.5	10.2	8.6	22.4	8.0	25.4	8.9	....	16.0	8.4	12.4	6.9	11.6
Mar	9.8	10.9	29.8	10.1	8.6	22.4	8.0	26.2	8.8	....	16.7	7.5	12.6	6.9	11.3
Apr	9.9	10.8	29.1	10.1	8.8	22.1	8.2	25.7	9.0	....	16.4	6.8	12.4	6.7	11.0
May	9.6	10.4	28.3	9.7	8.8	25.1	8.0	26.7	8.8	....	15.4	7.5	12.3	6.8	11.6
June	9.4	10.4	29.4	9.8	8.3	22.4	7.7	25.9	8.6	....	15.2	7.7	12.4	6.8	12.1
July	9.5	10.4	29.0	9.6	8.5	22.7	7.9	25.9	8.6	....	15.7	8.2	12.2	6.5	13.4
Aug	9.6	10.4	29.0	9.7	8.6	22.5	8.0	25.8	8.7	....	16.1	7.2	12.1	6.7	13.4
Sept	9.5	10.3	28.9	9.6	8.5	22.7	7.9	25.8	8.6	....	16.0	6.4	12.4	6.6	12.9
Oct	9.5	10.2	29.1	9.5	8.8	24.9	8.1	27.0	8.6	....	15.9	7.1	12.5	6.8	12.4
Nov	9.8	10.5	26.4	9.9	9.0	22.4	8.4	24.5	8.9	....	16.1	7.6	13.1	6.9	13.0
Dec	9.4	10.0	27.8	9.4	8.6	22.6	8.1	25.2	8.5	....	15.8	7.2	12.9	6.5	12.0
2011: Jan	9.1	9.6	27.2	8.9	8.5	23.6	7.9	25.4	8.1	....	15.7	6.9	12.0	5.9	12.7
Feb	9.0	9.4	25.9	8.8	8.5	21.8	7.9	23.9	8.0	....	15.4	6.8	11.6	5.8	13.0
Mar	8.9	9.4	26.4	8.7	8.3	22.6	7.8	24.5	7.9	....	15.6	7.1	11.3	6.0	12.3
Apr	9.0	9.5	28.1	8.8	8.4	21.6	7.9	24.9	8.1	....	16.2	6.4	11.8	6.1	11.7
May	9.0	9.5	27.0	8.9	8.5	21.3	8.0	24.1	8.0	....	16.2	7.0	11.8	6.0	12.7
June	9.1	9.7	27.4	9.0	8.5	21.7	8.0	24.6	8.1	....	16.2	6.8	11.6	6.1	12.8
July	9.1	9.6	27.2	8.9	8.5	22.5	7.9	24.9	8.1	....	15.9	7.7	11.3	6.1	12.1
Aug	9.1	9.5	28.1	8.8	8.5	22.4	7.9	25.3	7.9	....	16.7	7.1	11.3	5.8	11.9
Sept	9.0	9.4	27.8	8.7	8.6	21.1	8.1	24.5	7.9	....	15.9	7.8	11.3	5.8	12.4
Oct	8.9	9.4	27.3	8.7	8.4	20.6	7.9	24.0	8.0	....	15.0	7.3	11.4	5.8	12.3
Nov	8.7	8.9	26.6	8.3	8.3	20.7	7.8	23.7	7.6	....	15.5	6.5	11.4	5.3	12.4
Dec	8.5	8.7	26.6	8.0	8.3	19.3	7.9	23.1	7.5	....	15.8	6.8	11.0	5.1	12.9

[1] Unemployed as percent of civilian labor force in group specified.
[2] See footnote 1, Table B–37.
[3] Not seasonally adjusted (NSA).
[4] Persons whose ethnicity is identified as Hispanic or Latino may be of any race.

Note: Data relate to persons 16 years of age and over.
See footnote 5 and Note, Table B–35.

Source: Department of Labor (Bureau of Labor Statistics).

[Percent [1]; monthly data seasonally adjusted]

Year or month	All civilian work-ers	White [2] Total	White Males Total	White Males 16–19 years	White Males 20 years and over	White Females Total	White Females 16–19 years	White Females 20 years and over	Black or African American [2] Total	Black Males Total	Black Males 16–19 years	Black Males 20 years and over	Black Females Total	Black Females 16–19 years	Black Females 20 years and over
1972	5.6	5.1	4.5	14.2	3.6	5.9	14.2	4.9	10.4	9.3	31.7	7.0	11.8	40.5	9.0
1973	4.9	4.3	3.8	12.3	3.0	5.3	13.0	4.3	9.4	8.0	27.8	6.0	11.1	36.1	8.6
1974	5.6	5.0	4.4	13.5	3.5	6.1	14.5	5.1	10.5	9.8	33.1	7.4	11.3	37.4	8.8
1975	8.5	7.8	7.2	18.3	6.2	8.6	17.4	7.5	14.8	14.8	38.1	12.5	14.8	41.0	12.2
1976	7.7	7.0	6.4	17.3	5.4	7.9	16.4	6.8	14.0	13.7	37.5	11.4	14.3	41.6	11.7
1977	7.1	6.2	5.5	15.0	4.7	7.3	15.9	6.2	14.0	13.3	39.2	10.7	14.9	43.4	12.3
1978	6.1	5.2	4.6	13.5	3.7	6.2	14.4	5.2	12.8	11.8	36.7	9.3	13.8	40.8	11.2
1979	5.8	5.1	4.5	13.9	3.6	5.9	14.0	5.0	12.3	11.4	34.2	9.3	13.3	39.1	10.9
1980	7.1	6.3	6.1	16.2	5.3	6.5	14.8	5.6	14.3	14.5	37.5	12.4	14.0	39.8	11.9
1981	7.6	6.7	6.5	17.9	5.6	6.9	16.6	5.9	15.6	15.7	40.7	13.5	15.6	42.2	13.4
1982	9.7	8.6	8.8	21.7	7.8	8.3	19.0	7.3	18.9	20.1	48.9	17.8	17.6	47.1	15.4
1983	9.6	8.4	8.8	20.2	7.9	7.9	18.3	6.9	19.5	20.3	48.8	18.1	18.6	48.2	16.5
1984	7.5	6.5	6.4	16.8	5.7	6.5	15.2	5.8	15.9	16.4	42.7	14.3	15.4	42.6	13.5
1985	7.2	6.2	6.1	16.5	5.4	6.4	14.8	5.7	15.1	15.3	41.0	13.2	14.9	39.2	13.1
1986	7.0	6.0	6.0	16.3	5.3	6.1	14.9	5.4	14.5	14.8	39.3	12.9	14.2	39.2	12.4
1987	6.2	5.3	5.4	15.5	4.8	5.2	13.4	4.6	13.0	12.7	34.4	11.1	13.2	34.9	11.6
1988	5.5	4.7	4.7	13.9	4.1	4.7	12.3	4.1	11.7	11.7	32.7	10.1	11.7	32.0	10.4
1989	5.3	4.5	4.5	13.7	3.9	4.5	11.5	4.0	11.4	11.5	31.9	10.0	11.4	33.0	9.8
1990	5.6	4.8	4.9	14.3	4.3	4.7	12.6	4.1	11.4	11.9	31.9	10.4	10.9	29.9	9.7
1991	6.8	6.1	6.5	17.6	5.8	5.6	15.2	5.0	12.5	13.0	36.3	11.5	12.0	36.0	10.6
1992	7.5	6.6	7.0	18.5	6.4	6.1	15.8	5.5	14.2	15.2	42.0	13.5	13.2	37.2	11.8
1993	6.9	6.1	6.3	17.7	5.7	5.7	14.7	5.2	13.0	13.8	40.1	12.1	12.1	37.4	10.7
1994	6.1	5.3	5.4	16.3	4.8	5.2	13.8	4.6	11.5	12.0	37.6	10.3	11.0	32.6	9.8
1995	5.6	4.9	4.9	15.6	4.3	4.8	13.4	4.3	10.4	10.6	37.1	8.8	10.2	34.3	8.6
1996	5.4	4.7	4.7	15.5	4.1	4.7	12.9	4.1	10.5	11.1	36.9	9.4	10.0	30.3	8.7
1997	4.9	4.2	4.2	14.3	3.6	4.2	12.8	3.7	10.0	10.2	36.5	8.5	9.9	28.7	8.8
1998	4.5	3.9	3.9	14.1	3.2	3.9	10.9	3.4	8.9	8.9	30.1	7.4	9.0	25.3	7.9
1999	4.2	3.7	3.6	12.6	3.0	3.8	11.3	3.3	8.0	8.2	30.9	6.7	7.8	25.1	6.8
2000	4.0	3.5	3.4	12.3	2.8	3.6	10.4	3.1	7.6	8.0	26.2	6.9	7.1	22.8	6.2
2001	4.7	4.2	4.2	13.9	3.7	4.1	11.4	3.6	8.6	9.3	30.4	8.0	8.1	27.5	7.0
2002	5.8	5.1	5.3	15.9	4.7	4.9	13.1	4.4	10.2	10.7	31.3	9.5	9.8	28.3	8.8
2003	6.0	5.2	5.6	17.1	5.0	4.8	13.3	4.4	10.8	11.6	36.0	10.3	10.2	30.3	9.2
2004	5.5	4.8	5.0	16.3	4.4	4.7	13.6	4.2	10.4	11.1	35.6	9.9	9.8	28.2	8.9
2005	5.1	4.4	4.4	16.1	3.8	4.4	12.3	3.9	10.0	10.5	36.3	9.2	9.5	30.3	8.5
2006	4.6	4.0	4.0	14.6	3.5	4.0	11.7	3.6	8.9	9.5	32.7	8.3	8.4	25.9	7.5
2007	4.6	4.1	4.2	15.7	3.7	4.0	12.1	3.6	8.3	9.1	33.8	7.9	7.5	25.3	6.7
2008	5.8	5.2	5.5	19.1	4.9	4.9	14.4	4.4	10.1	11.4	35.9	10.2	8.9	26.8	8.1
2009	9.3	8.5	9.4	25.2	8.8	7.3	18.4	6.8	14.8	17.5	46.0	16.3	12.4	33.4	11.5
2010	9.6	8.7	9.6	26.3	8.9	7.7	20.0	7.2	16.0	18.4	45.4	17.3	13.8	40.5	12.8
2011	8.9	7.9	8.3	24.5	7.7	7.5	18.9	7.0	15.8	17.8	43.1	16.7	14.1	39.4	13.2
2010: Jan	9.7	8.7	9.9	27.8	9.2	7.4	18.3	6.9	16.5	19.0	46.4	17.8	14.2	37.6	13.2
Feb	9.8	8.9	9.8	25.7	9.2	7.8	20.1	7.3	16.0	19.0	44.9	17.9	13.2	40.3	12.2
Mar	9.8	8.8	9.7	27.3	9.0	7.8	20.3	7.3	16.7	20.2	47.9	19.0	13.4	34.5	12.6
Apr	9.9	9.0	10.0	27.1	9.3	7.9	19.5	7.3	16.4	18.4	36.6	17.6	14.6	39.8	13.7
May	9.6	8.8	9.4	26.6	8.8	8.0	22.8	7.3	15.4	17.5	35.9	16.8	13.5	41.5	12.3
June	9.4	8.6	9.4	27.0	8.8	7.6	19.3	7.1	15.2	18.3	44.3	17.3	12.5	37.6	11.6
July	9.5	8.6	9.4	26.1	8.8	7.6	20.2	7.1	15.7	17.9	45.6	16.8	13.7	37.3	12.9
Aug	9.6	8.7	9.5	26.6	8.9	7.6	20.1	7.1	16.1	18.4	50.1	17.0	14.0	38.1	13.2
Sept	9.5	8.6	9.4	26.5	8.7	7.7	20.2	7.1	16.0	18.6	48.0	17.4	13.7	48.6	12.6
Oct	9.5	8.6	9.3	25.6	8.7	7.8	20.9	7.2	15.9	17.9	52.4	16.4	14.1	44.8	13.0
Nov	9.8	8.9	9.7	23.2	9.2	8.0	18.6	7.6	16.1	18.0	48.9	16.6	14.4	43.8	13.3
Dec	9.4	8.5	9.1	25.9	8.5	7.7	19.4	7.2	15.8	17.7	41.4	16.8	14.2	46.3	13.0
2011: Jan	9.1	8.1	8.5	24.3	7.9	7.5	20.7	7.0	15.7	17.9	47.2	16.6	13.8	42.3	12.8
Feb	9.0	8.0	8.4	22.9	7.9	7.6	19.7	7.1	15.4	17.3	41.6	16.4	13.7	35.2	13.0
Mar	8.9	7.9	8.3	23.4	7.8	7.4	19.5	6.9	15.6	17.8	40.3	16.8	13.7	43.5	12.5
Apr	9.0	8.1	8.5	24.9	8.0	7.5	19.4	7.0	16.2	18.1	45.5	17.0	14.4	37.3	13.5
May	9.0	8.0	8.4	22.5	7.9	7.5	18.3	7.1	16.2	18.5	44.8	17.4	14.1	36.3	13.4
June	9.1	8.1	8.6	25.0	8.0	7.5	18.6	7.0	16.2	17.8	41.3	16.9	14.6	38.3	13.7
July	9.1	8.1	8.5	25.3	7.9	7.6	20.8	7.0	15.9	17.8	37.9	17.0	14.2	40.3	13.4
Aug	9.1	7.9	8.4	26.8	7.7	7.5	18.5	7.0	16.7	19.1	44.9	18.0	14.5	48.0	13.4
Sept	9.0	7.9	8.3	24.9	7.7	7.5	17.4	7.1	15.9	17.7	43.5	16.6	14.3	43.6	13.2
Oct	8.9	8.0	8.5	25.5	7.8	7.4	17.7	7.0	15.0	16.9	38.7	16.0	13.4	36.4	12.6
Nov	8.7	7.6	7.9	24.6	7.3	7.3	18.0	6.9	15.5	17.3	42.7	16.4	13.9	36.8	13.0
Dec	8.5	7.5	7.6	23.2	7.1	7.2	17.3	6.8	15.8	17.1	48.3	15.7	14.6	34.6	13.9

[1] Unemployed as percent of civilian labor force in group specified.
[2] See footnote 1, Table B–37.

Note: Data relate to persons 16 years of age and over.
See footnote 5 and Note, Table B–35.

Source: Department of Labor (Bureau of Labor Statistics).

TABLE B–44. Unemployment by duration and reason, 1965–2011

[Thousands of persons, except as noted; monthly data seasonally adjusted [1]]

Year or month	Un-employ-ment	Duration of unemployment						Reason for unemployment					
		Less than 5 weeks	5–14 weeks	15–26 weeks	27 weeks and over	Average (mean) duration (weeks) [3]	Median duration (weeks)	Job losers [4]			Job leavers	Re-entrants	New entrants
								Total	On layoff	Other			
1965	3,366	1,628	983	404	351	11.8	....	....	....	....	....	....	....
1966	2,875	1,573	779	287	239	10.4	....	....	....	....	....	....	....
1967 [2]	2,975	1,634	893	271	177	8.7	2.3	1,229	394	836	438	945	396
1968	2,817	1,594	810	256	156	8.4	4.5	1,070	334	736	431	909	407
1969	2,832	1,629	827	242	133	7.8	4.4	1,017	339	678	436	965	413
1970	4,093	2,139	1,290	428	235	8.6	4.9	1,811	675	1,137	550	1,228	504
1971	5,016	2,245	1,585	668	519	11.3	6.3	2,323	735	1,588	590	1,472	630
1972	4,882	2,242	1,472	601	566	12.0	6.2	2,108	582	1,526	641	1,456	677
1973	4,365	2,224	1,314	483	343	10.0	5.2	1,694	472	1,221	683	1,340	649
1974	5,156	2,604	1,597	574	381	9.8	5.2	2,242	746	1,495	768	1,463	681
1975	7,929	2,940	2,484	1,303	1,203	14.2	8.4	4,386	1,671	2,714	827	1,892	823
1976	7,406	2,844	2,196	1,018	1,348	15.8	8.2	3,679	1,050	2,628	903	1,928	895
1977	6,991	2,919	2,132	913	1,028	14.3	7.0	3,166	865	2,300	909	1,963	953
1978	6,202	2,865	1,923	766	648	11.9	5.9	2,585	712	1,873	874	1,857	885
1979	6,137	2,950	1,946	706	535	10.8	5.4	2,635	851	1,784	880	1,806	817
1980	7,637	3,295	2,470	1,052	820	11.9	6.5	3,947	1,488	2,459	891	1,927	872
1981	8,273	3,449	2,539	1,122	1,162	13.7	6.9	4,267	1,430	2,837	923	2,102	981
1982	10,678	3,883	3,311	1,708	1,776	15.6	8.7	6,268	2,127	4,141	840	2,384	1,185
1983	10,717	3,570	2,937	1,652	2,559	20.0	10.1	6,258	1,780	4,478	830	2,412	1,216
1984	8,539	3,350	2,451	1,104	1,634	18.2	7.9	4,421	1,171	3,250	823	2,184	1,110
1985	8,312	3,498	2,509	1,025	1,280	15.6	6.8	4,139	1,157	2,982	877	2,256	1,039
1986	8,237	3,448	2,557	1,045	1,187	15.0	6.9	4,033	1,090	2,943	1,015	2,160	1,029
1987	7,425	3,246	2,196	943	1,040	14.5	6.5	3,566	943	2,623	965	1,974	920
1988	6,701	3,084	2,007	801	809	13.5	5.9	3,092	851	2,241	983	1,809	816
1989	6,528	3,174	1,978	730	646	11.9	4.8	2,983	850	2,133	1,024	1,843	677
1990	7,047	3,265	2,257	822	703	12.0	5.3	3,387	1,028	2,359	1,041	1,930	688
1991	8,628	3,480	2,791	1,246	1,111	13.7	6.8	4,694	1,292	3,402	1,004	2,139	792
1992	9,613	3,376	2,830	1,453	1,954	17.7	8.7	5,389	1,260	4,129	1,002	2,285	937
1993	8,940	3,262	2,584	1,297	1,798	18.0	8.3	4,848	1,115	3,733	976	2,198	919
1994	7,996	2,728	2,408	1,237	1,623	18.8	9.2	3,815	977	2,838	791	2,786	604
1995	7,404	2,700	2,342	1,085	1,278	16.6	8.3	3,476	1,030	2,446	824	2,525	579
1996	7,236	2,633	2,287	1,053	1,262	16.7	8.3	3,370	1,021	2,349	774	2,512	580
1997	6,739	2,538	2,138	995	1,067	15.8	8.0	3,037	931	2,106	795	2,338	569
1998	6,210	2,622	1,950	763	875	14.5	6.7	2,822	866	1,957	734	2,132	520
1999	5,880	2,568	1,832	755	725	13.4	6.4	2,622	848	1,774	783	2,005	469
2000	5,692	2,558	1,815	669	649	12.6	5.9	2,517	852	1,664	780	1,961	434
2001	6,801	2,853	2,196	951	801	13.1	6.8	3,476	1,067	2,409	835	2,031	459
2002	8,378	2,893	2,580	1,369	1,535	16.6	9.1	4,607	1,124	3,483	866	2,368	536
2003	8,774	2,785	2,612	1,442	1,936	19.2	10.1	4,838	1,121	3,717	818	2,477	641
2004	8,149	2,696	2,382	1,293	1,779	19.6	9.8	4,197	998	3,199	858	2,408	686
2005	7,591	2,667	2,304	1,130	1,490	18.4	8.9	3,667	933	2,734	872	2,386	666
2006	7,001	2,614	2,121	1,031	1,235	16.8	8.3	3,321	921	2,400	827	2,237	616
2007	7,078	2,542	2,232	1,061	1,243	16.8	8.5	3,515	976	2,539	793	2,142	627
2008	8,924	2,932	2,804	1,427	1,761	17.9	9.4	4,789	1,176	3,614	896	2,472	766
2009	14,265	3,165	3,828	2,775	4,496	24.4	15.1	9,160	1,630	7,530	882	3,187	1,035
2010	14,825	2,771	3,267	2,371	6,415	33.0	21.4	9,250	1,431	7,819	889	3,466	1,220
2011	13,747	2,677	2,993	2,061	6,016	39.3	21.4	8,106	1,230	6,876	956	3,401	1,284
2010: Jan	14,953	2,909	3,383	2,603	6,322	30.3	20.1	9,327	1,477	7,851	908	3,640	1,187
Feb	15,039	2,760	3,369	2,718	6,207	29.8	19.9	9,570	1,545	8,025	884	3,465	1,208
Mar	15,128	2,691	3,258	2,495	6,556	31.4	20.4	9,508	1,629	7,879	897	3,567	1,171
Apr	15,221	2,696	3,055	2,341	6,730	33.1	22.0	9,328	1,350	7,978	930	3,753	1,203
May	14,876	2,775	3,110	2,210	6,687	33.9	22.5	9,220	1,452	7,768	975	3,417	1,209
June	14,517	2,758	3,149	2,263	6,652	34.5	25.0	9,085	1,393	7,692	891	3,249	1,168
July	14,609	2,829	3,057	2,192	6,503	33.7	21.8	9,029	1,234	7,795	899	3,419	1,204
Aug	14,735	2,730	3,549	2,166	6,242	33.6	20.5	9,191	1,486	7,706	867	3,377	1,272
Sept	14,574	2,819	3,321	2,301	6,093	33.5	20.1	9,170	1,341	7,828	805	3,410	1,180
Oct	14,636	2,664	3,370	2,451	6,215	34.3	21.5	8,916	1,261	7,655	849	3,493	1,277
Nov	15,104	2,875	3,310	2,427	6,320	34.2	21.5	9,462	1,450	8,012	857	3,443	1,274
Dec	14,393	2,701	3,167	2,191	6,421	34.9	22.3	8,877	1,366	7,511	920	3,406	1,306
2011: Jan	13,919	2,659	3,012	2,253	6,205	37.1	21.7	8,463	1,241	7,222	914	3,351	1,337
Feb	13,751	2,408	3,080	2,195	6,014	37.4	21.1	8,337	1,261	7,076	904	3,354	1,315
Mar	13,628	2,437	2,927	1,991	6,130	38.9	21.6	8,244	1,209	7,035	900	3,278	1,335
Apr	13,792	2,725	2,931	2,058	5,860	38.3	20.8	8,181	1,241	6,941	944	3,387	1,322
May	13,892	2,687	2,912	1,994	6,204	39.6	21.9	8,250	1,218	7,031	919	3,436	1,229
June	14,024	3,068	2,976	1,874	6,263	39.8	22.1	8,233	1,253	6,980	971	3,431	1,227
July	13,908	2,675	3,063	1,972	6,162	40.2	21.2	8,146	1,246	6,900	936	3,424	1,274
Aug	13,920	2,734	3,019	2,203	6,015	40.3	21.7	8,120	1,237	6,883	973	3,519	1,249
Sept	13,897	2,743	2,902	2,029	6,197	40.4	21.8	8,028	1,195	6,833	972	3,484	1,323
Oct	13,759	2,676	3,285	2,029	5,839	39.2	20.8	7,924	1,226	6,699	1,068	3,387	1,291
Nov	13,323	2,510	2,896	2,087	5,680	40.9	21.5	7,599	1,181	6,418	1,005	3,355	1,276
Dec	13,097	2,669	2,858	2,039	5,588	40.8	21.0	7,602	1,216	6,386	953	3,399	1,280

[1] Because of independent seasonal adjustment of the various series, detail will not sum to totals.

[2] For 1967, the sum of the unemployed categorized by reason for unemployment does not equal total unemployment.

[3] Beginning with January 2011, includes unemployment durations of up to 5 years; prior data are for up to 2 years.

[4] Beginning with January 1994, job losers and persons who completed temporary jobs.

Note: Data relate to persons 16 years of age and over.

See footnote 5 and Note, Table B–35.

Source: Department of Labor (Bureau of Labor Statistics).

[Thousands of persons, except as noted]

Year or month	All programs [1]		Regular State programs						
	Insured unemployment (weekly average) [2]	Total benefits paid (millions of dollars)	Covered employment [3]	Insured unemployment (weekly average) [2]	Initial claims (weekly average)	Exhaustions (weekly average) [4]	Insured unemployment as percent of covered employment	Benefits paid	
								Total (millions of dollars)	Average weekly check (dollars) [5]
1980	3,521	16,668	86,918	3,356	488	59	3.9	14,887	99.06
1981	3,248	15,910	87,783	3,045	460	57	3.5	14,568	106.61
1982	4,836	26,649	86,148	4,059	583	80	4.7	21,769	119.34
1983	5,216	31,615	86,867	3,395	438	80	3.9	19,025	123.59
1984	3,160	18,201	91,378	2,475	377	50	2.7	13,642	123.47
1985	2,751	16,444	94,027	2,617	397	49	2.8	14,941	128.09
1986	2,667	16,325	95,946	2,621	378	52	2.7	16,188	135.65
1987	2,349	14,632	98,760	2,300	328	46	2.3	14,561	140.39
1988	2,122	13,500	101,987	2,081	310	38	2.0	13,483	144.74
1989	2,158	14,618	104,750	2,156	330	37	2.1	14,603	151.43
1990	2,527	18,452	106,325	2,522	388	45	2.4	18,413	161.20
1991	3,514	27,004	104,642	3,342	447	67	3.2	25,924	169.56
1992	4,906	39,669	105,187	3,245	408	74	3.1	26,048	173.38
1993	4,188	34,649	107,263	2,751	341	62	2.6	22,599	179.41
1994	2,941	24,261	110,526	2,670	340	57	2.4	22,338	181.91
1995	2,648	22,026	113,504	2,572	357	51	2.3	21,925	187.04
1996	2,656	22,397	116,078	2,595	356	53	2.2	22,349	189.27
1997	2,372	20,333	119,159	2,323	323	48	1.9	20,287	192.84
1998	2,264	20,091	122,427	2,222	321	44	1.8	20,017	200.58
1999	2,223	21,037	125,280	2,188	298	44	1.7	21,001	212.10
2000	2,143	21,005	128,054	2,110	301	41	1.6	20,983	221.01
2001	3,012	32,227	127,923	2,974	404	54	2.3	32,135	238.07
2002	4,453	53,350	126,545	3,585	407	85	2.8	42,266	256.79
2003	4,400	53,352	126,084	3,531	404	85	2.8	41,896	261.67
2004	3,103	36,495	127,618	2,950	345	68	2.3	35,034	262.50
2005	2,709	32,154	129,929	2,661	328	55	2.0	32,098	266.63
2006	2,521	30,917	132,177	2,476	313	51	1.9	30,852	277.20
2007	2,612	33,212	133,688	2,572	324	51	1.9	33,156	287.73
2008	3,898	51,798	133,076	3,306	424	66	2.5	43,764	297.10
2009	9,122	141,384	126,763	5,724	568	145	4.5	80,564	308.73
2010	9,724	150,029	125,816	4,487	454	122	3.6	59,771	299.31
2011 p	7,717	107,452	126,603	3,681	406	93	2.9	48,520	295.79
2010: Jan	12,364	14,455.6	123,206	6,114	640	157	5.0	6,230.0	306.25
Feb	11,357	13,847.3	123,394	5,530	484	137	4.5	5,963.6	305.81
Mar	12,804	16,198.3	124,351	6,050	496	159	4.9	6,739.1	304.77
Apr	10,599	12,782.8	125,714	4,949	482	141	3.9	5,207.6	303.64
May	10,746	12,280.0	126,685	4,782	421	137	3.8	4,754.0	301.68
June	10,315	12,514.1	127,112	4,758	497	141	3.7	5,038.8	297.98
July	9,201	10,700.9	124,897	4,551	502	130	3.6	4,445.0	294.37
Aug	11,335	13,585.1	125,379	4,936	440	135	3.9	4,796.8	290.59
Sept	9,366	11,124.3	126,504	4,046	402	114	3.2	4,070.5	295.30
Oct	9,222	10,494.1	127,389	3,944	442	111	3.1	3,763.2	294.44
Nov	9,672	11,265.4	127,591	4,256	498	117	3.3	4,261.1	292.07
Dec	9,436	10,781.2	127,569	4,413	595	112	3.5	4,501.3	296.28
2011: Jan	10,646	11,116.8	124,494	5,209	598	121	4.2	5,085.6	296.92
Feb	8,971	9,904.7	125,059	4,450	397	100	3.6	4,643.6	299.06
Mar	9,328	10,780.0	125,943	4,545	416	111	3.6	4,982.6	299.68
Apr	8,113	8,846.7	127,392	3,862	428	107	3.0	3,950.1	298.18
May	8,831	9,302.9	128,197	4,094	407	109	3.2	4,033.2	295.89
June	7,885	8,812.7	128,530	3,688	447	97	2.9	3,808.6	293.63
July	7,958	8,127.3	....	3,887	439	101	....	3,662.3	289.72
Aug	8,252	9,125.4	....	4,013	398	103	....	4,115.5	289.00
Sept	6,849	7,589.3	....	3,305	366	85	....	3,348.4	296.37
Oct	7,406	7,610.1	....	3,582	403	94	....	3,435.7	295.07
Nov	8,746	8,109.3	....	3,533	459	92	....	3,662.3	296.08
Dec p	7,330	8,126.4	....	3,688	517	89	....	3,791.7	298.39

[1] Includes State Unemployment Insurance (State), Unemployment Compensation for Federal Employees (UCFE), Unemployment Compensation for Ex-service members (UCX), and Federal and State extended benefit programs. Also includes temporary Federal emergency programs: Federal Supplemental Compensation (1982-1985), Emergency Unemployment Compensation (EUC, 1991-1994), Temporary Extended Unemployment Compensation (2002-2004), EUC 2008 (2008-2011), and Federal Additional Compensation (2009-2010).

[2] The number of people continuing to receive benefits.

[3] Workers covered by regular State Unemployment Insurance programs.

[4] Individuals receiving final payments in benefit year.

[5] For total unemployment only. Excludes partial payments.

Note: Includes data for the District of Columbia, Puerto Rico, and the Virgin Islands.

Source: Department of Labor (Employment and Training Administration).

TABLE B–46. Employees on nonagricultural payrolls, by major industry, 1967–2011

[Thousands of persons; monthly data seasonally adjusted]

		Private industries									
			Goods-producing industries						Private service-providing industries		
Year or month	Total nonagricultural employment	Total private	Total	Mining and logging	Construction	Manufacturing			Total	Trade, transportation, and utilities [1]	
						Total	Durable goods	Nondurable goods		Total	Retail trade
1967	65,931	54,406	21,882	679	3,305	17,897	10,952	6,945	32,524	12,950	6,711
1968	68,023	56,050	22,292	671	3,410	18,211	11,137	7,074	33,759	13,334	6,977
1969	70,512	58,181	22,893	683	3,637	18,573	11,396	7,177	35,288	13,853	7,295
1970	71,006	58,318	22,179	677	3,654	17,848	10,762	7,086	36,139	14,144	7,463
1971	71,335	58,323	21,602	658	3,770	17,174	10,229	6,944	36,721	14,318	7,657
1972	73,798	60,333	22,299	672	3,957	17,669	10,630	7,039	38,034	14,788	8,038
1973	76,912	63,050	23,450	693	4,167	18,589	11,414	7,176	39,600	15,349	8,371
1974	78,389	64,086	23,364	755	4,095	18,514	11,432	7,082	40,721	15,693	8,536
1975	77,069	62,250	21,318	802	3,608	16,909	10,266	6,643	40,932	15,606	8,600
1976	79,502	64,501	22,025	832	3,662	17,531	10,640	6,891	42,476	16,128	8,966
1977	82,593	67,334	22,972	865	3,940	18,167	11,132	7,035	44,362	16,765	9,359
1978	86,826	71,014	24,156	902	4,322	18,932	11,770	7,162	46,858	17,658	9,879
1979	89,932	73,864	24,997	1,008	4,562	19,426	12,220	7,206	48,868	18,303	10,180
1980	90,528	74,154	24,263	1,077	4,454	18,733	11,679	7,054	49,891	18,413	10,244
1981	91,289	75,109	24,118	1,180	4,304	18,634	11,611	7,023	50,991	18,604	10,364
1982	89,677	73,695	22,550	1,163	4,024	17,363	10,610	6,753	51,145	18,457	10,372
1983	90,280	74,269	22,110	997	4,065	17,048	10,326	6,722	52,160	18,668	10,635
1984	94,530	78,371	23,435	1,014	4,501	17,920	11,050	6,870	54,936	19,653	11,223
1985	97,511	80,978	23,585	974	4,793	17,819	11,034	6,784	57,393	20,379	11,733
1986	99,474	82,636	23,318	829	4,937	17,552	10,795	6,757	59,318	20,795	12,078
1987	102,088	84,932	23,470	771	5,090	17,609	10,767	6,842	61,462	21,302	12,419
1988	105,345	87,806	23,909	770	5,233	17,906	10,969	6,938	63,897	21,974	12,808
1989	108,014	90,087	24,045	750	5,309	17,985	11,004	6,981	66,042	22,510	13,108
1990	109,487	91,072	23,723	765	5,263	17,695	10,737	6,958	67,349	22,666	13,182
1991	108,375	89,829	22,588	739	4,780	17,068	10,220	6,848	67,241	22,281	12,896
1992	108,726	89,940	22,095	689	4,608	16,799	9,946	6,853	67,845	22,125	12,828
1993	110,844	91,855	22,219	666	4,779	16,774	9,901	6,872	69,636	22,378	13,021
1994	114,291	95,016	22,774	659	5,095	17,020	10,132	6,889	72,242	23,128	13,491
1995	117,298	97,865	23,156	641	5,274	17,241	10,373	6,868	74,710	23,834	13,897
1996	119,708	100,169	23,409	637	5,536	17,237	10,486	6,751	76,760	24,239	14,143
1997	122,776	103,113	23,886	654	5,813	17,419	10,705	6,714	79,227	24,700	14,389
1998	125,930	106,021	24,354	645	6,149	17,560	10,911	6,649	81,667	25,186	14,609
1999	128,993	108,686	24,465	598	6,545	17,322	10,831	6,491	84,221	25,771	14,970
2000	131,785	110,995	24,649	599	6,787	17,263	10,877	6,386	86,346	26,225	15,280
2001	131,826	110,708	23,873	606	6,826	16,441	10,336	6,105	86,834	25,983	15,239
2002	130,341	108,828	22,557	583	6,716	15,259	9,485	5,774	86,271	25,497	15,025
2003	129,999	108,416	21,816	572	6,735	14,510	8,964	5,546	86,600	25,287	14,917
2004	131,435	109,814	21,882	591	6,976	14,315	8,925	5,390	87,932	25,533	15,058
2005	133,703	111,899	22,190	628	7,336	14,226	8,956	5,271	89,709	25,959	15,280
2006	136,086	114,113	22,531	684	7,691	14,155	8,981	5,174	91,582	26,276	15,353
2007	137,598	115,380	22,233	724	7,630	13,879	8,808	5,071	93,147	26,630	15,520
2008	136,790	114,281	21,334	767	7,162	13,406	8,463	4,943	92,947	26,293	15,283
2009	130,807	108,252	18,557	694	6,016	11,847	7,284	4,563	89,695	24,906	14,522
2010	129,818	107,337	17,755	705	5,526	11,524	7,067	4,457	89,582	24,605	14,414
2011 *p*	131,159	109,080	18,037	787	5,526	11,723	7,284	4,439	91,043	24,921	14,564
2010: Jan	129,281	106,793	17,717	667	5,585	11,465	6,999	4,466	89,076	24,536	14,383
Feb	129,246	106,772	17,667	672	5,533	11,462	6,994	4,468	89,105	24,525	14,384
Mar	129,438	106,916	17,701	680	5,550	11,471	7,010	4,461	89,215	24,559	14,408
Apr	129,715	107,145	17,762	687	5,566	11,509	7,039	4,470	89,383	24,581	14,424
May	130,173	107,193	17,763	698	5,529	11,536	7,065	4,471	89,430	24,584	14,421
June	129,981	107,258	17,763	704	5,511	11,548	7,079	4,469	89,495	24,587	14,409
July	129,932	107,351	17,791	711	5,500	11,580	7,114	4,466	89,560	24,609	14,419
Aug	129,873	107,461	17,790	719	5,520	11,551	7,092	4,459	89,671	24,601	14,413
Sept	129,844	107,570	17,784	725	5,514	11,545	7,095	4,450	89,786	24,627	14,430
Oct	130,015	107,713	17,785	734	5,512	11,539	7,097	4,442	89,928	24,670	14,457
Nov	130,108	107,841	17,793	735	5,504	11,554	7,113	4,441	90,048	24,684	14,441
Dec	130,260	108,008	17,797	734	5,498	11,565	7,126	4,439	90,211	24,746	14,447
2011: Jan	130,328	108,102	17,835	739	5,478	11,618	7,183	4,435	90,267	24,740	14,478
Feb	130,563	108,363	17,916	744	5,517	11,655	7,211	4,444	90,447	24,775	14,478
Mar	130,757	108,582	17,956	759	5,522	11,675	7,232	4,443	90,626	24,791	14,472
Apr	130,974	108,823	17,999	770	5,526	11,703	7,253	4,450	90,824	24,870	14,536
May	131,027	108,922	18,019	780	5,529	11,710	7,271	4,439	90,903	24,893	14,539
June	131,047	108,997	18,035	789	5,522	11,724	7,288	4,436	90,962	24,919	14,551
July	131,174	109,170	18,088	798	5,532	11,758	7,313	4,445	91,082	24,942	14,579
Aug	131,278	109,242	18,075	800	5,518	11,757	7,308	4,449	91,167	24,957	14,582
Sept	131,488	109,462	18,111	806	5,549	11,756	7,314	4,442	91,351	24,978	14,605
Oct	131,600	109,596	18,117	812	5,539	11,766	7,329	4,437	91,479	25,010	14,620
Nov *p*	131,700	109,716	18,111	817	5,527	11,767	7,342	4,425	91,605	25,052	14,659
Dec *p*	131,900	109,928	18,159	825	5,544	11,790	7,365	4,425	91,769	25,142	14,687

[1] Includes wholesale trade, transportation and warehousing, and utilities, not shown separately.

Note: Data in Tables B–46 and B–47 are based on reports from employing establishments and relate to full- and part-time wage and salary workers in nonagricultural establishments who received pay for any part of the pay period that includes the 12th of the month. Not comparable with labor force data (Tables B–35 through B–44), which include proprietors, self-employed persons, unpaid family workers, and private household workers; which count persons as employed when they are not at work because of industrial disputes, bad weather, etc., even if they are not paid for the time off; which are based on a sample of the

See next page for continuation of table.

[Thousands of persons; monthly data seasonally adjusted]

| Year or month | Private industries—Continued | | | | | | Government | | | |
| | Private service-providing industries—Continued | | | | | | | | | |
	Information	Financial activities	Professional and business services	Education and health services	Leisure and hospitality	Other services	Total	Federal	State	Local
1967	1,955	3,087	4,720	3,986	4,269	1,558	11,525	2,852	2,302	6,371
1968	1,991	3,234	4,918	4,191	4,453	1,638	11,972	2,871	2,442	6,660
1969	2,048	3,404	5,156	4,428	4,670	1,731	12,330	2,893	2,533	6,904
1970	2,041	3,532	5,267	4,577	4,789	1,789	12,687	2,865	2,664	7,158
1971	2,009	3,651	5,328	4,675	4,914	1,827	13,012	2,828	2,747	7,437
1972	2,056	3,784	5,523	4,863	5,121	1,900	13,465	2,815	2,859	7,790
1973	2,135	3,920	5,774	5,092	5,341	1,990	13,862	2,794	2,923	8,146
1974	2,160	4,023	5,974	5,322	5,471	2,078	14,303	2,858	3,039	8,407
1975	2,061	4,047	6,034	5,497	5,544	2,144	14,820	2,882	3,179	8,758
1976	2,111	4,155	6,287	5,756	5,794	2,244	15,001	2,863	3,273	8,865
1977	2,185	4,348	6,587	6,052	6,065	2,359	15,258	2,859	3,377	9,023
1978	2,287	4,599	6,972	6,427	6,411	2,505	15,812	2,893	3,474	9,446
1979	2,375	4,843	7,312	6,767	6,631	2,637	16,068	2,894	3,541	9,633
1980	2,361	5,025	7,544	7,072	6,721	2,755	16,375	3,000	3,610	9,765
1981	2,382	5,163	7,782	7,357	6,840	2,865	16,180	2,922	3,640	9,619
1982	2,317	5,209	7,848	7,515	6,874	2,924	15,982	2,884	3,640	9,458
1983	2,253	5,334	8,039	7,766	7,078	3,021	16,011	2,915	3,662	9,434
1984	2,398	5,553	8,464	8,193	7,489	3,186	16,159	2,943	3,734	9,482
1985	2,437	5,815	8,871	8,657	7,869	3,366	16,533	3,014	3,832	9,687
1986	2,445	6,128	9,211	9,061	8,156	3,523	16,838	3,044	3,893	9,901
1987	2,507	6,385	9,608	9,515	8,446	3,699	17,156	3,089	3,967	10,100
1988	2,585	6,500	10,090	10,063	8,778	3,907	17,540	3,124	4,076	10,339
1989	2,622	6,562	10,555	10,616	9,062	4,116	17,927	3,136	4,182	10,609
1990	2,688	6,614	10,848	10,984	9,288	4,261	18,415	3,196	4,305	10,914
1991	2,677	6,558	10,714	11,506	9,256	4,249	18,545	3,110	4,355	11,081
1992	2,641	6,540	10,970	11,891	9,437	4,240	18,787	3,111	4,408	11,267
1993	2,668	6,709	11,495	12,303	9,732	4,350	18,989	3,063	4,488	11,438
1994	2,738	6,867	12,174	12,807	10,100	4,428	19,275	3,018	4,576	11,682
1995	2,843	6,827	12,844	13,289	10,501	4,572	19,432	2,949	4,635	11,849
1996	2,940	6,969	13,462	13,683	10,777	4,690	19,539	2,877	4,606	12,056
1997	3,084	7,178	14,335	14,087	11,018	4,825	19,664	2,806	4,582	12,276
1998	3,218	7,462	15,147	14,446	11,232	4,976	19,909	2,772	4,612	12,525
1999	3,419	7,648	15,957	14,798	11,543	5,087	20,307	2,769	4,709	12,829
2000	3,630	7,687	16,666	15,109	11,862	5,168	20,790	2,865	4,786	13,139
2001	3,629	7,808	16,476	15,645	12,036	5,258	21,118	2,764	4,905	13,449
2002	3,395	7,847	15,976	16,199	11,986	5,372	21,513	2,766	5,029	13,718
2003	3,188	7,977	15,987	16,588	12,173	5,401	21,583	2,761	5,002	13,820
2004	3,118	8,031	16,394	16,953	12,493	5,409	21,621	2,730	4,982	13,909
2005	3,061	8,153	16,954	17,372	12,816	5,395	21,804	2,732	5,032	14,041
2006	3,038	8,328	17,566	17,826	13,110	5,438	21,974	2,732	5,075	14,167
2007	3,032	8,301	17,942	18,322	13,427	5,494	22,218	2,734	5,122	14,362
2008	2,984	8,145	17,735	18,838	13,436	5,515	22,509	2,762	5,177	14,571
2009	2,804	7,769	16,579	19,193	13,077	5,367	22,555	2,832	5,169	14,554
2010	2,711	7,630	16,688	19,564	13,020	5,364	22,482	2,968	5,142	14,372
2011 ᵖ	2,670	7,613	17,186	19,987	13,219	5,447	22,080	2,832	5,098	14,150
2010: Jan	2,737	7,666	16,513	19,371	12,931	5,322	22,488	2,866	5,140	14,482
Feb	2,731	7,657	16,544	19,399	12,932	5,317	22,474	2,872	5,143	14,459
Mar	2,718	7,643	16,546	19,455	12,963	5,331	22,522	2,926	5,142	14,454
Apr	2,716	7,648	16,615	19,482	12,998	5,343	22,570	2,985	5,138	14,447
May	2,715	7,640	16,640	19,508	12,995	5,348	22,980	3,413	5,135	14,432
June	2,701	7,628	16,683	19,535	13,018	5,343	22,723	3,184	5,134	14,405
July	2,706	7,618	16,681	19,571	13,013	5,362	22,581	3,041	5,154	14,386
Aug	2,711	7,616	16,711	19,612	13,051	5,369	22,412	2,927	5,132	14,353
Sept	2,701	7,616	16,719	19,631	13,103	5,389	22,274	2,850	5,138	14,286
Oct	2,697	7,617	16,759	19,695	13,072	5,418	22,302	2,847	5,146	14,309
Nov	2,699	7,616	16,844	19,732	13,057	5,416	22,267	2,844	5,144	14,279
Dec	2,694	7,617	16,902	19,760	13,074	5,418	22,252	2,853	5,140	14,259
2011: Jan	2,687	7,607	16,953	19,789	13,071	5,420	22,226	2,850	5,136	14,240
Feb	2,684	7,606	16,991	19,832	13,125	5,434	22,200	2,853	5,121	14,226
Mar	2,683	7,611	17,066	19,865	13,171	5,439	22,175	2,854	5,119	14,202
Apr	2,684	7,612	17,111	19,905	13,200	5,442	22,151	2,846	5,109	14,196
May	2,684	7,625	17,155	19,926	13,175	5,445	22,105	2,845	5,093	14,167
June	2,682	7,609	17,155	19,944	13,202	5,451	22,050	2,829	5,091	14,130
July	2,677	7,606	17,194	19,998	13,217	5,448	22,004	2,824	5,076	14,104
Aug	2,627	7,612	17,239	20,036	13,240	5,456	22,036	2,818	5,086	14,132
Sept	2,659	7,610	17,293	20,088	13,264	5,459	22,026	2,817	5,094	14,115
Oct	2,659	7,617	17,323	20,125	13,291	5,454	22,004	2,819	5,079	14,106
Nov ᵖ	2,652	7,622	17,342	20,158	13,321	5,458	21,984	2,815	5,077	14,092
Dec ᵖ	2,658	7,624	17,354	20,187	13,342	5,462	21,972	2,817	5,077	14,078

Note (cont'd): working-age population; and which count persons only once—as employed, unemployed, or not in the labor force. In the data shown here, persons who work at more than one job are counted each time they appear on a payroll.

Establishment data for employment, hours, and earnings are classified based on the 2007 North American Industry Classification System (NAICS). For further description and details see *Employment and Earnings*.

Source: Department of Labor (Bureau of Labor Statistics).

TABLE B–47. Hours and earnings in private nonagricultural industries, 1965–2011 [1]

[Monthly data seasonally adjusted]

Year or month	Average weekly hours			Average hourly earnings			Average weekly earnings, total private			
	Total private	Manufacturing		Total private		Manufacturing (current dollars)	Level		Percent change from year earlier	
		Total	Overtime	Current dollars	1982–84 dollars[2]		Current dollars	1982–84 dollars[2]	Current dollars	1982–84 dollars[2]
1965	38.6	41.2	3.6	$2.63	$8.30	$2.49	$101.52	$320.25	4.2	2.6
1966	38.5	41.4	3.9	2.73	8.37	2.60	105.11	322.42	3.5	.7
1967	37.9	40.6	3.3	2.85	8.48	2.71	108.02	321.49	2.8	–.3
1968	37.7	40.7	3.5	3.02	8.63	2.89	113.85	325.29	5.4	1.2
1969	37.5	40.6	3.6	3.22	8.73	3.07	120.75	327.24	6.1	.6
1970	37.0	39.8	2.9	3.40	8.72	3.23	125.80	322.56	4.2	–1.4
1971	36.8	39.9	2.9	3.63	8.92	3.45	133.58	327.32	6.2	1.5
1972	36.9	40.6	3.4	3.90	9.26	3.70	143.91	341.83	7.7	4.4
1973	36.9	40.7	3.8	4.14	9.26	3.97	152.77	341.77	6.2	.0
1974	36.4	40.0	3.2	4.43	8.93	4.31	161.25	325.10	5.6	–4.9
1975	36.0	39.5	2.6	4.73	8.74	4.71	170.28	314.75	5.6	–3.2
1976	36.1	40.1	3.1	5.06	8.85	5.09	182.67	319.35	7.3	1.5
1977	35.9	40.3	3.4	5.44	8.93	5.55	195.30	320.69	6.9	.4
1978	35.8	40.4	3.6	5.88	8.96	6.05	210.50	320.88	7.8	.1
1979	35.6	40.2	3.3	6.34	8.67	6.57	225.70	308.76	7.2	–3.8
1980	35.2	39.7	2.8	6.85	8.26	7.15	241.12	290.86	6.8	–5.8
1981	35.2	39.8	2.8	7.44	8.14	7.86	261.89	286.53	8.6	–1.5
1982	34.7	38.9	2.3	7.87	8.12	8.36	273.09	281.83	4.3	–1.6
1983	34.9	40.1	2.9	8.20	8.22	8.70	286.18	286.75	4.8	1.7
1984	35.1	40.7	3.4	8.49	8.22	9.05	298.00	288.48	4.1	.6
1985	34.9	40.5	3.3	8.74	8.18	9.40	305.03	285.34	2.4	–1.1
1986	34.7	40.7	3.4	8.93	8.22	9.59	309.87	285.33	1.6	.0
1987	34.7	40.9	3.7	9.14	8.12	9.77	317.16	281.92	2.4	–1.2
1988	34.6	41.0	3.8	9.44	8.07	10.05	326.62	279.16	3.0	–1.0
1989	34.5	40.9	3.8	9.80	7.99	10.35	338.10	275.77	3.5	–1.2
1990	34.3	40.5	3.9	10.20	7.91	10.78	349.75	271.12	3.4	–1.7
1991	34.1	40.4	3.8	10.52	7.83	11.13	358.51	266.95	2.5	–1.5
1992	34.2	40.7	4.0	10.77	7.79	11.40	368.25	266.46	2.7	–.2
1993	34.3	41.1	4.4	11.05	7.78	11.70	378.91	266.65	2.9	.1
1994	34.5	41.7	5.0	11.34	7.79	12.04	391.22	268.70	3.2	.8
1995	34.3	41.3	4.7	11.65	7.78	12.34	400.07	267.07	2.3	–.6
1996	34.3	41.3	4.8	12.04	7.81	12.75	413.28	268.19	3.3	.4
1997	34.5	41.7	5.1	12.51	7.94	13.14	431.86	274.02	4.5	2.2
1998	34.5	41.4	4.9	13.01	8.15	13.45	448.56	280.88	3.9	2.5
1999	34.3	41.4	4.9	13.49	8.27	13.85	463.15	283.79	3.3	1.0
2000	34.3	41.3	4.7	14.02	8.30	14.32	481.01	284.79	3.9	.4
2001	34.0	40.3	4.0	14.54	8.38	14.76	493.79	284.61	2.7	–.1
2002	33.9	40.5	4.2	14.97	8.51	15.29	506.75	288.09	2.6	1.2
2003	33.7	40.4	4.2	15.37	8.55	15.74	518.06	288.13	2.2	.0
2004	33.7	40.8	4.6	15.69	8.50	16.14	529.09	286.77	2.1	–.5
2005	33.8	40.7	4.6	16.13	8.45	16.56	544.33	284.99	2.9	–.6
2006	33.9	41.1	4.4	16.76	8.50	16.81	567.87	288.11	4.3	1.1
2007	33.9	41.2	4.2	17.43	8.60	17.26	590.04	290.99	3.9	1.0
2008	33.6	40.8	3.7	18.08	8.57	17.75	607.95	288.06	3.0	–1.0
2009	33.1	39.8	2.9	18.63	8.89	18.24	617.18	294.41	1.5	2.2
2010	33.4	41.1	3.8	19.07	8.91	18.61	636.91	297.67	3.2	1.1
2011 [p]	33.6	41.4	4.1	19.44	8.77	18.94	653.16	294.78	2.6	–1.0
2010: Jan	33.3	40.8	3.6	18.91	8.86	18.44	629.70	295.03	2.7	–.7
Feb	33.2	40.4	3.5	18.93	8.86	18.48	628.48	294.32	2.2	–.6
Mar	33.3	41.0	3.7	18.93	8.86	18.49	630.37	295.16	2.8	–.2
Apr	33.4	41.2	3.8	18.98	8.89	18.51	633.93	296.86	3.4	.4
May	33.4	41.5	4.0	19.03	8.93	18.59	635.60	298.29	3.5	1.0
June	33.4	41.0	3.8	19.05	8.97	18.59	636.27	299.45	3.8	2.4
July	33.5	41.1	3.8	19.08	8.94	18.60	639.18	299.50	3.7	2.0
Aug	33.5	41.1	3.8	19.13	8.94	18.63	640.86	299.57	3.6	2.1
Sept	33.5	41.3	3.9	19.14	8.93	18.65	641.19	299.12	3.8	2.3
Oct	33.5	41.2	3.9	19.23	8.94	18.71	644.21	299.62	4.0	2.5
Nov	33.5	41.2	4.0	19.24	8.94	18.75	644.54	299.46	3.3	2.0
Dec	33.5	41.3	4.0	19.23	8.89	18.80	644.21	297.74	2.9	1.3
2011: Jan	33.4	41.1	4.1	19.31	8.88	18.91	644.95	296.74	2.4	.6
Feb	33.6	41.3	4.2	19.32	8.83	18.89	649.15	296.82	3.3	.8
Mar	33.6	41.4	4.2	19.32	8.78	18.91	649.15	294.90	3.0	–.1
Apr	33.6	41.4	4.2	19.37	8.76	18.91	650.83	294.21	2.7	–.9
May	33.6	41.4	4.1	19.42	8.77	18.94	652.51	294.55	2.7	–1.3
June	33.6	41.4	4.0	19.43	8.80	18.91	652.85	295.72	2.6	–1.2
July	33.6	41.4	4.1	19.49	8.78	18.96	654.86	294.88	2.5	–1.5
Aug	33.5	41.3	4.1	19.47	8.73	18.92	652.25	292.48	1.8	–2.4
Sept	33.6	41.3	4.0	19.49	8.71	18.89	654.86	292.55	2.1	–2.2
Oct	33.7	41.5	4.1	19.53	8.74	19.00	658.16	294.43	2.2	–1.7
Nov [p]	33.6	41.4	4.1	19.54	8.75	18.98	656.54	293.93	1.9	–1.8
Dec [p]	33.7	41.5	4.1	19.54	8.75	19.05	658.50	294.83	2.2	–1.0

[1] For production or nonsupervisory workers; total includes private industry groups shown in Table B–46.
[2] Current dollars divided by the consumer price index for urban wage earners and clerical workers on a 1982–84=100 base.

Note: See Note, Table B–46.

Source: Department of Labor (Bureau of Labor Statistics).

TABLE B–48. Employment cost index, private industry, 1997–2011

Year and month	Total private			Goods-producing			Service-providing [1]			Manufacturing		
	Total compensation	Wages and salaries	Benefits [2]	Total compensation	Wages and salaries	Benefits [2]	Total compensation	Wages and salaries	Benefits [2]	Total compensation	Wages and salaries	Benefits [2]
Indexes on SIC basis, December 2005=100; not seasonally adjusted												
December:												
1997	74.9	77.6	68.5	74.5	78.3	67.3	75.1	77.4	69.2	74.6	78.6	67.4
1998	77.5	80.6	70.2	76.5	81.1	68.1	78.0	80.5	71.4	76.6	81.3	67.9
1999	80.2	83.5	72.6	79.1	83.8	70.5	80.6	83.4	73.8	79.2	84.1	70.3
2000	83.6	86.7	76.7	82.6	87.1	74.3	84.2	86.6	78.1	82.3	87.1	73.6
2001	87.1	90.0	80.6	85.7	90.2	77.3	87.8	89.9	82.5	85.3	90.2	76.3
Indexes on NAICS basis, December 2005=100; not seasonally adjusted												
2001 [3]	87.3	89.9	81.3	86.0	90.0	78.5	87.8	89.8	82.4	85.5	90.2	77.2
2002	90.0	92.2	84.7	89.0	92.6	82.3	90.4	92.1	85.8	88.7	92.8	81.3
2003	93.6	95.1	90.2	92.6	94.9	88.2	94.0	95.2	91.0	92.4	95.1	87.3
2004	97.2	97.6	96.2	96.9	97.2	96.3	97.3	97.7	96.1	96.9	97.4	96.0
2005	100.0	100.0	100.0	100.0	100.0	100.0	100.0	100.0	100.0	100.0	100.0	100.0
2006	103.2	103.2	103.1	102.5	102.9	101.7	103.4	103.3	103.7	101.8	102.3	100.8
2007	106.3	106.6	105.6	105.0	106.0	103.2	106.7	106.8	106.6	103.8	104.9	101.7
2008	108.9	109.4	107.7	107.5	109.0	104.7	109.4	109.6	108.9	105.9	107.7	102.5
2009	110.2	110.8	108.7	108.6	110.0	105.8	110.8	111.1	109.9	107.0	108.9	103.6
2010	112.5	112.8	111.9	111.1	111.6	110.1	113.0	113.1	112.6	110.0	110.7	108.8
2011: Mar	113.3	113.2	113.7	112.0	112.2	111.7	113.8	113.5	114.5	111.4	111.5	111.1
June	114.3	113.8	115.4	113.2	112.7	114.1	114.6	114.1	115.9	112.7	112.0	114.0
Sept	114.6	114.3	115.4	113.4	113.2	113.9	115.0	114.6	116.0	112.8	112.5	113.4
Indexes on NAICS basis, December 2005=100; seasonally adjusted												
2010: Mar	111.1	111.4	110.3	109.6	110.4	108.0	111.5	111.7	111.2	108.2	109.4	106.1
June	111.6	111.9	110.9	110.2	110.9	108.8	112.1	112.2	111.8	109.0	109.9	107.3
Sept	112.1	112.3	111.6	110.9	111.4	110.0	112.5	112.6	112.3	109.9	110.5	108.7
Dec	112.7	112.8	112.2	111.3	111.7	110.7	113.1	113.2	112.8	110.4	110.9	109.6
2011: Mar	113.3	113.2	113.5	111.9	112.1	111.4	113.8	113.5	114.4	111.1	111.4	110.6
June	114.2	113.8	115.3	113.2	112.7	114.0	114.6	114.1	115.8	112.6	112.0	113.8
Sept	114.6	114.2	115.4	113.3	113.1	113.8	115.0	114.6	116.0	112.8	112.5	113.4
Percent change from 12 months earlier, not seasonally adjusted												
December:												
SIC:												
1997	3.5	3.9	2.2	2.5	3.0	1.4	3.9	4.3	2.8	2.3	3.0	1.4
1998	3.5	3.9	2.5	2.7	3.6	1.2	3.9	4.0	3.2	2.7	3.4	.7
1999	3.5	3.6	3.4	3.4	3.3	3.5	3.3	3.6	3.4	3.4	3.4	3.5
2000	4.2	3.8	5.6	4.4	3.9	5.4	4.5	3.8	5.8	3.9	3.6	4.7
2001	4.2	3.8	5.1	3.8	3.6	4.0	4.3	3.8	5.6	3.6	3.6	3.7
NAICS:												
2001 [3]	4.1	3.8	5.2	3.6	3.6	3.7	4.4	3.8	5.6	3.4	3.6	3.5
2002	3.1	2.6	4.2	3.5	2.9	4.8	3.0	2.6	4.1	3.7	2.9	5.3
2003	4.0	3.1	6.5	4.0	2.5	7.2	4.0	3.4	6.1	4.2	2.5	7.4
2004	3.8	2.6	6.7	4.6	2.4	9.2	3.5	2.6	5.6	4.9	2.4	10.0
2005	2.9	2.5	4.0	3.2	2.9	3.8	2.8	2.4	4.1	3.2	2.7	4.2
2006	3.2	3.2	3.1	2.5	2.9	1.7	3.4	3.3	3.7	1.8	2.3	.8
2007	3.0	3.3	2.4	2.4	3.0	1.5	3.2	3.4	2.8	2.0	2.5	.9
2008	2.4	2.6	2.0	2.4	2.8	1.5	2.5	2.6	2.2	2.0	2.7	.8
2009	1.2	1.3	.9	1.0	.9	1.1	1.3	1.4	.9	1.0	1.1	1.1
2010	2.1	1.8	2.9	2.3	1.5	4.1	2.0	1.8	2.5	2.8	1.7	5.0
2011: Mar	2.0	1.6	3.0	2.1	1.5	3.0	2.0	1.6	2.9	2.8	1.9	4.2
June	2.3	1.7	4.0	2.6	1.6	4.7	2.2	1.6	3.6	3.3	1.8	6.1
Sept	2.1	1.7	3.3	2.2	1.5	3.5	2.1	1.7	3.3	2.6	1.7	4.3
Percent change from 3 months earlier, seasonally adjusted												
2010: Mar	0.6	0.5	1.2	0.7	0.2	1.6	0.5	0.4	1.0	0.7	0.3	1.8
June	.5	.4	.5	.5	.5	.7	.5	.4	.5	.7	.5	1.1
Sept	.4	.4	.6	.6	.5	1.1	.4	.4	.4	.8	.5	1.3
Dec	.5	.4	.5	.4	.3	.6	.5	.5	.4	.5	.4	.8
2011: Mar	.5	.4	1.2	.5	.4	.6	.6	.3	1.4	.6	.5	.9
June	.8	.5	1.6	1.2	.5	2.3	.7	.5	1.2	1.4	.5	2.9
Sept	.4	.4	.1	.1	.4	−.2	.3	.4	.2	.2	.4	−.4

[1] On Standard Industrial Classification (SIC) basis, data are for service-producing industries.
[2] Employer costs for employee benefits.
[3] Data on North American Industry Classification System (NAICS) basis available beginning with 2001; not strictly comparable with earlier data shown on SIC basis.

Note: Changes effective with the release of March 2006 data (in April 2006) include changing industry classification to NAICS from SIC and rebasing data to December 2005=100. Historical SIC data are available through December 2005.

Data exclude farm and household workers.

Source: Department of Labor (Bureau of Labor Statistics).

Table B-49. Productivity and related data, business and nonfarm business sectors, 1962–2011

[Index numbers, 2005=100; quarterly data seasonally adjusted]

Year or quarter	Output per hour of all persons		Output [1]		Hours of all persons [2]		Compensation per hour [3]		Real compensation per hour [4]		Unit labor costs		Implicit price deflator [5]	
	Business sector	Nonfarm business sector	Business sector	Nonfarm business sector	Business sector	Nonfarm business sector	Business sector	Nonfarm business sector	Business sector	Nonfarm business sector	Business sector	Nonfarm business sector	Business sector	Nonfarm business sector
1962	38.8	41.3	21.6	21.5	55.7	52.0	9.2	9.6	54.4	56.5	23.8	23.2	22.2	21.7
1963	40.3	42.7	22.6	22.5	56.1	52.6	9.6	9.9	55.6	57.7	23.7	23.2	22.3	21.8
1964	41.7	44.0	24.0	24.0	57.7	54.5	9.9	10.2	57.0	58.7	23.8	23.2	22.6	22.1
1965	43.1	45.4	25.7	25.7	59.6	56.6	10.3	10.6	58.2	59.7	23.9	23.3	22.9	22.4
1966	44.9	47.0	27.5	27.5	61.2	58.6	11.0	11.2	60.4	61.5	24.5	23.8	23.5	22.9
1967	45.9	47.8	28.0	28.0	61.0	58.6	11.6	11.8	61.9	63.1	25.3	24.8	24.1	23.6
1968	47.4	49.4	29.4	29.5	61.9	59.6	12.5	12.8	64.2	65.3	26.4	25.8	25.1	24.6
1969	47.7	49.5	30.3	30.4	63.5	61.3	13.4	13.6	65.1	66.2	28.1	27.5	26.2	25.7
1970	48.6	50.2	30.3	30.3	62.2	60.4	14.5	14.6	66.3	67.1	29.7	29.1	27.4	26.8
1971	50.6	52.3	31.4	31.5	62.1	60.2	15.4	15.5	67.5	68.4	30.3	29.8	28.5	28.0
1972	52.3	54.0	33.5	33.6	64.0	62.2	16.3	16.6	69.6	70.5	31.2	30.7	29.6	28.8
1973	53.9	55.7	35.8	36.0	66.5	64.7	17.7	17.9	71.0	71.8	32.9	32.2	31.1	29.9
1974	53.0	54.8	35.3	35.5	66.6	64.8	19.4	19.7	70.1	71.0	36.6	35.9	34.1	32.9
1975	54.8	56.3	34.9	34.9	63.7	62.0	21.4	21.6	70.8	71.6	39.0	38.4	37.4	36.5
1976	56.6	58.2	37.2	37.4	65.8	64.2	23.2	23.5	72.7	73.4	41.1	40.3	39.4	38.5
1977	57.5	59.1	39.3	39.5	68.3	66.8	25.1	25.4	73.7	74.5	43.6	42.9	41.8	40.9
1978	58.2	59.9	41.8	42.1	71.8	70.3	27.3	27.6	74.9	75.8	46.9	46.1	44.7	43.7
1979	58.1	59.6	43.2	43.4	74.3	72.8	29.9	30.2	74.9	75.7	51.4	50.7	48.5	47.4
1980	58.0	59.5	42.7	42.9	73.6	72.2	33.1	33.4	74.6	75.4	57.0	56.2	52.9	51.9
1981	59.2	60.3	43.9	43.8	74.1	72.7	36.2	36.7	74.5	75.5	61.1	60.8	57.8	56.9
1982	58.7	59.7	42.6	42.4	72.5	71.1	38.8	39.3	75.4	76.3	66.1	65.8	61.1	60.4
1983	60.8	62.3	44.8	45.1	73.7	72.5	40.4	40.9	75.3	76.2	66.4	65.7	63.1	62.4
1984	62.5	63.5	48.7	48.9	78.0	76.9	42.1	42.6	75.4	76.2	67.4	67.0	65.0	64.1
1985	63.9	64.6	51.0	51.0	79.8	78.9	44.1	44.5	76.3	76.9	69.0	68.9	66.5	66.0
1986	65.7	66.6	52.9	52.9	80.5	79.5	46.4	46.8	78.8	79.5	70.5	70.3	67.6	67.1
1987	65.9	66.8	54.6	54.7	82.9	81.9	48.0	48.5	79.0	79.7	72.9	72.7	69.2	68.7
1988	66.9	67.9	57.0	57.2	85.2	84.3	50.5	50.9	80.1	80.8	75.5	75.1	71.4	70.8
1989	67.6	68.4	59.1	59.2	87.4	86.6	51.9	52.2	78.9	79.4	76.7	76.4	74.0	73.4
1990	69.0	69.6	60.0	60.1	86.9	86.3	55.2	55.5	80.0	80.3	80.0	79.7	76.7	76.1
1991	70.1	70.7	59.5	59.5	84.9	84.2	58.0	58.4	81.1	81.6	82.8	82.6	79.2	78.7
1992	73.0	73.5	61.8	61.8	84.7	84.0	61.1	61.5	83.3	83.9	83.7	83.7	80.7	80.3
1993	73.4	73.9	63.8	63.9	86.9	86.4	62.5	62.7	83.1	83.5	85.1	84.9	82.3	81.9
1994	74.1	74.7	67.0	66.9	90.4	89.6	63.4	63.9	82.6	83.2	85.6	85.5	83.7	83.4
1995	74.1	75.0	68.8	69.0	92.9	92.0	64.7	65.2	82.4	82.9	87.4	86.9	85.2	84.8
1996	76.3	76.9	72.0	72.1	94.4	93.7	66.9	67.4	82.9	83.4	87.8	87.5	86.6	86.0
1997	77.6	78.1	75.7	75.7	97.5	96.9	69.1	69.4	83.8	84.2	89.1	88.9	87.9	87.6
1998	79.9	80.4	79.5	79.6	99.4	99.0	73.3	73.6	87.7	88.0	91.7	91.5	88.5	88.3
1999	82.7	83.1	83.9	84.1	101.4	101.2	76.6	76.8	89.8	89.9	92.6	92.4	89.2	89.1
2000	85.6	85.9	87.7	87.8	102.4	102.2	82.3	82.5	93.3	93.5	96.1	96.0	90.9	90.9
2001	88.2	88.4	88.4	88.6	100.3	100.2	86.1	86.2	95.0	95.0	97.7	97.5	92.5	92.4
2002	92.2	92.4	90.2	90.3	97.8	97.6	88.8	88.9	96.4	96.5	96.4	96.2	93.2	93.2
2003	95.7	95.8	93.0	93.0	97.2	97.1	93.0	93.1	98.7	98.8	97.2	97.1	94.5	94.4
2004	98.4	98.4	96.7	96.7	98.3	98.3	96.2	96.2	99.5	99.4	97.8	97.8	96.9	96.6
2005	100.0	100.0	100.0	100.0	100.0	100.0	100.0	100.0	100.0	100.0	100.0	100.0	100.0	100.0
2006	100.9	100.9	103.0	103.1	102.1	102.2	103.8	103.8	100.5	100.5	102.8	102.8	102.9	103.0
2007	102.4	102.4	105.1	105.3	102.6	102.7	108.1	107.9	101.7	101.6	105.5	105.3	105.6	105.4
2008	103.2	103.1	103.7	103.7	100.5	100.6	111.7	111.6	101.2	101.2	108.2	108.2	107.5	107.3
2009	105.7	105.5	98.7	98.5	93.4	93.3	113.5	113.4	103.3	103.3	107.4	107.5	108.3	108.4
2010	110.0	109.8	102.5	102.4	93.2	93.2	115.8	115.8	103.6	103.7	105.3	105.4	109.6	109.6
2008: I	103.1	103.0	105.2	105.2	102.1	102.1	111.3	111.3	102.1	102.1	108.0	108.0	106.5	106.2
II	103.6	103.6	105.3	105.3	101.6	101.7	111.0	110.9	100.5	100.4	107.1	107.1	107.2	107.0
III	103.4	103.4	103.8	103.9	100.4	100.5	111.9	111.9	99.8	99.8	108.3	108.2	108.2	108.0
IV	102.6	102.5	100.5	100.4	98.0	98.0	112.4	112.5	102.7	102.7	109.6	109.7	108.0	108.0
2009: I	103.0	102.8	98.3	98.2	95.5	95.5	111.7	111.7	102.6	102.6	108.5	108.6	108.4	108.6
II	105.0	104.8	98.1	97.9	93.4	93.4	113.5	113.5	103.8	103.8	108.1	108.3	108.1	108.2
III	106.8	106.5	98.5	98.2	92.3	92.2	114.2	114.2	103.5	103.5	107.0	107.2	108.1	108.4
IV	108.2	107.9	99.7	99.6	92.2	92.2	114.6	114.5	103.1	103.1	105.9	106.1	108.4	108.5
2010: I	109.3	109.2	101.0	100.8	92.4	92.4	114.9	114.9	103.1	103.1	105.1	105.3	108.9	109.0
II	109.6	109.5	102.1	102.0	93.2	93.1	115.6	115.6	103.9	103.9	105.5	105.6	109.4	109.5
III	110.3	110.1	103.1	102.9	93.5	93.5	116.2	116.2	104.1	104.0	105.4	105.6	109.7	109.7
IV	110.7	110.7	103.9	103.8	93.8	93.8	116.3	116.3	103.5	103.5	105.0	105.1	110.4	110.2
2011: I	110.4	110.5	104.0	104.0	94.2	94.2	117.9	117.9	103.5	103.6	106.8	106.7	111.2	110.8
II	110.4	110.5	104.4	104.5	94.6	94.6	117.9	117.9	102.5	102.5	106.8	106.7	111.9	111.5
III	110.9	111.1	105.2	105.3	94.8	94.8	117.8	117.8	101.6	101.7	106.2	106.0	112.6	112.2

[1] Output refers to real gross domestic product in the sector.

[2] Hours at work of all persons engaged in sector, including hours of proprietors and unpaid family workers. Estimates based primarily on establishment data.

[3] Wages and salaries of employees plus employers' contributions for social insurance and private benefit plans. Also includes an estimate of wages, salaries, and supplemental payments for the self-employed.

[4] Hourly compensation divided by the consumer price index for all urban consumers for recent quarters. The trend from 1978–2010 is based on the consumer price index research series (CPI-U-RS).

[5] Current dollar output divided by the output index.

Source: Department of Labor (Bureau of Labor Statistics).

[Percent change from preceding period; quarterly data at seasonally adjusted annual rates]

Year or quarter	Output per hour of all persons		Output [1]		Hours of all persons [2]		Compensation per hour [3]		Real compensation per hour [4]		Unit labor costs		Implicit price deflator [5]	
	Business sector	Nonfarm business sector	Business sector	Nonfarm business sector	Business sector	Nonfarm business sector	Business sector	Nonfarm business sector	Business sector	Nonfarm business sector	Business sector	Nonfarm business sector	Business sector	Nonfarm business sector
1962	4.6	4.5	6.4	6.8	1.8	2.2	4.4	4.0	3.4	3.0	–0.1	–0.5	1.0	1.0
1963	3.9	3.5	4.6	4.7	.7	1.1	3.6	3.4	2.2	2.1	–.3	–.1	.5	.7
1964	3.4	2.9	6.3	6.7	2.9	3.7	3.8	3.1	2.4	1.8	.4	.2	1.1	1.3
1965	3.5	3.1	7.1	7.1	3.4	3.9	3.7	3.3	2.1	1.7	.2	.2	1.6	1.3
1966	4.1	3.6	6.8	7.1	2.6	3.5	6.7	5.9	3.8	3.0	2.6	2.3	2.5	2.3
1967	2.2	1.7	1.9	1.7	–.3	.0	5.7	5.8	2.5	2.7	3.4	4.0	2.7	3.2
1968	3.4	3.4	5.0	5.2	1.5	1.8	8.1	7.8	3.7	3.5	4.5	4.3	4.0	3.9
1969	.5	.2	3.1	3.0	2.5	2.9	7.0	6.8	1.4	1.3	6.4	6.6	4.6	4.5
1970	2.0	1.5	.0	–.1	–2.0	–1.6	7.7	7.2	1.9	1.4	5.6	5.6	4.3	4.4
1971	4.1	4.0	3.8	3.8	–.3	–.2	6.3	6.4	1.8	1.9	2.1	2.3	4.2	4.3
1972	3.2	3.3	6.4	6.6	3.1	3.2	6.3	6.5	3.0	3.2	3.0	3.1	3.6	3.2
1973	3.1	3.1	7.0	7.3	3.8	4.1	8.4	8.1	2.1	1.8	5.2	4.9	5.2	3.5
1974	–1.7	–1.6	–1.5	–1.5	.2	.1	9.6	9.8	–1.3	–1.2	11.5	11.6	9.7	10.3
1975	3.5	2.8	–.9	–1.6	–4.3	–4.3	10.2	10.1	1.0	.9	6.5	7.1	9.7	10.7
1976	3.2	3.3	6.6	7.0	3.3	3.6	8.6	8.4	2.7	2.5	5.3	4.9	5.3	5.5
1977	1.7	1.6	5.6	5.6	3.8	3.9	8.0	8.1	1.4	1.5	6.2	6.5	6.0	6.3
1978	1.1	1.3	6.3	6.6	5.1	5.2	8.7	8.8	1.5	1.7	7.5	7.4	7.1	6.7
1979	–.1	–.4	3.3	3.2	3.4	3.6	9.6	9.4	.0	–.1	9.6	9.9	8.5	8.5
1980	–.2	–.3	–1.1	–1.1	–.9	–.8	10.7	10.7	–.4	–.4	10.9	11.0	9.0	9.6
1981	2.1	1.4	2.8	2.1	.7	.7	9.5	9.7	.0	.1	7.3	8.1	9.2	9.6
1982	–.8	–1.1	–3.0	–3.2	–2.3	–2.2	7.2	7.1	1.1	1.0	8.1	8.3	5.7	6.2
1983	3.6	4.4	5.4	6.4	1.8	1.9	4.1	4.2	–.1	–.1	.5	–.2	3.4	3.2
1984	2.7	2.0	8.7	8.2	5.8	6.1	4.2	4.1	.1	.0	1.5	2.0	2.9	2.9
1985	2.3	1.6	4.6	4.3	2.3	2.6	4.7	4.4	1.2	1.0	2.4	2.8	2.4	2.9
1986	2.9	3.1	3.7	3.9	.8	.8	5.1	5.2	3.3	3.4	2.2	2.1	1.6	1.7
1987	.3	.3	3.3	3.3	3.0	3.0	3.6	3.6	.2	.2	3.3	3.3	2.4	2.4
1988	1.5	1.6	4.3	4.6	2.7	2.9	5.2	5.0	1.5	1.3	3.7	3.3	3.2	3.0
1989	1.0	.8	3.7	3.5	2.6	2.7	2.7	2.6	–1.6	–1.7	1.6	1.8	3.7	3.6
1990	2.1	1.8	1.5	1.4	–.6	–.4	6.4	6.2	1.4	1.1	4.2	4.3	3.6	3.7
1991	1.5	1.5	–.9	–.9	–2.4	–2.4	5.1	5.3	1.5	1.6	3.5	3.7	3.3	3.5
1992	4.2	4.0	3.9	3.8	–.2	–.2	5.3	5.4	2.7	2.8	1.1	1.3	1.9	2.0
1993	.5	.6	3.2	3.5	2.7	2.9	2.2	2.0	–.2	–.4	1.7	1.4	2.0	2.0
1994	.9	1.0	4.9	4.7	4.0	3.6	1.5	1.8	–.6	–.3	.6	.8	1.7	1.8
1995	.0	.4	2.8	3.2	2.8	2.8	2.1	2.1	–.3	–.3	2.0	1.7	1.8	1.8
1996	2.9	2.6	4.6	4.4	1.6	1.8	3.4	3.3	.7	.6	.5	.7	1.6	1.4
1997	1.8	1.5	5.2	5.1	3.4	3.5	3.2	3.1	1.1	.9	1.5	1.6	1.6	1.9
1998	3.0	2.9	5.0	5.1	2.0	2.1	6.1	6.0	4.6	4.5	3.0	3.0	.7	.8
1999	3.5	3.3	5.6	5.6	2.0	2.2	4.5	4.3	2.4	2.2	.9	.9	.8	1.0
2000	3.5	3.4	4.5	4.4	1.0	1.0	7.4	7.4	3.9	4.0	3.7	3.9	1.8	1.9
2001	3.0	2.9	.8	.9	–2.1	–2.0	4.7	4.5	1.8	1.6	1.7	1.5	1.8	1.7
2002	4.5	4.6	2.0	1.9	–2.4	–2.5	3.1	3.2	1.5	1.5	–1.3	–1.3	.8	.9
2003	3.9	3.7	3.1	3.1	–.7	–.6	4.8	4.7	2.5	2.4	.9	1.0	1.4	1.2
2004	2.8	2.6	4.0	4.0	1.2	1.3	3.5	3.3	.7	.6	.7	.7	2.6	2.4
2005	1.7	1.6	3.4	3.4	1.7	1.7	3.9	3.9	.5	.6	2.2	2.3	3.2	3.5
2006	.9	.9	3.0	3.1	2.1	2.2	3.8	3.8	.5	.5	2.8	2.8	2.9	3.0
2007	1.5	1.5	2.0	2.1	.5	.6	4.1	4.0	1.2	1.1	2.6	2.4	2.6	2.3
2008	.7	.6	–1.3	–1.5	–2.0	–2.1	3.3	3.4	–.5	–.4	2.6	2.8	1.8	1.8
2009	2.4	2.3	–4.9	–5.1	–7.1	–7.2	1.6	1.6	2.0	2.0	–.8	–.7	.7	1.1
2010	4.1	4.1	3.9	4.0	–.1	–.1	2.0	2.1	.4	.4	–2.0	–2.0	1.3	1.1
2008: I	–2.0	–2.4	–3.1	–3.6	–1.1	–1.2	5.8	6.1	1.1	1.4	8.0	8.7	1.5	1.5
II	2.2	2.2	.2	.4	–1.9	–1.7	–1.1	–1.4	–6.0	–6.3	–3.2	–3.5	2.9	3.1
III	–.8	–.7	–5.4	–5.2	–4.6	–4.5	3.4	3.5	–2.8	–2.7	4.3	4.3	3.5	3.7
IV	–3.1	–3.4	–12.0	–12.7	–9.2	–9.7	1.8	2.1	12.1	12.5	5.0	5.7	–.5	.2
2009: I	1.5	1.3	–8.5	–8.7	–9.8	–9.9	–2.7	–2.7	–.4	–.4	–4.1	–4.0	1.4	2.0
II	8.0	8.0	–1.0	–1.1	–8.4	–8.4	6.6	6.7	4.6	4.7	–1.3	–1.2	–1.2	–1.2
III	7.0	6.5	1.8	1.4	–4.9	–4.8	2.7	2.3	–.9	–1.3	–4.0	–3.9	.3	.6
IV	5.3	5.5	5.0	5.6	–.3	.1	1.2	1.2	–1.6	–1.5	–3.9	–4.1	1.1	.5
2010: I	4.3	4.6	5.1	5.2	.8	.5	1.2	1.4	.0	.2	–2.9	–3.1	1.8	1.6
II	1.1	1.2	4.7	4.6	3.6	3.4	2.4	2.6	2.9	3.1	1.2	1.4	1.9	2.0
III	2.5	2.1	3.7	3.5	1.2	1.4	2.2	1.9	.7	.4	–.3	–.2	1.1	.7
IV	1.7	2.2	3.2	3.8	1.5	1.5	.4	.6	–2.2	–2.1	–1.3	–1.6	2.2	1.7
2011: I	–1.4	–.6	.3	.9	1.7	1.5	5.4	5.6	.1	.3	6.8	6.2	2.9	2.2
II	.1	–.1	1.7	1.8	1.6	2.0	.2	–.2	–3.8	–4.1	.1	–.1	2.9	2.7
III	1.9	2.3	3.0	3.2	1.0	.8	–.5	–.2	–3.5	–3.2	–2.4	–2.5	2.5	2.3

[1] Output refers to real gross domestic product in the sector.

[2] Hours at work of all persons engaged in the sector. See footnote 2, Table B–49.

[3] Wages and salaries of employees plus employers' contributions for social insurance and private benefit plans. Also includes an estimate of wages, salaries, and supplemental payments for the self-employed.

[4] Hourly compensation divided by a consumer price index. See footnote 4, Table B–49.

[5] Current dollar output divided by the output index.

Note: Percent changes are calculated using index numbers to three decimal places and may differ slightly from percent changes based on indexes in Table B–49, which are rounded to one decimal place.

Source: Department of Labor (Bureau of Labor Statistics).

TABLE B–51. Industrial production indexes, major industry divisions, 1963–2011

[2007=100; monthly data seasonally adjusted]

Year or month	Total industrial production [1]	Manufacturing				Mining	Utilities
		Total [1]	Durable	Nondurable	Other (non-NAICS) [1]		
1963	26.8	24.0					
1964	28.6	25.6					
1965	31.5	28.4					
1966	34.2	31.0					
1967	35.0	31.6					
1968	36.9	33.4					
1969	38.6	34.8					
1970	37.3	33.3					
1971	37.9	33.8					
1972	41.5	37.3	25.4	57.2	71.9	106.4	46.4
1973	44.9	40.7	28.6	59.9	74.1	107.0	49.1
1974	44.8	40.6	28.4	60.2	74.6	105.5	48.9
1975	40.8	36.4	24.7	55.8	71.0	103.0	49.8
1976	44.0	39.6	27.0	60.9	73.2	103.7	52.1
1977	47.4	43.0	29.7	65.1	80.2	106.1	54.2
1978	50.0	45.6	32.0	67.4	83.0	109.4	55.6
1979	51.5	47.1	33.6	67.8	84.8	112.7	56.8
1980	50.2	45.4	32.1	65.7	87.7	114.7	57.3
1981	50.8	45.9	32.5	66.3	89.9	117.7	58.1
1982	48.2	43.4	29.7	65.3	90.8	111.9	56.2
1983	49.5	45.5	31.2	68.4	93.4	106.0	56.7
1984	54.0	49.9	35.6	71.5	97.6	112.8	60.0
1985	54.6	50.7	36.4	71.9	101.5	110.6	61.3
1986	55.2	51.8	37.0	74.0	103.5	102.6	61.8
1987	58.0	54.8	39.2	78.0	109.5	103.6	64.7
1988	61.0	57.7	42.1	80.6	109.0	106.2	68.4
1989	61.5	58.2	42.6	81.1	107.4	105.0	70.6
1990	62.1	58.6	42.7	82.4	106.1	106.5	71.9
1991	61.2	57.5	41.4	82.0	101.8	104.2	73.7
1992	62.9	59.5	43.5	84.2	99.7	101.9	73.6
1993	65.0	61.6	45.9	85.3	100.5	101.9	76.2
1994	68.4	65.3	49.8	88.3	99.6	104.2	77.7
1995	71.6	68.7	54.0	89.9	99.6	104.1	80.5
1996	74.8	72.0	58.8	90.1	98.7	105.8	82.8
1997	80.2	78.0	65.9	93.5	107.0	107.8	82.8
1998	84.9	83.2	72.8	94.8	113.4	105.8	84.9
1999	88.5	87.3	78.9	95.4	116.7	100.3	87.4
2000	92.1	91.0	84.8	95.9	116.4	103.0	89.9
2001	88.9	87.3	80.9	93.0	108.8	103.4	89.5
2002	89.1	87.6	80.8	94.2	105.2	98.6	92.3
2003	90.2	88.7	82.9	94.4	102.1	98.8	94.1
2004	92.3	91.2	86.2	95.9	102.9	98.2	95.3
2005	95.3	94.8	91.2	98.3	102.6	97.1	97.3
2006	97.4	97.2	95.4	98.8	101.4	99.5	96.7
2007	100.0	100.0	100.0	100.0	100.0	100.0	100.0
2008	96.3	95.0	96.3	94.0	89.4	100.8	99.9
2009	85.5	82.2	79.0	86.4	77.0	95.6	97.3
2010	90.1	86.6	85.3	89.6	74.0	101.2	101.3
2011 ᵖ	93.8	90.5	92.2	91.1	70.3	107.2	101.0
2010: Jan	87.7	84.2	81.6	88.3	75.5	96.6	102.0
Feb	87.9	84.3	81.6	88.5	74.5	97.3	102.4
Mar	88.4	85.1	82.8	88.9	74.7	99.0	99.3
Apr	88.7	85.7	83.9	89.2	74.2	100.5	95.8
May	89.9	86.7	85.3	89.6	75.5	100.1	100.5
June	90.0	86.6	85.3	89.5	74.4	99.9	102.4
July	90.8	87.3	86.6	89.7	74.5	101.2	103.1
Aug	91.0	87.4	86.3	90.1	74.3	102.7	102.7
Sept	91.2	87.5	86.6	90.3	72.7	103.9	102.6
Oct	91.1	87.7	87.2	90.2	72.5	104.7	98.8
Nov	91.4	87.9	87.6	90.0	72.8	104.5	100.6
Dec	92.6	88.8	88.4	91.2	72.7	104.6	105.1
2011: Jan	92.8	89.4	89.9	91.0	72.4	104.0	103.4
Feb	92.5	89.5	90.6	90.6	71.2	102.5	101.0
Mar	93.1	90.1	91.3	91.2	70.3	104.2	100.7
Apr	92.7	89.6	90.5	91.0	69.9	105.1	99.7
May	93.0	89.7	91.2	90.6	69.9	105.8	100.6
June	93.1	89.8	91.4	90.7	68.3	106.1	101.0
July	94.1	90.5	92.2	91.2	68.5	107.4	104.3
Aug ᵖ	94.4	90.7	92.7	91.1	70.4	108.6	103.1
Sept ᵖ	94.6	91.2	93.3	91.4	71.3	108.8	101.7
Oct ᵖ	95.1	91.6	94.0	91.7	71.1	110.5	101.5
Nov ᵖ	94.9	91.3	93.9	91.2	69.8	111.0	100.9
Dec ᵖ	95.3	92.1	94.7	91.9	71.3	111.4	98.2

[1] Total industry and total manufacturing series include manufacturing as defined in the North American Industry Classification System (NAICS) plus those industries—logging and newspaper, periodical, book, and directory publishing—that have traditionally been considered to be manufacturing and included in the industrial sector.

Note: Data based on NAICS; see footnote 1.

Source: Board of Governors of the Federal Reserve System.

TABLE B–52. Industrial production indexes, market groupings, 1963–2011

[2007=100; monthly data seasonally adjusted]

Year or month	Total industrial production	Final products									Nonindustrial supplies			Materials		
		Total	Consumer goods				Equipment				Total	Construction	Business	Total	Nonenergy	Energy
			Total	Automotive products	Other durable goods	Nondurable goods	Total[1]	Business	Defense and space							
1963	26.8	25.9	34.7	25.1	22.4	40.7	15.3	10.5	46.6	27.7	38.1	23.6	26.6	....	56.4
1964	28.6	27.4	36.6	26.3	24.4	42.7	16.1	11.8	45.1	29.5	40.4	25.2	28.8	....	58.7
1965	31.5	30.1	39.5	32.4	27.7	44.5	18.2	13.5	49.9	31.4	42.9	26.9	32.1	....	61.4
1966	34.2	32.9	41.5	32.3	30.5	46.6	21.3	15.6	58.7	33.3	44.7	29.0	35.0	....	65.3
1967	35.0	34.2	42.5	28.3	30.9	49.1	22.6	15.9	66.9	34.7	45.9	30.5	34.6	27.3	67.5
1968	36.9	35.9	45.1	33.8	33.1	51.0	23.2	16.6	67.1	36.7	48.2	32.4	36.9	29.3	70.6
1969	38.6	37.0	46.7	33.9	35.3	52.7	23.9	17.7	63.9	38.7	50.3	34.4	39.1	31.1	74.2
1970	37.3	35.7	46.2	28.5	34.2	53.6	22.2	17.1	54.1	38.1	48.5	34.6	37.7	29.3	77.9
1971	37.9	36.0	48.9	36.4	36.3	55.1	20.8	16.2	48.6	39.3	50.1	35.6	38.3	29.8	78.5
1972	41.5	39.1	52.8	39.2	41.5	58.7	22.7	18.5	47.3	43.9	56.8	39.2	42.2	33.4	81.5
1973	44.9	42.1	55.2	42.6	44.3	60.5	25.9	21.4	51.8	46.9	61.7	41.6	46.0	37.0	83.5
1974	44.8	42.1	53.6	36.8	41.7	60.5	27.2	22.7	53.5	46.5	60.2	41.6	45.8	36.9	83.2
1975	40.8	39.7	51.5	35.5	36.5	59.4	24.9	20.2	54.0	41.7	51.0	38.4	40.8	31.7	82.4
1976	44.0	42.5	55.7	40.4	41.0	63.1	26.2	21.6	52.3	44.6	54.9	40.9	44.4	35.3	84.2
1977	47.4	46.0	59.1	45.7	45.8	65.5	29.2	24.9	46.9	48.4	59.8	44.3	47.5	38.2	86.9
1978	50.0	48.8	61.0	45.4	47.9	67.8	32.5	28.1	47.8	51.1	63.2	46.7	49.9	40.7	88.0
1979	51.5	50.4	60.1	40.8	48.2	67.4	36.3	31.7	51.2	52.7	64.8	48.3	51.2	41.8	90.4
1980	50.2	50.2	57.8	31.4	44.7	67.4	38.0	32.4	60.8	50.6	60.0	47.2	49.3	39.4	91.1
1981	50.8	51.4	58.2	32.4	45.0	67.8	39.8	33.4	65.8	51.1	59.0	48.3	49.6	39.5	92.0
1982	48.2	50.3	58.1	31.5	41.7	68.9	37.9	30.5	78.7	49.3	53.5	47.7	45.8	35.6	88.0
1983	49.5	51.3	60.2	36.6	45.2	69.7	37.7	30.7	79.3	51.9	57.3	50.0	47.0	38.0	85.2
1984	54.0	55.5	63.0	40.9	50.5	71.1	43.0	35.3	90.8	56.5	62.3	54.3	51.4	42.4	90.6
1985	54.6	56.9	63.5	40.8	50.5	72.0	45.2	36.6	101.6	57.9	63.9	55.7	51.4	42.4	90.1
1986	55.2	57.8	65.7	43.9	53.5	73.7	44.5	36.0	107.9	59.8	66.1	57.6	51.3	43.2	86.5
1987	58.0	60.4	68.5	47.0	56.3	76.3	46.9	38.5	110.2	63.5	70.3	61.0	54.0	46.1	88.6
1988	61.0	63.7	71.1	49.2	59.3	78.9	50.7	42.5	111.2	65.6	71.9	63.3	57.0	49.0	91.7
1989	61.5	64.4	71.3	50.8	60.0	78.6	52.0	44.0	111.3	66.2	71.6	64.2	57.4	49.3	92.6
1990	62.1	65.0	71.7	47.8	59.9	79.9	53.0	45.5	107.3	67.2	71.0	65.7	57.8	49.4	94.4
1991	61.2	64.2	71.7	44.9	58.2	81.0	51.2	44.7	99.3	65.5	67.1	64.8	56.9	48.3	94.5
1992	62.9	65.8	73.7	52.0	60.8	81.7	51.9	46.6	92.1	67.4	69.9	66.3	58.8	50.7	93.7
1993	65.0	67.8	76.0	57.2	65.0	82.8	53.6	48.8	86.9	69.7	73.0	68.4	60.8	52.9	93.9
1994	68.4	70.7	79.2	62.8	70.4	84.8	55.9	52.0	81.6	73.1	78.3	71.1	64.7	57.2	95.4
1995	71.6	73.6	81.6	64.7	74.6	86.9	59.5	56.5	79.1	75.7	80.1	74.1	68.4	61.1	96.8
1996	74.8	76.4	83.1	65.8	78.1	88.0	64.2	62.1	76.6	78.8	83.6	76.9	71.9	64.9	98.3
1997	80.2	81.4	86.1	70.9	83.1	90.1	72.0	71.1	75.4	83.9	87.7	82.4	77.7	71.8	98.3
1998	84.9	86.1	89.3	76.2	89.7	92.0	78.9	78.8	78.6	88.6	92.3	87.1	82.4	77.2	98.5
1999	88.5	88.5	91.3	84.6	94.4	92.0	81.9	83.1	76.3	91.9	94.7	90.7	87.3	83.2	98.0
2000	92.1	91.1	93.0	86.1	98.1	93.4	86.3	89.3	67.8	95.2	96.8	94.4	91.8	88.3	99.6
2001	88.9	89.3	91.9	82.8	92.7	93.6	82.8	83.9	74.4	91.4	92.4	90.9	87.7	83.3	98.3
2002	89.1	88.7	93.8	90.9	94.3	94.2	77.5	78.3	75.0	91.5	92.4	91.1	88.6	84.6	98.0
2003	90.2	89.9	95.1	95.7	95.3	94.9	78.3	78.3	79.6	92.5	92.2	92.6	89.8	86.1	98.1
2004	92.3	91.6	96.1	95.7	98.4	95.7	81.5	82.2	77.7	94.4	94.4	94.4	92.3	89.7	97.8
2005	95.3	95.3	98.7	94.2	101.6	98.9	87.6	87.8	85.8	97.9	98.9	97.4	94.5	93.3	96.9
2006	97.4	97.7	99.2	93.0	103.0	99.5	94.5	96.0	84.5	99.3	101.3	98.4	96.5	95.6	98.1
2007	100.0	100.0	100.0	100.0	100.0	100.0	100.0	100.0	100.0	100.0	100.0	100.0	100.0	100.0	100.0
2008	96.3	96.2	94.8	84.6	92.6	96.8	99.3	97.5	107.9	93.6	90.3	95.1	97.3	95.3	100.6
2009	85.5	86.9	88.0	72.9	76.1	92.3	84.4	81.6	109.2	80.5	70.0	85.6	86.0	79.0	98.2
2010	90.1	91.5	91.7	87.7	77.9	94.6	91.2	87.9	114.6	82.0	72.7	86.6	91.5	84.9	102.8
2011 _p_	93.8	95.4	93.6	96.6	81.4	95.3	99.9	97.2	117.2	84.2	76.2	88.0	95.6	89.3	106.3
2010: Jan	87.7	89.6	90.9	86.4	75.2	94.2	86.4	83.2	110.7	80.4	68.5	86.2	88.6	82.1	99.7
Feb	87.9	89.3	90.4	84.4	75.7	93.8	86.7	83.2	111.5	80.3	68.7	85.9	89.3	82.5	101.1
Mar	88.4	89.9	90.6	85.2	76.6	93.8	88.1	84.2	114.0	80.6	70.2	85.7	89.7	83.2	100.9
Apr	88.7	89.6	89.7	84.2	78.1	92.5	89.5	85.5	114.7	81.7	72.9	85.9	90.3	84.0	101.1
May	89.9	91.4	91.7	87.8	78.9	94.4	90.9	87.3	114.7	82.4	73.3	86.9	91.1	84.6	102.1
June	90.0	91.5	91.7	86.5	78.6	94.7	91.0	87.9	113.6	82.6	73.6	87.0	91.2	84.8	101.9
July	90.8	92.7	92.8	93.8	79.0	95.0	92.3	89.0	115.7	82.6	73.3	87.1	91.9	85.3	103.1
Aug	91.0	92.6	92.6	88.3	78.4	95.6	92.8	89.3	116.7	82.8	73.8	87.1	92.3	85.6	103.8
Sept	91.2	92.7	92.4	88.9	78.1	95.3	93.4	90.1	116.1	82.6	73.8	86.9	92.9	85.9	104.9
Oct	91.1	92.8	92.3	90.3	78.0	94.9	94.2	91.0	116.5	82.2	74.3	86.1	92.7	86.0	104.1
Nov	91.4	92.7	92.0	87.7	79.2	94.8	94.3	91.3	115.8	83.0	75.0	86.9	93.2	86.4	104.7
Dec	92.6	93.8	93.3	88.2	79.2	96.4	95.1	92.4	115.3	83.3	74.4	87.6	94.6	87.8	106.2
2011: Jan	92.8	94.6	93.7	92.0	79.6	96.3	96.8	94.1	116.2	83.2	74.9	87.2	94.5	88.8	104.0
Feb	92.5	94.3	93.0	94.7	81.0	94.8	97.3	94.7	116.7	82.9	74.4	87.1	94.1	88.5	103.4
Mar	93.1	94.4	93.2	97.1	81.6	94.6	97.4	94.6	116.8	83.7	75.2	87.8	95.1	89.3	104.9
Apr	92.7	94.2	92.8	92.8	80.4	94.7	97.4	94.5	116.8	83.3	75.0	87.4	94.6	88.5	104.9
May	93.0	94.8	93.2	92.5	81.4	95.2	98.7	95.8	117.1	84.1	76.3	87.9	94.5	88.6	104.3
June	93.1	94.7	93.1	93.0	80.8	95.2	98.7	96.1	115.3	83.9	76.3	87.5	94.9	88.6	105.4
July	94.1	95.6	93.8	95.3	81.8	95.6	99.8	97.3	116.3	84.7	77.3	88.2	96.2	89.2	108.0
Aug _p_	94.4	96.1	94.1	96.7	81.6	95.8	100.9	98.4	117.1	84.9	77.0	88.7	96.1	89.0	108.2
Sept _p_	94.6	96.2	94.0	97.4	82.3	95.4	101.6	99.1	117.2	85.4	77.3	89.3	96.4	89.7	107.6
Oct _p_	95.1	97.0	94.6	101.0	82.1	95.8	102.9	100.4	118.5	85.1	77.3	88.9	96.9	90.0	108.6
Nov _p_	94.9	96.6	93.9	98.8	82.1	95.1	103.1	100.4	119.4	84.3	77.1	87.9	97.0	90.0	108.9
Dec _p_	95.3	96.8	94.1	99.2	82.2	95.4	103.5	101.1	117.9	84.8	77.9	88.1	97.5	91.2	108.2

[1] Includes other items not shown separately.

Note: See footnote 1 and Note, Table B–51.

Source: Board of Governors of the Federal Reserve System.

[2007=100; monthly data seasonally adjusted]

Year or month	Durable manufacturing								Nondurable manufacturing					
	Primary metals		Fabricated metal products	Machinery	Computer and electronic products		Transportation equipment		Apparel	Paper	Printing and support	Chemicals	Plastics and rubber products	Food
	Total	Iron and steel products			Total	Selected high-technology [1]	Total	Motor vehicles and parts						
1968	....	....	....	....	....	0.1	....	....	....	....	....	....	....	....
1969	....	....	....	....	....	.1	....	....	....	....	....	....	....	....
1970	....	....	....	....	....	.1	....	....	....	....	....	....	....	....
1971	....	....	....	....	....	.1	....	....	....	....	....	....	....	....
1972	109.9	113.8	60.4	56.8	0.7	.1	47.1	43.2	286.4	68.2	49.7	40.9	34.7	55.8
1973	128.0	136.4	66.8	65.7	.9	.2	53.8	49.4	295.1	73.8	52.3	44.8	39.0	55.9
1974	131.1	145.8	65.7	68.9	1.0	.2	49.6	42.5	274.7	76.9	50.7	46.5	38.0	56.5
1975	101.8	108.2	56.7	60.0	.9	.2	45.0	37.1	268.8	66.5	47.4	40.9	32.5	55.4
1976	108.1	112.2	60.7	62.6	1.1	.3	50.3	47.3	283.9	73.5	50.8	45.8	36.0	59.9
1977	109.2	109.6	65.9	68.4	1.3	.3	54.7	53.7	301.8	76.7	55.0	49.8	42.4	61.0
1978	116.3	117.7	69.1	73.7	1.6	.4	58.2	56.0	310.5	80.2	58.2	52.3	43.8	62.8
1979	119.0	121.9	72.2	77.8	2.0	.5	58.8	51.3	294.3	81.4	60.0	53.5	43.2	62.2
1980	104.6	103.4	68.1	74.0	2.5	.7	52.2	37.9	298.6	81.1	60.4	50.6	38.4	63.3
1981	104.7	107.2	67.6	73.3	2.8	.8	50.2	36.9	296.9	82.3	62.0	51.4	40.7	64.2
1982	74.0	65.9	60.6	61.3	3.2	.9	46.2	33.3	300.7	80.9	66.7	48.1	40.0	66.7
1983	75.9	66.4	61.0	55.3	3.7	1.1	51.0	42.5	309.5	86.2	71.6	51.4	43.5	67.4
1984	83.1	73.2	66.4	64.5	4.6	1.4	57.9	50.9	313.9	90.5	78.0	54.4	50.2	68.7
1985	76.8	67.9	67.4	64.7	4.8	1.5	60.9	52.9	301.7	88.8	81.1	54.0	52.2	71.3
1986	75.0	66.3	66.9	63.7	5.0	1.6	62.4	52.8	305.2	92.4	85.2	56.4	54.4	72.3
1987	80.8	75.5	68.2	65.0	5.7	1.9	64.6	54.7	307.3	95.4	91.5	60.8	60.3	73.8
1988	90.3	87.9	71.7	71.6	6.4	2.3	68.6	58.5	301.7	99.2	94.4	64.3	62.9	75.7
1989	88.2	84.8	71.1	74.3	6.6	2.4	70.0	57.9	286.9	100.3	94.8	65.5	65.1	75.9
1990	87.1	83.8	70.3	72.5	7.2	2.7	67.8	54.4	281.0	100.3	98.4	67.0	66.9	78.2
1991	81.8	76.6	67.1	68.0	7.4	2.9	65.1	52.0	282.5	100.5	95.3	66.8	66.1	79.7
1992	83.8	80.1	69.1	67.8	8.4	3.5	67.5	59.2	288.0	102.9	100.5	67.8	71.2	81.2
1993	87.8	84.9	71.7	72.9	9.2	4.1	69.5	65.4	294.8	104.1	100.8	68.6	76.2	83.3
1994	94.5	91.6	78.0	79.8	10.8	5.2	72.7	75.1	300.7	108.6	101.9	70.4	82.6	83.8
1995	95.5	93.1	82.8	85.5	14.0	7.3	72.7	77.3	301.0	110.2	103.4	71.5	84.7	86.0
1996	97.9	95.3	85.8	88.4	18.1	10.5	74.1	77.9	292.6	106.8	104.1	73.0	87.5	84.2
1997	102.0	98.2	89.6	93.3	24.2	15.5	80.8	84.0	289.2	109.0	106.3	77.3	92.9	86.5
1998	103.8	98.0	92.6	95.7	31.2	21.6	87.9	88.4	273.8	109.9	107.5	78.6	96.2	90.3
1999	103.8	98.4	93.2	93.7	40.8	31.0	92.7	98.1	261.7	110.7	107.5	80.1	101.3	91.4
2000	100.3	97.1	96.9	98.5	53.4	43.4	88.3	97.4	249.7	107.8	108.4	81.2	102.4	92.9
2001	91.4	88.2	89.9	87.1	54.2	44.5	84.9	88.8	214.9	101.7	104.8	79.8	96.5	93.0
2002	91.3	89.2	87.6	83.7	52.9	44.2	88.6	97.6	170.2	102.9	102.1	85.1	99.9	95.0
2003	89.8	89.8	86.6	83.3	60.3	53.3	89.5	101.1	156.8	100.4	98.1	86.5	99.9	95.6
2004	97.7	101.7	86.9	86.7	68.4	60.7	89.4	101.7	134.6	101.2	98.5	89.9	101.2	95.6
2005	95.2	94.3	90.9	92.1	77.0	70.9	93.1	102.3	129.1	100.7	98.6	92.9	102.3	98.6
2006	98.0	98.4	95.9	96.5	87.2	84.5	94.2	100.8	125.8	99.6	97.8	95.2	102.9	99.5
2007	100.0	100.0	100.0	100.0	100.0	100.0	100.0	100.0	100.0	100.0	100.0	100.0	100.0	100.0
2008	99.7	106.4	96.4	97.3	106.6	112.8	89.6	80.0	78.0	95.8	93.8	92.4	90.6	98.7
2009	69.5	63.1	74.2	75.6	97.5	102.4	75.4	59.5	59.8	85.4	79.8	83.7	75.8	98.1
2010	83.3	87.7	78.6	80.8	107.9	116.1	83.9	76.1	57.8	89.0	76.0	86.7	83.4	102.3
2011 [p]	91.2	95.3	87.1	90.9	115.8	124.1	91.0	82.9	57.8	87.7	73.6	88.5	87.2	102.9
2010: Jan	79.6	83.6	73.4	75.7	102.5	110.6	81.8	73.2	59.1	87.7	76.9	87.4	79.6	100.0
Feb	81.3	86.3	73.6	76.0	103.7	112.3	80.8	71.4	57.9	88.8	75.7	86.7	80.2	100.9
Mar	84.2	92.9	74.6	76.2	105.3	113.8	82.2	73.3	57.6	89.6	75.2	86.6	81.1	101.0
Apr	83.5	90.2	76.1	78.9	106.5	115.1	81.7	72.5	58.0	89.6	76.0	86.5	83.5	100.9
May	84.4	92.7	77.5	80.8	107.7	115.8	83.9	76.7	57.5	89.3	77.3	86.2	84.3	101.5
June	84.3	89.4	78.9	81.8	107.4	115.2	83.3	75.7	57.3	89.5	76.8	86.1	83.6	101.8
July	81.6	81.6	79.9	81.7	108.5	115.6	87.7	82.7	56.9	89.1	76.2	86.2	84.5	101.7
Aug	81.9	83.4	81.1	81.7	109.3	117.0	85.2	77.6	57.4	88.4	77.0	86.3	84.5	103.6
Sept	82.7	85.5	81.5	82.0	109.7	117.7	85.5	78.3	56.5	88.8	75.8	87.0	84.1	104.5
Oct	82.4	82.8	81.4	83.2	110.2	117.8	85.9	79.0	57.9	88.5	75.4	86.0	84.9	104.2
Nov	84.9	88.8	82.5	84.4	111.6	120.2	84.2	76.2	57.7	88.8	74.9	86.6	85.1	103.6
Dec	88.6	95.2	83.1	87.0	113.2	122.7	84.1	76.5	60.0	90.0	74.4	88.5	85.7	103.7
2011: Jan	90.1	98.2	83.6	90.3	115.3	125.3	86.1	79.5	59.3	90.7	73.9	88.3	86.5	103.4
Feb	89.3	95.5	83.9	90.0	115.5	124.9	88.0	82.5	59.4	89.1	74.7	88.0	86.4	103.2
Mar	91.7	97.5	84.9	89.1	115.3	124.2	89.9	85.0	57.9	89.4	74.4	89.5	86.2	102.9
Apr	91.1	93.4	85.7	88.6	114.7	123.9	87.7	79.4	58.2	88.6	74.7	88.6	86.9	103.5
May	90.4	91.4	86.5	90.0	115.4	124.4	88.1	79.0	59.2	87.7	74.6	87.8	87.2	102.4
June	88.9	91.9	87.9	91.4	114.3	124.5	88.6	79.2	58.1	87.5	73.6	87.9	86.5	102.7
July	90.3	90.9	88.6	91.4	115.8	124.5	90.4	81.6	57.7	87.3	74.4	88.3	87.8	102.3
Aug [p]	89.8	94.4	88.5	90.9	117.0	126.0	91.9	83.0	57.4	86.1	73.7	88.4	87.2	102.3
Sept [p]	92.0	93.1	88.1	91.3	117.2	125.2	92.4	83.2	55.9	86.9	73.1	89.3	87.3	102.3
Oct [p]	91.6	94.7	88.3	91.8	116.8	123.3	95.1	86.1	57.2	86.3	72.4	89.0	88.2	103.6
Nov [p]	93.6	98.7	88.9	92.2	116.4	123.0	94.4	83.9	55.8	87.1	71.5	88.1	87.6	102.9
Dec [p]	96.6	105.9	89.9	94.1	117.5	123.7	94.2	84.4	56.2	86.2	71.9	89.1	89.0	103.7

[1] Computers and peripheral equipment, communications equipment, and semiconductors and related electronic components.

Note: See footnote 1 and Note, Table B–51.

Source: Board of Governors of the Federal Reserve System.

TABLE B–54. Capacity utilization rates, 1963–2011

[Percent [1]; monthly data seasonally adjusted]

Year or month	Total industry [2]	Manufacturing				Mining	Utilities	Stage-of-process		
		Total [2]	Durable goods	Nondurable goods	Other (non-NAICS) [2]			Crude	Primary and semi-finished	Finished
1963	....	83.5	....	....	....	....	....	....	83.8	83.4
1964	....	85.6	....	....	....	....	....	....	87.8	84.6
1965	....	89.5	....	....	....	....	....	....	91.0	88.8
1966	....	91.1	....	....	....	....	....	....	91.4	91.1
1967	87.0	87.2	87.5	86.3	....	81.2	94.5	81.1	85.0	88.2
1968	87.3	87.1	87.3	86.5	....	83.6	95.1	83.4	86.8	87.1
1969	87.4	86.6	87.1	86.1	....	86.7	96.8	85.6	88.1	85.6
1970	81.2	79.4	77.7	82.1	....	89.2	96.3	85.1	81.5	78.1
1971	79.6	77.9	75.5	81.7	....	87.8	94.7	84.3	81.6	75.6
1972	84.6	83.4	82.0	85.2	85.7	90.7	95.3	88.4	88.1	79.6
1973	88.3	87.7	88.6	86.6	84.7	91.5	93.3	90.0	92.1	83.2
1974	85.1	84.4	84.6	84.1	82.7	91.0	86.9	90.9	87.3	80.2
1975	75.7	73.6	71.7	76.0	77.3	89.3	85.1	83.9	75.2	73.6
1976	79.7	78.3	76.4	81.1	77.6	89.4	85.5	86.9	80.1	76.7
1977	83.4	82.4	81.1	84.3	83.2	89.5	86.6	89.1	84.5	79.8
1978	85.0	84.3	83.8	85.1	85.1	89.7	86.9	88.7	86.2	82.1
1979	85.0	84.0	84.0	83.7	85.6	91.3	87.0	89.9	85.9	81.7
1980	80.8	78.7	77.6	79.6	86.8	91.4	85.5	89.4	78.8	79.3
1981	79.6	77.0	75.3	78.7	87.5	90.9	84.4	89.3	77.3	77.5
1982	73.6	70.9	66.6	76.3	87.4	84.2	80.2	82.4	70.6	73.1
1983	74.9	73.4	68.7	79.4	88.1	79.9	79.6	79.9	74.5	73.0
1984	80.4	79.3	76.8	82.1	89.7	85.9	82.2	85.7	81.2	77.1
1985	79.2	78.1	75.7	80.4	90.5	84.4	81.9	83.8	79.8	76.6
1986	78.6	78.4	75.4	81.7	89.0	77.6	81.1	79.2	79.7	77.1
1987	81.2	81.0	77.7	84.6	90.8	80.3	83.6	82.8	82.8	78.8
1988	84.3	84.0	82.2	86.0	88.5	84.3	86.7	86.3	85.8	81.7
1989	83.8	83.3	81.9	84.9	85.4	85.0	86.9	86.7	84.7	81.7
1990	82.5	81.7	79.6	84.2	83.7	86.6	86.5	87.6	82.7	80.8
1991	79.8	78.5	75.4	82.2	80.7	85.0	87.9	85.2	79.9	78.3
1992	80.6	79.6	77.3	82.7	79.8	84.6	86.4	85.4	81.6	78.2
1993	81.5	80.4	78.5	82.7	81.1	85.4	88.3	85.6	83.4	78.2
1994	83.6	82.8	81.6	84.6	81.4	86.9	88.4	87.8	86.5	79.2
1995	84.1	83.3	82.4	84.7	82.2	87.6	89.4	88.7	86.5	80.1
1996	83.5	82.3	81.7	83.4	80.6	90.3	90.9	89.1	85.7	79.4
1997	84.2	83.2	82.3	84.0	85.7	91.5	90.4	90.6	86.2	80.4
1998	82.8	81.6	80.5	82.4	87.0	89.0	92.7	87.2	84.3	80.1
1999	81.7	80.4	79.8	80.4	87.2	85.9	94.2	86.1	84.1	77.9
2000	81.4	79.7	79.3	79.2	87.3	90.6	93.9	88.6	83.9	76.7
2001	76.0	73.7	71.2	75.9	82.7	90.2	89.6	85.6	77.3	72.3
2002	74.8	72.9	69.7	76.3	81.4	85.9	87.7	82.9	77.0	70.7
2003	75.9	73.9	70.9	76.9	81.4	87.9	85.9	84.7	77.9	71.6
2004	77.9	76.1	73.6	78.5	82.9	88.2	84.7	86.1	79.9	73.1
2005	79.9	78.2	75.9	80.4	82.8	88.7	85.2	86.4	81.9	75.3
2006	80.4	78.6	77.0	80.3	81.4	90.3	83.2	87.8	81.4	76.1
2007	81.0	79.2	78.0	80.4	81.0	89.4	85.6	88.6	81.5	77.4
2008	77.8	74.9	74.2	75.3	77.7	89.5	83.8	87.0	76.8	74.5
2009	69.2	66.2	61.8	71.0	70.4	81.0	80.7	79.3	66.6	68.7
2010	74.5	71.7	68.3	75.9	67.7	86.2	82.1	85.3	71.8	73.3
2011 [p]	77.3	74.9	73.5	77.5	64.7	89.9	79.8	88.2	74.3	76.2
2010: Jan	71.9	69.0	64.7	74.1	69.1	81.8	84.1	82.3	69.1	71.4
Feb	72.2	69.3	64.9	74.4	68.1	82.5	84.3	82.8	69.8	71.2
Mar	72.8	70.0	66.0	74.9	68.3	84.1	81.4	84.0	70.0	71.9
Apr	73.2	70.7	67.0	75.3	67.9	85.5	78.3	84.9	70.2	72.2
May	74.3	71.7	68.3	75.8	69.0	85.3	82.0	84.4	71.9	73.2
June	74.5	71.7	68.4	75.9	68.1	85.2	83.2	84.5	72.3	73.1
July	75.3	72.4	69.6	76.1	68.1	86.4	83.5	85.5	72.8	74.0
Aug	75.5	72.6	69.4	76.6	68.0	87.7	82.8	86.3	72.8	74.2
Sept	75.7	72.7	69.7	76.8	66.6	88.6	82.4	87.1	72.8	74.4
Oct	75.7	73.0	70.2	76.8	66.4	89.3	79.2	87.1	72.2	74.9
Nov	75.8	73.1	70.5	76.7	66.7	88.9	80.4	86.8	73.0	74.5
Dec	76.8	73.8	71.1	77.6	66.6	88.9	83.7	87.5	74.4	75.0
2011: Jan	76.9	74.3	72.3	77.5	66.4	88.2	82.1	87.2	74.3	75.7
Feb	76.5	74.4	72.8	77.2	65.4	86.8	80.0	86.1	73.7	75.9
Mar	77.0	74.8	73.3	77.7	64.5	88.0	79.6	87.3	74.1	76.1
Apr	76.6	74.4	72.6	77.4	64.2	88.5	78.7	87.1	73.6	75.8
May	76.7	74.4	73.0	77.1	64.3	89.0	79.3	86.9	73.9	75.9
June	76.7	74.4	73.0	77.1	62.8	89.1	79.5	87.2	73.9	75.8
July	77.5	74.9	73.6	77.6	63.0	90.0	82.0	88.2	75.0	76.1
Aug [p]	77.6	75.0	73.9	77.4	64.8	90.8	81.0	88.6	74.8	76.4
Sept [p]	77.7	75.3	74.2	77.7	65.7	90.9	79.8	89.3	74.9	76.4
Oct [p]	78.1	75.6	74.6	77.8	65.6	92.2	79.6	90.2	74.7	77.1
Nov [p]	77.8	75.3	74.4	77.4	64.3	92.6	79.0	90.2	74.5	76.6
Dec [p]	78.1	75.9	75.0	78.0	65.8	92.8	76.8	90.4	74.8	76.9

[1] Output as percent of capacity.
[2] See footnote 1 and Note, Table B–51.

Source: Board of Governors of the Federal Reserve System.

[Value put in place, billions of dollars; monthly data at seasonally adjusted annual rates]

Year or month	Total new construction	Private construction									Public construction		
		Total	Residential buildings [1]		Nonresidential buildings and other construction						Total	Federal	State and local
			Total [2]	New housing units [3]	Total	Lodging	Office	Commercial [4]	Manufacturing	Other [5]			
1967	87.2	61.8	28.7	21.5	33.1						25.4	3.3	22.1
1968	96.8	69.4	34.2	26.7	35.2						27.4	3.2	24.2
1969	104.9	77.2	37.2	29.2	39.9						27.8	3.2	24.6
1970	105.9	78.0	35.9	27.1	42.1						27.9	3.1	24.8
1971	122.4	92.7	48.5	38.7	44.2						29.7	3.8	25.9
1972	139.1	109.1	60.7	50.1	48.4						30.0	4.2	25.8
1973	153.8	121.4	65.1	54.6	56.3						32.3	4.7	27.6
1974	155.2	117.0	56.0	43.4	61.1						38.1	5.1	33.0
1975	152.6	109.3	51.6	36.3	57.8						43.3	6.1	37.2
1976	172.1	128.2	68.3	50.8	59.9						44.0	6.8	37.2
1977	200.5	157.4	92.0	72.2	65.4						43.1	7.1	36.0
1978	239.9	189.7	109.8	85.6	79.9						50.1	8.1	42.0
1979	272.9	216.2	116.4	89.3	99.8						56.6	8.6	48.1
1980	273.9	210.3	100.4	69.6	109.9						63.6	9.6	54.0
1981	289.1	224.4	99.2	69.4	125.1						64.7	10.4	54.3
1982	279.3	216.3	84.7	57.0	131.6						63.1	10.0	53.1
1983	311.9	248.4	125.8	95.0	122.6						63.5	10.6	52.9
1984	370.2	300.0	155.0	114.6	144.9						70.2	11.2	59.0
1985	403.4	325.6	160.5	115.9	165.1						77.8	12.0	65.8
1986	433.5	348.9	190.7	135.2	158.2						84.6	12.4	72.2
1987	446.6	356.0	199.7	142.7	156.3						90.6	14.1	76.6
1988	462.0	367.3	204.5	142.4	162.8						94.7	12.3	82.5
1989	477.5	379.3	204.3	143.2	175.1						98.2	12.2	86.0
1990	476.8	369.3	191.1	132.1	178.2						107.5	12.1	95.4
1991	432.6	322.5	166.3	114.6	156.2						110.1	12.8	97.3
1992	463.7	347.8	199.4	135.1	148.4						115.8	14.4	101.5
1993	485.5	358.2	208.2	150.9	150.0	4.6	20.0	34.4	23.4	67.7	127.4	14.4	112.9
1994	531.9	401.5	241.0	176.4	160.4	4.7	20.4	39.6	28.8	66.9	130.4	14.4	116.0
1995	548.7	408.7	228.1	171.4	180.5	7.1	23.0	44.1	35.4	70.9	140.0	15.8	124.3
1996	599.7	453.0	257.5	191.1	195.5	10.9	26.5	49.4	38.1	70.6	146.7	15.3	131.4
1997	631.9	478.4	264.7	198.1	213.7	12.9	32.8	53.1	37.6	77.3	153.4	14.1	139.4
1998	688.5	533.7	296.3	224.0	237.4	14.8	40.4	55.7	40.5	86.0	154.8	14.3	140.5
1999	744.6	575.5	326.3	251.3	249.2	16.0	45.1	59.4	35.1	93.7	169.1	14.0	155.1
2000	802.8	621.4	346.1	265.0	275.3	16.3	52.4	64.1	37.6	104.9	181.3	14.2	167.2
2001	840.2	638.3	364.4	279.4	273.9	14.5	49.7	63.6	37.8	108.2	201.9	15.1	186.8
2002	847.9	634.4	396.7	298.8	237.7	10.5	35.3	59.0	22.7	110.2	213.4	16.6	196.9
2003	891.5	675.4	446.0	345.7	229.3	9.9	30.6	57.5	21.4	109.9	216.1	17.9	198.2
2004	991.4	771.2	532.9	417.5	238.3	12.0	32.9	63.2	23.2	107.0	220.2	18.3	201.8
2005	1,104.1	870.0	611.9	480.8	258.1	12.7	37.3	66.6	28.4	113.1	234.2	17.3	216.9
2006	1,167.2	911.8	613.7	468.8	298.1	17.6	45.7	73.4	32.3	129.2	255.4	17.6	237.8
2007	1,152.4	863.3	493.2	354.1	370.0	27.5	53.8	85.9	40.2	162.7	289.1	20.6	268.5
2008	1,067.6	758.8	350.3	230.1	408.6	35.4	55.5	82.7	52.8	182.3	308.7	23.7	285.0
2009	903.2	588.3	245.9	133.9	342.4	25.4	37.3	50.5	56.3	173.0	314.9	28.4	286.5
2010	803.6	500.6	238.8	127.2	261.8	10.9	24.2	37.6	37.5	151.5	303.0	30.8	272.2
2010: Jan	813.4	519.3	254.5	130.5	264.8	13.6	27.1	39.9	40.7	143.5	294.2	27.3	266.8
Feb	795.2	505.8	242.7	130.7	263.0	12.9	27.8	38.8	41.4	142.2	289.5	28.9	260.5
Mar	806.7	510.4	244.5	131.1	265.9	11.8	25.1	38.5	47.1	143.4	296.3	29.3	267.0
Apr	819.7	515.4	252.7	134.0	262.6	11.4	24.8	38.4	42.0	146.0	304.4	32.4	272.0
May	811.2	506.8	245.2	133.5	261.5	11.0	24.2	37.7	39.3	149.4	304.5	31.8	272.7
June	810.4	501.9	240.9	132.4	261.0	10.6	23.8	39.1	38.5	148.9	308.6	33.1	275.5
July	789.0	487.6	235.6	129.7	252.0	10.5	22.5	36.5	36.2	146.2	301.4	30.4	271.0
Aug	791.7	484.1	228.9	123.4	255.2	10.6	23.5	37.9	35.2	148.1	307.6	29.7	277.9
Sept	797.3	482.9	228.2	121.5	254.8	10.0	23.9	37.0	35.1	148.8	314.3	32.4	282.0
Oct	802.0	492.9	235.0	120.4	257.9	9.5	23.6	36.3	33.2	155.5	309.1	32.4	276.7
Nov	803.0	502.3	235.7	121.2	266.6	9.6	22.3	36.2	32.7	165.7	300.7	31.8	269.0
Dec	782.9	489.0	230.0	120.6	259.0	9.2	22.9	35.5	30.3	161.1	293.9	28.6	265.4
2011: Jan	772.0	482.1	237.6	121.5	244.5	8.1	22.1	37.0	29.2	148.0	289.9	30.3	259.6
Feb	764.2	478.7	233.4	120.7	245.3	8.0	21.6	37.3	30.1	148.3	285.5	30.2	255.3
Mar	762.6	477.2	227.3	119.4	249.9	8.2	21.8	37.0	31.5	151.3	285.4	30.0	255.4
Apr	768.2	488.4	238.3	119.3	250.1	7.7	21.4	38.0	32.3	150.7	279.8	29.2	250.6
May	787.4	508.9	249.0	119.1	259.8	7.7	22.7	39.7	33.2	156.4	278.5	29.8	248.7
June	799.6	515.9	243.9	119.2	271.9	8.1	23.5	42.0	37.7	160.6	283.7	29.2	254.5
July	773.3	496.0	225.3	120.7	270.7	7.8	23.2	42.5	35.4	161.8	277.3	28.2	249.2
Aug	790.3	506.1	229.9	122.3	276.2	7.9	22.7	42.3	39.5	163.8	284.2	29.7	254.5
Sept	799.0	513.6	233.4	122.1	280.2	8.0	22.8	41.5	39.5	168.5	285.4	28.3	257.1
Oct [p]	797.4	517.3	238.9	122.6	278.5	7.5	23.2	40.9	37.4	169.5	280.1	26.2	253.9
Nov [p]	807.1	522.3	243.7	124.4	278.6	7.6	22.8	40.6	36.9	170.7	284.9	27.6	257.3

[1] Includes farm residential buildings.
[2] Includes residential improvements, not shown separately.
[3] New single- and multi-family units.
[4] Including farm.
[5] Health care, educational, religious, public safety, amusement and recreation, transportation, communication, power, highway and street, sewage and waste disposal, water supply, and conservation and development.

Note: Data beginning with 1993 reflect reclassification.

Source: Department of Commerce (Bureau of the Census).

TABLE B–56. New private housing units started, authorized, and completed and houses sold, 1965–2011

[Thousands; monthly data at seasonally adjusted annual rates]

Year or month	New housing units started				New housing units authorized[1]				New housing units completed	New houses sold
	Type of structure				Type of structure					
	Total	1 unit	2 to 4 units[2]	5 units or more	Total	1 unit	2 to 4 units	5 units or more		
1965	1,472.8	963.7	86.7	422.5	1,240.6	709.9	84.7	445.9	....	575
1966	1,164.9	778.6	61.2	325.1	971.9	563.2	61.0	347.7	....	461
1967	1,291.6	843.9	71.7	376.1	1,141.0	650.6	73.0	417.5	....	487
1968	1,507.6	899.4	80.7	527.3	1,353.4	694.7	84.3	574.4	1,319.8	490
1969	1,466.8	810.6	85.1	571.2	1,322.3	624.8	85.2	612.4	1,399.0	448
1970	1,433.6	812.9	84.9	535.9	1,351.5	646.8	88.1	616.7	1,418.4	485
1971	2,052.2	1,151.0	120.5	780.9	1,924.6	906.1	132.9	885.7	1,706.1	656
1972	2,356.6	1,309.2	141.2	906.2	2,218.9	1,033.1	148.6	1,037.2	2,003.9	718
1973	2,045.3	1,132.0	118.2	795.0	1,819.5	882.1	117.0	820.5	2,100.5	634
1974	1,337.7	888.1	68.0	381.6	1,074.4	643.8	64.4	366.2	1,728.5	519
1975	1,160.4	892.2	64.0	204.3	939.2	675.5	63.8	199.8	1,317.2	549
1976	1,537.5	1,162.4	85.8	289.2	1,296.2	893.6	93.1	309.5	1,377.2	646
1977	1,987.1	1,450.9	121.7	414.4	1,690.0	1,126.1	121.3	442.7	1,657.1	819
1978	2,020.3	1,433.3	125.1	462.0	1,800.5	1,182.6	130.6	487.3	1,867.5	817
1979	1,745.1	1,194.1	122.0	429.0	1,551.8	981.5	125.4	444.8	1,870.8	709
1980	1,292.2	852.2	109.5	330.5	1,190.6	710.4	114.5	365.7	1,501.6	545
1981	1,084.2	705.4	91.2	287.7	985.5	564.3	101.8	319.4	1,265.7	436
1982	1,062.2	662.6	80.1	319.6	1,000.5	546.4	88.3	365.8	1,005.5	412
1983	1,703.0	1,067.6	113.5	522.0	1,605.2	901.5	133.7	570.1	1,390.3	623
1984	1,749.5	1,084.2	121.4	543.9	1,681.8	922.4	142.6	616.8	1,652.2	639
1985	1,741.8	1,072.4	93.5	576.0	1,733.3	956.6	120.1	656.6	1,703.3	688
1986	1,805.4	1,179.4	84.0	542.0	1,769.4	1,077.6	108.4	583.5	1,756.4	750
1987	1,620.5	1,146.4	65.1	408.7	1,534.8	1,024.4	89.3	421.1	1,668.8	671
1988	1,488.1	1,081.3	58.7	348.0	1,455.6	993.8	75.7	386.1	1,529.8	676
1989	1,376.1	1,003.3	55.3	317.6	1,338.4	931.7	66.9	339.8	1,422.8	650
1990	1,192.7	894.8	37.6	260.4	1,110.8	793.9	54.3	262.6	1,308.0	534
1991	1,013.9	840.4	35.6	137.9	948.8	753.5	43.1	152.1	1,090.8	509
1992	1,199.7	1,029.9	30.9	139.0	1,094.9	910.7	45.8	138.4	1,157.5	610
1993	1,287.6	1,125.7	29.4	132.6	1,199.1	986.5	52.4	160.2	1,192.7	666
1994	1,457.0	1,198.4	35.2	223.5	1,371.6	1,068.5	62.2	241.0	1,346.9	670
1995	1,354.1	1,076.2	33.8	244.1	1,332.5	997.3	63.8	271.5	1,312.6	667
1996	1,476.8	1,160.9	45.3	270.8	1,425.6	1,069.5	65.8	290.3	1,412.9	757
1997	1,474.0	1,133.7	44.5	295.8	1,441.1	1,062.4	68.4	310.3	1,400.5	804
1998	1,616.9	1,271.4	42.6	302.9	1,612.3	1,187.6	69.2	355.5	1,474.2	886
1999	1,640.9	1,302.4	31.9	306.6	1,663.5	1,246.7	65.8	351.1	1,604.9	880
2000	1,568.7	1,230.9	38.7	299.1	1,592.3	1,198.1	64.9	329.3	1,573.7	877
2001	1,602.7	1,273.3	36.6	292.8	1,636.7	1,235.6	66.0	335.2	1,570.8	908
2002	1,704.9	1,358.6	38.5	307.9	1,747.7	1,332.6	73.7	341.4	1,648.4	973
2003	1,847.7	1,499.0	33.5	315.2	1,889.2	1,460.9	82.5	345.8	1,678.7	1,086
2004	1,955.8	1,610.5	42.3	303.0	2,070.1	1,613.4	90.4	366.2	1,841.9	1,203
2005	2,068.3	1,715.8	41.1	311.4	2,155.3	1,682.0	84.0	389.3	1,931.4	1,283
2006	1,800.9	1,465.4	42.7	292.8	1,838.9	1,378.2	76.6	384.1	1,979.4	1,051
2007	1,355.0	1,046.0	31.7	277.3	1,398.4	979.9	59.6	359.0	1,502.8	776
2008	905.5	622.0	17.5	266.0	905.4	575.6	34.4	295.4	1,119.7	485
2009	554.0	445.1	11.6	97.3	583.0	441.1	20.7	121.1	794.4	375
2010	586.9	471.2	11.4	104.3	604.6	447.3	22.0	135.3	651.7	323
2011 [p]	606.9	428.6	10.8	167.4	610.7	413.6	20.7	176.4	583.9	302
2010: Jan	615	510	....	98	636	508	20	108	662	346
Feb	603	522	....	64	655	514	22	119	660	344
Mar	626	531	....	87	688	533	23	132	651	385
Apr	687	566	....	108	632	473	19	140	744	420
May	580	460	....	108	582	435	20	127	702	281
June	539	451	....	83	585	423	21	141	881	307
July	550	429	....	102	575	409	22	144	581	279
Aug	606	427	....	165	575	405	21	149	607	278
Sept	597	447	....	144	562	403	25	134	634	316
Oct	539	434	....	93	555	407	24	124	601	282
Nov	551	454	....	82	564	420	20	124	551	287
Dec	526	421	....	97	630	445	25	160	565	331
2011: Jan	636	437	....	187	568	419	20	129	509	310
Feb	518	388	....	112	534	382	15	137	611	281
Mar	593	418	....	164	574	392	16	166	597	305
Apr	549	411	....	124	563	395	21	147	543	316
May	553	416	....	131	609	406	20	183	549	308
June	615	449	....	160	617	402	21	194	574	303
July	615	430	....	176	601	403	21	177	641	295
Aug	585	425	....	153	625	418	25	182	621	290
Sept	646	422	....	218	589	413	20	156	608	302
Oct	628	437	....	175	644	428	23	193	576	307
Nov [p]	685	450	....	227	680	436	21	223	554	314
Dec [p]	657	470	....	164	671	441	24	206	605	307

[1] Authorized by issuance of local building permits in permit-issuing places: 20,000 places beginning with 2004; 19,000 for 1994–2003; 17,000 for 1984–93; 16,000 for 1978–83; 14,000 for 1972–77; 13,000 for 1967–71; and 12,000 for 1965–66.

[2] Monthly data do not meet publication standards because tests for identifiable and stable seasonality do not meet reliability standards.

Note: One-unit estimates prior to 1999, for new housing units started and completed and for new houses sold, include an upward adjustment of 3.3 percent to account for structures in permit-issuing areas that did not have permit authorization.

Source: Department of Commerce (Bureau of the Census).

[Amounts in millions of dollars; monthly data seasonally adjusted]

Year or month	Total manufacturing and trade			Manufacturing			Merchant wholesalers[1]			Retail trade			Retail and food services sales
	Sales[2]	Inventories[3]	Ratio[4]	Sales[2]	Inventories[3]	Ratio[4]	Sales[2]	Inventories[3]	Ratio[4]	Sales[2,5]	Inventories[3]	Ratio[4]	
SIC:[6]													
1970	108,221	178,594	1.65	52,805	101,599	1.92	24,167	33,354	1.38	31,249	43,641	1.40	
1971	116,895	188,991	1.62	55,906	102,567	1.83	26,492	36,568	1.38	34,497	49,856	1.45	
1972	131,081	203,227	1.55	63,027	108,121	1.72	29,866	40,297	1.35	38,189	54,809	1.44	
1973	153,677	234,406	1.53	72,931	124,499	1.71	38,115	46,918	1.23	42,631	62,989	1.48	
1974	177,912	287,144	1.61	84,790	157,625	1.86	47,982	58,667	1.22	45,141	70,852	1.57	
1975	182,198	288,992	1.59	86,589	159,708	1.84	46,634	57,774	1.24	48,975	71,510	1.46	
1976	204,150	318,345	1.56	98,797	174,636	1.77	50,698	64,622	1.27	54,655	79,087	1.45	
1977	229,513	350,706	1.53	113,201	188,378	1.66	56,136	73,179	1.30	60,176	89,149	1.48	
1978	260,320	400,931	1.54	126,905	211,691	1.67	66,413	86,934	1.31	67,002	102,306	1.53	
1979	297,701	452,640	1.52	143,936	242,157	1.68	79,051	99,679	1.26	74,713	110,804	1.48	
1980	327,233	508,924	1.56	154,391	265,215	1.72	93,099	122,631	1.32	79,743	121,078	1.52	
1981	355,822	545,786	1.53	168,129	283,413	1.69	101,180	129,654	1.28	86,514	132,719	1.53	
1982	347,625	573,908	1.67	163,351	311,852	1.95	95,211	127,428	1.36	89,062	134,628	1.49	
1983	369,286	590,287	1.56	172,547	312,379	1.78	99,225	130,075	1.28	97,514	147,833	1.44	
1984	410,124	649,780	1.53	190,682	339,516	1.73	112,199	142,452	1.23	107,243	167,812	1.49	
1985	422,583	664,039	1.56	194,538	334,749	1.73	113,459	147,409	1.28	114,586	181,881	1.52	
1986	430,419	662,738	1.55	194,657	322,654	1.68	114,960	153,574	1.32	120,803	186,510	1.56	
1987	457,735	709,848	1.50	206,326	338,109	1.59	122,968	163,903	1.29	128,442	207,836	1.55	
1988	497,157	767,222	1.49	224,619	369,374	1.57	134,521	178,801	1.30	138,017	219,047	1.54	
1989	527,039	815,455	1.52	236,698	391,212	1.63	143,760	187,009	1.28	146,581	237,234	1.58	
1990	545,909	840,594	1.52	242,686	405,073	1.65	149,506	195,833	1.29	153,718	239,688	1.56	
1991	542,815	834,609	1.53	239,847	390,950	1.65	148,306	200,448	1.33	154,661	243,211	1.54	
1992	567,176	842,809	1.48	250,394	382,510	1.54	154,150	208,302	1.32	162,632	251,997	1.52	
NAICS:[6]													
1992	540,573	836,934	1.53	242,002	378,651	1.57	147,261	196,914	1.31	151,310	261,369	1.67	168,261
1993	567,580	864,049	1.50	251,708	379,681	1.50	154,018	204,842	1.30	161,854	279,526	1.68	179,858
1994	610,253	927,272	1.46	269,843	399,852	1.44	164,575	221,978	1.29	175,835	305,442	1.66	194,638
1995	655,097	986,059	1.48	289,973	424,742	1.44	179,915	238,392	1.29	185,209	322,925	1.72	204,677
1996	687,350	1,005,436	1.46	299,766	430,446	1.44	190,362	241,053	1.27	197,222	333,937	1.67	217,463
1997	723,879	1,046,701	1.42	319,558	443,529	1.37	198,154	258,557	1.26	206,167	344,615	1.64	227,670
1998	742,837	1,078,659	1.43	324,984	448,974	1.39	202,260	272,416	1.32	215,592	357,269	1.62	238,275
1999	786,634	1,138,831	1.40	335,991	463,529	1.35	216,597	290,317	1.30	234,046	384,985	1.59	257,793
2000	834,325	1,197,344	1.41	350,715	481,233	1.35	234,546	309,299	1.29	249,063	406,812	1.59	274,511
2001	818,615	1,120,103	1.43	330,875	427,806	1.38	232,096	297,657	1.32	255,644	394,640	1.58	282,122
2002	823,714	1,140,578	1.36	326,227	422,953	1.29	236,294	301,440	1.26	261,194	416,185	1.55	288,834
2003	854,760	1,148,886	1.34	334,616	408,273	1.24	247,798	308,321	1.23	272,346	432,292	1.56	301,586
2004	925,785	1,242,087	1.30	359,081	440,780	1.19	276,668	339,971	1.18	290,036	461,336	1.56	321,253
2005	1,004,510	1,313,706	1.27	395,173	473,977	1.17	301,280	367,535	1.18	308,058	472,194	1.51	341,171
2006	1,066,641	1,406,860	1.28	417,963	522,693	1.20	325,334	397,823	1.18	323,345	486,344	1.49	358,681
2007	1,124,962	1,483,244	1.29	443,288	562,058	1.22	347,857	422,813	1.18	333,817	498,373	1.48	370,973
2008	1,154,686	1,465,304	1.32	455,675	550,196	1.27	369,601	438,461	1.21	329,411	476,647	1.51	367,458
2009	981,801	1,328,900	1.39	369,683	512,889	1.41	308,912	386,846	1.30	303,206	429,165	1.46	340,977
2010	1,074,129	1,442,548	1.29	401,654	557,617	1.32	348,353	429,439	1.16	324,122	455,492	1.37	362,954
2010: Jan	1,033,676	1,330,844	1.29	391,192	513,731	1.31	329,180	387,319	1.18	313,304	429,794	1.37	351,079
Feb	1,036,520	1,339,482	1.29	389,580	518,607	1.33	333,259	388,751	1.17	313,681	432,124	1.38	352,109
Mar	1,058,286	1,347,309	1.27	397,323	520,370	1.31	339,776	391,073	1.15	321,187	435,866	1.36	359,877
Apr	1,067,887	1,353,757	1.27	400,920	523,410	1.31	343,974	392,904	1.14	322,993	437,443	1.35	361,735
May	1,061,363	1,356,650	1.28	396,819	523,255	1.32	343,911	395,041	1.15	320,633	438,354	1.37	359,262
June	1,056,919	1,366,666	1.29	393,959	527,044	1.34	342,915	396,093	1.16	320,045	443,529	1.39	358,722
July	1,069,471	1,379,763	1.29	402,458	530,012	1.32	346,266	401,909	1.16	320,747	447,842	1.40	359,446
Aug	1,074,608	1,390,434	1.29	401,696	532,323	1.33	348,340	406,008	1.17	324,572	452,103	1.39	363,666
Sept	1,083,695	1,405,404	1.30	405,645	537,957	1.33	350,599	412,769	1.18	327,451	454,678	1.39	366,417
Oct	1,098,722	1,421,984	1.29	408,082	544,410	1.33	359,126	424,107	1.18	331,514	453,467	1.37	370,676
Nov	1,113,873	1,428,094	1.28	412,779	550,059	1.33	366,508	424,466	1.16	334,586	453,569	1.36	373,952
Dec	1,129,958	1,442,548	1.28	423,543	557,617	1.32	369,558	429,439	1.16	336,857	455,492	1.35	376,208
2011: Jan	1,152,600	1,456,470	1.26	431,064	565,167	1.31	381,889	433,785	1.14	339,647	457,518	1.35	379,257
Feb	1,156,451	1,467,232	1.27	431,886	571,854	1.32	380,832	438,114	1.15	343,733	457,264	1.33	384,044
Mar	1,184,017	1,485,581	1.25	445,386	580,076	1.30	392,436	443,611	1.13	346,195	461,894	1.33	386,960
Apr	1,185,358	1,499,705	1.27	443,493	588,509	1.33	394,549	448,319	1.14	347,316	462,877	1.33	387,705
May	1,183,605	1,513,687	1.28	443,344	592,935	1.34	393,520	456,028	1.16	346,741	464,724	1.34	387,522
June	1,189,393	1,519,853	1.28	446,021	595,119	1.33	396,023	458,883	1.16	347,349	465,851	1.34	388,284
July	1,197,413	1,527,659	1.28	451,182	598,758	1.33	397,264	462,401	1.16	348,967	466,500	1.34	389,934
Aug	1,202,502	1,533,170	1.27	451,411	600,709	1.33	401,187	462,699	1.15	349,904	469,762	1.34	391,074
Sept	1,209,576	1,533,506	1.27	452,874	601,587	1.33	402,383	462,842	1.15	354,319	469,077	1.32	396,049
Oct	1,217,102	1,545,123	1.27	454,918	607,016	1.33	405,640	468,281	1.15	356,544	469,826	1.32	398,645
Nov *p*	1,220,852	1,550,126	1.27	455,028	609,814	1.34	407,901	468,878	1.15	357,923	471,434	1.32	400,268

[1] Excludes manufacturers' sales branches and offices.

[2] Annual data are averages of monthly not seasonally adjusted figures.

[3] Seasonally adjusted, end of period. Inventories beginning with January 1982 for manufacturing and December 1980 for wholesale and retail trade are not comparable with earlier periods.

[4] Inventory/sales ratio. Monthly inventories are inventories at the end of the month to sales for the month. Annual data beginning with 1982 are the average of monthly ratios for the year. Annual data for 1970–81 are the ratio of December inventories to monthly average sales for the year.

[5] Food services included on Standard Industrial Classification (SIC) basis and excluded on North American Industry Classification System (NAICS) basis. See last column for retail and food services sales.

[6] Effective in 2001, data classified based on NAICS. Data on NAICS basis available beginning with 1992. Earlier data based on SIC. Data on both NAICS and SIC basis include semiconductors.

Source: Department of Commerce (Bureau of the Census).

[Millions of dollars; monthly data seasonally adjusted]

| Year or month | Shipments [1] | | | Inventories [2] | | | | | | | | |
| | Total | Durable goods industries | Non-durable goods industries | Total | Durable goods industries | | | | Nondurable goods industries | | | |
					Total	Materials and supplies	Work in process	Finished goods	Total	Materials and supplies	Work in process	Finished goods
SIC: [3]												
1970	52,805	28,156	24,649	101,599	66,651	19,149	29,745	17,757	34,948	13,168	5,271	16,509
1971	55,906	29,924	25,982	102,567	66,136	19,679	28,550	17,907	36,431	13,686	5,678	17,067
1972	63,027	33,987	29,040	108,121	70,067	20,807	30,713	18,547	38,054	14,677	5,998	17,379
1973	72,931	39,635	33,296	124,499	81,192	25,944	35,490	19,758	43,307	18,147	6,729	18,431
1974	84,790	44,173	40,617	157,625	101,493	35,070	42,530	23,893	56,132	23,744	8,189	24,199
1975	86,589	43,598	42,991	159,708	102,590	33,903	43,227	25,460	57,118	23,565	8,834	24,719
1976	98,797	50,623	48,174	174,636	111,988	37,457	46,074	28,457	62,648	25,847	9,929	26,872
1977	113,201	59,168	54,033	188,378	120,877	40,186	50,226	30,465	67,501	27,387	10,961	29,153
1978	126,905	67,731	59,174	211,691	138,181	45,198	58,848	34,135	73,510	29,619	12,085	31,806
1979	143,936	75,927	68,009	242,157	160,734	52,670	69,325	38,739	81,423	32,814	13,910	34,699
1980	154,391	77,419	76,972	265,215	174,788	55,173	76,945	42,670	90,427	36,606	15,884	37,937
1981	168,129	83,727	84,402	283,413	186,443	57,998	80,998	47,447	96,970	38,165	16,194	42,611
1982	163,351	79,212	84,139	311,852	200,444	59,136	86,707	54,601	111,408	44,039	18,612	48,757
1983	172,547	85,481	87,066	312,379	199,854	60,325	86,899	52,630	112,525	44,816	18,691	49,018
1984	190,682	97,940	92,742	339,516	221,330	66,031	98,251	57,048	118,186	45,692	19,328	53,166
1985	194,538	101,279	93,259	334,749	218,193	63,904	98,162	56,127	116,556	44,106	19,442	53,008
1986	194,657	103,238	91,419	322,654	211,997	61,331	97,000	53,666	110,657	42,335	18,124	50,198
1987	206,326	108,128	98,198	338,109	220,799	63,562	102,393	54,844	117,310	45,319	19,270	52,721
1988	224,619	118,458	106,161	369,374	242,468	69,611	112,958	59,899	126,906	49,396	20,559	56,951
1989	236,698	123,158	113,540	391,212	257,513	72,435	122,251	62,827	133,699	50,674	21,653	61,372
1990	242,686	123,776	118,910	405,073	263,209	73,559	124,130	65,520	141,864	52,645	22,817	66,402
1991	239,847	121,000	118,847	390,950	250,019	70,834	114,960	64,225	140,931	53,011	22,815	65,105
1992	250,394	128,489	121,905	382,510	238,105	69,459	104,424	64,222	144,405	54,007	23,532	66,866
NAICS: [3]												
1992	242,002	126,572	115,430	378,651	237,901	69,649	104,182	64,070	140,750	53,131	23,430	64,189
1993	251,708	133,712	117,996	379,681	238,721	72,624	102,013	64,084	140,960	54,204	23,401	63,355
1994	269,843	147,005	122,838	399,852	253,073	78,559	106,538	67,976	146,779	57,067	24,448	65,264
1995	289,973	158,568	131,405	424,742	267,362	85,528	106,647	75,187	157,380	60,753	25,780	70,847
1996	299,766	164,883	134,883	430,446	272,472	86,287	110,596	75,589	157,974	59,176	26,478	72,320
1997	319,558	178,949	140,610	443,529	281,013	92,298	109,922	78,793	162,516	60,169	28,535	73,812
1998	324,984	185,966	139,019	448,974	290,532	93,553	115,143	81,836	158,442	58,255	27,096	73,091
1999	335,991	193,895	142,096	463,529	296,483	97,858	114,006	84,619	167,046	61,065	28,774	77,207
2000	350,715	197,807	152,908	481,233	306,392	106,014	110,991	89,387	174,841	61,488	30,013	83,340
2001	330,875	181,201	149,674	427,806	267,626	91,223	93,820	82,583	160,180	55,766	27,058	77,356
2002	326,227	176,968	149,259	422,953	260,406	88,475	92,337	79,594	162,547	56,627	27,813	78,107
2003	334,616	178,549	156,067	408,273	246,868	82,289	88,641	75,938	161,405	56,916	27,011	77,478
2004	359,081	188,722	170,359	440,780	264,993	92,102	91,070	81,821	175,787	61,877	29,862	84,048
2005	395,173	202,070	193,103	473,977	283,820	98,504	98,716	86,600	190,157	66,922	32,788	90,447
2006	417,963	213,516	204,447	522,693	317,653	111,603	106,639	99,411	205,040	70,340	36,925	97,775
2007	443,288	223,919	219,369	562,058	334,850	116,458	117,731	100,661	227,208	75,202	44,825	107,181
2008	455,675	218,328	237,347	550,196	334,094	118,559	114,062	101,473	216,102	72,150	40,953	102,999
2009	369,683	173,124	196,559	512,889	304,120	102,429	111,422	90,269	208,769	71,318	41,588	95,863
2010	401,654	183,860	217,793	557,617	334,238	109,104	127,634	97,500	223,379	76,636	44,011	102,732
2010: Jan	391,192	179,956	211,236	513,731	304,916	102,004	112,356	90,556	208,815	70,675	40,926	97,214
Feb	389,580	176,370	213,210	518,607	307,170	103,189	113,659	90,322	211,437	71,900	41,657	97,880
Mar	397,323	178,329	218,994	520,370	308,422	103,493	114,026	90,903	211,948	72,338	41,991	97,619
Apr	400,920	182,666	218,254	523,410	311,159	103,925	115,845	91,389	212,251	71,434	42,118	98,699
May	396,819	183,181	213,638	523,255	314,559	104,885	117,055	92,619	208,696	69,622	40,851	98,223
June	393,959	182,195	211,764	527,044	318,655	106,455	118,580	93,620	208,389	69,802	40,634	97,953
July	402,458	189,034	213,424	530,012	320,521	106,219	119,444	94,858	209,491	70,670	40,380	98,441
Aug	401,696	186,085	215,611	532,323	323,178	106,511	120,768	95,899	209,145	69,984	40,579	98,582
Sept	405,645	186,539	219,106	537,957	326,081	106,728	122,594	96,759	211,876	71,397	40,632	99,847
Oct	408,082	186,013	222,069	544,410	328,558	107,458	123,683	97,417	215,852	72,514	41,862	101,476
Nov	412,779	185,931	226,848	550,059	331,583	108,190	125,272	98,121	218,476	73,908	42,371	102,197
Dec	423,543	190,248	233,295	557,617	334,238	109,104	127,634	97,500	223,379	76,636	44,011	102,732
2011: Jan	431,064	190,912	240,152	565,167	337,495	110,243	129,003	98,249	227,672	77,701	44,734	105,237
Feb	431,886	190,921	240,965	571,854	341,416	110,901	130,592	99,923	230,438	79,367	45,243	105,828
Mar	445,386	196,879	248,507	580,076	347,292	112,099	134,135	101,058	232,784	79,871	45,417	107,496
Apr	443,493	194,103	249,390	588,509	351,488	113,622	135,882	101,984	237,021	80,502	46,845	109,674
May	443,344	195,099	248,245	592,935	355,983	114,806	138,216	102,961	236,952	80,420	46,405	110,127
June	446,021	197,263	248,758	595,119	358,215	114,983	139,595	103,637	236,904	79,972	46,689	110,243
July	451,182	201,376	249,806	598,758	362,100	115,723	141,416	104,961	236,658	79,746	45,859	111,053
Aug	451,411	201,505	249,906	600,709	365,291	116,558	142,336	106,397	235,418	80,380	44,561	110,477
Sept	452,874	200,700	252,174	601,587	365,314	116,869	141,654	106,791	236,273	79,857	45,256	111,160
Oct	454,918	203,613	251,305	607,016	366,881	117,064	142,740	107,077	240,135	82,496	46,173	111,466
Nov *p*	455,028	202,919	252,109	609,814	369,001	117,551	144,160	107,290	240,813	82,390	46,343	112,080

[1] Annual data are averages of monthly not seasonally adjusted figures.
[2] Seasonally adjusted, end of period. Data beginning with 1982 are not comparable with earlier data.
[3] Effective in 2001, data classified based on North American Industry Classification System (NAICS). Data on NAICS basis available beginning with 1992. Earlier data based on Standard Industrial Classification (SIC). Data on both NAICS and SIC basis include semiconductors.

Source: Department of Commerce (Bureau of the Census).

TABLE B-59. Manufacturers' new and unfilled orders, 1970–2011

[Amounts in millions of dollars; monthly data seasonally adjusted]

Year or month	New orders [1] Total	Durable goods industries Total	Durable goods industries Capital goods, nondefense	Nondurable goods industries	Unfilled orders [2] Total	Unfilled orders [2] Durable goods industries	Unfilled orders [2] Nondurable goods industries	Unfilled orders to shipments ratio [2] Total	Unfilled orders to shipments ratio [2] Durable goods industries	Unfilled orders to shipments ratio [2] Nondurable goods industries
SIC: [3]										
1970	52,022	27,340	6,072	24,682	105,008	100,412	4,596	3.61	4.36	0.76
1971	55,921	29,905	6,682	26,016	105,247	100,225	5,022	3.32	4.00	.76
1972	64,182	35,038	7,745	29,144	119,349	113,034	6,315	3.26	3.85	.86
1973	76,003	42,627	9,926	33,376	156,561	149,204	7,357	3.80	4.51	.91
1974	87,327	46,862	11,594	40,465	187,043	181,519	5,524	4.09	4.93	.62
1975	85,139	41,957	9,886	43,181	169,546	161,664	7,882	3.69	4.45	.82
1976	99,513	51,307	11,490	48,206	178,128	169,857	8,271	3.24	3.88	.74
1977	115,109	61,035	13,681	54,073	202,024	193,323	8,701	3.24	3.85	.71
1978	131,629	72,278	17,588	59,351	259,169	248,281	10,888	3.57	4.20	.81
1979	147,604	79,483	21,154	68,121	303,593	291,321	12,272	3.89	4.62	.82
1980	156,359	79,392	21,135	76,967	327,416	315,202	12,214	3.85	4.58	.75
1981	168,025	83,654	21,806	84,371	326,547	314,707	11,840	3.87	4.68	.69
1982	162,140	78,064	19,213	84,077	311,887	300,798	11,089	3.84	4.74	.62
1983	175,451	88,140	19,624	87,311	347,273	333,114	14,159	3.53	4.29	.69
1984	192,879	100,164	23,669	92,715	373,529	359,651	13,878	3.60	4.37	.64
1985	195,706	102,356	24,545	93,351	387,196	372,097	15,099	3.67	4.47	.68
1986	195,204	103,647	23,982	91,557	393,515	376,699	16,816	3.59	4.41	.70
1987	209,389	110,809	26,094	98,579	430,426	408,688	21,738	3.63	4.43	.83
1988	228,270	122,076	31,108	106,194	474,154	452,150	22,004	3.64	4.46	.76
1989	239,572	126,055	32,988	113,516	508,849	487,098	21,751	3.96	4.85	.77
1990	244,507	125,583	33,331	118,924	531,131	509,124	22,007	4.15	5.15	.76
1991	238,805	119,849	30,471	118,957	519,199	495,802	23,397	4.08	5.07	.79
1992	248,212	126,308	31,524	121,905	492,893	469,381	23,512	3.51	4.30	.75
NAICS: [3]										
1992					451,078				5.14	
1993	246,668	128,672	40,681		425,743				4.66	
1994	266,641	143,803	45,175		434,795				4.21	
1995	285,542	154,137	51,011		447,180				3.97	
1996	297,282	162,399	54,066		488,462				4.15	
1997	314,986	174,377	60,697		512,714				4.04	
1998	317,345	178,327	62,133		495,995				3.97	
1999	329,770	187,674	64,392		505,322				3.76	
2000	346,789	193,881	69,278		549,291				3.87	
2001	322,088	172,413	57,667		506,479				4.18	
2002	318,226	168,968	51,861		471,832				4.07	
2003	330,943	174,876	53,102		494,444				4.03	
2004	356,941	186,583	57,304		541,253				4.13	
2005	396,372	203,269	67,552		629,707				4.20	
2006	423,199	218,752	73,977		762,287				4.71	
2007	449,200	229,831	79,850		904,425				5.25	
2008	453,146	215,799	73,192		943,517				6.03	
2009	352,806	156,247	50,342		800,448				6.81	
2010	398,235	180,442	64,531		831,740				6.15	
2010: Jan	385,593	174,357	58,327		801,598				6.28	
Feb	388,104	174,894	63,721		804,985				6.31	
Mar	391,734	172,740	58,169		803,337				6.17	
Apr	398,577	180,323	64,678		807,393				6.16	
May	393,090	179,452	63,864		809,577				6.14	
June	390,126	178,362	65,089		809,990				6.10	
July	397,922	184,498	65,293		812,369				6.02	
Aug	395,248	179,637	64,400		812,582				6.09	
Sept	410,063	190,957	72,841		823,141				6.12	
Oct	406,014	183,945	70,901		827,560				6.20	
Nov	411,543	184,695	64,878		832,652				6.20	
Dec	416,654	183,359	62,159		831,740				6.03	
2011: Jan	430,864	190,712	66,285		838,186				6.10	
Feb	429,658	188,693	69,496		842,152				6.13	
Mar	445,836	197,329	72,979		848,202				5.96	
Apr	441,740	192,350	69,144		853,164				6.11	
May	444,454	196,209	72,856		860,748				6.11	
June	442,711	193,953	71,136		863,541				6.05	
July	451,885	202,079	74,125		871,117				6.06	
Aug	452,121	202,215	78,159		878,731				6.07	
Sept	451,636	199,462	75,387		884,132				6.08	
Oct	450,932	199,627	72,748		887,233				6.07	
Nov *p*	459,177	207,068	78,606		898,328				6.16	

[1] Annual data are averages of monthly not seasonally adjusted figures.

[2] Unfilled orders are seasonally adjusted, end of period. Ratios are unfilled orders at end of period to shipments for period (excludes industries with no unfilled orders). Annual ratios relate to seasonally adjusted data for December.

[3] Effective in 2001, data classified based on North American Industry Classification System (NAICS). Data on NAICS basis available beginning with 1992. Earlier data based on the Standard Industrial Classification (SIC). Data on SIC basis include semiconductors. Data on NAICS basis do not include semiconductors.

Note: For NAICS basis data beginning with 1992, because there are no unfilled orders for manufacturers' nondurable goods, manufacturers' nondurable new orders and nondurable shipments are the same (see Table B–58).

Source: Department of Commerce (Bureau of the Census).

TABLE B-60. Consumer price indexes for major expenditure classes, 1968–2011

[For all urban consumers; 1982–84=100, except as noted]

Year or month	All items	Food and beverages		Apparel	Housing	Transportation	Medical care	Recreation [2]	Education and communication [2]	Other goods and services	Energy [3]
		Total [1]	Food								
1968	34.8	36.2	35.3	53.7	32.0	34.3	29.9			36.9	24.2
1969	36.7	38.1	37.1	56.8	34.0	35.7	31.9			38.7	24.8
1970	38.8	40.1	39.2	59.2	36.4	37.5	34.0			40.9	25.5
1971	40.5	41.4	40.4	61.1	38.0	39.5	36.1			42.9	26.5
1972	41.8	43.1	42.1	62.3	39.4	39.9	37.3			44.7	27.2
1973	44.4	48.8	48.2	64.6	41.2	41.2	38.8			46.4	29.4
1974	49.3	55.5	55.1	69.4	45.8	45.8	42.4			49.8	38.1
1975	53.8	60.2	59.8	72.5	50.7	50.1	47.5			53.9	42.1
1976	56.9	62.1	61.6	75.2	53.8	55.1	52.0			57.0	45.1
1977	60.6	65.8	65.5	78.6	57.4	59.0	57.0			60.4	49.4
1978	65.2	72.2	72.0	81.4	62.4	61.7	61.8			64.3	52.5
1979	72.6	79.9	79.9	84.9	70.1	70.5	67.5			68.9	65.7
1980	82.4	86.7	86.8	90.9	81.1	83.1	74.9			75.2	86.0
1981	90.9	93.5	93.6	95.3	90.4	93.2	82.9			82.6	97.7
1982	96.5	97.3	97.4	97.8	96.9	97.0	92.5			91.1	99.2
1983	99.6	99.5	99.4	100.2	99.5	99.3	100.6			101.1	99.9
1984	103.9	103.2	103.2	102.1	103.6	103.7	106.8			107.9	100.9
1985	107.6	105.6	105.6	105.0	107.7	106.4	113.5			114.5	101.6
1986	109.6	109.1	109.0	105.9	110.9	102.3	122.0			121.4	88.2
1987	113.6	113.5	113.5	110.6	114.2	105.4	130.1			128.5	88.6
1988	118.3	118.2	118.2	115.4	118.5	108.7	138.6			137.0	89.3
1989	124.0	124.9	125.1	118.6	123.0	114.1	149.3			147.7	94.3
1990	130.7	132.1	132.4	124.1	128.5	120.5	162.8			159.0	102.1
1991	136.2	136.8	136.3	128.7	133.6	123.8	177.0			171.6	102.5
1992	140.3	138.7	137.9	131.9	137.5	126.5	190.1			183.3	103.0
1993	144.5	141.6	140.9	133.7	141.2	130.4	201.4	90.7	85.5	192.9	104.2
1994	148.2	144.9	144.3	133.4	144.8	134.3	211.0	92.7	88.8	198.5	104.6
1995	152.4	148.9	148.4	132.0	148.5	139.1	220.5	94.5	92.2	206.9	105.2
1996	156.9	153.7	153.3	131.7	152.8	143.0	228.2	97.4	95.3	215.4	110.1
1997	160.5	157.7	157.3	132.9	156.8	144.3	234.6	99.6	98.4	224.8	111.5
1998	163.0	161.1	160.7	133.0	160.4	141.6	242.1	101.1	100.3	237.7	102.9
1999	166.6	164.6	164.1	131.3	163.9	144.4	250.6	102.0	101.2	258.3	106.6
2000	172.2	168.4	167.8	129.6	169.6	153.3	260.8	103.3	102.5	271.1	124.6
2001	177.1	173.6	173.1	127.3	176.4	154.3	272.8	104.9	105.2	282.6	129.3
2002	179.9	176.8	176.2	124.0	180.3	152.9	285.6	106.2	107.9	293.2	121.7
2003	184.0	180.5	180.0	120.9	184.8	157.6	297.1	107.5	109.8	298.7	136.5
2004	188.9	186.6	186.2	120.4	189.5	163.1	310.1	108.6	111.6	304.7	151.4
2005	195.3	191.2	190.7	119.5	195.7	173.9	323.2	109.4	113.7	313.4	177.1
2006	201.6	195.7	195.2	119.5	203.2	180.9	336.2	110.9	116.8	321.7	196.9
2007	207.342	203.300	202.916	118.998	209.586	184.682	351.054	111.443	119.577	333.328	207.723
2008	215.303	214.225	214.106	118.907	216.264	195.549	364.065	113.254	123.631	345.381	236.666
2009	214.537	218.249	217.955	120.078	217.057	179.252	375.613	114.272	127.393	368.586	193.126
2010	218.056	219.984	219.625	119.503	216.256	193.396	388.436	113.313	129.919	381.291	211.449
2011	224.939	227.866	227.842	122.111	219.102	212.366	400.258	113.357	131.466	387.224	243.909
2010: Jan	216.687	219.223	218.874	116.678	215.925	190.512	382.688	113.310	129.072	377.652	208.026
Feb	216.741	219.140	218.778	118.869	215.841	189.577	385.907	113.345	129.105	377.992	204.455
Mar	217.631	219.378	219.032	122.073	216.023	192.130	387.142	113.339	129.236	378.808	209.999
Apr	218.009	219.536	219.218	122.143	215.798	193.994	387.703	113.781	129.344	378.911	212.977
May	218.178	219.693	219.374	121.006	215.981	194.761	387.762	113.684	129.270	379.714	214.363
June	217.965	219.562	219.218	118.319	216.778	192.651	388.199	113.802	129.263	380.926	211.660
July	218.011	219.539	219.121	115.248	217.076	193.038	387.898	113.689	129.586	383.247	212.372
Aug	218.312	219.877	219.491	116.667	216.976	193.454	388.467	113.521	130.599	383.685	212.663
Sept	218.439	220.586	220.216	121.011	216.602	192.412	390.616	113.120	131.154	383.663	210.003
Oct	218.711	221.005	220.616	122.454	216.100	194.283	391.240	112.984	130.959	382.764	210.947
Nov	218.803	220.991	220.617	121.498	215.830	195.659	391.660	112.839	130.894	383.633	211.970
Dec	219.179	221.278	220.946	118.071	216.142	198.280	391.946	112.345	130.548	384.502	217.953
2011: Jan	220.223	223.160	222.912	116.664	216.739	200.835	393.858	112.638	130.665	384.689	223.266
Feb	221.309	224.039	223.799	118.369	217.259	203.037	397.065	113.183	130.692	385.397	226.860
Mar	223.467	225.479	225.350	121.286	217.707	211.014	397.726	113.261	130.682	385.637	242.516
Apr	224.906	226.248	226.150	122.226	217.901	216.867	398.813	113.368	130.643	386.226	253.495
May	225.964	227.082	226.976	122.271	218.484	220.270	399.375	113.659	130.600	385.476	260.376
June	225.722	227.451	227.360	120.578	219.553	216.880	399.552	113.654	130.568	386.171	254.170
July	225.922	228.323	228.316	118.770	220.230	216.164	400.305	113.492	130.859	386.494	252.661
Aug	226.545	229.490	229.554	121.547	220.506	216.057	400.874	113.592	132.028	387.053	251.706
Sept	226.889	230.448	230.573	125.272	220.540	215.198	401.605	113.440	132.627	388.627	250.480
Oct	226.421	230.885	231.017	127.590	220.138	212.127	403.430	113.270	132.755	389.119	240.902
Nov	226.230	230.656	230.790	127.285	219.969	211.358	404.858	113.232	132.750	390.761	238.177
Dec	225.672	231.130	231.301	123.470	220.193	208.585	405.629	113.499	132.728	391.043	232.300

[1] Includes alcoholic beverages, not shown separately.
[2] December 1997=100.
[3] Household energy—gas (piped), electricity, fuel oil, etc.—and motor fuel. Motor oil, coolant, etc. also included through 1982.

Note: Data beginning with 1983 incorporate a rental equivalence measure for homeowners' costs.
Series reflect changes in composition and renaming beginning in 1998, and formula and methodology changes beginning in 1999.

Source: Department of Labor (Bureau of Labor Statistics).

[For all urban consumers; 1982–84=100, except as noted]

Year or month	Food and beverages				Housing						
	Total [1]	Food			Total [2]	Shelter			Fuels and utilities		
		Total	At home	Away from home		Total [2]	Rent of primary residence	Owners' equivalent rent of residences [3,4]	Total [2]	Household energy	
										Total [2]	Energy Services
1968	36.2	35.3	36.3	32.9	32.0	30.1	43.3		27.4	21.7	23.9
1969	38.1	37.1	38.0	34.9	34.0	32.6	44.7		28.0	22.1	24.3
1970	40.1	39.2	39.9	37.5	36.4	35.5	46.5		29.1	23.1	25.4
1971	41.4	40.4	40.9	39.4	38.0	37.0	48.7		31.1	24.7	27.1
1972	43.1	42.1	42.7	41.0	39.4	38.7	50.4		32.5	25.7	28.5
1973	48.8	48.2	49.7	44.2	41.2	40.5	52.5		34.3	27.5	29.9
1974	55.5	55.1	57.1	49.8	45.8	44.4	55.2		40.7	34.4	34.5
1975	60.2	59.8	61.8	54.5	50.7	48.8	58.0		45.4	39.4	40.1
1976	62.1	61.6	63.1	58.2	53.8	51.5	61.1		49.4	43.3	44.7
1977	65.8	65.5	66.8	62.6	57.4	54.9	64.8		54.7	49.0	50.5
1978	72.2	72.0	73.8	68.3	62.4	60.5	69.3		58.5	53.0	55.0
1979	79.9	79.9	81.8	75.9	70.1	68.9	74.3		64.8	61.3	61.0
1980	86.7	86.8	88.4	83.4	81.1	81.0	80.9		75.4	74.8	71.4
1981	93.5	93.6	94.8	90.9	90.4	90.5	87.9		86.4	87.2	81.9
1982	97.3	97.4	98.1	95.8	96.9	96.9	94.6		94.9	95.6	93.2
1983	99.5	99.4	99.1	100.0	99.5	99.1	100.1	102.5	100.2	100.5	101.5
1984	103.2	103.2	102.8	104.2	103.6	104.0	105.3	107.3	104.8	104.0	105.4
1985	105.6	105.6	104.3	108.3	107.7	109.8	111.8	113.2	106.5	104.5	107.1
1986	109.1	109.0	107.3	112.5	110.9	115.8	118.3	119.4	104.1	99.2	105.7
1987	113.5	113.5	111.9	117.0	114.2	121.3	123.1	124.8	103.0	97.3	103.8
1988	118.2	118.2	116.6	121.8	118.5	127.1	127.8	131.1	104.4	98.0	104.6
1989	124.9	125.1	124.2	127.4	123.0	132.8	132.8	137.4	107.8	100.9	107.5
1990	132.1	132.4	132.3	133.4	128.5	140.0	138.4	144.8	111.6	104.5	109.3
1991	136.8	136.3	135.8	137.9	133.6	146.3	143.3	150.4	115.3	106.7	112.6
1992	138.7	137.9	136.8	140.7	137.5	151.2	146.9	155.5	117.8	108.1	114.8
1993	141.6	140.9	140.1	143.2	141.2	155.7	150.3	160.5	121.3	111.2	118.5
1994	144.9	144.3	144.1	145.7	144.8	160.5	154.0	165.8	122.8	111.7	119.2
1995	148.9	148.4	148.8	149.0	148.5	165.7	157.8	171.3	123.7	111.5	119.2
1996	153.7	153.3	154.3	152.7	152.8	171.0	162.0	176.8	127.5	115.2	122.1
1997	157.7	157.3	158.1	157.0	156.8	176.3	166.7	181.9	130.8	117.9	125.1
1998	161.1	160.7	161.1	161.1	160.4	182.1	172.1	187.8	128.5	113.7	121.2
1999	164.6	164.1	164.2	165.1	163.9	187.3	177.5	192.9	128.8	113.5	120.9
2000	168.4	167.8	167.9	169.0	169.6	193.4	183.9	198.7	137.9	122.8	128.0
2001	173.6	173.1	173.4	173.9	176.4	200.6	192.1	206.3	150.2	135.4	142.4
2002	176.8	176.2	175.6	178.3	180.3	208.1	199.7	214.7	143.6	127.2	134.4
2003	180.5	180.0	179.4	182.1	184.8	213.1	205.5	219.9	154.5	138.2	145.0
2004	186.6	186.2	186.2	187.5	189.5	218.8	211.0	224.9	161.9	144.4	150.6
2005	191.2	190.7	189.8	193.4	195.7	224.4	217.3	230.2	179.0	161.6	166.5
2006	195.7	195.2	193.1	199.4	203.2	232.1	225.1	238.2	194.7	177.1	182.1
2007	203.300	202.916	201.245	206.659	209.586	240.611	234.679	246.235	200.632	181.744	186.262
2008	214.225	214.106	214.125	215.769	216.264	246.666	243.271	252.426	220.018	200.808	202.212
2009	218.249	217.955	215.124	223.272	217.057	249.354	248.812	256.610	210.696	188.113	193.563
2010	219.984	219.625	215.836	226.114	216.256	248.396	249.385	256.584	214.187	189.286	192.886
2011	227.866	227.842	226.201	231.401	219.102	251.646	253.638	259.570	220.367	193.648	194.386
2010: Jan	219.223	218.874	215.404	224.916	215.925	247.950	249.144	256.591	211.381	187.330	190.439
Feb	219.140	218.778	215.118	225.081	215.841	248.001	249.017	256.483	210.819	186.345	189.549
Mar	219.378	219.032	215.623	224.991	216.023	248.052	249.089	256.272	212.295	187.864	191.280
Apr	219.536	219.218	215.737	225.276	215.798	248.031	249.012	256.170	211.726	187.054	190.284
May	219.693	219.374	215.793	225.573	215.981	248.100	248.925	256.163	212.773	188.017	191.628
June	219.562	219.218	215.361	225.797	216.778	248.470	248.999	256.352	217.820	193.678	198.207
July	219.539	219.121	215.256	225.710	217.076	248.677	249.126	256.395	219.614	195.268	200.177
Aug	219.877	219.491	215.382	226.422	216.976	248.595	249.024	256.509	219.602	194.865	199.632
Sept	220.586	220.216	216.161	227.075	216.602	248.522	249.368	256.590	217.695	192.635	197.049
Oct	221.005	220.616	216.698	227.287	216.100	248.646	249.618	256.823	213.031	187.271	190.603
Nov	220.991	220.617	216.538	227.512	215.830	248.738	250.317	257.202	210.978	184.764	187.335
Dec	221.278	220.946	216.955	227.722	216.142	248.972	250.986	257.452	212.505	186.338	188.443
2011: Jan	223.160	222.912	220.016	228.181	216.739	249.462	251.555	257.775	214.045	187.704	189.088
Feb	224.039	223.799	221.241	228.606	217.259	249.886	251.829	258.073	215.587	189.006	189.837
Mar	225.479	225.350	223.430	229.282	217.707	250.310	252.145	258.263	216.672	190.071	190.213
Apr	226.248	226.150	224.233	230.082	217.901	250.447	252.221	258.400	217.254	190.622	190.459
May	227.082	226.976	225.356	230.501	218.484	250.745	252.393	258.587	219.956	193.498	193.698
June	227.451	227.360	225.588	231.097	219.553	251.422	252.592	259.010	225.022	199.122	200.191
July	228.323	228.316	226.891	231.580	220.230	252.155	253.085	259.573	226.643	200.587	202.002
Aug	229.490	229.554	228.354	232.513	220.506	252.546	254.003	260.178	226.493	200.144	201.564
Sept	230.448	230.573	229.739	233.032	220.540	252.647	254.628	260.459	226.409	199.814	201.270
Oct	230.885	231.017	230.196	233.459	220.138	253.101	255.651	261.034	220.450	193.058	193.843
Nov	230.656	230.790	229.380	234.046	219.969	253.312	256.367	261.503	218.199	190.444	190.572
Dec	231.130	231.301	229.982	234.435	220.193	253.716	257.189	261.982	217.674	189.711	189.891

[1] Includes alcoholic beverages, not shown separately.
[2] Includes other items not shown separately.
[3] December 1982=100.
[4] Beginning January 2010, includes expenditure weight for second homes. Prior data are for primary residence only.

See next page for continuation of table.

[For all urban consumers; 1982-84=100, except as noted]

		Transportation						Medical care		
		Private transportation								
Year or month	Total	Total [2]	New vehicles		Used cars and trucks	Motor fuel	Public trans-porta-tion	Total	Medical care com-modities	Medical care services
			Total [2]	New cars						
1968	34.3	34.8	50.7	50.7	....	26.8	28.7	29.9	45.0	27.9
1969	35.7	36.0	51.5	51.5	30.9	27.6	30.9	31.9	45.4	30.2
1970	37.5	37.5	53.1	53.0	31.2	27.9	35.2	34.0	46.5	32.3
1971	39.5	39.4	55.3	55.2	33.0	28.1	37.8	36.1	47.3	34.7
1972	39.9	39.7	54.8	54.7	33.1	28.4	39.3	37.3	47.4	35.9
1973	41.2	41.0	54.8	54.8	35.2	31.2	39.7	38.8	47.5	37.5
1974	45.8	46.2	58.0	57.9	36.7	42.2	40.6	42.4	49.2	41.4
1975	50.1	50.6	63.0	62.9	43.8	45.1	43.5	47.5	53.3	46.6
1976	55.1	55.6	67.0	66.9	50.3	47.0	47.8	52.0	56.5	51.3
1977	59.0	59.7	70.5	70.4	54.7	49.7	50.0	57.0	60.2	56.4
1978	61.7	62.5	75.9	75.8	55.8	51.8	51.5	61.8	64.4	61.2
1979	70.5	71.7	81.9	81.8	60.2	70.1	54.9	67.5	69.0	67.2
1980	83.1	84.2	88.5	88.4	62.3	97.4	69.0	74.9	75.4	74.8
1981	93.2	93.8	93.9	93.7	76.9	108.5	85.6	82.9	83.7	82.8
1982	97.0	97.1	97.5	97.4	88.8	102.8	94.9	92.5	92.3	92.6
1983	99.3	99.3	99.9	99.9	98.7	99.4	99.5	100.6	100.2	100.7
1984	103.7	103.6	102.6	102.8	112.5	97.9	105.7	106.8	107.5	106.7
1985	106.4	106.2	106.1	106.1	113.7	98.7	110.5	113.5	115.2	113.2
1986	102.3	101.2	110.6	110.6	108.8	77.1	117.0	122.0	122.8	121.9
1987	105.4	104.2	114.4	114.6	113.1	80.2	121.1	130.1	131.0	130.0
1988	108.7	107.6	116.5	116.9	118.0	80.9	123.3	138.6	139.9	138.3
1989	114.1	112.9	119.2	119.2	120.4	88.5	129.5	149.3	150.8	148.9
1990	120.5	118.8	121.4	121.0	117.6	101.2	142.6	162.8	163.4	162.7
1991	123.8	121.9	126.0	125.3	118.1	99.4	148.9	177.0	176.8	177.1
1992	126.5	124.6	129.2	128.4	123.2	99.0	151.4	190.1	188.1	190.5
1993	130.4	127.5	132.7	131.5	133.9	98.0	167.0	201.4	195.0	202.9
1994	134.3	131.4	137.6	136.0	141.7	98.5	172.0	211.0	200.7	213.4
1995	139.1	136.3	141.0	139.0	156.5	100.0	175.9	220.5	204.5	224.2
1996	143.0	140.0	143.7	141.4	157.0	106.3	181.9	228.2	210.4	232.4
1997	144.3	141.0	144.3	141.7	151.1	106.2	186.7	234.6	215.3	239.1
1998	141.6	137.9	143.4	140.7	150.6	92.2	190.3	242.1	221.8	246.8
1999	144.4	140.5	142.9	139.6	152.0	100.7	197.7	250.6	230.7	255.1
2000	153.3	149.1	142.8	139.6	155.8	129.3	209.6	260.8	238.1	266.0
2001	154.3	150.0	142.1	138.9	158.7	124.7	210.6	272.8	247.6	278.8
2002	152.9	148.8	140.0	137.3	152.0	116.6	207.4	285.6	256.4	292.9
2003	157.6	153.6	137.9	134.7	142.9	135.8	209.3	297.1	262.8	306.0
2004	163.1	159.4	137.1	133.9	133.3	160.4	209.1	310.1	269.3	321.3
2005	173.9	170.2	137.9	135.2	139.4	195.7	217.3	323.2	276.0	336.7
2006	180.9	177.0	137.6	136.4	140.0	221.0	226.6	336.2	285.9	350.6
2007	184.682	180.778	136.254	135.865	135.747	239.070	230.002	351.054	289.999	369.302
2008	195.549	191.039	134.194	135.401	133.951	279.652	250.549	364.065	296.045	384.943
2009	179.252	174.762	135.623	136.685	126.973	201.978	236.348	375.613	305.108	397.299
2010	193.396	188.747	138.005	138.094	143.128	239.178	251.351	388.436	314.717	411.208
2011	212.366	207.641	141.883	142.226	149.011	302.619	269.403	400.258	324.089	423.810
2010: Jan	190.512	186.308	138.743	139.290	139.174	234.106	241.058	382.688	310.494	404.937
Feb	189.577	185.274	138.851	139.198	140.218	227.674	241.967	385.907	312.864	408.447
Mar	192.130	187.796	138.600	138.712	140.797	237.671	244.766	387.142	314.023	409.687
Apr	193.994	189.503	138.174	138.170	141.315	244.801	249.135	387.703	314.535	410.256
May	194.761	190.071	137.750	137.896	142.537	246.671	253.275	387.762	314.923	410.173
June	192.651	187.593	137.503	137.759	144.399	234.868	257.825	388.199	314.888	410.802
July	193.038	188.028	137.323	137.462	146.379	234.642	257.337	387.898	314.113	410.710
Aug	193.454	188.616	137.119	137.180	147.909	235.690	254.717	388.467	314.881	411.182
Sept	192.412	187.646	137.365	137.423	146.065	232.518	252.525	390.616	315.804	413.807
Oct	194.283	189.674	137.849	137.880	144.040	240.303	251.435	391.240	316.082	414.564
Nov	195.659	190.915	138.222	138.015	142.250	245.165	254.995	391.660	316.794	414.850
Dec	198.280	193.545	138.567	138.147	142.454	256.025	257.172	391.946	317.199	415.079
2011: Jan	200.835	196.087	138.925	138.203	142.555	265.703	259.634	393.858	318.929	417.025
Feb	203.037	198.073	140.158	139.584	142.937	271.843	265.327	397.065	321.186	420.567
Mar	211.014	206.165	140.860	140.311	144.072	303.565	270.366	397.726	322.691	420.852
Apr	216.867	212.210	141.462	141.154	145.968	326.024	272.187	398.813	324.241	421.716
May	220.270	215.829	142.494	142.717	148.361	337.359	271.417	399.375	324.399	422.438
June	216.880	212.216	143.054	143.812	151.776	318.242	272.297	399.552	324.102	422.813
July	216.164	211.432	142.763	143.707	154.184	313.488	272.868	400.305	324.159	423.847
Aug	216.057	211.315	142.327	143.283	155.823	311.962	272.949	400.874	324.395	424.546
Sept	215.198	210.513	142.334	143.414	153.586	309.745	271.199	401.605	325.130	425.258
Oct	212.127	207.404	142.535	143.419	151.494	296.944	269.158	403.430	325.962	427.467
Nov	211.358	206.635	142.736	143.489	149.230	294.049	268.478	404.858	326.624	429.191
Dec	208.585	203.809	142.953	143.619	148.140	282.501	266.958	405.629	327.254	430.005

Source: Department of Labor (Bureau of Labor Statistics).

[For all urban consumers; 1982–84=100, except as noted]

Year or month	All items (CPI-U) [1]	Commodities		Services	Special indexes				All items		
		All commodities	Commodities less food		All items less food	All items less energy	All items less food and energy	All items less medical care	CPI-U-X1 (Dec. 1982 = 97.6) [2]	CPI-U-RS (Dec. 1977 = 100) [3]	C-CPI-U (Dec. 1999 = 100) [4]
1968	34.8	38.1	40.0	30.3	34.9	35.9	36.3	35.1	37.7		
1969	36.7	39.9	41.7	32.4	36.8	38.0	38.4	37.0	39.4		
1970	38.8	41.7	43.4	35.0	39.0	40.3	40.8	39.2	41.3		
1971	40.5	43.2	45.1	37.0	40.8	42.0	42.7	40.8	43.1		
1972	41.8	44.5	46.1	38.4	42.0	43.4	44.0	42.1	44.4		
1973	44.4	47.8	47.7	40.1	43.7	46.1	45.6	44.8	47.2		
1974	49.3	53.5	52.8	43.8	48.0	50.6	49.4	49.8	51.9		
1975	53.8	58.2	57.6	48.0	52.5	55.1	53.9	54.3	56.2		
1976	56.9	60.7	60.5	52.0	56.0	58.2	57.4	57.2	59.4		
1977	60.6	64.2	63.8	56.0	59.6	61.9	61.0	60.8	63.2		
1978	65.2	68.8	67.5	60.8	63.9	66.7	65.5	65.4	67.5	104.4	
1979	72.6	76.6	75.3	67.5	71.2	73.4	71.9	72.9	74.0	114.4	
1980	82.4	86.0	85.7	77.9	81.5	81.9	80.8	82.8	82.3	127.1	
1981	90.9	93.2	93.1	88.1	90.4	90.1	89.2	91.4	90.1	139.2	
1982	96.5	97.0	96.9	96.0	96.3	96.1	95.8	96.8	95.6	147.6	
1983	99.6	99.8	100.0	99.4	99.7	99.6	99.6	99.6	99.6	153.9	
1984	103.9	103.2	103.1	104.6	104.0	104.3	104.6	103.7	103.9	160.2	
1985	107.6	105.4	105.2	109.9	108.0	108.4	109.1	107.2	107.6	165.7	
1986	109.6	104.4	101.7	115.4	109.8	112.6	113.5	108.8	109.6	168.7	
1987	113.6	107.7	104.3	120.2	113.6	117.2	118.2	112.6	113.6	174.4	
1988	118.3	111.5	107.7	125.7	118.3	122.3	123.4	117.0	118.3	180.8	
1989	124.0	116.7	112.0	131.9	123.7	128.1	129.0	122.4	124.0	188.6	
1990	130.7	122.8	117.4	139.2	130.3	134.7	135.5	128.8	130.7	198.0	
1991	136.2	126.6	121.3	146.3	136.1	140.9	142.1	133.8	136.2	205.1	
1992	140.3	129.1	124.2	152.0	140.8	145.4	147.3	137.5	140.3	210.3	
1993	144.5	131.5	126.3	157.9	145.1	150.0	152.2	141.2	144.5	215.5	
1994	148.2	133.8	127.9	163.1	149.0	154.1	156.5	144.7	148.2	220.1	
1995	152.4	136.4	129.8	168.7	153.1	158.7	161.2	148.6	152.4	225.4	
1996	156.9	139.9	132.6	174.1	157.5	163.1	165.6	152.8	156.9	231.4	
1997	160.5	141.8	133.4	179.4	161.1	167.1	169.5	156.3	160.5	236.4	
1998	163.0	141.9	132.0	184.2	163.4	170.9	173.4	158.6	163.0	239.7	
1999	166.6	144.4	134.0	188.8	167.0	174.4	177.0	162.0	166.6	244.7	
2000	172.2	149.2	139.2	195.3	173.0	178.6	181.3	167.3	172.2	252.9	102.0
2001	177.1	150.7	138.9	203.4	177.8	183.5	186.1	171.9	177.1	260.0	104.3
2002	179.9	149.7	136.0	209.8	180.5	187.7	190.5	174.3	179.9	264.2	105.6
2003	184.0	151.2	136.5	216.5	184.7	190.6	193.2	178.1	184.0	270.1	107.8
2004	188.9	154.7	138.8	222.8	189.4	194.4	196.6	182.7	188.9	277.4	110.5
2005	195.3	160.2	144.5	230.1	196.0	198.7	200.9	188.7	195.3	286.7	113.7
2006	201.6	164.0	148.0	238.9	202.7	203.7	205.9	194.7	201.6	296.1	117.0
2007	207.342	167.509	149.720	246.848	208.098	208.925	210.729	200.080	207.342	304.5	119.957
2008	215.303	174.764	155.310	255.498	215.528	214.751	215.572	207.777	215.303	316.2	124.433
2009	214.537	169.698	147.071	259.154	214.008	218.433	219.235	206.555	214.537	315.0	123.850
2010	218.056	174.566	152.990	261.274	217.828	220.458	221.337	209.689	218.056	320.2	125.663
2011	224.939	183.862	162.409	265.762	224.503	224.806	225.008	216.325	224.939	330.3	
2010: Jan	216.687	173.646	152.035	259.459	216.362	219.287	220.086	208.499	216.687	318.2	124.997
Feb	216.741	173.419	151.767	259.792	216.440	219.708	220.602	208.432	216.741	318.3	124.973
Mar	217.631	174.798	153.516	260.196	217.430	220.133	221.059	209.301	217.631	319.6	125.528
Apr	218.009	175.333	154.163	260.420	217.839	220.252	221.166	209.669	218.009	320.1	125.740
May	218.178	175.333	154.106	260.756	218.010	220.298	221.193	209.841	218.178	320.4	125.815
June	217.965	173.899	152.247	261.756	217.788	220.336	221.265	209.605	217.965	320.1	125.613
July	218.011	173.503	151.754	262.241	217.857	220.316	221.258	209.664	218.011	320.1	125.568
Aug	218.312	173.925	152.182	262.421	218.147	220.619	221.551	209.952	218.312	320.6	125.718
Sept	218.439	174.282	152.395	262.320	218.179	221.030	221.907	210.001	218.439	320.8	125.782
Oct	218.711	175.225	153.508	261.927	218.431	221.236	222.079	210.257	218.711	321.2	125.977
Nov	218.803	·175.415	153.761	261.921	218.538	221.235	222.077	210.336	218.803	321.3	126.013
Dec	219.179	176.015	154.443	262.074	218.921	221.045	221.795	210.712	219.179	321.9	126.228
2011: Jan	220.223	177.480	155.682	262.701	219.820	221.666	222.177	211.714	220.223	323.4	126.811
Feb	221.309	178.874	157.221	263.480	220.937	222.506	223.011	212.709	221.309	325.0	127.429
Mar	223.467	182.728	161.804	263.956	223.192	223.315	223.690	214.907	223.467	328.2	128.618
Apr	224.906	185.311	164.964	264.256	224.731	223.798	224.118	216.346	224.906	330.3	129.408
May	225.964	186.804	166.657	264.883	225.826	224.275	224.534	217.414	225.964	331.8	129.943
June	225.722	185.266	164.461	265.928	225.485	224.635	224.891	217.158	225.722	331.5	129.841
July	225.922	184.931	163.664	266.660	225.566	225.010	225.164	217.336	225.922	331.8	129.930
Aug	226.545	185.566	164.059	267.271	226.092	225.797	225.874	217.955	226.545	332.7	130.258
Sept	226.889	186.015	164.287	267.510	226.329	226.303	226.289	218.281	226.889	333.2	130.449
Oct	226.421	185.236	163.084	267.352	225.717	226.754	226.743	217.730	226.421	332.5	130.204
Nov	226.230	184.791	162.572	267.413	225.532	226.818	226.859	217.479	226.230	332.2	130.066
Dec	225.672	183.345	160.453	267.737	224.805	226.795	226.740	216.875	225.672	331.4	129.719

[1] Consumer price index, all urban consumers.

[2] CPI-U-X1 reflects a rental equivalence approach to homeowners' costs for the CPI-U for years prior to 1983, the first year for which the official index incorporates such a measure. CPI-U-X1 is rebased to the December 1982 value of the CPI-U (1982–84=100) and is identical with CPI-U data from December 1982 forward. Data prior to 1967 estimated by moving the series at the same rate as the CPI-U for each year.

[3] Consumer price index research series (CPI-U-RS) using current methods introduced in June 1999. Data for 2011 are preliminary. All data are subject to revision annually.

[4] Chained consumer price index (C-CPI-U) introduced in August 2002. Data for 2010 and 2011 are subject to revision.

Source: Department of Labor (Bureau of Labor Statistics).

[For all urban consumers; percent change]

Year or month	All items		All items less food		All items less energy		All items less food and energy		All items less medical care	
	Dec. to Dec.[1]	Year to year	Dec. to Dec.[1]	Year to year	Dec. to Dec.[1]	Year to year	Dec. to Dec.[1]	Year to year	Dec. to Dec.[1]	Year to year
1968	4.7	4.2	5.0	4.5	4.9	4.4	5.1	4.6	4.7	4.2
1969	6.2	5.5	5.6	5.4	6.5	5.8	6.2	5.8	6.1	5.4
1970	5.6	5.7	6.6	6.0	5.4	6.1	6.6	6.3	5.2	5.9
1971	3.3	4.4	3.0	4.6	3.4	4.2	3.1	4.7	3.2	4.1
1972	3.4	3.2	2.9	2.9	3.5	3.3	3.0	3.0	3.4	3.2
1973	8.7	6.2	5.6	4.0	8.2	6.2	4.7	3.6	9.1	6.4
1974	12.3	11.0	12.2	9.8	11.7	9.8	11.1	8.3	12.2	11.2
1975	6.9	9.1	7.3	9.4	6.6	8.9	6.7	9.1	6.7	9.0
1976	4.9	5.8	6.1	6.7	4.8	5.6	6.1	6.5	4.5	5.3
1977	6.7	6.5	6.4	6.4	6.7	6.4	6.5	6.3	6.7	6.3
1978	9.0	7.6	8.3	7.2	9.1	7.8	8.5	7.4	9.1	7.6
1979	13.3	11.3	14.0	11.4	11.1	10.0	11.3	9.8	13.4	11.5
1980	12.5	13.5	13.0	14.5	11.7	11.6	12.2	12.4	12.5	13.6
1981	8.9	10.3	9.8	10.9	8.5	10.0	9.5	10.4	8.8	10.4
1982	3.8	6.2	4.1	6.5	4.2	6.7	4.5	7.4	3.6	5.9
1983	3.8	3.2	4.1	3.5	4.5	3.6	4.8	4.0	3.6	2.9
1984	3.9	4.3	3.9	4.3	4.4	4.7	4.7	5.0	3.9	4.1
1985	3.8	3.6	4.1	3.8	4.0	3.9	4.3	4.3	3.5	3.4
1986	1.1	1.9	.5	1.7	3.8	3.9	3.8	4.0	.7	1.5
1987	4.4	3.6	4.6	3.5	4.1	4.1	4.2	4.1	4.3	3.5
1988	4.4	4.1	4.2	4.1	4.7	4.4	4.7	4.4	4.2	3.9
1989	4.6	4.8	4.5	4.6	4.6	4.7	4.4	4.5	4.5	4.6
1990	6.1	5.4	6.3	5.3	5.2	5.2	5.2	5.0	5.9	5.2
1991	3.1	4.2	3.3	4.5	3.9	4.6	4.4	4.9	2.7	3.9
1992	2.9	3.0	3.2	3.5	3.0	3.2	3.3	3.7	2.7	2.8
1993	2.7	3.0	2.7	3.1	3.1	3.2	3.2	3.3	2.6	2.7
1994	2.7	2.6	2.6	2.7	2.6	2.7	2.6	2.8	2.5	2.5
1995	2.5	2.8	2.7	2.8	2.9	3.0	3.0	3.0	2.5	2.7
1996	3.3	3.0	3.1	2.9	2.9	2.8	2.6	2.7	3.3	2.8
1997	1.7	2.3	1.8	2.3	2.1	2.5	2.2	2.4	1.6	2.3
1998	1.6	1.6	1.5	1.4	2.4	2.3	2.4	2.3	1.5	1.5
1999	2.7	2.2	2.8	2.2	2.0	2.0	1.9	2.1	2.6	2.1
2000	3.4	3.4	3.5	3.6	2.6	2.4	2.6	2.4	3.3	3.3
2001	1.6	2.8	1.3	2.8	2.8	2.7	2.7	2.6	1.4	2.7
2002	2.4	1.6	2.6	1.5	1.8	2.3	1.9	2.4	2.2	1.4
2003	1.9	2.3	1.5	2.3	1.5	1.5	1.1	1.4	1.8	2.2
2004	3.3	2.7	3.4	2.5	2.2	2.0	2.2	1.8	3.2	2.6
2005	3.4	3.4	3.6	3.5	2.2	2.2	2.2	2.2	3.3	3.3
2006	2.5	3.2	2.6	3.4	2.5	2.5	2.6	2.5	2.5	3.2
2007	4.1	2.8	4.0	2.7	2.8	2.6	2.4	2.3	4.0	2.8
2008	.1	3.8	−.8	3.6	2.4	2.8	1.8	2.3	−.1	3.8
2009	2.7	−.4	3.3	−.7	1.4	1.7	1.8	1.7	2.7	−.6
2010	1.5	1.6	1.5	1.8	.9	.9	.8	1.0	1.4	1.5
2011	3.0	3.2	2.7	3.1	2.6	2.0	2.2	1.7	2.9	3.2

Percent change from preceding month

Year or month	Unadjusted	Seasonally adjusted	Unadjusted	Seasonally adjusted	Unadjusted	Seasonally adjusted	Unadjusted	Seasonally adjusted	Unadjusted	Seasonally adjusted
2010: Jan	0.3	0.1	0.3	0.1	0.1	−0.1	0.0	−0.1	0.3	0.1
Feb	.0	.0	.0	.0	.2	.1	.2	.1	.0	.0
Mar	.4	.0	.5	.0	.2	.1	.2	.0	.4	.0
Apr	.2	.0	.2	.0	.1	.1	.0	.0	.2	.0
May	.1	−.1	.1	−.2	.0	.1	.0	.1	.1	−.2
June	−.1	−.2	−.1	−.2	.0	.1	.0	.1	−.1	−.2
July	.0	.3	.0	.4	.0	.1	.0	.1	.0	.4
Aug	.1	.2	.1	.2	.1	.1	.1	.1	.1	.2
Sept	.1	.2	.0	.1	.2	.1	.2	.0	.0	.1
Oct	.1	.2	.1	.3	.1	.0	.1	.0	.1	.3
Nov	.0	.1	.0	.1	.0	.1	.0	.1	.0	.1
Dec	.2	.4	.2	.5	−.1	.1	−.1	.1	.2	.4
2011: Jan	.5	.4	.4	.4	.3	.2	.2	.2	.5	.4
Feb	.5	.5	.5	.5	.4	.3	.4	.2	.5	.6
Mar	1.0	.5	1.0	.5	.4	.2	.3	.1	1.0	.6
Apr	.6	.4	.7	.4	.2	.2	.2	.2	.7	.4
May	.5	.2	.5	.1	.2	.3	.2	.3	.5	.2
June	−.1	−.2	−.2	−.3	.2	.2	.2	.3	−.1	−.3
July	.1	.5	.0	.5	.2	.3	.1	.2	.1	.5
Aug	.3	.4	.2	.4	.3	.3	.3	.2	.3	.4
Sept	.2	.3	.1	.3	.2	.1	.2	.1	.1	.3
Oct	−.2	−.1	−.3	−.1	.2	.1	.2	.1	−.3	−.1
Nov	−.1	.0	−.1	.0	.0	.2	.1	.2	−.1	.0
Dec	−.2	.0	−.3	.0	.0	.2	−.1	.1	−.3	.0

[1] Changes from December to December are based on unadjusted indexes.

Source: Department of Labor (Bureau of Labor Statistics).

[For all urban consumers: percent change]

Year	All items Dec. to Dec.[1]	All items Year to year	Commodities Total Dec. to Dec.[1]	Commodities Total Year to year	Commodities Food Dec. to Dec.[1]	Commodities Food Year to year	Services Total Dec. to Dec.[1]	Services Total Year to year	Services Medical care Dec. to Dec.[1]	Services Medical care Year to year	Medical care[2] Dec. to Dec.[1]	Medical care[2] Year to year	Energy[3] Dec. to Dec.[1]	Energy[3] Year to year
1940	0.7	0.7	1.4	0.7	2.5	1.7	0.8	0.8	0.0	0.0	0.0	1.0		
1941	9.9	5.0	13.3	6.7	15.7	9.2	2.4	.8	1.2	.0	1.0	.0		
1942	9.0	10.9	12.9	14.5	17.9	17.6	2.3	3.1	3.5	3.5	3.8	2.9		
1943	3.0	6.1	4.2	9.3	3.0	11.0	2.3	2.3	5.6	4.5	4.6	4.7		
1944	2.3	1.7	2.0	1.0	.0	-1.2	2.2	2.2	3.2	4.3	2.6	3.6		
1945	2.2	2.3	2.9	3.0	3.5	2.4	.7	1.5	3.1	3.1	2.6	2.6		
1946	18.1	8.3	24.8	10.6	31.3	14.5	3.6	1.4	9.0	5.1	8.3	5.0		
1947	8.8	14.4	10.3	20.5	11.3	21.7	5.6	4.3	6.4	8.7	6.9	8.0		
1948	3.0	8.1	1.7	7.2	-.8	8.3	5.9	6.1	6.9	7.1	5.8	6.7		
1949	-2.1	-1.2	-4.1	-2.7	-3.9	-4.2	3.7	5.1	1.6	3.3	1.4	2.8		
1950	5.9	1.3	7.8	.7	9.8	1.6	3.6	3.0	4.0	2.4	3.4	2.0		
1951	6.0	7.9	5.9	9.0	7.1	11.0	5.2	5.3	5.3	4.7	5.8	5.3		
1952	.8	1.9	-.9	1.3	-1.0	1.8	4.4	4.5	5.8	6.7	4.3	5.0		
1953	.7	.8	-.3	-.3	-1.1	-1.4	4.2	4.3	3.4	3.5	3.5	3.6		
1954	-.7	.7	-1.6	-.9	-1.8	-.4	2.0	3.1	2.6	3.4	2.3	2.9		
1955	.4	-.4	-.3	-.9	-.7	-1.4	2.0	2.0	3.2	2.6	3.3	2.2		
1956	3.0	1.5	2.6	1.0	2.9	.7	3.4	2.5	3.8	3.8	3.2	3.8		
1957	2.9	3.3	2.8	3.2	2.8	3.2	4.2	4.3	4.8	4.3	4.7	4.2		
1958	1.8	2.8	1.2	2.1	2.4	4.5	2.7	3.7	4.6	5.3	4.5	4.6	-0.9	0.0
1959	1.7	.7	.6	.0	-1.0	-1.7	3.9	3.1	4.9	4.5	3.8	4.4	4.7	1.9
1960	1.4	1.7	1.2	.9	3.1	1.0	2.5	3.4	3.7	4.3	3.2	3.7	1.3	2.3
1961	.7	1.0	.0	.6	-.7	1.3	2.1	1.7	3.5	3.6	3.1	2.7	-1.3	.4
1962	1.3	1.0	.9	.9	1.3	.7	1.6	2.0	2.9	3.5	2.2	2.6	2.2	.4
1963	1.6	1.3	1.5	.9	2.0	1.6	2.4	2.0	2.8	2.9	2.5	2.6	-.9	.0
1964	1.0	1.3	.9	1.2	1.3	1.3	1.6	2.0	2.3	2.3	2.1	2.1	.0	-.4
1965	1.9	1.6	1.4	1.1	3.5	2.2	2.7	2.3	3.6	3.2	2.8	2.4	1.8	1.8
1966	3.5	2.9	2.5	2.6	4.0	5.0	4.8	3.8	8.3	5.3	6.7	4.4	1.7	1.7
1967	3.0	3.1	2.5	1.9	1.2	.9	4.3	4.3	8.0	8.8	6.3	7.2	1.7	2.1
1968	4.7	4.2	4.0	3.5	4.4	3.5	5.8	5.2	7.1	7.3	6.2	6.0	1.7	1.7
1969	6.2	5.5	5.4	4.7	7.0	5.1	7.7	6.9	7.3	8.2	6.2	6.7	2.9	2.5
1970	5.6	5.7	3.9	4.5	2.3	5.7	8.1	8.0	8.1	7.0	7.4	6.6	4.8	2.8
1971	3.3	4.4	2.8	3.6	4.3	3.1	4.1	5.7	5.4	7.4	4.6	6.2	3.1	3.9
1972	3.4	3.2	3.4	3.0	4.6	4.2	3.4	3.8	3.7	3.5	3.3	3.3	2.6	2.6
1973	8.7	6.2	10.4	7.4	20.3	14.5	6.2	4.4	6.0	4.5	5.3	4.0	17.0	8.1
1974	12.3	11.0	12.8	11.9	12.0	14.3	11.4	9.2	13.2	10.4	12.6	9.3	21.6	29.6
1975	6.9	9.1	6.2	8.8	6.6	8.5	8.2	9.6	10.3	12.6	9.8	12.0	11.4	10.5
1976	4.9	5.8	3.3	4.3	.5	3.0	7.2	8.3	10.8	10.1	10.0	9.5	7.1	7.1
1977	6.7	6.5	6.1	5.8	8.1	6.3	8.0	7.7	9.0	9.9	8.9	9.6	7.2	9.5
1978	9.0	7.6	8.8	7.2	11.8	9.9	9.3	8.6	9.3	8.5	8.8	8.4	7.9	6.3
1979	13.3	11.3	13.0	11.3	10.2	11.0	13.6	11.0	10.5	9.8	10.1	9.2	37.5	25.1
1980	12.5	13.5	11.0	12.3	10.2	8.6	14.2	15.4	10.1	11.3	9.9	11.0	18.0	30.9
1981	8.9	10.3	6.0	8.4	4.3	7.8	13.0	13.1	12.6	10.7	12.5	10.7	11.9	13.6
1982	3.8	6.2	3.6	4.1	3.1	4.1	4.3	9.0	11.2	11.8	11.0	11.6	1.3	1.5
1983	3.8	3.2	2.9	2.9	2.7	2.1	4.8	3.5	6.2	8.7	6.4	8.8	-.5	.7
1984	3.9	4.3	2.7	3.4	3.8	3.8	5.4	5.2	5.8	6.0	6.1	6.2	.2	1.0
1985	3.8	3.6	2.5	2.1	2.6	2.3	5.1	5.1	6.8	6.1	6.8	6.3	1.8	.7
1986	1.1	1.9	-2.0	-.9	3.8	3.2	4.5	5.0	7.9	7.7	7.7	7.5	-19.7	-13.2
1987	4.4	3.6	4.6	3.2	3.5	4.1	4.3	4.2	5.6	6.6	5.8	6.6	8.2	.5
1988	4.4	4.1	3.8	3.5	5.2	4.1	4.8	4.6	6.9	6.4	6.9	6.5	.5	.8
1989	4.6	4.8	4.1	4.7	5.6	5.8	5.1	4.9	8.6	7.7	8.5	7.7	5.1	5.6
1990	6.1	5.4	6.6	5.2	5.3	5.8	5.7	5.5	9.9	9.3	9.6	9.0	18.1	8.3
1991	3.1	4.2	1.2	3.1	1.9	2.9	4.6	5.1	8.0	8.9	7.9	8.7	-7.4	.4
1992	2.9	3.0	2.0	2.0	1.5	1.2	3.6	3.9	7.0	7.6	6.6	7.4	2.0	.5
1993	2.7	3.0	1.5	1.9	2.9	2.2	3.8	3.9	5.9	6.5	5.4	5.9	-1.4	1.2
1994	2.7	2.6	2.3	1.7	2.9	2.4	2.9	3.3	5.4	5.2	4.9	4.8	2.2	.4
1995	2.5	2.8	1.4	1.9	2.1	2.8	3.5	3.4	4.4	5.1	3.9	4.5	-1.3	.6
1996	3.3	3.0	3.2	2.6	4.3	3.3	3.3	3.2	3.2	3.7	3.0	3.5	8.6	4.7
1997	1.7	2.3	.2	1.4	1.5	2.6	2.8	3.0	2.9	2.9	2.8	2.8	-3.4	1.3
1998	1.6	1.6	.4	.1	2.3	2.2	2.6	2.7	3.2	3.2	3.4	3.2	-8.8	-7.7
1999	2.7	2.2	2.7	1.8	1.9	2.1	2.6	2.5	3.6	3.4	3.7	3.5	13.4	3.6
2000	3.4	3.4	2.7	3.3	2.8	2.3	3.9	3.4	4.6	4.3	4.2	4.1	14.2	16.9
2001	1.6	2.8	-1.4	1.0	2.8	3.2	3.7	4.1	4.8	4.8	4.7	4.6	-13.0	3.8
2002	2.4	1.6	1.2	-.7	1.5	1.8	3.2	3.1	5.6	5.1	5.0	4.7	10.7	-5.9
2003	1.9	2.3	.5	1.0	3.6	2.2	2.8	3.2	4.2	4.5	3.7	4.0	6.9	12.2
2004	3.3	2.7	3.6	2.3	2.7	3.4	3.1	2.9	4.9	5.0	4.2	4.4	16.6	10.9
2005	3.4	3.4	2.7	3.6	2.3	2.4	3.8	3.3	4.5	4.8	4.3	4.2	17.1	17.0
2006	2.5	3.2	1.3	2.4	2.1	2.4	3.4	3.8	4.1	4.1	3.6	4.0	2.9	11.2
2007	4.1	2.8	5.2	2.1	4.9	4.0	3.3	3.3	5.9	5.3	5.2	4.4	17.4	5.5
2008	.1	3.8	-4.1	4.3	5.9	5.5	3.0	3.5	3.0	4.2	2.6	3.7	-21.3	13.9
2009	2.7	-.4	5.5	-2.9	-.5	1.8	.9	1.4	3.4	3.2	3.4	3.2	18.2	-18.4
2010	1.5	1.6	2.0	2.9	1.5	.8	1.2	.8	3.4	3.5	3.3	3.4	7.7	9.5
2011	3.0	3.2	4.2	5.3	4.7	3.7	2.2	1.7	3.6	3.1	3.5	3.0	6.6	15.4

[1] Changes from December to December are based on unadjusted indexes.
[2] Commodities and services.
[3] Household energy—gas (piped), electricity, fuel oil, etc.—and motor fuel. Motor oil, coolant, etc. also included through 1982.

Source: Department of Labor (Bureau of Labor Statistics).

TABLE B–65. Producer price indexes by stage of processing, 1965–2011

[1982=100]

| Year or month | Total finished goods | Consumer foods | | | Finished goods excluding consumer foods | | | | Capital equipment | Total finished consumer goods |
| | | Total | Crude | Processed | Total | Consumer goods | | | | |
						Total	Durable	Nondurable		
1965	34.1	36.8	39.0	36.8	....	33.6	43.2	28.8	33.8	34.2
1966	35.2	39.2	41.5	39.2	....	34.1	43.4	29.3	34.6	35.4
1967	35.6	38.5	39.6	38.8	35.0	34.7	44.1	30.0	35.8	35.6
1968	36.6	40.0	42.5	40.0	35.9	35.5	45.1	30.6	37.0	36.5
1969	38.0	42.4	45.9	42.3	36.9	36.3	45.9	31.5	38.3	37.9
1970	39.3	43.8	46.0	43.9	38.2	37.4	47.2	32.5	40.1	39.1
1971	40.5	44.5	45.8	44.7	39.6	38.7	48.9	33.5	41.7	40.2
1972	41.8	46.9	48.0	47.2	40.4	39.4	50.0	34.1	42.8	41.5
1973	45.6	56.5	63.6	55.8	42.0	41.2	50.9	36.1	44.2	46.0
1974	52.6	64.4	71.6	63.9	48.8	48.2	55.5	44.0	50.5	53.1
1975	58.2	69.8	71.7	70.3	54.7	53.2	61.0	48.9	58.2	58.2
1976	60.8	69.6	76.7	69.0	58.1	56.5	63.7	52.4	62.1	60.4
1977	64.7	73.3	79.5	72.7	62.2	60.6	67.4	56.8	66.1	64.3
1978	69.8	79.9	85.8	79.4	66.7	64.9	73.6	60.0	71.3	69.4
1979	77.6	87.3	92.3	86.8	74.6	73.5	80.8	69.3	77.5	77.5
1980	88.0	92.4	93.9	92.3	86.7	87.1	91.0	85.1	85.8	88.6
1981	96.1	97.8	104.4	97.2	95.6	96.1	96.4	95.8	94.6	96.6
1982	100.0	100.0	100.0	100.0	100.0	100.0	100.0	100.0	100.0	100.0
1983	101.6	101.0	102.4	100.9	101.8	101.2	102.8	100.5	102.8	101.3
1984	103.7	105.4	111.4	104.9	103.2	102.2	104.5	101.1	105.2	103.3
1985	104.7	104.6	102.9	104.8	104.6	103.3	106.5	101.7	107.5	103.8
1986	103.2	107.3	105.6	107.4	101.9	98.5	108.9	93.3	109.7	101.4
1987	105.4	109.5	107.1	109.6	104.0	100.7	111.5	94.9	111.7	103.6
1988	108.0	112.6	109.8	112.7	106.5	103.1	113.8	97.3	114.3	106.2
1989	113.6	118.7	119.6	118.6	111.8	108.9	117.6	103.8	118.8	112.1
1990	119.2	124.4	123.0	124.4	117.4	115.3	120.4	111.5	122.9	118.2
1991	121.7	124.1	119.3	124.4	120.9	118.7	123.9	115.0	126.7	120.5
1992	123.2	123.3	107.6	124.4	123.1	120.8	125.7	117.3	129.1	121.7
1993	124.7	125.7	114.4	126.5	124.4	121.7	128.0	117.6	131.4	123.0
1994	125.5	126.8	111.3	127.9	125.1	121.6	130.9	116.2	134.1	123.3
1995	127.9	129.0	118.8	129.8	127.5	124.0	132.7	118.8	136.7	125.6
1996	131.3	133.6	129.2	133.8	130.5	127.6	134.2	123.3	138.3	129.5
1997	131.8	134.5	126.6	135.1	130.9	128.2	133.7	124.3	138.2	130.2
1998	130.7	134.3	127.2	134.8	129.5	126.4	132.9	122.2	137.6	128.9
1999	133.0	135.1	125.5	135.9	132.3	130.5	133.0	127.9	137.6	132.0
2000	138.0	137.2	123.5	138.3	138.1	138.4	133.9	138.7	138.8	138.2
2001	140.7	141.3	127.7	142.4	140.4	141.4	134.0	142.8	139.7	141.5
2002	138.9	140.1	128.5	141.0	138.3	138.8	133.0	139.8	139.1	139.4
2003	143.3	145.9	130.0	147.2	142.4	144.7	133.1	148.4	139.5	145.3
2004	148.5	152.7	138.2	153.9	147.2	150.9	135.0	156.6	141.4	151.7
2005	155.7	155.7	140.2	156.9	155.5	161.9	136.6	172.0	144.6	160.4
2006	160.4	156.7	151.3	157.1	161.0	169.2	136.9	182.6	146.9	166.0
2007	166.6	167.0	170.2	166.7	166.2	175.6	138.3	191.7	149.5	173.5
2008	177.1	178.3	175.5	178.6	176.6	189.1	141.2	210.5	153.8	186.3
2009	172.5	175.5	157.8	177.3	171.1	179.4	144.3	194.1	156.7	179.1
2010	179.8	182.4	172.6	183.3	178.3	190.4	144.9	210.1	157.3	189.1
2011 p	190.6	193.9	182.3	195.0	188.9	205.6	147.4	231.7	159.7	203.4
2010: Jan	178.0	180.1	178.3	180.1	176.7	187.7	145.4	205.9	157.5	186.5
Feb	177.0	180.9	180.7	180.7	175.3	185.6	145.2	202.8	157.3	185.1
Mar	179.1	185.6	223.6	181.0	176.9	188.2	145.0	206.8	157.1	188.3
Apr	179.5	184.2	196.8	182.6	177.6	189.4	144.8	208.7	157.1	188.8
May	179.8	184.1	176.0	184.8	178.1	190.0	145.0	209.6	157.2	189.2
June	179.0	179.5	146.0	183.2	178.1	190.1	144.3	210.1	157.0	188.2
July	179.5	180.5	157.8	182.9	178.5	190.8	144.2	211.2	156.9	188.9
Aug	179.9	180.1	151.9	183.2	179.1	191.6	144.3	212.3	157.1	189.4
Sept	180.0	181.9	152.2	185.2	178.7	191.1	144.2	211.5	157.0	189.5
Oct	181.2	182.1	149.9	185.6	180.1	192.7	145.8	213.2	158.0	190.8
Nov	181.6	183.9	168.8	185.5	180.2	193.0	145.6	213.7	157.8	191.4
Dec	182.6	186.0	189.4	185.4	181.0	194.2	145.3	215.7	157.8	192.9
2011: Jan	184.4	186.9	190.5	186.3	183.0	197.0	145.7	219.7	158.4	195.2
Feb	186.6	193.4	230.7	188.9	184.2	198.7	146.0	222.1	158.7	198.2
Mar	189.1	192.9	198.9	191.9	187.4	203.7	146.2	229.5	158.8	201.8
Apr	191.4	193.0	182.6	194.0	190.1	207.8	146.8	235.2	159.2	204.8
May	192.5	191.0	160.0	194.3	191.9	210.5	146.6	239.4	159.2	206.3
June	191.4	192.4	170.8	194.7	190.3	207.8	146.9	235.2	159.5	204.7
July	192.2	193.5	165.8	196.5	191.0	208.8	147.2	236.6	159.7	205.7
Aug	191.7	195.7	169.1	198.5	189.8	207.0	147.3	233.8	159.7	204.9
Sept [1]	192.5	196.5	175.9	198.6	190.7	208.4	147.1	236.0	159.6	206.1
Oct [1]	191.9	195.8	174.9	197.9	190.2	206.8	149.5	232.3	161.2	204.7
Nov [1]	192.0	198.2	187.1	199.2	189.7	206.0	149.5	231.1	161.2	204.8
Dec [1]	191.3	197.3	180.9	199.0	189.1	204.9	149.4	229.5	161.4	203.8

[1] Data have been revised through August 2011; data are subject to revision four months after date of original publication.

See next page for continuation of table.

[1982=100]

Year or month	Intermediate materials, supplies, and components								Crude materials for further processing				
	Total	Foods and feeds [2]	Other	Materials and components		Processed fuels and lubricants	Containers	Supplies	Total	Foodstuffs and feedstuffs	Other		
				For manufacturing	For construction						Total	Fuel	Other
1965	31.2	....	30.7	33.6	32.8	16.5	33.5	35.0	31.1	39.2	....	10.6	27.7
1966	32.0	....	31.3	34.3	33.6	16.8	34.5	36.5	33.1	42.7	....	10.9	28.3
1967	32.2	41.8	31.7	34.5	34.0	16.9	35.0	36.8	31.3	40.3	21.1	11.3	26.5
1968	33.0	41.5	32.5	35.3	35.7	16.5	35.9	37.1	31.8	40.9	21.6	11.5	27.1
1969	34.1	42.9	33.6	36.5	37.7	16.6	37.2	37.8	33.9	44.1	22.5	12.0	28.4
1970	35.4	45.6	34.8	38.0	38.3	17.7	39.0	39.7	35.2	45.2	23.8	13.8	29.1
1971	36.8	46.7	36.2	38.9	40.8	19.5	40.8	40.8	36.0	46.1	24.7	15.7	29.4
1972	38.2	49.5	37.7	40.4	43.0	20.1	42.7	42.5	39.9	51.5	27.0	16.8	32.3
1973	42.4	70.3	40.6	44.1	46.5	22.2	45.2	51.7	54.5	72.6	34.3	18.6	42.9
1974	52.5	83.6	50.5	56.0	55.0	33.6	53.3	56.8	61.4	76.4	44.1	24.8	54.5
1975	58.0	81.6	56.6	61.7	60.1	39.4	60.0	61.8	61.6	77.4	43.7	30.6	50.0
1976	60.9	77.4	60.0	64.0	64.1	42.3	63.1	65.8	63.4	76.8	48.2	34.5	54.9
1977	64.9	79.6	64.1	67.4	69.3	47.7	65.9	69.3	65.5	77.5	51.7	42.0	56.3
1978	69.5	84.8	68.6	72.0	76.5	49.9	71.0	72.9	73.4	87.3	57.5	48.2	61.9
1979	78.4	94.5	77.4	80.9	84.2	61.6	79.4	80.2	85.9	100.0	69.6	57.3	75.5
1980	90.3	105.5	89.4	91.7	91.3	85.0	89.1	89.9	95.3	104.6	84.6	69.4	91.8
1981	98.6	104.6	98.2	98.7	97.9	100.6	96.7	96.9	103.0	103.9	101.8	84.8	109.8
1982	100.0	100.0	100.0	100.0	100.0	100.0	100.0	100.0	100.0	100.0	100.0	100.0	100.0
1983	100.6	103.6	100.5	101.2	102.8	95.4	100.4	101.8	101.3	101.8	100.7	105.1	98.8
1984	103.1	105.7	103.0	104.1	105.6	95.7	105.9	104.1	103.5	104.7	102.2	105.1	101.0
1985	102.7	97.3	103.0	103.3	107.3	92.8	109.0	104.4	95.8	94.8	96.9	102.7	94.3
1986	99.1	96.2	99.3	102.2	108.1	72.7	110.3	105.6	87.7	93.2	81.6	92.2	76.0
1987	101.5	99.2	101.7	105.3	109.8	73.3	114.5	107.7	93.7	96.2	87.9	84.1	88.5
1988	107.1	109.5	106.9	113.2	116.1	71.2	120.1	113.7	96.0	106.1	85.5	82.1	85.9
1989	112.0	113.8	111.9	118.1	121.3	76.4	125.4	118.1	103.1	111.2	93.4	85.3	95.8
1990	114.5	113.3	114.5	118.7	122.9	85.9	127.7	119.4	108.9	113.1	101.5	84.8	107.3
1991	114.4	111.1	114.6	118.1	124.5	85.3	128.1	121.4	101.2	105.5	94.6	82.9	97.5
1992	114.7	110.7	114.9	117.9	126.5	84.5	127.7	122.7	100.4	105.1	93.5	84.0	94.2
1993	116.2	112.7	116.4	118.9	132.0	84.7	126.4	125.0	102.4	108.4	94.7	87.1	94.1
1994	118.5	114.8	118.7	122.1	136.6	83.1	129.7	127.0	101.8	106.5	94.8	82.4	97.0
1995	124.9	114.8	125.5	130.4	142.1	84.2	148.8	132.1	102.7	105.8	96.8	72.1	105.8
1996	125.7	128.1	125.6	128.6	143.6	90.0	141.1	135.9	113.8	121.5	104.5	92.6	105.7
1997	125.6	125.4	125.7	128.3	146.5	89.3	136.0	135.9	111.1	112.2	106.4	101.3	103.5
1998	123.0	116.2	123.4	126.1	146.8	81.1	140.8	134.8	96.8	103.9	88.4	86.7	84.5
1999	123.2	111.1	123.9	124.6	148.9	84.6	142.5	134.2	98.2	98.7	94.3	91.2	91.1
2000	129.2	111.7	130.1	128.1	150.7	102.0	151.6	136.9	120.6	100.2	130.4	136.9	118.0
2001	129.7	115.9	130.5	127.4	150.6	104.5	153.1	138.7	121.0	106.1	126.8	151.4	101.5
2002	127.8	115.5	128.5	126.1	151.3	96.3	152.1	138.9	108.1	99.5	111.4	117.3	101.0
2003	133.7	125.9	134.2	129.7	153.6	112.6	153.7	141.5	135.3	113.5	148.2	185.7	116.9
2004	142.6	137.1	143.0	137.9	166.4	124.3	159.3	146.7	159.0	127.0	179.2	211.4	149.2
2005	154.0	133.8	155.1	146.0	176.6	150.0	167.1	151.9	182.2	122.7	223.4	279.7	176.7
2006	164.0	135.2	165.4	155.9	188.4	162.8	175.0	157.0	184.8	119.3	230.6	241.5	210.0
2007	170.7	154.4	171.5	162.4	192.5	173.9	180.3	161.7	207.1	146.7	246.3	236.8	238.7
2008	188.3	181.6	188.7	177.2	205.4	206.2	191.8	173.8	251.8	163.4	313.9	298.3	308.5
2009	172.5	166.0	173.0	162.7	202.9	161.9	195.8	172.2	175.2	134.5	197.5	166.3	211.1
2010	183.4	171.7	184.4	174.0	205.7	185.2	201.2	175.0	212.2	152.4	249.3	188.0	280.8
2011 [p]	200.0	192.3	200.6	190.0	212.8	215.5	205.5	184.2	249.6	188.4	284.5	181.6	342.7
2010: Jan	179.4	168.7	180.2	169.4	202.3	180.2	194.2	172.9	212.8	142.0	260.3	232.3	269.0
Feb	179.2	168.3	180.1	171.0	203.5	174.9	196.1	173.1	208.5	142.3	252.2	222.3	262.4
Mar	181.2	167.7	182.3	172.6	204.6	180.0	198.8	173.3	212.7	146.9	255.5	201.8	281.6
Apr	183.2	168.5	184.4	175.0	206.1	183.1	200.1	173.8	211.0	148.6	250.7	174.8	292.1
May	184.3	170.8	185.4	175.4	207.4	185.9	201.6	174.7	208.3	153.0	241.5	180.3	273.2
June	183.3	169.7	184.4	173.6	206.6	185.2	204.1	174.5	203.7	146.3	239.3	182.1	268.4
July	183.1	170.0	184.2	172.6	206.3	186.3	204.4	174.8	208.7	150.7	244.4	195.6	267.6
Aug	183.9	171.2	184.9	173.1	206.2	188.4	205.0	175.1	211.8	152.5	248.5	195.3	274.6
Sept	184.1	173.5	184.9	174.0	205.9	187.5	202.3	175.5	209.2	158.6	237.7	166.4	276.4
Oct	185.3	175.5	186.1	175.5	205.9	188.9	202.4	176.4	215.3	160.8	247.0	168.0	290.6
Nov	186.4	178.3	187.0	177.0	206.3	189.5	202.5	177.5	217.2	162.3	249.1	155.8	302.2
Dec	187.8	178.3	188.6	178.4	207.0	192.2	202.7	178.1	227.0	164.6	265.2	181.3	311.3
2011: Jan	190.6	180.2	191.4	181.5	208.3	196.2	203.4	179.6	235.9	171.6	274.9	186.5	323.8
Feb	193.7	185.0	194.4	185.2	209.5	200.9	203.9	180.9	242.8	184.4	275.5	190.0	322.2
Mar	197.6	189.1	198.2	187.7	210.9	212.0	204.4	182.3	248.2	185.7	284.4	176.9	345.7
Apr	201.0	192.5	201.7	191.1	212.1	218.6	204.9	183.9	261.3	193.1	301.7	187.3	367.0
May	203.2	192.9	204.0	192.6	212.8	224.3	206.4	184.5	255.5	190.3	293.6	189.7	352.1
June	203.3	194.1	204.0	192.4	213.7	224.2	206.8	185.2	256.8	195.3	291.3	190.8	347.5
July	204.1	195.3	204.8	193.3	214.7	225.1	207.1	185.7	256.9	192.6	293.9	191.0	351.7
Aug	202.8	197.9	203.1	192.7	214.6	219.5	205.9	186.1	251.2	196.3	279.7	190.1	329.2
Sept [1]	203.5	198.6	203.8	193.4	213.9	221.6	206.5	186.5	253.0	192.1	287.2	180.2	348.1
Oct [1]	200.7	194.1	201.1	191.4	214.2	213.3	206.0	185.4	242.5	186.4	273.2	172.3	330.4
Nov [1]	200.7	194.8	201.1	190.2	214.1	216.1	205.9	185.4	250.0	188.0	285.5	165.0	355.6
Dec [1]	199.3	193.1	199.7	188.4	214.4	213.7	205.2	185.0	241.6	184.6	273.0	159.3	339.0

[2] Intermediate materials for food manufacturing and feeds.

Source: Department of Labor (Bureau of Labor Statistics).

[1982=100]

Year or month	Finished goods						Intermediate materials, supplies, and components				Crude materials for further processing			
				Excluding foods and energy										
	Total	Foods	Energy	Total	Capital equipment	Consumer goods excluding foods and energy	Total	Foods and feeds [1]	Energy	Other	Total	Foodstuffs and feedstuffs	Energy	Other
1974	52.6	64.4	26.2	53.6	50.5	55.5	52.5	83.6	33.1	54.0	61.4	76.4	27.8	83.3
1975	58.2	69.8	30.7	59.7	58.2	60.6	58.0	81.6	38.7	60.2	61.6	77.4	33.3	69.3
1976	60.8	69.6	34.3	63.1	62.1	63.7	60.9	77.4	41.5	63.8	63.4	76.8	35.3	80.2
1977	64.7	73.3	39.7	66.9	66.1	67.3	64.9	79.6	46.8	67.6	65.5	77.5	40.4	79.8
1978	69.8	79.9	42.3	71.9	71.3	72.2	69.5	84.8	49.1	72.5	73.4	87.3	45.2	87.8
1979	77.6	87.3	57.1	78.3	77.5	78.8	78.4	94.5	61.1	80.7	85.9	100.0	54.9	106.2
1980	88.0	92.4	85.2	87.1	85.8	87.8	90.3	105.5	84.9	90.3	95.3	104.6	73.1	113.1
1981	96.1	97.8	101.5	94.6	94.6	94.6	98.6	104.6	100.5	97.7	103.0	103.9	97.7	111.7
1982	100.0	100.0	100.0	100.0	100.0	100.0	100.0	100.0	100.0	100.0	100.0	100.0	100.0	100.0
1983	101.6	101.0	95.2	103.0	102.8	103.1	100.6	103.6	95.3	101.6	101.3	101.8	98.7	105.3
1984	103.7	105.4	91.2	105.5	105.2	105.7	103.1	105.7	95.5	104.7	103.5	104.7	98.0	111.7
1985	104.7	104.6	87.6	108.1	107.5	108.4	102.7	97.3	92.6	105.2	95.8	94.8	93.3	104.9
1986	103.2	107.3	63.0	110.6	109.7	111.1	99.1	96.2	72.6	104.9	87.7	93.2	71.8	103.1
1987	105.4	109.5	61.8	113.3	111.7	114.2	101.5	99.2	73.0	107.8	93.7	96.2	75.0	115.7
1988	108.0	112.6	59.8	117.0	114.3	118.5	107.1	109.5	70.9	115.2	96.0	106.1	67.7	133.0
1989	113.6	118.7	65.7	122.1	118.8	124.0	112.0	113.8	76.1	120.2	103.1	111.2	75.9	137.9
1990	119.2	124.4	75.0	126.6	122.9	128.8	114.5	113.3	85.5	120.9	108.9	113.1	85.9	136.3
1991	121.7	124.1	78.1	131.1	126.7	133.7	114.4	111.1	85.1	121.4	101.2	105.5	80.4	128.2
1992	123.2	123.3	77.8	134.2	129.1	137.3	114.7	110.7	84.3	122.0	100.4	105.1	78.8	128.4
1993	124.7	125.7	78.0	135.8	131.4	138.5	116.2	112.7	84.6	123.8	102.4	108.4	76.7	140.2
1994	125.5	126.8	77.0	137.1	134.1	139.0	118.5	114.8	83.0	127.1	101.8	106.5	72.1	156.2
1995	127.9	129.0	78.1	140.0	136.7	141.9	124.9	114.8	84.1	135.2	102.7	105.8	69.4	173.6
1996	131.3	133.6	83.2	142.0	138.3	144.3	125.7	128.1	89.8	134.0	113.8	121.5	85.0	155.8
1997	131.8	134.5	83.4	142.4	138.2	145.1	125.6	125.4	89.0	134.2	111.1	112.2	87.3	156.5
1998	130.7	134.3	75.1	143.7	137.6	147.7	123.0	116.2	80.8	133.5	96.8	103.9	68.6	142.1
1999	133.0	135.1	78.8	146.1	137.6	151.7	123.2	111.1	84.3	133.1	98.2	98.7	78.5	135.2
2000	138.0	137.2	94.1	148.0	138.8	154.0	129.2	111.7	101.7	136.6	120.6	100.2	122.1	145.2
2001	140.7	141.3	96.7	150.0	139.7	156.9	129.7	115.9	104.1	136.4	121.0	106.1	122.3	130.7
2002	138.9	140.1	88.8	150.2	139.1	157.6	127.8	115.5	95.9	135.8	108.1	99.5	102.0	135.7
2003	143.3	145.9	102.0	150.5	139.5	157.9	133.7	125.9	111.9	138.5	135.3	113.5	147.2	152.5
2004	148.5	152.7	113.0	152.7	141.4	160.3	142.6	137.1	123.2	146.5	159.0	127.0	174.6	193.0
2005	155.7	155.7	132.6	156.4	144.6	164.3	154.0	133.8	149.2	154.6	182.2	122.7	234.0	202.4
2006	160.4	156.7	145.9	158.7	146.9	166.7	164.0	135.2	162.8	163.8	184.8	119.3	226.9	244.5
2007	166.6	167.0	156.3	161.7	149.5	170.0	170.7	154.4	174.6	168.4	207.1	146.7	232.8	282.6
2008	177.1	178.3	178.7	167.2	153.8	176.4	188.3	181.6	208.1	180.9	251.8	163.4	309.4	324.4
2009	172.5	175.5	146.9	171.5	156.7	181.6	172.5	166.0	162.5	173.4	175.2	134.5	176.8	248.4
2010	179.8	182.4	166.9	173.6	157.3	185.1	183.4	171.7	187.8	180.8	212.2	152.4	216.7	329.1
2011 [p]	190.6	193.9	193.4	177.7	159.7	190.7	200.0	192.3	220.2	192.1	249.6	188.4	240.6	391.4
2010: Jan	178.0	180.1	162.7	173.0	157.5	183.9	179.4	168.7	183.2	176.8	212.8	142.0	241.5	304.0
Feb	177.0	180.9	157.7	173.0	157.3	184.0	179.2	168.3	177.4	178.3	208.5	142.3	229.8	306.0
Mar	179.1	185.6	163.3	173.0	157.1	184.2	181.2	167.7	182.9	179.6	212.7	146.9	226.8	324.6
Apr	179.5	184.2	165.9	173.0	157.1	184.2	183.2	168.5	185.8	181.5	211.0	148.6	216.0	335.3
May	179.8	184.1	166.7	173.3	157.2	184.6	184.3	170.8	188.5	181.9	208.3	153.0	205.9	330.0
June	179.0	179.5	166.8	173.2	157.0	184.7	183.3	169.7	187.3	181.0	203.7	146.3	207.7	317.1
July	179.5	180.5	168.0	173.3	156.9	184.9	183.1	170.0	188.4	180.4	208.7	150.7	216.1	313.2
Aug	179.9	180.1	169.6	173.5	157.1	185.1	183.9	171.2	190.8	180.5	211.8	152.5	217.7	324.1
Sept	180.0	181.9	168.1	173.5	157.0	185.3	184.1	173.5	189.8	180.9	209.2	158.6	199.0	334.5
Oct	181.2	182.1	170.0	174.7	158.0	186.6	185.3	175.5	191.5	181.9	215.3	160.8	207.9	344.0
Nov	181.6	183.9	170.5	174.7	157.8	186.6	186.4	178.3	192.4	182.9	217.2	162.3	207.3	352.5
Dec	182.6	186.0	172.9	174.8	157.8	186.9	187.8	178.3	195.7	183.9	227.0	164.6	225.1	364.0
2011: Jan	184.4	186.9	177.4	175.8	158.4	188.2	190.6	180.2	199.5	186.4	235.9	171.6	232.0	381.1
Feb	186.6	193.4	180.6	176.1	158.7	188.7	193.7	185.0	204.7	188.7	242.8	184.4	229.1	391.6
Mar	189.1	192.9	191.6	176.4	158.8	189.0	197.6	189.1	216.6	190.2	248.2	185.7	241.5	387.8
Apr	191.4	193.0	200.0	176.9	159.2	189.5	201.0	192.5	223.6	192.5	261.3	193.1	260.6	399.1
May	192.5	191.0	206.1	176.9	159.2	189.7	203.2	192.9	229.4	193.8	255.5	190.3	251.9	393.8
June	191.4	192.4	199.5	177.2	159.5	189.9	203.3	194.1	229.1	193.9	256.8	195.3	246.9	399.6
July	192.2	193.5	200.3	177.9	159.7	191.0	204.1	195.3	230.8	194.4	256.9	192.6	249.9	401.0
Aug	191.7	195.7	195.6	178.1	159.7	191.4	202.8	197.9	224.1	194.2	251.2	196.3	231.0	402.2
Sept [2]	192.5	196.5	199.1	177.9	159.6	191.1	203.5	198.6	226.6	194.4	253.0	192.1	239.8	403.7
Oct [2]	191.9	195.8	192.9	179.6	161.2	192.9	200.7	194.1	218.5	193.3	242.5	186.4	228.0	384.3
Nov [2]	192.0	198.2	190.7	179.7	161.2	193.1	200.7	194.8	221.2	192.4	250.0	188.0	246.8	375.7
Dec [2]	191.3	197.3	187.5	180.1	161.4	193.6	199.3	193.1	218.7	191.4	241.6	184.6	230.0	376.6

[1] Intermediate materials for food manufacturing and feeds.

[2] Data have been revised through August 2011; data are subject to revision four months after date of original publication.

Source: Department of Labor (Bureau of Labor Statistics).

[1982=100]

Year or month	Farm products and processed foods and feeds			Industrial commodities				
	Total	Farm products	Processed foods and feeds	Total	Textile products and apparel	Hides, skins, leather, and related products	Fuels and related products and power	Chemicals and allied products
1965	39.0	40.7	38.0	30.9	48.8	35.9	13.8	33.9
1966	41.6	43.7	40.2	31.5	48.9	39.4	14.1	34.0
1967	40.2	41.3	39.8	32.0	48.9	38.1	14.4	34.2
1968	41.1	42.3	40.6	32.8	50.7	39.3	14.3	34.1
1969	43.4	45.0	42.7	33.9	51.8	41.5	14.6	34.2
1970	44.9	45.8	44.6	35.2	52.4	42.0	15.3	35.0
1971	45.8	46.6	45.5	36.5	53.3	43.4	16.6	35.6
1972	49.2	51.6	48.0	37.8	55.5	50.0	17.1	35.6
1973	63.9	72.7	58.9	40.3	60.5	54.5	19.4	37.6
1974	71.3	77.4	68.0	49.2	68.0	55.2	30.1	50.2
1975	74.0	77.0	72.6	54.9	67.4	56.5	35.4	62.0
1976	73.6	78.8	70.8	58.4	72.4	63.9	38.3	64.0
1977	75.9	79.4	74.0	62.5	75.3	68.3	43.6	65.9
1978	83.0	87.7	80.6	67.0	78.1	76.1	46.5	68.0
1979	92.3	99.6	88.5	75.7	82.5	96.1	58.9	76.0
1980	98.3	102.9	95.9	88.0	89.7	94.7	82.8	89.0
1981	101.1	105.2	98.9	97.4	97.6	99.3	100.2	98.4
1982	100.0	100.0	100.0	100.0	100.0	100.0	100.0	100.0
1983	102.0	102.4	101.8	101.1	100.3	103.2	95.9	100.3
1984	105.5	105.5	105.4	103.3	102.7	109.0	94.8	102.9
1985	100.7	95.1	103.5	103.7	102.9	108.9	91.4	103.7
1986	101.2	92.9	105.4	100.0	103.2	113.0	69.8	102.6
1987	103.7	95.5	107.9	102.6	105.1	120.4	70.2	106.4
1988	110.0	104.9	112.7	106.3	109.2	131.4	66.7	116.3
1989	115.4	110.9	117.8	111.6	112.3	136.3	72.9	123.0
1990	118.6	112.2	121.9	115.8	115.0	141.7	82.3	123.6
1991	116.4	105.7	121.9	116.5	116.3	138.9	81.2	125.6
1992	115.9	103.6	122.1	117.4	117.8	140.4	80.4	125.9
1993	118.4	107.1	124.0	119.0	118.0	143.7	80.0	128.2
1994	119.1	106.3	125.5	120.7	118.3	148.5	77.8	132.1
1995	120.5	107.4	127.0	125.5	120.8	153.7	78.0	142.5
1996	129.7	122.4	133.3	127.3	122.4	150.5	85.8	142.1
1997	127.0	112.9	134.0	127.7	122.6	154.2	86.1	143.6
1998	122.7	104.6	131.6	124.8	122.9	148.0	75.3	143.9
1999	120.3	98.4	131.1	126.5	121.1	146.0	80.5	144.2
2000	122.0	99.5	133.1	134.8	121.4	151.5	103.5	151.0
2001	126.2	103.8	137.3	135.7	121.3	158.4	105.3	151.8
2002	123.9	99.0	136.2	132.4	119.9	157.6	93.2	151.9
2003	132.8	111.5	143.4	139.1	119.8	162.3	112.9	161.8
2004	142.0	123.3	151.2	147.6	121.0	164.5	126.9	174.4
2005	141.3	118.5	153.1	160.2	122.8	165.4	156.4	192.0
2006	141.2	117.0	153.8	168.8	124.5	168.4	166.7	205.8
2007	157.8	143.4	165.1	175.1	125.8	173.6	177.6	214.8
2008	173.8	161.3	180.5	192.3	128.9	173.1	214.6	245.5
2009	161.4	134.6	176.2	174.8	129.5	157.0	158.7	229.4
2010	171.2	151.0	182.3	187.0	131.7	181.4	185.8	246.6
2011 [p]	193.8	186.7	197.5	202.2	141.8	200.0	216.4	275.6
2010: Jan	166.0	142.5	178.9	184.6	130.1	165.9	185.6	239.9
Feb	166.2	142.3	179.3	183.6	130.3	173.3	178.9	244.2
Mar	169.2	150.3	179.5	185.6	131.0	176.1	183.4	246.1
Apr	169.3	149.1	180.4	187.0	131.1	176.3	184.4	248.9
May	171.2	150.0	182.8	187.2	131.5	182.7	184.6	246.9
June	167.1	141.6	181.1	186.4	131.5	182.9	184.1	244.1
July	169.0	146.8	181.2	186.7	131.5	184.2	186.3	243.3
Aug	170.0	148.4	181.8	187.5	131.8	185.1	188.4	244.3
Sept	173.4	154.1	183.9	186.8	131.9	184.9	184.5	245.8
Oct	175.5	157.4	185.3	188.4	132.3	187.6	187.6	248.8
Nov	177.8	162.1	186.4	189.2	133.3	187.8	188.4	252.1
Dec	179.7	166.8	186.6	191.3	134.0	189.6	193.6	254.7
2011: Jan	182.9	173.3	187.9	194.2	136.1	192.8	198.4	262.2
Feb	191.0	189.8	191.3	196.4	137.7	196.3	201.9	267.3
Mar	191.4	185.1	194.5	200.4	139.7	198.3	214.2	270.3
Apr	195.2	191.1	197.1	204.2	141.1	202.9	223.9	276.4
May	193.5	186.0	197.3	205.7	143.0	203.6	227.6	280.6
June	196.2	192.6	197.8	205.0	143.3	203.0	224.0	279.7
July	195.7	188.4	199.4	205.9	143.3	203.4	225.5	280.5
Aug	198.4	192.2	201.6	203.7	143.6	202.9	217.4	280.1
Sept [1]	198.0	190.1	202.0	204.8	143.8	203.2	221.2	281.8
Oct [1]	194.2	183.6	199.9	202.3	143.4	200.9	213.2	278.7
Nov [1]	195.8	186.3	200.8	202.8	143.4	196.7	217.2	276.8
Dec [1]	193.7	181.6	200.1	201.1	142.8	195.4	211.7	272.8

[1] Data have been revised through August 2011; data are subject to revision four months after date of original publication.

See next page for continuation of table.

Year or month	Industrial commodities—Continued									Miscellaneous products
	Rubber and plastic products	Lumber and wood products	Pulp, paper, and allied products	Metals and metal products	Machinery and equipment	Furniture and household durables	Non-metallic mineral products	Transportation equipment		
								Total	Motor vehicles and equipment	
1965	39.7	33.7	33.3	32.0	33.7	46.8	30.4	....	39.2	34.7
1966	40.5	35.2	34.2	32.8	34.7	47.4	30.7	....	39.2	35.3
1967	41.4	35.1	34.6	33.2	35.9	48.3	31.2	....	39.8	36.2
1968	42.8	39.8	35.0	34.0	37.0	49.7	32.4	....	40.9	37.0
1969	43.6	44.0	36.0	36.0	38.2	50.7	33.6	40.4	41.7	38.1
1970	44.9	39.9	37.5	38.7	40.0	51.9	35.3	41.9	43.3	39.8
1971	45.2	44.7	38.1	39.4	41.4	53.1	38.2	44.2	45.7	40.8
1972	45.3	50.7	39.3	40.9	42.3	53.8	39.4	45.5	47.0	41.5
1973	46.6	62.2	42.3	44.0	43.7	55.7	40.7	46.1	47.4	43.3
1974	56.4	64.5	52.5	57.0	50.0	61.8	47.8	50.3	51.4	48.1
1975	62.2	62.1	59.0	61.5	57.9	67.5	54.4	56.7	57.6	53.4
1976	66.0	72.2	62.1	65.0	61.3	70.3	58.2	60.5	61.2	55.6
1977	69.4	83.0	64.6	69.3	65.2	73.2	62.6	64.6	65.2	59.4
1978	72.4	96.9	67.7	75.3	70.3	77.5	69.6	69.5	70.0	66.7
1979	80.5	105.5	75.9	86.0	76.7	82.8	77.6	75.3	75.8	75.5
1980	90.1	101.5	86.3	95.0	86.0	90.7	88.4	82.9	83.1	93.6
1981	96.4	102.8	94.8	99.6	94.4	95.9	96.7	94.3	94.6	96.1
1982	100.0	100.0	100.0	100.0	100.0	100.0	100.0	100.0	100.0	100.0
1983	100.8	107.9	103.3	101.8	102.7	103.4	101.6	102.8	102.2	104.8
1984	102.3	108.0	110.3	104.8	105.1	105.7	105.4	105.2	104.1	107.0
1985	101.9	106.6	113.3	104.4	107.2	107.1	108.6	107.9	106.4	109.4
1986	101.9	107.2	116.1	103.2	108.8	108.2	110.0	110.5	109.1	111.6
1987	103.0	112.8	121.8	107.1	110.4	109.9	110.0	112.5	111.7	114.9
1988	109.3	118.9	130.4	118.7	113.2	113.1	111.2	114.3	113.1	120.2
1989	112.6	126.7	137.8	124.1	117.4	116.9	112.6	117.7	116.2	126.5
1990	113.6	129.7	141.2	122.9	120.7	119.2	114.7	121.5	118.2	134.2
1991	115.1	132.1	142.9	120.2	123.0	121.2	117.2	126.4	122.1	140.8
1992	115.1	146.6	145.2	119.2	123.4	122.2	117.3	130.4	124.9	145.3
1993	116.0	174.0	147.3	119.2	124.0	123.7	120.0	133.7	128.0	145.4
1994	117.6	180.0	152.5	124.8	125.1	126.1	124.2	137.2	131.4	141.9
1995	124.3	178.1	172.2	134.5	126.6	128.2	129.0	139.7	133.0	145.4
1996	123.8	176.1	168.7	131.0	126.5	130.4	131.0	141.7	134.1	147.7
1997	123.2	183.8	167.9	131.8	125.9	130.8	133.2	141.6	132.7	150.9
1998	122.6	179.1	171.7	127.8	124.9	131.3	135.4	141.2	131.4	156.0
1999	122.5	183.6	174.1	124.6	124.3	131.7	138.9	141.8	131.7	166.6
2000	125.5	178.2	183.7	128.1	124.0	132.6	142.5	143.8	132.3	170.8
2001	127.2	174.4	184.8	125.4	123.7	133.2	144.3	145.2	131.5	181.3
2002	126.8	173.3	185.9	125.9	122.9	133.5	146.2	144.6	129.9	182.4
2003	130.1	177.4	190.0	129.2	121.9	133.9	148.2	145.7	129.6	179.6
2004	133.8	195.6	195.7	149.6	122.1	135.1	153.2	148.6	131.0	183.2
2005	143.8	196.5	202.6	160.8	123.7	139.4	164.2	151.0	131.5	195.1
2006	153.8	194.4	209.8	181.6	126.2	142.6	179.9	152.6	131.0	205.6
2007	155.0	192.4	216.9	193.5	127.3	144.7	186.2	155.0	132.2	210.3
2008	165.9	191.3	226.8	213.0	129.7	148.9	197.1	158.6	134.1	216.6
2009	165.2	182.8	225.6	186.8	131.3	153.1	202.4	162.2	137.0	217.5
2010	170.7	192.7	236.9	207.6	131.1	153.2	201.8	163.4	137.6	221.5
2011 *p*	182.7	194.4	245.4	226.1	132.8	156.4	205.1	166.1	139.4	229.0
2010: Jan	166.8	185.8	227.2	200.5	131.1	153.0	200.7	163.7	138.4	218.4
Feb	167.4	190.2	229.7	200.8	131.1	152.5	201.4	163.6	138.3	218.7
Mar	168.5	193.2	233.1	205.0	131.2	152.6	201.6	163.1	137.7	219.6
Apr	169.9	197.2	234.6	210.3	131.1	152.8	201.9	163.4	137.9	219.8
May	170.6	200.6	237.3	210.1	131.2	153.0	202.3	163.4	137.9	220.9
June	171.7	195.7	237.5	207.4	131.1	153.5	202.5	162.9	137.0	221.6
July	171.9	194.0	238.7	205.0	131.2	153.3	202.3	162.5	136.4	222.3
Aug	171.8	192.1	238.5	206.5	131.1	153.7	202.3	162.9	136.8	222.7
Sept	171.8	191.4	240.3	208.2	131.1	153.6	201.9	162.8	136.6	222.6
Oct	171.9	190.5	241.1	210.4	131.0	153.7	201.6	164.4	138.5	223.1
Nov	172.5	190.3	242.2	212.2	130.9	153.6	201.6	164.2	138.1	223.6
Dec	173.2	191.2	242.8	214.8	131.1	153.3	201.8	164.0	137.8	225.0
2011: Jan	175.2	193.4	243.0	219.8	131.6	153.7	202.3	164.7	138.4	225.7
Feb	176.5	194.7	243.2	224.2	132.0	154.4	202.6	164.9	138.5	226.6
Mar	178.2	195.8	244.3	225.7	132.2	155.1	202.9	165.0	138.5	227.1
Apr	180.3	195.6	245.0	229.2	132.5	155.5	203.5	165.5	139.0	227.4
May	182.5	194.3	245.6	228.3	132.6	155.7	204.9	165.3	138.7	227.5
June	185.2	193.4	246.2	228.4	132.9	156.2	205.7	165.6	138.9	228.0
July	186.2	193.6	247.1	230.0	133.0	157.0	206.6	165.8	139.0	229.9
Aug	186.2	194.7	247.2	229.0	133.1	157.1	206.6	166.1	139.1	230.0
Sept [1]	186.2	194.1	248.0	228.2	133.3	157.4	205.9	165.5	138.4	230.6
Oct [1]	186.3	194.5	247.1	224.4	133.3	158.1	206.4	168.2	141.3	230.7
Nov [1]	184.8	194.1	244.3	222.7	133.2	158.3	206.2	168.1	141.2	232.0
Dec [1]	184.4	194.8	244.1	222.7	133.5	158.3	206.8	168.3	141.3	232.3

Source: Department of Labor (Bureau of Labor Statistics).

[Percent change]

Year or month	Total finished goods — Dec. to Dec.[1]	Total finished goods — Year to year	Finished consumer foods — Dec. to Dec.[1]	Finished consumer foods — Year to year	Finished goods excluding consumer foods — Total — Dec. to Dec.[1]	Total — Year to year	Consumer goods — Dec. to Dec.[1]	Consumer goods — Year to year	Capital equipment — Dec. to Dec.[1]	Capital equipment — Year to year	Finished energy goods — Dec. to Dec.[1]	Finished energy goods — Year to year	Finished goods excluding foods and energy — Dec. to Dec.[1]	Finished goods excluding foods and energy — Year to year
1972	3.9	3.2	7.9	5.4	2.3	2.0	2.1	1.8	2.1	2.6	....	....	....	....
1973	11.7	9.1	22.7	20.5	6.6	4.0	7.5	4.6	5.1	3.3	....	....	....	....
1974	18.3	15.4	12.8	14.0	21.1	16.2	20.3	17.0	22.7	14.3	....	....	17.7	11.4
1975	6.6	10.6	5.6	8.4	7.2	12.1	6.8	10.4	8.1	15.2	16.3	17.2	6.0	11.4
1976	3.8	4.5	-2.5	-.3	6.2	6.2	6.0	6.2	6.5	6.7	11.6	11.7	5.7	5.7
1977	6.7	6.4	6.9	5.3	6.8	7.1	6.7	7.3	7.2	6.4	12.0	15.7	6.2	6.0
1978	9.3	7.9	11.7	9.0	8.3	7.2	8.5	7.1	8.0	7.9	8.5	6.5	8.4	7.5
1979	12.8	11.2	7.4	9.3	14.8	11.8	17.6	13.3	8.8	8.7	58.1	35.0	9.4	8.9
1980	11.8	13.4	7.5	5.8	13.4	16.2	14.1	18.5	11.4	10.7	27.9	49.2	10.8	11.2
1981	7.1	9.2	1.5	5.8	8.7	10.3	8.6	10.3	9.2	10.3	14.1	19.1	7.7	8.6
1982	3.6	4.1	2.0	2.2	4.2	4.6	4.2	4.1	3.9	5.7	-.1	-1.5	4.9	5.7
1983	.6	1.6	2.3	1.0	.0	1.8	-.9	1.2	2.0	2.8	-9.2	-4.8	1.9	3.0
1984	1.7	2.1	3.5	4.4	1.1	1.4	.8	1.0	1.8	2.3	-4.2	-4.2	2.0	2.4
1985	1.8	1.0	.6	-.8	2.2	1.4	2.1	1.1	2.7	2.2	-.2	-3.9	2.7	2.5
1986	-2.3	-1.4	2.8	2.6	-4.0	-2.6	-6.6	-4.6	2.1	2.0	-38.1	-28.1	2.7	2.3
1987	2.2	2.1	-.2	2.1	3.2	2.1	4.1	2.2	1.3	1.8	11.2	-1.9	2.1	2.4
1988	4.0	2.5	5.7	2.8	3.2	2.4	3.1	2.4	3.6	2.3	-3.6	-3.2	4.3	3.3
1989	4.9	5.2	5.2	5.4	4.8	5.0	5.3	5.6	3.8	3.9	9.5	9.9	4.2	4.4
1990	5.7	4.9	2.6	4.8	6.9	5.0	8.7	5.9	3.4	3.5	30.7	14.2	3.5	3.7
1991	-.1	2.1	-1.5	-.2	.3	3.0	-.7	2.9	2.5	3.1	-9.6	4.1	3.1	3.6
1992	1.6	1.2	1.6	-.6	1.6	1.8	1.6	1.8	1.7	1.9	-.3	-.4	2.0	2.4
1993	.2	1.2	2.4	1.9	-.4	1.1	-1.4	.7	1.8	1.8	-4.1	.3	.4	1.2
1994	1.7	.6	1.1	.9	1.9	.6	2.0	-.1	2.0	2.1	3.5	-1.3	1.6	1.0
1995	2.3	1.9	1.9	1.7	2.3	1.9	2.3	2.0	2.2	1.9	1.1	1.4	2.6	2.1
1996	2.8	2.7	3.4	3.6	2.6	2.4	3.7	2.9	.4	1.2	11.7	6.5	.6	1.4
1997	-1.2	.4	-.8	.7	-1.2	.3	-1.5	.5	-.6	-.1	-6.4	.2	.0	.3
1998	.0	-.8	.1	-.1	-.1	-1.1	-.1	-1.4	.0	-.4	-11.7	-10.0	2.5	.9
1999	2.9	1.8	.8	.6	3.5	2.2	5.1	3.2	.3	.0	18.1	4.9	.9	1.7
2000	3.6	3.8	1.7	1.6	4.1	4.4	5.5	6.1	1.2	.9	16.6	19.4	1.3	1.3
2001	-1.6	2.0	1.8	3.0	-2.6	1.7	-3.9	2.2	.0	.6	-17.1	2.8	.9	1.4
2002	1.2	-1.3	-.6	-.8	1.7	-1.5	2.9	-1.8	-.6	-.4	12.3	-8.2	-.5	.1
2003	4.0	3.2	7.7	4.1	3.0	3.0	4.1	4.3	.8	.3	11.4	14.9	1.0	.2
2004	4.2	3.6	3.1	4.7	4.5	3.4	5.5	4.3	2.4	1.4	13.4	10.8	2.3	1.5
2005	5.4	4.8	1.7	2.0	6.4	5.6	8.8	7.3	1.2	2.3	23.9	17.3	1.4	2.4
2006	1.1	3.0	1.7	.6	1.0	3.5	.4	4.5	2.3	1.6	-2.0	10.0	2.0	1.5
2007	6.2	3.9	7.6	6.6	5.8	3.2	7.7	3.8	1.4	1.8	17.8	7.1	2.0	1.9
2008	-.9	6.3	3.2	6.8	-2.1	6.3	-4.8	7.7	4.3	2.9	-20.3	14.3	4.5	3.4
2009	4.3	-2.6	1.2	-1.6	4.9	-3.1	7.4	-5.1	-.1	1.9	19.4	-17.8	.9	2.6
2010	3.8	4.2	3.4	3.9	3.8	4.2	5.4	6.1	.4	.4	10.8	13.6	1.4	1.2
2011 p	4.8	6.0	6.1	6.3	4.5	5.9	5.5	8.0	2.3	1.5	8.4	15.9	3.0	2.4

Percent change from preceding month

Year or month	Total finished goods — Unadjusted	Total finished goods — Seasonally adjusted	Finished consumer foods — Unadjusted	Finished consumer foods — Seasonally adjusted	FG excl consumer foods, Total — Unadjusted	Total — Seasonally adjusted	Consumer goods — Unadjusted	Consumer goods — Seasonally adjusted	Capital equipment — Unadjusted	Capital equipment — Seasonally adjusted	Finished energy goods — Unadjusted	Finished energy goods — Seasonally adjusted	FG excl foods and energy — Unadjusted	FG excl foods and energy — Seasonally adjusted
2010: Jan	1.1	1.1	0.2	-0.1	1.4	1.4	1.9	2.0	0.3	0.1	4.3	4.5	0.3	0.3
Feb	-.6	-.4	.4	.5	-.8	-.6	-1.1	-.9	-.1	-.1	-3.1	-2.3	.0	.0
Mar	1.2	.7	2.6	2.5	.9	.3	1.4	.5	-.1	.1	3.6	.7	.0	.2
Apr	.2	-.1	-.8	-.2	.4	.0	.6	-.1	.0	.1	1.6	-.2	.0	.1
May	.2	-.2	-.1	-.4	.3	-.1	.3	-.2	.1	.2	.5	-1.0	.2	.2
June	-.4	-.3	-2.5	-2.4	.0	.1	.1	.2	-.1	.0	.1	.2	-.1	.1
July	.3	.1	.6	.7	.2	-.1	.4	-.2	-.1	.2	.7	-1.0	.1	.2
Aug	.2	.6	-.2	-.1	.3	.7	.4	1.1	.1	.1	1.0	2.5	.1	.1
Sept	.1	.3	1.0	.9	-.2	.1	-.3	.2	-.1	.1	-.9	.0	.0	.2
Oct	.7	.6	.1	.5	.8	.6	.8	1.0	.6	-.4	1.1	3.0	.7	-.3
Nov	.2	.5	1.0	.8	.1	.4	.2	.7	-.1	-.1	.3	1.6	.0	.0
Dec	.6	.9	1.1	.8	.4	.8	.6	1.2	.0	.1	1.4	2.5	.1	.2
2011: Jan	1.0	1.0	.5	.4	1.1	1.2	1.4	1.5	.4	.3	2.6	2.8	.6	.5
Feb	1.2	1.5	3.5	3.5	.7	1.0	.9	1.3	.2	.3	1.8	2.9	.2	.2
Mar	1.3	.7	-.3	-.4	1.7	1.0	2.5	1.3	.1	.3	6.1	2.8	.2	.3
Apr	1.2	.8	.1	.5	1.4	.9	2.0	1.1	.3	.3	4.4	2.2	.3	.3
May	.6	.1	-1.0	-1.2	.9	.4	1.3	.6	.0	.1	3.1	1.1	.0	.1
June	-.6	-.3	.7	.6	-.8	-.5	-1.3	-.8	.2	.4	-3.2	-2.3	.2	.3
July	.4	.3	.6	.8	.4	.2	.5	.0	.1	.4	.4	-1.0	.4	.6
Aug	-.3	.2	1.1	1.2	-.6	-.1	-.9	-.1	.0	.0	-2.3	-.7	.1	.2
Sept[2]	.4	.7	.4	.4	.5	.8	.7	1.1	-.1	.1	1.8	2.8	-.1	.0
Oct[2]	-.3	-.3	-.4	.1	-.3	-.4	-.8	-.5	1.0	-.1	-3.1	-1.4	1.0	.0
Nov[2]	.1	.3	1.2	1.0	-.3	.1	-.4	.1	.0	.1	-1.1	.1	.1	.1
Dec[2]	-.4	-.1	-.5	-.8	-.3	.0	-.5	-.1	.1	.2	-1.7	-.8	.2	.3

[1] Changes from December to December are based on unadjusted indexes.
[2] Data have been revised through August 2011; data are subject to revision four months after date of original publication.

Source: Department of Labor (Bureau of Labor Statistics).

Money Stock, Credit, and Finance

Table B-69. Money stock and debt measures, 1972–2011

[Averages of daily figures, except debt end-of-period basis; billions of dollars, seasonally adjusted]

Year and month	M1 — Sum of currency, demand deposits, travelers checks, and other checkable deposits (OCDs)	M2 — M1 plus retail MMMF balances, savings deposits (including MMDAs), and small time deposits [2]	Debt [1] — Debt of domestic nonfinancial sectors	Percent change — From year or 6 months earlier [3] M1	Percent change — From year or 6 months earlier [3] M2	Percent change — From previous period [4] Debt
December:						
1972	249.2	802.3	1,711.2	9.2	13.0	10.0
1973	262.9	855.5	1,895.5	5.5	6.6	10.7
1974	274.2	902.1	2,069.9	4.3	5.4	9.2
1975	287.1	1,016.2	2,261.8	4.7	12.6	9.3
1976	306.2	1,152.0	2,505.3	6.7	13.4	10.8
1977	330.9	1,270.3	2,826.6	8.1	10.3	12.8
1978	357.3	1,366.0	3,211.2	8.0	7.5	13.8
1979	381.8	1,473.7	3,603.0	6.9	7.9	12.2
1980	408.5	1,599.8	3,953.5	7.0	8.6	9.5
1981	436.7	1,755.5	4,361.7	6.9	9.7	10.4
1982	474.8	1,909.3	4,783.4	8.7	8.8	10.4
1983	521.4	2,125.7	5,359.2	9.8	11.3	12.0
1984	551.6	2,308.8	6,146.2	5.8	8.6	14.8
1985	619.8	2,494.6	7,123.1	12.4	8.0	15.6
1986	724.7	2,731.6	7,966.3	16.9	9.5	11.9
1987	750.2	2,831.0	8,670.1	3.5	3.6	9.1
1988	786.7	2,992.8	9,450.7	4.9	5.7	9.0
1989	792.9	3,156.7	10,152.1	.8	5.5	7.2
1990	824.7	3,274.9	10,834.9	4.0	3.7	6.5
1991	897.0	3,374.8	11,301.4	8.8	3.1	4.3
1992	1,024.9	3,427.1	11,816.5	14.3	1.5	4.5
1993	1,129.8	3,477.4	12,391.4	10.2	1.5	4.7
1994	1,150.8	3,491.5	12,973.6	1.9	.4	4.6
1995	1,127.5	3,634.2	13,667.5	−2.0	4.1	5.2
1996	1,081.4	3,814.3	14,399.8	−4.1	5.0	5.4
1997	1,072.5	4,028.5	15,210.8	−.8	5.6	5.6
1998	1,095.7	4,369.6	16,216.4	2.2	8.5	6.6
1999	1,122.4	4,628.9	17,291.3	2.4	5.9	6.4
2000	1,087.8	4,911.6	18,165.4	−3.1	6.1	5.0
2001	1,182.8	5,424.9	19,297.5	8.7	10.5	6.3
2002	1,220.6	5,768.7	20,716.1	3.2	6.3	7.4
2003	1,307.0	6,058.6	22,443.8	7.1	5.0	8.1
2004	1,376.7	6,404.4	25,264.5	5.3	5.7	9.2
2005	1,375.0	6,667.9	27,588.5	−.1	4.1	9.2
2006	1,367.2	7,059.7	29,979.4	−.6	5.9	8.7
2007	1,375.4	7,484.5	32,525.7	.6	6.0	8.5
2008	1,606.9	8,231.7	34,463.7	16.8	10.0	6.0
2009	1,697.8	8,514.2	35,430.4	5.7	3.4	3.0
2010	1,840.3	8,796.4	36,931.6	8.4	3.3	4.1
2011	2,173.9	9,640.1	....	18.1	9.6	....
2010: Jan	1,684.3	8,479.9	....	2.7	.5	....
Feb	1,705.0	8,531.0	....	6.0	2.5	....
Mar	1,712.5	8,524.4	35,798.6	6.2	2.1	3.5
Apr	1,701.7	8,549.5	....	3.2	2.0	....
May	1,706.0	8,596.3	....	3.1	2.3	....
June	1,722.4	8,616.4	36,145.9	2.9	2.4	3.9
July	1,724.6	8,613.1	....	4.8	3.1	....
Aug	1,743.7	8,639.2	....	4.5	2.5	....
Sept	1,762.1	8,673.7	36,484.6	5.8	3.5	3.7
Oct	1,777.0	8,726.2	....	8.8	4.1	....
Nov	1,822.6	8,756.0	....	13.7	3.7	....
Dec	1,840.3	8,796.4	36,931.6	13.7	4.2	4.9
2011: Jan	1,868.4	8,860.4	....	16.7	5.7	....
Feb	1,878.9	8,903.5	....	15.5	6.1	....
Mar	1,891.2	8,949.9	37,147.2	14.7	6.4	2.3
Apr	1,903.8	8,996.9	....	14.3	6.2	....
May	1,931.6	9,046.1	....	12.0	6.6	....
June	1,945.2	9,120.8	37,438.5	11.4	7.4	3.1
July	2,004.7	9,293.2	....	14.6	9.8	....
Aug	2,106.3	9,483.1	....	24.2	13.0	....
Sept	2,122.7	9,502.6	37,844.2	24.5	12.4	4.3
Oct	2,138.9	9,549.8	....	24.7	12.3	....
Nov	2,158.3	9,596.1	....	23.5	12.2	....
Dec	2,173.9	9,640.1	....	23.5	11.4	....

[1] Consists of outstanding credit market debt of the U.S. Government, State and local governments, and private nonfinancial sectors.

[2] Money market mutual fund (MMMF). Money market deposit account (MMDA).

[3] Annual changes are from December to December; monthly changes are from six months earlier at a simple annual rate.

[4] Annual changes are from fourth quarter to fourth quarter. Quarterly changes are from previous quarter at annual rate.

Note: For further information on the composition of M1 and M2, see the H6 release of the Federal Reserve Board. The Federal Reserve no longer publishes the M3 monetary aggregate and most of its components. Institutional money market mutual funds is published as a memorandum item in the H.6 release, and the component on large-denomination time deposits is published in other Federal Reserve Board releases. For details, see H.6 release of March 23, 2006.

Source: Board of Governors of the Federal Reserve System.

[Averages of daily figures; billions of dollars, seasonally adjusted]

Year and month	Currency	Nonbank travelers checks	Demand deposits	Other checkable deposits (OCDs)		
				Total	At commercial banks	At thrift institutions
December:						
1972	56.2	1.2	191.6	0.2	0.0	0.2
1973	60.8	1.4	200.3	.3	.0	.3
1974	67.0	1.7	205.1	.4	.2	.4
1975	72.8	2.1	211.3	.9	.4	.5
1976	79.5	2.6	221.5	2.7	1.3	1.4
1977	87.4	2.9	236.4	4.2	1.8	2.3
1978	96.0	3.3	249.5	8.5	5.3	3.1
1979	104.8	3.5	256.6	16.8	12.7	4.2
1980	115.3	3.9	261.2	28.1	20.8	7.3
1981	122.5	4.1	231.4	78.7	63.0	15.6
1982	132.5	4.1	234.1	104.1	80.5	23.6
1983	146.2	4.7	238.5	132.1	97.3	34.8
1984	156.1	5.0	243.4	147.1	104.7	42.4
1985	167.7	5.6	266.9	179.5	124.7	54.9
1986	180.4	6.1	302.9	235.2	161.0	74.2
1987	196.7	6.6	287.7	259.2	178.2	81.0
1988	212.0	7.0	287.1	280.6	192.5	88.1
1989	222.3	6.9	278.6	285.1	197.4	87.7
1990	246.5	7.7	276.8	293.7	208.7	85.0
1991	267.1	7.7	289.6	332.5	241.6	90.9
1992	292.1	8.2	340.0	384.6	280.8	103.8
1993	321.7	8.0	385.4	414.6	302.6	112.0
1994	354.7	8.6	383.6	404.0	297.4	106.6
1995	372.8	9.0	389.0	356.6	249.0	107.6
1996	394.6	8.8	402.2	275.8	172.1	103.7
1997	425.2	8.4	393.7	245.2	148.3	96.9
1998	460.4	8.5	376.8	250.0	143.9	106.1
1999	517.9	8.6	352.8	243.2	139.7	103.5
2000	531.4	8.3	309.9	238.3	133.2	105.2
2001	581.3	8.0	335.9	257.6	142.0	115.6
2002	626.3	7.8	307.1	279.4	154.3	125.1
2003	662.5	7.7	326.6	310.2	175.2	134.9
2004	697.6	7.6	343.6	328.0	186.9	141.0
2005	724.0	7.2	325.1	318.7	180.6	138.1
2006	749.5	6.7	306.0	304.9	176.3	128.6
2007	760.0	6.3	303.8	305.3	172.0	133.3
2008	816.1	5.5	474.9	310.4	177.3	133.1
2009	863.3	5.1	447.4	382.0	232.1	149.9
2010	918.0	4.7	519.4	398.3	236.7	161.6
2011	1,000.0	4.3	759.2	410.5	235.2	175.3
2010: Jan	863.8	5.1	439.3	376.1	223.7	152.4
Feb	868.0	5.0	447.8	384.1	230.6	153.5
Mar	871.4	5.0	447.7	388.3	235.7	152.6
Apr	875.6	4.9	449.8	371.3	217.1	154.3
May	879.4	4.9	446.8	374.8	218.7	156.1
June	882.5	4.8	456.7	378.4	224.1	154.3
July	887.0	4.8	455.2	377.6	223.1	154.5
Aug	892.6	4.7	466.1	380.2	224.5	155.7
Sept	899.1	4.7	474.0	384.3	228.9	155.4
Oct	907.1	4.7	477.4	387.7	229.4	158.3
Nov	914.0	4.7	506.8	397.1	237.5	159.5
Dec	918.0	4.7	519.4	398.3	236.7	161.6
2011: Jan	922.6	4.7	539.1	402.0	237.0	165.1
Feb	930.2	4.6	539.7	404.5	237.8	166.7
Mar	938.6	4.6	542.8	405.1	237.6	167.6
Apr	947.6	4.6	552.4	399.3	231.2	168.1
May	956.2	4.6	567.4	403.4	235.5	168.0
June	963.0	4.5	575.7	401.9	235.8	166.2
July	969.2	4.5	627.3	403.8	236.2	167.6
Aug	975.8	4.4	713.6	412.5	239.7	172.8
Sept	981.7	4.4	727.1	409.5	237.5	172.1
Oct	986.2	4.4	738.5	409.9	235.8	174.1
Nov	993.1	4.3	750.0	410.8	235.6	175.3
Dec	1,000.0	4.3	759.2	410.5	235.2	175.3

See next page for continuation of table.

[Averages of daily figures; billions of dollars, seasonally adjusted]

Year and month	Savings deposits [1]			Small-denomination time deposits [2]			Retail money funds	Institutional money funds [3]
	Total	At commercial banks	At thrift institutions	Total	At commercial banks	At thrift institutions		
December:								
1972	321.4	124.8	196.6	231.6	108.2	123.5	....	....
1973	326.8	128.0	198.7	265.8	116.8	149.0	0.1	....
1974	338.6	136.8	201.8	287.9	123.1	164.8	1.4	0.2
1975	388.9	161.2	227.6	337.9	142.3	195.5	2.4	.5
1976	453.2	201.8	251.4	390.7	155.5	235.2	1.8	.6
1977	492.2	218.8	273.4	445.5	167.5	278.0	1.8	1.0
1978	481.9	216.5	265.4	521.0	185.1	335.8	5.8	3.5
1979	423.8	195.0	228.8	634.3	235.5	398.7	33.9	10.4
1980	400.3	185.7	214.5	728.5	286.2	442.3	62.5	16.0
1981	343.9	159.0	184.9	823.1	347.7	475.4	151.7	38.2
1982	400.1	190.1	210.0	850.9	379.9	471.0	183.4	48.8
1983	684.9	363.2	321.7	784.1	350.9	433.1	135.3	40.9
1984	704.7	389.3	315.4	888.8	387.9	500.9	163.8	63.7
1985	815.3	456.6	358.6	885.7	386.4	499.3	173.8	66.7
1986	940.9	533.5	407.4	858.4	369.4	489.0	207.6	87.3
1987	937.4	534.8	402.6	921.0	391.7	529.3	222.3	94.4
1988	926.4	542.4	383.9	1,037.1	451.2	585.9	242.6	95.8
1989	893.7	541.1	352.6	1,151.3	533.8	617.6	318.8	114.1
1990	922.9	581.3	341.6	1,173.3	610.7	562.6	354.0	143.3
1991	1,044.5	664.8	379.6	1,065.3	602.2	463.1	368.1	192.9
1992	1,187.2	754.2	433.1	867.7	508.1	359.7	347.3	218.4
1993	1,219.3	785.3	434.0	781.5	467.9	313.6	346.8	223.7
1994	1,151.3	752.8	398.5	817.5	503.6	313.9	371.9	219.6
1995	1,135.9	774.8	361.0	932.4	575.8	356.5	438.5	273.8
1996	1,274.9	906.1	368.8	947.9	594.2	353.7	510.2	334.7
1997	1,401.6	1,022.8	378.8	967.6	625.5	342.2	586.7	408.6
1998	1,605.2	1,188.6	416.6	951.3	626.4	324.9	717.4	563.4
1999	1,739.7	1,288.6	451.1	955.2	636.9	318.3	811.6	667.9
2000	1,878.3	1,424.3	454.0	1,046.0	700.8	345.2	899.4	822.7
2001	2,309.7	1,738.8	570.9	974.5	636.0	338.5	957.9	1,231.1
2002	2,771.8	2,058.5	713.3	894.5	591.2	303.4	881.8	1,287.4
2003	3,160.9	2,336.5	824.4	817.8	541.8	276.0	772.9	1,143.0
2004	3,506.7	2,631.1	875.6	827.9	551.7	276.2	693.1	1,092.1
2005	3,601.0	2,772.7	828.3	993.2	646.5	346.8	698.6	1,161.3
2006	3,688.8	2,906.6	782.3	1,205.6	780.4	425.1	798.1	1,371.3
2007	3,861.6	3,035.7	825.9	1,275.8	858.7	417.1	971.7	1,922.7
2008	4,086.2	3,318.2	768.0	1,457.4	1,078.2	379.3	1,081.2	2,404.4
2009	4,813.1	3,977.6	835.5	1,182.6	862.7	319.9	820.7	2,218.0
2010	5,324.7	4,409.4	915.3	927.6	656.6	271.0	703.9	1,868.5
2011	6,023.2	5,024.3	998.9	759.7	530.5	229.1	683.3	1,738.5
2010: Jan	4,840.6	3,996.1	844.5	1,154.2	838.4	315.8	800.9	2,178.4
Feb	4,902.5	4,042.2	860.3	1,134.3	822.9	311.4	789.3	2,115.1
Mar	4,933.9	4,062.0	871.8	1,112.8	805.5	307.2	765.3	2,042.6
Apr	5,003.7	4,130.1	873.6	1,092.6	790.4	302.2	751.5	1,957.5
May	5,068.5	4,184.1	884.4	1,072.4	774.7	297.7	749.4	1,910.2
June	5,090.6	4,199.9	890.7	1,053.1	759.9	293.2	750.2	1,883.0
July	5,109.3	4,216.8	892.5	1,035.9	746.5	289.5	743.3	1,889.8
Aug	5,145.8	4,248.9	896.8	1,018.4	732.1	286.4	731.3	1,901.9
Sept	5,191.7	4,293.0	898.6	995.7	713.3	282.5	724.2	1,909.3
Oct	5,261.0	4,354.4	906.6	972.3	693.5	278.8	715.9	1,897.8
Nov	5,275.5	4,365.6	909.9	948.5	673.9	274.5	709.5	1,894.4
Dec	5,324.7	4,409.4	915.3	927.6	656.6	271.0	703.9	1,868.5
2011: Jan	5,379.6	4,453.7	925.9	910.0	644.1	265.8	702.4	1,821.2
Feb	5,432.1	4,492.9	939.2	897.7	634.9	262.8	694.8	1,797.4
Mar	5,483.2	4,527.8	955.4	884.3	624.0	260.3	691.2	1,820.0
Apr	5,533.8	4,573.7	960.1	872.0	614.7	257.3	687.3	1,846.7
May	5,571.1	4,597.9	973.2	858.3	604.0	254.3	685.1	1,866.9
June	5,647.2	4,674.5	972.7	843.4	592.7	250.7	685.0	1,841.6
July	5,777.1	4,800.0	977.1	828.2	581.3	246.9	683.3	1,808.8
Aug	5,868.9	4,889.4	979.5	811.8	569.1	242.6	696.1	1,720.1
Sept	5,893.0	4,913.8	979.2	796.9	558.1	238.8	690.0	1,744.8
Oct	5,935.4	4,948.6	986.9	782.7	547.8	234.9	692.8	1,739.3
Nov	5,983.1	4,988.4	994.7	768.7	537.3	231.3	686.1	1,730.6
Dec	6,023.2	5,024.3	998.9	759.7	530.5	229.1	683.3	1,738.5

[1] Savings deposits including money market deposit accounts (MMDAs); data prior to 1982 are savings deposits only.

[2] Small-denomination deposits are those issued in amounts of less than $100,000.

[3] Institutional money funds are not part of non-M1 M2.

Note: See also Table B–69.

Source: Board of Governors of the Federal Reserve System.

[Averages of daily figures [1]; millions of dollars; seasonally adjusted, except as noted]

| Year and month | Adjusted for changes in reserve requirements [2] | | | | | Borrowings from the Federal Reserve (NSA) [3] | | | Other borrowings from the Federal Reserve [5] | | | |
| | Reserves of depository institutions | | | | | | | | | | | |
	Total	Non-borrowed	Required	Excess (NSA) [3]	Monetary base	Total [4]	Term auction credit	Primary	Primary dealer and other broker-dealer credit [6]	Asset-backed commercial paper money market mutual fund liquidity facility	Credit extended to American International Group, Inc., net [7]	Term asset-backed securities loan facility, net [8]
December:												
1982	23,600	22,966	23,100	500	160,127	634						
1983	25,367	24,593	24,806	561	175,467	774						
1984	26,913	23,727	26,078	835	187,252	3,186						
1985	31,569	30,250	30,505	1,063	203,555	1,318						
1986	38,840	38,014	37,667	1,173	223,416	827						
1987	38,913	38,135	37,893	1,019	239,829	777						
1988	40,453	38,738	39,392	1,061	256,897	1,716						
1989	40,486	40,221	39,545	941	267,761	265						
1990	41,766	41,440	40,101	1,665	293,340	326						
1991	45,516	45,324	44,526	990	317,521	192						
1992	54,421	54,298	53,267	1,154	350,884	124						
1993	60,566	60,484	59,497	1,069	386,715	82						
1994	59,466	59,257	58,295	1,171	418,468	209						
1995	56,483	56,226	55,193	1,290	434,648	257						
1996	50,185	50,030	48,766	1,418	451,941	155						
1997	46,875	46,551	45,189	1,687	479,825	324						
1998	45,170	45,053	43,658	1,512	513,826	117						
1999	42,108	41,787	40,814	1,294	593,506	[9]320						
2000	38,675	38,465	37,349	1,325	584,997	210						
2001	41,404	41,338	39,761	1,643	635,642	67						
2002	40,287	40,207	38,279	2,008	681,540	80						
2003	42,565	42,519	41,519	1,046	720,182	46		17				
2004	46,462	46,400	44,555	1,908	759,106	63		11				
2005	45,002	44,833	43,102	1,900	787,340	169		97				
2006	43,132	42,941	41,270	1,862	812,342	191		111				
2007	43,156	27,726	41,372	1,784	824,753	15,430	11,613	3,787				
2008	820,217	166,651	52,899	767,318	1,654,873	653,565	438,327	88,245	47,631	32,102	47,206	
2009	1,138,685	968,758	63,486	1,075,199	2,018,795	169,927	82,014	19,025	0	0	22,023	46,310
2010	1,077,351	1,031,863	70,716	1,006,636	2,010,240	45,488	0	41			20,394	25,025
2011	1,597,185	1,587,659	94,868	1,502,317	2,610,864	9,526	0	103				9,400
2010: Jan	1,109,019	966,876	63,219	1,045,800	1,989,485	142,142	54,209	16,407	0	0	23,213	47,342
Feb	1,224,805	1,113,578	62,954	1,161,851	2,110,262	111,227	23,677	14,258	0	0	25,544	46,874
Mar	1,185,953	1,094,309	65,584	1,120,369	2,074,581	91,644	7,286	11,136			25,252	47,306
Apr	1,116,551	1,036,326	66,336	1,050,215	2,008,764	80,225	796	6,468			25,739	46,617
May	1,109,769	1,034,144	64,991	1,044,779	2,005,681	75,626	0	4,198			26,397	44,565
June	1,099,619	1,029,721	64,693	1,034,926	1,998,540	69,897	0	288			25,937	43,401
July	1,087,924	1,022,077	66,278	1,021,646	1,991,401	65,847	0	39			24,185	41,548
Aug	1,085,946	1,025,862	66,387	1,019,559	1,994,517	60,083	0	22			22,064	37,913
Sept	1,047,969	995,448	67,138	980,831	1,962,566	52,521	0	32			19,791	32,620
Oct	1,040,101	991,528	66,510	973,590	1,962,813	48,573	0	37			19,478	29,012
Nov	1,038,835	992,146	67,270	971,565	1,968,357	46,689	0	89			19,912	26,665
Dec	1,077,351	1,031,863	70,716	1,006,636	2,010,240	45,488	0	41			20,394	25,025
2011: Jan	1,106,507	1,074,261	70,040	1,036,467	2,044,170	32,246	0	51			8,368	23,818
Feb	1,262,697	1,240,764	72,686	1,190,012	2,207,724	21,933	0	28				21,902
Mar	1,436,146	1,416,264	73,985	1,362,161	2,389,892	19,882	0	11				19,864
Apr	1,526,480	1,508,637	74,514	1,451,966	2,489,298	17,842	0	14				17,820
May	1,587,576	1,572,431	75,072	1,512,505	2,559,321	15,146	0	10				15,115
June	1,666,349	1,653,106	77,615	1,588,734	2,644,620	13,243	0	24				13,178
July	1,696,473	1,684,077	78,344	1,618,129	2,680,642	12,395	0	7				12,315
Aug	1,666,490	1,655,115	83,584	1,583,365	2,657,378	11,834	0	5				11,737
Sept	1,642,710	1,631,135	91,718	1,550,992	2,638,581	11,575	0	19				11,474
Oct	1,638,605	1,627,394	93,287	1,545,318	2,639,137	11,210	0	19				11,140
Nov	1,591,978	1,581,637	94,059	1,497,919	2,598,949	10,341	0	20				10,301
Dec	1,597,185	1,587,659	94,868	1,502,317	2,610,864	9,526	0	103				9,400

[1] Data are prorated averages of biweekly (maintenance period) averages of daily figures.

[2] Aggregate reserves incorporate adjustments for discontinuities associated with regulatory changes to reserve requirements. For details on aggregate reserves series see *Federal Reserve Bulletin*.

[3] Not seasonally adjusted (NSA).

[4] Includes secondary, seasonal, other credit extensions, adjustment credit, and extended credit not shown separately.

[5] Does not include credit extensions made by the Federal Reserve Bank of New York to Maiden Lane LLC, Maiden Lane II LLC, Maiden Lane III LLC, and Commercial Paper Funding Facility LLC.

[6] Includes credit extended through the Primary Dealer Credit Facility and credit extended to certain other broker-dealers.

[7] Includes outstanding principal and capitalized interest net of unamortized deferred commitment fees and allowance for loan restructuring. Excludes credit extended to consolidated LLCs as described in footnote 5.

[8] Includes credit extended by Federal Reserve Bank of New York to eligible borrowers through the Term Asset-Backed Securities Loan Facility.

[9] Total includes borrowing under the terms and conditions established for the Century Date Change Special Liquidity Facility in effect from October 1, 1999 through April 7, 2000.

Source: Board of Governors of the Federal Reserve System.

[Monthly average; billions of dollars, seasonally adjusted [1]]

Year and month	Total bank credit	Securities in bank credit [2]			Loans and leases in bank credit						
		Total securities	U.S. Treasury and agency securities	Other securities	Total loans and leases [3]	Commercial and industrial loans	Real estate loans			Consumer loans [6]	Other loans and leases [7]
							Total [4]	Revolving home equity loans	Commercial loans [5]		
December:											
1974	707.5	172.1	88.2	83.9	535.4	191.3	129.8			102.1	112.2
1975	737.8	204.9	118.1	86.8	532.9	183.4	134.1			104.3	111.1
1976	798.6	226.7	137.5	89.1	571.9	185.2	148.5			115.8	122.3
1977	885.6	234.3	137.5	96.8	651.3	204.7	175.1			138.0	133.5
1978	1,003.8	240.3	138.4	101.9	763.6	237.2	210.5			164.4	151.4
1979	1,118.2	258.0	146.1	111.9	860.2	279.7	241.7			183.8	155.0
1980	1,216.9	293.5	171.5	122.0	923.4	312.0	262.3			178.7	170.4
1981	1,297.7	306.9	179.8	127.1	990.8	350.4	283.6			182.1	174.7
1982	1,397.6	333.8	202.4	131.4	1,063.8	392.2	299.6			187.9	184.1
1983	1,549.6	398.2	260.3	137.8	1,151.4	414.0	330.3			212.9	194.2
1984	1,715.6	401.1	259.9	141.1	1,314.5	473.4	376.1			253.8	211.1
1985	1,877.4	440.3	263.7	176.5	1,437.2	499.2	421.9			291.1	225.0
1986	2,072.8	498.9	310.0	188.9	1,573.9	539.3	490.4			314.8	229.3
1987	2,222.3	526.1	336.1	190.0	1,696.2	565.1	585.5	30.4		327.1	218.5
1988	2,396.2	549.6	360.4	189.2	1,846.6	604.4	663.1	41.1		355.3	223.8
1989	2,560.2	570.9	401.5	169.4	1,989.3	636.5	760.6	51.4		373.5	218.6
1990	2,698.4	619.3	460.0	159.3	2,079.1	639.4	842.5	63.5		375.4	221.8
1991	2,810.0	728.7	565.0	163.8	2,081.2	617.8	869.3	72.0		363.4	230.6
1992	2,910.1	825.4	664.8	160.7	2,084.7	597.5	888.4	75.1		354.7	244.1
1993	3,064.8	897.4	731.3	166.2	2,167.4	584.5	929.4	74.2		386.2	267.3
1994	3,236.7	894.2	721.9	172.3	2,342.5	643.8	987.8	76.0		443.7	267.1
1995	3,465.3	896.1	703.3	192.8	2,569.2	715.2	1,062.1	79.9		484.5	307.4
1996	3,638.5	895.9	698.6	197.3	2,742.6	778.7	1,122.6	86.3		507.3	334.0
1997	3,963.4	990.2	751.7	238.5	2,973.2	845.7	1,220.6	98.8		500.3	406.5
1998	4,368.6	1,096.3	795.3	301.0	3,272.3	939.1	1,311.4	97.3		497.8	524.0
1999	4,629.6	1,145.0	811.1	333.9	3,484.6	1,001.8	1,461.0	101.3		506.8	515.0
2000	5,024.9	1,175.4	787.7	387.7	3,849.6	1,087.1	1,639.4	129.5		556.1	567.1
2001	5,209.2	1,308.7	838.8	469.9	3,900.6	1,023.9	1,758.8	154.0		574.3	543.5
2002	5,640.2	1,490.0	1,004.1	485.9	4,150.2	962.3	2,009.6	212.5		610.5	567.7
2003	6,000.1	1,622.4	1,088.6	533.8	4,377.6	889.5	2,207.0	278.6		665.0	616.1
2004	6,582.6	1,741.6	1,145.6	596.0	4,841.0	913.3	2,552.4	395.1	1,075.6	691.1	684.1
2005	7,301.0	1,853.0	1,135.2	717.8	5,448.0	1,043.7	2,922.3	443.1	1,207.3	702.8	779.1
2006	8,085.6	1,983.6	1,187.2	796.4	6,102.0	1,191.7	3,364.1	467.9	1,436.6	736.8	809.4
2007	8,889.9	2,101.8	1,108.8	993.0	6,788.1	1,431.3	3,590.0	484.6	1,521.9	798.4	968.5
2008	9,370.9	2,105.9	1,240.6	865.3	7,265.0	1,579.9	3,814.1	588.8	1,498.5	875.5	995.4
2009	9,005.5	2,336.2	1,443.3	892.9	6,669.3	1,283.7	3,772.7	602.5	1,529.1	835.9	777.0
2010	9,205.1	2,438.3	1,632.9	805.5	6,766.8	1,215.5	3,607.3	581.2	1,527.4	1,117.8	826.1
2011	9,416.5	2,510.5	1,695.7	814.8	6,906.0	1,339.0	3,476.2	547.4	1,515.4	1,096.9	993.9
2010: Jan	8,937.2	2,335.7	1,448.0	887.8	6,601.4	1,259.6	3,754.1	600.0	1,527.2	818.7	769.0
Feb	8,880.0	2,338.3	1,462.0	876.3	6,541.6	1,244.4	3,720.9	599.0	1,502.7	810.9	765.4
Mar	8,938.7	2,326.2	1,470.6	855.7	6,612.5	1,231.2	3,705.5	599.4	1,496.7	886.6	789.2
Apr	9,260.7	2,329.6	1,510.2	819.4	6,931.1	1,227.2	3,716.0	601.1	1,513.6	1,162.6	825.3
May	9,206.1	2,312.5	1,509.4	803.1	6,893.6	1,216.6	3,701.4	599.3	1,514.6	1,154.1	821.6
June	9,175.5	2,304.3	1,503.5	800.8	6,871.2	1,212.2	3,683.5	597.1	1,511.4	1,147.8	827.6
July	9,208.2	2,361.9	1,556.3	805.6	6,846.2	1,212.6	3,658.0	596.2	1,500.5	1,147.8	827.8
Aug	9,227.4	2,392.6	1,583.5	809.1	6,834.8	1,210.0	3,653.3	594.5	1,507.7	1,142.7	828.7
Sept	9,214.3	2,412.5	1,601.3	811.3	6,801.8	1,205.3	3,642.2	591.7	1,512.2	1,128.6	825.6
Oct	9,232.6	2,441.3	1,629.7	811.6	6,791.3	1,202.9	3,623.3	588.4	1,511.9	1,120.8	844.3
Nov	9,225.7	2,456.6	1,645.3	811.3	6,769.1	1,205.8	3,615.1	585.3	1,518.9	1,117.0	831.1
Dec	9,205.1	2,438.3	1,632.9	805.5	6,766.8	1,215.5	3,607.3	581.2	1,527.4	1,117.8	826.1
2011: Jan	9,181.8	2,438.8	1,638.6	800.1	6,743.0	1,220.3	3,597.4	577.4	1,532.7	1,080.0	845.4
Feb	9,145.3	2,432.1	1,633.6	798.5	6,713.2	1,223.5	3,568.3	574.5	1,514.1	1,074.3	847.2
Mar	9,140.2	2,441.9	1,644.5	797.4	6,698.3	1,234.2	3,537.5	571.8	1,496.6	1,073.7	853.0
Apr	9,178.6	2,463.3	1,678.3	785.0	6,715.2	1,244.2	3,516.4	569.0	1,487.2	1,079.0	875.6
May	9,175.9	2,451.5	1,676.2	775.3	6,724.3	1,257.8	3,503.8	566.2	1,482.7	1,079.3	883.4
June	9,183.5	2,445.1	1,663.5	781.5	6,738.5	1,265.8	3,497.2	563.6	1,485.2	1,085.7	889.8
July	9,224.7	2,445.9	1,655.4	790.4	6,778.8	1,277.1	3,490.4	560.0	1,490.9	1,090.8	920.6
Aug	9,269.2	2,458.5	1,660.8	797.8	6,810.7	1,297.6	3,485.4	557.7	1,497.3	1,089.0	938.7
Sept	9,276.9	2,465.0	1,664.9	800.1	6,811.9	1,302.2	3,482.0	555.8	1,500.9	1,086.6	941.0
Oct	9,338.6	2,474.5	1,676.0	798.5	6,864.1	1,316.9	3,485.2	552.3	1,515.8	1,089.5	972.4
Nov	9,389.9	2,487.8	1,685.6	802.2	6,902.1	1,325.0	3,487.1	550.3	1,520.5	1,091.3	998.7
Dec	9,416.5	2,510.5	1,695.7	814.8	6,906.0	1,339.0	3,476.2	547.4	1,515.4	1,096.9	993.9

[1] Data are prorated averages of Wednesday values for domestically chartered commercial banks, branches and agencies of foreign banks, New York State investment companies (through September 1996), and Edge Act and agreement corporations.

[2] Includes securities held in trading accounts, held-to-maturity, and available for sale. Excludes all non-security trading assets, such as derivatives with a positive fair value or loans held in trading accounts.

[3] Excludes unearned income. Includes the allowance for loan and lease losses. Excludes Federal funds sold to, reverse repurchase agreements (RPs) with, and loans to commercial banks. Includes all loans held in trading accounts under a fair value option.

[4] Includes closed-end residential loans, not shown separately.

[5] Includes construction, land development, and other land loans, and loans secured by farmland, multifamily (5 or more) residential properties, and nonfarm nonresidential properties.

[6] Includes credit cards and other consumer loans.

[7] Includes other items, not shown separately.

Note: Data in this table are shown as of January 20, 2012.

Source: Board of Governors of the Federal Reserve System.

[Percent per annum]

Year and month	U.S. Treasury securities					Corporate bonds (Moody's)		High-grade municipal bonds (Standard & Poor's)	New-home mortgage yields [4]	Prime rate charged by banks [5]	Discount window (Federal Reserve Bank of New York) [5,6]		Federal funds rate [7]
	Bills (at auction) [1]		Constant maturities [2]			Aaa [3]	Baa				Primary credit	Adjustment credit	
	3-month	6-month	3-year	10-year	30-year								
1940	0.014	....	....	....	....	2.84	4.75	2.50	....	1.50	....	1.00	....
1941	.103	....	....	....	....	2.77	4.33	2.10	....	1.50	....	1.00	....
1942	.326	....	....	....	....	2.83	4.28	2.36	....	1.50	....	[8]1.00	....
1943	.373	....	....	....	....	2.73	3.91	2.06	....	1.50	....	[8]1.00	....
1944	.375	....	....	....	....	2.72	3.61	1.86	....	1.50	....	[8]1.00	....
1945	.375	....	....	....	....	2.62	3.29	1.67	....	1.50	....	[8]1.00	....
1946	.375	....	....	....	....	2.53	3.05	1.64	....	1.50	....	[8]1.00	....
1947	.594	....	....	....	....	2.61	3.24	2.01	....	1.50–1.75	....	1.00	....
1948	1.040	....	....	....	....	2.82	3.47	2.40	....	1.75–2.00	....	1.34	....
1949	1.102	....	....	....	....	2.66	3.42	2.21	....	2.00	....	1.50	....
1950	1.218	....	....	....	....	2.62	3.24	1.98	....	2.07	....	1.59	....
1951	1.552	....	....	....	....	2.86	3.41	2.00	....	2.56	....	1.75	....
1952	1.766	....	....	....	....	2.96	3.52	2.19	....	3.00	....	1.75	....
1953	1.931	....	2.47	2.85	....	3.20	3.74	2.72	....	3.17	....	1.99	....
1954	.953	....	1.63	2.40	....	2.90	3.51	2.37	....	3.05	....	1.60	....
1955	1.753	....	2.47	2.82	....	3.06	3.53	2.53	....	3.16	....	1.89	1.79
1956	2.658	....	3.19	3.18	....	3.36	3.88	2.93	....	3.77	....	2.77	2.73
1957	3.267	....	3.98	3.65	....	3.89	4.71	3.60	....	4.20	....	3.12	3.11
1958	1.839	....	2.84	3.32	....	3.79	4.73	3.56	....	3.83	....	2.15	1.57
1959	3.405	3.832	4.46	4.33	....	4.38	5.05	3.95	....	4.48	....	3.36	3.31
1960	2.93	3.25	3.98	4.12	....	4.41	5.19	3.73	....	4.82	....	3.53	3.21
1961	2.38	2.61	3.54	3.88	....	4.35	5.08	3.46	....	4.50	....	3.00	1.95
1962	2.78	2.91	3.47	3.95	....	4.33	5.02	3.18	....	4.50	....	3.00	2.71
1963	3.16	3.25	3.67	4.00	....	4.26	4.86	3.23	5.89	4.50	....	3.23	3.18
1964	3.56	3.69	4.03	4.19	....	4.40	4.83	3.22	5.83	4.50	....	3.55	3.50
1965	3.95	4.05	4.22	4.28	....	4.49	4.87	3.27	5.81	4.54	....	4.04	4.07
1966	4.88	5.08	5.23	4.93	....	5.13	5.67	3.82	6.25	5.63	....	4.50	5.11
1967	4.32	4.63	5.03	5.07	....	5.51	6.23	3.98	6.46	5.63	....	4.19	4.22
1968	5.34	5.47	5.68	5.64	....	6.18	6.94	4.51	6.97	6.31	....	5.17	5.66
1969	6.68	6.85	7.02	6.67	....	7.03	7.81	5.81	7.81	7.96	....	5.87	8.21
1970	6.43	6.53	7.29	7.35	....	8.04	9.11	6.51	8.45	7.91	....	5.95	7.17
1971	4.35	4.51	5.66	6.16	....	7.39	8.56	5.70	7.74	5.73	....	4.88	4.67
1972	4.07	4.47	5.72	6.21	....	7.21	8.16	5.27	7.60	5.25	....	4.50	4.44
1973	7.04	7.18	6.96	6.85	....	7.44	8.24	5.18	7.96	8.03	....	6.45	8.74
1974	7.89	7.93	7.84	7.56	....	8.57	9.50	6.09	8.92	10.81	....	7.83	10.51
1975	5.84	6.12	7.50	7.99	....	8.83	10.61	6.89	9.00	7.86	....	6.25	5.82
1976	4.99	5.27	6.77	7.61	....	8.43	9.75	6.49	9.00	6.84	....	5.50	5.05
1977	5.27	5.52	6.68	7.42	7.75	8.02	8.97	5.56	9.02	6.83	....	5.46	5.54
1978	7.22	7.58	8.29	8.41	8.49	8.73	9.49	5.90	9.56	9.06	....	7.46	7.94
1979	10.05	10.02	9.70	9.43	9.28	9.63	10.69	6.39	10.78	12.67	....	10.29	11.20
1980	11.51	11.37	11.51	11.43	11.27	11.94	13.67	8.51	12.66	15.26	....	11.77	13.35
1981	14.03	13.78	14.46	13.92	13.45	14.17	16.04	11.23	14.70	18.87	....	13.42	16.39
1982	10.69	11.08	12.93	13.01	12.76	13.79	16.11	11.57	15.14	14.85	....	11.01	12.24
1983	8.63	8.75	10.45	11.10	11.18	12.04	13.55	9.47	12.57	10.79	....	8.50	9.09
1984	9.53	9.77	11.92	12.46	12.41	12.71	14.19	10.15	12.38	12.04	....	8.80	10.23
1985	7.47	7.64	9.64	10.62	10.79	11.37	12.72	9.18	11.55	9.93	....	7.69	8.10
1986	5.98	6.03	7.06	7.67	7.78	9.02	10.39	7.38	10.17	8.33	....	6.32	6.80
1987	5.82	6.05	7.68	8.39	8.59	9.38	10.58	7.73	9.31	8.21	....	5.66	6.66
1988	6.69	6.92	8.26	8.85	8.96	9.71	10.83	7.76	9.19	9.32	....	6.20	7.57
1989	8.12	8.04	8.55	8.49	8.45	9.26	10.18	7.24	10.13	10.87	....	6.93	9.21
1990	7.51	7.47	8.26	8.55	8.61	9.32	10.36	7.25	10.05	10.01	....	6.98	8.10
1991	5.42	5.49	6.82	7.86	8.14	8.77	9.80	6.89	9.32	8.46	....	5.45	5.69
1992	3.45	3.57	5.30	7.01	7.67	8.14	8.98	6.41	8.24	6.25	....	3.25	3.52
1993	3.02	3.14	4.44	5.87	6.59	7.22	7.93	5.63	7.20	6.00	....	3.00	3.02
1994	4.29	4.66	6.27	7.09	7.37	7.96	8.62	6.19	7.49	7.15	....	3.60	4.21
1995	5.51	5.59	6.25	6.57	6.88	7.59	8.20	5.95	7.87	8.83	....	5.21	5.83
1996	5.02	5.09	5.99	6.44	6.71	7.37	8.05	5.75	7.80	8.27	....	5.02	5.30
1997	5.07	5.18	6.10	6.35	6.61	7.26	7.86	5.55	7.71	8.44	....	5.00	5.46
1998	4.81	4.85	5.14	5.26	5.58	6.53	7.22	5.12	7.07	8.35	....	4.92	5.35
1999	4.66	4.76	5.49	5.65	5.87	7.04	7.87	5.43	7.04	8.00	....	4.62	4.97
2000	5.85	5.92	6.22	6.03	5.94	7.62	8.36	5.77	7.52	9.23	....	5.73	6.24
2001	3.44	3.39	4.09	5.02	5.49	7.08	7.95	5.19	7.00	6.91	....	3.40	3.88
2002	1.62	1.69	3.10	4.61	5.43	6.49	7.80	5.05	6.43	4.67	....	1.17	1.67
2003	1.01	1.06	2.10	4.01	....	5.67	6.77	4.73	5.80	4.12	2.12	....	1.13
2004	1.38	1.57	2.78	4.27	....	5.63	6.39	4.63	5.77	4.34	2.34	....	1.35
2005	3.16	3.40	3.93	4.29	....	5.24	6.06	4.29	5.94	6.19	4.19	....	3.22
2006	4.73	4.80	4.77	4.80	4.91	5.59	6.48	4.42	6.63	7.96	5.96	....	4.97
2007	4.41	4.48	4.35	4.63	4.84	5.56	6.48	4.42	6.41	8.05	5.86	....	5.02
2008	1.48	1.71	2.24	3.66	4.28	5.63	7.45	4.80	6.05	5.09	2.39	....	1.92
2009	.16	.29	1.43	3.26	4.08	5.31	7.30	4.64	5.14	3.25	.50	....	.16
2010	.14	.20	1.11	3.22	4.25	4.94	6.04	4.16	4.80	3.25	.72	....	.18
2011	.06	.10	.75	2.78	3.91	4.64	5.66	4.29	4.56	3.25	.75	....	.10

[1] High bill rate at auction, issue date within period, bank-discount basis. On or after October 28, 1998, data are stop yields from uniform-price auctions. Before that date, they are weighted average yields from multiple-price auctions.

See next page for continuation of table.

[Percent per annum]

Year and month	Bills (at auction) [1]		Constant maturities [2]			Corporate bonds (Moody's)		High-grade municipal bonds (Standard & Poor's)	New-home mortgage yields [4]	Prime rate charged by banks [5]	Discount window (Federal Reserve Bank of New York) [5,6]		Federal funds rate [7]
	3-month	6-month	3-year	10-year	30-year	Aaa [3]	Baa				Primary credit	Adjustment credit	
										High-low	High-low	High-low	
2007: Jan	4.96	4.93	4.79	4.76	4.85	5.40	6.34	4.29	6.35	8.25–8.25	6.25–6.25		5.25
Feb	5.02	4.96	4.75	4.72	4.82	5.39	6.28	4.21	6.31	8.25–8.25	6.25–6.25		5.26
Mar	4.96	4.90	4.51	4.56	4.72	5.30	6.27	4.18	6.22	8.25–8.25	6.25–6.25		5.26
Apr	4.87	4.87	4.60	4.69	4.87	5.47	6.39	4.32	6.21	8.25–8.25	6.25–6.25		5.25
May	4.77	4.80	4.69	4.75	4.90	5.47	6.39	4.37	6.22	8.25–8.25	6.25–6.25		5.25
June	4.63	4.77	5.00	5.10	5.20	5.79	6.70	4.64	6.54	8.25–8.25	6.25–6.25		5.25
July	4.83	4.85	4.82	5.00	5.11	5.73	6.65	4.64	6.70	8.25–8.25	6.25–6.25		5.26
Aug	4.34	4.56	4.34	4.67	4.93	5.79	6.65	4.73	6.73	8.25–8.25	6.25–5.75		5.02
Sept	4.01	4.13	4.06	4.52	4.79	5.74	6.59	4.57	6.58	8.25–7.75	5.75–5.25		4.94
Oct	3.96	4.08	4.01	4.53	4.77	5.66	6.48	4.41	6.55	7.75–7.50	5.25–5.00		4.76
Nov	3.49	3.63	3.35	4.15	4.52	5.44	6.40	4.45	6.42	7.50–7.50	5.00–5.00		4.49
Dec	3.08	3.29	3.13	4.10	4.53	5.49	6.65	4.22	6.21	7.50–7.25	5.00–4.75		4.24
2008: Jan	2.86	2.84	2.51	3.74	4.33	5.33	6.54	4.00	6.02	7.25–6.00	4.75–3.50		3.94
Feb	2.21	2.09	2.19	3.74	4.52	5.53	6.82	4.35	5.96	6.00–6.00	3.50–3.50		2.98
Mar	1.38	1.53	1.80	3.51	4.39	5.51	6.89	4.67	5.92	6.00–5.25	3.50–2.50		2.61
Apr	1.32	1.54	2.23	3.68	4.44	5.55	6.97	4.43	5.98	5.25–5.00	2.50–2.25		2.28
May	1.71	1.82	2.69	3.88	4.60	5.57	6.93	4.34	6.01	5.00–5.00	2.25–2.25		1.98
June	1.89	2.15	3.08	4.10	4.69	5.68	7.07	4.48	6.13	5.00–5.00	2.25–2.25		2.00
July	1.72	1.99	2.87	4.01	4.57	5.67	7.16	4.88	6.29	5.00–5.00	2.25–2.25		2.01
Aug	1.79	1.96	2.70	3.89	4.50	5.64	7.15	4.90	6.33	5.00–5.00	2.25–2.25		2.00
Sept	1.46	1.78	2.32	3.69	4.27	5.65	7.31	5.03	6.09	5.00–5.00	2.25–2.25		1.81
Oct	.84	1.39	1.86	3.81	4.17	6.28	8.88	5.68	6.10	5.00–4.00	2.25–1.25		.97
Nov	.30	.86	1.51	3.53	4.00	6.12	9.21	5.28	6.16	4.00–4.00	1.25–1.25		.39
Dec	.04	.32	1.07	2.42	2.87	5.05	8.43	5.53	5.67	4.00–3.25	1.25–0.50		.16
2009: Jan	.12	.31	1.13	2.52	3.13	5.05	8.14	5.13	5.11	3.25–3.25	0.50–0.50		.15
Feb	.31	.46	1.37	2.87	3.59	5.27	8.08	5.00	5.09	3.25–3.25	0.50–0.50		.22
Mar	.25	.43	1.31	2.82	3.64	5.50	8.42	5.15	5.10	3.25–3.25	0.50–0.50		.18
Apr	.17	.37	1.32	2.93	3.76	5.39	8.39	4.88	4.96	3.25–3.25	0.50–0.50		.15
May	.19	.31	1.39	3.29	4.23	5.54	8.06	4.60	4.92	3.25–3.25	0.50–0.50		.18
June	.17	.32	1.76	3.72	4.52	5.61	7.50	4.84	5.17	3.25–3.25	0.50–0.50		.21
July	.19	.29	1.55	3.56	4.41	5.41	7.09	4.69	5.40	3.25–3.25	0.50–0.50		.16
Aug	.18	.27	1.65	3.59	4.37	5.26	6.58	4.58	5.32	3.25–3.25	0.50–0.50		.16
Sept	.13	.22	1.48	3.40	4.19	5.13	6.31	4.13	5.26	3.25–3.25	0.50–0.50		.15
Oct	.08	.17	1.46	3.39	4.19	5.15	6.29	4.20	5.14	3.25–3.25	0.50–0.50		.12
Nov	.06	.16	1.32	3.40	4.31	5.19	6.32	4.35	5.08	3.25–3.25	0.50–0.50		.12
Dec	.07	.17	1.38	3.59	4.49	5.26	6.37	4.16	5.01	3.25–3.25	0.50–0.50		.12
2010: Jan	.06	.15	1.49	3.73	4.60	5.26	6.25	4.22	5.04	3.25–3.25	0.50–0.50		.11
Feb	.10	.18	1.40	3.69	4.62	5.35	6.34	4.23	5.08	3.25–3.25	0.75–0.50		.13
Mar	.15	.22	1.51	3.73	4.64	5.27	6.27	4.22	5.09	3.25–3.25	0.75–0.75		.16
Apr	.15	.24	1.64	3.85	4.69	5.29	6.25	4.24	5.21	3.25–3.25	0.75–0.75		.20
May	.16	.23	1.32	3.42	4.29	4.96	6.05	4.15	5.12	3.25–3.25	0.75–0.75		.20
June	.12	.19	1.17	3.20	4.13	4.88	6.23	4.18	5.00	3.25–3.25	0.75–0.75		.18
July	.16	.20	.98	3.01	3.99	4.72	6.01	4.11	4.87	3.25–3.25	0.75–0.75		.18
Aug	.15	.19	.78	2.70	3.80	4.49	5.66	3.91	4.67	3.25–3.25	0.75–0.75		.19
Sept	.15	.19	.74	2.65	3.77	4.53	5.66	3.76	4.52	3.25–3.25	0.75–0.75		.19
Oct	.13	.17	.57	2.54	3.87	4.68	5.72	3.83	4.40	3.25–3.25	0.75–0.75		.19
Nov	.13	.17	.67	2.76	4.19	4.87	5.92	4.30	4.26	3.25–3.25	0.75–0.75		.19
Dec	.15	.20	.99	3.29	4.42	5.02	6.10	4.72	4.44	3.25–3.25	0.75–0.75		.18
2011: Jan	.15	.18	1.03	3.39	4.52	5.04	6.09	5.02	4.75	3.25–3.25	0.75–0.75		.17
Feb	.14	.17	1.28	3.58	4.65	5.22	6.15	4.92	4.94	3.25–3.25	0.75–0.75		.16
Mar	.11	.16	1.17	3.41	4.51	5.13	6.03	4.70	4.98	3.25–3.25	0.75–0.75		.14
Apr	.06	.12	1.21	3.46	4.50	5.16	6.02	4.71	4.91	3.25–3.25	0.75–0.75		.10
May	.04	.08	.94	3.17	4.29	4.96	5.78	4.34	4.86	3.25–3.25	0.75–0.75		.09
June	.04	.10	.71	3.00	4.23	4.99	5.75	4.22	4.61	3.25–3.25	0.75–0.75		.09
July	.03	.08	.68	3.00	4.27	4.93	5.76	4.24	4.55	3.25–3.25	0.75–0.75		.07
Aug	.05	.09	.38	2.30	3.65	4.37	5.36	3.92	4.29	3.25–3.25	0.75–0.75		.10
Sept	.02	.05	.35	1.98	3.18	4.09	5.27	3.79	4.36	3.25–3.25	0.75–0.75		.08
Oct	.02	.06	.47	2.15	3.13	3.98	5.37	3.94	4.19	3.25–3.25	0.75–0.75		.07
Nov	.01	.05	.39	2.01	3.02	3.87	5.14	3.95	4.26	3.25–3.25	0.75–0.75		.08
Dec	.02	.05	.39	1.98	2.98	3.93	5.25	3.76	4.18	3.25–3.25	0.75–0.75		.07

[2] Yields on the more actively traded issues adjusted to constant maturities by the Department of the Treasury. The 30-year Treasury constant maturity series was discontinued on February 18, 2002, and reintroduced on February 9, 2006.

[3] Beginning with December 7, 2001, data for corporate Aaa series are industrial bonds only.

[4] Effective rate (in the primary market) on conventional mortgages, reflecting fees and charges as well as contract rate and assuming, on the average, repayment at end of 10 years. Rates beginning with January 1973 not strictly comparable with prior rates.

[5] For monthly data, high and low for the period. Prime rate for 1947–1948 are ranges of the rate in effect during the period.

[6] Primary credit replaced adjustment credit as the Federal Reserve's principal discount window lending program effective January 9, 2003.

[7] Since July 19, 1975, the daily effective rate is an average of the rates on a given day weighted by the volume of transactions at these rates. Prior to that date, the daily effective rate was the rate considered most representative of the day's transactions, usually the one at which most transactions occurred.

[8] From October 30, 1942 to April 24, 1946, a preferential rate of 0.50 percent was in effect for advances secured by Government securities maturing in one year or less.

Sources: Department of the Treasury, Board of Governors of the Federal Reserve System, Federal Housing Finance Agency, Moody's Investors Service, and Standard & Poor's.

[Billions of dollars; quarterly data at seasonally adjusted annual rates]

Item	2003	2004	2005	2006	2007	2008	2009	2010
NONFINANCIAL SECTORS								
Domestic	1,683.5	2,068.7	2,324.1	2,392.5	2,539.8	1,938.0	1,050.9	1,445.1
By instrument	1,683.5	2,068.7	2,324.1	2,392.5	2,539.8	1,938.0	1,050.9	1,445.1
Commercial paper	−37.3	15.3	−7.7	22.4	11.3	7.7	−73.1	24.5
Treasury securities	398.4	362.5	307.3	183.7	237.5	1,239.0	1,443.7	1,579.6
Agency- and GSE-backed securities [1]	−2.4	−.6	−.4	−.3	−.4	.2	.1	.7
Municipal securities	137.6	212.9	193.6	168.3	235.9	95.3	154.5	97.7
Corporate bonds	151.9	75.5	56.7	215.6	311.2	204.6	377.2	420.6
Bank loans n.e.c.	−76.3	5.2	134.5	175.3	240.2	192.5	−296.0	−33.0
Other loans and advances	10.3	58.6	119.3	159.8	311.0	74.9	−154.2	−85.3
Mortgages	995.3	1,222.1	1,420.4	1,372.3	1,053.8	85.0	−286.2	−515.5
Home	817.1	1,016.5	1,116.8	1,065.3	714.3	−110.3	−200.4	−342.4
Multifamily residential	71.6	43.7	60.8	37.0	84.4	46.2	7.5	−10.2
Commercial	118.8	149.5	233.7	266.7	250.4	127.1	−90.0	−167.8
Farm	−12.2	12.5	9.1	3.3	4.6	22.0	−3.4	4.9
Consumer credit	105.9	117.2	100.4	95.4	139.3	38.8	−115.3	−44.2
By sector	1,683.5	2,068.7	2,324.1	2,392.5	2,539.8	1,938.0	1,050.9	1,445.1
Household sector	1,011.5	1,044.3	1,174.3	1,167.2	867.3	14.7	−232.0	−278.4
Nonfinancial business	155.4	475.7	705.6	943.7	1,288.5	664.1	−272.5	77.0
Corporate	76.5	214.8	356.8	520.9	819.2	337.3	−133.4	279.1
Nonfarm noncorporate	91.6	245.2	331.6	408.6	454.8	321.8	−132.7	−213.2
Farm	−12.6	15.8	17.3	14.2	14.6	5.1	−6.3	11.1
State and local governments	120.5	186.8	137.2	98.3	146.9	20.0	111.5	66.2
Federal Government	396.0	361.9	306.9	183.4	237.1	1,239.2	1,443.9	1,580.2
Foreign borrowing in the United States	43.0	155.3	113.0	332.6	170.3	−226.2	211.7	88.2
Commercial paper	18.9	69.2	38.6	98.4	−69.3	−71.0	59.4	−2.7
Bonds	28.7	85.8	64.5	227.8	218.7	−158.8	163.2	72.8
Bank loans n.e.c.	−2.5	3.8	14.5	13.8	24.1	5.1	−11.2	17.9
Other loans and advances	−2.1	−3.6	−4.6	−7.4	−3.2	−1.5	.3	.2
Nonfinancial domestic and foreign borrowing	1,726.5	2,224.0	2,437.1	2,725.1	2,710.1	1,711.8	1,262.6	1,533.2
FINANCIAL SECTORS								
By instrument	1,071.6	971.3	1,116.5	1,300.0	1,793.9	901.9	−1,844.0	−968.5
Open market paper	−63.5	21.7	214.2	196.3	−111.4	−125.6	−448.2	−101.7
GSE issues [1]	250.9	75.0	−84.0	35.6	282.4	271.7	−475.3	−233.8
Agency- and GSE-backed mortgage pool securities [1]	335.4	40.8	164.5	292.6	623.3	497.0	415.3	186.9
Corporate bonds	487.3	668.2	744.6	810.0	698.3	−277.4	−589.1	−591.8
Bank loans n.e.c.	21.4	66.0	18.8	−62.3	70.9	496.1	−467.5	−90.2
Other loans and advances	31.2	74.1	44.4	21.2	225.8	33.3	−282.6	−144.7
Mortgages	8.9	25.5	14.1	6.6	4.7	6.8	3.4	6.9
By sector	1,071.6	971.3	1,116.5	1,300.0	1,793.9	901.9	−1,844.0	−968.5
U.S.-chartered commercial banks	13.2	18.7	36.9	107.5	131.8	79.1	−152.6	−133.5
Foreign banking offices in the United States	−0.1	.1	.0	−.3	.0	−.2	.0	.0
Bank holding companies	35.4	59.5	48.2	68.7	129.4	84.0	−10.3	−42.6
Savings institutions	35.3	91.4	22.5	−108.2	104.1	−67.1	−169.6	−29.0
Credit unions	2.2	2.3	3.3	4.2	13.4	8.3	−14.1	−.4
Life insurance companies	2.9	3.0	.4	2.7	14.5	26.2	−6.6	−3.2
Government-sponsored enterprises	250.9	75.0	−84.0	35.6	282.4	271.7	−475.3	−233.8
Agency- and GSE-backed mortgage pools [1]	335.4	40.8	164.5	292.6	623.3	497.0	415.3	186.9
Asset-backed securities issuers	249.8	439.3	731.1	811.2	339.4	−408.0	−740.1	−515.2
Finance companies	111.1	134.3	33.5	34.8	34.9	−79.4	−156.2	−173.9
REITs [2]	32.3	94.6	55.4	15.5	10.2	−53.8	−50.0	4.6
Brokers and dealers	6.4	15.2	.1	6.4	−4.0	77.7	−49.7	36.9
Funding corporations	−3.2	−2.9	104.7	29.1	114.5	466.4	−434.8	−65.3
ALL SECTORS, BY INSTRUMENT								
Total	2,798.0	3,195.3	3,553.6	4,025.1	4,504.1	2,613.7	−581.5	564.8
Open market paper	−82.0	106.2	245.1	317.1	−169.4	−189.0	−461.9	−79.9
Treasury securities	398.4	362.5	307.3	183.7	237.5	1,239.0	1,443.7	1,579.6
Agency- and GSE-backed securities [1]	583.8	115.2	80.0	327.9	905.3	768.9	−59.9	−46.2
Municipal securities	137.6	212.9	193.6	168.3	235.9	95.3	154.5	97.7
Corporate and foreign bonds	668.0	829.5	865.8	1,253.4	1,228.2	−231.6	−48.6	−98.4
Bank loans n.e.c.	−57.4	75.1	167.8	126.9	335.1	693.7	−774.6	−105.4
Other loans and advances	39.4	129.2	159.1	173.6	533.6	106.7	−436.5	−229.8
Mortgages	1,004.2	1,247.6	1,434.5	1,378.8	1,058.5	91.7	−282.8	−508.6
Consumer credit	105.9	117.2	100.4	95.4	139.3	38.8	−115.3	−44.2

[1] Government-sponsored enterprises (GSE).
[2] Real estate investment trusts (REITs).

See next page for continuation of table.

[Billions of dollars; quarterly data at seasonally adjusted annual rates]

Item	2010				2011		
	I	II	III	IV	I	II	III
NONFINANCIAL SECTORS							
Domestic	1,247.9	1,389.3	1,354.7	1,788.4	862.1	1,143.6	1,622.9
By instrument	1,247.9	1,389.3	1,354.7	1,788.4	862.1	1,143.6	1,622.9
Commercial paper	50.3	62.7	43.8	−58.7	31.7	55.4	35.6
Treasury securities	1,604.8	1,848.7	1,390.4	1,474.4	740.4	826.2	1,380.7
Agency- and GSE-backed securities [1]	0.3	1.1	.5	.8	1.2	.2	1.9
Municipal securities	126.3	−4.8	76.9	192.4	−74.3	−110.3	−9.6
Corporate bonds	432.4	231.6	510.6	507.7	392.0	447.1	294.0
Bank loans n.e.c.	−54.7	−55.0	−84.3	62.0	110.9	212.0	141.8
Other loans and advances	−122.4	−96.7	−50.3	−71.9	−8.3	15.5	60.7
Mortgages	−691.5	−516.2	−479.4	−374.9	−383.9	−386.6	−311.7
Home	−557.7	−313.4	−292.1	−206.4	−296.4	−271.4	−203.4
Multifamily residential	−19.9	−14.5	.8	−7.4	7.1	2.9	3.8
Commercial	−118.8	−193.3	−193.1	−166.1	−90.6	−113.9	−108.0
Farm	4.9	4.9	5.0	5.0	−4.1	−4.1	−4.2
Consumer credit	−97.6	−82.1	−53.5	56.5	52.5	84.1	29.5
By sector	1,247.9	1,389.3	1,354.7	1,788.4	862.1	1,143.6	1,622.9
Household sector	−419.2	−296.9	−298.8	−98.7	−243.7	−85.0	−158.8
Nonfinancial business	−10.2	−147.6	200.6	265.4	464.2	508.8	398.0
Corporate	366.6	119.7	353.3	277.0	475.7	515.3	343.1
Nonfarm noncorporate	−376.2	−271.4	−176.0	−29.0	−17.8	10.8	71.7
Farm	−0.5	4.1	23.3	17.5	6.3	−17.3	−16.8
State and local governments	72.2	−15.9	62.0	146.6	−99.9	−106.5	1.0
Federal Government	1,605.1	1,849.8	1,390.9	1,475.1	741.5	826.4	1,382.6
Foreign borrowing in the United States	119.1	−43.5	132.0	145.1	221.4	−17.4	−191.8
Commercial paper	−24.9	−55.6	13.9	55.8	128.9	−43.2	−248.2
Bonds	143.0	−.6	89.8	58.9	44.2	13.4	15.0
Bank loans n.e.c.	−0.5	13.8	28.2	29.9	47.9	13.7	41.3
Other loans and advances	1.5	−1.1	.1	.5	.5	−1.4	.1
Nonfinancial domestic and foreign borrowing	1,367.1	1,345.8	1,486.6	1,933.4	1,083.6	1,126.2	1,431.0
FINANCIAL SECTORS							
By instrument	−1,257.2	−1,107.8	−703.5	−805.3	−151.5	−994.2	−499.2
Open market paper	−201.7	−189.0	189.6	−206.0	92.2	−99.8	31.0
GSE issues [1]	−60.1	−248.6	−372.1	−254.3	11.1	−479.9	−138.3
Agency- and GSE-backed mortgage pool securities [1]	169.7	228.6	159.7	189.6	263.7	146.5	124.0
Corporate bonds	−932.7	−640.9	−336.5	−457.1	−438.5	−366.2	−339.4
Bank loans n.e.c.	−86.6	−108.8	−103.4	−62.1	−46.7	−115.8	−39.7
Other loans and advances	−146.6	−151.1	−244.0	−37.3	−40.4	−97.4	−141.2
Mortgages	0.8	1.9	3.1	21.8	7.1	18.4	4.2
By sector	−1,257.2	−1,107.8	−703.5	−805.3	−151.5	−994.2	−499.2
U.S.-chartered commercial banks	−118.7	−127.7	−175.6	−111.9	−15.6	−67.1	−94.9
Foreign banking offices in the United States	0.0	.0	.0	.0	.0	.0	.0
Bank holding companies	−75.4	−118.4	204.4	−180.9	44.3	−186.9	−107.7
Savings institutions	−60.2	−41.6	−61.9	47.9	−39.9	−33.3	−63.1
Credit unions	−4.4	−1.6	.8	3.6	−9.6	−3.5	3.7
Life insurance companies	−10.8	.0	−1.2	−.8	1.8	2.4	.9
Government-sponsored enterprises	−60.1	−248.6	−372.1	−254.3	11.1	−479.9	−138.3
Agency- and GSE-backed mortgage pools [1]	169.7	228.6	159.7	189.6	263.7	146.5	124.0
Asset-backed securities issuers	−632.7	−551.2	−465.7	−411.2	−369.0	−242.0	−252.7
Finance companies	−309.9	−176.2	−143.0	−66.5	−9.7	−169.8	35.6
REITs [2]	4.6	−8.6	35.7	−13.4	44.5	75.9	25.9
Brokers and dealers	−2.4	34.6	−19.2	134.4	−5.9	−72.7	−43.5
Funding corporations	−156.9	−97.1	134.5	−141.8	−67.1	36.3	10.9
ALL SECTORS, BY INSTRUMENT							
Total	109.9	238.0	783.1	1,128.1	932.0	132.0	931.8
Open market paper	−176.3	−181.9	247.3	−208.8	252.7	−87.5	−181.6
Treasury securities	1,604.8	1,848.7	1,390.4	1,474.4	740.4	826.2	1,380.7
Agency- and GSE-backed securities [1]	109.9	−18.9	−211.8	−64.0	276.0	−333.3	−12.4
Municipal securities	126.3	−4.8	76.9	192.4	−74.3	−110.3	−9.6
Corporate and foreign bonds	−357.3	−409.8	263.8	109.6	−2.3	94.3	−30.4
Bank loans n.e.c.	−141.8	−150.1	−159.5	29.8	112.1	109.9	143.4
Other loans and advances	−267.5	−248.8	−294.2	−108.7	−48.2	−83.3	−80.3
Mortgages	−690.7	−514.3	−476.3	−353.1	−376.8	−368.1	−307.5
Consumer credit	−97.6	−82.1	−53.5	56.5	52.5	84.1	29.5

Source: Board of Governors of the Federal Reserve System.

TABLE B–75. Mortgage debt outstanding by type of property and of financing, 1954–2011

[Billions of dollars]

End of year or quarter	All proper-ties	Farm proper-ties	Nonfarm properties				Nonfarm properties by type of mortgage					
							Government underwritten				Conventional [2]	
			Total	1- to 4-family houses	Multi-family proper-ties	Com-mercial proper-ties	Total [1]	1- to 4-family houses			Total	1- to 4-family houses
								Total	FHA-insured	VA-guar-anteed		
1954	113.6	8.2	105.4	75.7	13.5	16.3	36.2	32.1	12.8	19.3	69.3	43.6
1955	129.9	9.0	120.9	88.2	14.3	18.3	42.9	38.9	14.3	24.6	78.0	49.3
1956	144.5	9.8	134.6	99.0	14.9	20.7	47.8	43.9	15.5	28.4	86.8	55.1
1957	156.5	10.4	146.1	107.6	15.3	23.2	51.6	47.2	16.5	30.7	94.6	60.4
1958	171.8	11.1	160.7	117.7	16.8	26.1	55.2	50.1	19.7	30.4	105.5	67.6
1959	191.6	12.1	179.5	131.6	18.7	29.2	59.3	53.8	23.8	30.0	120.2	77.7
1960	208.3	12.8	195.4	142.7	20.3	32.4	62.3	56.4	26.7	29.7	133.1	86.3
1961	229.1	13.9	215.1	155.8	23.0	36.4	65.6	59.1	29.5	29.6	149.5	96.7
1962	252.7	15.2	237.5	170.5	25.8	41.1	69.4	62.2	32.3	29.9	168.1	108.3
1963	280.0	16.8	263.1	187.9	29.0	46.2	73.4	65.9	35.0	30.9	189.7	122.0
1964	307.4	18.9	288.4	204.8	33.6	50.0	77.2	69.2	38.3	30.9	211.3	135.6
1965	334.7	21.2	313.5	221.9	37.2	54.5	81.2	73.1	42.0	31.1	232.4	148.8
1966	357.9	23.1	334.8	234.4	40.3	60.1	84.1	76.1	44.8	31.3	250.7	158.3
1967	382.5	25.0	357.4	248.7	43.9	64.8	88.2	79.9	47.4	32.5	269.3	168.8
1968	412.1	27.3	384.8	266.1	47.3	71.4	93.4	84.4	50.6	33.8	291.4	181.6
1969	442.5	29.2	413.3	283.9	52.3	77.1	100.2	90.2	54.5	35.7	313.1	193.7
1970	474.5	30.5	444.0	298.0	60.1	85.8	109.2	97.3	59.9	37.3	334.7	200.8
1971	525.0	32.4	492.7	326.4	70.1	96.2	120.7	105.2	65.7	39.5	371.9	221.2
1972	598.2	35.4	562.9	367.0	82.8	113.1	131.1	113.0	68.2	44.7	431.7	254.1
1973	673.9	39.8	634.1	408.7	93.2	132.3	135.0	116.2	66.2	50.0	499.1	292.4
1974	734.0	44.9	689.1	441.5	100.0	147.5	140.2	121.3	65.1	56.2	548.8	320.2
1975	793.9	49.9	744.0	483.2	100.7	160.1	147.0	127.7	66.1	61.6	597.0	355.5
1976	881.1	55.4	825.7	546.4	105.9	173.4	154.0	133.5	66.5	67.0	671.6	412.9
1977	1,013.0	63.8	949.2	642.5	114.3	192.3	161.7	141.6	68.0	73.6	787.4	500.9
1978	1,165.5	72.8	1,092.8	753.7	125.2	213.9	176.4	153.4	71.4	82.0	916.4	600.3
1979	1,331.5	86.8	1,244.7	870.8	135.0	238.8	199.0	172.9	81.0	92.0	1,045.7	697.9
1980	1,467.6	97.5	1,370.1	969.7	141.1	259.3	225.1	195.2	93.6	101.6	1,145.1	774.5
1981	1,591.5	107.2	1,484.3	1,046.5	139.2	298.6	238.9	207.6	101.3	106.2	1,245.4	838.9
1982	1,676.1	111.3	1,564.8	1,091.1	141.1	332.6	248.9	217.9	108.0	109.9	1,315.9	873.3
1983	1,871.7	113.7	1,757.9	1,214.9	154.3	388.6	279.8	248.8	127.4	121.4	1,478.1	966.1
1984	2,120.6	112.4	2,008.2	1,358.9	177.4	471.9	294.8	265.9	136.7	129.1	1,713.4	1,093.0
1985	2,370.3	94.1	2,276.2	1,528.8	205.9	541.5	328.3	288.8	153.0	135.8	1,947.8	1,240.0
1986	2,657.9	84.0	2,573.9	1,732.8	239.3	601.7	370.5	328.6	185.5	143.1	2,203.4	1,404.2
1987	2,996.2	75.8	2,920.4	1,960.9	262.1	697.4	431.4	387.9	235.5	152.4	2,489.0	1,573.0
1988	3,313.1	70.8	3,242.3	2,194.7	279.0	768.6	459.7	414.2	258.8	155.4	2,782.6	1,780.5
1989	3,585.4	68.8	3,516.6	2,428.1	289.9	798.6	486.8	440.1	282.8	157.3	3,029.8	1,988.0
1990	3,788.2	67.6	3,720.6	2,613.6	288.3	818.8	517.9	470.9	310.9	160.0	3,202.7	2,142.7
1991	3,929.8	67.5	3,862.4	2,771.9	284.1	806.4	537.2	493.3	330.6	162.7	3,325.2	2,278.6
1992	4,043.4	67.9	3,975.5	2,942.0	270.9	762.6	533.3	489.8	326.0	163.8	3,442.2	2,452.2
1993	4,174.8	68.4	4,106.4	3,100.9	267.7	737.8	513.4	469.5	303.2	166.2	3,592.9	2,631.4
1994	4,339.0	69.9	4,269.1	3,278.2	268.2	722.7	559.3	514.2	336.8	177.3	3,709.8	2,764.0
1995	4,524.8	71.7	4,453.0	3,445.4	273.9	733.8	584.3	537.1	352.3	184.7	3,868.8	2,908.3
1996	4,792.4	74.4	4,718.0	3,668.4	286.1	763.5	620.3	571.2	379.2	192.0	4,097.7	3,097.3
1997	5,104.4	78.5	5,025.9	3,902.5	297.9	825.5	656.7	605.7	405.7	200.0	4,369.2	3,296.8
1998	5,589.5	83.1	5,506.4	4,259.0	332.0	915.4	674.1	623.8	417.9	205.9	4,832.4	3,635.2
1999	6,195.1	87.2	6,107.9	4,683.1	372.8	1,052.0	731.5	678.8	462.3	216.5	5,376.4	4,004.3
2000	6,752.6	84.7	6,667.9	5,106.6	402.1	1,159.2	773.1	720.0	499.9	220.1	5,894.8	4,386.6
2001	7,460.4	88.5	7,371.9	5,658.5	444.3	1,269.0	772.7	718.5	497.4	221.2	6,599.2	4,940.0
2002	8,361.2	95.4	8,265.8	6,413.3	483.3	1,369.2	759.3	704.0	486.2	217.7	7,506.5	5,709.3
2003	9,377.5	83.2	9,294.3	7,240.5	557.3	1,496.5	709.2	653.3	438.7	214.6	8,585.1	6,587.2
2004	10,639.5	95.7	10,543.9	8,271.4	604.5	1,667.9	661.5	605.4	398.1	207.3	9,882.4	7,666.0
2005	12,074.1	104.8	11,969.3	9,388.2	665.2	1,915.9	606.6	550.4	348.4	202.0	11,362.7	8,837.8
2006	13,449.5	108.0	13,341.4	10,453.4	701.6	2,186.3	600.2	543.5	336.9	206.6	12,741.3	9,910.0
2007	14,512.9	112.7	14,400.2	11,167.8	784.6	2,447.9	609.2	552.6	342.6	210.0	13,791.1	10,615.2
2008	14,604.6	133.0	14,471.6	11,067.4	837.7	2,566.4	807.2	750.7	534.0	216.7	13,664.3	10,316.7
2009	14,321.8	132.1	14,189.8	10,864.7	847.0	2,478.1	1,005.0	944.3	752.6	191.7	13,184.7	9,920.4
2010	13,813.2	136.2	13,677.0	10,522.0	837.7	2,317.3	1,227.7	1,156.2	934.4	221.8	12,449.2	9,365.8
2010: I	14,148.0	133.4	14,014.6	10,726.4	842.4	2,445.9	1,069.5	1,006.1	806.9	199.1	12,945.1	9,720.3
II	14,032.6	133.7	13,898.9	10,660.3	838.8	2,399.8	1,129.9	1,063.0	856.7	206.3	12,769.0	9,597.3
III	13,910.3	135.0	13,775.3	10,581.4	839.6	2,354.4	1,182.4	1,113.4	898.5	214.9	12,592.9	9,468.0
IV	13,813.2	136.2	13,677.0	10,522.0	837.7	2,317.3	1,227.7	1,156.2	934.4	221.8	12,449.2	9,365.8
2011: I	13,718.7	135.2	13,583.5	10,450.4	838.9	2,294.2	1,269.2	1,196.6	966.4	230.2	12,314.3	9,253.8
II	13,641.3	134.2	13,507.1	10,395.5	839.7	2,271.9	1,307.7	1,233.3	994.6	238.7	12,199.4	9,162.2
III p	13,559.1	133.1	13,426.0	10,336.1	840.9	2,249.0	1,360.0	1,283.5	1,035.2	248.2	12,066.0	9,052.6

[1] Includes Federal Housing Administration (FHA)–insured multi-family properties, not shown separately.
[2] Derived figures. Total includes multi-family and commercial properties with conventional mortgages, not shown separately.

Source: Board of Governors of the Federal Reserve System, based on data from various Government and private organizations.

[Billions of dollars]

End of year or quarter	Total	Major financial institutions				Other holders	
		Total	Savings institutions [1]	Commercial banks [2]	Life insurance companies	Federal and related agencies [3]	Individuals and others [4]
1954	113.6	85.7	41.1	18.6	26.0	4.7	23.2
1955	129.9	99.3	48.9	21.0	29.4	5.3	25.3
1956	144.5	111.2	55.5	22.7	33.0	6.2	27.1
1957	156.5	119.7	61.2	23.3	35.2	7.7	29.1
1958	171.8	131.5	68.9	25.5	37.1	8.0	32.3
1959	191.6	145.5	78.1	28.1	39.2	10.2	35.9
1960	208.3	157.5	86.9	28.8	41.8	11.5	39.3
1961	229.1	172.6	98.0	30.4	44.2	12.2	44.2
1962	252.7	192.5	111.1	34.5	46.9	12.6	47.6
1963	280.0	217.1	127.2	39.4	50.5	11.8	51.0
1964	307.4	241.0	141.9	44.0	55.2	12.2	54.1
1965	334.7	264.6	154.9	49.7	60.0	13.5	56.6
1966	357.9	280.7	161.8	54.4	64.6	17.5	59.7
1967	382.5	298.7	172.3	58.9	67.5	20.9	62.8
1968	412.1	319.7	184.3	65.5	70.0	25.1	67.3
1969	442.5	338.9	196.4	70.5	72.0	31.1	72.4
1970	474.5	355.9	208.3	73.3	74.4	38.3	80.2
1971	525.0	394.2	236.2	82.5	75.5	46.3	84.5
1972	598.2	449.9	273.6	99.3	76.9	54.5	93.8
1973	673.9	505.4	305.0	119.1	81.4	64.7	103.9
1974	734.0	542.6	324.2	132.1	86.2	82.2	109.2
1975	793.9	581.2	355.8	136.2	89.2	101.1	111.5
1976	881.1	647.5	404.6	151.3	91.6	116.7	116.9
1977	1,013.0	745.2	469.4	179.0	96.8	140.5	127.3
1978	1,165.5	848.2	528.0	214.0	106.2	170.6	146.8
1979	1,331.5	938.2	574.6	245.2	118.4	216.0	177.3
1980	1,467.6	996.8	603.1	262.7	131.1	256.8	214.0
1981	1,591.5	1,040.5	618.5	284.2	137.7	289.4	261.6
1982	1,676.1	1,021.3	578.1	301.3	142.0	355.4	299.4
1983	1,871.7	1,108.1	626.6	330.5	151.0	433.3	330.2
1984	2,120.6	1,247.8	709.7	381.4	156.7	490.6	382.3
1985	2,370.3	1,363.5	760.5	431.2	171.8	580.9	425.8
1986	2,657.9	1,476.5	778.0	504.7	193.8	733.7	447.7
1987	2,996.2	1,667.6	860.5	594.8	212.4	857.9	470.7
1988	3,313.1	1,834.3	924.5	676.9	232.9	937.8	541.1
1989	3,585.4	1,935.2	910.3	770.7	254.2	1,067.3	582.9
1990	3,788.2	1,918.8	801.6	849.3	267.9	1,258.9	610.5
1991	3,929.8	1,846.2	705.4	881.3	259.5	1,422.5	661.2
1992	4,043.4	1,770.4	627.9	900.5	242.0	1,558.1	714.9
1993	4,174.8	1,770.1	598.4	947.8	223.9	1,682.8	721.8
1994	4,339.0	1,824.7	596.2	1,012.7	215.8	1,788.0	726.4
1995	4,524.8	1,900.1	596.8	1,090.2	213.1	1,878.7	746.0
1996	4,792.4	1,981.9	628.3	1,145.4	208.2	2,006.1	804.5
1997	5,104.4	2,084.0	631.8	1,245.3	206.8	2,111.4	909.0
1998	5,589.5	2,194.6	644.0	1,337.0	213.6	2,310.9	1,084.1
1999	6,195.1	2,394.3	668.1	1,495.4	230.8	2,613.3	1,187.5
2000	6,752.6	2,619.0	723.0	1,660.1	235.9	2,833.2	1,300.5
2001	7,460.4	2,790.9	758.0	1,789.8	243.0	3,203.8	1,465.8
2002	8,361.2	3,089.3	781.0	2,058.3	250.0	3,590.9	1,681.0
2003	9,377.5	3,387.3	870.6	2,255.8	260.9	4,037.4	1,952.8
2004	10,639.5	3,926.3	1,057.4	2,595.6	273.3	4,087.2	2,626.0
2005	12,074.1	4,396.2	1,152.7	2,958.0	285.5	4,213.9	3,464.0
2006	13,449.5	4,783.6	1,076.8	3,403.1	303.8	4,528.6	4,137.3
2007	14,512.9	5,064.6	1,094.0	3,644.4	326.2	5,189.9	4,258.5
2008	14,604.6	5,044.4	860.6	3,841.3	342.4	5,762.6	3,797.6
2009	14,321.8	4,778.1	633.3	3,818.6	326.1	6,192.8	3,351.0
2010	13,813.2	4,583.5	614.8	3,651.2	317.5	6,267.0	2,962.6
2010: I	14,148.0	4,711.9	629.3	3,761.2	321.4	6,191.7	3,244.4
II	14,032.6	4,644.0	619.3	3,706.8	317.9	6,239.3	3,149.4
III	13,910.3	4,610.3	617.8	3,674.4	318.2	6,238.3	3,061.6
IV	13,813.2	4,583.5	614.8	3,651.2	317.5	6,267.0	2,962.6
2011: I	13,718.7	4,469.6	600.2	3,550.9	318.4	6,349.3	2,899.8
II	13,641.3	4,436.0	590.9	3,521.9	323.1	6,363.8	2,841.6
III _p_	13,559.1	4,433.8	589.3	3,515.3	329.2	6,351.2	2,774.1

[1] Includes savings banks and savings and loan associations. Data reported by Federal Savings and Loan Insurance Corporation–insured institutions include loans in process for 1987 and exclude loans in process beginning with 1988.

[2] Includes loans held by nondeposit trust companies but not loans held by bank trust departments.

[3] Includes Government National Mortgage Association (GNMA or Ginnie Mae), Federal Housing Administration, Veterans Administration, Farmers Home Administration (FmHA), Federal Deposit Insurance Corporation, Resolution Trust Corporation (through 1995), and in earlier years Reconstruction Finance Corporation, Homeowners Loan Corporation, Federal Farm Mortgage Corporation, and Public Housing Administration. Also includes U.S.-sponsored agencies such as Federal National Mortgage Association (FNMA or Fannie Mae), Federal Land Banks, Federal Home Loan Mortgage Corporation (FHLMC or Freddie Mac), Federal Agricultural Mortgage Corporation (Farmer Mac, beginning 1994), Federal Home Loan Banks (beginning 1997), and mortgage pass-through securities issued or guaranteed by GNMA, FHLMC, FNMA, FmHA, or Farmer Mac. Other U.S. agencies (amounts small or current separate data not readily available) included with "individuals and others."

[4] Includes private mortgage pools.

Source: Board of Governors of the Federal Reserve System, based on data from various Government and private organizations.

[Amount outstanding (end of month); millions of dollars, seasonally adjusted]

Year and month	Total consumer credit [1]	Revolving	Nonrevolving [2]
December:			
1960	60,025.31		60,025.31
1961	62,248.53		62,248.53
1962	68,126.72		68,126.72
1963	76,581.45		76,581.45
1964	85,959.57		85,959.57
1965	95,954.72		95,954.72
1966	101,788.22		101,788.22
1967	106,842.64		106,842.64
1968	117,399.09	2,041.54	115,357.55
1969	127,156.18	3,604.84	123,551.35
1970	131,551.55	4,961.46	126,590.09
1971	146,930.18	8,245.33	138,684.84
1972	166,189.10	9,379.24	156,809.86
1973	190,086.31	11,342.22	178,744.09
1974	198,917.84	13,241.26	185,676.58
1975	204,002.00	14,495.27	189,506.73
1976	225,721.59	16,489.05	209,232.54
1977	260,562.70	37,414.82	223,147.88
1978	306,100.39	45,690.95	260,409.43
1979	348,589.11	53,596.43	294,992.67
1980	351,920.05	54,970.05	296,950.00
1981	371,301.44	60,928.00	310,373.44
1982	389,848.74	66,348.30	323,500.44
1983	437,068.86	79,027.25	358,041.61
1984	517,278.98	100,385.63	416,893.35
1985	599,711.23	124,465.80	475,245.43
1986	654,750.24	141,068.15	513,682.08
1987	686,318.77	160,853.91	525,464.86
1988 [3]	731,917.76	184,593.12	547,324.64
1989	794,612.18	211,229.83	583,382.34
1990	808,230.57	238,642.62	569,587.95
1991	798,028.97	263,768.55	534,260.42
1992	806,118.69	278,449.67	527,669.02
1993	865,650.58	309,908.02	555,742.56
1994	997,301.74	365,569.56	631,732.19
1995	1,140,744.36	443,920.09	696,824.27
1996	1,253,437.09	507,516.57	745,920.52
1997	1,324,757.33	540,005.56	784,751.77
1998	1,420,996.44	581,414.78	839,581.66
1999	1,531,105.96	610,696.47	920,409.49
2000	1,716,969.72	682,646.37	1,034,323.35
2001	1,867,852.87	714,840.73	1,153,012.14
2002	1,972,112.21	750,947.45	1,221,164.76
2003	2,077,360.69	768,258.31	1,309,102.38
2004	2,192,246.17	799,552.18	1,392,693.99
2005	2,290,928.13	829,518.36	1,461,409.78
2006	2,384,905.42	871,024.51	1,513,880.91
2007	2,522,548.77	941,852.88	1,580,695.89
2008	2,561,810.03	957,484.09	1,604,325.94
2009	2,450,146.97	865,497.83	1,584,649.14
2010	2,408,335.19	800,226.54	1,608,108.65
2010: Jan	2,445,629.19	856,247.67	1,589,381.52
Feb	2,435,717.83	848,732.38	1,586,985.45
Mar	2,426,343.06	842,563.18	1,583,779.88
Apr	2,415,822.44	832,580.37	1,583,242.07
May	2,411,110.86	831,131.00	1,579,979.86
June	2,406,399.97	826,306.08	1,580,093.89
July	2,399,442.23	819,347.78	1,580,094.45
Aug	2,394,941.35	813,209.33	1,581,732.01
Sept	2,393,620.01	805,398.86	1,588,221.15
Oct	2,399,504.10	801,545.69	1,597,958.41
Nov	2,402,026.97	798,048.77	1,603,978.20
Dec	2,408,335.19	800,226.54	1,608,108.65
2011: Jan	2,408,942.15	794,655.72	1,614,286.43
Feb	2,417,131.18	792,785.39	1,624,345.79
Mar	2,421,459.15	792,837.73	1,628,621.42
Apr	2,425,173.67	790,302.10	1,634,871.57
May	2,431,166.37	793,318.77	1,637,847.60
June	2,442,872.56	795,896.81	1,646,975.75
July	2,454,261.23	793,160.98	1,661,100.25
Aug	2,443,774.05	791,556.20	1,652,217.85
Sept	2,451,280.62	791,985.20	1,659,295.42
Oct	2,457,303.07	792,671.13	1,664,631.94
Nov [p]	2,477,676.79	798,267.21	1,679,409.58

[1] Covers most short- and intermediate-term credit extended to individuals. Credit secured by real estate is excluded.

[2] Includes automobile loans and all other loans not included in revolving credit, such as loans for mobile homes, education, boats, trailers, or vacations. These loans may be secured or unsecured. Beginning with 1977, includes student loans extended by the Federal Government and by SLM Holding Corporation.

[3] Data newly available in January 1989 result in breaks in these series between December 1988 and subsequent months.

Source: Board of Governors of the Federal Reserve System.

TABLE B–78. Federal receipts, outlays, surplus or deficit, and debt, fiscal years, 1945–2013

[Billions of dollars; fiscal years]

Fiscal year or period	Total			On-budget			Off-budget			Federal debt (end of period)		Addendum: Gross domestic product
	Receipts	Outlays	Surplus or deficit (–)	Receipts	Outlays	Surplus or deficit (–)	Receipts	Outlays	Surplus or deficit (–)	Gross Federal	Held by the public	
1945	45.2	92.7	–47.6	43.8	92.6	–48.7	1.3	0.1	1.2	260.1	235.2	221.4
1946	39.3	55.2	–15.9	38.1	55.0	–17.0	1.2	.2	1.0	271.0	241.9	222.6
1947	38.5	34.5	4.0	37.1	34.2	2.9	1.5	.3	1.2	257.1	224.3	233.2
1948	41.6	29.8	11.8	39.9	29.4	10.5	1.6	.4	1.2	252.0	216.3	256.6
1949	39.4	38.8	.6	37.7	38.4	–.7	1.7	.4	1.3	252.6	214.3	271.3
1950	39.4	42.6	–3.1	37.3	42.0	–4.7	2.1	.5	1.6	256.9	219.0	273.1
1951	51.6	45.5	6.1	48.5	44.2	4.3	3.1	1.3	1.8	255.3	214.3	320.2
1952	66.2	67.7	–1.5	62.6	66.0	–3.4	3.6	1.7	1.9	259.1	214.8	348.7
1953	69.6	76.1	–6.5	65.5	73.8	–8.3	4.1	2.3	1.8	266.0	218.4	372.5
1954	69.7	70.9	–1.2	65.1	67.9	–2.8	4.6	2.9	1.7	270.8	224.5	377.0
1955	65.5	68.4	–3.0	60.4	64.5	–4.1	5.1	4.0	1.1	274.4	226.6	395.9
1956	74.6	70.6	3.9	68.2	65.7	2.5	6.4	5.0	1.5	272.7	222.2	427.0
1957	80.0	76.6	3.4	73.2	70.6	2.6	6.8	6.0	.8	272.3	219.3	450.9
1958	79.6	82.4	–2.8	71.6	74.9	–3.3	8.0	7.5	.5	279.7	226.3	460.0
1959	79.2	92.1	–12.8	71.0	83.1	–12.1	8.3	9.0	–.7	287.5	234.7	490.2
1960	92.5	92.2	.3	81.9	81.3	.5	10.6	10.9	–.2	290.5	236.8	518.9
1961	94.4	97.7	–3.3	82.3	86.0	–3.8	12.1	11.7	.4	292.6	238.4	529.9
1962	99.7	106.8	–7.1	87.4	93.3	–5.9	12.3	13.5	–1.3	302.9	248.0	567.8
1963	106.6	111.3	–4.8	92.4	96.4	–4.0	14.2	15.0	–.8	310.3	254.0	599.2
1964	112.6	118.5	–5.9	96.2	102.8	–6.5	16.4	15.7	.6	316.1	256.8	641.5
1965	116.8	118.2	–1.4	100.1	101.7	–1.6	16.7	16.5	.2	322.3	260.8	687.5
1966	130.8	134.5	–3.7	111.7	114.8	–3.1	19.1	19.7	–.6	328.5	263.7	755.8
1967	148.8	157.5	–8.6	124.4	137.0	–12.6	24.4	20.4	4.0	340.4	266.6	810.0
1968	153.0	178.1	–25.2	128.1	155.8	–27.7	24.9	22.3	2.6	368.7	289.5	868.4
1969	186.9	183.6	3.2	157.9	158.4	–.5	29.0	25.2	3.7	365.8	278.1	948.1
1970	192.8	195.6	–2.8	159.3	168.0	–8.7	33.5	27.6	5.9	380.9	283.2	1,012.7
1971	187.1	210.2	–23.0	151.3	177.3	–26.1	35.8	32.8	3.0	408.2	303.0	1,080.0
1972	207.3	230.7	–23.4	167.4	193.5	–26.1	39.9	37.2	2.7	435.9	322.4	1,176.5
1973	230.8	245.7	–14.9	184.7	200.0	–15.2	46.1	45.7	.3	466.3	340.9	1,310.6
1974	263.2	269.4	–6.1	209.3	216.5	–7.2	53.9	52.9	1.1	483.9	343.7	1,438.5
1975	279.1	332.3	–53.2	216.6	270.8	–54.1	62.5	61.6	.9	541.9	394.7	1,560.2
1976	298.1	371.8	–73.7	231.7	301.1	–69.4	66.4	70.7	–4.3	629.0	477.4	1,738.1
Transition quarter	81.2	96.0	–14.7	63.2	77.3	–14.1	18.0	18.7	–.7	643.6	495.5	459.4
1977	355.6	409.2	–53.7	278.7	328.7	–49.9	76.8	80.5	–3.7	706.4	549.1	1,973.5
1978	399.6	458.7	–59.2	314.2	369.6	–55.4	85.4	89.2	–3.8	776.6	607.1	2,217.5
1979	463.3	504.0	–40.7	365.3	404.9	–39.6	98.0	99.1	–1.1	829.5	640.3	2,501.4
1980	517.1	590.9	–73.8	403.9	477.0	–73.1	113.2	113.9	–.7	909.0	711.9	2,724.2
1981	599.3	678.2	–79.0	469.1	543.0	–73.9	130.2	135.3	–5.1	994.8	789.4	3,057.0
1982	617.8	745.7	–128.0	474.3	594.9	–120.6	143.5	150.9	–7.4	1,137.3	924.6	3,223.7
1983	600.6	808.4	–207.8	453.2	660.9	–207.7	147.3	147.4	–.1	1,371.7	1,137.3	3,440.7
1984	666.4	851.8	–185.4	500.4	685.6	–185.3	166.1	166.2	–.1	1,564.6	1,307.0	3,844.4
1985	734.0	946.3	–212.3	547.9	769.4	–221.5	186.2	176.9	9.2	1,817.4	1,507.3	4,146.3
1986	769.2	990.4	–221.2	568.9	806.8	–237.9	200.2	183.5	16.7	2,120.5	1,740.6	4,403.9
1987	854.3	1,004.0	–149.7	640.9	809.2	–168.4	213.4	194.8	18.6	2,346.0	1,889.8	4,651.4
1988	909.2	1,064.4	–155.2	667.7	860.0	–192.3	241.5	204.4	37.1	2,601.1	2,051.6	5,008.5
1989	991.1	1,143.7	–152.6	727.4	932.8	–205.4	263.7	210.9	52.8	2,867.8	2,190.7	5,399.5
1990	1,032.0	1,253.0	–221.0	750.3	1,027.9	–277.6	281.7	225.1	56.6	3,206.3	2,411.6	5,734.5
1991	1,055.0	1,324.2	–269.2	761.1	1,082.5	–321.4	293.9	241.7	52.2	3,598.2	2,689.0	5,930.5
1992	1,091.2	1,381.5	–290.3	788.8	1,129.2	–340.4	302.4	252.3	50.1	4,001.8	2,999.7	6,242.0
1993	1,154.3	1,409.4	–255.1	842.4	1,142.8	–300.4	311.9	266.6	45.3	4,351.0	3,248.4	6,587.3
1994	1,258.6	1,461.8	–203.2	923.5	1,182.4	–258.8	335.0	279.4	55.7	4,643.3	3,433.1	6,976.6
1995	1,351.8	1,515.7	–164.0	1,000.7	1,227.1	–226.4	351.1	288.7	62.4	4,920.6	3,604.4	7,341.1
1996	1,453.1	1,560.5	–107.4	1,085.6	1,259.6	–174.0	367.5	300.9	66.6	5,181.5	3,734.1	7,718.3
1997	1,579.2	1,601.1	–21.9	1,187.2	1,290.5	–103.2	392.0	310.6	81.4	5,369.2	3,772.3	8,211.7
1998	1,721.7	1,652.5	69.3	1,305.9	1,335.9	–29.9	415.8	316.6	99.2	5,478.2	3,721.1	8,663.0
1999	1,827.5	1,701.8	125.6	1,383.0	1,381.1	1.9	444.5	320.8	123.7	5,605.5	3,632.4	9,208.4
2000	2,025.2	1,789.0	236.2	1,544.6	1,458.2	86.4	480.6	330.8	149.8	5,628.7	3,409.8	9,821.0
2001	1,991.1	1,862.8	128.2	1,483.6	1,516.0	–32.4	507.5	346.8	160.7	5,769.9	3,319.6	10,225.3
2002	1,853.1	2,010.9	–157.8	1,337.8	1,655.2	–317.4	515.3	355.7	159.7	6,198.4	3,540.4	10,543.9
2003	1,782.3	2,159.9	–377.6	1,258.5	1,796.9	–538.4	523.8	363.0	160.8	6,760.0	3,913.4	10,980.2
2004	1,880.1	2,292.8	–412.7	1,345.4	1,913.3	–568.0	534.7	379.5	155.2	7,354.7	4,295.5	11,676.0
2005	2,153.6	2,472.0	–318.3	1,576.1	2,069.7	–493.6	577.5	402.2	175.3	7,905.3	4,592.2	12,428.6
2006	2,406.9	2,655.1	–248.2	1,798.5	2,233.0	–434.5	608.4	422.1	186.3	8,451.4	4,829.0	13,206.5
2007	2,568.0	2,728.7	–160.7	1,932.9	2,275.0	–342.2	635.1	453.6	181.5	8,950.7	5,035.1	13,861.4
2008	2,524.0	2,982.5	–458.6	1,865.9	2,507.8	–641.8	658.0	474.8	183.3	9,986.1	5,803.1	14,334.4
2009	2,105.0	3,517.7	–1,412.7	1,451.0	3,000.7	–1,549.7	654.0	517.0	137.0	11,875.9	7,544.7	13,937.5
2010	2,162.7	3,456.2	–1,293.5	1,531.0	2,901.5	–1,370.5	631.7	554.7	77.0	13,528.8	9,018.9	14,359.7
2011	2,303.5	3,603.1	–1,299.6	1,737.7	3,104.5	–1,366.8	565.8	498.6	67.2	14,764.2	10,128.2	14,958.6
2012 (estimates)	2,468.6	3,795.5	–1,326.9	1,896.5	3,290.4	–1,393.9	572.1	505.2	67.0	16,350.9	11,578.1	15,601.5
2013 (estimates)	2,902.0	3,803.4	–901.4	2,224.5	3,169.3	–944.7	677.4	634.1	43.3	17,547.9	12,636.7	16,335.0

Note: Fiscal years through 1976 were on a July 1–June 30 basis; beginning with October 1976 (fiscal year 1977), the fiscal year is on an October 1–September 30 basis. The transition quarter is the three-month period from July 1, 1976 through September 30, 1976.

See *Budget of the United States Government, Fiscal Year 2013,* for additional information.

Sources: Department of Commerce (Bureau of Economic Analysis), Department of the Treasury, and Office of Management and Budget.

TABLE B–79. Federal receipts, outlays, surplus or deficit, and debt, as percent of gross domestic product, fiscal years 1939–2013

[Percent; fiscal years]

Fiscal year or period	Receipts	Outlays		Surplus or deficit (−)	Federal debt (end of period)	
		Total	National defense		Gross Federal	Held by public
1939	7.1	10.3	....	−3.2	54.0	46.5
1940	6.8	9.8	1.7	−3.0	52.4	44.2
1941	7.6	12.0	5.6	−4.3	50.4	42.3
1942	10.1	24.3	17.8	−14.2	54.9	47.0
1943	13.3	43.6	37.0	−30.3	79.1	70.9
1944	20.9	43.6	37.8	−22.7	97.6	88.3
1945	20.4	41.9	37.5	−21.5	117.5	106.2
1946	17.7	24.8	19.2	−7.2	121.7	108.7
1947	16.5	14.8	5.5	1.7	110.3	96.2
1948	16.2	11.6	3.5	4.6	98.2	84.3
1949	14.5	14.3	4.8	.2	93.1	79.0
1950	14.4	15.6	5.0	−1.1	94.1	80.2
1951	16.1	14.2	7.4	1.9	79.7	66.9
1952	19.0	19.4	13.2	−.4	74.3	61.6
1953	18.7	20.4	14.2	−1.7	71.4	58.6
1954	18.5	18.8	13.1	−.3	71.8	59.5
1955	16.5	17.3	10.8	−.8	69.3	57.2
1956	17.5	16.5	10.0	.9	63.9	52.0
1957	17.7	17.0	10.1	.8	60.4	48.6
1958	17.3	17.9	10.2	−.6	60.8	49.2
1959	16.2	18.8	10.0	−2.6	58.6	47.9
1960	17.8	17.8	9.3	.1	56.0	45.6
1961	17.8	18.4	9.4	−.6	55.2	45.0
1962	17.6	18.8	9.2	−1.3	53.4	43.7
1963	17.8	18.6	8.9	−.8	51.8	42.4
1964	17.6	18.5	8.5	−.9	49.3	40.0
1965	17.0	17.2	7.4	−.2	46.9	37.9
1966	17.3	17.8	7.7	−.5	43.5	34.9
1967	18.4	19.4	8.8	−1.1	42.0	32.9
1968	17.6	20.5	9.4	−2.9	42.5	33.3
1969	19.7	19.4	8.7	.3	38.6	29.3
1970	19.0	19.3	8.1	−.3	37.6	28.0
1971	17.3	19.5	7.3	−2.1	37.8	28.1
1972	17.6	19.6	6.7	−2.0	37.1	27.4
1973	17.6	18.7	5.9	−1.1	35.6	26.0
1974	18.3	18.7	5.5	−.4	33.6	23.9
1975	17.9	21.3	5.5	−3.4	34.7	25.3
1976	17.1	21.4	5.2	−4.2	36.2	27.5
Transition quarter	17.7	20.9	4.8	−3.2	35.0	27.0
1977	18.0	20.7	4.9	−2.7	35.8	27.8
1978	18.0	20.7	4.7	−2.7	35.0	27.4
1979	18.5	20.1	4.7	−1.6	33.2	25.6
1980	19.0	21.7	4.9	−2.7	33.4	26.1
1981	19.6	22.2	5.2	−2.6	32.5	25.8
1982	19.2	23.1	5.7	−4.0	35.3	28.7
1983	17.5	23.5	6.1	−6.0	39.9	33.1
1984	17.3	22.2	5.9	−4.8	40.7	34.0
1985	17.7	22.8	6.1	−5.1	43.8	36.4
1986	17.5	22.5	6.2	−5.0	48.2	39.5
1987	18.4	21.6	6.1	−3.2	50.4	40.6
1988	18.2	21.3	5.8	−3.1	51.9	41.0
1989	18.4	21.2	5.6	−2.8	53.1	40.6
1990	18.0	21.9	5.2	−3.9	55.9	42.1
1991	17.8	22.3	4.6	−4.5	60.7	45.3
1992	17.5	22.1	4.8	−4.7	64.1	48.1
1993	17.5	21.4	4.4	−3.9	66.1	49.3
1994	18.0	21.0	4.0	−2.9	66.6	49.2
1995	18.4	20.6	3.7	−2.2	67.0	49.1
1996	18.8	20.2	3.4	−1.4	67.1	48.4
1997	19.2	19.5	3.3	−.3	65.4	45.9
1998	19.9	19.1	3.1	.8	63.2	43.0
1999	19.8	18.5	3.0	1.4	60.9	39.4
2000	20.6	18.2	3.0	2.4	57.3	34.7
2001	19.5	18.2	3.0	1.3	56.4	32.5
2002	17.6	19.1	3.3	−1.5	58.8	33.6
2003	16.2	19.7	3.7	−3.4	61.6	35.6
2004	16.1	19.6	3.9	−3.5	63.0	36.8
2005	17.3	19.9	4.0	−2.6	63.6	36.9
2006	18.2	20.1	4.0	−1.9	64.0	36.6
2007	18.5	19.7	4.0	−1.2	64.6	36.3
2008	17.6	20.8	4.3	−3.2	69.7	40.5
2009	15.1	25.2	4.7	−10.1	85.2	54.1
2010	15.1	24.1	4.8	−9.0	94.2	62.8
2011	15.4	24.1	4.7	−8.7	98.7	67.7
2012 (estimates)	15.8	24.3	4.6	−8.5	104.8	74.2
2013 (estimates)	17.8	23.3	4.3	−5.5	107.4	77.4

Note: See Note, Table B–78.

Sources: Department of the Treasury and Office of Management and Budget.

TABLE B–80. Federal receipts and outlays, by major category, and surplus or deficit, fiscal years 1945–2013

[Billions of dollars; fiscal years]

Fiscal year or period	Receipts (on-budget and off-budget)					Outlays (on-budget and off-budget)										Surplus or deficit (–) (on-budget and off-budget)
	Total	Individual income taxes	Corporation income taxes	Social insurance and retirement receipts	Other	Total	National defense Total	National defense Department of Defense, military	International affairs	Health	Medicare	Income security	Social security	Net interest	Other	
1945	45.2	18.4	16.0	3.5	7.3	92.7	83.0	....	1.9	0.2	....	1.1	0.3	3.1	3.1	–47.6
1946	39.3	16.1	11.9	3.1	8.2	55.2	42.7	....	1.9	.2	....	2.4	.4	4.1	3.6	–15.9
1947	38.5	17.9	8.6	3.4	8.5	34.5	12.8	....	5.8	.2	....	2.8	.5	4.2	8.2	4.0
1948	41.6	19.3	9.7	3.8	8.8	29.8	9.1	....	4.6	.2	....	2.5	.6	4.3	8.5	11.8
1949	39.4	15.6	11.2	3.8	8.9	38.8	13.2	....	6.1	.2	....	3.2	.7	4.5	11.1	.6
1950	39.4	15.8	10.4	4.3	8.9	42.6	13.7	....	4.7	.3	....	4.1	.8	4.8	14.2	–3.1
1951	51.6	21.6	14.1	5.7	10.2	45.5	23.6	....	3.6	.3	....	3.4	1.6	4.7	8.4	6.1
1952	66.2	27.9	21.2	6.4	10.6	67.7	46.1	....	2.7	.3	....	3.7	2.1	4.7	8.1	–1.5
1953	69.6	29.8	21.2	6.8	11.7	76.1	52.8	....	2.1	.3	....	3.8	2.7	5.2	9.1	–6.5
1954	69.7	29.5	21.1	7.2	11.9	70.9	49.3	....	1.6	.3	....	4.4	3.4	4.8	7.1	–1.2
1955	65.5	28.7	17.9	7.9	11.0	68.4	42.7	....	2.2	.3	....	5.1	4.4	4.9	8.9	–3.0
1956	74.6	32.2	20.9	9.3	12.2	70.6	42.5	....	2.4	.4	....	4.7	5.5	5.1	10.1	3.9
1957	80.0	35.6	21.2	10.0	13.2	76.6	45.4	....	3.1	.5	....	5.4	6.7	5.4	10.1	3.4
1958	79.6	34.7	20.1	11.2	13.6	82.4	46.8	....	3.4	.5	....	7.5	8.2	5.6	10.3	–2.8
1959	79.2	36.7	17.3	11.7	13.5	92.1	49.0	....	3.1	.7	....	8.2	9.7	5.8	15.5	–12.8
1960	92.5	40.7	21.5	14.7	15.6	92.2	48.1	....	3.0	.8	....	7.4	11.6	6.9	14.4	.3
1961	94.4	41.3	21.0	16.4	15.7	97.7	49.6	....	3.2	.9	....	9.7	12.5	6.7	15.2	–3.3
1962	99.7	45.6	20.5	17.0	16.5	106.8	52.3	50.1	5.6	1.2	....	9.2	14.4	6.9	17.2	–7.1
1963	106.6	47.6	21.6	19.8	17.6	111.3	53.4	51.1	5.3	1.5	....	9.3	15.8	7.7	18.3	–4.8
1964	112.6	48.7	23.5	22.0	18.5	118.5	54.8	52.6	4.9	1.8	....	9.7	16.6	8.2	22.6	–5.9
1965	116.8	48.8	25.5	22.2	20.3	118.2	50.6	48.8	5.3	1.8	....	9.5	17.5	8.6	25.0	–1.4
1966	130.8	55.4	30.1	25.5	19.8	134.5	58.1	56.6	5.6	2.5	0.1	9.7	20.7	9.4	28.5	–3.7
1967	148.8	61.5	34.0	32.6	20.7	157.5	71.4	70.1	5.6	3.4	2.7	10.3	21.7	10.3	32.1	–8.6
1968	153.0	68.7	28.7	33.9	21.7	178.1	81.9	80.4	5.3	4.4	4.6	11.8	23.9	11.1	35.1	–25.2
1969	186.9	87.2	36.7	39.0	23.9	183.6	82.5	80.8	4.6	5.2	5.7	13.1	27.3	12.7	32.6	3.2
1970	192.8	90.4	32.8	44.4	25.2	195.6	81.7	80.1	4.3	5.9	6.2	15.7	30.3	14.4	37.2	–2.8
1971	187.1	86.2	26.8	47.3	26.8	210.2	78.9	77.5	4.2	6.8	6.6	22.9	35.9	14.8	40.0	–23.0
1972	207.3	94.7	32.2	52.6	27.8	230.7	79.2	77.6	4.8	8.7	7.5	27.7	40.2	15.5	47.3	–23.4
1973	230.8	103.2	36.2	63.1	28.3	245.7	76.7	75.0	4.1	9.4	8.1	28.3	49.1	17.3	52.8	–14.9
1974	263.2	119.0	38.6	75.1	30.6	269.4	79.3	77.9	5.7	10.7	9.6	33.7	55.9	21.4	52.9	–6.1
1975	279.1	122.4	40.6	84.5	31.5	332.3	86.5	84.9	7.1	12.9	12.9	50.2	64.7	23.2	74.8	–53.2
1976	298.1	131.6	41.4	90.8	34.3	371.8	89.6	87.9	6.4	15.7	15.8	60.8	73.9	26.7	82.7	–73.7
Transition quarter	81.2	38.8	8.5	25.2	8.8	96.0	22.3	21.8	2.5	3.9	4.3	15.0	19.8	6.9	21.4	–14.7
1977	355.6	157.6	54.9	106.5	36.6	409.2	97.2	95.1	6.4	17.3	19.3	61.1	85.1	29.9	93.0	–53.7
1978	399.6	181.0	60.0	121.0	37.7	458.7	104.5	102.3	7.5	18.5	22.8	61.5	93.9	35.5	114.7	–59.2
1979	463.3	217.8	65.7	138.9	40.8	504.0	116.3	113.6	7.5	20.5	26.5	66.4	104.1	42.6	120.2	–40.7
1980	517.1	244.1	64.6	157.8	50.6	590.9	134.0	130.9	12.7	23.2	32.1	86.6	118.5	52.5	131.3	–73.8
1981	599.3	285.9	61.1	182.7	69.5	678.2	157.5	153.9	13.1	26.9	39.1	100.3	139.6	68.8	133.0	–79.0
1982	617.8	297.7	49.2	201.5	69.3	745.7	185.3	180.7	12.3	27.4	46.6	108.2	156.0	85.0	125.0	–128.0
1983	600.6	288.9	37.0	209.0	65.6	808.4	209.9	204.4	11.8	28.6	52.6	123.0	170.7	89.8	121.8	–207.8
1984	666.4	298.4	56.9	239.4	71.8	851.8	227.4	220.9	15.9	30.4	57.5	113.4	178.2	111.1	117.9	–185.4
1985	734.0	334.5	61.3	265.2	73.0	946.3	252.7	245.1	16.2	33.5	65.8	129.0	188.6	129.5	131.0	–212.3
1986	769.2	349.0	63.1	283.9	73.2	990.4	273.4	265.4	14.1	35.9	70.2	120.6	198.8	136.0	141.4	–221.2
1987	854.3	392.6	83.9	303.3	74.5	1,004.0	282.0	273.9	11.6	40.0	75.1	124.1	207.4	138.6	125.2	–149.7
1988	909.2	401.2	94.5	334.3	79.2	1,064.4	290.4	281.9	10.5	44.5	78.9	130.4	219.3	151.8	138.7	–155.2
1989	991.1	445.7	103.3	359.4	82.7	1,143.7	303.6	294.8	9.6	48.4	85.0	137.4	232.5	169.0	158.3	–152.6
1990	1,032.0	466.9	93.5	380.0	91.5	1,253.0	299.3	289.7	13.8	57.7	98.1	148.7	248.6	184.3	202.5	–221.0
1991	1,055.0	467.8	98.1	396.0	93.1	1,324.2	273.3	262.3	15.8	71.2	104.5	172.5	269.0	194.4	223.5	–269.2
1992	1,091.2	476.0	100.3	413.7	101.3	1,381.5	298.3	286.8	16.1	89.5	119.0	199.6	287.6	199.3	172.1	–290.3
1993	1,154.3	509.7	117.5	428.3	98.8	1,409.4	291.1	278.5	17.2	99.4	130.6	210.0	304.6	198.7	157.9	–255.1
1994	1,258.6	543.1	140.4	461.5	113.7	1,461.8	281.6	268.6	17.1	107.1	144.7	217.2	319.6	202.9	171.5	–203.2
1995	1,351.8	590.2	157.0	484.5	120.1	1,515.7	272.1	259.4	16.4	115.4	159.9	223.8	335.8	232.1	160.2	–164.0
1996	1,453.1	656.4	171.8	509.4	115.4	1,560.5	265.7	253.1	13.5	119.4	174.2	229.7	349.7	241.1	167.2	–107.4
1997	1,579.2	737.5	182.3	539.4	120.1	1,601.1	270.5	258.3	15.2	123.8	190.0	235.0	365.3	244.0	157.3	–21.9
1998	1,721.7	828.6	188.7	571.8	132.6	1,652.5	268.2	255.8	13.1	131.4	192.8	237.8	379.2	241.1	188.9	69.3
1999	1,827.5	879.5	184.7	611.8	151.5	1,701.8	274.8	261.2	15.2	141.0	190.4	242.5	390.0	229.8	218.1	125.6
2000	2,025.2	1,004.5	207.3	652.9	160.6	1,789.0	294.4	281.0	17.2	154.5	197.1	253.7	409.4	222.9	239.7	236.2
2001	1,991.1	994.3	151.1	694.0	151.7	1,862.8	304.7	290.2	16.5	172.2	217.4	269.8	433.0	206.2	243.1	128.2
2002	1,853.1	858.3	148.0	700.8	146.0	2,010.9	348.5	331.8	22.3	196.5	230.9	312.7	456.0	170.9	273.1	–157.8
2003	1,782.3	793.7	131.8	713.0	143.9	2,159.9	404.7	387.1	21.2	219.5	249.4	334.6	474.7	153.1	302.6	–377.6
2004	1,880.1	809.0	189.4	733.4	148.4	2,292.8	455.8	436.4	26.9	240.1	269.4	333.1	495.5	160.2	311.8	–412.7
2005	2,153.6	927.2	278.3	794.1	154.0	2,472.0	495.3	474.1	34.6	250.5	298.6	345.8	523.3	184.0	339.8	–318.3
2006	2,406.9	1,043.9	353.9	837.8	171.2	2,655.1	521.8	499.3	29.5	252.7	329.9	352.5	548.5	226.6	393.5	–248.2
2007	2,568.0	1,163.5	370.2	869.6	164.7	2,728.7	551.3	528.5	28.5	266.4	375.4	366.0	586.2	237.1	317.9	–160.7
2008	2,524.0	1,145.7	304.3	900.2	173.7	2,982.5	616.1	594.6	28.9	280.6	390.8	431.3	617.0	252.8	365.2	–458.6
2009	2,105.0	915.3	138.2	890.9	160.5	3,517.7	661.0	636.7	37.5	334.3	430.1	533.2	683.0	186.9	651.6	–1,412.7
2010	2,162.7	898.5	191.4	864.8	207.9	3,456.2	693.6	666.7	45.2	369.1	451.6	622.2	706.7	196.2	371.6	–1,293.5
2011	2,303.5	1,091.5	181.1	818.8	212.1	3,603.1	705.6	678.1	45.7	372.5	485.7	597.4	730.8	230.0	435.5	–1,299.6
2012 (estimates)	2,468.6	1,164.7	236.8	840.7	226.5	3,795.5	716.3	688.3	56.3	361.6	484.5	579.6	778.6	224.8	593.9	–1,326.9
2013 (estimates)	2,902.0	1,359.3	347.7	959.1	235.9	3,803.4	701.8	672.9	59.6	385.9	530.2	559.4	825.9	247.7	492.9	–901.4

Note: See Note, Table B–78.

Sources: Department of the Treasury and Office of Management and Budget.

[Millions of dollars; fiscal years]

Description	Actual				Estimates	
	2008	2009	2010	2011	2012	2013
RECEIPTS, OUTLAYS, AND SURPLUS OR DEFICIT						
Total:						
Receipts	2,523,991	2,104,989	2,162,724	2,303,466	2,468,599	2,901,956
Outlays	2,982,544	3,517,677	3,456,213	3,603,061	3,795,547	3,803,364
Surplus or deficit (–)	–458,553	–1,412,688	–1,293,489	–1,299,595	–1,326,948	–901,408
On-budget:						
Receipts	1,865,945	1,450,980	1,531,037	1,737,678	1,896,459	2,224,545
Outlays	2,507,793	3,000,661	2,901,531	3,104,455	3,290,381	3,169,287
Surplus or deficit (–)	–641,848	–1,549,681	–1,370,494	–1,366,777	–1,393,922	–944,742
Off-budget:						
Receipts	658,046	654,009	631,687	565,788	572,140	677,411
Outlays	474,751	517,016	554,682	498,606	505,166	634,077
Surplus or deficit (–)	183,295	136,993	77,005	67,182	66,974	43,334
OUTSTANDING DEBT, END OF PERIOD						
Gross Federal debt	9,986,082	11,875,851	13,528,807	14,764,222	16,350,885	17,547,936
Held by Federal Government accounts	4,183,032	4,331,144	4,509,926	4,636,016	4,772,802	4,911,247
Held by the public	5,803,050	7,544,707	9,018,882	10,128,206	11,578,083	12,636,689
Federal Reserve System	491,127	769,160	811,669	1,664,660	....	....
Other	5,311,923	6,775,547	8,207,213	8,463,546	....	....
RECEIPTS BY SOURCE						
Total: On-budget and off-budget	2,523,991	2,104,989	2,162,724	2,303,466	2,468,599	2,901,956
Individual income taxes	1,145,747	915,308	898,549	1,091,473	1,164,650	1,359,260
Corporation income taxes	304,346	138,229	191,437	181,085	236,801	347,741
Social insurance and retirement receipts	900,155	890,917	864,814	818,792	840,650	959,057
On-budget	242,109	236,908	233,127	253,004	268,510	281,646
Off-budget	658,046	654,009	631,687	565,788	572,140	677,411
Excise taxes	67,334	62,483	66,909	72,381	79,415	88,055
Estate and gift taxes	28,844	23,482	18,885	7,399	11,377	12,738
Customs duties and fees	27,568	22,453	25,298	29,519	30,817	33,488
Miscellaneous receipts	49,997	52,117	96,832	102,817	104,889	101,617
Deposits of earnings by Federal Reserve System	33,598	34,318	75,845	82,546	81,339	80,409
All other	16,399	17,799	20,987	20,271	23,550	21,208
OUTLAYS BY FUNCTION						
Total: On-budget and off-budget	2,982,544	3,517,677	3,456,213	3,603,061	3,795,547	3,803,364
National defense	616,073	661,049	693,586	705,625	716,300	701,767
International affairs	28,857	37,529	45,195	45,685	56,252	59,556
General science, space, and technology	26,772	28,417	30,098	29,466	30,991	31,265
Energy	628	4,749	11,613	12,174	23,270	13,914
Natural resources and environment	31,817	35,568	43,662	45,470	42,829	41,312
Agriculture	18,387	22,237	21,356	20,661	19,173	25,624
Commerce and housing credit	27,870	291,535	–82,298	–12,575	79,624	–25,001
On-budget	25,453	291,231	–86,998	–13,383	84,744	–20,381
Off-budget	2,417	304	4,700	808	–5,120	–4,620
Transportation	77,616	84,289	91,972	92,965	102,552	114,228
Community and regional development	23,952	27,650	23,804	23,816	31,685	34,983
Education, training, employment, and social services	91,287	79,749	127,710	101,233	139,212	122,135
Health	280,599	334,335	369,054	372,500	361,625	385,868
Medicare	390,758	430,093	451,636	485,653	484,486	530,246
Income security	431,313	533,224	622,210	597,352	579,578	559,413
Social security	617,027	682,963	706,737	730,811	778,574	825,872
On-budget	17,830	34,071	23,317	101,933	140,065	61,840
Off-budget	599,197	648,892	683,420	628,878	638,509	764,032
Veterans benefits and services	84,653	95,429	108,384	127,189	129,605	140,117
Administration of justice	48,097	52,581	54,385	56,055	62,016	62,792
General government	20,323	22,017	23,031	25,507	31,763	26,266
Net interest	252,757	186,902	196,194	229,968	224,784	247,715
On-budget	366,475	304,856	314,696	345,949	337,380	356,552
Off-budget	–113,718	–117,954	–118,502	–115,981	–112,596	–108,837
Allowances	....	....	....	....	125	1,575
Undistributed offsetting receipts	–86,242	–92,639	–82,116	–86,494	–98,897	–96,283
On-budget	–73,097	–78,413	–67,180	–71,395	–83,270	–79,785
Off-budget	–13,145	–14,226	–14,936	–15,099	–15,627	–16,498

Note: See Note, Table B–78.

Sources: Department of the Treasury and Office of Management and Budget.

TABLE B–82. Federal and State and local government current receipts and expenditures, national income and product accounts (NIPA), 1963–2011

[Billions of dollars; quarterly data at seasonally adjusted annual rates]

Year or quarter	Total government			Federal Government			State and local government			Addendum: Grants-in-aid to State and local governments
	Current receipts	Current expenditures	Net government saving (NIPA)	Current receipts	Current expenditures	Net Federal Government saving (NIPA)	Current receipts	Current expenditures	Net State and local government saving (NIPA)	
1963	162.2	151.2	11.0	111.8	106.5	5.3	56.0	50.3	5.7	5.6
1964	166.6	159.3	7.3	111.8	110.9	.9	61.3	54.9	6.4	6.5
1965	180.3	170.6	9.8	121.0	117.7	3.2	66.5	60.0	6.5	7.2
1966	202.8	192.8	10.0	138.0	135.7	2.3	74.9	67.2	7.8	10.1
1967	217.7	220.0	−2.3	146.9	156.2	−9.3	82.5	75.5	7.0	11.7
1968	252.1	247.0	5.1	171.3	173.7	−2.4	93.5	86.0	7.5	12.7
1969	283.5	267.0	16.5	192.7	184.1	8.6	105.5	97.5	8.0	14.6
1970	286.9	295.2	−8.4	186.1	201.6	−15.5	120.1	113.0	7.1	19.3
1971	303.6	325.8	−22.2	191.9	220.6	−28.7	134.9	128.5	6.5	23.2
1972	347.0	356.3	−9.3	220.3	245.2	−24.9	158.4	142.8	15.6	31.7
1973	390.4	386.5	3.9	250.8	262.6	−11.8	174.3	158.6	15.7	34.8
1974	431.8	436.9	−5.2	280.0	294.5	−14.5	188.1	178.7	9.3	36.3
1975	442.1	510.2	−68.2	277.6	348.3	−70.6	209.6	207.1	2.5	45.1
1976	505.9	552.2	−46.3	323.0	376.7	−53.7	233.7	226.3	7.4	50.7
1977	567.3	600.3	−33.0	364.0	410.1	−46.1	259.9	246.8	13.1	56.6
1978	646.1	656.3	−10.2	424.0	452.9	−28.9	287.6	268.9	18.7	65.5
1979	728.9	729.9	−1.0	486.9	500.9	−14.0	308.4	295.4	13.0	66.3
1980	798.7	846.5	−47.8	532.8	589.5	−56.6	338.2	329.4	8.8	72.3
1981	917.7	966.9	−49.2	619.9	676.7	−56.8	370.2	362.7	7.6	72.5
1982	939.3	1,076.8	−137.5	617.4	752.6	−135.3	391.4	393.6	−2.2	69.5
1983	1,000.3	1,171.7	−171.4	643.3	819.5	−176.2	428.6	423.7	4.9	71.6
1984	1,113.5	1,261.0	−147.5	710.0	881.5	−171.5	480.2	456.2	23.9	76.7
1985	1,214.6	1,370.9	−156.3	774.4	953.0	−178.6	521.1	498.7	22.4	80.9
1986	1,290.1	1,464.0	−173.9	816.0	1,010.7	−194.6	561.6	540.9	20.7	87.6
1987	1,403.2	1,540.5	−137.4	896.5	1,045.9	−149.3	590.6	578.6	12.0	83.9
1988	1,502.4	1,623.6	−121.2	958.5	1,096.9	−138.4	635.5	618.3	17.2	91.6
1989	1,627.2	1,741.0	−113.8	1,038.0	1,172.0	−133.9	687.5	667.4	20.1	98.3
1990	1,709.3	1,879.5	−170.3	1,082.8	1,259.2	−176.4	738.0	731.8	6.2	111.4
1991	1,759.7	1,984.0	−224.2	1,101.9	1,320.3	−218.4	789.4	795.2	−5.8	131.6
1992	1,845.1	2,149.0	−303.9	1,148.0	1,450.5	−302.5	846.2	847.6	−1.4	149.1
1993	1,948.2	2,229.4	−281.2	1,224.1	1,504.3	−280.2	888.2	889.1	−.9	164.0
1994	2,091.9	2,304.0	−212.2	1,322.1	1,542.5	−220.4	944.8	936.6	8.2	175.1
1995	2,215.5	2,412.5	−197.0	1,407.8	1,614.0	−206.2	991.9	982.7	9.2	184.2
1996	2,380.4	2,505.7	−125.3	1,526.4	1,674.7	−148.2	1,045.1	1,022.1	23.0	191.1
1997	2,557.2	2,581.1	−23.8	1,656.2	1,716.3	−60.1	1,099.5	1,063.2	36.3	198.4
1998	2,729.8	2,649.3	80.5	1,777.9	1,744.3	33.6	1,164.5	1,117.6	46.9	212.6
1999	2,902.5	2,761.9	140.6	1,895.0	1,796.2	98.8	1,240.4	1,198.6	41.8	232.9
2000	3,132.4	2,906.0	226.5	2,057.1	1,871.9	185.2	1,322.6	1,281.3	41.3	247.3
2001	3,118.2	3,093.6	24.6	2,020.3	1,979.8	40.5	1,374.0	1,389.9	−15.9	276.1
2002	2,967.9	3,274.7	−306.9	1,859.3	2,112.1	−252.8	1,412.7	1,466.8	−54.1	304.2
2003	3,043.4	3,458.6	−415.2	1,885.1	2,261.5	−376.4	1,496.3	1,535.1	−38.8	338.0
2004	3,265.7	3,653.5	−387.8	2,013.9	2,393.4	−379.5	1,601.0	1,609.3	−8.4	349.2
2005	3,659.3	3,916.4	−257.1	2,290.1	2,573.1	−283.0	1,730.4	1,704.5	25.9	361.2
2006	3,995.2	4,147.9	−152.7	2,524.5	2,728.3	−203.8	1,829.7	1,778.6	51.0	359.0
2007	4,197.0	4,430.0	−233.0	2,654.7	2,900.0	−245.2	1,923.1	1,910.8	12.2	380.8
2008	4,051.6	4,737.3	−685.7	2,502.2	3,115.7	−613.5	1,944.8	2,017.0	−72.2	395.5
2009	3,703.7	4,999.7	−1,296.0	2,232.5	3,450.4	−1,217.9	1,953.6	2,031.7	−78.0	482.4
2010	3,962.8	5,261.8	−1,299.0	2,429.6	3,703.3	−1,273.7	2,064.7	2,090.0	−25.3	531.5
2011 ᵖ		5,409.8			3,753.6			2,148.7		492.5
2008: I	4,196.2	4,627.5	−431.3	2,640.1	3,028.9	−388.8	1,942.9	1,985.4	−42.5	386.8
II	4,006.7	4,800.9	−794.2	2,409.8	3,174.2	−764.4	1,993.2	2,023.0	−29.8	396.3
III	4,052.9	4,793.7	−740.9	2,501.4	3,140.4	−639.1	1,945.6	2,047.4	−101.8	394.1
IV	3,950.4	4,727.0	−776.6	2,457.7	3,119.4	−661.7	1,897.5	2,012.4	−114.9	404.8
2009: I	3,680.8	4,792.8	−1,112.1	2,225.9	3,219.8	−993.9	1,893.3	2,011.4	−118.1	438.4
II	3,663.4	5,041.7	−1,378.3	2,214.0	3,516.9	−1,303.0	1,952.8	2,028.2	−75.3	503.4
III	3,704.4	5,083.8	−1,379.4	2,221.6	3,527.0	−1,305.4	1,969.2	2,043.2	−74.0	486.4
IV	3,766.2	5,080.4	−1,314.2	2,268.5	3,537.9	−1,269.4	1,999.2	2,044.0	−44.8	501.4
2010: I	3,883.9	5,188.0	−1,304.0	2,364.8	3,636.6	−1,271.8	2,034.0	2,066.2	−32.3	514.8
II	3,927.0	5,233.2	−1,306.2	2,407.8	3,685.8	−1,278.0	2,043.3	2,071.6	−28.2	524.2
III	4,015.4	5,278.4	−1,262.9	2,475.4	3,733.1	−1,257.7	2,082.1	2,087.4	−5.2	542.1
IV	4,025.0	5,347.8	−1,322.8	2,470.5	3,757.8	−1,287.3	2,099.3	2,134.8	−35.5	544.9
2011: I	4,106.0	5,364.3	−1,258.3	2,527.9	3,729.0	−1,201.1	2,092.5	2,149.7	−57.2	514.5
II	4,154.4	5,470.0	−1,315.6	2,554.1	3,829.5	−1,275.4	2,128.0	2,168.2	−40.2	527.7
III	4,163.3	5,418.9	−1,255.6	2,571.8	3,744.2	−1,172.4	2,062.1	2,145.3	−83.2	470.6
IV ᵖ		5,386.2			3,711.8			2,131.5		457.1

Note: Federal grants-in-aid to State and local governments are reflected in Federal current expenditures and State and local current receipts. Total government current receipts and expenditures have been adjusted to eliminate this duplication.

Source: Department of Commerce (Bureau of Economic Analysis).

[Billions of dollars; quarterly data at seasonally adjusted annual rates]

Year or quarter	Current receipts									Current expenditures					Net government saving
	Total	Current tax receipts				Contributions for government social insurance	Income receipts on assets	Current transfer receipts	Current surplus of government enterprises	Total [2]	Consumption expenditures	Current transfer payments	Interest payments	Subsidies	
		Total [1]	Personal current taxes	Taxes on production and imports	Taxes on corporate income										
1963	162.2	134.4	54.6	53.4	26.2	21.7	3.4	1.3	1.4	151.2	102.7	34.3	12.0	2.2	11.0
1964	166.6	137.5	52.1	57.3	28.0	22.5	3.7	1.6	1.3	159.3	108.6	35.1	12.9	2.7	7.3
1965	180.3	149.5	57.7	60.7	30.9	23.5	4.1	1.9	1.3	170.6	115.9	38.0	13.7	3.0	9.8
1966	202.8	163.5	66.4	63.2	33.7	31.4	4.7	2.2	1.0	192.8	131.8	42.0	15.1	3.9	10.0
1967	217.7	173.8	73.0	67.9	32.7	35.0	5.5	2.5	.9	220.0	149.5	50.3	16.4	3.8	−2.3
1968	252.1	203.1	87.0	76.4	39.4	38.8	6.4	2.6	1.2	247.0	165.7	58.4	18.8	4.2	5.1
1969	283.5	228.4	104.5	83.9	39.7	44.3	7.0	2.7	1.0	267.0	178.2	64.1	20.2	4.5	16.5
1970	286.9	229.2	103.1	91.4	34.4	46.6	8.2	2.9	.0	295.2	190.1	77.3	23.1	4.8	−8.4
1971	303.6	240.3	101.7	100.5	37.7	51.5	9.0	3.1	−.2	325.8	204.7	92.2	24.5	4.7	−22.2
1972	347.0	273.8	123.6	107.9	41.9	59.6	9.5	3.6	.5	356.3	220.8	103.0	26.3	6.6	−9.3
1973	390.4	299.3	132.4	117.2	49.3	76.0	11.6	3.9	−.4	386.5	234.8	115.2	31.3	5.2	3.9
1974	431.8	328.1	151.0	124.9	51.8	85.8	14.4	4.5	−.9	436.9	261.7	135.9	35.6	3.3	−5.2
1975	442.1	334.3	147.6	135.3	50.9	89.9	16.1	5.1	−3.2	510.2	294.6	171.3	40.0	4.5	−68.2
1976	505.9	383.6	172.3	146.4	64.2	102.0	16.3	5.8	−1.8	552.2	316.6	184.3	46.3	5.1	−46.3
1977	567.3	431.0	197.5	159.7	73.0	113.9	18.4	6.8	−2.7	600.3	346.6	195.9	50.8	7.1	−33.0
1978	646.1	484.8	229.4	170.9	83.5	132.1	23.2	8.2	−2.2	656.3	376.5	210.9	60.2	8.9	−10.2
1979	728.9	537.9	268.7	180.1	88.0	153.7	30.8	9.4	−2.9	729.9	412.3	236.0	72.9	8.5	−1.0
1980	798.7	585.6	298.9	200.3	84.8	167.2	39.9	11.1	−5.1	846.5	465.9	281.7	89.1	9.8	−47.8
1981	917.7	663.5	345.2	235.6	81.1	196.9	50.2	12.7	−5.6	966.9	520.6	318.1	116.7	11.5	−49.2
1982	939.3	659.5	354.1	240.9	63.1	210.1	58.9	15.3	−4.5	1,076.8	568.1	354.7	138.9	15.0	−137.5
1983	1,000.3	694.1	352.3	263.3	77.2	227.2	65.3	16.9	−3.2	1,171.7	610.5	382.5	156.9	21.3	−171.4
1984	1,113.5	762.5	377.4	289.8	94.0	258.8	74.3	19.7	−1.9	1,261.0	657.6	395.3	187.3	21.1	−147.5
1985	1,214.6	823.9	417.3	308.1	96.5	282.8	84.0	23.4	.6	1,370.9	720.1	420.4	208.8	21.4	−156.3
1986	1,290.1	868.8	437.2	323.4	106.5	304.9	89.7	25.9	.9	1,464.0	776.1	446.6	216.3	24.9	−173.9
1987	1,403.2	965.7	489.1	347.5	127.1	324.6	85.6	27.0	.2	1,540.5	815.1	464.4	230.8	30.3	−137.4
1988	1,502.4	1,018.9	504.9	374.5	137.2	363.2	89.9	27.9	2.6	1,623.6	852.8	493.6	247.7	29.5	−121.2
1989	1,627.2	1,109.2	566.1	398.9	141.5	386.9	93.7	32.5	4.9	1,741.0	902.9	538.1	272.5	27.4	−113.8
1990	1,709.3	1,161.3	592.7	425.0	140.6	412.1	98.0	36.3	1.6	1,879.5	966.0	592.4	294.2	27.0	−170.3
1991	1,759.7	1,179.9	586.6	457.1	133.6	432.2	97.0	44.9	5.7	1,984.0	1,015.8	628.9	311.7	27.5	−224.2
1992	1,845.1	1,239.7	610.5	483.4	143.1	457.1	89.6	50.5	8.2	2,149.0	1,050.4	756.3	312.3	30.1	−303.9
1993	1,948.2	1,317.8	646.5	503.1	165.4	479.6	86.8	55.3	8.7	2,229.4	1,075.4	804.6	312.7	36.7	−281.2
1994	2,091.9	1,425.6	690.5	545.2	186.7	510.7	86.0	60.0	9.6	2,304.0	1,108.9	839.9	322.7	32.5	−212.2
1995	2,215.5	1,516.7	743.9	557.9	211.0	535.5	91.8	58.4	13.1	2,412.5	1,141.4	882.4	353.9	34.8	−197.0
1996	2,380.4	1,641.5	832.0	580.8	223.6	557.9	99.9	66.8	14.4	2,505.7	1,176.7	929.2	364.6	35.2	−125.3
1997	2,557.2	1,780.0	926.2	611.6	237.1	590.3	103.6	69.3	14.1	2,581.1	1,222.1	954.6	370.6	33.8	−23.8
1998	2,729.8	1,910.8	1,026.4	639.5	239.2	627.8	102.7	75.3	13.3	2,649.3	1,263.2	978.1	371.6	36.4	80.5
1999	2,902.5	2,035.8	1,107.5	673.6	248.8	664.6	106.4	81.7	14.1	2,761.9	1,343.9	1,014.9	357.9	45.2	140.6
2000	3,132.4	2,202.8	1,232.3	708.6	254.7	709.4	118.8	92.3	9.1	2,906.0	1,426.6	1,071.5	362.0	45.8	226.5
2001	3,118.2	2,163.7	1,234.8	727.7	193.5	736.9	114.6	98.9	4.0	3,093.6	1,524.4	1,169.0	341.5	58.7	24.6
2002	2,967.9	2,002.1	1,050.4	762.8	181.3	755.2	99.9	104.3	6.3	3,274.7	1,639.9	1,280.9	312.6	41.4	−306.9
2003	3,043.4	2,047.9	1,000.3	806.8	231.8	782.8	96.8	108.9	7.0	3,458.6	1,756.8	1,354.8	298.0	49.1	−415.2
2004	3,265.7	2,213.2	1,047.8	863.4	292.0	831.7	100.3	119.3	1.2	3,653.5	1,860.4	1,440.1	306.6	46.4	−387.8
2005	3,659.3	2,546.8	1,208.6	930.2	395.9	877.4	111.9	126.7	−3.5	3,916.4	1,977.9	1,534.9	342.7	60.9	−257.1
2006	3,995.2	2,807.4	1,352.4	986.8	454.2	926.4	129.6	136.0	−4.2	4,147.9	2,093.3	1,631.0	372.2	51.4	−152.7
2007	4,197.0	2,951.2	1,488.7	1,027.2	420.6	964.2	144.2	149.2	−11.8	4,430.0	2,217.8	1,743.4	414.3	54.6	−233.0
2008	4,051.6	2,774.1	1,435.7	1,038.6	281.0	992.1	137.5	163.9	−16.0	4,737.3	2,381.0	1,903.1	400.2	52.9	−685.7
2009	3,703.7	2,423.0	1,141.4	1,017.9	249.1	969.0	141.4	185.2	−14.9	4,999.7	2,412.2	2,169.3	358.6	59.7	−1,296.0
2010	3,962.8	2,648.7	1,193.9	1,054.0	387.4	991.7	144.0	194.1	−15.7	5,261.8	2,497.5	2,316.8	390.2	57.3	−1,299.0
2011 [p]			1,404.8	1,098.3		924.6	145.2	197.2	−14.6	5,409.8	2,547.5	2,370.8	428.5	63.1	
2008: I	4,196.2	2,914.6	1,536.0	1,035.0	327.1	994.7	143.8	158.4	−15.2	4,627.5	2,337.0	1,826.2	412.3	51.9	−431.3
II	4,006.7	2,730.7	1,351.8	1,047.3	315.4	991.3	141.7	158.8	−15.9	4,800.9	2,373.8	1,959.7	415.6	51.9	−794.2
III	4,052.9	2,781.0	1,432.1	1,046.7	284.9	993.5	135.2	159.3	−16.1	4,793.7	2,421.8	1,893.2	426.2	52.5	−740.9
IV	3,950.4	2,670.1	1,422.8	1,025.5	196.8	989.0	129.1	178.9	−16.8	4,727.0	2,391.3	1,933.5	346.9	55.4	−776.6
2009: I	3,680.8	2,407.1	1,198.0	1,008.0	185.4	970.9	135.9	183.5	−16.8	4,792.8	2,372.3	2,052.0	312.1	56.4	−1,112.1
II	3,663.4	2,369.6	1,120.3	1,011.8	221.8	971.8	143.0	194.4	−15.3	5,041.7	2,405.7	2,203.7	375.5	56.8	−1,378.3
III	3,704.4	2,433.1	1,120.6	1,020.4	279.0	967.0	140.4	177.9	−14.0	5,083.8	2,425.4	2,211.1	378.8	68.4	−1,379.4
IV	3,766.2	2,482.3	1,126.4	1,031.3	310.2	966.4	146.1	185.0	−13.6	5,080.4	2,445.1	2,210.3	368.0	57.1	−1,314.2
2010: I	3,883.9	2,587.0	1,146.4	1,040.9	386.4	980.8	141.2	189.6	−14.7	5,188.0	2,477.0	2,282.1	372.5	56.4	−1,304.0
II	3,927.0	2,615.4	1,175.4	1,050.6	376.3	990.6	143.8	192.7	−15.5	5,233.2	2,497.7	2,283.3	395.4	56.8	−1,306.2
III	4,015.4	2,691.7	1,212.8	1,059.0	406.8	996.3	145.8	197.6	−16.0	5,278.4	2,505.6	2,325.3	390.5	57.0	−1,262.9
IV	4,025.0	2,700.6	1,240.9	1,065.5	380.2	999.0	145.4	196.6	−16.5	5,347.8	2,509.7	2,376.4	402.6	59.1	−1,322.8
2011: I	4,106.0	2,864.7	1,365.9	1,087.4	397.2	915.9	145.2	195.7	−15.6	5,364.3	2,530.7	2,361.8	411.7	60.0	−1,258.3
II	4,154.4	2,907.0	1,396.2	1,101.1	394.4	921.9	144.0	196.1	−14.6	5,470.0	2,560.4	2,389.6	457.4	62.7	−1,315.6
III	4,163.3	2,909.9	1,408.5	1,100.0	384.3	925.7	145.1	197.1	−14.5	5,418.9	2,561.0	2,370.0	423.7	64.2	−1,255.6
IV [p]			1,448.5	1,104.6		934.7	146.3	199.9	−13.9	5,386.2	2,537.7	2,361.7	421.2	65.6	

[1] Includes taxes from the rest of the world, not shown separately.
[2] Includes an item for the difference between wage accruals and disbursements, not shown separately.

Source: Department of Commerce (Bureau of Economic Analysis).

TABLE B–84. Federal Government current receipts and expenditures, national income and product accounts (NIPA), 1963–2011

[Billions of dollars; quarterly data at seasonally adjusted annual rates]

Year or quarter	Current receipts	Current tax receipts				Contributions for government social insurance	Income receipts on assets	Current transfer receipts	Current surplus of government enterprises	Current expenditures	Consumption expenditures	Current transfer payments[3]	Interest payments	Subsidies	Net Federal Government saving
	Total	Total[1]	Personal current taxes	Taxes on production and imports	Taxes on corporate income					Total[2]					
1963	111.8	88.6	49.1	14.7	24.6	21.1	1.8	0.6	−0.3	106.5	60.8	34.2	9.3	2.2	5.3
1964	111.8	87.7	46.0	15.4	26.1	21.8	1.8	.7	−.3	110.9	62.8	35.4	10.0	2.7	.9
1965	121.0	95.6	51.1	15.4	28.9	22.7	1.9	1.1	−.3	117.7	65.7	38.5	10.6	3.0	3.2
1966	138.0	104.7	58.6	14.4	31.4	30.6	2.1	1.2	−.6	135.7	75.7	44.4	11.6	3.9	2.3
1967	146.9	109.8	64.4	15.2	30.0	34.1	2.5	1.1	−.6	156.2	87.0	52.8	12.7	3.8	−9.3
1968	171.3	129.7	76.4	16.9	36.1	37.9	2.9	1.1	−.3	173.7	95.3	59.7	14.6	4.1	−2.4
1969	192.7	146.0	91.7	17.8	36.1	43.3	2.7	1.1	−.4	184.1	98.3	65.5	15.8	4.5	8.6
1970	186.1	137.9	88.9	18.1	30.6	45.5	3.1	1.1	−1.5	201.6	98.6	80.5	17.7	4.8	−15.5
1971	191.9	138.6	85.8	19.0	33.5	50.3	3.5	1.1	−1.6	220.6	101.9	96.1	17.9	4.6	−28.7
1972	220.3	158.2	102.8	18.5	36.6	58.3	3.6	1.3	−1.1	245.2	107.6	112.7	18.8	6.6	−24.9
1973	250.8	173.0	109.6	19.8	43.3	74.5	3.8	1.3	−1.8	262.6	108.8	125.9	22.8	5.1	−11.8
1974	280.0	192.1	126.5	20.1	45.1	84.1	4.2	1.4	−1.8	294.5	117.9	146.9	26.0	3.2	−14.5
1975	277.6	186.8	120.7	22.1	43.6	88.1	4.9	1.5	−3.6	348.3	129.5	185.6	28.9	4.3	−70.6
1976	323.0	217.9	141.2	21.4	54.6	99.8	5.9	1.6	−2.2	376.7	137.1	200.9	33.8	4.9	−53.7
1977	364.0	247.2	162.2	22.7	61.6	111.1	6.7	2.0	−3.0	410.1	150.7	215.5	37.1	6.9	−46.1
1978	424.0	286.6	188.9	25.3	71.4	128.7	8.5	2.7	−2.5	452.9	163.3	235.7	45.3	8.7	−28.9
1979	486.9	325.9	224.6	25.7	74.4	149.8	10.7	3.1	−2.6	500.9	178.9	258.0	55.7	8.2	−14.0
1980	532.8	355.5	250.0	33.7	70.3	163.6	13.7	3.9	−3.9	589.5	207.4	302.9	69.7	9.4	−56.6
1981	619.9	407.7	290.6	49.9	65.7	193.0	18.3	4.1	−3.2	676.7	238.3	333.5	93.9	11.1	−56.8
1982	617.4	386.3	295.0	41.0	49.0	206.0	22.2	5.7	−2.9	752.6	263.3	363.0	111.8	14.6	−135.3
1983	643.3	393.2	286.2	44.4	61.3	223.1	23.8	6.1	−3.0	819.5	286.4	387.2	124.6	20.9	−176.2
1984	710.0	425.2	301.4	47.3	75.2	254.1	26.6	7.4	−3.4	881.5	309.9	400.8	150.3	20.7	−171.5
1985	774.4	460.2	336.0	46.1	76.3	277.9	29.1	9.7	−2.6	953.0	338.3	424.0	169.4	21.0	−178.6
1986	816.0	479.2	350.0	43.7	83.8	298.9	31.3	8.5	−1.9	1,010.7	358.0	449.9	178.2	24.6	−194.6
1987	896.5	543.6	392.5	45.9	103.2	317.4	27.5	11.0	−3.0	1,045.9	373.7	457.6	184.6	30.0	−149.3
1988	958.5	566.2	402.8	49.8	111.1	354.8	29.4	10.5	−2.3	1,096.9	381.7	486.8	199.3	29.2	−138.4
1989	1,038.0	621.2	451.5	49.7	117.2	378.0	28.0	12.7	−1.7	1,172.0	398.5	527.1	219.3	27.1	−133.9
1990	1,082.8	642.2	470.1	50.9	118.1	402.0	29.6	14.2	−5.3	1,259.2	419.0	576.2	237.5	26.6	−176.4
1991	1,101.9	635.6	461.3	61.8	109.9	420.6	29.1	18.2	−1.6	1,320.3	438.3	604.0	250.9	27.1	−218.4
1992	1,148.0	659.9	475.2	63.3	118.8	444.0	24.8	19.4	.0	1,450.5	444.1	725.4	251.3	29.7	−302.5
1993	1,224.1	713.0	505.5	66.4	138.5	465.5	25.5	21.3	−1.3	1,504.3	441.2	773.4	253.4	36.3	−280.2
1994	1,322.1	781.4	542.5	79.0	156.7	496.2	22.7	22.8	−.9	1,542.5	440.7	808.3	261.3	32.2	−220.4
1995	1,407.8	844.6	585.8	75.6	179.3	521.9	23.3	18.4	−.3	1,614.0	440.1	849.0	290.4	34.5	−206.2
1996	1,526.4	931.9	663.3	72.9	190.6	545.4	26.5	23.8	−1.2	1,674.7	446.5	896.0	297.3	34.9	−148.2
1997	1,656.2	1,030.1	744.2	77.8	203.0	579.4	25.4	21.3	−.1	1,716.3	457.5	925.4	300.0	33.4	−60.1
1998	1,777.9	1,115.8	825.2	80.7	204.2	617.4	21.2	22.6	.8	1,744.3	454.6	954.9	298.8	35.9	33.6
1999	1,895.0	1,195.4	893.0	83.4	213.0	654.8	20.6	23.4	.8	1,796.2	473.3	995.4	282.7	44.8	98.8
2000	2,057.1	1,309.6	995.6	87.3	219.4	698.6	24.5	25.7	−1.2	1,871.9	496.0	1,047.4	283.3	45.3	185.2
2001	2,020.3	1,249.4	991.8	85.3	164.7	723.3	24.5	27.0	−4.0	1,979.8	530.2	1,140.0	258.6	51.1	40.5
2002	1,859.3	1,073.5	828.6	86.8	150.5	739.3	20.3	26.1	.2	2,112.1	590.5	1,252.1	229.1	40.5	−252.8
2003	1,885.1	1,070.2	774.2	89.3	197.8	762.8	22.8	25.6	3.7	2,261.5	660.3	1,339.4	212.9	49.0	−376.4
2004	2,013.9	1,153.8	799.2	94.3	250.3	807.6	23.2	29.0	.3	2,393.4	721.4	1,405.0	221.0	46.0	−379.5
2005	2,290.1	1,383.7	931.9	98.8	341.0	852.6	23.7	33.6	−3.5	2,573.1	765.8	1,491.3	255.4	60.5	−283.0
2006	2,524.5	1,558.3	1,049.9	99.4	395.0	904.6	26.1	38.3	−2.9	2,728.3	811.0	1,587.1	279.2	51.0	−203.8
2007	2,654.7	1,637.6	1,165.6	94.5	362.8	945.3	29.8	44.8	−2.7	2,900.0	848.9	1,690.4	313.2	47.4	−245.2
2008	2,502.2	1,447.7	1,101.3	94.0	233.7	973.1	30.7	54.4	−3.7	3,115.7	931.7	1,841.9	292.1	49.9	−613.5
2009	2,232.5	1,170.2	856.6	97.3	201.7	948.9	48.1	69.8	−4.4	3,450.4	986.6	2,153.6	251.9	58.3	−1,217.9
2010	2,429.6	1,340.7	896.4	101.5	329.6	970.9	53.1	69.7	−4.8	3,703.3	1,054.0	2,313.7	279.9	55.8	−1,273.7
2011 *p*	....	....	1,075.9	110.9	....	902.9	55.5	67.6	−1.4	3,753.6	1,072.5	2,306.1	312.4	62.6	....
2008: I	2,640.1	1,586.2	1,200.2	92.6	276.9	975.9	31.5	49.6	−3.0	3,028.9	908.6	1,766.7	305.7	47.9	−388.8
II	2,409.8	1,358.4	982.6	95.7	263.8	972.5	32.6	49.8	−3.6	3,174.2	918.7	1,899.8	306.8	48.9	−764.4
III	2,501.4	1,450.2	1,106.3	94.5	232.1	974.4	30.6	49.7	−3.7	3,140.4	946.2	1,826.2	317.6	50.4	−639.1
IV	2,457.7	1,396.1	1,116.0	93.2	161.7	969.7	27.9	68.4	−4.4	3,119.4	953.5	1,874.9	238.4	52.6	−661.7
2009: I	2,225.9	1,169.7	915.7	90.5	147.7	951.2	39.0	71.1	−5.1	3,219.8	955.2	2,006.2	204.1	54.4	−993.9
II	2,214.0	1,137.1	844.6	100.0	176.7	951.7	49.6	80.2	−4.7	3,516.9	981.2	2,210.4	269.8	55.6	−1,303.0
III	2,221.6	1,168.7	830.8	99.0	225.9	946.6	48.7	61.6	−4.0	3,527.0	997.8	2,189.9	272.1	67.2	−1,305.4
IV	2,268.5	1,205.4	835.2	99.6	256.3	945.9	54.9	66.1	−3.9	3,537.9	1,012.4	2,207.9	261.8	55.9	−1,269.4
2010: I	2,364.8	1,290.3	856.5	98.3	322.3	960.3	49.8	69.1	−4.7	3,636.6	1,033.9	2,283.0	264.9	54.8	−1,271.8
II	2,407.8	1,322.0	888.7	102.0	318.1	969.9	52.3	68.6	−4.9	3,685.8	1,056.0	2,289.0	286.2	54.7	−1,278.0
III	2,475.4	1,377.8	912.3	103.6	348.9	975.5	55.3	71.6	−4.8	3,733.1	1,066.6	2,331.9	279.1	55.4	−1,257.7
IV	2,470.5	1,372.8	927.8	101.9	329.1	977.9	55.0	69.7	−4.9	3,757.8	1,059.6	2,350.7	289.4	58.2	−1,287.3
2011: I	2,527.9	1,513.3	1,046.8	106.7	345.4	894.6	54.6	68.1	−2.7	3,729.0	1,059.1	2,312.7	298.0	59.2	−1,201.1
II	2,554.1	1,532.7	1,065.4	112.0	340.0	900.3	54.9	67.4	−1.2	3,829.5	1,077.5	2,346.9	342.8	62.2	−1,275.4
III	2,571.8	1,546.5	1,082.7	112.3	334.5	904.0	55.5	66.9	−1.1	3,744.2	1,084.9	2,289.0	306.6	63.8	−1,172.4
IV *p*	....	....	1,108.6	112.5	....	912.9	56.9	67.9	−.8	3,711.8	1,068.5	2,275.9	302.3	65.1	....

[1] Includes taxes from the rest of the world, not shown separately.
[2] Includes an item for the difference between wage accruals and disbursements, not shown separately.
[3] Includes Federal grants-in-aid to State and local governments. See Table B–82 for data on Federal grants-in-aid.

Source: Department of Commerce (Bureau of Economic Analysis).

[Billions of dollars; quarterly data at seasonally adjusted annual rates]

Year or quarter	Current receipts									Current expenditures					Net State and local government saving
	Total	Current tax receipts				Contributions for government social insurance	Income receipts on assets	Current transfer receipts [1]	Current surplus of government enterprises	Total [2]	Consumption expenditures	Government social benefit payments to persons	Interest payments	Subsidies	
		Total	Personal current taxes	Taxes on production and imports	Taxes on corporate income										
1963	56.0	45.8	5.4	38.7	1.7	0.6	1.6	6.4	1.6	50.3	41.9	5.7	2.7	0.0	5.7
1964	61.3	49.8	6.1	41.8	1.8	.7	1.9	7.3	1.6	54.9	45.8	6.2	2.9	.0	6.4
1965	66.5	53.9	6.6	45.3	2.0	.8	2.2	8.0	1.7	60.0	50.2	6.7	3.1	.0	6.5
1966	74.9	58.8	7.8	48.8	2.2	.8	2.6	11.1	1.6	67.2	56.1	7.6	3.4	.0	7.8
1967	82.5	64.0	8.6	52.8	2.6	.9	3.0	13.1	1.5	75.5	62.6	9.2	3.7	.0	7.0
1968	93.5	73.4	10.6	59.5	3.3	.9	3.5	14.2	1.5	86.0	70.4	11.4	4.2	.0	7.5
1969	105.5	82.5	12.8	66.0	3.6	1.0	4.3	16.2	1.5	97.5	79.8	13.2	4.4	.0	8.0
1970	120.1	91.3	14.2	73.3	3.7	1.1	5.2	21.1	1.5	113.0	91.5	16.1	5.3	.0	7.1
1971	134.9	101.7	15.9	81.5	4.3	1.2	5.5	25.2	1.4	128.5	102.7	19.3	6.5	.0	6.5
1972	158.4	115.6	20.9	89.4	5.3	1.3	5.9	34.0	1.6	142.8	113.2	22.0	7.5	.1	15.6
1973	174.3	126.3	22.8	97.4	6.0	1.5	7.8	37.3	1.5	158.6	126.0	24.1	8.5	.1	15.7
1974	188.1	136.0	24.5	104.8	6.7	1.7	10.2	39.3	.9	178.7	143.7	25.3	9.6	.1	9.3
1975	209.6	147.4	26.9	113.2	7.3	1.8	11.2	48.7	.4	207.1	165.1	30.8	11.1	.2	2.5
1976	233.7	165.7	31.1	125.0	9.6	2.2	10.4	55.0	.4	226.3	179.5	34.1	12.5	.2	7.4
1977	259.9	183.7	35.4	136.9	11.4	2.8	11.7	61.4	.3	246.8	195.9	37.0	13.7	.2	13.1
1978	287.6	198.2	40.5	145.6	12.1	3.4	14.7	71.1	.3	268.9	213.2	40.8	14.9	.2	18.7
1979	308.4	212.0	44.0	154.4	13.6	3.9	20.1	72.7	−.3	295.4	233.3	44.3	17.2	.3	13.0
1980	338.2	230.0	48.9	166.7	14.5	3.6	26.3	79.5	−1.2	329.4	258.4	51.2	19.4	.4	8.8
1981	370.2	255.8	54.6	185.7	15.4	3.9	32.0	81.0	−2.4	362.7	282.3	57.1	22.8	.4	7.6
1982	391.4	273.2	59.1	200.0	14.0	4.0	36.7	79.1	−1.6	393.6	304.9	61.2	27.1	.5	−2.2
1983	428.6	300.9	66.1	218.9	15.9	4.1	41.4	82.4	−.2	423.7	324.1	66.9	32.3	.4	4.9
1984	480.2	337.3	76.0	242.5	18.8	4.7	47.7	89.0	1.5	456.2	347.7	71.2	37.0	.4	23.9
1985	521.1	363.7	81.4	262.1	20.2	4.9	54.8	94.5	3.2	498.7	381.8	77.3	39.4	.3	22.4
1986	561.6	389.5	87.2	279.7	22.7	6.0	58.4	105.0	2.8	540.9	418.1	84.3	38.2	.3	20.7
1987	590.6	422.1	96.6	301.6	23.9	7.2	58.2	100.0	3.1	578.6	441.4	90.7	46.2	.3	12.0
1988	635.5	452.8	102.1	324.6	26.0	8.4	60.5	109.0	4.8	618.3	471.0	98.5	48.4	.4	17.2
1989	687.5	488.0	114.6	349.1	24.2	9.0	65.7	118.1	6.7	667.4	504.5	109.3	53.2	.4	20.1
1990	738.0	519.1	122.6	374.1	22.5	10.0	68.5	133.5	6.9	731.8	547.0	127.7	56.8	.4	6.2
1991	789.4	544.3	125.3	395.3	23.6	11.6	68.0	158.2	7.3	795.2	577.5	156.5	60.8	.4	−5.8
1992	846.2	579.8	135.3	420.1	24.4	13.1	64.8	180.3	8.3	847.6	606.2	180.0	61.0	.4	−1.4
1993	888.2	604.7	141.1	436.8	26.9	14.1	61.3	198.1	9.9	889.1	634.2	195.2	59.4	.4	−.9
1994	944.8	644.2	148.0	466.3	30.0	14.5	63.3	212.3	10.5	936.6	668.2	206.7	61.4	.3	8.2
1995	991.9	672.1	158.1	482.4	31.7	13.6	68.5	224.2	13.5	982.7	701.3	217.6	63.5	.3	9.2
1996	1,045.1	709.6	168.7	507.9	33.0	12.5	73.4	234.0	15.6	1,022.1	730.2	224.3	67.3	.3	23.0
1997	1,099.5	749.9	182.0	533.8	34.1	10.8	78.2	246.4	14.2	1,063.2	764.5	227.6	70.6	.4	36.3
1998	1,164.5	794.9	201.2	558.8	34.9	10.4	81.5	265.3	12.5	1,117.6	808.6	235.8	72.8	.4	46.9
1999	1,240.4	840.4	214.5	590.2	35.8	9.8	85.8	291.1	13.3	1,198.6	870.6	252.3	75.2	.4	41.8
2000	1,322.6	893.2	236.7	621.3	35.2	10.8	94.3	313.9	10.4	1,281.3	930.6	271.4	78.8	.5	41.3
2001	1,374.0	914.3	243.0	642.4	28.9	13.7	90.0	348.0	8.0	1,389.9	994.2	305.1	83.0	7.7	−15.9
2002	1,412.7	928.7	221.8	676.0	30.9	15.9	79.6	382.3	6.1	1,466.8	1,049.4	333.0	83.5	.9	−54.1
2003	1,496.3	977.7	226.2	717.5	34.0	20.1	74.0	421.3	3.3	1,535.1	1,096.5	353.4	85.1	.1	−38.8
2004	1,601.0	1,059.4	248.6	769.1	41.7	24.1	77.1	439.4	1.0	1,609.3	1,139.1	384.3	85.6	.4	−8.4
2005	1,730.4	1,163.1	276.7	831.4	54.9	24.8	88.3	454.3	.1	1,704.5	1,212.0	404.8	87.3	.4	25.9
2006	1,829.7	1,249.0	302.5	887.4	59.2	21.8	103.5	456.7	−1.3	1,778.6	1,282.3	402.9	93.0	.4	51.0
2007	1,923.1	1,313.6	323.1	932.7	57.8	18.9	114.5	485.1	−9.1	1,910.8	1,368.9	433.7	101.1	7.1	12.2
2008	1,944.8	1,326.4	334.4	944.6	47.4	19.0	106.8	505.0	−12.3	2,017.0	1,449.2	456.7	108.1	3.0	−72.2
2009	1,953.6	1,252.8	284.8	920.6	47.4	20.2	93.3	597.8	−10.5	2,031.7	1,425.5	498.1	106.7	1.4	−78.0
2010	2,064.7	1,307.9	297.5	952.6	57.9	20.8	90.9	655.9	−10.8	2,090.0	1,443.5	534.6	110.4	1.6	−25.3
2011 p	....	....	328.9	987.4	....	21.6	89.7	622.1	−13.2	2,148.7	1,475.0	557.1	116.1	.5	....
2008: I	1,942.9	1,328.4	335.9	942.4	50.1	18.7	112.4	495.6	−12.2	1,985.4	1,428.4	446.3	106.6	4.0	−42.5
II	1,993.2	1,372.3	369.2	951.6	51.5	18.8	109.1	505.3	−12.3	2,023.0	1,455.1	456.1	108.8	2.9	−29.8
III	1,945.6	1,330.7	325.7	952.2	52.8	19.0	104.6	503.7	−12.4	2,047.4	1,475.6	461.0	108.6	2.2	−101.8
IV	1,897.5	1,274.0	306.8	932.2	35.0	19.4	101.2	515.3	−12.4	2,012.4	1,437.8	463.4	108.4	2.8	−114.9
2009: I	1,893.3	1,237.4	282.3	917.5	37.6	19.7	96.9	550.9	−11.7	2,011.4	1,417.1	484.2	108.1	2.0	−118.1
II	1,952.8	1,232.5	275.7	911.8	45.0	20.1	93.4	617.5	−10.6	2,028.2	1,424.6	496.6	105.8	1.2	−75.3
III	1,969.2	1,264.4	289.9	921.4	53.1	20.3	91.7	602.7	−9.9	2,043.2	1,427.6	507.7	106.7	1.2	−74.0
IV	1,999.2	1,276.8	291.3	931.7	53.9	20.5	91.2	620.3	−9.7	2,044.0	1,432.7	503.8	106.2	1.2	−44.8
2010: I	2,034.0	1,296.7	289.9	942.6	64.2	20.6	91.4	635.4	−10.0	2,066.2	1,443.1	513.9	107.6	1.6	−32.3
II	2,043.3	1,293.4	286.6	948.6	58.2	20.7	91.5	648.3	−10.6	2,071.6	1,441.8	518.5	109.2	2.1	−28.2
III	2,082.1	1,313.8	300.5	955.4	57.9	20.9	90.5	668.1	−11.1	2,087.4	1,438.9	535.5	111.4	1.6	−5.2
IV	2,099.3	1,327.8	313.1	963.6	51.1	21.1	90.3	671.8	−11.6	2,134.8	1,450.1	570.6	113.2	1.0	−35.5
2011: I	2,092.5	1,351.4	319.0	980.7	51.7	21.3	90.6	642.1	−12.9	2,149.7	1,471.7	563.6	113.7	.9	−57.2
II	2,128.0	1,374.2	330.8	989.1	54.4	21.6	89.1	656.4	−13.3	2,168.2	1,482.9	570.4	114.5	.4	−40.2
III	2,062.1	1,363.4	325.8	987.8	49.8	21.7	89.6	600.8	−13.4	2,145.3	1,476.1	551.6	117.1	.4	−83.2
IV p	....	....	339.9	992.1	....	21.8	89.5	589.1	−13.2	2,131.5	1,469.2	542.9	118.9	.5	....

[1] Includes Federal grants-in-aid. See Table B–82 for data on Federal grants-in-aid.
[2] Includes an item for the difference between wage accruals and disbursements, not shown separately.

Source: Department of Commerce (Bureau of Economic Analysis).

TABLE B–86. State and local government revenues and expenditures, selected fiscal years, 1946–2009

[Millions of dollars]

Fiscal year [1]	General revenues by source [2]							General expenditures by function [2]				
	Total	Property taxes	Sales and gross receipts taxes	Individual income taxes	Corporation net income taxes	Revenue from Federal Government	All other [3]	Total [4]	Education	Highways	Public welfare [4]	All other [4,5]
1946	12,356	4,986	2,986	422	447	855	2,660	11,028	3,356	1,672	1,409	4,591
1948	17,250	6,126	4,442	543	592	1,861	3,686	17,684	5,379	3,036	2,099	7,170
1950	20,911	7,349	5,154	788	593	2,486	4,541	22,787	7,177	3,803	2,940	8,867
1952	25,181	8,652	6,357	998	846	2,566	5,762	26,098	8,318	4,650	2,386	10,744
1953	27,307	9,375	6,927	1,065	817	2,870	6,253	27,910	9,390	4,987	2,914	10,619
1954	29,012	9,967	7,276	1,127	778	2,966	6,898	30,701	10,557	5,527	3,060	11,557
1955	31,073	10,735	7,643	1,237	744	3,131	7,583	33,724	11,907	6,452	3,168	12,197
1956	34,670	11,749	8,691	1,538	890	3,335	8,467	36,715	13,224	6,953	3,139	13,399
1957	38,164	12,864	9,467	1,754	984	3,843	9,252	40,375	14,134	7,816	3,485	14,940
1958	41,219	14,047	9,829	1,759	1,018	4,865	9,701	44,851	15,919	8,567	3,818	16,547
1959	45,306	14,983	10,437	1,994	1,001	6,377	10,514	48,887	17,283	9,592	4,136	17,876
1960	50,505	16,405	11,849	2,463	1,180	6,974	11,634	51,876	18,719	9,428	4,404	19,325
1961	54,037	18,002	12,463	2,613	1,266	7,131	12,562	56,201	20,574	9,844	4,720	21,063
1962	58,252	19,054	13,494	3,037	1,308	7,871	13,488	60,206	22,216	10,357	5,084	22,549
1963	62,891	20,089	14,456	3,269	1,505	8,722	14,850	64,815	23,776	11,135	5,481	24,423
1963–64	68,443	21,241	15,762	3,791	1,695	10,002	15,952	69,302	26,286	11,664	5,766	25,586
1964–65	74,000	22,583	17,118	4,090	1,929	11,029	17,251	74,678	28,563	12,221	6,315	27,579
1965–66	83,036	24,670	19,085	4,760	2,038	13,214	19,269	82,843	33,287	12,770	6,757	30,029
1966–67	91,197	26,047	20,530	5,825	2,227	15,370	21,198	93,350	37,919	13,932	8,218	33,281
1967–68	101,264	27,747	22,911	7,308	2,518	17,181	23,599	102,411	41,158	14,481	9,857	36,915
1968–69	114,550	30,673	26,519	8,908	3,180	19,153	26,117	116,728	47,238	15,417	12,110	41,963
1969–70	130,756	34,054	30,322	10,812	3,738	21,857	29,973	131,332	52,718	16,427	14,679	47,508
1970–71	144,927	37,852	33,233	11,900	3,424	26,146	32,372	150,674	59,413	18,095	18,226	54,940
1971–72	167,535	42,877	37,518	15,227	4,416	31,342	36,156	168,549	65,813	19,021	21,117	62,598
1972–73	190,222	45,283	42,047	17,994	5,425	39,264	40,210	181,357	69,713	18,615	23,582	69,447
1973–74	207,670	47,705	46,098	19,491	6,015	41,820	46,542	199,222	75,833	19,946	25,085	78,358
1974–75	228,171	51,491	49,815	21,454	6,642	47,034	51,735	230,722	87,858	22,528	28,156	92,180
1975–76	256,176	57,001	54,547	24,575	7,273	55,589	57,191	256,731	97,216	23,907	32,604	103,004
1976–77	285,157	62,527	60,641	29,246	9,174	62,444	61,125	274,215	102,780	23,058	35,906	112,472
1977–78	315,960	66,422	67,596	33,176	10,738	69,592	68,435	296,984	110,758	24,609	39,140	122,478
1978–79	343,236	64,944	74,247	36,932	12,128	75,164	79,822	327,517	119,448	28,440	41,898	137,731
1979–80	382,322	68,499	79,927	42,080	13,321	83,029	95,467	369,086	133,211	33,311	47,288	155,276
1980–81	423,404	74,969	85,971	46,426	14,143	90,294	111,599	407,449	145,784	34,603	54,105	172,957
1981–82	457,654	82,067	93,613	50,738	15,028	87,282	128,925	436,733	154,282	34,520	57,996	189,935
1982–83	486,753	89,105	100,247	55,129	14,258	90,007	138,008	466,516	163,876	36,655	60,906	205,080
1983–84	542,730	96,457	114,097	64,871	16,798	96,935	153,571	505,008	176,108	39,419	66,414	223,068
1984–85	598,121	103,757	126,376	70,361	19,152	106,158	172,317	553,899	192,686	44,989	71,479	244,745
1985–86	641,486	111,709	135,005	74,365	19,994	113,099	187,314	605,623	210,819	49,368	75,868	269,568
1986–87	686,860	121,203	144,091	83,935	22,425	114,857	200,350	657,134	226,619	52,355	82,650	295,510
1987–88	726,762	132,212	156,452	88,350	23,663	117,602	208,482	704,921	242,683	55,621	89,090	317,527
1988–89	786,129	142,400	166,336	97,806	25,926	125,824	227,838	762,360	263,898	58,105	97,879	342,479
1989–90	849,502	155,613	177,885	105,640	23,566	136,802	249,996	834,818	288,148	61,057	110,518	375,094
1990–91	902,207	167,999	185,570	109,341	22,242	154,099	262,955	908,108	309,302	64,937	130,402	403,467
1991–92	979,137	180,337	197,731	115,638	23,880	179,174	282,376	981,253	324,652	67,351	158,723	430,526
1992–93	1,041,643	189,744	209,649	123,235	26,417	198,663	293,935	1,030,434	342,287	68,370	170,705	449,072
1993–94	1,100,490	197,141	223,628	128,810	28,320	215,492	307,099	1,077,665	353,287	72,067	183,394	468,916
1994–95	1,169,505	203,451	237,268	137,931	31,406	228,771	330,677	1,149,863	378,273	77,109	196,703	497,779
1995–96	1,222,821	209,440	248,993	146,844	32,009	234,891	350,645	1,193,276	398,859	79,092	197,354	517,971
1996–97	1,289,237	218,877	261,418	159,042	33,820	244,847	371,233	1,249,984	418,416	82,062	203,779	545,727
1997–98	1,365,762	230,150	274,883	175,630	34,412	255,048	395,639	1,318,042	450,365	87,214	208,120	572,343
1998–99	1,434,029	239,672	290,993	189,309	33,922	270,628	409,505	1,402,369	483,259	93,018	218,957	607,134
1999–2000	1,541,322	249,178	309,290	211,661	36,059	291,950	443,186	1,506,797	521,612	101,336	237,336	646,512
2000–01	1,647,161	263,689	320,217	226,334	35,296	324,033	477,592	1,626,066	563,575	107,235	261,622	693,634
2001–02	1,684,879	279,191	324,123	202,832	28,152	360,546	490,035	1,736,866	594,694	115,295	285,464	741,413
2002–03	1,763,212	296,683	337,787	199,407	31,369	389,264	508,702	1,821,917	621,335	117,696	310,783	772,102
2003–04	1,887,397	317,941	361,027	215,215	33,716	423,112	536,386	1,908,543	655,182	117,215	340,523	795,622
2004–05	2,026,034	335,779	384,266	242,273	43,256	438,558	581,902	2,012,110	688,314	126,350	365,295	832,151
2005–06	2,197,475	364,559	417,735	268,667	53,081	452,975	640,458	2,123,663	728,917	136,502	373,846	884,398
2006–07	2,329,356	388,701	440,331	290,278	60,626	464,585	684,834	2,259,899	773,676	144,714	388,277	953,232
2007–08	2,423,024	408,972	451,776	304,901	56,932	477,983	722,460	2,404,549	825,486	153,734	408,419	1,016,911
2008–09	2,413,384	424,014	433,556	270,518	45,980	536,760	702,556	2,479,895	850,674	152,067	435,854	1,041,301

[1] Fiscal years not the same for all governments. See Note.

[2] Excludes revenues or expenditures of publicly owned utilities and liquor stores and of insurance-trust activities. Intergovernmental receipts and payments between State and local governments are also excluded.

[3] Includes motor vehicle license taxes, other taxes, and charges and miscellaneous revenues.

[4] Includes intergovernmental payments to the Federal Government.

[5] Includes expenditures for libraries, hospitals, health, employment security administration, veterans' services, air transportation, sea and inland port facilities, parking facilities, transit subsidies, police protection, fire protection, correction, protective inspection and regulation, sewerage, natural resources, parks and recreation, housing and community development, solid waste management, financial administration, judicial and legal, general public buildings, other government administration, interest on general debt, and other general expenditures, not elsewhere classified.

Note: Except for States listed, data for fiscal years listed from 1963–64 to 2008–09 are the aggregation of data for government fiscal years that ended in the 12-month period from July 1 to June 30 of those years; Texas used August and Alabama and Michigan used September as end dates. Data for 1963 and earlier years include data for government fiscal years ending during that particular calendar year.

Data prior to 1952 are not available for intervening years.

Source: Department of Commerce (Bureau of the Census).

[Billions of dollars]

End of year or month	Total Treasury securities outstanding [1]	Marketable							Nonmarketable				
		Total [2]	Treasury bills	Treasury notes	Treasury bonds	Treasury inflation-protected securities			Total	U.S. savings securities [3]	Foreign series [4]	Government account series	Other [5]
						Total	Notes	Bonds					
Fiscal year:													
1973	456.4	263.0	100.1	117.8	45.1	....	....	....	193.4	59.4	28.5	101.7	3.7
1974	473.2	266.6	105.0	128.4	33.1	....	....	....	206.7	61.9	25.0	115.4	4.3
1975	532.1	315.6	128.6	150.3	36.8	....	....	....	216.5	65.5	23.2	124.2	3.6
1976	619.3	392.6	161.2	191.8	39.6	....	....	....	226.7	69.7	21.5	130.6	4.9
1977	697.6	443.5	156.1	241.7	45.7	....	....	....	254.1	75.4	21.8	140.1	16.8
1978	767.0	485.2	160.9	267.9	56.4	....	....	....	281.8	79.8	21.7	153.3	27.1
1979	819.0	506.7	161.4	274.2	71.1	....	....	....	312.3	80.4	28.1	176.4	27.4
1980	906.4	594.5	199.8	310.9	83.8	....	....	....	311.9	72.7	25.2	189.8	24.2
1981	996.5	683.2	223.4	363.6	96.2	....	....	....	313.3	68.0	20.5	201.1	23.7
1982	1,140.9	824.4	277.9	442.9	103.6	....	....	....	316.5	67.3	14.6	210.5	24.1
1983	1,375.8	1,024.0	340.7	557.5	125.7	....	....	....	351.8	70.0	11.5	234.7	35.6
1984	1,559.6	1,176.6	356.8	661.7	158.1	....	....	....	383.0	72.8	8.8	259.5	41.8
1985	1,821.0	1,360.2	384.2	776.4	199.5	....	....	....	460.8	77.0	6.6	313.9	63.3
1986	2,122.7	1,564.3	410.7	896.9	241.7	....	....	....	558.4	85.6	4.1	365.9	102.8
1987	2,347.8	1,676.0	378.3	1,005.1	277.6	....	....	....	671.8	97.0	4.4	440.7	129.8
1988	2,599.9	1,802.9	398.5	1,089.6	299.9	....	....	....	797.0	106.2	6.3	536.5	148.0
1989	2,836.3	1,892.8	406.6	1,133.2	338.0	....	....	....	943.5	114.0	6.8	663.7	159.0
1990	3,210.9	2,092.8	482.5	1,218.1	377.2	....	....	....	1,118.2	122.2	36.0	779.4	180.6
1991	3,662.8	2,390.7	564.6	1,387.7	423.4	....	....	....	1,272.1	133.5	41.6	908.4	188.5
1992	4,061.8	2,677.5	634.3	1,566.3	461.8	....	....	....	1,384.3	148.3	37.0	1,011.0	188.0
1993	4,408.6	2,904.9	658.4	1,734.2	497.4	....	....	....	1,503.7	167.0	42.5	1,114.3	179.9
1994	4,689.5	3,091.6	697.3	1,867.5	511.8	....	....	....	1,597.9	176.4	42.0	1,211.7	167.8
1995	4,950.6	3,260.4	742.5	1,980.3	522.6	....	....	....	1,690.2	181.2	41.0	1,324.3	143.8
1996	5,220.8	3,418.4	761.2	2,098.7	543.5	....	....	....	1,802.4	184.1	37.5	1,454.7	126.1
1997	5,407.5	3,439.6	701.9	2,122.2	576.2	24.4	24.4	....	1,967.9	182.7	34.9	1,608.5	141.9
1998	5,518.7	3,331.0	637.6	2,009.1	610.4	58.8	41.9	17.0	2,187.7	180.8	35.1	1,777.3	194.4
1999	5,647.2	3,233.0	653.2	1,828.8	643.7	92.4	67.6	24.8	2,414.2	180.0	31.0	2,005.2	198.1
2000	5,622.1	2,992.8	616.2	1,611.3	635.3	115.0	81.6	33.4	2,629.3	177.7	25.4	2,242.9	183.3
2001 [1]	5,807.5	2,930.7	734.9	1,433.0	613.0	134.9	95.1	39.7	2,876.7	186.5	18.3	2,492.1	179.9
2002	6,228.2	3,136.7	868.3	1,521.6	593.0	138.9	93.7	45.1	3,091.5	193.3	12.5	2,707.3	178.4
2003	6,783.2	3,460.7	918.2	1,799.5	576.9	166.1	120.0	46.1	3,322.5	201.6	11.0	2,912.2	197.7
2004	7,379.1	3,846.1	961.5	2,109.6	552.0	223.0	....	....	3,533.0	204.2	5.9	3,130.0	192.9
2005	7,932.7	4,084.9	914.3	2,328.8	520.7	307.1	....	....	3,847.8	203.6	3.1	3,380.6	260.5
2006	8,507.0	4,303.0	911.5	2,447.2	534.7	395.6	....	....	4,203.9	203.7	3.0	3,722.7	274.5
2007	9,007.7	4,448.1	958.1	2,458.0	561.1	456.9	....	....	4,559.5	197.1	3.0	4,026.8	332.6
2008	10,024.7	5,236.0	1,489.8	2,624.8	582.9	524.5	....	....	4,788.7	194.3	3.0	4,297.7	293.8
2009	11,909.8	7,009.7	1,992.5	3,773.8	679.8	551.7	....	....	4,900.1	192.5	4.9	4,454.3	248.4
2010	13,561.6	8,498.3	1,788.5	5,255.9	849.9	593.8	....	....	5,063.3	188.8	4.2	4,645.3	225.0
2011	14,790.3	9,624.5	1,477.5	6,412.5	1,020.4	705.7	....	....	5,165.8	185.2	3.0	4,793.9	183.7
2010: Jan	12,278.6	7,226.6	1,689.5	4,229.5	731.4	564.3	....	....	5,052.1	190.9	5.4	4,616.2	239.6
Feb	12,440.1	7,406.4	1,736.5	4,337.3	749.2	571.4	....	....	5,033.7	190.7	5.4	4,601.8	235.8
Mar	12,773.1	7,757.0	1,843.5	4,566.1	762.4	573.2	....	....	5,016.1	190.3	4.9	4,580.6	240.3
Apr	12,948.7	7,901.3	1,847.5	4,704.3	776.3	561.2	....	....	5,047.5	190.1	4.5	4,611.7	241.2
May	12,992.5	7,958.4	1,855.5	4,734.0	793.7	563.2	....	....	5,034.2	189.9	4.4	4,598.7	241.1
June	13,201.8	8,102.4	1,782.5	4,938.4	806.8	564.5	....	....	5,099.4	189.7	4.0	4,669.9	235.8
July	13,237.7	8,178.9	1,790.5	4,981.4	819.8	576.9	....	....	5,058.9	189.4	3.4	4,638.6	227.4
Aug	13,449.7	8,404.5	1,825.5	5,148.3	836.8	583.6	....	....	5,045.2	189.0	4.2	4,627.5	224.5
Sept	13,561.6	8,498.3	1,788.5	5,255.9	849.9	593.8	....	....	5,063.3	188.8	4.2	4,645.3	225.0
Oct	13,668.8	8,542.7	1,768.5	5,296.3	863.0	604.7	....	....	5,126.1	188.7	4.2	4,706.4	226.9
Nov	13,860.8	8,748.3	1,775.5	5,467.8	879.5	615.4	....	....	5,112.5	188.4	4.2	4,693.9	226.0
Dec	14,025.2	8,863.3	1,772.5	5,571.7	892.6	616.1	....	....	5,162.0	188.0	4.0	4,745.2	224.7
2011: Jan	14,131.1	8,964.7	1,760.5	5,672.2	905.9	615.8	....	....	5,166.3	187.5	4.0	4,755.8	219.0
Feb	14,194.8	9,048.2	1,738.5	5,750.8	922.3	626.3	....	....	5,146.6	187.3	3.8	4,741.3	214.1
Mar	14,270.1	9,132.7	1,698.5	5,847.9	935.3	640.8	....	....	5,137.4	186.9	3.8	4,733.0	213.7
Apr	14,287.6	9,136.6	1,638.5	5,903.5	948.9	635.4	....	....	5,151.1	186.6	3.8	4,748.0	212.7
May	14,344.7	9,262.2	1,578.5	6,054.7	964.9	653.8	....	....	5,082.4	186.4	3.7	4,684.8	207.5
June	14,343.1	9,334.6	1,531.5	6,151.3	977.9	665.5	....	....	5,008.4	186.1	3.7	4,620.4	198.3
July	14,342.4	9,377.6	1,492.5	6,204.3	990.9	681.5	....	....	4,964.7	185.8	3.1	4,588.2	187.7
Aug	14,684.3	9,521.8	1,493.5	6,318.7	1,007.4	693.8	....	....	5,162.5	185.4	3.0	4,791.3	182.8
Sept	14,790.3	9,624.5	1,477.5	6,412.5	1,020.4	705.7	....	....	5,165.8	185.2	3.0	4,793.9	183.7
Oct	14,993.7	9,746.5	1,482.5	6,507.0	1,033.4	715.2	....	....	5,247.2	185.6	3.0	4,872.2	186.4
Nov	15,110.5	9,878.3	1,512.5	6,579.0	1,050.6	727.8	....	....	5,232.2	185.5	3.0	4,857.2	186.5
Dec	15,222.9	9,936.9	1,520.5	6,605.1	1,064.1	738.8	....	....	5,286.1	185.3	3.0	4,913.9	183.9

[1] Data beginning with January 2001 are interest-bearing and non-interest-bearing securities; prior data are interest-bearing securities only.

[2] Data from 1986 to 2002 and 2005 to 2011 include Federal Financing Bank securities, not shown separately.

[3] Through 1996, series is U.S. savings bonds. Beginning 1997, includes U.S. retirement plan bonds, U.S. individual retirement bonds, and U.S. savings notes previously included in "other" nonmarketable securities.

[4] Nonmarketable certificates of indebtedness, notes, bonds, and bills in the Treasury foreign series of dollar-denominated and foreign-currency-denominated issues.

[5] Includes depository bonds; retirement plan bonds; Rural Electrification Administration bonds; State and local bonds; special issues held only by U.S. Government agencies and trust funds and the Federal home loan banks; for the period July 2003 through February 2004, depositary compensation securities; and beginning August 2008, Hope bonds for the HOPE For Homeowners Program.

Note: Through fiscal year 1976, the fiscal year was on a July 1–June 30 basis; beginning with October 1976 (fiscal year 1977), the fiscal year is on an October 1–September 30 basis.

Source: Department of the Treasury.

TABLE B–88. Maturity distribution and average length of marketable interest-bearing public debt securities held by private investors, 1973–2011

End of year or month	Amount outstanding, privately held	Maturity class					Average length [1]
		Within 1 year	1 to 5 years	5 to 10 years	10 to 20 years	20 years and over	
		Millions of dollars					Months
Fiscal year:							
1973	167,869	84,041	54,139	16,385	8,741	4,564	37
1974	164,862	87,150	50,103	14,197	9,930	3,481	35
1975	210,382	115,677	65,852	15,385	8,857	4,611	32
1976	279,782	150,296	90,578	24,169	8,087	6,652	31
1977	326,674	161,329	113,319	33,067	8,428	10,531	35
1978	356,501	163,819	132,993	33,500	11,383	14,805	39
1979	380,530	181,883	127,574	32,279	18,489	20,304	43
1980	463,717	220,084	156,244	38,809	25,901	22,679	41
1981	549,863	256,187	182,237	48,743	32,569	30,127	43
1982	682,043	314,436	221,783	75,749	33,017	37,058	43
1983	862,631	379,579	294,955	99,174	40,826	48,097	44
1984	1,017,488	437,941	332,808	130,417	49,664	66,658	49
1985	1,185,675	472,661	402,766	159,383	62,853	88,012	54
1986	1,354,275	506,903	467,348	189,995	70,664	119,365	59
1987	1,445,366	483,582	526,746	209,160	72,862	153,016	65
1988	1,555,208	524,201	552,993	232,453	74,186	171,375	66
1989	1,654,660	546,751	578,333	247,428	80,616	201,532	70
1990	1,841,903	626,297	630,144	267,573	82,713	235,176	70
1991	2,113,799	713,778	761,243	280,574	84,900	273,304	70
1992	2,363,802	808,705	866,329	295,921	84,706	308,141	69
1993	2,562,336	858,135	978,714	306,663	94,345	324,479	69
1994	2,719,861	877,932	1,128,322	289,998	88,208	335,401	66
1995	2,870,781	1,002,875	1,157,492	290,111	87,297	333,006	63
1996	3,011,185	1,058,558	1,212,258	306,643	111,360	322,366	62
1997	2,998,846	1,017,913	1,206,993	321,622	154,205	298,113	64
1998	2,856,637	940,572	1,105,175	319,331	157,347	334,212	68
1999	2,728,011	915,145	962,644	378,163	149,703	322,356	72
2000	2,469,152	858,903	791,540	355,382	167,082	296,246	75
2001	2,328,302	900,178	650,522	329,247	174,653	273,702	73
2002	2,492,821	939,986	802,032	311,176	203,816	235,811	66
2003	2,804,092	1,057,049	955,239	351,552	243,755	196,497	61
2004	3,145,244	1,127,850	1,150,979	414,728	243,036	208,652	59
2005	3,334,411	1,100,783	1,279,646	499,386	281,229	173,367	58
2006	3,496,359	1,140,553	1,295,589	589,748	290,733	179,736	59
2007	3,634,666	1,176,510	1,309,871	677,905	291,963	178,417	58
2008	4,745,256	2,042,003	1,468,455	719,347	352,430	163,022	49
2009	6,228,565	2,604,676	2,074,723	994,688	350,550	203,928	49
2010	7,676,335	2,479,518	2,955,561	1,529,283	340,861	371,112	57
2011	7,951,366	2,503,926	3,084,882	1,543,847	309,151	509,559	60
2010: Jan	6,412,960	2,324,877	2,334,184	1,147,170	349,376	257,353	54
Feb	6,591,769	2,372,965	2,420,971	1,173,496	342,995	281,343	54
Mar	6,968,331	2,492,450	2,579,109	1,258,977	343,413	294,381	54
Apr	7,112,555	2,496,967	2,644,691	1,320,051	343,461	307,386	54
May	7,139,816	2,493,411	2,659,209	1,324,688	353,276	309,233	55
June	7,315,100	2,432,122	2,800,261	1,406,962	353,499	322,256	55
July	7,360,528	2,453,077	2,797,309	1,421,267	353,608	335,267	56
Aug	7,607,853	2,504,906	2,922,651	1,481,051	341,136	358,109	56
Sept	7,676,335	2,479,518	2,955,561	1,529,283	340,861	371,112	57
Oct	7,859,482	2,470,906	2,930,452	1,537,902	338,278	381,945	57
Nov	7,827,328	2,510,845	3,012,545	1,572,551	334,655	396,733	57
Dec	7,831,450	2,544,760	2,981,135	1,568,471	330,178	406,906	57
2011: Jan	7,825,784	2,559,917	2,968,708	1,552,207	328,998	415,954	57
Feb	7,810,240	2,568,072	2,962,896	1,527,039	329,050	423,183	57
Mar	7,781,983	2,555,954	2,937,225	1,528,474	329,019	431,311	58
Apr	7,653,649	2,522,043	2,870,226	1,496,984	324,243	440,152	58
May	7,721,626	2,499,253	2,953,201	1,499,893	317,188	452,090	59
June	7,706,588	2,474,344	2,961,638	1,486,856	315,369	468,382	59
July	7,674,300	2,481,706	2,924,762	1,471,149	315,618	481,063	60
Aug	7,861,156	2,495,843	3,048,014	1,510,394	310,042	496,863	60
Sept	7,951,366	2,503,926	3,084,882	1,543,847	309,151	509,559	60
Oct	8,074,439	2,546,549	3,164,655	1,539,649	307,001	516,584	60
Nov	8,196,987	2,615,920	3,234,816	1,535,457	292,136	518,658	59
Dec	8,205,749	2,641,533	3,251,453	1,505,074	289,711	517,978	59

[1] Average length calculations are to call date. Treasury inflation-protected securities—notes, first offered in 1997, and bonds, first offered in 1998—are included in the average length calculation from 1997 forward.

Note: Through fiscal year 1976, the fiscal year was on a July 1–June 30 basis; beginning with October 1976 (fiscal year 1977), the fiscal year is on an October 1–September 30 basis.

Data shown in this table are as of January 20, 2012.

Source: Department of the Treasury.

TABLE B-89. Estimated ownership of U.S. Treasury securities, 1998–2011

[Billions of dollars]

End of month	Total public debt [1]	Federal Reserve and Intragovernmental holdings [2]	Held by private investors									
						Pension funds						
			Total privately held	Depository institutions [3]	U.S. savings bonds [4]	Private [5]	State and local governments	Insurance companies	Mutual funds [6]	State and local governments	Foreign and international [7]	Other investors [8]
1998: Mar	5,542.4	2,104.9	3,437.5	308.3	181.2	141.3	212.1	169.5	234.6	238.1	1,250.5	701.9
June	5,547.9	2,198.6	3,349.3	290.9	180.7	139.0	213.2	160.6	230.8	258.5	1,256.0	619.8
Sept	5,526.2	2,213.0	3,313.2	244.5	180.8	135.5	207.8	151.4	231.7	271.8	1,224.2	665.4
Dec	5,614.2	2,280.2	3,334.0	237.4	180.3	133.2	212.6	141.7	257.6	280.8	1,278.7	611.7
1999: Mar	5,651.6	2,324.1	3,327.5	247.4	180.6	135.5	211.5	137.5	245.0	288.4	1,272.3	609.4
June	5,638.8	2,439.6	3,199.2	240.6	180.0	142.9	213.8	133.6	228.1	298.6	1,258.8	502.7
Sept	5,656.3	2,480.9	3,175.4	241.2	180.0	150.9	204.8	128.0	222.5	299.2	1,281.4	467.3
Dec	5,776.1	2,542.2	3,233.9	248.7	179.3	153.0	198.8	123.4	228.7	304.5	1,268.7	528.8
2000: Mar	5,773.4	2,590.6	3,182.8	237.7	178.6	150.2	196.9	120.0	222.3	306.3	1,085.0	685.7
June	5,685.9	2,698.6	2,987.3	222.2	177.7	149.0	194.9	116.5	205.4	309.3	1,060.7	551.7
Sept	5,674.2	2,737.9	2,936.3	220.5	177.7	147.9	185.5	113.7	207.8	307.9	1,038.8	536.5
Dec	5,662.2	2,781.8	2,880.4	201.5	176.9	145.0	179.1	110.2	225.7	310.0	1,015.2	516.9
2001: Mar	5,773.7	2,880.9	2,892.8	188.0	184.8	153.4	177.3	109.1	225.3	316.9	1,012.5	525.4
June	5,726.8	3,004.2	2,722.6	188.1	185.5	148.5	183.1	108.1	221.0	324.8	983.3	380.2
Sept	5,807.5	3,027.8	2,779.7	189.1	186.5	149.9	166.8	106.8	234.1	321.2	992.2	433.1
Dec	5,943.4	3,123.9	2,819.5	181.5	190.4	145.8	155.1	105.7	261.9	328.4	1,040.1	410.6
2002: Mar	6,006.0	3,156.8	2,849.2	187.6	192.0	152.7	163.3	114.0	266.1	327.6	1,057.2	388.8
June	6,126.5	3,276.7	2,849.8	204.7	192.8	152.1	153.9	122.0	253.8	333.6	1,123.1	313.7
Sept	6,228.2	3,303.5	2,924.8	209.3	193.3	154.5	156.3	130.4	256.8	338.6	1,188.6	296.9
Dec	6,405.7	3,387.2	3,018.5	222.6	194.9	153.8	158.9	139.7	281.0	354.7	1,235.6	277.4
2003: Mar	6,460.8	3,390.8	3,070.0	153.6	196.9	165.8	162.1	139.5	296.6	350.0	1,275.2	330.2
June	6,670.1	3,505.4	3,164.7	145.4	199.2	170.2	161.3	138.7	302.3	347.9	1,371.9	327.8
Sept	6,783.2	3,515.3	3,267.9	146.8	201.6	167.7	155.5	137.4	287.1	357.7	1,443.3	371.0
Dec	6,998.0	3,620.1	3,377.9	153.1	203.9	172.2	148.6	136.5	280.9	364.2	1,523.1	395.4
2004: Mar	7,131.1	3,628.3	3,502.8	162.8	204.5	169.8	143.6	172.4	280.8	374.1	1,670.0	324.8
June	7,274.3	3,742.8	3,531.5	158.6	204.6	173.3	134.9	174.6	258.7	381.2	1,735.4	310.1
Sept	7,379.1	3,772.0	3,607.1	138.5	204.2	174.0	140.8	182.9	255.0	381.7	1,794.5	335.5
Dec	7,596.1	3,905.6	3,690.5	125.0	204.5	173.7	151.0	188.5	254.1	389.1	1,849.3	355.4
2005: Mar	7,776.9	3,921.6	3,855.3	141.8	204.2	177.3	158.0	193.3	261.1	412.0	1,952.2	355.5
June	7,836.5	4,033.5	3,803.0	126.9	204.2	181.0	171.3	195.0	248.7	444.0	1,877.5	354.4
Sept	7,932.7	4,067.8	3,864.9	125.3	203.6	184.2	164.8	200.7	244.7	467.6	1,929.6	344.3
Dec	8,170.4	4,199.8	3,970.6	117.1	205.2	184.9	153.8	202.3	251.3	481.4	2,033.9	340.6
2006: Mar	8,371.2	4,257.2	4,114.0	113.0	206.0	186.7	153.0	200.3	248.7	473.3	2,082.1	450.9
June	8,420.0	4,389.2	4,030.8	119.5	205.2	192.1	150.9	196.1	244.2	484.2	1,977.8	460.9
Sept	8,507.0	4,432.8	4,074.2	113.6	203.7	201.9	154.7	196.8	235.7	484.9	2,025.3	457.5
Dec	8,680.2	4,558.1	4,122.1	114.8	202.4	207.5	156.2	197.9	250.7	506.8	2,103.1	382.7
2007: Mar	8,849.7	4,576.6	4,273.1	119.8	200.3	221.7	158.3	185.4	264.5	546.2	2,194.8	382.0
June	8,867.7	4,715.1	4,152.6	110.4	198.6	232.5	159.3	168.9	267.7	569.3	2,192.0	253.7
Sept	9,007.7	4,738.0	4,269.7	119.7	197.1	246.7	138.9	155.1	306.3	526.8	2,235.3	343.7
Dec	9,229.2	4,833.5	4,395.7	129.8	196.5	257.6	141.6	141.9	362.9	525.1	2,353.2	287.2
2008: Mar	9,437.6	4,694.7	4,742.9	125.0	195.4	270.5	142.0	152.1	484.4	524.9	2,506.3	342.2
June	9,492.0	4,685.8	4,806.2	112.7	195.0	276.7	141.8	159.4	477.2	513.4	2,587.4	342.5
Sept	10,024.7	4,692.7	5,332.0	130.0	194.3	292.5	143.9	163.4	656.1	493.9	2,802.4	455.5
Dec	10,699.8	4,806.4	5,893.4	105.0	194.1	297.2	146.4	171.4	768.8	475.1	3,077.2	658.3
2009: Mar	11,126.9	4,785.2	6,341.7	125.6	194.0	330.9	150.2	191.0	715.9	508.0	3,265.7	860.4
June	11,545.3	5,026.8	6,518.5	140.8	193.6	353.4	159.9	200.0	695.6	504.7	3,460.8	809.7
Sept	11,909.8	5,127.1	6,782.7	198.1	192.5	398.1	167.3	210.2	644.9	492.3	3,570.6	908.7
Dec	12,311.3	5,276.9	7,034.4	202.4	191.3	429.8	174.5	222.0	666.2	493.9	3,685.1	969.1
2010: Mar	12,773.1	5,259.8	7,513.3	269.4	190.3	462.2	179.1	225.7	646.4	499.9	3,877.9	1,162.5
June	13,201.8	5,345.1	7,856.7	266.1	189.7	531.9	182.0	231.8	632.1	504.8	4,070.0	1,248.4
Sept	13,561.6	5,350.5	8,211.1	322.9	188.8	595.2	185.5	240.6	607.4	498.1	4,324.2	1,248.5
Dec	14,025.2	5,656.2	8,368.9	319.1	188.0	615.9	185.6	248.4	637.9	503.6	4,435.6	1,234.9
2011: Mar	14,270.0	5,958.9	8,311.1	321.2	186.9	632.9	187.9	246.9	641.1	496.8	4,473.6	1,123.8
June	14,343.1	6,220.4	8,122.7	279.3	186.1	658.7	186.9	246.1	653.1	479.3	4,511.1	922.1
Sept	14,790.3	6,328.0	8,462.4	292.2	185.2	689.6	188.7	253.7	699.0	460.8	4,667.0	1,026.2
Dec	15,222.8	6,439.6	8,783.3	....	185.3	....	....	....	....	....	....	....

[1] Face value.
[2] Federal Reserve holdings exclude Treasury securities held under repurchase agreements.
[3] Includes commercial banks, savings institutions, and credit unions.
[4] Current accrual value.
[5] Includes Treasury securities held by the Federal Employees Retirement System Thrift Savings Plan "G Fund."
[6] Includes money market mutual funds, mutual funds, and closed-end investment companies.
[7] Includes nonmarketable foreign series, Treasury securities, and Treasury deposit funds. Excludes Treasury securities held under repurchase agreements in custody accounts at the Federal Reserve Bank of New York. Estimates reflect benchmarks to this series at differing intervals; for further detail, see *Treasury Bulletin* and http://www.treas.gov/tic/ticsec2.shtml.
[8] Includes individuals, Government-sponsored enterprises, brokers and dealers, bank personal trusts and estates, corporate and noncorporate businesses, and other investors.

Note: Data shown in this table are as of January 20, 2012.

Source: Department of the Treasury.

TABLE B–90. Corporate profits with inventory valuation and capital consumption adjustments, 1963–2011

[Billions of dollars; quarterly data at seasonally adjusted annual rates]

Year or quarter	Corporate profits with inventory valuation and capital consumption adjustments	Taxes on corporate income	Corporate profits after tax with inventory valuation and capital consumption adjustments		
			Total	Net dividends	Undistributed profits with inventory valuation and capital consumption adjustments
1963	68.3	26.4	42.0	16.2	25.7
1964	75.5	28.2	47.4	18.2	29.2
1965	86.5	31.1	55.5	20.2	35.3
1966	92.5	33.9	58.7	20.7	38.0
1967	90.2	32.9	57.3	21.5	35.8
1968	97.3	39.6	57.6	23.5	34.1
1969	94.5	40.0	54.5	24.2	30.3
1970	82.5	34.8	47.7	24.3	23.4
1971	96.1	38.2	57.9	25.0	32.9
1972	111.4	42.3	69.1	26.8	42.2
1973	124.5	50.0	74.5	29.9	44.6
1974	115.1	52.8	62.3	33.2	29.1
1975	133.3	51.6	81.7	33.0	48.7
1976	161.6	65.3	96.3	39.0	57.3
1977	191.8	74.4	117.4	44.8	72.6
1978	218.4	84.9	133.6	50.8	82.8
1979	225.4	90.0	135.3	57.5	77.8
1980	201.4	87.2	114.2	64.1	50.2
1981	223.3	84.3	138.9	73.8	65.2
1982	205.7	66.5	139.2	77.7	61.5
1983	259.8	80.6	179.2	83.5	95.7
1984	318.6	97.5	221.1	90.8	130.3
1985	332.5	99.4	233.1	97.6	135.6
1986	314.1	109.7	204.5	106.2	98.3
1987	367.8	130.4	237.4	112.3	125.1
1988	426.6	141.6	285.0	129.9	155.1
1989	425.6	146.1	279.5	158.0	121.5
1990	434.4	145.4	289.0	169.1	120.0
1991	457.3	138.6	318.7	180.7	138.0
1992	496.2	148.7	347.5	188.0	159.5
1993	543.7	171.0	372.7	202.9	169.7
1994	628.2	193.1	435.1	235.7	199.4
1995	716.2	217.8	498.3	254.4	243.9
1996	801.5	231.5	570.0	297.7	272.3
1997	884.8	245.4	639.4	331.2	308.2
1998	812.4	248.4	564.1	351.5	212.6
1999	856.3	258.8	597.5	337.4	260.1
2000	819.2	265.1	554.1	377.9	176.3
2001	784.2	203.3	580.9	370.9	210.0
2002	872.2	192.3	679.9	399.3	280.6
2003	977.8	243.8	734.0	424.9	309.2
2004	1,246.9	306.1	940.8	550.3	390.5
2005	1,456.1	412.4	1,043.7	557.3	486.4
2006	1,608.3	473.3	1,135.0	704.8	430.3
2007	1,510.6	445.5	1,065.2	794.5	270.7
2008	1,248.4	309.0	939.4	786.9	152.5
2009	1,362.0	272.4	1,089.6	620.0	469.6
2010	1,800.1	411.1	1,389.1	737.3	651.7
2011 ᵖ				814.6	
2008: I	1,360.0	355.2	1,004.8	835.9	168.9
II	1,333.7	344.1	989.7	803.4	186.3
III	1,328.6	312.5	1,016.1	780.5	235.5
IV	971.2	224.3	746.9	727.6	19.2
2009: I	1,175.2	208.8	966.4	671.9	294.5
II	1,262.3	244.8	1,017.5	600.9	416.6
III	1,438.8	301.6	1,137.3	584.1	553.1
IV	1,571.6	334.4	1,237.2	623.0	614.2
2010: I	1,724.2	409.7	1,314.5	684.8	629.7
II	1,785.8	399.6	1,386.3	729.3	657.0
III	1,833.1	430.3	1,402.8	760.5	642.3
IV	1,857.4	404.7	1,452.7	774.8	677.9
2011: I	1,876.4	422.3	1,454.1	793.8	660.3
II	1,937.6	420.5	1,517.1	807.4	709.6
III	1,970.1	411.4	1,558.7	821.4	737.3
IV ᵖ				835.6	

Source: Department of Commerce (Bureau of Economic Analysis).

TABLE B–91. Corporate profits by industry, 1963–2011

[Billions of dollars; quarterly data at seasonally adjusted annual rates]

		Corporate profits with inventory valuation adjustment and without capital consumption adjustment												
		Domestic industries												Rest of the world
Year or quarter	Total	Total	Financial			Nonfinancial								
			Total	Federal Reserve banks	Other	Total	Manufactur-ing[1]	Transporta-tion[2]	Utilities	Whole-sale trade	Retail trade	Infor-mation	Other	
SIC:[3]														
1963	62.1	58.1	8.3	1.0	7.3	49.8	29.7	9.5	....	2.8	3.6	....	4.1	4.1
1964	68.6	64.1	8.8	1.1	7.6	55.4	32.6	10.2	....	3.4	4.5	....	4.7	4.5
1965	78.9	74.2	9.3	1.3	8.0	64.9	39.8	11.0	....	3.8	4.9	....	5.4	4.7
1966	84.6	80.1	10.7	1.7	9.1	69.3	42.6	12.0	....	4.0	4.9	....	5.9	4.5
1967	82.0	77.2	11.2	2.0	9.2	66.0	39.2	10.9	....	4.1	5.7	....	6.1	4.8
1968	88.8	83.2	12.8	2.5	10.3	70.4	41.9	11.0	....	4.6	6.4	....	6.6	5.6
1969	85.5	78.9	13.6	3.1	10.5	65.3	37.3	10.7	....	4.9	6.4	....	6.1	6.6
1970	74.4	67.3	15.4	3.5	11.9	52.0	27.5	8.3	....	4.4	6.0	....	5.8	7.1
1971	88.3	80.4	17.6	3.3	14.3	62.8	35.1	8.9	....	5.2	7.2	....	6.4	7.9
1972	101.6	92.1	19.2	3.3	15.8	72.9	42.2	9.5	....	6.9	7.4	....	7.0	9.5
1973	115.4	100.5	20.5	4.5	16.1	80.0	47.2	9.1	....	8.2	6.7	....	8.8	14.9
1974	109.6	92.1	20.2	5.7	14.5	71.9	41.4	7.6	....	11.5	2.3	....	9.1	17.5
1975	135.0	120.4	20.2	5.6	14.6	100.2	55.2	11.0	....	13.8	8.2	....	12.0	14.6
1976	165.6	149.1	25.0	5.9	19.1	124.1	71.4	15.3	....	12.9	10.5	....	14.0	16.5
1977	194.8	175.7	31.9	6.1	25.8	143.8	79.4	18.6	....	15.6	12.4	....	17.8	19.1
1978	222.4	199.6	39.5	7.6	31.9	160.0	90.5	21.8	....	15.6	12.3	....	19.8	22.9
1979	232.0	197.4	40.4	9.4	30.9	157.0	89.8	17.0	....	18.8	9.9	....	21.6	34.6
1980	211.4	175.9	34.0	11.8	22.2	142.0	78.3	18.4	....	17.2	6.2	....	21.8	35.5
1981	219.1	189.4	29.1	14.4	14.7	160.3	91.1	20.3	....	22.4	9.9	....	16.7	29.7
1982	191.1	158.5	26.0	15.2	10.8	132.5	67.1	23.1	....	19.6	13.5	....	9.3	32.6
1983	226.6	191.5	35.5	14.6	21.0	156.0	76.2	29.5	....	21.0	18.8	....	10.4	35.1
1984	264.6	228.1	34.4	16.4	18.0	193.7	91.8	40.1	....	29.5	21.1	....	11.1	36.6
1985	257.5	219.4	45.9	16.3	29.5	173.5	84.3	33.8	....	23.9	22.2	....	9.2	38.1
1986	253.0	213.5	56.8	15.5	41.2	156.8	57.9	35.8	....	24.1	23.5	....	15.5	39.5
1987	306.9	258.8	61.6	16.2	45.3	197.3	87.5	42.4	....	19.0	24.0	....	24.4	48.0
1988	367.7	310.8	68.8	18.1	50.7	242.0	122.5	48.9	....	20.4	21.0	....	29.3	57.0
1989	374.1	307.0	80.2	20.6	59.5	226.8	112.1	43.8	....	22.1	22.1	....	26.7	67.1
1990	398.8	322.7	92.3	21.8	70.5	230.4	114.4	44.7	....	19.6	21.6	....	30.1	76.1
1991	430.3	353.8	122.1	20.7	101.4	231.7	99.4	53.8	....	22.2	27.7	....	28.7	76.5
1992	471.6	398.5	142.7	18.3	124.4	255.8	100.8	59.2	....	25.5	29.2	....	41.1	73.1
1993	515.0	438.1	133.4	16.7	116.7	304.7	116.8	70.2	....	26.7	40.6	....	50.4	76.9
1994	586.6	508.6	129.2	18.5	110.7	379.5	150.1	85.2	....	31.8	47.2	....	65.2	78.0
1995	666.0	573.1	160.1	22.9	137.2	413.0	176.7	87.9	....	28.0	44.8	....	75.5	92.9
1996	743.8	641.8	167.5	22.5	144.9	474.4	192.0	93.7	....	40.6	53.7	....	94.5	102.0
1997	815.9	708.3	187.4	24.3	163.2	520.9	212.2	86.5	....	48.2	65.9	....	108.1	107.6
1998	738.6	635.9	159.6	25.6	134.0	476.2	173.4	81.1	....	51.7	74.7	....	95.5	102.8
1999	776.6	655.0	190.4	26.7	163.8	464.6	174.6	59.1	....	51.7	75.6	....	103.6	121.5
2000	755.7	610.0	194.4	31.2	163.2	415.7	166.5	45.8	....	55.6	71.4	....	76.4	145.6
NAICS:[3]														
1998	738.6	635.9	159.5	25.6	133.9	476.4	155.8	21.3	33.5	52.8	67.3	21.9	123.7	102.8
1999	776.6	655.0	189.3	26.7	162.6	465.7	148.8	16.5	33.7	54.8	65.7	12.5	133.6	121.5
2000	755.7	610.0	189.6	31.2	158.4	420.4	143.9	15.2	25.6	58.7	60.7	−15.5	131.8	145.6
2001	720.8	551.1	228.0	28.9	199.1	323.1	49.7	1.2	25.2	51.3	72.6	−24.4	147.4	169.7
2002	762.8	604.9	265.2	23.5	241.7	339.7	47.7	−.1	12.3	49.1	81.6	−3.8	153.0	157.9
2003	892.2	726.4	311.8	20.1	291.8	414.6	69.4	7.4	12.4	54.8	88.9	4.9	176.7	165.8
2004	1,195.1	990.1	362.3	20.0	342.3	627.8	154.1	14.4	19.4	75.6	93.4	45.6	225.2	205.0
2005	1,609.5	1,370.0	443.6	26.6	417.0	926.4	247.2	29.0	29.8	92.2	122.6	81.3	324.3	239.4
2006	1,784.7	1,527.8	448.0	33.8	414.1	1,079.9	304.5	42.1	54.4	103.7	133.2	92.4	349.6	256.8
2007	1,691.1	1,340.2	345.5	36.0	309.5	994.7	271.3	27.7	50.3	99.9	117.8	93.6	334.2	350.9
2008	1,315.5	908.9	122.2	35.1	87.1	786.7	195.5	31.9	30.7	86.3	81.6	75.1	285.7	406.6
2009	1,456.3	1,095.9	401.8	47.3	354.5	694.1	125.2	23.5	22.2	83.3	106.0	81.2	252.8	360.4
2010	1,780.4	1,398.5	494.7	71.6	423.2	903.7	217.1	34.4	25.0	85.8	122.6	87.7	331.2	381.9
2009: I	1,285.7	925.7	241.3	27.1	214.2	684.4	109.2	24.4	18.2	102.7	101.6	75.7	252.5	360.1
II	1,359.7	1,015.1	395.0	43.3	351.7	620.1	107.4	13.6	21.6	77.4	103.8	70.8	225.6	344.6
III	1,525.0	1,162.5	481.2	54.2	427.0	681.2	130.8	27.0	15.5	73.0	107.7	80.2	247.1	362.6
IV	1,654.6	1,280.3	489.6	64.7	425.0	790.6	153.4	29.2	33.4	79.9	110.9	97.9	285.8	374.3
2010: I	1,797.0	1,428.0	479.8	71.5	408.3	948.2	216.2	32.5	46.5	93.4	128.6	91.4	339.6	368.9
II	1,859.9	1,469.3	490.6	73.9	416.7	978.7	237.3	37.7	18.2	111.0	125.4	93.5	355.6	390.6
III	1,812.6	1,417.3	487.8	71.4	416.4	929.5	227.2	39.3	28.0	89.4	119.0	86.6	340.0	395.3
IV	1,652.2	1,279.3	520.8	69.5	451.3	758.5	187.7	28.2	7.1	49.5	117.3	79.1	289.6	372.9
2011: I	1,761.1	1,350.3	491.5	72.7	418.8	858.8	217.6	23.5	14.9	71.6	120.2	98.9	312.0	410.8
II	1,830.2	1,384.9	438.9	80.7	358.3	945.9	249.9	26.8	15.2	90.8	112.7	103.6	346.9	445.4
III	1,867.4	1,416.6	448.7	77.6	371.0	967.9	268.2	33.5	10.7	85.6	110.6	97.1	362.2	450.8

[1] See Table B–92 for industry detail.

[2] Data on Standard Industrial Classification (SIC) basis include transportation and public utilities. Those on North American Industry Classification System (NAICS) basis include transporation and warehousing. Utilities classified separately in NAICS (as shown beginning 1998).

[3] SIC-based industry data use the 1987 SIC for data beginning in 1987 and the 1972 SIC for prior data. NAICS-based data use 2002 NAICS.

Note: Industry data on SIC basis and NAICS basis are not necessarily the same and are not strictly comparable.

Source: Department of Commerce (Bureau of Economic Analysis).

TABLE B–92. Corporate profits of manufacturing industries, 1963–2011

[Billions of dollars; quarterly data at seasonally adjusted annual rates]

| Year or quarter | Total manufacturing | Corporate profits with inventory valuation adjustment and without capital consumption adjustment | | | | | | | | | | | |
| | | Durable goods [2] | | | | | | | Nondurable goods [2] | | | | |
		Total [1]	Fabricated metal products	Machinery	Computer and electronic products	Electrical equipment, appliances, and components	Motor vehicles, bodies and trailers, and parts	Other	Total	Food and beverage and tobacco products	Chemical products	Petroleum and coal products	Other
SIC: [3]													
1963	29.7	16.4	1.3	2.6	....	1.6	4.9	4.0	13.3	2.7	3.7	2.2	4.7
1964	32.6	18.1	1.5	3.3	....	1.7	4.6	4.4	14.5	2.7	4.1	2.4	5.3
1965	39.8	23.3	2.1	4.0	....	2.7	6.2	5.2	16.5	2.9	4.6	2.9	6.1
1966	42.6	24.1	2.4	4.6	....	3.0	5.2	5.2	18.6	3.3	4.9	3.4	6.9
1967	39.2	21.3	2.5	4.2	....	3.0	4.0	4.9	18.0	3.3	4.3	4.0	6.4
1968	41.9	22.5	2.3	4.2	....	2.9	5.5	5.6	19.4	3.2	5.3	3.8	7.1
1969	37.3	19.2	2.0	3.8	....	2.3	4.8	4.9	18.1	3.1	4.6	3.4	7.0
1970	27.5	10.5	1.1	3.1	....	1.3	1.3	2.9	17.0	3.2	3.9	3.7	6.1
1971	35.1	16.6	1.5	3.1	....	2.0	5.2	4.1	18.5	3.6	4.5	3.8	6.6
1972	42.2	22.9	2.2	4.6	....	2.9	6.0	5.6	19.3	3.0	5.3	3.4	7.7
1973	47.2	25.2	2.7	4.9	....	3.2	5.9	6.2	22.1	2.5	6.2	5.4	7.9
1974	41.4	15.3	1.8	3.3	....	.6	.7	4.0	26.1	2.6	5.3	10.9	7.3
1975	55.2	20.6	3.3	5.1	....	2.6	2.3	4.7	34.5	8.6	6.4	10.1	9.5
1976	71.4	31.4	3.9	6.9	....	3.8	7.4	7.3	39.9	7.1	8.2	13.5	11.1
1977	79.4	38.0	4.5	8.6	....	5.9	9.4	8.5	41.4	6.9	7.8	13.1	13.6
1978	90.5	45.4	5.0	10.7	....	6.7	9.0	10.5	45.1	6.2	8.3	15.8	14.8
1979	89.8	37.2	5.3	9.5	....	5.6	4.7	8.5	52.6	5.8	7.2	24.8	14.7
1980	78.3	18.9	4.4	8.0	....	5.2	−4.3	2.7	59.5	6.1	5.7	34.7	13.1
1981	91.1	19.5	4.5	9.0	....	5.2	.3	−2.6	71.6	9.2	8.0	40.0	14.5
1982	67.1	5.0	2.7	3.1	....	1.7	.0	2.1	62.1	7.3	5.1	34.7	15.0
1983	76.2	19.5	3.1	4.0	....	3.5	5.3	8.4	56.7	6.3	7.4	23.9	19.1
1984	91.8	39.3	4.7	6.0	....	5.1	9.2	14.6	52.6	6.8	8.2	17.6	20.1
1985	84.3	29.7	4.9	5.7	....	2.6	7.4	10.1	54.6	8.8	6.6	18.7	20.5
1986	57.9	26.3	5.2	.8	....	2.7	4.6	12.1	31.7	7.5	7.5	−4.7	21.3
1987	87.5	41.3	5.5	5.6	....	6.1	3.8	17.7	46.2	11.2	14.6	−1.4	21.9
1988	122.5	54.8	6.6	11.3	....	7.8	6.3	16.7	67.7	9.7	18.8	12.9	26.4
1989	112.1	51.8	6.4	12.4	....	9.5	2.8	14.3	60.3	11.2	18.3	6.6	24.2
1990	114.4	44.5	6.1	12.0	....	8.7	−1.8	16.1	69.9	14.4	17.0	16.5	22.0
1991	99.4	35.1	5.3	5.8	....	10.2	−5.3	17.5	64.3	18.3	16.3	7.4	22.3
1992	100.8	41.2	6.3	7.6	....	10.6	−.9	17.6	59.6	18.4	16.1	−.8	25.9
1993	116.8	56.5	7.4	7.6	....	15.4	6.1	19.6	60.4	16.5	16.0	2.8	25.0
1994	150.1	75.8	11.2	9.3	....	23.2	8.0	21.7	74.3	20.4	23.6	1.5	28.9
1995	176.7	82.3	11.9	14.9	....	22.0	.2	26.1	94.4	27.6	28.2	7.4	31.2
1996	192.0	92.0	14.6	17.0	....	20.7	4.5	29.5	99.9	22.7	26.6	15.3	35.3
1997	212.2	104.8	17.1	16.9	....	26.0	5.2	33.3	107.4	25.2	32.4	17.6	32.3
1998	173.4	86.7	16.1	19.6	....	9.1	5.9	29.8	86.6	22.0	26.2	7.1	31.4
1999	174.6	77.9	16.1	12.0	....	5.3	7.5	34.8	96.6	28.1	24.8	4.6	39.2
2000	166.5	64.6	15.5	16.2	....	5.1	−1.4	28.1	101.9	26.0	15.3	29.7	30.9
NAICS: [3]													
1998	155.8	82.7	16.4	15.3	4.2	6.2	6.4	34.2	73.1	22.1	25.0	5.3	20.7
1999	148.8	71.2	16.4	11.7	−6.8	6.4	7.7	35.9	77.6	30.9	22.8	2.2	21.7
2000	143.9	60.0	15.8	7.7	4.2	5.9	−.7	27.1	83.9	26.0	13.8	27.6	16.5
2001	49.7	−26.9	9.8	2.0	−48.6	1.9	−8.9	16.8	76.6	28.2	11.6	29.7	7.1
2002	47.7	−7.7	9.1	1.4	−34.4	.0	−4.5	20.7	55.4	25.3	17.8	1.3	11.0
2003	69.4	−4.3	8.0	1.0	−14.7	2.2	−11.7	10.8	73.8	24.0	18.9	23.5	7.4
2004	154.1	40.7	12.2	7.1	−4.3	.6	−6.8	31.9	113.4	24.3	24.7	49.1	15.3
2005	247.2	95.6	18.1	14.5	9.0	−1.4	1.1	54.2	151.7	27.3	25.7	79.4	19.3
2006	304.5	118.9	18.7	19.2	17.4	11.5	−6.8	58.9	185.7	32.5	52.5	76.6	24.0
2007	271.3	96.1	20.5	22.1	11.0	−1.2	−16.4	60.2	175.2	30.7	48.3	73.5	22.7
2008	195.5	56.8	15.8	16.6	12.2	4.6	−33.1	40.7	138.6	29.9	23.9	77.8	7.1
2009	125.2	20.5	10.5	7.8	15.4	8.4	−45.1	23.6	104.7	41.5	38.3	9.4	15.5
2010	217.1	95.0	11.7	15.3	39.5	7.0	−12.7	34.1	122.1	37.8	34.7	36.0	13.7
2009: I	109.2	.1	16.2	10.1	7.0	8.8	−64.1	22.2	109.1	39.2	29.6	29.5	10.8
II	107.4	7.9	11.4	6.7	15.2	7.7	−53.6	20.4	99.5	44.1	43.2	−4.5	16.6
III	130.8	22.2	8.6	5.9	17.0	7.9	−37.1	19.9	108.6	43.6	44.6	3.3	17.1
IV	153.4	51.7	5.9	8.3	22.3	9.0	−25.5	31.7	101.7	39.1	35.6	9.5	17.5
2010: I	216.2	99.8	11.4	13.3	39.5	8.8	−14.9	41.7	116.5	41.1	28.8	31.3	15.3
II	237.3	100.4	9.3	14.3	37.4	9.3	−6.9	36.9	136.9	40.8	29.4	52.8	13.9
III	227.2	95.2	12.5	16.8	39.0	7.6	−9.9	29.2	132.0	39.6	45.5	31.7	15.2
IV	187.7	84.5	13.5	16.9	41.9	2.4	−19.1	28.8	103.2	29.6	35.0	28.4	10.2
2011: I	217.6	90.8	14.6	20.0	29.0	4.3	−12.0	34.8	126.9	33.5	36.1	37.9	19.3
II	249.9	97.1	15.6	20.3	34.5	2.0	−12.2	36.8	152.9	34.7	32.4	71.3	14.4
III	268.2	113.6	17.5	24.5	35.4	1.9	−10.9	45.1	154.7	28.5	38.0	72.2	16.0

[1] For Standard Industrial Classification (SIC) data, includes primary metal industries, not shown separately.

[2] Industry groups shown in column headings reflect North American Industry Classification System (NAICS) classification for data beginning 1998. For data on SIC basis, the industry groups would be industrial machinery and equipment (now machinery), electronic and other electric equipment (now electrical equipment, appliances, and components), motor vehicles and equipment (now motor vehicles, bodies and trailers, and parts), food and kindred products (now food and beverage and tobacco products), and chemicals and allied products (now chemical products).

[3] See footnote 3 and Note, Table B–91.

Source: Department of Commerce (Bureau of Economic Analysis).

TABLE B–93. Sales, profits, and stockholders' equity, all manufacturing corporations, 1970–2011

[Billions of dollars]

Year or quarter	All manufacturing corporations				Durable goods industries				Nondurable goods industries			
	Sales (net)	Profits Before income taxes[1]	Profits After income taxes	Stockholders' equity[2]	Sales (net)	Profits Before income taxes[1]	After income taxes	Stockholders' equity[2]	Sales (net)	Profits Before income taxes[1]	After income taxes	Stockholders' equity[2]
1970	708.8	48.1	28.6	306.8	363.1	23.0	12.9	155.1	345.7	25.2	15.7	151.7
1971	751.1	52.9	31.0	320.8	381.8	26.5	14.5	160.4	369.3	26.5	16.5	160.5
1972	849.5	63.2	36.5	343.4	435.8	33.6	18.4	171.4	413.7	29.6	18.0	172.0
1973	1,017.2	81.4	48.1	374.1	527.3	43.6	24.8	188.7	489.9	37.8	23.3	185.4
1973: IV	275.1	21.4	13.0	386.4	140.1	10.8	6.3	194.7	135.0	10.6	6.7	191.7
New series:												
1973: IV	236.6	20.6	13.2	368.0	122.7	10.1	6.2	185.8	113.9	10.5	7.0	182.1
1974	1,060.6	92.1	58.7	395.0	529.0	41.1	24.7	196.0	531.6	51.0	34.1	199.0
1975	1,065.2	79.9	49.1	423.4	521.1	35.3	21.4	208.1	544.1	44.6	27.7	215.3
1976	1,203.2	104.9	64.5	462.7	589.6	50.7	30.8	224.3	613.7	54.3	33.7	238.4
1977	1,328.1	115.1	70.4	496.7	657.3	57.9	34.8	239.9	670.8	57.2	35.5	256.8
1978	1,496.4	132.5	81.1	540.5	760.7	69.6	41.8	262.6	735.7	62.9	39.3	277.9
1979	1,741.8	154.2	98.7	600.5	865.7	72.4	45.2	292.5	876.1	81.8	53.5	308.0
1980	1,912.8	145.8	92.6	668.1	889.1	57.4	35.6	317.7	1,023.7	88.4	56.9	350.4
1981	2,144.7	158.6	101.3	743.4	979.5	67.2	41.6	350.4	1,165.2	91.3	59.6	393.0
1982	2,039.4	108.2	70.9	770.2	913.1	34.7	21.7	355.5	1,126.4	73.6	49.3	414.7
1983	2,114.3	133.1	85.8	812.8	973.5	48.7	30.0	372.4	1,140.8	84.4	55.8	440.4
1984	2,335.0	165.6	107.6	864.2	1,107.6	75.5	48.9	395.6	1,227.5	90.0	58.8	468.5
1985	2,331.4	137.0	87.6	866.2	1,142.6	61.5	38.6	420.9	1,188.8	75.6	49.1	445.3
1986	2,220.9	129.3	83.1	874.7	1,125.5	52.1	32.6	436.3	1,095.4	77.2	50.5	438.4
1987	2,378.2	173.0	115.6	900.9	1,178.0	78.0	53.0	444.3	1,200.3	95.1	62.6	456.6
1988 [3]	2,596.2	215.3	153.8	957.6	1,284.7	91.6	66.9	468.7	1,311.5	123.7	86.8	488.9
1989	2,745.1	187.6	135.1	999.0	1,356.6	75.1	55.5	501.3	1,388.5	112.6	79.6	497.7
1990	2,810.7	158.1	110.1	1,043.8	1,357.2	57.3	40.7	515.0	1,453.5	100.8	69.4	528.9
1991	2,761.1	98.7	66.4	1,064.1	1,304.0	13.9	7.2	506.8	1,457.1	84.8	59.3	557.4
1992 [4]	2,890.2	31.4	22.1	1,034.7	1,389.8	−33.7	−24.0	473.9	1,500.4	65.1	46.0	560.8
1993	3,015.1	117.9	83.2	1,039.7	1,490.2	38.9	27.4	482.7	1,524.9	79.0	55.7	557.1
1994	3,255.8	243.5	174.9	1,110.1	1,657.6	121.0	87.1	533.3	1,598.2	122.5	87.8	576.8
1995	3,528.3	274.5	198.2	1,240.6	1,807.7	130.6	94.3	613.7	1,720.6	143.9	103.9	627.0
1996	3,757.6	306.6	224.9	1,348.0	1,941.6	146.6	106.1	673.9	1,816.0	160.0	118.8	674.2
1997	3,920.0	331.4	244.5	1,462.7	2,075.8	167.0	121.4	743.4	1,844.2	164.4	123.1	719.3
1998	3,949.4	314.7	234.4	1,482.9	2,168.8	175.1	127.8	779.9	1,780.7	139.6	106.5	703.0
1999	4,148.9	355.3	257.8	1,569.3	2,314.2	198.8	140.3	869.6	1,834.6	156.5	117.5	699.7
2000	4,548.2	381.1	275.3	1,823.1	2,457.4	190.7	131.8	1,054.3	2,090.8	190.5	143.5	768.7
2000: IV	1,163.6	69.2	46.8	1,892.4	620.4	31.2	19.3	1,101.5	543.2	38.0	27.4	790.9
NAICS: [5]												
2000: IV	1,128.8	62.1	41.7	1,833.8	623.0	26.9	15.4	1,100.0	505.8	35.2	26.3	733.8
2001	4,295.0	83.2	36.2	1,843.0	2,321.2	−69.0	−76.1	1,080.5	1,973.8	152.2	112.3	762.5
2002	4,216.4	195.5	134.7	1,804.0	2,260.6	45.9	21.6	1,024.8	1,955.8	149.6	113.1	779.2
2003	4,397.2	305.7	237.0	1,952.2	2,282.7	117.6	88.2	1,040.8	2,114.5	188.1	148.9	911.5
2004	4,934.1	447.5	348.2	2,206.3	2,537.3	200.0	156.5	1,212.9	2,396.7	247.5	191.6	993.5
2005	5,411.5	524.2	401.3	2,410.4	2,730.5	211.3	161.2	1,304.0	2,681.0	312.9	240.2	1,106.5
2006	5,782.7	604.6	470.3	2,678.6	2,910.2	249.1	192.8	1,384.0	2,872.5	355.5	277.5	1,294.6
2007	6,060.0	602.8	442.7	2,921.8	3,015.7	246.8	159.4	1,493.1	3,044.4	356.1	283.3	1,428.7
2008	6,374.1	388.1	266.3	2,980.4	2,969.5	97.7	43.3	1,480.6	3,404.6	290.4	223.1	1,499.8
2009	5,109.8	360.6	286.5	2,781.1	2,426.9	84.5	54.9	1,342.5	2,683.0	276.1	231.6	1,438.5
2010	5,759.5	584.2	477.7	3,175.3	2,710.7	287.1	232.3	1,558.4	3,048.8	297.1	245.4	1,616.9
2009: I	1,196.7	48.5	33.8	2,598.4	584.1	−6.4	−10.2	1,239.7	612.6	54.9	44.0	1,358.7
II	1,253.8	80.8	60.0	2,647.9	592.3	11.7	3.4	1,250.1	661.5	69.1	56.6	1,397.8
III	1,305.9	120.5	98.1	2,870.6	613.2	40.6	32.6	1,412.1	692.6	79.9	65.5	1,458.5
IV	1,353.4	110.8	94.6	3,007.4	637.3	38.5	29.1	1,468.3	716.2	72.3	65.5	1,539.1
2010: I	1,349.2	138.7	108.3	3,043.5	625.2	59.3	45.7	1,489.4	724.0	79.4	62.6	1,554.1
II	1,461.7	141.8	117.2	3,117.5	688.8	81.5	65.8	1,528.1	772.9	60.3	51.4	1,589.4
III	1,463.5	155.6	127.5	3,219.3	696.3	74.9	60.6	1,578.2	767.2	80.7	66.9	1,641.1
IV	1,485.1	148.1	124.8	3,320.9	700.4	71.4	60.3	1,637.8	784.7	76.6	64.5	1,683.1
2011: I	1,537.8	179.1	143.9	3,435.9	698.5	82.8	65.9	1,694.3	839.3	96.4	78.0	1,741.6
II	1,664.2	203.3	164.6	3,560.2	738.0	92.2	75.8	1,758.8	926.2	111.1	88.8	1,801.5
III	1,658.0	186.7	152.0	3,552.0	748.9	87.2	71.7	1,758.0	909.1	99.5	80.3	1,794.0

[1] In the old series, "income taxes" refers to Federal income taxes only, as State and local income taxes had already been deducted. In the new series, no income taxes have been deducted.

[2] Annual data are average equity for the year (using four end-of-quarter figures).

[3] Beginning with 1988, profits before and after income taxes reflect inclusion of minority stockholders' interest in net income before and after income taxes.

[4] Data for 1992 (most significantly 1992:I) reflect the early adoption of Financial Accounting Standards Board Statement 106 (Employer's Accounting for Post-Retirement Benefits Other Than Pensions) by a large number of companies during the fourth quarter of 1992. Data for 1993 (1993:I) also reflect adoption of Statement 106. Corporations must show the cumulative effect of a change in accounting principle in the first quarter of the year in which the change is adopted.

[5] Data based on the North American Industry Classification System (NAICS). Other data shown are based on the Standard Industrial Classification (SIC).

Note: Data are not necessarily comparable from one period to another due to changes in accounting principles, industry classifications, sampling procedures, etc. For explanatory notes concerning compilation of the series, see *Quarterly Financial Report for Manufacturing, Mining, Trade, and Selected Service Industries*, Department of Commerce, Bureau of the Census.

Source: Department of Commerce (Bureau of the Census).

Year or quarter	Ratio of profits after income taxes (annual rate) to stockholders' equity—percent [1]			Profits after income taxes per dollar of sales—cents		
	All manufacturing corporations	Durable goods industries	Nondurable goods industries	All manufacturing corporations	Durable goods industries	Nondurable goods industries
1962	9.8	9.6	9.9	4.5	4.4	4.7
1963	10.3	10.1	10.4	4.7	4.5	4.9
1964	11.6	11.7	11.5	5.2	5.1	5.4
1965	13.0	13.8	12.2	5.6	5.7	5.5
1966	13.4	14.2	12.7	5.6	5.6	5.6
1967	11.7	11.7	11.8	5.0	4.8	5.3
1968	12.1	12.2	11.9	5.1	4.9	5.2
1969	11.5	11.4	11.5	4.8	4.6	5.0
1970	9.3	8.3	10.3	4.0	3.5	4.5
1971	9.7	9.0	10.3	4.1	3.8	4.5
1972	10.6	10.8	10.5	4.3	4.2	4.4
1973	12.8	13.1	12.6	4.7	4.7	4.8
1973: IV	13.4	12.9	14.0	4.7	4.5	5.0
New series:						
1973: IV	14.3	13.3	15.3	5.6	5.0	6.1
1974	14.9	12.6	17.1	5.5	4.7	6.4
1975	11.6	10.3	12.9	4.6	4.1	5.1
1976	13.9	13.7	14.2	5.4	5.2	5.5
1977	14.2	14.5	13.8	5.3	5.3	5.3
1978	15.0	16.0	14.2	5.4	5.5	5.3
1979	16.4	15.4	17.4	5.7	5.2	6.1
1980	13.9	11.2	16.3	4.8	4.0	5.6
1981	13.6	11.9	15.2	4.7	4.2	5.1
1982	9.2	6.1	11.9	3.5	2.4	4.4
1983	10.6	8.1	12.7	4.1	3.1	4.9
1984	12.5	12.4	12.5	4.6	4.4	4.8
1985	10.1	9.2	11.0	3.8	3.4	4.1
1986	9.5	7.5	11.5	3.7	2.9	4.6
1987	12.8	11.9	13.7	4.9	4.5	5.2
1988 [2]	16.1	14.3	17.8	5.9	5.2	6.6
1989	13.5	11.1	16.0	4.9	4.1	5.7
1990	10.6	7.9	13.1	3.9	3.0	4.8
1991	6.2	1.4	10.6	2.4	.5	4.1
1992 [3]	2.1	−5.1	8.2	.8	−1.7	3.1
1993	8.0	5.7	10.0	2.8	1.8	3.7
1994	15.8	16.3	15.2	5.4	5.3	5.5
1995	16.0	15.4	16.6	5.6	5.2	6.0
1996	16.7	15.7	17.6	6.0	5.5	6.5
1997	16.7	16.3	17.1	6.2	5.8	6.7
1998	15.8	16.4	15.2	5.9	5.9	6.0
1999	16.4	16.1	16.8	6.2	6.1	6.4
2000	15.1	12.5	18.7	6.1	5.4	6.9
2000: IV	9.9	7.0	13.9	4.0	3.1	5.1
NAICS: [4]						
2000: IV	9.1	5.6	14.3	3.7	2.5	5.2
2001	2.0	−7.0	14.7	.8	−3.3	5.7
2002	7.5	2.1	14.5	3.2	1.0	5.8
2003	12.1	8.5	16.3	5.4	3.9	7.0
2004	15.8	12.9	19.3	7.1	6.2	8.0
2005	16.7	12.4	21.7	7.4	5.9	9.0
2006	17.6	13.9	21.4	8.1	6.6	9.7
2007	15.2	10.7	19.8	7.3	5.3	9.3
2008	8.9	2.9	14.9	4.2	1.5	6.6
2009	10.3	4.1	16.1	5.6	2.3	8.6
2010	15.0	14.9	15.2	8.3	8.6	8.0
2009: I	5.2	−3.3	13.0	2.8	−1.7	7.2
II	9.1	1.1	16.2	4.8	.6	8.6
III	13.7	9.2	18.0	7.5	5.3	9.5
IV	12.6	7.9	17.0	7.0	4.6	9.1
2010: I	14.2	12.3	16.1	8.0	7.3	8.6
II	15.0	17.2	12.9	8.0	9.6	6.6
III	15.8	15.3	16.3	8.7	8.7	8.7
IV	15.0	14.7	15.3	8.4	8.6	8.2
2011: I	16.8	15.6	17.9	9.4	9.4	9.3
II	18.5	17.2	19.7	9.9	10.3	9.6
III	17.1	16.3	17.9	9.2	9.6	8.8

[1] Annual ratios based on average equity for the year (using four end-of-quarter figures). Quarterly ratios based on equity at end of quarter.
[2] See footnote 3, Table B–93.
[3] See footnote 4, Table B–93.
[4] See footnote 5, Table B–93.

Note: Based on data in millions of dollars.
See Note, Table B–93.

Source: Department of Commerce (Bureau of the Census).

Table B–95. Historical stock prices and yields, 1949–2003

Year	Common stock prices [1]									Common stock yields (Standard & Poor's) (percent) [5]	
	Composite (Dec. 31, 2002= 5,000) [3]	New York Stock Exchange (NYSE) indexes [2]					Dow Jones industrial average [2]	Standard & Poor's composite index (1941–43=10) [2]	Nasdaq composite index (Feb. 5, 1971=100) [2]	Dividend-price ratio [6]	Earnings-price ratio [7]
		December 31, 1965=50									
		Composite	Industrial	Transportation	Utility [4]	Finance					
1949		9.02					179.48	15.23		6.59	15.48
1950		10.87					216.31	18.40		6.57	13.99
1951		13.08					257.64	22.34		6.13	11.82
1952		13.81					270.76	24.50		5.80	9.47
1953		13.67					275.97	24.73		5.80	10.26
1954		16.19					333.94	29.69		4.95	8.57
1955		21.54					442.72	40.49		4.08	7.95
1956		24.40					493.01	46.62		4.09	7.55
1957		23.67					475.71	44.38		4.35	7.89
1958		24.56					491.66	46.24		3.97	6.23
1959		30.73					632.12	57.38		3.23	5.78
1960		30.01					618.04	55.85		3.47	5.90
1961		35.37					691.55	66.27		2.98	4.62
1962		33.49					639.76	62.38		3.37	5.82
1963		37.51					714.81	69.87		3.17	5.50
1964		43.76					834.05	81.37		3.01	5.32
1965		47.39					910.88	88.17		3.00	5.59
1966	487.92	46.15	46.18	50.26	90.81	44.45	873.60	85.26		3.40	6.63
1967	536.84	50.77	51.97	53.51	90.86	49.82	879.12	91.93		3.20	5.73
1968	585.47	55.37	58.00	50.58	88.38	65.85	906.00	98.70		3.07	5.67
1969	578.01	54.67	57.44	46.96	85.60	70.49	876.72	97.84		3.24	6.08
1970	483.39	45.72	48.03	32.14	74.47	60.00	753.19	83.22		3.83	6.45
1971	573.33	54.22	57.92	44.35	79.05	70.38	884.76	98.29	107.44	3.14	5.41
1972	637.52	60.29	65.73	50.17	76.95	78.35	950.71	109.20	128.52	2.84	5.50
1973	607.11	57.42	63.08	37.74	75.38	70.12	923.88	107.43	109.90	3.06	7.12
1974	463.54	43.84	48.08	31.89	59.58	49.67	759.37	82.85	76.29	4.47	11.59
1975	483.55	45.73	50.52	31.10	63.00	47.14	802.49	86.16	77.20	4.31	9.15
1976	575.85	54.46	60.44	39.57	73.94	52.94	974.92	102.01	89.90	3.77	8.90
1977	567.66	53.69	57.86	41.09	81.84	55.25	894.63	98.20	98.71	4.62	10.79
1978	567.81	53.70	58.23	43.50	78.44	56.65	820.23	96.02	117.53	5.28	12.03
1979	616.68	58.32	64.76	47.34	76.41	61.42	844.40	103.01	136.57	5.47	13.46
1980	720.15	68.10	78.70	60.61	74.69	64.25	891.41	118.78	168.61	5.26	12.66
1981	782.62	74.02	85.44	72.61	77.81	73.52	932.92	128.05	203.18	5.20	11.96
1982	728.84	68.93	78.18	60.41	79.49	71.99	884.36	119.71	188.97	5.81	11.60
1983	979.52	92.63	107.45	89.36	93.99	95.34	1,190.34	160.41	285.43	4.40	8.03
1984	977.33	92.46	108.01	85.63	92.89	89.28	1,178.48	160.46	248.88	4.64	10.02
1985	1,142.97	108.09	123.79	104.11	113.49	114.21	1,328.23	186.84	290.19	4.25	8.12
1986	1,438.02	136.00	155.85	119.87	142.72	147.20	1,792.76	236.34	366.96	3.49	6.09
1987	1,709.79	161.70	195.31	140.39	148.59	146.48	2,275.99	286.83	402.57	3.08	5.48
1988	1,585.14	149.91	180.95	134.12	143.53	127.26	2,060.82	265.79	374.43	3.64	8.01
1989	1,903.36	180.02	216.23	175.28	174.87	151.88	2,508.91	322.84	437.81	3.45	7.42
1990	1,939.47	183.46	225.78	158.62	181.20	133.26	2,678.94	334.59	409.17	3.61	6.47
1991	2,181.72	206.33	258.14	173.99	185.32	150.82	2,929.33	376.18	491.69	3.24	4.79
1992	2,421.51	229.01	284.62	201.09	198.91	179.26	3,284.29	415.74	599.26	2.99	4.22
1993	2,638.96	249.58	299.99	242.49	228.90	216.42	3,522.06	451.41	715.16	2.78	4.46
1994	2,687.02	254.12	315.25	247.29	209.06	209.73	3,793.77	460.42	751.65	2.82	5.83
1995	3,078.56	291.15	367.34	269.41	220.30	238.45	4,493.76	541.72	925.19	2.56	6.09
1996	3,787.20	358.17	453.98	327.33	249.77	303.89	5,742.89	670.50	1,164.96	2.19	5.24
1997	4,827.35	456.54	574.52	414.60	283.82	424.48	7,441.15	873.43	1,469.49	1.77	4.57
1998	5,818.26	550.26	681.57	468.69	378.12	516.35	8,625.52	1,085.50	1,794.91	1.49	3.46
1999	6,546.81	619.16	774.78	491.60	473.73	530.86	10,464.88	1,327.33	2,728.15	1.25	3.17
2000	6,805.89	643.66	810.63	413.60	477.65	553.13	10,734.90	1,427.22	3,783.67	1.15	3.63
2001	6,397.85	605.07	748.26	443.59	377.30	595.61	10,189.13	1,194.18	2,035.00	1.32	2.95
2002	5,578.89	527.62	657.37	431.10	260.85	555.27	9,226.43	993.94	1,539.73	1.61	2.92
2003 [3]	5,447.46		633.18	436.51	237.77	565.75	8,993.59	965.23	1,647.17	1.77	3.84

[1] Averages of daily closing prices.

[2] Includes stocks as follows: for NYSE, all stocks listed; for Dow Jones industrial average, 30 stocks; for Standard & Poor's (S&P) composite index, 500 stocks; and for Nasdaq composite index, over 5,000.

[3] The NYSE relaunched the composite index on January 9, 2003, incorporating new definitions, methodology, and base value. (The composite index based on December 31, 1965=50 was discontinued.) Subset indexes on financial, energy, and health care were released by the NYSE on January 8, 2004 (see Table B–96). NYSE indexes shown in this table for industrials, utilities, transportation, and finance were discontinued.

[4] Effective April 1993, the NYSE doubled the value of the utility index to facilitate trading of options and futures on the index. Annual indexes prior to 1993 reflect the doubling.

[5] Based on 500 stocks in the S&P composite index.

[6] Aggregate cash dividends (based on latest known annual rate) divided by aggregate market value based on Wednesday closing prices. Monthly data are averages of weekly figures; annual data are averages of monthly figures.

[7] Quarterly data are ratio of earnings (after taxes) for four quarters ending with particular quarter-to-price index for last day of that quarter. Annual data are averages of quarterly ratios.

Sources: New York Stock Exchange, Dow Jones & Co., Inc., Standard & Poor's, and Nasdaq Stock Market.

Year or month	Common stock prices[1]							Common stock yields (Standard & Poor's) (percent)[4]	
	New York Stock Exchange (NYSE) indexes (December 31, 2002=5,000)[2,3]				Dow Jones industrial average[2]	Standard & Poor's composite index (1941–43=10)[2]	Nasdaq composite index (Feb. 5, 1971=100)[2]	Dividend-price ratio[5]	Earnings-price ratio[6]
	Composite	Financial	Energy	Health care					
2000	6,805.89				10,734.90	1,427.22	3,783.67	1.15	3.63
2001	6,397.85				10,189.13	1,194.18	2,035.00	1.32	2.95
2002	5,578.89				9,226.43	993.94	1,539.73	1.61	2.92
2003	5,447.46	5,583.00	5,273.90	5,288.67	8,993.59	965.23	1,647.17	1.77	3.84
2004	6,612.62	6,822.18	6,952.36	5,924.80	10,317.39	1,130.65	1,986.53	1.72	4.89
2005	7,349.00	7,383.70	9,377.84	6,283.96	10,547.67	1,207.23	2,099.32	1.83	5.36
2006	8,357.99	8,654.40	11,206.94	6,685.06	11,408.67	1,310.46	2,263.41	1.87	5.78
2007	9,648.82	9,321.39	13,339.99	7,191.79	13,169.98	1,477.19	2,578.47	1.86	5.29
2008	8,036.88	6,278.38	13,258.42	6,171.19	11,252.62	1,220.04	2,161.65	2.37	3.54
2009	6,091.02	3,987.04	10,020.30	5,456.63	8,876.15	948.05	1,845.38	2.40	1.86
2010	7,230.43	4,744.05	10,943.85	6,230.62	10,662.80	1,139.97	2,349.89	1.98	6.04
2011	7,871.41	4,641.01	12,880.35	6,847.80	11,966.36	1,268.89	2,680.42	2.05	
2008: Jan	9,165.10	7,776.77	14,222.14	7,068.98	12,538.12	1,378.76	2,418.09	2.06	
Feb	9,041.52	7,577.54	13,931.92	6,674.75	12,419.57	1,354.87	2,325.83	2.10	
Mar	8,776.21	7,155.51	14,000.91	6,318.44	12,193.88	1,316.94	2,254.82	2.17	4.57
Apr	9,174.10	7,579.73	15,159.35	6,381.98	12,656.63	1,370.47	2,368.10	2.09	
May	9,429.04	7,593.63	16,365.23	6,405.40	12,812.48	1,403.22	2,483.24	2.07	
June	8,996.98	6,798.20	16,272.67	6,243.42	12,056.67	1,341.25	2,427.45	2.15	4.01
July	8,427.37	6,207.89	14,899.86	6,412.48	11,322.38	1,257.33	2,278.14	2.27	
Aug	8,362.20	6,304.58	13,772.04	6,618.92	11,530.75	1,281.47	2,389.27	2.23	
Sept	7,886.29	6,159.18	12,562.82	6,316.05	11,114.08	1,217.01	2,205.20	2.36	3.94
Oct	6,130.39	4,733.74	9,515.71	5,434.03	9,176.71	968.80	1,730.32	2.83	
Nov	5,527.63	3,779.86	9,262.07	5,088.99	8,614.55	883.04	1,542.70	3.11	
Dec	5,525.70	3,673.95	9,136.33	5,090.83	8,595.56	877.56	1,525.89	3.00	1.65
2009: Jan	5,477.14	3,337.14	9,295.97	5,256.13	8,396.20	865.58	1,537.20	3.01	
Feb	5,051.42	2,823.74	8,785.04	5,106.78	7,690.50	805.23	1,485.98	3.07	
Mar	4,739.72	2,633.65	8,266.81	4,596.81	7,235.47	757.13	1,432.23	2.92	.86
Apr	5,338.39	3,313.47	8,839.95	4,771.71	7,992.12	848.15	1,641.15	2.60	
May	5,823.10	3,819.95	9,848.66	5,051.78	8,398.37	902.41	1,726.08	2.41	
June	5,985.64	3,924.19	10,189.64	5,224.16	8,593.00	926.12	1,826.99	2.35	.82
July	6,026.55	4,000.66	9,765.09	5,410.22	8,679.75	935.82	1,873.84	2.31	
Aug	6,577.18	4,646.60	10,295.91	5,706.96	9,375.06	1,009.72	1,997.16	2.12	
Sept	6,839.88	4,844.93	10,791.73	5,838.22	9,634.97	1,044.55	2,084.75	2.06	1.19
Oct	6,986.35	4,918.07	11,342.57	5,931.28	9,857.34	1,067.66	2,122.85	2.02	
Nov	7,079.38	4,848.04	11,486.95	6,155.21	10,227.55	1,088.07	2,143.53	1.99	
Dec	7,167.51	4,734.07	11,335.23	6,430.25	10,433.44	1,110.38	2,220.60	1.95	4.57
2010: Jan	7,257.37	4,795.75	11,548.08	6,523.83	10,471.24	1,123.58	2,267.77	1.92	
Feb	6,958.36	4,567.29	10,840.96	6,320.43	10,214.51	1,089.16	2,194.44	2.00	
Mar	7,349.86	4,942.17	11,194.52	6,453.81	10,677.52	1,152.05	2,362.24	1.90	5.21
Apr	7,607.49	5,187.03	11,690.25	6,391.99	11,052.15	1,197.32	2,475.72	1.84	
May	7,010.08	4,689.81	10,491.24	5,929.68	10,500.19	1,125.06	2,319.24	1.98	
June	6,767.75	4,484.05	9,960.54	5,838.56	10,159.27	1,083.36	2,235.23	2.09	6.51
July	6,814.61	4,553.76	10,007.16	5,867.77	10,222.24	1,079.80	2,210.27	2.10	
Aug	6,922.30	4,588.87	10,186.03	5,939.69	10,350.40	1,087.28	2,205.28	2.10	
Sept	7,149.32	4,694.66	10,423.43	6,208.29	10,598.07	1,122.08	2,298.35	2.06	6.30
Oct	7,482.15	4,778.71	11,164.11	6,456.56	11,044.49	1,171.58	2,441.30	1.97	
Nov	7,608.40	4,770.65	11,639.37	6,389.44	11,198.31	1,198.89	2,530.99	1.94	
Dec	7,837.43	4,875.84	12,180.49	6,447.34	11,465.26	1,241.53	2,631.56	1.90	6.15
2011: Jan	8,093.40	5,097.71	12,861.65	6,570.59	11,802.37	1,282.62	2,717.21	1.84	
Feb	8,361.70	5,292.98	13,680.69	6,658.62	12,190.00	1,321.12	2,783.54	1.80	
Mar	8,274.78	5,157.33	13,896.16	6,696.08	12,081.48	1,304.49	2,722.29	1.90	6.13
Apr	8,470.07	5,177.21	14,197.31	6,989.18	12,434.88	1,331.51	2,797.07	1.92	
May	8,414.33	5,067.79	13,534.36	7,345.34	12,579.99	1,338.31	2,815.08	1.95	
June	8,108.71	4,814.06	13,118.75	7,214.22	12,097.31	1,287.29	2,687.76	2.04	6.35
July	8,286.83	4,846.73	13,678.27	7,290.81	12,512.33	1,325.18	2,810.58	1.99	
Aug	7,342.37	4,215.95	11,964.10	6,587.04	11,326.62	1,185.31	2,504.62	2.20	
Sept	7,099.58	3,958.64	11,370.24	6,578.35	11,175.45	1,173.88	2,524.14	2.25	7.69
Oct	7,255.05	4,048.81	11,760.87	6,666.64	11,515.93	1,207.22	2,594.78	2.28	
Nov	7,348.85	3,991.61	12,243.52	6,696.20	11,804.33	1,226.41	2,606.29	2.22	
Dec	7,401.26	4,023.34	12,258.25	6,880.58	12,075.68	1,243.32	2,601.67	2.24	

[1] Averages of daily closing prices.

[2] Includes stocks as follows: for NYSE, all stocks listed (in 2011, over 1,800); for Dow Jones industrial average, 30 stocks; for Standard & Poor's (S&P) composite index, 500 stocks; and for Nasdaq composite index, in 2011, over 2,500.

[3] The NYSE relaunched the composite index on January 9, 2003, incorporating new definitions, methodology, and base value. Subset indexes on financial, energy, and health care were released by the NYSE on January 8, 2004.

[4] Based on 500 stocks in the S&P composite index.

[5] Aggregate cash dividends (based on latest known annual rate) divided by aggregate market value based on Wednesday closing prices. Monthly data are averages of weekly figures, annual data are averages of monthly figures.

[6] Quarterly data are ratio of earnings (after taxes) for four quarters ending with particular quarter-to-price index for last day of that quarter. Annual data are averages of quarterly ratios.

Sources: New York Stock Exchange, Dow Jones & Co., Inc., Standard & Poor's, and Nasdaq Stock Market.

TABLE B–97. Farm income, 1950–2011

[Billions of dollars]

Year	Gross farm income Total [1]	Cash marketing receipts Total	Cash marketing receipts Livestock, dairy, and poultry	Cash marketing receipts Crops [2]	Value of inventory changes [3]	Direct Government payments [4]	Production expenses	Net farm income
1950	33.1	28.5	16.1	12.4	0.8	0.3	19.5	13.6
1951	38.3	32.9	19.6	13.2	1.2	.3	22.3	15.9
1952	37.8	32.5	18.2	14.3	.9	.3	22.8	15.0
1953	34.4	31.0	16.9	14.1	−.6	.2	21.5	13.0
1954	34.2	29.8	16.3	13.6	.5	.3	21.8	12.4
1955	33.5	29.5	16.0	13.5	.2	.2	22.2	11.3
1956	34.0	30.4	16.4	14.0	−.5	.6	22.7	11.3
1957	34.8	29.7	17.4	12.3	.6	1.0	23.7	11.1
1958	39.0	33.5	19.2	14.2	.8	1.1	25.8	13.2
1959	37.9	33.6	18.9	14.7	.0	.7	27.2	10.7
1960	38.6	34.0	19.0	15.0	.4	.7	27.4	11.2
1961	40.5	35.2	19.5	15.7	.3	1.5	28.6	12.0
1962	42.3	36.5	20.2	16.3	.6	1.7	30.3	12.1
1963	43.4	37.5	20.0	17.4	.6	1.7	31.6	11.8
1964	42.3	37.3	19.9	17.4	−.8	2.2	31.8	10.5
1965	46.5	39.4	21.9	17.5	1.0	2.5	33.6	12.9
1966	50.5	43.4	25.0	18.4	−.1	3.3	36.5	14.0
1967	50.5	42.8	24.4	18.4	.7	3.1	38.2	12.3
1968	51.8	44.2	25.5	18.7	.1	3.5	39.5	12.3
1969	56.4	48.2	28.6	19.6	.1	3.8	42.1	14.3
1970	58.8	50.5	29.5	21.0	.0	3.7	44.5	14.4
1971	62.1	52.7	30.5	22.3	1.4	3.1	47.1	15.0
1972	71.1	61.1	35.6	25.5	.9	4.0	51.7	19.5
1973	98.9	86.9	45.8	41.1	3.4	2.6	64.6	34.4
1974	98.2	92.4	41.3	51.1	−1.6	.5	71.0	27.3
1975	100.6	88.9	43.1	45.8	3.4	.8	75.0	25.5
1976	102.9	95.4	46.3	49.0	−1.5	.7	82.7	20.2
1977	108.8	96.2	47.6	48.6	1.1	1.8	88.9	19.9
1978	128.4	112.4	59.2	53.2	1.9	3.0	103.2	25.2
1979	150.7	131.5	69.2	62.3	5.0	1.4	123.3	27.4
1980	149.3	139.7	68.0	71.7	−6.3	1.3	133.1	16.1
1981	166.3	141.6	69.2	72.5	6.5	1.9	139.4	26.9
1982	164.1	142.6	70.3	72.3	−1.4	3.5	140.3	23.8
1983	153.9	136.8	69.6	67.2	−10.9	9.3	139.6	14.3
1984	168.0	142.8	72.9	69.9	6.0	8.4	142.0	26.0
1985	161.1	144.0	70.1	73.9	−2.3	7.7	132.6	28.5
1986	156.1	135.4	71.6	63.8	−2.2	11.8	125.0	31.1
1987	168.4	141.8	76.0	65.8	−2.3	16.7	130.4	38.0
1988	177.9	151.3	79.6	71.6	−4.1	14.5	138.3	39.6
1989	191.6	160.5	83.6	76.9	3.8	10.9	145.1	46.5
1990	197.8	169.3	89.1	80.2	3.3	9.3	151.5	46.3
1991	192.0	168.0	85.8	82.2	−.2	8.2	151.8	40.2
1992	200.6	171.5	85.8	85.7	4.2	9.2	150.4	50.2
1993	205.0	178.3	90.5	87.8	−4.2	13.4	158.3	46.7
1994	216.1	181.4	88.3	93.1	8.3	7.9	163.5	52.6
1995	210.8	188.2	87.2	101.0	−5.0	7.3	171.1	39.8
1996	235.8	199.4	92.9	106.5	7.9	7.3	176.9	58.9
1997	238.0	207.8	96.5	111.3	.6	7.5	186.7	51.3
1998	232.6	196.5	94.2	102.2	−.6	12.4	185.5	47.1
1999	234.9	187.8	95.7	92.1	−.2	21.5	187.2	47.7
2000	241.7	192.1	99.6	92.5	1.6	23.2	191.0	50.7
2001	249.9	200.0	106.7	93.4	1.1	22.4	195.0	54.9
2002	230.6	194.6	93.9	100.7	−3.5	12.4	191.4	39.1
2003	258.7	216.0	105.7	110.3	−2.7	16.5	197.7	61.0
2004	294.9	237.9	123.5	114.4	11.2	13.0	207.5	87.4
2005	298.5	240.9	124.9	116.0	−.4	24.4	219.7	78.8
2006	290.2	240.6	118.5	122.1	−3.1	15.8	232.7	57.4
2007	339.6	288.5	138.5	150.1	.6	11.9	269.5	70.0
2008	377.9	316.7	141.6	175.0	6.6	12.2	293.2	84.7
2009	342.7	288.6	120.3	168.3	−1.1	12.2	281.1	61.6
2010	364.7	314.4	141.4	172.9	−2.0	12.4	285.6	79.1
2011 ᵖ	420.8	365.9	165.4	200.6	1.5	10.6	320.0	100.9

[1] Cash marketing receipts, Government payments, value of changes in inventories, other farm-related cash income, and nonmoney income produced by farms including imputed rent of operator dwellings.

[2] Crop receipts include proceeds received from commodities placed under Commodity Credit Corporation loans.

[3] Physical changes in beginning and ending year inventories of crop and livestock commodities valued at weighted average market prices during the year.

[4] Includes only Government payments made directly to farmers.

Note: Data for 2011 are forecasts.

Source: Department of Agriculture (Economic Research Service).

[Billions of dollars]

| End of year | Total assets | Physical assets | | | | | Financial assets | | | Claims | | | Farm equity |
		Real estate	Livestock and poultry [1]	Machinery and motor vehicles	Crops stored [2]	Purchased inputs [3]	Total [4]	Investments in cooperatives	Other [4]	Total claims	Real estate debt [5]	Non-real estate debt [6]	
1952	133.1	85.1	14.8	15.0	7.9	....	10.3	3.2	7.1	133.1	6.2	7.1	119.8
1953	128.7	84.3	11.7	15.6	6.8	....	10.3	3.3	7.0	128.7	6.6	6.3	115.8
1954	132.6	87.8	11.2	15.7	7.5	....	10.4	3.5	6.9	132.6	7.1	6.7	118.8
1955	137.0	93.0	10.6	16.3	6.5	....	10.6	3.7	6.9	137.0	7.8	7.3	121.9
1956	145.7	100.3	11.0	16.9	6.8	....	10.7	4.0	6.7	145.7	8.5	7.4	129.8
1957	154.5	106.4	13.9	17.0	6.4	....	10.8	4.2	6.6	154.5	9.0	8.2	137.3
1958	168.7	114.6	17.7	18.1	6.9	....	11.4	4.5	6.9	168.7	9.7	9.4	149.6
1959	172.9	121.2	15.2	19.3	6.2	....	11.0	4.8	6.2	172.9	10.6	10.7	151.6
1960	174.4	123.3	15.6	19.1	6.4	....	10.0	4.2	5.8	174.4	11.3	11.1	151.9
1961	181.6	129.1	16.4	19.3	6.5	....	10.4	4.5	5.9	181.6	12.3	11.8	157.5
1962	188.9	134.6	17.3	19.9	6.5	....	10.5	4.6	5.9	188.9	13.5	13.2	162.2
1963	196.7	142.4	15.9	20.4	7.4	....	10.7	5.0	5.7	196.7	15.0	14.6	167.1
1964	204.2	150.5	14.5	21.2	7.0	....	11.0	5.2	5.8	204.2	16.9	15.3	172.1
1965	220.8	161.5	17.6	22.4	7.9	....	11.4	5.4	6.0	220.8	18.9	16.9	185.0
1966	234.0	171.2	19.0	24.1	8.1	....	11.6	5.7	6.0	234.0	20.7	18.5	194.8
1967	246.1	180.9	18.8	26.3	8.0	....	12.0	5.8	6.1	246.1	22.6	19.6	203.9
1968	257.2	189.4	20.2	27.7	7.4	....	12.4	6.1	6.3	257.2	24.7	19.2	213.2
1969	267.8	195.3	22.8	28.6	8.3	....	12.8	6.4	6.4	267.8	26.4	20.0	221.4
1970	278.8	202.4	23.7	30.4	8.7	....	13.6	7.2	6.5	278.8	27.2	21.3	230.3
1971	301.8	217.6	27.3	32.4	10.0	....	14.5	7.9	6.7	301.8	28.8	24.0	248.9
1972	339.9	243.0	33.7	34.6	12.9	....	15.7	8.7	6.9	339.9	31.4	26.7	281.8
1973	418.5	298.3	42.4	39.7	21.4	....	16.8	9.7	7.1	418.5	35.2	31.6	351.7
1974 [7]	449.2	335.6	24.6	48.5	22.5	....	18.1	11.2	6.9	449.2	39.6	35.1	374.5
1975	510.8	383.6	29.4	57.4	20.5	....	19.9	13.0	6.9	510.8	43.8	39.8	427.3
1976	590.7	456.5	29.0	63.3	20.6	....	21.3	14.3	6.9	590.7	48.5	45.7	496.6
1977	651.5	509.3	31.9	69.3	20.4	....	20.5	13.5	7.0	651.5	55.8	52.6	543.1
1978	777.7	601.8	50.1	78.8	23.8	....	23.2	16.1	7.1	777.7	63.4	60.4	653.9
1979	914.7	706.1	61.4	91.9	29.9	....	25.4	18.1	7.3	914.7	75.8	71.7	767.2
1980	1,000.4	782.8	60.6	97.5	32.8	....	26.7	19.3	7.4	1,000.4	85.3	77.2	838.0
1981	997.9	785.6	53.5	101.1	29.5	....	28.2	20.6	7.6	997.9	93.9	83.8	820.2
1982	962.5	750.0	53.0	103.9	25.9	....	29.7	21.9	7.8	962.5	96.8	87.2	778.5
1983	959.3	753.4	49.5	101.7	23.7	....	30.9	22.8	8.1	959.3	98.1	88.1	773.1
1984	897.8	661.8	49.5	125.8	26.1	2.0	32.6	24.3	8.3	897.8	101.4	87.4	709.0
1985	775.9	586.2	46.3	86.1	22.9	1.2	33.3	24.3	9.0	775.9	94.1	78.1	603.8
1986	722.0	542.4	47.8	79.0	16.3	2.1	34.4	24.4	10.0	722.0	84.1	67.2	570.7
1987	756.5	563.7	58.0	78.7	17.8	3.2	35.2	25.3	9.9	756.5	75.8	62.7	618.0
1988	788.5	582.3	62.2	81.0	23.7	3.5	35.9	25.6	10.4	788.5	70.8	62.3	655.4
1989	813.7	600.1	66.2	84.1	23.9	2.6	36.8	26.3	10.4	813.7	68.8	62.3	682.7
1990	840.6	619.1	70.9	86.3	23.2	2.8	38.3	27.5	10.9	840.6	67.6	63.5	709.5
1991	844.2	624.8	68.1	85.9	22.2	2.6	40.5	28.7	11.8	844.2	67.4	64.4	712.3
1992	867.8	640.8	71.0	84.8	24.2	3.9	43.0	29.4	13.6	867.8	67.9	63.7	736.2
1993	909.2	677.6	72.8	85.4	23.3	3.8	46.3	31.0	15.3	909.2	68.4	65.9	774.9
1994	934.7	704.1	67.9	86.8	23.3	5.0	47.6	32.1	15.5	934.7	69.9	69.0	795.8
1995	965.7	740.5	57.8	87.6	27.4	3.4	49.1	34.1	15.0	965.7	71.7	71.3	822.8
1996	1,002.9	769.5	60.3	88.0	31.7	4.4	49.0	34.9	14.1	1,002.9	74.4	74.2	854.3
1997	1,051.3	808.2	67.1	88.7	32.7	4.9	49.7	35.7	13.9	1,051.3	78.5	78.4	894.4
1998	1,083.4	840.4	63.4	89.8	29.9	5.0	54.7	40.5	14.2	1,083.4	83.1	81.5	918.7
1999	1,138.8	887.0	73.2	89.8	28.3	4.0	56.5	41.9	14.6	1,138.8	87.2	80.5	971.1
2000	1,203.2	946.4	76.8	90.1	27.9	4.9	57.1	43.0	14.1	1,203.2	84.7	79.2	1,039.3
2001	1,255.9	996.2	78.5	92.8	25.2	4.2	58.9	43.6	15.3	1,255.9	88.5	82.1	1,085.3
2002	1,259.7	998.7	75.6	96.2	23.1	5.6	60.4	44.7	15.8	1,259.7	95.4	81.8	1,082.5
2003	1,383.4	1,112.1	78.5	100.3	24.4	5.6	62.4	45.6	16.9	1,383.4	83.2	81.0	1,219.2
2004	1,588.0	1,305.2	79.4	107.8	24.4	5.7	65.5	....	....	1,588.0	95.7	86.3	1,406.1
2005	1,779.4	1,487.0	81.1	113.1	24.3	6.5	67.5	....	....	1,779.4	104.8	91.6	1,583.0
2006	1,923.6	1,625.8	80.7	114.2	22.7	6.5	73.7	....	....	1,923.6	108.0	95.5	1,720.0
2007	2,055.3	1,751.4	80.6	114.7	22.7	7.0	78.8	....	....	2,055.3	112.7	101.4	1,841.2
2008	2,023.3	1,703.0	80.6	123.4	27.6	7.2	81.6	....	....	2,023.3	134.7	106.9	1,781.7
2009	2,054.4	1,724.4	79.8	126.0	32.9	7.2	84.1	....	....	2,054.4	131.3	110.6	1,812.5
2010	2,190.9	1,853.7	81.4	127.9	35.6	7.3	84.9	....	....	2,190.9	136.3	110.6	1,944.0
2011 [p]	2,339.8	1,987.2	80.2	133.5	39.6	7.6	91.8	....	....	2,339.8	132.1	110.3	2,097.3

[1] Excludes commercial broilers; excludes horses and mules beginning with 1959 data; excludes turkeys beginning with 1986 data.
[2] Non–Commodity Credit Corporation (CCC) crops held on farms plus value above loan rate for crops held under CCC.
[3] Includes fertilizer, chemicals, fuels, parts, feed, seed, and other supplies.
[4] Beginning with 2004, data available only for total financial assets. Data through 2003 for other financial assets are currency and demand deposits.
[5] Includes CCC storage and drying facilities loans.
[6] Does not include CCC crop loans.
[7] Beginning with 1974 data, farms are defined as places with sales of $1,000 or more annually.

Note: Data exclude operator households.
Data for 2011 are forecasts.

Source: Department of Agriculture (Economic Research Service).

[2005=100]

Year	Farm output				Productivity indicators	
	Total	Livestock and products	Crops	Farm-related output	Farm output per unit of total input	Farm output per unit of labor input
1950	39	47	35	25	39	10
1951	40	49	36	24	40	11
1952	41	50	38	24	41	11
1953	42	50	38	23	42	12
1954	42	52	37	23	43	12
1955	43	54	38	25	43	13
1956	44	56	38	25	43	14
1957	43	55	38	27	43	15
1958	46	56	41	30	45	17
1959	47	58	42	37	46	17
1960	49	59	44	39	48	19
1961	50	62	44	38	49	20
1962	50	62	45	37	49	20
1963	52	64	46	38	50	21
1964	51	65	45	34	51	22
1965	53	64	47	33	52	23
1966	53	65	46	30	51	25
1967	54	67	49	30	53	28
1968	55	67	50	29	54	28
1969	56	67	52	27	55	29
1970	55	69	49	24	54	30
1971	60	72	55	25	58	33
1972	60	73	55	25	58	34
1973	62	73	59	27	60	35
1974	58	70	53	28	56	33
1975	62	68	61	29	61	36
1976	63	71	61	28	60	37
1977	67	72	66	28	63	40
1978	68	72	68	30	60	41
1979	71	73	74	31	62	43
1980	69	75	67	31	60	42
1981	74	75	77	27	67	45
1982	75	75	78	56	69	50
1983	65	76	60	57	60	44
1984	74	75	75	52	71	51
1985	77	77	79	66	75	58
1986	75	78	74	64	74	55
1987	76	79	74	65	75	55
1988	72	80	66	77	72	52
1989	77	80	75	80	78	57
1990	80	82	80	76	81	64
1991	81	84	79	81	82	64
1992	86	86	87	76	88	69
1993	82	87	78	76	83	69
1994	91	91	93	74	89	66
1995	86	93	82	84	82	63
1996	89	91	89	79	89	70
1997	94	94	94	91	91	74
1998	94	95	93	105	90	79
1999	96	98	94	113	90	81
2000	97	98	95	103	94	90
2001	97	97	95	110	95	90
2002	95	99	91	106	94	88
2003	97	100	95	99	97	93
2004	101	98	104	104	102	101
2005	100	100	100	100	100	100
2006	99	102	95	106	101	105
2007	102	103	102	92	99	106
2008	103	103	104	88	104	110
2009	106	102	110	84	106	119

Note: Farm output includes primary agricultural activities and certain secondary activities that are closely linked to agricultural production for which information on production and input use cannot be separately observed. Secondary output (alternatively, farm-related output) includes recreation activities, the imputed value of employer-provided housing, land rentals under the Conservation Reserve, and services such as custom machine work and custom livestock feeding.

See Table B–100 for farm inputs.

Source: Department of Agriculture (Economic Research Service).

Year	Farm employment (thousands)[1]			Crops harvested (millions of acres)[4]	Total farm input	Capital input (2005=100)		Labor input (2005=100)			Intermediate input (2005=100)				
	Total	Self-employed and unpaid family workers[2]	Hired workers[3]			Total[5]	Durable equipment	Total	Hired labor	Self-employed and unpaid family labor	Total	Farm Origin[6]	Energy and lubricants[7]	Agricultural chemicals	Purchased services
1950	9,283	6,965	2,318	345	99	120	84	388	310	435	50	52	81	30	51
1951	8,653	6,464	2,189	344	100	122	94	373	299	417	52	54	84	28	56
1952	8,441	6,301	2,140	349	100	124	102	365	292	408	52	53	88	28	59
1953	7,904	5,817	2,087	348	100	125	107	350	284	389	52	54	90	26	56
1954	7,893	5,782	2,111	346	98	126	113	343	268	388	50	52	89	26	55
1955	7,719	5,675	2,044	340	101	126	115	335	263	378	54	57	92	27	57
1956	7,367	5,451	1,916	324	101	126	116	314	240	358	56	60	92	29	59
1957	6,966	5,046	1,920	324	101	125	115	291	230	327	58	63	90	27	61
1958	6,667	4,705	1,962	324	102	123	113	278	232	304	61	67	88	28	63
1959	6,565	4,621	1,944	324	104	123	114	276	227	305	64	68	89	32	74
1960	6,155	4,260	1,895	324	102	123	115	260	227	280	63	68	90	33	71
1961	5,994	4,135	1,859	302	101	123	113	254	226	270	63	67	93	35	70
1962	5,841	3,997	1,844	295	103	122	111	255	225	272	65	70	94	33	70
1963	5,500	3,700	1,800	298	103	123	111	244	225	255	67	72	95	36	69
1964	5,206	3,585	1,621	298	101	123	113	229	203	245	66	70	97	39	67
1965	4,964	3,465	1,499	298	101	123	115	224	191	243	66	70	98	41	68
1966	4,574	3,224	1,350	294	102	124	118	208	172	229	70	76	100	46	69
1967	4,303	3,036	1,267	306	102	124	122	195	160	216	71	76	99	49	72
1968	4,207	2,974	1,233	300	101	125	128	195	155	218	70	77	100	39	69
1969	4,050	2,843	1,207	290	102	125	130	191	156	212	72	81	101	42	67
1970	3,951	2,727	1,224	293	102	124	131	183	157	198	74	82	101	49	64
1971	3,868	2,665	1,203	305	102	124	132	180	155	195	75	83	99	51	64
1972	3,870	2,664	1,206	294	104	123	133	179	155	194	78	87	98	54	64
1973	3,947	2,702	1,245	321	104	123	135	178	157	190	78	86	99	58	68
1974	3,919	2,588	1,331	328	103	124	143	177	167	183	77	83	95	61	66
1975	3,818	2,481	1,337	336	102	125	149	174	170	176	75	80	112	55	70
1976	3,741	2,369	1,372	337	106	127	153	171	172	171	80	83	126	64	73
1977	3,660	2,347	1,313	345	105	129	158	167	167	166	79	83	132	60	73
1978	3,682	2,410	1,272	338	112	130	162	164	157	168	89	93	139	64	87
1979	3,549	2,320	1,229	348	115	131	168	167	163	169	92	96	127	71	91
1980	3,605	2,302	1,303	352	115	133	174	162	162	163	92	96	124	79	82
1981	3,497	2,241	1,256	366	111	132	175	162	161	163	87	91	119	75	78
1982	3,335	2,142	1,193	362	109	130	172	151	145	154	87	94	112	63	84
1983	3,282	1,991	1,291	306	108	128	165	149	160	142	87	94	108	60	83
1984	3,091	1,930	1,161	348	105	124	157	144	149	141	84	87	112	68	81
1985	2,760	1,753	1,007	342	103	122	149	133	135	132	83	88	101	66	84
1986	2,693	1,740	953	325	101	118	139	135	130	139	83	89	93	71	76
1987	2,681	1,717	964	302	101	114	129	138	133	141	83	88	104	69	79
1988	2,727	1,725	1,002	297	100	112	122	140	137	141	82	87	104	60	79
1989	2,637	1,709	928	318	98	110	116	135	128	139	81	84	103	63	85
1990	2,568	1,649	919	322	99	108	113	126	128	125	86	90	103	70	81
1991	2,591	1,682	909	318	99	108	110	127	127	127	86	89	103	70	85
1992	2,505	1,640	865	319	97	106	107	124	121	126	84	89	102	64	81
1993	2,367	1,510	857	308	98	105	103	119	120	118	88	91	102	66	91
1994	2,613	1,774	839	321	102	104	99	137	117	149	90	92	105	69	95
1995	2,597	1,730	867	314	105	104	96	137	121	148	95	96	110	72	100
1996	2,433	1,602	831	326	100	102	94	127	116	134	91	89	110	77	95
1997	2,432	1,557	875	333	103	102	92	126	122	129	96	93	113	82	102
1998	2,284	1,405	879	326	105	102	91	120	124	117	100	98	114	86	107
1999	2,239	1,326	913	327	107	101	92	119	129	112	105	103	115	91	110
2000	2,126	1,249	877	325	102	101	92	107	109	106	101	101	113	93	103
2001	2,084	1,211	873	321	102	100	91	107	110	105	100	98	110	93	105
2002	2,115	1,243	872	316	101	100	93	108	111	106	98	97	120	85	99
2003	2,066	1,181	885	324	100	99	94	104	109	102	99	101	100	99	96
2004	2,012	1,188	824	321	99	99	96	101	100	101	98	99	108	97	95
2005	1,988	1,208	780	321	100	100	100	100	100	100	100	100	100	100	100
2006	1,900	1,148	752	312	98	100	102	94	96	93	99	101	95	88	102
2007	1,832	1,082	750	322	103	99	102	96	104	91	108	105	108	103	112
2008	1,786	1,054	732	327	99	101	104	94	99	90	101	97	98	104	105
2009	1,757	1,018	739	319	100	101	107	89	98	84	103	98	119	106	101
2010	....	....	....	322	....	....	....	....	....	....	....	....	....	....	....
2011 [p]	....	....	....	311	....	....	....	....	....	....	....	....	....	....	....

[1] Persons involved in farmwork.
[2] Data from Current Population Survey (CPS) conducted by the Department of Commerce, Census Bureau, for the Department of Labor, Bureau of Labor Statistics.
[3] Data from national income and product accounts from Department of Commerce, Bureau of Economic Analysis.
[4] Acreage harvested plus acreages in fruits, tree nuts, and vegetables and minor crops. Includes double-cropping.
[5] Consists of durable equipment, service buildings, land, and inventories.
[6] Consists of seed, feed, and purchased livestock.
[7] Consists of petroleum fuels, natural gas, electricity, hydraulic fluids, and lubricants.

Source: Department of Agriculture (Economic Research Service).

TABLE B–101. Agricultural price indexes and farm real estate value, 1975–2011

[1990-92=100, except as noted]

| Year or month | Prices received by farmers | | | Prices paid by farmers | | | | | | | | | | | Addendum: Average farm real estate value per acre (dollars)[4] |
	All farm products	Crops	Livestock and products	All commodities, services, interest, taxes, and wage rates[1]	Total[2]	Feed	Livestock and poultry[3]	Fertilizer	Agricultural chemicals	Fuels	Farm machinery	Farm services	Rent	Wage rates	
1975	73	88	62	47	55	83	39	87	72	40	38	48		44	340
1976	75	87	64	50	59	83	47	74	78	43	43	52		48	397
1977	73	83	64	53	61	82	48	72	71	46	47	57		51	474
1978	83	89	78	58	67	80	65	72	66	48	51	60		55	531
1979	94	98	90	66	76	89	88	77	67	61	56	66		60	628
1980	98	107	89	75	85	98	85	96	71	86	63	81		65	737
1981	100	111	89	82	92	110	80	104	77	98	70	89		70	819
1982	94	98	90	86	94	99	78	105	83	97	76	96		74	823
1983	98	108	88	86	92	107	76	100	87	94	81	82		76	788
1984	101	111	91	89	94	112	73	103	90	93	85	86		77	801
1985	91	98	86	86	91	95	74	98	90	93	85	85		78	713
1986	87	87	88	85	86	88	73	90	89	76	83	83		81	640
1987	89	86	91	87	87	83	85	86	87	76	85	84		85	599
1988	99	104	93	91	90	104	91	94	89	77	89	85		87	632
1989	104	109	100	96	95	110	93	99	93	83	94	91		95	668
1990	104	103	105	99	99	103	102	97	95	100	96	96	96	96	683
1991	100	101	99	100	100	98	102	103	101	104	100	98	100	100	703
1992	98	101	97	101	101	99	96	100	103	96	104	103	104	105	713
1993	101	102	100	104	104	102	104	96	109	93	107	110	100	108	736
1994	100	105	95	106	106	106	94	105	112	89	113	110	108	111	798
1995	102	112	92	109	108	103	82	121	116	89	120	115	117	114	844
1996	112	127	99	115	115	129	75	125	119	102	125	116	128	117	887
1997	107	115	98	118	119	125	94	121	121	106	128	116	136	123	926
1998	102	107	97	115	113	111	88	112	122	84	132	115	120	129	974
1999	96	97	95	115	111	100	95	105	121	94	135	114	113	135	1,030
2000	96	96	97	119	115	102	110	110	120	129	139	118	110	140	1,090
2001	102	99	106	123	120	109	111	123	121	121	144	120	117	146	1,150
2002	98	105	90	124	119	112	102	108	119	115	148	120	120	153	1,210
2003	106	110	103	128	124	114	109	124	121	140	151	125	123	157	1,270
2004	118	115	122	134	132	121	128	140	121	165	162	127	126	160	1,340
2005	114	110	119	142	140	117	138	164	123	216	173	133	129	165	1,610
2006	115	120	111	150	148	124	134	176	128	239	182	139	141	171	1,830
2007	136	142	130	161	160	149	131	216	129	264	191	146	147	177	2,010
2008	149	169	130	183	190	194	124	392	139	344	209	146	165	183	2,170
2009	131	150	112	178	182	186	115	275	149	229	222	156	184	187	2,110
2010	141	153	130	183	188	180	133	252	144	284	230	161	191	189	2,200
2011	177	201	152	203	214	223	154	328	145	361	241	167	203	191	2,350
2010: Jan	136	149	121	180	185	185	121	232	143	279	226	160	191	191	
Feb	132	145	122	180	184	178	126	236	143	271	226	159	191	191	
Mar	137	150	127	181	185	175	131	238	143	276	226	160	191	191	
Apr	135	146	128	182	187	171	140	246	144	288	227	160	191	187	
May	138	148	131	182	187	171	137	250	144	289	228	160	191	187	
June	135	144	129	181	186	170	134	249	145	275	228	162	191	187	
July	138	147	132	181	186	172	135	247	145	272	230	162	191	186	
Aug	141	151	134	182	187	174	133	247	146	278	230	162	191	186	
Sept	143	152	134	183	188	180	130	255	146	279	231	162	191	186	
Oct	151	163	134	185	191	188	132	266	146	291	232	161	191	192	
Nov	154	172	134	187	194	195	134	276	144	299	235	161	191	192	
Dec	153	170	134	189	197	200	142	286	144	309	235	161	191	192	
2011: Jan	166	189	137	196	204	204	151	305	144	320	237	165	203	195	
Feb	171	200	144	198	207	212	155	304	145	335	238	165	203	195	
Mar	173	198	152	201	212	212	159	318	145	363	239	166	203	195	
Apr	176	200	156	204	215	223	159	326	144	379	240	166	203	189	
May	175	203	152	204	215	228	149	327	144	382	241	167	203	189	
June	179	208	153	204	215	229	146	329	144	371	241	168	203	189	
July	180	206	155	204	216	229	151	333	145	369	241	168	203	189	
Aug	184	210	158	205	216	235	147	331	145	366	241	168	203	189	
Sept	179	203	152	205	217	237	146	330	148	365	242	168	203	189	
Oct	184	203	154	205	216	225	155	343	149	357	244	167	203	193	
Nov	184	206	157	206	218	223	164	346	147	366	245	167	203	193	
Dec	176	191	158	205	217	221	167	350	145	357	246	166	203	193	

[1] Includes items used for family living, not shown separately.
[2] Includes other production items, not shown separately.
[3] Includes cattle, hogs, dairy, and poultry.
[4] Average for 48 States. Annual data are: March 1 for 1975, February 1 for 1976–81, April 1 for 1982–85, February 1 for 1986–89, January 1 for 1990–2009, and annual average for 2010-2011.

Source: Department of Agriculture (National Agricultural Statistics Service).

TABLE B–102. U.S. exports and imports of agricultural commodities, 1950–2011

[Billions of dollars]

| Year | Exports | | | | | | | Imports | | | | | Agricultural trade balance |
	Total[1]	Feed grains	Food grains[2]	Oilseeds and products	Cotton	Tobacco	Animals and products	Total[1]	Fruits, nuts, and vegetables[3]	Animals and products	Coffee	Cocoa beans and products	
1950	2.9	0.2	0.6	0.2	1.0	0.3	0.3	4.0	0.2	0.7	1.1	0.2	−1.1
1951	4.0	.3	1.1	.3	1.1	.3	.5	5.2	.2	1.1	1.4	.2	−1.1
1952	3.4	.3	1.1	.2	.9	.2	.3	4.5	.2	.7	1.4	.2	−1.1
1953	2.8	.3	.7	.2	.5	.3	.4	4.2	.2	.6	1.5	.2	−1.3
1954	3.1	.2	.5	.3	.8	.3	.5	4.0	.2	.5	1.5	.3	−.9
1955	3.2	.3	.6	.4	.5	.4	.6	4.0	.2	.5	1.4	.2	−.8
1956	4.2	.4	1.0	.5	.7	.3	.7	4.0	.2	.4	1.4	.2	.2
1957	4.5	.3	1.0	.5	1.0	.4	.7	4.0	.2	.5	1.4	.2	.6
1958	3.9	.5	.8	.4	.7	.4	.5	3.9	.2	.7	1.2	.2	*
1959	4.0	.6	.9	.6	.4	.3	.6	4.1	.2	.8	1.1	.2	−.1
1960	4.8	.5	1.2	.6	1.0	.4	.6	3.8	.2	.6	1.0	.2	1.0
1961	5.0	.5	1.4	.6	.9	.4	.6	3.7	.2	.7	1.0	.2	1.3
1962	5.0	.8	1.3	.7	.5	.4	.6	3.9	.2	.9	1.0	.2	1.2
1963	5.6	.8	1.5	.8	.6	.4	.7	4.0	.3	.9	1.0	.2	1.6
1964	6.3	.9	1.7	1.0	.7	.4	.8	4.1	.3	.8	1.2	.2	2.3
1965	6.2	1.1	1.4	1.2	.5	.4	.8	4.1	.3	.9	1.1	.1	2.1
1966	6.9	1.3	1.8	1.2	.4	.5	.7	4.5	.4	1.2	1.1	.1	2.4
1967	6.4	1.1	1.5	1.3	.5	.5	.7	4.4	.5	1.1	1.0	.2	1.9
1968	6.2	.9	1.4	1.3	.5	.5	.7	5.0	.6	1.3	1.2	.2	1.2
1969	5.9	.9	1.2	1.3	.3	.6	.8	5.0	.7	1.4	.9	.2	1.0
1970	7.2	1.1	1.4	1.9	.4	.5	.9	5.7	.7	1.6	1.2	.3	1.5
1971	7.7	1.0	1.3	2.2	.6	.5	1.0	5.8	.7	1.6	1.2	.2	1.9
1972	9.4	1.5	1.8	2.5	.5	.7	1.1	6.4	.8	1.9	1.3	.2	2.9
1973	17.6	3.6	4.7	4.4	.9	.7	1.6	8.4	1.0	2.6	1.7	.3	9.3
1974	21.9	4.7	5.4	5.8	1.4	.8	1.8	10.2	1.0	2.2	1.6	.5	11.7
1975	21.9	5.2	6.1	4.6	1.0	.9	1.7	9.3	1.0	1.8	1.7	.5	12.6
1976	23.0	6.0	4.7	5.2	1.1	.9	2.4	11.0	1.2	2.4	2.9	.6	12.0
1977	23.6	4.9	3.6	6.8	1.5	1.1	2.7	13.4	1.5	2.4	4.3	1.0	10.2
1978	29.4	5.9	5.5	8.4	1.7	1.4	3.1	14.8	1.8	3.1	4.1	1.4	14.6
1979	34.7	7.7	6.3	9.4	2.2	1.2	3.8	16.7	2.0	3.9	4.2	1.2	18.0
1980	41.2	9.8	7.9	10.0	2.9	1.3	3.8	17.4	2.0	3.8	4.2	.9	23.9
1981	43.3	9.4	9.6	10.1	2.3	1.5	4.3	16.8	2.5	3.5	2.9	.9	26.6
1982	36.6	6.4	7.9	9.8	2.0	1.5	4.0	15.2	2.8	3.7	2.9	.7	21.4
1983	36.1	7.3	7.4	9.4	1.8	1.5	3.8	16.6	2.9	3.8	2.8	.8	19.5
1984	37.8	8.1	7.5	9.1	2.4	1.5	4.3	19.3	3.7	4.0	3.3	1.1	18.5
1985	29.0	6.0	4.5	6.4	1.6	1.5	4.2	20.0	4.1	4.2	3.3	1.4	9.1
1986	26.2	3.1	3.9	7.3	.8	1.2	4.6	21.4	4.2	4.4	4.6	1.1	4.8
1987	28.7	3.8	3.8	7.2	1.6	1.1	5.2	20.4	4.3	4.8	2.9	1.2	8.3
1988	37.1	5.9	5.9	8.5	2.0	1.3	6.5	20.9	4.4	5.1	2.5	1.0	16.2
1989[4]	40.0	7.7	7.1	6.4	2.2	1.3	6.4	21.9	4.8	5.1	2.4	1.0	18.2
1990	39.5	7.0	4.8	5.7	2.8	1.4	6.6	22.9	5.5	5.7	1.9	1.1	16.6
1991	39.4	5.7	4.2	6.4	2.5	1.4	7.0	22.9	5.4	5.5	1.9	1.1	16.5
1992	43.2	5.8	5.4	7.3	2.0	1.6	7.9	24.8	5.5	5.7	1.7	1.1	18.5
1993	43.0	5.0	5.7	7.3	1.6	1.3	8.0	25.1	5.6	5.9	1.5	1.0	17.9
1994	46.2	4.7	5.3	7.2	2.6	1.3	9.2	27.0	6.0	5.8	2.5	1.0	19.1
1995	56.2	8.1	6.7	8.9	3.7	1.4	10.9	30.3	6.5	6.0	3.3	1.1	26.0
1996	60.4	9.4	7.4	10.8	2.7	1.4	11.1	33.5	7.5	6.1	2.8	1.4	26.9
1997	57.1	6.0	5.3	12.1	2.7	1.5	11.3	36.1	7.8	6.5	3.9	1.5	21.0
1998	51.8	5.0	5.0	9.5	2.6	1.5	10.6	36.9	8.4	6.9	3.4	1.7	14.9
1999	48.4	5.5	4.7	8.1	1.0	1.3	10.4	37.7	9.3	7.3	2.9	1.5	10.7
2000	51.3	5.2	4.3	8.6	1.9	1.2	11.6	39.0	9.3	8.4	2.7	1.4	12.3
2001	53.7	5.2	4.2	9.2	2.2	1.3	12.4	39.4	9.7	9.2	1.7	1.5	14.3
2002	53.1	5.5	4.5	9.6	2.0	1.0	11.1	41.9	10.4	9.0	1.7	1.8	11.2
2003	59.4	5.4	5.0	11.7	3.4	1.0	12.2	47.4	11.6	8.9	2.0	2.4	12.0
2004	61.4	6.4	6.3	10.4	4.2	1.0	10.4	54.0	13.1	10.6	2.3	2.5	7.4
2005	63.2	5.4	5.7	10.2	3.9	1.0	12.2	59.3	14.4	11.5	3.0	2.8	3.9
2006	70.9	7.7	5.5	11.3	4.5	1.1	13.5	65.3	15.8	11.5	3.3	2.7	5.6
2007	90.0	10.9	9.9	15.6	4.6	1.2	17.2	71.9	18.1	12.4	3.8	2.7	18.1
2008	114.8	14.9	13.6	23.7	4.8	1.2	21.3	80.5	19.5	12.0	4.4	3.3	34.3
2009	98.5	9.4	7.7	24.1	3.3	1.2	18.0	71.7	18.9	10.1	4.1	3.5	26.8
2010	115.8	10.6	9.2	27.2	5.7	1.2	22.3	81.9	21.3	11.2	4.9	4.3	34.0
Jan-Nov:													
2010	103.3	9.5	8.3	23.7	4.8	1.1	20.2	74.6	19.3	10.2	4.4	3.9	28.7
2011	124.6	13.4	12.5	23.6	7.9	1.0	25.4	90.5	21.9	11.2	7.3	4.3	34.0

* Less than $50 million.

[1] Total includes items not shown separately.
[2] Rice, wheat, and wheat flour.
[3] Includes fruit, nut, and vegetable preparations and fruit juices.
[4] In 1989, the World Customs Organization established new trade codes that harmonized reporting of commodity trade around the world. Significant changes were made in individual commodity groupings. Those changes are reflected in the data from 1989 forward.

Note: Data derived from official estimates released by the Department of Commerce, Census Bureau. Agricultural commodities are defined as (1) nonmarine food products and (2) other products of agriculture that have not passed through complex processes of manufacture. Export value, at U.S. port of exportation, is based on the selling price and includes inland freight, insurance, and other charges to the port. Import value, defined generally as the market value in the foreign country, excludes import duties, ocean freight, and marine insurance.

Source: Department of Agriculture (Economic Research Service).

TABLE B-103. U.S. international transactions, 1953–2011

[Millions of dollars; quarterly data seasonally adjusted. Credits (+), debits (−)]

| Year or quarter | Goods [1] | | | Services | | | Balance on goods and services | Income receipts and payments | | | Unilateral current transfers, net [2] | Balance on current account |
	Exports	Imports	Balance on goods	Net military transactions [2]	Net travel and transportation	Other services, net		Receipts	Payments	Balance on income		
1953	12,412	−10,975	1,437	1,753	−238	307	3,259	2,736	−624	2,112	−6,657	−1,286
1954	12,929	−10,353	2,576	902	−269	305	3,514	2,929	−582	2,347	−5,642	219
1955	14,424	−11,527	2,897	−113	−297	299	2,786	3,406	−676	2,730	−5,086	430
1956	17,556	−12,803	4,753	−221	−361	447	4,618	3,837	−735	3,102	−4,990	2,730
1957	19,562	−13,291	6,271	−423	−189	482	6,141	4,180	−796	3,384	−4,763	4,762
1958	16,414	−12,952	3,462	−849	−633	486	2,466	3,790	−825	2,965	−4,647	784
1959	16,458	−15,310	1,148	−831	−821	573	69	4,132	−1,061	3,071	−4,422	−1,282
1960	19,650	−14,758	4,892	−1,057	−964	639	3,508	4,616	−1,238	3,379	−4,062	2,824
1961	20,108	−14,537	5,571	−1,131	−978	732	4,195	4,999	−1,245	3,755	−4,127	3,822
1962	20,781	−16,260	4,521	−912	−1,152	912	3,370	5,618	−1,324	4,294	−4,277	3,387
1963	22,272	−17,048	5,224	−742	−1,309	1,036	4,210	6,157	−1,560	4,596	−4,392	4,414
1964	25,501	−18,700	6,801	−794	−1,146	1,161	6,022	6,824	−1,783	5,041	−4,240	6,823
1965	26,461	−21,510	4,951	−487	−1,280	1,480	4,664	7,437	−2,088	5,350	−4,583	5,431
1966	29,310	−25,493	3,817	−1,043	−1,331	1,497	2,940	7,528	−2,481	5,047	−4,955	3,031
1967	30,666	−26,866	3,800	−1,187	−1,750	1,742	2,604	8,021	−2,747	5,274	−5,294	2,583
1968	33,626	−32,991	635	−596	−1,548	1,759	250	9,367	−3,378	5,990	−5,629	611
1969	36,414	−35,807	607	−718	−1,763	1,964	91	10,913	−4,869	6,044	−5,735	399
1970	42,469	−39,866	2,603	−641	−2,038	2,330	2,254	11,748	−5,515	6,233	−6,156	2,331
1971	43,319	−45,579	−2,260	653	−2,345	2,649	−1,303	12,707	−5,435	7,272	−7,402	−1,433
1972	49,381	−55,797	−6,416	1,072	−3,063	2,965	−5,443	14,765	−6,572	8,192	−8,544	−5,795
1973	71,410	−70,499	911	740	−3,158	3,406	1,900	21,808	−9,655	12,153	−6,913	7,140
1974	98,306	−103,811	−5,505	165	−3,184	4,231	−4,292	27,587	−12,084	15,503	−9,249	1,962
1975	107,088	−98,185	8,903	1,461	−2,812	4,854	12,404	25,351	−12,564	12,787	−7,075	18,116
1976	114,745	−124,228	−9,483	931	−2,558	5,027	−6,082	29,375	−13,311	16,063	−5,686	4,295
1977	120,816	−151,907	−31,091	1,731	−3,565	5,680	−27,246	32,354	−14,217	18,137	−5,226	−14,335
1978	142,075	−176,002	−33,927	857	−3,573	6,879	−29,763	42,088	−21,680	20,408	−5,788	−15,143
1979	184,439	−212,007	−27,568	−1,313	−2,935	7,251	−24,565	63,834	−32,961	30,873	−6,593	−285
1980	224,250	−249,750	−25,500	−1,822	−997	8,912	−19,407	72,606	−42,532	30,073	−8,349	2,317
1981	237,044	−265,067	−28,023	−844	144	12,552	−16,172	86,529	−53,626	32,903	−11,702	5,030
1982	211,157	−247,642	−36,485	112	−992	13,209	−24,156	91,747	−56,583	35,164	−16,544	−5,536
1983	201,799	−268,901	−67,102	−563	−4,227	14,124	−57,767	90,000	−53,614	36,386	−17,310	−38,691
1984	219,926	−332,418	−112,492	−2,547	−8,438	14,404	−109,073	108,819	−73,756	35,063	−20,335	−94,344
1985	215,915	−338,088	−122,173	−4,390	−9,798	14,483	−121,880	98,542	−72,819	25,723	−21,998	−118,155
1986	223,344	−368,425	−145,081	−5,181	−8,779	20,502	−138,538	97,064	−81,571	15,494	−24,132	−147,177
1987	250,208	−409,765	−159,557	−3,844	−8,010	19,728	−151,684	108,184	−93,891	14,293	−23,265	−160,655
1988	320,230	−447,189	−126,959	−6,320	−3,013	21,725	−114,566	136,713	−118,026	18,687	−25,274	−121,153
1989	359,916	−477,665	−117,749	−6,749	3,551	27,805	−93,142	161,287	−141,463	19,824	−26,169	−99,486
1990	387,401	−498,438	−111,037	−7,599	7,501	30,270	−80,864	171,742	−143,192	28,550	−26,654	−78,968
1991	414,083	−491,020	−76,937	−5,274	16,561	34,516	−31,135	149,214	−125,084	24,130	9,904	2,898
1992	439,631	−536,528	−96,897	−1,448	19,969	39,164	−39,212	133,766	−109,531	24,234	−36,636	−51,613
1993	456,943	−589,394	−132,451	1,385	19,714	41,041	−70,310	136,057	−110,741	25,316	−39,812	−84,806
1994	502,859	−668,690	−165,831	2,570	16,305	48,463	−98,493	166,521	−149,375	17,146	−40,265	−121,612
1995	575,204	−749,374	−174,170	4,600	21,772	51,414	−96,384	210,244	−189,353	20,891	−38,074	−113,567
1996	612,113	−803,113	−191,000	5,385	25,015	56,535	−104,065	226,129	−203,811	22,318	−43,017	−124,764
1997	678,366	−876,794	−198,428	4,968	22,152	63,035	−108,273	256,804	−244,195	12,609	−45,062	−140,726
1998	670,416	−918,637	−248,221	5,220	10,210	66,651	−166,140	261,819	−257,554	4,265	−53,187	−215,062
1999	698,218	−1,034,389	−336,171	−7,245	6,606	73,649	−263,159	295,423	−283,492	11,931	−50,428	−301,656
2000	784,781	−1,230,568	−445,787	−6,488	2,462	73,065	−376,749	352,478	−333,300	19,178	−58,767	−416,338
2001	731,189	−1,152,464	−421,276	−8,324	−3,389	71,219	−361,771	292,430	−262,702	29,728	−64,561	−396,603
2002	697,439	−1,171,930	−474,491	−12,719	−4,465	74,242	−417,432	282,701	−257,526	25,175	−64,990	−457,248
2003	729,816	−1,270,225	−540,409	−17,060	−12,451	78,934	−490,984	322,411	−278,721	43,691	−71,796	−519,089
2004	821,986	−1,485,492	−663,507	−17,359	−16,225	91,734	−605,356	415,793	−350,712	65,081	−88,243	−628,519
2005	911,686	−1,692,416	−780,730	−15,594	−14,549	102,249	−708,624	537,339	−468,748	68,591	−105,741	−745,774
2006	1,039,406	−1,875,095	−835,689	−11,743	−11,276	105,420	−753,288	684,620	−640,438	44,182	−91,515	−800,621
2007	1,163,957	−1,982,843	−818,886	−10,826	2,599	130,386	−696,728	833,834	−732,349	101,485	−115,061	−710,303
2008	1,307,499	−2,137,608	−830,109	−13,600	16,365	129,006	−698,338	813,903	−666,814	147,089	−125,885	−677,135
2009	1,069,491	−1,575,400	−505,910	−13,863	13,981	124,521	−381,272	599,495	−471,494	128,001	−123,280	−376,551
2010	1,288,699	−1,934,555	−645,857	−12,908	20,384	138,355	−500,027	663,240	−498,016	165,224	−136,095	−470,898
2010: I	304,572	−457,404	−152,832	−3,409	4,834	31,765	−119,642	158,857	−122,473	36,384	−35,034	−118,292
II	315,954	−481,912	−165,958	−3,092	5,039	33,486	−130,523	165,030	−121,859	43,170	−32,947	−120,300
III	325,514	−493,336	−167,822	−3,077	4,678	35,109	−131,113	167,115	−121,375	45,740	−34,754	−120,127
IV	342,659	−501,904	−159,245	−3,330	5,831	37,996	−118,749	172,239	−132,309	39,930	−33,360	−112,179
2011: I	361,544	−543,767	−182,222	−3,339	5,844	39,746	−139,972	180,258	−127,600	52,658	−32,277	−119,591
II	373,045	−563,609	−190,564	−3,071	7,422	40,008	−146,205	191,212	−134,276	56,936	−35,449	−124,719
III p	382,718	−564,469	−181,750	−2,805	8,629	40,345	−135,580	188,373	−130,068	58,305	−33,006	−110,281

[1] Adjusted from Census data to align with concepts and definitions used to prepare the international and national economic accounts. The adjustments are necessary to supplement coverage of Census data, to eliminate duplication of transactions recorded elsewhere in the international accounts, to value transactions according to a standard definition, and for earlier years, to record transactions in the appropriate period.

[2] Includes transfers of goods and services under U.S. military grant programs.

[3] Consists of gold, special drawing rights, foreign currencies, and the U.S. reserve position in the International Monetary Fund (IMF).

See next page for continuation of table.

[Millions of dollars; quarterly data seasonally adjusted. Credits (+), debits (–)]

Year or quarter	Capital account trans- actions, net	Financial account							Financial deriva- tives, net	Statistical discrepancy	
		U.S.-owned assets abroad, excluding financial derivatives [increase/financial outflow (–)]				Foreign-owned assets in the U.S., excluding financial derivatives [increase/financial inflow (+)]				Total (sum of the items with sign reversed)	Of which: Seasonal adjustment discrep- ancy
		Total	U.S. official reserve assets [3]	Other U.S. Govern- ment assets	U.S. private assets	Total	Foreign official assets	Other foreign assets			
1953			1,256								
1954			480								
1955			182								
1956			–869								
1957			–1,165								
1958			2,292								
1959			1,035								
1960		–4,099	2,145	–1,100	–5,144	2,294	1,473	821		–1,019	
1961		–5,538	607	–910	–5,235	2,705	765	1,939		–989	
1962		–4,174	1,535	–1,085	–4,623	1,911	1,270	641		–1,124	
1963		–7,270	378	–1,662	–5,986	3,217	1,986	1,231		–360	
1964		–9,560	171	–1,680	–8,050	3,643	1,660	1,983		–907	
1965		–5,716	1,225	–1,605	–5,336	742	134	607		–457	
1966		–7,321	570	–1,543	–6,347	3,661	–672	4,333		629	
1967		–9,757	53	–2,423	–7,386	7,379	3,451	3,928		–205	
1968		–10,977	–870	–2,274	–7,833	9,928	–774	10,703		438	
1969		–11,585	–1,179	–2,200	–8,206	12,702	–1,301	14,002		–1,516	
1970		–9,337	2,481	–1,589	–10,229	7,226	7,775	–550		–219	
1971		–12,475	2,349	–1,884	–12,940	23,687	27,596	–3,909		–9,779	
1972		–14,497	–4	–1,568	–12,925	22,171	11,185	10,986		–1,879	
1973		–22,874	158	–2,644	–20,388	18,388	6,026	12,362		–2,654	
1974		–34,745	–1,467	366	–33,643	35,227	10,546	24,682		–2,444	
1975		–39,703	–849	–3,474	–35,380	16,870	7,027	9,843		4,717	
1976		–51,269	–2,558	–4,214	–44,498	37,839	17,693	20,147		9,134	
1977		–34,785	–375	–3,693	–30,717	52,770	36,816	15,954		–3,650	
1978		–61,130	732	–4,660	–57,202	66,275	33,678	32,597		9,997	
1979		–66,054	–1,133	–3,746	–61,176	40,693	–12,526	53,218		25,647	
1980		–86,967	–8,155	–5,162	–73,651	62,037	16,649	45,388		22,613	
1981		–114,147	–5,175	–5,097	–103,875	85,684	6,053	79,631		23,433	
1982		–127,882	–4,965	–6,131	–116,786	95,056	3,593	91,464		38,362	
1983		–66,373	–1,196	–5,006	–60,172	87,399	5,845	81,554		17,666	
1984		–40,376	–3,131	–5,489	–31,757	116,048	3,140	112,908		18,672	
1985		–44,752	–3,858	–2,821	–38,074	144,231	–1,119	145,349		18,677	
1986		–111,723	312	–2,022	–110,014	228,330	35,648	192,681		30,570	
1987		–79,296	9,149	1,006	–89,450	247,100	45,387	201,713		–7,149	
1988		–106,573	–3,912	2,967	–105,628	244,833	39,758	205,075		–17,107	
1989	–207	–175,383	–25,293	1,233	–151,323	222,777	8,503	214,274		52,299	
1990	–7,220	–81,234	–2,158	2,317	–81,393	139,357	33,910	105,447		28,066	
1991	–5,130	–64,388	5,763	2,924	–73,075	108,221	17,389	90,833		–41,601	
1992	1,449	–74,410	3,901	–1,667	–76,644	168,349	40,477	127,872		–43,775	
1993	–714	–200,552	–1,379	–351	–198,822	279,758	71,753	208,005		6,314	
1994	–1,111	–178,937	5,346	–390	–183,893	303,174	39,583	263,591		–1,514	
1995	–222	–352,264	–9,742	–984	–341,538	435,102	109,880	325,222		30,951	
1996	–7	–413,409	6,668	–989	–419,088	547,885	126,724	421,161		–9,705	
1997	–256	–485,475	–1,010	68	–484,533	704,452	19,036	685,416		–77,995	
1998	–8	–353,829	–6,783	–422	–346,624	420,794	–19,903	440,697		148,105	
1999	–4,176	–504,062	8,747	2,750	–515,559	742,210	43,543	698,667		67,684	
2000	–1	–560,523	–290	–941	–559,292	1,038,224	42,758	995,466		–61,361	
2001	13,198	–382,616	–4,911	–486	–377,219	782,870	28,059	754,811		–16,849	
2002	–141	–294,646	–3,681	345	–291,310	795,161	115,945	679,216		–43,126	
2003	–1,821	–325,424	1,523	537	–327,484	858,303	278,069	580,234		–11,969	
2004	3,049	–1,000,870	2,805	1,710	–1,005,385	1,533,201	397,755	1,135,446		93,138	
2005	13,116	–546,631	14,096	5,539	–566,266	1,247,347	259,268	988,079		31,942	
2006	–1,788	–1,285,729	2,374	5,346	–1,293,449	2,065,169	487,939	1,577,230	29,710	–6,742	
2007	384	–1,453,604	–122	–22,273	–1,431,209	2,064,642	481,043	1,583,599	6,222	92,660	
2008	6,010	332,109	–4,848	–529,615	866,571	431,406	554,634	–123,228	–32,947	–59,443	
2009	–140	–139,330	–52,256	541,342	–628,417	335,793	480,237	–144,444	49,456	130,773	
2010	–152	–1,005,182	–1,834	7,540	–1,010,888	1,245,736	349,754	895,982	13,735	216,761	
2010: I	–3	–313,010	–773	9,433	–321,669	329,340	89,751	239,589	16,152	85,813	13,688
II	–2	–168,537	–165	–2,441	–165,931	186,636	66,736	119,900	9,980	92,223	–6,531
III	–146	–286,834	–1,096	788	–286,526	463,115	135,477	327,638	–11,893	–44,116	–21,959
IV	–2	–236,802	200	–240	–236,762	266,646	57,790	208,856	–504	82,841	14,802
2011: I	–29	–334,359	–3,619	–547	–330,193	487,194	48,764	438,430	3,220	–36,436	14,497
II	–829	25,115	–6,267	–1,358	32,740	2,767	95,143	–92,376	7,504	90,161	–5,740
III [p]	0	–70,833	–4,079	–1,265	–65,490	254,742	24,371	230,371		–73,627	–24,678

Note: Data are on a balance of payments basis. Beginning with data for 1999, exports of goods under the U.S. Foreign Military Sales program and imports of petroleum abroad by U.S. military agencies are included in goods and excluded from net military transactions. Beginning with data for 1999, fuel purchases by air and ocean carriers in foreign ports are included in goods exports and imports and excluded from net travel and transportation.

Source: Department of Commerce (Bureau of Economic Analysis).

[Billions of dollars; quarterly data seasonally adjusted]

Year or quarter	Exports							Imports						
			Nonagricultural products							Nonpetroleum products				
	Total	Agricultural products	Total	Industrial supplies and materials	Capital goods except automotive	Automotive	Other	Total	Petroleum and products	Total	Industrial supplies and materials	Capital goods except automotive	Automotive	Other
1965	26.5	6.3	20.2	7.6	8.1	1.9	2.6	21.5	2.0	19.5	9.1	1.5	0.9	8.0
1966	29.3	6.9	22.4	8.2	8.9	2.4	2.9	25.5	2.1	23.4	10.2	2.2	1.8	9.2
1967	30.7	6.5	24.2	8.5	9.9	2.8	3.0	26.9	2.1	24.8	10.0	2.5	2.4	9.9
1968	33.6	6.3	27.3	9.6	11.1	3.5	3.2	33.0	2.4	30.6	12.0	2.8	4.0	11.8
1969	36.4	6.1	30.3	10.3	12.4	3.9	3.7	35.8	2.6	33.2	11.8	3.4	4.9	13.0
1970	42.5	7.4	35.1	12.3	14.7	3.9	4.3	39.9	2.9	36.9	12.4	4.0	5.5	15.0
1971	43.3	7.8	35.5	10.9	15.4	4.7	4.5	45.6	3.7	41.9	13.8	4.3	7.4	16.4
1972	49.4	9.5	39.9	11.9	16.9	5.5	5.6	55.8	4.7	51.1	16.3	5.9	8.7	20.2
1973	71.4	18.0	53.4	17.0	22.0	6.9	7.6	70.5	8.4	62.1	19.6	8.3	10.3	23.9
1974	98.3	22.4	75.9	26.3	30.9	8.6	10.0	103.8	26.6	77.2	27.8	9.8	12.0	27.5
1975	107.1	22.2	84.8	26.8	36.6	10.6	10.8	98.2	27.0	71.2	24.0	10.2	11.7	25.3
1976	114.7	23.4	91.4	28.4	39.1	12.1	11.7	124.2	34.6	89.7	29.8	12.3	16.2	31.4
1977	120.8	24.3	96.5	29.8	39.8	13.4	13.5	151.9	45.0	106.9	35.7	14.0	18.6	38.6
1978 [1]	142.1	29.9	112.2	34.2	47.5	15.2	15.3	176.0	42.6	133.4	40.7	19.3	25.0	48.4
1979	184.4	35.5	149.0	52.2	60.2	17.9	18.7	212.0	60.4	151.6	47.5	24.6	26.6	52.8
1980	224.3	42.0	182.2	65.1	76.3	17.4	23.4	249.8	79.5	170.2	53.0	31.6	28.3	57.4
1981	237.0	44.1	193.0	63.6	84.2	19.7	25.5	265.1	78.4	186.7	56.1	37.1	31.0	62.4
1982	211.2	37.3	173.9	57.7	76.5	17.2	22.4	247.6	62.0	185.7	48.6	38.4	34.3	64.3
1983	201.8	37.1	164.7	52.7	71.7	18.5	21.8	268.9	55.1	213.8	53.7	43.7	43.0	73.3
1984	219.9	38.4	181.5	56.8	77.0	22.4	25.3	332.4	58.1	274.4	66.1	60.4	56.5	91.4
1985	215.9	29.6	186.3	54.8	79.3	24.9	27.2	338.1	51.4	286.7	62.6	61.3	64.9	97.9
1986	223.3	27.2	196.2	59.4	82.8	25.1	28.9	368.4	34.3	334.1	69.9	72.0	78.1	114.2
1987	250.2	29.8	220.4	63.7	92.7	27.6	36.4	409.8	42.9	366.8	70.8	85.1	85.2	125.7
1988	320.2	38.8	281.4	82.6	119.1	33.4	46.3	447.2	39.6	407.6	83.1	102.2	87.9	134.4
1989 [1]	359.9	41.1	318.8	90.5	136.9	35.1	56.3	477.7	50.9	426.8	84.6	112.3	87.4	142.5
1990	387.4	40.2	347.2	97.0	153.0	36.2	61.0	498.4	62.3	436.1	83.0	116.4	88.2	148.5
1991	414.1	40.1	374.0	101.6	166.6	39.9	65.9	491.0	51.7	439.3	81.3	121.1	85.5	151.4
1992	439.6	44.1	395.6	101.7	176.4	46.9	70.6	536.5	51.6	484.9	89.1	134.8	91.5	169.6
1993	456.9	43.6	413.3	105.1	182.7	51.6	74.0	589.4	51.5	537.9	100.8	153.2	102.1	182.0
1994	502.9	47.1	455.8	112.7	205.7	57.5	79.9	668.7	51.3	617.4	113.6	185.0	118.1	200.6
1995	575.2	57.2	518.0	135.6	234.4	61.4	86.5	749.4	56.0	693.3	128.5	222.1	123.7	219.0
1996	612.1	61.5	550.6	138.7	254.0	64.4	93.6	803.1	72.7	730.4	136.1	228.4	128.7	237.1
1997	678.4	58.5	619.9	148.6	295.8	73.4	102.0	876.8	71.8	805.0	144.9	253.6	139.4	267.1
1998	670.4	53.2	617.3	139.4	299.8	72.5	105.5	918.6	50.9	867.7	151.6	269.8	148.6	297.7
1999	698.2	49.7	648.6	143.7	311.2	75.3	118.4	1,034.4	72.1	962.3	157.8	296.1	178.2	330.1
2000	784.8	52.8	732.0	168.4	357.0	80.4	126.3	1,230.6	126.1	1,104.4	183.5	347.7	195.0	378.3
2001	731.2	54.9	676.3	154.6	321.7	75.4	124.5	1,152.5	109.4	1,043.0	174.1	299.2	188.7	381.1
2002	697.4	54.5	642.9	151.4	290.4	78.9	122.1	1,171.9	109.3	1,062.7	166.3	284.9	202.8	408.6
2003	729.8	60.9	668.9	167.5	293.7	80.6	127.1	1,270.2	140.4	1,129.8	183.2	297.6	209.2	439.8
2004	822.0	62.9	759.0	199.1	327.5	89.2	143.2	1,485.5	189.9	1,295.6	234.5	346.1	227.3	487.6
2005	911.7	64.9	846.8	230.8	358.4	98.4	159.2	1,692.4	263.2	1,429.2	274.9	382.8	238.7	532.8
2006	1,039.4	72.9	966.5	275.0	404.0	107.3	180.2	1,875.1	316.7	1,558.4	302.5	422.6	256.0	577.3
2007	1,164.0	92.1	1,071.8	315.5	433.0	121.3	202.1	1,982.8	346.7	1,636.2	310.8	449.1	258.5	617.8
2008	1,307.5	118.0	1,189.5	389.5	457.7	121.5	220.9	2,137.6	476.1	1,661.5	335.5	458.7	233.2	634.1
2009	1,069.5	101.0	968.5	294.5	390.5	81.7	201.9	1,575.4	267.7	1,307.7	211.1	372.7	159.2	564.8
2010	1,288.7	119.0	1,169.7	388.0	446.6	112.0	223.1	1,934.6	353.7	1,580.8	270.1	450.0	225.6	635.2
2008: I	323.4	29.2	294.1	95.2	113.6	30.6	54.8	539.4	117.3	422.2	82.8	116.2	64.5	158.6
II	342.6	31.6	311.0	105.2	117.7	31.6	56.5	562.6	130.0	432.5	87.8	119.1	63.1	162.4
III	346.9	31.5	315.4	107.9	118.3	32.6	56.7	565.9	138.6	427.3	91.1	116.6	57.3	162.3
IV	294.6	25.6	269.0	81.3	108.0	26.7	52.9	469.8	90.3	379.5	73.7	106.7	48.3	150.7
2009: I	254.4	23.4	231.0	66.2	98.2	17.2	49.4	376.7	55.0	321.7	55.5	92.8	32.8	140.6
II	253.9	25.6	228.3	68.3	93.9	17.0	49.1	365.8	60.1	305.7	47.4	87.9	32.2	138.3
III	270.3	25.1	245.2	77.3	95.9	22.1	49.9	399.8	73.1	326.7	50.7	92.4	43.7	139.9
IV	290.9	27.0	263.9	82.6	102.4	25.4	53.5	433.1	79.6	353.5	57.5	99.6	50.4	146.0
2010: I	304.6	28.8	275.8	89.6	105.6	26.8	53.9	457.4	88.2	369.2	64.1	102.4	51.7	151.0
II	316.0	27.1	288.8	96.3	110.4	27.8	54.3	481.9	89.1	392.8	67.6	111.5	56.2	157.5
III	325.5	29.0	296.5	97.7	114.1	28.4	56.3	493.3	86.9	406.4	68.2	116.2	59.1	163.0
IV	342.7	34.0	308.7	104.5	116.6	29.0	58.6	501.9	89.5	412.4	70.3	119.9	58.6	163.7
2011: I	361.5	37.1	324.4	117.1	117.6	32.0	57.6	543.8	111.3	432.4	76.6	123.4	64.0	168.4
II	373.0	35.8	337.2	123.2	122.2	32.2	59.6	563.6	120.0	443.6	82.5	128.6	58.2	174.3
III [p]	382.7	33.1	349.6	129.5	125.6	34.5	60.1	564.5	114.4	450.0	83.3	129.2	66.8	170.8

[1] End-use commodity classifications beginning 1978 and 1989 are not strictly comparable with data for earlier periods. See *Survey of Current Business*, June 1988 and July 2001.

Note: Data are on a balance of payments basis. Beginning with data for 1999, exports of goods under the U.S. Foreign Military Sales program are included in "other" exports and imports of petroleum abroad by U.S. military agencies are included in imports of petroleum and products; prior to 1999, these transactions are included in services. Beginning with data for 1978, re-exports are assigned to detailed end-use categories in the same manner as exports of domestic goods.

Source: Department of Commerce (Bureau of Economic Analysis).

TABLE B–105. U.S. international trade in goods by area, 2003–2011

[Millions of dollars]

Item	2003	2004	2005	2006	2007	2008	2009	2010	2011 first 3 quarters at annual rate[1]
EXPORTS									
Total, all countries	729,816	821,986	911,686	1,039,406	1,163,957	1,307,499	1,069,491	1,288,699	1,489,743
Europe	175,033	194,296	213,452	247,642	288,916	331,868	263,849	289,463	334,845
Euro area[2]	114,263	127,373	138,294	156,150	180,691	203,542	164,895	178,055	197,749
France	17,257	21,157	22,612	24,009	27,217	29,681	26,987	27,365	28,959
Germany	29,018	31,782	34,874	41,919	50,115	55,322	43,943	48,523	49,191
Italy	10,569	10,903	11,627	12,750	14,372	15,755	12,427	14,387	16,397
United Kingdom	33,979	36,158	38,870	45,673	51,104	54,873	46,823	49,027	57,497
Canada	169,992	190,042	212,340	231,346	249,819	262,282	205,457	250,132	283,775
Latin America and Other Western Hemisphere	149,699	172,629	193,679	223,288	243,863	289,785	239,204	302,768	364,011
Brazil	11,224	13,870	15,343	19,008	24,304	32,435	26,085	35,341	42,736
Mexico	97,467	110,837	120,444	133,998	136,166	151,610	129,078	163,398	196,323
Venezuela	2,842	4,788	6,439	9,017	10,218	12,638	9,337	10,648	11,985
Asia and Pacific	203,880	226,576	244,220	280,513	312,005	339,342	291,483	369,034	414,037
China	28,646	34,833	41,874	54,813	64,313	71,346	70,631	93,014	101,069
India	5,040	6,170	8,014	9,775	15,048	17,845	16,479	19,334	21,537
Japan	51,805	53,458	54,817	59,276	62,796	67,178	52,937	61,537	67,129
Korea, Republic of	24,851	26,835	28,639	33,515	35,874	36,746	29,703	39,795	45,472
Singapore	16,569	19,606	20,755	24,172	25,932	28,576	22,648	29,108	31,852
Taiwan	17,847	22,264	22,794	23,817	26,854	26,177	19,387	26,762	27,817
Middle East	19,913	24,357	32,151	37,754	45,533	55,755	44,921	48,899	58,237
Africa	11,299	14,086	15,844	18,863	23,817	28,468	24,577	28,402	34,837
Memorandum: Members of OPEC[3]	17,463	22,570	31,781	39,265	48,757	65,386	50,419	54,533	63,051
IMPORTS									
Total, all countries	1,270,225	1,485,492	1,692,416	1,875,095	1,982,843	2,137,608	1,575,400	1,934,555	2,229,127
Europe	287,020	323,567	358,581	386,870	414,509	446,750	333,052	385,293	450,079
Euro area[2]	189,121	211,259	231,450	248,580	270,765	281,395	213,846	244,296	287,083
France	29,394	31,830	34,210	37,431	41,865	44,556	34,382	38,703	39,583
Germany	68,311	77,556	85,321	89,613	94,792	98,299	71,678	82,852	97,697
Italy	25,501	28,239	31,226	32,869	35,268	36,567	26,686	28,768	34,231
United Kingdom	42,984	46,418	51,469	54,087	57,215	59,418	47,776	50,699	51,264
Canada	224,336	259,377	293,960	305,822	319,498	341,640	227,175	281,851	323,237
Latin America and Other Western Hemisphere	219,280	257,925	297,364	337,128	351,251	382,247	288,626	365,031	441,493
Brazil	17,989	21,250	24,571	26,547	25,831	30,719	20,208	24,201	30,039
Mexico	140,005	158,598	173,771	202,434	215,350	220,856	179,788	232,719	267,053
Venezuela	17,152	24,946	34,006	37,206	39,997	51,531	28,149	32,825	44,521
Asia and Pacific	465,210	546,224	614,121	691,217	725,995	738,752	603,545	740,863	812,872
China	152,974	197,456	244,699	289,246	322,975	339,580	297,795	366,052	394,377
India	13,091	15,625	18,896	21,969	24,233	25,888	21,335	29,680	37,000
Japan	119,335	131,500	140,380	150,847	148,271	142,393	97,754	122,876	127,501
Korea, Republic of	37,671	46,757	44,142	46,386	48,648	49,312	39,918	49,533	58,175
Singapore	15,426	15,713	15,556	18,381	18,919	16,873	16,317	18,451	20,561
Taiwan	32,292	35,193	35,350	38,699	38,814	36,857	28,723	35,966	42,377
Middle East	42,315	52,721	63,112	73,523	79,473	114,613	60,502	76,270	104,620
Africa	32,062	45,678	65,278	80,535	92,116	113,605	62,501	85,248	96,828
Memorandum: Members of OPEC[3]	69,007	95,215	125,501	146,507	176,145	245,143	113,100	151,466	195,463
BALANCE (excess of exports +)									
Total, all countries	−540,409	−663,507	−780,730	−835,689	−818,886	−830,109	−505,910	−645,857	−739,381
Europe	−111,987	−129,271	−145,129	−139,228	−125,593	−114,882	−69,203	−95,829	−115,233
Euro area[2]	−74,857	−83,887	−93,156	−92,430	−90,074	−77,853	−48,951	−66,240	−89,333
France	−12,137	−10,674	−11,598	−13,422	−14,649	−14,875	−7,394	−11,338	−10,624
Germany	−39,293	−45,774	−50,447	−47,694	−44,677	−42,977	−27,736	−34,328	−48,507
Italy	−14,932	−17,336	−19,599	−20,119	−20,896	−20,812	−14,259	−14,382	−17,833
United Kingdom	−9,005	−10,260	−12,599	−8,414	−6,110	−4,545	−954	−1,672	6,232
Canada	−54,344	−69,335	−81,620	−74,476	−69,679	−79,359	−21,718	−31,719	−39,464
Latin America and Other Western Hemisphere	−69,581	−85,297	−103,685	−113,839	−107,388	−92,462	−49,422	−62,263	−77,480
Brazil	−6,765	−7,380	−9,228	−7,539	−1,528	1,716	5,877	11,140	12,699
Mexico	−42,538	−47,761	−53,327	−68,436	−79,184	−69,246	−50,711	−69,322	−70,731
Venezuela	−14,310	−20,157	−27,567	−28,189	−29,779	−38,893	−18,812	−22,178	−32,537
Asia and Pacific	−261,331	−319,648	−369,901	−410,705	−413,990	−399,410	−312,062	−371,829	−398,833
China	−124,328	−162,623	−202,825	−234,433	−258,662	−268,234	−227,164	−273,038	−293,308
India	−8,052	−9,455	−10,882	−12,194	−9,185	−8,043	−4,856	−10,346	−15,463
Japan	−67,531	−78,042	−85,562	−91,571	−85,475	−75,214	−44,817	−61,339	−60,372
Korea, Republic of	−12,821	−19,922	−15,503	−12,872	−12,774	−12,566	−10,215	−9,739	−12,703
Singapore	1,143	3,893	5,199	5,791	7,013	11,703	6,331	10,657	11,291
Taiwan	−14,445	−12,928	−12,555	−14,883	−11,959	−10,680	−9,335	−9,204	−14,560
Middle East	−22,402	−28,364	−30,961	−35,769	−33,940	−58,859	−15,581	−27,371	−46,383
Africa	−20,763	−31,593	−49,434	−61,672	−68,298	−85,137	−37,923	−56,846	−61,989
Memorandum: Members of OPEC[3]	−51,544	−72,645	−93,720	−107,242	−127,389	−179,757	−62,680	−96,933	−132,411

[1] Preliminary; seasonally adjusted.

[2] Euro area consists of: Austria, Belgium, Cyprus (beginning in 2008), Estonia (beginning in 2011), Finland, France, Germany, Greece (beginning in 2001), Ireland, Italy, Luxembourg, Malta (beginning in 2008), Netherlands, Portugal, Slovakia (beginning in 2009), Slovenia (beginning in 2007), and Spain.

[3] Organization of Petroleum Exporting Countries, consisting of Algeria, Angola (beginning in 2007), Ecuador (beginning in 2007), Indonesia (ending in 2008), Iran, Iraq, Kuwait, Libya, Nigeria, Qatar, Saudi Arabia, United Arab Emirates, and Venezuela.

Note: Data are on a balance of payments basis. For further details, and additional data by country, see *Survey of Current Business*, January 2012.

Source: Department of Commerce (Bureau of Economic Analysis).

[Billions of dollars; monthly data seasonally adjusted]

Year or month	Goods: Exports (f.a.s. value)[1,2] Total, BOP basis[3,4]	Census basis (by end-use category) Total, Census basis[3,5]	Foods, feeds, and beverages	Industrial supplies and materials	Capital goods except automotive	Automotive vehicles, parts, and engines	Consumer goods (nonfood) except automotive	Goods: Imports (customs value)[6] Total, BOP basis[4]	Census basis (by end-use category) Total, Census basis[5]	Foods, feeds, and beverages	Industrial supplies and materials	Capital goods except automotive	Automotive vehicles, parts, and engines	Consumer goods (nonfood) except automotive	Services (BOP basis) Exports[4]	Imports[4]
1983	201.8	205.6	30.9	56.7	67.2	16.8	13.4	268.9	258.0	18.2	107.0	40.9	40.8	44.9	64.3	55.0
1984	219.9	224.0	31.5	61.7	72.0	20.6	13.3	332.4	7330.7	21.0	123.7	59.8	53.5	60.0	71.2	67.7
1985	215.9	8218.8	24.0	58.5	73.9	22.9	12.6	338.1	7336.5	21.9	113.9	65.1	66.8	68.3	73.2	72.9
1986	223.3	8227.2	22.3	57.3	75.8	21.7	14.2	368.4	365.4	24.4	101.3	71.8	78.2	79.4	86.7	80.1
1987	250.2	254.1	24.3	66.7	86.2	24.6	17.7	409.8	406.2	24.8	111.0	84.5	85.2	88.7	98.7	90.8
1988	320.2	322.4	32.3	85.1	109.2	29.3	23.1	447.2	441.0	24.8	118.3	101.4	87.7	95.9	110.9	98.5
1989	359.9	363.8	37.2	99.3	138.8	34.8	36.4	477.7	473.2	25.1	132.3	113.3	86.1	102.9	127.1	102.5
1990	387.4	393.6	35.1	104.4	152.7	37.4	43.3	498.4	495.3	26.6	143.2	116.4	87.3	105.7	147.8	117.7
1991	414.1	421.7	35.7	109.7	166.7	40.0	45.9	491.0	488.5	26.5	131.6	120.7	85.7	108.0	164.3	118.5
1992	439.6	448.2	40.3	109.1	175.9	47.0	51.4	536.5	532.7	27.6	138.6	134.3	91.8	122.7	177.3	119.6
1993	456.9	465.1	40.6	111.8	181.7	52.4	54.7	589.4	580.7	27.9	145.6	152.4	102.4	134.0	185.9	123.8
1994	502.9	512.6	42.0	121.4	205.0	57.8	60.0	668.7	663.3	31.0	162.0	184.4	118.3	146.3	200.4	133.1
1995	575.2	584.7	50.5	146.2	233.0	61.8	64.4	749.4	743.5	33.2	181.8	221.4	123.8	159.9	219.2	141.4
1996	612.1	625.1	55.5	147.7	253.0	65.0	70.1	803.1	795.3	35.7	204.5	228.1	128.9	172.0	239.5	152.6
1997	678.4	689.2	51.5	158.2	294.5	74.0	77.4	876.8	869.7	39.7	213.8	253.3	139.8	193.8	256.1	165.9
1998	670.4	682.1	46.4	148.3	299.4	72.4	80.3	918.6	911.9	41.2	200.1	269.5	148.7	217.0	262.8	180.7
1999	698.2	695.8	46.0	147.5	310.8	75.3	80.9	1,034.4	1,024.6	43.6	221.4	295.7	179.0	241.9	268.8	195.8
2000	784.8	781.9	47.9	172.6	356.9	80.4	89.4	1,230.6	1,218.0	46.0	299.0	347.0	195.9	281.8	288.0	219.0
2001	731.2	729.1	49.4	160.1	321.7	75.4	88.3	1,152.5	1,141.0	46.6	273.9	298.0	189.8	284.3	276.5	217.0
2002	697.4	693.1	49.6	156.8	290.4	78.9	84.4	1,171.9	1,161.4	49.7	267.7	283.3	203.7	307.8	283.4	226.4
2003	729.8	724.8	55.0	173.0	293.7	80.6	89.9	1,270.2	1,257.1	55.8	313.8	295.9	210.1	333.9	293.7	244.3
2004	822.0	814.9	56.6	203.9	327.5	89.2	103.2	1,485.5	1,469.7	62.1	412.8	343.6	228.2	372.9	341.2	283.0
2005	911.7	901.1	59.0	233.0	358.4	98.4	115.3	1,692.4	1,673.5	68.1	523.8	379.3	239.4	407.2	375.8	303.6
2006	1,039.4	1,026.0	66.0	276.0	404.0	107.3	129.1	1,875.1	1,853.9	74.9	602.0	418.3	256.6	442.6	420.4	338.0
2007	1,164.0	1,148.2	84.3	316.4	433.0	121.3	146.0	1,982.8	1,957.0	81.7	634.7	444.5	256.7	474.6	490.6	368.4
2008	1,307.5	1,287.4	108.3	388.0	457.7	121.5	161.3	2,137.6	2,103.6	89.0	779.5	453.7	231.2	481.6	535.2	403.4
2009	1,069.5	1,056.0	93.9	296.7	390.5	81.7	150.0	1,575.4	1,559.6	81.6	462.5	369.3	157.6	428.4	505.5	380.9
2010	1,288.7	1,278.3	107.7	391.7	446.6	112.0	165.9	1,934.6	1,913.2	91.7	602.7	449.2	225.0	483.3	548.9	403.0
2010: Jan	99.6	98.6	8.8	29.1	34.5	8.8	13.6	148.5	146.8	7.2	47.2	33.6	17.1	36.7	44.0	32.6
Feb	100.3	99.3	8.7	29.5	35.1	9.0	13.1	151.7	150.0	7.2	48.9	34.0	16.4	38.4	43.7	33.2
Mar	104.7	104.0	8.7	31.6	35.9	9.0	13.9	157.1	155.4	7.4	51.2	34.6	18.1	39.0	44.2	32.9
Apr	103.9	103.0	8.3	32.2	36.0	9.2	13.1	156.6	155.0	7.5	51.4	36.1	17.5	37.8	43.8	32.6
May	106.7	105.7	8.2	32.8	37.6	9.2	13.6	161.0	159.3	7.6	50.3	37.5	19.1	40.0	45.4	33.2
June	105.3	104.5	8.0	32.0	36.8	9.4	13.6	164.3	162.4	7.7	49.6	37.8	19.5	42.6	46.0	33.9
July	108.3	107.5	8.1	32.7	38.7	9.4	13.6	162.0	160.3	7.7	49.5	37.6	19.4	41.1	46.4	34.3
Aug	108.5	107.6	9.0	33.3	37.5	9.5	13.8	166.1	164.3	7.8	50.2	38.6	20.2	42.2	46.4	34.3
Sept	108.8	108.1	9.4	32.6	37.9	9.5	13.9	165.2	163.4	7.9	50.1	39.8	19.3	41.3	46.9	34.4
Oct	112.6	112.0	10.1	34.5	38.5	9.8	14.1	164.9	163.0	7.8	49.1	39.2	19.5	42.2	46.9	34.1
Nov	113.8	112.7	10.2	35.1	38.5	9.4	15.0	166.3	164.4	7.9	50.7	40.3	19.4	40.8	47.4	33.8
Dec	116.3	115.4	10.3	36.3	39.6	9.8	14.6	170.7	168.7	8.1	54.5	40.0	19.6	41.2	47.7	33.7
2011: Jan	119.5	118.1	10.4	39.6	38.9	10.8	14.1	181.1	179.0	8.4	59.8	42.0	22.0	42.0	48.3	34.6
Feb	117.4	115.7	10.5	38.7	38.9	9.9	13.8	177.1	174.8	8.6	57.6	39.8	20.0	44.0	48.3	34.3
Mar	124.6	122.9	11.2	41.3	39.8	11.3	14.5	185.6	183.3	8.6	64.4	41.2	21.9	41.9	49.4	34.8
Apr	126.6	125.1	11.0	43.4	41.0	10.6	14.7	184.7	182.4	9.0	63.0	41.9	19.1	44.0	49.7	35.2
May	125.3	123.8	11.0	41.5	41.4	10.8	14.3	190.7	188.1	9.1	67.6	43.2	19.6	43.3	50.5	35.6
June	121.2	119.7	10.1	39.5	39.9	10.8	15.1	188.3	185.7	9.2	65.0	43.0	19.4	43.3	50.6	35.6
July	126.8	125.4	10.1	42.2	42.1	12.1	14.4	188.0	185.7	8.9	62.7	43.2	22.7	43.3	51.0	35.8
Aug	126.7	125.4	10.3	43.0	41.7	11.1	14.7	187.6	185.2	8.9	63.5	42.9	21.7	42.4	51.4	35.7
Sept	129.3	127.7	10.3	44.4	41.8	11.3	15.4	188.8	186.2	9.2	64.6	42.5	22.3	42.4	51.4	36.0
Oct	128.1	126.7	10.2	43.1	42.3	11.2	14.9	186.6	184.1	9.4	61.0	43.7	21.5	43.2	51.3	36.0
Nov P	126.6	125.1	10.1	41.4	42.0	11.0	15.7	189.7	187.5	9.3	63.8	43.8	22.3	42.5	51.3	35.9

[1] Department of Defense shipments of grant-aid military supplies and equipment under the Military Assistance Program are excluded from total exports through 1985 and included beginning 1986.

[2] F.a.s. (free alongside ship) value basis at U.S. port of exportation for exports.

[3] Beginning with data for 1989, exports have been adjusted for undocumented exports to Canada and are included in the appropriate end-use categories. For prior years, only total exports include this adjustment.

[4] Beginning with data for 1999, exports of goods under the U.S. Foreign Military Sales program and fuel purchases by foreign air and ocean carriers in U.S. ports are included in goods exports (BOP basis) and excluded from services exports. Beginning with data for 1999, imports of petroleum abroad by U.S. military agencies and fuel purchases by U.S. air and ocean carriers in foreign ports are included in goods imports (BOP basis) and excluded from services imports.

[5] Total includes "other" exports or imports, not shown separately.

[6] Total arrivals of imported goods other than in-transit shipments.

[7] Total includes revisions not reflected in detail.

[8] Total exports are on a revised statistical month basis; end-use categories are on a statistical month basis.

Note: Goods on a Census basis are adjusted to a BOP basis by the Bureau of Economic Analysis, in line with concepts and definitions used to prepare international and national accounts. The adjustments are necessary to supplement coverage of Census data, to eliminate duplication of transactions recorded elsewhere in international accounts, to value transactions according to a standard definition, and for earlier years, to record transactions in the appropriate period.

Data include international trade of the U.S. Virgin Islands, Puerto Rico, and U.S. Foreign Trade Zones.

Source: Department of Commerce (Bureau of the Census and Bureau of Economic Analysis).

TABLE B–107. International investment position of the United States at year-end, 2004–2010

[Millions of dollars]

Type of investment	2004	2005	2006	2007	2008	2009	2010 [p]
NET INTERNATIONAL INVESTMENT POSITION OF THE UNITED STATES	−2,253,026	−1,932,149	−2,191,653	−1,796,005	−3,260,158	−2,396,426	−2,470,989
Financial derivatives, net [1]	....	57,915	59,836	71,472	159,635	134,749	110,421
Net international investment position, excluding financial derivatives	−2,253,026	−1,990,064	−2,251,489	−1,867,477	−3,419,793	−2,531,175	−2,581,410
U.S.-OWNED ASSETS ABROAD	9,340,634	11,961,552	14,428,137	18,399,676	19,464,717	18,487,042	20,315,359
Financial derivatives, gross positive fair value [1]	....	1,190,029	1,238,995	2,559,332	6,127,450	3,500,786	3,652,909
U.S.-owned assets abroad, excluding financial derivatives	9,340,634	10,771,523	13,189,142	15,840,344	13,337,267	14,986,256	16,662,450
U.S. official reserve assets	189,591	188,043	219,853	277,211	293,732	403,804	488,673
Gold [2]	113,947	134,175	165,267	218,025	227,439	284,380	367,537
Special drawing rights	13,628	8,210	8,870	9,476	9,340	57,814	56,824
Reserve position in the International Monetary Fund	19,544	8,036	5,040	4,244	7,683	11,385	12,492
Foreign currencies	42,472	37,622	40,676	45,466	49,270	50,225	51,820
U.S. Government assets, other than official reserve assets	83,062	77,523	72,189	94,471	624,099	82,774	75,235
U.S. credits and other long-term assets [3]	80,308	76,960	71,635	70,015	69,877	71,830	74,399
Repayable in dollars	80,035	76,687	71,362	69,742	69,604	71,557	74,126
Other [4]	273	273	273	273	273	273	273
U.S. foreign currency holdings and U.S. short-term assets [5]	2,754	563	554	24,456	554,222	10,944	836
U.S. private assets	9,067,981	10,505,957	12,897,100	15,468,662	12,419,436	14,499,678	16,098,542
Direct investment at current cost	2,498,494	2,651,721	2,948,172	3,553,095	3,748,512	4,067,501	4,429,426
Foreign securities	3,545,396	4,329,259	5,604,475	6,835,079	3,985,712	5,565,636	6,222,864
Bonds	984,978	1,011,554	1,275,515	1,587,089	1,237,284	1,570,341	1,737,271
Corporate stocks	2,560,418	3,317,705	4,328,960	5,247,990	2,748,428	3,995,295	4,485,593
U.S. claims on unaffiliated foreigners reported by U.S. nonbanking concerns [6]	793,556	1,018,462	1,184,073	1,233,341	930,909	861,914	873,667
U.S. claims reported by U.S. banks and securities brokers, not included elsewhere	2,230,535	2,506,515	3,160,380	3,847,147	3,754,303	4,004,627	4,572,585
FOREIGN-OWNED ASSETS IN THE UNITED STATES	11,593,660	13,893,701	16,619,790	20,195,681	22,724,875	20,883,468	22,786,348
Financial derivatives, gross negative fair value [1]	....	1,132,114	1,179,159	2,487,860	5,967,815	3,366,037	3,542,488
Foreign-owned assets in the United States, excluding financial derivatives	11,593,660	12,761,587	15,440,631	17,707,821	16,757,060	17,517,431	19,243,860
Foreign official assets in the United States	2,019,508	2,313,295	2,832,999	3,411,831	3,943,862	4,402,762	4,863,623
U.S. Government securities	1,509,986	1,725,193	2,167,112	2,540,062	3,264,139	3,588,574	3,957,204
U.S. Treasury securities	1,251,943	1,340,598	1,558,317	1,736,687	2,400,516	2,879,611	3,320,694
Other	258,043	384,595	608,795	803,375	863,623	708,963	636,510
Other U.S. Government liabilities [7]	23,896	22,869	26,053	31,860	40,694	99,095	110,243
U.S. liabilities reported by U.S. banks and securities brokers, not included elsewhere	270,387	296,647	297,012	406,031	256,355	187,482	178,107
Other foreign official assets	215,239	268,586	342,822	433,878	382,674	527,611	618,069
Other foreign assets	9,574,152	10,448,292	12,607,632	14,295,990	12,813,198	13,114,669	14,380,237
Direct investment at current cost	1,742,716	1,905,979	2,154,062	2,345,923	2,397,396	2,441,705	2,658,932
U.S. Treasury securities	561,610	643,793	567,861	639,755	852,458	791,765	1,064,594
U.S. securities other than U.S. Treasury securities	3,995,506	4,352,998	5,372,339	6,190,018	4,620,661	5,319,867	5,860,093
Corporate and other bonds	2,035,149	2,243,135	2,824,871	3,289,070	2,770,606	2,825,591	2,868,460
Corporate stocks	1,960,357	2,109,863	2,547,468	2,900,948	1,850,055	2,494,276	2,991,633
U.S. currency	271,953	280,400	282,627	271,952	301,139	313,771	342,090
U.S. liabilities to unaffiliated foreigners reported by U.S. nonbanking concerns	600,161	658,177	799,471	863,140	740,553	707,401	747,795
U.S. liabilities reported by U.S. banks and securities brokers, not included elsewhere	2,402,206	2,606,945	3,431,272	3,985,202	3,900,991	3,540,160	3,706,733
Memoranda:							
Direct investment abroad at market value	3,362,796	3,637,996	4,470,343	5,274,991	3,102,418	4,330,914	4,843,325
Direct investment in the United States at market value	2,717,383	2,817,970	3,293,053	3,551,307	2,486,446	3,026,781	3,451,405

[1] A break in series in 2005 reflects the introduction of U.S. Department of the Treasury data on financial derivatives.

[2] U.S. official gold stock is valued at market prices.

[3] Also includes paid-in capital subscriptions to international financial institutions and resources provided to foreigners under foreign assistance programs requiring repayment over several years. Excludes World War I debts that are not being serviced.

[4] Includes indebtedness that the borrower may contractually, or at its option, repay with its currency, with a third country's currency, or by delivery of materials or transfer of services.

[5] Beginning in 2007, includes foreign-currency-denominated assets obtained through temporary reciprocal currency arrangements between the Federal Reserve System and foreign central banks.

[6] A break in series in 2005 reflects the addition of previously unreported claims of U.S. financial intermediaries on their foreign parents associated with the issuance of asset-backed commercial paper in the United States.

[7] Includes U.S. Government liabilities associated with military sales contracts and U.S. Government reserve-related liabilities from allocations of special drawing rights (SDRs).

Note: For details regarding these data, see *Survey of Current Business*, July 2011.

Source: Department of Commerce (Bureau of Economic Analysis).

TABLE B-108. Industrial production and consumer prices, major industrial countries, 1985–2011

Year or quarter	United States [1]	Canada	Japan	France	Germany [2]	Italy	United Kingdom
	Industrial production (Index, 2007=100) [3]						
1985	54.6	64.8	74.1	73.4	62.8	72.1	79.0
1986	55.2	64.3	73.9	74.3	64.0	75.0	81.0
1987	58.0	67.0	76.5	75.8	64.3	77.3	84.2
1988	61.0	71.5	83.8	78.8	66.5	82.2	88.3
1989	61.5	71.2	88.7	81.7	69.7	85.2	90.1
1990	62.1	69.3	92.3	86.6	73.3	85.4	89.8
1991	61.2	66.8	93.9	86.2	78.2	84.6	86.8
1992	62.9	67.7	88.2	84.6	76.5	83.7	87.1
1993	65.0	70.9	84.9	81.1	70.7	81.7	89.0
1994	68.4	75.4	85.7	84.6	72.8	86.6	93.8
1995	71.6	78.8	88.3	86.8	73.6	91.8	95.5
1996	74.8	79.7	90.1	86.6	73.6	90.2	96.8
1997	80.2	84.3	93.8	90.0	75.8	93.7	98.1
1998	84.9	87.2	87.2	93.2	78.6	94.9	99.6
1999	88.5	92.3	87.6	94.7	79.5	94.7	100.9
2000	92.1	100.3	92.2	98.1	83.9	98.7	102.9
2001	88.9	96.3	86.2	98.9	84.2	97.5	101.3
2002	89.1	97.8	85.1	97.5	83.3	96.0	99.8
2003	90.2	97.9	87.6	96.5	83.7	95.5	99.5
2004	92.3	99.5	91.8	97.7	86.3	95.2	100.3
2005	95.3	101.4	93.2	97.9	89.2	94.7	99.5
2006	97.4	100.8	97.1	98.8	94.3	98.2	99.5
2007	100.0	100.0	100.0	100.0	100.0	100.0	100.0
2008	96.3	95.5	96.6	97.1	100.0	96.3	97.2
2009	85.5	84.5	75.5	84.9	83.7	78.3	88.5
2010	90.1	89.7	88.1	88.8	92.6	83.4	90.1
2011 p	93.8						
2010: I	88.0	87.7	88.1	87.4	87.7	81.9	89.2
II	89.5	89.7	88.7	89.1	92.3	83.1	90.2
III	91.0	90.4	87.8	88.8	94.0	84.0	90.4
IV	91.7	90.8	87.7	90.0	96.6	84.5	90.6
2011: I	92.8	93.0	85.9	91.5	98.3	83.8	90.4
II	92.9	92.2	82.5	90.8	99.9	84.3	89.1
III	94.4	93.5	86.0	91.3	101.6	83.9	89.2
IV p	95.1						
	Consumer prices (Index, 1982–84=100)						
1985	107.6	108.9	104.2	114.3	104.9	121.8	111.1
1986	109.6	113.5	104.8	117.2	104.7	128.9	114.9
1987	113.6	118.4	105.0	121.1	105.0	135.0	119.7
1988	118.3	123.2	105.7	124.3	106.3	141.9	125.6
1989	124.0	129.3	108.1	128.7	109.2	150.8	135.4
1990	130.7	135.5	111.4	133.1	112.2	160.4	148.2
1991	136.2	143.1	115.1	137.3	116.7	170.6	156.9
1992	140.3	145.2	117.0	140.6	122.7	179.4	162.7
1993	144.5	147.9	118.5	143.6	128.1	187.3	165.3
1994	148.2	148.2	119.3	146.0	131.6	194.9	169.4
1995	152.4	151.4	119.2	148.6	133.9	205.2	175.1
1996	156.9	153.8	119.3	151.5	135.8	213.2	179.4
1997	160.5	156.2	121.4	153.3	138.4	217.6	185.0
1998	163.0	157.8	122.2	154.3	139.7	221.9	191.4
1999	166.6	160.5	121.8	155.2	140.5	225.5	194.3
2000	172.2	164.9	121.0	157.8	142.5	231.2	200.0
2001	177.1	169.1	120.1	160.3	145.3	237.7	203.7
2002	179.9	172.9	119.0	163.4	147.4	243.5	207.0
2003	184.0	177.7	118.7	166.9	148.9	250.1	213.0
2004	188.9	181.0	118.7	170.4	151.4	255.6	219.3
2005	195.3	185.0	118.4	173.4	153.7	260.6	225.6
2006	201.6	188.7	118.6	176.3	156.2	266.1	232.8
2007	207.342	192.7	118.7	178.9	159.7	270.9	242.7
2008	215.303	197.3	120.3	184.0	163.9	280.0	252.4
2009	214.537	197.9	118.7	184.1	164.5	282.2	251.1
2010	218.056	201.4	117.9	186.9	166.3	286.5	262.7
2011 p	224.939	207.2	117.5	190.9	170.2	294.5	276.3
2010: I	217.020	199.6	118.0	185.7	165.3	284.3	257.6
II	218.051	200.9	118.2	187.3	166.0	286.2	262.6
III	218.254	202.0	117.5	187.0	166.6	287.4	263.7
IV	218.898	203.1	117.7	187.8	167.3	288.1	266.7
2011: I	221.666	204.8	117.4	189.1	168.8	291.0	271.3
II	225.531	207.6	117.7	191.2	169.9	293.8	276.0
III	226.452	208.0	117.7	191.1	170.7	295.5	277.5
IV p	226.108	208.6	117.4	192.3	171.2	297.7	280.4

[1] See Note, Table B–51 for information on U.S. industrial production series.
[2] Prior to 1991 data are for West Germany only.
[3] All data exclude construction. Quarterly data are seasonally adjusted.

Note: National sources data have been rebased for industrial production and consumer prices.

Sources: As reported by each country, Board of Governors of the Federal Reserve System, and Department of Labor (Bureau of Labor Statistics).

[Quarterly data seasonally adjusted]

Year or quarter	United States	Canada	Japan	France	Germany [1]	Italy	United Kingdom
			Civilian unemployment rate (Percent) [2]				
1985	7.2	10.1	2.5	9.1	7.2	6.0	11.4
1986	7.0	9.2	2.7	9.1	6.6	[3]7.5	11.4
1987	6.2	8.4	2.6	9.2	6.3	7.9	10.5
1988	5.5	7.4	2.4	8.9	6.3	7.9	8.6
1989	5.3	7.1	2.2	8.3	5.7	7.8	7.3
1990	[3]5.6	7.7	2.0	8.0	5.0	7.0	7.1
1991	6.8	9.8	2.0	8.3	[3]5.6	[3]6.9	8.9
1992	7.5	10.6	2.1	9.1	6.7	7.3	10.0
1993	6.9	10.8	2.4	10.2	8.0	[3]9.8	10.4
1994	[3]6.1	[3]9.6	2.6	10.8	8.5	10.7	9.5
1995	5.6	8.6	2.9	10.2	8.2	11.3	8.7
1996	5.4	8.8	3.1	10.7	9.0	11.3	8.1
1997	4.9	8.4	3.1	10.9	9.9	11.4	7.0
1998	4.5	7.7	3.8	10.5	9.3	11.5	6.3
1999	4.2	7.0	4.2	10.1	[3]8.5	11.0	6.0
2000	4.0	6.1	4.4	8.6	7.8	10.2	5.5
2001	4.7	6.5	4.5	7.9	7.9	9.2	5.1
2002	5.8	7.0	4.9	8.0	8.6	8.7	5.2
2003	6.0	6.9	4.6	8.6	9.3	8.5	5.0
2004	5.5	6.4	4.2	9.0	10.3	8.1	4.8
2005	5.1	6.0	3.8	9.0	[3]11.2	7.8	4.9
2006	4.6	5.5	3.6	8.9	10.3	6.9	5.5
2007	4.6	5.2	3.6	8.1	8.7	6.2	5.4
2008	5.8	5.3	3.7	7.5	7.6	6.8	5.7
2009	9.3	7.3	4.8	9.2	7.8	7.9	7.7
2010	9.6	7.1	4.8	9.4	7.2	8.6	7.9
2011	8.9						
2010: I	9.8	7.4	4.7	9.6	7.6	8.6	8.0
II	9.6	7.2	4.8	9.5	7.3	8.7	7.9
III	9.5	7.0	4.7	9.5	7.1	8.3	7.8
IV	9.6	6.7	4.7	9.3	7.0	8.4	7.9
2011: I	9.0	6.7	4.4	9.3	6.8	8.3	7.8
II	9.1	6.5	4.3	9.2	6.6	8.2	7.9
III	9.1	6.3	4.1	9.2	6.5	8.3	8.3
IV	8.7						
			Manufacturing hourly compensation in U.S. dollars (Index, 2002=100) [4]				
1985	51.4	64.6	32.7	39.9	32.8	44.8	33.2
1986	53.8	64.6	48.2	54.0	46.3	61.2	40.8
1987	55.6	69.3	57.8	64.7	58.4	75.9	50.5
1988	57.5	78.1	66.8	67.6	62.2	81.2	58.6
1989	59.3	85.0	65.7	66.7	61.1	85.0	57.6
1990	62.1	91.9	66.8	81.7	76.4	104.8	70.4
1991	65.8	100.2	76.6	83.4	79.1	110.1	78.6
1992	68.9	99.5	84.3	93.4	92.0	118.0	78.4
1993	70.5	94.3	98.9	91.0	92.2	96.3	68.9
1994	72.2	91.6	109.5	96.3	98.4	99.1	72.0
1995	73.4	93.4	123.1	110.5	117.4	103.7	75.2
1996	74.6	95.4	107.3	109.6	117.0	115.5	74.2
1997	76.5	96.3	99.7	99.5	103.4	109.5	81.1
1998	81.2	94.5	94.4	99.3	103.4	105.5	88.3
1999	84.8	96.4	108.6	98.3	101.4	103.3	91.7
2000	91.3	99.5	113.9	89.7	92.4	91.9	91.0
2001	94.8	98.1	102.3	89.3	92.4	92.1	90.6
2002	100.0	100.0	100.0	100.0	100.0	100.0	100.0
2003	108.0	116.6	105.6	122.8	122.4	124.2	114.5
2004	108.9	130.3	114.3	139.3	135.2	141.2	134.4
2005	112.5	146.2	113.2	144.4	137.1	145.9	141.4
2006	114.8	162.4	106.1	151.4	144.0	150.4	151.2
2007	118.5	177.4	103.1	168.5	158.7	168.8	170.1
2008	123.6	181.0	119.1	185.9	175.1	188.7	160.9
2009	129.1	166.5	133.0	181.1	174.1	184.8	140.7
2010	131.2	184.4	140.1	175.9	162.8	179.6	143.2

[1] Prior to 1991 data are for West Germany only.

[2] Civilian unemployment rates, approximating U.S. concepts. Quarterly data for Germany should be viewed as less precise indicators of unemployment under U.S. concepts than the annual data.

[3] There are breaks in the series for Canada (1994), Germany (1991, 1999, and 2005), Italy (1986, 1991, and 1993), and the United States (1990 and 1994). For details, see *International Comparisons of Annual Labor Force Statistics, Adjusted to U.S. Concepts, 10 Countries, 1970–2010*, March 30, 2011, Appendix B, at http://www.bls.gov/fls/flscomparelf/notes.htm#country_notes.

[4] Hourly compensation in manufacturing, U.S. dollar basis; data relate to all employed persons (employees and self-employed workers). For details, see *International Comparisons of Manufacturing Productivity and Unit Labor Cost Trends, 2010*, October 13, 2011.

Source: Department of Labor (Bureau of Labor Statistics).

TABLE B–110. Foreign exchange rates, 1992–2011

[Foreign currency units per U.S. dollar, except as noted; certified noon buying rates in New York]

Period	Australia (dollar)[1]	Canada (dollar)	China, P.R. (yuan)	EMU Members (euro)[1,2]	Germany (mark)[2]	Japan (yen)	Mexico (peso)	South Korea (won)	Sweden (krona)	Switzer-land (franc)	United Kingdom (pound)[1]
March 1973	1.2716	0.9967	2.2401	....	2.8132	261.90	0.013	398.85	4.4294	3.2171	2.4724
1992	.7352	1.2085	5.5206	....	1.5618	126.78	3.095	784.66	5.8258	1.4064	1.7663
1993	.6799	1.2902	5.7795	....	1.6545	111.08	3.116	805.75	7.7956	1.4781	1.5016
1994	.7316	1.3664	8.6397	....	1.6216	102.18	3.385	806.93	7.7161	1.3667	1.5319
1995	.7407	1.3725	8.3700	....	1.4321	93.96	6.447	772.69	7.1406	1.1812	1.5785
1996	.7828	1.3638	8.3389	....	1.5049	108.78	7.600	805.00	6.7082	1.2361	1.5607
1997	.7437	1.3849	8.3193	....	1.7348	121.06	7.918	953.19	7.6447	1.4514	1.6376
1998	.6291	1.4836	8.3008	....	1.7597	130.99	9.152	1,400.40	7.9522	1.4506	1.6573
1999	.6454	1.4858	8.2783	1.0653	....	113.73	9.553	1,189.84	8.2740	1.5045	1.6172
2000	.5815	1.4855	8.2784	.9232	....	107.80	9.459	1,130.90	9.1735	1.6904	1.5156
2001	.5169	1.5487	8.2770	.8952	....	121.57	9.337	1,292.01	10.3425	1.6891	1.4396
2002	.5437	1.5704	8.2771	.9454	....	125.22	9.663	1,250.31	9.7233	1.5567	1.5025
2003	.6524	1.4008	8.2772	1.1321	....	115.94	10.793	1,192.08	8.0787	1.3450	1.6347
2004	.7365	1.3017	8.2768	1.2438	....	108.15	11.290	1,145.24	7.3480	1.2428	1.8330
2005	.7627	1.2115	8.1936	1.2449	....	110.11	10.894	1,023.75	7.4710	1.2459	1.8204
2006	.7535	1.1340	7.9723	1.2563	....	116.31	10.906	954.32	7.3718	1.2532	1.8434
2007	.8391	1.0734	7.6058	1.3711	....	117.76	10.928	928.97	6.7550	1.1999	2.0020
2008	.8537	1.0660	6.9477	1.4726	....	103.39	11.143	1,098.71	6.5846	1.0816	1.8545
2009	.7927	1.1412	6.8307	1.3935	....	93.68	13.498	1,274.63	7.6539	1.0860	1.5661
2010	.9200	1.0298	6.7696	1.3261	....	87.78	12.624	1,155.74	7.2053	1.0432	1.5452
2011	1.0332	.9887	6.4630	1.3931	....	79.70	12.427	1,106.94	6.4878	.8862	1.6043
2010: I	.9041	1.0401	6.8271	1.3821	....	90.66	12.759	1,142.84	7.1928	1.0583	1.5575
II	.8842	1.0273	6.8237	1.2740	....	92.08	12.553	1,164.80	7.5737	1.1073	1.4931
III	.9062	1.0386	6.7680	1.2938	....	85.74	12.789	1,181.06	7.2501	1.0308	1.5521
IV	.9879	1.0129	6.6570	1.3586	....	82.54	12.389	1,132.56	6.7843	.9740	1.5804
2011: I	1.0055	.9856	6.5783	1.3699	....	82.24	12.060	1,118.58	6.4779	.9404	1.6027
II	1.0626	.9677	6.4986	1.4399	....	81.56	11.723	1,082.63	6.2607	.8699	1.6309
III	1.0496	.9803	6.4155	1.4123	....	77.62	12.332	1,084.50	6.4783	.8247	1.6102
IV	1.0133	1.0227	6.3584	1.3476	....	77.34	13.638	1,144.16	6.7460	.9127	1.5718

Trade-weighted value of the U.S. dollar

Period	Nominal				Real[7]		
	G-10 index (March 1973=100)[3]	Broad index (January 1997=100)[4]	Major currencies index (March 1973=100)[5]	OITP index (January 1997=100)[6]	Broad index (March 1973=100)[4]	Major currencies index (March 1973=100)[5]	OITP index (March 1973=100)[6]
1992	86.6	76.91	87.00	53.13	87.79	82.20	104.96
1993	93.2	83.78	89.90	63.37	89.13	85.46	102.33
1994	91.3	90.87	88.43	80.54	88.96	85.10	102.34
1995	84.2	92.65	83.41	92.51	86.51	81.24	102.40
1996	87.3	97.46	87.25	98.24	88.52	86.14	99.40
1997	96.4	104.43	93.93	104.64	93.23	93.41	100.45
1998	98.8	115.89	98.45	125.89	101.20	98.47	113.61
1999	....	116.16	97.06	129.20	100.33	98.14	112.18
2000	....	119.55	101.76	129.81	104.18	104.80	112.31
2001	....	126.06	107.87	135.92	110.17	112.23	116.82
2002	....	126.82	106.18	140.41	110.32	110.62	119.26
2003	....	119.26	93.15	143.57	103.65	97.60	120.84
2004	....	113.76	85.51	143.38	99.01	90.62	119.41
2005	....	110.84	83.86	138.87	97.34	90.37	115.73
2006	....	108.70	82.60	135.40	96.22	90.30	113.02
2007	....	103.58	77.96	130.23	91.63	86.14	107.44
2008	....	99.90	74.42	126.80	87.78	83.15	102.21
2009	....	105.69	77.69	135.91	91.39	86.24	106.70
2010	....	101.85	75.39	130.37	87.13	83.87	100.15
2011	....	97.17	70.88	125.76	82.66	79.58	94.99
2010: I	....	102.13	74.90	131.65	88.03	83.52	102.37
II	....	103.58	77.63	131.19	88.71	86.38	101.03
III	....	102.42	75.90	130.92	87.49	84.48	100.31
IV	....	99.26	72.98	127.68	84.28	81.11	96.90
2011: I	....	97.77	71.86	125.82	83.21	80.32	95.43
II	....	95.32	69.61	123.29	81.23	78.10	93.46
III	....	95.92	69.77	124.46	81.75	78.67	93.99
IV	....	99.65	72.38	129.47	84.43	81.24	97.08

[1] U.S. dollars per foreign currency unit.
[2] European Economic and Monetary Union (EMU) members consists of Austria, Belgium, Cyprus (beginning in 2008), Estonia (beginning in 2011), Finland, France, Germany, Greece (beginning in 2001), Ireland, Italy, Luxembourg, Malta (beginning in 2008), Netherlands, Portugal, Slovakia (beginning in 2009), Slovenia (beginning in 2007), and Spain.
[3] G-10 index discontinued after December 1998.
[4] Weighted average of the foreign exchange value of the U.S. dollar against the currencies of a broad group of major U.S. trading partners.
[5] Subset of the broad index. Consists of currencies of the Euro area, Australia, Canada, Japan, Sweden, Switzerland, and the United Kingdom.
[6] Subset of the broad index. Consists of other important U.S. trading partners (OITP) whose currencies do not circulate widely outside the country of issue.
[7] Adjusted for changes in consumer price indexes for the United States and other countries.

Source: Board of Governors of the Federal Reserve System.

TABLE B–111. International reserves, selected years, 1992–2011

[Millions of special drawing rights (SDRs); end of period]

Area and country	1992	2002	2007	2008	2009	2010	2011 October	2011 November
World [1]	760,933	1,893,554	4,306,246	4,842,754	5,481,411	6,295,460	6,765,590	6,904,817
Advanced economies [1]	557,729	1,160,395	1,587,985	1,674,763	1,954,426	2,196,883	2,334,558	2,404,358
United States	52,995	59,160	46,820	52,396	85,519	87,977	97,212	97,443
Japan	52,937	340,088	603,794	656,178	652,926	690,127	737,040	814,111
United Kingdom	27,300	27,973	31,330	29,142	35,881	44,728	51,101	51,380
Canada	8,662	27,225	25,944	28,426	34,601	37,015	41,141	42,252
Euro area (incl. ECB) [1]		195,771	148,621	154,221	192,559	207,103	210,652	212,785
Austria	9,703	7,480	7,079	6,101	5,491	6,542	7,676	7,547
Belgium	10,914	9,010	6,827	6,306	10,403	10,970	11,573	11,698
Cyprus	764	2,239	3,888	416	524	350	362	356
Estonia	127	736	2,065	2,574	2,534	1,660	136	139
Finland	3,862	6,885	4,525	4,587	6,250	4,813	5,302	5,297
France	22,522	24,268	31,855	24,630	32,487	38,974	36,087	34,123
Germany	69,489	41,516	31,896	31,846	42,059	44,277	46,162	46,470
Greece	3,606	6,083	526	350	1,118	976	1,020	955
Ireland	2,514	3,989	499	572	1,245	1,203	1,183	916
Italy	22,438	23,798	20,721	26,838	31,955	33,722	33,722	34,119
Luxembourg	66	114	93	220	469	488	591	570
Malta	927	1,625	2,396	239	340	348	301	292
Netherlands	17,492	7,993	7,198	8,140	12,088	12,683	13,837	13,711
Portugal	14,474	8,889	1,226	1,281	1,996	2,802	2,044	1,997
Slovak Republic		6,519	11,450	11,631	477	503	570	569
Slovenia	520	5,143	624	567	620	605	599	535
Spain	33,640	25,992	7,582	8,376	11,930	12,749	15,363	18,837
Australia	8,429	15,307	15,764	20,015	24,935	25,193	27,055	26,150
China, P.R.: (Hong Kong)	25,589	82,308	96,593	118,468	163,152	174,446	177,564	182,025
Czech Republic		17,342	21,878	23,812	26,268	27,227	25,969	26,189
Denmark	8,090	19,924	20,663	26,347	47,464	47,803	56,395	52,731
Iceland	364	326	1,634	2,284	2,435	3,703	5,380	5,888
Israel	3,729	17,714	18,047	27,601	38,663	46,043	48,490	48,437
Korea	12,463	89,272	165,908	130,607	172,201	189,293	195,274	197,575
New Zealand	2,239	3,650	10,914	7,175	9,947	10,859	13,885	12,667
Norway	8,725	23,579	38,500	33,079	31,166	34,284	31,831	29,772
San Marino		135	410	459	504	292		
Singapore	29,048	60,478	103,121	113,092	119,796	146,565	154,824	155,392
Sweden	16,667	12,807	17,281	16,967	27,481	27,781	28,129	28,316
Switzerland	27,100	31,693	29,432	30,426	63,810	146,285	183,784	170,444
Taiwan Province of China	60,333	119,381	171,532	189,864	222,586	248,527	248,490	250,526
Emerging and developing economies	196,119	729,317	2,714,485	3,164,230	3,523,429	4,094,846	4,427,324	4,496,743
By area:								
Developing Asia	63,596	368,405	1,355,391	1,654,908	1,973,767	2,370,440	2,583,566	2,630,147
China, P.R. (Mainland)	15,441	214,815	969,055	1,266,206	1,542,335	1,862,240		
India	4,584	50,174	169,356	161,036	169,782	179,375	183,700	181,633
Europe	13,684	107,521	503,928	480,811	501,200	550,712	575,647	570,015
Russia		32,840	295,872	267,908	266,503	288,925	301,728	299,188
Middle East and North Africa	45,316	107,687	480,435	602,353	596,194	659,340	697,196	715,737
Sub-Saharan Africa	8,421	27,004	92,324	102,270	101,816	102,731	109,444	111,301
Western Hemisphere	65,102	118,700	282,407	323,888	350,452	411,624	461,881	469,955
Brazil	16,457	27,593	113,585	125,239	151,448	186,434	221,403	225,736
Mexico	13,800	37,223	55,128	61,766	63,536	78,101	88,311	91,142
Memoranda:								
Export earnings: Fuel	40,861	131,380	793,421	900,280	866,829	943,765	1,013,081	1,027,937
Export earnings: Nonfuel	155,257	597,937	1,921,064	2,263,949	2,656,599	3,151,081	3,414,243	3,468,806

[1] Includes data for European Central Bank (ECB) beginning 1999. Detail does not add to totals shown.

Note: International reserves consists of monetary authorities' holdings of gold (at SDR 35 per ounce), SDRs, reserve positions in the International Monetary Fund, and foreign exchange.

U.S. dollars per SDR (end of period) are: 1.37500 in 1992; 1.35952 in 2002; 1.58025 in 2007; 1.54027 in 2008; 1.56769 in 2009; 1.54003 in 2010; 1.58590 in October 2011; and 1.55156 in November 2011.

Source: International Monetary Fund, *International Financial Statistics*.

TABLE B–112. Growth rates in real gross domestic product, 1993–2012

[Percent change]

Area and country	1993–2002 annual average	2003	2004	2005	2006	2007	2008	2009	2010	2011 [1]	2012 [1]
World	3.3	3.6	4.9	4.6	5.3	5.4	2.8	−.7	5.2	3.8	3.3
Advanced economies	2.8	1.9	3.1	2.7	3.1	2.8	.1	−3.7	3.2	1.6	1.2
Of which:											
United States	3.4	2.5	3.5	3.1	2.7	1.9	−.3	−3.5	3.0	1.8	1.8
Euro area [2]	2.1	.7	2.2	1.7	3.2	3.0	.4	−4.3	1.9	1.6	−.5
Germany	1.4	−.4	.7	.8	3.9	3.4	.8	−5.1	3.6	3.0	.3
France	2.0	.9	2.3	1.9	2.7	2.2	−.2	−2.6	1.4	1.6	.2
Italy	1.6	.0	1.5	.7	2.0	1.5	−1.3	−5.2	1.5	.4	−2.2
Spain	3.2	3.1	3.3	3.6	4.0	3.6	.9	−3.7	−.1	.7	−1.7
Japan	0.8	1.4	2.7	1.9	2.0	2.4	−1.2	−6.3	4.4	−.9	1.7
United Kingdom	3.1	2.8	3.0	2.2	2.8	2.7	−.1	−4.9	2.1	.9	.6
Canada	3.5	1.9	3.1	3.0	2.8	2.2	.7	−2.8	3.2	2.3	1.7
Memorandum:											
Newly industrialized Asian economies [3]	5.4	3.2	5.9	4.8	5.8	5.9	1.8	−.7	8.4	4.2	3.3
Emerging and developing economies	4.1	6.2	7.5	7.3	8.2	8.9	6.0	2.8	7.3	6.2	5.4
Regional groups:											
Central and eastern Europe	3.2	4.8	7.3	5.8	6.4	5.5	3.1	−3.6	4.5	5.1	1.1
Commonwealth of Independent States [4]	−1.2	7.7	8.1	6.7	8.9	8.9	5.3	−6.4	4.6	4.5	3.7
Russia	−0.9	7.3	7.2	6.4	8.2	8.5	5.2	−7.8	4.0	4.1	3.3
Developing Asia	7.1	8.1	8.5	9.5	10.3	11.5	7.7	7.2	9.5	7.9	7.3
China	9.8	10.0	10.1	11.3	12.7	14.2	9.6	9.2	10.4	9.2	8.2
India	5.8	6.9	7.6	9.0	9.5	10.0	6.2	6.8	9.9	7.4	7.0
Latin America and the Caribbean	2.7	2.1	6.0	4.6	5.6	5.8	4.3	−1.7	6.1	4.6	3.6
Brazil	2.9	1.1	5.7	3.2	4.0	6.1	5.2	−.6	7.5	2.9	3.0
Mexico	2.7	1.4	4.0	3.2	5.2	3.2	1.2	−6.2	5.4	4.1	3.5
Middle East and North Africa	3.3	7.3	5.9	5.4	6.0	6.7	4.6	2.6	4.3	3.1	3.2
Sub-Saharan Africa	3.7	4.9	7.1	6.2	6.4	7.1	5.6	2.8	5.3	4.9	5.5

[1] All figures are forecasts as published by the International Monetary Fund. For the United States, advance estimates by the Department of Commerce show that real GDP rose 1.7 percent in 2011.

[2] Euro area consists of: Austria, Belgium, Cyprus, Estonia, Finland, France, Germany, Greece, Ireland, Italy, Luxembourg, Malta, Netherlands, Portugal, Slovak Republic, Slovenia, and Spain.

[3] Consists of Hong Kong SAR (Special Administrative Region of China), Korea, Singapore, and Taiwan Province of China.

[4] Includes Georgia and Mongolia, which are not members of the Commonwealth of Independent States but are included for reasons of geography and similarities in economic structure.

Note: For details on data shown in this table, see *World Economic Outlook*, September 2011, and *World Economic Outlook Update*, January 2012, published by the International Monetary Fund.

Sources: Department of Commerce (Bureau of Economic Analysis) and International Monetary Fund.